JIM MURRAY'S
WHISKY
BIBLE
2019

Keep the faith!

J Murray

This edition first published 2018 by Dram Good Books Ltd

10 9 8 7 6 5 4 3 2 1

The "Jim Murray's" logo and the "Whisky Bible" logo are trade marks of Jim Murray.

For information regarding using tasting notes from Jim Murray's Whisky Bible contact:
Dram Good Books Ltd, Unit 2, Barnstones Business Park, Litchborough, U.K., NN12 8JJ
Tel: 44 (0)117 317 9777. Or contact us via www.whiskybible.com

A CIP catalogue record for this book is available from the British Library

ISBN: 978-0-9932986-3-9

Printed in Italy by L.E.G.O SPA

Written by: Jim Murray
Edited by: Peter Mayne and David Rankin
Design: Rob-indesign, Jim Murray and Vincent Flint-Hill
Maps: James Murray, Rob-indesign and Vincent Flint-Hill
Production: Rob-indesign, Vincent Flint-Hill and Jane Garnett
Chief Researcher: Vincent Flint-Hill
Sample Research: Vincent Flint-Hill, Ally Telfer, Julia Nourney, Mick Secor
Other Research: Emma Thomson
Sales: sales@whiskybible.com
European Dictionary: Julie Nourney, Tom Wyss, Mariette Duhr-Merges, Stefan Baumgart,
Erik Molenaar, Jürgen Vromans, Henric Molin and Kalle Valkonen.

Author's Note
I have used the spelling "whiskey" or "whisky" depending on how the individual distillers
prefer. All Scotch is "whisky". So is Canadian. All Irish, these days, is "whiskey", though
that was not always the case. In Kentucky, bourbon and rye are spelt "whiskey", with the
exception of the produce of the early Times/Old Forester Distillery and Maker's Mark which
they bottle as "whisky". In Tennessee, it is a 50-50 split: Dickel is "whisky", while Daniel's is
"whiskey".

JIM MURRAY'S
WHISKY
BIBLE
2019

DRAM GOOD BOOKS

Contents

Introduction

Bizarrely, eerily, as I sat contemplating the very first words to begin this Introduction, the traditional finale, the home chapter of this latest Whisky Bible, a World War Two B17 Flying Fortress bomber rumbled low and dramatically over my village, its engines pulsing shockwaves deep into my body.

Sitting in my garden, warmed by the late summer sun in a cloudless September sky and with chickens pecking contentedly at the badger-ravaged lawn, an ancient, 900-year-old church just yards to my right and a 300-year-old cottage before me, it was as though I had been transported 75 years back to 1944.

There was the same unmistakable timelessness that you feel when you are in the company of the greatest whiskies of them all. For rarely is it a faddy whisky trying to make the most of a latest fashion that wins either the heart or the prize. The whiskies which seem to reverberate around your body, like the throbbing pistons of that B17, are the whiskies which stick to tradition and go to the greatest pain of getting it right. Simply, but effectively.

The sudden, nerve-tingling presence of that B17, quite literally out of the blue, could not have been more appropriate or better timed had it tried. It was as though one all-powerful giant of America was paying homage to another, in this case a fortress of a bourbon called William Larue Weller which for the first time ever I have named World Whisky of the Year. And, for good measure, a rye Thomas Handy Sazerac grabbed third spot: First and Third best whiskies for Kentucky...and not, it has to be said, for the first time. In fact, it was the third consecutive year the USA had produced the world's finest whisky. Astonishing. And a triumph for Buffalo Trace which produced both whiskeys. With that B17 roaring a few hundred feet above, for those passing moments it was Ancient Age again...

In my younger days I was a reasonable middle distance and cross country runner, picking up a few gold and silver medals along the way and qualifying for the British trials. But to find gold for this year's Whisky Bible World Whisky of the Year I had to take up the marathon...a four-month daily slog through over 1,250 of the world's whiskies.

With the increase of older and older whiskies into the marketplace the demands on time required for objective, professional analysis is getting greater. And this year was unquestionably the greatest since the Whisky Bible began 15 years ago. Talking to executives within various whisky companies in recent months, it appears there is little prospect of this altering as the demand for the contents of the longest laid down casks shows little sign of abating.

At least I didn't have to spend quite so long this year having to waste an hour or two cleaning my palate from the unpleasant effects of dire, sulphur-treated sherry butts. However, there are still plenty still out there, so remain on your guard. But for the first time I have noticed that the number of clean sherry casks has reached significant numbers. The clean-up operation of a problem an industry still fails to publicly recognise is taking effect, though a lot more could be done to take tainted casks out of the system, rather than making the false and misguided economy of using them a second or even third time.

Now, wherever I go in the world, irrespective of country or even continent, I am told with a degree of certainty that I must have the luckiest and most enjoyable job on the planet. And I suppose I have. This is the 15th Jim Murray's Whisky Bible and to produce them I have tasted in excess of 17,500 different whiskies. That, in case you are not too sure about this, is quite a lot of whisky. What I didn't expect all those whiskies to do was have me spending last Christmas Day lying on the floor of my cottage in complete and total agony unable to sit or stand. And I apologise to those of you I was supposed to meet in the first few months of 2018, but I had to cancel any shows or book signings. But, it was the whisky what got me!

You see, 15 years of spitting whisky for this book (and that doesn't include the tasting worldwide I do away from the Bible) – and remember each whisky is tasted a minimum five times, usually six – that is some 100,000 mouthfuls of whisky sent hurling into my spittoon. However, for those 15 years the spittoon had been in the same position to my right. And this continuous action over so great a time apparently led to a contraction of my right back muscle, which became so severe and pronounced that is sent my spine and hip in opposite directions and way out of alignment – to agonising and devastating effect. So thanks to my brilliant chiropractor, Katie, and moving the spittoon to the left (next year there will be one on either side) I was able to write this year's Bible. And am fit enough to resume to journey around the world's whisky distilleries.

I hope I see you somewhere along my travels.

Jim Murray
Willow Cottage
Somewhere in rural Northamptonshire
September 2018

How to Read The Bible

The whole point of this book is for the whisky lover – be he or she an experienced connoisseur or, better fun still, simply starting out on the long and joyous path of discovery – to have ready access to easy-to-understand information about as many whiskies as possible. And I mean a lot. Thousands.

This book does not quite include every whisky on the market... just by far and away the vast majority. And those that have been missed this time round – either through accident, logistics or design – will appear in later editions once we can source a sample.

WHISKY SCORING

The marking for this book is tailored to the consumer and scores run out just a little higher than I use for my own personal references. But such is the way it has been devised that it has not affected my order of preference.

Each whisky is given a rating out of 100. Twenty-five marks are given to each of four factors: nose (n), taste (t), finish (f), balance and overall complexity (b). That means that 50% of the marks are given for flavour alone and 25% for the nose, often an overlooked part of the whisky equation. The area of balance and complexity covers all three previous factors and a usually hidden one besides:

Nose: this is simply the aroma. Often requires more than one inspection as hidden aromas can sometimes reveal themselves after time in the glass, increased contact with air and changes in temperature. The nose very often tells much about a whisky, but – as we shall see – equally can be quite misleading.

Taste: this is the immediate arrival on the palate and involves the flavour profile up to, and including, the time it reaches maximum intensity and complexity.

Finish: often the least understood part of a tasting. This is the tail and flourish of the whisky's signature, often revealing the effects of ageing. The better whiskies tend to finish well and linger without too much oak excess. It is on the finish, also, that certain notes which are detrimental to the whisky may be observed. For instance, a sulphur-tarnished cask may be fully revealed for what it is by a dry, bitter residue on the palate which is hard to shake off. It is often worth waiting a few minutes to get the full picture of the finish before having a second taste of a whisky.

Balance: This is the part it takes a little experience to appreciate but it can be mastered by anyone. For a whisky to work well on the nose and palate, it should not be too one-sided in its character. If you are looking for an older whisky, it should have evidence of oak, but not so much that all other flavours and aromas are drowned out. Likewise, a whisky matured or finished in a sherry butt must offer a lot more than just wine alone and the greatest Islay malts, for instance, revel in depth and complexity beyond the smoky effects of peat.

Each whisky has been analysed by me without adding water or ice. I have taken each whisky as it was poured from the bottle and used no more than warming in an identical glass to extract and discover the character of the whisky. To have added water would have been pointless: it would have been an inconsistent factor as people, when pouring water, add different amounts at varying temperatures. The only constant with the whisky you and I taste will be when it has been poured directly from the bottle.

Even if you and I taste the same whiskies at the same temperature and from identical glasses – and even share the same values in whisky – our scores may still be different. Because a factor that is built into my evaluation is drawn from expectation and experience. When I sample a whisky from a certain distillery at such-and-such an age or from this type of barrel or that, I would expect it to offer me certain qualities. It has taken me 30 years to acquire this knowledge (which I try to add to day by day!) and an enthusiast cannot be expected to learn it overnight. But, hopefully, Jim Murray's Whisky Bible will help...!

SCORE CHART

Within the parentheses () is the overall score out of 100.

0–50.5 Nothing short of absolutely diabolical.
51–64.5 Nasty and well worth avoiding.
65–69.5 Very unimpressive indeed.
70–74.5 Usually drinkable but don't expect the earth to move.
75–79.5 Average and usually pleasant though sometimes flawed.
80–84.5 Good whisky worth trying.
85–89.5 Very good to excellent whiskies definitely worth buying.
90–93.5 Brilliant.
94–97.5 Superstar whiskies that give us all a reason to live.
98–100 Better than anything I've ever tasted!

KEY TO ABBREVIATIONS & SYMBOLS

% Percentage strength of whisky measured as alcohol by volume. **b** Overall balance and complexity. **bott** Date of bottling. **db** Distillery bottling. In other words, an expression brought out by the owners of the distillery. **dist** Date of distillation or spirit first put into cask. **f** Finish. **n** Nose. **nc** Non-coloured. **ncf** Non-chill-filtered. **sc** Single cask. **t** Taste. ◇ New entry for 2019. ⊙ Retasted – no change. ⊙⊕ Retasted and re-evaluated. **v** Variant WB19-001 Code for Whisky Club bottling.

Finding Your Whisky

Worldwide Malts: Whiskies are listed alphabetically throughout the book. In the case of single malts, the distilleries run A–Z style with distillery bottlings appearing at the top of the list in order of age, starting with youngest first. After age comes vintage. After all the "official" distillery bottlings are listed, next come other bottlings, again in alphabetical order. Single malts without a distillery named (or perhaps named after a dead one) are given their own section, as are vatted malts.

Worldwide Blends: These are simply listed alphabetically, irrespective of which company produces them. So "Black Bottle" appears ahead of "White Horse" and Japanese blends begin with "Ajiwai Kakubin" and end with "Za". In the case of brands being named after companies or individuals the first letter of the brand will dictate where it is listed. So William Grant, for instance, will be found under "W" for William rather "G" for Grant.

Bourbon/Rye: One of the most confusing types of whiskey to list because often the name of the brand bears no relation to the name of the distillery that made it. Also, brands may be sold from one company to another, or shortfalls in stock may see companies buying bourbons from another. For that reason all the brands have been listed alphabetically with the name of the bottling distiller being added at the end.

Irish Whiskey: There are four types of Irish whiskey: (i) pure pot still; (ii) single malt; (iii) single grain and (iv) blended. Some whiskies may have "pure pot still" on the label, but are actually single malts. So check both sections.

Bottle Information

As no labels are included in this book I have tried to include all the relevant information you will find on the label to make identification of the brand straightforward. Where known I have included date of distillation and bottling. Also the cask number for further recognition. At the end of the tasting notes I have included the strength and, if known, number of bottles (sometimes abbreviated to btls) released and in which markets.

PRICE OF WHISKY

You will notice that Jim Murray's Whisky Bible very rarely refers to the cost of a whisky. This is because the book is a guide to quality and character rather than the price tag attached. Also, the same whiskies are sold in different countries at varying prices due to market forces and variations of tax, so there is a relevance factor to be considered. Equally, much depends on the size of an individual's pocket. What may appear a cheap whisky to one could be an expensive outlay to another. With this in mind prices are rarely given in the Whisky Bible.

How to Taste Whisky

It is of little use buying a great whisky, spending a comparative fortune in doing so, if you don't get the most out of it.

So when giving whisky tastings, no matter how knowledgeable the audience may be I take them through a brief training schedule in how to nose and taste as I do for each sample included in the Whisky Bible.

I am aware that many aspects are contrary to what is being taught by distilleries' whisky ambassadors. And for that we should be truly thankful. However, at the end of the day we all find our own way of doing things. If your old tried and trusted technique suits you best, that's fine by me. But I do ask you try out the instructions below at least once to see if you find your whisky is talking to you with a far broader vocabulary and clearer voice than it once did. I strongly suspect you will be pleasantly surprised – amazed, even - by the results.

Amusingly, someone tried to teach me my own tasting technique some years back in an hotel bar. He was not aware who I was and I didn't let on. It transpired that a friend of his had been to one of my tastings a few years earlier and had passed on my words of "wisdom". I'd be lying if I said I didn't smile when he informed me it was called "The Murray Method." It was the first time I had heard the phrase... though certainly not the last!

"THE MURRAY METHOD"

1. Drink a black, unsweetened, coffee or chew on 90% minimum cocoa chocolate to cleanse the palate, especially of sugars.

2. Find a room free from distracting noises as well as the aromas of cooking, polish, flowers and other things which will affect your understanding and appreciation of the whisky.

3. Make sure you have not recently washed your hands using heavily scented soap or are wearing a strong aftershave or perfume.

4. Use a tulip shaped glass with a stem. This helps contain the alcohols at the bottom yet allows the more delicate whisky aromas you are searching for to escape.

5. Never add ice. This tightens the molecules and prevents flavours and aromas from being released. It also makes your whisky taste bitter. There is no better way to get the least from your whisky than by freezing it.

6. Likewise, ignore any advice given to put the bottle in the fridge before drinking.

7. Don't add water! Whatever anyone tells you. It releases aromas but can mean the whisky falls below 40%... so it is no longer whisky. Also, its ability to release flavours and aromas diminishes quite quickly. Never add ridiculous "whisky rocks" or other supposed tasting aids.

8. Warm the undiluted whisky in the glass to body temperature before nosing or tasting. Hence the stem, so you can cradle in your hand and curve the curve of the thin base. This excites the molecules and unravels the whisky in your glass, maximising its sweetness and complexity.

9. Keep an un-perfumed hand over the glass to keep the aromas in while you warm. Only a minute or two after condensation appears at the top of your glass should you extend your arms, lift your covering hand and slowly bring the glass to your nose, so the alcoholic vapours have been released before the glass reaches your face.

10. Never stick your nose in the glass. Or breathe in deeply. Allow glass to gently touch your top lip, leaving a small space below the nose. Move from nostril to nostril, breathing normally. This allows the aromas to break up in the air, helping you find the more complex notes.

11. Take no notice of your first mouthful. This is a marker for your palate.

12. On second, bigger mouthful, close your eyes to concentrate on the flavour and chew the whisky - moving it continuously around the palate. Keep your mouth slightly open to let air in and alcohol out. It helps if your head is tilted back very slightly.

13. Occasionally spit – if you have the willpower! This helps your senses to remain sharp for the longest period of time.

14. Look for the balance of the whisky. That is, which flavours counter others so none is too dominant. Also, watch carefully how the flavours and aromas change in the glass over time.

15. Assess the "shape" and mouth feel of the whisky, its weight and how long its finish. And don't forget to concentrate on the first flavours as intensely as you do the last. Look out for the way the sugars, spices and other characteristics form.

16. Never make your final assessment until you have tasted it a third or fourth time.

17. Be honest with your assessment: don't like a whisky because someone (yes, even me!), or the label, has tried to convince you how good it is.

18. When you cannot discriminate between one whisky and another, stop immediately.

Immortal Drams:
The Whisky Bible
Winners 2004-2018

	World Whisky of the Year	Second Finest Whisky of the Year	Third Finest Whisky of the Year
2004	George T Stagg	N/A	N/A
2005	George T Stagg	N/A	N/A
2006	George T Stagg	Glen Moray 1986 Cask 4696	N/A
2007	Old Parr Superior 18 Years Old	Buffalo Trace Twice Barreled	N/A
2008	Ardbeg 10 Years Old	The Ileach Single Islay Malt Cask Strength	N/A
2009	Ardbeg Uigedail	Nikka Whisky Single Coffey Malt 12 Years	N/A
2010	Sazerac Rye 18 Years Old (bottled Fall 2008)	Ardbeg Supernova	Amrut Fusion
2011	Ballantine's 17 Years Old	Thomas H Handy Sazerac Rye (129 proof)	Wiliam Larue Weller (134.8 proof)
2012	Old Pulteney Aged 21 Years	George T Stagg	Parker's Heritage Collection Aged 10 Years
2013	Thomas H Handy Sazerac Rye (128.6 proof)	William Larue Weller (133.5 proof)	Ballantine's 17 Years Old
2014	Glenmorangie Ealanta 1993	William Larue Weller (123.4 proof)	Thomas Handy Sazerac Rye (132.4 proof)
2015	Yamazaki Single Malt Sherry 2013	William Larue Weller (68.1 abv)	Sazerac Rye 18 Years Old (bottled Fall 2013)
2016	Crown Royal Northern Harvest Rye	Pikesville 110 Proof Straight Rye	Midleton Dair Ghaelach
2017	Booker's Rye 13 Years, 1 Month, 12 Days	Glen Grant 18 Year Old	William Larue Weller (134.6 proof)
2018	Colonel E.H. Taylor 4 Grain Aged 10 Years	Redbreast Aged 21 Years	Glen Grant 18 Year Old

Who has won this year? Find out on page 14

Bible Thumping
For its Price is
Far Above Rubies...

It seems like a long time ago now, but I remember the days when you bought a bottle of whisky...and then drank it.

Now I know the sentence above will probably cause a little bit of scratching of heads or the coming to a conclusion that this is just the work of a writer using a vivid imagination and setting out to shock. But, no, I can assure you: it really did happen.

This is how it worked. You would walk into a shop, one which normally sold wine and/or beer and ask what whiskies they had. Usually you would be shown a number of blends and among them might be sticking out a Glenfiddich or a Glenmorangie. On rare days you might even see a Macallan, Talisker or Laphroaig under the mounting dust. Or if the shop did well in its sale of Bells and had a good relationship with the "rep", an Inchgower, Blair Athol or Dufftown might be offered to you. Now you knew these were single malts and were a bit special because they were double the price; even possibly more.

So you would take them home, unwrap them from the layers of tissue paper in which they have been carefully rolled, find yourself a suitable glass, somewhere quiet, open the bottle and settle down to see what all the fuss was about.

If you were in Scotland or somewhere with a slightly higher class wine merchants to hand – mine in the early 1980s would have been on Cross Street, Manchester - then you might spot the chocolate brown and cream labels of Gordon and MacPhail displaying weird and unpronounceable names from years that weren't far off when I was born. And you would take a couple of these home each week after opening your wallet to hand over banknotes (that was a thing made of paper which had different values printed on them) and your journey of discovery would continue.

The best fun of all was when I was driving along the backroads of Scotland, in those days barely much above farm tracks, and would turn up at some lonely village with its inevitable store. And there on ancient, creaking shelves behind the store keeper would be a number of bottles, the odd one carrying the all too familiar Gordon and MacPhail label, and your heart would quicken if it was of a type long obsolete. Because it meant the whisky had sat on that shelf for maybe a decade and contained liquid from a distillery long closed and at exactly the same price it had been when in a moment of youthful madness and confidence, the storekeeper had agreed to stock it thinking certain people would beat a path to his door. They hadn't and there it still was, as much a part of the shop's furniture as the till but now with a decade's worth of grime to be wiped away with a degree of embarrassment, handed over.... and still you would get change from a ten-pound note.

So, after storing the bottle safely away in the car where it was least likely to get smashed, you would take it home to be examined as might a creature in Area 51. And after cracking the cap open you were breathing in the aromas of yesteryear, a malt distilled in the early 1960s from a distillery now as unloved as the bottle had been on the shelves for all those years.

The thought of keeping it never even crossed my mind. The whisky had to be tasted and experienced. Oh, how well I remember in the late 1980s finding a bottle Glenugie in circumstances almost exactly as described above. So I drove to Peterhead, found what little remained of the distillery, located in a cruelly taunting situation close to a prison in just the same way the Manchester brewery Boddington's was. And on the remains of the site breached the bottle and slowly savoured the distillery's spirit both figuratively and physically.

There was no other consideration other than to taste the whisky, to experience the moments. I can taste it now....

Likewise, some 35 years ago I remember bringing from the Port Ellen Co-op my usual two cases of Ardbeg 10-year-old, which itself represented a not insignificant percentage of the Ardbeg allowed to be sold in the UK: in those days it nearly all went to Italy.

Rather than hoarding the whisky for myself, I kept a case of six bottles to last me through the year. And took the other case of this then entirely unknown and unappreciated balm of the gods to my newspaper office where I would sell it at the same price I paid for it – simply because I wanted others to share in my joy...

One Sunday my News Editor came to my desk to collect his bottle and handed over the £10 which I had paid for the bottle. A few moments later the voice of a female colleague on the desk opposite bristled over my typewriter with north-eastern disgust: "You bastard! You unspeakable, greedy bastard!"

Puzzled, I asked what the matter could be. My enquiry was met by another volley of expletives and then accusations. I had, I was bluntly told, been ripping off my colleagues.

I asked how. The answer was equally blunt: "No fucking whisky costs £10! How can you sit there and rip off your friends and colleagues?" Her voice was now raised with an emotional blend of undisguised anger, indignation and odium and the usual hubbub of the newsroom was beginning to die down to a bemused and quizzical whisper.

I reminded my colleague that, being a journalist, it probably wouldn't be a bad idea if she actually checked her facts before making such accusations. I suggested, surprisingly gently in the circumstances, that maybe a call to the Co-op at Port Ellen might confirm that I was, indeed, passing on the whisky for the same amount I had paid for it.

My colleague considered this for a moment or two, picked up the phone put it down again before dialling, got up walked around the desk and then, being a well-built lass, punched me off my chair splitting my lip open....to the shocked silence of a national newspaper newsroom.

So, as you can see: I have been spilling blood for the good name of whisky for nearly four decades now....

When I privately tell people in the industry of that story, they thought I was mad to allow such a truly great whisky to go to others: I should have kept it all for myself. Indeed, when I became Ardbeg's first designated blender 20 years ago I found that the highest quality stocks were held in barrels dating back to 1974 – the ten-year-old Ardbeg that had caused all the controversy was actually from sister casks of that year's output.

Even since that last Whisky Bible was written I was asked after after a tasting I had given if I would part with any of those 1984 bottled 10-year-old and was offered the equivalent of about £3,500 for each one. Oh, had my erstwhile, pugilistic colleague been beside me then to witness such an offer made.

But that wasn't really the point. I had not bought those two cases to make money on them. They were not an investment. I had purchased them to enjoy, and so I could share my enjoyment with others: this whisky was so good, I remember thinking at the time, I really want to convert others into whisky drinkers.

And this, now, is the problem. Ten years ago, maybe one in 50 of the questions asked me at the end of one of my shows would have been about which bottles to buy as an investment. Now, depending which country I am in, that question may crop up one in five times.

Or I would stand there while a whisky enthusiast would reel off a list of whiskies that he had bought in the last few years, often involving Macallan, Ardbeg, Highland Park, Glen Grant and other glittering names from the Scottish highlands and islands and usually at ages which defied the distilleries' natural life expectancy. Having mentally noted the best I could of this roll call of extraordinary whiskies, I would ask which of those this person personally preferred. Usually the reply would be: "Oh, I have not tasted them. I have collected them. I can't afford to taste them." Once, while I was writing this Bible, it was: "No, I've bought them as an investment. I thought I'd ask you which ones I should keep longest as they would be most likely to rise in value."

Naturally, the whisky industry has noticed this trend also. So the prices for older whiskies have risen exponentially. Be they independent bottlers or the distillers themselves, they know that a fancy bottle of something relatively ancient, and of one of the prized malts in particular, can fetch amounts of money now which they would not have dreamed possible five, certainly ten years ago.

Without question the rise of the Chinese economy and that country's love affair with whisky has much to do with that. As has diminishing stocks of whiskies at certain ages due to greater and unforeseen demand.

It really does not seem that long ago I was traipsing around warehouses with blenders and distillery managers. Where there would be barrels of 20-, 30-, 40-year old whiskies and they had no idea what to do with them as the demand simply wasn't there for older stock; nor the confidence that they could sell it if bottled. Also, the quality varied, so there was a matter of trust in the product. I remember one blender looking at a stack of whiskies nearing 30 years and saying to me: "My god! Our 15-year-old's going to taste a bit special for the next couple of years".

Once, I used to attend whisky auctions, or, rather, get someone to represent me and bid incognito on my behalf. There is no point now. I bought the whiskies to taste, learn from and enjoy. Now I am up against the investor who will pay way above the actual worth in terms of quality. So now some whiskies have gone the same way as stamps or paintings. Something to be kept privately or on public display to impress. I have no great problem with that as we should live in a society where people can choose to spend their own money as they wish. But I have visited some private collections and one can only stand there and admire not just the whiskies, but the care and devotion – and very considerable expense – that has gone into turning what was once an ordinary room into an elegant shrine for Scotland's many malts. The thing I have noticed, though, was that when I first started being shewn around these libraries, I was encouraged to taste from the bottles, most, if not all, of which would be open and the contents at widely varying levels. In the last couple of years, the bottles have remained sealed and my offering would be from a choice of maybe one or two whiskies which had been opened but were not part of the collection.

And another thing I have noticed in recent years has been that these private display shelves are now no longer the domain of Scotch single malts. Increasingly Japanese single malts have barged their way into the frame, and Kentucky bourbon and rye also. But mainly Japanese. I know that when I awarded the Yamazaki World Whisky of the Year back in 2015 its price had gone up tenfold in a week and by a factor of 50 by the end of the year. Last month while in Shanghai someone asked me to value their collection of Japanese malt and rare, top range blends: I declined, telling them, honestly, I wouldn't even know where to start. And joked that by the time I'd finished, my valuation would be out of date. When I asked him if he drank any, he said he loved Hibiki 17. But now that had been discontinued due to stock shortages, he was trying to find as many as he could: not to drink, but put to add to his investment collection. "I'll probably never drink it again," he said...then told me he had six bottles to his name. I found that quite sad on more than one level.

Surely, this is not what whisky should be about. Yes, I have told people to hold on to a whisky and not open it. But then only because it was sherry cask from a distillery that would almost certainly be offering up some sulphurous rubbish rather than a dram that could be properly explored and savoured. Then, yes, by all means hang on to it and try and get a return.

But for whiskies that pre-date the sulphur treated sherry butts – or have not undergone ridiculous "freshening" in sulphur-tainted casks – then please, I beg you, try the whisky for what it was intended: drinking. That, surely, is what whisky is about: discovering flavours and nuances you could barely imagine possible, or comparing one distillery against another. Or enjoying the blossoming of malt through the years until it has reached a point of no return. No amount of money can make up for moments as magical and mercurial as that.

Oh, how a part of me mourns for those days when people would hunt for a whisky not to see how much money they could make on it in three or five-years-time. But for when they would gather up a group of like-minded friends and they would open the bottle like Howard Carter would breach a newly discovered tomb in Valley of the Kings, peer inside and find what hidden and long-forgotten jewels may be discovered.

Certainly the days of visiting little corner shops and unearthing forgotten gems are over. But the chance to discover is still there. Providing you are brave and your valuation of a whisky is determined by the pleasure, the mystery and mastery it offers you on the nose and palate, not how much money you can eventually make from it....

Jim Murray's Whisky Bible Awards 2019

All things come to those who wait, so they say. And that can certainly be said for Jim Murray's Whisky Bible 2019 World Whisky of the Year, William Larue Weller.

This immense, wheated bourbon has three times previously been Whisky Bible runner up. And twice came third: together, an extraordinary record. But the coveted top prize had so far eluded it...until now. Even more remarkable was that last year it didn't make the top three at all, a very rare event. But this year it re-ticked the boxes it had failed twelve months earlier and replaced its Buffalo Trace stablemate, Col E. H. Taylor, as the World's Finest.

This year was an extraordinary whisky judging year in many way. The far above average age and quality of of the 1,263 whiskies tasted meant that it took me nearly two months longer than last year to complete my analysis: the more complex the whisky the greater time required to fully understand its nuances and idiosyncrasies. Even the Canadians came up with an astonishing 41-year-old. Yet, that said, for the first time in several years only five whiskies made it to the final taste off; in other words, only five out of 1,263 whiskies had that indefinable star quality which put them on a platform capable of challenging for the title of the world's very finest. Those missing out on the prizes were the Irish Pot Still Redbreast 12 Cast Strength and the Ballantine's 17, that most gentle of irremovable forces among Scottish blends.

The battle for third place between the rye and the Irish pot still was, perhaps, from a technical and professional viewpoint, the most fascinating. Rye and pure Irish Pot Still have a number of similar characteristics. However, it was the slightest over-elaboration of the gorgeously unsullied sherry butts which did for the Redbreast: the richness of the fruit very slightly obscured the crisp tendencies of the Pot Still just a little too enthusiastically, while the Thomas Handy was able to show the grain to the max, thereby coming home in third place almost literally by a nose. The margin was a fraction of a fraction, but in this rarified atmosphere of near whisky perfection, that is all it takes.

Once more the stunning Glen Grant 18-years-old single malt from Speyside carried the banner for Scotland, claiming runner-up prize for the second year running, and underlining how the delicacy of this distillery's malt depends on the usage of bourbon cask.

And, on the subject of Scotland, what a year for the Islay distilleries! Official bottlings from Laphroaig, Lagavulin and Bowmore have won major Whisky Bible awards: Laphroaig, indeed, has come away with two gongs with their Lore for the No Age Statement category and their timeless 10-year-old for the up to 10 years section. Another mainstay brand, Lagavulin 12, carried off the 11-15 years section. While a mind-blowing 19-year-old single cask from Bowmore was one of the highlights of my tasting year. And, not to be outdone, another island whisky, Talisker, ran away with the 22-27 Years segment with a sublime 25-year-old. Even the dead Islay distillery Port Ellen got in on the act with Gleann Mor's staggering over 33-years-old bottling. This was, without question, a vintage year for peat lovers.

2019 World Whisky of the Year
William Larue Weller 128.2 Proof

Second Finest Whisky in the World
Glen Grant Aged 18 Years

Third Finest Whisky in the World
Thomas Handy Sazerac Rye 127.2 Proof

Single Cask of the Year
Blanton's Gold Edition Single Barrel

SCOTCH

Scotch Whisky of the Year
Glen Grant Aged 18 Years Rare Edition
Single Malt of the Year (Multiple Casks)
Glen Grant Aged 18 Years Rare Edition
Single Malt of the Year (Single Cask)
The Last Drop Glenrothes 1969 Cask 16207
Scotch Blend of the Year
Ballantine's 17 Years Old
Scotch Grain of the Year
Berry Bros & Rudd Cambus 26 Years Old
Scotch Vatted Malt of the Year
Collectivum XXVIII

Single Malt Scotch

No Age Statement
Laphroaig Lore
10 Years & Under (Multiple Casks)
Laphroaig 10 Years Old
10 Years & Under (Single Cask)
Berry Bros & Rudd Ardmore 9 Years Old
11-15 Years (Multiple Casks)
Lagavulin 12 Year Old
11-15 Years (Single Cask)
Cadenhead's Rum Cask Mortlach 14 Years Old
16-21 Years (Multiple Casks)
Glen Grant Aged 18 Years Rare Edition
16-21 Years (Single Cask)
Bowmore Aged 19 Years The Feis Ile Collection
22-27 Years (Multiple Casks)
Talisker 25 Years Old
22-27 Years (Single Cask)
Scotch Malt Whisky Society Glen Grant Cask
9.128 24 Year Old
28-34 Years (Multiple Casks)
Convalmore 32 Year Old
28-34 Years (Single Cask)
Gleann Mor Port Ellen Aged Over 33 Years
35-40 Years (Multiple Casks)
Benromach 39 Year Old 1977 Vintage
35-40 Years (Single Cask)
Glenfarclas The Family Casks 1979
41 Years & Over (Multiple Casks)
Tomatin Warehouse 6 Collection 1972
41 Years & Over (Single Cask)
The Last Drop Glenrothes 1969 Cask 16207

BLENDED SCOTCH

No Age Statement (Standard)
Ballantine's Finest
5-12 Years
Johnnie Walker Black Label 12 Years Old
13-18 Years
Ballantine's 17 Years Old
19 - 25 Years
Royal Salute 21 Years Old
26 - 50 Years
Royal Salute 32 Years Old Union of the Crowns

IRISH WHISKEY

Irish Whiskey of the Year
Redbreast Aged 12 Years Cask Strength
Irish Pot Still Whiskey of the Year
Redbreast Aged 12 Years Cask Strength

Irish Single Malt of the Year
Bushmills Distillery Reserve Aged 12 Years
Irish Blend of the Year
Bushmills Black Bush
Irish Single Cask of the Year
The Irishman Aged 17 Years

AMERICAN WHISKEY

Bourbon of the Year
William Larue Weller 128.2 Proof
Rye of the Year
Thomas H. Handy Sazerac 127.2 Proof
US Micro Whisky of the Year
Garrison Brothers Balmorhea
US Micro Whisky of the Year (Runner Up)
Balcones Peated Texas Single Malt

BOURBON

No Age Statement (Multiple Barrels)
Blanton's Gold Edition Single Barrel
No Age Statement (Multiple Barrels)
William Larue Weller
Up To 10 Years
Eagle Rare 10 Years Old
11 - 15 Years
Pappy Van Winkle Family Reserve 15 Years Old
16 - 20 Years
Abraham Bowman Sweet XVI Bourbon
11 Years & Over
Orphan Barrel Rhetoric Aged 24 Years

RYE

No Age Statement
Thomas H. Handy Sazerac 127.2 Proof
Up to 10 Years
Knob Creek Cask Strength
11 Years & Over
Sazerac 18 Years Old

CANADIAN WHISKY

Canadian Whisky of the Year
Canadian Club Chronicles: Issue No. 1 Water of
Windsor Aged 41 Years

JAPANESE WHISKY

Japanese Whisky of the Year
The Hakushu Paul Rusch

EUROPEAN WHISKY

European Whisky of the Year (Multiple)
Nestville Master Blender 8 Years Old Whisky
European Whisky of the Year (Single)
The Norfolk Farmers Single Grain
Whisky (England)

WORLD WHISKIES

Asian Whisky of the Year
Amrut Greedy Angels 8 Years Old (India)
Southern Hemisphere Whisky of the Year
Belgrove Peated Rye (Australia)

**Overall age category and/or section
winners are presented in **bold**.*

The Whisky Bible Liquid Gold Awards (97.5-94)

Jim Murray's Whisky Bible is delighted to again make a point of celebrating the very finest whiskies you can find in the world. So we salute the distillers who have maintained or even furthered the finest traditions of whisky making and taken their craft to the very highest levels. And the bottlers who have brought some of them to us.

After all, there are over 4,600 different brands and expressions listed in this guide and from every corner of the planet. Those which score 94 and upwards represents only a very small fraction of them. These whiskies are, in my view, the élite: the finest you can currently find on the whisky shelves of the world. Rare and precious, they are Liquid Gold.

So it is our pleasure to announce that all those scoring 94 and upwards automatically qualify for the Jim Murray's Whisky Bible Liquid Gold Award. Congratulations!

97.5
Scottish Single Malt
Glenmorangie Ealanta 1993 Vintage
Old Pulteney Aged 21 Years
Scottish Blends
Ballantine's 17 Years Old
Irish Pure Pot Still
Midleton Dair Ghaelach Grinsell's Wood
Ballagtobin Estate
Bourbon
Colonel E.H. Taylor Four Grain Bottled in Bond
George T Stagg
William Larue Weller
William Larue Weller 128.2 Proof
William Larue Weller bott Spring 2001
American Straight Rye
Booker's Rye 13 Years, 1 Month, 12 Days
Pikesville Straight Rye Whiskey aged at least 6 years
Thomas H. Handy Sazerac Straight Rye Whiskey
Canadian Blended
Crown Royal Northern Harvest Rye
Japanese Single Malt
Yamazaki Single Malt Whisky Sherry Cask

97
Scottish Single Malt
Ardbeg 10 Years Old
Bowmore Aged 19 Years The Feis Ile Collection
Glenfiddich 50 Years Old
Glen Grant Aged 18 Years Rare Edition
Gordon & MacPhail Rare Vintage Glen Grant 1957
Scottish Grain
Cambus Aged 40 Years
Xtra Old Particular Cambus 40 Years Old
Scottish Blends
Compass Box The Double Single
Johnnie Walker Blue Label The Casks Edition
The Last Drop 1971 Blended Scotch Whisky
The Last Drop 50 Year Old
Old Parr Superior 18 Years Old
Irish Pure Pot Still
Midleton Dair Ghaelach
Redbreast Aged 12 Years Cask Strength
Redbreast Aged 21 Years
Bourbon
George T. Stagg
George T. Stagg 129.2 Proof
Parker's Heritage Collection Wheated Mash Bill Bourbon Aged 10 Years
William Larue Weller
American Straight Rye
Colonel E.H. Taylor Straight Rye

Thomas H. Handy Sazerac 127.2 Proof
Sazerac Rye 18 Year Old Fall 2013
Sazerac Rye 18 Years Old Spring 2015
Canadian Blended
Canadian Club Chronicles: Issue No. 1 Water of Windsor Aged 41 Years
Crown Royal Northern Harvest Rye
Japanese Single Malt
Nikka Whisky Single Coffey Malt 12 Years
The Yamazaki Single Malt Whisky Mizunara
Taiwanese Single Malt
Kavalan Single Malt Amontillado Sherry

96.5
Scottish Single Malt
Ardbeg 20 Something
Ardbeg 21 Years Old
Ardbeg Corryvreckan
Ardbeg Supernova
Berry Bros & Rudd Ardmore 9 Years Old
Gordon & MacPhail Cask Strength Ardmore 2002
Balblair 1965
Bowmore Black 50 Year Old
Brora Aged 38 Years
Octomore Edition 7.1 Aged 5 years
Caol Ila 30 Year Old
That Boutique-y Whisky Company Clynelish 15 Year Old
Convalmore 32 Year Old
Glencadam Aged 18 Years
The Glendronach Aged 10 Years PX Casks
Cadenhead's Small Batch International Glendullan 20 Year Old
Gordon & MacPhail Rare Vintage Glen Grant 1960
Scotch Malt Whisky Society Cask 9.128 24 Year Old
The Glenlivet Cipher
Glenmorangie Sonnalta PX
Old Particular Glen Moray 25 Years Old
The Last Drop Glenrothes 1968 cask no. 13504
Whisky Illuminati Glentauchers 20 Year Old
Highland Park 50 Years Old
WoodWinters Northern Star 21 Year Old
Berry Bros & Rudd Arran 21 Years Old
Simon Brown Arran Distillery 1997
Kilchoman Private Cask Release
AnCnoc Cutter 20.5 ppm
AnCnoc Rutter 11 ppm
Laphroaig Aged 27 Years
Loch Lomond Organic Aged 17 Years
The Cooper's Choice Lochside 1967 Aged 44 Years

Cadenhead's Rum Cask Mortlach 14 Years Old
Gleann Mor Port Ellen Aged Over 33 Years
Talisker Aged 25 Years
Tomatin 36 Year Old
Tullibardine 1970
Port Askaig 100 Proof
Alos Sansibar Whisky Speyside Region 1975
Glen Castle Aged 28 Years
Scottish Vatted Malt
Compass Box Flaming Heart Fifteenth
Anniversary
Collectivum XXVIII
Scottish Grain
Berry Bros & Rudd Cambus 26 Years Old
Xtra Old Particular Cameronbridge 32 Years Old
The Sovereign Dumbarton 29 Years Old
The Whisky Barrel Dumbarton 30 Year Old
Scottish Blends
The Antiquary Aged 35 Years
The Last Drop 1965
Royal Salute 32 Years Old Union of the
Crowns
Teacher's Aged 25 Years
Irish Pure Pot Still
Powers John's Lane Release
Aged 12 Years
Redbreast Aged 32 Years Dream Cask
Irish Single Malt
Dunville's VR First Edition Aged 15 Years
Single Malt
Bourbon
Blanton's Gold Edition Single Barrel
Blanton's Gold Original Single Barrel
Blanton's Uncut/Unfiltered
Elmer T. Lee Bourbon 1919 - 2013
George T. Stagg 69.05%
George T. Stagg 71.4%
George T. Stagg 69.1%
Virgin Bourbon 7 Years Old
American Straight Rye
Knob Creek Cask Strength
Sazerac Rye 18 Year Old
Thomas H. Handy Sazerac
American Microdistilleries
Balcones Texas Blue Corn Straight Bourbon
Whisky Aged At Least 24 Months
Garrison Brothers Balmorhea
The Notch Aged 12 Years
Japanese Single Malt
Chichibu 'The Peated' 2013
The Hakushu Single Malt Whisky
Sherry Cask
Yamazaki Single Malt Sherry Cask 2016
English Single Malt
The Norfolk Farmers Single Grain Whisky
The Norfolk Single Grain Parched
Welsh Single Malt
Penderyn Icons of Wales No 5/50 Bryn Terfel
Australian Single Malt
Belgrove Distillery Peated Rye Whisky
Limeburners Single Malt Darkest Winter
Indian Single Malt
Amrut Greedy Angels 10 Years Old
Paul John Edited

96
Scottish Single Malt
Gordon & MacPhail Connoisseurs Choice
Aberfeldy 1993
Aberlour A'Bunadh Batch No. 54
Ardbeg 1977
Ardbeg Provenance 1974

Golden Cask Ardmore Aged 17 Years
Old Malt Cask Ardmore Aged 20 Years
Old Malt Cask Ardmore Aged 21 Years
Old Particular Ardmore 21 Years Old
Kingsbury Gold Bowmore 18 Year Old
Bruichladdich Ocotomore 7.1 5 Years Old
Octomore 5 Years Old
Bruichladdich Octomore 7.1 5 Years Old
Gordon & MacPhail Cask Strength
Bunnahabhain 2009
Liquid Treasures Entomology Bunnahabhain
Over 28 Years Old
Caol Ila 18 Year Old
Old Particular Caol Ila 19 Years Old
Gordon & MacPhail Connoisseurs Choice
Clynelish 2004
The Dalmore Candela Aged 50 Years
Gordon & MacPhail Rare Vintage Glen
Albyn 1976
Gordon & MacPhail Cask Strength
Glenburgie 1995
Glenfarclas The Family Casks 1989 S18
Release
Glenfarclas The Family Casks 1998 S18
Release
Kirsch Import Glenfarclas 2008
The Last Drop Glen Garioch 47 Year Old
Glen Grant Aged 10 Years
Gordon & MacPhail Rare Vintage
Glen Grant 1948
Sansibar Whisky Glen Moray 25 Year Old
The Last Drop Glenrothes 1969 cask no. 16207
Cadenhead's Cask Strength Glentauchers
Aged 41 Years
The Glenturret Fly's 16 Masters Edition
That Boutique-y Whisky Company
Glenturret 35 Year Old
Highland Park Loki Aged 15 Years
Highland Park Aged 25 Years
Highland Park 2002
Highland Park Sigurd
Old Particular Arran 20 Years Old
Kilchoman 10 Years Old
Lagavulin 12 Years Old
Laphroaig Lore
Laphroaig PX Cask
Laphroaig Quarter Cask
Scotch Malt Whisky Society Cask 29.191 16
Year Old
Gordon & MacPhail Connoisseurs Choice
Macduff 2004
Old Pulteney Aged 25 Years
Rosebank 25 Years Old
Gordon & MacPhail Rare Vintage Strathisla 1960
The First Editions Teaninich Aged 18 Years
Ledaig Dùsgadh 42 Aged 42 Years
The Cooper's Choice Tormore Sweet & Smoky
Ben Bracken Islay Single Malt 22 Years Old
Lotus Lord 28 Year Old 1988
SaarWhisky Gruwehewwel Edition 3
Scottish Vatted Malt
Compass Box 3 Year Old Deluxe
Glen Castle Blended Malt 1992 Sherry Cask Matured
Scottish Grain
That Boutique-y Whisky Company
Caledonian 29 Year Old
Single Cask Collection Dumbarton 30 Years Old
The Cooper's Choice Garnheath 48 Year Old
Port Dundas 52 Year Old
The Sovereign Blended Grain 28 Years Old
Scottish Blends
Ballantine's Aged 30 Years

Ballantine's Finest
Ballantine's Limited
Grant's Aged 12 Years
Islay Mist Aged 17 Years
Oishii Wisukii Aged 36 Years
Royal Salute 21 Years Old
That Boutique-y Whisky Company
Blended Whisky No. 1 50 Year Old

Irish Pure Pot Still
Powers Aged 12 Years John's Lane Release
Redbreast Aged 12 Years Cask Strength
Redbreast Aged 21 Years

Irish Single Malt
Glendalough 13 Year Old Irish Single Malt
Mizunara Finish
Teeling Whiskey Single Malt Aged 26 Years

Irish Blends
Powers Gold label

Bourbon
1792 High Rye Kentucky Straight Bourbon
Ancient Ancient Age 10 Years Old
Buffalo Trace Experimental Collection
Organic 6 Grain Whiskey 7 Years, 1 Month
Buffalo Trace Single Oak Project Barrel #101
Colonel E.H. Taylor Single Barrel Bottled in Bond
Mayor Pingree Aged 9 Years Straight
Bourbon Whiskey batch no. 16-314
Old Weller Antique 107
Pappy Van Winkle's Family Reserve 15 YO
Parker's Heritage Collection 24 Year Old
Bottled in Bond Bourbon dist Spring 91
Stagg Jr
Very Old Barton 100 Proof
William Larue Weller

American Straight Rye
Bulleit 95 Rye
John David Albert's Taos Lightning
Very Rare 21 YO Barrel 28
Rittenhouse Rye Single Barrel No 19
Sazerac 18 Years Old bott Summer 2017

American Microdistilleries
Balcones Peated Texas Single Malt Aged
26 Months
Balcones True Blue Cask Strength
291 E Colorado Bourbon Whiskey Aged 333 Days
Garrison Brothers Cowboy Bourbon Barrel
Proof Aged Four Years

American/Kentucky Whiskey Blends
High West Double Rye

American White Dog
Buffalo Trace White Dog Rye Mash

Canadian Blended
Crown Royal Noble Collection 13 Year Old
Bourbon Mash
Crown Royal Northern Harvest Rye
Crown Royal Special Reserve
J. P. Wiser's 35 Year Old
Lot No. 40 Rye Whisky

Japanese Single Malt
Paul Rusch 120th Anniversary of Birth
ePower Komagatake
The Yamazaki Single Malt Aged 18 Years

Japanese Single Grain
Nikka Coffey Malt Whisky

English Single Malt
Hicks & Healey Cornish Whiskey 2004
The English Whisky Co. Chapter 14

Welsh Single Malt
Penderyn Madeira Finish
Penderyn Single Cask Tawny Portwood

Austrian Single Malt
J.H. 13 Years Old Single Malt

Belgian Single Malt
Belgian Owl Single Malt Intense 41 Months
Belgian Owl Single Malt Whisky The
Private Angels Aged 36 Months

Czech Republic Single Malt
Gold Cock Single Malt Whisky 2008 Virgin
Oak

French Single Malt
Kornog Saint Erwan 2017

German Single Malt
Blaue Maus New Make

Australian Single Malt
The Good Convict Port Cask
Heartwood @*$% · &*
Heartwood Calm Before The Storm 2009
Heartwood Shade of Night Single Malt
Redlands Distillery Single Malt
Timboon Single Malt Whisky 2010
Timboon Single Malt Whisky Port
Expression

Indian Single Malt
Amrut Greedy Angels 8 Years Old
Amrut Greedy Angels 10 Years Old
Paul John Kanya
Paul John Select Cask Peated

95.5
Scottish Single Malt
Ardbeg An Oa
Ardbeg Grooves Committee Release
Kingsbury Gold Ardmore 6 Year Old 2008
Old Particular Ardmore 16 Years Old
Hunter Laing's Old & Rare Auchentoshan
Aged 24 Years
Balblair 2000 2nd Release
Gordon & MacPhail Discovery Range
Balblair Aged 12 Years
The Single Malts of Scotland Balblair 19
Years Old 1997
Fadandel.dk Ben Nevis 21 Years Old
The BenRiach Aged 12 Years Matured In
Sherry Wood
The BenRiach Aged 18 Years Dunder
Benromach 30 Years Old
Benromach Organic 2010
Bowmore 20 Years Old 1997
Dramfool 13 Port Charlotte 2001 Aged 15
Years
Caol Ila Aged 15 Years
Caol Ila Aged 25 Years
Gordon & MacPhail Connoisseurs Choice
Caol Ila 1990
Kingsbury Gold Caol Ila 21 Years Old
Xtra Old Particular Islay Caol Ila 36 Years Old
Xtra Old Particular Clynelish 21 Years Old
The Dalmore Visitor Centre Exclusive
Old Malt Cask Glencadam Aged 19 Years
Gordon & MacPhail Connoisseurs Choice
Glendullan 2004
Glenfarclas 105
Glenfarclas 1994
The Glenfiddich Unique Solera Reserve
Aged 15 Years
Glenfiddich Project XX
Glengoyne 25 Year Old
Glengoyne 25 Year Old
The Glenlivet Archive 21 Years of Age
The Glenlivet Nàdurra First Fill Selection
The Glenlivet Nàdurra Peated Whisky Cask
Finish Batch No. PW0715
Cadenhead's Single Cask International
Glenlossie 23 Years Old

Glenmorangie 25 Years Old
Glenmorangie Grand Vintage 1993
Glenmorangie Private Edition 9 Spios
Scotch Malt Whisky Society Cask 35.185
Cadenhead's Authentic Collection
Glen Ord 11 Year Old
   Scotch Malt Whisky Society Cask 3092 24 Year Old
   The Last Drop Glenrothes 1968 cask no. 13508
   The Last Drop Glenrothes 1969 cask no. 16203
Cadenhead's Sherry Cask Glen Scotia 15
Year Old
   Old Particular Glentauchers 20 Years Old
   Old Particular Glenturret 28 Years Old
   Old Particular Highland Glenturret 28
Years Old
   Gordon & MacPhail Rare Old Glenury Royal 1984
   Highland Park Aged 18 Years
   Acla Special Selection No. 4 Highland Park
24 Years Old
   Kilchoman 100% Islay 5th edition
AnCnoc 1999
Lagavulin Aged 8 Years
Lagavulin 12 Year Old 57.7%
Lagavulin 12 Year Old 56.5%
Dramfool Avian Gull 8 Year Old
The Whisky Barrel Isle of Islay 10 Year Old
That Boutique-y Whisky Company
Linkwood 26 Year Old
   Hunter Laing's Old & Rare Longmorn Aged
30 Years
   The Macallan Fine Oak 12 Years Old
   The Macallan Oscuro
   Spirit of Caledonia Macduff 9 Years Old
   Old Pulteney Aged 15 Years
   Rosebank 21 Year Old
   Cù Bòcan Highland Single Malt 1989 Vintage
   Scotch Malt Whisky Society Cask 11.32
   Elements of Islay OC5
The Whisky Agency Speyside Region
Single Malt 1973

Scottish Vatted Malt
   Compass Box The Lost Blend
   Compass Box The Spice Tree
   Glen Castle Blended Malt 1992 Sherry Cask
Matured
   Wemyss Malts Spice King Batch Strength
Scottish Grain
   Glen Fahrn Airline No. 17 Cambus 1991
   MacAlabur Cambus 25 Years Old
   That Boutique-y Whisky Company Girvan
52 Year Old
   The Pearls of Scotland North of Scotland 1971
Scottish Blends
   Ballantine's Aged 30 Years
   The Chivas 18 Ultimate Cask Collection
First Fill American Oak
   Chivas Regal Aged 25 Years
   Glenalba Aged 34 Years Sherry Cask Finish
   Johnnie Walker Black Label 12 Years Old
   Royal Salute "62 Gun Salute"
Irish Pure Pot Still
   Bushmills Distillery Reserve Aged 12 Years
   Redbreast Aged 12 Years Cask Strength B1/13
Irish Single Malt
   The Tyrconnell Single Cask 11 Year Old
   Bushmills Aged 21 Years
   Acla Special Selection No. 6 County of
Antrim 24 Years Old
   Eiling Lim Irish Single Malt
22 Years Old 1991
   The Irishman Aged 17 Years
   Teeling Whiskey Single Malt Aged 24 Years

Bourbon
   Abraham Bowman Limited Edition Viriginia
Sweet XVI Bourbon
   Blade and Bow 22 Year Old
   Blanton's Single Barrel
   Buffalo Trace Single Oak Project Barrel #27
   Buffalo Trace Single Oak Project Barrel #30
   Buffalo Trace Single Oak Project Barrel #63
   Buffalo Trace Single Oak Project Barrel #183
   Charter 101
   Eagle Rare Aged 10 Years
   Elijah Craig Barrel Proof Bourbon 12 Years
   Knob Creek Aged 9 Years
   Parker's Heritage Collection 24 Year Old
Bottled in Bond Bourbon dist Fall 90
   Weller Antique 107
   Willet Pot Still Reserve
American Straight Rye
   George Dickel Rye
   Michter's No. 1 Straight Rye
   Michter's Single Barrel Kentuck Straight
Rye 10 Years Old
   Sazerac 18 Years Old bott Spring 2016
   Sazerac Kentucky Straight Rye 18 Years Old
   Sazerac Rye
   Thomas H. Handy Sazerac 63.45%
   Thomas H. Handy Sazerac 64.6%
American Straight Wheat
   Parker's Heritage Collection Original Batch
Kentucky Straight Wheat Whiskey Aged
13 Years
American Microdistilleries
   291 E Colorado 100% Rye Malt Whiskey
Aged 291 Days
   291 M Colorado Whiskey Rye Malt
   Hillrock Single Malt Whiskey
   Iron Smoke Apple Wood Smoked Whiskey
batch no. 10
   Reservoir Distillery Rye Whiskey
   Stranahan's Snowflake Cab Franc
American/Kentucky Whiskey Blends
   High West Campfire
Canadian Single Malt
   Lohin McKinnon Peated Single Malt Whisky
Canadian Blended
   Alberta Premium
   Crown Royal Northern Harvest Rye
   Forty Creek Port Wood Reserve
   Gibson's Finest Rare Aged 18 Years
   Masterson's 10 Year Old Straight Rye
Whiskey
Japanese Single Malt
   Ichiro's Malt Aged 20 Years
Japanese Single Grain
   Kawasaki Single Grain
Austrian Single Malt
   Peter Affenzeller Single Malt Whisky 7
Years Old
English Single Malt
   Bimber Single Malt New-Make Test Batch
Sample
Welsh Single Malt
   Penderyn Legend
   Penderyn Single Cask Rich Madeira
German Single Malt
   Valerie Single Malt Amarone Cask Strength
   Derrina Purpur Ur-Weizen Schwarzwälder
   The Glen Els Claret Aged 5 Years
Liechtenstein Single Malt
   Telser Liechtenstein Single Malt X+1 Pinot Noir
Slovakian Single Malt
   Nestville Master Blender 8 Years Old Whisky

Swedish Single Malt
Gute Single Malt Whisky
Smögen Svensk Single Malt Single Cask 18
Swiss Single Malt
Langatun Cardeira Cask Finish Single Malt
Langatun Old Deer Cask Strength
Langatun Sherry Cask Finish
Australian Single Malt
Belgrove Distillery Rye Whisky
Heartwood 2 of /3 Tasmanian Malt Whisky
Indian Blends
Rendezvous

95 (New Entries Only)
Scottish Single Malt
Ardbeg Grooves
Spirit of Caledonia Ben Nevis 18 Years Old
Cadenhead's Bowmore 16 Years Old
Edradour 13 Year Old
Gordon & MacPhail Connoisseurs Choice Glendullan 1993
Glenfarclas The Family Casks 1979 S18 Release
Glenfarclas The Family Casks 1986 S18 Release
Glen Grant Aged 12 Years
Fadandel.dk Glen Grant Aged 22 Years
Scotch Malt Whisky Society Cask 9.140
Glen Scotia 18 Year Old
Fadandel.dk Glentauchers 19 Years Old
Scotch Malt Whisky Society Cask 63.46
Gordon & MacPhail Connoisseurs Choice Highland Park 1999 Cask No. 4265
Old Particular Laphroaig 18 Years Old
Inchmoan 1992 Peated
Endangered Drams Macduff 19 Year Old
Gordon & MacPhail Connoisseurs Choice Pulteney 1998
Gordon & MacPhail Connoisseurs Choice Strathmill 2004
Old Ballantruan Aged 15 Years
Elements of Islay C110
Port Askaig 14 Year Old Bourbon Cask
Scottish Grain
The First Editions Girvan Aged 38 Years
Cave Aquila A Knight's Dram Invergordon 44 Years Old
Irish Single Malt
Bushmills Single Malt The Steamship Collection #3 Bourbon Cask
Acla Special Selection No. 2 Somewhere in Ireland 24 Years Old
Teeling Whiskey Brabazon Bottling Single Malt Series 02
Bourbon
Blanton's Single Barrel
Elijah Craig Barrel Proof Kentucky Straight Bourbon
Orphan Barrel Rhetoric Aged 24 Years
Pappy Van Winkle's Family Reserve 20 Years Old
Rock Hill Farms Single Barrel Bourbon
American Microdistilleries
Bainbridge Battle Point Two Islands Organic Wheat Whiskey
77 Whiskey Bonded Rye & Corn Aged 4 Years
Cooper's Legacy Bourbon Whiskey Grant's Recipe
291 Barrel Proof Colorado Whiskey Aged Less Than 2 Years
A.D. Law Secale Straight Rye Whiskey
Other American Whiskey
Basil Hayden's Two by Two Rye
English Single Malt
Bimber Single Malt Test Batch Sample 22 Months Old

Cotswolds Single Malt Whisky Inaugural Release
Cotswolds Single Malt Whisky 2014 Odyssey Barley Batch No. 02/2017
Cotswolds Single Malt Whisky 2014 Odyssey Barley Batch No. 03/2018
The English Whisky Co. Single Cask Unpeated Bourbon Cask
Belgian Single Malt
Belgian Owl Single Malt 12.5 Years Old
Danish Single Malt
Stauning Web Kaos
Finnish Single Malt
Teerenpeli Islay Cask
French Single Malt
Glann Ar Mor Maris Otter Barley
German Single Malt
Rieger & Hofmeister Schwäbischer Rye Roggenmalz-Whisky
The Nine Springs Single Malt Whisky Peated Breeze Edition
Australian Single Malt
Belgrove Distillery Rye Whisky 10% Rye
Timboon Single Malt Whisky Christie's Cut

94.5 (New Entries Only)
Scottish Single Malt
Gordon & MacPhail Connoisseurs Choice Aberfeldy 2003
The Duchess Ardbeg Malin 25 Year Old
Auchentoshan The Bartender's Malt
Old Particular Auchentoshan 20 Years Old
Balblair 1991 3rd Release
Kingsbury Gold Ben Nevis 20 Years Old
Scotch Malt Whisky Society Cask 50.95
Hidden Spirits Lochindaal 10 Year Old
Gordon & MacPhail Cask Strength Caol Ila 2006
Glenfarclas The Family Casks 1990 S18 Release
Glenfarclas The Family Casks 2002 S18 Release
Glenmorangie Grand Vintage 1991
Scotch Malt Whisky Society Cask 125.74 11 Year Old
The Whisky Chamber Glenrothes 21 Years Old 1996
Glen Scotia Aged 10 Years Peated
Gordon & MacPhail Connoisseurs Choice Glen Spey 1995
Gordon & MacPhail Connoisseurs Choice Highland Park 1999 Cask No. 4262
Gordon & MacPhail Connoisseurs Choice Highland Park 2004
Golden Cask Arran Aged 21 Years
Kingsbury Gold Linkwood 25 Years Old
Gordon & MacPhail Distillery Label Longmorn 2003
Old Particular Miltonduff 23 Years Old
Hunter Laing's Old & Rare Port Ellen Aged 33 Years
The Loch Fyne Springbank 29 Year Old
Gordon & MacPhail Cask Strength Ledaig 2004
The Whisky Cask Company Tormore 21 Year Old
Elements of Islay Lg7
Glen Castle Islay Single Malt 1990
Scottish Vatted Malt
Le Gus't Selection X Speyside Blended Malt 39 Years Old
Scottish Grain
Cadenhead's Single Cask International Invergordon 43 Years Old
Berry Bros & Rudd North British 20 Years Old
Scottish Blends
Buchanan's Master

Bourbon
Blanton's Single Barrel
Colonel E.H. Taylor Small Batch Bottled in Bond
Eagle Rare 17 Years Old bott Summer 2017
Elmer T Lee Single Barrel
Old Forester
Pappy Van Winkle's Family Reserve 23 Years Old

American Straight Rye
Colonel E.H. Taylor Straight Rye Bottled in Bond

American Microdistilleries
Balcones Texas Blue Corn Bourbon Aged At Least 30 Months
Balcones True Blue Straight 100 Proof

American White Dog
Buffalo Trace White Dog Wheated Mash

Canadian Blended
Crown Royal Bourbon Mash Bill

English Single Malt
The English Whisky Co. Original

Welsh Single Malt
Penderyn Single Cask Ex-Ruby Port 2007 Vintage

Belgian Single Malt
Belgian Owl Single Malt 42 Months
Belgian Owl Single Malt Intense 42 Months

Danish Single Malt
Mosgaard New Make Spirit Organic

Finnish Single Malt
Teerenpeli Peated New Make

French Single Malt
Glann Ar Mor 2018
Glenn ar Mor Maris Otter Barley 2017
Kornog Saint Ivy 2017
Elsass Single Malt Whisky Premium Aged 8 Years

German Single Malt
Finch Single Malt Kronberger Genuss-Messe 2017 4 Years & 353 Days
The Spirit of St. Kilian Single Malt Batch No. 2 15 Months Old

Swedish Single Malt
Spirit of Hven Seven Stars No. 6:1 Mizar

Indian Single Malt
Amrut Double Cask
Cadenhead's Paul John 5 Years Old

94 (New Entries Only)
Scottish Single Malt
Le Gus't Selection XIV Ardmore 8 Years Old
Cadenhead's Sherry Cask Aultmore 28 Year Old
Acla Selection Ben Nevis 17 Years Old
Howard Cai Selected Ben Nevis 19 Years
Benromach 39 Year Old 1977 Vintage
Golden Cask Bowmore Aged 16 Years
Scotch Malt Whisky Society Cask 10.145
Gordon & MacPhail Connoisseurs Choice Clynelish 2005
Golden Cask Craigellachie Aged 10 Years
The Duchess Glendronach 13 Year Old Virgin Oak
Glenfarclas The Family Casks 1988 S18 Release
Glen Grant Aged 15 Years Batch Strength 1st Edition
Glen Scotia Aged 25 Years
Kingsbarns 2 Year Old Spirit Drink
Lagavulin Aged 12 Years
Laphroaig 10 Year Old
Old Particular Linkwood 20 Years Old
Endangered Drams Loch Lomond 10 Year Old
Golden Cask Longmorn Aged 9 Years
Old Malt Cask Macduff Aged 20 Years

Old Particular Mortlach 12 Years Old
Berry Bros & Rudd Speyside 21 Years Old
Cadenhead's Authentic Collection Speyside 26 Year Old
Hunter Laing's Old & Rare Springbank Aged 20 Years
Cadenhead's Islay 9 Years Old

Scottish Vatted Malt
Elements of Islay Peat Islay Blended Malt Selkie batch no. 001

Scottish Grain
The Sovereign Dumbarton 30 Years Old
The First Editions Invergordon Aged 45 Years
Old Particular Strathclyde 26 Years Old

Irish Pure Pot Still
Method and Madness Single Pot Irish Whiskey

Irish Blend
The Dublin Liberties Oak Devil
Great Oaks New Frontiers Irish Whiskey
Teeling Whiskey Stout Cask Small Batch

Bourbon
1792 Small Batch
Ancient Age
Early Times Bottled-in-Bond Straight Bourbon

American Microdistilleries
Balcones Brimstone Redux
Iron Smoke Four Grain Bourbon
A.D. Law Four Grain Straight Bourbon Whiskey
Rock Town Arkansas Bourbon Whiskey
Rock Town Arkansas Rye Whiskey
Rock Town Single Barrel Bourbon Whiskey
Rock Town Whiskey from Wheat Mash
Westland Peat Week 4th Year

American White Dog
Buffalo Trace White Dog Mash #1

Canadian Single Malt
Two Brewers Yukon Single Malt Release 07 Peated

Canadian Blended
Gooderham & Worts 11 Souls
Hiram Walker Legends Series Wendel Clark
J. P Wiser's Canada 2018 Commemorative Series

English Single Malt
Cotswolds Single Malt Whisky 3 Years Old
Cotswolds Single Malt Whisky 2014 Odyssey Barley Batch No. 04/2017
The English Whisky Co. Smokey

Welsh Single Malt
Penderyn Celt
Penderyn Madeira Finish
Penderyn Myth

Austrian Single Malt
Waldviertler Haferwhisky Classic
Bodding Lokn Single Malt Blended Malt Nr. 2
J H. 12 Years Single Malt Single Cask

Belgian Single Malt
Belgian Owl Single Malt Passion 42 Months
Belgian Owl Single Malt Passion 47 Months

German Single Malt
Eifel Roggen Whisky Regional Serie Ahrtaler
The Glen Els PX Sherry Casks Aged 10 Years
The Spirit of St. Kilian Single Malt Batch No. 3 8 Months Old

Slovakian Single Malt
Nestville Cast Strength Single Barrel 2011

Australian Single Malt
Hobart Whisky Tasmanian Single Malt First Release

Scottish Malts

For those of you deciding to take the plunge and head off into the labyrinthine world of Scotch malt whisky, a piece of advice. And that is, be careful who you take your advice from. Because, too often, I hear that you should leave the Islays until you have tackled the featherlight Speysiders and the bolder, weightier Highlanders. This is just complete, patronising nonsense. The only time that rings true is if you are tasting a number of whiskies in one day. Then leave the smoky ones till last, so the lighter chaps get a fair hearing.

I know many people who didn't like whisky until they got a Talisker from Skye inside them, or a Lagavulin to swamp their tastebuds with oily iodine. The fact is, you can take your map of malt whisky, start at any point and head in whichever direction you feel. There are no hard and fast rules. Certainly with over 2,000 tasting notes for Scottish malts here you should have some help in picking where this journey of a lifetime begins.

It is also worth remembering not always to be seduced by age. It is true that many of the highest scores are given to big-aged whiskies. The truth is that the majority of malts, once they have lived beyond 25 years or so, suffer from oak influence rather than benefit. Part of the fun of discovering whiskies is to see how malts from different distilleries perform to age and type of cask. Happy discovering.

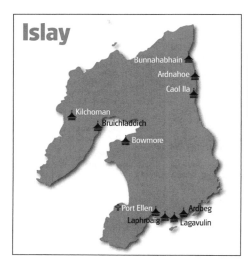

Abhainn Dearg

LEWIS

Isle of Harris

Isle of Ra

SKYE

Talisker

Torabhaig

Ardnamu

Tobermory

Ncn'ea

MULL

Oban

Isle of Ju

ISLAY

Isle of A

Springbank
Glen Scotia
Glengyle

Islay

Bunnahabhain

Ardnahoe

Caol Ila

Kilchoman

Bruichladdich

Bowmore

Port Ellen

Laphroaig

Ardbeg

Lagavulin

ORKNEY
ISLANDS

Highland Park
Scapa

Wolfburn

Pultney

Clynelish
✝Brora

Dornoch
Balblair
Glenmorangie
Dalmore
Teaninich
Invergordon
Glen Ord
Banff ✝
GlenWyris
Glenglassaugh
Macduff
Knockdhu
Inverness
Royal Brackla
Glen Albyn
Glendronach
Glenugie
Glen Mhor ✝
Tomatin
Ardmore
Millburn ✝
Glen Garioch

Speyside see page 24

The Speyside Distillery
Royal Lochnagar

Aberdeen

Dalwhinnie
✝ Glenury Royal
Fettercairn

Blair Athol
Glencadam
North Port
Glenesk ✝
Fort William
Edradour
✝Lochside
Ben Nevis
Aberfeldy
Arbikie
Glenlochy ✝
Strathearn
Lindores
Dundee
Abbey
Glenturret
Perth
Aberargie
Daftmill
Kingsbarns
Tullibardine
Eden Mill
Cameronbridge
Deanston
InchDairnie
Glengoyne
✝Rosebank
Glenkinchie
✝ St. Magdelene
Loch Lomond
Edinburgh
✝Dumbarton
Starlaw
North British
✝Interleven
Glasgow
✝Littlemill
Glasgow
Auchentoshan
Strathclyde
Port Dundas
Kinclaith ✝

Borders

Girvan
Ailsa Bay
Ladyburn ✝

Annandale

Bladnoch

Key

● **Major Town or City**

▲ Single Malt Distillery

▲ (*Italics*) Grain Distillery

✝ Dead Distillery

Speyside

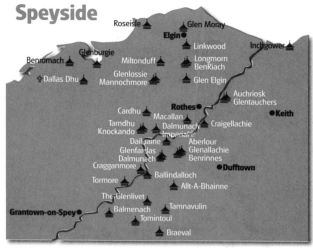

Distilleries by Town

SINGLE MALTS
ABERFELDY

Highlands (Perthshire), 1898. Bacardi. Working.

Aberfeldy 12 Year Old db (81) n21 t21 f19 b20. A puzzling malt. Aberfeldy makes and matures some of the greatest whisky on this planet, make no mistake. So why this conservative, ultra safe toffee-sultana-fudge offering when their warehouses are crammed with casks which could blow the world away? Pleasant. But so relentlessly dull and disappointing. And 40% abv...? Really...? 40% WB16/031

Aberfeldy 16 Year Old db (89.5) n22.5 Light, leathery and with a citrus freshness; t23.5 succulent, with a ripe melon sweetness meeting an earthier, almost semi-phenolic, substrata; a beautiful match; f21.5 should recede in layers. Yet, despite some lingering sugars, fades with a surprising flatness; b22 finishes far too fast and tamely. But the thrust of the malt is wonderful. 40%

Aberfeldy 21 Year Old db (88) n22 t22.5 f21.5 b22 The kind of malt I wish I could be let loose on...this really could be world class. But... 40% WB16/032

Aberfeldy Aged 25 Years db (85) n24 t21 f19 b21. Just doesn't live up to the nose. When Tommy Dewar wrote, "We have a great regard for old age when it is bottled," as quoted on the label, I'm not sure he had as many as 25 years in mind. 40%.

⬥ **Gordon & MacPhail Connoisseurs Choice Aberfeldy 1993** first fill sherry puncheon, cask no. 4056, dist 6 Jun 93, bott 21 Feb 18 (96) n24 a beautiful nuttiness underlines both the age and the sherried origins of the cask. Amazingly, this is 100% clean: not the slightest whiff of an off note. The dry, demure shape of the fruit spells elegance at every turn, a light maltiness floats for a second or two, before being submerging beneath the rising butterscotch and Dundee cake; t24.5 oh, such texture! Soft, succulent yet busily spicy – again with a quick malt burst which vanishes as quickly as it arrives. The sugars are meagre, but distinctly of a molassed type, slightly spent and bending for a moment towards liquorice; dry grape skin is abundant; f23.5 the spices and vanillas work beautifully; some further malt and grape skin mix stretch a point but the spices pulse as the light coffee notes reveal the oak as a major player after all; b24 a completely untainted sherry puncheon in full, clean richness: not sure whether to run outside and dance naked by the light of the moon. Perhaps after going to quite nearby ancient Rollright Stones. For this is a very rare and special event, these days seemingly prehistoric. 58.7%. nc ncf sc. 589 bottles.

⬩ **Gordon & MacPhail Connoisseurs Choice Aberfeldy 2003** bott 14 Mar 17 (94.5) n23.5 warm suet pudding with no shortage of fat sultanas; the vaguest pinch of salt accompanies the spice and light molten chocolate rather well...; t23.5 one very voluptuous delivery: the malt is first up, but the palate is awash with an oily, ever-fattening oaky toastiness, comprising vanillas and demerara sugar – and again that curious sultana sweetness; f23.5 dries on cue, the chocolate being of the cocoa-powdered truffle variety, with a little spice sizzle to keep things interesting; b24 just bursting from the bottle with personality. Big, at times muscular, but never coarse... 46%.

ABERLOUR
Speyside, 1826. Chivas Brothers. Working.

Aberlour 10 Years Old db (87.5) n22.5 t22 f21 b22. Remains a lusty fellow though here nothing like as sherry-cask faultless as before, nor displaying its usual honeyed twinkle. 43%

Aberlour 10 Years Old Sherry Cask Finish db (85) n21 t21 f21 b22. Bipolar and bitter-sweet with the firmness of the grain in vivid contrast to the gentle grape. 43%

⬩ **Aberlour 12 Years Old Double Cask** db (89) n22 nutty, but lightened by cherry blossom; t23 salivating with a slow unravelling of ever-intensifying tannin. Quite pithy and chalky on the fruity front; f21.5 dries further towards cocoa powder; a little bitter but the firmness of the malt is impressive; late spice; b22.5 a delicately poised malt which makes as much ado about the two different oak types as it does the fruit-malt balancing act. 40%

Aberlour 12 Years Old Double Cask Matured db (88.5) n22 t22.5 f22 b22. Voluptuous and mouth-watering in some areas, firmer and less expansive in others. Pretty tasty in all of them. 43%

Aberlour 12 Years Old Non Chill-Filtered db (87) n22.5 t22 f21 b21.5. There are many excellent facets to this malt, not least the balance between barley and grape and the politeness of the gristy sugars. But a sulphured butt has crept into this one, taking the edge off the excellence and bringing down the score like a cold front drags down the thermometer. 48%. ncf.

Aberlour 12 Years Old Sherry Cask Matured db (88) n23 t22 f21 b22. Could do with some delicate extra sweetness to take it to the next level. Sophisticated nonetheless. 40%

Aberlour 15 Years Cuvee Marie d'Ecosse db (91) n22 t24 f22 b23. This always was a deceptive lightweight, and it's got lighter still. It is sold primarily in France, and one can assume only that this is God's way of making amends for that pretentious, over-rated, caramel-ridden rubbish called Cognac they've had to endure. 43%

Aberlour 15 Year Old Double Cask Matured db (84) n23 t22 f19 b20. Brilliant nose full of vibrant apples and spiced sultana, but then, after a complex, chewy, malt-enriched kick-off, falls surprisingly flat on its face. 40%

Aberlour 15 Year Old Sherry Finish db (91) n24 t22 f23 b22 Quite unique: freaky, even. Really a whisky to be discovered and ridden. Once you acclimatize, you'll adore it. 43%

Aberlour 18 Years Old db (91) n22 thick milkshake with various fruits and vanilla; t22 immediate fresh juice which curdles beautifully as the vanilla is added; f24 wonderful fruit-chocolate fudge development: long, and guided by a gentle oiliness; b23 another high performance distillery age-stated bottling. 43%

Aberlour 100 Proof db (91) n23 t23 f22 b23. Stunning, sensational whisky, the most extraordinary Speysider of them all...which it was when I wrote those official notes for the bottling back in '97, I think. Other malts have superseded it now, but on re-tasting I stand by those original notes, though I disassociate myself entirely with the rubbish: "In order to savour Aberlour 100 at its best add 1/3 to 1/2 pure water." 57.1%

Aberlour A'Bunadh Batch No. 53 db (95) n23 t24 f24 b24 A truly beautiful whisky. But, oh! had only Batch 54 been this sulphur free we would have entered a new experience of whisky perfection. 59.7%

Aberlour A'Bunadh Batch No. 54 db (96) n23.5 t25 f23 b24.5 For just the delivery, no whisky will be better this year, or probably next. It had even crossed my mind to give it 25.5! A privilege to experience... 60.7%

Aberlour A'Bunadh Batch No. 57 Spanish Oloroso sherry butts db (81) n20.5 t22.5 f18 b20 Read my notes to batch 47, and we have a similar malt, though here there is not quite so much sparkle on delivery and there may be two rather than one butt at fault. 60.7%. ncf.

⬩ **Aberlour A'Bunadh Batch No. 61** Spanish Oloroso sherry butts db (95) n23 stunning honey melds with intense grape must. Ridiculously roasty and brooding despite the Manuka on show, and show real sizzling spice, too...; decidedly Kentuckian in part; t24 the first ten seconds register among the best deliveries of the year! A blend of concentrated Manuka and ulmo honey absorbs malt and grape in equal quantities and then blasts off into the palate while simultaneously a bourbon-style liquorice and hickory note merges with a surprisingly demure fruitiness; the spices, though telling, refuse to overplay their hand; f23.5 long, immensely roasty and honeyed with oak still in lightly spiced command; b24.5 although matured in 100% sherry butts – and clean, sulphur-free ones at that – one of the most remarkable, and delicious, features of this malt is the bourbon-esque quality of the oak notes mixing in with the grape. Wow! 60.8%. ncf.

◇ **Aberlour Casg Annamh** batch no. 0001 db (84.5) n21.5 t22.5 f19 b21.5 The nose is at first promising with nutty sherry tones dominating, then dry but with the most subtle countering muscovado and black cherry sweetness. Then comes the threat of the S word... which is confirmed on the rough, furry finish. The delivery stars with those sugars well into their stride, arriving early and mingling with the spice. Dates and figs represent the fruit with panache. 48%. ncf.

The Whisky Chamber Aberlour 10 Year Old bourbon cask, dist 2006 (94.5) n23 t24 f23.5 b24 Think of a boxer painting in finest detail a primrose...while he is still wearing his gloves. 54.1%.

ABHAINN DEARG
Highlands (Outer Hebrides), 2008. Marko Tayburn. Working.

Abhainn Dearg New Make db (92.5) n23 t23 f23.5 b23. Exceptionally well made with no feints and no waste, either. Oddly salty – possibly the saltiest new make I have encountered, and can think of no reason why it should be – with excellent weight as some extra copper from the new still takes hold. Given a good cask, no reason this impressive new born son of the Outer Hebrides won't go on to become something significant. 67%

AILSA BAY
Lowland, 2007. William Grant & Sons. Working.

Ailsa Bay db (92.5) n23.5 t23.5 f22.5 b23 I remember years back being told they wanted to make an occasional peaty malt at this new distillery different in style to Islay's. They have been only marginally successful: only the finish gives the game away. But they have certainly matched the island when it comes to the average high quality. A resounding success of a first effort, though I'd like to see the finish offer a little more than it currently does. Early days, though. 48.9%.

ALLT-Á-BHAINNE
Speyside, 1975. Chivas Brothers. Working.

◇ **Chapter 7 Allt-A-Bhainne 9 Year Old** 1st fill bourbon finish, cask no. 170, dist 2008 (78) n18 t19 f21 b20 Hot and tuneless, it takes time for find its rhythm and range and finally settles down for a big malty, if slightly austere finish. Younger than its years, also. 60.7%. sc.

The Cooper's Choice Allt-A-Bhainne 22 Year Old port finish, dist 1993 (92.5) n23 t23 f23.5 b23 Takes some time to show its true credentials. But stick with it because...wow...!!! 46%. nc ncf sc. The Vintage Malt Whisky Co.

◇ **The First Editions Allt-A-Bhainne Aged 24 Years 1995** refill bourbon barrel, cask no. 14120, bott 2017 (93) n22.5 richly perfumed, and all from the oak. Slices of vanilla merge with intense red liquorice; t23 a beautiful mouth feel: the oils have just enough weight to ensure the flavours of the busy tannins are not overindulged. Big oak from early on met elegantly by a light fudge; the spices build but never dominate; f23 dries as the toastier oak notes go on show; the spices tingle on; b23.5 a really big oak input here is surprisingly well received by a usually light spirit: a surprise package, indeed! 52.9%. nc ncf sc. 180 bottles.

◇ **Golden Cask Allt-A-Bhainne Aged 8 Years** cask no. CM230, dist 2008, bott 2016 (74.5) n18 t19 f18.5 b19 The firm, juicy, boisterous maltiness to this is undone by a cask-induced tang to both the nose and finish. A pity. 60.9%. sc. 306 bottles.

Hepburn's Choice Allt-A-Bhainne 7 Years Old sherry butt, dist 2008, bott 2016 (85) n21.5 t21 f21 b21.5 A slightly dull cove with the youth of the malt entirely and, surprisingly, blunted by a gentle cream sherry theme. Some late spices do no harm at all. 46%. nc ncf sc. 615 bottles.

Liquid Sun Allt-a-Bhainne 22 Years Old dist 1993 (92.5) n23.5 t23 f22.5 b23.5 A malt to go nuts about. 50.2%.

Old Malt Cask Allt-A-Bhainne Aged 18 Years refill hogshead, cask no. 10198, dist Nov 95, bott Oct 14 (91) n22.5 t23 f22.5 b23 How charming is that...??? 50%. nc ncf sc. 138 bottles.

◇ **Old Particular Allt-A-Bhainne 16 Years Old** sherry butt, cask no. 11338, dist Jul 00, bott Sept 16 (92) n23 classic Spotted Dick, the sultanas in good voice; t23.5 chewy and sumptuous, a little ulmo honey fills in the cracks; the barley powers into the middle at full throttle; f22.5 retains its shape beautifully and the spice build impresses; b23 a really good, unspoiled sherry butt at work here, adding just the right degree of balance and complexity. 48.4%. nc ncf sc. 273 bottles.

⬩ **Old Particular Allt-A-Bhainne 21 Years Old** refill hogshead, cask no. 12038, dist Nov 95, bott Aug 17 (91.5) n23 about as clean, fresh and malty as you can imagine a beautifully distilled 21-y-o to nose; you'd expect a degree of citrus – and there it is...; t23 a slow procession of lighter sugars dissolving on the palate, all of them with a light maltiness attached; f22.5 the length the malt stretches is ridiculous. Remains clean and entirely intact to the end, even as the polite oak makes an overdue entrance; b23 just sings "Speyside" to you. Just so clean and malty: you feel your teeth will sparkle after tasting it... 496%. nc ncf sc. 287 bottles.

⬩ **Scotch Malt Whisky Society Cask 108.10 9 Year Old** 1st fill ex-bourbon barrel, dist 12 Mar 08 (91) n22.5 the malt bunches up to give a sharp sweetness to the cream toffee which pours from the oak; a lighter diced apple and Demerara sugar strand binds the bigger players; t23 a fat malt, much oilier than normally associated with this distillery. A vague Manuka honey element combines with a surprisingly salty kick as the barley turns a little biscuity; a milk chocolate middle; f22.5 dries, but keeps to the cocoa contours; b23 recent bottlings from AAB from this period have been disappointing, to put it mildly. No fear with this one, which makes the most of both the big malt and the high- quality barrel. 61.2%. sc.

ANNANDALE
Lowlands, 2014. Annandale Distillery Company Ltd. Working.

⬩ **Annandale Man O' Sword** cask no. 100, dist 2014 (92.5) n23.5 youthful certainly. But so wonderfully clean: obviously enormous work has gone into getting the cuts this on the mark. A plethora of citrus notes – lemon and grapefruit mainly, adding further sharpness to the gristy phenols; t23 truly pre-pubescent, but there is such a charm to the semi-new makey malt that you can only sit back and enjoy the salivating freshness, underpinned by the chewy and ever-increasing phenols; f21.5 at this age the finish is the hardest bit to get right, and here the tannins and malt are barely on the same wave-length; b23.5 the strangest thing...I nosed this and thought: Jim Swan. This delightful style has the late, great whisky consultant's finger prints all over it. A young malt from a brand new distillery already punching way above its weight age-wise and in terms of complexity. Welcome to the whisky world, Annandale. And what a worthy addition you have already become. Now you just have to keep up this standard: no pressure at all... 61.6%. sc. 256 bottles.

⬩ **Annandale Man O' Words** cask no. 140, dist 2014 db (89.5) n22.5 a thick, weighty nose. Clean yet with definite oils making an impact, intensifying the malt but mixing it in with the butterscotch also. Young but with substance, also...; t22.5 much juicier than the nose lets on, then the malt positively cascades onto the palate, a ridiculous amount of spices hanging on to its coat-tails; a little citrus does lighten the load here and there; f22 here the ultra-youthful new make traits kick in, but the malt still has an attractive vitality; b22.5 a malty delight. Had been meaning to take in Annan Athletic FC and Annandale Distillery over the last four years but my diary just wouldn't allow it. Somehow I have to make it happen. This distillery promises great things. 61.6%. sc. 273 bottles.

ARDBEG
Islay, 1815. Glenmorangie Plc. Working.

Ardbeg 10 Years Old db (97) n24 t24 f24 b25 Like when you usually come across something that goes down so beautifully and with such a nimble touch and disarming allure, just close your eyes and enjoy... 46%

Ardbeg 10 bottling mark L10 152 db (95) n24.5 t23.5 f23.5 b23.5 A bigger than normal version, but still wonderfully delicate. Fabulous and faultless. 46%. Canadian market bottling in English and French dual language label.

Ardbeg 17 Years Old earlier bottlings db (92) n23 t22 f23 b24. OK, I admit I had a big hand in this, creating it with the help of Glenmorangie Plc's John Smith. It was designed to take the weight off the better vintages of Ardbeg whilst ensuring a constant supply around the world. Certainly one of the more subtle expressions you are likely to find, though criticised by some for not being peaty enough. As the whisky's creator, all I can say is they are missing the point. 40%

Ardbeg 17 Years Old later bottlings db (90) n22 t23 f22 b23. The peat has all but vanished and cannot really be compared to the original 17-year-old: it's a bit like tasting a Macallan without the sherry: fascinating to see the naked body underneath, and certainly more of a turn on. Peat or no peat, great whisky by any standards. 40%

⬩ **Ardbeg 19 Years Old** db (93) n23 lower than usual phenols drift dream-like away from the glass. Look carefully and you'll find that lightly salted Digestive biscuit tannins enjoy the same foothold and the citrus has its usual seat at the table; t23 that biscuit saltiness acts as a brief spur to ramp up the early juice levels. But is fleeting and the whole dries quickly as the powdery phenols assert themselves; f23.5 the oils have thinned but have enough purchase to ensure the minty chocolate is on an equal footing with the friendly phenols; **b23.5** one of the sensuously understated Ardbegs that could be found in style (though with a different peat imprint) from time to time during the 1960s. 46.2%.

⬧ **Ardbeg 20 Something** db **(96.5) n24** no doubting that a once heavyweight smoke signature has lightened over the years an aged but deft aroma of extraordinary poise: a bit like unearthing the preserved footsteps of a giant dinosaur... The very first hint of exotic fruit also underlines that this is heading towards antique mode...; **t24** one suspects from the nose that may be some differing ages in play and the fabulous structure on the palate only confirms this. Despite the peat, nothing heavy, no aggression. Just layering, like one snow fall on top of another, revealing the vanilla and ethereal tannins drifting away. Those little nudges again towards exotic fruit once more remind you of the many passing years; **f24** late salivation as the almost sherbet like lemon kicks over the smoky traces; like the 19-year-old a vague minty-chocolate trace fits in effortlessly; **b24.5** such mastery over the phenols...such elegance! It is though the whisky was distilled from gossamer... 46%.

Ardbeg 21 Years Old db **(96.5) n24** it is as though there are three levels of smokiness working in tandem: the layering is ridiculously well-structured. The deepest notes are earthy, rich with even a hint of unpicked tomato; the middle layer is flightier and spiced, seemingly in league with the gristier notes. And a third layer of phenols are sooty and wispy, like thin clouds scudding across on a windy day...amazing....; **t24** the delivery by contrast is only two-toned. The malt, sans smoke, is gristy, lemon tinged and juices up with intense barley as the sugars strike home. But it is kept in check by the phenols which hit first with a combined weight, but then scatters about the palate until it reforms later on in liquorice and chocolate vogue; **f24** much more ethereal now, though we have moved more towards crystalline sugars only too willing to melt and discreet spices which occasionally nip. To say the finish is long is a little bit of an understatement...; **b24.5** tap into Ardbeg with great care, like someone has done here, and there is no describing what beauty can be unleashed. For much of the time, the smoke performs in brilliant fashion somewhere between the ethereal and profound. 46%

Ardbeg 23 Year Old db **(93) n22.5** takes time for the strongarm oak to get anything less than too firm a grip of proceedings: if there is smoke in there, it has taken cover...; vague citrus pops its head up for a quick look – then quickly down again as it hides with the phenols...; **t24** yep, full on tannin...at first. The fragile citrus and more ample barley begins the job of restoring balance, which it does with typical Ardbegian elegance. There is a delicate smokiness which can be found lightly brushed over the milky, vaguely minty mocha which has gathered up enough dark sugars to form the nucleus of the resistance movement; just enough gristy barley lurks about to ensure a degree of defiant salivation, too; **f23** those big tannins return to mount a guard, but some lovely chocolate malt and spice manage to get through without being spotted...; **b23.5** a malt forever treading on eggshells, trying not to disturb the tannins. As a dram, makes a nervous wreck of you, as you spend the entire time waiting for the shallow truce to be broken and the oak to declare war and come pouring in. Thankfully, it never quite happens. As all whiskies, not taken with water. But, in this instance, a tranquiliser might not go amiss... 46.3%.

Ardbeg 1977 db **(96) n25 t24 f23 b24.** When working through the Ardbeg stocks, I earmarked '77 a special vintage, the sweetest of them all. So it has proved. Only the '74 absorbed that extra oak that gave greater all-round complexity. Either way, the quality of the distillate is beyond measure: simply one of the greatest experiences – whisky or otherwise – of your life. 46%

Ardbeg 1978 db **(91) n23 t24 f22 b22.** An Ardbeg on the edge of losing it because of encroaching oak, hence the decision made by John Smith and me to bottle this vintage early alongside the 17-year-old. Nearly ten years on, still looks a pretty decent bottling, though slightly under strength! 43%

Ardbeg An Oa db **(95.5) n24 t24 f23.5 b24** I'd never say "whoa" if someone poured me an Oa... 46%.

Ardbeg Aurivedes American oak casks with specially toasted cask lids. db **(91.5) n22 t22.5 f24 b23** I have spoken to nobody at Ardbeg about this one but from the slight bourbon character of the nose and the heavy vanilla, this version appears to be about the casks, possibly the char of the barrels. Fascinating, enjoyable...but whatever this is, the usual complexity of the peat feels compromised in the same way a wine cask might. Except here I detect no real curiosity, whatever it is... 49.9%. Moet Hennessy.

Ardbeg Blasda db **(90.5) n23.5 t22.5 f22 b22.5** A beautiful, if slightly underpowered malt, which shows Ardbeg's naked self to glowing effect. Overshadowed by some degree in its class by the SMWS bottling, but still something to genuinely make the heart flutter. 40%

Ardbeg Corryvreckan db **(96.5) n23 t24.5 f24 b25** As famous writers – including the occasional genius film director (stand up wherever you are my heroes Powell and Pressburger) – appear to be attracted to Corryvreckan, the third most violent whirlpool found in the world and just off Islay, to boot, - I selected this as my 1,500th whisky tasted for the historic Jim Murray Whisky Bible 2009. I'm so glad I did because many have told me they thought Blasda ahead of this. To me, it's not even a contest. Currently I have only a sample. Soon I shall have a bottle. I doubt if even the feared whirlpool is this deep and perplexing. *57.1%. 5000 bottles.*

Ardbeg Dark Cove db (86) n22.5 t22.5 f19.5 b21.5. For whatever reason, this is a much duller version than the Committee Edition. And strength alone can't explain it, or solely the loss of the essential oils from reduction. There is a slight nagging to this one so perhaps any weakness to the sherry butts has been accentuated by the reduction of oil, if it has been bottled from the same vatting – which I doubt. Otherwise, the tasting notes are along the lines of below, except with just a little less accent on the sugars. *46.5%*

Ardbeg Dark Cove Committee Edition db (90.5) n23.5 oh, sherry! And some! Gives the wrong signal about the depth of the peat involvement, as the grape is sticky enough to hide some of the phenols, though not the more sooty types. Liquorice and dates at play. Sticky, indeed...; t23 an immediate blast of dark molassed sugars point towards Melton Hunt Cake at first, but the smoke arrives in droves to drive you off that particular scent. Spices begin to compensate; chewy until your jaw hurts...; f21.5 just leans towards a slight burnt bitterness and a cloying of the fruit; b22.5 big sherry and bigger peat always struggle somewhere along the line. This one does pretty well until we reach the finale when it unravels slightly. But sulphur-free. And challenging. *55%*

⟫ **Ardbeg Grooves** db (95) n24 such a rare nose! Some decent tannin at work here from seriously revitalised casks, and though the peat is full on there is no head-on collision and the two forces amalgamate with amazing gentleness; t23.5 onrushing caramels from the casks ensure the gentlest of deliveries which the smoke slowly devours; cocoa powder and smoke is dotted around the drying middle, though a little bourbon-style molasses ensures a weighty sweetness is maintained; f23.5 more of the same as it dries, with the usual Ardbeg sleight of hand and complexity; b24 groovy. *46%.*

⟫ **Ardbeg Grooves Committee Release** db (95.5) n24 as above, except: oilier phenols adding extra depth and weight; t23.5 as above except: a more rounded gloss to the same traits and development and much greater lustre to the sugars; f24 as above except: longer finale and now a more apparent spice; b24 even groovier! *51.6%.*

Ardbeg Guaranteed 30 Years Old db (91) n24 t23 f21 b23. An unsual beast, one of the last ever bottled by Allied. The charm and complexity early on is enormous, but the fade rate is surprising. That said, still a dram of considerable magnificence. *40%*

Ardbeg Kelpie db (95) n24 t23.5 f23.5 b24 Beautifully crafted and cleverly – and intriguingly - structured. An understated Ardbeg for true Ardbeg lovers... *46%.*

Ardbeg Kelpie Committee Edition db (94) n24 as Kelpie (above) but extra oils disperse a slightly broader span of sugars...; t24 as above (again!). Except, once more a different, richer texture does nothing to detract from the juiciness, but certainly makes the toffee a little more chewy; f22.5 different from the 46% version in that here some bitterness is extracted from the oak to lay alongside the big caramels; b23.5 as Burns might have said: I'se no speer nae to anither helpie o' Kelpie... *51.7%.*

Ardbeg Mor db (95) n24 t24 f23 b24 Quite simply... more the merrier... *57.5%*

Ardbeg Perpetuum db (94.5) n23.5 t23.5 f23.5 b24 what a beautifully structured malt. There is no escaping the youth of some of the phrases. But you can't help enjoying what it says. *47.4%. ncf.*

Ardbeg Provenance 1974 bott 1999 db (96) n24 t25 f23 b24. This is an exercise in subtlety and charisma, the beauty and the beast drawn into one. Until I came across the 25-year-old OMC verson during a thunderstorm in Denmark, this was arguably the finest whisky I had ever tasted: I opened this and drank from it to see in the year 2000. When I went through the Ardbeg warehouse stocks in 1997 I earmarked the '74 and '77 vintages as something special. This bottling has done me proud. *55.6%*

Ardbeg Renaissance db (92) n22.5 t22.5 f23 b23.5. How fitting that the 1,200th (and almost last) new-to-market whisky I sampled for the 2009 Bible was Renaissance... because that's what I need after tasting that lot...!! This is an Ardbeg that comes on strong, is not afraid to wield a few hefty blows and yet, paradoxically, the heavier it gets the more delicate, sophisticated and better-balanced it becomes. Enigmatically Ardbegian. *55.9%*

Ardbeg Uigeadail db (89) n25 t22 f20 b22. A curious Ardbeg with a nose to die for. Some tinkering - please guys, as the re-taste is not better - regarding the finish may lift this to being a true classic *54.1%*

⟫ **The Duchess Ardbeg Malin 25 Year Old** cask no. 649, dist 1991, bott 2016 (94.5) n24 huge coastal kick to this, with the seaweed and salt over every movement the gentle phenols make. Islay in a sniff...; t23.5 salivating despite the massive age, with the salt pressing hard against the tastebuds and gristy sugars in slowly to lessen the coastal attack. The smoke is almost moribund, having seemingly reached the end of the road as the tannins take over; f23.5 long with the lightest trace of smoke but now the cocoa and liquorice is more in touch with the salty spices; b23.5 really, a beautiful show with the peat fading but the elegance and class unimpeached. 49.8%. sc. The Shieldmaiden Series.

ARDMORE
Speyside, 1899. Beam Suntory. Working.

Ardmore 12 Year Old Port Wood Finish db (90) n21.5 t23.5 f22 b23 Here we have a lovely fruit-rich malt, but one which has compromised on the very essence of the complexity which sets this distillery apart. Lovely whisky I am delighted to say...but, dammit, by playing to its unique nuances it could have been so much better...I mean absolutely sensational...!46%. ncf.

◇ **Ardmore Aged 20 Years 1996 Vintage** 1st fill ex-bourbon & ex-Islay casks, bott code: L723657A db (89.5) n22 a major degree of tannin ups the peppery content, which clashes with a slightly harder-edged smokiness. Some excellent tropical fruit nimbly softens the impact; t23 a good, though unusually intense, delivery for an Ardmore: like on the nose the unusual liquorice-led, sharp and salivating tannins hammer home early on, the oiliness ensuring there is stickiness to the mix of muscovado sugars and at times muscular peat. The spices are a delight; f22 quietens rather quickly, though that fruit on the nose does seep down very late on; b22.5 slightly confused by this malt, for all its charm. At 20 years old this distillery projects, through its usual ex-bourbon cask portfolio of varied usages, a quite disarming complexity. To bolster it with extra oak and smoke slightly undermines the inherent subtlety of this malt which sets it apart from all others. Highly enjoyable, nonetheless. 49.3%. ncf.

Ardmore 25 Years Old db (89.5) n21 t23.5 f22.5 b22.5 A 25-y-o box of chocolates: coffee creams, fudge, orange cream...they are all in there. The nose may be ordinary: what follows is anything but. 51.4%. ncf.

Ardmore 30 Years Old Cask Strength db (94) n23.5 t23.5 f23 b24 I remember when the present owners of Ardmore launched their first ever distillery bottling. Over a lunch with the hierarchy there I told them, with a passion, to ease off with the caramel so the world can see just how complex this whisky can be. This brilliant, technically faultless, bottling is far more eloquent and persuasive than I was that or any other day... 53.7%. nc ncf. 1428 bottles.

Ardmore 1996 db (87) n22 t22 f21 b22. Very curious Ardmore, showing little of its usual dexterity. Perhaps slightly more heavily peated than the norm, but there is also much more intense heavy caramel extracted from the wood. Soft, very pleasant and easy drinking it is almost obsequious. 43%.

Ardmore Fully Peated Quarter Casks db (89) n21 t23 f23 b22. Firstly, Ardmore has rarely been filled in ex-bourbon and that oak type is having an effect on the balance and smoke weight; also they have unwisely added caramel, which has flattened things further. I don't expect the caramel to be in later bottlings and, likewise, I think the bourbon edge might be purposely blunted a little. But for a first attempt this is seriously big whisky that shows enormous promise. When they get this right, it could – and should – be a superstar. Now I await the more traditional vintage bottlings... 46%. ncf.

◇ **Ardmore Legacy** bott code: L713757B db (88) n22.5 some young citrusy notes enjoy a whirlwind courtship with punchier phenols. Some anthracite dust mingles with a little pineapple; t23 charming and lucid peat draws upon the gristy sugars to make the softest of landings, all kinds of vanilla at work through the middle; f20.5 hmm, just a little tangy and off balance; b22 that's much more like it! The initial bottling of this brand was a travesty to the distillery, seemingly making a point omitting all of the personality which makes this potentially one of the great whiskies of the world. No such problem here: a much more sympathetic rendition, though the finish is perhaps a little sharper than ideally desired. So, a massive improvement but still room for further improvement. 40%.

Ardmore Traditional Cask db (88.5) n21.5 t22 f23 b22. Not quite what I expected. "Jim. Any ideas on improving the flavour profile?" asked the nice man from Ardmore distillery when they were originally launching the thing. "Yes. Cut out the caramel." "Ah, right..." So what do I find when the next bottling comes along? More caramel. It's good to have influence... Actually, I can't quite tell if this is a result of natural caramelization from the quarter casking or just an extra dollop of the stuff in the bottling hall. The result is pretty similar: some of the finer complexity is lost. My guess, due to an extra fraction of sweetness and spice, is that it is the former. All that said, the overall experience remains quite beautiful. And this remains one of my top ten distilleries in the world. 46%. ncf.

◇ **Berry Bros & Rudd Ardmore 9 Years Old** cask no. 708628, dist 2008, bott 2018 (96.5) n24 not sure a smoky whisky can get much more delicate than this: the smoke, though offering a presence, refuses to dominate the available ground, allowing a coy nutty and vaguely fruity sub plot to build towards a vaguely minty maltiness: so complex! t24 it's not just the flavours which grab the attention here, but the mouth feel which is so ridiculously lush. Ardmore at its most gristy and vibrant early on, so the smoke is slowly released onto the palate. This allows breathing space for the melon and papaya fruit salad to offer its genteel fruitiness; f24 splendidly oily, ensuring the sugars and coffee-clad smoke maximum length; b24.5 confirmation of just what a stupendous distillery this is. For a 9-year-old, the balance defies belief. Few single malts under ten years will match this bottling this year. 52.3%. nc ncf sc.

Best Dram Ardmore 8 Year Old ex-Laphroaig barrel, dist 2008, bott 2016 (88.5) n21.5 t22.5 f22.5 b22 What a fascinating if random dram. Ardmore is that peaty malt which makes a little phenol go a long way. Here, just by altering the type of cask in favour of smoke, you can see just how fragile the ecosystem of this malt really is. 59.2%.

C & S Dram Collection Ardmore 8 Years Old bourbon barrel, cask no. 702425, dist 19 Jun 08, bott 20 Feb 17 (89) n22 t22.5 f22 b22.5 A fragile, well-used cask adds only a limited degree of depth. 58.3%. sc. 261 bottles.

Golden Cask Ardmore 14 Years Old cask no. CM 217, dist 2000, bott 2015 (91) n23 t22.5 f22.5 b23 a fierce, yet brutally and sometimes deliciously honest, account of the distillery in its more fiery mode. No frills, but plenty of thrills. 57.3%. sc. 178 bottles.

◇ **Golden Cask Ardmore Aged 16 Years** cask no. CM231, dist 2000, bott 2016 (92.5) n22.5 a weighty aroma of some milky fudge with a spikey smokiness; t23.5 wow! This clatters about the palate like smoky ghost in chains. A rock hard, thumping delivery which spices up early – and to impressive effect – as the dark sugars and light cocoa tones purvey the more delicate nuances of the smoke; brilliantly salivating throughout; f23 vanilla comes into play with gusto, yet the smokes and spice refuses to be entirely silenced; b23.5 one seriously chunky dram. Love this classy act. 55.8%. sc. 80 bottles.

◇ **Golden Cask Ardmore Aged 17 Years** cask no. CM242, dist 2000, bott 2017 (96) n24 the seemingly diminished effect of the peat is an illusion: it is there all the time shaping the weight of the sugars and light cedar wood, both lightening and adding weight at the same time...: a seasoned nose for all seasons...; t24 soft...so amazingly soft...wow...! Seems like spices acting alone as a juicy malty gristiness emboldens the richness. But it is not: it is the peat playing tricks and with equal sleight of hand it offers an earthy quality to the vanillas representing the simple oaks; f23.5 several levels and layers of cocoa, from simple bourbon cream biscuit to a fine Columbian bean mix with the vanilla. And all slightly imbued with a delicate, spicy smoke...; b24.5 I really admire the quality of Golden Cask's bottlings. Here's one that is a little different for an Ardmore, with the peaty bits seemingly shaved off to ensure the phenols always come across as secondary influence – though, on close inspection, you'll find it is actually the first. One of the most nuanced malts you'll encounter this year. Stunning. 55.3%. sc. 136 bottles.

Gordon & MacPhail Cask Strength Ardmore 2002 bott 27 Oct 16 (96.5) n24 t24 f24 b24.5 Ardmore revelling in all its understated genius. 57.5%.

Hidden Spirits Ardmore 6 Year Old cask no. AM016, dist 2010, bott 2016 (85.5) n21.5 t22 f21 b21 A youngster very much at an awkward age. The peat, sugars and early tannin tang all seems to be out of sync. Brusque. 50%. sc

Kingsbury Gold Ardmore 6 Year Old 2008 hogshead, cask no. 800006 (95.5) n24 t23.5 f24 b24 young, adorable and fabulous example of why this is one of the great blending malts in the world at this age. Truly faultless. 59.5%. sc. 187 bottles.

◇ **Le Gus't Selection XIV Ardmore 8 Years Old** bourbon cask, cask no. 705804 (94) n23 punchy phenols take the lead, rather than being comfortable in the back seat as of yore; profers a good dry-sweet balance, though with the smoke being in both camps, alongside some hickory; t23.5 chunky and chewy, the phenols first swamp and then buzz the taste buds with its peppery offshoot; despite the youth and a slight new make aside a little ulmo honey works cunningly in tandem with the vanilla concentrate; f23.5 the spices refuse to take their foot off the gas: in fact quite the opposite. Both a peppery and phenolic buzz to the finish alongside the cocoa and red liquorice; b24 evidence that the eating level at Ardmore may have risen a tad in recent years: much more smoke at work here than in the old days. For its age, outstanding... 60.9%. sc. 242 bottles.

Old Malt Cask Ardmore Aged 20 Years refill hogshead, cask no. 12929, dist Oct 96, bott Nov 16 (96) n24 t24 f24 b24 If you really want to learn something about great whisky, worth investing in First editions cask 12930 and this bottling...and then spending a good week comparing the subtle differences of the two. It will be one of the best weeks of your life... 50%. nc ncf sc. 148 bottles.

◇ **Old Malt Cask Ardmore Aged 20 Years** refill hogshead, cask no. 13770, dist Oct 96, bott Apr 17 (90.5) n23 the peat is barely heard background music to the fruit salad candy; t23 light, juicy, intensely malty with a just-so degree of radiating spice; f22 just a little ash detected amid the drying oak; b22.5 smoke happily plays third fiddle to the fruit and spice. Charming. 50%. nc ncf sc. 278 bottles.

Old Malt Cask Ardmore Aged 21 Years refill hogshead, cask no. 14466, dist Apr 96, bott Nov 17 (96) n24 although the nose appears understated, a few minutes study is rewarded with the discovery that the peat is operating on two completely different levels: its duel personality means that it both provides the background grumble as well as the flutier higher notes on which the spices travel; diced green apple and liquorice add further variation in tone; t24 it will be hard to find a better malt of this age when it comes to near perfect levels of oils, sugars, phenols and spice. The interplay and crossover in tone and temperament deserves a good 20 minutes to untangle and savour; f24 long, with the oak now playing a part, but the tannins of the highest quality with not a bitter note to be had. Still complex, a little malt sticky and lightly smoked, even on the final fade; b24 as elegant as it is articulate. An unambiguous, must-find great from this distillery. 50%. nc ncf sc. 167 bottles.

Old Particular Ardmore 16 Years Old refill barrel, cask no. 11168, dist May 00, bott Jun 16 (95.5) n24 t24 f23.5 b24 A blinding example of the distillery at this healthy age: truly magnificent malt. 44.5%. nc ncf sc. 283 bottles.

Old Particular Ardmore 21 Years Old refill hogshead, cask no. 12196, dist Oct 96, bott Nov 17 (96) n23.5 the peat is obviously designed to be on the lower side here. Yet such is gentle nature of the ulmo honey, beeswax and varied floral notes, the smoke appears a little larger than it actually is...like the moon rising over the evening's horizon...; t24 ticks every box you require from a delivery...and adds a few extra. Melts in the mouth – ever-growing barley intensity – spreading smokiness, slow and even – a growing awareness of light honey and butterscotch...all this, but delivered in slow motion and with near perfect weight; f24.5 a fabulous mocha finale with a vague saltiness and a late, delightful, dovetailing of vanilla and barley with a vague hint of orange blossom honey; b24 near faultless. If you want to discover how a relatively low dose of peat can bring a level of balance and complexity to die for, just sample this truly great whisky... 52%. nc ncf sc. 310 bottles.

Provenance Ardmore Aged 8 Years refill barrel, cask no. 11329, dist Jul 08, bott Aug 16 (88.5) n22 t22.5 f23.5 b22 At these younger ages the smoke is more happily and emphatically pronounced. 46%. nc ncf sc. 301 bottles.

Provenance Ardmore Aged 8 Years refill barrel, cask no. 11536, dist Jul 08, bott Nov 16 (89.5) n22.5 t22 f22.5 b22.5 A better balanced offering than the starker cask 11329. 46%. nc ncf sc.

Provenance Ardmore Aged 8 Years refill barrel, cask no. 11632, dist Jul 08, bott Feb 17 (91) n23 makes no secret of its young age and profers varied floral notes, especially violets and bluebells, to accompany the trim, crisp, phenols; t23 much softer on the palate and simple dissolves on delivery. The gristy phenols and buzzing spice make a magnificent combination; the youthful is evident but never a hindrance; f22.5 a simple vanilla-clad fade; b22.5 that is one adorable whisky: forget the age, the charm and quality are stupendous. 46%. nc ncf sc. 306 bottles.

Romantic Rhine Collection Ardmore 9 Year Old cask no. 1915843, dist 2008, bott 2017 (89) n22.5 light peat drifts over the comfortable vanilla; t21 a simplistic delivery: takes time to find its mark then starts to unload a delicate peatiness; the spirit is a little firm here; f23 at last relaxes into sublime mode: coffee Swiss roll is at the centre of a scrumptious, now lightly oiled fade; b22 takes time to find its feet, but the quality is always there. 52.8%. nc ncf sc.

Scotch Malt Whisky Society Cask 66.101 9 Year Old refill ex-bourbon barrel, dist 15 May 07 (89.5) n22.5 t22.5 f22 b22.5 At the low end of Ardmore's phenol spectrum. 60.1%.

Scotch Malt Whisky Society Cask 66.111 8 Year Old refill ex-bourbon barrel, dist 4 Jun 09 (89.5) n23 suspicions of a phenol level above their normal 9ppm here: they have not only upped the peat, but the tannins are flying, too, for a malt so obviously young; t22 two-toned: incredibly oily for Ardmore but has to be to withstand the impact of the spice and oak. Young and slightly on the aggressive side with hickory asserting the oak's position against the smoke; f22.5 a dry, far more even fade; b22 pretty creamy by Ardmore standards. 58.9%. sc.

Spirit of Caledonia Ardmore Peated 8 Years Old cask no. 707029 (85.5) n21.5 t22.5 f20 b21.5 Absolutely nothing wrong with the spirit itself, which shows Ardmore in its most salivating and smoky light. However, the contribution of the oak leaves a little to be desired, its vaguely milky weakness particularly noticeable at the death. 61.3%. sc.

Teacher's Highland Single Malt quarter cask finish db (89) n22.5 t23 f21.5 b22. This is Ardmore at its very peatiest. And had not the colouring levels been heavily tweaked to meet the flawed perceptions of what some markets believe makes a good whisky, this malt would have been better still. As it is: superb. With the potential of achieving greatness if only they have the confidence and courage... 40%. India/Far East Retail exclusive.

That Boutique-y Whisky Company Ardmore 10 Year Old batch 1 (94.5) n23.5 t24 f23.5 b23.5 A beautiful age for Ardmore to show off its smoky dexterity. And this bottling shows the distillery at the higher end of its phenol spectrum. 55.5%. 350 bottles.

Whisky Krüger Ardmore 2010 6 Years Old bott 2016 (88.5) n22 t21.5 f23 b22 Not a bad cask. But one that has a minor problem in maximising and brodcasting its positive points. 60.8%.

AUCHENTOSHAN

Lowlands, 1800. Morrison Bowmore. Working.

Auchentoshan 10 Years Old db (81) n22 t21 f19 b19. Much better, maltier, cleaner nose than before. But after the initial barley surge on the palate it shows a much thinner character. 40%

Auchentoshan 12 Years Old db (91.5) n22.5 sexy fruit element – citrus and apples in particular – perfectly lightens the rich, oily barley; t23.5 oily and buttery; intense barley carrying delicate marzipan and vanilla; f22.5 simplistic, but the oils keep matters lush and the delicate sugars do the rest; b23 a delicious malt very much happier with itself than it has been for a while. 40%

Auchentoshan 14 Years Old Cooper's Reserve db (83.5) n20 t21.5 f21 b21. Malty, a little nutty and juicy in part. 46%. ncf.

Auchentoshan 18 Years Old db (78) n21 t21.5 f17 b19. Although matured for 18 years in ex-bourbon casks, as according to the label, this is a surprisingly tight and closed malt in far too many respects. Some heart-warming sugars early on, but the finish is bitter and severely limited in scope. 43%

Auchentoshan 21 Years Old db (93) n23.5 t23 f23 b23.5 One of the finest Lowland distillery bottlings of our time. A near faultless masterpiece of astonishing complexity to be cherished and discussed with deserved reverence. So delicate, you fear that sniffing too hard will break the poor thing...! 43%.

Auchentoshan 1975 db (88) n22.5 t22.5 f21 b22 Goes heavy on the natural caramels. Does not even remotely show its enormous age for this distillery. I detest the word "smooth". But for those who prefer that kind of malt...well, your dreams have come true...; 45.6%

⬩ **Auchentoshan 1979** db (94) n23.5 t24 f23 b23.5 It's amazing what a near faultless sherry butt can do. 50.1%

⬩ **Auchentoshan 1990 27 Year Old** db (94) n23.5 t23 f24 b23.5 The fact this is triple-distilled malt has a major bearing on the structure of this excellent dram. Lighter malty and citrus notes seem able to fly above the more ingrained grape. The result is a two-toned, salivating little charmer which carries its years in a way 'Toshan was never really expected to. The mocha starts creeping in from about the halfway point, laying down a weightiness which is still in keeping with the lighter fruit. Such a delight and elegant experience with the kind of finish blenders can only dream of.... 53.1%. Selected for CWS.

Auchentoshan 1998 Sherry Cask Matured fino sherry cask db (81.5) n21 t22 f18.5 b20. A genuine shame. Before these casks were treated in Jerez, I imagine they were spectacular. Even with the obvious faults apparent, the nuttiness is profound and milks every last atom of the oils at work to maximum effect. The sugars, also, are delicate and gorgeously weighted. There is still much which is excellent to concentrate on here. 54.6%. ncf. 6000 bottles.

Auchentoshan American Oak db (85.5) n21.5 t22 f20.5 b21.5. Very curious: reminds me very much of Penderyn Welsh whisky before it hits the Madeira casks. Quite creamy with some toasted honeycomb making a brief cameo appearance. 40%

Auchentoshan Blood Oak French red wine & American bourbon casks db (76.5) n20.5 t19 f18 b19. That's funny: always thought blood tasted a little sweet. This is unremittingly bitter. 48%. ncf.

Auchentoshan Classic db (80) n19 t20 f21 b20. Classic what exactly...? Some really decent barley, but goes little further. 40%

Auchentoshan Noble Oak Aged 24 Years Oloroso sherry casks & American bourbon hogsheads db (87.5) n22 t23 f21 b21.5. Normally a skinny soul on account of its triple distillation, unusual to find a 'Toshan with so much muscle. The fruit from the sherry is piled on high, yet it is a massive toffee effect which takes the firmest grip, presumably tannins from the oak. So the finish is a little flat. But the good news is that this is one fruit cake that is happily sulphur-free. 50.3%. ncf. 2015 Limited Release.

Auchentoshan Select db (85) n20 t21.5 f22 b21.5. Has changed shape of late, if not quality. Much more emphasis on the enjoyable juicy barley sharpness these days. 40%

Auchentoshan Solera db (88) n23 t22 f22 b21. Enormous grape input and enjoyable for all its single mindedness. Will benefit when a better balance with the malt is struck. 48%. ncf.

⬩ **Auchentoshan The Bartender's Malt** batch 01, bott code: L172249 db (94.5) n23.5 busy and complex: beautiful ripe gooseberries and rhubarb cake; a little cedar bites as the oak gets to work in earnest; t24 a charmingly manicured delivery: the malt still has much to say though speaks modestly; it is the third and fourth flavour waves which dazzle as the complex sugars, or more to the point, thinned honeys (ulmo and heather in particular) go head to head with a fabulous oak-lusting spice surge; a thick smoothie of fruit firms the final dimension; f23 plenty of chocolate as the vanilla fills in any tiring gaps, while the spices quietly buzz; a tame fuzziness late on suggests a mildly out or sorts cask and costs half a point; **b24** seeing as this was assembled by a dozen bartenders from around the world, namely Messrs Alvarado, Billing, Halsius, Heinrich, Jehli, Klus, Magro, Morgan, Schurmann, Shock, Stern and Wareing surely this is the Bartenders' Malt, not Bartender's Malt. Still, I digress. Good job, boys and (presumably) girls. Some might mark this down as a clever marketing ploy (which it may well be...). I'd rather record it as an exceptionally fine Auchentoshan. And by the way, bartenders, you have proved a point I have been making for the last 25 years: the finest cocktail is a blend of whiskies...even if from the same distillery...Now don't you go ruining this by putting ice, water, or anything else in it... 47%.

Auchentoshan Three Wood db (76) n20 t18 f20 b18. Takes you directly into the rough. Refuses to harmonise, except maybe for some late molassed sugar. 43%

Auchentoshan Virgin Oak db (92) n23.5 like a busy bourbon with the accent on the buzzing small grains: all the regulation manuka honey and liquorice there in respectful amounts; t23 big, sugary delivery, but a cushion of hickory and vanilla keeps the sweetness under control; a little molasses adds extra weight to the middle; f22.5 pretty dry, with a bit of a coppery sheen, as though some work had recently been done to a still; b23 not quite how I've seen 'Toshan perform before: but would love to see it again! 46%

Cadenhead's Small Batch Cask Strength Auchentoshan 17 Year Old bourbon casks, dist 1999 (92.5) n22.5 t23.5 f23 b23.5 The kind of dram that makes you emit a little groan of pleasure... 55.5%.

Hunter Laing's Old & Rare Auchentoshan Aged 24 Years refill hogshead, dist Oct 91, bott Apr 16 (95.5) n24.5 t24 f24 b24 There are refill hogshead and then there are refill hogsheads... And this is some refill hogshead...!! As it happens, this was my 69th whisky for the 2018 Bible...and, my word, this one went down beautifully... 58.4%. nc ncf sc. 216 bottles.

Old Malt Cask Auchentoshan Aged 19 Years refill hogshead, cask no. 13300, dist May 97, bott Feb 17 (89) n22.5 a little bourbonesque but a hint of coriander and nutmeg; t22 after the initial sweet barley burst almost a gin-like botanical feel to this: dry gin at that...; f22 continues along its herbal way...; b22.5 for serious malt lovers you'll just have to gin and bear it... 50%. nc ncf sc. 285 bottles.

◈ **Old Particular Auchentoshan 16 Years Old** refill hogshead, cask no. 11591, dist Sept 00, bott Mar 17 (89.5) n22.5 busy, with slight Cognacy pretensions not least because an austere pithy countenance; t23 fresh, salivating and the build up of barley taking on epic proportions; f22 minimal oak other than spice and toasty vanilla; quite thin towards the finale; b22 after the big, breathtaking barley statement definitely veers on the side of an austere aloofness. 48.4%. nc ncf sc. 319 bottles.

Old Particular Auchentoshan 18 Years Old virgin oak hogshead, cask no. 11203, dist Dec 97, bott Jun 16 (89.5) n22.5 brittle but some real bite to the spice; t23 superb delivery of barley concentrate, natural caramels and intense vanilla; spices fizz quietly in the background; f22 a little butterscotch and lot of tart; bitters out a tad; b22 slightly confused here: doesn't give the impression of having spent 18 years in virgin oak. 48.4%. nc ncf sc. 278 bottles.

◈ **Old Particular Auchentoshan 18 Years Old** refill hogshead, cask no. 11829, dist Nov 98, bott Jun 17 (87) n21 t22 f22 b22 Warming, barley-intense and salivating there are some surprisingly good oils on this. A little bit of tired oak tang, also. 47.5%. nc ncf sc. 251 bottles.

◈ **Old Particular Auchentoshan 20 Years Old** refill hogshead, cask no. 12032, dist May 97, bott Aug 17 (94.5) n24 the triple distillation appears to have cleared the decks for the oak to have taken on the odd oak character which seems a lot older than its 20 years, tempered with something younger. Clean, superbly structured and weighted and the barley showing both a fruit and out-and-out grassy disposition; t23 concentrated gooseberry keeps the fruit-side of its character from the off, then revels in the polished, salivating barley; f23.5 the nose told you there would be spices present and these take a little longer to arrive than suspected; also late oils enforce grassiness and a little ulmo honey; b24 a real sparkling gem of a dram. 51.5%. nc ncf sc. 279 bottles.

◈ **Provenance Auchentoshan Aged 14 Years** refill hogshead, cask no. 11906, dist Oct 02, bott Jun 17 (84) n21 t22 f20 b21 Well, bless my soul! A vaguely smoky, oily 'Toshan. Now there's a first. Either I have been sent a rogue sample or they went 2D at one stage to try to experiment. Either way, the cask is a bit shot and doesn't add anything positive. 46%. nc ncf sc. 852 bottles.

AUCHROISK

Speyside, 1974. Diageo. Working.

Auchroisk Aged 10 Years db (84) n20 t22 f21 b21. Tangy orange on the nose, the malt amplified by a curious saltiness on the palate. 43%. Flora and Fauna.

Auchroisk Aged 25 Years dist 1990 db (89) n22 t22.5 f22 b22.5 One of the most rampant Aucroisks I've encountered since the distillery issued its first-ever bottling. The full strength helps galvanise the malt and accentuate the barley sugar. A little rough, but very satisfying. *51.2%. 3,954 bottles. Diageo Special Releases 2016.*

⬗ **Cadenhead's Wine Cask Auchroisk 16 Years Old** Chateau Lafitte cask, dist 2001 (84.5) n21 t22 f21 b20 Lafitte, but not elite. Filling a very average spirit with very limited body into this cask probably didn't much help. Only the fruit shows amid the spices and cocoa. The malt itself vanishes, overwhelmed. *554%. sc. 246 bottles.*

⬗ **The First Editions Auchroisk Aged 19 Years** refill hogshead, cask no. 14661, bott 2018 (90.5) n22.5 French toast...with a little pepper added..; t22.5 soothing delivery lacking the usual Auchroiskian fire. The malt arrives in force, with an unusual early backup of slight oils to generate extra weight. The oaky vanilla is entirely proportionate; f23 layered and helped by those surprise oils to add extra length and even a butterscotch tart depth; b22.5 a thoroughly enjoyable bottling showing an unusual degree of complexity for this distillery. *54.2%. nc ncf sc. 290 bottles.*

⬗ **The First Editions Auchroisk Aged 22 Years 1994** refill hogshead, cask no. 12429, bott 2016 (89) n21.5 thin malt shouting meekly above the toasty vanilla; t22.5 clean, juicy, elegant, ethereal sugar barley. Apart from the quick spice delivery, nothing more or less; f22 the oak continues with a clarity as precise as the barley; b23 one of Speyside's lightest malts has put little weight on 22 years. But there is no faulting its delightful elegance. *571%. nc ncf sc. 110 bottles.*

Hepburn's Choice Auchroisk 7 Years Old refill hogshead, dist 2009, bott 2017 (86.5) n21.5 t22.5 f21 b21.5 Malt dominates the story. However, a little sharpness on the nose and finish where the copper and oak don't se e eye to eye interrupts the flow. *46%. nc ncf sc. 405 bottles.*

Hepburn's Choice Auchroisk 7 Years Old refill hogshead, dist 2009, bott 2017 (88) n22 t22.5 f21.5 b22 Forget the age: gentle and deliciously moreish. *46%. nc ncf sc. 406 bottles.*

⬗ **Hepburn's Choice Auchroisk 8 Years Old** red wine cask, dist 2009, bott 2017 (67) n16 t18 f16 b17 Can someone tell the wine cask people that sulphur is not a good idea when it comes to whisky. *46%. nc ncf sc. 272 bottles.*

⬗ **Old Malt Cask Auchroisk Aged 15 Years** refill hogshead, cask no. 14747, dist Nov 02, bott Feb 18 (87) n21 t22 f21.5 b21.5 A malty skeleton on which hangs very little meat. Light, delicately spiced, the occasional snippet of barley sugar. *50%. nc ncf sc. 337 bottles.*

Old Malt Cask Auchroisk Aged 22 Years refill hogshead, cask no. 13302, dist Feb 94, bott Feb 17 (90) n22 t23.5 f22 b22.5 Rare that an Auchroisk keeps its integrity quite so well. The early moments of the delivery are sublime. *50%. nc ncf sc. 287 bottles.*

Provenance Auchroisk Aged 8 Years refill hogshead, cask no. 11190, dist Apr 08, bott May 16 (85) n21 t22 f21 b21 Faultlessly clean and mouth-watering. But a little too clean and lightweight, perhaps, allowing the lingering new-makey aspect a little too much rope. Attractive late cocoa. *46%. nc ncf sc.*

Provenance Auchroisk Aged 8 Years refill hogshead, cask no. 11489, dist Apr 08, bott Nov 16 (84) n21 t21.5 f20.5 b21 Very similar to cask 11190, though perhaps lacking a little of the sparkle on the maltiness. *46%. nc ncf sc. 249 bottles.*

Whisky Castle Auchroisk 7 Year Old bourbon hogshead, dist 2009, bott 2017 (94) n23 t23.5 f23.5b24 In this kind of cask Auchroisk is probably at its optimum age as the marriage between its vibrancy and still measured elements of the oak is at its happiest. Well worth a trip to Tomintoul to grab this one, as this, for me, is numbered among the best ever bottlings from the distillery. *46%. Bottled by Morrison and Mackay Ltd.*

AULTMORE
Speyside, 1896. Bacardi. Working.

Aultmore 12 Year Old db (85.5) n22 t22 f20 b21.5. Not quite firing on all cylinders due to the uncomfortably tangy oak. But relish the creamy malt for the barley is the theme of choice and for its sheer intensity alone, it doesn't disappoint; a little ulmo honey and marzipan doff their cap to the kinder vanillas. *46% WB16/028*

Aultmore 18 Year Old db (88.5) n22.5 soft, though with a vague spice nip. Otherwise, a mix of ulmo honey, treacle and cream toffee combine; t22.5 the barley makes the first play on delivery, a grassy volley which slowly vanishes into a mist of caramel; f22 that caramel persists – again of Toffo variety - but at least the spices can be heard; b21.5 charming, but could do with having the toffee blended out... *46%*

Aultmore 25 Year Old db (92.5) n23 t23.5; f23 b23 Now here's a curiosity: this is the first brand I have ever encountered which on the label lists the seasons the distillery was silent (1917-19, 1943-45, 1970-71) like a football club would once list on the front page of their official programme the years they won the FA Cup! Strange, but rather charming. And as for the whisky: succulent stuff!! *46% WB16/029*

⬗ **Aultmore Exceptional Cask Series 21 Years Old 1996** db (94.5) n24 t23.5 f23.5 b23.5 There is age creaking from every pore of this whisky. The nose is magnificently sensual with its orange blossom honey theme, spicy toasty tannins lurking at every corner. And those tannins carry on their impressive work, yet at the same time allowing a delicious alloy of malt and sultanas to not only thrive but fully fill the palate. Toward the end we are back to those insistent tannins which, if anything display an age greater than its given years. A malt plucked at the very right time from the warehouse: it would never have made half as good a 25-year-old. 54%. Selected for CWS.

⬧ **Cadenhead's Sherry Cask Aultmore 28 Year Old** dist 1989 (94) n23.5 no doubting the cask's provenance: also obviously from pre sulphur tainting days, as this the fruit is rich and unsullied, though also demure and happy to mingle with the oak; t23.5 though the oak taps out an aged theme, this remains mouth-watering. Like a Dundee cake, a nuttiness joining the burnt raisin and buttery barley; f23 the spices which had started long earlier continue to pulse, a little muscovado sugar and treacle in the background; b24 another sure- footed oldie from Cadenhead. 43.4%. sc.

⬧ **Chapter 7 Aultmore 9 Year Old** Oloroso Finish, cask no. 900160, dist 2008 (93) n22.5 intense moist Genoa fruitcake, with a strange mix of pencil shavings and pepper for company; t24 that was one outstanding oloroso butt, because the grape juices form a thick guad f honour for the light malt which can makes its way through. Weighty, viscous and sensual; f22.5 drier as a surprising degree of tannin marks its mark; a little bitterness, not unlike burnt fruitcake, mingles with the spices and late barley tones; b24 a clean, sulphur-free cask allows the whisky to develop naturally and in a beautifully relaxed manner – something of genuine rarity. Just enough malt gets through to keep the balance happy. 62.2%. sc.

⬧ **Endangered Drams Aultmore 9 Year Old** cask no. 900152, dist Apr 08, bott Jun 17 (77) n19 t20 f19 b19 Malty. But unlikely to win any gongs at the Speyside Distillers' Technical Distilling Excellence Awards anytime soon... 51.6%. nc ncf sc.

⬧ **Hepburn's Choice Aultmore 6 Years Old** bourbon barrel, dist 2010, bott 2017 (82.5) n21 t20 f21 b20.5 A curious malt which noses and tastes like a savagely undercooked bourbon. 46%. nc ncf sc. 345 bottles.

⬧ **Hepburn's Choice Aultmore 7 Years Old** refill butt, dist 2010, bott 2017 (85) n21 t22 f21 b21 Young, decent, no nonsense Speyside with a light banana milkshake sweetness to it. 46%. nc ncf sc. 792 bottles.

⬧ **Hidden Spirits Aultmore 11 Year Old** Amarone cask finish, dist 2006, bott 2018 (93) n22.5 a slight milkiness from an old cask is soon overshadowed by a sharp, grapey nuance which gets forever spicier; t24 a delivery of, and for, your dreams: breathtaking weight and sheen to the arrival with the malt and fruit on pretty much equal terms; the sugars melt towards a honeyed stance while the spices begin to jab and prickle with obvious intent; f23 although only eleven, the oak really does turn out in force, though always controlled and as back up to the busy spices which work so well with the hickory and plums; b23.5 a vague hint of tightness on the nose turns out to be a false warning. Instead we are treated to a malt of rare intensity, a swashbuckling, cut and thrusting dram if ever there was one: Amarone for all, all for Amarone...! 51.6%.

Liquid Treasures Aultmore 10 Year Old bourbon cask, dist 2006, bott 2017 (83) n20 t21 f21 b21 Not quite the greatest cask at work here makes for a jerky and uncomfortable ride. Some tangy salt and thick malt does offer compensation. 58.7%. Artist Edition.

⬧ **Provenance Aultmore Aged 6 Years** refill hogshead, cask no. 12072, dist May 11, bott Aug 17 (77) n19 t21 f18 b19 There is borderline genius in the way this malt fails either on the nose on palate to find the remotest degree of harmony with the vaguely smoky notes veering this way and that and out of control against the puckering barley and off key milky finish. 46%. nc ncf sc. 452 bottles.

Scotch Malt Whisky Society Cask 73.82 14 Year Old virgin char, heavy toasted heads American barrel, dist 23 Sept 02 (91.5) n21.5 t23.5 f23 b23.5 About as subtle as a punch in the kisser. Very different and no shortage of magnificent moments. 55.3%.

Whisky Broker Aultmore 23 Year Old (89) n22 22.5 f22 b22.5 A novel Aultmore displaying in a way unusual even by its own non-conformist standards. Both on nose and finish there is a tang I cannot place for certain. 51.1%.

⬧ **The Whisky Chamber Aultmore 9 Years Old 2008** bourbon hogshead (92) n23.5 spellbindingly complex: beautiful honey tones partner the ever-warming spices while the malt and vanilla are equally hand in glove; t23 salivating, intense and increasingly rich as the oils gather. As on the nose, the light acacia honey is always detectable and supports the massive barley with aplomb. The spice is more subdued than expected but that adds to the excellence of the balance; f22.5 a wonderfully warming cocoa powder fade...; b23 an exceptionally fine bourbon cask helps the whisky blossom to a complexity above its years. 61%. sc.

World of Orchids Aultmore 10 Year Old bourbon cask, dist 2006 (86) n21.5 t22 f21.5 b21 Magnificent colour for a bourbon cask of this vintage. However, the tannins and malt are at times happily as one, then at odds with each other. It is like picking a fruit ripe on one side, over-ripe on another and then under-ripe in the middle. Some attractive orange-citrus thrust, intense barley and chocolate, but all are quite divorced from each other. 55.7%.

BALBLAIR
Highlands (Northern), 1872. Inver House Distillers. Working.

Balblair 10 Years Old db (86) n21 t22 f22 b21. Such an improved dram away from the clutches of caramel. 40%

Balblair Aged 16 Years db (84) n22 t22 f20 b20. Definitely gone up a notch in the last year. The lime on the nose has been replaced by dim Seville oranges; the once boring finish reveals elements of fruit and spice. It's the barley- rich middle that shines, though, and some more work will belt this up into the high 90s where this great distillery belongs. 40%

Balblair 1965 db (96.5) n23 t24.5 f24.5 b24.5 Many malts of this age have the spirit hanging on in there for grim life. This is an exception: the malt is in joint control and never for a moment allows the oak to dominate. It is almost too beautiful for words. 52.3%

Balblair 1969 db (94.5) n22.5 t23.5 f24 b24.5. A charmer. Don't even think about touching this until it has stood in the glass for ten minutes. And if you are not prepared to give each glass a minimum half hour of your time (and absolutely no water), then don't bother getting it for, to be honest, you don't deserve it... 41.4%

Balblair 1975 db (94.5) n24.5 t23.5 f23 b23.5. Essential Balblair. 46%

Balblair 1978 db (94) n24 t24 f23 b23. Just one of those drams that exudes greatness and charm in equal measures. Some malts fall apart when hitting thirty: this one is totally intact and in command. A glorious malt underlining the greatness of this mostly under-appreciated distillery. 46%

Balblair 1983 Vintage 1st Release dist 1983, bott 2014 db (95) n23.5 t23 f24.5 b24 the last Balblair 83 I tasted fair won my heart and undying devotion with its beauty and complexity. This may also be a beautiful and shapely morsel, but the over exuberance of the oak means this is more of a spicy, pleasure-indulging, hedonistic one night-stand than lasting, tender love. Mind you... 46%. nc ncf.

Balblair 1989 db (91) n23 t23 f22.5 b22.5. Don't expect gymnastics on the palate or the pyrotechnics of the Cadenhead 18: in many ways a simple malt, but one beautifully told. Almost Cardhu-esque in the barley department. 43%

Balblair 1989 db (88) n21.5 t22 f22.5 b22. A clean, pleasing malt, though hardly one that will induce anyone to plan a night raid on any shop stocking it... 46%

Balblair 1990 db (92.5) n24 t23.5 f22 b23. Tangy in the great Balblair tradition. Except here this is warts and all with the complexity and greatness of the distillery left in no doubt. 46%

◈ **Balblair 1991 3rd Release** bott 2018, bott code L18/044 R18/5054IB db (94.5) n23.5 orange blossom honey drifts on the malty wind. Deft and understated, the oak noticeable now and again like trees drifting down a monsoon-swollen river; t23.5 for a malt of such antiquity, the landing could hardly be softer, nor the barley more intact. This is mouth-filling, juicy stuff. Slowly, though, tannins build as well as spices and sugar. All very correct and frightfully polite; f23.5 a little liquorice to accompany the now quietly fizzing spice and mocha; b24 a malt embracing its passing years and has aged, silver temples and all, with great style and panache. 46%. nc ncf.

Balblair 1997 2nd Release db (94) n23.5 t23.5 f23 b24 a very relaxed well-made and matured malt, comfortable in its own skin, bursting with complexity and showing an exemplary barley-oak ratio. A minor classic. 46%. nc ncf.

Balblair 1999 Vintage 2nd Release dist 1999, bott 2015 db (91.5) n23.5 t22.5 f23 b22.5 Always subtle and sensual. 46%. nc ncf.

Balblair 2000 db (87.5) n21.5 t22.5 f21.5 b22. No toffee yet still a clever degree of chewy weight for all the apparent lightness. 43%

◈ **Balblair 2000 2nd Release** bott 2017, bott code L17/R121 db (95.5) n24.5 a blitz of oaky tones, offering the full gamut from dry, slightly burned toast to intense dark cherry, via polished oak floors en-route. There are dark Jamaican rum notes, full of molasses, mixing it with marzipan; t24 superb layering of oils coat the palate, the roof of the mouth in particular, and extract every last nuance from that toasty oak; liquorice, natural vanillas and butterscotch form a delicious alliance; light, molten muscovado sugars balance the tannins brilliantly; f23 gentle oaky spices tingle while the oils allow the tannins to come to a flickering, but never overly bitter, conclusion; b24 first encountered this malt at a tasting I gave in Corsica earlier in the year. It blew away my audience while equally seducing me. Sampled back in the tasting lab, if anything it is even more stunning. The stock of this under-appreciated distillery rises by the day... 46%. nc ncf.

Balblair 2001 db (90.5) n23.5 t23.5 f21.5 b22.5 A typically high quality whisky from this outrageously underestimated distillery. 46%

Balblair 2003 Vintage 1st Release dist 2003, bott 2015 db (89) n21 t23 f22.5 b22.5 just like their 2013 bottling, gets off to an uncertain start on the nose but makes its mark on delivery. 46%. nc ncf.

Balblair 2005 Vintage 1st Release dist 2005, bott 2015 db (86.5) n20 t23 f21.5 b22. The nose is tight and has problems expanding, while the finish is short and quickly out of puff. But the delivery and follow through are superb with the malt really on maximum volume, and not without a little saline sharpness. Some good citrus, too. 46%. nc ncf.

⬦ **Gordon & MacPhail Connoisseurs Choice Balblair 1993** first fill sherry puncheon, cask no. 1965, dist 28 Jun 93, bott 20 Feb 18 (89) n22.5 curiously, amid the dark cherries, kumquats, and crushed physallis is a drowsy smoky note, though it could just be the oak acting in a rather strange way...; t22. sweeter delivery than the nose admits to, though after those early gristy sugars that odd note on the nose re-emerges and throws the fruit around a bit; f22.5 settled into a lovely, lightly spiced chocolate fruit and nut finale with a late vanilla surge; b22 a decent sherry puncheon, but struggles to find a rhythm. 51.6%. nc ncf sc. 624 bottles.

⬦ **Gordon & MacPhail Discovery Range Balblair Aged 12 Years** (95.5) n24 black cherry is normally associated with wine casks, but it is here from presumably American oak this time as a semi-bourbon signature strikes up an aroma of bewildering complexity. Leather and liquorice point to an older malt, yet the faultless integrity of the barley takes you on a trip around many different honey pots...; t24 just about a perfect mouth feel, even though reduced to 43%. Thinned ulmo and acacia honey add extra dimensions to the salivating barley; f23.5 now it passes the rice for the lesser strength as the finish is shorter than it should be, though still the vanilla and barley is happy to remain on its honeyed course; b24 Balblair is continuing its move to become recognised as one of the world's truly great distilleries. An understated epic whisky. 43%.

⬦ **The Single Malts of Scotland Balblair 19 Years Old 1997** cask no. 10117 (95.5) n23.5 classically dry thanks to the oak squeezing the malt into tight corners. The signature distillery notes are unmistakable, even though all the spices buzz with a degree of bourbon intensity; t24.5 truly fabulous delivery with the oak etched into every scene. The sugars are weighted beautifully to counter the spice attack. In pockets between the malt is in concentrated, briefly juicy, form, with the Balblair accent at its most pronounced; f23.5 as with the nose, goes into a semi austere, almost suave, lockdown mode with the dry tannins in quiet control; b24 every nuance has "Balblair" stamped all over it. A minor classic for this distillery. 56.2%. sc.

BALMENACH
Speyside, 1824. Inver House Distillers. Working.

Balmenach Aged 25 Years Golden Jubilee db (89) n21 t23 f22 b23. What a glorious old charmer this is! An essay in balance despite the bludgeoning nature of the beast early on. Takes a little time to get to know and appreciate: persevere with this belter because it is classic stuff for its age. 58%. Around 800 decanters.

Cadenhead's Small Batch International Balmenach 11 Year Old sherry cask, dist 2005 (92.5) n22.5 t24 f22.5 b23.5 A malt which doesn't sit still on the palate for a second. 46%.

⬦ **Hepburn's Choice Balmenach 12 Years Old** refill hogshead, dist 2004, bott 2017 (88) n23 just love that nose: has a bit of spirity hiss to it, but the punchiness of the barley is superb, especially the mix of citrus and celery; t22.5 salivating, clean, barley intense and warming; f20.5 thins a tad over eagerly; b22 drink in that nose...! 46%. nc ncf sc. 396 bottles.

Provenance Balmenach Aged 10 Years refill hogshead, cask no. 11247, dist Nov 05, bott May 16 (85.5) n21.5 t22.5 f21 b21 Intensely malty but perhaps a little one-dimensional. Dries with a slightly bitter twist. 46%. nc ncf sc.

Provenance Balmenach Aged 10 Years refill hogshead, cask no. 11636, dist Mar 07, bott Mar 17 (83.5) n21 t21.5 f20 b21 A little new makey and wide cut from top to bottom, so never sits quite right. 46%. nc ncf sc. 408 bottles.

Scotch Malt Whisky Society Cask 48.89 11 Year Old first fill ex-bourbon barrel, dist 29 Mar 05 (93) n23 t23.5 f23 b23.5 Beautiful, high-grade malt that fills the mouth with all kinds of goodies. 57.9%.

THE BALVENIE
Speyside, 1892. William Grant & Sons. Working.

The Balvenie Aged 10 Years Founders Reserve db (90) n23 t24 f20 b23 just one of those all-time-great standard 10-year-olds from a great distillery – pity they've decided to kill it off. 40%

The Balvenie Double Wood Aged 12 Years db (80.5) n22 t20.5 f19 b19. OK. So here's the score: Balvenie is one of my favourite distilleries in the world, I confess. I admit it. The original Balvenie 10 is a whisky I would go to war for. It is what Scotch malt whisky is all about. It invented complexity; or at least properly introduced me to it. But I knew that it was going to die, sacrificed on the altar of ageism. So I have tried to get to love Double Wood. And I have tasted and/or drunk it every month for the last couple of years to get to know it and, hopefully fall in love. But still I find it rather boring company. We may have kissed and canoodled. But still there is no spark. No romance whatsoever. 40%

The Balvenie 14 Years Old Cuban Selection db (86) n20 t22 f22.5 b21.5. Unusual malt. No great fan of the nose but the roughness of the delivery grows on you; there is a jarring, tongue-drying quality which actually works quite well and the development of the inherent sweetness is almost in slow motion. Some sophistication here, but also the odd note which, on the nose especially, is a little out of tune. 43%

The Balvenie 14 Years Old Golden Cask db (91) n23.5 t23 f22 b22.5 A confident, elegant malt which doesn't stint one iota on complexity. Worth raiding the Duty Free shops for this little gem alone. 475%

⟫ **The Balvenie Single Barrel Sherry Cask Aged 15 Years** db cask no 2075 (58) n14 t16 f14 b14 Lovely distillery. Shame about this shockingly sulphured cask. 478%. sc.

The Balvenie 16 Year Old Triple Cask db (84.5) n22 t22.5 f19 b21 Well, after their single cask and then double wood, who saw this coming...? There is nothing about this whisky you can possibly dislike: no diminishing off notes (OK, well maybe at the very death) and a decent injection of sugar, especially early on. The trouble is, when you mix together sherry butts (even mainly good ones, like here) and first fill bourbon casks, the intense toffee produced tends to make for a monosyllabic, toffeed, dullish experience. And so it proves here. 40% WB16/030

The Balvenie Double Wood Aged 17 Years db (84) n22 t21 f20 b21. Balvenie does like 17 years as an age to show off its malt at its most complex, & understandably so as it is an important stage in its development before its usual premature over maturity: the last years or two when it remains full of zest and vigour. Here, though, the oak from the bourbon cask has offered a little too much of its milkier, older side while the sherry is a fraction overzealous and a shade too tangy. Enjoyable, but like a top of the range Mercedes engine which refuses to run evenly. 43%

The Balvenie Double Wood Aged 17 Years bott 2012 db (91) n22.5 t23.5 f22 b23 A far friskier date than the 12-year-old. Here, maturity equals sophistication. Still not as outrageously sexy as a straightforward high grade bourbon cask offering from the distillery. But easily enough to get you hot under the collar. Lip smacking, high quality entertainment. 43%

The Balvenie Roasted Malt Aged 14 Years db (90) n21 t23 f22 b24. Balvenie very much as you've never seen it before. An absolute, mouth-filling cracker! 471%

The Balvenie Rum Wood Aged 14 Years db (88) n22 t23 f21 b22. Tasted blind I would never have recognized the distillery: I'm not sure if that's a good thing. 471%

Balvenie 17 Years Old Rum Cask db (88.5) n22 t22.5 f22 b22 For all the best attentions of the rum cask at times this feels all its 17 years, and perhaps a few Summers more. Impossible not to love, however. 43%

Balvenie New Wood Aged 17 Years db (85) n23 t22 f19 b21. A naturally good age for Balvenie; the nose is lucid and exciting, the early delivery is thick with rich malt. This, though, has sucked out lots of caramel from the wood to leave an annoyingly flat finish. 40%

The Balvenie 17 Year Old Sherry Oak db (88) n23 t22.5 f21 b21.5. Clean as a nut. High-class sherry it may be but the price to pay is a flattening out of the astonishing complexity one normally finds from this distillery. Bitter-sweet in every respect. 43%

The Balvenie Aged 21 Years Port Wood db (94.5) n24 t24 f23 b23.5 What a magnificently improved malt. Last time out I struggled to detect the fruit. Here, there's no escaping. 40%

The Balvenie Thirty Years Aged 30 Years db (92) n24 t23 f22 b23 Rarely have I come across a bottling of a whisky of these advanced years which is so true to previous ones. Amazing. 473%

The Balvenie Tun 1509 Batch 1 db (89) n23 t22.5 f21.5 b22 Balvenie is a distillery which struggles with age. And this is hanging on for life by its bloodied claws... 471%

The Balvenie TUN 1509 batch 2 db (94) n23.5 t24 f23 b23.5 A far happier and all round better balanced bottling than Batch 1. A big whisky, though you won't at first realise it... 50.3%

BANFF

Speyside, 1863–1983. Diageo. Demolished.

⟫ **Gleann Mor Banff Aged Over 42 Years** dist 1975 (91) n23 age may have wearied it, yet lovely, though sharp, raspberry note appears from somewhere to breathe life back into the barley; t23.5 it isn't all about the malty richness. It is more about the mouth feel... the light oils which both intensify and spread the positive notes. Almost like porridge with jam and demerara sugar melted on top...; f22.5 the oak begins to put up a wearied display, but creamy barley still retains pole position; b22 this was distilled in the same year I visited my first distillery in Scotland...and that was a bloody long time ago. Not many casks have made it from then to today, and those that have are in varying states of quality: old age does not always mean an improvement in a whisky's fortunes...often the reverse. This is a classic example of a malt which should have been bottled a little time back. But it is still massively enjoyable, throwing up the odd surprise here and there and keeping to the malty script despite the militant oak. Quite an experience.... *41.1%.*

Gordon & MacPhail Rare Old Banff 1966 (90) n22.5 t23 f22 b22.5 Quite a remarkable tail off in quality from their last bottling – but the age is going now into unknown territory for this lost distillery. Still excellent, though, and so much to enjoy... *46%.*

BEN NEVIS
Highlands (Western), 1825. Nikka. Working.

Ben Nevis 10 Years Old db (88) n21 t22 f23 b22. A massive malt that has steadied itself in recent bottlings, but keep those knives and forks to hand! *46%*

Ben Nevis Synergy 13 Years Old db (88) n22 t22 f21.5 b22.5 One of the sweetest Ben Nevises for a long time, but as chewy as ever! A bit of a lady's dram to be honest. *46%*

Best Dram Ben Nevis 18 Years Old (86.5) n21 t22.5 f21.5 b21.5. The huge oak takes absolutely no prisoners here. There is an imbalance of tannin over barley from the word go and the malt seems at least double its 18 years. Still, the chunky sugars do their best to take the sting from the oak, though it proves an unequal battle. *51.2%*

⁓ **Acla Selection Ben Nevis 17 Years Old** hogshead, dist 1998, bott 2016 (94) n23 beautifully toasty, complete with lightly salted butter...and even a hint of marmalade. The slight mint is a bit of a poser...; t23.5 distinctly confident delivery: the spices arrive almost rudely early while the barley ups in intensity for quite a while; f23.5 sophisticated finale: the oak is layered and dries in no great hurry. The spices are reinvigorated to startling effect while a little citrus laps around the edges; b24 very fine Ben Nevis, indeed. *48.3%. sc. 89 bottles.*

⁓ **Acla Selection Ben Nevis 19 Years Old** refill butt, dist 1996, bott 2016 (87.5) n22 t22.5 f21 b22 A nutty, slightly salty offering. Expands on delivery with a velvety fruitiness. But elsewhere is just a fraction tight, though there is no faulting the delicate cocoa and spice. *47.3%. sc. 90 bottles.*

Best Dram Ben Nevis 20 Year Old refill sherry butt, dist 1996, bott 2017 (81.5) n21 t23.5 f17 b20 There are those who will not feel the sulphur in this, like those who cannot tell the shudder of a minor earthquake rippling through their apartment. But it is there, sadly. A shame, as the early signals of plum pudding and Melton Hunt cake, all topped off with fabulous spiced sultana, were very promising. *57.1%.*

⁓ **Cadenhead's Ben Nevis Rum Cask 18 Years Old** dist 1998 (89.5) n22 a hard, brittle nose in danger of fragmenting. Here and there isolated barley escapes...; t22 the malt is intense and salivating in the delivery, but hits the palate like a brick. A little toasted fudge-like quality begins to reveal itself; f23 far more relaxed now with the malt shewing exceptionally deft qualities and the oak easily inclined towards mocha and praline; b22.5 rum casks can close a whisky slightly due to the sugars, as well as open. For the start, the doors to this malt remain shut, but the slow blossoming is a delight. *50.2%. sc. 210 bottles. 175th Anniversary bottling.*

⁓ **Cask 88 Ben Nevis 45 Year Old** sherry hogshead, dist 1972 (88.5) n22.5 its burnt toast and marmalade character shows it has almost given up the ghost, but just enough positive oak has hung around to bring out the best in the residual fruit; t22 an extra dose of muscovado sugar and molasses is required to see off the excesses of the puckering old oak; overall, gives a bigger ancient bourbon kick than malt one; f22 lively spices breath in fresh life; no shortage of toasty fudge; b22 a malt whisky tiring by the minute but gamely hanging on in there. *42%. nc ncf sc. 228 bottles.*

The Cooper's Choice Ben Nevis 19 Year Old port finish, dist 1996, bott 2016 (73) n18 t19 f18 b18 Seems more like a sherry wood to me, alas... *46%. nc ncf sc. The Vintage Malt Whisky Co.*

The Cooper's Choice Ben Nevis 19 Year Old sherry wood, dist 1996, bott 2016 (87) n20.5 t23 f22 b22.5 Somewhat on the tight side, especially on the nose, but really wraps out a lush, grapey malt of good weight with a big toffee undertone. *50%. nc ncf sc. The Vintage Malt Whisky Co.*

Deerstalker Ben Nevis 18 Years 3 Months dist Jan 99 (90) n23 t22.5 f22 b22.5 By no means your usual Ben Nevis at work; and not the usual ultra-delicate Deerstalker, either. A surprise package, and a delicious one at that...! *52%. sc.*

⁓ **Fadandel.dk Ben Nevis 21 Years Old** refill sherry cask, cask no. 18/1996, dist 9 Feb 96, bott 31 May 17 (95.5) n24 I could nose this all day, every day. The spices are operating sharply off two levels, one of almost sneezable pepperiness, the other deeper and warming. The fruit is of under-ripe apple; the oak come in gentle waves of red liquorice but never affects the overall dryness and sophistication; t24 what a delivery: fingers of fruit caress the taste buds with a degree of undisguised eroticism; the barley is more forthright and confident than apparent on the nose; the brown, toasty sugars delicate and low in profile but significant in contribution; f23.5 a buzzing spice attaches to the vanilla and butterscotch...; b24 that rarest of things: a beautiful clean sherry butt pulling the strings with panache. 51.1%. sc. 487 bottles.

The First Editions Ben Nevis Aged 20 Years 1996 refill hogshead, cask no. 13188, bott 2017 (94) n23.5 t24 f23 b23.5 Top of the range Ben Nevis... 56.9%. nc ncf sc. 66 bottles.

Hepburn's Choice Ben Nevis 6 Years Old refill barrel, dist 2011, bott 2017 (86) n21.5 t22 f21.5 b21 A fresh citrus theme combines with the light oils and sugars to loosen some of the tighter notes. 46%. nc ncf sc. 353 bottles.

Hepburn's Choice Ben Nevis 6 Years Old refill barrel, dist 2011, bott 2017 (87.5) n21 t22.5 f22.5 b21.5 This is the slightly paler version of two Hepburn Choice Ben Nevis of the same vintage. That lighter shade is reflected by the more distinct new make nose, though the clean, unfettered gristiness throughout is a joy. 46%. nc ncf sc. 359 bottles.

◈ **Hidden Spirits Ben Nevis 12 Year Old** heavily peated sherry cask, cask no. BN618, dist 2006, bott 2018 (76) n19 t21 f18 b18 The peat may be piled on high, but it can't disguise the failings of the sherry butt. 55.4%. sc.

Hidden Spirits Ben Nevis 13 Year Old cask no. BN417, dist 2004, bott 2017 (90.5) n22.5 t23.5 f22 b22.5 All the usual Nevis idiosyncrasies plus a delicious smoked storyline. 57.5%. sc.

◈ **Howard Cai Selected Ben Nevis 19 Years** sherry cask no 198 db (94) n23 from the very dry, noble school of oloroso; t23.5 every bit as mouth-filling as the nose suggests, though against the aroma early sugars emerge – very much of the muscovado variety. Despite the big fruit presence the malt still powers through. A great combination and genuinely delicious! f23.5 reverts to its drier self but with a gorgeous interplay between the tannins of the grape and the tannins of the oak; b24 really uplifts the heart when great distillate combines with a faultless sherry butt and have the best art of two decades to work their magic. 50.4%. 260 bottles.

◈ **Kingsbury Gold Ben Nevis 20 Years Old** butt, cask no. 70, dist 1997 (94.5) n23.5 the sugars from the oloroso are so sharp, it almost boasts a rye-style personality. And for a 20-year-old, the crisp green apple touch is amazing; t23.5 pure silk on delivery: the grape s juicy and sublime, but light enough to let first the oak then the barley into the act; f23.5 my Pavlovian response is to wait for sulphur...but it doesn't come. Instead I just enjoy the two-toned spice: one pulsing, the other tingling. And the rich toffee apple and moist fruitcake finale; b24 so rare to find a Scotch from this period with unspoiled sherry maturation. Superb. And not a bad way to mark my 750th whisky for the 2019 Bible... 573%. 247 bottles.

Kintra Whisky Ben Nevis Aged 15 Years sherry butt, cask no. 152, dist 23 Apr 01, bott 17 Nov 16 (91) n23 t23.5 f21.5 b23 A near faultless sherry butt and an outrageously flavoursome whisky! About as sophisticated as a punch in the kisser... 53.7%. nc ncf sc. Bottled by Whiskybroker Ltd.

Le Gus't Selection VI Ben Nevis 2006 sherry butt, cask no. 3, bott 2016 (84) n22 t22.5 f19 b20.5 Stupendously rich oloroso at play here – and from a faultless butt, also. The grape lends the malt a glossiness of texture which is hardly matched by the whisky's eccentric personality. Never quite sits still or allows the tannins and fruit to happily fuse, it is a dram always on the march. At times delicious, sometimes fascinating, always frustrating! 51.3%. 762 bottles.

Liquid Treasures Ben Nevis 19 Year Old bourbon cask, dist 1997, bott 2016 (86.5) n21 t22.5 f22 b21 A massive mouth-puckering, eye-watering dram where balance and elegance step back from taking part very early on. But for sheer mouth-watering juicy barley bludgeoning, this wins hands down. 51.9%. Fairy Tales Edition.

Old Malt Cask Ben Nevis Aged 15 Years refill hogshead, cask no. 13297, dist Nov 01, bott Feb 17 (81.5) n19 t22.5 f20 b20 The nose warns with a strident voice that all is not well. And once the first malty rays are extinguished, the off-key oak begins to take its toll. 50%. nc ncf sc. 77 bottles.

◈ **Old Malt Cask Ben Nevis Aged 16 Years** refill hogshead, cask no. 14755, dist Nov 01, bott Feb 18 (89.5) n22.5 gooseberry tart; some stewed apples steam on a side dish; t23 anything other than a salivating delivery would have made a mockery of the nose. Both sharp and sweet in pretty equal measure; much drier mid-ground as the oak slams home; f21.5 a very straightforward cocoa and vanilla fade with a touch of bitterness; b22.5 a really good, honest cask showing Ben Nevis is its forthright glory. 50%. nc ncf sc. 280 bottles.

◈ **Old Malt Cask Ben Nevis Aged 21 Years** refill hogshead, cask no. 14287, dist May 96, bott Sept 17 (91.5) n22 the oak comes like a plank in its thickness; salty barley adds bite; t23 that saltiness ups the richness of the malt from the first moment. Barley, barley everywhere – spice and molasses on the prowl; f23 even more spice and a real Milky Way chocolate nougat finale; b23.5 typically and pleasingly chunky and chewy for this distillery: just choc-a-bloc with character. 50%. nc ncf sc. 318 bottles.

Old Particular Ben Nevis 20 Years Old refill hogshead, cask no. 11354, dist Nov 96, bott Nov 16 (87) n20 t22.5 f22.5 b22 A beautifully bright whisky which celebrates the crystalline clarity of the crisp, sugary barley. Yet somehow fails to offer up the trimmings you might expect from a malt of this age. Still, well balanced and charming with none of the usual Ben Nevis weightiness. 49.8%. nc ncf sc. 260 bottles.

⁘ **Old Particular Ben Nevis 21 Years Old** refill butt, cask no. 11767, dist Apr 96, bott Jun 17 (91) n23 a refill it may be, but something of the Cream Sherry to this one. Surprisingly rich and complex; t23 a true translation from nose to delivery: oily and intense the light, juicy fruit mingles with the malt to make a handsome couple; f22.5 takes time, but the spices and oak make an elegant contribution; b22.5 unusually creamy and sweet for a Nevis: no complaints from me! 51.5%. nc ncf sc. 583 bottles.

Saar Whisky N°8 dist 1998, bott 2018 (79.5) n19 t21.5 f19 b20 One of the most oily single malts I have encountered for a while: the barley is huge on this and the spices are inevitable. But also a slightly feinty malt, unusually for a Scotch. 54.2%. ncf sc.

Sansibar Whisky Ben Nevis 1996 bott 2016 (82) n20 t22 f19 b21 Has all the directional skills of a North Korean missile. Both the nose and finish veer wildly off course but the sugars on delivery are explosive. 51.9%.

⁘ **The Single Malts of Scotland Ben Nevis 20 Years Old 1996** cask no. 1528 (92.5) n22.5 anyone with a love for spiced nuts and dates will be drawn to this; t23.5 on its day Ben Nevis has balls enough to just grab your taste buds and hammer them into a different dimension: this is one of those days. There is nothing subtle about the delivery, nor is it intended to be. Just one huge wave after another thumping remorselessly into the palate, the mix of dates and molasses offering a sweet respectability to the gung-ho, shoot on sight spices. Somewhere – somehow – the remnants of the barley can be detected, but the oak is now really starting to grab hold; f23 the spices try to batter all else before, but we are soothed by late, delicious, waves of minty chocolate; b23.5 strap yourself into the chair for this one: it is some ride...! 53.1%. sc.

⁘ **Spirit of Caledonia Ben Nevis 18 Years Old** sherry cask, cask no. 24 (95) n23.5 what a wonderful experience: Parkin Cake and Christmas Pudding rolled into one, with a little lavender just for good measure; the spices are throbbing from the glass; t24 anything other than a big delivery would make a liar of the nose: though the mouth feel is distinctly rounded and full, the spices have no difficulty puncturing the dense, fruity cloud to explode on impact on the palate; just towards the middle a little barley shows its hand, plus a little molasses, too; f23.5 sublime mix of mint and chocolate, not an unknown style with this idiosyncratic distillery...; b24 look what happens when you work with a perfect, unspoiled sherry butt... 51.7%. sc.

The Whisky Agency Ben Nevis 1988 (85) n20.5 t21.5 f22 b21 Malty, fat and initially well short of the sugars required for balance. But, slowly the big juices arrive and with it some residual grist to do battle with the spiced oak. 50.9%.

The Whisky Agency Ben Nevis 17 Years Old dist 1999 (85.5) n21 t22 f21.5 b21 No prizes for its gait, wit or elegance: this is a hobbling, lumpy old scruff of a thing. But there is something very appealing about the sharpness of the barley and its rough texture, like an old piece of tweed. 50.9%. Bottled for Casa de Vinos, Australia.

The Whisky Agency Ben Nevis 18 Years Old dist 1996 (89) n21.5 t22 f23.5 b22 A blending malt this would do a very useful job stirring up the lowish m knuckle-dragger, ungainly and looking for a fight at any moment. There is something almost endearing about its roughhouse style and the intensity of its maltiness deserves a standing ovation. 50.5%.

The Whisky Agency Ben Nevis 18 Years Old dist 1996 (92.5) n23.5 t23.5 22.5 b23 wonderfully coastal and alive! 51.2%.

⁘ **The Whisky Embassy Ben Nevis Aged 20 Years** cask no. 615, dist May 97, bott Aug 17 (90.5) n22 imagine spicy new cut grass and you've got this...; t22.5 succulent delivery with the barley fresh and lively despite the years. A little heather honey meets the encroaching oak head on; f23 a light roast coffee with a molassed polish b23 as sweet as a nut. 51.4%. nc ncf sc.

BENRIACH
Speyside, 1898. Brown-Forman. Working.

BenRiach 10 Year Old db (87.5) n20 t23 f22.5 b22. A much fatter spirit than from any time when I worked those stills. The dry nose never quite decides where it is going. But there's no doubting the creamy yet juicy credentials on the palate. Malty, with graceful fruit sugars chipping in delightfully. 43%

The BenRiach Aged 12 Years db (82.5) n21 t20 f21 b20.5. More enjoyable than the 43% I last tasted. But still an entirely inoffensive malt determined to offer minimal complexity. 40%

The BenRiach Aged 12 Years Matured In Sherry Wood db (95.5) n23.5 t24 f24 b24 Since previously experiencing this the number of instances of sampling a sherry wood whisky and not finding my taste buds caked in sulphur has nosedived dramatically. Therefore, to start my tasting day at 7am with something as honest as this propels one with myriad reasons to continue the day. A celebration of a malt whisky in more ways than you could believe. 46%. nc ncf.

The BenRiach Aged 16 Years db (83.5) n21.5 t21 f20 b21. Although maltily enjoyable, if over dependent on caramel flavours, you get the feeling that a full works 46% version would offer something more gripping and true to this great distillery. 40%

The BenRiach Aged 16 Years db (83.5) n21.5 t21 f20 b21. Pleasant malt but now without the dab of peat which gave it weight; also a marked reduction of the complexity that once gave this such a commanding presence. 43%. nc ncf.

The BenRiach Aged 17 Years Pedro Ximénez Sherry Wood Finish db (81) n21 t22.5 f17.5 b20 A prevailing problem with PX casks is that the influence of the hyper-sweet grape can have an overwhelming effect on a whisky. So while a number of eye-watering, succulent tones might arrive thanks to the grape influence, the overall picture of the malt may be obscured. That has happened to an extent here, and the bitter blood-orange finale doesn't help, either. 46%.

The BenRiach Aged 17 Years "Septendecim" Peated Malt db (93.5) n24 t24.5 f23 b24 proof, not that it is now needed, that Islay is not alone in producing phenomenal phenols... 46%. nc ncf.

The BenRiach Aged 18 Years Albariza db (92.5) n23 t23.5 f23 b23.5 Always preferable to see a fruit influence that is floored rather than flawed... 46%.

The BenRiach Aged 18 Years Dunder db (95.5) n24 t24 f23 b24.5 It may be Dunder, but it certainly ain't the pits...! 46%.

The BenRiach Aged 18 Years Latada db (92) n24 t23 f22 b23 The nose and delivery are the best I have encountered so far today...and I began tasting some nine hours ago.... 46%.

The BenRiach Aged 20 Years db (85.5) n21.5 t23 f19 b22. A much more attractive version than the American Release 46%. The barley offers a disarming intensity and sweetness which makes the most of the light oils. Only a bittering finish shuts the gate on excellence. 43%. nc ncf.

The BenRiach Aged 20 Years db (78) n19 t20 f19 b20. This is big, but not necessarily for the right reasons or in the right places. A big cut of oiliness combines with some surging sugars for a most un-BenRiachy ride. 46%. US Market.

The BenRiach Aged 21 Years Tawny Port Wood Finish db (87.5) n22 t21 f22 b21.5 I'm not sure if the cask finish was designed to impart a specific fruitiness profile or simply repair some tired old oak. In either case, it has been a partial success only. The intemperance of the tannin makes its mark in no small measure both on nose and delivery and it is only in the finish that the sugars bond strongly enough together to form a balance with the woody input. 46%.

The BenRiach Aged 22 years Moscatel Wood Finish db (81) n21 t23 f17 b20 Not sure any wine finish I have tasted this year has thrown up so many huge, one might even say challenging, perfumed notes which score so highly for sheer lip-smacking effect. Had this cask not given the impression of being sulphur treated what an enormous score it would have amassed...! 46%.

The BenRiach 25 Years Old db (87.5) n21.5 t23 f21 b22. The tranquillity and excellent balance of the middle is the highlight by far. 50%

The BenRiach Aged 25 Years Authenticus db (91) n23 t23 f22 b23 Every moment feels as old as a Roman senator...who is eventually stabbed in the back by Oakicus. 46%.

BenRiach 35 Year Old db (90) n23 juicy dates and plums are tipped into a weighty fruitcake; t24 sit right back in your armchair (no..? Then go and find one...!!) having dimmed the lights and silenced the room and just let your taste buds run amok: those plums and toasted raisins really do get you salivating, with the spices also whipping up a mid-life storm; f21.5 angular oak dries and bitters at a rate of knots; b22 sexy fruit, but has late oaky bite. 42.5%

BenRiach Cask Strength batch 1 db (93) n22.5 t24 f23 b23.5 If you don't fall in love with this one, you should stick to vodka... 57.2%

The BenRiach Curiositas Aged 10 Years Single Peated Malt db (90.5) n23 t23 f22 b22.5 "Hmmmm. Why have my research team marked this down as a 'new' whisky" I wondered to myself. Then immediately on nosing and tasting I discovered the reason without having to ask: the pulse was weaker, the smoke more apologetic...it had been watered down from the original 46% to 40%. This is excellent malt. But can we have our truly great whisky back, please? As lovely as it is, this is a bit of an imposter. As Emperor Hadrian might once have said: "ifus itus aintus brokus..." 40%

The BenRiach "Heart of Speyside" db (85.5) n21.5 t22 f21 b21. A decent, non-fussy malt where the emphasis is on biscuity barley. At times juicy and sharp. Just a tease of very distant smoke here and there adds weight. 40%

The BenRiach Peated Cask Strength batch 1 db (95) n24 the gentle, zesty lemon offers a clinically precise degree of lightness to the rolling smoke. A hint of acrid burnt toast in the air but of no greater intensity than the subtle dark sugars which perform a textbook balancing act; t23 youthful gristiness shows those Demerara sugars up to the max; the smoke is layered though each next one is deeper and with spices mounting...; f24 as a buttery dimension develops it just gets better and better...; b24 stunning whisky magnificently distilled and, though relatively young, almost perfectly matured. 56%.

BenRiach Peated Quarter Casks db (93) n23.5 there's a lot of peat in them barrels. The citrus is vital...; t24 a plethora of sugars and caramel leached from the casks make for a safe landing when the smoke and malt – with a slightly new make feel - arrive in intensive form; f22.5 the caramel continues, now with spice; b23 though seemingly youthful in some phases, works a treat! 46%

The BenRiach "Solstice" db (94) n23.5 t24 f23 b23.5. On midsummer's day 2011, the summer solstice, I took a rare day off from writing this book. With the maximum light available in my part of the world for the day I set off at daybreak to see how many miles I could walk along remote country paths stopping, naturally, only at a few remote pubs on the way. It was a fraction under 28 miles. Had this spellbinding whisky been waiting for me just a little further down the road, I am sure, despite my troubled left knee and blistered right foot, I would have made it 30... 50%. nc ncf.

Birnie Moss Intensely Peated db (90) n22 youthful, full of fresh barley and lively, clean smoke; t23.5 juicy, fabulously smoked, wet-behind the ears gristy sugars; f22 some vanillas try to enter a degree of complexity; b22.5 before Birnie Moss started shaving... or even possibly toddling. Young and stunning. 48%. nc ncf.

⬥ **Chapter 7 Benriach 9 Year Old** bourbon hogshead, cask no. 133, dist 2008 (85.5) n22 t22 f20 b21.5 As bourbon casks go, this is highly unusual. The usual markers have been removed and in their stead is a languid fruitiness, avec tang (which is quite dominant late on), determined to outgun the prolific spice. Those who remember fruit fudge will recognise the main thrust of this – though it never came this warm 59.8%. sc.

⬥ **Chapter 7 Benriach 9 Year Old** bourbon hogshead, cask no. 134, dist 2008 (88.5) n21.5 still some young notes scattered amid the barley; t22 salivating youthful gristiness which builds in weight and intensity: a touch of the Mars bar candy in midstream; the spices work hard to disguise the light new make character; f22.5 far better sugar distribution as a little molasses merge with the vanilla; b22.5 no disguising its comparative tender years. But juicily delicious all the same. 60%. sc.

⬥ **Endangered Drams Benriach 9 Year Old** cask no. 61, dist Apr 08, bott Jun 17 (86.5) n21.5 t22 f21.5 b21.5 A sparkling, simplistic Speysider. Light, but the barley is out in force with vanilla a generous sidekick. 57.8%. nc ncf sc.

⬥ **Hepburn's Choice Benriach 7 Years Old** refill hogshead, dist 2010, bott 2018 (84.5) n20 t23 f20 b21.5 Nothing essentially wrong with this whisky: packed to the gunnels with serious malty intent: indeed, it hits a beautiful spot two or three waves in after the delivery. Yet, like Bambi, its looks cute but is unsteady on its feet and falls flat on its face as often as not. 46%. nc ncf sc. 465 bottles.

BENRINNES
Speyside, 1826. Diageo. Working.

Benrinnes Aged 15 Years db (70) n16 t19 f17 b18. What a shame that in the year the independent bottlers at last get it right for Benrinnes, the actual owners of the distillery make such a pig's ear of it. Sulphured and sicklysweet, this bottling has little to do with the very good whisky made there day in day out by its talented team. Depressing. 43%. Flora and Fauna.

Benrinnes 21 Year Old ex-sherry European oak casks, dist 1992 db (83.5) n21 t22 f19 b21.5. Salty and soapy. Some superb cocoa moments mixing with the muscovado sugars as it peaks. But just a little too furry and bitter at the finish. 56.9%. 2,892 bottles. Diageo Special Releases 2014.

⬥ **Acla Selection Benrinnes 18 Years Old** hogshead, cask no. 819, dist 1997, bott 2015 (89) n22 t22.5 f22.5 b22 The distillery showing much richer fettle than normal with there being distinct depth to the barley and quite excellent cocoa on the warming fade. May have been bottled a few years back, but still around and worth finding as an above-average version of this distillery. 52.2%. sc. 138 bottles.

⬥ **The First Editions Benrinnes Aged 20 Years** refill hogshead, cask no. 14985, bott 2018 (78.5) n19 t21 f19 b19.5 An untidy whisky which never finds its purpose or rhythm. Cloying sweetness and sharp, jagged edges to annoy and ends in a stark bitterness. A first edition hardly worthy of a reprint. 45.4%. nc ncf sc. 94 bottles.

⬥ **Golden Cask Benrinnes Aged 21 Years** cask no. CM241, dist 1995, bott 2017 (87) n22.5 t22 f21 b21.5 Rips into the palate at full throttle but boasts a honey and marzipan padding which absorbs much, though not all, of the warmer moments. 55.8%. sc. 290 bottles.

⬥ **Hepburn's Choice Benrinnes 7 Years Old** refill hogshead, dist 2010, bott 2017 (84.5) n21 t21 f21 b21.5 Nothing wrong with this whisky whatsoever: sound distillate, if on the light side and ultra clean barley is never far from the surface from nose to finish. But never for a moment loses its new make tag. 46%. nc ncf sc. 378 bottles.

Hepburn's Choice Benrinnes 8 Years Old rosé wine finished refill hogshead, dist 2007, bott 2016 (72) n14 t20 f19 b19 A thorn among roses: plenty of prickle. 46%. nc ncf sc. 373 botts.

⬩ **Hepburn's Choice Benrinnes 8 Years Old** wine cask, dist 2009, bott 2017 (85.5) n21 t21.5 f21.5 b21.5 Threatens at times to be a spitfire of a dram but the passive maltiness calms things down for a decent if unexciting ride. The spices can't be tamed late on, though... 46%. nc ncf sc. 300 bottles.

⬩ **Kingsbury Gold Benrinnes 20 Years Old** hogshead, cask no. 11711, dist 1996 (91.5) n22 at first sniff a little gluey and thin. Slowly, though, the oak begins to spin a little magic and some vague bourbony notes sit prettily with the cake mix; t23.5 superb mouth feel, and even better deployment of ultra-intense barley. A little ulmo honey makes a telling contribution and offers the perfect landing ground for the forceful spices; f22.5 a more demure finale, complete with that trademark Benrinnes austerity at the death. But still well weighted and charming; b23.5 being Benrinnes you'd expect a bit of fire and attitude. But that character trait works well with the honey which has been assembled over the passing 20 years. 56.5%. 225 bottles.

Old Malt Cask Benrinnes Aged 19 Years refill hogshead, cask no. 13272, dist Oct 97, bott Feb 17 (86) n22 t22.5 f20.5 b21 An attractively lively Benrinnes, making the very best of the fresh grist and citrus start. Afterwards the oak gains a niggardly foothold. Even so, a better example of the distillery's work. 50%. nc ncf sc. 316 bottles.

Provenance Benrinnes Aged 8 Years refill hogshead, cask no. 11326, dist Feb 08, bott Aug 16 (83.5) n20 t21.5 f21 b21 Youthful, malty and attractively fat. You can see why this is so useful in a blend. 46%. nc ncf sc. 435 bottles.

Scotch Malt Whisky Society Cask 36.121 9 Year Old first fill ex-bourbon barrel, dist 8 Nov 06 (90) n22.5 t23 f22 b22.5 An outstanding cask influence results in the distillery at the top of its game for this age. All the usual bite and haphazardness. But some top drawer honey tones, too. 57.8%.

⬩ **Scotch Malt Whisky Society Cask 36.138 19 Year Old** refill ex-bourbon barrel, dist 15 Aug 97 (86) n21 t22 f21.5 b21.5 Benrinnes doing what Benrinnes does: a bit thin and hot in parts, but still plenty of attractive barley on the scene to make for an pleasantly mouth-watering dram. Decent oak helps. 60.9%. sc.

⬩ **Scyfion Choice Benrinnes 1997** Artania cask finished, bott 2017 (86.5) n22 t21.5 f21.5 b21.5 Not a flavour profile I have often experienced. Mouth-puckering and eye-watering fare where the effects of the cask seem to be above what poor old Benrinnes, hardly the most sturdy of malts, can cope with. Strangely enjoyable, in the same way you might enjoy a spin on the dodgems: expect the occasional very heavy jolt from any angle! 46%. nc ncf. 226 bottles.

Stronachie 18 Years Old (83.5) n21.5 t21 f20 b21. This is so much like the older brother of the Stronachie 12: shows the same hot temper on the palate and even sharper teeth. Also, the same slim-line body. Have to say, though, something strangely irresistible about the intensity of the crisp malt.46%

⬩ **The Whisky Embassy Benrinnes Aged 20 Years** cask no. 969, dist 1997, bott 2017 (86.5) n22 t22.5 f20.5 b21.5 A shame about the tangy fade. Until then the malt had acquitted itself well by keeping its occasional violent tendencies in check and maximising the sweetness of the malt. 48.9%. nc ncf.

Whisky-Fässle Benrinnes 18 Year Old hogshead, dist 1997, bott 2016 (89) n22.5 t22.5 f22 b22 As fettles go, this is Benrinnes in its finest... 52.2%.

BENROMACH
Speyside, 1898. Gordon & MacPhail. Working.

Benromach 10 Years Old matured in hand selected oak casks db (87.5) n22 t22 f21.5 b22. For a relatively small still using peat, the experience is a delicately light one. 43%

Benromach 15 Year Old db (78) n20 t22 f17 b19. Some charming early moments, especially when the grape escapes its marker and reveals itself in its full juicy and sweet splendour. But it is too short lived as the sulphur, inevitably takes over. 43%

Benromach 21 Years Old db (91.5) n22 t23.5 f23 b23 An entirely different, indeed lost, style of malt from the old, now gone, big stills. The result is an airier whisky which has embraced such good age with a touch of panache and grace. 43%

Benromach 22 Years Old Finished in Port Pipes db (86) n22 t23 f20 b21. Slightly Jekyll and Hyde. 45%. 3500 bottles.

Benromach 25 Years Old db (92) n24 t22 f23 b23 A classic old-age Speysider, showing all the quality you'd hope for. 43%

Benromach 30 Years Old db (95.5) n23.5 t24 f24 b24 You will struggle to find a 30-year-old with fewer wrinkles than this.. Magnificent: one of the outstanding malts of the year. 43%

⬩ **Benromach 39 Year Old 1977 Vintage** db (94) n23.5 just love that! The oak keeps threatening to go OTT but never quite manages, being pulled back by grapefruit, red liquorice and heather honey; t24 just love that! The oak keeps threatening to go OTT, but is pulled back by salivating barley, toasty sugars – fudge almost – and now hickory on top of burnt treacle tart; that citrus on the nose dribbles through from time to time; f23 just love that! A swathe of caramel comforts any tiring oak and blends in beautifully with the intact barley; b23.5 just love it when a whisky creaks and complains and lets you know just how old it is...but then produces the magic that keeps alive, well and captivatingly complex after all these years. 56%.

Benromach 100° Proof db (94) n23 t23.5 f23.5 b24 For any confused US readers, the strength is based on the old British proof strength, not American! What is not confusing is the undisputed complexity and overall excellence of this malt. 57%

◇ **Benromach 20th Anniversary Bottling** db (81) n19 t22 f19 b21 Bit of a clumsy whisky never really feeling right on the nose or palate, though has its better moments with a big malt crescendo and a delicate minty-chocolate movement towards the late middle and early finish. 56.2%.

Benromach 2005 Sassicaia Finish db (92.5) n22.5 t24 f23 b23. A sassy dram in every way... 45%

Benromach Cask Strength 1981 db (91) n21.5 t23 f23.5 b23. Really unusual with that seaweedy aroma awash with salt: stunningly delicious stuff. 54.2%

Benromach Cask Strength 2001 db (89) n21.5 t23 f22 b22.5. Just fun whisky which has been very well made and matured with total sympathy to the style. Go get. 59.9%

Benromach Cask Strength 2003 db (92) n22.5 t23.5 f23 b23.5 Hats off to the most subtle and sophisticated Benromach I have tasted in a while. 59.4%.

Benromach Heritage 35 Year Old db (87) n22 t21.5 f22 b21.5. A busy exchange of complex tannin notes, some backed by the most faded spice and caramel. All charming and attractive, but the feeling of decay is never far away. 43%

Benromach Heritage 1974 db (93) n23.5 t23 f23 b23.5 Made in the year I left school to become a writer, this appears to have survived the years in better nick than I... 49.1%

Benromach Heritage 1975 db (89) n22 t22.5 f22 b22.5 A bottling where the malt is hanging on for grim death against the passing of time. But the discreet light honey notes do just the trick. 49.9%.

Benromach Heritage 1976 db (86.5) n21.5 t21 f22.5 b21.5 There are times when you can have a little too much tannin and this has crossed the Rubicon. That said, look closely on the nose for some staggering lime and redcurrant notes which escape the onslaught as well as the gorgeous butterscotch on the finish as the sugars fight back at the death in style. Some moments of genius in the oakiest of frames. 53.5%.

Benromach Madeira Wood db (92) n22 t24 f23 b23. If you want a boring, safe, timid malt, stay well away from this one. Fabulous: you are getting the feeling that the real Benromach is now beginning to stand up. 45%

Benromach Marsala Wood db (86.5) n21.5 t22 f22 b21. Solid, well made, enjoyable malt, which in some ways is too solid: the imperviousness of both the peat and grape appears not to allow much else get through. Not a dram to say no to, however, and the spices in particular are a delight. 45%

Benromach Organic db (91) n23 t23 f22 b23. Young and matured in possibly first fill bourbon or, more likely, European (even Scottish) oak; you cannot do other than sit up and take notice of this guns-blazing big 'un. An absolute treat! 43%. nc ncf.

Benromach Organic Special Edition db (85.5) n22 t21 f21.5 b21. The smoky bacon crisp aroma underscores the obvious youth. Also, one of the driest malts of the year. Overall, pretty. But pretty pre-pubescent, too... 43%

Benromach Organic 2010 db (95.5) n24 a charming, understated essay in which malt, salted spice and barley sugar are described to perfection; the most delicate lavender and mint sub strata does no harm, either; t24 the melting of the gristy sugars on the palate is truly a work of art: one of the great moments of the 2017 whisky year and possible the most awe inspiring few moments since the distillery returned to production: barley simply doesn't come better defined or weighted than this. The delicate spice which follows is also straight off the blueprint; f23 the malt recaptures its intensity to dominate over the developing vanilla and butterscotch. The spices stay on course, also; b24.5 gentle, refined and exquisitely elegant. 43%.

Benromach Peat Smoke Batch 3 db (90.5) n22 t23 f22.5 b23 An excellent malt that has been beautifully made. Had it been bottled at 46 we would have seen it offer an extra degree of richness. 40%

Benromach Peat Smoke 2008 db (85.5) n22 t22 f20.5 b21 Well, that was certainly different! The nose has the oily hallmark of a Caol Ila, though without the phenol intensity. The palate, those oils apart, is a very different tale. A unique flavour profile for sure: a kind of smoked toffee fudge which actually makes your tongue ache while tasting! And there is a bitterness, also. Normally I can spot exactly from where it originates...this one leaves me baffled...though I'd go from the distillation if pushed. 46%.

Benromach Traditional db (86) n22 t21 f21.5 b21.5. Deliciously clean and smoky. But very raw and simplistic, too. 40%

◇ **Benromach Triple Distilled** db (88) n23 the firmness to the malt has an almost Irish pot still quality: sharp, yet with a firm, brooding disposition; t22.5 salivating and ultra-clean. Gristy sugars melt into the mix with vanilla upping the weight; f21.5 a slight oak-sponsored bitterness from the more antiquated casks makes its mark; b22 the finish part, a really charming barley character pervades throughout. 50%.

Benromach Vintage 1976 db (89.5) n23 t23.5 f21 b22 hardly complex and shows all the old age attributes to be expected. That said...a very comfortable and satisfying ride. 46%

Benromach Wood Finish 2007 Sassicaia db (86.5) n22 t22 f21 b21.5. Now back to the new distillery. Problem with this wood finish is that even when free from any taint, as this is, it is a harsh taskmaster and keeps a firm grip of any malty development – even on a dram so young. A brave cask choice. 45%

BLADNOCH
Lowlands, 1817. David Prior. Working.

Bladnoch Aged 6 Years Bourbon Matured db (91) n21.5 t22.5 f24 b23 The fun starts with the late middle, where those extra oils congregate and the taste buds are sent rocking. Great to see a Lowlander bottled at an age nearer its natural best and even the smaller cut, in a roundabout way, ensures a mind-blowing dram. 57.3%

Bladnoch Aged 6 Years Lightly Peated db (93) n23 t23 f23.5 b23.5 The peat has nothing to do with the overall score here: this is a much better-made whisky with not a single off-note and the cut is spot on. And although it claims to be lightly peated, that is not exactly true: such is the gentle nature of the distillate, the smoke comes through imperiously and on several levels. "Spirit of the Lowlands" drones the label. Since when has outstanding peated malt been associated with that part of the whisky world...?? 58.5%

Bladnoch Aged 6 Years Sherry Matured db (73.5) n18 t19 f18.5 b18. A sticky, lop-sided malt where something, or a group of somethings, conjures up a very unattractive overture. Feints on the palate but no excellent bourbon cask to the rescue here. 56.9%

Bladnoch Aged 10 Years db (94) n23 t24 f23 b24 This is probably the ultimate Bladnoch, certainly the best I have tasted in over 25 years. This Flora and Fauna bottling by then owners United Distillers should be regarded as the must-get-at-all-costs Bladnoch. If the new owner can create something even to hang on to this one's coat-tails then he has excelled himself. For those few of us lucky enough to experience this, this dram is nothing short of a piece of Lowland legend and folklore. 43%.

Bladnoch Aged 15 Years db (91) n22.5 t22.5 f23 b23 Quite outstanding Lowland whisky which, I must admit, is far better than I would have thought possible at this age. 55%

Bladnoch 18 Years Old db (88.5) n21 t23.5 f22 b22. The juiciness and clarity to the barley, and especially the big gooseberry kick, early on makes this a dram well worth finding. 55%

Kirsch Import Bladnoch 1989 refill bourbon barrel, cask no. 1297, bott 2016 (93) n23 t23.5 f23 b23.5 A malt which carried it great age with pride and honour. Delicious! 48.7%. 156 bottles.

Scotch Malt Whisky Society Cask 50.84 25 Year Old refill ex-bourbon barrel, dist 15 May 90 (89.5) n22.5 t23 f22 b22 A malt which takes on you on a long, convoluted journey spending most of its time trying not to crash into oak. 55.1%.

◇ **Scotch Malt Whisky Society Cask 50.95 27 Year Old** refill ex-bourbon barrel, dist 26 Jan 90 (94.5) n23.5 wonderful halfway-house between a liquorice-crusted bourbon and dyed-in-the-wool ultra malt. Sharp, clean yet powerful; t24 the barley first blood with a juicy malty, onslaught. But riding on its husk are those very same liquorice tones apparently on the nose as the bourbon character tries to keep in the game; a compromise of oak-dried ulmo honey fills the middle ground; f23 settles into a more sombre and grown up period of barley-oak layering; b24 Bladnoch revving up a malty intensity massive even for their own scale... Sublime. 59.8%. sc.

◇ **Scotch Malt Whisky Society Cask 50.96 27 Year Old** refill ex-bourbon barrel, dist 26 Jan 90 (86) n22.5 t21.5 f21 b21 An aggressive delivery with the oak taking few prisoners. Many pointers towards a tired cask: the citrus takes on the sharpness usually reserved for limescale remover, though the malt does its best to hold its ground, especially by launching a defence of concentrated, oily barley. Enjoyable, providing you don't mind the scratches. 53.7%. sc.

The Whisky Agency Bladnoch 25 Years Old dist 1990 (88) n22 t22.5 f21.5 b22 I suspect five or six years ago this malt was at its zenith. 52.2%.

BLAIR ATHOL
Highlands (Perthshire), 1798. Diageo. Working.

Blair Athol Aged 12 Years db (77) n18 t19 f21 b19. Thick, fruity, syrupy and a little sulphury and heavy. The finish has some attractive complexity among the chunkiness. 43%.

⬧ **Blair Athol 23 Year Old** ex-bodega European oak butts db (90.5) n23 it's all about the cask: the malt adds nothing positive, but the oak and fruitcake effect is sublime; t23.5 and there you go! Intense fruit sloshing around the palate with a spice kick for good measure f21.5 duller here as the malt itself does have some input. The spices continue to kick. A very slow dryness develops; b22.5 very often you think: "Aha! Here's an un-sulphur-treated sherry-matured malt!" And then find long into the finish that the taint turns up and sticks with you for another 20 minutes. Is there a slight trace on this late on? Yes. But it is one of the lightest and least concerning I have encountered this year. Which leaves you with plenty of luscious grape to enjoy... 58.4%. 5,514 bottles. Diageo Special Releases 2017.

⬧ **Acla Selection Blair Athol 28 Years Old** hogshead, cask no. 4863, dist 1988, bott 2016 (91) n23.5 this is huge and wildly convoluted. The massive, full on barley-fruit mix is tempered with the sugary strains of the old top shelf of a sweet shop: balls of lemon, lime and aniseed mixing with dusty Demerara; t22.5 so mouth-watering. Back to a fruity theme again, now watermelon with barley sugar and little ginger; f22 tires, leaving the oak to leave a light cocoa dusting; b23 a huge malt indicative of the unwieldly new make this would have been 28 years ago but now, in old age, find some charm to match the charisma. 47.3%. sc. 90 bottles.

Alos Sansibar Whisky Blair Athol 1988 bott 2016 (89) n22.5 t22.5 f22 b22 Hardly textbook, but enjoyable. 50.4%.

Best Dram Blair Athol 26 Years Old wine treated butt (66.5) n17 t18.5 f15 b16. I think they meant "sulphur ruined butt". 57.8%

Cadenhead's Small Batch International Blair Athol 28 Year Old bourbon casks, dist 1988 (87) n22.5 t22 f21 b21.5 Everything from the nose to the finish tells you that this bottling peaked a few years earlier as the sugars you'd expect to find have now turned to dry tannin. But there remain green shoots still where there is a late flowering, highlighting the richer, remaining elements of the barley itself. A fascinating display of contrary indicators. 53.6%.

The First Editions Blair Athol Aged 19 Years 1997 refill sherry butt, cask no. 12823, bott 2016 (83) n22 t21 f20 b20 Tight and sugary. A malt performing as though in a straightjacket, seemingly unable to relax. Good spices, though. 50.7%. nc ncf sc. 241 bottles.

⬧ **The First Editions Blair Athol Aged 22 Years** sherry butt, cask no. 14656, bott 2018 (87.5) n21.5 t23 f21.5 b21.5 A superior Blair Athol where the sherry influence is profound – in a juicy, spicy, nutty and all-round positive kind of way. However, the spirit itself is a little uncompromising in its hefty weight, meaning charm and elegance are at a premium. 57.7%. nc ncf sc. 234 bottles.

⬧ **Gordon & MacPhail Connoisseurs Choice Blair Athol 1997** refill American hogshead, cask no. 5720, dist 25 Aug 97, bott 21 Feb 18 (83) n21 t21.5 f20.5 b20 Nothing too wrong with the cask. The spirit, however, is determined to test you. Hops around the palate refusing to find a happy narrative, occasionally happening upon a lick of honey. But too often a dour bitterness. 54.5%. nc ncf sc. 255 bottles.

⬧ **Gordon & MacPhail Connoisseurs Choice Blair Athol 2008** bott 28 Mar 17 (84) n19 t21 f23 b21 You know how irritating and disappointing Blair Tony is. Yep, at times it's as bad as that. Though, entirely unlike Britain's former Prime Minister, it does actually have something interesting and relevant to say late on that is worth listening to. That spice and honey helped along with some subtle layers of cocoa makes for an elegant, insightful fade before finally shutting up. Mr Blair, grab a bottle and please take note. 46%.

⬧ **Hepburn's Choice Blair Athol 7 Years Old** wine cask, dist 2009, bott 2016 (86.5) n21 t23 f22 b20.5 A real sweetie. Sugars abound, some of a gristy nature, others of a more fruity origin. Enjoyable, especially on delivery, but don't expect too much in the way of balance. 46%. nc ncf sc. 413 bottles.

Hepburn's Choice Blair Athol 7 Years Old refill butt, dist 2009, bott 2017 (87) n21 t23 f21 b22 A chocolaty affair where, thankfully, the butt (though not quite perfect) does little damage. Instead the barley makes an early impact, complete with sugary oils and spices before making its sumptuous praline-laden crescendo. 46%. nc ncf sc. 714 bottles.

⬧ **Old Malt Cask Blair Athol Aged 21 Years** sherry butt, cask no. 14245, dist Oct 95, bott Sept 17 (85.5) n21 t22.5 f21 b21 Initially sweet on the tongue, there is also an eye-watering tartness which somehow matches the light mossy note on the nose. 50%. nc ncf sc. 366 bottles.

⬧ **Old Malt Cask Blair Athol Aged 22 Years** sherry butt, cask no. 14455, dist Sept 95, bott Nov 17 (87.5) n22 t22 f21 b22.5 Elements of walnut brown sherry to this. No off notes, but the original spirit has a Spartan feel, though the malt does surge through in places. Attractively unusual. 50%. nc ncf sc. 328 bottles.

⬧ **Old Malt Cask Blair Athol Aged 22 Years** sherry butt, cask no. 14657, dist Mar 95, bott Feb 18 (88) n22 intense oloroso concentrate; t22.5 salivating as the huge fruit entirely coats the mouth; uncompromising grape and molasses mysteriously moving off into a non-descript maltiness; f21.5 burnt raisins; b22 thick enough on the palate to paint walls with.

Enormous presence on the palate with the sugars and fruit flying in every direction. Hardly a sophisticated dram. But, very decent fun all the same. *50%. nc ncf sc. 292 bottles.*

◇ **Old Particular Blair Athol 15 Years Old** refill hogshead, cask no. 12106, dist Sept 02, bott Sept 17 **(86)** n22 t22.5 f20 b21.5 Lively and salivating with the barley sharp, focused and healthy. Just strays towards a certain tautness at the death. *48.4%. nc ncf sc. 357 bottles.*

Old Particular Blair Athol 21 Years Old sherry butt, cask no. 11355, dist Sept 95, bott Sept 16 **(89.5)** n23.5 t23 f21 b22 Not quite a flawless cask, but in today's terms this one's a bit of a belter! *51.5%. nc ncf sc. 204 bottles.*

◇ **Old Particular Blair Athol 21 Years Old** sherry butt, cask no. 11788, dist Nov 95, bott Jun 17 **(86.5)** n22 t22.5 f21 b21 By no means a bad sherry butt, offering much on the delivery before the slight awkwardness of the spirit itself begins to form a cloying persona. The tannins are also at times formidable. *51.2%. nc ncf sc. 321 bottles.*

Provenance Blair Athol Aged 14 Years refill hogshead, cask no. 11488, dist Oct 02, bott Nov 16 **(89.5)** n22.5 t22.5 f22 b22.5 Blair Athol at its most clean, malty and refreshing. Great fun! *46%. nc ncf sc. 379 bottles.*

Sansibar Whisky Blair Athol 1998 bott 2016 **(83.5)** n21.5 t22 f19 b21 No apparent flight plan for this malt, so it lands haphazardly offering random flavours, some fruity and malt-creamy, some, alas, unattractively bitter. *50.7%.*

BOWMORE
Islay, 1779. Morrison Bowmore. Working.

Bowmore Aged 10 Years Spanish oak sherry casks & hogsheads, bott code: L172033 db **(92.5)** n23.5 wow...!! This is some nose: the peat is as hefty and cinderish as I have come across from a Bowmore in an age. The fruit s clean and actually backs the phenols, rather than hinders them: superb! t23.5 a silky mouth feel is first enriched by muscovado sugars and molasses and then a gradual but unrelenting build up in peat. Very gratifying, indeed...; f22.5 the phenols return to the ashes suggested on the nose and a little oak, marmalade and burnt sugar bitterness creeps in, also...; b23 a very happy marriage between some full on peat and decent sherry butts makes for the intense malt promised on the label. *40%.*

Bowmore Aged 12 Years db **(91)** n22.5 t23.5 f22 b23.5 This new bottling still proudly carries the Fisherman's Friend cough sweet character, but the coastal, saline properties here are a notch or three up: far more representative of Islay and the old distillery style. Easily by far the truest Bowmore I have tasted in a long while with myriad complexity. Even going back more than a quarter of a century, the malt at this age rarely showed such relaxed elegance. Most enjoyable. *40%*

Bowmore "Enigma" Aged 12 Years db **(82)** n19 t22 f20 b21. Sweet, molassed and with that tell-tale Fisherman's Friend tang representing the light smoke. This Enigma hasn't quite cracked it, though. *40%. Duty Free.*

Bowmore Gold Reef oak casks db **(79)** n19.5 t21 f19 b19.5. Simple, standard (and rather boring and safe) fare for the masses gagged by toffee. *43% WB15/280*

Bowmore Aged 15 Years 1st fill bourbon casks, bott code: L172034 031 db **(88)** n23.5 t22 f21 b21.5 This was going swimmingly until the caramel just went nuts. I know first-fill bourbon casks are at work here, but hard to believe that was all natural... *43%.*

Bowmore Aged 15 Years sherry cask finish, bott code: L172073 db **(91)** n23 t22.5 f22.5 b23 A sherry influenced whisky outpointing a bourbon cask one....how often will you find that in this book...? *43%.*

Bowmore Aged 17 Years db **(77)** n18 t22 f18 b19. For all the attractiveness of the sweet fruit on delivery, the combination of butt and cough sweet makes for pretty hard going. *43%*

Bowmore Aged 18 Years db **(79)** n20 t21 f19 b19. Pleasant, drinkable Fisherman's Friend style – like every Bowmore it appears around this age. But why so toffee-dull? *43%*

Bowmore Aged 18 Years Oloroso & Pedro Ximénez casks, bott code: L172067 060 db **(82)** n20.5 t22.5 f19 b20 A dirty old nose – and I don't just mean the peat – pre-warns of the furry finish. But there is no denying the sheer joy of the voluptuous grape grappling with the phenols on delivery and in the wonderful moments just after. *43%.*

◇ **Bowmore Aged 19 Years The Feis Ile Collection** first fill sherry puncheon, cask no. 57,dist 13 Jan 98, bott 27 May 17 db **(97)** n24 as though the puncheon was sat in the sea with the waves lapping against it: everything is there, the tannins give a faux Kentucky kick, the thick grape to imbue the richest of fruitcakes, the hazy layering of smoke which appears to sandwich the fruit, oak and salt and hold it all together. Just so much... t24.5 the grape steals a march on the smoke, though this soon not only catches up but overtakes: indeed, the phenols, so relaxed yet purposeful on the nose make a solid statement here, refusing to bend to the will of the sherry. All the time the salt sharpens the flavours into a salivating mass, bringing out the sweetness, also, especially the muscovado and molasses; f24 at last settles into a more delicate narrative, though all the flavour points present before still busy and working hard. Toastier now with some overcooked Melton Hunt Cake at its burnt raisin best...; **b24.5** if there was an award for the Best Cask Chosen by a Distillery Manager 2019, then it would go to this extraordinary bottling. A problem with sherry butts, even if entirely free from sulphur as this delightfully is, is their propensity to mask the actual distillery from which the whisky comes. Not here: this is as instantly and unmistakably recognisable as a Bowmore as the first three notes are as the signature of 'Goldfinger'. The salt from the No 1 warehouse, the light layering of smoke...well done distillery manager David Turner take a bow for your Bowmore....the finest I have ever tasted...! 54.3%. sc. Distillery Exclusive

⬧ **Bowmore 20 Years Old 1997** sherry cask, bott 2017 db **(95.5) n24 t24 f23.5 b24** The curtain of thick musky peat which descends on the nose leaves no doubt that we are in for one big sherried, oaky experience. And so it proves, although not quite in the fashion you might expect. For the softness on delivery is at odds with the boldness on the nose though, slowly, rung by rung the oak begins to take an increasingly more powerful hold: it is like experiencing whisky in slow motion. The fruit is a mix of blood orange and concentrated plum, the oak (here taken to its max) and smoke together creating a peaty chocolate spine. A malt of breath-taking enormity and beauty...to be devoured in slow-motion. 54.5%. sc. 231 bottles. Selected for CWS.

Bowmore Aged 23 Years Port Matured db **(86) n22 t22 f21 b21.** Have you ever sucked Fisherman's Friends and fruit pastels at the same time, and thrown in the odd Parma Violet for good measure...? 50.8%

Bowmore Aged 25 Years db **(86) n21 t22 f21 b22.** Not the big, chunky guy of yore: the age would surprise you if tasted blind. 43%

Bowmore Aged 25 Years Small Batch Release db **(85.5) n21 t22 f21 b21.5.** Distilled at the very heart of Bowmore's peculiar and uniquely distinctive Fisherman's Friend cough sweet era. You will never find a more vivid example. 43%

⬧ **Bowmore 29 Years Old 1989** db **(81.5) n20.5 t21 f20 b20** From that uniquely disjointed: Fisherman's Friend" period of their production history. 44%. sc. 170 bottles. Exclusive to The Whisky Shop.

Bowmore Aged 30 Years db **(94) n23 t24 f23 b24** A Bowmore that no Islay scholar should be without. Shows the distillery at its most intense yet delicate; an essay in balance and how great oak, peat and fruit can combine for those special moments in life. Unquestionably one of the best Bowmores bottled this century. 43%

Bowmore Black 50 Year Old db **(96.5) n25 t24 f23 b24.5** a little known fact: a long time ago, before the days of the internet and a world of whisky experts which outnumbers the stars that puncture the sky on the very darkest of nights, I actually tasted the first Black Bowmore in their very basic blending lab and gave it the required seal of approval before they allowed it to hit the shelves. It wasn't a 50-year-old beast like this one, though. And it proves that though something may have reached half a century, it knows how to give pleasure on at least a par with anything younger ... 41%

Bowmore 1985 db **(89) n21.5 t24 f22 b21.5.** I may have tasted a sweeter Islay. Just not sure when. This whisky is so wrong..it's fantastically right...! 52.6%

Bowmore 100 Degrees Proof db **(90.5) n22** low key smoke. Anyone who has been to Arbroath looking for where the Smokies are cured and homed in on the spot by nose alone will recognise this aroma...; **t23** delicate in all departments, including the peat. The barley is sweet but it is the tenderness of the oils which stars; **f22.5** long with a tapering muscovado finale; **b23** proof positive! A real charmer. 57.1%. ncf.

Bowmore Black Rock oak casks db **(87.5) n22.5 t22 f21 b22.** A friendly, full bodied dram whose bark is worse than its bite. Smoked toasted fudge is the main theme. But that would not work too well without the aid of a vague backdrop cinnamon and marmalade. If you are looking for a gentle giant, they don't come more wimpish than this. 40% WB15/336

Bowmore Devil's Casks III db **(92.5) n23 t23 f23.5 b23.5** a whisky created by Charles Williams, surely. So, at last....I'm in league with the devil....! Hawwww-hhaaaa-haaaaaa!!!! 56.7%

Bowmore Laimrig Aged 15 Years db **(90.5) n22.5 t23.5 f22 b22.5** first things first: absolutely spot on sherry butts at work here with not a hint of an off note. But often it is hard to get smoke and sherry to gel. The exercise here is not without success, but you feel it is straining at every sinew to hit the high spots. 53.7%. 18,000 bottles.

Bowmore Laimrig III db **(92) n23.5 t23.5 f22.5 b23** I must ask my research team: where the hell are Laimrigs I and II....? 53.7%

Bowmore Legend db **(88) n22 t22.5 f22 b22.5.** Not sure what has happened here, but it has gone through the gears dramatically to offer a substantial dram with both big peat and excellent balancing molasses. Major stuff. 40%

Bowmore Mizunara Cask Finish db **(90.5) n22.5 t22 f23.5 b22.5** A Bowmore like no other: not always happy in its own skin, but when it relaxes towards the finish, it positively pulses its Islay credentials. 53.9%. 2,000 bottles.

Bowmore No.1 first fill bourbon casks, bott code: L172026 db (91.5) n23 t23 f22.5 b23 Bowmore was never the most peaty of Islay's malts. But here the phenols are at their shyest. Delicate and all a rather sexy tease... 40%.

Bowmore Small Batch "Bourbon Cask Matured" db (86) n22 t22 f21 b21. A big improvement on the underwhelming previous Small Batch from this distillery, then called "Reserve", though there appears to be a naivety to the proceeding which both charm and frustrate. The smoke, hanging on the grist, is very low key. 40%.

Bowmore Small Batch Reserve db (80.5) n20 t21 f19 b20.5. With a name like "Small Batch Reserve" I was expecting a marriage between intense Kentucky and Islay. Alas, this falls well short of the mark. 40%

Bowmore White Sands Aged 17 Years db (88) n20 t22 f23 b23 A muzzled malt which shouldn't work – but somehow does. 43%

◇ **Cadenhead's Bowmore 16 Years Old** dist 2001 (95) n23.5 the phenol levels seem a little more challenging than normal and the sugary clarity of the peat reek really is something to celebrate; even a hint of well matured melon; t24 the delivery injects an instant dose of peat commensurate with the big phenols on the nose, then....quietness. The phenols fade back down to expected Bowmorian levels, but the excellent oak stirs up both the grist, the red liquorice and the praline; f23.5 what a fabulous fade of salted, smoked muscovado sugar. The gentle butterscotch kiss at the finale is a touch of class; b24 Mesmerisingly beautiful. 54.8%. 175th Anniversary bottling.

◇ **Cave Aquila The Eagles Collection Islay Single Malt 10 Years Old** batch no. 1 (88.5) n22 light and fruity, with a little diced banana amid the delicate phenol; a strange juniper note; t22.5 soft and pleasing delivery. The spices and basic sugars are just about in equal measure, the vanilla arriving to cool things down; f22 dries almost with a gin-like quality; b22 errs on the cautious, understated side of things. But tip toes elegantly around. 43%.

◇ **Dramfool 15 Bowmore 21 Years Old** bourbon hogshead, dist 1996 (93.5) n22.5 when distilled perhaps not at its finest: definite traces of Fisherman's Friend crazy days. But some extra vanilla and time has calmed things; t23.5 so salivating! The malt comes through with a wonderful light spearmint glaze to the mocha and sweet smoke; f23.5 not an ounce of bitterness, or reduction in grace. b24 has come of age in every sense: has a beautifully distinguished air. 52.9%. nc ncf. 299 bottles.

◇ **The First Editions Bowmore Aged 21 Years** refill hogshead, cask no. 14868, bott 2018 (90.5) n22.5 sooty and spicy; t22.5 excellent lift off into spice, followed by several waves of vanilla and butterscotch as the smoke thickens and Demerara sweetens; f22.5 complex and multi-layered with some delicate oils b23 so similar in personality to its sister OMC cask, except here it benefits substantially from better oak. 52.8%. nc ncf sc. 290 bottles.

◇ **Golden Cask Bowmore Aged 16 Years** cask no. CM232, dist 2000, bott 2016 (94) n23.5 a slightly more robust smokiness than is the norm, certainly above its usual 25ppm mark. Attractively crisp and clipped in its phenolic utterances, gloriously spiced, too; t23.5 salivating and warming with the sugary maltiness refusing to be dominated by the macho smoke; f23 superb spices, clean and lean but just enough oils to ensure a lingering, smoky fade. Distinctly biscuity; b24 very high quality, clean Bowmore, not instantly recognisable thanks to the extra peaty weight. 59.2%. sc. 234 bottles.

Kingsbury Gold Bowmore 18 Year Old hogshead, cask no. 800336, dist 1997 (96) n24 t24 f24 b24.5 A Bowmore with no little poise and very comfortable in its own skin. Above all, though, the complexity and balance shoots off the scale. A must find malt. 53.5%. 243 bottles. sc.

Old Malt Cask Bowmore Aged 14 Years refill hogshead, cask no. 12765, bott Oct 16 (90) n22.5 t22 f22.5 b23 The peat buds on my nose must be missing... 50%. nc ncf sc. 341 bottles.

Old Malt Cask Bowmore Aged 20 Years refill hogshead, cask no. 13284, bott Feb 17 (90.5) n22 t23 f22.5 b23 Superb sugar involvement and balance. 50%. nc ncf sc. 239 bottles.

Old Malt Cask Bowmore Aged 20 Years refill hogshead, cask no. 13301, dist Sept 96, bott Feb 17 (87) n22 t22.5 f21 b21.5 Enjoy the milk chocolate mousse middle, smoked of course. And with a good spoonful of Demerara sugar mixed in. Elsewhere there are a few bumps and grinds as the gears are not quite found. 50%. nc ncf sc. 275 bottles.

◇ **Old Malt Cask Bowmore Aged 21 Years** refill hogshead, cask no. 14267, dist Sept 96, bott Sept 17 (93.5) n23.5 a three pipe nose, needing a decent amount of time and reflection to get to the bottom of. The sugars are crisp, vaguely of a Demerara hue. But there is a beeswax note, too, sitting alongside the almost apologetic smokiness; t23.5 lies the nose, repays constant re-examination and rigid concentration. Seemingly in the reedy and sparse side, but further afield the sugars flex their muscles and a surprising degree of oils form a coherent backdrop. Surprisingly juicy and no great weight for the spices; f23 a slow burn of spice and an elegant oakiness; b23.5 a polished malt brimming with quality. 50%. nc ncf sc. 270 bottles.

⟨⟨⟨ **Old Malt Cask Bowmore Aged 21 Years** refill hogshead, cask no. 14867, dist Dec 96, bott Mar 18 (87) n22 t22.5 f21 b21.5 Plenty of sugars at work here, the majority of a muscovado variety, fitting snugly with the spice and coffee-themed smoke. But the oak is a bit on the rough side. 50%. nc ncf sc. 300 bottles.

⟨⟨⟨ **Old Particular Bowmore 15 Years Old** refill hogshead, cask no. 11804, dist Dec 01, bott Jun 17 (89.5) n22.5 fat aroma with the smoke in modest but attractive quantities; t22.5 relaxed sugars early on with the peat carried on very light oils; traces of lychee at the mid-point; f22 slow spice build, plus lovely cocoa; b22.5 unspectacular, but a really attractive and moreish shape to it. 48.4%. nc ncf sc. 321 bottles.

⟨⟨⟨ **Old Particular Bowmore 15 Years Old** refill hogshead, cask no. 12058, dist Sept 02, bott Sept 17 (86) n21.5 t22 f21 b21.5 Two peas in a pod, but clearly not identical. Compared to the OP cask 11804, this is a little shyer with the smoke and generally more austere, on the finish especially. 48.4%. nc ncf sc. 360 bottles.

Old Particular Bowmore 20 Years Old refill hogshead, cask no. 11590, dist Dec 96, bott Mar 17 (90.5) n22.5 t23 f22.5 b22.5 Unusually creamy Bowmore with a plethora of delicate, satisfying moments. 51.5%. nc ncf sc. 291 bottles.

Scotch Malt Whisky Society Cask 3.274 20 Year Old refill ex-bourbon hogshead, dist 6 Apr 95 (93) n23.5 t23 f23 b23.5 Huge profile, as though the salt has brought the flavours out to their maximum effect. A beautiful and significant cask. 53.1%.

⟨⟨⟨ **The Single Malts of Scotland Bowmore 22 Years Old 1994** cask no. 224 (89.5) n22.5 a whispered peatiness along with the crushed hazelnut and toffee; t22.5 as solid as a rock on the Bowmore shoreline. The smoke builds in intensity, aided by crystalline and crunchy Demerara sugars; f22 dries and spices up oakily and peatily on cue...; b22.5 sturdy and warming very much like in the lost style of its sister distillery Bowmore. 52.8%. sc.

The Whisky Barrel Burns Malt Bowmore 15 Year Old 2001 bourbon barrel, cask no. 31931 (94) n23 t24 f23 b24 Bowmore not a million miles in style to 35 years ago...and the smoke appears to be at the high end, too. 52.5%. sc.

WoodWinters The Four Isle Solera Aged 16 Years (83.5) n22 t22 f19 b20.5 Yes, I know: some people will sell their grandmother on eBay to raise the money for this. The huge, juicy grape locking horns with the peat; mega burnt fruitcake abounding. Yes, a Bowmore collectors' item and all that. But this is one of those malts where you have too much of a good thing and integration is at a premium. Also, the furry finish doesn't help... 58.1%. sc. 700 bottles.

BRAEVAL
Speyside, 1974. Chivas Brothers. Working.

The First Editions Braes of Glenlivet Aged 27 Years 1989 refill hogshead, cask no. 13310, bott 2017 (86) n21.5 t22.5 f21 b21 Works tirelessly hard to overcome the age-induced oaky imbalance. A little orange blossom honey infuses with the house-style big malty juiciness. But the thudding oak – though not without a vague mocha softness – has the biggest say. 54.9%. nc ncf sc. 144 bottles.

⟨⟨⟨ **Golden Cask Braes O'Glenlivet Aged 21 Years** cask no. CM234, dist 1994, bott 2016 (89.9) n22.5 I have nosed many a young bourbon which has less bourbon character than this malt: just love the mix of red liquorice and redcurrant sewn together by a fragrant grassy maltiness; t22.5 soft icing sugar melts on delivery before successive waves of tame malt lap gently at the taste buds. The mid-ground is more about the oak, a tangy, mouth-watering and lazily spicy return to understated bourbony ways; f22 a long, relaxed fade with more accent now on the spice; b22.5 there is a Kentucky twist to this malt which at times makes it as enjoyable as it is fascinating. 51.3%. sc. 195 bottles.

Gordon & MacPhail Connoisseurs Choice Braeval 1998 (90.5) n23 t23 f22 b22.5 A distillery which, through its delicate nature, wears its heart on its sleeves. And this is a very old heart... 46%.

⟨⟨⟨ **Gordon & MacPhail Connoisseurs Choice Braeval 1998** refill American hogshead, dist 1998, bott 22 Feb 18 (84.5) n21.5 t22 f20 b21 Not the first malt I have tasted this year which has the unmistakable hallmarks of a rushed distillate, where the stills have been fired a little too enthusiastically than is best for the whisky. The thinness to both nose and body coupled with the huge sugary outpouring as the grist and sweeter elements of the oak dominate. Then that flickering, faulting finale....59%. nc ncf sc. 185 bottles.

⟨⟨⟨ **Howard Cai Selected Braeval** (86) n21 t23.5 f21 b20.5 Many Chinese whisky lovers tend to be on the young side: now they have a whisky to match. This is a pre-pubescent Speysider in a stunningly beautiful, entirely blemish-free, clean-as-a-whistle sherry butt. Don't look for balance, as there isn't any of note. But just savour the delivery and first two or three flavour waves which are simply full of the joys of fruity, spicy, juicy young whisky. 46.1%. 1,800 bottles.

Hunter Laing's Distiller's Art Braeval Aged 14 Years refill hogshead, dist Dec 01, bott 2016 (89) n22.5 t22 f22 b22.5 This distillery does that understated Speysidey thing so well... 48%. nc ncf sc. 480 bottles.

Kingsbury Gold Braes of Glenlivet 21 Year Old barrel, cask no. 165589, dist 1994 (88.5) n21.5 t23 f21.5 b22.5 A malt full of malty energy but sometimes runs before it can walk. All very entertaining but, for a 21-year-old, surprisingly unkempt. 52.2%. 195 bottles. sc.

◇ **Le Gus't Selection XII Braeval 22 Years Old** bourbon cask, cask no. 165365 (85) n22 t22 f20.5 b21.5 An extremely malty procession, salivating and spicy at first then slightly wearing and tired towards the end. Not quick enough oomph to see off the slight oak bitterness that creeps in late on. 53.2%. sc. 178 bottles.

Old Malt Cask Braeval Aged 15 Years sherry butt, cask no. 13270, dist Dec 01, bott Feb 17 (85.5) n22 t21.5 f20.5 b21.5 Not sure whether to be pleased or disappointed with this. Anything marked "sherry butt" is enough to have me twitching in the chair and expecting the worst when raising my glass to the nose. But the aroma is initially clean and sulphur free: instead, a floral, salty tannin tone with a lovely toffee popcorn edge can be found. Slowly, though, the first traces of the S word are apparent...which can be found again on the finish after duller than expected delivery. Even so, a malt not without its salivating and delicious moments. 50%. nc ncf sc. 677 bottles.

Old Malt Cask Braeval Aged 25 Years refill hogshead, cask no. 12815, dist Aug 91, bott Oct 16 (95) n24 t24 f23 b24 An elegant gem of a dram. 50%. nc ncf sc. 238 bottles.

Old Particular Braeval 15 Years Old sherry butt, cask no. 11562, dist May 01, bott Nov 16 (90) n22 t23 f22.5 b22.5 Don't be put off by the colour or, rather, lack of it. Obvious this sherry butt was probably carved by Jesus' dad and now emptied is probably found somewhere in the British Museum. But because it is of such antiquity it pre-dates the Great Scottish Sulphur Cock-up and here we can experience Braeval in its most charming malty form. Really lovely stuff. 48.4%. nc ncf sc. 377 bottles.

Old Particular Braeval 18 Years Old sherry butt, cask no. 11205, dist Dec 97, bott Jun 16 (92) n23.5 t22 f23 b23.5 Effortlessly satisfying with sublime use of the sweeter elements. A Speysider for Speyside affectionados. 48.4%. nc ncf sc. 323 bottles.

The Single Cask Braeval Aged 22 Years cask no. 165641, dist 1994 (93) n23.5 t23 f23 b23.5 A typical example of a malt from a distillery which, at this age, is very comfortable in its own skin. 55%. nc ncf sc.

Wemyss Malts Braeval 1994 Oak For All Seasons first fill barrel, bott 2016 (91) n22.5 t23 f22.5 b23 A high quality, surprising dram which offers less colour and more smoke than you might expect from a first fill Speysider. 46%. sc. 255 bottles.

Whisky Broker Braes of Glenlivet 22 Year Old barrel, cask no. 65683, dist 20 Dec 94, bott 16 May 17 (90) n22.5 t23 f22 b22.5 Until the oak makes some slightly unwelcome late inroads, this is a story of delightful barley. 48.9%.

BRORA
Highlands (Northern), 1819–1983. Diageo. Closed.

◇ **Brora 34 Year Old** refill American oak hogsheads db (88.5) n22.5 skeletal fingers of age are all over this nose: citrus offers sinue and a little smoke the flesh...but time is catching up...(best nosed from an empty glass about half an hour later 24/25); t22 just as the nose transmits, the tannin is first up, but shewing signs of wear and tear. Grape juice quickly livens things up, but it is brief, a hit and run. The smoke tries to add extra weight, but the power is gone; f22 very tired, though the smoke battles on gamely, but in depleted numbers; a little chocolate fills in; b22 the nose kinds of sums things up perfectly: skeletal fingers of age are all over this: citrus offers sinew and a little smoke the flesh...but time is catching up... 51.9%. 3,000 bottles. Diageo Special Releases 2017.

Brora Aged 38 Years dist 1977 db (96.5) n24 t24 f24 b24.5 Where the 2015 bottling was a battle to keep the braying tannins in harness, this version has managed to link up both the peat and oak in thoroughbred pose. Soul-kissingly beautiful. 48.6%. 2,984 bottles. Diageo Special Releases 2016.

BRUICHLADDICH
Islay, 1881. Rémy Cointreau. Working.

Bruichladdich 10 Years Old db (90) n22 t23 f23 b22 More oomph than previous bottlings, yet still retaining its fragile personality. Truly great stuff for a standard bottling. 46%

Bruichladdich 12 Years Old 2nd Edition db (88) n23 t22 f22 b21. A similar type of wine involvement to "Waves", but this is oilier in the old-fashioned 'Laddie style and lacks a little of the sparkle. The fruit on the finish is outstanding, though, and I don't think you or I would turn down a third glass... 46%

Bruichladdich 15 Years Old 2nd Edition db (86) n22 t23 f20 b21. Delicious, as usual, but something, possibly fruity, appears to be holding back the show. 46%

Bruichladdich 16 Years Old bourbon cask db (89) n22.5 t22.5 f22 b22. Plucked from the cask in the nick of time. In this state rather charming, but another Summer or two might have seen the oak take a more sinister turn. 46%

Bruichladdich XVII Aged 17 Years bourbon/renegade rum db (92) n23 t23.5 f22 b23.5. Always good to see the casks of drier, more complexly structured rums being put to such intelligent use. My sample doesn't tell me which rum casks were used, but I was getting vivid flashbacks here of Ruby-Topaz Hummingbirds flitting from flower to flower in the gardens of the now closed Eigflucht distillery in Guyana in the long gone days when I used to scramble around the warehouses there. That distinctive dryness though is pure Enmore, though some Barbadian rum can offer a similar effect. Something very different and a top quality experience. 46%. nc ncf.

Bruichladdich 18 Years Old bourbon/cognac cask db (84.5) n23.5 t21 f20 b20. Big oak-spice buzz but thin. Sublime grapey nose, for sure, but pays a certain price, ultimately, for associating with such an inferior spirit... 46%

Bruichladdich 2004 Islay Barley Valinch fresh sherry butt db (89.5) n22.5 t24 f21 b22. Yet another quite fabulous bottling form Bruichladdich, this one really cranking up the flavours to maximum effect. Having said all that, call me mad if you will...but seeing as this is Islay barley, would it not have been a good idea to shove it into a bourbon barrel, so we could see exactly what it tastes like? Hopefully that is on its way... 57.5%

Bruichladdich Bere Barley 2009 7 Years Old bourbon barrel, cask no. 16/102 db (94) n23 t23.5 f23.5 b24 Bruichladdich wearing very different colours. Fabulous. 50%.

Bruichladdich Infinity Third Edition refill sherry tempranillo db (94.5) n24 t24 f23 b23.5. I dare anybody who says they don't like smoky whisky not to be blown away by this. Go on...I dare you... 50%

Bruichladdich Islay Barley Aged 5 Years db (86) n21 t22.5 f21.5 b21. The nose suggests a trainee has been let loose at the stills. But it makes amends with an almost debauched degree of barley on delivery which lasts the entirety of the experience. Heavens! This is different. But I have to say: it's bloody fun, too! 50%. nc ncf.

Bruichladdich Classic Laddie cask no. 16/175 db (93) n22.5 t23.5 f23.5 b23.5 Well, call me an ol' stick in the peat. But I'd regard a Classic Laddie as unsmoked....then, I must be of a certain age now, I suppose. This youthful cracker'll more than do, though... 50%.

Bruichladdich Islay Barley 2010 7 Years Old bourbon/French wine cask, cask no. 17/011 db (87.5) n21.5 t23.5 f21 b22 There is a rawness to this which brings a tear to the eye. Both the nose and finish are perhaps a little hamstrung, most probably by the French influence. But the delivery is something else! Brilliantly youthful, the peat doesn't even try to integrate, but comes at you full force. The grist still shews a fresh barley side to its nature divorced from the phenols, while a red liquorice and ulmo honey middle reveals a light degree of oak and sticky sweetness. But it is that no-holds-barred delivery which will win your smoky heart. 50%.

Bruichladdich The Laddie Eight Years Old American & European oak, cask no. 16/070 db (83) n21.5 t22 f19 b20.5 Doesn't chime anything like so well as the Classic Laddie, for instance. The sugars surge and soar in impressive manner, the mid-range smokiness benefitting. But there is a tightness which does very few favours. 50%.

Bruichladdich Laddie Classic Edition 1 db (89.5) n23 t23 f21 b22.5. You probably have to be a certain vintage yourself to fully appreciate this one. Hard to believe, but I can remember the days when the most popular malt among those actually living on Islay was the Laddie 10. That was a staunchly unpeated dram offering a breezy complexity. Not sure of the age on this Retroladdich, but the similarities almost bring a lump to the throat... 46%

Bruichladdich Scottish Barley The Classic Laddie db (78.5) n20 t21.5 f18 b19. Not often a Laddie fluffs its lines. But despite some obviously complex and promising moves, the unusual infiltration of some sub-standard casks has undone the good of the local barley. If you manage to tune out of the off-notes, some sublime moments can still be had. 50%. nc ncf sc.

Bruichladdich Sherry Classic Fusion: Fernando de Castilla bourbon/Jerez de la Frontera db (91) n23 t23 f22 b23. What a fantastically stylish piece of work! I had an overwhelming urge to sing Noel Coward songs while tasting this: for the Dry Martini drinkers out there who have never thought of moving on to Scotch... 46%

Bruichladdich X4 db (82) n18 t22 f21 b21. Frankly, like no new make I have ever come across in Scotland before. Thankfully, the taste is sweet, malty and compact: far, far better than the grim, cabbage water nose. Doesn't really have the X-Factor yet, though. 50%

The Laddie Ten American oak db (94.5) n24 t23.5 f23 b24 This, I assume, is the 2012 full strength version of an Islay classic which was the preferred choice of the people of Islay throughout the 70s, 80s and early 90s. And I have to say that this is already a classic in its own right... 46%. nc ncf.

The Laddie Sixteen American oak db (88) n22 huge natural caramels dipped in brine; t22.5 very even and gentle with a degree of citrus perking it up; f21.5 reverts to caramels before the tannins strike hard; b22 oak 'n' salt all the way... *46%*

The Laddie Twenty Two db (90.5) n24 a breakfast plate of three pieces of toast: one with salted butter, another with ulmo honey and the last one with marmalade; light spices, too. Busy yet understated; t23 silky salted butters again on delivery immediately backed by intense barley sugar; f21.5 the oak cranks up significantly; b22 fabulous coastal malt, though the oak is a presence always felt. *46%*

Octomore 5 Years Old db (96) n23.5 t24.5 f24 b24. Forget about the age. Don't be frightened by the phenol levels. Great whisky is not about numbers. It is about excellent distillation and careful maturation. Here you have a memorable combination of both... *63.5%*

Octomore Edition 5.1 db (91.5) n23 t22.5 f23 b23. A slightly less complex version, probably because of the obvious lack of years. Great fun, though. *59.9%*

Octomore Edition 6.1 Aged 5 Years bourbon cask db (91.5) n24 t23 f22 b22.5 A slightly different Octomore, a little more tart than usual and wears its youth with pride. *57%*

Octomore Edition 6.2 Aged 5 Years Cognac cask db (90) n22.5 t23.5 f22 b22 One of the sweetest bottlings from this distillery of all time. Some warming late spice, too; *58.2%*.

Octomore Edition 7.1 Aged 5 years (208 ppm) db (96.5) n24 t24.5 f24 b24 A gargantuan malt which will make short work of the feint hearted... This, also, was the whisky which Islay whisky maker par excellence Jim McEwen decided to bow out on. Farewell, Jim, my dear old friend of some 35 years.You have been to Scotch whisky what Jock Stein was to Scottish football; what Octomore is to Islay malt.... *59.5%*

Bruichladdich Ocotomore 7.1 5 Years Old ex-bourbon casks, cask no. 16/080 db (96) n23.5 t24.5 f24 b24 Fan-bloody-tastic...!! A kid of a whisky which sorts the men from the boys... *57%*.

Bruichladdich Ocotomore 7.2 5 Years Old bourbon & Syrah casks, cask no. 15/058 db (81.5) n21 t23 f18 b19.5 I love the fact that the sample bottles I have been sent under "education." Brilliant! An hilarious first. But here, if anything is to be learned by those who for some reason don't already know, is the fact that you don't piss around with perfection. Five-year-old Octomore in bourbon cask is a joy that has just about proved beyond description for me. Pointlessly add wine casks – and the sulphur which so often accompanies them – and you get a whisky very much reduced in quality and stature. Some superb moments on this, especially round the time of the warts-and-all delivery. But as it settles the faults of the Syrah casks slowly become clear. What a shame. And waste of great whisky. An education, indeed! *58.5%*.

Octomore 10 db (95) n24 t24 f23 b24 When I am tasting an Octomore, it means I am in the home straight inside the stadium after running (or should I say nosing and tasting) a marathon. After this, there are barely another 20 more Scotch malts to go and I am closing in on completing my 1,200 new whiskies for the year. So how does this fair? It is Octomore. It is what I expect and demand. It gives me the sustenance and willpower to get to that crossing line. For to tell you guys about a whisky like this is always worth it...whatever the pain and price. Because honesty and doing the right thing is beyond value. Just ask David Archer... *50%*.

Port Charlotte 2007 CC:01 Aged 8 Years bourbon/Cognac casks, cask no. 16/072 db (94.5) n23.5 t23.5 f23.5 b24 I think today I have tasted no less than seven Cognac/French wine finishes; a record. I had forgotten, but it turns out to be the day the French have elected a new president. Odd that. Here the Cognac can do little to lessen the impact of the huge peat and even offers a comforting, firm sweetness. However, the success of this over the PC 16/002 is the intensity of the phenol rather than the magic of the Cognac cask alone, though it certainly contributes. *578%*.

Port Charlotte Heavily Peated db (94.5) n23 t24 f23.5 b24 Rearrange the following two words: "giant" and "gentle". *50%*

Port Charlotte Scottish Barley cask no. 16/002 db (93.5) n23.5 t24 f23 b23 Sweet, youthful and a deceptively light smokiness: it sometimes appears heavier than it actually is! *50%*.

⟐ **Dramfool Port Charlotte 2009 8 Years Old** rum barrel (91) n22.5 an incredibly restrained nose: you can sense there is enormous peat at play, but it has been shackled...; spicy and a little salt, too; t24 the first four or five flavour waves are dull, as though the peat has been gagged. Then, suddenly, the dam bursts and the sweetest wave of phenols you can imagine bursts upon the palate. For a moment, there is a peaty whiteout as the nerve ending adjusts. Then you are aware of a searing sweetness, castor sugar gone nuclear; rich oils guide the growing vanilla towards the exit doors; f21.5 after such sweetness, the bitterness of the oak is too easy to detect..; b23 a very strange – one might say brave – choice of cask. Rum casks have the propensity to both bottle up the nose, as though putting a sugary straightjacket on, and greatly sweeten a whisky. And if something is already young and gristy... Still, it is enjoyable. And very different.. *62.7%*. 218 bottles.

◇ **Dramfool 8 Bruichladdich 6 Years Old** bloodtub, cask no. 4091 (86.5) n23 t22 f20 b21.5 Starts well with the youthfulness of the 'Laddie being played to brilliant, full-flavoured advantage. But after the first initial fruitcake and molasses kick off, descends into an unfortunate bitterness. 56.9%. nc ncf sc. 42 bottles

◇ **Dramfool 9 Bruichladdich 10 Years Old** bourbon barrel, cask no. 657, dist 25 Apr 07, bott 12 Oct 17 (89.5) n21 a lively aroma dominated by some wilder bourbon tones – red liquorice on steroids. The barley tries to speak but is a little intimidated by the tannin; t23.5 much better delivery: fat lush barley has the taste buds on full mastication alert. A little golden syrup makes an entrance just as the oak begins to reassert itself; f22.5 an impressive landing, full of bourbon-tannin codes as it becomes toastier by the moment. Some barley flickers, but briefly as the vanilla grabs hold again; b22.5 a beautiful dram, though there is a little hesitancy in the marriage between the barley and oak. 62.2%. nc ncf sc. 258 bottles.

◇ **Dramfool 13 Port Charlotte 2001 Aged 15 Years** bourbon hogshead, cask no. 847, dist Dec 01, bott Dec 16 (95.5) n23.5 huge salty peat nose: has the tingle factor as spices pop and nip. Yet from somewhere a little hickory squeezes in to represent the oak; t24 surprising layers of lemon and lime soften the huge peaty attack like a Swiss Roll acting as a sponge to soak up the smoke; f24 long? How long is a piece of Port Charlotte...? Oh, and that lemon and lime swiss roll really does make its mark at the death...in a peaty kind of way, of course...; b24.5 you know that I there was space for another atom in this improbably thick and fruity dram...it'd be a fruity peaty one... 58.3%. nc ncf sc. 195 bottles. *Spirit of Speyside 2018 release.*

◇ **Dramfool 14 Octomore 2011 6 Years Old** bourbon barrel (86) n22.5 t21 f21.5 b21 Too young for such enormity. Despite the excellent nose, bottled at a point when the peat shouts and screams but struggles to harmonise with any other characters in the play. Enjoyable if it is a peat fix you are after, but disappointing if you are looking for a balanced malt. 58.3%. nc ncf. 253 bottles. *Spirit of Speyside 2018 release.*

Fadandel.dk Bruichladdich 14 Year Old cask no. 569, dist Nov 01, bott Jul 16 (92) n22.5 t24 f22.5 b23 Has that wonderful feel of a malt taken directly, and that second, from the cask. Excellent. 57.2%. nc ncf sc. 276 bottles.

◇ **Hidden Spirits Lochindaal 10 Year Old** dist 2007, bott 2018 (94.5) n23.5 just enough oak to frame perfectly the citrusy lightness of the peat; t23.5 and yet more lemon squeezed all over the grist which just radiates its delicate sugars and ever-intensifying peat; f23.5 getting to the oaky – and salty - end of matters: a little more age than previously seen as the smoke joins forces with the distinctive Maryland cookie fade; b24 the one thing not hidden about this spirit is its unambiguous beauty. 53.1%.

◇ **Hidden Spirits Port Charlotte 14 Year Old** dist 2003, bott 2017 (64) n16 t17 f15 b16 And the latest score in during this World Cup summer: Sulphur 6, Peat 0. When even a PC in all its massively peaty glory cannot douse the ugly excesses of a sulphur-treated sherry butt, it shows you the enormity of the problem, however much people try to gloss over it. With my taste buds obliterated, that, I'm afraid, is my tasting day prematurely finished... 55.5%. sc.

Liquid Treasures Bruichladdich 26 Year Old bourbon cask, dist 1990, bott 2017 (91.5) n23.5 t23 f22 b23 Traditional unpeated style – and doesn't look any the worse for it. 47.3%.

◇ **Old Particular Bruichladdich 12 Years Old** 1st fill bourbon barrel, cask no. 12013, dist May 05, bott Aug 17 (88) n22 one of the nuttiest noses of the year; a little tannin goes a long way as the body is quite thin; t22.5 simplistic sweet maltiness. On the nose, the natural oils are limited giving the malt a bit of edge and the oak some bite; f21.5 quite hot now although a little chocolate and nut does help soften things; b22 distilled from hazelnuts? 48.4%. nc ncf sc. 253 bottles.

◇ **Old Particular Bruichladdich 12 Years Old** sherry hogshead, cask no. 12197, dist Jun 05, bott Nov 17 (74) n20 t20 f16 b18 The peat and grape find about as much common ground as the Presidents of the USA and Mexico. Bitter, harsh and unforgiving. 48.4%. nc ncf sc. 184 bottles.

That Boutique-y Whisky Company Bruichladdich 12 Year Old batch 3 (94) n24 23.5 f23 b23.5 must be a first fill bourbon in there somewhere as this is showing good age. Great to see a Laddie so close to its old-fashioned form: a treat of a dram. 52.4%. 275 bottles.

Xtra Old Particular Islay Bruichladdich 25 Years Old refill hogshead, cask no. 11204, dist May 91, bott Jun 16 (94.5) n23 t24 f23 b23.5 Old school Laddie: peat-free and living entirely off its considerable charm. 54.6%. nc ncf sc. 197 bottles.

BUNNAHABHAIN
Islay, 1881. Burn Stewart Distillers. Working.

Bunnahabhain Aged 12 Years db (85.5) n20 t23 f21 b21.5. Lovers of Cadbury's Fruit and Nut will adore this. There is, incongruously, a big bourbony kick alongside some smoke, too. A lusty fellow who is perhaps a bit too much of a bruiser for his own good. Some outstanding moments, though. But, as before, still a long way removed from the magnificent Bunna 12 of old... 46.3%. nc ncf.

Bunnahabhain Aged 16 Years Manzanilla Sherry Wood Finish db (87) n20.5 t23 f21.5 b22. The kind of undisciplined but fun malt which just makes it up as it goes along... 53.2%

Bunnahabhain Aged 18 Years db (93.5) n24 t24.5 f22 b23 Only an odd cask has dropped this from being a potential award winner to something that is merely magnificent... 46.3%. nc ncf.

Bunnahabhain XXV Aged 25 Years db (94) n23 t24 f23 b24 No major blemishes here at all. Carefully selected sherry butts of the highest quality (well, except maybe one) and a malt with enough personality to still gets its character across after 25 years. Who could ask for more...? 46.3%. nc ncf.

Bunnahabhain 46 Year Old db (91) n24 bourbon...Kentucky-by-the-Sea!! Salty big liquorice-shaped tannins with a mix of molasses and fruit which gets greater as the whisky oxidises in the glass. So many bourbon tones, yet as though it has been reduced by water from a rock pool...; t23 big age kick, but the more militant of the tannins are quietened by the sugars; f21.5 the oak shows one creak too many, though salty caramel moves in fill the cracks; b22.5 needs a good half hour in the glass to open up and have justice done to it. Perishes towards the end, but the nose and build up to that are remarkably beautiful for a whisky which normally doesn't age very well at all.... 42.1%.

Bunnahabhain Ceòbanach db (87.5) n21.5 t22.5 f21.5 b22. An immensely chewable and sweet malt showing little in years but much in character. A charming liquorice and acacia honey lead then a developing, dry smokiness. Great fun. 46.3%

Bunnahabhain Darach Ùr Batch no. 4 db (95) n24 t24.5 f23 b23.5 Because of my deep love for this distillery, with my association with it spanning some 30 years, I have been its harshest critic in recent times. This, though, is a stunner.. 46.3%. nc ncf.

Bunnahabhain Moine 7 Year Old Oloroso Finish db (85) n22 t23.5 f18 b21.5 Some three decades ago Bunna's warehouse manager and I would spend the odd long summer evening, year after year, going through samples of maturing stock, many of which were coming to life in dripping sherry butts. But that was a different whisky to this entirely: there was no peat. And the sulphur craze which was to dent the quality of so much Scotch had not yet arrived on Islay's shores, or even Scotland's. So the 7-year-old would taste nothing like this – instead it was usually maltier, a little creamier and showing the very first hints of a saltiness. It was even and relaxed. Which, sadly, this isn't. The faults are apparent on both nose and finish especially. But the grape intensity of the delivery is, momentarily, something special. 60.1%.

Bunnahabhain Toiteach db (78) n19 t21 f19 b19. Cloying, sweet, oily, disjointedly smoky. Had you put me in a time capsule at the distillery 30 years ago, whizzed me forward to the present day and given me this, it would have needed some serious convincing for me to believe this to be a Bunna. 46%

Bunnahabhain Toiteach Un-Chillfiltered db (75.5) n18 t21 f17.5 b19. A big gristy, peaty confrontation on the palate doesn't hide the technical fault lines of the actual whisky. 46%. ncf.

◈ **Drams by Dramtime Bunnahabhain Staoisha Edition 4 Years Old** dist 2013 (89) n22.5 sooty and dry with an undercurrent of sweeter grist and a little salt; t23 huge phenols make an immediate impact. Oily and soft on one hand, thumping phenols on the other, always with a big gristy, malty back up; f21.5 natural vanillas, caramels and peat, but all too youthful and unrefined to make much sense; late buzzing spice; b22 a ridiculously young, outlandish peaty whippersnapper. What fun! 59.5%.

Gordon & MacPhail Cask Strength Bunnahabhain 2007 bott 22 Nov 16 (93.5) n23.5 t23.5; f23 b23.5 Some magnificent cask selection at play here. Well done G&M!! 55.8%.

◈ **Gordon & MacPhail Cask Strength Bunnahabhain 2009** cask nos. 323 & 325, bott 21 Mar 17 (96) n24.5 a fabulous fruitiness haunts, the salty, ocean-rich aroma. Cleanly made, but though comparatively young it is already adorned with many complexities. Truly mesmerising: one of the best noses of the year...; t24 first, it is the texture which gets you, but almost immediately the taste buds are under attack (in the most delicious way possible!) from the most extraordinary salt and honey complexity which gets your juices flowing like few others have managed before: somehow, inexplicably your senses are telling you this is a very dry, yet very salivating malt – which makes no sense. However, the intensity of the barley does, as do the mallow-like vanillas which keeps it company; f23 near enough impossible to follow a delivery like that, so it doesn't try. Instead, it settles for a salty, malty, Malteser candy-like fade, though the spices continue to buzz; b24 a superbly dextrous Bunna, twisting and turning into many shapes and textures on the palate. A new age masterpiece. 60.5%.

◈ **Gordon & MacPhail Cask Strength Bunnahabhain 2009** cask nos. 326, 327 & 329, bott 14 Jun 17 (86.5) n22.5 t23.5 f19 b21.5 Bunna in bottled form as I have never quite seen it before. Unrecognisable from the "Westering Home" malt of the early 1980s. There is young spirit at work here which ensures the most salivating delivery of any Bunna known to mankind. Saltiness, too. But the overwhelming fruitiness does offer spice but at the cost of balance. *59%.*

⬥ **Gordon & MacPhail Cask Strength Bunnahabhain 2009** cask nos. 337 & 338, bott 20 Sept 17 (86.5) n21.5 t21.5 f22 b21.5 This is so far removed from the 12-year-old Bunna I grew up on, it is hard to know exactly where to start! This is very tart and for the start of its life on the palate unsure of its direction. Only when a vaguely salty, malty and distinctively chocolatey persona begins to form does it relax into something distinguished. *59%.*

Hunter Laing's Old & Rare Bunnahabhain Aged 27 Years refill hogshead, dist Oct 89, bott Jan 17 (93) n23.5 t23 f23.5; b23 The great age of this malt is etched into every sniff and mouthful. More than the temples are grey, but it remains distinguished nonetheless. *50.8%. nc ncf sc. 198 bottles.*

⬥ **Kingsbury Gold Bunnahabhain 19 Years Old** rum cask, cask no. 5386, dist 1997 (87.5) n22 t23 f21 b21.5 Was working rather beautifully and effortlessly until the bitter, unkempt finish arrived. But still plenty of scope to enjoy the docile, seemingly accidental, smokiness pitted against rich vanilla streaked with acacia honey: bliss. *54.3%. 198 bottles.*

⬥ **Le Gus's Selection XIII Bunnahabhain 6 Years Old** hogshead, cask no. 704139 (92.5) n23 youthful, breezy but displaying a disarming piquancy to the smoke; t23 all the big sugary grists are aboard and after riding those very large waves it settles down into a much more structured and better balanced malt. Lots of vanilla at play with trace ulmo honey; f23 the smoke has a buttery, doughy countenance now, like a lightly peated, undercooked muffin; b23.5 though the freshness of youth is there to see, this has grown up sufficiently to be regarded as a serious peated whisky of no little sophistication. *59.7%. sc. 278 bottles.*

⬥ **Liquid Treasures Entomology Bunnahabhain Over 28 Years Old** ex-bourbon cask, dist 1989, bott 2018 (96) n24.5 the light salty encrusting reveals a number of honey types when cracked, heather honey at the forefront. Old leather armchairs underline antiquity, then a slow deployment of orange blossom honey. The oak is far from dormant, supplying teasing spice and more creaking leather; t24 sublime texture: just a small amount melts on the plate to unveil slowly the lightest ulmo honey and barley sugars. Though gentle, a light saltiness ups the mouth-watering qualities. Red liquorice now points towards the oak while the spices for the first time become a little louder than the tapestry of gentle malt-shaped flavours; f23.5 even at the death the texture remains rich and complex, the ulmo honey travelling far. The spices remain mercurial, busy and seemingly refusing to end...; b24 old school Bunna. Spectacularly beautiful and one of the malts of the year. *44.9%.*

⬥ **The Loch Fyne Bunnahabhain 12 Year Old** sherry cask, cask no. 1312, dist Sept 05, bott Oct 17 (92) n23.5 nutty and dry, this is old-fashioned oloroso at its best. The molasses peep through in their roastiest form, for we are now heading into serious Melton Hunting Cake country. And few whiskies can lay claim to that today....; t23.5 magnificent. The delivery is well weighted without becoming remotely stodgy, the fruit growing in intensity without shutting down all other flavour avenues. Spices enter the fray with a spring in their step and gather intensity without undue haste; f22 a sulphur candle has been waved around briefly in the butt, but much shorter in time than normal. The resulting buzz is secondary to the fruit; b23 a way above average sherry butt, not something normally associated with Buna. For a 12-y-o, the delivery and follow-through could hardly be any better. Superb! *46%. sc. 950 bottles.*

⬥ **The Loch Fyne Bunnahabhain 16 Year Old** sherry cask, cask no. 3687, dist Dec 01, bott May 18 (86) n22 t24.5 f19.5 b20 Obviously has a bit of a weakness and it is all in the finish (other than the bit on the nose). But until it arrives, just suck on that amazing honey: it is though the sherry butt was filled with English summer flower honey (especially a type specialised in around Hook Norton, Oxfordshire). Worth going through the pain of the finish for the sheer ecstasy of the delivery. *57%. sc. 850 bottles.*

Old Malt Cask Bunnahabhain Aged 26 Years refill hogshead, cask no. 12626, dist Oct 89, bott Jun 16 (92.5) n23.5 t23.5 f22.5; b23 The half-hearted smokiness ensures an attractively understated yet complex dram. *49.8%. nc ncf sc. 127 bottles.*

Old Particular Bunnahabhain 15 Years Old sherry butt, cask no. 11604, dist Dec 01, bott Mar 17 (87) n22 t23 f20 b22 A clammy malt, moist and sticky on the palate, especially when the fruitcake kicks in. Not at all bad, but there is a slightly jarring bitterness out of keeping with the excellent dates and raisins. *48.4%. nc ncf sc. 611 bottles.*

Provenance Bunnahabhain Aged 8 Years refill hogshead, cask no. 11561, dist Jun 08, bott Nov 16 (83.5) n21.5 t22 f20 b20 A malty cove, quite literally. But just a little too new make heavy for any serious balance to be achieved or for the rougher edges to be blunted. *46%. nc ncf sc. 451 bottles.*

⬥ **Provenance Bunnahabhain Aged 10 Years** refill hogshead, cask no. 12220, dist Oct 07, bott Dec 17 (84) n20 t22 f21 b21 Sweet, smoky, young but lacking coastal character and overly simplistic. *46%. nc ncf sc. 658 bottles.*

◇ **Provenance Bunnahabhain Aged 12 Years** refill barrel, cask no. 11899, dist May 05, bott Aug 17 (87) n21 t22 f22 b22 A well-oiled dram revealing delicate peating levels and a high cocoa character. 46%. nc ncf sc. 275 bottles.

◇ **Romantic Rhine Collection Bunnahabhain 9 Year Old** cask no. 3813596, dist 2008, bott 2017 (78) n19 t19 f20 b20 Poorly made malt filled into a less than brilliant cask: about as romantic as coming home to find your partner in bed with your best friend. 52.3%. nc ncf sc.

◇ **Scotch Malt Whisky Society Cask 10.145 9 Year Old** refill ex-bourbon barrel, dist 07 Feb 08 (94) n23 superbly weighted phenols ensure the smoke has a certain calmness, like clouds filling a valley below a mountain road hiding the terrain below...; t24 a mix of gristy, ultra-malty sugars and maple syrup make for a friendly, sweet start...and then the peat begins to take hold, first with gentle caresses, then more forthright squeezes and finally, aided by spice, it starts to molest you...; f23 a very late fault in the oak barely detracts from the joy of the smoked Werther's Originals...; b24 Bunna in rip-roaring form...! 61.7%. sc.

◇ **Scotch Malt Whisky Society Cask 10.146 9 Year Old** refill ex-bourbon barrel, dist 07 Feb 08 (91) n22.5 the liveliness of the spice underlines the docile nature of the prevailing smoke and vanilla; t23.5 deliciously salivating kick off though, oddly, vanilla shows ahead of the barley. The smoke creeps up while your attention is diverted; f22 remarkably gristy to the very end, the sweetness countering a late light bitterness; b23 a very charmingly etched peated malt. 60.1%. sc.

The Single Cask Bunnahabhain Aged 25 Years cask no. 5429, dist 1991 (86) n21.5 t22 f21 b21.5 I'm struggling to find a narrative here and must rank this as a completely new branch of Bunna personality in the 35 years I have been tasting this stuff! 48.8%. nc ncf sc.

Wemyss Malts Bunnahabhain 1990 Haven Trail hogshead, bott 2016 (87) n22.5 t23.5 f20 b21 Forget the tannin overdose at the death and concentrate on the brief magnificence of the acacia and ulmo honeys mingling with the salted barley concentrate. Just for the odd nano second you think you detect perfection....and then, regrettably, the oak moves in... 46%. sc.

The Whisky Agency Bunnahabhain 1989 (94) n23.5 t23.5 f23 b24 Rare to see a Bunna handle so many passing years with such aplomb, though hardly with ease. 44%.

◇ **The Whisky Embassy Bunnahabhain Aged 9 Years** cask no. 3813649, dist 2008, bott 2017 (82.5) n21 t21 f20 b20.5 Malty but seriously struggles to find a happy combination despite a big vanilla intervention. 52.5%. nc ncf sc.

Whisky Broker Bunnahabhain 26 Year Old hogshead, cask no. 7728, dist 22 Dec 89, bott 18 Nov 16 (89) n22.5 t23 f21.5 b22 Lovely in to start with but wilts under the oak influence. 44.6%.

Wilson & Morgan Barrel Selection Bunnahabhain 15 Year Old 2016 sherry wood, cask no. 1431, dist 2001 (88) n23 t22.5 f21 b21.5 Just about gets away with the sulphur treatment: it is in there, lightly, but is out-muscled by the intense grape. 60.2%. sc.

World of Orchids Bunnahabhain 25 Year Old bourbon cask, dist 1990 (94) n24 t23 f23.5 b23.5 Bunna in all its old-fashioned unpeated, old school excellence. And, not only that, unusually for the distillery, it has thrived in its great age 47.7%.

CAOL ILA
Islay, 1846. Diageo. Working.

Caol Ila Aged 10 Years "Unpeated Style" bott Aug 09 db (93.5) n24 t23.5 f23 b23 Always fascinating to see a traditional peaty Islay stripped bare and in full naked form. Shapely and very high class indeed. 65.4%. Only available at the Distillery.

Caol Ila Aged 12 Years db (89) n23 t23 f21 b22. A telling improvement on the old 12-y-o with much greater expression and width. 43%

Caol Ila Aged 15 Years dist 2000 db (95.5) n24 t24 f23.5 b24 Any smoke detected here is token and a mere reflection of the distillery rather than substance. Instead we have a naked malt lustfully showing its beauty and proving there can be fire without smoke... 61.5%. Diageo Special Releases 2016.

Caol Ila 17 Year Old American oak ex-bourbon casks, dist 1997 db (90) n23 t23.5 f21.5 b22 a charming malt. But not one the serious Peat Heads out there will much appreciate. 55.9%. Diageo Special Releases 2015.

Caol Ila Aged 18 Years db (80) n21 t20 f19 b20. Another improvement on the last bottling, especially with the comfortable integration of citrus. But still too much oil spoils the dram, particularly at the death. 43%

◇ **Caol Ila 18 Year Old** refill American oak hogsheads db (96) n23.5 hickory acts as a dais from which the still confident phenol makes its impressive speech; mild mint and eucalyptus adds to the honeyed, oaky depth; t24.5 so, so beautiful...The peat appears to be absorbed into the oak, which in turns radiates honey and spice until you re reduced to a purring mass...; f23.5 coconut in golden syrup...with a light smoky lustre; b24.5 pretty sure there is no colouring or chill-filtration. This is the way Caol Ila should be: so true to the distillery. And whisky. 59.8%. Diageo Special Releases 2017.

◇ **Caol Ila Aged 25 Years** bott code: L71860M000 db (95.5) n24 quite a beefy, meaty phenol kick, with something of the farmyard for good measure. Unusually for Caol Ila, a little salty, too; t24 soft and buttery on delivery, the usual oils having taken on a more greasy feel. The sugars start to mount up impressively, while the spices become positively warm f23.5 the smoke rumbles along with spicy mischief; b24 even after all these years this malt can not only lay on its Islay credentials with its eyes closed, but does so with an almost haughty air, cocking a smoky snook at the passing quarter of a century... 43%.

Caol Ila 30 Year Old refill American oak & European oak casks, dist 1983 db (96.5) n24 wow! Like being back on Islay: the peat mixes quite brilliantly with rock pools with the tide out...you half expect to see crabs running about and starfish trying not to get stranded..; t24.5 one of the deliveries of the year: the silky oil one expects from this distillery, landing at first with a wave of rounded, understated peat plus salt and malt galore, then thickening with rich fruitcake and ulmo honey. The coastal saltiness bolsters the flavour profile, but not to the extent of overcooking it; f24 just more of the same, but with the slowest of fades...; b24 indisputably, one of the most complex, well-rounded and complete Caol Ilas I have tasted since they rebuilt the distillery... 55.1%. 7,638 bottles. Diageo Special Releases 2014.

Caol Ila Moch db (87) n22 t22 f21 b22. Easy drinking, but I think they mean "Mocha"... 43%

Caol Ila Stitchell Reserve "Unpeated Style" bott 2013 db (89) n23 t24 f20 b22 Not really a patch on the 2012 bottling, mainly due to inferior sherry butts, any smoke which does appear is like a half-imagined movement in the shadows. The delivery, though, is superb! 59.6% WB15/344

◇ **Cave Aquila The Eagles Collection Islay Single Malt 10 Years Old** batch no. 2 (90.5) n22.5 dry, ashy, a little brine of the citrus and the smoke on the gentle side; t23 a very comfortable balance between the peat and oak with the spices taking up the slack; f22.5 a surprising confidence to the oak ensures a dry finish; b22.5 lovely example of the distillery at this age with everything where it should be except for the heavier oils which appear to be hiding. 43%.

◇ **Dramfool 11 Cola Ali 9 Years Old** 1st fill Oloroso hogshead finish (88) n22.5 no doubting the cask type: dripping in fruit – though there is a light off note; the peat levels might be a little scary to the uninitiated...; t23.5 have to say the delivery really is on the money: a massive yet controlled explosion, or a friendly fisticuffs between fruit and phenol, one seemingly intent on outdoing the other; f20 big, sugary peat, but that sulphur note comes through at the end; b22 not a perfect butt, but worth experiencing for the delivery alone... 58.4%. nc ncf. 150 bottles.

◇ **Endangered Drams Caol Ila 9 Year Old** cask no. 4016823, dist 2008, bott 2018 (90) n22 remarkably clean and young, giving the peat extra space to reveal its light citrus muscle...; t23 gorgeous delivery. Off the charts in the salivation measurements. Busy, spicy grist full of phenols, then a sudden drop off in intensity, as the peat turns from fire to smoke...; f22.5 vanilla under a heavy shower of soot...; b22.5 a bottle of this is in danger of being drunk in a matter of hours... 53%. nc ncf sc.

◇ **Golden Cask Caol Ila Aged 25 Years** cask no. CM238, dist 1991, bott 2017 (94.5) n23 as can be the case with Caol Ila at this age, a real trip to the farmyard, the cattle byre in particular...; t24 even after all these years, melt-in-the-mouth grist heads us into acacia honey territory; the smoke remains true and significant, the spices delicate; f23.5 now the spices warm up. Yet still the smoke has a big say while the natural caramels are soft and buttery with a light layer of ulmo honey – even at this late stage; b24 a real smoky, complex stunner. 51.5%. sc. 121 bottles.

◇ **Gordon & MacPhail Connoisseurs Choice Caol Ila 1990** refill sherry hogshead, cask no. 1112, dist 31 Jan 90, bott 26 Feb 18 (86.5) n22.5 t22 f21 b21 A huge amount going on here; one might say too much. The nose warns that the oak is showing signs of advanced age and is not entirely checked and balanced by the still healthy fruit. Spiced, attractive, but fractionally out of sync. Those who like big oak and smoke will score this more highly. 49.6%. nc ncf sc. 176 bottles.

◇ **Gordon & MacPhail Connoisseurs Choice Caol Ila 1990** refill sherry hogshead, cask no. 1118, dist 31 Jan 90, bott 26 Feb 18 (95.5) n24 time has lightened the peat now to an unmistakable outline, TCP in the next room while melons and physalis make quiet noises of age; t24 eye-wateringly juicy, but that has a little do with age, as the oak is also initially sharp before the whole settles. Salty, a vague oil and light smokiness rolls around the plate; some Brazilian biscuit and more confident spices fill the middle; f23.5 beautifully pulsing spices match the most brilliant array of vanillas, confirming at this point oak of outstanding quality; b24.5 from the days when sherry hogsheads were sherry hogshead and not stink bombs and the oak was seasoned for the good of all. Sheer, unadulterated elegance... 50.7%. nc ncf sc. 191 bottles.

◇ **Gordon & MacPhail Connoisseurs Choice Caol Ila 2000** first fill bourbon barrel, cask no. 309606, dist 27 Oct 00, bott 26 Feb 18 (93) n23 good, positive age has crept into this: floral and earthy: an aroma those of us up at 6am in dark and dank Spring woods know only too well; the peat level is lower than some might expect or hope for, but it works well in context; t23 soft and yielding body, then fruity caresses as the oak takes a turn for the exotic fruitiness; f23.5 the phenols re now trace, thought the mint chocolate "Wizard" ice cream lolly effect charms; b23.5 elegant and understated from first to last moment. *57.5%. nc ncf sc. 180 bottles.*

◇ **Gordon & MacPhail Connoisseurs Choice Caol Ila 2003** first fill bourbon barrel, cask no. 302260, dist 10 Sept 03, bott 26 Feb 18 (88) n22.5 unusually firm, with few of the usual oils apparent. The peat is controlled mid-range for Caol Ila and offering a light spice accompaniment; t23 the huge sugar stampede on delivery is at odds with the nose. Lightly smoked molten muscovado and barley grist; f20.5 bitters out a little too quickly; b22 a very decent spirit slightly undone by the oak. *57.7%. nc ncf sc. 212 bottles.*

◇ **Gordon & MacPhail Connoisseurs Choice Caol Ila 2004** Hermitage wood finish, dist 2004, bott 13 Mar 18 (67) n16 t19 f16 b16 Oh dear. The "s" word strikes with a vengeance. *45%. nc ncf. 3,950 bottles.*

◇ **Gordon & MacPhail Cask Strength Caol Ila 2005** cask nos. 301522, 301530 & 301532, bott 30 Jan 17 (88.5) n22.5 exceptionally dry for a Caol Ila: there is a nipping astringency to the phenols; t22 the peat is surprisingly restrained: nothing like the usual 35ppm phenol blast. The sugars kick off brightly but are soon brought to heel by an austere, salty twist of the oak; f22 at last a little oil turns up – pretty late – and softens the previous granity ground; b22 a little tight and ashy with the sugars and oils unusually constrained. *56.8%.*

◇ **Gordon & MacPhail Cask Strength Caol Ila 2006** cask nos. 306183, 306184, 306186 & 306187, bott 30 May 17 (94.5) n23.5 beautifully adroit on the phenol front, the smoke coming across as both dry and sweet as it lends itself to a gristy curve; the little lightening citrus is welcome; t23.5 that delicate citrus shows more prominently on delivery and though the oils gather, there is something breezy about the structure. The sugars and spices go head to head in delightful fashion; a little Brazil nut and caramelised biscuit ensure a sturdy middle; the smoke both dive-bombs the palate and acts as surround sound; f24 now that is a quality finale: just carried on forever with playful spice on friendly terms with the gentle grist and smoky, minty milk chocolate; b23.5 succulent and lively. Ever increasing complexity. *60.2%.*

◇ **Gordon & MacPhail Discovery Range Caol Ila Aged 13 Years** (87.5) n22 t22 f21.5 b22 This is almost a re-run of their 2005 cask Strength Caol Ila (see above), probably drawn from the same family of casks, though at the reduced strength the breaking down of the oils means the intensity and complexity levels are significantly lowered. *43%.*

Hepburn's Choice Caol Ila 5 Years Old refill hogshead, dist 2011, bott 2017 (87) n22 t22 f21.5 b21.5 Anyone with a penchant for heavily peated, freshly ground grist will be kicking the doors down for this. Very limited complexity, but spices do ensure there is never a dull moment. *46%. nc ncf sc. 393 bottles.*

Hepburn's Choice Caol Ila 5 Years Old refill hogshead, dist 2011, bott 2017 (86) n22 t22 f20.5 b21.5 Pretty modest smoke by Caol Ila standards, and especially at an age when it is normally more forceful. Citrus, but tagged by a bitter tannin note. The palate is soft and salivating with a beautifully deft vanilla and gristy-phenol mix before the bitterness of the nose at last arrives for the finish *46%. nc ncf sc. 392 bottles.*

◇ **Hepburn's Choice Caol Ila 6 Years Old** refill hogshead, dist 2010, bott 2017 (87) n23 t22.5 f20 b21.5 A lovely peat-head's nose, brimming with oily phenols and the delivery ticks the right smoky boxes, also. The finish, though, is incomplete. *46%. nc ncf sc. 390 bottles.*

◇ **Hepburn's Choice Caol Ila 8 Years Old** wine cask, dist 2009, bott 2017 (89.5) n22.5 semi-acrid peat and dry grape peel: an attractive mix; t23 salivatingly sweet with a little orange blossom honey amid the oiled phenols; f21.5 dries and spices up significantly; b22.5 quite a polarising bottling. Not so much among drinkers, but in its distinct make up of very early sweetness on the palate dramatically set flush against the eye-wateringly dry finale. The peat appears to move on a slightly different plane, above it all but always on the dry, ashy side. *46%. nc ncf sc. 438 bottles.*

◇ **Hidden Spirits Young Rebels Collection Caol Ila 9 Year Old** dist 2008, bott 2017 (90.5) n22.5 lovely weave of peppermint and smoke; t23 sweet, youthful grist heralds the semi-brutal arrival of the thumping phenols and thickening oils; a slightly digestive biscuity dryness to the seeping barley and vanilla; f22 a little drying molasses can be found beneath and smoke and spice; b23 a straight down the line, no frills, exceptionally clean and technically solid example of a youngish Caol Ila. *52%.*

Hunter Laing's Old & Rare Caol Ila Aged 25 Years refill hogshead, dist Mar 91, bott Jan 17 (84.5) n22 t21.5 f20 b21 The nose radiates some meaningful smoke. But there is a bite beyond the spices that hints of mild potential oak problems further down the line...which are realised. *53.3%. nc ncf sc. 276 bottles.*

Scottish Malts

Hunter Laing's Old & Rare Caol Ila Aged 35 Years refill hoggy, dist Sept 80, bott Apr 16 **(88.5)** n22.5 t22 f22 b22 Probably needed a Zimmer to help the cask down the warehouse. 54.6%. sc.

⟷ **Kingsbury Gold Caol Ila 21 Years Old** hogshead, cask no. 791, dist 1996 **(95.5)** n24 time has muzzled the smoke but the remaining phenols offer sufficient weight and add ballast to the orange blossom honey and salt...; the oak rolls gently over the nose like a cotton bud cloud over a distant hill, offering both depth and a lovely degree of sophistication; t24 the honey springs into immediate action before a series of waves of concentrated barley thicken the malty soup. Again salt and spice are even-handedly added while the ancient phenols swirl contentedly; f23.5 a range of varying vanilla notes rounded with a little molasses and those laid back phenols; b24 if you could picture a 21-year-old Caol Ila in your mind, it wouldn't be far off this. Truly delightful. 56%. 247 bottles.

⟷ **Kingsbury Gold Caol Ila 35 Years Old** hogshead, cask no. 703, dist 1982 **(87)** n21 t22.5 f22 b21.5 The entire experience is shaped by oak which at times offers a degree of tannin that bristles a little too haughtily. Orange peel and gentle smoke offers succour. 46.1%. 80 bottles.

Kirsch Import Caol Ila 1997 refill American hogshead, cask no. 12522, bott 2016 **(94)** n24 t23.5 f23 b23.5 A standard well-casked Caol Ila...which means it's bloody good..!! 54.4%.

Le Gus's Selection IX Caol Ila 2008 first fill bourbon, dist 16 Jun 08, bott 28 Feb 17 **(93)** n23.5 t23.5 f23 b23 Just a lovely age for a Caol Ila when its vibrancy can still be captured – and not a single flaw. 59.5%. 235 bottles.

Old Malt Cask Caol Ila Aged 7 Years refill hogshead, cask no. 13267, dist Dec 09, bott Feb 17 **(90)** n22.5 t23 f22 b22.5 Even at such tender years this with its wings hardly spread this whisky has travelled a long way. 50%. nc ncf sc. 365 bottles.

Old Malt Cask Caol Ila Aged 7 Years refill hogshead, cask no. 13334, dist Dec 09, bott Feb 17 **(86)** n22 t22 f20.5 b21.5 Much tighter than its sister cask with the sugars muzzled late on especially, resulting in a starker, less enveloping dram altogether. 50%. nc ncf sc. 403 bottles.

Old Malt Cask Caol Ila Aged 8 Years refill hogshead, cask no. 13095, dist Nov 08, bott Nov 16 **(91.5)** n22.5 light, vaguely earthy and floral with the smoke drifting gently and without intent; t23 crisp barley ramps up the juice levels; the barley-sugar dissolves into the burgeoning phenols; f22.5 much drier with some clever peppery notes offering life and depth beyond its eight years; b23.5 initially docile on the smoke front, but swims in its own charm. Lovely stuff. 50%. nc ncf sc. 158 bottles.

⟷ **Old Malt Cask Caol Ila Aged 9 Years** refill hogshead, cask no. 14413, dist Nov 08, bott Nov 17 **(91)** n22.5 youthful, but just enough age to take off the edge. Fat, smoky and sweet; t23.5 sweet, gristy, oaky and spices – yummy!! f22.5 the earlier sugars dissolves leaving an ashy residue; b22.5 if you need proof of how beautifully made Caol Ila is, try this. Limited oak means the oils and peat superb structure is fully exposed. 50%. nc ncf sc. 242 bottles.

Old Particular Caol Ila 19 Years Old refill hogshead, cask no. 11208, dist Sept 96, bott Jun 16 **(96)** n23.5 t24 f24 b24.5 A magnificent example of this distillery in full song. 50.7%. sc.

Old Particular Caol Ila 20 Years Old refill hogshead, cask no. 11498, dist Sept 96, bott Nov 16 **(94.5)** n24 t23.5 f23.5 b24 Sheer class. Helped by some very understanding oak which interferes to a minimal degree. 51.5%. nc ncf sc. 316 bottles.

Provenance Caol Ila Aged 5 Years refill hogshead, cask no. 11346, dist Mar 11, bott Nov 16 **(91)** n23 t23 f22.5 b22.5 So young, but oh so beautiful...! 46%. nc ncf sc. 428 bottles.

⟷ **Provenance Caol Ila Aged 6 Years** refill hogshead, cask no. 11746, dist Nov 10, bott May 17 **(86.5)** n21.5 t23 f 20.5 b21.5 Distinctly new makey. Not only six years old but filled into casks hardly in the flush of youth. At least the vigorous eat and the salivating barley gets unfettered and delicious access to your taste buds. 46%. nc ncf sc. 387 bottles.

Spirits Shop Selection Caol Ila 1990 bourbon cask, bott 2016 **(91.5)** n23 t23.5 f22 b23 So rare a Caol Ila dependent on its honey and oak tones rather than peat for success. A genuine surprise – and delicious - package. 42.9%. 210 bottles. A joint bottling with Sansibar Whisky.

The Whisky Agency Caol Ila 2007 **(88)** n22.5 t22 f22 b21.5 A Caol Ila where the usual oils are remarkable by their absence. 53.7%.

Whisky-Fässle Caol Ila 10 Year Old hogshead, dist 2006, bott 2017 **(87)** n22 t22 f21.5 b21.5 The nose suggests a bitter tightness from the barrel may be on the cards further down the line. As it happens, those restrictions arrive sooner than forecast. Luckily, the full-bodied smokiness has sugars in reserve to still make for an attractive malt overall. 53.6%.

⟷ **Whiskyjace Caol Ila 5 Years Old** 1st fill Marsala cask, dist May 11, bott Feb 17 **(76)** n19 t21 f18 b18 Sorry, chaps, that I can't be more upbeat about such an unusual bottling: the age and cask type were a bit of a gamble. But from the sweaty armpit nose to the off-key finish it is a battle, though one where the cask treatment wins out in the end. 59%. 20 bottles.

Xtra Old Particular Islay Caol Ila 36 Years Old refill hogshead, cask no. 11491, dist Sept 80, bott Nov 16 **(95.5)** n23 t24 f24 b24.5 Caol Ila has the propensity to creak quite noisily when it hits a certain age – often one younger than this. But a superb cask - and a ladle full of honey - has ensured that life has gone on not just with dignity but aplomb. 57.4%. nc ncf sc. 172 bottles.

CAPERDONICH

Speyside, 1898. Chivas Brothers. Closed.

Acla Selection Caperdonich 21 Years Old bourbon hogshead, dist 1992, bott 2013 (87) n21.5 t22 f22 b21.5. Some older Caperdonichs have been among the most complex malts ever listed in the history of the Whisky Bible. However, this tends towards the other direction: simplistically malty. Actually, the malt itself is unerringly attractive. The hot bite which accompanies it is perhaps not quite so desired. 52.3%. nc ncf.

Hunter Laing's Old & Rare Caperdonich Aged 21 Years refill hogshead, dist Jul 94, bott Apr 16 (86.5) n21 t22 f21.5 b22 Technically, not the most gifted of single malts. But I have to admit I fully enjoyed this, starting with its attractive bonfire nose, the confiding nature of its ever intensifying malt and then its sweeping Tunnock's Teacake finale. Ignore the nip and fury of the delivery and the incisored bite of the finale: there are other things besides. 59.6%. nc ncf sc. 200 bottles.

CARDHU

Speyside, 1824. Diageo. Working.

Cardhu 12 Years Old db (83) n22 t22 f18 b21. What appears to be a small change in the wood profile has resulted in a big shift in personality. What was once a guaranteed malt love-in is now a drier, oakier, fruitier affair. Sadly, though, with more than a touch of something furry. 40%

⬧ **Cardhu Aged 15 Years** bott code: L8070IX00 db (87) n22 t23 f20.5 b21.5 Decent and easy going. But hang on: this is Cardhu! It should be offering a lot more than that. Does fine until the finish when the caramel kicks in without mercy, and other off-key moments develop. But love the citrus and pineapple on the nose and the oak layering on the delivery. This is a malt which should be 100% bourbon cask, preferably no colouring and allowing its natural brilliance to dazzle. 40%.

Cardhu 18 Year Old db (88) n22.5 t23 f20.5 b22 Very attractive at first. But when you consider what a great distillery Cardhu is and how rare stocks of 18 year old must be, have to say that I am disappointed. The fruit masks the more intricate moments one usually experiences on a Cardhu to ensure an acceptable blandness and accounts for a poor finish. Why, though, it is bottled at a pathetic 40% abv instead of an unchillfiltered 46% – the least this magnificent distillery deserves – is a complete mystery to me.40%

Cardhu Amber Rock db (87.5) n22 t23 f21 b21.5. Amber is the right colour for this: it appears stuck between green and red, not sure whether to go or not. The delivery, in which the tangerine cream is in full flow reflects the better elements of the nose. But the finish is all about being stuck in neutral. Not helped by the useless 40% abv, you get the feeling that a great whisky is trying to get out. The odd tweak and we'll have a winner. That said, very enjoyable indeed. Just even more frustrating! 40%. Diageo.

⬧ **Cardhu Gold Reserve** bott code: L8024IX02 db (86.5) n22 t22 f21 b21.5 Once, maybe two decades ago, Cardhu single malt was synonymous with malted barley shining at you from the glass in a lightly golden, gristy complexity, in near perfect harmony with bourbon casks in which it had been stored for a dozen years or so. It was very delicate in colour and even more fragile on the palate, flitting around like some exotic form of whisky sprite. The character of this malt is far removed from those halcyon days: this is dull and box-ticking, rather than its old inspiration self. That said, for a few brief moments, there is a fleeting glimpse into its past style, when a gently honeyed sheen flares and then fades. 40%.

CLYNELISH

Highlands (Northern), 1968. Diageo. Working.

⬧ **Clynelish Aged 14 Years** bott code: L7285CM008 db (86.5) n22 some malt nips though with a vaguely salty theme. Where is the usual honey? t22.5 soft, but a degree of caramel running through this might answer a previous question. A salty vanilla coupled with a lively maltiness lifts the mid-ground; f20 much duller with an over reliance on caramel; b21 very strange. This is one of the world's true Super Distilleries, in the top five of the most beautifully complex in Scotland. Yet from this very subdued, relatively character-bypassed bottling it would be hard to tell. 46%.

Clynelish Aged 15 Years "The Distillers Edition" double matured in oloroso-seco casks Cl-Br: 169-1f, bott code L6264CM000 03847665, dist 1991, bott 2006 db (79) n20 t20 f19 b20. Big in places, distinctly oily in others but the overall feel is of a potentially brilliant whisky matured in unsympathetic barrels. 46%

Clynelish Select Reserve ex-bourbon, rejuvenated & refilled American oak, and ex-bodega & refill European oak casks db (92) n23 t24 f22 b23 Does anyone do honey as well as Clynelish? The fact they can even pull it off with European oak involvement underlines the distillery's brilliance. 54.9%. 2,964 bottles. Diageo Special Releases 2014.

Gordon & MacPhail Connoisseurs Choice Clynelish 2004 bott 29 Nov 16 (96) n24 t24 f24 b24 Technically faultless. If every distillery was Clynelish, every bottler carried the stocks of Gordon and MacPhail...if every single bottle of whisky was like this, what a world we would live in... 46%.

⬙ **Gordon & MacPhail Connoisseurs Choice Clynelish 2005** refill sherry butt, cask no. 308764, dist 14 Jun 05, bott 21 Feb 18 (94) n24 a hefty, nutty nose. Very dry for this distillery but a little ground pistachio and mocha make it through the grip of the grapey influence; t25 this is a sensational delivery, something of rare, controlled enormity. The mouth feel is absolutely perfect: just enough viscosity to ensure the mix of sweet, muscovado and molasses-enriched fruit clings to the plate, yet allows the chocolate (actually, anyone who remember Payne's Chocolate and Raisin Poppets will be in raptures here) to make a vital incursion. The mid-ground fills up with the most intense and beautifully spiced vanilla; f21.5 sadly, the sherry butt wasn't 100% free of sulphur, but the treatment was light enough not to spoil the delivery and follow-through, though it does make its mark slightly at the death; b23.5 such is the fragile complexity of Clynelish my first choice for bottling would never be a sherry butt, even if in entirely tip-top nick. Well, I would have been wrong. Because had this butt not latterly shown signs of sulphur it would most certainly have picked up a major award in this year's Bible. So, forget the imperfections and, once a week, treat yourself to the ecstasy of a mouthful of this outrageously orgasmic organoleptic odyssey. 55.1%. nc ncf sc. 518 bottles.

Hunter Laing's Old & Rare Clynelish Aged 20 Years refill hogshead, dist Dec 96, bott Jan 17 (95) n24 t23.5 f23.5 b24 Some distilleries just have "it" without even trying. Here is such a case... Brilliant – and so relaxed is this you get the feeling it has barely reached second gear! 55.5%. nc ncf sc. 295 bottles.

Kingsbury Gold Clynelish 19 Year Old hogshead, cask no. 7101, dist 1997 (90) n22 t23.5 f22.5 b22.5 Unusual to find a Clynelish feel the effects of time after less than 20 years quite the way this does. But its charisma is barely dented. 53.9%. 210 bottles. sc.

Old Particular Clynelish 18 Years Old refill hogshead, dist Jul 97, bott Dec 15 (88) n22 t23 f21 b22 Unusually for a Clynelish is there is a little bit of tiredness in the cask taking the edge off the malt's undoubted beauty. 48.4%. nc ncf sc. 298 bottles.

That Boutique-y Whisky Company Clynelish 15 Year Old batch 3 (96.5) n24 t24 f24 b24.5 If I took a glass of this to bed with me, not sure whether to drink it or screw it into the middle of next week... 49.3%. 134 bottles.

⬙ **Whisky Illuminati Clynelish 20 Year Old** American oak hogshead, cask no. 6921, dist 1997 (91) n22.5 dark and earthy: bluebell woods and primroses. Busy spice bite and a light layering of treacle tart; t23 much more salivating than the nose suggests, the malt really blossoming, as does the light heather honey. Digestive biscuit, complete with salt, as it dries and thickens, the tannins getting roastier by the moment; f22.5 butterscotch, vanilla and spice by the barrel-load; b23 goes about producing excellence in a quiet and dignified way. 55.3%. sc. 251 bottles. Candlelight Series.

⬙ **Xtra Old Particular Clynelish 21 Years Old** refill hogshead, cask no. 12014, dist Oct 95, bott Sept 17 (95.5) n23.5 ah, the first true Clynelish nose I have encountered in bottled form this year – including, alas, the distillery's own bottling. The heather honey mixes with the malt like a great hostess mingles with her guests...; t24 ah, the first true Clynelish on the palate: remarkably like a Highland Park at its best with a complex interplay between heather honey and delicate phenols. But not quite the same weight, allowing the marzipan and maple syrup a lovely glide towards the finish; f23.5 long, malty with incredible refinement to the continued nutty, praline-style sweetness; b24 so true to this magnificent distillery in full flow. 54.6%. nc ncf sc. 265 bottles.

CONVALMORE
Speyside, 1894–1985. William Grant & Sons. Closed.

⬙ **Convalmore 32 Year Old** refill American oak hogsheads db (96.5) n24 no damage to the nose from the passing of time: instead, we have an incredible richness to the oaky vanilla as the malt has become interwoven into its make up while a dry high quality marzipan generates the delicate sweetness. If you can spot the vaguest vegetable aroma, that is the residue from the distillery character– once a black mark, now little more than an echo of a past life; t24 the malt starts quietly, then builds and builds until even the texture changes and the palate is bathed in rich, slightly juicy barley. The sugars are soothing, of the maple syrup and light treacle variety while the high integrity of the casks has worked wonders here, imparting such stunningly nuanced oak tones: none harsh or overly weighty. But always finding the right depth to ensure the cocoa and natural caramels remains on the same level and intensity as the malt: truly brilliant! f24 the malt and sugars have receded but the oak refuses to become bitter or over-aged and instead spices up gently and calls on the remaining oils to lengthen and balance the experience; b24.5 being 32 years old and bottled in 2017, these must be casks from among the very last production of the distillery before it was closed for the final time in 1985. The new spirit then, from what I remember, was not the greatest: thin and with an occasional tendency to be on the rough house side. Time, though, is a great healer. And forgiver. It has passed the last three decades turning from ugly duckling to the most elegant of swans. A sub-species, though, that is on the brink of extinction... 48.2%. 3,972 bottles. Diageo Special Releases 2017.

Gordon & MacPhail Rare Old Convalmore 1975 (94) n23 t24 f23 b24 The rarest of the rare. And in tasting, the flavour map took me back 30 years, to when I used to buy bottles of this from Gordon and MacPhail as a 10-year-old...probably distilled around 1975. The unique personality and DNA is identical on the palate as it was then; except now, of course, there is far more oak to contend with. Like finding an old lover 30 years further on: a little greyer, not quite in the same lithe shape as three decades earlier...but instantly recognisable and still very beautiful... 46%

CRAGGANMORE
Speyside, 1870. Diageo. Working.

Cragganmore db (81) n23 t24 f16 b18 A whisky which asks some major questions: such as should I just sit here and sob, or bang my head repeatedly on my tasting table? This had begun as such a promising and sturdy addition to the Cragganmore lexicon, with the complexity of the early sugars really upping the expectations. But the dreaded "s" word arrived in abundance from, presumably, a sherry butt involvement and things went downhill rapidly after that. Tragic. 55.7%. 4,932 bottles. Diageo Special Releases 2016.

Cragganmore Aged 12 Years db (81.5) n20 t21 f20 b20.5. I have a dozen bottles of Cragganmore in my personal cellar dating from the early 90s when the distillery was first bottled as a Classic Malt. Their astonishing dexterity and charm, their naked celebration of all things Speyside, casts a sad shadow over this drinkable but drab and instantly forgettable expression. 40%

Acla Selection Cragganmore 12 Years Old bourbon hogshead, dist 2004, bott 2016 (88.5) n22 a dozen years has passed, but the grist continues its sugary massage...and message; decent oak spice; t23 salivating and satisfying. Dominated by clean, grassy barley without much of a backbone. The spices still nip slightly; f21.5 an unhelpful late tang from the oak finds little resistance; b22 a competent bottling shewing the distillery in its malty clarity without bothering too much about complexity. 54.6%. sc. Joint bottling with The Whisky Agency.

Hunter Laing's Old & Rare Cragganmore Aged 30 Years refill hogshead, dist Jun 86, bott Jan 17 (89) n23 t22.5 f21.5 b22 A malt, caked in vanilla and tannin, coming to the end of its natural life span but having one last golden hurrah... 59.7%. nc ncf sc. 167 bottles.

The Whisky Agency Cragganmore 1989 (89) n22 t23 f22 b22 Plucked from the cask just as the oak began closing in: a narrow escape! 52.1%.

The Whisky Agency Cragganmore 12 Years Old dist 2004 (95) n24 t24 f23.5 b23.5 There are some malts which appear to carry the perfect DNA of the Speyside style: this is one such bottling. 54.6%.

Whisky-Fässle Cragganmore 27 Year Old sherry butt, dist 1989, bott 2016 (88) n23.5 t23 f19.5 b22 For a Cragganmore, the malt is conspicuous by its absence. Not exactly the perfect sherry butt, but it could have been worse. Those who don't pick up sulphur will adore this. 48.7%.

CRAIGELLACHIE
Speyside, 1891. Bacardi. Working.

Craigellachie 13 Year Old db (78.5) n20 t22 f18 b18.5. Oily and intense, it shovels the malt for all it is worth. That said, the sulphur notes are its undoing. 46%

Craigellachie 17 Year Old db (88.5) n22 chocolate Liquorice Allsort! A tad oily and boiled vegetable. But enough malt to make the difference; t22.5 just love that delivery. Not the cleanest. But a mix of those heavy duty oils and an almost biting vanilla-barley note is attractive in an unkempt kind of way; f22 almost like an oil slick in a sea of oak-splintered barley; b22 technically falls flat on its face. Yet the whole is way better than the sum parts...46%

Craigellachie 23 Year Old db (91.5) n23.5 t23 f22 b23.5 Expected a little house smoke on this (the malt made here in the early 1990s always had delicate phenol), but didn't show. The honey is nothing like so shy. 46% WB16/035

Craigellachie Exceptional Cask Series 1994 bott May 18 db (91.5) n22.5 t23 f23 b23 How fascinating. Yes, a sherry butt and yes: there is sulphur. But this time it is not from the sherry, as the nose reveals a particular character from the condenser which does accentuate a mild sulphur character. Yet the clean wine casks tell a different, at once puckering yet juicy, story. Beautifully structured and a jaw-aching chewing malt with an unusual late salivation point. 54.8%. Bottled for Whisky L! & Fine Spirits Show.

The First Editions Craigellachie Aged 19 Years 1995 sherry butt, cask no. 12362, bott 2016 (87) n21 t23 f21 b22 Fruity, and though not a vintage period for sherry butts from this distillery this has enough honest fruit cake character to ensure some rich and enjoyable moments. Not quite technically perfect, the toasted raisin is there to be savoured in full. 54.4%. nc ncf sc. 305 bottles.

The First Editions Craigellachie Aged 21 Years 1995 sherry butt, cask no. 13305, bott 2017 (73) n18 t20 f17 b18 Yes, some massive, eye-watering grape. But furs up considerably. 59%. nc ncf sc. 282 bottles.

⬧ **The First Editions Craigellachie Aged 22 Years** sherry butt, cask no. 14461, bott 2017 (85.5) n21.5 t22 f21 b21 Earnest and intense in, first, its malty endeavours then, latterly, on the fruit scene. But a degree of bitterness ensures the desired balance proves elusive. 54.7%. nc ncf sc. 180 bottles.

⬧ **Golden Cask Craigellachie Aged 10 Years** cask no. CM237, dist 2006, bott 2017 (94) n23 surprisingly coastal, with a series of breezy, salty rock pool notes; t23.5 the way the acacia honey blends with the Manuka honey to make for a thumping crescendo with the spice has the hallmarks of Ricard Strauss at his most romantic...; f23.5 is that a little vein of smoke I detect in the dry, oaky wreckage? Light praline and so much salty vanilla, too; b24 another golden cask from Golden Cask...awash with honey and character. 54.2%. sc. 134 bottles.

⬧ **Gordon & MacPhail Connoisseurs Choice Craigellachie 1991** refill American hogshead, cask no. 9465, dist 13 Nov 91, bott 19 Feb 18 (89.5) n23 celebrates a heather honey theme to the max; t22.5 eye-watering on impact: a surprising salt surge really wrings every last nuance out of the malt and tannin mix; f22 the oak still holds the upper hand and lets you know it...; b22 while the oak tires, the spirit itself appears to want to carry on forever. 56.5%. nc ncf sc. 172 bottles.

⬧ **Hepburn's Choice Craigellachie 9 Years Old** wine cask, dist 2008, bott 2017 (86.5) n20 t22 f22.5 b22 Those who like those bitter and sharp green fruit pastels will most probably appreciate this lively little number. 46%. nc ncf sc. 296 bottles.

⬧ **Hepburn's Choice Craigellachie 11 Years Old** sherry butt, dist 2006, bott 2017 (92) n22.5 hurrah....! A 2006 distillation and no great off notes from the wine cask; instead an entertaining array of earthy, fruity tones – and a distinct bluebell forest floor after a rain-burst – makes for an enjoyable serenade; t23.5 conspicuously malty on delivery, despite the cask type, though a light greengage note does blossom; f23 remains doggedly malty, and even offers a late degree of salty salivation; b23 an absolute joy of a sherry-influenced whisky. 46%. nc ncf sc. 300 bottles.

⬧ **The Loch Fyne Craigellachie 10 Year Old** sherry cask, cask no. 311, dist Sept 07, bott Nov 17 (81) n18 t21 f20 b20 This is one of the most naturally sulphur-producing distilleries in Scotland without getting a helping hand from the sherry butt. An attractive malt-doused delivery considering. 46%. sc. 1,205 bottles.

Old Malt Cask Craigellachie Aged 21 Years sherry butt, cask no. 13304, dist Sept 95, bott Feb 17 (73.5) n20.5 t18 f17 b18 Yikes! Blood orange on steroids. A bitter-sweet experience...without the sweetness... 50%. nc ncf sc. 331 bottles.

⬧ **Old Malt Cask Craigellachie Aged 21 Years** sherry butt, cask no. 13740, dist Sept 95, bott Apr 17 (78.5) n21.5 t21.5 f17.5 b18 A malt which makes a bit of a ham fist at engaging your attention. Lollops along with an essentially malty theme interrupted by some very ordinary sherry-influenced moments, not all of them as fruit rich as you might like. 50%. nc ncf sc. 587 bottles.

⬧ **Old Malt Cask Craigellachie Aged 22 Years** sherry butt, cask no. 14405, dist Sept 95, bott Nov 17 (93.5) n23 excellent oak spice displays early...this is a good sign for an old sherry butt...; fruit cough sweets and a little barley sugar; t23.5 a sumptuous, toasted raisin delivery, the roastiness increasing by the second with a little Manuka honey making a foray; the spices ping gamely around the palate as chocolate begins to arrive in force; f23.5 plain chocolate fruit and nut...just so yummy...! b23.5 clean sherry...!!! And does it repay the palate in kind...! 50%. nc ncf sc. 122 bottles.

⬧ **Old Malt Cask Craigellachie Aged 22 Years** sherry butt, cask no. 14460, dist Sept 95, bott Nov 17 (90.5) n22 a slight sweaty sock earthiness to the Genoa cake; t23.5 excellent mouth feel: the oils are well weighted, the malty structure intact and a vague smokiness to the fruit intrigues as the spices build; f22 the peppers pepper...; b23 weighty and satisfying. 50%. nc ncf sc. 450 bottles.

⬧ **Old Particular Craigellachie 18 Years Old** sherry butt, cask no. 12218, dist Jul 99, bott Dec 17 (84.5) n20 t22 f21 b21.5 Firm both on nose and delivery with no shortage of heat, either. Juicy, but never quite relaxes a little bit of tightness throughout. 48.4%. nc ncf sc. 295 bottles.

Old Particular Craigellachie 21 Years Old sherry butt, cask no. 11343, dist Sept 95, bott Sept 16 (89) n22 t23 f22 b22 A malt still offering vitality and very much at ease with itself... 51.5%. nc ncf sc. 504 bottles.

◇ **Old Particular Craigellachie 21 Years Old** sherry butt, cask no. 11769, dist Oct 95, bott Jun 17 (87.5) n21.5 t22 f21.5 b22.5 Crisp and bitter-sweet. The barley is harnessed tightly by the oak while a little butterscotch, acacia honey and cocoa quietens the spice. 51.5%. nc ncf sc. 390 bottles.

◇ **Provenance Craigellachie Aged 8 Years** refill hogshead, dist Jan 08, bott Mar 16 (80) n19 t21 f20 b20 An interesting malt as the naturally sulphury character of the malt can be seen here in full spate. 46%. nc ncf sc.

◇ **Provenance Craigellachie Aged 8 Years** refill hogshead, cask no. 12202, dist Feb 09, bott Dec 17 (78.5) n18 t19 f21.5 b19 The same notes as for the bottling above, except here the sulphur is slightly more pronounced, the barley takes longer to convene while an extra dose of cocoa comes to the rescue. 46%. nc ncf sc. 660 bottles.

Scotch Malt Whisky Society Cask 44.76 14 Year Old virgin heavy toast medium char oak hogshead, dist 6 Nov 02 (89) n22.5 t23 f22 b21.5 Subtlety plays no part in this malt. 57.5%.

◇ **Scotch Malt Whisky Society Cask 44.82 13 Year Old** refill ex-bourbon barrel, dist 27 Jun 03 (84.5) n21.5 t22 f20 b21 Huge amounts of natural cream toffee to chew on from the cask; at times the sweetness is all-engulfing. But the distillery's usual bite and attitude are not put off that easily. 56.7%. sc.

DAILUAINE
Speyside, 1854. Diageo. Working.

Dailuaine 1997 The Manager's Choice db (87.5) n21.5 t23 f21 b22. One of the most enjoyable (unpeated!!) Dailuaines I've come across in an age. There is the usual distillery biff to this, but not without a honeyed safety net. Great fun. 58.6%

Dailuaine Aged 16 Years bott lot no. L4334 db (79) n19 t21 f20 b19. Syrupy, almost grotesquely heavy at times; the lighter notes of previous bottlings have been lost under an avalanche of sugary, over-ripe tomatoes. One for those who want a massive dram. 43%

◇ **Berry Bros & Rudd Dailuaine 21 Years Old** cask no. 10608, dist 1996, bott 2018 (91.5) n23 not what I expected: this is structured beautifully with crisp barley notes in league with boiled fruit candy. And – and this is worth the extra mark – the most docile base note of smoke...; t22.5 the nose promises a full- on salivating delivery – and that's just what you get! Again, the barley and those non-specific boiled fruit sweets strike up a delicious harmony with wave upon wave of spice (unusual in that the first is the most powerful, then followed by more gentle waves); custardy vanilla fills the softening middle ground; f22.5 the spices are more singular as the sugars recede. Again, the vaguest hint of smoke seeps into play...; b23.5 not often you come across a Dailuaine that is a real joy, so hearty congratulations for BBR buyer Doug McIvor for spotting this collectors' item. And if you want to know how rare: a highly decent Dailuaine like this comes along about as often as a Charlton victory over Millwall: practically never... 46%. nc ncf sc.

Douglas Laing's Premier Barrel Selection Dailuaine Aged 7 Years (60) n16 t17 f17 b16 I could go into all the things that's wrong with this. But, frankly, it doesn't deserve my time. 46%. nc ncf sc. 400 bottles.

◇ **Gordon & MacPhail Connoisseurs Choice Dailuaine 1998** refill American hogshead, dist 11 Aug 98, bott 14 Mar 18 (82) n21.5 t21 f19 b20.5 Not even some well above average oak, imparting at times spice and cocoa, can disguise the fact that this is a lesser, unsophisticated whisky: a Trabant engine inside a Jaguar F Type. 46%. nc ncf. 661 bottles.

Gordon & MacPhail Connoisseurs Choice Dailuaine 2006 bott 14 Mar 17 (82.5) n20 t22 f20 b20.5 A very average distillery displaying very ordinary malt. Nothing offensive, but not a single thing to set the heart racing either. Typically clunky and out of tune. 46%.

Hepburn's Choice Dailuaine 7 Years Old wine cask, dist 2009, bott 2016 (88) n21 t22.5 f22 b22.5 Well done good people of Hepburn's Choice. Your selection of wine cask is impressive. 46%. nc ncf sc. 280 bottles.

◇ **Hepburn's Choice Dailuaine 7 Years Old** rum barrel, dist 2009, bott 2017 (85) n21 t21.5 f21 b21.5 An attractive, mouth-watering and vaguely spicy little cove benefitting from the sugary dusting bestowed upon it by the rum. 46%. nc ncf sc. 138 bottles.

◇ **Hepburn's Choice Dailuaine 10 Years Old** sherry butt, dist 2007, bott 2018 (77.5) n19 t20 f19 b19.5 Only a quick, passing dose of barley sugar saves us from encountering a Dailuaine in one of its well-known off key and belligerent moods. 46%. nc ncf sc. 789 bottles.

◇ **Old Particular Dailuaine 15 Years Old** sherry butt, cask no. 12016, dist Mar 02, bott Aug 17 (80) n21 t20 f19 b19 Not even a sympathetic sherry butt can entirely save this fiery malt which is as excellent an example of an overheated spirit still as you are ever likely to find. 48.4%. nc ncf sc. 356 bottles.

⟡ **Provenance Dailuaine Aged 8 Years** refill hogshead, cask no. 12037, dist Aug 09, bott Aug 17 (80.5) n20.5 t20 f20 b20 Not untypically for this distillery, this has to be the bare basics of malt whisky. No faults as such, but beyond the intense, youthful malt itself it goes nowhere – and makes no attempt to. 46%. nc ncf sc. 400 bottles.

Provenance Dailuaine Aged 9 Years sherry butt, cask no. 11250, dist Mar 07, bott May 16 (87.5) n21 t22 f22.5 b22 An entirely clean butt offers up little in the way of fruit but helps herd the more intense malty qualities into an area where it offers maximum effect. Some lovely late spice, too! 46%. nc ncf sc.

Provenance Dailuaine Aged 9 Years refill hogshead, cask no. 11504, dist Jan 07, bott Nov 16 (85) n20 t22 f21.5 b21.5 Some not unattractive cream soda qualities to this. For a Dailuaine, quite juicy and characterful. 46%. nc ncf sc. 347 bottles.

Scotch Malt Whisky Society Cask 41.92 13 Year Old first fill ex-bourbon barrel, dist 14 Aug 03 (80) n21 t20 f19 b20 More bite than a rabid Jack Russell. Eye-watering, tangy, malty...but just not a great experience. 61%.

Simon Brown Dailuaine 2008 ex-bourbon cask, cask no. 20, dist Feb 08, bott Jan 16 (86) n21.5 t22 f21 b21.5 The distillery nutshelled: a typical rawness to the nose where the oak has a slightly discordant say. And this is repeated on the finish. The highlight is the massively oily and intensely malty delivery which really does possess star quality. 43%. nc ncf sc.

Whisky Castle Dailuaine 12 Year Old sherry butt, cask no. 13454, dist Jan 05, bott Mar 17 (87.5) n21 t22 f22.5 b22 Dailuaine, over the years one of Scotland's most consistently inept malts – bottled in a sherry butt! A case of two negatives making a positive, right? Well, probably not far off. The sherry offers up no sulphur at all and the distillate does, for a short while, generate some distinctly attractive malt before vanishing under an avalanche of natural caramel and even spice. Pleasantly surprised. 50%. Bottled by Hunter Laing.

DALLAS DHU
Speyside, 1899–1983. Closed. Now a museum.

Gordon & MacPhail Rare Vintage Dallas Dhu 1979 (94.5) n23 t23.5 f23.5 b24 I can hardly recall the last time a bottling from this distillery popped along – depressing to think I am old enough to remember when they were so relatively common they were being sold on special offer! It was always a class act; its closure an act of whisky vandalism, whether it be preserved as a museum or not. This, even after all these years, shows the extraordinary quality we are missing day in, day out. 43%

DALMORE
Highands (Northern), 1839. Whyte and Mackay. Working.

The Dalmore 12 Years Old db (90) n22 t23 f22.5 b22.5 Has changed character of late yet remains underpowered and with a shade too much toffee. But such is the quality of the malt in its own right it can overcome any hurdles placed before it to ensure a real mouth-filling, rumbustious dram. 40%

The Dalmore 15 Years Old db (83.5) n21 t21 f20.5 b21. Another pleasant Dalmore that coasts along the runway but simply fails to get off the ground. The odd off note here and there, but it's the blood orange which shines brightest. 40%

The Dalmore 18 Years Old db (76.5) n19 t21 f18 b18.5. Heaps of caramel and the cask choice might have been better. 43%

The Dalmore 21 Year Old db (88.5) n22 date and walnut cake...though light on the walnuts...; t23 fat, chewy, mouth-watering and complex...though light on the complexity; f21.5 remains chewy, bitter and sweet...though light on the sweetness; b22 fat, unsubtle, but pretty enjoyable. 42%

The Dalmore 25 db (88) n23.5 hugely attractive with a sherry-trifle signature; t22.5 a glossy delivery with the accent very much on fruit, plums in particular; an attractive degree of sharpness throughout; f20 just a little dry with a tell-tale tang towards the end; b22 the kind of neat and tidy, if imperfect, whisky which, were it in human form, would sport a carefully trimmed and possibly darkened little moustache, a pin-striped suit, matching tie and square and shiny black shoes. 42%. Whyte & Mackay Ltd.

The Dalmore 30 Year Old db (94) n24 the grape drifts across the glass; not quite perfect but enough panache and class to carry an aura of slight wonder...; t24 so thick, so long, so dripping in fruit....; subtle spice and a slow realisation of aged, confident tannin;f22.5 undone very slightly by a very late degree of bitterness; b23.5 a malt, quite literally for the discerning whisky lover. Essays in complexity are rarely so well written in the glass as found here... 45%

The Dalmore 50 Years Old db (88) n21 t19 f25 b23. Takes a while to warm up, but when it does becomes a genuinely classy and memorable dram befitting one of the world's great and undervalued distilleries. 52%

The Dalmore 62 Years Old db (95) n23 t25 f24 b24 If I am just half as beautiful, elegant and fascinating as this by the time I reach 62, I'll be a happy man. Somehow I doubt it. A once-in-a-lifetime whisky – something that comes around every 62 years, in fact. Forget Dalmore Cigar Malt – even I might be tempted to start smoking just to get a full bottle of this. 40.5%

The Dalmore 1263 King Alexander III db (86) n22 t22.5 f20 b21.5. Starts brightly with all kinds of barley sugar, fruit and decent age and oak combinations, plus some excellent spice prickle. So far, so good...and obviously thoughtfully and complexly structured. But then vanishes without trace on finish. 40%

The Dalmore 1980 db (81.5) n19 t21 f20.5 b21. Wonderful barley intensity on delivery does its best to overcome the so-so nose and finale. 40%

The Dalmore 1981 Amoroso Sherry Finesse amoroso sherry wood cask db (85.5) n21 t22 f21.5 b21. A very tight, fruity, dram which gives away its secrets with all the enthusiasm of an agent under torture. Enjoyable to a degree... but bloody hard work. 42%

The Dalmore Astrum Aged 40 Years db (89) n23.5 t21 f22 b22.5. This guy is all about the nose. The oak is too big for the overall framework and the balance hangs by a thread. Yet somehow the overall effect is impressive. Another summer and you suspect the whole thing would have snapped... 42%

The Dalmore Aurora Aged 45 Years db (90.5) n25 t22 f21.5 b22. Sophisticated for sure. But so huge is the oak on the palate, it cannot hope to match the freakish brilliance of the nose. 45%

The Dalmore Candela Aged 50 Years db (96) n25 t24 f23.5 b23.5. Just one of those whiskies which you come across only a handful of times in your life. All because a malt makes it to 50 does not mean it will automatically be great. This, however, is a masterpiece, the end of which seemingly has never been written. 50% (bottled at 45%).

The Dalmore Cabernet Sauvignon db (79) n22 t19 f19 b19. Too intense for its own good. 45%

The Dalmore Ceti db (91.5) n24 a nose for fruitcake lovers everywhere: ripe cherries and blood orange abound and work most attractively with the slightly suety, muscovado enriched body...; t23.5 the nose demands a silky delivery and that's exactly what you get. Rich fruit notes form the principle flavour profile but the backing salivating barley and spice is spot on; the mid ground becomes a little saltier and more coastal...;f21.5 a vague bitterness to the rapidly thinning finale, almost a pithy element, which is slightly out of sync with the joys of before; b22.5 a Ceti which warbles rather well... 44.7%

The Dalmore Cigar Malt Reserve Limited Edition db (73.5) n19 t19.5 f17 b18. One assumes this off key sugarfest is for the cigar that explodes in your face... 44%

The Dalmore Dominium db (89.5) n22.5 thick, full-on grape; t23 lush delivery which becomes progressively more chewy. A few spiced sultanas in there; f22 big on the caramel; b22 like so many Dalmores, starts brightly but as the caramels gather it just drifts into a soupy lump. Still, no taint to the fruit and though the finish is dull you can say it is never less than very attractive. 43%. Fortuna Meritas Collection

The Dalmore Luceo db (87) n22 t22 f21.5 b21.5. Pleasantly malty, exceptionally easy going and perfect for those of you with a toffeed tooth. 40%. Fortuna Meritas Collection

The Dalmore Valour db (85.5) n21 t22 f21 b21.5. Not often you get the words "Valour" and "fudge" in the same sentence. 40%. Fortuna Meritas Collection

The Dalmore Regalis db (86.5) n22.5 t21.5 f21 b21.5. For a brief moment, grassy and busy. Then dulls, other than the spice. The caramel held in the bottling hall is such a great leveller. 40%. Fortuna Meritas Collection

The Dalmore Visitor Centre Exclusive db (95.5) n25 t24 f22.5 b24 Not exactly the easiest distillery to find but a bottle of this is worth the journey alone. I have tasted some sumptuous Dalmores over the last 30-odd years. But this one stands among the very finest. 46%

The Dalmore Quintessence db (91) n22 t23.5 f22 b23.5 A late night dram after a hard day. Slump into your favourite chair, dim the lights, pour yourself a glass of this, warm in the hand and then study, quietly, for the next half hour. 45%.

⬦ **The Whisky Chamber Dalmore 10 Years Old 2007** sherry refill hogshead (79) n19 t21 f19 b20 Some serious dollops of honey go a long way to disrupt the tangy influence of the cask. A forthright dram taking no prisoners. 55.9%. sc.

DALWHINNIE
Highlands (Central), 1898. Diageo. Working.

Dalwhinnie 15 Years Old db (95) n24 t24 f23 b24 A malt it is hard to decide whether to drink or bath in: I suggest you do both. One of the most complete mainland malts of them all. Know anyone who reckons they don't like whisky? Give them a glass of this – that's them cured. Oh, if only the average masterpiece could be this good. 43%

Dalwhinnie Winter's Gold db (95) n23.5 for such a remote and inland distillery, the coastal saltiness to this is remarkable... golden syrup and earthy heather-honey also at work here;

t24 something of the Johnnie Walker Gold about this: there is a clarity to the malt, the citrus and vanilla which reminds one of the air when looking far away into the mountains on a cool winter's morn; f23.5 earthy to the end with the honey (ulmo, naturally!) still the dominating theme; just a late hint of bitterness; b24 whichever blender came up with this deserves a pat on the back. 43%

DEANSTON
Highlands (Perthshire), 1966. Burn Stewart Distillers. Working.

Deanston 6 Years Old db (83) n20 t21 f22 b20. Great news for those who remember how good Deanston was a decade or two ago: it's on its way back. A delightfully clean dram with its trademark honey character restored. A little beauty slightly undermined by caramel. 40%

Deanston 10 Year Old PX Finish db (83.5) n21 t22.5 f20 b20 Displays the uncompromising sweetness of a whisky liqueur. A must-have malt for those who like their sherry influence to be way over the top. The finish, like the nose, reveals minor a dry, furry element. 57.5%

Deanston 12 Years Old db (74) n18 t19 f18.5 b18.5. It is quite bizarre how you can interchange this with Tobermory in style; or, rather, at least the faults are the same. 46%. ncf.

Deanston Aged 12 Years db (75) n18 t21.5 f17.5 b18. The delivery is, for a brief moment, a malty/orangey delight. But the nose is painfully out of sync and finish is full of bitter, undesirable elements. A lot of work still required to get this up to a second grade malt, let alone a top flight one. 46.3%. ncf. Burn Stewart.

Deanston 18 Year Old batch 2 db (89.5) n23 celebrates a very healthy degree of ulmo honey: soft and sexy; t22.5 big malt kick early on; soft oils bring on the vanillas; juicy and just a touch of lime to lighten things; f22 a little spicier and deeper toned as the tannin takes charge; b22 a soft treat for the palate... 46.3%. nc ncf.

Deanston 20 Year Old db (61) n15 t16 f15 b15 Riddled with sulphur. 55.4%. nc ncf.

Deanston 40 Year Old PX Finish db (87.5) n22 t23 f21 b21.5 The PX is doubtless in use here to try and give a sugary wrap around the over-aged malt. Some success, though limited. This type of cask has the unfortunate habit of restricting complexity in a whisky by embracing it too tightly with its wealth of syrupy top notes. The aromas and flavours which do escape often seem brittle and clipped, and this is the case here: the whisky has no chance to tell of its 40 years in the cask – the period that counts most now is the time it has spent in PX. Love the spices, though, and the overall mouth feel. Whatever its limitations, this still does offer a lovely dram. 45.6%.

Deanston Virgin Oak db (90) n22.5 t23 f22.5 b22 Quirky. Don't expect this to taste anything like Scotch... 46.3%

Old Malt Cask Deanston Aged 21 Years refill hogshead, cask no. 12816, dist Aug 95, bott Oct 16 (88) n21.5 t23 f21.5 b22 A clean, sparkling, honest malt. 50%. nc ncf sc. 263 bottles.

◇ **The Single Cask Deanston 20 Years Old** cask no. 1982 (84) n22.5 t21.5 f21 b21.5 Not an easy task to find great Deanston. And I have failed again here. But despite its inherent roughness, hotness and wayward personality, have to say I rather like the intense, malty nuttiness. For a Deanston, not a bad shout at all. 52.7%.

DUFFTOWN
Speyside, 1898. Diageo. Working.

Singleton of Dufftown 12 Years Old db (71) n18 t18 f17 b18. A roughhouse malt that's finesse-free. For those who like their tastebuds Dufft up a bit... 40%

◇ **The Singleton of Dufftown Aged 18 Years** bott code: L7094DM000 db (86.5) n21 t22 f21.5 b22 To be honest, I was expecting a bit of dud here, based on some 30-years-experience of this distillery. And though, for an 18-year-old, it can't be said really to hit the heights, it has – as so many less than brilliant distilleries over the years – mellowed enough with age to show a certain malty gentleness worthy of respect. 40%.

The Singleton of Dufftown Spey Cascade db (80) n19 t20 f21 b20. A dull whisky, stodgy and a little dirty on the nose. Improves the longer it stays on the palate thanks mainly to sympathetic sugars and an ingratiating oiliness. But if you are looking for quality, prepare to be disappointed. 40%

The Singleton of Dufftown "Sunray" db (77) n20 t20 f18 b19. One can assume only that the sun has gone in behind a big toffeed cloud. Apparently, according to the label, this is "intense". About as intense as a ham sandwich. Only not as enjoyable. 40%. WB15/121

The Singleton of Dufftown "Tailfire" db (79) n20 t20 f19 b20. Tailspin, more like. 40%.

Cadenhead's Authentic Collection Dufftown 38 Year Old bourbon hogshead, dist 1978 (89.5) n22.5 t23 f21.5 b22.5 It is curious that during this period Dufftown, like Littlemill and Fettercairn, was making some of the least impressive whisky in Scotland. Yet nearly four decades on, the malt, if matured in the right cask, can have a genuinely attractive – albeit very different – personality. This is one such cask. 44.6%. sc.

◇ **Gordon & MacPhail Connoisseurs Choice Dufftown 1999** first fill bourbon barrel, cask no. 8789, dist 18 Aug 99, bott 19 Feb 18 (85.5) n21.5 t22 f21 b21 A typical Dufftown offering, the thick, glutinous sugars riding roughshod over the palate. The odd phase of high intensity barley does offer the occasional fascinating interlude. 54.5%. nc ncf sc. 163 bottles.

◇ **Gordon & MacPhail Connoisseurs Choice Dufftown 2008** bott 29 Mar 17 (77) n19 t20 f19 b19 Pretty standard for a Dufftown: unctuous and irritating. Had the distillery been built by the time of his writing, you'd wonder if Trollope had based his Mr Slope on its output. 46%.

Hepburn's Choice Dufftown 9 Years Old refill hogshead, dist 2007, bott 2017 (84) n21 t22 f21 b20 An interesting bottling as the oak offers very little of any meaning. So it is possible to see that the basic spirit is a lot cleaner than it once was and the gristy barley is very evident. Beyond that it has little to say. 46%. nc ncf sc. 358 bottles.

◇ **Hepburn's Choice Dufftown 10 Years Old** refill hogshead, dist 2007, bott 2018 (84.5) n21 t22.5 f20 b21 Oily barley sugar with an acceptable chewability and simplistic outlook. The finish can't help itself but the journey there is surprisingly pleasant. 46%. nc ncf sc. 409 bottles.

EDRADOUR

Highlands (Perthshire), 1837. Signatory Vintage. Working.

Edradour Aged 10 Years db (79) n18 t20 f22 b19. A dense, fat malt that tries offer something along the sherry front but succeeds mainly in producing a whisky cloyingly sweet and unfathomable. Some complexity to the finish compensates. 43%

◇ **Edradour 13 Year Old** 1st fill oloroso sherry butt, dist 4 Dec 95, bott 4 May 18 db (95) n24 t23.5 f23.5 b24 When this whisky was distilled it was made at, then, Scotland's smallest distillery. Well, that may be so, but there is no denying that this is one absolutely huge whisky. And not only that, one where no degree of understated enormity is out step with any other: it is a giant, but a beautifully proportioned one. The spicy, sherry trifle on steroids nose will entrap you. The staggering complexity of the sturdy tannin and muscular fruit will keep you there, spellbound. The chocolate on the finish is almost an arrogant flourish. This really is Edradour from the old school, where its old manager Puss Mitchell had laid down the law on the type of sherry butt the hefty malt had to be filled into. Were he with us now, he'd be purring... 54.2%. 661 bottles. Bottled for Whisky L! & Fine Spirits Show.

FETTERCAIRN

Highland (Eastern), 1824. Whyte and Mackay. Working.

Fettercairn 12 Year Old db (66) n14 t19 f16 b17. If the nose doesn't get you, what follows probably will...Grim doesn't quite cover it. 40%

Fettercairn 30 Years Old db (73) n19 t18 f18 b18. A bitter disappointment. Literally. 46.3%

Fettercairn 40 Years Old db (92) n23 t24 f22 b23 Yes, everyone knows my views on this distillery. But I'll have to call this spade a wonderfully big, old shovel you can't help loving... just like the memory of me tattooed ol' granny... 40%. 463 bottles.

Fettercairn 1824 db (69) n17 t19 f16 b17. By Fettercairn standards, not a bad offering. Relatively free from its inherent sulphury and rubbery qualities, this displays a sweet nutty character not altogther unattractive – though caramel plays a calming role here. Need my arm twisting for a second glass, though. 40%

Alos Sansibar Whisky Fettercairn 1988 bott 2016 (75.5) n18.5 t20.5 f18 b18.5 You almost feel like applauding this malt's bloody-minded stubbornness, even after nearly three decades in what appears a half decent barrel, to try and lift itself as high as even below average. Grim. 50.6%.

◇ **Berry Bros & Rudd Fettercairn 11 Years Old** cask no. 107750, dist 2006, bott 2018 (80) n21 t20 f19 b20 Pretty survivable for a Fettercairn. Lots of barley weirdness as you might expect. And that vaguely rubbery, nutty noise you always get in the background, especially at the death. But the oak is good, which helps, and the sugars and spices are in just about equal measure. Way above average. 46%. nc ncf sc.

Bdram Fettercairn 7 Year Old bourbon barrel, cask no. 1119, dist Mar 09, bott Jan 17 (81) n21 t22.5 f18.5 b19 For a Fettercairn of this age, as opposed to an ordinary malt, it is pretty impressive. Yes, it is as hot as Hades – and that has nothing to do with the strength, rather the poor spirit itself. And the finish has its usual zero character, other than the torturous burn. But for a few moments and malt and nuts combine to rise above the roaring flames and offer, thanks to a degree of additional heather honey, something to fleetingly cherish. 60.5%.

Cadenhead's Small Batch International Fettercairn 28 Year Old bourbon casks, dist 1988 (84) n22 t21.5 f20 b20.5 Good old Fettercairn! Lovely nose with malt and butterscotch. But the delivery and beyond reminds you that you can polish an object all you like, it ends up exactly what it started as...only with a sheen. 55.4%.

◇ **Fadandel.dk Fettercairn Aged 21 Years** hogshead, cask no. 1803, dist 27 Sept 96, bott 26 Feb 18 (85.5) n21.5 t22 f21 b21 A sticky, glutinous, cloying, nutty dram though the improbable, salivating qualities of the malt is worth the exploration. As Fettercairns go, not too bad at all. 63.5%. sc. 24 bottles.

Hepburn's Choice Fettercairn 7 Years Old European oak quarter cask, dist 2008, bott 2016 (73) n17 t18 f19 b19 You can dress Cowdenbeath FC's third team in a Real Madrid kit. But they still will be Cowdenbeath's third team... 46%. nc ncf sc. 140 bottles.

Hepburn's Choice Fettercairn 7 Years Old European oak quarter cask, dist 2008, bott 2016 (70.5) n15 t20 f17 b18.5 At times a far better experience than the dreadful nose promises with the oils doing some Stirling Albion work until the finish kicks in begins to rip at your throat with frenzied relish. Would lose against a Cowdenbeath third team in all white... 46%. nc ncf sc. 85 bottles.

Hepburn's Choice Fettercairn 8 Years Old sherry hogshead, dist 2008, bott 2016 (59) n14 t15 f16 b14 I was tempted to shoot the bottle to put it out of its misery... 46%. nc ncf sc. 407 bottles.

⬥ **Hepburn's Choice Fettercairn 9 Years Old** wine cask, dist 2008, bott 2017 (63) n15 t17 f15 b16 Poor spirit and not a great cask. Proof that two negatives don't make a positive. 46%. nc ncf sc. 371 bottles.

⬥ **Hepburn's Choice Fettercairn 10 Years Old** wine cask, dist 2008, bott 2018 (63) n15 t17 f15 b16 This may have been bottled in a different year, but the result is exactly the same... 46%. nc ncf sc. 406 bottles.

Hunter Laing's Distiller's Art Fettercairn Aged 14 Years refill hogshead, dist Jun 02, bott 2016 (79) n19 t21 f19 b19 A sweet but harsh malt enjoyable a few attractive date and walnut moments. 48%. nc ncf sc. 317 bottles.

⬥ **Old Malt Cask Fettercairn Aged 20 Years** refill hogshead, cask no. 13736, dist Jan 97, bott Apr 17 (81) n20 t22 f19 b20 A barley-sugared beastie. So similar to Littlemill here in its flat malty projection and cardboard backdrop that, just like that lost distillery, it shows that good age can greatly improve an originally poor spirit. 50%. nc ncf sc. 328 bottles.

Provenance Fettercairn Aged 8 Years refill hogshead, cask no. 11512, dist May 08, bott Nov 16 (87) n21.5 t22 f21.5 b22 Fettercairn in finest fettle. The muscovado and thin marzipan link with the grist quite deliciously. Perhaps a little tang towards the end but marginal and certainly none of the usual nonsense surrounding the distillery: an exceptional and very enjoyable bottling. 46%. nc ncf sc. 393 bottles.

⬥ **Provenance Fettrcairn Aged 10 Years** refill hogshead, cask no. 11776, dist Feb 07, bott May 17 (75) n18 t20.5 f18 b18.5 Big and malt intense but, like so many Fettercairns before, a part of its DNA is just plain wrong... 46%. nc ncf sc. 379 bottles.

The Whisky Agency Fettercairn 28 Years Old dist 1988 (64) n16 t17 f15 b16 Nutty and dirty with a distinct feints kick. Why anyone would want to bottle this nonsense is beyond me. 49.9%. Bottled for La Maison du Whisky.

The Whisky Chamber Fettercairn 10 Year Old bourbon cask, dist 2006 (84.5) n20 t23 f20 b21.5 That rarest of beasts: a thoroughly drinkable and enjoyable Fettercairn. OK, it won't win any beauty prizes and the nose, like the finish, is hardly something to actually savour. But the delivery and middle – a beautiful malt and muscovado romp – really does have the odd moment of true excellence. 55.2%.

GLEN ALBYN
Highlands (Northern) 1846–1983. Diageo. Demolished.

Gordon & MacPhail Rare Vintage Glen Albyn 1976 (96) n22.5 t24.5 f24.5 b24.5 Wow! My eyes nearly popped out of my head when I spotted this in my sample room. Glen Albyns come round as rarely as a Scotsman winning Wimbledon. Well, almost. When I used to buy this (from Gordon and MacPhail in their early Connoisseur's Choice range, as it happens) when the distillery was still alive (just) I always found it an interesting if occasionally aggressive dram. This masterpiece, though, is something else entirely. And the delivery really does take us to places where only the truly great whiskies go... 43%

GLENALLACHIE
Speyside, 1968. The GlenAllachie Distillers Co Limited. Working.

Glenallachie 15 Years Old Distillery Edition db (81) n20 t21 f19 b19. Real battle between nature and nurture: an exceptional sherry butt has silk gloves and honied marzipan, while a hot-tempered bruiser lurks beneath. 58%

The First Editions Glenallachie Aged 21 Years 1995 refill hogshead, cask no. 13309, bott 2017 (86) n21.5 t22.5 f20.5 b21.5 Worther's original nose and very presentable barley on delivery. Simple but attractive. 58.7%. nc ncf sc. 242 bottles.

Old Malt Cask Glenallachie Aged 21 Years refill hogshead, cask no. 13299, dist Mar 95, bott Feb 17 (87.7) n22 t23 f20.5 b22 Cut from almost identical cloth as the First Editions 1995, except this has much more oomph in the barley department. 50%. nc ncf sc. 229 bottles.

⟨⟩ **Old Particular Glenallachie 25 Years Old** refill barrel, cask no. 11771, dist Feb 92, bott Jun 17 **(83) n21.5 t21 f20 b20.5** Some half a century ago, when I watched my old dad replace my neighbour's window I had sent a cricket ball through earlier in the day (missing their new born baby by only a matter of inches), I remember the indelible smell of the putty that he grumpily applied to the frame as he eased the new glass into place. It was something very much like this. Whether it tasted of strained barley or not, and was this hot, history will never record.... *50.6%. nc ncf sc. 210 bottles.*

Provenance Glenallachie Aged 7 Years refill hogshead, cask no. 11187, dist Apr 09, bott May 16 **(69.5) n18 t17 f17 b17.5** Oddly enough, there are no faults with this as such. It is just a very poor quality whisky – though standard for the distillery – matured in a tiring cask. Harsh and thin. *46%. nc ncf sc.*

⟨⟩ **Rest & Be Thankful Glenallachie 2004** hogshead sherry, cask no. 900641, dist 05 Oct 04, bott 27 Jul 17 **(90) n23** think of the fruitiest cake you've ever encountered, put it in the oven until it is just on the cusp of burning and there you have this celebration of toasty fruitiness; the barley barely lays a glove...; **t23.5** actually, it is the malt which hits first, in a lopsided, less than impressive way. The big fruit comes to the rescue with a succession of raisins, plum, dates and muscovado notes; **f21.5** dries as the malt tries to reconnect. But the bid is a little pathetic and the toasted raisins carry on their good work; **b22.5** bravo, Rest and Be Thankful people. That is the rarest of sherry casks you have unearthed there. The only blemish comes from the malt itself, which (thankfully) has virtually disappeared under the grape like a village might under the waters of a reservoir. *52.2%. nc ncf sc. 607 bottles.*

⟨⟩ **Whiskyjace Glenallachie 8 Years Old** 1st fill sherry butt, dist Nov 08, bott Aug 17 **(87) n22.5 t22 f21 b21.5** No problem here with the sherry butt which really punches out the clean grape to sensuous effect, especially on the nose where a hint of cinnamon and ginger adds further to the fruit-spattered spices. But the spirit and cask are not yet in sync, so the usual foibles of the malt are fully exposed. Hopefully the cask has not been entirely emptied as this will improve massively over the forthcoming years. *52.5%. 20 bottles.*

GLENBURGIE
Speyside, 1810. Chivas Brothers. Working.

Glenburgie Aged 15 Years bott code L00/129 db **(84) n22 t23 f19 b20**. Doing so well until the spectacularly flat, bitter finish. Orangey citrus and liquorice had abounded. *46%*

⟨⟩ **Ballantine's The Glenburgie Aged 15 Years Series No. 001** American oak casks, bott code: LKRM1245 2018/04/03 **(86) n21.5 t22 f21 b21.5** Clunking caramels clog up the nose and finish big time. But there are some interesting tannin-laden spice notes in full swing as well. *40%..*

C & S Dram Collection Glenburgie 5 Years Old bourbon barrel, cask no. 800538, dist 31 Oct 10, bott 23 Jan 17 **(89) n22 t23 f22 b22** A youngster for sure, but a beauty for all that. *61.4%. sc. 240 bottles.*

⟨⟩ **Glenkeir Treasures Glenburgie 7 Year Old** cask filled 26/9/10, bott 20/2/18 **(90) n22.5** youthful with a zesty maltiness; **t23** salivating, fresh, with a sublime malt intensity that for the initial few moments explodes off the scale; **f22** typically nutty and dry at the death **b22.5** a beautiful malt that is exactly as expected from this age in (probably) second fill cask. A spot-on blender's dream. *% strength not given on bottle. Bizarre!*

Gordon & MacPhail Cask Strength Glenburgie 1995 bott 29 Sept 16 **(96) n24 t24.5 f23.5 b24** If you want to encounter nigh-on faultless sherry influence at its most positive, grab a bottle of this...quick! For this is how a sherry cask whisky used to taste...and there is now, tragically, an entire generation of whisky drinkers out there today who really have no idea... *57.9%.*

⟨⟩ **Hepburn's Choice Glenburgie 8 Years Old** bourbon wine barrel, dist 2007, bott 2016 **(91.5) n22.5 t23.5 f22.5 b23** Serene and silky. *46%. nc ncf sc. 283 bottles.*

⟨⟩ **Hepburn's Choice Glenburgie 8 Years Old** bourbon barrel, dist 2007, bott 2016 **(86.5) n22 t22 f21 b21.5** What it lacks in complexity it more than makes up for with classic Speyside grassy juiciness. *46%. nc ncf sc. 320 bottles.*

Hunter Laing's Old & Rare Glenburgie Aged 36 Years refill hogshead, dist Nov 80, bott Jan 17 **(93) n24.5 t23 f22.5 b23** Spend as much time with that nose as you possible can... *47.4%. nc ncf sc. 257 bottles.*

Old Malt Cask Glenburgie Aged 18 Years refill hogshead, cask no. 12806, dist Feb 98, bott Aug 16 **(90.5) n21.5 t24 f22 b23** The nose is flat, but beyond that this is a very sweet and pretty boy with a long tail. Perhaps it should be called Glenbudgie... *50%. nc ncf sc. 139 bottles.*

Old Malt Cask Glenburgie Aged 21 Years refill hogshead, cask no. 12358, dist Apr 95, bott Apr 16 **(83.5) n21.5 t22 f20 b20.5** A significant degree of cask tang knocks the big barley surge off track. *50%. nc ncf sc. 170 bottles.*

⟨⟩ **Old Malt Cask Glenburgie Aged 21 Years** refill hogshead, cask no. 14246, dist Jul 99, bott Sept 17 **(91) n22.5** a little lemon sherbet gives a zesty edge; **t23** pure Burgie: the oak is scant but this particular the malty make up is very well known by blenders at this age who use it to offer barley-rich sheen; **f22.5** the spices are warming yet aligned with the delicate butterscotch tart and gentle toffee; **b23** offers a beautiful lustre and depth and brims with malty confidence. *50%. nc ncf sc. 330 bottles.*

⟫ **Old Particular Glenburgie 25 Years Old** refill hogshead, cask no. 11772, dist Apr 92, bott Jun 17 (**93**) **n23.5** attractively two-toned: the oak holds its position well without domineering, allowing gentle bourbon-style liquorice and even a degree of light coconut to mingle with the proud, clean barley; rarely is the sweetness of a malt so finely tuned; **t23** the barley is in the driving seat on delivery and less inclined to make way than on the nose; **f22** the vaguest spice ambles into view as the vanilla tries to match the fading grist; **b22.5** barley-dominant Bergie in excelsis...Just wonderful. *51.5%. nc ncf sc. 270 bottles.*

Provenance Glenburgie Aged 8 Years refill hogshead, cask no. 11628, dist Jun 08, bott Feb 17 (**87**) **n21.5 t22 f22 b21.5** Makes no great effort to hide its youth; indeed celebrates its limited scope by concentrating on what it can best: project a lovely custard-rich gristy personality with the aid of a pear-drop sharpness. *46%. nc ncf sc. 234 bottles.*

Whisky Castle Glenburgie 18 Year Old first fill bourbon, dist 22 Jul 98, bott Aug 16 (**94.5**) **n23 t24 f23.5 b24** My kind of Burgie: brilliant! *55.8%. Bottled by Gordon & MacPhail.*

⟫ **The Whisky Embassy Glenburgie Aged 22 Years** cask no. 6520, dist 15 Jun 95, bott 12 Feb 18 (**90.5**) **n23** ridiculously fresh for its age with a lovely bitten toffee apple sharpness; **t23** you expect salivating and you get salivating. Except there is an extra dose of natural caramel to go with the green apple: toffee apple, indeed! **f22** the malt still has an amazing amount to say as it cosies up to the butterscotch; **b22.5** another gorgeous Burgie bottling benefitting from excellent oak. *56.7%. nc ncf sc.*

GLENCADAM
Highlands (Eastern), 1825. Angus Dundee. Working.

Glencadam Aged 10 Years db (**95**) **n24** crystal clarity to the sharp, ultra fresh barley. Clean, uncluttered by excessive oak, the apparent lightness is deceptive; the intensity of the malt carries its own impressive weight and the citrus note compliments rather than thins. Enticing; **t24** immediately zingy and eye-wateringly salivating with a fabulous layering of sweet barley. Equally delicate oak chimes in to ensure a lightly spiced balance and a degree of attitude; **f23** longer than the early barley freshness would have you expecting, with soft oils ensuring an extended, tapering, malty edge to the gentle, clean oak; **b24** sophisticated, sensual, salivating and seemingly serene, this malt is all about juicy barley and balance. Just bristles with character and about as puckeringly elegant as single malt gets...and even thirst-quenching. My God: the guy who put this one together must be a genius, or something... *46%*

⟫ **Glencadam Aged 10 Years Special Edition** batch no. 1, bott code: L1702608 CB2 db (**90.5**) **n22.5** soft with slightly unusual degrees of natural caramels wafting around. Thinned molasses and orange blossom honey vie with red liquorice, a slightly more morose and less ebullient nose than usual; **t23.5** that is one magnificent delivery: the barley cascades onto the palate to form a lake of the juiciest malt imaginable – just exactly how a Glencadam 10 should be. There is a lemon sherbet fizz, too. But, suddenly, the dam breaks, the lake empties and we are left with a vanilla and caramel tidemark; **f22** just a little flat after the ecstasy of the delivery. A little spice now as the vanilla and extra tannins pulse; **b22.5** a weightier, oakier version of the standard Glencadam 10. Fascinating to see this level of oak involvement, though it further underlines what a delicate creature its spirit is... *48.2%. nc ncf. Special edition for The Whisky Shop.*

Glencadam Aged 13 Years db (**94**) **n23.5 t24 f23 b23.5** Tasting this within 24 hours of Brechin City, the cheek by jowl neighbours of this distillery winning promotion after a penalty shoot out success in their play off final. This malt, every bit as engrossing and with more twists and turns than their seven-goal-thriller yesterday, is the perfect way to toast their success. *46%. nc ncf. 6,000 bottles.*

Glencadam Aged 15 Years db (**90.5**) **n22.5 t23 f22 b23** The spices keep the taste buds on full alert but the richness and depth of the barley defies the years. Another exhibition of Glencadam's understated elegance. Some more genius malt creation... *46%*

Glencadam Aged 17 Years Triple Cask Portwood Finish db (**93.5**) **n23 t24.5 f22; b24** A 17-year-old whisky truffle. A superb late night or after dinner dram, where even the shadowy sulphur cannot spoil its genius. *46%. nc ncf. 1128 bottles.*

Glencadam Aged 18 Years db (**96.5**) **n24.5 t24 f23.5 b24.5** So, here we go again: head down and plough on with the Whisky Bible 2018. This is the first whisky tasted in anger for the new edition and I select Glencadam for the strangest of reasons: it is the closest distillery to a football ground (North British, apart) I can think of, being a drop kick from Brechin City's pretty Glebe Park ground. And why is that relevant? Well today is a Saturday and I should really be at a game but decided to start off a weekend when there are fewest interruptions and I can get back into the swing of things before settling into the rhythm of a six day tasting week. Also, Glencadam, though criminally little known beyond readers of the Whisky Bible, is among the world's greatest distilleries producing one of the most charming whiskies of them all. So, hopefully, it will be a little reward for me. And offering the bourbon cask induced natural, light gold - which perfectly matches the buzzard which has just drifted on the winds into my garden - this enticingly fills the gap between their 17- and 19- years old. Strikes me there is a fraction more first fill cask at play here than usual, ensuring not just a distinctively honeyed, bourbony edge but a drier element also. Distinguished and elegant this is a fabulous, almost unbelievable way to start the new Bible as it has the hallmarks of a malt likely to end up winning some kind of major award. Somehow I think the bar set here, one fashioned from gold, will be far too high for the vast majority that will follow over the next five months... *46%. nc ncf.*

Glencadam Aged 19 Years Oloroso Sherry Cask Finish db (84) n21.5 t22 f19.5 b21. Mainly, though not quite, free of sulphur so the whisky after 19 years gets a good chance to speak relatively ungagged, though somewhat muffled. *46%. nc ncf. 6,000 bottles.*

Glencadam Aged 21 Years "The Exceptional" bott 2011 db (94) n23.5 t24 f23 b23.5. This distillery is emerging out of the shadows from its bad old Allied days as one of the great Scottish single malt distilleries. So good is some of their whisky, this "exceptional" bottling is almost becoming the norm. *46%. nc ncf.*

Glencadam Aged 25 Years db (95) n25 t24 f22 b24 Imagine the best-balanced team Mourinho ever produced for Chelsea. Well, it was never as good as this nose... *46%. nc ncf. 1,600 bottles.*

Old Malt Cask Glencadam Aged 19 Years refill hogshead, cask no. 12775, dist Nov 96, bott Aug 16 (95.5) n25 t23.5 f23; b24 The palate, though a thorough delight, still struggles to live up to the perfection of the nose. There again, very few whiskies would... *50%. nc ncf sc. 145 bottles.*

Old Particular Glencadam 18 Years Old refill hogshead, cask no. 11474, dist May 98, bott Nov 16 (92.5) n23.5 t23.5 f22 b23.5 Wallows in charm. *48.4%. nc ncf sc. 310 bottles.*

GLENCRAIG
Speyside, 1958. Chivas Brothers. Silent.

Cadenhead's Single Malt Glencraig 31 Years Old (92) n22.5 t23.5 f23 b23 Well done Cadenhead in coming up with one of the last surviving Glencraig casks on the planet. The feintiness shows why it was eventually done away with. But this is a malt with great distinction, too. *50.8%*

GLENDRONACH
Highlands, 1826. Brown-Forman. Working.

GlenDronach 8 Year Old The Hielan db (82) n20 t22 f20 b20. Intense malt. But doesn't quite feel as happy with the oil on show as it might. *46%*

Glendronach Aged 10 Years PX Casks bott code 2016/09/20 LK31312 db (96.5) n24.5 t24 f24 b24 If you find a more intense, clean, sulphur-free exhibition of PX this year, then I need to see it. As astonishing as it is beautiful! This was the 1,197th new whisky I tasted for the 2018 Bible, and not a single PX cask has come anywhere near as close to this for unbridled excellence. If there was a Whisky Bible award for Sheer Voluptuousness among single malts, this would win hands down... *48%.*

The GlenDronach 12 Years Old db (92) n22 t24 f22.5 b23.5 An astonishingly beautiful malt despite the fact that a rogue sherry butt has come in under the radar. But for that, this would have been a mega scorer: potentially an award-winner. Fault or no fault, seriously worth discovering this bottling of this too long undiscovered great distillery *43%*

The GlenDronach Aged 12 Years "Original" db (86.5) n21 t22 f22 b21.5. One of the more bizarre moments of the year: thought I'd got this one mixed up with a German malt whisky I had tasted earlier in the day. There is a light drying tobacco feel to this and the exact same corresponding delivery on the palate. That German version is distilled in a different type of still; this is made in probably the most classic stillhouse on mainland Scotland. Good, enjoyable whisky. But I see a long debate with distillery owner Billy Walker on the near horizon, though it was in Allied's hands when this was produced. *43%*

GlenDronach 12 Year Old Sauternes db (93.5) n23 t24 f23 b23.5 Despite the magnificently delicate fruit, it is the malt which wins on points. Superb! *46%*

The GlenDronach 14 Years Old Virgin Oak db (87) n22.5 t22 f21 b21.5. Charming, pretty, but perhaps lacking in passion... *46%. nc ncf.*

The GlenDronach Aged 18 Years "Allardice" db (83.5) n19 t22 f21 b21.5. Huge fruit. But a long-running bitter edge to the toffee and raisin sits awkwardly on the palate. *46%*

The GlenDronach Aged 18 Years Tawny Port Wood Finish db (94.5) n23.5 t24 f23 b24 A malt with not just an excellent flavour profile but sits on the palate as comfortably as you might snuggle into an old Jag. 46%.

The GlenDronach Aged 21 Years Parliament db (76) n23 t21.5 f15 b16.5 Red-hued, myopically one dimensional, rambles on and on, sulphur-tongued, bitter and does its best to leave a bad taste in the mouth while misrepresenting its magnificent land. Now, who does that remind me of...? 48%.

GlenDronach Cask Strength batch 5 db (89.5) n22 gentle vanillas are straight and unerring; t23 salivating as the malt takes command on delivery; the middle is more intense malt with a Victoria sponge edge; f22 butterscotch tart with a pinch of spice; b22.5 a very safe malt which does everything to keep its shape intact. 55.3%.

The GlenDronach Cask Strength Batch 6 db (92) n23.5 t24 f22 b22.5 With the exception of the very last phase, this shows Glendronach in a deliciously shining light. 56.1%.

◇ **The GlenDronach Kingsman Editon 1992 Vintage** sherry casks db (59) n16 t15 f14 b14 Should be called the Klinsmann: it certainly takes a dramatic dive when the sulphur makes a tackle. 48.2%.

GlenDronach Peated db (93.5) n23.5 t23.5 f23 b23.5 I rarely mark the smoky whisky from a distillery which makes peat as an afterthought higher than its standard distillate. But here it is hard not to give massive marks. Only a failing cask at the very death docks a point or so... 46%

◇ **The Duchess Glendronach 13 Year Old Virgin Oak** cask no. 1751, dist 14 Jan 03, bott May 16 (94) n23 as expected a caramel-rich tannin tweaks the nose, though it is a playful one. More bourbon-style honeyed sugars and liquorice on display, the malt a little overawed; t24 sublime mouth feel: just enough oils to ensure the malt gets a big say here. But the slow build, thin layer after thin layer, of delicate tannins, specially captures the heart. Such amazing control of the honey notes; f23.5 suspicion of work being done on the stills or condensers at this time as a rich coppery notes unite beautifully with the fragile ulmo honey and vanilla fade; b23.5 this virgin Duchess is a beauty. 53.9%. sc.

◇ **Scotch Malt Whisky Society Cask 96.14 11 Year Old** refill ex-bourbon barrel, dist 08 Jun 06 (87) n22 t21.5 f22 b21.5 A warming, semi-aggressive 'Dronach high on sharp, juicy malt but low on tact, patience and complexity. 57.1%. sc.

GLENDULLAN (see also below)
Speyside, 1972. Diageo. Working.

Glendullan Aged 8 Years db (89) n20 t22 f24 b23. This is just how I like my Speysiders: young fresh and uplifting. A truly charming malt. 40%

Singleton of Glendullan 12 Years Old db (87) n22 t22 f21 b22. Much more age than is comfortable for a 12-y-o. 40%

◇ **The Singleton of Glendullan 15 Years of Age** bott code: L7228DM001 db (89.5) n22 a gentle framework of vanilla, malt and toffee; t23 the sweetest delivery of any Glendullan I have tasted in some 40 years. A chink of malty light bursts through, then an explosion of intense molasses and fudge; f22.5 the fudge, once burnt, is now creamier; b22 mixed feelings. Designed for a very specific market, I suspect, and impossible not to really like. But would the real Glendullan with all its intrinsic Speyside characteristics please stand up. 40%.

◇ **The Singleton of Glendullan 18 Years of Age** bott code: L6186DM000 db (89) n23 decent mix of Demerara sugars, dates and walnuts: have a problem locating the malt; t22.5 a soft, sugary ultra-friendly delivery. A mix of red liquorice, light molasses and toffee; some welcome juiciness; f21.5 the big caramel I'm afraid puts the dull in Glendullan...; b22 a very pleasant if safe whisky where the real character of the malt is hard to unearth. 40%.

Singleton of Glendullan Liberty db (73) n17 t19 f18 b19. For showing such a really unforgiving off key bitter furriness, it should be clamped in irons... 40% WB16/036

Singleton of Gendullan Trinity db (92.5) n24 t23 f22.5 b23 Designed for airports, this complex little beauty deserves to fly off the shelves... 40% WB16/037

Cadenhead's Small Batch International Glendullan 20 Year Old Lafitte cask, dist 1996 (96.5) n24.5 t24 f24 b24 A malt which is truly Lafitte for purpose... 52.4%. sc.

◇ **Gordon & MacPhail Connoisseurs Choice Glendullan 1993** refill American hogshead, cask no. 8339, dist 2 Sept 93, bott 22 Feb 18 (95) n23.5 boiled under-ripe gooseberries; early morning German bakers with the mix of sweet, fresh dough and various apple cakes, cinnamon vaguely included; t24. Ever felt a parachute? Well, the mouth feel is even silkier than that. And the landing a lot less jarring as serious tannins keep their nerve and structure to absorb the concentrated malt and apple and pear fruits. Big, spiced appropriately and makes you gasp in all the right places; f23.5 a more genteel relaxed fade with the accent on hickory and Demerara, the earlier battles over; b24 nothing remotely dull about this Glendullan: this is a whisky story spanning 25 years brilliantly and vividly told. 56.6%. nc ncf sc. 171 bottles.

Gordon & MacPhail Connoisseurs Choice Glendullan 2004 bott 18 Nov 16 **(95.5)** n24 t24 f23 b24.5 Another GlenStunning... 46%.

◈ **Simon Brown Traders Glendullan 2010** ex-bourbon cask, dist Oct 10, bott Feb 17 **(92.5)** n23 beautifully layered nose, the malt and the light vanilla of the oak being of about equal depth, both stark and three-dimensional; a light, wispy puff of smoke here and there; t23 light, refreshing, mildly juicy delivery, the barley seemingly yielding on the soft oils, then suddenly firm up. Light citrus notes welcome in the oak; f23.5 dries decisively. Light mocha and lemon drizzle cake and the very vaguest hint of late phenols; b23 a really gorgeous bottling that shows the shape of a whisky like a diaphanous dress of the early 1930s revealed the shape of the wearer. Just enough oak content to show depth as well as the spirit's integrity. A thin, teasing layer of smoke, too... 43%. nc ncf sc.

GLEN ELGIN
Speyside, 1900. Diageo. Working.

Glen Elgin Aged 12 Years db **(89)** n23 t24 f20 b22. Absolutely murders Cragganmore as Diageo's top dog bottled Speysider. The marks would be several points further north if one didn't get the feeling that some caramel was weaving a derogatory spell. Brilliant stuff nonetheless. States Pot Still on label – not to be confused with Irish Pot Still. This is 100% malt... and it shows! 43%

◈ **Glen Elgin 18 Year Old** ex-bodega European oak butts db **(89)** n23.5 a bit like honey-covered cornflakes, though with bite, an extra sprinkle of Demerara sugar spotted dog pudding still warm in the oven; t24 the complex, malt-rich sugar positively sparkle. More maple syrup now as the malt shows its gristy side; the fruit is happy to take a back seat; f19 a build-up of imperfect furry bitterness as the succulent malt and vanilla play out the long game; b22.5 before the bitterness kicks in, Speyside at its most subtly rich. 58.4%. 5,352 bottles. Diageo Special Releases 2017.

◈ **Gordon & MacPhail Connoisseurs Choice Glen Elgin 1997** first fill sherry butt, cask no. 4331, dist 14 Oct 97, bott 20 Feb 18 **(81.5)** n20.5 t21 f19 b21 A pea-souper of a malt but somewhat tight, something not quite right. 55.7%. nc ncf sc. 602 bottles.

Old Particular Glen Elgin 21 Years Old refill hogshead, cask no. 11596, dist Dec 95, bott Mar 17 **(94.5)** n23.5 t23.5 f23.5 b24 A distillery which rarely lets you down if in a decent cask. Playfully, almost coquettishly adorable. 51.5%. nc ncf sc. 226 bottles.

World of Orchids Glen Elgin 21 Year Old bourbon cask, dist 1995 **(95)** n23.5 t23.5 f23.5 b24.5 One of those rare malts where the mouth feel matches the malt in pure excellence. A blender's malt if ever there was one... 50.3%.

GLENESK
Highlands (Eastern), 1897–1985. Diageo. Demolished.

The Cooper's Choice Glen Esk 31 Year Old dist 1984, bott 2016 **(92)** n22.5 t23 f23 b23.5 A very simple, un-taxing but well preserved, unblemished, quietly delicious and poignant malt from the last days of a small and little known distillery. 50%. nc ncf sc. The Vintage Malt Whisky Co.

Gordon & MacPhail Rare Old Glenesk 1980 (95) n23.5 t24 f23.5 b24 What a charmer: better dead than when alive, some might argue. But this has weathered the passing three and half decades with ease and really does have something of an ice cream feel to it from beginning to the end...well I suppose the distillery was located close to the seaside...One of the most understated but beautiful lost distillery bottlings of the year. 46%.

GLENFARCLAS
Speyside, 1836. J&G Grant. Working.

Glenfarclas 8 Years Old db **(86)** n21 t22 f22 b21. Less intense sherry allows the youth of this malt to stand out. Mildly quirky as a Glenfarclas and enormous entertainment. 40%

Glenfarclas 10 Years Old db **(80)** n19 t20 f22 b19. Always an enjoyable malt, but for some reason this version never seems to fire on all cylinders. There is a vague honey sheen which works well with the barley, but struggles for balance and the nose is a bit sweaty. Still has distinctly impressive elements but an odd fish. 40%

Glenfarclas 12 Years Old db **(94)** n23.5 a wonderfully fresh mix of grape and mint; t24 light, youthful, playful, mouthwatering. Less plodding honey, more vibrant Demerara and juiced-up butterscotch; f23 long, with soft almost ice-cream style vanillas with a grapey topping; b23.5 a superb re-working of an always trustworthy malt. This dramatic change in shape works a treat and suits the malt perfectly. What a sensational success!! 43%

Glenfarclas 15 Years Old db **(85.5)** n21.5 t23 f20 b21. One thing is for certain: working with sherry butts these days is a bit like working with ACME dynamite....you are never sure when it is about to blow up in your face. There is only minimal sulphur here, but enough to take the edge off a normally magnificent whisky, at the death. Instead it is now merely, in part, quite lovely. The talent at Glenfarclas is unquestionably among the highest in the industry: I'll be surprised to see the same weaknesses with the next bottling. 46%

Glenfarclas 17 Years Old db (93) n23 t23 f23 b24 an excellent age for this distillery, allowing just enough oak in to stir up the complexity. A stupendous addition to the range. 40%

Glenfarclas 17 Years Old db (94.5) n23 t24 f23 b24 When a malt is this delicate, it is surprising the difference that just 3% can make to the oils and keeping the structure together. A dram for those with a patient disposition. 43%.

Glenfarclas 18 Years Old db (84) n21 t22 f20 b21. Tight, nutty and full of crisp muscovado sugar. 43%. Travel Retail Exclusive.

Glenfarclas 21 Years Old db (83) n20 t23 f19 b21. A chorus of sweet, honied malt and mildly spiced, teasing fruit on the fabulous mouth arrival and middle compensates for the few blips. 43%

Glenfarclas 25 Years Old db (84) n20 t22 f20 b22. A curious old bat: by no means free from imperfect sherry but compensating with some staggering age – seemingly way beyond the 25-year statement. Enjoys the deportment of a doddering old classics master from a family of good means and breeding. 43%.

Glenfarclas 30 Years Old db (85) n20 t22 f21 b22. Flawed yet juicy. 43%

Glenfarclas 40 Years Old db (95) n24.5 t23.5 f23 b24 A few moments ago an RAF plane flew low over my usually quiet cottage, violently shaking the windows, silencing my parrot and turning a great spotted woodpecker feeding in my garden to stone: it was too shocked to know whether to stay or fly. And I thought, immediately: Glenfarclas 40! For when, a long time ago now, John Grant paid me the extraordinary compliment of opening his very first bottle of Glenfarclas 40 so we could taste it together, a pair of RAF fighters chose that exact moment to roar feet above his distillery forcing the opened bottle from John's startled hands and onto the lush carpet...into which the initial measures galloopingly poured, rather than our waiting glasses. And it so happened I had a new sample to hand. So, with this whisky I made a fond toast: to John. And to the RAF. 43%

Glenfarclas 40 Years Old db (94) n23 t23 f24 b24 Couldn't help but laugh: this sample was sent by the guys at Glenfarclas after they spotted that I had last year called their disappointing 40-year-old a "freak". I think we have both proved a point... 46%

Glenfarclas 50 Years Old db (92) n24 t23 f22 b23 Most whiskies cannot survive such great age. This one really does bloom in the glass and the earthy, peaty aspect make it all the more memorable. It has taken 50 years to reach this state. Give a glass of this at least an hour's inquisition, as I have. Your patience will be rewarded many times over. 44.4%

Glenfarclas 50 Years Old lll ex-Oloroso sherry casks db (88.5) n23.5 t21 f22 b22 You can actually hear it wheezing as it has run out of puff. But it is easy to recognise the mark of an old champion... 41.1%. ncf. 937 bottles.

Glenfarclas 105 db (95.5) n23.5 the youthful grape comes in clean, juicy bunches; the herbs and spices on a rack on the kitchen wall; t24 any lovers of the old Jennings books will here do a Mr Wilkins explosive snort as the magnificent barley-grape mix is propelled with the force of dynamite into the taste buds; survivors of this experience still able to speak may mention something about cocoa notes forming; f24 long, luxurious, with a pulsing vanilla-grape mix and a build up of spices; light oils intensify and elongate; b24 I doubt if any restorative on the planet works quite as well as this one does. Or if any sherry cask whisky is so clean and full of the joys of Jerez. A classic malt which has upped a gear or two and has become exactly what it is: a whisky of pure brilliance... 60%

Glenfarclas £511.19s.0d Family Reserve db (88) n22.5 t22.5 f21 b22 Not the best, but this still ain't no two bob whisky, mister, and make no mistake... 43%

Glenfarclas 1994 db (95.5) n23.5 t24.5f23.5 b24 Very close in character and quality with to distillery's latest official 1994 release. Which means it's not far off God's gift to present day sherried malt whisky... 43%. 1200 bottles. The Whisky Shop exclusive.

Glenfarclas Family Cask 2002 sherry butt, cask no. 3770 db (93) n23.5 t23.5 f23 b23 Like some of the sexiest things in life have... a faultless butt... 53%.

◇ **Glenfarclas The Family Casks 1977 S18 Release** 4th fill hogshead, cask no. 7292 (93) n22.5 there is a pungency to the oak that tells both of great age and an intact malt that though inland, drifts close to the sea: a delicate brine to sharpen the citrus and tannin; t23.5 a creamy disposition does no harm to the still beautifully intact malt. Indeed, salivating in part – which wasn't expected from the nose – with again a slight salty tang as the malt levels rise; f23 for a moment there is a threat over-eager tannin taking over, but the light demerara sugars respond to dampened down the dryness; a late malty mocha finale; b24 so fourth fill in 1977...we are talking some ancient oak in league with the malt here. As fascinating as it is delicately attractive. Has travelled the 40 years beautifully... 63.5%. sc.

◇ **Glenfarclas The Family Casks 1978 S18 Release** 4th fill hogshead, cask no. 747 (87) n21 t21.5 f23 b21.5 By no means a common occurrence to get such a serious dose of ancient tannin thrust at you at such strength! Normally, this amount of oak pokes at you annoyingly and feebly at about 48%, if that. But here it wallops you. Not too great an experience at first, but as the mocha first kicks in and then wallows in its concentrated form, you can't help kind of falling in love a little bit.... 63.6%. sc.

◇ **Glenfarclas The Family Casks 1979 S18 Release** 4th fill hogshead, cask no. 8796 (95) n23.5 lovely dry custard powder and malted barley biscuit; cocoa power sprinkled in; low voltage peat; t23.5 superb delivery! So lively with a saltiness joining the light fruit and intense yet clean barley to send your salivation levels through the roof; f24 gristy even now, blending in gorgeously with the sublimely layered vanillas. Just the vaguest hint of sherry trifle at work here late on, plus that delicate hint of smoke; b24 retains its integrity with aplomb while the complexity stuns. 63.6%. sc.

◇ **Glenfarclas The Family Casks 1980 S18 Release** refill hogshead, cask no. 1413 (87.5) n22 t22 f21.5 b22 The oak is a little more tired here. But there is nothing to stop you enjoying the richness of the malt or the usual salivating qualities, though the tannins do grip a little tightly. Decent strands of mocha and blood orange, though. 63.4%. sc.

◇ **Glenfarclas The Family Casks 1985 S18 Release** refill sherry hogshead, cask no. 2601 (93.5) n22 a little bit of a kick to the tannin and citrus; t23.5 ahh...settles as soon as the malt makes its impact. Light ulmo honey intensifies into muscovado sugars; the vanilla giving weight rather than flightiness; f24 vanilla together sublimely at the death: spices join the fray, plus a little orange and cocoa; the oils gather up slightly more than the usual 'Farclas to ensure improbably length and depth; b24 so yummy! One of those rare whiskies that just gets better as it goes along... 63.5%. sc.

◇ **Glenfarclas The Family Casks 1986 S18 Release** refill butt, cask no. 4775 (95) n23.5 like the leather of an old Jag meeting Melton Hunt Cake: now there's an idea for a day out...; t24 such succulence! The mouth feel, a beautifully toned and weighted oil seemingly brushed with crushed sultana, works so well here. Juicy and chewy in equal measure, a little Manuka and ulmo honey flashes through before broader tannins takes its place; oh, and did I mention the spice...? There from the moment and slowly makes way for the developing complexity; f23.5 long with a return of the spice and chocolate raisin fade; b24 this sulphur-free cask full of weights and counter-weights and seeming sleight of hand is just how a sherry-influenced malt should be. 63.4%. sc.

◇ **Glenfarclas The Family Casks 1988 S18 Release** refill sherry butt, cask no. 7054 (94) n23 a big-breasted, matronly fruitiness bustles purposefully around the nose; t24 fat, hugely spiced and an outbreak of the bourbons despite the massive grape signature; an undercurrent of liquorice and molasses impresses; f23 a relatively simplistic fruit and vanilla fade, pepped up by the continuing bourbon-style spice; b24 a voluptuous and beautiful malt which, oddly enough, because it shows far fresher fruit than, say, the 1986, works fractionally less well overall as it simply cannot match its understated complexity. That said, this is amazing stuff: it is like comparing Liverpool with Manchester City.... 63.6%. sc.

◇ **Glenfarclas The Family Casks 1989 S18 Release** sherry butt, cask no. 13005 (96) n23.5 almost rum-like in the mix of esters and and intensity of the muscovado sugar. But a Christmas cake fruitiness slowly emerges with no shortage of marzipan; t24 right...! Only one kind of sherry butt gives that kind of delivery...and you won't find it today. Everything is toasty – the raisins are a tad burnt, the vanillas singed, the tannins charred, the sugars mollassed: there is not a delicate note to be had, yet somehow everything fits without too much aggression; f24 the hugely toasty take continues with the fruitcake almost burnt and the spices on full blast; b24.5 darker in colour and personality than a moonless night in the ghostly Northamptonshire countryside. This is from one of those big, lusty, grape-soaked sherry butts dong the rounds in the late '80s but had vanished off the scene within a couple of years. Gives a very different aspect to the Glenfarclas portfolio. And reminds us of the amazing, almost self-parodying (in this case absolutely 100% sulphur-free) sherry butts that were once available to the industry...but no more. 63.6%. sc.

◇ **Glenfarclas The Family Casks 1990 S18 Release** sherry butt, cask no. 9468 (94.5) n23.5 grape must holds sway, but a little upfront mocha, too; t24 all-consuming grape at first leaves no room whatsoever for the malt. But when the sherry is this rumbustious and lusty and spices so muscular and enthralling, you can forgive the over-exuberance...; f23.5 as I feared. Once the grape has receded, there is surprisingly little left behind, so simple vanillas and the toastier tannins have to fill in; b23.5 about as butch a sherry butt as you'll ever find. And, no: not a single trace of sulphur to be had. 63.4%. sc.

◇ **Glenfarclas The Family Casks 1994 S18 Release** refill sherry butt, cask no. 1580 (93) n23 a slight untidiness to the fruit by comparison the previous two years: slightly fragmented but the spices stick to a game plan; t23.5 while the previous bottlings were all about the sherry, this is all about the levels of spice. Warming from the off, there is an important oiliness which ramps up the amps. Sugars abound – a mix of barley sugar sweets and distant fruit bonbons – with huge vanilla surging into the open spaces; f23 spicy and vanilla heavy to the very last; b23.5 a perfect malt for those with a penchant for spiced boiled fruit candy... 63.5%. sc.

⬦ **Glenfarclas The Family Casks 1995 S18 Release** sherry butt, cask no. 6649 (86.5) n22 t22.5 f20.5 b21.5 Lots of delicious jammy notes – spread onto slightly burnt toast, of course - but a little too bitter on the finish for comfort. 63.5%. sc.

⬦ **Glenfarclas The Family Casks 1998 S18 Release** 4th fill butt, cask no. 3587 (96) n24 not so much a nose as a series of fruity sighs...gentle, playfully sweet with citrus and grape notes intertwangling; t24 pure silk, though with a meaningful nip. The muscovado sugars are molten, the spices offering the only backbone and solidity to the delicious entanglement; f24 long, languid and with an ever-increasing degree of cocoa; the spices break down into minute, peppery particles it seems; b24 an inherent subtle sweetness almost suggests a Sauternes cask finish at its finest. The fact this is fourth use sherry from way back when gives you some idea of the enormity and brilliance of this butt in its earliest days. 63.5%. sc.

⬦ **Glenfarclas The Family Casks 2000 S18 Release** refill sherry butt, cask no. 4076 (86) n21.5 t22 f21 b21.5 Juicy and at times minty but sometimes hard to get past that little threat on the fruit, which is confirmed on the furry finish. 63.5%. sc.

⬦ **Glenfarclas The Family Casks 2001 S18 Release** refill sherry butt, cask no. 3353 (92.5) n23 young with promiscuous grape. Fresh, clean with the juices still dripping...; t23 a very surprising dose of young malt appears on the radar – or is it just that with tasting the 'Farclas Family Casks, you become accustomed to old age! Even so, the complexity is wonderful, especially when the big barley powers through, a little lemon sherbet livening things further; f23 the naughtier tannins have had enough of the youngsters and ensured a weighty finish; b23.5 such a lovely, refreshing malt showing a series of fascinating age facets in this one vintage. 63.5%. sc.

⬦ **Glenfarclas The Family Casks 2002 S18 Release** sherry butt, cask no. 3769 (94.5) n23.5 so busy: the tannins work overtime to generate vanilla and spice while the more docile fruit does as little as possible; t23.5 like the 2001 there is a degree of juicy juvenility to malt, but the barley is forthright enough to make its mark and the fruit of an entirely different intensity. The grape and tannin seem to be on a combined wavelength apart, really ramping up the muscovado sugars and spices; f23.5 toasty, warming and spicy: almost like a spiced plum jam...; b24 it's amazing what you can do with a rich, unsulphured sherry butt. Create stunning whisky like this, for a start... 67.8%. sc.

Eiling Lim Glenfarclas 37 Year Old cask no. 88/8, dist 1979, bott 2016 (90) n23 t23 f22 b22 The tannins' attempted take-over sums up this malt: utterly fascinating... 46.9%. 188 bottles.

Kirsch Import Glenfarclas 2008 oloroso sherry hoggy, cask nos. 2132 & 2178, bott 2016 (96) n23.5 t25 f23.5 b24 Clean as a whistle: how sherry matured whisky should always be. 60.2%.

GLENFIDDICH
Speyside. 1887. William Grant & Sons. Working.

Glenfiddich 12 Years Old db (85.5) n21 t22 f21 b21.5. A malt now showing a bit of zap and spark. Even displays a flicker of attractive muscovado sugars. Simple, untaxing and safe. 40%

Glenfiddich 12 Years Old Toasted Oak Reserve db (92.5) n22.5 t23.5 f22.5 b24. Another bottling to confound the critics of Glenfiddich. This is as fine an essay in balance, charm and sophistication as you are likely to find in the whole of Speyside this year. Crack open a bottle... but only when you have a good hour to spend. 40%

Glenfiddich Caoran Reserve Aged 12 Years db (89) n22.5 t22 f21.5 b23. Has fizzed up a little in the last year or so with some salivating charm from the barley and a touch of cocoa from the oak. A complex little number. 40%

Glenfiddich Rich Oak Over 14 Years Old new American & new Spanish oak finish db (90.5) n23 t22 f23.5 b22. Delicious, thoughtful whisky and one to tick off on your journey of malt whisky discovery. Though a pity we don't see it at 46% and in full voluptuous nudity: you get the feeling that this would have been something really exceptional to conjure with. 40%.

Glenfiddich 15 Years Old db (94.5) n23 t23 f24.5 b24 If an award were to be given for the most consistently beautiful dram in Scotland, this would win more often than not. This underrated distillery has won more friends with this masterpiece than probably any other brand. 40%

Glenfiddich Aged 15 Years Cask Strength db (85.5) n20 t23 f21 b21.5. Improved upon the surprisingly bland bottlings of old, especially on the fabulously juicy delivery. Still off the pace due to an annoying toffee-ness towards the middle and at the death. 51%

Glenfiddich Distillery Edition 15 Years Old db (93.5) n24.5 t24 f22 b23. Had this exceptional whisky been able to maintain the pace through to the finish, this would have been a single malt of the year contender - at least. 51%. ncf.

◈ **The Glenfiddich Unique Solera Reserve Aged 15 Years** bott code: L2B 6562 db (95.5) n24.5 probably the most rounded nose in Scottish whisky: the fruit, the oak, the malt meld into one. Light roasted hazelnut, firm brown sugars, some plums on the grape.... easy, gently does it...; t24 salivating barley with crisp firm sugars as promised on the nose melting into even more salivating fruits. The oak rises like a Hunter's Moon, shining brightly before showering the proceedings with spice...; f23 toasty, drying quite dramatically towards the end; b24 some aspects of this are as good as it gets in Scotch whisky. The nose and delivery are the stuff of a blender's wet dream. Memorable. *40% (80 proof) imported by Wm Grant & Sons New York.*

Glenfiddich 18 Years Old db (95) n23.5 the smoke, which for long marked this aroma, appears to have vanished. But the usual suspects of blood orange and various other fruit appear to thrive in the lightly salted complexity; t24.5 how long are you allowed to actually keep the whisky held on the palate before you damage your teeth? One to really close your eyes and study because here we have one of the most complex deliveries Speyside can conjure: the peat may have gone, but there is coal smoke around as the juicy barley embeds with big fat sultanas, plums, dates and grapes. Despite the distinct lack of oil, the mouthfeel is entirely yielding to present one of the softest and most complete essays on the palate you can imagine, especially when you take the bitter-sweet ratio and spice into balance; f23 long, despite the miserly 40% offered, with plenty of banana-custard and a touch of pear; b24 at the moment, the ace in the Glenfiddich pack. If this was bottled at 46%, unchilfiltered etc, I dread to think what the score might be... *40%*

Glenfiddich Age Of Discovery Aged 19 Years Bourbon Cask Reserve db (92) n23.5 t24 f22 b22.5. For my money Glenfiddich turns from something quite workaday to a malt extraordinaire between the ages of 15 and 18. So, depending on the casks chosen, a year the other side of that golden age shouldn't make too much difference. The jury is still out on whether it was helped by being at 40%, which means the natural oils have been broken down somewhat, allowing the intensity and richness only an outside chance of fully forming. *40%*

Glenfiddich Age Of Discovery Aged 19 Years Madeira Cask Finish db (88.5) n22.5 t22.5 f21 b22.5. Oddly enough, almost a breakfast malt: it is uncommonly soft and light yet carries a real jam and marmalade character. *40%*

Glenfiddich 21 Years Old db (86) n21 t23 f21 b21. A much more uninhibited bottling with loads of fun as the mouth-watering barley comes rolling in. But still falls short on taking the hair-raisingly rich delivery forward and simply peters out. *40%*

Glenfiddich 30 Years Old db (93.5) n23 t23.5 f23.5 b23.5 a 'Fiddich which has changed its spots. Much more voluptuous than of old and happy to mine a grapey seam while digging at the sweeter bourbon elements for all it is worth. Just one less than magnificent butt away from near perfection and a certain Bible Award... *40%*

Glenfiddich Rare Collection 40 Years Old db (86.5) n22.5 t23 f20 b21. A quite different version to the last with the smoke having all but vanished, allowing the finish to show the full weight of its considerable age. The nose and delivery are superb, though. The barley sheen on arrival really deserves better support. *43.5%*

Glenfiddich 50 Years Old db (97) n25 t24 f24 b24 For the record, my actual words, after tasting my first significant mouthful, were: "fuck! This is brilliant." It was an ejaculation of genuine surprise, as any fly on the wall of my Tasting Room at 1:17am on Tuesday 4th August would testify. Because I have tasted many 50-year-old whiskies over the years, quite possibly as many as anyone currently drawing breath. For not only have I tasted those which have made it onto the whisky shelves, but, privately, or as a consultant, an untold number which didn't: the heroic but doomed oak-laden failures. This, however, is a quite different animal. We were on the cusp of going to press when this was released, so we hung back. William Grant blender David Stewart, whom I rank above all other blenders on this planet, has known me long and well enough to realise that the surrounding hype, with this being the most expensive whisky ever bottled at £10,000 a go or a sobering £360 a pour, would bounce off me like a pebble from a boulder. "Honestly, David," he told my chief researcher with a timorous insistence, "please tell Jim I really think this isn't too oaky." He offered almost an apology for bringing into the world this 50-year-old babe. Well, as usual David Stewart, doyen of the blending lab and Ayr United season ticket holders, was absolutely spot on. And, as is his wont, he was rather understating his case. For the record, David, next time someone asks you how good this whisky is, for just once do away with the Ayeshire niceness installed by generations of very nice members of the Stewart family and tell them: "Actually, it's bloody brilliant if I say so myself! And I don't give a rat's bollocks what Murray thinks." *46.1%*

Glenfiddich Cask Collection Select Cask db (78.5) n19 t22.5 f18 b19. Bourbon and wine casks may be married together...but they are on course for a messy divorce. The honeymoon on delivery is pretty rich and exotic. But it is all too short-lived as things soon turn pretty bitter. *40%*

Glenfiddich Cask Collection Reserve Cask db (83) n20 t22 f20 b21. Soft, chewy, occasionally sparkling but the overdose of toffee and a disappointing degree of late furriness means its speech is distinctly limited in its topic. 40% WB16/040

Glenfiddich IPA Experiment Experimental Series No 1 bott code: L34A4972141211 db (86) n21.5 t22.5 f21 b21 IPA and XX...all very Greene King brewery of the early 1980s... An IPA is, by definition, extra hopped in order to preserve the beer on a long journey (to India, originally). I can't say I am picking out hop here, exactly, unless it is responsible for the off-key bitter finale. Something is interfering with the navigation and after an attractive early malty blast on delivery everything goes a little bland. 43%.

Glenfiddich Malt Master's Edition double matured in oak and sherry butts db (84) n21 t22 f20 b21. I would have preferred to have seen this double matured in bourbon barrels and bourbon barrels... The sherry has done this no great favours. 43%

Glenfiddich Millennium Vintage dist 2000, bott 2012 db (83.5) n21.5 t22 f20 b20. Short and not very sweet. Good juicy delivery though, reminiscent of the much missed original old bottling. 40%

Glenfiddich Project XX Experimental Series No 2 bott code: L34B4041170207 db (95.5) n24 t24 f23.5 b24 "20 minds, one unexpected whisky" goes the blurb on the label. And, in fairness, they have a point. It has been a long time since I have encountered a distillery-produced malt this exceptionally well rounded and balanced. All 20 involved should take a bow: this is Glenfiddich as it should be...xxellent, in fact! 47%.

GLEN GARIOCH
Highlands (Eastern), 1798. Morrison Bowmore. Working.

Glen Garioch 8 Years Old db (85.5) n21 t22 f21 b21.5. A soft, gummy, malt – not something one would often write about a dram of this or any age from Geary! However, this may have something to do with the copious toffee which swamps the light fruits which try to emerge. 40%

Glen Garioch 10 Years Old db (80) n19 t22 f19 b20. Chunky and charming, this is a malt that once would have ripped your tonsils out. Much more sedate and even a touch of honey to the rich body. Toffeed at the finish. 40%

Glen Garioch 12 Years Old db (88.5) n22 t23 f21.5 b22. A significant improvement on the complexity front. The return of the smoke after a while away was a surprise and treat. 43%

Glen Garioch 12 Years Old db (88) n22.5 t22.5 f21.5 b22. Sticks, broadly, to the winning course of the original 43% version, though here there is a fraction more toffee at the expense of the smoke. 48%. ncf.

Glen Garioch 15 Years Old db (86.5) n20.5 t22 f22 b22. In the a bottling I sampled last year the peat definitely vanished. Now it's back again, though in tiny, if entertaining, amounts. 43%

◇ **Glen Garioch Aged 16 Years The Renaissance 2nd Chapter** bott code: L162292 db (81) n21 t23 f18 b19 For a wonderful moment, actually two: once on the nose and then again on the delivery, you think you are heading towards some kind of Sauternes-type magnificence...then it all goes wrong. Yes, there are fleeting moments of borderline perfection. But those dull, bitter notes have by far the bigger and longer say. Perhaps the biggest disappointment of the year... 51.4%.

Glen Garioch 21 Years Old db (91) n21 a few wood shavings interrupt the toasty barley; t23 really good bitter-sweet balance with honeycomb and butterscotch leading the line; pretty juicy, busy stuff; f24 dries as it should with some vague spices adding to the vanilla and hickory; b23 an entirely re-worked, now smokeless, malt that has little in common with its predecessors. Quite lovely, though. 43%

◇ **Glen Garioch 30 Years Old** No. 503 dist 1987, bott 2017 db (89) n22.5 t23 f21.5 b22 This is from the exotic fruit school of ancient whiskies, the oak's tannin now out-manoeuvering the fruit. Perhaps moved on a little too far down a chalky, tannin-rich route though a little smoke does cushion the blow. Ancient, but still very attractive. 47.1%. Selected for CWS.

Glen Garioch 1797 Founders Reserve db (87.5) n21 t22 f22.5 b22. Impressively fruity and chewy: some serious flavour profiles in there. 48%

Glen Garioch 1958 db (90) n24 t21 f23 b22. The distillery in its old smoky clothes: and quite splendid it looks! 43%. 328 bottles.

Glen Garioch 1995 db (86) n21 t22 f21.5 b21.5. Typically noisy on the palate, even though the malty core is quite thin. Some big natural caramels, though. 55.3%. ncf.

Glen Garioch 1997 db (89) n22 t22.5 f22 b22.5 had you tasted this malt as a 15-year-old back in 1997, you would have tasted something far removed from this, with a peaty bite ripping into the palate. To say this malt has evolved is an understatement. 56.5%. Whisky Shop Exclusive.

Glen Garioch 1997 db (89.5) n22 t23 f22 b22.5. I have to say: I have long been a bit of a voice in the wilderness among whisky professionals as regards this distillery. This not so subtly muscled malt does my case no harm whatsoever. 56.7%. ncf.

Glen Garioch 1998 db (89.5) n21 t23.5 f22.5 b23 with dates this good, a chocolate-loving, non-Islamic Tuareg will adore this one...one of the best flawed whiskies I have tasted in a while... 48% WB16/039

◇◇◇ **Glen Garioch 2000 Bourbon Cask** db (93.5) n23 a wonderful mix of malt and ulmo honey, bringing into play the natural caramels more normally associated with Kentucky; t24 the barley sets the palate into salivation mode within a nanosecond of delivery. Immediately, though, another avenue of flavours is triggered, spicier, hickory-laden and with a mix of caramels and molasses; f23 a gentle fade, the busy spices keeping their head down as the vanilla and butterscotch ensure a soothing final passage; b23.5 the distance this malt has travelled from the days when it was lightly peated firewater is almost beyond measure. A bourbony delight of a Highland malt. 57.3%. ncf.

The First Editions Glen Garioch Aged 25 Years 1991 refill hogshead, cask no. 12828, bott 2016 (88) n21 sharp, aggressive, of the paint-stripping mould..; t22.5 malty and salivating: simple and effective; f22 excellent oils stretch out the intense barley ad sugars; b22.5 a macho malt of limited scope but fully benefitting from its full strength status. 56.2%. nc ncf sc. 129 bottles.

The Last Drop Glen Garioch 47 Year Old hogshead, cask no. 662 dist 23 Mar 67(96) n24 t23.5 f24 b24.5 When this distillery produced the whisky in the bottle before me it was making probably the smokiest malt on mainland Scotland. Which is just as well for this grizzled old greybeard. Because things preserve rather well in peat – and this Glen Garioch is no exception. Just a standard low- or non-peated malt would have vanished behind the layers of tannins which have formed a crust around some of the lighter components of the dram. But here the smoke softens the oaky blows until they become only caresses. It is a quite extraordinary - and in many ways lucky – experience. 45.4%.

Old Malt Cask Glen Garioch Aged 25 Years refill hogshead, cask no. 12811, dist Apr 91, bott Aug 16 (87.5) n21.5 t22 f22 b22 Nutty throughout, though the main statement here is lack of peat. This was a smoky malt almost right up to the time this was made and the lack of phenols fully exposes the more fiery nature of the spirit. No shrinking violet, this... 50%. nc ncf sc. 121 bottles.

◇◇◇ **Whiskyjace Glen Garioch 22 Years Old** sherry cask, dist 1994, bott 2016 (90.5) n23 seriously chunky grape, not unlike green grape jam; vaguest hints of nutmeg and allspice, too; t23 typically bold delivery with the usual bite, but the fruit is elevated in the process to aid in the big juicy kick. The spices, which start off quietly enough are soon of epic proportion; f22.5 those spices sizzle on...gosh! b22 perhaps the most warming single malt you will encounter this year: the searing spices should have a health warning. Be brave....be very brave... 55.4%. 20 bottles.

GLENGLASSAUGH
Speyside, 1875. Brown-Forman. Working.

Glenglassaugh 30 Year Old db (87) n22.5 t23 f20 b21.5. A gentle perambulation around soft fruitcake. Moist and nutty it still has a major job on its hands overcoming the enormity of the oak. The buzzing spices underline the oak involvement. Meek, charming though a touch furry on the finish. 44.8%.

Glenglassaugh Evolution db (85) n21 t22 f21 b21. Cumbersome, oily and sweet, this youngster is still evolving. 50%.

Glenglassaugh Madeira db (93) n23.5 spices rarely come sexier: busy, pulsing and of varying tone and heat; mainly appear to be oak led, though the sultana concentrate makes its mark, also; t23.5 thick grape dulls the expected spice kick; the sugars, at first beaming, are also quickly subdued, though of a lightly molassed style; supremely chewy, though, with just so sugar impact; f22.5 a gorgeous creamy mocha with a tea spoon of molasses; a slightly muffled, furry finale; b23.5 a deliciously rich but surprising malt in that the spices fanfared on the nose never quite arrive. Love it, warts and all. 44.8% nc ncf sc. 437 bottles.

Glenglassaugh Octaves Classic db (91.5) n23 beautiful: like molten jammy dodger biscuits; t23.5 pristine malt backed up by Demerara sugar and a light touch of ulmo honey; f22 quietens as the vanillas begin to take control; b23 very high quality malt with a clean, intense persona which makes the most of any sweetness going. 44%

Glenglassaugh Octaves Peated db (93) n23.5 the phenols offer only the most subtle of anchors; t23.5 fabulously crisp: Demerara sugars meet with much loftier, more fruity dark muscovado; again, the peat rumbles – though nothing like it might...; f22.5 the oak at last gets a word in with a volley of caramels; b23.5 because of the apparent extra degree of oil, this really is a treat. Quite splendid and scarily seductive malt. 44%

Glenglassaugh Revival new, refill and Oloroso sherry casks db (75) n19 t20 f17 b19. Rule number one: if you are going to spend a lot of money to rebuild a distillery and make great whisky, then ensure you put the spirit into excellent oak. Which is why it is best avoiding present day sherry butts at all costs as the chances of running into sulphur is high. There is some stonkingly good malt included in this bottling, and the fabulous chocolate raisin is there to see. But I look forward to seeing a bottling from 100% ex-bourbon. 46%. nc ncf.

Glenglassaugh Torfa db (**90**) n23.5 not stinting on the phenols: the peat appears to have been shovelled into the furnace like a fireman feeding coals to the Flying Scotsman; t22.5 crisp, sugary delivery with some meaningful smoke layering. Some Parma Violet candy nuzzles alongside the treacle-cocnut; f22 good phenolic grist fade; b22 appears happy and well suited in its new smoky incarnation. 50%.

GLENGOYNE
Highlands (Southwest), 1833. Ian Macleod Distillers. Working.

Glengoyne 10 Years Old db (**90**) n22 t23 f22 b23 Proof that to create balance you do not have to have peat at work. The secret is the intensity of barley intertwangling with oak. Not a single negative note from first to last and now a touch of oil and coffee has upped the intensity further. 40%

Glengoyne 12 Years Old db (**91.5**) n22.5 salty, sweet, lightly fruity; t23 one of the softest deliveries on the market: the fruit, gristy sugars and malt combine to melt in the mouth: there is not a single hint of firmness; f23 a graduation of spices and vanilla. Delicate and delightful...; b23 the nose has a curiously intimate feel but the tasting experience is a wonderful surprise. 43%

Glengoyne 12 Years Old Cask Strength db (**79**) n18 t22 f19 b20. Not quite the happiest Glengoyne I've ever come across with the better notes compromised. 57.2%. nc ncf.

Glengoyne 15 Years sherry casks db (**81**) n19 t20 f21 b21. Brain-numbingly dull and heavily toffeed in style. Just don't get what is trying to be created here. Some late spices remind me I'm awake, but still the perfect dram to have before bed – simply to send you to sleep. Or maybe I just need to see a Doctor... 43%. nc. Ian Macleod Distillers.

Glengoyne 17 Years Old db (**86**) n21 t23 f21 b21. Some of the guys at Glengoyne think I'm nuts. They couldn't get their head around the 79 I gave it last time. And they will be shaking my neck not my hand when they see the score here...Vastly improved but there is an off sherry tang which points to a naughty butt or two somewhere. Elsewhere mouth-watering and at times fabulously intense. 43%

Glengoyne 18 Years first-fill sherry casks db (**82**) n22 t22 f18 b20. Bunches of lush grape on nose and delivery, where there is no shortage of caramel. But things go downhill once the dreaded "s" word kicks in. 43%. nc. Ian Macleod Distillers.

Glengoyne 21 Years Old db (**90**) n21 t22 f24 b23 A vastly improved dram where the caramel has vanished and the tastebuds are constantly assailed and questioned. A malt which builds in pace and passion to delivery a final, wonderful coup-de-grace. Moments of being quite cerebral stuff. 43%

Glengoyne 21 Years Old Sherry Edition db (**93**) n22 t24 f23 b24. The nose at first is not overly promising, but it settles at it warms and what follows on the palate is at times glorious. Few whiskies will match this for its bitter-sweet depth which is pure textbook. Glengoyne as few will have seen it before. 43%

Glengoyne 25 Year Old db (**95.5**) n24 t24.5 f22.5 b23.5 A beautiful sherry-matured malt from the pre-cock up sulphur days. Not a single off note of note and a reminder of what a sherry cask malt meant to those of us who were involved in whisky a quarter of a century ago... 48%

Glengoyne 40 Years Old db (**83**) n23 t21 f19 b20. Thick fruit intermittently pads around the nose and palate but the oak is pretty colossal. Apparent attempts to reinvigorate it appear to have backfired. 45.9%

The First Editions Glengoyne Aged 20 Years 1995 refill hogshead, cask no. 12825, bott 2016 (**92**) n23 t24 f22.5 b22.5 A seriously malty beast for the herds of Glengoyne collectors out there. 60.4%. nc ncf sc. 83 bottles.

The First Editions Glengoyne Aged 21 Years 1995 refill barrel, cask no. 13308, bott 2017 (**95**) n23.5 t24 f23.5 b24 Huge: a Glengoyne classic. 55.9%. nc ncf sc. 215 bottles.

◇◇ **Gleann Mor Glengoyne Aged Over 21 Years** dist 1995 (**88**) n21.5 when they say over 21, there are noses younger than this at 30...; t22.5 huge malt and tannin delivery. Maltesers and Fisherman's Friend hickory arm wrestle as the spices mount; f22 remains malty, but the oak has kicked in sharply here; b22 the tannin really does have a big say and another year in cask might well have been one too many. But the malt, somehow never loses its structure or goal. Will divide opinion, but I certainly wouldn't turn down a second glass... 53%.

Hepburn's Choice Glengoyne 8 Years Old refill hogshead, dist 2008, bott 2017 (**80.5**) n19 t21.5 f20 b20 Young it may be, but old enough to have a broken nose. Struggles to find any meaningful balance though the barley sugar concentrate does offer some respite. 46%. nc ncf sc. 390 bottles.

Hepburn's Choice Glengoyne 8 Years Old refill hogshead, dist 2008, bott 2016 (85) n21.5 t21.5 f21 b21 Has plenty of the New Make infancy about it with restricted oak access and maximum malty busy-ness. 46%. nc ncf sc. 372 bottles.

Old Malt Cask Glengoyne Aged 21 Years refill hogshead, cask no. 13266, dist Dec 95, bott Feb 17 (86) n21 t23.5 f20 b21.5 What can you say? Inoffensive. Unless you are offended by a 21-year-old having relatively so little to tell. There is a sherbet sharpness to this which celebrates the intense effervescence of the maltiness and gristy sugars. But beyond that... 50%. nc ncf sc. 282 bottles.

Old Particular Glengoyne 20 Years Old refill hogshead, cask no. 11212, dist Apr 96, bott Jun 16 (92) n22.5 t23.5 f23 b23 An eccentric dram which appears to throw the rule book out of the window: all the flavour profiles refuse to follow the accepted course. A wonderfully intriguing journey. 51.5%. nc ncf sc. 245 bottles.

Old Particular Glengoyne 20 Years Old refill hogshead, cask no. 11629, dist Dec 96, bott Mar 17 (90.5) n22.5 so charmingly elegant: a floral outlook at first, then slowly the malt and spice up the complexity; t23 still barley fresh after two decades thanks to a sugary, gristy posting of clean malt. Little tannin is evident beyond the spice, though a few gentle oils arrive to add texture and chewability; f22.5 very even pairing between the unmasked malt and the genteel spice; b22.5 a quiet dram which discusses the 20 passing years gently and with little beating of the chest. 50%. nc ncf sc. 287 bottles.

Provenance Glengoyne Aged 9 Years refill hogshead, cask no. 11339, dist Mar 09, bott Mar 16 (83) n21 t21 f20 b21 Not unpleasant, as there is plenty of decent malt to be going on with. But seriously undercooked. 46%. nc ncf sc.

Provenance Glengoyne Aged 10 Years refill hogshead, cask no. 11754, dist Apr 07, bott May 17 (87.5) n21 t22.5 f22 b22 The new manic nose is, thankfully, not quite matched by the beautiful clean barley which cascades over the taste buds. All kinds of barley sugar and thin honey in delightful evidence. 46%. nc ncf sc. 335 bottles.

Provenance Glengoyne Aged 10 Years refill hogshead, cask no. 12104, dist Apr 07, bott Sept 17 (87) n20.5 t22 f22.5 b22 Very similar to cask 11754 above in its original malty outlook, except here some serious spice assembles from the mid-point onwards. 46%. nc ncf sc. 670 bottles.

GLEN GRANT
Speyside, 1840. Campari. Working.

Glen Grant db (87) n21.5 t23 f21 b21.5. This is a collector's malt for the back label alone: truly one of the most bizarre I have ever seen. "James Grant, 'The Major'" it cheerfully chirrups, "was only 25 when he set about achieving his vision of a single malt with a clear colour. The unique flavour and appearance was due to the purifiers and the tall slender stills he designed and the decision to retain its natural colour..." Then underneath is written: "Farven Justeter Med Karamel/Mit Farbstoff"" Doh! Or, as they say in German: "Doh!" Need any more be said about the nonsense, the pure insanity, of adding colouring to whisky. 40%

Glen Grant 5 Years Old db (89) n22.5 t22 f21.5 b23. Elegant malt which has noticeably grown in stature and complexity of late. 40%

Glen Grant Aged 10 Years db (96) n23.5 t24 f23.5 b24 Unquestionably the best official 10-y-o distillery bottling I have tasted from this distillery. Absolutely nails it! Oh, and had they bottled this at 46% abv and without the trimmings...my word! Might well have been a contender for Scotch of the Year. It won't be long before word finally gets around about just how bloody good this distillery is. 40%

Glen Grant Aged 10 Years db (96) n24.5 t24 f23.5 b24 This is the new bottling purely for the UK market without, alas for a traditionalist like me, the famous, magnificent white label. The bottle design may not be a patch on the beautifully elegant one that had served the distillery with distinction for so long, but the malt effortlessly stands up to all scrutiny. The only difference between this and the original bottling available world-wide is a slight reduction in the work of the sugars, the muscovado ones in particular, and an upping in the green, grassy, sharper barley. Overall, this is a little drier yet slightly tarter, more reserved and stylish. My one and only regret is that it is not yet upped to 46% so the people of Britain could see a whisky, as I have so many times in the private and privileged enclave of my blending lab, as close to perfection as it comes... 40%.

Glen Grant Aged 12 Years db (95) n23.5 a subtle nose: a little cream toffee, but a wonderful sleight of hand for a citrus slant as well as a totally unexpected hint of weak lavender; t24 sharp malt, as though barley sugar candy has been melted down – with a bunch of grist stirred in for good measure; slightly more oils than expected; f23.5 remains refreshing and determined to show the fresh barley is all its stunning dimensions; some very late mocha gives a nod to the oak; far more spices than the norm for a Gen Grant adding, with those oils, some welcome extra length; **b24** beautifully distilled, thoughtfully matured and deeply satisfying malt. 43%.

◈ **Glen Grant Aged 12 Years** bott code. LRO/FE 03 db (95) **n24** concentrated malt, clean other than a light salty edge. The gentle caramels which used to drift across the nose appear to have vanished, revealing even more malt and extra floral qualities; **t24** a typical GG delivery: the malt is intense and truly riveting, then melts in the mouth. The sweetness just about perfect with the most elegant Demerara involvement; juicy despite the gradual arrival of drier tannins; **f23** an oily, vaguely coppery edge now as spices, which began to quietly form around the midpoint, stretch further and to warming effect; **b24** a slightly different slant to previous 12-year-olds but still within the expected and brilliant spectrum. Fabulous. 43%.

Glen Grant Aged 12 Years Non Chill-Filtered db (91.5) **n23** some lovely oils give the startling barley much extra; **t23** a much weightier cove than your average Glen Grant with the oils maximising the fruity qualities of the muscovado sugars which brood and enrich in equal measure; **f22.5** the tannins have much more to say than normal, perhaps also reflected by the above average spice. And there is also that persistent fruity note which even hints at the faintest degree of furriness. This is a rumbler: a very long finish indeed which just refuses to go quietly...or soon...; **b23** in so many ways speaks volumes about what non-filtration can do to one of the world's truly great distilleries... 48%. *Exclusive to travel retail.*

◈ **Glen Grant Aged 15 Years Batch Strength 1st Edition** bott code. LRO/FG 21 db (94) **n23.5** not sure a 15-year-old malt gets any more endearingly gentle than this: clean, but with a light milk chocolate attachment to the thoroughbred malt giving it an unmistakable Malteser candy effect; **t24** oh-my-word...If you think the nose is gentle, wait until you taste this. This is like a grist just melting on the tongue, spreading icing sugar in all directions, then ulmo honey and malted milk shake. A third the way in the spices arrive and with a plan, too...; **f23** just a fraction of bitterness from the oak, but the malt and ulmo honey sooth and kiss their way to the end; **b23.5** one of the maltiest malts of the year! Just a joy! 50%.

Glen Grant Aged 16 Years bott Mar 10 db (91.5) **n23 t23.5 f21.5 b22** Again the finish doesn't do justice to the earlier jousting on the nose and palate. The label talks about orchard fruits, and they are absolutely spot on. Apples are order of the day, but not sure about the ripe bit: they appear slightly green to me...and that suits the nature of the crisp malt. A gorgeous whisky I fully expect to see improve over coming batches: it's one that has potential to hit superstar status. 43%

Glen Grant Aged 18 Years Rare Edition db (97) **n24.5** the hardest decision to make here: full marks or not. Actually, no: an even harder decision is trying to work out the leading forces behind this extraordinary nose. This is so in tune and well balanced it is impossible to nail exactly what leads and which follows. Instead, one is left mesmerised by the incredible brittleness of the barley, which seems to snap if you sniff slightly too hard; the sugars at once delicate and fruity yet with the crafted sharpness of a newly forged sword. And those tannins, somehow caught up in the overall firmness, the friability of it all. Has to be the essential Speyside nose...; **t24.5** oh, wow! When the barley does arrive this beautifully manicured, not a malty molecule out of place? The sugars are as clipped as a 1940's English actor's enunciation, and probably more precise. From somewhere light oils ooze to the surface to ensure some velvet caresses the sword. The oak builds up some steam, but the tannins never once outpoint the sugars and by the mid-ground, when a little cocoa can be detected, honours are even...; so complex it was on about the fifth go I realised just what a vital role those big early spices play; **f23.5** the firmness here is so complete, that I have only tasted whisky like this in commercially bottled form in pure Irish Pot still and rye, though here without the same intensity of spice you find in either. That said, the spices teasingly impact all the same...; **b24.5** the most crystalline, technically sublime Speysider I have tasted in a very long time... I didn't expect to find a better distillery bottled Glen Grant than their superlative 10-year-old. I was wrong... 43%.

◈ **Glen Grant Aged 18 Years** bott code. LRO/EE04 db (97) **n24.5 t24.5 f23.5 b24.5** See tasting notes to the Glen Grant 18 above. A different bottling, but not a single alteration in character, other than maybe just a fraction extra spice at the very end. Another Glen Grant knocking on the door of perfection. 43%.

Glen Grant 40 Year Old db (83.5) **n22.5 t21 f20 b20**. Probably about ten summers too many. The nose threatens an oakfest, though there are enough peripheral sugars for balance and hope. Sadly, on the palate the cavalry never quite gets there. 40%.

Glen Grant 170th Anniversary db (89) **n23.5 t23.5 f20 b22**. The odd mildly sulphured cask has slipped through the net here to reduce what was shaping to be something magnificent. Still enjoyable, though. 46%

Glen Grant Five Decades bott 2013 db (92) **n24** the kind of aroma which leaves you transfixed: the trademark crisp, juicy barley is there in force, but the darker, deeper tones rumble with a spiced orange lead: sublimely complex; **t23.5** the delivery is full of the usual malty zest for life. There is a unique clarity to the barley of Glen Grant and here, on delivery and for a few a few moments after, this goes into overdrive. The mid ground is more muddled with tannin and burnt raisin making their presence felt; **f21.5** tangy marmalade; **b23** a nose and delivery of astonishing complexity. Hardly surprising the fade cannot keep up the pace. *46%*

Glen Grant The Major's Reserve bott Mar 10 db (85.5) **n21.5 t23 f20 b21.** Forget about the so-so nose and finish. This is one of those drams that demands you melt into your chair on delivery, such is the fresh beauty of the malt and stunning honeycomb threads which tie themselves around every taste bud. Pity about the ultra dry, caramel-rich finish, but apparently nearly all the sherry butts have now been used up at the distillery. Thank gawd for that. *40%*

Cadenhead's Authentic Collection Glen Grant 31 Year Old sherry casks, dist 1985 (94) **n22.5 t24 f23.5 b24** Defies the odds to deliver a really marvellous old malt. *44.8%.*

◇ **Fadandel.dk Glen Grant Aged 22 Years** bourbon barrel, cask no. 1802, dist 27 Jul 95, bott 26 Feb 18 (95) **n23.5** typical Glen Grant: despite the age, a precise, sparkling, entirely intact and pristine barley note holds its position irrespective of all else going on around it; the oak is gentle without being too placid, creating a spicy vanilla dais on which the malt appears to raise itself higher by the minute...; **t24** mercurial and magical... Age is apparent from the very first sip as the oak stands proud. But so incredibly pure is the barley note the oak is stopped in its tracks and instead mingles so neither dominate; the mid-ground spices up as the vanilla and fudge sweeten; **f23.5** lightly oiled and a languid continuation of the middle, except for a very late non-specific fruit note; **b24** it is as if every bottling of Glen Grant, even a single barrel, these days is a newly composed phrase by Beethoven.... *51.9%. sc. 24 bottles.*

The First Editions Glen Grant Aged 25 Years 1992 refill hogshead, cask no. 13358, bott 2017 (92) **n23 t23.5 f22.5 b23** Just an astonishing exhibition of flavoursome malt tones. *48.2%. nc ncf sc. 180 bottles.*

◇ **Gordon & MacPhail Cask Strength Glen Grant 2008** cask nos. 900011 & 900014, bott 1 Jun 17 (86) **n22 t21 f22 b21** This may not make sense. But it has not been marked down slightly for showing sulphur – it doesn't: these are perfectly good casks at work. But because there is is just too much fruit on show: it is too big, too aggressive; one might even say it is loud and brash. And that just isn't Glen Grant, a distillery which is the epitome of understated elegance. I learned that from the Gordon and MacPhail bottlings of the late 1970s. This, for all its juicy oomph, whizz and bang, doesn't quite get it. *56.7%.*

Gordon & MacPhail Distillery Label Glen Grant 2008 bott 7 Dec 16 (84.5) **n22 t22 f20 b20.5** For a Glen Grant this is remarkably short in stature but long in caramel. The toffee notes close just as the fresh barley grapples free of the early vanillas. A late bitterness also drags down the complexity. Easy drinking but none of the usual Glen Grant sparkle. *43%.*

Gordon & MacPhail Rare Vintage Glen Grant 1948 (96) **n24.5 t23.5 f24 b24** In the week I tasted this I placed my 95-year-old mother in an old people's home for the very first time. A poignant whisky, indeed. And I admit, without shame, that I write this with a tear in the eye. This is, indeed, the perfect whisky to reflect what this spirit represents so vividly and like no other: the passing of time... *40%.*

Gordon & MacPhail Rare Vintage Glen Grant 1949 (94) **n23.5 t24 f23 b23.5** True brinkmanship. True brilliance. A malt seemingly on the edge but steps back from the brink to give one final, magnificent performance. You can still see the special, indelible wow factor which clings to it like the natural beauty on an aged film star... *40%.*

Gordon & MacPhail Rare Vintage Glen Grant 1957 (97) **n24 t24.5 f23.5 b25** In November 2017 I reach a significant milestone in my life. So to bring up the 1,000th whisky tasted for Jim Murray's Whisky Bible 2017 it had to be a whisky from the year of my birth from a distillery which has won as many of my awards as any in Scotland. And this is the 15th edition of the Bible...which means I have been writing this book for exactly a quarter of my life....with almost 20,000 different whiskies tasted in that time it seems like longer.... much longer... Right, back to this whisky. What an inspired choice that was...! Pour, but don't touch for about 20 minutes. Like a First Growth Bordeaux, let the whisky open and oxidize. And when you do finally taste – not with ice or water, but by the Murray Method, though go easy on the heat - watch carefully as each sniff and small mouthful gives a slightly different result...for the first hour for the better each time. A whisky to be worshipped... *40%.*

Gordon & MacPhail Rare Vintage Glen Grant 1960 (96.5) **n24 t24 f24 b24.5** I think this how every whisky lover pictures an ancient malt...but dare not imagine they'd ever be lucky enough to find. Well done the good people who manned Glen Grant 57 years ago. Congratulations Gordon and MacPhail!! *40%.*

Gordon & MacPhail Rare Vintage Glen Grant 1961 (95) **n24 t24 f23 b24** Defies its years without breaking sweat. A remarkable whisky in countless ways... *40%.*

Gordon & MacPhail Rare Vintage Glen Grant 1963 (89.5) **n23 t22.5 f21.5 b22.5** A malt so hard trying to keep the tannins at bay that the narrative is sometimes lost. Some stunning moments, nonetheless. *40%.*

Gordon & MacPhail Rare Vintage Glen Grant 1965 (94) n23 t23.5 f24 b23.5 The casks in use here have sorely tested the resolve of this obviously high quality distillate. It nearly buckles under, but not quite... 40%

Gordon & MacPhail Rare Vintage Glen Grant 1966 (93.5) n22.5 t23.5 f24b23.5 Tired, yes. Asleep, by no means... 40%.

Kingsbury Gold Glen Grant 20 Year Old hogshead, cask no. 110775, dist 1996 (92.5) n23 t23.5 f22.5 b23.5 You can hardly go wrong with Glen Grant in a decent bourbon cask. And Kingsbury haven't. Charming. 53.8%. 263 bottles. sc.

Liquid Treasures Glen Grant 20 Year Old bourbon cask, dist 1996, bott 2016 (88.5) n21.5 t23 f21.5 b22.5 A workaday Glen Grant which would offer a malty lustre to any blend. 54.4%. Fairy Tales Edition.

⬥ **Scotch Malt Whisky Society Cask 9.128 24 Year Old** refill ex-bourbon cask, dist 16 Nov 92 (96.5) n25 not sure, after nearly a quarter of a century in the cask, how this maintains such a clear and crystalline perspective of barley sugar. The oak must have been long seasoned for it to ad such a delicate degree of tannin, nothing which adds weight, just backbone and structure. Likewise, the citrus notes are fresh but fleeting. This is a half hour nose: it is perfect...; t24.5 the grain tumbles around the palate like a small, lofty stream might trickle its pure mountain water onto rocks below, the fresh, salivating grassy barley melting into the ulmo honey; f23 the very lightest oak bitterness encroaches on the delicate butterscotch and barley. Light spices take to the air; b24 only Glen Grant could be responsible for this... 51.3%. sc.

⬥ **Scotch Malt Whisky Society Cask 9.140 24 Year Old** refill ex-bourbon cask, dist 16 Nov 92 (95) n24 a slightly duskier version of above, with the addition of a little maple syrup replacing the citrus; t23.5 a big honeyed delivery, the malt being swept up in its sticky arms; a suggestion of smokiness but the spices are real enough; f23.5 long, thanks to the extra oils. The vanilla and ulmo honey drift contently on the extra oils like a bother on a Lilo; b24 talk about peas from the same pod: rarely after 24 years in cask have I seen two casks as similar as SMWS's 9.128 and 9.140. But, just like twins, though they may have the same features and mannerisms, one may be heftier than the other. This is the bigger one. 51.4%. sc.

⬥ **The Single Cask Glen Grant 22 Years Old** cask no. 119461 (92.5) n22.5 a slight saline slant to the citrus enlivened malt; t23.5 fascinating and delicious interplay between busy, juicy malt and citrus-vanilla mix: mouth-watering, momentarily mouth-puckering; f23 spices at last announce the oak in fuller form, as does the malty mocha; b23.5 effortlessly elegant. 52%.

GLENGYLE
Campbeltown, 2004. J&A Mitchell & Co. Working.

Kilkerran 12 Year Old db (90.5) n22.5 very polite phenols offer a surprisingly fresh mintiness to the countenance. Wafer light body, and a wafer light caramel has been extracted from the genteel oak; t23 despite the dozen years in cask, this still retains a degree of youth about it. But the malts are confident and take advantage of the overall lack of body to spread out and blossom; f22.5 light, with a chocolate chip mint finale; b22.5 a malt far more comfortable at this age than some of the previous, younger, bottlings from a few years back. Has a fragile feel to it and the air of a malt which must be treated gently and with respect. 46%

GLEN KEITH
Speyside, 1957. Chivas Brothers. Working (re-opened 14th June 2013).

Glen Keith 10 Years Old db (80) n22 t21 f18 b19. A malty if thin dram that finishes with a whimper after an impressively refreshing, grassy start. 43%

⬥ **Cave Aquila A Knight's Dram Glen Keith 21 Years Old** hogshead, cask no. 100264, dist Nov 95, bott Dec 16 (88) n21 untidy and the odd sign of less than a less than great cask at play; t23.5 Glen Keith can do scary-intense barely like few others distilleries on the planet when it feels like it – and here it is with the malt at its most hubristic and noisy. The oak contribution is not helping, But the barley is irresistible; f21.5 warms in a slightly threatening manner; the tannins are tight and unfriendly. But the barley and its retinue of light honey tones saves the day...; b22 once a knight is enough for a delightful rough house like this... 48.6%. sc.

The Cooper's Choice Glen Keith 22 Year Old Madeira finish, dist 1993, bott 2015 (92.5) n23 t22.5 f23.5 b23.5 Good, clean fruit gives a clipped feel to this highly attractive malt. 46%. nc ncf sc. The Vintage Malt Whisky Co.

The First Editions Glen Keith Aged 21 Years 1995 refill hogshead, cask no. 13122, bott 2016 (90) n22.5 t23 f22.5 b22 Straight down the line, no-nonsense Speysider. Love it! 53.8%. nc ncf sc. 119 bottles.

⬥ **The First Editions Glen Keith Aged 21 Years** sherry butt, cask no. 14986, bott 2018 (87.5) n21 t23 f21.5 b22 A spicy guy which makes the most of the big malt and citrus theme. Just a fraction off key, alas, but plenty of storming, juicy moments to enjoy. 57.2%. nc ncf sc. 346 bottles.

Kingsbury Gold Glen Keith 23 Year Old hogshead, cask no. 82796, dist 1993 (91.5) n23 t23.5 f22 b23 Glen Keith in absolutely top form. So satisfying! 53.7%. 205 bottles.

Old Malt Cask Glen Keith Aged 20 Years refill butt, cask no. 13359, dist Aug 96, bott Feb 17 (86.5) n21.5 t22.5 f21 b21.5 No problems regarding the butt, which is always a relief. Yet despite the good age, the malt displays a freshness and concentrated gristy character of a malt probably little more than half its age. Ridiculously easy drinking. 50%. nc ncf sc. 726 bottles.

Old Malt Cask Glen Keith Aged 21 Years refill hogshead, cask no. 13125, dist Nov 95, bott Nov 16 (87) n22 t22.5 f21 b21.5 A very similar feller to the First Editions bottling. Except here we see what happens when the cask is just a little less relaxed and doesn't give a leg up to the malt in the right places. 50%. nc ncf sc. 181 bottles.

◇ **Old Particular Glen Keith 21 Years Old** sherry butt, cask no. 12198, dist Aug 96, bott Nov 17 (85.5) n22 t21.5 f20 b21.5 Marked down not just because of odd off notes from the butt. But more because of the overall flatness of the personality. 51.5%. nc ncf sc. 261 bottles.

The Whisky Agency Glen Keith 1993 (92.5) n22.5 t24 f23 b23 Amazing to find a Glen Keith handling this kind of age without breaking sweat. Delicious. 48.6%.

◇ **Whisky-Fässle Glen Keith 24 Year Old** barrel, dist 1993, bott 2017 (90.5) n23 grapefruit, anyone? t23 gorgeously mouth-watering with the still fresh, malty gristy notes harmonising with the grapefruit and lime; f22 a light spice gives a nod to the gentle oak; b22.5 a very clean malt which revels in its delicate citrus persona. 47.6%.

World of Orchids Glen Keith 19 Year Old bourbon cask, dist 1995 (89.5) n22.5 t23.5 f21 b22.5 The intensely passionate moments are truly outstanding. 53.5%.

GLENKINCHIE
Lowlands, 1837. Diageo. Working.

Glenkinchie 12 Years Old db (85) n19 t22.5 f21.5 b22. The last 'Kinchie 12 I encountered was beyond woeful. This is anything but. Still not firing on all cylinders and can definitely do better. But there is a fabulous vibrancy to this which nearly all the bottlings I have tasted in the last few years have sadly lacked. Impressive. 43%

Glenkinchie Aged 15 Years The Distillers Edition Amontillado finished, dist 1992, bott 2007 db (94) n23.5 t24 f23 b23.5. Now this is absolutely top class wine cask finishing. One of my last whiskies of the night, and one to take home with me. Sophisticated, intelligent and classy. 46%

Glenkinchie 20 Years Old db (85.5) n21 t22 f21 b21. When I sampled this, I thought: "hang on, haven't I tasted this one before?" When I checked with my tasting notes for one or two independents who bottled around this age a year or two ago, I found they were nigh identical to what I was going to say here. Well, you can't say it's not a consistent dram. The battle of the citrus-barley against the welling oak is a rich and entertaining one. 58.4%

Glenkinchie Aged 24 Years dist 1991 db (95) n24 t24 f23 b24 The old managers at Glenkinchie a generation ago felt their malt didn't quite have the body to become a big aged malt. At the time – roughly about the time this was made – you could see why from the evidence of the fragile 12-years-old. This, though, reveals the distillery in a new light and I'd love to see those responsible for making this aware of joyous fruits of their labours. 57.2%. 5,928 bottles. Diageo Special Releases 2016.

Glenkinchie 1992 The Manager's Choice db (78) n19 t22 f18 b19. Has a lot going for it on delivery with a barley explosion which rocks you back in your chair and has you salivating like a rabies victim. But the rest of it is just too off key. 58.1%. Diageo.

◇ **Glenkinchie The Distillers Edition** Amontillado cask-wood, dist 2005, bott 2017, bott code: L7222CM000 db (91.5) n23 the nuttiness of the Amontillado influence immediately impacts lending a restrained dryness to the sweeter grist and thin molasses; t23.5 a gorgeous subtlety to the delivery: so many layers of delicate sweetness. The grape offers both sugary and earthier qualities, the tannins are a light pulse of vanilla and Manuka honey; the malt thickens: seriously charming; f21.5 soft spices mix it with the residual nuttiness; unfortunately, a murmur of sulphur towards the finish; b23 now that is one very elegant whisky. 43%.

THE GLENLIVET
Speyside, 1824. Chivas Brothers. Working.

◇ **The Glenlivet 12 Years of Age** bott 2017/03/30 db (92.5) n23 marries its usual Speyside higher, fluty notes with a warmer-than-the-norm rumble of oak: confidently delicate...; t23 the delivery offers a spectacular blast of malt concentrate, sugars and grist going in all direction. As the dust settles the oak again makes a far greater impression than usual making for an impressive balance; the oils nestle into every taste bud, making it obvious we are in for the long haul; f23 long with an extended introduction of warming, oak-induced spices b23.5 probably the best Glenlivet 12 I have tasted for quite a while...lucky Americans! An extra few percentage points of first fill bourbon cask has gone a long way here. Excellent and satisfying. 40% (80 proof)

The Glenlivet Aged 12 Years db (79.5) n22 t21 f18 b18.5. Wonderful nose and very early development but then flattens out towards the kind of caramel finish you just wouldn't traditionally associate with this malt, and further weakened by a bitter, furry finale. 40%

The Glenlivet Aged 12 Years Old First Fill Matured db (91) n22.5 t22.5 f23 b23. A quite wonderful whisky, far truer to The Glenlivet than the standard 12 and one which every malt whisky lover should try once in their journey through the amber stuff. Forget the tasting notes on the bottle, which bear little relation to what is inside. A gem of a dram. 40%

The Glenlivet Excellence 12 Year Old db (87) n22 t21.5 f22 b21.5. Low key but very clean. The emphasis is on delicate. 40%. Visitor Centre and Asian exclusive.

The Glenlivet 15 Years of Age db (80) n19 t21 f20 b20. Undeniable charm to the countless waves of malt and oak. But don't expect much in the way of complexity or charisma. 40%

The Glenlivet Aged 18 Years bott Feb 10 db (91) n22 t23.5 f23 b23 A hugely improved bottling seriously worth discovering in this form. Appears to have thrown off its old shackles and offers up an intensity that leaves you giving a little groan of pleasure. 43%

The Glenlivet 18 Years of Age bott code: 2017/02/02 LKPL0386 db (83.5) n22 t22 f19 b20.5 This is a rather flat version of a usually rich malt. Has the odd honey-charmed moment and the spices aren't hiding, either. But way too much caramel has turned the usual undulations on the palate to something of pancake proportions. A little furry at the death, also. 43%.

The Glenlivet Alpha db (92) n23.5 t24 f21.5 b23. You get the feeling some people have worked very hard at creating a multi-toned, complex creature celebrating the distillery's position at the centre of Speyside. They have succeeded. Just a cask selection or two away from a potential major Bible award. Maybe for the next bottling.... 50%

The Glenlivet Archive 21 Years of Age batch no. 0513M db (95.5) n24 t24 f23.5 b24 Less archive and more achieve. For getting so many honey tones to work together without it getting overly sweet or syrupy really is a major achievement. 43%

⬧ **The Glenlivet Captain's Reserve** finished in Cognac casks db (89.5) n22 oddly, there is a bit more bite than the usual 40%abv malt, which seems to favour the rich intent of the oak; t23 silky and playfully soft, the malt and caramel appear bound in a crusty sugary shell; the spices hinted on the nose really pulse through towards the middle; f22 a tad bitter, as always seems the case after a sugary onslaught, though those spices tingle on regardless; b22.5 a laid-back malt playing games being simultaneously spicy and super-soft. 40%.

The Glenlivet Cipher db (96.5) n24.5 t24 f23.5 b24.5 It has taken over half an hour to distil these tasting notes into something that will fit the book: we have more new entries than normal and I'm running out of room. Few whiskies I taste this year, however, will compare to this. 48%

The Glenlivet Conglass 14 db (92.5) n22 t23 f23.5 b24 A joyous barley and high quality oak interplay: probably what this distillery does best of all. 59.8% WB16/043

The Glenlivet Founder's Reserve db (78.5) n20 t21.5 f18 b19. Really can't believe what a shy and passionless whisky this is (not to mention flawed). The strength gives the game away slightly as to where the malt is positioned. But I had hoped for a little more than malty tokenism. 40%

The Glenlivet Founder's Reserve bott code: 2017/04/04 LCPL 0591 db (88.5) n23 t22 f21.5 b22 Anyone who can remember the less than impressive start to this brand will be pretty amazed at just how deliciously approachable it is now. 40%.

The Glenlivet French Oak Reserve 15 Years of Age Limousin oak casks db (91) n22.5 t23 f22.5 b23. I have to say that after tasting nearly 800 cask strength whiskies, to come across something at the ancient 40% is a shock to the system. My taste buds say merci... And, what is more, a bottle of this shall remain in my dining room for guests. Having, a lifetime ago, lived with a wonderful French girl for three years I suspect I know how her country folk will regard that... Oh, and forgive a personal message to a literary friend: Bobby-Ann...keep a bottle of this beside the Ancient Age... 40%

The Glenlivet 15 Years of Age French Oak Reserve bott code: 2016/12/19 LCPK 2465 db (93) n23.5 t23 f23 b23.5 Many years ago when this first came out it wasn't very good, to be honest. Then it was re-shaped, upped a gear and became a very enjoyable dram, indeed. Now, having apparently been steered on a slightly different course again, it is just excellent...An expression that has evolved slowly but quite beautifully. 40%.

The Glenlivet The Guardians' Chapter db (81.5) n20 t21 f20 b20.5. Read the chapter – but can make neither head nor tail of it. A brief moment of honeyed enjoyment. But nothing else really adds up. Just doesn't gel. 48.7%. WB15/120

The Glenlivet The Master Distiller's Reserve bott code: 2016/10/04 LCPK 1866 db (86.5) n22.5 t22 f20.5 b21 It is a shame the malty sparkle on the nose and delivery isn't matched by what follows. A pleasant, safe dram. But too toffee-rich and doesn't develop as this great distillery should. 40%.

The Glenlivet The Master Distiller's Reserve Small Batch batch no. 9378/006 db (**93**) n23.5 t24 f22.5 b23.5 By far the best Master Distillers Reserve in Glenlivet's armoury. 40%

The Glenlivet The Master Distiller's Reserve Solera Vatted bott code: 2017/03/01 LCPL 0371 db (**89.5**) n22.5 t23 f22 b22 Pretty much in line with the 2015 bottling above, except there is slightly more caramel here shaving the top off the higher notes. 40%.

The Glenlivet Nàdurra First Fill Selection batch no. FF0714, first fill American white oak casks, bott 07/14 db (**95.5**) n23.5 t24.5 f23.5 b24 Now that is what I call a whisky... 63.1%. ncf.

The Glenlivet Nàdurra First Fill Selection Batch No. FF0117 first fill American white oak casks, bott Jan 17 db (**91**) n22.5 t23.5 f22.5 b22.5 For those who adore their Speysides honeyed and spiced, Mind, what I'd give for them to bring out a Nadurra from 100% second fill bourbon cask – then what fun time could be had creating a perfect vatting of the two...and what a whisky would result! 59.1%. ncf.

The Glenlivet Nàdurra Oloroso Matured Batch No. OI0317 first fill Oloroso sherry casks, bott Mar 17 db (**83**) n21 t21 f19 b20 Spicy, honey and succulent. But a slight fault: three guesses... 60.3%. ncf.

The Glenlivet Nàdurra Peated Whisky Cask Finish Batch No. PW0715 heavily peated whisky casks, bott Jul 15 db (**95.5**) n23.5 t24 f24 b24 An indubitably beautiful whisky, and one which might even win over a few non-peated devotees... 61.5%. ncf.

The Glenlivet XXV Twenty Five Years of Age batch no. 0115B, finished in first fill Oloroso sherry casks db (**88**) n24.5 t22 f20 b21.5 What a shame this is not at 46% or even 50% to allow the oils to keep slightly tighter control. The nose, though: wow! 43%

Gordon & MacPhail Distillery Label Glenlivet 2002 bott 1 Mar 17 (**91.5**) n23 grassy and flighty: clean, cut glass...; t23 salivating, bubbling barley at first, then chalky vanilla; f22.5 a light cocoa sign off; b23 delicious, but annoyingly under powered. 43%.

Simon Brown Glenlivet Distillery 1995 ex-bourbon cask, cask no. HE112013-01, dist Sept 95, bott Nov 13 (**90**) n23.5 t23 f21 b22.5 Suffers a little from being bottled at too weak a strength: the oils are fractured allowing the oak far too chalky a say, though the nose may have benefitted slightly. Lovely complex stuff, all the same.... 43%. nc ncf sc.

◇ **The Whisky Barrel Glenlivet 11 Year Old 2006** 1st fill sherry hogshead, cask no. 900552, dist 30 May 06, bott 25 Aug 17 (**92.5**) n22.5 solid grape: a whole bunch of them lightly sprinkled in cinnamon and intense vanilla; t23.5 a breath-taking delivery to celebrate. Succulent and salivating, the malt and fruit appear to be even-handed...but so huge and juicy; f22.5 the spices throb, the cinnamon dries yet helps sweeten; b23.5 if you think of Glenlivet as this little gentle old distillery in the heart of Speyside responsible for gentle old malts, then think again. This is a prize bull of a dram. And it's snorting in your glass... 63.5%. nc ncf sc. 316 bottles. Bottled by Signatory Vintage.

GLENLOCHY
Highlands (Western), 1898–1983. Diageo. Closed.

Gordon & MacPhail Rare Old Glenlochy 1979 (**95**) n23.5 t24 f23.5 b24 it has been many years since a bottle from this long lost distillery turned up and that was such a classic, I can remember every nuance of it even now. This shows far greater age, but the way with which the malt takes it in its stride will become the stuff of legend. I held back on tasting this until today, August 2nd 2013, because my lad David this afternoon moved into the first home he has bought, with new wife Rachael and little Abi. It is near Fort William, the remote west coast Highland town in which this whisky was made, and where David will be teaching next year. His first job after moving in, though, will be to continue editing this book, for he worked on the Whisky Bible for a number of editions as researcher and editor over the years. So I can think of no better way of wishing David a happy life in his new home than by toasting him with what turned out to be a stunningly beautiful malt from one of the rarest of all the lost distilleries which, by strange coincidence, was first put up for sale exactly 100 years ago. So, to David, Rachael & little Abigail... your new home! And this time I swallowed..46%. ncf.

GLENLOSSIE
Speyside, 1876. Diageo. Working.

◇ **Cadenhead's Single Cask International Glenlossie 23 Years Old** dist 1993 (**95.5**) n23.5 creamy vanilla ice cream with a lemon sauce topping; t24.5 oh....wow! The malt appears to have been redistilled into concentrated form within the bottle: massive barley sugar and heather honey. Bt the oak has much to say, though none of it too loud and sets down the anchor; f23 dancing spices, but still that citrusy malt hangs around; b24.5 hard to imagine a malt more glassy as it slides effortlessly and seemingly without friction around the palate...Magnificent! 56.8%. sc. 175th Anniversary bottling.

⟨⟩ **Gordon & MacPhail Cask Strength Glenlossie 2008** cask no. 6775, bott 11 Jul 17 (83.5) n20 t21.5 f21 b21 At times appears to have all the right attributes. But from the dim nose onwards, things fail to gel. Very hit and miss and un-Lossie-like. 61.7%. sc.

⟨⟩ **Hepburn's Choice Glenlossie 9 Years Old** refill hogshead, dist 2007, bott 2017 (84.5) n21.5 t21 f21 b21 Grassy, simple but very flat textured. 46%. nc ncf sc. 375 bottles.

⟨⟩ **Kingsbury Gold Glenlossie 20 Years Old** hogshead, cask no. 2059, dist 1997 (93) n23 unusual to nose a 20-year-old this clean and well refined: light spices apart, the entire aroma consists of a gentle interplay between ulmo honey and a citrus-tinged vanilla; t23.5 just classic stuff! Malt offers a gristy sweetness which develops more into a thinned maple syrup, thicker heather honey and liquorice. Spices prickle perfectly; f23 darker and weightier as the mocha and butterscotch join the spices; b23.5 Lossie ladelling out the honey and malt in just about equal dollops. Just lovely! 55.1%. 255 bottles.

⟨⟩ **Old Particular Glenlossie 19 Years Old** refill hogshead, cask no. 12017, dist Nov 97, bott Aug 17 (93.5) n24 dank putty, powdered white chocolate and sweetened aniseed amid the barley; t23.5 another melt-in-the-mouth merchant with the gristiness about as intense as it gets. Lightweight lime and ulmo honey rising on the delicate but important oils; f22.5 everything gives way to the gentle tannins; b23.5 if you ever wondered why I think this is a great distillery, grab a glass of this... 50.9%. nc ncf sc. 140 bottles.

Scotch Malt Whisky Society Cask 46.45 23 Year Old refill ex-bourbon hogshead, dist 17 Nov 92 (89.5) n22.5 t22.5 f22 b22.5 What a glossy Lossie...! 52.7%.

⟨⟩ **Scotch Malt Whisky Society Cask 46.55 24 Year Old** refill ex-bourbon barrel, dist 16 Nov 92 (90.5) n23 delicate strands of citrus – marmalade especially – wend their way through the cake mix: memories of childhood licking of bowls here...; t22 the first couple of waves are stoically bold barley. But these are soon disrupted by a tannin attack which gradually increases in severity; f23 dark chocolate mousse; b22.5 big oak means this malt is hanging on a bit at times but comes through beautifully in the end. 52.7%. sc.

⟨⟩ **The Whisky Embassy Glenlossie Aged 20 Years** cask no. 6766, dist 20 Nov 97, bott 24 Nov 17 (87.5) n22 t22.5 f21 b22 A little ulmo honey and marzipan counters the muscular, dry oak. Some lovely hickory presence as the odd bourbon note seeps through. 51.7%. nc ncf sc.

WoodWinters Drochaid 10 Year Old (92.5) n23 t23.5 f23 b23 Given the right cask and 'Lossie can be as lively as they come. And this is the right cask...! 60.7%. sc. 345 bottles.

GLEN MHOR
Highlands (Northern), 1892–1983. Diageo. Demolished.

Glen Mhor 1976 Rare Malt db (92.5) n23 t24 f22 b23.5. You just dream of truly great whisky sitting in your glass from time to time. But you don't expect it, especially from such an old cask. This was the best example from this distillery I've tasted in 30 years...until the Glenkeir version was unleashed! If you ever want to see a scotch that has stretched the use of oak as far it will go without detriment, here it is. What a pity the distillery has gone because the Mhor the merrier... 52.2%

GLENMORANGIE
Highlands (Northern), 1843. Glenmorangie Plc. Working.

Glenmorangie 10 Years Old db (94) n24 t22 f24 b24 You might find the occasional "orange variant", where the extra degree of oak, usually from a few too many first-fill casks, has flattened out the more extreme peaks and toughs of complexity (scores about 89). But these are pretty rare – almost a collector's item – and overall this remains one of the great single malts: a whisky of uncompromising aesthetic beauty from the first enigmatic whiff to the last teasing and tantalising gulp. Complexity at its most complex. 40%

Glenmorangie 15 Years Old db (90.5) n23 chunky and fruity: something distinctly sugar candy about this one; the barley's no slouch, either; and, just to raise the eyebrows, just the faintest waft of something smoky...; t23 silky, a tad sultry, and serious interplay between oak and barley; a real, satisfying juiciness to this one; f22 dries towards the oaky side of things, but just a faint squeeze of liquorice adds extra weight; b22.5 exudes quality. 43%

Glenmorangie 15 Years Old Sauternes Wood Finish db (68) n16 t18 f17 b17 I had hoped – and expected – an improvement on the sulphured version I came across last time. Oh, whisky! Why are you such a cruel mistress...? 46%

Glenmorangie 18 Years Old db (91) n22 pleasant if unconvincing spotted dick; t23 sharp, eye-watering mix of fruit and mainly honeyed barley; nutty and, with the confident vanillas, forming a breakfast cereal completeness; f23. Cocoa Krispies; b23 having thrown off some previous gremlins, now a perfect start to the day whisky... 43%

Glenmorangie 19 Year Old db (94) n24 light fruit ensures an ethereal feel totally making a mockery of nearly two decades in the cask: fresh, subtle and sophisticated; t23.5 the most brittle and vulnerable malt I have experienced from this distillery. Every note is gossamer thin, the grist can fracture any moment; the delicate fruit shatter into millions of pieces if you chew too hard...bitters...? **f22.5** yes, a slight bitter notes creeps in briefly. But it creeps out again as the light gooseberry and lighter barley notes play their game of peek-a-boo...; **b24** fruity or malty...? I can't decide...but then I don't think for a moment that you're supposed to be able to... 43%.

Glenmorangie 25 Years Old db **(95.5) n24 t24 f23.5 b24** Every bit as statesmanlike and elegant as a whisky at this age from such a blinding distillery should be. Ticks every single box for a 25-year-old and is Morangie's most improved malt by the distance of Tain to Wellingborough. There is a hint of genius with each unfolding wave of flavours with this one: a whisky that will go in 99/100 whisky lover's top 50 malts of all time. And that includes the Peatheads. 43%

Glenmorangie 30 Years Old db **(72) n17 t18 f19 b18.** From the evidence in the glass the jury is out on whether it has been spruced up a little in a poor sherry cask — and spruce is the operative word: lots of pine on this wrinkly. 44.1%

Glenmorangie Vintage 1975 db **(89) n23 t23 f21 b22.** A charming, fruity and beautifully spiced oldie. 43%

⬦ **Glenmorangie Allta** db **(89) n22.5** incredibly fat nose, almost with a vanilla pod shoved up your nostril to give a very melted ice cream persona. Lightly spiced...and intriguing; **t23** as fat as it is on the nose, that is nothing to the delivery: I would never have recognised this as 'Morangie in blind tasting in a million years. Again the sweetened vanilla is on overdrive, though there is a juicy, non-specific fruity lustre (push comes to shove, a strange strawberry tinge, perhaps) and even a light chocolate caramel towards the middle; **f21.5** just a fraction too tangy and bitter; **b22** this is a very different 'Morangie: the Allta, could well be for Alternative. Because while the distillery is rightly famed for its cask innovation, there is no barrel style I can think of on the planet which can shape the malt in this unique way. So either grain or yeast is the deciding factor here — perhaps a mixture of both (and you can rule out water!). My money is on yeast, as the only ever time I've come across something quite like this was in a lab in Kentucky with some experimental stuff. The perfect Glenmorangie to confuse your friends by... 51.2%.

Glenmorangie Artisan Casks db **(93) n23 t23.5 f23 b23.5.** If whisky could be sexed, this would be a woman. Every time I encounter Morangie Artisan, it pops up with a new look, a different perfume. And mood. It appears not to be able to make up its mind. But does it know how to pout, seduce and win your heart...? Oh yes. 46%

Glenmorangie Astar db **(93) n24 t23.5 f22 b23.5** Astar has moved a long way from the first bottling which left me scratching my head. This is one of the maltiest of all their range, though the lightness of touch means that any bitterness can be too easily detected. 52.5%.

Glenmorangie Bacalta db **(87) n22 t22.5 f21 b21.5.** Unusually for a Glenmorangie the narrative is muffled and indistinct. Has some lovely moments, but a bit sharp and lacking in places. 46%

Glenmorangie Burgundy Wood Finish db **(72) n17.5 t19.5 f18 b18.** Sulphured whisky de table. 43%

Glenmorangie Cadboll db **(86.5) n21 t23.5 f20.5 b21.5** Every year a challenging new breed of Glenmorangie appears to be thrown into the mix, as though to fully test the taste buds. This is this year's offering: different again, with neither the nose nor finish quite up to par with the outstanding delivery — indeed, the finale is pretty bitter, indeed. But the texture and intensity of the barley on arrival is borderline brilliant, as is the most wonderful caramel which frames it with a buttery sweetness. 43.1%.

Glenmorangie Cellar 13 Ten Years Old db **(88.5) n22 t22.5 f22 b22** Oh, if only I could lose weight as efficiently as this appears to have done... oh, I have! My love and thanks to Nancy, Nigel and Ann Marie. 43%

Glenmorangie Companta Clos de Tart & Rasteau casks, dist 27 Jan 99, bott 14 Nov 13 db **(74) n17 t20 f18 b19.** "I don't think you'll be a fan of this one, Jim" said the Glenmorangie blender to me, letting me know the sample was on its way. How right he was. Have to say there is some breath-taking fruit to be had before the sulphur does its worst. 46%. ncf.

Glenmorangie Dornoch db **(94) n23.5 t23 f23.5 b24** A rare Glenmorangie which this time does not put the emphasis on fruit or oak influence. But this appears to concentrate on the malt itself, taking it through a routine which reveals as many angles and facets as it can possibly conjure. Even if the casks are from a central warehouse, at times a seascape has been created by a light salty influence — so befitting the whisky's name. A real treat. 43%

Glenmorangie Ealanta 1993 Vintage db **(97.5) n24 t24 f24.5 b25** When is a bourbon not a bourbon? When it is a Scotch single malt...And here we have potentially the World Whisky of the Year. Free from the embarrassing nonsense which passes for today's sherry butt, and undamaged by less than careful after use care of second-hand bourbon casks, we see what happens when the more telling aspects of oak, the business end which gives bourbon that extra edge, blends with the some of the very finest malt made in Scotland. Something approaching one of the best whiskies of my lifetime is the result... 46%

Glenmorangie Elegance db (92) n22 quite herbal and soothing; t24 the thinnest layer of icing sugar coats the silk-soft malt; every bit as gentle as the nose suggests; f22 medium to short with some attractive rolling vanilla; b24 a surprise package that is not entirely dissimilar to the Golden Rum, only a tad sweeter. 43%

Glemorangie Finealta db (84.5) n21 t22 f20.5 b21. Plump and thick, one of the creamiest malts around. For what it lacks in fine detail it makes up for in effect, especially the perky oaky spices. 46%

Glenmorangie Grand Vintage Malt 1989 db (94) n23.5 t23.5 f23 b24 A stunning, silky blend of a single malt where the flavour profile – and even texture - has obviously been sculpted. As much a work of art as a dram... 43.1%

Glenmorangie Grand Vintage Malt 1990 db (94) n24 t24 f22.5 b23.5 Grand by name, grand by nature...almost. For a malt this outstandingly good, it really should have been at 46% minimum... 43%

◇◇ **Glenmorangie Grand Vintage 1991** db (94.5) n23.5 brilliant mix of blackcurrant and lush dates. That before you get to the toasted raisins...; t24 you think, momentarily, this is going to be a dry, toasty affair...then in rush the muscovado sugars and the fruit is transformed into a sweet, juicy chewathon, spices prickling and tickling at will. The tannins are firm but never tire; f23 a little salty, though the malt finally surfaces; b24 some years back – indeed, at around the time this whisky was distilled - I was reliably informed by the blender at Glenmorangie that his whisky was not designed for this kind of great age, hence it was bottled at 10 and, at a push and with sherried sticking plaster and grapey crutches, at 18. This has past 25 years without apparent damage and with seemingly many more years still left on the clock. How times have changed... 43%.

◇◇ **Glenmorangie Grand Vintage 1993** db (95.5) n24 the saltiest, almost earthiest Glenmorangie for a very long while: the tannins really thump out the vanilla and butterscotch notes; t24 salted honey....? An almost unique flavour profile there: you are expecting fruit to come roaring at you – well it does, to a degree – but then you are aware of this unlikely but delicious combination pulling the strings first appearing on delivery, disappearing for a bit as some fruitier sugars take brief hold, then re-emerging to show who exactly is in command; f23.5 buzzy, busy and brilliant; b24.5 I have known their bender Bill Lumsden long enough to know that he doesn't like to play safely or by the book: if he can bowl a googly (throw a curve ball to our friends Stateside) he will. I'm not exactly sure what he's done with this, but whatever it was I'll be happy for him to do it again. By the way, Bill, if you are reading this: I'd create this by selecting some 1991 casks that are well past their sell by date and kicking out some salty tannin and reinvigorating them with others that are still juicy and younger than their years. It's a hard trick to pull off, because you have to get the percentages almost exactly spot on (there may be a 3% give either way to hit the required balance), but Dr. Lumsden is one of only a handful of blenders able to pull off the manoeuvre without crashing. 43%.

Glenmorangie Lasanta sherry casks db (68.5) n16 t19 f16 b17.5. The sherry problem has increased dramatically rather than being solved. 46%

Glenmorangie Lasanta Aged 12 Years sherry cask finish db (93) n23.5 t24 f22 b23.5 A delightful surprise: every bottling of Lasanta I'd ever tasted had been sulphur ruined. But this new 12-y-o incarnation has got off to a flying start. Although a little bit of a niggle on the finish, I can live with that in the present climate. Here's to a faultless second bottling... 43%

Glenmorangie Legends The Duthac db (91.5) n23.5 t23.5 f21.5 b23 Not spoken to their blender, Bill Lumsden, about this one. But he's been busy on this, though not so busy as to get rid of the unwelcome you-know-what from the wine casks. Educated guess: some kind of finish involving virgin oak, or at least first fill bourbon, and sherry, probably PX on account of the intensity of the crisp sugar. 43%. ncf.

Glenmorangie Madeira Wood Finish db (78) n19.5 t20.5 f19 b19. One of the real problems with wine finishes is getting the point of balance right when the fruit, barley and oak are in harmony. Here it is on a par with me singing in the shower, though frankly my aroma would be a notch or two up. 43%

Glenmorangie Margaux Cask Finish db (88) n22 t22 f22 b22. Even taking every whisky with an open mind, I admit this was better than my subconscious might have considered. Certainly better than the near undrinkable Ch. Margaux '57 I used to bring out for my birthday each year some 20-odd years ago... 46%

Glenmorangie Milsean db (94) n23 t23.5 f23.5 b24 A quite beautiful malt which goes out of its way to put the orangey in 'Morangie. 46%

Glenmorangie Nectar D'or Sauternes Finish db (94) n23 t24 f23 b24 Great to see French casks that actually complement a whisky – so rare! This has replaced the Madeira finish. But there are some similar sweet-fruit characteristics. An exercise in outrageously good sweet-dry balancing. 46%

Glenmorangie Private Edition 9 Spios db (95.5) n23 t24.5 f23.5 b24.5 Glenmorangie displaying countless layers of brilliance. Breathtakingly beautiful. 46%.

Glenmorangie Quinta Ruban Port Finish db (92) n24 t23 f22 b23 This replacement of the original Port finish shows a genuine understanding of the importance of grape-oak balance. Both are portrayed with clarity and confidence. This is a form of cask finishing that has progressed from experimentation to certainty. 46%

Glenmorangie Sherry Wood Finish db (84) n23 t21 f20 b20. Stupendous clean sherry nose, then disappoints with a somewhat bland display on the palate. 43%

Glenmorangie Signet db (80.5) n20 t21.5 f19 b20. A great whisky holed below the waterline by oak of unsatisfactory quality. Tragic. 46%. Travel Retail Exclusive.

Glenmorangie Sonnalta PX db (96.5) n24t24 f24.5b24 Remains a giant among the tall stills. A mesmeric whisky... 46%

Glenmorangie Taghta db (92) n23 t23 f23 b23 A curious Glenmorangie which, unusually, appears not to be trying to make a statement or force a point. This is an old Sunday afternoon film of a dram: an old-fashioned black and whitie, (home grown and not an Ealing, or Bogie or Edward G Robinson) where, whether we have seen it before or not, we know pretty much what is going to happen, in a reassuring kind of a way... 46%

Glenmorangie Tarlogan db (95) n24 t24 f22.5 b23.5 Interesting. I have just tasted three new Dalmore. Identical colour and some very similar toffeed characteristics. I allowed a whisky-loving visitor to taste them, without telling him what they were. He could barely tell them apart. Here, I have three new Glenmorangies. All of a different hue. I may not like them all; we will see. But at least I know there will be remarkable differences between them. This fabulous malt radiates the countryside in a way few drams have done before. As refreshing as an early morning dip in a Scottish pond... 43%

Glenmorangie Traditional db (90.5) n22 orange blossom, barley sugar and chalk dust; t23 delicate delivery revelling in gentle complexity: really playful young-ish malt makes for a clean start and middle; f22.5 soft mocha notes play out a quiet finish; b23 an improved dram with much more to say, but does so quietly. 57.1%

Glenmorangie Tayne db (87.5) n21 t22.5 f22 b22. Tangy back story. But also a curious early combination between butterscotch and Werther's Original candy. The malt – topped with a splash of double cream - in the centre ground, though, is the star showing. 43%. Travel Retail Exclusive.

Glenmorangie Tùsail Private Edition db (92) n24.5 if you sniff this too hard, you might break the whisky into a thousand pieces... just so gentle, wafer-thin shards of barley, butterscotch, boiled pear, vanilla, marzipan...and all watched over by brittle spices; t23 the delivery mirrors the nose: the first six or seven waves are simply sketches of most of the things you find in the aroma, yet with no weight or substance at all...the mid-ground becomes little more simple and vanilla-driven, though with a delicate ulmo honey thread; f21.5 lightweight vanilla and barley; only the spices make a noise; bitters very slightly at death; b23 doesn't quite live up to the nose. But that would have been a big ask! From the Understated School of Glenmorangie.46%. ncf.

⬧ **Scotch Malt Whisky Society Cask 125.74 11 Year Old** 1st fill ex-bourbon barrel, dist 07 Aug 05 (94.5) n23 a light, at times ethereal, maltiness still has sufficient clout to mix it with the confident chocolate-liquorice; t23.5 big structured with impressive oils and delicate (slightly molassed) sugars, the malt really does ramp up the intensity. But even that has to give way to the developing hickory, liquorice and chocolate which fill every inch of the middle ground; the spices are playful and in tune; f24 a lightly malted, increasingly intense plain chocolate mousse; b24 Glenchocolatie. 57.9%. sc.

GLEN MORAY
Speyside, 1897. La Martiniquaise. Working.

Glen Moray Classic 8 Years Old db (86) n20 t22 f21 b23. A vast improvement on previous bottlings with the sluggish fatness replaced by a thinner, barley-rich, slightly sweeter and more precise mouthfeel. 40%

Glen Moray 10 Years Old Chardonnay Matured db (73.5) n18.5 t19 f18 b18. Tighter than a wine cork. 40%

Glen Moray 12 Years Old db (90) n22.5 t22 f23 b22.5 I have always regarded this as the measuring stick by which all other malty and clean Speysiders should be tried and tested. It is still a fabulous whisky, full of malty intricacies. Something has fallen off the edge, perhaps, but minutely so. Still think a trick or two is being missed by bottling this at 40%: the natural timbre of this malt demands 46% and no less.... 40%

Glen Moray 16 Years Old db (74) n19 t19 f18 b19. A serious dip in form. Drab. 40%

Glen Moray 20 Years Old db (80) n22 t22 f18 b18. With so much natural cream toffee, it is hard to believe that this has so many years on it. After a quick, refreshing start it pans out, if anything, a little dull. 40%

Glen Moray Aged 25 Years Port Cask Finish dist 1988 db (88) n23 t22.5 f20.5 b22 Thought I'd celebrate Andy Murray's second Wimbledon victory, which he completed just a few minutes ago, by having another go at a Glen Moray 25-year-old (Moray is pronounced Murray). I remember last time being slightly disappointed with this expression. Well this later bottling is a little better, but nowhere near the brilliance Murray displayed in gaining revenge for Canada last year getting World Whisky of the Year. Curiously, if this is a 25-year-old and was distilled in 1988, then presumably it was bottled in 2013...the first time Murray won Wimbledon!43%

Glen Moray 25 Year Old Port Cask Finish batch 2 db (95) n23.5 t23.5 f24 b24 Some quite first rate port pipes are involved here. Absolutely clean as a whistle and without any form of off-note. A distillery I have a very soft spot for showing very unusual depth – and age. Brilliant. 43%. 3295 bottles.

Glen Moray Aged 25 Years Portwood Finish Rare Vintage Limited Edition bott code. 3153, dist 1986 db (87.5) n22.5 t22 f21 b22. Just get the feeling that the Port pipe has not quite added what was desired. 43%

Glen Moray Aged 25 Years Port Cask Finish dist 1988, bott code L709759A 2017/04/07 db (94) n23 t23.5 f23.5 b24 A lovely intense malt where the Port casks leave big fruity fingerprints at every turn. 43%.

Glen Moray 30 Years Old db (92.5) n23.5 it's probably the deftness of the old-fashioned Speyside smoke in tandem with the structured fruits that makes this so special; t23.5 for a light Speysider, the degree of barley to oak is remarkable: soft, oil-gilde d barley is met by a wonderful, if brief, spice prickle; f22.5 deft layering of vanilla and cocoa; a sprinkle of muscovado sugar repels any darker oak notes; b23 for all its years, this is comfortable malt, untroubled by time. There is no mistaking quality. 43%

Glen Moray 1984 db (83) n20 t22 f20 b21. Mouthwatering and incredibly refreshing malt for its age. 40%

Glen Moray 1989 db (86) n23 t22 f20 b21. Doesn't quite live up to the fruit smoothie nose but I'm being a little picky here. 40%

Glen Moray Bourbon Cask 1994 cask no. 42/0, bott code. 25/04/17 170635 db (93.5) n23.5 t23.5 f23 b23.5 For most people in England Glen Moray is a highly productive goalscorer for Brighton. But it would be great if the world woke up to just what lovely whisky can come from this much under-rated distillery. 56.4%. sc.

Glen Moray Classic db (86.5) n22 t21.5 f21.5 b21.5. The nose is the star with a wonderful, clean barley-fruit tandem, but what follows cannot quite match its sure-footed wit. 40%

Glen Moray Classic Port Cask Finish db (89.5) n21 t21.5 f23.5 b23.5 A malt which has to somehow work its way to the exit...and finally does so with supreme confidence and a touch of class along the way... 40%

Glen Moray Classic Chardonnay Cask Finish db (73) n19 t19 f17 b18. Juicy. But sulphur-dulled. 40%

Glen Moray Elgin Classic Sherry Cask Finish db (85) n21 t22 f20.5 b21.5. Must be a cream sherry, because this is one exceptionally creamy malt. A bit of a late sulphur tang wipes off a few marks, but the delicious grapey positives outweigh the negatives. 40%

Glen Moray Elgin Heritage Aged 15 Years db (74) n19 t20 f17 b18. Dulled by some poor, sulphur-laden sherry butts. Glen Moray is one of the maltiest drams on God's earth and at its most evocative in ex-bourbon. Who needs sherry? 40%

Glen Moray Elgin Heritage Aged 18 Years db (94) n23.5 t24 f23 b23.5 Absolutely true to the Glen Moray style. Superb. 47%

Glen Moray Mastery db (89.5) n23.5 t22.5 f21.5 b22 Has an expensive feel to this, to be honest. But, though a huge GM fan, have to say that for all its very clean, attractive, unblemished fruit; for all its juiciness I'm afraid it's just a little bit too one-dimensional. No doubting its charm and elegance, however. 52.3%.

Glen Moray Peated Cask 1994 cask no. 904/70, bott code. 25/04/17 170637 db (91) n22.5 the sweet smoke has as much mintiness about it as it does Arbroath Smokie; t23 delicate smoke has been absorbed into the slightly liquorice and fudge sweetness; soft mouth feel yet interestingly peppered with spice from an early point; f22 lightly smoked butterscotch; b23.5 a minor masterclass in smoky subtlety if ever there was one... 56.3%. sc.

Glen Moray Peated Classic db (87.5) n21.5 t22.5 f21.5 b22. Really never thought I'd see this distillery, once the quintessential Speyside unpeated dram, gone all smoky... A little bit of a work in progress. And a minor word to the wise to their blenders: by reducing to 40% you've broken up the oils a shade – but tellingly - too much, which can be crucial in peaty whiskies. Up to 46% next bottling and I think you'll find things fall into place – and not apart... Some minor erotic moments, though, especially on the fourth or fifth beats, when the sugars and smoked vanilla do work well together. Too fleeting, though. *40%*

Glen Moray Sherry Cask Finish 1994 cask no. 904/57, bott code. 25/04/17 170636 db **(92)** n23.5 t23 f22 b23.5 Old-fashioned, traditional dry oloroso influence in its most resounding form. A must find malt for those looking to broaden their positive whisky experiences.*56.7%. sc.*

Alos Sansibar Whisky Glen Moray 1988 bott 2016 **(94)** n23.5 t24 f23 b23.5 Imagine Glen Moray as a bar of chocolate... *45.1%.*

Best Dram Glen Moray 18 Year Old Lagavulin PX Octave finish, bott 2016 **(87)** n22.5 t23 f21 b20.5 Glen Moray as, undoubtedly, you will never have seen it before: certainly I haven't! An intriguing if slightly confusing mish-mash of styles, though offering a creaminess alien to the distillery. Enjoyable, but the over enthusiastic sweetness often seems forced and unsteady while the tang at the end does few favours. Good spices and sulphur-free, though. *54.9%.*

Demijohn Glen Moray 9 Year Old cask no. 5858, bott 20 Jan 17 **(95)** n23.5 t24 f23.5 b24 A Glen Moray exactly how it should be considering cask type and age: wonderful! *60.2%. sc.*

⟨ **The First Editions Glen Moray Aged 21 Years 1995** refill hogshead, cask no. 12831, bott 2016 **(93)** n23.5 so classy – and glassy! Such a firm, crystalline character to the delicate sugars. Diced green apple and even the light nuttiness of a pear mixed in with the usual malty onslaught; t23 at once salivating, yet crisp. Like the nose, the sugars are brittle – not dissimilar to Glen Grant in some ways – but nothing contain the huge malt surge; f23 the vaguest of spice mingles with the modest muscovado and vanilla; b23.5 an unusual Glen Moray, as this contains its usual big malt character, but everything seems encased in a sugar outer shell. Fabulous. *51.9%. nc ncf sc. 102 bottles.*

Hepburn's Choice Glen Moray 9 Years Old refill bourbon barrel, dist 2007, bott 2016 **(87.5)** n22 t23 f21 b21.5 Massive caramel credentials. The nose and delivery is one huge malt and cream toffee fest, with Glen Moray in is most single style mode. Only a little oak bitterness at the death interfers with these simple delights. *46%. nc ncf sc. 370 bottles.*

⟨ **Hepburn's Choice Glen Moray 10 Years Old** refill barrel, dist 2007, bott 2018 **(91.5)** n22.5 egg custard, a splash of lemon, a twist of black pepper, a flake or three of vanilla....and lots and lots of barley...; t23 lots of mouth-watering, palate peppering lively malt in a clean, spicy way; f23 ...and lots of big spicy malt...; b23 nails the distillery succinctly. A lovely little treat of a dram. *46%. nc ncf sc. 372 bottles.*

Old Malt Cask Glen Moray Aged 21 Years refill hogshead, cask no. 12819, dist Mar 95, bott Aug 16 **(89.5)** n22 t23 f22 b22.5 Moray at its most charming. *50%. nc ncf sc. 111 bottles.*

⟨ **Old Particular Glen Moray 25 Years Old** refill hogshead, cask no. 11831, dist Oct 91, bott Jun 17 **(96.5)** n24.5 a 15-minute nose, minimum, before tasting: complex, gentle and alluring it relies on pastel shading with no aroma dominant. The malt is grassy and ethereal, the sweetness is diffuse, noticeable only because it is obvious that there is nothing bitter about this either. A slow nosing reveals the lightest of orange blossom honey and molten Demerara, as well as the vaguest of gristy tones; t24 just melts in the mouth – as you just knew it would. The light grist on the nose is more apparent here, but it is the aroma again this time in physical form. All in slow motion, all in near perfect parcels of personality; f23.5 the lightest of spices mingle with the Malteser candy and butterscotch; b24.5 a malt which even an old pro like me finds very difficult to spit. Mesmerizingly beautiful. *51.5%. nc ncf sc. 247 bottles.*

Provenance Glen Moray Aged 8 Years refill hogshead, cask no. 11621, dist Jun 08, bott Feb 17 **(86)** n21.5 t22.5 f21 b21 Just not really enough in the tank to raise this above being young, lively but undercooked – especially on the nose and finish. *46%. nc ncf sc. 367 bottles.*

Provenance Glen Moray Aged 10 Years refill hogshead, cask no. 11186, dist Jun 05, bott Mar 16 **(86)** n21.5 t22 f21 b21.5 A beautifully made, salivating malt with the barley coming at you from all directions. But the antiquity of the cask means little meaningful is added oak-wise. *46%. nc ncf sc.*

Provenance Glen Moray Aged 12 Years refill hogshead, cask no. 11622, dist May 04, bott Feb 17 **(90.5)** n21 t23.5 f23 b23 The nose hints at a malt not yet ready for bottling. The delivery reveals something entirely different! Lovely. *46%. nc ncf sc. 379 bottles.*

Sansibar Whisky Glen Moray 25 Year Old dist 1991, bott 2016 **(96)** n24 t24 f24 b24 A great distillery overcoming the years with extraordinary panache. One of the great Moray 25s... *50.9%.*

Scotch Malt Whisky Society Cask 35.185 22 Year Old toasted oak hogshead, dist 17 Nov 94 **(95.5)** n24 t24 f23 b24.5 Some of these heavily toasted experimental casks have not quite hit the heights one hopes for. This one, by happy contrast, has far exceeded expectation... *575%.*

⟨ **The Whisky Chamber Glen Moray 12 Years Old 2005** sherry refill hogshead **(82.5)** n21 t21.5 f19 b21 A shockingly tart malt which puckers the taste buds to previously unknown levels. That said, no particularly offensive sulphur at work (well, maybe not until the very end), so the fruit does get a chance to shine. But not for the feint-hearted. *55.2%. sc.*

Wilson & Morgan Barrel Selection Glen Moray 13 Year Old 2016 1st fill bourbon barrel, dist 2007 (92.5) n22.5 t24 f22 b23 A distillery which feels so at home at this age in a decent bourbon barrel. 48%.

GLEN ORD
Highlands (Northern), 1838. Diageo. Working.

Glen Ord Aged 12 Years db (81) n20 t23 f18 b20. Just when you thought it safe to go back...for a while Diageo ditched the sherry-style Ord. It has returned. Better than some years ago, when it was an unhappy shadow of its once-great self, but without the sparkle of the vaguely-smoked bottling of a year or two back. Nothing wrong with the rich arrival, but the finish is a mess. I'll open the next bottling with trepidation... 43%

◇◇◇ **The Singleton of Glen Ord Aged 15 Years** European & American oak casks, bott code: L8038DM003 db (90.5) n23 Fox's chocolate ginger biscuits circa 1977; some warmed, extra spiced Melton Hunt cake sits nearby; t23.5 silky thanks to a beautiful infusion of intense barley and plummy fruit. You can pick this out as being neither sweet nor dry: it is either, depending on which particular flavour chain you are following at any given moment. But the controlled juiciness on delivery contains not just profuse barley, but that ginger and chocolate backdrop, too...; f21.5 just a little too dry and furry, though warming cocoa means there is plenty still to grab on to; b22.5 the fun of the label on many a bottle of whisky is just how far removed the described tasting notes are to what is actually poured from the bottle. Here, there are no quibbles from me: the promised ginger and chocolate come true! 40%.

Glen Ord 25 Years Old dist 1978 db (95) n24 t24 f23 b24. Stupendous vatting here: cask selection at its very highest to display Ord in all its far too rarely seen magnificence. 58.3%

Glen Ord 28 Years Old db (90) n22 t23 f22 b23. This is mega whisky showing slight traces of sap, especially on the nose, but otherwise a concentrate of many of the qualities I remember from this distillery before it was bottled in a much ruined form. Blisteringly beautiful. 58.3%

Glen Ord 30 Years Old db (87) n22 t21 f23 b21. Creaking with oak, but such is the polish to the barley some serious class is on show. 58.8%

Singleton of Glen Ord 12 Years Old db (89) n22.5 t22.5 f22 b22 A fabulous improvement on the last bottling I encountered. Still possesses blood oranges to die for, but greatly enhanced by some sublime spices and a magnificent juiciness. 40%

Singleton of Glen Ord 32 Year Old db (91) n23.5 t23 f22 b22.5. Delicious. But if ever a malt has screamed out to be at 46%, this is it. 40%

Cadenhead's Small Batch International Glen Ord 11 Year Old dist 2005 (87.5) n21.5 t22.5 f22 b21.5 Glen Ord at its most intense and, in this case, most wild. This is a slow developer for an 11-year-old so a degree of fresh young malt has a say at every turn. The result is a salivating, biting wildcat of a dram which is magnificent fun but hardly one for the purists!56.2%.

Old Malt Cask Glen Ord Aged 12 Years refill hogshead, cask no. 12812, dist Sept 04, bott Oct 16 (88.5) n22.5 t22 f22 b22 Malty and quietly satisfying. 50%. nc ncf sc. 337 bottles.

◇◇◇ **Old Particular Glen Ord 13 Years Old** refill hogshead, cask no. 12060, dist Sept 94, bott Sept 17 (90) n23 sheer entertainment! A plate of custard cream biscuits, with a lemon cream biscuit to keep them company; oh, and some racy barley, too...; t22.5 yep! That's just how you want a malt surge to be: surging and very malty! Barley doesn't come cleaner or with a more intense maltiness that appears to benefit from a lightly salted edge; f22 much drier as the oak takes its place; additionally, the mouth feel is outstanding; b22.5 an obviously well-made malt showing exceptionally fine structure. 48.4%. nc ncf sc. 312 bottles.

Provenance Glen Ord Aged 11 Years refill hogshead, cask no. 11215, dist Sept 04, bott May 16 (92) n23 t23 f23 b23 It is a rare whisky which can leech so little from the cask yet be quite so full blooded... 46%. nc ncf sc.

GLENROTHES
Speyside, 1878. Edrington. Working.

Glenrothes 2001 dist 25 May 01, bott 13 db (72) n16 t21 f17 b18. The sulphur in Spain makes this whisky very plain. 43% WB15/297

The Glenrothes Alba Reserve db (87.5) n22 t22 f21.5 b22. You know that smartly groomed, polite but rather dull chap you invariably get at dinner parties? 40%

The Glenrothes Elders' Reserve db (75.5) n19 t20.5 f17.5 b18.5. Now when I was a young man, young man, Scotch single malt whisky tasted a lot better than this, you know. Well, could hardly have tasted worse, could it?! That nice young Mr Lloyd George wouldn't have put up with this rubbish, oh no. He would have sent in the troops and nationalised the industry, that's what he would have done. Hanged anyone guilty of using sherry butts stinking of sulphur. Or shot 'em. Only fair. These young blenders... Blenders?!? Don't know they are born... In my day.... 43% WB16/046

The Glenrothes Manse Reserve db (74) n18.5 t20 f17 b18.5. More like Mansfield Reserves... 43% WB16/045

The Glenrothes Minister's Reserve db (91) n22.5 trace sulphur, but by Genrothes standards this is pretty amazing: the grape really does come through with a spring in its juicy step; t23.5 absolutely top dollar sherry at work: a gorgeous sultana-laden sweetness but backed by the most luscious mouth feel, aided by a little liquorice from the oak; f22 a little manuka honey fights off successfully the late bitterness from the obligatory dodgy butt; b23 I think the Minister had a little word with someone upstairs... 43% WB16/047

The Glenrothes Sherry Cask Reserve db (68) n16 t19 f16 b17. Inevitable, I suppose... The tragedy is that before some bloke stuffed lighted sulphur candles into these sherry butts, thereby ruining them and the whisky which would later mature in them, they were obviously the dog's...; and had they been left unmolested we would have been nosing and tasting something of intense brilliance. Exasperating doesn't even begin to cover it. 40% WB16/044

Cadenhead's Small Batch International Glenrothes 27 Year Old bourbon & rum casks, dist 1989 (93.5) n22.5 t24.5f23 b23.5 I think only Cadenhead's could have come up with this minor classic. 53.7%.

◇ **The Duchess Glenrothes Lagertha 20 Year Old** cask no. 10/1996, dist 23 Oct 96, bott 24 Mar 17 (93) n23 from the nutty, crushed pip school of aromas; t23.5 silky, sumptuous and salivating, the balance between the salivating barley and equally salivating spice deserves a round of applause; f23 dries uniformly, leaving a hint of cocoa and a very obvious oaky spice buzz; b23.5 impossible not to enjoy. Oh, and salivating.. 52.8%. sc. The Shieldmaiden Series.

◇ **Kingsbury Gold Glenrothes 20 Years Old** hogshead, cask no. 48, dist 1996 (93) n22.5 concentrated malt; big age spice, too; t23.5 massive malt – and I really mean massive - with a superb vanilla and caramel halo, though this is obviously the gift of top-class oak at work; spices abound, but never overstate the mark, nor the Mars bar chocolate nougat; f23 an undulating interplay between intense malt and lazy spices...; b24 understated greatness. Seemingly simple, but don't be taken in. Give it as much time as you can as there so much more... 52.3%. 329 bottles.

◇ **The Last Drop Glenrothes 1968** cask no. 13504 (96.5) n24 from the mercurial school of exotic fruit comes a Speysider which celebrates its antiquity in style. This is low lying, thick and rich without ever being pungent. The gentlest hint of eucalyptus underlines the great age t24 ridiculous. Just utterly ridiculous! Some 50 years in the cask and the first element to show on delivery is the most nubile yet thickset malt which revels in its intensity; there are chalky citrus notes, too, as well as a slow emergence of exotic fruit advertised on the nose; scampering, bitty spices prickle the mid-ground; f24 at last the tannins fight back. But instead of a bitter onslaught of tired oak, as might be expected, we have heather and Manuka honey mixing together with burnt fudge and toasty treacle. Aided by gentle oils it is a far softer finale than could ever be expected; b24.5 no whisky has any right to be in such command of its faculties after half a century. No over-tiredness, no breakdown in balance or structure. Just incredible whisky of which one glass can fill an hour of anybody's time with malty pleasures and complexity 51.3%. sc. 168 bottles.

◇ **The Last Drop Glenrothes 1968** cask no. 13508 (95.5) n24 a slightly saltier edge to this appears to lift the same aroma profiles apparent on 13508. Does not make it any better or worse, just a touch more angular and emboldened. And every bit as sexy; t23.5 ah, that salt on the nose is replicated on the lush delivery, but this time it means the older aspects of the malt are highlighted further. But the recovery is prompt with an improbably rich vein of barley surging through the middle, to which light ulmo honey and molasses attach without a second thought; f24 this old dog has learned a new trick: just when the tannins return once more and come on a little too strong, a fabulous dose of chocolate mousse offers delicious, vaguely salty, compensation. And also the spices kick in to lengthen the finish majestically; b24 a wonderful old cask plucked from the back of the warehouse just in time. Another summer might have proved fatal. But here, in this mode, we see an aged malt at its very peak of defiance... 50.2%. sc. 141 bottles.

◇ **The Last Drop Glenrothes 1969** cask no. 16203 (95.5) n24.5 fruit toffee ensures there is a surprising creamy softness to a malt distilled at a time when man was first venturing to the moon: no surprises then that for its age it is out of this world, with not a hint of tiredness or an aged blemish; that doesn't mean to say that we don't have a light mint and eucalyptus sub-strata, because we do, or exotic fruit on cue, and the most docile spice. All the hallmarks of antiquity are here, they just happen to be without aggression or tiredness; t23.5 fruit toffee leads on the nose and soft, oaky caramels on delivery. Indeed, the oak is the busiest guy in town, working hard to create layers of vanilla and the lightest liquorice with upsetting taking away from the short burst of juicy barley which arrives about a third of the way in; f23.5 still no sign of tiredness with a long, dry wafer effect; b24 a malt which appears to have spent nearly 50 years treading on eggshells: certainly here everything is gentle and carefully positioned so there nothing collapses after so many passing year. Brilliant. 45.7%. sc. 160 bottles.

Scottish Malts

⟫ **The Last Drop Glenrothes 1969** cask no. 16207 (96) n24 a hint of sharper kiwi fruit stands out from the older exotic fruit tones. Ulmo honey and fudge props up the sugars and emboldens the chalkier vanillas; t24 a kiss, a caress and a sigh on the palate as the malty sugars land like snowflakes. Weak heather honey intertwines with the sturdier tannins and spices form as the sugars melt away; so much toasted fudge now; f24 spicy, with rich tannin first on that fudgy theme then moving towards the ultimate in controlled toastiness...; b24 jst a ridiculous whisky for its years. This should have collapsed in upon itself, so well defined are the older oaks. Yet, somehow, the sugars appear at just the right time and in just-so amounts not just to see off a catastrophe, but help create something rather special. 46.6%. sc. 140 bottles.

Liquid Treasures Glenrothes 19 Year Old refill butt, dist 1997, bott 2017 (89) n22 salty, citrusy barley; t22.5 salivating, salty, citrusy barley; f22 now spicy, citrusy barley – with a simple dry oak finale; b22.5 makes no attempt at great complexity, but does the malt thing rather well. 59.4%. Faces of Angkor Edition.

⟫ **The Loch Fyne Glenrothes 12 Year Old** sherry cask, cask no. 2012, dist Jan 05, bott Sept 17 (77) n19 t20 f19 b19 Dull. Just so dull, dull, dull and, well....dull! 46%. sc. 1,035 bottles.

⟫ **Old Malt Cask Glenrothes Aged 12 Years** sherry butt, cask no. 14095, dist Mar 05, bott Aug 17 (86) n22 t22.5 f20 b21.5 Not too bad by Glenrothes sherry butt standards. Certainly tightens and gives any sugars present a vigorous working over as it dries. But also possesses early on some really excellent moments to savour on delivery as the malt and fruit appear to be in perfect harmony. 50%. nc ncf sc. 492 bottles.

Old Malt Cask Glenrothes Aged 20 Years refill hogshead, cask no. 13093, dist Jul 96, bott Nov 16 (92.5) n22.5 citrus and putty: oddly attractive; t23.5 intense, clean, salivating barley. So much to chew on and the early spices raise the stakes further; f23 a superb fade. A little salt is rubbed into the gathering tannin but it is the layering of the barley that stars; b23.5 a beautiful Speysider just dripping in personality. 50%. nc ncf sc. 180 bottles.

Old Particular Glenrothes 12 Years Old sherry butt, cask no. 11170, dist May 04, bott Jun 16 (79.5) n20 t21.5 f18 b20 Despite the obvious sulphur at play, some of the richer oloroso tones carry enough Demerara sugar to help with damage limitation. 48.4%. nc ncf sc. 490 bottles.

Old Particular Glenrothes 12 Years Old sherry butt, cask no. 11601, dist Feb 05, bott Mar 17 (71) n17 t19 f17 b18 One guess... The perfect gift for Mrs Merkel... 48.4%. nc ncf sc. 402 bottles.

⟫ **Old Particular Glenrothes 12 Years Old** sherry butt, cask no. 11792, dist Mar 05, bott Jun 17 (81) n20 t22 f19 b20 The odd fruitcake moment both on nose and delivery. Slightly bitter on the finish, but the journey there takes you through a field of spice and stubbornly juicy barley. The sherry influence is a slight distraction. 48.4%. nc ncf sc. 808 bottles.

Scotch Malt Whisky Society Cask 30.92 24 Year Old ex-bourbon barrel, dist 21 Feb 92 (95.5) n24 t24 f23 b24.5 Pure malty magic! For the distillery and age, just about perfection. 46.7%.

The Single Cask Glenrothes Aged 19 Years cask no. L1097, dist 8 Oct 97, bott 13 Jan 17 (79) n18 t22 f19 b20 Dripping in fruit and coffee but, sadly, one strictly for the German and central European market where this type of s-affected cask might be appreciated. 58.5%. nc ncf sc.

The Single Cask Glenrothes Aged 19 Years cask no. T497, dist 28 Apr 97, bott 13 Jan 17 (90.5) n22 t23 f23.5 b22 About as subtle as a sherry pie in the face. Almost a self-lampooning of a sherry-matured Speysider, but at least swamped with fruit rather than sulphur. So amen to that...!!! 58%. nc ncf sc. 86 bottles.

The Whisky Barrel Burns Malt Glenrothes 19 Year Old 1997 sherry butt, cask no. 7157 (88) n23 t23.5 f20 b21.5 Tragically close to a potential award-winning malt. Sherry butts rarely come along this beautifully structured. But those very late furry notes cannot be ignored (though those unable to detect sulphur might just have found one of their whiskies of the year). Still, what a pity...53.5%. sc.

⟫ **The Whisky Chamber Glenrothes 21 Years Old 1996** ex bourbon cask (94.5) n23.5 how often do you find stunning praline on the nose...? t23.5 and just as stunning praline on the palate...that is after your taste buds has been bathed in the most juicy, intense and complete malted barley; a wonderful short-wave molasses sub plot adds so much; f23.5 ulmo honey and malt leads into a Demerara a barley sugar fade: one of the most beautifully sweetened finishes of the year..with matching spices, of course; b24 mmm....ex-bourbon Glenrothes! Why can't they all be like that from this distillery...? All those dreadful, dud sherry butts, when they could have been like this! 53%. sc.

⟫ **Whisky-Fässle Glenrothes 20 Year Old** sherry butt, dist 1997, bott 2017 (58) n14 t15 f14 b15 Massively sulphured in classic Glenrothes mid-1990s style. Just horrible. 47.9%.

⟫ **Whisky-Fässle Glenrothes 20 Year Old** sherry butt, dist 1997, bott 2017 (84.5) n22 t22.5 f19 b21 A collectors' item: a Glenrothes sherry cask under 25 years of age not entirely riddled with sulphur. Have to say that the sherry does rather over fruit the experience and is all over the malt like an oversized raincoat. The flaw is evident at the death, but still much to enjoy otherwise...providing you like very juicy grape... 50.1%.

GLEN SCOTIA
Campbeltown, 1832. Loch Lomond Distillers. Working

Glen Scotia Aged 10 Years bourbon cask, bott Dec 12 db (90.5) n22.5 t23.5 f22 b22.5. Fabulous to see Scotia back in this excellent nick again. 46%. nc ncf.

◇ **Glen Scotia Aged 10 Years Peated** first fill bourbon barrels db (94.5) n24 what can you say...? The sharpness to the phenols suggests a chemical composition that used to be common (and is now almost entirely lost) when distilleries used their own local turf. If this is from Port Elen maltings, they are using a different peat source for this. Delicate diced apple and pear, also. Beautiful...; t23 just like the nose, the delivery has its very own signature: at first gentle, submissive smoke quickly replaced by a darkening, busy, crisp sugary phenol quality intensifying in spice very quickly; f23.5 long, relatively languid thanks to a pacifying hickory intervention; fades out with rolling smoke and lilting vanilla; b24 this entire whisky style is a throwback to the very first peated whiskies I tasted 40 years ago. Indeed, anyone still alive and able to remember Glen Garioch when it was heavily peated through its own kilns will raise an eyebrow of happy recognition... One of the greatest Glen Scotias of all time. 46%. nc ncf.

◇ **Glen Scotia 11 Years Old 2006** cask no. 532, dist Dec 06, bott Apr 18 db (92.5) n22.5 wonderful battle between spicy oak and in your face unpeated malt: this will be fun...; t23.5 brilliant delivery! A real bite to this, the barley pumped up and thickening by the second, the gristy sugars radiating a measured sweetness; f23 calms down as the high grade oaky butterscotch begins to intertwangle with the indomitable malt. Still revels in a little roughhouse antics; b23.5 absolutely typical Glen Scotia, proudly displaying its rugged charm. 55.6%. sc. 212 bottles. Bottled for The Whisky Shop.

Glen Scotia 12 Years Old db (73.5) n18 t19 f18 b18.5. Ooops! I once said you could write a book about this called "Murder by Caramel." Now it would be a short story called "Murder by Flavours Unknown." What is happening here? Well, a dozen years ago Glen Scotia was not quite the place to be for consistent whisky, unlike now. Here, the caramel is the only constant as the constituent parts disintegrate. 40%

Glen Scotia Aged 12 Years bourbon cask, bott Dec 12 db (89) n22 t22 f23 b22. Simplistic but delicious. 46%. nc ncf.

◇ **Glen Scotia 13 Years Old 2005** cask no. 17/412-10, dist Mar 05, bott Apr 18 db (91.5) n22.5 a dense smokiness and spice prickle. The odd (in best senses of the word) touch of anthracite and kiwi fruit: not an everyday combination; t23 palate gripping in old-fashioned and delicious GS style as the phenols tear into the taste buds. Thin bodied but fattened by Manuka honey joining the smoke; f23 major complexity now as the peat backs off enough to allow the oak to come through clearly now with chalky vanilla building steadily; b23 a peaty whisky for sure, but so much else happening, too. What entertainment! 55.6%. sc. 330 bottles. Bottled for Loch Fyne Whiskies.

Glen Scotia 14 Year Old Peated bourbon cask db (87) n21.5 t22 f21.5 b22. A very straight bat played by this one: a malty up and downer with few frills others than a slow though ineffective build up of smoke. 50%. nc ncf.

Glen Scotia Aged 15 Years American oak barrels db (91.5) n22.5 a serious buzz of lively, working tannin to this. All dark sugars and spice, it suggests a malt which means business; t23 mouth-filling deep, roasty, slightly fat, vaguely salty, massively chewy. A kind of molasses feel with the sweetness reduced; f23 long, with a lovely, buttery oiliness giving a sheen to the late liquorice; the spices really do come into their own; b23 great to see this rather special little distillery produce something quite so confident and complete. 46%. ncf.

Glen Scotia Aged 16 Years bourbon cask, bott Dec 12 db (87) n22 t22 f21 b22. Signs of a less than brilliant distillate which has been ironed out to some good effect in the cask. 46%. nc ncf.

◇ **Glen Scotia Aged 16 Years** American oak barrels, bott code: L12 087 18 db (92.5) n23.5 beautiful blood orange (not what one normally expects from bourbon casks) and caramel meet a spicy, quasi-phenolic resistance; t23.5 ah...! So ridiculously succulent! Juicy and full bodied thanks to a brilliant degree of barley getting in first. The caramels and spices form a substantial sub division; f22.5 just dies a little on the palate as caramel wins through, though the spices do keep matters alive; b23 doesn't stint on character. 46%. nc ncf.

Glen Scotia Aged 18 Years bourbon cask, bott Dec 12 db (77) n20 t21 f17 b19. Malty but hot as Hades: a reminder of a less than glorious period in the distillery's history. 46%. nc ncf.

◇ **Glen Scotia 18 Year Old** American oak casks & first fill oloroso casks, bott code: L2/221/17 db (95) n24 wow...clean grape! Not an off note...not a hint or threat of an off note. Just rich grape on best behaviour pinning a fruitcake spicy sweetness to the thick malt core; t24 you can almost swoon at this kind of delivery: fabulous muscovado sugars, fat sultana, plum and also a build-up of warming spices. Again, malt is present and correct, though now more regimented by the firmer oak; f23 though a slight bitterness evolves, this is kept in line by busy spice and the continuation of a moist sultana fruitcake chewiness; **b24** my Panama is doffed in grateful thanks for the excellent use of un-sulphured clean sherry butts which give this malt a genuine lustre. And as three dimensional as its sister PX bottling is just one... *51.3%. ncf.*

Glen Scotia Aged 21 Years bourbon cask, bott Dec 12 db (86.5) **n21.5 t22.5 f21 b21.5.** Appears nothing like its age: the very vaguely smoked malt is entirely on top and offers little deviation. A playful spice reminds you oak is involved somewhere. *46%. nc ncf.*

◈ **Glen Scotia Aged 25 Years** American oak barrels, bott 2017, bott code: L8/187/17 db (94) **n23.5** a happy and lively marriage here between a salty, crisp maltiness and far sweeter bourbon characteristics, with Demerara and red liquorice leading the way; elements of lime and kiwi fruit add further sharpness; **t24** on delivery, the bourbon side of the family wins: the tannins are upfront and bold, but the edge blunted by Manuka honey and spice; a wonderful sub-plot of barley sugar sneaks in when seemingly uninvited; **f23** those spices continue to zing – with a broad American accent; **b23.5** so beautiful! Truly adorable – and displaying a Scotia as you have never quite seen it before. Incredibly rare to find a Scotch single malt so under the thumb of a bourbon character: this must have been filled into very fresh first-fill bourbon barrels to come up with this highly American effect. Trump that! *48.8%. ncf.*

◈ **Glen Scotia Campbeltown 1832** American oak barrels, finished in Pedro Ximenez sherry casks, bott code: L2 087 18 db (85.5) **n22.5 t22 f20 b21** Yes, pleasant enough I suppose...but so dull! As usual there is a bitterness to a PX finish as any foibles in the oak is exaggerated massively by the sweetness of the grape, which in turn fills in all the natural ridge and furrows of the malt and leaves the flattest of whiskies. The sooner distillers and bottlers get over this PX fad the better... *46%. nc ncf.*

Glen Scotia Double Cask finished in American oak & Pedro Ximenez sherry casks db (85.5) **n22 t22 f20.5 b21.** When blending, I do not like to get too involved with PX casks, unless I know for certain I can shape the effect to further or enrich the storyline on the palate. The reason is that PX means the complexity of a malt can easily come to a sticky end. That has happened here with both the malt and grape cancelling each other out. Soft and easy drinking with an excellent early delivery spike of intensity. But dull middle and finish. And dull has never been a word I have associated with this distillery. Ever. *46%. ncf.*

◈ **Glen Scotia Malts Festival 2018 Ruby Port Finish 2008 Vintage Peated** bott code: L2 127 18 db (88.5) **n21.5** both the smoke and fruit is angular and on the attack: charm is not on the agenda; **t23** deliciously eye-watering and tart, but perhaps too much so; both the peat and grape is profound, and both are punching the living daylights out of each other; **f22** aggressively spicy and a tad bitter; **b22** interesting: in effect, the Glen Scotia 10 Peated (see above) finished in Port. And the winner is...the standard version by a knockout. Here the Port gets in the way of the charm and classiness of the American cask bottling and thrusts fruit at you with all the gum-chewing, flesh-flashing subtlety a lady of the night might try to seduce a punter. *57.8%. nc ncf.*

Glen Scotia Single Cask Distillery Edition 001 cask no. 196, dist Dec 02, bott May 15 db (94) **n23 t24 f23.5 b23.5** A delicious malt which makes the most of what is available. Love it! *56.1%. sc.*

Glen Scotia Single Cask Distillery Edition No. 002 cask no. 332/543-1, dist Jun 03, bott Aug 15 db (94.5) **n23 t24 f23.5 b24** So busy and alive with internecine battling for control. No overall winners, other than the lucky person tasting this. *56.4%. ncf sc.*

Glen Scotia Single Cask Distillery Edition No. 003 cask no. 536, dist Dec 06, bott Apr 16 db (85) **n20 t21.5 f22 b21.5.** Malty, juicy and all that. And good light molasses, too. But someone was in a big hurry to get home for Christmas by the look of this thin offering: appears as though the stills were run like the clappers...or do I mean sleigh bells.... *56.9%. ncf sc.*

Glen Scotia Victoriana db (89.5) **n23 t23 f21.5 b22** An unusual malt for a cask strength. Beyond the nose there is limited layering, instead concentrating on the malt-toffee intertwangling. *51.5%*

Cadenhead's Sherry Cask Glen Scotia 15 Year Old dist 2000, bott Apr 16 (95.5) **n24 t24 f23.5 b24** A clean, rich sherry butt. A malt spirit brimming with character. What's not to like...? Again, Cadenhead come up with something just a little special... *50.5%. sc. 252 bottles.*

Maltbarn Glen Scotia 1992 ex-bourbon cask, bott 2016 (88.5) **n22 t22.5 f22 b22** What it lacks in finesse, it makes up for in personality. *53.3%. sc. 144 bottles.*

◈ **The Whisky Embassy Glen Scotia Aged 10 Years** cask no. 16/558-3, dist Nov 06, bott Aug 17 (87) **n21 t22 f22 b22** An unusually perfumed malt bulging with barley on the juicy delivery. Quietly satisfying with a pronounced sugar and spice finale. *54.7%. nc ncf sc.*

GLEN SPEY
Speyside, 1885. Diageo. Working.

Glen Spey Aged 12 Years db (90) **n23** the kind of firm, busy malt you expect from this distillery plus some lovely spice; **t22** mouthwatering and fresh, a layer of honey makes for an easy three or four minutes; **f22** drier vanilla, but the pulsing oak is controlled and stylish; **b23**

very similar to the first Glen Spey I can remember in this range, the one before the over-toffeed effort of two years ago. Great to see it back to its more natural, stunningly beautiful self. 43%

The First Editions Glen Spey Aged 25 Years 1990 refill hogshead, cask no. 12824, bott 2016 (89) n21.5 t23.5 f22 b22 Some serious signs of great age here. But the malt stands just firm enough to give an illusion of effortless control...though I suspect it was very hard work! 53.9%. nc ncf sc. 78 bottles.

The First Editions Glen Spey Aged 25 Years 1991 refill hogshead, cask no. 13307, bott 2017 (93) n22.5 t23.5 f22.5 b23 A blueprint showing how an old Speyside whisky, even one as fragile as Glen Spey, can still be delicate and wonderfully layered. 50.7%. nc ncf sc. 132 bottles.

◇ **Gordon & MacPhail Connoisseurs Choice Glen Spey 1995** refill American hogshead, dist 6 Oct 95, bott 14 Mar 18 (94.5) n23.5 probably the most delicate and fragile nose you will encounter this year from any distillery: the structure is a thin tapestry of unsullied barley and genteel oaky-vanilla; t24 dissolves on impact, imparting the most wonderful barley sugar outline framed only by an oakiness of equal elegance; a little grassiness nudges up the salivating qualities very gently; f23 light traces of barley and oak plus some natural caramels and the very lightest of oils to form a light cream toffee fade; b24 a truly classic nose and profile well known and revered by creators of older blends. Spellbinding. 46%. nc ncf sc. 615 bottles.

Liquid Sun Glen Spey 26 Years Old dist 1988 (87) n23 t21.5 f21 b21.5 The nose star bills with a fabulous lemon curd tart and crème brule double header. Sadly, there is not enough weight and structure to the malt to be able to comfortably hold the weight of the oak which dominates and crushes. Still some orange blossom honey does its best at damage limitation.41.1%.

Old Malt Cask Glen Spey Aged 25 Years refill hogshead, cask no. 13306, dist Dec 91, bott Feb 17 (89) n22 t23 f22 b22 An attractive and slightly quirky bottling. 50%. nc ncf sc. 182 bottles.

Old Particular Glen Spey 18 Years Old refill hogshead, cask no. 11336, dist Dec 97, bott Sept 16 (90.5) n22 t22 f23.5 b23 After a faltering, insecure start blossoms into a real charmer. 48.4%. nc ncf sc. 328 bottles.

GLENTAUCHERS
Speyside, 1898. Chivas Brothers. Working.

◇ **Ballantine's The Glentauchers Aged 15 Years Series No.003** traditional oak casks, bott code: LKRM0071 2018/02/13 (86) n22 t22 f21 b21 Alarm bells ring when confronted by the dull nose with a neutral fruit and caramel edge. When the palate offers something fat and glossy (that's a new one for 'Tauchers) with a dull spice development to accompany the vague fruit and caramel, the heart sinks and flashing lights join the ringing alarm. The big, boring caramel finish drives you to distraction.... If anyone on this planet has championed Glentauchers longer or louder than me, or with more heart-felt gusto, then I would like to meet them. For well over 20 years I have been telling anyone who cares to listen – and many who don't – that this is one of Scotland's finest distilleries worthy of its own proprietary bottling. It finally arrives, and instead of a malt which scores in the mid-90s, as it should (and so often has done with independent bottlings in Whisky Bibles past), we have before us something pleasant, bland and not instantly recognisable as a 'Tauchers. Frankly, it could be from any Scottish distillery as the blueprint for the nose and flavour profile is shared by many: too many. As I say, pleasant whisky. But, knowing just how good this whisky really is (using 100% bourbon cask, no colour, no chill-filtration) what a huge and crushing disappointment. A bit like going to see the Sistine Chapel and finding someone had whitewashed over it.... 40%.

◇ **Cadenhead's Cask Strength Glentauchers Aged 41 Years** dist 1976 (96) n23.5 the big age is unequivocal: all the classic aromas are there to confirm it. Light eucalyptus, mint, concentrated liquorice, the driest hickory. It is all there. Yet so, miraculously, is the malt ensuring balance and splendour; t24.5 oh...just close your eyes and let the abundant sugars caress your palate: muscovado and maple syrup in particular....but both dipped in concentrated malt; the oils attached to the mouth feel defies reality – stunning! f23.5 toasty now (as it should be!) with an overcooked butterscotch tart feel, curiously oily spices and ulmo honey even at this ridiculously late stage; b24.5 one of the world's truly great distilleries fittingly honoured in its advanced age. 42%. sc. 126 bottles.

◇ **Fadandel.dk Glentauchers 19 Years Old** cask no. 3825, dist 16 Jul 97, bott 14 Feb 17 (95) n23.5 all kinds of exploding fat sultanas at play here: a spotted dog pudding with attitude; t24 everything is right about this delivery: the huge heather honey presence mixing with concentrated golden syrup, figs, burnt raisins and, invariably, spice; f23.5 toasty, warming and a few late strands of malt to go with the moist syrup and sultana cake blend; b24 a 'Tauchers fruit cake...with many added extras. Magnificent. 53.3%. sc. 187 bottles.

Gordon & MacPhail Distillery Label Glentauchers 1997 bott 13 Dec 16 (82.5) n20 t22 f19 b21.5 An awkward and uncomfortable 'Tauchers well below par for the distillery. Muffled and muted throughout, the nose and finish struggle to find the right key and a little furry. Even the mid-ground, usually so full of convoluted malt, is flat and toffee dominant. *43%.*

⬥ **Gordon & MacPhail Cask Strength Glentauchers 2003** cask nos. 650 & 652, bott 15 May 17 (92.5) n22.5 a heavy fruit presence, mainly citrus – dried orange peel in particular – is met by heavy tannin and busy spice: weighty stuff; t23.5 those tannins strike early and without a second thought: the sugars are a front of massed molasses with liquorice and natural caramels filling in the cracks; f23 dry, toasty oak with a little ulmo honey taking off the excess; plenty of hickory to see us out; b23.5 one of the most heavy and uncompromising 'Tauchers I've encountered for a while. When the malt speaks, it's all rather muffled. For those who usually savour and celebrate the distillery's treble will have to be satisfied with the base. *55.6%.*

Hepburn's Choice Glentauchers 7 Years Old refill hogshead, dist 2009, bott 2016 (88.5) n22 t22.5 f22 b22 A simple, well-made malt. *46%. nc ncf sc. 320 bottles.*

Hidden Spirits Glentauchers 20 Year Old cask no. GT617, dist 1996, bott 2017 (90) n22 t23 f22.5 b22.5 A very safe and conservative Tauchers allowing the natural caramels a free hand. *55.3%. sc.*

⬥ **The Loch Fyne Glentauchers 10 Year Old** sherry cask, cask no. 606, dist Mar 07, bott Nov 17 (88) n22 grapes kept in the fruit bowl a week or two too long...; t23 beautifully malty, salivating sweetness on immediate delivery, then a chewy fruity curtain descends; f21 just a little fruity furriness amid the vanilla; b22 a relatively clean sherry butt. Hurrah! However, the grape fills in the gaps and robs us of the rare complexity which makes 'Tauchers that little bit special... *46%. sc. 1,184 bottles.*

Old Particular Glentauchers 20 Years Old refill barrel, cask no. 11635, dist Dec 96, bott Mar 17 (95.5) n24 t24 f23.5 b24 Have to admit: will be drinking a mouthful of this before bed tonight. This is the perfect Speyside experience! *51.5%. nc ncf sc. 223 bottles.*

Provenance Glentauchers Aged 7 Years refill hogshead, cask no. 11330, dist Apr 09, bott Aug 16 (87) n22 t21 f22 b22 A less than taxing malt-fest which intriguingly seems to have something of the American "White Dog" about it.... *46%. nc ncf sc. 402 bottles.*

Scotch Malt Whisky Society Cask 63.36 26 Year Old refill ex-bourbon barrel, dist 19 Dec 89 (92) n23.5 t23 f22.5 b23 So consistent, this distillery: just makes it look all so easy... *51.8%.*

⬥ **Scotch Malt Whisky Society Cask 63.46 9 Year Old** refill ex-bourbon barrel, dist 6 Dec 07 (95) n23 superbly weighted malt and gentle vanilla (oak) balance; t24 the first two flavour waves confirm this as something a little special: the vivacity of the barley shows in both crisp and more gentle tones. But these are vital markers of a malt absolutely bang in tune; salivating to a breathtaking degree; f24 considering the oils are modest, the finish goes on seemingly without end. The barley, though dominating, remains deft and happy to absorb the slow march of vanilla and spice; b24 this is close to perfection as an example of 'Tauchers in well used first/good nick second fill bourbon barrel. An all too easy to overlook gem: a true benders' dream. *61%. sc.*

⬥ **Single Cask Collection Glentauchers Aged 10 Years** 1st fill sherry hogshead, cask no. 900302, dist 10 May 07, bott 21 Dec 17 (87) n22 t22.5 f21.5 b21 Bitter from first delivery, making a big, fruity but puckering impression from the off. 'Tauchers is one of the most complex malts in Speyside, but the enormity of the sherry really does overbear all. Not a bad sherry butt by modern day standards, but simply too muscular. *55%. nc ncf sc. 237 bottles.*

Single Cask Collection Glentauchers 17 Years Old 1996 bourbon hogshead (91) n22.5 t23 f22.5 b23 Shows this underrated distillery in bright mood. *55.2%. sc.*

Single Cask Collection Glentauchers 20 Year Old bourbon barrel, cask no. 3620, dist 04 Apr 96, bott 06 Sept 16 (91.5) n23.5 t22.5 f22.5 b23 Much more like it: after tasting a few 'Tauchers which barely did this wonderful distillery justice, here is a bottling at last which encapsulates its splendidly subtle fare. Holds its age well. *49.1%. 170 bottles. sc.*

The Whisky Barrel Burns Malt Glentauchers 8 Year Old 2008 sherry butt, cask no. 900184 (77) n21 t21 f17 b18 Plenty of toffee apple. But the bitterness bites deep and hard. *50%. sc.*

⬥ **The Whisky Embassy Glentauchers Aged 9 Years** cask no. 8515933, dist 2008, bott 2017 (89) n22 lightweight and zesty; t22 youthful barley but the malt intensifies to startling and juicy effect; f22.5 a light wave of orange blossom honey gives way to a malty vanilla: simplistic but effective; very late praline; b22.5 even when the cask is a little lazy, so good is the spirit of 'Tauchers it carries the ensemble through beautifully. *52.6%. nc ncf sc.*

⬥ **Whisky Illuminati Glentauchers 20 Year Old** American oak hogshead, cask no. 3844, dist 1997 (96.5) n24.5 a 15 minute nose minimum: the interplay between the complex layering of malt and the breathtakingly varied oak tones is the reason whisky was invented: everything is at half volume and in full need of concentration – but, by god, it's worth it! The delicate marmalade notes intertwangle with barely believable deftness with the sandpapered old oak, demerara-sweetened allspice and freshly baked Parkin cake. Just, wow...!!! t24.5 the mouthfeel is the stuff of dream and legends: seemingly thin, but bold enough to carry every hint and nuance of incredibly varied malt tones on display. Likewise, the sugars range from icing sugar with marzipan attached to a light Manuka honey, via ulmo honey. And all the time the spices buzz like contented bees on a distant lavender bush; **f23.5** still malty, with a chalky butterscotch fade. Oh and so much else besides...; **b24** simple question: why can't the official bottling be this beautiful and so true to the distillery? Or even close...? *50.3%. sc. 150 bottles. Candlelight Series.*

Whisky Krüger Glentauchers 10 Years Old bott 2016 **(94.5) n24 t23.5 f23 b24** One very substantial, high quality and truly sophisticated malt. *62.9%.*

GLENTURRET

Highlands (Perthshire), 1775. Edrington. Working.

Glenturret Aged 8 Years db **(88) n21 t22 f23 b22.** Technically no prizewinner. But the dexterity of the honey is charming, as this distillery has a tendency sometimes to be. *40%*

The Glenturret Aged 10 Years db **(76) n19 t18 f20 b19.** Lots of trademark honey but some less than impressive contributions from both cask and the stillman. *40%*

The Glenturret Aged 15 Years db **(87) n21 t22 f22 b22.** A beautifully clean, small-still style dram that would have benefitted from being bottled at a fuller strength. A discontinued bottling now: if you see it, it is worth the small investment. *40%*

The Glenturret Fly's 16 Masters Edition db **(96) n24.5 t24 f23.5 b24.5** When I first found Glenturret some 30 years so ago, their whisky was exceptionally rare – on account of their size and having been closed for a very long time – but the few bottlings they produced had a very distinctive, indeed unique, feel. Then it changed as they used more Highland Distillers sherry butts which were, frankly, the kiss of death. Here, though, we appear to have reverted back to exactly how it tasted half a lifetime ago. Rich, kissed with copper and stirred with honey. It is, as is fitting to old Fly, the dog's bollocks... *44%. 1,740 bottles.*

Glenturret 30 Year Old db **(94) n23** my word, this is a tired old malt: the oak has ganged up in its most funereal, sawdusty, chalky manner but has been thwarted in its attempt to bury whisky thanks to some heroic honey and citrus notes which simply refuse to die. Better still, they rally for a copper-rich orange-blossom honey and lime juice hurrah...! **t24** the fabulous honey and maple syrup tones again combine with that coppery sheen to cock a snook at the oak which gathers like vultures just the other side of the lightly-smoked curtain; **f23** miraculously, a little malt enters the fray to add some unexpected lightness to the spicy gloom: once more the rabid oak is thwarted; **b24** the ultimate exhibition of brinkmanship, surely: hangs on to its integrity by a cat's whisker... *43.4%.*

Glenturret Peated Drummond db **(87) n21 t23.5 f21 b21.5** The wide cut from the small still means the odd feint creeps into this one; the peat is too much on the sparse side to paper over the cracks. However, the delivery is something that has to be experienced. A new make freshness can be found all over the show, but even that gives way as the golden syrup and smoke mingle for one of the briefest yet most beautiful star quality moments of the whisky year. *58.9%*

The Glenturret Peated Edition db **(86) n20.5 t22 f21.5 b22.** Pleasant enough, for sure, even if the nose is a bit rough. But in the grand scheme of things, just another peated malt and one of no special distinction. Surely they should concentrate on being Glenturret: there is only one of those.... *43%*

The Glenturret Sherry Edition db **(78) n19 t21 f19 b19.** Not sure if this sherry lark is the best direction for this great distillery to take. *43%*

The Glenturret Triple Wood Edition db **(84) n20 t22.5 f20 b21.5.** Not the happiest of whiskies, but recovers from its obvious wounds by concentrating on the juicy grain, rather than the grape. *43%*

The Cooper's Choice Glenturret 30 Year Old dist 1986, bott 2017 **(93.5) n23 t23.5 f23 b24** What a charming and evocative cask this is. *48.5%. nc ncf sc. The Vintage Malt Whisky Co.*

Gordon & MacPhail Connoisseurs Choice Glenturret 1999 first fill sherry hogshead, cask no. 690, dist 16 Aug 99, bott 22 Feb 18 **(86) n22.5 t23.5 f19 b21** usually, the term "First Fill Sherry" associated with any of the old Highland Distillers distilleries has you running to the fallout shelter. Well, yes, there is sulphur on board, and comes through definitively at the finale. But first you can luxuriate in the stunning, honey-riddled delivery. Toasted honeycomb, cinnamon and maple syrup combine stunningly with the roasted tannins for a brilliant opening salvo. Shame about the late sulphur. *51.6%. nc ncf sc. 265 bottles.*

The MacPhail's Collection Glenturret 2004 (84) n20.5 t22.5 f20 b21 A tad heavy on the cut here, which makes for a thick, enjoyable dram but one that doesn't entirely convince; nor, indeed does the late oak involvement. The usual honey notes are at a premium, though there is little shortage of malt and caramel. *43%.*

Old Particular Highland Glenturret 28 Years Old cask no. 11028, dist Nov 87 **(95.5) n24 t23.5 f24 b24** As near as damn it faultless so far as a single cask of Glenturret goes. *51.5%*

Old Particular Glenturret 28 Years Old refill hogshead, cask no. 11199, dist Nov 87, bott Jun 16 **(95.5)** n24 t24 f23 b24.5 Simply delicious: the little distillery in very big form. The distillery style distilled, quite literary. *45.9%. nc ncf sc. 171 bottles.*

That Boutique-y Whisky Company Glenturret 35 Year Old **(96)** n24.5 t24.5 f23 b24 Thank heaven they've bottled just enough to keep any self-respecting whisky lover going for a year... *47.7%. 365 bottles.*

Whisky Broker Glenturret 26 Year Old Barolo wine barrique, cask no. 220, dist 11 May 94, bott 23 Feb 17 **(88.5)** n22 t22 f22.5 b22 The colour of rust – and there is a distinct steeliness to this one. *55.5%.*

GLENUGIE
Highlands (Eastern). 1834–1983. Whitbread. Closed.

Deoch an Doras Glenugie 30 Years Old dist 1980, bott 2011 db **(87)** n22 t23.5 f19.5 b22. It is now 2017 and it has been six long years since this arrived in my tasting room - something I didn't expect to see again: a distillery bottling of Glenugie. Well, technically, anyway, as Glenugie was part of the Chivas group when it died in the 1980s. As far as I can remember they only brought it out once, either as a seven- or five-year-old. I think that went to Italy, so when I walked around the old site just after it closed, it was a Gordon and MacPhail bottling I drank from and it tasted nothing like this! Just a shame there is a very slight flaw in the sherry butt, but just great to see it in bottle again. *52.13%. nc ncf.*

GLENURY ROYAL
Highlands (Eastern), 1868–1985. Diageo. Demolished.

Glenury Royal 36 Years Old db **(89)** n21 t23 f22 b23. An undulating dram, hitting highs and lows. The finish, in particular, is impressive: just when it looks on its last legs, it revives delightfully. The whole package, though far from perfect, is pretty astounding. *50.2%*

Glenury Royal 40 Year Old Limited Edition dist 1970, bott 2011 db **(84)** n20.5 t20 f22 b21.5. Glenury is these days so rare I kept this back as a treat to savour as I neared the end of the book. The finale throws up a number of interesting citrus equations. But the oak, for the most part, is too rampant here and makes for a puckering experience. *59.4%. 1,500 bottles.*

Gordon & MacPhail Rare Old Glenury Royal 1984 **(95.5)** n23 t24 f23.5 b25 In the rare instances of the early 1980s I tasted a young Glenury, it was never this good and hardly looked up for 30 years in the cask. But this incredibly rare bottling of the malt, the best I have ever encountered from Glenury and distilled in the final days of its 117 year existence, stands its ground proudly and performs, unforgettably, the Last Post with magical honeyed notes... *46%.*

HAZELBURN *(see Springbank)*

HIGHLAND PARK
Highlands (Island–Orkney), 1795. Edrington. Working.

Highland Park 8 Years Old db **(87)** n22 t22 f22 b21. A journey back in time for some of us: this is the orginal distillery bottling of the 70s and 80s, bottles of which are still doing the rounds in obscure Japanese bars and specialist outlets such as the Whisky Exchange. *40%*

Highland Park 10 Year Old Ambassador's Choice db **(74)** n17.5 t20 f17.5 b19. Some of the casks are so badly sulphured, I'm surprised there hasn't been a diplomatic incident... *46%*

Highland Park Aged 12 Years db **(78)** n19 t21 f19 b19. Let's just hope that the choice of casks for this bottling was a freak. To be honest, this was one of my favourite whiskies of all time, one of my desert island drams, and I could weep. *40% WB16/048*

Highland Park Aged 15 Years db **(85)** n21 t22 f21 b21. Had to re-taste this several times, surprised as I was by just how relatively flat this was. A hill of honey forms the early delivery, but then... *40%*

Highland Park Earl Magnus Aged 15 Years 1st edition db **(76.5)** n20 t21 f17.5 b18. Tight and bitter. *52.6%. 5976 bottles.*

Highland Park Loki Aged 15 Years db **(96)** n24 t24 f23.5 b24.5 the weirdness of the heather apart, a bit of a trip back in time. A higher smoke ration than the bottlings of more recent years which new converts to the distillery will be unfamiliar with, but reverting to the levels regularly found in the 1970s and 80s, probably right through to about 1993/94. Which is a very good thing because the secret of the peat at HP was that, as puffed out as it could be in the old days, it never interfered with the overall complexity, other than adding to it. Which is exactly the case here. Beyond excellent! *48.7%. Edrington.*

Highland Park 16 Years Old db **(88)** n23 t23 f20 b22. I tasted this the day it first came out at one of the Heathrow whisky shops. I thought it a bit flat and uninspiring. This sample, maybe from another bottling, is more impressive and showing true Highland Park colours, the finish apart. *40%. Exclusively available in Duty Free/Travel Retail.*

Highland Park Thor Aged 16 Years db (87.5) n22.5 t23.5 f19 b22.5. Now, from what I remember of my Norse gods, Thor was the God of Thunder. Which is a bit spooky seeing as hailstones are crashing down outside as I write this and lightning is striking overhead. Certainly a whisky built on power. Even taking into account the glitch in one or two of the casks, a dram to be savoured on delivery. *52.1%. 23,000 bottles.*

Highland Park Ice Edition Aged 17 Years db (87) n22 t23 f21 b21. The smoke drifts around unit it finds some spices. Frustrating: you expect it to kick on but it stubbornly refuses to. Caramel and vanilla up front, then bitters out. *53.9%.*

Highland Park Aged 18 Years db (95.5) n23.5 t24 f24 b24 If familiarity breeds contempt, then it has yet to happen between myself and HP 18. This is a must-have dram. I show it to ladies the world over to win their hearts, minds and tastebuds when it comes to whisky. And the more time I spend with it, the more I become aware and appreciative of its extraordinary consistency. The very latest bottlings have been astonishing, possibly because colouring has now been dropped, and wisely so. Why in any way reduce what is one of the world's great whisky experiences? Such has been the staggering consistency of this dram I have thought of late of promoting the distillery into the world's top three: only Ardbeg and Buffalo Trace have been bottling whisk(e)y of such quality over a wide range of ages in such metronomic fashion. Anyway, enough: a glass of something honeyed and dazzling calls... *43%*

Highland Park Aged 21 Years db (82.5) n20.5 t22 f19 b21. Good news and bad news. The good news is that they appear to have done away with the insane notion of reducing this to 40% abv. The bad news: a sulphured sherry butt has found its way into this bottling. *47.5%*

Highland Park Aged 25 Years db (96) n24 t24 f24 b24 I am a relieved man: the finest HP 25 for a number of years which displays the distillery's unmistakable fingerprints with a pride bordering on arrogance. One of the most improved bottlings of the year: an emperor of a dram. *48.1%*

Highland Park Aged 30 Years db (90) n22 t22.5 f23 b22.5 A very dramatic shift from the last bottling I tasted; this has taken a fruitier route. Sheer quality, though. *48.1%*

Highland Park 40 Years Old db (90.5) n20.5 t22.5 f24 b23.5 Picking splinters from my nose with this one. Some of the casks used here have obviously choked on oak, and I feared the worst. But such is the brilliance of the resilience by being on the money with the honey, you can say only that it has pulled off an amazing feat with the peat. Sheer poetry... *48.3%*

Highland Park 50 Years Old dist Jan 60 db (96.5) n24.5 t24 f24 b24 Old whiskies tend to react to unchartered territory as far as time in the oak is concerned in quite different ways. This grey beard has certainly given us a new slant. Nothing unique about the nose. But when one is usually confronted with those characteristics on the nose, what follows on the palate moves towards a reasonably predictable path. Not here. Truly unique – as it should be after all this time. *44.8%. sc. 275 bottles.*

◈ **Highland Park 2002** cask no. 3374-HCF064 db (96) n23 decidedly coastal with a seaweedy brine effect for once out-punching the honey; t24.5 a brilliant recovery! Unmistakably HP with the trademark heather honey and light smoke combing to create something of stunning beauty. Lovers of Milky Way candy bars will particularly enjoy this, not least because of the milk chocolate middle – ironic, as I took a break from tasting for 15 minutes to marvel at Mars (two days out from its closest meeting with Earth for 17 years), Jupiter, showing three of its moons and Saturn with rings straighter than they have been or a little while; oh, and the spices...wow! f24 what an finish: incorruptible, with the heather honey now not only set but slowly growing in intensity, the smoke now just a little more definite and the new more perfect maltiness in astonishing harness with the cocoa; b24.5 I have always through HP peaked at around 18 in mixed casks rather than 25. This is breathtaking to the point of whisky life changing and revels in its refined, complex sweetness to make a mockery of my theory. The nose apart, this has all the things that makes HP one of the world's great distilleries, and piles it on to an extent it has rarely been witnessed before. Such awesome beauty... *58.4%. sc. Bottled for Loch Fyne Whiskies.*

◈ **Highland Park 2006** cask no. 2132-HCF067 db (91) n22.5 rather than the usual lightly smoked heather honey, we have a different style of HP, with lightly smoked salty vanilla, instead; t23 this strength just means the HP velvet is thicker still. The lightest trace of honey (Bruyere rather than heather) dissolves into a morass of malt. Again, a degree of brine surfaces as well as some muscular oaky tones which becomes increasingly toasty; f23 at last the malt gets a look in, but the delicate honey keeps tabs; b22.5 you'd be hard pushed to recognise this as an HP unless you were told. Has many of the signature traits, but they don't click into place to create that unique style. An atypical HP, but typically delicious. *67%. sc. Bottled for The W Club.*

Highland Park Dark Origins db (80) n19 t23 f18 b20. Part of that Dark Origin must be cocoa, as there is an abundance of delicious high grade chocolate here. But the other part is not so much dark as yellow, as sulphur is around on the nose and finish in particular - and does plenty of damage. Genuinely disappointing to see one of the world's greatest distilleries refusing to play to its strengths and putting so much of its weight on its Achilles heel. 46.8%. ncf.

Highland Park Earl Haakon db (92) n22.5 t24 f22.5 b23. A fabulous malt offering some of the best individual moments of the year. But appears to run out of steam about two thirds in. 54.9%. 3,300 bottles.

Highland Park Einar db (90.5) n23 soft, warmingly smoky, toffee apple; t23 fresh, salivating delivery but bordered by tannin and imbued with spice; vague heather honey; f22 dry with the tannins and spices buzzing to the end; b22.5 a curious style of HP which shows most of its usual traits but possesses an extra sharpness. 40% WB15/328

Highland Park Freya 1st fill ex-bourbon casks db (88.5) n22 t23 f21.5 b22. The majestic honey on delivery makes up for some of the untidier moments. 52.10%.

Highland Park Harald db (74.5) n19 t20 f17 b18.5. Warrior Harald has been wounded by sulphur. Fatally. 40% WB15/337

Highland Park Hjärta db (79.5) n18.5 t22 f19 b20. In part, really does celebrate the honeycomb character of Highland Park to the full. But obviously a major blemish or two in there as well. 58.1%. 3924 bottles.

Highland Park King Christian db (83.5) n22 t22.5 f18.5 b20.5. A hefty malt with a massive fruit influence. But struggles for balance and to keep full control of the, ultimately, off-key grapey input. Despite the sub-standard finale, there is much to enjoy with the early malt-fruit battles on delivery that offer a weighty and buttery introduction to the diffused molasses and vanilla. But with the spice arrives the Achilles heel... 46.8%

Highland Park Leif Eriksson bourbon and American oak db (86) n22 t22 f21 b21. The usual distillery traits have gone AWOL while all kinds of caramel notes have usurped them. That said, this has to be one of the softest drams you'll find. 40%. Edrington.

Highland Park Ragnavald db (87.5) n21.5 t22 f22 b22. Thickset and muscular, this malt offers a slightly different type of earthiness to the usual HP. Even the malt has its moment in the sun. But the overall portrait hangs from the wall at a slight tilt... 45.05%

Highland Park Sigurd db (96) n23.5 t24.5 f23.5 b24.5 Breathtaking, star-studded and ridiculously complex reminder that this distillery is capable of serving up some of the best whisky the world can enjoy. 43%

Highland Park Svein db (87) n22 t22 f21.5 b21.5. A soft, friendly dram with good spice pick up. But rather too dependent on a tannin-toffee theme. 40% WB15/318

◈ **Acla Special Selection No. 4 Highland Park 24 Years Old** hogshead, dist 1992, bott 2016 (95.5) n24 not just textbook: this could be the blueprint of the distillery at 24: soft heather honey brushed gently with almost erotic smoky fingertips; dashing tannin holding on to the wisps of vanilla and orange blossom; t24 the nose suggests complexity and even the delivery obliges; the smoke has now adopted a slightly sterner voice: while the nose woos the flavours command. The tannin is forceful but meets its match in the punchier, spicier phenols; the honey melts fast and is replaced by a more dogmatic molassed heaviness; f23.5 the tannins try to win back control and do so to fade with a creamy mocha flourish, a whole lot softer, showing the traditional HP oils, than the firm goings on of before; b24 it is so wonderful to see a HP of this vintage exactly as it should be: a picture of controlled complexity. A gem to warm the heart and soul. 50%. sc. 82 bottles.

Cadenhead's Authentic Collection Highland Park 28 Year Old port cask, dist 1988 (94) n23.5 t24 f23.5 b24 Not often you find a wine cask which works with HP, as this is such a complex whisky the fruit can prevent the most subtle notes being heard. But this is still a very busy and beautifully proportioned dram of the highest order... 49.6%. sc.

The Cooper's Choice Highland Park 21 Year Old dist 1995, bott 2017 (89.5) n22 t23 f22 b22.5 Not sure if this cask was stored just off the Atlantic...or in it... 49.5%. nc ncf sc.

◈ **Gordon & MacPhail Connoisseurs Choice Highland Park 1999 Cask No. 4262** first fill bourbon barrel, dist 30 Aug 99, bott 21 Feb 18 (94.5) n23 a lighter, more citrusy version of the HP theme, the smoke more fragile, the honey a little crisper. But beautifully integrated; t23.5 a light, juicy, timid start, then suddenly we are off on a journey far more prickly and spicy than the norm for an HP, with ulmo honey instead of the usual heather version; the smoke, as usual acts as both bath and soother-in-chief; f24 butterscotch, vanilla, hickory and mocha, all topped deliciously, with a vague smoked honey; b24 a lighter HP, but still beautifully hefty for all that with its magical mouth feel. And further proof that, given the right cask, HP remains one of the greatest distilleries in the world. 56%. nc ncf sc. sc.

◈ **Gordon & MacPhail Connoisseurs Choice Highland Park 1999 Cask No. 4265** first fill bourbon barrel, dist 30 Aug 99, bott 21 Feb 18 (95) n23.5 all the usual HP attributes on the nose which at first stubbornly refuse to mesh; but with sufficient cajoling from heat (Gawd bless the Murray Method!) suddenly things click into place and the smoke and honey combine to create something approaching a whisky Valhalla....; **t24** aaah! Instant harmony. In a nanosecond the delivery manages what the nose constantly failed to do; a massive dose of luxurious heather honey followed by a chocolatey smoky spiciness, all inter-linked, arm-in-arm...: stunning. **f23.5** a more docile fade, with none of the engulfing brilliance of the delivery. Instead, those light honey and vaguely smoky notes simply drift away on the lightly salted tide...; **b24** sweeping, cascading, beautiful soul-touching chords: if this were a film score it would have been written by John Barry. 55.6%. nc ncf sc. 210 bottles.

⬦ **Gordon & MacPhail Connoisseurs Choice Highland Park 2004** first fill sherry butt, cask no. 3812, dist 2004, bott 22 Feb 18 (94.5) **n23** dry and nutty, the tannin contribution is a prickly one. The grape is subdued and concentrates mainly on adding weight; lots of chalky-dry wheat flour, too; **t24** two flavour beats in and the sweetness lacking so obviously on the nose turns up in droves. Not the distillery's normal heather honey style: slightly more Manuka mixed in with muscovado. The fruit element is both restrained and refined before the late mid-ground takes up a fudge and raisin chewiness; **f23.5** long, the most vague wisp of smoke, then a litany of two or three oak-heavy tones recurring ad infinitum; **b24** come out from behind your sofas: this sherry butt is 100% free from sulphur. And, my word, does it show...!! 60%. nc ncf sc. 655 bottles.

Gordon & MacPhail Cask Strength Highland Park 2007 bott 2 Nov 16 (88) **n22 t22.5 f21.5 b22** HP in insecure mode: how many will not have quite seen it before... 58.8%.

Hunter Laing's Old & Rare Highland Park Aged 18 Years refill hogshead, dist Sept 97, bott Apr 16 (95) **n23.5 t24 f23.5; b24** Really, this could come from only one distillery in the world... almost a parody of itself. Beautiful. 54.6%. nc ncf sc. 266 bottles.

The MacPhail's Collection Highland Park 1989 (92) **n23.5 t23 f22.5 b23** So many of the distillery's more recognisable traits on delicious display. 43%.

Spirits Shop Selection Highland Park 1992 bourbon cask, bott 2016 (93) **n24 t23.5 f22.5 b23** The nose and delivery are as close to the archetypal HP 25-year-old – well near 25! – as you are likely to find. 51.4%. 278 bottles. A joint bottling with Sansibar Whisky.

⬦ **The Whisky Embassy Highland Park Aged 14 Years** cask no. 5016993, dist 2003, bott 2017 (88.5) **n23** low key malt ad honey: so low key the gentle smoke has the biggest say; **t22** unusually sharp delivery for an HP, but steadies itself as a light maple syrup makes its mark; **f21.5** a tad bitter from the oak but the Lubeck marzipan compensates; **b22** bit of a spluttering HP, but still has all the trademark gags... 52.8%. nc ncf sc.

⬦ **The Whisky Embassy Highland Park Aged 14 Years** cask no. 5017013, dist 2003, bott 2017 (93.5) **n23.5 t23.5 f23 b23.5** Almost identical in style to their 6993 cask, but without all the oaky flaws. The greater intensity and integration results in the smoke dovetailing with a richer, now heather honey, sweetness rather than being aloof. The lack of bitterness allows the story to be told without interruption. 53.8%. nc ncf sc.

WoodWinters Northern Star 21 Year Old dist 1995 (96.5) **n24 t24 f24 b24.5** For me, 21 was always the optimum age for HP...and always, without exception, in an ex bourbon cask. Or, at least, non-sherry. With a stunning bottling like this, surely some kind of award winner this year, it is hard to argue... 60.7%. sc. 278 bottles.

IMPERIAL
Speyside, 1897. Chivas Brothers. Silent.

Imperial Aged 15 Years "Special Distillery Bottling" db (69) **n17 t18 f17 b17.** At least one very poor cask, hot spirit and overly sweet. Apart from that it's wonderful. 46%

⬦ **Gordon & MacPhail Distillery Label Imperial 1997** bott 9 Aug 17 (87.5) **n23 t21 f22 b21.5** A breezy light over-simplistic dram on the palate perhaps due to the wafer thin structure of the body. However, the nose is a different matter altogether and excels by offering a beautifully balanced mix of dates, plums and warming malt which fits gloriously with the lightly splintered, toasty oak. 43%.

Kingsbury Gold Imperial 21 Year Old hogshead, cask no. 50408, dist 1995 (84.5) **n20.5 t22.5 f20 b21.5** The nose alone would stop most blenders from making this a force in their creation. But the slow burn of the malt on the palate has many delightful and surprising qualities, especially the sleight of hand so far as the humble sugars are concerned. Light but attractive. 51.7%. 171 bottles. sc.

⬦ **Kingsbury Gold Imperial 21 Years Old** hogshead, cask no. 50406, dist 1995 (87) **n22 t22.5 f21 b21.5** Plenty of yap, nip and bite. The big malt has some ulmo honey to assist early on, but the teeth get a little sharper, the structure a tad thinner as things progress. 50.7%. 256 bottles.

INCHGOWER
Speyside, 1872. Diageo. Working.

Inchgower 1993 The Manager's Choice db (84.5) **n21 t21.5 f21 b21.** Like your malts subtle, delicate, clean and sophisticated? Don't bother with this one if you do. This has all the feel of a malt that's been spray painted onto the taste buds: thick, chewy and resilient. Can't help but like that mix of hazelnut and Demerara, though. You can stand a spoon in it. 61.9%

Cadenhead's Authentic Collection Inchgower 27 Year Old bourbon casks, dist 1989 (89.5) n22.5 t22 f22; b23 The Inchgower spirit distilled back in about 1990 was a real roughhouse pretty much devoid of shape and meaning thanks to years of neglect of the overworked stills. As often as not, this type of spirit over good time becomes a genuinely fascinating and entertaining malt. Here is such a case: an excellent reflection oof the distillery in its day. 53.2%.

◇ **The First Editions Inchgower Aged 20 Years 1997** refill hogshead, cask no. 14219, bott 2017 (83.5) n21 t21 f20.5 b21 Not atypical of the period with the malt and oak crushed and confined, sometimes uncomfortably, by the heat of the spirit. The sugars which come to the rescue appear to carry the most distant hint of smoke. 56.1%. nc ncf sc. 154 bottles.

◇ **Gleann Mor Inchgower Aged Over 14 Years** dist 2003 (89) n21 Good lord! Smoke...!!! Not much, but enough to take those who have known Inchgower a good few decades by pleasant surprise. There is also a vague hint of juniper here (suspicious, on the bottling hall front – as is the smoke) as well as orange peel; t23 I would never have recognised this as an Inchgower in a million years: the delivery is oily (fair enough) but that seems to collect not just the intense malt but an ever-increasing degree of chocolatey smoke, then a little juniper in the mid-stream; f22.5 dries as the oak coagulates; muscovado sugars meld with the late cocoa; b22.5 the light powdering of phenols is a pleasant surprise and does nothing to subtract from this distillery's all-round, though not instantly recognisable, charm. 53.3%.

Hepburn's Choice Inchgower 7 Years Old sherry hogshead, dist 2008, bott 2016 (86.5) n22.5 t21.5 f21 b21.5 Good old Inchgower! If you are looking for a good, earthy malt with a bit of attitude, this is so often your man! Some weak but recognisable oily grape stars in the mid-points. 46%. nc ncf sc. 380 bottles.

◇ **Hepburn's Choice Inchgower 8 Years Old** Oloroso sherry finished butt, dist 2008, bott 2016 (69) n17 t18 f17 b17 The sulphur is unremittingly grim. 46%. nc ncf sc. 663 bottles.

Hepburn's Choice Inchgower 9 Years Old refill hogshead, dist 2008, bott 2017 (84) n20 t22 f21 b21 Chalk.... 46%. nc ncf sc. 365 bottles.

Hepburn's Choice Inchgower 9 Years Old refill hogshead, dist 2008, bott 2017 (91.5) n22.5 t23 f22.5 b23.5 Cheese. Hard to believe that this and the other Hepburn's Inchgower 2017 bottling are related: they have so little in common. Where the other is dry overall and often grating and tangy, this version abounds in controlled malty sweetness. It possesses the lot: fresh grist, sugared lemon and well-weighted spices. And even some oak-shaved butterscotch to complete the balance. Superb. 46%. nc ncf sc. 278 bottles.

Old Malt Cask Inchgower Aged 20 Years sherry butt, cask no. 12301, dist Sept 95, bott Feb 16 (88.5) n22 t23 f21 b22.5 Not a faultless cask. But the malt itself has the balls to take on any off-key messages and bang them back into line. 50%. nc ncf sc. 377 bottles.

◇ **Old Malt Cask Inchgower Aged 21 Years** sherry butt, cask no. 14253, dist Oct 95, bott Sept 17 (88) n22 a touch of the sherry trifles about this, complete with jelly; t22.5 sweet, sumptuous mouth-feel with sugars dominant early on, before the salivating barley and green grape begin to be nudged by the spices; f21.5 a little tang at the death as the spices and oaky notes dominate; b22 not quite the perfect butt, but character enough to see it through the obvious flaws. 50%. nc ncf sc. 708 bottles.

◇ **Old Particular Inchgower 18 Years Old** sherry butt, cask no. 12102, dist Sept 98, bott Sept 17 (89) n22.5 attractive light must; excellent spice prickle and a little ginger, too; t22 salivating barley soon gibes way to the marauding spice; f22 long, malty with surmising rise in oils; b22.5 an unruined sherry butt helps offer a light fruity glaze to the malt. 48.4%. nc ncf sc. 365 bottles.

Provenance Inchgower Aged 8 Years refill hogshead, cask no. 11227, dist Mar 09, bott May 16 (90.5) n23.5 t22.5 f22 b22.5 Forget the age: this is pure, unsophisticated enjoyment! 46%. nc ncf sc.

◇ **Provenance Inchgower Aged 9 Years** refill hogshead, cask no. 12028, dist Feb 08, bott Aug 17 (85) n22 t22.5 f20 b20.5 A full-flavoured beast which cranks up the malt early on, even with accompanying Demerara sugars, but dramatically falls flat at the death. 46%. nc ncf sc. 416 bottles.

INVERLEVEN
Lowland, 1938–1991. Demolished.

Deoch an Doras Inverleven 36 Years Old dist 1973 (94.5) n24 t23.5 f23 b24 As light on the palate as a morning mist. This distillery just wasn't designed to make a malt of this antiquity, yet this is to the manor born. 48.85%. nc ncf. Chivas Brothers. 500 bottles.

ISLE OF ARRAN

Highlands (Island–Arran), 1995. Isle of Arran Distillers. Working.

Isle of Arran Machrie Moor 5th Edition bott 2014 db (91.5) n22.5 t24 f22 b23 A few tired old bourbon barrels have taken the score down slightly on last year. But the spirit itself is nothing short of brilliant. 46% WB16/049

The Arran Malt 10 Year Old db (87) n22.5 t22.5 f20 b22. It has been a while since I last officially tasted this. If they are willing to accept some friendly advice, I think the blenders should tone down on raising any fruit profile and concentrate on the malt, which is amongst the best in the business. 46%. nc ncf.

The Arran Malt 12 Years Old db (85) n21.5 t22 f20.5 b21 Hmmmm. Surprise one, this. There must be more than one bottling already of this. The first I tasted was perhaps slightly on the oaky side but otherwise intact and salt-honeyed where need be. This one has a bit of a tang: very drinkable, but definitely a less than brilliant cask around. 46%

The Arran Malt Aged 14 Years db (89.5) n22 t23.5 f21.5 b22.5. A superb whisky, but the evidence that there has been a subtle shift in emphasis, with the oak now taking too keen an interest, is easily attained. 46%. ncf.

The Arran Malt Aged 17 Years db (91.5) n23.5 t23.5 f21.5 b23 "Matured in the finest ex-Sherry casks" trills the back label. And, by and large, they are right. Maybe a single less than finest imparts the light furriness to the finish. But by present day sherry butt standards, a pretty outstanding effort. 46%. nc ncf. 9000 bottles. WB15/152

The Arran Malt Fino Sherry Cask Finish db (82.5) n21 t20 f21 b20.5. Pretty tight with the bitterness not being properly compensated for. 50%

◇ **Berry Bros & Rudd Arran 21 Years Old** cask no. 370, dist 1996, bott 2018 (96.5) n24 such a seductive dram: light, green peaches meld with lush, moist grass and grist; a gentle salt sprinkling opens up the aromas further t24 just so refined: the oils near bring a tear to my eye, as they display the exact small still quality desired when the distillery opened, and this in turn helps exhibit the malt at its most rounded and gorgeously chewy; f24 there is no let up to the complexity: now the spices which had started to make barely detectable noises earlier have no constraints whatsoever and apparently delight in teasing the tastebuds; still the oils persist in concentrating the mind on the intense malt, though a little butterscotch and fudge-edged tannin also linger on the viscosity; b24.5. When my dear old friend Harold Currie built this distillery in the mid-1990s he wanted the spirit to be as close in style to Macallan as he could get it. So, when I selected the very first cuts for the very first distillation, it was Harold's wish I had I mind. This bottling was almost certainly made to the cutting points I chose and my only sadness is that Harold is no longer with us to enjoy his malt whisky coming of age. Though this is probably not from oloroso (or if it was, it was so old that very restrained fruit is imparted) – and that is just as well, as most early oloroso butts from the distillery are poor quality – it certainly matches the profile of Macallan of the same age matured in top end second fill bourbon. This is, unquestionably one of the single malt bottlings of the year. 46.4%. nc ncf sc.

◇ **Golden Cask Arran Aged 21 Years** cask no. CM240, dist 1996, bott 2017 (94.5) n23.5 heather honey with a twist of black pepper; t24 near perfect delivery: the malt is in super-concentrated form, but the sugars so rich the heather-honey nose is recreated on the palate; the oak attacks in well-ordered waves, the pepperiness intensifying with each pulse; f23 after the most luscious honey storm comes the lull where a slightly dry, vaguely chalky finale is kept busy by the spice; b24 impeccable Arran. 51.6%. sc. 254 bottles.

◇ **Gordon & MacPhail Connoisseurs Choice Arran 1996** refill sherry hogshead, cask no. 37, dist 24 Jan 96, bott 22 Feb 18 (92) n23.5 big, muscular malt enjoying the spicy fruit: a cross between Dundee and Manor House style as much Arran...; a powerful bourbon oakiness is equally evident; t23.5 brilliant delivery: the spices fizz, crackle and sparkle, aided and abetted by the crisp Demerara; juicy dates and plums abound...yet the barley itself is still to be celebrated at the halfway point and remains faithfully salivating; f22 dries with a burnt toast and marmalade finale; b23 a sound sherry cask at work means this is a rare view of Arran at this great age at its very fruitiest. 49.2%. nc ncf sc. 283 bottles.

◇ **Gordon & MacPhail Connoisseurs Choice Arran 2009** bott 21 Mar 17 (92.5) n22.5 a real creamy rice pudding with molten Demerara sugars on top; light spices not unlike crushed caramelised biscuit; t23.5 succulent and salivating barley with the vaguest hint of a mix of honey and marmalade on slightly overcooked toast; f23 the dryness is a shock as the more sawdusty elements of the oak bite fast and hard. Still the oils act as balm – and inject some late barley sugars, some even creating a moment or two of late salivation; b23.5 the initial drop on palate from sweetness to dryness is an unusual cliff edge variety with few warnings close to the precipice. No doubts helps to make this exciting malt from a great distillery. 46%.

The Grey Wolf Isle of Arran 21 Year Old 1996 sherry hogshead, cask no. 82 **(90.5)** n23.5 t24 f23 b23 Though obviously flawed, still not too bad a sherry cask with the dreaded "s" word on slow burn and arriving long after the party... Just live for that delivery... *50.7%. sc. 334 bottles.*

⬦ **H*A*S*H Barley Bree Isle of Arran Aged 21 Years** ex-sherry puncheon, cask no. 96/1327, dist 17 Sept 96, bott 16 Nov 17 **(85.5)** n21.5 t22.5 f20 b21.5 A rich though slightly laboured malt which is a bit of a battle between the obvious brilliance of the original whisky and the slight failings of the cask. Plenty of good things at work and early on the fruit has a generous, salty depth. But soon tightens and sharpens making the finale a bit of an uphill struggle. *50.2%. sc. 556 bottles.*

Old Particular Arran 20 Years Old refill hogshead, cask no. 11345, dist Aug 96, bott Sept 16 **(96)** n24.5 t24 f23 b24.5 An energetic, vibrant yet sensual malt which is defying the years, especially to those who doubted it would stand up to this kind of ageing with such finesse... and that includes me...! This is quite brilliant whisky. *51.5%. nc ncf sc. 287 bottles.*

Old Particular Arran 21 Years Old refill hogshead, cask no. 11608, dist Jan 97, bott Mar 17 **(92.5)** n23 t23 f23 b23 A cask beyond its sell by date...but here we're taking a distillery into previously unexplored territory. Truly amazing, historic dramming...*44.4%. nc ncf sc. 136 bottles.*

Scotch Malt Whisky Society Cask 121.89 16Year Old refill ex-bourbon hogshead, dist 2 Dec 99 **(92)** n23.5 t23 f22.5 b23 By Arran standards, not the greatest bourbon oak. But the quality is undiminished. *54.1%.*

Simon Brown Arran Distillery 1997 barrel, cask no. 97/1504, dist Aug 97, bott Feb 14 **(96.5)** n24.5 t24.5 f23.5 b24 Isle of Arran distillery when wisely kept away from sherry butts (which as often as not renders it malt ordinaire) often boasts all the attributes of a world superdistillery. This wonderful bottling shows exactly why. *46%. nc ncf sc.*

⬦ **Single Cask Collection Arran 21 Years Old Platin Edition** sherry edition **(88.5)** n22.5 more cherry cake than the usual fruit cake; a tad salty with dry vanilla wafer; t22.5 juicy, though thickened by a big vanilla and malt combination; f21.5 sherry trifle; b22 a mainly clean sherry butt doles out the fruit. *51%. sc.*

That Boutique-y Whisky Company Arran 19 Year Old batch 6 **(94)** n23.5 t24 f23 b23.5 I was convinced Arran would struggle to reach this kind of age intact. This, and other recent bottlings of a similar vintage, have proved me quite wrong. *49.7%. 250 bottles.*

⬦ **The Whisky Chamber Arran 17 Years Old 2000** sherry cask 1099 **(87)** n22 t23 f20.5 b21.5 Not the Chamber of from a sherry butt as I had feared. But still a little tight in places That said, the delivery horrors I had feared conjure up all kinds of spicy tricks, most of them involving some busy, prickly tannins. A real mouthful...with plenty of oak-dried sultanas on show *.52.4%. sc.*

ISLE OF JURA

Highlands (Island–Jura), 1810. Whyte and Mackay. Working.

Isle Of Jura Aged 10 Years db **(79.5)** n19 t22 f19 b19.5. Perhaps a little livelier than before, but still miles short of where you might hope it to be. *40%*

Isle Of Jura Aged 16 Years db **(90.5)** n21.5 t23.5 f23 b23 A massive improvement, this time celebrating its salty, earthy heritage to good effect. The odd strange, less than harmonious note. But by far and away the most improved Jura for a long, long while. *40%*

Isle of Jura 21 Years Old Cask Strength db **(92)** n22 t24 f23 b23. Every mouthful exudes class and quality. A must-have for Scottish Island collectors... or those who know how to appreciate a damn fine malt *58.1%*

Isle of Jura 30 Years Old db **(89)** n22.5 t22.5 f22 b22. A relaxed dram with the caramel dousing the higher notes just as they started to get very interesting. If there is a way of bringing down these presumably natural caramels – it is a 30 years old, so who in their right mind would add colouring? – this would score very highly, indeed. *40%*

Isle of Jura 40 Years Old finished in oloroso wood db **(90)** n23 t22 f22 b23 Throw the Jura textbooks away. This is something very different. Completely out of sync in so many ways, but... *40%*

Jura Elements "Air" db **(76)** n19.5 t19 f18.5 b19. Initially, I thought this was earth: there is something strangely dirty and flat about both nose and delivery. Plenty of fruits here and there but just doesn't get the pulse racing at all. *45%*

Jura Elements "Earth" db **(89)** n23.5 t22 f21.5 b22. I haven't spoken to blender Richard Paterson about these whiskies yet. No doubt I'll be greeted with a knee on the nuts for declaring two as duds. My guess is that this is the youngest of the quartet by a distance and that is probably why it is the best. The peat profile is very different and challenging. I'd still love to see this in its natural plumage as the caramel really does put the brakes on the complexity and development. Otherwise we could have had an elementary classic. *45%*

Jura Elements "Fire" db **(86.5)** n22.5 t21.5 f21 b21.5. Pleasant fare, the highlight coming with the vaguely Canadian-style nose thanks to a classic toffee-oak mix well known east of the Rockies. Some botanicals also there to be sniffed at while a few busy oaky notes pep up the barley-juiced other, too. Sadly, just a shade too toffee dependent. 45%

Jura Elements "Water" db (73.5) n18.5 t19 f18 b18. Oranges by the box-full trying to get out but the mouth is sent into puckering spasm by the same sulphur which spoils the nose. 50%

⬥ **Jura One and All Aged 20 Years** db (83.5) n21 t22 f19.5 b21 A metallic tang to this. Nutty with tart, fruity borders but nothing to get excited about. Doesn't quite add up. 51%. nc ncf.

Jura One For The Road Aged 22 Years Pinot Noir finish db (89) n23 t23 f21 b22 Enjoyable though ultimately a bit too straight and, just like the single road on Jura, goes nowhere... 47%. nc ncf.

⬥ **Jura One For You** db (87.5) n22 t22.5 f21.5 b21.5 A straight up and down maltfest with a vaguely salty edge. Very pleasant in its own limited way, but don't spend too much time looking for complexity. 52.5%. nc ncf.

Jura Prophecy profoundly peated db (90.5) n23.5 t23 f22 b22 Youthful, well made and I prophesy this will be one of Jura's top scorers of 2011... 46%

Jura Superstition db (73.5) n17 t19 f18 b18.5. I thought this could only improve. I was wrong. One to superstitiously avoid. 43%

Jura Tastival 2016 triple sherry finish db (67) n17 t18 f15 b17. Sulphur. In triplicate. 51%. ncf.

⬥ **Jura Tastival 2017** db (90.5) n22 surprising grassy and fresh; diced apple; sharp, almost distant bonfire without trying to be phenolic; t23 fat and beautifully structured with an enormous malty mott to the demerara sugar bailey; f22.5 slightly metallic and spicy; b23 one of the better Juras I've encountered in recent times. 51%. nc ncf.

Jura Turas-Mara db (82.5) n20.5 t22 f19 b21. Some irresistible Jaffa Cake moments. But the oils are rather too severe and tangy. 42%. Travel Retail Exclusive.

Hepburn's Choice Jura 8 Years Old refill hogshead, dist 2008, bott 2017 (87) n20 t23.5 f21.5 b22 A bipolar malt: after a truly average, off-key nose the delivery – full of voluptuous barley both gristy and even boasting sensual ulmo honey – makes for one of the surprise package whiskies this year. The finish, though, is not all it might be despite the vague spices. 46%. nc ncf sc. 332 bottles.

⬥ **Hepburn's Choice Jura 10 Years Old** refill hogshead, dist 2007, bott 2017 (81.5) n20 t21.5 f19 b21 The limitations of this distillery are in evidence here. That said, the odd attractive nutty and spicy thread to this. 46%. nc n cf sc. 420 bottles.

Old Malt Cask Jura Aged 25 Years refill hogshead, cask no. 13274, dist Feb 91, bott Feb 17 (81.5) n20.5 t22 f19 b20 Just not enough character or panache to see off the more tangy, faltering elements of the oak. Still, ride that tidal wave of malt when it arrives just after delivery... 50%. nc ncf. 168 bottles.

Provenance Jura Aged 8 Years refill hogshead, cask no. 11628, dist Jul 08, bott Feb 17 (87) n22 t22 f21 b22 Nuttier than a squirrel's jockstrap. 46%. nc ncf sc. 380 bottles.

Provenance Jura Aged 10 Years refill hogshead, cask no. 11353, dist Apr 06, bott Nov 16 (87.5) n22 t22 f22 b21.5 Great to see Jura at its classic age sans caramel. But it is also lacking on the oak front. Which means we have the malt in its most naked form and though still blushing in its new-make freshness, has body enough to maximise the barley and spices for a very enjoyable experience. Clean, salivating with some excellent muscovado sugars ensuring weight to the texture. 46%. nc ncf sc. 397 bottles.

⬥ **Provenance Jura Aged 10 Years** refill hogshead, cask no. 12033, dist Mar 07, bott Aug 17 (82) n19.5 t21 f20.5 b21 A little bit of extra oil softens the blows. Some decent sweet malt here and there. 46%. nc ncf sc. 375 bottles.

KILCHOMAN
Islay, 2005. Kilchoman Distillery Co. Working.

⬥ **Kilchoman 10 Years Old** cask no. 150/2007, dist 20 Jul 07, bott 11 Jun 18 db (96) n24 two-toned nose: sweeter grist notes dovetail with the dry, sooty phenols; t24 that is a delivery and a half: fabulous oils – quite unlike the Caol Ila style – which brilliantly capture the harmony of the smoke and sugars. The vanilla is also stunningly intense and sits somewhere between the two main character points; f23.5 with oils like this, you'd expect a long finish – and you get one. Deft vanilla still, but the peat, if anything, gathers in intensity and forms a gorgeous chocolate crust at the very finale; b24.5 has controlled the oils beautifully. Class in a glass. 56.5%. sc. 238 bottles. Bottled for The Whisky Shop.

⬥ **Kilchoman 10 Years Old 100% Islay** cask no. 84/2008, dist 6 Mar 08, bott 19 Mar 18 db (91) n23.5 vanilla dominant: the peat is relatively shy; t23 smokier on delivery, but the crisp Demerara sugars virtually crackle on the plate; f22 a light smoky farewell; the oak s not performing as you might hope; b22.5 such is the high class of Kilchomen, even an exceptionally good malt on the whisky stage is not quite up to the distillery's normal performance. Not a bad place to be... 53.2%. sc. 239 bottles. Bottled for Loch Fyne Whiskies.

◇ **Kilchoman 12 Years Old** bourbon cask, cask no. 36/2006, dist 4 May 06, bott 21 Jun 18 db (93.5) n23.5 a spattering of citrus over the peaty embers; t23.5 seriously sweet: the smoke takes a back seat to the sharp, salivating almost lemon sherbet eye-watering buzz on the palate: a big dose of vanilla at the mid-point; f23 the phenols begin to reconfigure, though not before some mocha has turned up; some late hickory accompanies the spice; b23.5 high grade malt taking a slightly different course from this distillery's normal style. 56.9%. sc. 228 bottles. Bottled for Loch Fyne Whiskies.

Kilchoman 100% Islay The 5th Edition db (95.5) n23.5 t24 f24 b24 100% stunning. 50%. nc ncf.

Kilchoman 100% Islay 7th Edition db (88) n22.5 t22.5 f21.5 b21.5 At times a lovely experience, and one showing some older ages than normal. But ultimately unlikely to go down in the annals of Kilchoman as one of their great vintages... Looks like this was taken from the casks right in the middle of the flavours not quite harmonising – it is possible the previous month they had and another two months on they might well have again: an unfortunately timed bottling. 50%.

Kilchoman Machir Bay bott 2015 db (94.5) n23 t24 f23.5 b24 A thudding, thumping dram hitting you like a Dave Mackay tackle. Big peat, perfectly representing a big malt. 50%. nc ncf.

◇ **Kilchoman Private Cask Release** bourbon cask, cask no. 431/2007, dist 13 Dec 07, bott 26 Feb 18 db (96.5) n24.5 when, like me, you have tasted and professionally analysed over a thousand whiskies in a matter of a few months, and then you taste six bad 'uns on the trot you begin to lose the will to live: nose this and suddenly life, this Bible, has a meaning again. This is a 20 minute nose. Thirty, easy. The layering of the peat is exemplary and seductive: how can you get a whisky this dry and still find pockets of sweetness to ensure balance...? Sublime...; t24 if you want to set up all the things you want to find in a heavily peated malt, this will still give you the run around, as it will tick every single box and create a few of its own. In broad terms, we have big smoke balanced with a ridiculously precise degree of ulmo honey and spicy vanilla; f24 the oils have been restrained but they have built up now for a grand finale, taking the malt into distant territories. A light liquorice note can be found which moves onto hickory and heather honey. Every note restrained and elegant; b24.5 someone fell on their feet when they bought this cask: holy crap, this is seriously good whisky! 57.2%. sc. Bottled exclusively for The Whisky Club.

◇ **Kilchoman PX Finish Cask Vatting** dist 2011/12, bott 20 Sept 17 db (86.5) n22 t22.5 f21.5 b20.5 A peat and sticky fruit soup. Some people, I know, will probably sell their home for a bottle of this. But to me, pleasant, especially on delivery, but ultimately just too much... of everything. 56.7%. Bottled for the Swedish Whisky Federation.

Kilchoman Sanaig bourbon & sherry casks, bott 2016 db (89.5) n23 full on smoke, slightly rounded down by the fruit; t22 a distinctly muzzled delivery: the peat clears its throat to make a statement when soft grape intervenes, so little is said until the middle ground is reached and an oily smokiness is announced; f22 slightly thin, despite the oils, and a little light grape accompanying the gentle smoke; b22.5 never quite seen a Kilchoman toe the line this way before... 46%. nc ncf.

KINCLAITH
Lowlands, 1957–1975. Closed. Dismantled.

Mo Òr Collection Kinclaith 1969 41 Years Old first fill bourbon hogshead, cask no. 301453A, dist 28 May 69, bott 29 Oct 10 (85.5) n22 t22 f20.5 b21. Hangs on gamely to the last vestiges of life, though the oak, without being overtly aggressive, is squeezing all the breath of out of it. 46%. nc ncf sc. Release No. 2. The Whisky Talker. 164 bottles.

KINGSBARNS
Lowland, 2014. Wemyss. Working.

Kingsbarns Spirit Drink bott code L 25 02 16 db (95) n23.5 t24 f23.5 b24 This is the new make spirit from the fledgling Lowlander, Kingsbarns. And whatever their cuts points and running speeds were for this: take note and abide by them! An exceptionally high quality cut which obviously benefits from the added transient richness of a new still but enjoys a sublime sweetness to both the barley and the late cocoa. How promising... 63.5%.

◇ **Kingsbarns 2 Year Old Spirit Drink** 1st fill ex-bourbon barrels db (94) n23 t23.5 f24 b23.5 Thought I'd bring up my 1,200th tasting note for the 2019 Whisky Bible with this maturing malt from Kingsbarns. It was an inspired choice. For although the youth is more than apparent – as it should be! – there is a surprising degree of complexity to this and balances out far better than most two year olds. For a start, the distillate was beautifully created with the cut points spot on, seemingly clean enough or the malt to flourish, but with a broadness o allow complexity to develop. Even on the nose a wonderful Cadbury's hazelnut and milk chocolate promises good things ahead and you are not remotely disappointed as the barley strikes up proudly before marzipan and mocha make their mark. Delicious! *62.8%. 1,800 bottles.*

KNOCKANDO
Speyside, 1898. Diageo. Working.

◇ **Knockando Aged 12 Years** bott code: L7229CM000 db **(82)** n20 t22.5 f19 b20.5 My dear, late friend and mentor Jim Milne was for a very long time J&B blender and for decades this malt came under his clever jurisdiction. It was Jim who persuaded me, over a quarter of a century ago now, to publish my views on whisky, something I felt I was underqualified to do. He vehemently disagreed, so I took his advice and the rest, as they say, is history. I knew Jim's work intimately, so I know he would not be happy with his beloved Knockando in this incarnation. His Knockando was dry, making the most of the interaction between bourbon cask and delicate malt. This is sweet and, worse still, sulphur tarnished by the sherry: I doubt he would ever let grape get this kind of grip, thus negating the distillery's fragile style. Some lovely moments here for sure. But just too fleeting. *43%.*

Knockando 1990 db **(83)** n21 t22 f20 b20. The most fruity Knockando I've come across with some attractive salty notes. Dry, but a little extra malty sweetness these days. *40%*

KNOCKDHU
Speyside, 1894. Inver House Distillers. Working.

AnCnoc 12 Year Old db **(94.5)** n24 t23 f23.5 b24.5 A more complete or confident Speyside-style malt you are unlikely to find. Shimmers with everything that is great about Scotch whisky... always a reliable dram, but this is stupendous. *40%*

AnCnoc 16 Years Old db **(91.5)** n22 sharp, pithy, salty, busy...; t23.5 those salts crash headlong into the taste buds and then give way to massive spice and barley; soft sugars and vanilla follow at a distance; f23 salted mocha and spice; b23 unquestionably the spiciest AnCnoc of all time. Has this distillery been moved to the coast..? *46%*

AnCnoc 18 Years Old db **(88.5)** n22.5 t23 f21 b22 Cleaner sherry at work here. But again, the contours of the malt have been flattened out badly. *46%. nc ncf.*

AnCnoc 22 Year Old db **(87)** n22 t21.5 f22 b21.5. Often a malt which blossoms before being a teenager, as does the fruits of Knockdhu; struggles to cope comfortably with the inevitable oakiness of old age. Here is such a case. *46%. Inverhouse Distillers.*

AnCnoc 24 Years Old db **(94)** n23 t24.5 f22.5 b24 Big, broad-shouldered malt which carries a lot of weight but hardly veers away from the massively fruity path. For sherry loving whisky drinkers everywhere... *46%. nc ncf.*

AnCnoc 26 Years Old Highland Selection db **(89)** n23 t22 f23 b21. There is a little flat moment between the middle and finish for which I have chipped off a point or two. That apart, superb. *48.2%*

AnCnoc 30 Years Old db **(85)** n21 t23 f19 b22. Seat-of-the-pants whisky that is just on the turn. Still has a twinkle in the eye, though. *49%*

AnCnoc 35 Years Old db **(86)** n21 t21 f22.5 b21.5. Tries to take the exotic fruit route to antiquity but headed off at the pass by a massive dollop of natural caramels. The slow burn on the spice is an unexpected extra treat, though. *43%*

AnCnoc 35 Years Old bourbon and sherry casks db **(88)** n22.5 t22 f21.5 b22. The usual big barley sheen has dulled with time here. Some attractive cocoa notes do compensate. *44.3%. nc ncf.*

AnCnoc 1975 bott 2014 db **(90)** n23.5 creaking, crumbling oak at every turn. Fortunately there's enough sugar at play – a blend of maple syrup and molasses – to see off any negative points. When some form of equality is established, the rich fruitcake comes out to play...; t23 all kinds of timber notes up front but the fruit gushes in quickly to form a lush cushion. Two year old Melton Hunt Cake with fully burned raisin; f21.5 just a little bit of awkward bitterness – and an odd furriness – joins the fruit; b22.5 if it showed any more signs of age, it'd need its own Zimmer frame. But the deep, fruity sugars are a superb restorative. *44.2%. nc ncf.*

An Cnoc 1993 db **(89)** n22 t21 f24 b22. Quite an odd one this. I have tasted it a couple of times with different samples and there is a variance. This one takes an oakier path and then invites the barley to do its stuff. Delicious, but underscores the deft touch of the standard 12-year-old. *46%*

AnCnoc 1994 db **(88.5)** n22.5 t22.5 f21.5 b22. Coasts through effortlessly, showing the odd flash of brilliance here and there. Just get the feeling that it never quite gets out of third gear... *46%. ncf.*

AnCnoc 1995 db **(84.5)** n21 t22 f20.5 b21. Very plump for a Knockdhu with caramel notes on a par with the citrus and burgeoning bourbon. Some barley juice escapes on delivery but the finish is peculiarly dry for the distillery. *46%*

AnCnoc 1999 db (95.5) n24 t24 f23.5 b24 I noticed as I was putting the bottle away that on their back label their description includes "Colour: soft, very aromatic with a hint of honey and lemon in the foreground" and "Nose: amber with a slight yellow hue." Which would make this malt pretty unique. But this is worth getting for far more than just the collectors' item typo: this is brilliant whisky – one of their best vintage malts for a very long time. In fact, one of their best ever bottlings...period.46%. nc ncf. WB15/160

AnCnoc 2001 bott Dec 15 db (92) n23.5 not sure I can get enough of those citrus notes..wow! t23.5 tell me, 'cos I can't decide: is it the malt or that citrus that is making me drown in my own saliva...? f22 at last the tannins get a word in, though still pretty muted as plenty of toffee makes for a chewy finish; b23 cruises effortlessly along like a 2001 Jag... 46%. nc ncf.

AnCnoc 2002 bott Mar 17, bott code: L17/089 R17/5104 IB db (86) n21.5 t23 f20.5 b21 Overall, it is enjoyable and well spiced, but a mushy, tangy, untidy finish shows up the failings of the odd cask used. This is a distillery whose spirit yearns for ex-bourbon so its stunning naked form can be worshipped, loved and salivated over. 46%.

AnCnoc Barrow 13.5 ppm phenols db (88) n22 t21 f23 b22 A quite peculiar Knockdhu. The usual subtle richness of texture is curiously absent. As are friendly sugars. The strange angles of the phenols fascinate, however. 46%. nc ncf. Exclusive to travel retail.

AnCnoc Blas db (67) n16 t18 f16 b17. Blast! Great chocolate. Shame about the sulphur.... 54%. nc ncf.

AnCnoc Black Hill Reserve db (81) n20 t22 f19 b20. The furriness threatened on the nose and realised at the finish does this great distillery no favours at all. 46%. nc ncf. Exclusive to travel retail.

AnCnoc Cutter 20.5 ppm phenols db (96.5) n24 t24 f24 b24.5 Brilliant! An adjective I am far more used to associating with anCnoc than some of the others I have had to use this year. The most Ardbeg-esque mainland malt I have ever encountered. 46%. nc ncf.

AnCnoc Flaughter 14.8 ppm phenols db (88.5) n23 t22 f21.5 b22 interesting to compare the relative heavy handedness of this against the Rutter. A lovely whisky this may be, but has nothing like the poise or balance. 46%. ncf nc. WB15/345

⬨ **AnCnoc Peatheart** batch no. 1, 40ppm, bott code: L17/301 R17/5394 db (91.5) n22 not what you'd expect from such a high dose of phenols: the oaky caramel appears to be out-performing the smoke; t23.5 much more like it...eventually. Again, a soft cream toffee kick off before the phenols begin to arrive in sizeable waves; vaguely salty and chalky, too; serious salivating tendencies as barley plays up hard; f23 classy finish: excellent understated oak at play and here it benefits from both non-filtration and non-colouring as the more intimate and complex late liquorice notes gel; a light spice works well with a light buttered toast – and smoke – finale; b23 won't be long before Peatheart becomes the peataholics' sweetheart. Curiously underperforming nose, but makes amends in style on the palate. 46%.

AnCnoc Peter Arkle Limited Edition db (87.5) n22.5 t22.5 f20.5 b22. A floral nose, with lavender and honeysuckle in abundance. Also offers dried orange peel. But the malt doesn't move on from there as one might hope, becoming just a little too sugary and caramel stodgy for the malt to do itself justice. All that said, a great dram to chew on for a few minutes! 46%. ncf nc. WB15/321

AnCnoc Rùdhan bott code: L16/273 R16/5391 db (94.5) n24 t23.5 f23.5 b24 Hard to imagine a mainland Scottish distillery producing a more complex, elegant and wholly ingratiating peated malt... What a gem this is! 46%.

AnCnoc Rutter 11 ppm phenols db (96.5) n24.5 t24.5 f23.5 b24 I remember vividly, at this great distillery's Centenary party exactly 20 years ago this summer, mentioning to the then distillery manager that I thought that the style of the malt produced at Knockdhu was perfectly geared to make a lightly malted peat along the lines of its neighbour, Ardmore. Only for a few weeks of the year I ventured. I'm pretty certain this malt was not a result of that observation, but it is heartening to see that my instincts were right: it's a sensation! 46%. ncf nc. WB15/320

LADYBURN

Lowlands, 1966–2000. William Grant & Sons. Closed.

Mo Òr Collection Rare Ayrshire 1974 36 Years Old first fill bourbon barrel, cask no. 2608, dist 10 May 74, bott 1 Nov 11 (89.5) n22 t23.5 f22 b22.5. I had a feeling it'd be this distillery when I saw the title on the label... it couldn't be much else! Fascinating to think that I was in final countdown for my 'O' levels when this was made. It appears to have dealt with the passing years better than I have. Even so, I had not been prepared for this. For years during the very early 1990s Grant's blender David Stewart sent me samples of this stuff and it was, to put it mildly, not great. Some were the oakiest malt I ever tasted in my life. And, to compound matters further, the distillery's own bottling was truly awful. But this cask has re-written history. 46%. nc ncf sc. Release No. 4. The Whisky Talker. 261 bottles.

LAGAVULIN
Islay, 1816. Diageo. Working.

Lagavulin Aged 8 Years bott code: L7285CM013 db (95.5) n25 it is as though the whisky has sat in a rock pool for the last eight years, breathing in the spume of the waves, absorbing the brine and ozone. Youthful citrus tones and, strangely, grated chocolate, too. And there is, of course, the peat.... It is, quite literally, faultless...; t23.5 just as it should for its tender years, the gristy sugars are displayed first and come through with a vivacious elegance. The oak-fuelled vanilla is never more than delicate, the smoke simply a caress rather than a blast; f23 now the spices tingle and play while the grist still has energy and sugar enough to keep the balance; b24.5 having gone from the colouring-spoiled Cardhu to this chardonnay-hued Lagavulin in all its bourbon cask nakedness, you have to wonder: why don't they do this for all their whiskies. This was the age I first tasted Lagavulin possibly the best part of 40 years ago. It was love at first flight, and my passions – with the whisky in this beautifully natural form, though not as heavily peated now as then – have not been remotely doused. 48%.

Lagavulin 12 Year Old refill American oak casks db (95.5) n23.5 t24 f24 b24 at the age I cut my Lagavulin teeth on, long before the 16-year-old was even the twinkle in a blender's eye. Not as peaty as then, to be honest. But for subtlety, this doesn't compare unfavourably... 48.8%. Diageo Special Releases 2015.

Lagavulin 12 Years Old db (96) n24 t24 f23.5 b24.5 Just so beautifully made and matured and such a faultless exhibition of weight maximisation from a minimalist impact. Brilliant! 57.7%. Diageo Special Releases 2016.

Lagavulin Aged 12 Years bott 2017, bott code: L7089CM000 db (94) n23.5 ashy dry phenols: the still warm embers of the peat fire from the night before; chicory preambles a low level degree of sweetness; t23.5 a sublime gristy sweetness paves the way for the big peat fanfare. Medium weight and oils means it's the phenols that do the flying, leaving a vapour trail of vanilla; a delicate molasses note adds extra weight; f23 the smoke is subdued as the vanilla mops up the finish; b24 when I first tasted Lagavulin at this age, the phenol levels were around the 50ppm mark and not the present day 35. That meant the finish offered just a little extra Islay. Even so, I challenge you not to adore this. 56.5%.

Lagavulin 12 Year Old refill American oak hogsheads db (96) n24.5 the rise of the oak has rendered this malt not quite as intricately breezy as the 8-year-old but the complex layering of the phenols against the vanilla and distant marmalade ensure something very special indeed; t24 as mouth feels go, this is just about perfect. Neither too light, nor too heavy; oily but not too oily; smoky but not so all-consuming as to not allow the marshmallow sweetness to glide into view... And so salivating, too, with the smoke still on the end of some sublime grist and sugars ranging from melt-in-the-mouth icing to maple syrup: glorious...; f23.5 this is the point where lesser whiskies normally reveal the weakness of a slight bitterness. Not here...; b24 I think whisky like this was invented by the whisky gods to be experienced at this full strength. Even people who do not regard themselves as peat lovers are likely to be seduced by this one. Talk about controlled power.... 56.5%. Diageo Special Releases 2017.

Lagavulin 16 Years Old db (95) n24 t24 f23 b24 Although i have enjoyed this whisky countless times socially, it is the first time for a while I have dragged it into the Tasting Room for professional analysis for the Bible. If anyone has noticed a slight change in Lagavulin, they would be right. The peat remains profound but much more delicate than before, while the oils appear to have receded. A different shape and weight dispersal for sure. But the sky-high quality remains just the same. 43%

Dramfool Avian Gull 8 Year Old bourbon cask (95.5) n24 t23.5 f24 b24 If Diageo don't bring out an 8-year-old Lagavulin exclusive bourbon cask after this, they must be mad... 59.2%. sc.

Dramfool 10 Avian Gull Too 9 Years Old 1st fill Oloroso Octave finish (91) n22.5 a heavyweight, as to be expected. But the grape is proportionate to the smoke, so there is structure and layering to enjoy; t23 fat, flavoursome and fulsome. Huge delivery, benefitting from its relative youth. Once the eyes stop watering, burnt fruitcake on delivery, though the grape soon wanders off leaving the phenols a clear but dry and spicy run; f22.5 now the burnt fruit cake has smoke coming from it...; b23 no detectable sulphur (hurrah!) and definitely a better and more measured version of this too often OTT style of malt. I admit: I thoroughly enjoyed this classy malt. 57.9%. nc ncf. 66 bottles.

Gleann Mor Lagavulin dist 08 May 06 (95) n24 t24 f23 b24 A near faultless bottling. If only we could see Lagavulin like this more often: Diageo are missing a trick... 58.6%.

The Whisky Barrel Isle of Islay 10 Year Old refill hogshead, cask no. 200703, dist 17 Oct 07, bott Feb 18 (95.5) n24 fabulous how a little glistening oil turns the peat soot into an aroma that outwardly seems dry yet offers something a little more rounded; t24 brings you to your knees in sheer delight and wonder: that sheen on the nose translates into a glorious celebration of controlled peaty enormity – this appears closer to its old 50ppm, than the present day 35. The sugars and oils are magnificent checks and balances on the smoke, keeping it grounded and ensuring a degree of (young-ish) maltiness gets into the act; f23.5 such is the intensity of the delivery and aftermath, the finish seems unusually subdued by comparison. A generally enjoyable chocolate mint fade, siting with the smoke very comfortably; b24 if this is Lagavulin, then this is how it should be commercially bottled: 100% ex-bourbon at full strength and ten years old. It is like being given the elixir of life... 57.1%. sc. 285 bottles.

LAPHROAIG
Islay, 1815. Beam Suntory. Working.

Laphroaig 10 Years Old db (90) n24 t23 f20.5 b22.5 Has reverted back slightly towards a heavier style in more recent bottling, though I would like to see that old oomph at the very death. Even so, this is, indisputably, a classic whisky. The favourite of Prince Charles apparently: he will make a wise king... 40%

◇ **Laphroaig 10 Year Old** bott code: L80099MB1 db (94) n23.5 t23.5 f23.5 b24 An essay in voluptuousness. The oils speak volumes here, gathering the two-toned phenols and landing them in all corners of the palate and ensuring they stick there. The iodine kick off on the nose is like a salty trademark, the balance between the sootier phenols and jucier Demera notes a joy to experience. The finish is not so much enourmous as controlled and long, with a sublime degree of mocha moving in for the last blissful moments. Glorious, still after all these years... 40%.

Laphroaig 10 Years Old Original Cask Strength db (92) n22 t24 f23 b23 Caramel apart, this is much truer to form than one or two or more recent bottlings, aided by the fresh, gristy sweetness and explosive spices. Wonderful! 55.7%

◇ **Laphroaig 12 Year Old 2005** bott 2017 db (91.5) n21.5 t23.5 f23 b23.5 Here we go: one of the exceptions in whisky that proves the rule. I have long wailed about the usage of PX cask and peaty malt together. And from the nose, you think your case will be won again, for here is another example of one giant nullifying another: both the smoke and fruit cancelling the other out. Yet, confound it, the delivery shows signs of proving me wrong and the finish continues in the same fashion. For once a PX cask is allowing the peat to breath and sing. And what's more itself kick up a juicy encore. Beyond the nose a PX and smoky giant that walks tall. Who would have thought...? 55.3%. Selected for CWS.

Laphroaig Aged 15 Years db (79) n20 t20 f19 b20. A hugely disappointing, lacklustre dram that is oily and woefully short on complexity. Not what one comes to expect either from this distillery or age. 43%

Laphroaig 18 Years Old db (94) n24 t23.5 f23 b23.5 This is Laphroaig's replacement to the woefully inadequate and gutless 15-year-old. And talk about taking a giant step in the right direction. Absolutely brimming with character and panache, from the first molecules escaping the bottle as you pour to the very final ember dying on the middle of your tongue. 48%

Laphroaig Aged 25 Years db (94) n23 t24 f23.5 b23.5 Like the 27-y-o, an Islay which doesn't suffer for sherry involvement. Very different from a standard, bourbon barrel-aged Laphroaig with much of the usually complexity reined in, though its development is first class. This one's all about effect - and it works a treat! 40%

◇ **Laphroaig Aged 27 Years** dist Oct 88 to Nov 89, bott Mar 17, bott code: L7062VB1 db (96.5) n24.5 such a remarkable balance between smoke and age. Which plays the biggest part? The peat? The lime? The ginger? The butterscotch? The mint? Blessed if I know. And I'm certain you won't have a clue, either, no matter how long you take to decide...; t24 you hope for a silky delivery –and that's exactly what you get. That despite the oak making a bigger noise on delivery than it ever dares on the nose. The smoke moves in gently to keep the balance and help inject some liquorice and thin Manuka honey so relaxed sugars massage the tannins; f23.5 long, of course; the oak now more than content to rumble along with its sugary and smoky guard of honour; b24.5 the 27 passing years and the added interference of fresh ex-bourbon barrels and quarter casks has taken its toll on the potency of the peat. Instead of Laphroaig pulsing with its renowned style of sea-soaked phenols, we are now faced with a dram which is more than content to allow age and gentility to be the guiding hand; so now less febrile and more cerebral. Such an honour to taste whiskies of this extraordinary yet understated magnitude. I can think of no other presently available whisky which so eloquently demonstrates that you don't have to stand a spoon up in in the peat for the phenols to have such a vital input. 41.7%. ncf.

Laphroaig Aged 30 Years db (94) n24 t23 f23 b24. The best Laphroaig of all time? Nope, because the 40-y-o is perhaps better still... just. However, Laphroaig of this subtlety and charm gives even the very finest Ardbeg a run for its money. A sheer treat that should be bottled at greater strength. 43%

Laphroaig Aged 40 Years db (94) n23 t24 f23 b24. Mind-blowing. A malt that defies all logic and theory to be in this kind of shape at such age. The Jane Fonda of Islay whisky. 43%

Laphroaig The 1815 Legacy Edition bott code: L7059VB1 2070 db (92.5) n24 t24 f21 b23.5 a sherry butt away from one of the best new whiskies of the year. 48%. *Travel Retail Exclusive.*

Laphroaig Au Cuan Mòr db (95) n24 t24 f23 b24 You don't need to squint at the back label to be told that first fill bourbon barrels are at work here: this is where Kentucky, Jerez and Islay merges with breath-taking ease and harmony. 48%. *Travel retail exclusive.*

◈ **Laphroaig Brodir Port Wood Finish** bott code: L6157MB1 db (91.5) n24 probably one of the most old-fashioned Islay warehouse aromas I have ever encountered: that incomparable mix of smoke, oak and grape hanging thickly in a moist, salty air...; t22 the usual gristy sugars have been silenced by the intense, moody fruit; f23 much better balance late on as a little liquorice and treacle joins the clouds of phenols to ensure complexity; b22.5 this is a big Laphroaig at its most brooding and taciturn. Not for when you are at your most frivolous. 48%.

Laphroaig Four Oak bott code: L6327VB1 2359 db (88) n22 t22.5 f21.5 b22 Attractive, but the smoke seems a little in awe of the oak as it is unusually quiet. 40%. *Travel Retail Exclusive.*

Laphroaig Lore db (94) n23.5 t24 f23 b23.5 Seeing how much I adore this distillery – and treasure my near 40 years of tasting its exceptional malt and visiting its astonishing home – I left this to become my 750th new whisky for the 2016 Whisky Bible. "Our richest expression ever" the label promised. It isn't. Big, fat and chunky? Tick. Bounding with phenols? Yep. Enjoyable? Aye! Richest expression ever. Nah. Not quite. Still, a friendly beast worth cuddling up with. And, whatever they say on the label, this is a stunner! 48%. ncf.

◈ **Laphroaig Lore** bott code: L7229VB1 db (96) n23.5 a friendly, complex and stylish aroma making the best use of a varied set of sugar traits, the most telling being a hickory note entirely in tune with the gentle phenols; t24 the delivery is friendlier still and once more the hickory is leading the way. Softly oiled so there is not a squeak to be heard as this incredibly well rounded Islay moves seamlessly around the palate, one moment displaying its smokier ego, then an improbable dexterity with the dark sugars; f24 incredible. In the time I have written this, I have watched Venus setting across my south-western skyline, dropping left to right between the outline of two silhouetted trees. Such is the complexity of this finish, it has taken much of that time to try and find words to describe something uniquely beyond description. Suffice to say, Venus has now vanished: the finish, with its myriad oscillating levels of smoke, sweetness and oak tones, is still with me...; b24.5 Laphroaig how I've never quite seen it before – and we are talking some 40 years of intimately studying this malt: truly a lore into itself... 48%.

Laphroaig PX Cask bourbon, quarter and Pedro Ximenez casks db (96) n23.5 t24.5 f24 b24. I get the feeling that this is a breathtaking success despite the inclusion of Pedro Ximenez casks. This ultra sweet wine is often paired with smoky malt, often with disastrous consequences. Here it has worked, but only because the PX has been controlled itself by absolutely outstanding oak. And the ability of the smoke to take on several roles and personas simultaneously. A quite beautiful whisky and unquestionably one of the great malts of the year...in spite of itself. 48%. *Travel Retail exclusive.*

Laphroaig Quarter Cask db (96) n23 t24 f24 b25 A great distillery back to its awesome, if a little sweet, self. Layer upon layer of sexed-up peatiness. The previous bottling just needed a little extra complexity on the nose for this to hit mega malt status. Now it has been achieved... 48%

Laphroaig Select db (89) n22 t22 f23 b22 Missed a trick by not being unchillfiltered at 46%. An après-taste squint at the back label revealed some virgin oak casks had been used here, which explains much! 40%. WB15/117

Laphroaig Triple Wood ex-bourbon, quarter and European oak casks db (86) n21 t21.5 f21.5 b21. A pleasing and formidable dram. But one where the peat takes perhaps just too much of a back seat. Or, rather, is somewhat neutralised to the point of directional loss. The sugars, driven home by the heavy weight of oak, help give the whisky a gloss almost unrecognisable to this distillery. Even so, an attractive whisky in many ways. 48%. ncf.

◈ **The Exclusive Malts Laphroaig Aged 6 Years** refill sherry hogshead, cask no. 195, dist 05 May 11 (87) n21.5 t22 f22 b21.5 Sherry and peat are seldom comfortable bedfellows and here we can see, despite all the phenolic beating of chests and the thumping alcohol present, why. The complexity is reduced a little by the light fruit and the peat cancelling each other out. There is no denying the brilliance of the spice, though, or the attractiveness of the oils and meandering dark sugars. Enjoyable for sure, but you get the feeling that had the age been doubled so, too, would the complexity. 58.7%. nc ncf sc. 237 bottles. Bottled by the Creative Whisky Co.

The First Editions Laphroaig Aged 16 Years 2000 refill butt, cask no. 13277, bott 2017 (81) n21 t23 f18 b19 A very different animal to its sister cask 12276. There a tightness on the nose suggests there may be some sherry cask interference further down the line, which duly occurs. But not after a sensational phenolic blast off involving Fisherman's Friends and liquorice. 58.1%. nc ncf sc. 306 bottles.

Old Malt Cask Laphroaig Aged 12 Years refill hogshead, cask no. 13433, dist Sept 04, bott Feb 17 (92) n23.5 t24 f21.5 b23 Not perfect: enough faults to underline it was made by man. But seriously big! 50%. nc ncf sc. 324 bottles.

◇ **Old Malt Cask Laphroaig Aged 12 Years** refill hogshead, cask no. 14099, dist Sept 04, bott Aug 17 (93) n24 billowing peat reek. Clean, uncomplicated but gets the coastal peat element absolutely bang on; t23 simple sweet barley sub strata, but the peat and light oils filling the mouth with a satisfying, timeless Islay quality; f22.5 dry with the phenols sticking to the oak shavings; b23.5 old school Laphroaig: the kind of malt which keeps the Peatheads very happy, indeed...and with very good reason. Impressive. 50%. nc ncf sc. 339 bottles.

Old Malt Cask Laphroaig Aged 16 Years refill butt, cask no. 13276, dist Apr 00, bott Feb 17 (93) n23 t23.5 f23 b23.5 A refill butt that's a clean as a whistle. Just as well, for this is superb! 50%. nc ncf sc. 359 bottles.

◇ **Old Malt Cask Laphroaig Aged 16 Years** refill butt, cask no. 13741, dist Feb 01, bott Apr 17 (89) n23 a real salty and phenolic beast fully accentuating a coastal character; t22 the usual sweetness on delivery arrives but vanishes more quickly than normal. Dry and exceptionally dusty on the palate; f22 good smoke fade, but just a little too dull on the sugar front; b22 big on the peat but closes up just a little too early for greatness. 50%. nc ncf sc. 742 bottles.

◇ **Old Particular Laphroaig 18 Years Old** refill hogshead, cask no. 11634, dist Dec 98, bott Mar 17 (95) n24 a wonderful example of when complex, aged oak notes walk hand-in-hand with fading phenols: exceptional complexity and weight with a light salt sprinkle to rouse the tones into a higher plane; t23.5 so sweet: there are non-specific sugars on the nose. But here it manifests itself in a lightly smoked ulmo honey sparring playfully with a spiciness which appears to be induced by both the phenols and the tannin; f23.5 an exhibition of spicy smoke of the highest order; b24 glorious! 48.4%. nc ncf sc. 262 bottles.

Provenance Laphroaig Aged 10 Years refill hogshead, cask no. 11333, dist Nov 05, bott Aug 16 (87) n21.5 t22 f21.5 b22 Seriously sooty and just a little on the bitter side. Patchy, though not without some big smoky moments. 46%. nc ncf sc. 403 bottles.

Provenance Laphroaig Aged 12 Years refill hogshead, cask no. 11686, dist Sept 04, bott Feb 17 (87.5) n22 t22 f22 b21.5 Big and gristy. The spices can't make their mind up whether to attack or sit back. The cask offers little and the all-round picture seems blurred and out of focus. Still a treat of peataholics, though... 46%. nc ncf sc. 350 bottles.

Scotch Malt Whisky Society Cask 29.191 16 Year Old refill ex-bourbon barrel, dist 1 Jul 99 (96) n24.5 t24 f23 b24.5 A 16-year-old Laphroaig – interesting to compare with a Lagavulin...! Though not many single casks will outpoint this true classic: indeed, it is nigh impossible to extract more from a single barrel. 59%. 234 bottles.

◇ **Scotch Malt Whisky Society Cask 29.232 18 Year Old** refill ex-bourbon barrel, dist 11 Nov 98 (92) n23.5 one of those noses which stops you in your tracks: smoky, of course, spicy, yes...everything in order. But it is the gentle meeting of the smoke with the oak which works so well. And the gentlest squeeze of lemon to lighten things a little.. and is that banana...? t23 silky soft oils, almost out of the Caol Ila textbook, plants the smoke from where it can hardly move. Bourbon chocolate cream biscuits and spices do the rest..; f22.5 fades with little desire to go. A tad bitter at the death, but the smoked mallows before you get there are a joy; b23 Laphroaig being Laphroaig. 59.1%. sc.

◇ **Scotch Malt Whisky Society Cask 29.237 18 Year Old** refill ex-bourbon barrel, dist 11 Nov 98 (84.5) n22.5 t22 f19 b21 The shyness of the nose does at least give some warning of the fiery phenols to follow. The cask has not done the spirit justice, resulting in a hot and unstructured malt with a very dim finish. 60.9%. sc.

That Boutique-y Whisky Company Laphroaig 12 Year Old batch 1 (72.5) n16 t21 f17.7 b18 Is the modern parlance "whisky fail"? 52.4%. 421 bottles.

LINKWOOD
Speyside, 1820. Diageo. Working.

Linkwood 12 Years Old db (94.5) n23.5 t24 f23 b24 Possibly the most improved distillery bottling in recent times. Having gone through a period of dreadful casks, it appears to have come through to the other side very much on top and close to how some of us remember it a quarter of a century ago. Sublime malt: one of the most glittering gems in the Diageo crown. 43%

Linkwood Aged 37 Years dist 1978 db (87.5) n23 t22 f21 b21.5 This is old whisky from a distillery rarely exposed to this kind of antiquity. Rather, this would end up giving succour to a high class blend. The lightness of the spirit means that some of its faults a little too clearly exposed here, especially the bitterness at the death. But there would have to be something wrong with you not to savour the blood orange and marmalade thread which ensures the oak doesn't get all its own way. 50.3%. 6,114 bottles. Diageo Special Releases 2016.

Gordon & MacPhail Distillery Label Linkwood 15 Year Old (83) n20 t23 f19 b21 Lots of big, biscuity malt. But a bitterness on the nose and finish is out of keeping with the rich delivery. 43%.

◇ **Gordon & MacPhail Private Collection Linkwood 1956** first fill sherry hogshead, cask no. 20, bott 23 Aug 17 (90.5) n23.5 changes its story, weight and tones many times over 60 minutes. From fruity, still moderately fresh but with huge, unambiguous olororo notes when first poured to a far more age-induced burnt toast and marmalade leviathan further down the oxidisation road. Throughout this time scale a plethora of other notes rise and fall, reappear and disappear again many, unsurprisingly, involving hickory and mocha...; t23 fresh fruit and muscovado sugars when tasted early on but infinitely more gravitas as it oxidises and warms; f22 tires quite dramatically and bitters significantly at the end, irrespective of where in the glass evolution process the whisky is; late on, though, the bitter cocoa is quite astonishing, if not that easy to take though, once you become accustomed, is slightly delicious; b22 always heart-warming to come across a new bottling of a whisky older than me: once quite a common occurrence but in recent years an increasingly and depressingly rare event. Well this is the only one; and also my 1,250th whisky for the 2019 Bible. And which of us has aged better...? I'll let you decide... 49.4%. sc.

Gordon & MacPhail Rare Vintage Linkwood 1954 (87) n22 t21 f22.5 b21.5 Still hangs on in there, a bit on its last legs....but alive and kicking. Oak – lashings of tannin – is there by the small copse load. Sawdust and pencil shaving for all. But the last pulses of grape offer enough fruit and succour – and succulence – to get the malt through to the end without being further scathed. Some good liquorice and Manuka honey further helps the cause. 40%.

Gordon & MacPhail Rare Vintage Linkwood 1972 (90.5) n22.5 t22 f23 b23 A beautiful malt which takes its time to tame the big age statement but then does so with surprising ease... 43%.

Gordon & MacPhail Rare Vintage Linkwood 1973 (93) n23.5 t23 f23.5 b23 Don't know about late night dram: one for first thing in the morning instead of your coffee... 43%.

Hepburn's Choice Linkwood 10 Years Old refill hogshead, dist 2006, bott 2017 (87.5) n21.5 t22.5 f21.5 b22 The very limited shaping from oak means this is another malt where the barley has an almost disproportionate say. Fortunately, the little oak present is for the good and just gives a slight vanilla and spiced aspect to the grist. Dries attractively. 46%. nc ncf sc. 382 bottles.

◇ **Hepburn's Choice Linkwood 10 Years Old** refill hogshead, dist 2006, bott 2017 (89) n22 a lovely marriage of gristy malt and apple blossom; t23 almost too delicate for this world: the gentle malt fractures, then dissolves on the palate, a Love Heart candy fizz follows through; f22 drier as the butterscotch tart proves crusty; b22 delightfully simple. 46%. nc ncf sc. 372 bottles.

◇ **Kingsbury Gold Linkwood 25 Years Old** sherry hogshead, cask no. 10434, dist 1991 (94.5) n23.5 spiced grape. Dark cherry at play, also – indeed, not unlike some European cherry brandy; t24 still the cherry theme persists, even widens. So silky on the palate, the malt also finding a clean voice which becomes increasingly loud. The age begins to reveal itself at the midpoint as toasty tannins emerge; f23 satisfyingly spicy; ridiculously malty, too; b24 well played Kingsbury: you have again managed to find a Speyside malt matured in sherry but without a hint of sulphur. That really does take some doing these days. Linkwood in sherry – or should that be cherry? - as it should be. 54.1%. 229 bottles.

Old Malt Cask Linkwood Aged 19 Years refill hogshead, cask no. 13269, dist Jun 97, bott Jan 17 (91.5) n22.5 t23.5 f22.5 b23 The lovey citrus sub-plot enthrals. 50%. nc ncf sc. 303 bottles.

◇ **Old Malt Cask Linkwood Aged 20 Years** refill hogshead, cask no. 14098, dist Jun 97, bott Aug 17 (90) n22.5 confident, green malt despite the age just blasting the nose with grass and citrus; t23 just a green note on delivery, the barley in full salivation mode aided by the most delicate of oils. Oak doesn't wait too long before entering with a little dry vanilla; f22 green olive; b22.5 when working on an 18- or 21-year-old blend, this is the type of malt blenders get pretty excited about: a sample which offers a vivid richness to the malt make up and punching the barley through on both nose and delivery. 50%. nc ncf sc. 297 bottles.

◇ **Old Particular Linkwood 20 Years Old** refill hogshead, cask no. 12036, dist Jun 97, bott Aug 17 (94) n23 dry, sophisticated green olive and vanilla with barley trace; t23.5 a surprising injection of grassy barley fused with light cocoa and a slow acceleration of spice; f23.5 complex, long and more of the same; b24 real understated class. 51.5%. nc ncf sc. 326 bottles.

Old Particular Linkwood 21 Years Old refill hogshead, cask no. 11599, dist Jun 95, bott Mar 17 (92) n22.5 t23 f23.5 b23 Now that is how you want a 21-year-old Linkwood to taste...!! 51.5%. nc ncf sc. 234 bottles.

Scyfion Linkwood Troyanda Zakapattya Wine Cask Finish 19 Years Old (88.5) n22.5 t23 f21 b22 Fascinating: multi-layered, though doesn't work on all fronts. But enough major plusses to make for a pleasing experience. 46%.

Scotch Malt Whisky Society Cask 39.132 15 Year Old virgin heavy toast medium char oak butt, dist 1 Jun 00 (87) n21.5 t23 f21 b21.5 An up and down malt with a massive variance in the way in which it conducts itself. Many people will be bored by the single-minded aspect of the intense cream toffee which dominates the late middle and finish. But that is to overlook the aftermath of the delivery which peaks dramatically with an infusion of spice and salivating barley. Even then the toffee is well represented. *58.6%*.

⬦ **Scotch Malt Whisky Society Cask 39.166 27 Year Old** (92.5) n23 t23.5 f23 b23 From the nose you'd be expecting a spiced up, oaky chap with a little bit of the devil. Instead you get a well-constructed, lush, chewy and beautifully paced malt with little of the spice so evident on the aroma until the very measured end. So much natural caramel at work here, too, sitting very comfortably with the fruit to produce a chewy fruit toffee candy effect. *56.6%. sc. Bottled for Whisky L! & Fine Spirits Show.*

That Boutique-y Whisky Company Linkwood 26 Year Old batch 3 (95.5) n24 t24 f23.5 b24 Old school Linkwood at its most intense and effervescent. Brilliant. *52.3%. 54 bottles.*

⬦ **Whisky Illuminati Linkwood 19 Year Old** American oak hogshead, cask no. 10926, dist 1998 (88.5) n21.5 slightly uncomfortable: even after all this time the oak and barley have problems in finding common ground; just a little too grassy for its own good; t22.5 ah...that's more like it! Big, salivating and very clean barley hit: indeed, the malt is huge – something of the Glen Morays about this...; f22 gutters with a malty flicker; b22.5 I could wax lyrical about this Malt Fest. Enjoy! *58.5%. sc. 269 bottles. Candlelight Series.*

LITTLEMILL
Lowland, 1772. Loch Lomond Distillers. Demolished.

Littlemill 21 Year Old 2nd Release bourbon cask db (87) n22 t21.5 f21.5 b22. So thin you expect it to fragment into a zillion pieces on the palate. But the improvement on this as a new make almost defies belief. The sugars are crisp enough to shatter on your teeth, the malt is stone hard and fractured and, on the finish, does show some definite charm before showing its less attractive teeth....and its roots... Overall, though, more than enjoyable. *47%. ncf.*

Littlemill 25 Year Old db (92.5) n22 t24 f23 b23.5 Another example of a malt which was practically undrinkable in its fiery, punkish youth but that is now a reformed, gentle character in older age. *52%*

Littlemill 1964 db (82) n21 t20 f21 b20. A soft-natured, bourbony chap that shows little of the manic tendencies that made this one of Scotland's most-feared malts. Talk about mellowing with age... *40%*

⬦ **Littlemill 2017 Private Cellar 27 Year Old** db (93) n23 ginger and allspice dance with the malt and pepper tannins; no shortage of caramel, either; t23.5 reformed bad boy now kisses the palate where once it would rip with deadly talons. The usual fire is now a gorgeous spice attached to the glassy manuka and heather honeys. Then, amazingly, like the sun appearing from behind dramatic cloud, arrives the malt...; f23 a salty edge to the finale, though the oaky sugars refuse to relinquish control; b23.5 how ironic and sad that the last casks of what were unloved – and unusable - firewater when distilled have now, after nearly three decades, calmed into a malt which is the matured embodiment of grace and finesse. *51.3%.*

Glen Fahrn Airline Nr. 16 Littlemill 23 Year Old cask no. 16215, dist 1989 (95) n23.5 t24.5 f23.5 b24 Another Littlemill that has not only passed the test of time but has a Masters degree... And a must have for those with a penchant for sado-erotic whisky... *52.9%. sc.*

Gordon & MacPhail Rare Old Littlemill 1991 (87) n21 t22.5 f21.5 b22 This is a very odd whisky. Make no mistake: it has its fair share of deliciousness. But its make up means it is so hard to relax to as the pages and chapters of its story on the palate fly past. There is, for instance, a strange fruitiness to this of a style I can't quite pinpoint. Not from the sugars, for sure. A kind of washed out lime. Then there are the big malt notes, enormous and seriously delicious. But just as one is about mark highly, in comes a secondary flavour wave of bitter, unkempt tannin...and malt. But from where...? An enjoyable conundrum. *46%.*

Hunter Laing's Old & Rare Littlemill Aged 27 Years refill hogshead, dist Nov 88, bott Apr 16 (95) n23 t24 f23.5 b24.5 Always intriguing to see how one of Scotland's most singular former late distilleries is faring as its stocks around the warehouses begin to thin. And it gladdens my heart to say that this cask is of rare good quality: indeed, it is absolutely delicious – not something that could be said of the spirit when the near uncontrollable stills remained in use a generation ago. Unquestionably one of the greatest Littlemills ever made available to the public: perhaps the surprise turn of the Whisky Bible 2018. Only 93 bottles, eh? Better get one, then... *573%.*

LOCH LOMOND
Highlands (Southwestern), 1966. Loch Lomond Distillers. Working.

Loch Lomond Aged 12 Years db (93.5) n22.5 a triangular battle between spices, malt and an almost coppery-metallic fruitiness; t23.5 so succulent! Not sure if the distiller at the time was playing about with some high propane yeast which just explodes with fruit, but there is a richness to this malt which really does deserve applause; f23.5 good grief! I've been through some Loch Lomond casks over the years but not sure where they dug these up from. Never before seen spice quite like it, or such a sublime balance with the fruity malt. And when I say fruit, please don't think grape..; **b24** great to see they now have the stocks to allow this malt to really flex its muscles... *46%. ncf.*

Loch Lomond 14 Year Old Peated bourbon cask db (83) **n21 t21.5 f20.5 b20**. Lomond can do a lot, lot better than this. Huge malts but entirely out of sync and never comfortable with the oils present. This isn't the Loch Lomond I know and love. *46% nc ncf.*

◇ **Loch Lomond 15 Year Old** db (87.5) **n21.5 t22 f22 b22** Spends a lot of its time waving its malty flag. But a slight tartness on both nose and on palate means it never quite settles into a comfortable narrative *46%.*

Loch Lomond Aged 18 Years db (89.5) **n22 t23 f22.5 b22.5** There is always something slightly irresistible when you come across a single malt where the peat beats a gentle rhythm rather than its own chest... *46%. ncf.*

Loch Lomond 21 Years Old db (89.5) **n22.5 t23 f22 b22**. A little while since I last tasted this, and pretty close to exactly how I remember it. Seems to revel in its own enormity! *43%*

◇ **Loch Lomond The Open Special Edition** db (80) **n20 t21 f19 b20** Straight into the rough. *46%.*

◇ **Loch Lomond The Open 18 Year Old Course Collection Carnoustie 1999** db (92) **n23** superb mix of barley and Love Heart-oaky tannin; **t23.5** two-toned delivery: firm and salivating while soft and soothing. Still the malt calls the shots **f22** just a little spicy and fuzzy, dropping a shot or two; **b23.5** decided to wait until the 2018 Open at Carnoustie was in full swing before checking to see if this is up to par. Well, it is beyond that: a true double birdie as rarely is Loch Lomond this clean and malt rich. Would grace any 19th hole... *47.2%.*

Loch Lomond Organic 12 Year Old bourbon cask db (83.5) **n19 t20 f23 b21.5**. A malty beast. But in some respects has more in common with a German still than a traditional pot. Definite traces of feint. *48%. nc ncf.*

◇ **Loch Lomond Organic Aged 17 Years** bott code: L2 120 18 db (96.5) **n24** about as close a single malt Scotch gets to becoming a bourbon: the natural caramels, red liquorice, mild hickory meander and murmur beautifully, never wanting to out point the beautifully clean and intense malt; the spices come in with just the right pitch; **t24.5** where do you find fault...? Not with the mouthfeel, which generates just enough oils to ensure that the flavours not only radiate to maximum effect but hang around for maximum time; not with the pace of flavour development, which is patient and allows all strata from Demerara sugar tannins through varying forms of malt, molasses and manuka honey to become sexposed and explored; not with the balance; **f23.5** just more of the same, only at half intensity and pace; **b24.5** organic...? Orgasmic, more like! A dram which will win the hearts, minds and souls of both bourbon and scotch whisky lovers. In fact, if you don't like this, whatever the cut of your jib, you might as well give up now. *54.9%. nc ncf.*

Loch Lomond Original bourbon casks db (81.5) **n20 t21 f20 b20.5**. Hmmm. Surprisingly feinty, though the really wide cut does ensure a huge number of flavours. A distinctly German style to this. *40%*

Glengarry 12 Year Old db (92.5) **n22.5 t23.5 f23 b23.5** Probably the most intense malt on the market today. Astonishing. And stunning. *46%. ncf.*

◇ **Inchmoan Aged 10 Years Peated** bott code: L2 106 18 db (83) **n20 t21.5 f20.5 b21** Living, as I do, in the country, I know a cattle byre when I nose one. And here it is most certainly on show. This can be achieved sometimes when the cut isn't quite right and reacting with the peated malt. Or can just be from the type of peat itself. Well, here is the former case. *46%. nc ncf. Loch Lomond Island Collection.*

◇ **Inchmoan Aged 12 Years Peated** recharred American oak & refill bourbon casks, bott code: L2/188/17 db (89) **n20** a feinty, nougat-rich touch to this: a kind of distillery trademark. But the peat is pungent while the recharging appears to have unleashed a boiled redcurrant quality to counter the bourbon-style tannins; **t23.5** a white knuckle ride of a delivery! Astonishingly keen peat grips every part of the palate while wonderful Demerara and muscovado sugars try to soothe; the spices are up fast an inject heat; **f22.5** a touch oily, lengthening the smoke. But the liquorice and hickory bourbon character hangs around, also, as does the Manuka honey and spice; an inevitable late feinty tang; **b23.5** that little bit of nougat marks this out as distinctively Inchmoan while the vibrancy of the peat offers a bit of a beast... *46%. ncf. Loch Lomond Island Collection.*

◇ **Inchmoan 1992 Peated** refill bourbon barrels db (95) **n23** such a gentle presence of smoke: just a caress; the oak is finely tuned towards a fruity bourbon style with greengages amid the abundant red liquorice; **t24.5** a sublime, faultless, silky-textured delivery which is about as good as anything I have ever encountered out of the Loch Lomond stable. The oak dominates politely at first with all kinds of tropical fruit at work, then increasingly intense waves of peat until the smoke gives way to spice; **f23.5** so much chocolate sweetened with smoked raisins; the oils hold all the fruits, phenols and light spices in constellation for an impressively long time; b24 I do believe I was at Loch Lomond distillery in 1992 while they were producing the Inchmoan strand of their output. So to see it after all this time is astonishing. No less astonishing is the sheer excellence of the malt, which here is almost a cross between a light rye-recipe bourbon and a smoky island scotch. This is a true Loch Lomond classic 48.6%. ncf. *Loch Lomond Island Collection.*

Inchmurrin 12 Years Old db (86.5) n21.5 t22 f21.5 b21.5. A significantly improved dram which is a bit of a malt soup. Love the Demerara injection. 40%

Inchmurrin Aged 15 Years bourbon cask, bott Dec 12 db (86) n22 t21.5 f21 b21.5. Slightly tangy with an edge to the cask which interferes with the usual malty procession. 46%. nc ncf.

Inchmurrin Aged 18 Years bourbon cask, bott Dec 12 db (92.5) n22.5 t23.5 f23.5 b23. Loch Lomond distillery in its brightest colours. 46%. nc ncf. *Glen Catrine Bonded Warehouse Ltd.*

Inchmurrin Aged 21 Years bourbon cask, bott Dec 12 db (90) n22 t23 f22.5 b22.5. This has spent 21 years in a very exceptional cask. Not exactly breathtaking complexity, but what it does is completed with aplomb. 46%. nc ncf. *Glen Catrine Bonded Warehouse Ltd.*

Inchmurrin Loch Lomond Island Collection 12 Year Old db (87) n21.5 t22 f21.5 b22. A thick malty offering with a weighty grist and maple syrup infusion. Big and clumsy. 46%. ncf.

Inchmurrin Island Collection Aged 18 Years db (87) n21 t22.5 f21.5 b22. Wow! That is quite a tangle of flavours and messages. Not quite sure where the "summer grass" on the label comes from. But date and walnut cake...now that would have made sense. Big and rather beautiful in an ugly kind of way... 46%. ncf. *Loch Lomond Whiskies*

Inchmurrin Island Collection Madeira Wood Finish db (77) n17 t23 f18 b19. Alas, it wasn't only sherry butts which were sulphur damaged. Mind you, the explosion of golden sultana on delivery is worth the discomfort. 46%. ncf. *Loch Lomond Whiskies*

◇ **Acla Selection Croftengea 10 Years Old** hogshead, cask no. 495, dist 2006, bott 2016 (84.5) n20 t22 f21.5 b21 Old school Croftengea – unlike the two 6-year-old offerings below – full of the distillery's myriad idiosyncrasies. Chunky, hefty on the peat, lush on the cocoa and not afraid to reveal a little feinty oiliness. 51.6%. sc. 90 bottles.

◇ **Endangered Drams Loch Lomond 10 Year Old** bourbon cask, dist Mar 03, bott 2017 (94) n23.5 really sooty and dry, the clean smoke offering just basic sugars; t23.5 the delivery offers up Sooty and Sweet (apologies!) with Demerara sugars then; when the smoke has cleared, muscovado; f23 beautiful spices dovetails with the phenols; b24 endangered smoky Loch Lomond...? I should say, so: I didn't know they did one. Now an Inchmoan or Croftengea, maybe... But, right enough: it is in the clean Loch Lomond style... 58.5%. nc ncf.

◇ **Golden Cask Croftengea Aged 6 Years** cask no. CM233, dist 2010, bott 2016 (92) n23 none of the usual oils – just wave upon wave of seductive, ashy peat; t23.5 powerful phenols charge around the palate on a wave of sweet, ultra-clean oils, the sugars slowly dissolving leaving tide marks of hefty ash and light oak; youthful traits abound; f22.5 smoked cocoa with ever-increasing spice; b23 the cleanest, most Islay-style Croftengea I've ever encountered. A real style shock and totally delicious. 58.5%. sc. 319 bottles.

Old Malt Cask Inchmurrin Aged 32 Years refill hogshead, cask no. 13362, dist Jun 84, bott Feb 17 (87.5) n21.5 t23 f21 b22 Some beautiful moments to this one, a malt so thick you feel you need to stir it with a spoon. Not for first time an Inchmurrin fortified with butterscotch and fudge which makes for a big chewy experience. Let down slightly only on the bittering finish. 46.5%.

Scotch Malt Whisky Society Cask 112.15 16 Year Old second fill ex-bourbon barrel, dist 25 Jul 00 (91) n23.5 t22.5 f22 b23 More saline to this Inchmurrin than is the norm. 56%.

Simon Brown Croftengea ex-bourbon cask, dist Mar 06, bott Jul 16 (84.5) n19 t22.5 f21.5 b21.5 Nothing wrong with the cask. Just not the greatest cut ever taken from a run. A dirty nose flags there are problems and for all the smoky Peak Frean biscuits and dashing smoked maple syrup, it never quite finds its equilibrium. 43%. nc ncf sc.

Single Cask Collection Croftengea Aged 10 Years bourbon hogshead (92) n22.5 t23.5 f23 b23 Loch Lomond stills at their most bruising, but this really is a fabulous dram full of weight and charisma. A rare treat! 53.8%. sc.

◇ **Spirit of Caledonia Croftengea 6 Years Old** cask no. 340 (91.5) n22.5 Islay by another name...; t23.5 stunning, oiled-up phenols with early, then diminishing sugar, leaving layers of oak and ash; f22.5 the spices hang on to see off the final waves of smoke; b23 like the Golden Cask Croftengea, almost more Islay-like than an Islay... 58.3%. sc.

LOCHSIDE
Highlands (Eastern), 1957–1992. Chivas Brothers. Demolished.

The Cooper's Choice Lochside 1967 Aged 44 Years cask no. 807 (96.5) n24.5 t24.5 f23.5 b24 It is amazing that I had to travel 6,000 miles to find this in British Columbia. But, this is the kind of whisky you would travel four times that kind of distance to experience. Easily one of the top ten single casks I have tasted in the last five years. 41.5%. 354 bottles.

LONGMORN

Speyside, 1895. Chivas Brothers. Working.

Longmorn 15 Years Old db (93) n23 t24 f22 b24 These latest bottlings are the best yet: previous ones had shown just a little too much oak but this has hit a perfect compromise. An all-time Speyside great. 45%

Longmorn 16 Years Old db (84.5) n20.5 t22 f21 b21. This was one of the disappointments of the 2008 edition, thanks to the lacklustre nose and finish. This time we see a cautious nudge in the right direction: the colour has been dropped fractionally and the nose celebrates with a sharper barley kick with a peppery accompaniment. The non-existent (caramel apart) finale of yore now offers a distinct wave of butterscotch and thinned honey...and still some spice. Only the delivery has dropped a tad...but a price worth paying for the overall improvement. Still a way to go before the real Longmorn 16 shines in our glasses for all to see and fall deeply in love with. Come on lads in the Chivas lab: we know you can do it... 48%

Longmorn 23 Year Old db (93) n23 the natural caramels carry a slightly Canadian feel to this; thick vanilla but the layering of malt is stunning; a very slight earthy vegetable note gives weight; t24 dull ulmo honey weaves about the butterscotch and barley sugar like a bat around a tree, flitting here and dipping there; occasional juicy malty shews amazing clarity; f23 in comes the timber and spices, though both are on their best behaviour and offer the barley and butterscotch full respect; b23.5 I can just imagine how this would be such rich top dressing for the finest blend I could concoct: as a single malt it is no less a delight. 48%. ncf.

◇ **Golden Cask Longmorn Aged 9 Years** cask no. CM228, dist 2007, bott 2016 (94) n23 despite a little earthiness, the fresh barley builds in muscle and depth. A little spice prickle mixes with light lime; t23.5 the first three or four flavour waves point unambiguously to the freshness and comparative youth of the barley; slowly, though, the vanillas fills in the gaps; f23.5 surprising depth to the oak, with just-so accompanying spice; b24 Longmorn at this age is criminally neglected for bottling – not least by the distillery owners. This shows the malt in, first, its most playful then most serious and statesmanlike light. Superb. 594%. sc. 115 bottles.

Gordon & MacPhail Rare Vintage Longmorn 1967 (87.5) n21.5 t21.5 f22.5 b22 The sheer force of the tannin on the nose warns of a malt which will be taking few prisoners, and so it proves. Many whiskies remind you of certain breakfast experiences, though the one here is burnt toast! It is not until about the fifth mouthful that the palate acclimatises sufficiently to see the sugars, a bit like making out figures in the dark. But as you get accustomed, those sugars turn into more attractive honey tones and no small degree of balance – as well as pleasure – is found. 43%.

◇ **Gordon & MacPhail Distillery Label Longmorn 2003** bott 18 May 17 (94.5) n23.5 a gentle, rhythmic pulsing of butterscotch and ulmo honey: almost too soft to be true; the very faintest hint of light smoke; t23.5 the malt gangs up early to form a thick core with a sprightly spiciness jostling around the edges; f23.5 a curiously sticky finish: the viscosity has built up to good effect. More butterscotch before a beautiful Malteser candy intensity with a little dollop of extra tannin for good measure which fits well with the late, delicate smoke burst; b24 anyone for butterscotch and Worther's Originals had better get their skates on before all this has gone... 43%.

Hunter Laing's Old & Rare Longmorn Aged 30 Years refill hogshead, dist Oct 85, bott May 16 (95.5) n24.5 t24 f23 b24 Mesmerically beautiful: a rare bottling that does the distillery full justice. This is a work of art. 49.2%. nc ncf sc. 157 bottles.

Old Particular Longmorn 20 Years Old refill hogshead, cask no. 11626, dist Oct 96, bott Mar 17 (90) n22.5 t23 f22 b22.5 Longmorn unplugged. Away from the awful caramel straightjacket in which it is normally found, you can see why blenders love to use this to make the malt in a blend talk very loudly. 51.5%. nc ncf sc. 263 bottles.

Old Particular Longmorn 21 Years Old refill hogshead, cask no. 11334, dist Dec 94, bott Sept 16 (91) n22 t23.5 f22.5 b23 Always a treat to taste the distillery's fruits without it being under a toffee blanket. And also slightly younger than its years thanks to a polite though not too indulgent cask... 51.5%. nc ncf sc. 265 bottles.

WoodWinters Fiadhaich 27 Year Old (95) n24 t24 f23 b24 Superb! 54.6%. sc. 278 bottles.

THE MACALLAN

Speyside, 1824. Edrington. Working.

The Macallan 7 Years Old db (89) n23 t23 f21 b22. An outstanding dram that underlines just how good young malts can be. Fun, fabulous and in recent bottlings has upped the clarity of the sherry intensity to profound new heights. 40%

The Macallan Fine Oak 8 Years Old db (82.5) n20.5 t22 f20 b20. A slight flaw has entered the mix here. Even so, the barley fights to create a distinctive sharpness. However, a rogue sherry butt has put paid to any hopes the honey and spice normally found in this brand. 40%

The Macallan 10 Years Old db (91) n23 t23 f21.5 b23.5 For a great many of us, it is with the Mac 10 our great Speyside odyssey began. It has to be said that in recent years it has been something of a shadow of its former great self. However, this is the best version I have come across for a while. Not perhaps in the same league as those bottlings in the 1970s which made us re-evaluate the possibilities of single malt. But fine enough to show just how great this whisky can be when the butts have not been tainted and, towards the end, the balance between barley and grape is a relatively equal one. 40%

The Macallan 10 Years Old Cask Strength db (85) n20 t22 f22 b21. Enjoyable and a would give chewing gum a run for its money. But over-egged the sherry here and not a patch on the previous bottling. 58.8%. Duty Free.

The Macallan Fine Oak 10 Years Old db (90) n23 t22.5 f21.5 b22 Much more on the ball than the last bottling of this I came across. Malts really come as understated or clever than this. 40%

◇ **Macallan 12 Year Old** db (61) n15 t16 f15 b15 An uncompromising and comprehensive essay in the present day sulphured sherry butt problem. 43% US tag CP981113

The Macallan Sherry Oak 12 Years Old db (93) n24 t23.5 f22.5 b23 I have to say that some Macallan 12 I have tasted on the road has let me down in the last year or so. This is virtually faultless. Virtually a time machine back to another era... 40%

The Macallan 12 Years Old Sherry Oak Elegancia db (86) n23 t22 f20 b21. Promises, but delivers only to an extent. 40%

The Macallan Fine Oak 12 Years Old db (95.5) n24 t24 f23.5 b24 A whisky whose quality has hit the stratosphere since I last tasted it. I encountered a disappointing one early in the year. This has restored my faith to the point of being a disciple... 40%

Macallan Gran Reserva Aged 12 Years db (92) n23 t24 f22 b23 Well, you don't get many of these to the pound. A real throwback. The oloroso threatens to overwhelm but there is enough intrigue to make for a quite lovely dram which, as all good whiskies should, never quite tells the story the same way twice. Not entirely without blemish, but I'm being picky. A Macallan soaked in oloroso which traditionalists will swoon over. 45.6%

The Macallan Fine Oak 15 Years Old db (79.5) n19 t21.5 f19 b20. As the stock of the Fine oak 12 rises, so its 15-y-o brother, once one of my favourite drams, falls. Plenty to enjoy, but a few sulphur stains remove the gloss. 43%

The Macallan Fine Oak 17 Years Old db (82) n19.5 t22 f19.5 b21. Where once it couldn't quite make up its mind on just where to sit, it has now gone across to the sherry benches. Sadly, there are a few dissenters. 43%

The Macallan Sherry Oak 18 Years Old db (87) n24 t22 f20 b21. Underpowered. The body doesn't even come close to matching the nose which builds up the expectancy to enormous levels and, by comparison to the Independents, this at 43% appears weak and unrepresentative. Why this isn't at 46% at the very least and unambiguously uncoloured, I have no idea. 43%

The Macallan Fine Oak 18 Years Old db (94.5) n23.5 t24 f23 b24 Is this the new Fine Oak 15 in terms of complexity? That original bottling thrived on the balance between casks types. This is much more accentuated on a cream sherry persona. But this sample is sulphur-free and quite fabulous. 43%

The Macallan Fine Oak 21 Years Old db (84) n21 t22 f20 b21. An improvement on the characterless dullard I last encountered. But the peaks aren't quite high enough to counter the sulphur notes and make this a great malt. 43%

The Macallan 25 Years Old db (84.5) n22 t21 f20.5 b21. Dry with an even drier oloroso residue; blood orange adds to the fruity mix. Something, though, is not entirely right about this and one fears from the bitter tang at the death that a rogue butt has gained entry to what should be the most hallowed of dumping troughs. 43%

The Macallan Fine Oak 25 Years Old db (90) n22 t23.5 f22 b22.5 The first time I tasted this brand a few years back I was knocked off my perch by the peat reek which wafted about with cheerful abandon. Here the smoke is tighter, more shy and of a distinctly more anthracitic quality. Even so, the sweet juiciness of the grape juxtaposes gamely with the obvious age to create a malt of obvious class. 43%

The Macallan Fine Oak 25 Years Old db (89) n23 t23 f21 b22. Very similar to the Fine Oak 18. However, the signature smoke has vanished, as I suppose over time it must. Not entirely clean sherry, but much remains to enjoy. 43%

The Macallan Fine Oak 30 Years Old db (81.5) n22 t22 f18 b19.5. For all its manyriches on delivery, especially those moments of great bourbon-honey glory, it has been comprehensively bowled middle stump by the sherry. Gutted. 43%

The Macallan Millennium 50 Years Old (1949) db (90) n23 t22 f22 b23. Magnificent finesse and charm despite some big oak makes this another Macallan to die for. 40%

The Macallan Lalique III 57 Years Old db (95) n24.5 t23 f23.5 b24 No experience with this whisky under an hour pays sufficient tribute to what it is all about. Checking my watch, I am writing this just two minutes under two hours after first nosing this malt. The score started at 88.5. With time, warmth, oxidation and understanding that score has risen to 95. It has spent 57 years in the cask; it deserves two hours to be heard. It takes that time, at least, to not just hear what it has to say to interpret it, but to put it into context. And for certain notes, once locked away and forgotten, to be slowly released. The last Lalique was good. But simply not this good. 48.5%

The Macallan 1824 db (88) n24 t23.5 f19 b21.5. Absolutely magnificent whisky, in part. But there are times my job is depressing...and this is one of them.. 48%

The Macallan 1824 Estate Reserve db (90.5) n22 excellent clean grape with an intriguing dusting of mint; t23 almost a Jamaican pot still rum sheen and sweetness; beautiful weight and even some barley present; f22.5 satisfying, gorgeously clean with very good vanilla-grape balance; b23 don't know about Reserve: definitely good enough for the First Team. 45.7%

The Macallan 1824 Select Oak db (82) n19 t22 f20 b21. Soft, silky, sometimes sugary... and tangy. Not convinced every oak selected was quite the right one. 40%

The Macallan 1851 Inspiration db (77) n19.5 t19.5 f19 b19. Flat and uninspirational in 2008. 41%

Macallan Cask Strength db (94) n22 t24 f24 b24. One of those big sherry babies; it's like surfacing a massive wave of barley-sweetened sherry. Go for the ride. 58.6%. USA.

The Macallan Estate Reserve db (84) n22 t22 f20 b20. Doh! So much juice lurking about, but so much bitterness, too. ...grrrrr!!!! 45.7%

The Macallan Fine Oak Master's Edition db (91) n23 t23 f22 b23 Adorable. 42.8%

The Macallan Fine Oak Whisky Maker's Selection db (92) n22 t23 f23 b24. This is a dram of exquisite sophistication. Coy, mildly cocoaed dryness, set against just enough barley and fruit sweetness here and there to see off any hints of austerity. Some great work has gone on in the lab to make this happen: fabulous stuff! 42.8%. Duty Free.

The Macallan Gold sherry oak cask db (89.5) n22 t23.5 f21.5 b22.5. No Macallan I have tasted since my first in 1975 has been sculpted to show the distillery in such delicate form. 40%

The Macallan Oscuro db (95.5) n24.5 t24 f23 b24. Oh, if all sherried whiskies could be that kind - and taste bud-blowingly fabulous! 46.5%

The Macallan Ruby sherry oak cask db (92.5) n23 t24 f22 b23.5. Those longer in the tooth who remember the Macallan 10 of 30 years ago will nod approvingly at this chap. Perhaps one butt away from a gong! 43%.

The Macallan Sienna sherry cask db (94.5) n23 t24 f23.5 b24. The pre-bottling sample presented to me was much more vibrant than this early on, but lacked the overall easy charm and readily flowing general complexity of the finished article. A huge and pleasing improvement. 43%.

The Macallan Rare Cask Black db (83.5) n21.5 t22 f19 b21. Pretty rich and some intense, molasses, black cherry and liquorice notes to die for. But some pretty off-key ones, too. Overall, average fare. 48%.

The Macallan Royal Marriage db (89) n23.5 t22.5 f21 b22. Some amazing moments to remember. 46.8%

The Macallan Select Oak db (83) n23 t21 f19 b20. Exceptionally dry and tight; and a little furry despite the early fruitiness. 40%

The Macallan Whisky Makers Edition db (76) n19 t20 f18 b19. Distorted and embittered by the horrific "S" element... 42.8%

The Macallan Woodlands Limited Edition Estate Bottling db (86) n21 t23 f21 b21. Toffee towards the finish brings a premature halt to a wonderfully mollased early delivery. 40%

Gleann Mor Macallan 1985 dist 18 Jun 85 (94.5) n23.5 t24 f23 b24 One deliciously attractive and spicy Macallan. 53.8%.

Hunter Laing's Old & Rare Macallan Aged 25 Years refill hogshead, dist Mar 91, bott Jan 17 (91) n23 t23 f22 b23 Fabulous weight. 51.2%. nc ncf sc. 222 bottles.

That Boutique-y Whisky Company Macallan 29 Year Old batch 6 (89) n22.5 t23.5 f21 b22 You get the feeling the optimum time for this cask may have been five or six years ago. Still, big and full of trademark Macallan richness and, thankfully, no sulphur present. 43.5%. 293 bottles.

Xtra Old Particular Speyside Macallan 25 Years Old refill butt, cask no. 11489, dist Mar 91, bott Nov 16 (94) n23.5 t23.5 f23 b24 Always melts the heart to find an unsullied Macallan showing such marvellously effortless timing and depth. Gorgeous. 51.1%. nc ncf sc. 231 bottles.

MACDUFF
Speyside, 1963. Bacardi. Working.

The Deveron 12 Year Old db (87.5) n22 t22 f21.5 b22. Buttery and pleasant. But feels like driving a Ferrari with a Fiat Uno engine. Woefully underpowered and slightly too flat in too many places where it should be soaring. The trademark honey notes cannot be entirely defied, however. 40%

The Deveron 18 Year Old db (94) n24.5 oh well, this is a 20 minuter. Evolves as it warms and oxidises. Almost a sherbet lemon kick at times, with freshly diced apple and halved Chinese gooseberry. The malt is present, but happy for delicate exotic fruits to quietly dominate the show; t23.5 silky, with much more malt at the helm. A vague bitter tannin note, too; f22.5 spiced honey alongside that vaguely bitter tannin; b23.5 each bottle should be stamped" Class: handle with care"... 40%

◇ **Endangered Drams Macduff 19 Year Old** cask no. 5253, dist Sept 97, bott Jun 17 (95) n24 ethereal, yet at its weightiest gooseberry tart with custard; spices caress rather than prickle; t24 amazingly delicate in its texture, it is not long before this heads off to its referred honey-rich territory. The acacia honey and barley sugar strands would fracture even if you looked at them too hard; f23 gentle spices herd the vanillas and playful barley b24 there are times I would like to simply kiss this distillery. Its adorably gentle, sweet nature is perfectly captured in this delightful, slightly sexy and entirely seductive dram. 54.9%. nc ncf sc.

◇ **Fadandel.dk Macduff Aged 14 Years** refill sherry butt, cask no. 1801, dist 18 Mar 03, bott 27 Feb 18 (88.5) n22 a bit of nip to the fruitcake; t22.5 a fat maple syrup sweetness vies with the spotted dick pudding; f21.5 slightly dull as a little furriness from the butt moves in; b22.5 an almost, though not quite, clean sherry butt, but the actual shape of the malt itself has been obfuscated by the fruit. 60.3%. sc. 24 bottles.

◇ **Golden Cask Macduff Aged 25 Years** cask no. CM235, dist 1992, bott 2017 (94) n23 apple and pear crumble works beautifully with the clean malt; t23.5 again, a soft fruit outline but the star of the show is the barley and butterscotch thrust which switches salivation on to full blast and maximises the depth and integrity of the rich, honeyed oak; spices are inevitable and operate with both vim and panache; f23.5 long, mildly viscous and still flying the malt flag; b24 an absolute gem of a cask. 56%. sc. 248 bottles.

◇ **Gordon & MacPhail Connoisseurs Choice Macduff 2004** bott 28 Mar 17 (96) n23.5 a little anthracite coal smoke adds a delicate extra ballast to the honey and red liquorice theme; t24 sooo beautiful! Everything comes together like a dream: the weight, pace of the dissolving sugars, the unhurried dissolving then reassembly of the malt, the slightly coppery sharpness against the peppery warming; all the while a finger of ulmo honey can be detected and clung on to; f24 one of those where you are not sure where the end begins, so long is this wonderful experience. The light smoke begins to take on a little weight, though by now the spices are busier and a little more flighty, stretching the width of the sensations. Malt still plays an intriguing game, accompanied now by the last elements of the honey...; b24.5 this year has been a truly great year for MacDuff bottlings. Another peach of a dram showing the distillery in all its subtly honeyed and understatedly smoky brilliance. Early days, but any whisky which outpoints this for an award must be of the very rarest brilliance. 46%.

Hepburn's Choice Macduff 8 Years Old refill hogshead, dist 2008, bott 2016 (85.5) n21 t22 f21 b21.5 A very bitty dram, though where it takes off on delivery, with a big fruit note lumping with a slightly salty barley, it soars very high, indeed! 46%. nc ncf sc. 405 bottles.

◇ **Kingsbury Gold Macduff 20 Years Old** hogshead, cask no. 4130, dist 1997 (88.5) n22.5 doughy, early morning German bakers, crusty rolls; a strange light honey and yeast mix, too; t22 ye gods! There is a blaze on the palate as the hotness of the spirit burns deep. The fire is extinguished by some hugely intense barley with thumping in close attendance; f22 gorgeous, lingering cocoa tones...but still a little warm; b22 surprisingly aggressive for a MacDuff – the distiller must have been in one hell of a hurry to get home. Plenty of pointers to some hidden excellence, though. 54.9%. 257 bottles.

◇ **Old Malt Cask Macduff Aged 20 Years** refill barrel, cask no. 14414, dist Oct 97, bott Nov 17 (94) n23.5 a surprise smokiness to this works well with the spiced apple pie and demerara sugars; t23.5 ridiculously soft landing. Dusty oakiness early on, then a building of juicier barley and black pepper; f23 chili and Venezuelan cocoa gets a late topping of thin ulmo honey... and vague smoke notes once more; b24 so pleasingly complex and gloriously manicured. A real triumph of a dram, not least with the surprise smoke element. 50%. nc ncf sc. 134 bottles.

Old Particular Macduff 25 Years Old refill hogshead, cask no. 11358, dist Dec 90, bott Sept 16 (88.5) n22.5 t22.5 f21.5 b22 This is a curious soul: the honey is truly resplendent. But there is a little tired oak tang which just chips away at the finer points of what would have been a stunning malt. 49.1%. nc ncf sc. 136 bottles.

The Single Cask Macduff Aged 19 Years cask no. 5278, dist 1991 (88.5) n22 t23 f21.5 b22 One of the most simplistic MacDuffs I've encountered in years. The overall malt thrust, though, is excellent. 53.5%. nc ncf sc.

◇ **Single Cask Collection Macduff 10 Years Old** bourbon barrel (91) n22 a tangy nose with blood orange on the sharp barley; t23.5 with a mix of fearsome spice and honey. The malt also stands out like organ stops, the base note coming from the oak; **f22.5** the spiciest of tail offs; lightly coppery and metallic at the death; **b23** evidence of a new still, or part of, here as there is a distinct sharpness t both the barley and sugars. *56.8%. sc.*

◇ **Spirit of Caledonia Macduff 9 Years Old** cask no. 101732 (95.5) **n23.5** outstanding oak deposits for a malt so young: spiced, nutty and full of bourbon style red liquorice. The secret of its success is its understated ulmo honey, relaxed pace and genteel layering; **t24.5** what a delightful marriage of rich, succulent malt with vanilla and barley sugar in equal measure; the oak makes a classy and spicy entrance; like the nose, the pacing is exceptional; **f23.5** spice and honey dovetailing towards a light, chalky and gristy finale; **b24** a distillery which, given half a chance and the right circumstances, loves to show its honeyed edge. And it does so here, beautifully and all the while pulsing pure elegance. As 9-year-olds go, it doesn't get much better... *56.5%. sc.*

That Boutique-y Whisky Company Macduff 11 Year Old (93) **n23** orange blossom honey mixes with a blend of vanilla and grist; **t23.5** classy start: the barley is not just lush but also in near concentrated form. The vanilla offers strands of over-ripe banana and spice; **f23** long, with a very distant puff of phenol on the lingering spice; attractive praline on the fade, also; **b23.5** a lilting, pleasantly oiled dram which makes the best from its sugary contours. The most vague hint of smoke pops up randomly. *49.1%. 164 bottles.*

That Boutique-y Whisky Company Macduff 18 Year Old batch 3 (88.5) **n22 t23 f21.5 b22** A delicious dram which never seems to settle into a comfortable rhythm but finds the right tune. *48.6%. 372 bottles.*

◇ **The Whisky Embassy Macduff Aged 20 Years** cask no. 4081, dist 12 Jun 97, bott 16 Nov 17 (88) **n22.5** spiced marmalade on toast; **t22** big juicy barley lift off, but the oak soon intervenes with a slightly muddled, tangy presence; **f21.5** any amount of vanilla and citrus; still tangy; **b22** some tangy oak interference can't entirely distract from the elegance of the malt itself. *55.7%. nc ncf sc.*

MANNOCHMORE
Speyside, 1971. Diageo. Working.

Mannochmore Aged 12 Years db (84) **n22 t21 f20 b21.** As usual the mouth arrival fails to live up to the great nose. Quite a greasy dram with sweet malt and bitter oak. *43%.*

Mannochmore Aged 25 Years dist 1990 db (90) **n22 t23.5 f22 b23** Less a whisky and more a battle, starting on your nose and spreading over onto your palate (a little ironic, seeing as this is whisky number 633 for the year). Will the evil tannins destroy all before them, or can enough sugars be conjured up to keep them at bay? Some may feel the evil forces prevailed, others that it was a victory for the goodies. You decide... *53.4%. 3954 bottles. Diageo Special Releases 2016.*

◇ **Gordon & MacPhail Connoisseurs Choice Mannochmore 1996** bott 28 Mar 17 (88.5) **n22** bold, crisp barley sugar with a little Manuka honey and molasses but with some firm oak propping everything else up; **t22** aggressive barley makes for an eye-watering and mouth-puckering kick off, but for the masochistic there is plenty to be enjoyed by this malty and liquorice-laden whipping; **f22.5** still plenty of bite but settles with a buttery fruit biscuit finale which goes well with the light praline; **b22** even 20 years in the cask can't douse some of the flames... *46%.*

The Whisky Agency Mannochmore 28 Years Old dist 1988 (93.5) **n23.5 t23.5 f23 b23.5** Quite superb. *46%. Bottled for La Maison du Whisky.*

Whisky-Fässle Mannochmore 10 Year Old hogshead, dist 1988, bott 2016 (92) **n23.5 t23.5 f22 b23** Impressively confident and solid. A real malty-plus treat. *46%.*

MILLBURN
Highlands (Northern), 1807–1985. Diageo. Demolished.

Millburn 1969 Rare Malt db (77) **n19 t21 f18 b19.** Some lovely bourbon-honey touches but sadly over the hill and declining fast. Nothing like as interesting or entertaining as the massage parlour that was firebombed a few yards from my office twenty minutes ago. Or as smoky... *51.3%*

MILTONDUFF
Speyside, 1824. Chivas Brothers. Working.

Miltonduff Aged 15 Years bott code L00/123 db (86) **n23 t22 f20 b21.** Some casks beyond their years have crept in and unsettled this one. But some real big salty moments to savour, too. *46%*

◇ **Ballantine's The Miltonduff Aged 15 Years Series No.002** American oak casks, bott code: LKRM1193 2018/03/27 (88.5) **n23** antique oak, liquorice and blood orange; **t22** malt assembles early on offering a delicate salivating quality. Big – too big - caramel surge, but as it dissipates the complex bourbon-style stars form, light hickory and burnt mallow especially; the spices flit around like bats in the glow of the sunset; **f21.5** vanishes under caramel; **b22** soft, spicy, attractive but far too much one-dimensional caramel for complexity or greatness. Some decent bourbon notes filter through, though. (The Murray Method brings out the caramels further – best enjoyed at cool bottle temperature). 40%.

Cadenhead's Authentic Collection Miltonduff 38 Year Old bourbon casks, dist 1978 **(93)** **n23.5 t23.5 f23 b23** A great distillery and a great bottling once it comes to terms with its advanced old age... 46.5%.

Gordon & MacPhail Cask Strength Miltonduff 1994 bott 29 Sept 16 **(93.5) n24 t23.5 f22.5 b23.5** A stunning, enveloping malt. 60.4%.

◇ **Gordon & MacPhail Cask Strength Miltonduff 1997** cask no. 9179, bott 25 Sept 17 **(92) n23** some aggro on the nose with the odd sharp, spicy, fruity slap: Miltonduffed-up, more like...; **t23.5** ahhh, so salivating and mouth cleansing. The fruity notes seem to rant at the palate, hitting home with one belligerent wave after another...wonderful; **f22.5** the muscovado sugars seem a bit played out now leaving a more molassed sweetness in its wake; **b23** this uplifting and upbeat little beauty has some serious attitude... Hit me again..! 58.8%. sc.

◇ **Gordon & MacPhail Discovery Range Miltonduff Aged 10 Years (89.5) n23** well, you can certainly discover the oak: the toasty tannins are everywhere...!; **t22** salivating and increasingly spicy as the malt gives way to the healthy oak; **f22** gentle mocha; **b22.5** packs in a huge amount for a 10-year-old. 43%.

◇ **Hepburn's Choice Miltonduff 7 Years Old** sherry finished hogshead, dist 2009, bott 2017 **(81.5) n21 t21.5 f19 b20** Beautifully made, zesty malt, still smacking of new make tendencies. A bit sulphurous here and there, but nothing too disastrous. 46%. nc ncf sc. 288 bottles.

Hunter Laing's Distiller's Art Miltonduff Aged 22 Years refill hogshead, dist Apr 94, bott 2016 **(91) n22 t23 f23 b23** A liquorice chew... 48%. nc ncf sc. 287 bottles.

Hunter Laing's Old & Rare Miltonduff Aged 34 Years refill hogshead, dist Jun 82, bott Jun 16 **(93) n23.5 t23.5 f23 b23** Just enough tannin has made a mark here to leave no doubt about the geriatric quality of this malt. Indeed, in lesser whiskies it might have been regarded as too much. But such is the overall high quality, the occasional pulses of big oak can be seen as a proud war wound... 50.8%. nc ncf sc. 196 bottles.

Liquid Sun Miltonduff 20 Years Old dist 1995 **(92) n23 t23.5 f22.5 b23** True Miltonduff in both essence and esprit. 51.1%.

◇ **Liquid Treasures Entomology Miltonduff 22 Years Old** ex-bourbon cask, dist 1995, bott 2017 **(92) n23** cream caramel and crushed Malteser mix; **t23.5** infinitely more full bodied and juicy than the nose remotely suggests. Even a degree of treacle tart here, underscoring the bourbon cask influence, yet the integrity of the malt is always shining brightest of all; **f22.5** the vanilla and butterscotch blend that seemed almost inevitable; **b23** well measured and beautifully paced. Impeccable malt. 56.1%.

◇ **Old Malt Cask Miltonduff Aged 20 Years** refill hogshead, cask no. 11234, dist Feb 95, bott Feb 15 **(91) n23** very good age on the nose, the oak offering light bourbon-style tannins: no shortage of red liquorice and hickory; a little floral, too...; **t23.5** mmm...so lush and salivating. Excellent light oils carry the grassy element while a subversive spice note rumbles in contrast. Muscovado sugars and vanilla fill in the mid-ground; **f22** a slight bitterness of the Allied old school but the persistent spices compensate; **b22.5** a very satisfying Speysider. 50%. nc ncf sc. 171 bottles.

Old Malt Cask Miltonduff Aged 21 Years refill hogshead, cask no. 13271, dist Apr 95, bott Feb 17 **(85) n22.5 t21.5 f20 b21** More than a hint of Cream Soda. Despite some average oak influence the malt comes through mainly unscathed. Disjointed and tangy, though. 50%. nc ncf sc. 269 bottles.

Old Particular Miltonduff 21 Years Old refill barrel, cask no. 11537, dist Feb 95, bott Nov 16 **(88.5) n22 t23 f21.5 b22** A malt which is such ambrosia to a good blender needs just a little more tannin than this to do itself justice when fully exposed. An understated delight, all the same. 51.5%. nc ncf sc. 244 bottles.

◇ **Old Particular Miltonduff 23 Years Old** refill hogshead, cask no. 12200, dist Apr 94, bott Nov 17 **(94.5) n24** the nose of a Miltonduff screaming to be added to an award-winning blend: clean, sharply-focused malt and elegant though by no means overpowering oak; the diced pear adds to the charm, vague smokiness the intrigue; **t24** exemplary barley, just full of gristy sugars even after all these years, backed further by acacia honey and **f23** you could not ask more from the mix of busy, warming spice and butterscotch and the vaguest of light smoke deposits; **b23.5** nimble and sprightly for its age, full of agile malt throughout. Class with every nuance. 50.6%. nc ncf sc. 262 bottles.

◇ **Scotch Malt Whisky Society Cask 72.56 35 Year Old** refill ex-bourbon barrel, dist 11 Jun 82 **(82.5) n24 t21.5 f18 b19** Fabulous nose which warns of the over-oaking to come but retains some serious quality. Butterscotch tart goes without saying, and acts as the background for a succession of faux fruity notes, mostly of a boiled sweet variety. The lightest sliver of acacia honey and marzipan. But there is also a tell-tale warning of an off oak note. And this becomes more than apparent once the initial sweetness on delivery has died. The finish, I warn you, is grim. *49.5%. sc.*

◈ **The Whisky Embassy Miltonduff Aged 9 Years** cask no. 8316533, dist 2008, bott 2017 (86) n21.5 t22 f21 b21.5 Malty, rich but not entirely at home with itself. Delicious in part, bit still some growing to do. *53.6%. nc ncf sc.*

MORTLACH
Speyside, 1824. Diageo. Working.

Mortlach Aged 16 Years db (87) n20 t23 f22 b22. Once it gets past the bold if very mildly sulphured nose, the rest of the journey is superb. Earlier Mortlachs in this range had a slightly unclean feel to them and the nose here doesn't inspire confidence. But from arrival on the palate onwards, it's sure-footed, fruity and even refreshing... and always delicious. *43%*

Mortlach 18 Year Old db (75) n19 t19 f18 b19. When I first tasted Mortlach, probably over 30 years ago now, it really wasn't even close to this. Something went very wrong in the late '80s, I can tell you...*43.4%. Diageo.*

Mortlach 25 Year Old db (91.5) n23 just love the lemon grass alongside the liquorice and hickory; t23.5 thick and palate-encompassing. The sugars are pretty toasty with a light mocha element in play; f22.5 crisp finale with a return of the citrus, sitting confidently with the late spice; b22.5 much more like it. The sugars may be pretty full on, but there is enough depth and complexity for a narrative to be told. Very much a better Mortlach on so many levels. *43.4%.*

Mortlach Rare Old db (79) n20 t21 f19 b19. Not rare enough... *43.4%. Diageo.*

Mortlach Special Strength db (79.5) n20 t21.5 f19 b19. Does whisky come any more cloyingly sweet than Mortlach...? Not in my experience.... *49%. Diageo.*

◈ **Cadenhead's Rum Cask Mortlach 14 Years Old** Guyana rum cask, dist 2003 (96.5) n25 take your time with this one and rarely will the Murray Method of tasting be better rewarded: at body temperature you are lost in a maze of complex yet hefty aromas, ranging from diced Brazil nut to moist date. Despite the Demerara rum background to this cask, there is also a distinctive bourbony thrust from the oak, the red liquorice element in full spate; The spices are less mesmerising, hiding behind and then reappearing before the pulsing malt. I could ramble on indefinitely: I will leave it to you to discover the vast richness of this truly faultless nose; t24.5 fabulously succulent with an array of concentrated barley, orange-blossom honey and virile spice: an almost perfect follow on from the improbably brilliance of the nose; f23 just dries a touch too boisterously as the oak takes hold. But never loses sight of its greatness and elegance...or the spice; b24 mind-blowingly beautiful. This really is what malt whisky should be all about. Thank you Cadenhead! *55%. sc. 240 bottles.*

◈ **Gordon & MacPhail Cask Strength Mortlach 1994** cask no. 8192, bott 19 Apr 17 (85.5) n21.5 t22 f21 b21 A Mortlach of its time: 23 years ago they were producing an outrageously sweet, bouncy matl lacking shape and depth. Even though matured here in good wood, which is in itself a rarity for this distillery and vintage only so much salvation can be achieved. A loud, unruly spirit which offers a little bit of fun, but will do nothing to win the heart of the whisky purist. *54.2%. sc.*

Hepburn's Choice Mortlach 7 Years Old refill hogshead, dist 2010, bott 2017 (85) n21.5 t22.5 f21 b20 The oak has made a no show, allowing the gristy barley the entire run of the glass. Barely any colour or complexity, it is just as well the spirit is of decent Speyside standard. *46%.*

◈ **Hepburn's Choice Mortlach 7 Years Old** refill hogshead, dist 2010, bott 2017 (87) n22 t22 f21.5 b21.5 An attractive, essentially juicy, entirely agreeable malt with an easy-going, untaxing freshness. *46%. nc ncf sc. 420 bottles.*

Hepburn's Choice Mortlach 8 Years Old bourbon barrel, dist 2007, bott 2016 (90.5) n22.5 t23 f22.5 b22.5 Great to see this distillery returning to its old excellent self after two decades of grimness. *46%. nc ncf sc. 298 bottles.*

◈ **Hepburn's Choice Mortlach 8 Years Old** refill hogshead, dist 2010, bott 2018 (86) n21.5 t22 f21 b21.5 A rotund, sweet whisky but for all its massive gristy, malty front fails to really find a direction. The finish disintegrates slightly. *46%. nc ncf sc. 387 bottles.*

◈ **Kingsbury Gold Mortlach 22 Years Old** hogshead, cask no. 4873, dist 1995 (86.5) n21.5 t22 f21.5 b22 Outwardly a chunky whisky, a little on the nutty side but with a surprising hotness to the thinner core. When the early muddle has settled a highly pleasing ultra-malty blast makes for a satisfying all round finale. *53.2%. 255 bottles.*

◈ **Old Malt Cask Mortlach Aged 10 Years** refill hogshead, cask no. 14406, dist Jul 07, bott Nov 17 (93) n23 clean enough to allow the barley to sparkle; t23.5 satisfyingly salivating on delivery with a surprise spice package arriving very early on; always grassy in the most traditional of Speyside ways; **f23** drier as an elegant, high quality oakiness spotlights the delicate sophistication; **b23.5** a refined, dignified malt complete with cut grass accent. *50%. nc ncf sc. 317 bottles.*

Old Malt Cask Mortlach Aged 12 Years refill hogshead, cask no. 13298, dist Jan 05, bott Feb 17 **(89) n22** intense malt with a dollop of vanilla; **t22** intense malt with two dollops of vanilla; **f23** intense malt with three dollops of vanilla and a squirt of spice; **b22** with a bit of a one trick pony, I agree. But some trick! *50%. nc ncf sc. 315 bottles.*

Old Particular Mortlach 12 Years Old refill hogshead, cask no. 11595, dist Mar 05, bott Apr 17 **(90) n22 t23 f22.5 b22.5** One very fat Speysider...! *48.4%. nc ncf sc. 329 bottles.*

⬦ **Old Particular Mortlach 12 Years Old** refill hogshead, cask no. 11797, dist Mar 05, bott Jun 17 **(94) n22.5** very elementary yet enticing malt; **t24** superb delivery! The barley is in its most concentrated form and links up with the light oils, thin acacia honey and spices in a way the join cannot be seen; **f23.5** what a beautifully orchestrated retreated by the malt, leaving the vanilla nd light spice to play on; **b24** same age and strength as cask 12219 below, yet this contains so much more malty whoomph and pzazz and all round brilliance... *48.4%. nc ncf sc. 367 bottles.*

⬦ **Old Particular Mortlach 12 Years Old** refill hogshead, cask no. 12219, dist Mar 05, bott Dec 17 **(87) n21 t22.5 f21.5 b22** A modest nose but intensity and dash of the rich malt on delivery, with the confident barley controlling the show, reveals when this distillery started turning the corner in again making *48.4%. nc ncf sc. 341 bottles.*

⬦ **Platinum Old & Rare Mortlach 25 Year Old** sherry butt db **(93) n23** thick, glutinous, grape. Sweet, too, with toasty Manuka honey at work; warming spices; **t23.5** thick, glutinous grape. Sweet, too, with toasty Manuka honey at work; warming spices; **f23** thick, glutinous grape. Sweet, too, with toasty Manuka honey at work; warming spices **b23.5** yes, it one of those famous old Mortlachs that appears to have been distilled from raisins. Oh, and not an atom of sulphur on the scene. *58.8%. sc. 319 bottles. Bottled for The Whisky Shop.*

⬦ **Provenance Mortlach Aged 10 Years** refill hogshead, cask no. 11828, dist Nov 06, bott May 17 **(88.5) n21.5** a tad youthful; **t22.5** sticky malt with spice and toffee; **f22** dries towards a spiced cocoa finale; **b22** simplistic but effective *46%. nc ncf sc. 366 bottles.*

Scotch Malt Whisky Society Cask 76.131 15 Year Old first fill French oak hogshead, dist 30 Sept 01 **(86.5) n22.5 t21.5 f21 b21.5** You can use the best oak on the planet...it will take you so far: probably in this case from about 81 points to nearly 87. This is indifferent distillate and only the boldness yet restrained elegance of the tannin saves the day. Excellent chocolate nut. *57.8%.*

⬦ **Scotch Malt Whisky Society Cask 76.137 35 Year Old** refill ex-bourbon barrel, dist 29 Sept 87 **(87) n22 t21.5 f22 b22** A true tsunami of malt on both nose and palate. But the sweetness is a shade too cloying for greatness while the gluey elements shew a countering thinness which is magnified by the thick, sugary onslaught. Enjoyable, providing you have arms to your chair. *50.5%. sc.*

That Boutique-y Whisky Company Mortlach 18 Year Old batch 3 **(85.5) n21 t22 f21 b21.5** Not quite this distillery's finest vintage. Heavy and sticky on the palate having been cumbersome on the nose. Furry on the finish. Love the mucky molasses, though! *48.9%. 363 bottles.*

That Boutique-y Whisky Company Mortlach 22 Year Old batch 4 **(87.5) n21 t23 f21.5 b22** Unusually malty and intense for a Mortlach of this period with some massive barley sugar notes. Some of the gluey untidiness that is the distillery's signature but the big malt wins! *52.6%. 200 bottles.*

⬦ **Whisky Illuminati Mortlach 19 Year Old** Spanish oak sherry butt, cask no. 3657, dist 1998 **(85) n22 t21.5 f21.5 b20** Being entirely sulphur free, a whisky I should wax lyrical about. But Mortlach at this time was perhaps not the best spirit distilled in Speyside, tending to be on the fat and unruly side. Add to that a sherry butt that appears to be dripping in grape and you get a rather 'in your face' malt where balance is at a premium and subtlety is nil. Gutters at the death. *56.9%. sc. 476 bottles. Candlelight Series.*

MOSSTOWIE
Speyside, 1964–1981. Chivas Brothers. Closed.

Rare Old Mosstowie 1979 **(84.5) n21.5 t21 f21 b21.** Edging inextricably well beyond its sell by date. But there is a lovely walnut cream cake (topped off with brown sugar and spices) to this which warms the cockles. Bless... *43%. Gordon & MacPhail.*

NORTH PORT
Highlands (Eastern), 1820–1983. Diageo. Demolished.

Brechin 1977 db **(78) n19 t21 f18 b20.** Fire and brimstone was never an unknown quantity with the whisky from this doomed distillery. Some soothing oils are poured on this troubled – and sometimes attractively honeyed – water of life. *54.2%*

OBAN

Highlands (Western), 1794. Diageo. Working.

Oban 14 Years Old db (79) n19 t22 f18 b20. Absolutely all over the place. The cask selection sits very uncomfortably with the malt. I look forward to the resumption of normality to this great but ill-served distillery. 43%

Oban The Distillers Edition special release OD 162.FX, dist 1998, bott 2013 db (87.5) n22.5 t22.5 f21 b21.5. Some attractive kumquat and blood orange makes for a fruity and rich malt, though just a little furry towards the finish. Decent Demerara early on, too. 43%

Oban Little Bay db (87.5) n21 t23 f21.5 b22. A pleasant, refreshing simple dram. Clean and juicy in part and some wonderful oak-laden spice to stir things up a little. Just a little too much chewy toffee near the end, though. 43%

PITTYVAICH

Speyside, 1975–1993. Diageo. Demolished.

Pittyvaich Aged 12 Years db (64) n16 t18 f15 b15. It was hard to imagine this whisky getting worse. But somehow it has achieved it. From fire-water to cloying undrinkability. What amazes me is not that this is such bad whisky: we have long known that Pittyvaich can be as grim as it gets. It's the fact they bother bottling it and inflicting it on the public. Vat this with malt from Fettercairn and neighbouring Dufftown and you'll have the perfect dram for masochists. Or those who have entirely lost the will to live. Jesus... 43%. Flora and Fauna.

Pittyvaich 25 Year Old refill American oak hogsheads & first fill ex-bourbon barrels, dist 1989 db (80) n21 t20 f19 b20. No matter what collar you put on it, once a Rottweiler, always a Rottweiler... 49.9%. 5,922 bottles. Diageo Special Releases 2015.

PORT ELLEN

Islay, 1825–1983. Diageo. Closed.

Port Ellen 1979 db (93) n22 t23 f24 b24 Takes so long to get out of the traps, you wonder if anything is going to happen. But when it does, my word...it's glorious! 57.5%

Port Ellen Aged 37 Years dist 1978 db (91) n24.5 t22.5 f22 b22 The bark is far better than the bite: one of the great noses of the year cannot be backed up on the palate as the oak is simply too demanding. An historical experience, but ensure you spend as much time nosing as you do tasting... 55.2%. 2,940 bottles. Diageo Special Releases 2016.

◇ **Port Ellen 37 Year Old** refill American oak hogsheads & refill American oak butts db (88) n23 a surprisingly robust degree of smoke despite the oak trying to get in on the act every which way; t21.5 salivating delivery with a brief glimpse of the trademark gristiness before the oak rishes in taking few prisoners; f22 settles into a spicier mode where the smoke is more comfortable; b21.5 the oak scars the overall beauty of the malt. 51%. 2,988 bottles. Diageo Special Releases 2017.

◇ **Gleann Mor Port Ellen Aged Over 33 Years** dist 1983 (96.5) n25 well, that's my nosing done for the night: very hard to get past this. And what could possibly follow it? Port Ellen, after three decades still displaying its unique gristy charms: peaty whisky gets no more delicate or complex than this. Words are inadequate. If you track this down, half an hour minimum, please, before you taste...and fill in the description for yourself...; t24 melts on the palate, like a Kobe steak might; or the love of your life into your arms. The salivation is unstoppable. Even now the peat acts as the driver, the base and even the higher notes: it is omnipitant. The sugars, very much a mix of molasses and icing, dissolve with the grist yet embrace rather than obliterate the tannins; f23.5 long...so long. With the chalky, hickory-type tannin met atom for atom with the gentlest of peats imaginable; b24 if a whisky can bring a tear to your eye, then this one will. It is too elegant and beautiful for this world... 57%. sc.

Gordon & MacPhail Rare Old Port Ellen 1979 (90.5) n22 t23 f22.5 b23 Really not helped by being reduced to 46%, the oils have been broken up to allow the oak a much drier more sawdusty personality. Somehow pulls itself together to present a pretty, if dishevelled, figure... 46%.

◇ **Hunter Laing's Old & Rare Port Ellen Aged 33 Years** sherry butt, dist Mar 83, bott Nov 16 (94.5) n23.5 a real sweaty sock experience – and I don't mean Scottish! – with the smoke and salt bound together tightly. A little raisin peeps through, but it is shackled; t23.5 one of the most volatile deliveries from a Port Ellen I've experienced for maybe 15 years or so. The salty fruit bites deep, then the spices attack harder still. A little heather honey breaks out as the smokiness recedes and the sweetness increases; f23.5 an endearing rumble and murmur of smoke, the tiring tannins always stating the age; b24 very enjoyable malt. But odd to see Port Ellen in sherry: so much of their output was in bourbon. Had to actually pick up and define the character f the distillery itself. That said, a punchy and enjoyable dram. 56.8%. nc ncf sc. 174 bottles.

PULTENEY

Highlands (Northern), 1826. Inver House Distillers. Working.

Old Pulteney Aged 12 Years db (90.5) n22 t23 f22.5 b23 A cleaner, zestier more joyous composition than the old 43%, though that has less to do with strength than overall construction. A dramatic whisky which, with further care, could get even closer to the truth of this distillery. 40%

Old Pulteney Aged 12 Years bott code L15/030 R15/5046 IB db (91) n22.5 t23 f22.5 b23 Remarkably consistent from the bottling above. The salt continues to ensure lustre, though this bottling has a little extra – and welcome – barley gristiness. 40%. ncf.

Old Pulteney Aged 12 Years db (85) n22 t23 f19 b21. There are few malts whose finish dies as spectacularly as this. The nose and delivery are spot on with a real buzz and panache. The delivery in particular just bowls you over with its sharp barley integrity: real pulse-racing stuff! Then... toffee...!!! Grrrr!!! If it is caramel causing this, then it can be easily remedied. And in the process we'd have a malt absolutely basking in the low 90s...! 43%

◇ **Old Pulteney Aged 15 Years** db (95.5) n24 salty in an...umm...erotic kind of way....oh, gosh...; t24 absolutely full blown intensity on delivery. Hard to imagine how the malt could be any maltier, the oak any more controlled in its toastiness; the nuttiness any more hazelnuttier and the vanilla any more vanilliaer...And that's just on the delivery...! The mid-ground is almost like a salty bourbon...; f23.5 the sugars from the grist are still hanging around, the integrity of the bourbon barrels truly stunning; b24 more than a night cap. One you should definitely take to bed with you... 46%.

Old Pulteney Aged 15 Years db (91) n21 t24 f23 b23 Only on about the fourth or fifth mouthful do you start getting the picture here: enormously complex with a genuine coastal edge to this. The complexity is awesome. 54.9%

Old Pulteney Aged 17 Years db (95) n22 t25 f24 b24 The nose confirms that some of the casks at work here are not A1. Even so, the whisky performs to the kind of levels some distillers could only dream of. 46%

Old Pulteney Aged 17 Years bott code: L15/329 R15/5530 IB db (82) n20.5 t22.5 f19 b20 This is usually one of the greatest whiskies bottled anywhere in the world. But not even something of Pulteney 17's usually unfathomable excellence and charisma can withstand this degree of sulphur. Much greater care has to be taken in the bottling hall to preserve the integrity of what should be one of Scotland's most beautiful offerings to the world. 46%. ncf.

◇ **Old Pulteney Aged 18 Years** db (81) n19 t21.5 f20 b20.5 If you are going to work with sherry butts you have to be very careful. And here we see a whisky that is not careful enough as the sulphur does its usual damage. For those in central Europe without the "sulphur gene", then no problem as the fruit is still intact. 46%.

Old Pulteney Aged 21 Years db (97.5) n25 t24 f24 b24.5 By far and away one of the great whiskies of 2012, absolutely exploding from the glass with vitality, charisma and class. One of Scotland's great undiscovered distilleries about to become discovered, I think... and rightly so! 46%

◇ **Old Pulteney Aged 25 Years** American & Spanish oak casks, bott code: L17/282 R17/5353 IB db (96) n25 few distilleries do noses quite like Pulteney, and here it is pretty much close to perfection. There may be sherry casks in use, but none possess an atom of sulphur as this this is fruit and chalky mocha in saline at its very best. But that is just a simple round-up: a half hour inspecyion will take you down paths of gentle smoke, others of Jaffa Cake or Lubek marzipan (note the presence of the dark chocolate in each case), slightly damp sheep, praline...and so much more. This is my 1,1172nd whisky for the 2018 Bible, and the best nose so far...; t23.5 surprisingly, it is the lightest smokiness which shows first on delivery, soon followed by that chocolate promised on the nose. The malt is even and still to the lightly oiled palate effortlessly; the vanillas of a mixed bunch, ringing fro the odd shard of sturdier tannin to relaxed vanilla; f23.5 delicate spice but, alas, that atom of sulphur missing on the nose surfaces here: nothing drastic, but there nonetheless....and perhaps the difference between the best whisky of 2019 and one that came very, very close...; b24 a quiet but incredibly complex reminder why this distillery is capable of producing World Whisky of the Year. Age is all around you, but degradation there is none. 46%.

Old Pulteney 30 Years Old db (92) n23.5 t23.5 f22 b23 I had to laugh when I tasted this: indeed, it had me scrambling for a copy of the 2009 Bible to check for sure what I had written. And there it was: after bemoaning the over oaking I conjectured, "As Pulteney has the fascinating tendency to radically shift style over not too long a period, I can't wait for the next instalment." And barely a year on, here it is. Pretty far removed from last year's offering and an absolute peach of a dram that laughs in the face of its 30 years... 45%

Old Pulteney 35 Year Old db (89) n23 t21.5 f22.5 b22 A malt on the perimeter of its comfort zone. But there are enough gold nuggets included to make this work. Just. 46%.
Inverhouse Distilleries.

Old Pulteney Aged 40 Years db (95) n23.5 t23.5 f24 b24 This malt still flies as close to the sun as possible. But some extra fruit, honey and spice now grasps the tannins by the throat to ensure a whisky of enormous magnitude and complexity *51.3%*

Old Pulteney 1990 Vintage American oak ex bourbon & Spanish oak ex sherry butts. db (85) n21 t23 f21 b20. As you know, anything which mentions sherry butts gets me nervous – and for good reason. Even with a World Great distillery like Pulteney. Oddly enough, this bottling is, as near a dammit, free of sulphur. Yee-hah! The bad news, though, is that it is also untroubled by complexity as well. It reminded me of some heavily sherried peaty jobs...and then I learned that that ex Islay casks were involved. That may or may not be it. But have to say, beyond the first big, salivating, lightly spiced moments on delivery you wait for the story to unfurl...and it all turns out to be dull rumours. *46%. Inverhouse Distilleries.*

◇ **Old Pulteney 2006 Vintage** first fill ex-bourbon casks, bott 2017, bott code: L17/279 R17/5452 IB db (93) n23 there is something so timelessly familiar about high quality malt in top quality bourbon barrels...and so enticing, too when as faultless as this; t23.5 stunningly intense malt. Immediately backed up by a firm oaky backbone. Ridiculously silky with an ever-increasing spice buzz; f23 a beautiful finale of intense yet controlled tannin and a silky, creamy Swiss roll. Dries as it should, the tannins weighty but by no means oppressive; b23.5 a beautiful, lightly salted ceremony of malt with the glycerine feel of raspberry and cream Swiss rolls. Just so love it! *46%.*

Old Pulteney Duncansby Head Lighthouse bourbon and sherry casks db (90.5) n23 t23 f22 b22.5 Beginning to wonder if Pulteney is into making whisky or cakes. And malt straight from the oven. *46% WB15/329*

Old Pulteney Dunnet Head Lighthouse bourbon & sherry casks db (90.5) n22 t23.5 f22 b23 Loads to chew over with this heavyweight.*46%. nc ncf. Exclusive to travel retail.*

◇ **Old Pulteney Huddart** db (88.5) n22 citrus nibble and salty light, lazy smoke; t22.5 the malt at times ramps up on the salivation levels while the peat remains strangely bitty and incomplete, neither forceful enough take the style forward or heavy enough to give weight. Strange, but pretty tasty, though, and demands a second taste...; f22 chalky, youthful with a lightly peated spice buzz; b22 hopefully not named after my erstwhile physics teacher of 45 years ago, Ernie Huddart, who, annoyingly, for an entire year insisted on calling me Murphy rather than Murray, despite my constant correcting his mistake. One day he told me off for my not remembering some or other Law of Physics. When he finished berating me quite unpleasantly at high volume before my fellow classmates, I simply said: "Well, sir, that's fine coming from you. You've had a year to learn that my name is Murray and not Murphy, and still you failed!" He was so lost for words at this impudence I got away with it, though if his glare could have killed... Anyway, back to the whisky: this seemingly young, lightly smoked version shows all the hallmarks of being finished in peaty casks, as opposed to being distilled from phenolic malt, hence the slightly mottled and uneven feel to this. Odd, but attractive. Oh, and Huddart...? I think that's actually the name of the nondescript old street on which the distillery sits *46%.*

Old Pulteney Navigator bourbon & sherry casks db (80) n19 t23 f18 b20. Sherry butts have clearly been added to this. Not sure why, as the sulphur only detracts from the early honey riches. The compass is working when the honey and cocoa notes briefly harmonise in beautiful tandem. But otherwise, badly off course. *46%. nc ncf.*

Old Pulteney Navigator bourbon & sherry casks, bott code: L15/207 R15/5318 IB db (78) n19 t22 f18 b19 Even further lost in sulphurous territory than before... *46%. ncf.*

Old Pulteney Noss Head Lighthouse bourbon casks db (84) n22.5 t22 f19 b20.5. If Noss Head was as light as this dram, it'd be gone half way through its first half decent storm. An apparent slight overuse of third and less sturdy second fill casks means the finale bitters out considerably. A shame, as the nose and delivery is about as fine a display of citrus maltiness as you'll find. *46%. Travel retail exclusive. WB15/327*

Old Pulteney Pentland Skerries Lighthouse db (85) n21 t22 f20.5 b21.5. A chewy dram with an emphasis on the fruit. Sound, evens enjoys the odd chocolate-toffee moment. But a little sulphur, apparent on the nose, creeps in to take the gloss off. *46%. WB15/323*

Cadenhead's Authentic Collection Old Pulteney 11 Year Old bourbon hogshead, dist 2006 (87) n22.5 t23 f23 b22.5 Never quite encountered a Pulteney like this! Certainly the most spiced at this age I have seen in some 30 years and though from bourbon there is a profound fruitiness and pithy quality. A very strange but truly delicious experience. But I wouldn't have recognised this as a Pulteney in 50 years... *56.1%. sc.*

◇ **Cadenhead's Small Batch Old Pulteney 11 Year Old** dist 2006 (84) n21.5 t22 f20 b20.5 An odd mix of salivating salt and citrus but the oak isn't quite up to the standard of the spirit. *55.8%.*

⟨⟩ **Gordon & MacPhail Connoisseurs Choice Pulteney 1998** first fill bourbon barrels, dist 1998, bott 15 Mar 18 (95) n23.5 how many levels of sweetness? The banana in custard? The chocolate ginger? The rhubarb tart...? t24 first you are met by a definitively yielding mouth feel. Then a slightly salty element to the layered malt; an interplay of red liquorice and rape seed honey...; f24 now it's the oak's turn. With the spices. And the sugars...and the malt...and leathery butterscotch...and so it goes on; b24 so many facets to win your heart with this one. Just sit back and let this Pulteney go about its beautiful business.... 46%. nc ncf. 528 bottles.

⟨⟩ **Hidden Spirits Pulteney 5 Year Old** dist 2012, bott 2017 (86.5) n21 t23 f21 b21 A young, bright barley thumping malt fest showing one of the world's greatest distilleries more or less at the moment its maturing whisky starts to walk... Don't expect any complexity. 50%.

ROSEBANK
Lowlands, 1840–1993. Diageo. Closed- soon to re-open. (The gods have answered!)

Rosebank Aged 12 Years db (95) n24 t24 f23 b24. Infinitely better than the last bottling, this is quite legendary stuff, even better than the old 8-y-o version, though probably a point or two down regarding complexity. The kind of whisky that brings a tear to the eye... for many a reason... 43%. Flora and Fauna.

Rosebank 21 Year Old refill American oak casks, dist 1992 db (95.5) n23.5 t24 f24 b24 Rosebank is at its very best at eight-years-old. Well, that won't happen again, so great to see it has proven successful at 21... 55.3%. 4,530 bottles. Diageo Special Releases 2014.

Rosebank 21 Years Old Special Release db (94) n24 t23.5 f23 b23.5 Can any Lowland be compared to a fully blossomed Rosebank? This is whisky to both savour and worship for this is nectar in a Rose... 53.8%. nc ncf.

Rosebank 25 Years Old db (96) n24.5 t23.5 f24 b24. I had to sit back, take a deep breath and get my head around this. It was like Highland Park but with a huge injection of sweetened chocolate on the finale and weight – and even smoke – from a Rosebank I had never quite seen before. And believe me, as this distillery's greatest champion, I've tasted a few hundred, possibly thousands, of casks of this stuff over the last 25 years. Is this the greatest of all time? I am beginning to wonder. Is it the most extraordinary since the single malt revolution took off? Certainly. Do I endorse it? My god, yes! 61.4%

⟨⟩ **Scotch Malt Whisky Society Cask 25.70 26 Year Old** refill ex-bourbon barrel, dist 14 Nov 90 (79.5) n20 t21.5 f19 b19 "A perfumed garden" apparently. Must be the odd dead oak in there. This is a pretty exhausted cask far beyond its sell by date despite the odd defiant note of honey on delivery. 58.3%. sc.

ROYAL BRACKLA
Speyside, 1812. Bacardi. Working.

Royal Brackla Aged 10 Years db (73) n18 t20 f17 b18. A distinct lowering of the colours since I last tasted this. What on earth is going on? 40%

Royal Brackla 12 Year Old db (82.5) n21.5 t21 f20 b20. Just one of those bottlings which is pleasant enough if you are just looking for something to drink without too much thought, but there is a frustrating lack of harmony and purpose in this for those of us looking to be entertained. 40%

Royal Brackla 21 Year Old db (91) n23.5 wonderful dried lychee kick sets the tone for the sweetness of the malt; t23 silky malt, with a shade of coastal salt ensuring the full flavours are wrung out; f22 creamy chocolate ice cream before the spices arrive; b22.5 now that's much more like it! 40%

⟨⟩ **Hepburn's Choice Royal Brackla 8 Years Old** refill barrel, dist 2009, bott 2018 (87) n20.5 t22.5 f22 b22 While the nose may be a little youthful and untidy, the same can't be said for the experience in the palate. A disciplined celebration of juicy, lightly oiled maltiness, though if it does have a fault it is that it clings to the barley track without attempting too hard to find a branch line. 46%. nc ncf sc. 356 bottles.

⟨⟩ **MacAlabur Royal Brackla 11 Year Old** sherry hogshead, cask no. 310875, dist 7 Nov 06, bott 4 Dec 17 (91) n22.5 boiled fruit candy upon a malty bed; t23.5 impressively sharp fruit goes on instant, salivating attack: quite brilliant...literally. The second phase is a pleasurable mix of big vanilla and malt; f22 back to fruit candy: a mix of wine gum, barley sugar and a Worther's Original being sucked simultaneously; seems like a little feint at the death: surely not! b23 excellent untainted sherry butt which provides controlled hugeness. 56.8%. nc ncf sc. 161 bottles.

Old Malt Cask Royal Brackla Aged 18 Years refill barrel, cask no. 13429, dist May 98, bott Feb 17 (92.5) n23 t22.5 f23.5 b23.5 An excellent cask has ensured harmony. Superb! 50%.

ROYAL LOCHNAGAR
Highlands (Eastern), 1826. Diageo. Working.

Royal Lochnagar Aged 12 Years db (84) n21 t22 f20 b21. More care has been taken with this than some other bottlings from this wonderful distillery. But I still can't understand why it never quite manages to get out of third gear...or is the caramel on the finish the giveaway...? 40%

ST. MAGDALENE
Lowlands, 1798–1983. Diageo. Demolished.

Linlithgow 30 Years Old dist 1973 db (70) n18 t18 f16 b18. A brave but ultimately futile effort from a malt that is way past its sell-by date. 59.6%

SCAPA
Highlands (Island–Orkney), 1885. Chivas Brothers. Working.

Scapa 12 Years Old db (88) n23 t22 f21 b22. Always a joy. 40%

Scapa 14 Years Old db (88) n22 t22.5 f21.5 b22. Enormous variation from bottling to bottling. In Canada I have tasted one that I gave 94 to: but don't have notes or sample here. This one is a bit of dis-service due to the over-the-top caramel added which appears to douse the usual honeyed balance. Usually, this is one of the truly great malts of the Chivas empire and a classic islander. 40%

Scapa 16 Years Old db (81) n21 t20.5 f19.5 b20. For it to be so tamed and toothless is a crime against a truly great whisky which, handled correctly, would be easily among the finest the world has to offer. 40%

Scapa Skiren db (89.5) n22.5 t22.5 f22 b22.5 Chaps who created this: lovely, you really have to power this one up a bit... 40%

SPEYBURN
Speyside, 1897. Inver House Distillers. Working.

Speyburn Aged 10 Years bott code: L16/303 R165434 IB db (84.5) n21 t21.5 f21 b21 Appears to celebrate and even emphasises its remarkable thinness of body. As usual, juicy with a dominant toffee character. 40.5%

◇ **Speyburn Aged 10 Years Travel Exclusive** American oak ex-bourbon & ex-sherry casks, bott code L18/055 R18/5069 IB db (89.5) n21.5 gentle, almost neutral – but clean; t22.5 nothing neutral about the juicy delivery and follow through: the oak is peppering the palate with quite a rich tannin backbone while the wine gently engulfs, softening and soothing, with a definite sweet grape aside; f22.5 still spicy, the bourbon casks winning through to the finish, even adding a slight mocha finale; b23 really imaginative use of excellent sherry butts. An understatedly complex and delicious malt. 46%. ncf.

◇ **Speyburn Aged 15 Years** American oak & Spanish oak casks, bott code L1717/253 R17/5323 IB db (91) n22 marmalade and chocolate; t23.5 full throttle fruit, or so it seems at first with the huge oily muscovado sugars and blood orange/Jaffa cake kick off. But somehow the malt – usually so thin – here appears to power through in concentrated form and with outstanding clarity, also adding to the rich weight of the texture. The middle is biscuity, malty, yet increasingly spicy; f22 back to the muscovado sugars as the sweet, spicy fruit lingers; b23.5 well done: not an off sherry butt in sight, helping to make this an enjoyably rich and fulsome malt. One of the most inventive and sympathetic Speyburns of all time. 46%.

◇ **Speyburn Aged 18 Years** db (86) n22 t22.5 f20 b21.5 Nutty, malty and displaying a cocoa tendency. But the finish is a bit on the bitter side. 46%.

Speyburn Aged 25 Years db (92) n22 t24 f23 b23. Either they have re-bottled very quickly or I got the diagnosis dreadfully wrong first time round. Previously I wasn't overly impressed; now I'm taken aback by its beauty. Some change. 46%

Speyburn Arranta Casks first fill ex-bourbon casks bott code: L16/097 R16/5130 IB db (90) n22 t23 f22 b23 Speyburn at its most vocal and interesting: rather beautifully constructed. 46%.

Speyburn Bradon Orach bott code: L17/039 R17/5048 IB db (75) n19 t19 f18.5 b18.5 Remains one of the most curious distillery bottlings on Speyside and one still unable to find either its balance or a coherent dialogue. 46%.

◇ **Speyburn Hopkins Reserve Travel Exclusive** bott code R18/5066 IB db (92) n23 young (very young!) with some clean, hairy-chested smoke; t23 youthful, salivating grist offers up a big dose of sweet malt and floaty smoke; f22.5 gentle, lightly smoky grist all the way...; b23.5 the kind of ultra-simplistic raw, smoky Speysider that the distillery's founder John Hopkins would have recognised – and drooled over - over a century ago... 46%. ncf.

◇ **The First Editions Speyburn Aged 12 Years** sherry butt, cask no. 14654, bott 2018 (89.5) n22.5 simple malt and not so simple Parkin cake; t22.5 much more body than the usual Speyburn with the malt really making a mark. Buttery and lithe...; f22 custard cream biscuits...and inescapable, intense malt...; **b22.5** despite its typically warming stance, there is a wonderful lustre to the malt. 56.2%. nc ncf sc. 326 bottles.

Gordon & MacPhail Cask Strength Speyburn 2006 bott 27 Oct 16 (91.5) **n22 t23.5 f22.5 b23.5** Comfortably out performs the distillery's own 10-year-old bottling...truly magnificent 59.2%.

◇ **Gordon & MacPhail Connoisseurs Choice Speyburn 1989** refill bourbon barrels, dist 2004, bott 14 Mar 18 (88) **n22** apricots in amid a malty haze; **t22.5** unusually vibrant delivery – and even more unusual is the slightly oily back up giving unexpected weight; malt dominates, always with a slight juicy fruit hint; the malt abounds and with a light butterscotch coating controls the midpoint; **f21.5** back to usual more prosaic and untidy simplicity; **b22** Speyburn at both its most attractive and full bodied. A pleasant surprise. 46%. nc ncf. 528 bottles.

◇ **Old Malt Cask Speyburn Aged 12 Years** sherry butt, cask no. 14655, dist Oct 05, bott Feb 18 (87) **n21 t22.5 f21.5 b22** Sister cask to the First Editions 12 above. Huge malty signature but thins out much more in the distillery's usual style, More spice at work but less overall complexity. Very pleasant, though. 50%. nc ncf sc. 387 bottles.

◇ **Provenance Speyburn Aged 8 Years** refill hogshead, cask no. 11785, dist Sept 08, bott May 17 (82) **n20 t21.5 f20 b20.5** Intense, sweet, feisty, basic Speyside malt at its most raw and unprepossessing. 46%. nc ncf sc. 390 bottles.

Provenance Speyburn Aged 10 Years refill hogshead, cask no. 11641, dist Jan 07, bott Feb 17 (88) **n21.5 t22.5 f22 b22** Speyburn rarely win prizes for complexity – and this doesn't. But for sheer malty riches, this is one enjoyable bottling. 46%. nc ncf sc. 359 bottles.

The Whisky Chamber Speyburn 11 Year Old ex-brandy cask, dist 2005 (89.5) **n21.5 t23 f22.5 b22.5** Speyburn is a such a fragile, threadbare soul at the best of times that I wondered how it would fare against the persistent, almost hostile, fruitiness of a brandy cask. No surprises, the brandy won. Or to be more precise, the malt extracted the best out the brandy, especially the sugars, to bolster its its own meagre personality. 60.4%.

THE SPEYSIDE DISTILLERY
Speyside, 1990. Speyside Distillers. Working.

Spey 12 Years Old limited edition, finished in new oak casks db (85.5) **n21.5 t23 f19.5 b21.5**. One of the hardest whiskies I have had to define this year: it is a curious mixture of niggling faults and charming positives which come together to create a truly unique scotch. The crescendo is reached early after the delivery with an amalgamation of acacia honey, barley sugar and butter notes interlocking with something bordering classicism. However, the nose and finish, despite the chalky oak, reveals that something was lacking in the original distillate or, to be more precise, was rather more than it should have been. Still, some hard work has obviously gone into maximising the strengths of a distillery that had hitherto failed to raise the pulse and impresses for that alone. 40%. nc. 8,000 bottles.

Spey 18 Years Old ltd edition, fresh sherry casks db (82.5) **n19 t23.5 f19 b21**. What a shame this malt has been brushed with sulphur. Apparent on nose and finish, it still can't diminish from the joy of the juicy grape on delivery and the excellent weight as the liquorice and treacle add their gentle treasures and pleasures. So close to a true classic. 46%. nc.

Spey Chairman's Choice db (77) **n19 t21 f18 b19**. Their Chairman's Choice, maybe. But not mine... 40%

Spey Fumare db (90.5) **n22** minty phenols. Delicate with a light touch of grated milk chocolate; **t23.5** salivating, for a moment heads towards an oily richness then has second thoughts. Checks back to a more citrusy juiciness with the phenols taking their time to regain their intensity; **f22** a little sparse in part with the peat and sugars thinning out noticeably; **b23** a very different type of peaty malt with some surprising twists and turns. As fascinating as it is quietly delicious. I am looking at Speyside distillery in a new light...46%. nc ncf.

Spey Royal Choice db (87) **n21 t23 f21 b22**. "I'll have the slightly feinty one, Fortescue." "Of course, Your Highness. Would that be the slightly feinty one which has a surprising softness on the palate, a bit like a moist date and walnut cake? But with a touch too much oil on the finish?" "That's the blighter! No ice, Fortescue!" "Perish the thought, Sir." Or water, Forters. One must drink according to the Murray Method, don't you know!" "Very wise, Sir." 46%

Spey Tenné finished in Tawny Port casks db (90) **n22.5 t23 f22 b22.5** Upon pouring, the handsome pink blush tells you one of three things: i) someone has swiped the whisky and filled the bottle with Mateus Rose instead; ii) I have just located where I put the pink paraffin or iii) this whisky has been matured in brand spanking new port casks. Far from a technical paragon of virtue so far as distilling is concerned. But those Tawny Port casks have brought something rather magical to the table. And glass. 46%. nc. 18,000 bottles.

Spey Trutina bourbon casks db (90) n22.5 t23 f22 b22.5 The best Speyside Distillery bottling I have encountered for a very long time. Entirely feint free and beautifully made. 46%. nc ncf.

Beinn Dubh db (82) n20 t21 f21 b20. Mountains. Dogs. Who can tell the difference...? I suppose to a degree I can, as this has for more rummy undertones and is slightly less inclined to layering than the old Danish version. 43%

◇ **Berry Bros & Rudd Speyside 21 Years Old** cask no. 25, dist 1995, bott 2017 (94) n23.5 dripping with grapes, prunes (with juice), walnuts and molasses, this is not a nose to forget in a hurry. Perfect for a sherry butt? Not quite, but close enough. Oh, some outstanding black peppers, too; t24.5 so soft, perhaps a little under-strength for the power you know this could unleash: a bit like having a F-Type Jag on cruise control...The spices gather and multiply enough to dominate for a while. The fruit remains thick, refusing to let the malt play. The plums become a little dry while the dates take on aged, toffee quality; f22.5 a little sulphur comes into the mix. But so concerted is the duo of spice and vanilla-led tannin, its damage is thankfully limited; b23.5 I am agog... Usually I end the working tasting day with a sherry-matured malt as 49 times out of 50 my palate will have been addled with sulphur and I have an evening and night to remove the taste. Not so with this bottling: I will have to find another task. Is it entirely free of brimstone? Not exactly, but the trace sulphur is manageable, My main moan is that I would have preferred to have seen this at a minimum 50% abv... 46%. nc ncf sc.

◇ **Cadenhead's Authentic Collection Speyside 26 Year Old** bourbon cask, dist 1991 (94) n23.5 unlike some of their later make, this is perfectly distilled: not a crease or crevice to be found as the concentrated malt and ever sharpening citrus come together; t23.5 oh, if only all of Speyside's later make could have this degree of class: a tad oily, but then a slow rolling out of malt and (unsalted) buttered croissant; deft layering of lightly honeyed tannin; f23 an almost apologetic spiciness lifts the buttered malt; b24 the only time I have ever been stuck in a snow drift came when I was on my way back from the warehouses of Speyside distillery. I had reminded the then owner of the distillery that the very oldest barrels of his maturing spirit was about to hit its third birthday — a date he had completely overlooked. So I, accompanied by my then girlfriend and three children, drove up to Glasgow to be the first to sample the first casks on the very day they legally became Scotch whisky. And on the drive home the skies turned a whiter shade of grey, the snow begun to fall, the road chilled and for the one and only time in my life I became trapped, alongside my fellow prisoners. Now, at 2am of a balmy summer's night — in the middle of the biggest drought in recent British history - I am tasting the oldest malt from The Speyside distillery I have ever seen. Isn't life strange... 48.9%. sc.

◇ **Dramfool 12 Speyside 1995 22 Years Old** sherry butt (77.5) n19 t21 f18.5 b19 Plenty of grape. And a few other things besides. But, sadly, even that doesn't entirely obliterate the very poor spirit. 55%. nc ncf. 156 bottles. Spirit of Speyside 2018 release.

◇ **The First Editions Speyside Aged 24 Years** refill hogshead, cask no. 15001, bott 2018 (81) n21 t18 f22 b20 Not one of the better distilling days at Speyside in this period — and, in truth, good ones were few and far between. The stillman must have been wanting to get home quick for his tatties and neeps (or maybe just his leg over), as this is hotter than the core of the sun. Whatever his hurry was for, I hope was more enjoyable than this... Anyway, if you survive the radiation burns, the malt comes through pleasantly in the end. 59.4%. nc ncf sc. 123 bottles.

◇ **Old Malt Cask Speyside Aged 21 Years** refill hogshead, cask no. 14269, dist Sept 96, bott Sept 17 (88) n22 the cask is slightly in decline with a little milkiness coming through. But it is minimal and there are plenty of goodies to concentrate on, especially the malt and marmalade mix; t23 creamy-textured barley comes at you from all angles: delicious; f21 that slight oak kink flares up at the tangy death; b22 enjoyable despite the imperfections. 50%. nc ncf sc. 224 bottles.

Old Particular Speyside 15 Years Old refill hogshead, cask no. 11483, dist Dec 00, bott Nov 16 (83.5) n20 t22 f20 b21.5 Certainly no shortage of barley as the malt grips, sometimes with sharp fingernails digging into the palate. Hot and a spirit which patently wasn't too well cared for at birth.The oils and light vanilla caress are attractively redeeming features. 48.4%. nc ncf sc. 333 bottles.

◇ **Old Particular Speyside 21 Years Old** refill butt, cask no. 12019, dist Sept 96, bott Sept 17 (93) n23.5 refill it may be. But having established we are damaging sulphur free, you can then be only amazed at the rich influence of cream sherry: some new butts offer less...; t23.5 cream sherry, indeed! Lashings of it, plus spices and Demerara sugars enough to fully arm a Christmas cake; f22.5 plums and chocolate mix sumptuously, and there is still a juicy malt edge for good measure amid the late saltiness; a dull ache late on...; b23.5 a mostly clean sherry butt sees the distillery in an unusual and truly delicious light. 51.5%. nc ncf sc. 362 bottles.

SPRINGBANK

Campbeltown, 1828. J&A Mitchell & Co. Working.

Springbank Aged 10 Years db (89.5) n22 t23 f22 b22.5. Although the inherent youthfulness of the 10-y-o has not changed, the depth of body around it has. Keeps the taste buds on full alert. 46%

Springbank Aged 10 Years (100 Proof) db (86) n21.5 t22 f21 b21.5. Trying to map a Springbank demands all the skills required of a young 18th century British naval officer attempting to record the exact form and shape of a newly discovered land just after his sextant had fallen into the sea. There is no exact point on which you can fix...and so it is here. A shifting dram that never quite tastes the same twice, but one constant, sadly, is the bitterness towards the finale. Elsewhere, it's one hell of a journey...! 57%

Springbank Aged 15 Years db (88.5) n22.5 t22 f22 b22. Last time I had one of these, sulphur spoiled the party. Not this time. But the combination of oil and caramel does detract from the complexity a little. 46%

Springbank Aged 18 Years db (90.5) n23 busy in the wonderful Springbank way; delicate greengage and date; nippy; t23 yummy, mouthwatering barley and green banana. Fresh with excellent light acacia honey; f21.5 fabulous oak layering, including chocolate. A little off-key furriness from a sherry butt late on; b23 just one so-so butt away from bliss... 46%

Springbank Aged 21 Years db (90) n22 t23 f22.5 b22.5 A few years ago I was at Springbank when they were bottling a very dark, old-fashioned style 21-year-old. I asked if I could take a 10cl sample with me for inclusion in the Bible; they said they would send it on, though I tasted a glass there and then just for enjoyment's sake. They never did send it, which was a shame. For had they, they most probably would have carried off World Whisky of the Year. This, though very good, is not quite in the same class. But just to mark how special this brand has always been to me, I have made this the 500th new single malt scotch and 700th new whisky in all of the 2015 Whisky Bible. 46%. WB15/096

Hazelburn Aged 8 Years bourbon cask, bott 2011 db (94.5) n23 t24 f23.5 b24 A very curious coppery sheen adds extra lustre and does no harm to a very well made spirit filled into top grade oak. For an eight year old malt, something extra special. 46%

Longrow Aged 10 Years db (78) n19 t20 f19 b20. This has completely bemused me: bereft not only of the usual to-die-for smoke, its warts are exposed badly, as this is way too young. Sweet and malty, perhaps, and technically better than the marks I'm giving it – but this is Longrow, dammit! I am astonished. 46%

Longrow Aged 10 Years 100 Proof db (86) n20 t23 f22 b21. Still bizarrely smokeless – well, maybe a flicker of smoke as you may find the involuntary twitching of a leg of a dying fly – but the mouthfeel is much better here and although a bit too oily and dense for complexity to get going, a genuinely decent ride heading towards Hazelburn-esque barley intensity. Love it, because this oozes class. But where's the ruddy peat...?! 57%

Longrow 14 Years Old refill bourbon and sherry casks db (89) n24 t23.5 f19 b22.5. Again, a sherry butt proves the Achilles heel. But until then, a charmer. 46%

Longrow Aged 18 Years (94.5) n25 t23 f23 b23.5 If you gently peat a blend of ulmo, manuka and heather honey you might end up with something as breathtakingly stunning as this. But you probably won't... 46%. WB15/103

⬦ **Endangered Drams Springbank 15 Year Old** cask no. 596, dist 1993, bott 2018 (90) n22 probably the saltiest malt on the planet this year; t23 yep...your blood pressure might be rising as you taste this gristy malt and salt fest...; f22.5 coppery and sharp...but still the malt puckers on; b22.5 not sure exactly what is endangered about Springbank, one of the world's most complex single malts. That said, this delicious bottling will soon be endangered, as I can see it selling out and being consumed very quickly – even though it is a bit on the young and underdeveloped side for this Campbeltown leviathan. 55.2%. nc ncf sc.

⬦ **Hunter Laing's Old & Rare Springbank Aged 20 Years** sherry hogshead, dist Oct 96, bott Nov 16 (94) n23.5 hefty with the oak really adding on the planks; token grape but salty, too..; t24 now that is unmistakably Springbank. Few distilleries in the world can generate that level of ultra-concentrated malt....and here it is in all its glory. The fruit can do little more than become an add-on as the salt and malt writhe together in ecstasy; f23 spicy with a return to the unsubtle, plank-like oakiness. But the malt still acts as a buffer and controls any excess; b23.5 maybe a sherry hoggy, but any grape is, like us, little more than a dazzled bystander as the salty malt and oak hook p. 58.3%. nc ncf sc. 75 bottles.

⬦ **Kingsbury Gold Springbank 26 Years Old** hogshead, cask no. 321, dist 1991 (93) n24 anything less than half an hour to spare and don't even think of pouring this: this nose is a work of art with the tannins working off so many varying levels of weight and intensity the head spins even without the alcohol. Especially look out for the three different styles of honey on show, ranging from summer meadow blossom, through to ulmo and then heather. The odd sprig of mint underlines the age; **t23.5** a mix of ulmo honey and concentrated malt sees for the throat-kissing delivery; hard to imagine the malt being any more concentrated of the custard tart being more custardy; **f21.5** just a little bitterness on the tiring oak, but the spices distract brilliantly; **b23.5** a beauty but worth finding just for the nose alone! 40.7%. 93 bottles.

◇ **The Loch Fyne Springbank 29 Year Old** (94.5) **n24** old honey where the pollen has started to break down into constituent parts; eucalyptus. Talk about old polished oak floors...; **t23.5** the oak is a shade OTT on delivery but several waves of heather honey increases the sweetness content to desirably attractive levels; amazing silk-like qualities make this probably the softest whisky launched in 2018; **f23** at last faces up to reality and enters a bourbon-style status with red liquorice, maple syrup and molasses – all in diluted form – seeing us through to the gentle finale; **b23** this cask didn't really have much longer to live. Another summer and it could have ducked below 40%, and those outrageous oaky tones would have dropped some of the sugars to go it alone. This has to be almost the ultimate example of whisky brinkmanship. 40.07%. sc.

◇ **Whisky Foundation Springbank Aged 24 Years** ex-sherry cask (86.5) **n215 t22.5 f21 b21.5** Highly unusual to find a Springbank suffering from the ill-effects of old age when less than 25 years into maturation – that is when it is normally just getting into its stride. But there is no denying that this is tannin heavy and creased in all the wrong places. Some excellent maple syrup supplements the big malty middle. But it isn't quite enough to make this the kind of malt one had hoped for....or expected. 47.1%. sc. 244 bottles. Bottled by The Maltman.

Xtra Old Particular Campbeltown Springbank 21 Years Old refill butt, cask no. 11366, dist Jun 95, bott Aug 16 (91) **n23 t23 f22 b23** Don't worry: it may be a refill butt, but all is safe. As you'd expect from a Springbank, complex, demanding and intriguing in equal measure. 54.8%. sc.

STRATHISLA
Speyside, 1786. Chivas Brothers. Working.

Strathisla 12 Years Old db (85.5) **n21.5 t22 f21 b21.** A slight reduction in strength from the old bottling and a significant ramping up of toffee notes means this is a malt which will do little to exert your taste buds. Only a profusion of spice is able to cut through the monotonous style. Always sad to see such a lovely distillery so comprehensively gagged. 40%.

Strathisla Distillery Edition 15 Years Old db (94) **n23 t23 f24 b24** What a belter! The distillery is beautiful enough to visit: to take away a bottle of this as well would just be too good to be true! 53.7%

Gordon & MacPhail Rare Vintage Strathisla 1960 (96) **n23.5** a half-hour's worth of anyone time: outrageously fruity but has acted like a collector of tannins, so the raisins are seriously toasted – a bit like a fruit cake where every bit is the outside; that means molasses should abound...and it does! **t24** the tannins have been brought forward to have the first say. But before they can speak clearly, in whooshes the fruit and takes its breath away – and probably yours', too; **f24.5** one of those where the finish is so long, you are not sure quite where it starts: dried dates, old Flore plums, mocha as well as praline, liquorice, very thin eucalyptus, hickory and dried out molasses and Manuka honey...it rambles forever onwards...; **b24** this was a sherry cask style that 20 years ago I would have criticised for being far too heavy and over the top. In the two decades which have now passed such, has become the appalling state of Scottish sherry butt stock, that I now fling my arms around this style of whisky with love, glee and reverence. Yes, of course it is still over the top. But the enormity and lusciousness of the grape has protected the cask for the best part of 60 years now, allowing the tannins to go so far and no further. And, of course, there is not an atom of sulphur to be detected: the blenders of that day simply would never have allowed it. Worth raiding your piggy bank and exploring this now lost style. 43%.

◇ **Gordon & MacPhail Distillery Label Strathisla 2006** bott 28 Jun 17 (92.5) **n23** wonderful array of malt and vaguely fruity notes, under-ripe gooseberry leading the way in that direction. A little coal dust dries things a little and stirs up the spices; **t24** one of the most silky-textured deliveries of the year: like wrapping yourself in Egyptian cotton just after the bed had been re-laid. The massively intense barley simply caresses the taste buds, then that earlier hint of coal dust arrives from nowhere, still attached to the busy, prickly spice; the bitter-swet balance is pretty much perfect...; **f22** dries rather too austerely and beyond the spice and vanilla suddenly has little to say **b23.5** some moments of this malt are to be cherished. 43%.

◇ **Hidden Spirits Strathisla 15 Year Old** dist 2002, bott 2018 (89) **n21.5** honeyroast peanuts; **t23** the initial firm arrival seems to slip away after the Demerara sugars melt leaving the softer, gristier base malt exposed; the spices are controlled and polite, the Malteser-like malt dissolving like the earlier sugars; **f22** drier with light chocolate spread on toast fade; **b22.5** at times simplistic, at others attractively complex. 51.2%.

Scotch Malt Whisky Society Cask 58.19 10 Year Old virgin heavy toast medium char oak hogshead, dist 30 Mar 06 (79.5) **n20 t20.5 f19 b20** Tangy, off beam and, though the malt flashes wildly here and there, awfully disappointing - especially considering the distillery. 57.7%.

STRATHMILL
Speyside, 1891. Diageo. Working.

Strathmill 25 Year Old refill American oak casks, dist 1988 db (89) n23 t22 f22 b22 A blending malt which reveals the kind of big malty deal it offers older brands. *52.4%. 2,700 bottles. Diageo Special Releases 2014.*

◇ **Cadenhead's Cask Strength Strathmill Aged 22 Years** port cask, dist 1995 (89) n23 an interesting nose: like a rock solid Christmas pudding fruitiness. Very little give on the aroma at all, though it remains enticing; t22.5 no less relaxed on delivery: the malt and Demerara sugars virtually crackle on the palate; f21.5 just bitters and tightens slightly with a blood orange fade; b22 nothing like I envisaged. A very different take on the port wood theme. *50.8%. sc. 252 bottles.*

Cadenhead's Wine Cask Strathmill 19 Year Old Chateau Lafitte barrel, dist 1995 (72) n18 t19 f17 b18. Sulphur afoot with the Laffite *55.1%*

◇ **Gordon & MacPhail Connoisseurs Choice Strathmill 2004** bott 29 Mar 17 (95) n24 the intertwangling between the ridiculously busy oak and the elegant, crisp barley is a good ten minute nosing. After a while a wonderful confusion of delicate bourbon notes is located with a mix of thinned Manuka honey and liquorice backed with molasses. Always playful, always keeping your nose at full stretch with its whispered tones; t23.5 slightly more whoosh than you might expect from the nose, but it settles down quickly after the initial oak-enriched barley delivery has passed. Spices ping and nip from the off; the mid-ground is centred around Lubeck marzipan; at times a little grassy and just sings its Speyside origin; f23.5 light mocha and praline wafer; b24 rather beautiful bottlings like this cannot help but make you wonder why the turn of the 19th century status of this being a relatively widely available malt is not resurrected. *46%.*

◇ **Gordon & MacPhail Connoisseurs Choice Strathmill 2004** refill bourbon barrels, dist 2004, bott 15 Mar 18 (88) n22 light oak seasoning forms an elegant backdrop to the dominating malts. A little marzipan and putty adds the nuttier depth; t23 gristy sugars stroll into all corners of the palate in a beautifully soft, teasing manner. A study of intense malt, though things get a little rocky as the oak enters the fray; f21 disappointingly bitter as the oak no longer plays ball; b22 enjoyable enough, but one expects to see Strathmill in a better light. *46%. nc ncf. 990 bottles.*

TALISKER
Highlands (Island–Skye), 1832. Diageo. Working.

Talisker Aged 10 Years db (93) n23 t23 f24 b23 The deadening caramel that had crept into recent bottlings of the 10-y-o has retreated, and although that extraordinary, that wholly unique finale has still to be re-found in its unblemished, explosive entirety, this is much, much closer to the mark and a quite stupendous malt to be enjoyed at any time. But at night especially. *45.8%*

Talisker 12 Years Old Friends of the Classic Malts db (86) n22 t21.5 f21 b21.5. Decent, sweet, lightly smoked...but the explosion which made this distillery unique - the old kerpow! - appears kaput. *45.8%*

Talisker Aged 14 Years The Distillers Edition Jerez Amoroso cask, dist 1993, bott 2007 db (90.5) n23 t23 f22 b22.5. Certainly on the nose, one of the more old-fashioned peppery Taliskers I've come across for a while. Still I mourn the loss of the nuclear effect it once had, but the sheer quality of this compensates. *45.8%*

◇ **Talisker Aged 18 Years** bott code: L7201CM000 db (93.5) n23.5 once upon a time the smoke on this must have been slightly above the Talisker average, as, even in this genteel and non-threatening form, it comes across clearly, adding an attractive weight. This is a massaging of the nose...; t23.5 you get the feeling that brilliant oak is in play here, as the immediate marriage between the smoke and the tannins is something of rare interdependence. Molasses breaks down into Demerara as the sweetness is consumed by the building vanilla. The smoke is rarely little more than a wisp; f23 just a light shade of bitterness creeps in, but some metallic, smoky heather honey forms towards the finish; b23.5 after such a good age, you don't expect the roaring Talisker of younger days but might expect a little more than is available here. Delicious, nonetheless. *45.8%.*

Talisker Aged 20 Years db (95) n24 t24 f23 b24. I have been tasting Talisker for 28 years. This is the best bottling ever. Miss this and your life will be incomplete. *62%*

◇ **Talisker Aged 25 Years** bott 2017, bott code: L7023CM000 db (96.5) n24 if confirmation is required that the peat on Talisker had a bigger say yesteryear than today, then the way the phenols stand up to the pounding, grey-beard oak gives you just that; a light strawberry jam note, too; t4 such an elegant sweetness for a malt so old. A broad sweep of intense barley before icing sugar turns into lightly smoked Lubec marzipan – then a busy, peppery spiciness, once the trademark of this distillery hoves into view. Though only on quarter power, those spices still generate life and energy...and gladden the heart; f24 plenty of natural caramels begin to absorb a gently smoked mocha quality; light molasses drift though to the finish; b24.5 a malt of magnificent complexity that generously rewards time and concentration. So for some, it may not be easy to get through the forests of oak early on, but switching your senses on to full alert not only pays dividends, but is no less than this great old malt deserves or demands. 45.8%. 21,498 bottles.

Talisker 25 Years Old db (88) n22.5t22 f21.5 b22. Pretty taken aback by this one: it has taken a fancy to being a bit of a Bowmore, complete with a bountiful supply of Fisherman's Friends. 45.8%

Talisker 30 Years Old db (93.5) n23 t24 f23 b23.5 Much fresher and more infinitely entertaining than the 25 year old...!!! 45.8%

Talisker 30 Years Old db (84.5) n21 t21.5 f21 b21. Toffee-rich and pretty one dimensional. Did I ever expect to say that about a Talisker at 30...? 53.1%

Talisker 57 Degrees North db (95) n24 t24.5 f23 b23.5 A glowing tribute, I hope, for a glowing whisky... 57%

Talisker Dark Storm charred oak db (92) n22 t23.5 f23 b23.5 Much more like it! Unlike the Storm, which appeared to labour under some indifferent American oak, this is just brimming with vitality and purpose. 45.8%.

◇◇ **Talisker Neist Point** bott code: L6067CM000 db (87) n22 t21.5 f22 b21.5 Not exactly Nil Points, but for people like me who adore Talisker (indeed, it was a visit to this distillery 43 years ago that turned my appreciation of whisky into a passionate love affair), it tastes like the malt has barely got out of second gear. Where is the fizz and bite of the peppery phenols on impact? The journey through myriad styles of smoke? The breath-taking and life-giving oomph? Not to be found in this pleasantly tame and overly sweet version, though the spices do mount to something towards the very end. It is like observing a lion that has had its teeth forcibly removed. 45.8%.

Talisker Port Ruighe db (88) n22 t22 f22 b22. Sails into port without changing course 45.8%.

Talisker Skye (85) n21 t22 f21 b21. The sweetest, most docile Talisker I can ever remember with the spices working hard in the background but weirdly shackled. More Toffee Sky than Vanilla... 45.8% WB16/051

Talisker Storm db (85.5) n20 t23 f21 b21.5 The nose didn't exactly go down a storm in my tasting room. There are some deft seashore touches, but the odd poor cask −evident on the finish, also - has undone the good. But it does recover on the palate early on with an even, undemanding and attractively sweet display showing malt to a higher degree than I have seen any Talisker before. 45.8%.

Hepburn's Choice Talisker 5 Years Old refill hogshead, dist 2011, bott 2017 (86.5) n21.5 t22.5 f21 b21.5 Thought this would be a fascinating malt to mark the 200th new whisky tasted for Bible 2018. Just trace outlines of cask involvement and at times of peat also which takes a back seat to the rigid metallic backbone (actually,just discovered I described a similar Talisker bottling metallic over a week ago...beginning to see a theme here). Just nothing like the samples of Talisker 5 I tasted 20 years ago, but enough gristy sweetness to enjoy. 46%. nc ncf sc.

Hepburn's Choice Talisker 6 Years Old refill hogshead, dist 2010, bott 2016 (84.5) n21 t22.5 f20 b21 Very little is getting in the way of the peat here in a bottling which shows Talisker at its most phenolic. Struggles, though, for a satisfactory balance as the nose and finish are stark and metallic. 46%. nc ncf sc. 368 bottles.

Old Malt Cask Talisker Aged 7 Years refill hogshead, cask no. 13273, dist Nov 09, bott Feb 17 (88.5) n21.5 t23 f22 b22 Enjoyable. But still can't help wondering: what the hell has happened to the fire, that spiced inferno, of torturous pleasure which once made this distillery truly unique....? 50%. nc ncf sc. 393 bottles.

Provenance Talisker Aged 8 Years refill hogshead, cask no. 11178, dist Apr 08, bott May 16 (88.5) n22 t22.5 f22 b22 Not a Talisker 8 as those of us old enough will remember it from a lifetime ago. But rewardingly eccentric nonetheless. 46%. nc ncf sc.

TAMDHU

Speyside, 1897. Ian Macleod Distillers. Working (re-opened 3rd March 2013).

Tamdhu db (84.5) n20 t22.5 f21 b21. So-so nose, but there is no disputing the fabulous, stylistic honey on delivery. The silkiest Speyside delivery of them all. 40%

Tamdhu Aged 10 Years oak sherry cask db (69.5) n17 t18.5 f17 b17. A much better malt when they stick exclusively to ex-bourbon casks, as used to be the case. 40%

Tamdhu Aged 18 Years bott code L0602G L12 20/08 db (74.5) n19 t19 f18 b18.5. Bitterly disappointing. Literally. 43%.

Tamdhu 25 Years Old db (88) n22 t22 f21 b23. Radiates quality. 43%

Tamdhu Batch Strength db (80) n19.5 t21.5 f19 b20. A chunky bruiser of a dram. What it misses in sophistication, it makes up for with a brooding sugary, spicy oomph... 58.8%

The First Editions Tamdhu Aged 18 Years 1998 refill hogshead, cask no. 12826, bott 2016 (86.5) n21.5 t22 f21.5 b21.5 Something of the Grappa about this, though here on malty steroids. Almost brutal in part, this is where a seemingly gentle Speysider takes you down a quiet alleyway and roughs you up a bit... 52.2%. nc ncf sc. 126 bottles.

⬙ **The First Editions Tamdhu Aged 18 Years** first fill hogshead, cask no. 14732, bott 2018 (89) n22 tangy lemon drizzle cake; t22.5 attractive clean, busy malt with a slightly yeasty middle; the salivating starts dries quickly, then kicks off again as the spices arrive; f22 a little sharper and saltier; bourbon cream biscuit towards the finale; b22.5 about as complex a Tamdhu you'll ever happen across. 51.5%. nc ncf sc. 134 bottles.

Hepburn's Choice Tamdhu 9 Years Old refill hogshead, dist 2007, bott 2017 (84.5) n21.5 t22 f20 b21 Those of you living in the country and chewing straw from time to time will recognise the main properties of this malt. 46%. nc ncf sc. 354 bottles.

⬙ **Hepburn's Choice Tamdhu 10 Years Old** sherry butt, dist 2007, bott 2018 (85) n20.5 t22 f21 b21.5 The usual malty story but just a little untidy on both nose and finish. 46%. nc ncf sc. 452 bottles.

Hunter Laing's Distiller's Art Tamdhu Aged 18 Years refill hogshead, dist Aug 98, bott 2016 (88.5) n22 t22.5 f22 b22 No frills but plenty of malty thrills. 48%. nc ncf sc. 130 bottles.

⬙ **Old Malt Cask Tamdhu Aged 18 Years** refill hogshead, cask no. 14731, dist Apr 99, bott Feb 18 (87.5) n21 t22.5 f22 b22 Sister cask to the First Edition 18 (above) but this is a little tangier and more spice dependent. Enjoyably malty, but doesn't offer quite the same entertainment of its kin cask. 50%. nc ncf sc. 153 bottles.

Old Particular Tamdhu 18 Years Old refill hogshead, cask no. 11472, dist May 98, bott Nov 16 (86) n21 t22.5 f21 b21.5 Sharp, sweet, malty, well-oiled and revels in its bubble gum chewiness – and taste. 48.4%. nc ncf sc. 248 bottles.

⬙ **Old Particular Tamdhu 18 Years Old** refill hogshead, cask no. 11764, dist Apr 99, bott Jun 17 (84.5) n21 t21 f21.5 b21 A little on the dour side with the malts and sugars present but never able to stretch their wings or bring fun to the proceedings. 48.4%. nc ncf sc. 290 bottles.

⬙ **Old Particular Tamdhu 18 Years Old** refill hogshead, cask no. 12201, dist May 99, bott Nov 17 (90.5) n22 a charming mix of traditional Speyside citrussy elan and tannin-rich, bourbonesque showmanship; t22.5 gleeful barley mixes attractively with red liquorice and spice; f23 the faux bourbon theme continues with a series of layered drying oaky tones mixes with docile light brown sugar; b23 by no means a representative Tamdhu: some delicate bourbon elements give this a lift. 48.4%. nc ncf sc. 337 bottles.

Provenance Tamdhu Aged 9 Years refill hogshead, cask no. 11217, dist Nov 06, bott May 16 (83.5) n20.5 t21 f21 b21 Pleasant, malty, clean but stark. Rather overplays the limitations of a limited distillery. 46%. nc ncf sc.

Provenance Tamdhu Aged 10 Years refill hogshead, cask no. 11636, dist Nov 06, bott Feb 17 (87.5) n21.5 t22.5 f21.5 b22 A beautifully sticky malt. Not the most well-endowed in the complexity stakes, but carries its youthful and exuberant malt with an impressive degree of confidence. 46%. nc ncf sc. 445 bottles.

Provenance Tamdhu Aged 12 Years refill butt, cask no. 11337, dist Mar 04, bott Aug 16 (79) n20 t20 f19 b20 The malt works impressively to overcome the dulling effect of the sherry butt. A gentle, pleasing ride for those immune to sherry cask's little spells... 46%. nc ncf sc. 346 bottles.

TAMNAVULIN
Speyside. 1966. Whyte and Mackay. Working.

Tamnavulin 1966 Aged 35 Years cream sherry butt db (91) n24 t22 f23 b22. For those who love great old sherry, this is an absolute. Perhaps too much sherry to ever make it a true great, but there is no denying such quality. 52.6%

Tamnavulin Double Cask batch no. 0308 db (87.5) n22.5 t22.5 f21 b21.5 A bottling which deserves – and perhaps needs – to be at 46% at least. Reduced down to this strength it is levelled to a much chalkier, drier plane than it requires to fully project the oils, sugars and obvious intricacies. Entirely pleasant as it is, with an attractive clean maltiness to the thinned golden syrup as well as well-mannered spicing. But, overall, refuses to open out and develop as you might hope or expect. A 92-plus whisky just waiting to happen... 40%.

C & S Dram Collection Tamnavulin 7 Years Old hogshead, cask no. 2391, dist 15 Apr 09, bott 26 Sept 16 (88) n22 t23 f21.5 b21.5 A substantial malt all the more intense due to its tender years. 57.1%. sc. 310 bottles.

TEANINICH

Highlands (Northern), 1817. Diageo. Working.

⟶ **Teaninich 17 Year Old** refill American oak hogsheads & refill American oak barrels db (90) n22 light custard powder mixed in with the grist; t23 the star is not so much the taste but the mouth feel itself: the oils are gentle but rich enough to ensure the barley and citrus-tinged vanilla stick around long enough for growing delicate molasses to make a difference; f22 light spices before the vanilla and spent molasses notes takes hold; b23 a distillery rarely celebrated in bottle by its owners. Here they have selected an age and cask profile which gets the mix between simple barley and far from taxing oak just about right. Minimalistically elegant. 55.9%. Diageo Special Releases 2017.

⟶ **The First Editions Teaninich Aged 18 Years** refill hogshead, cask no. 14771, bott 2018 (96) n24 has the oaky hallmarks of a dram closer to a 25-year-old marmalade on slightly overdone toast; dank bluebell-laden woods with a salty sea breeze wafting in; the vaguest hint of medium roast Java coffee; t24 a near perfect mouthfeel: sympathetic oils help the malt slip into place with ease. At first a little gristy, the weight ratchets up a few points until a light mocha middle appears; f23.5 Demerara sugars counter the weightier tannins; the spices grumble, the mocha soothes; b24.5 just brilliant...!!! An 18-year-old successfully passing itself off as a 25- or 30-year-old top quality malt. 57.2%. nc ncf sc. 120 bottles.

⟶ **Golden Cask Teaninich Aged 9 Years** cask no. CM229, dist 2007, bott 2016 (89) n22 dry vanilla: barley and biscuit; t22 early, gushing barley dominance with a quick spice introduction; f23 biscuity but with a resounding spice and chocolatey bourbon cream sub strata; b22 stands up exceptionally tall and proud for its age. 62.3%. sc. 301 bottles.

⟶ **Hepburn's Choice Teaninich 9 Years Old** refill butt, dist 2008, bott 2017 (84.5) n21 t21.5 f21 b21 About as simplistic, untaxing a blending malt you'll ever find. 46%. nc ncf sc. 420 bottles.

⟶ **Hepburn's Choice Teaninich 10 Years Old** refill butt, dist 2007, bott 2018 (85.5) n22 t22 f21.5 b20 In my professional whisky career stretching over a quarter of a century I have tasted literally thousands of 10-year-old samples. Only a handful, though, would have been lesser troubled by oak than this offering. It is close to alcoholic barley water. The gristy malt dominant in every department from first to last. That said, as a pre-prandial dram on a warm day before a grilled fish supper, rather enchanting. 46%. nc ncf sc. 804 bottles.

⟶ **Old Malt Cask Teaninich Aged 18 Years** refill hogshead, cask no. 14770, dist Jul 99, bott Feb 18 (90) n23 maybe it's the oaky saltiness, but the malt is uplifted and flies at you as a vivid mass; earthy with bluebells and a promising spice prickle; t22.5 the malt really does come at you from every conceivable direction: salivating, initially clean but soon the tannins begin to get a gentle grip, again showing a slightly salty edge; a little late acacia honey blends in with fudge and caramel; f22 dries with a mocha finale; b22.5 has a real malty swagger about it. 50%. nc ncf sc. 148 bottles.

Scotch Malt Whisky Society Cask 59.54 32 Year Old refill ex-bourbon hogshead, dist 8 Nov 83 (87.5) n21 t23.5 f21 b22 An old malt with a short fuse. Positively bristles on delivery with the most explosive spices arriving early. The barley offers several degrees of change in a well layered malt presentation, but the intensity of the spice deflects attention from an otherwise lovely show. The natural caramels are huge and chewy, as are the tannins as it over enthusiastically shows its years. 46%.

TOBERMORY

Highlands (Island–Mull), 1795. Burn Stewart Distillers. Working.

Tobermory 10 Years Old db (73.5) n17.5 t19 f18 b19. The last time I tasted an official Tobermory 10 for the Bible, I was aghast with what I found. So I prodded this sample I had before me of the new 46.3% version with all the confidence Wile E Coyote might have with a failed stick of Acme dynamite. No explosions in the glass or on my palate to report. And though this is still a long way short, and I'm talking light years here, of the technical excellence of the old days, the uncomplicated sweet maltiness has a very basic charm. The nose and finish, though, are still very hard going. 46.3%

Tobermory Aged 15 Years db (93) n23.5 t23.5 f23 b23 A tang to the oils on both nose and finish suggests an ever widened middle. But such is the quality of the sherry butts and the intensity of the salt-stained malt, all is forgiven. 46.3%. nc ncf.

Tobermory Aged 15 Years Limited Edition db (72.5) n17 t18 f19 b18.5. Another poorly made whisky: the nose and delivery tells you all you need to know. 46.3%

Tobermory 42 Year Old db (94.5) n23.5 t23.5 f23.5 b24 A real journey back in time. Wonderful. 47.7%

Ledaig Aged 10 Years db (85.5) n20 t22.5 f21.5 b21.5. Almost a Bowmore in disguise, such are its distinctive cough sweet qualities. Massive peat: easily one of the highest phenol Ledaigs of all time. But, as usual, a slight hiccup on the technical front. Hard not to enjoy it, though. 46.3%.

Ledaig Aged 10 Years db (63) n14 t17 f15 b17. What the hell is going on? Butyric and peat in a ghoulish harmony on nose and palate that is not for the squeamish. *43%*

Ledaig Aged 12 Years db (90) n23 t23.5 f21.5 b22 It has ever been known that there is the finest of lines between genius and madness. A side-by-side comparison of the Ledaig 10 and 12 will probably be one of whisky's best examples of this of all time... *43%*

Ledaig 18 Year Old batch 2 db (71) n16 t20 f17 b18. There are many ways to describe this whisky. Well made, alas, is not one of them. The nose sets off many alarms, especially on the feinty front. And though some exceptional oak repairs some of the damage, it cannot quite do enough. Sugary, too – and occasionally cloyingly so. *46.3%. nc ncf.*

Ledaig 19 Year Old Marsala Finish db (92) n23.5 this is profound smoke, even more robust and concentrated than when Tobermory first begun distilling their peaty spirit a long, long time ago. There is also a raw element to it also: this is not soothed or couched in oils: the phenols are base and feral, the fruit barely has a chance to get a word in edgeways. It is hard not to become hooked to this unsophisticatedly acrid, sooty attack...; t23 oddly enough, where the fruit barely registers on the nose, it is the first on the palate's roll call. Also, there is softness here for the first time, though by the time the phenols arrive we are back to a rough battle with little finesse; f22.5 settles for a smoky, slightly spikey spice buzz, all the while the phenols rumbling in the background; b23 hardly textbook malt but a real gung-ho adventure story on the palate. *51%.*

Ledaig 42 Year Old db (93) n23.5 if the oak were a person, it'd have got a telegram from the Queen a long time ago...huge age yet the big peat acts like a sticking plaster – complete with Germolene. Under the smoky haze sweet spearmint and eucalyptus mark the passing years...; t24 bravo! There are muscovado sugars and untainted phenols enough to see off whatever oaky inroads might be made. Actually, the tannins take their time allowing the most salivating sugars and even barley to make a mockery of the passage of four decades; f22 begins to tighten as the toasty oak begin to march into town, dries and aggressively bitters by the moment; a little light spice brazens it out; b23.5 only on the nose and very finish do we encounter excessive age which is borderline OTT but somehow stays within levels of toleration. For the most part this is a triumph of smoky elegance over advancing years. *46.7%.*

Ledaig Dùsgadh 42 Aged 42 Years db (96) n25 t24.5 f22.5 b24 It has to be about 30 years ago I tasted my first-ever Ledaig – as a 12 year old peated malt. This must be from the same stocks, only this has been housed in exceptional casks. Who would have thought, three decades on, that it would turn into some of the best malt bottled in a very long time. A smoky experience unlikely to be forgotten. *46.3%*

Ledaig 1996 db (88) n21 some annoying barrels in there have seen better days and the tang distracts from what would have been a playful smokiness; t23.5 grip your seat, fling your head back, close your eyes and chew...we are in business. Absolutely sublime mouth feel: dense yet passable, lush yet never boggy. The dark sugars and barley intertwangle quite deliciously with the underplayed smoke...; f21 long, smoky bacon and still that lovely oil trace. Thins out towards a pasty austerity just when it starts getting really interesting.... damn it...!! b22.5 a malt you feel is at times reaching for the stars. But has to settle for an, ultimately, barren planet. *46.3%*

⬩ **Acla Selection Tobermory 20 Years Old** hogshead, cask no. 0342, dist 1995, bott 2015 (93) n23.5 a salty, oaky buzz seems to galvanise the already intense barley evident. Just jumps, three dimensionally, from the glass...; t23.5 just a fabulous delivery: there is an effervescence to both the barley and Demerara sugars which simply abound: the perfect antidote to the miserable, misty Spring morning outside; f23 delightful spice and malty tannin topped by a little acacia honey; b23.5 lively and hugely satisfying. *48.4%. sc. 114 bottles.*

Best Dram Ledaig 8 Year Old bourbon barrel, dist 2008, bott 2016 (94) n23 t23.5 f23.5 b24 Ledaig back to its adorable best. *57%.*

Cadenhead's Authentic Collection Ledaig 11 Year Old bourbon casks, dist 2005 (94.5) n24 t23.5 f23.5 b23.5 Much more like it: those who remember the first-ever bottlings of Ledaig will seriously appreciate this! *61.8%.*

⬩ **Cadenhead's Single Cask Ledaig 12 Year Old** dist 2005 (88.5) n22.5 dry and acidic. A sharper fruit note bores into the phenol; t22.5 succulent but also warming and semi-belligerent. The smoke wanders about without a cause; f21.5 very mixed and random: a kind of smoke and fruit lucky dip; a tad bitter, too; b22 good malt. Obviously very good sherry butt. But the smoke and grape don't always see eye to eye. *61.1%. sc.*

Dramfool Tobermory 21 Year Old bourbon cask, cask no. 127/1996 (86.5) n22 t21.5 f21.5 b21.5 Originally distilled at high speed off the still, the thinness and burn is pretty much there to be seen. As is the malt which stretched and sugary, but at least lasts the entire distance. Some excellent oak has helped repair the damage and add some welcome backbone and soothing buttery notes. *56.7%. sc. 247 bottles.*

◇◇ **Fadandel.dk Ledaig 10 Years Old** cask no. 700815-1716FD2, dist 2007, bott 2017 (71.5) n18.5 t20 f15 b17 This is a massively peated dram which has spent four months under a first fill PX octave influence. Sulphur has got into the system, which certainly catches in the finish. But, as is so often the case when PX and peat meat, it is like setting off a bomb with a sledgehammer. Still, if you are into cloyingly sweet smoke with a sulphur-riddled finish, this is your baby. 55.2%. sc. 72 bottles.

Fadandel.dk Ledaig 15 Year Old cask no. 71, dist Sept 00, bott Jun 16 (89.5) n23 t22.5 f21.5 b22.5 A sharp malt with its eyes on effect rather than complexity. 57%. nc ncf sc. 300 bottles.

◇◇ **Fadandel.dk Ledaig Aged 20 Years** refill sherry cask, cask no. FAP-1801, dist 24 Mar 97, bott 27 Feb 18 (86.5) n21.5 t22 f21.5 b21.5 A very interesting Ledaig made at a time when things in the still house were not perhaps as they are now. There is evidence this was not brought slowly to boil as the thinness of the body matches the bite which is further sharpened by the strength. Even after 20 years the grape and smoke have yet to make peace with the other and rather than forging a harmonised, balanced dram, our palate is used as little more than a battleground. Certainly not short on character, though! 60.7%. sc. 24 bottles.

◇◇ **The First Editions Tobermory Aged 21 Years** refill hogshead, cask no. 14407, bott 2017 (84.5) n21.5 t21 f21 b21 Puckeringly sharp and salty. If you don't salivate to this, then you are probably fatally dehydrated. 50.4%. nc ncf sc. 90 bottles.

◇◇ **Golden Cask Tobermory Aged 20 Years** cask no. CM227, dist 1995, bott 2016 (84) n21 t21.5 f20.5 b21 Mory at its most characterful. Certainly has a bit of spit and vim about it, aggression one might say, though the thin body and texture does ensure that the juiciness of the barley is accentuated. 578%. sc. 243 bottles.

◇◇ **Gordon & MacPhail Cask Strength Ledaig 2004** cask nos. 16600503 & 16600506, bott 22 Jun 17 (91.5) n23 the smoke takes a back seat to the spice prickle which accentuates the oak's involvement; t22.5 huh...! Didn't see that coming on the nose: a real wave of youthful malt, suggesting on blind-tasting a base malt younger than a 2004 vintage. Agreeable sugars work attractively with the oils; f23 more settled and weighty now: still many waves of toasted oak even at this late age. Inevitably spice follows this, though the smoke pops in and out as fancy takes it; b23 the slight aggressiveness here is not the work of the alcohol alone: the oak is keen and fights its corner. 55.5%.

◇◇ **Gordon & MacPhail Connoisseurs Choice Ledaig 2004** bott 19 Apr 17 (90.5) n22 dry in excelsis: it as though even the soot has been drained of any remaining moisture atoms...; t23 better balanced on delivery with the vaguely salivating, sugary grist working its way into the mouth-puckering phenols and hickory; the late mocha in the mid-ground is a relief; f22.5 any remaining oils soon burn off to leave lightly smoked parched vanilla; b23 less a dessert whisky and more a desert one... 46%.

◇◇ **Gordon & MacPhail Cask Strength Ledaig 2004** cask nos. 16600504 & 16600505, bott 20 Sept 17 (94.5) n23.5 intense yet strangely gentle peat: big phenols so beautifully couched in the lemon-drizzled vanilla and dry sawdusty oak; t23.5 immediately comes to life on delivery: gristy and caressing with the phenols and muscovado sugars locked in a friendly joust. Not too sure who wins the battle for supremacy; f23.5 superb spices on just right level. The sugars keep their shape, the smoke its depth; b24 a truly superior example of this malt and a serious blast from the past: Ledaig very much in the colours of when it was first launched...a long, long time ago now... 56.6%.

◇◇ **Gordon & MacPhail Private Collection Ledaig 2005** bott 23 Aug 17 (67) n17 t18 f16 b16 Sulphur laden. 45%.

Kingsbury Gold Ledaig 19 Year Old hogshead, cask no. 800106, dist 1997 (79.5) n19 t21 f20.5 b19 Not exactly a vintage time in this distillery's history. And although there is no denying the peaty impact, the overall disharmony and discontent amid the ranks is all too clear to see. 53.1%. 288 bottles. sc.

Old Malt Cask Tobermory Aged 20 Years refill hogshead, cask no. 13190, dist Jul 96, bott Jan 17 (89) n23 t22.5 f21.5 b22 Such a wonderful nose and delivery! 50%. nc ncf sc. 242 bottles.

Old Malt Cask Tobermory Aged 21 Years sherry butt, cask no. 11891, dist Jul 94, bott Sept 15 (73) n18 t19 f18 b18. Don't blame the sherry butt. That is fine – indeed, it has been wasted! It is all down to the bloody awful distillate made at the distillery. Almost worth rubber-necking for... 50%. nc ncf sc. 645 bottles.

◇◇ **Old Malt Cask Tobermory Aged 21 Years** refill hogshead, cask no. 14082, dist Jul 96, bott Aug 17 (87.5) n21 t23 f21.5 b22 Malty but a little stodgy, too. Some of the tannins ensure a busy spiciness but it is the juicy barley on delivery which stars. 50%. nc ncf sc. 272 bottles.

Old Particular Ledaig 15 Years Old refill hogshead, cask no. 11605, dist May 01, bott Mar 17 (85.5) n22.5 t21.5 f20 b21.5 The star turn has to be the nose, which is startlingly reminiscent of the air breathed in an island distillery warehouse on a dank December morn. However, despite the prompting of the modest peat, the dram never quite takes off and suffers from an unhelpful tangy residue. 48.4%. nc ncf sc. 355 bottles.

Old Particular Ledaig 18 Years Old refill butt, cask no. 11211, dist Apr 98, bott Jun 16 (83) n23 t23 f17 b20 Chunky, rip-roaring peat meets its match with a Melton Hunt Cake fruit onslaught : the marriage is turbulent, passionate and spellbindingly sexy...the divorce is messy and sulphur-laden.... 48.4%. nc ncf sc. 252 bottles.

Old Particular Tobermory 21 Years Old refill hogshead, cask no. 10950, dist Jul 94, bott Dec 15 (88) n21.5 t23 f21.5 b22 A little tangy in part, the soft smoke hides the majority of the cracks. 51.5%. nc ncf sc. 306 bottles.

◇ **Old Particular Tobermory 21 Years Old** 1st fill bourbon barrel, cask no. 11768, dist Apr 96, bott Jun 17 (89) n21.5 nutty and fresh; a little green apple, pear and....where's the oak....? t22.5 beautiful delivery with the intense barley encased in a sugared shell; some tannins seep apologetically through and set off a little spice attack; f22 drier, though the barley echoes through; b23 if this has been matured in first fill bourbon, then it has spent the last 21 years in a fridge...The oak contribution is negligible, even for a second fill after 21 years. Rather sexy all the same. 51.5%. nc ncf sc. 290 bottles.

◇ **Old Particular Tobermory 21 Years Old** refill hogshead, cask no. 11485, dist Apr 95, bott Nov 16 (87) n21.5 t22.5 f21 b22 Never quite reaches star status, but there is something admirable and enjoyable about the precision in the balance between very basic malt and elementary oak. 51.5%. nc ncf sc. 313 bottles.

Provenance Ledaig Aged 8 Years refill hogshead, cask no. 11327, dist Feb 08, bott Aug 16 (90.5) n23 t23 f22.5 b22 A high phenol level appears to be at play here, which makes this a must for peatophiles. 46%. nc ncf sc. 459 bottles.

◇ **Provenance Ledaig Aged 9 Years** refill barrel, cask no. 12022, dist May 08, bott Aug 17 (88.5) n22 dry coal tar and citrus; t22.5 untroubled by oak the gristy peat has it easy. Light oils and again delicate citrus; f22 dry and ashy; b22 a simple smoky number but most enjoyable. 46%. nc ncf sc. 313 bottles.

The Single Cask Tobermory Aged 22 Years cask no. A394, dist 29 Mar 94, bott 13 Jan 17 (94) n24 t23.5 f22.5 b24 What a fabulous example of the distillery at its most complex! 59.1%.

World of Orchids Tobermory 20 Year Old bourbon cask, dist 1994 (88) n22 t23 f21 b22 Take the off-beam finish out of the equation and this is a delightful malt. 47.9%.

TOMATIN
Speyside, 1897. Takara, Shuzo and Okura & Co. Working.

Tomatin 8 Years Old bourbon & sherry casks db (89) n22 polite, though youthful exuberance is easy to spot. So is the fruitiness which displays a distant tang; t23 fabulous delivery of wet-behind-the ears barley and under-ripe greengages: salivating and a lovely lead into the massive toffee; f21.5 just a little furriness to the latte coffee; b22.5 a malt very proud of its youth. 40%. Travel Retail Exclusive.

Tomatin 10 Year Old MacAlabur 10th Anniversary first fill ex-bourbon cask, cask no. 1874, dist 7 May 03, bott 28 Apr 14 db (92.5) n23 t24 f22.5 b23 That must have been one underused bourbon cask in Kentucky, because the tannins never release their grip. 58.4%. sc. 228 bottles. Bottled for the MacAlabur Barrel Society.

Tomatin 12 Years Old db (85.5) n21 t21.5 f22 b21. Reverted back to a delicately sherried style, or at least shows signs of a touch of fruit, as opposed to the single-minded maltfest it had recently been. So, nudge or two closer to the 18-y-o as a style and shows nothing other than good grace and no shortage of barley, either. 40%

Tomatin 12 Year Old finished in Spanish sherry casks db (91.5) n23 t23.5 f21.5 b23.5 For a great many years, Tomatin operated under severe financial restrictions. This meant that some of the wood brought to the distillery during this period was hardly of top-notch quality. This has made life difficult for those charged with moulding the stocks into workable expressions. I take my hat off to the creator of this: some great work is evident, despite the finish. 43%

Tomatin 14 Year Old Port Finish db (92.5) n23 under-ripe greengage shows some nip and spice; t24 salivating, as a Tomatin delivery so often is. But here we get all juiced up by succulent fruit, helped along by glazed muscavado; f22.5 the fruit tails off allowing the vanilla and spice an easy ride; b23 allows the top notch port a clear road. 46%. ncf.

Tomatin 15 Years Old American oak casks db (89.5) n22.5 grass and hay mixed together; malted breakfast cereal with a sprinkling of muscovado sugar; t22.5 concentrated malt delivery. Salivating, with a profound ulmo honey and vanilla mix; f22 remains steadfastly malty, though the oak shows just a little sign of wear and tear as a degree of bitterness emerges; the spices rise to the challenge; b22.5 a delicious exhibition of malt. 46%. Travel Retail Exclusive.

Tomatin Aged 15 Years ex bourbon cask, bott 2010 db (86) n21 t22 f21.5 b21.5. One of the most malty drams on the market today. Perhaps suffers a little from the 43% strength as some of the lesser oak notes get a slightly disruptive foothold. But the intense, juicy barley trademark remains clear and delicious. 43% Tomatin Distillery

Tomatin 15 Years Old bourbon barrels and Spanish Tempranillo wine casks db (88.5) n22 t23 f21 b22.5. Not free from the odd problem with the Spanish wine casks but gets away with it as the overall complexity and enjoyment levels are high. 52%

Tomatin 15 Year Old Cadenhead's Anniversary bourbon barrel, Pedro Ximenez first fill cask finish, cask 34876 dist 30 Nov 01, bott 11 Apr 16 db (93) n23.5 t23.5 f23 b23 I actually began nosing this in the dark, before I was aware of the distillery. But I certainly knew the cask type: the PX drips all over this malt like a murderer's fingers drip blood over a knife. Guys, you are meant to dump the PX before putting the whisky in, right...? Oh, no sulphur by the way...yippee...!! 56.1%. ncf sc. Bottled for Cadenhead's Switzerland.

Tomatin Aged 18 Years db (85) n22 t21 f21 b21. I have always held a torch for this distillery and it is good to see some of the official older stuff being released. This one has some serious zing to it, leaving your tastebuds to pucker up - especially as the oak hits. 40%

Tomatin 18 Years Old db (88) n22.5 t22 f21.5 b22. What a well-mannered malt. As though it grew up in a loving, caring family and behaves itself impeccably from first nose to last whimpering finale; 43%

Tomatin 25 Years Old db (89) n22 t23 f21.5 b22.5. Not a nasty bone in its body: understated but significant. 43%

Tomatin 30 Years Old db (91) n22 t23 f23.5 b22.5 Malts of this age rarely maintain such a level of viscosity. Soft oils can often be damaging to a whisky, because they often refuse to allow character to flourish. Yet here we have a whisky that has come to terms with its age with great grace. And no little class. 49.3%

Tomatin 30 Year Old European & American oak casks db (85.5) n21 t21 f22.5 b21. Unusually for an ancient malt, the whisky becomes more comfortable as it wears its aged shoes. The delivery is just a bit too enthusiastic on the oaky front, but the natural caramels soften the journey rather delightfully. 46%. ncf.

◈ **Tomatin 30 Years Old** bott 2018 db (93) n23 racked with old age, displaying outrageous tannin. Exotic fruit escape from every pore; the kiwi fruit sorbet is exceptional; t22.5 just a little too much oak on delivery, giving both the tongue and palate a bit of a torrid time. Slowly, though, malt and darker sugars work their magic, helped along by an indulgently silky mouth feel and the ever intensifying malt and cocoa; f24 now settles into something a little special. Yes the tannins haven't let go entirely, but the specially tailored Neapolitan ice cream – a mix of chocolate, vanilla and exotic fruit note - come together stupendously; b23.5 puts me in mind of a 29-year-old Springbank I have tasted for this Bible, which showed similar initial signs of wear and tear. But as the whisky warmed and oxidised, then so it grew in the glass and began to reveal previously hidden brilliance. This is not, perhaps, up to those gargantuan standards but what is achieved here shews the rewards for both patience and the use of the Murray Method. Patience and care are most certainly rewarded 46%.

Tomatin 36 Year Old American & European oak db (96.5) n24 t24.5 f23.5 b24.5 The difference between old oak and the newer stuff is brilliantly displayed here. Make no mistake: this is a masterpiece of a malt. 46%

Tomatin 40 Years Old db (89.5) n21.5 t22 f23 b23. Not quite sure how it's done it, but somehow it has made it through all those oaky scares to make for one very impressive 40-y-o!! Often it shows the character of a bourbon on a Zimmer. 42.9%

Tomatin 40 Years Old Oloroso sherry casks db (87.5) n21.5 t23 f21 b22 One of those malts which offers a graceful peep at the past, when sherry butts were clean and offered nothing to fear. But no matter how good the cask time takes its toll and the intense chalkiness reveals tannins that have got slightly the better of the barley. Thankfully the grape is still intact and brings us a beautiful raisin and date depth before the chalk returns a little more determined than before. 43%. Travel Retail Exclusive.

Tomatin 1995 Olorosso Sherry db (82) n21 t22 f19 b20 You can peel the grape off the malt. But one of the sherry butts wasn't quite as spotless as one might hope for. The inevitable tang arrives towards the finish. 46%

Tomatin 2002 Whisky L Beijing - Shanghai 2015 American oak hogshead, cask no. 33196, dist 25 Jan 02, bott 10 Jun 15 db (95) n23.5 t24 f23.5 b24 Spectacularly serious whisky! Takes the oak element to the max without tipping over the edge, thanks to an absolutely top quality bourbon cask. About as enormous as this distillery gets. 57.8%. sc. 288 bottles.

Tomatin Highland 1988 Vintage db (86.5) n22 t22 f21 b21.5. Few whiskies in the world shows off its malty muscle like Tomatin and here, briefly, it goes into overdrive. For the most part, a happy meeting of slightly salty malt and oak. 46%. ncf.

Tomatin Cabernet Sauvignon 2002 Edition db (82) n21 t22 f18 b21 Surprising degree of weight to this one. The fruit is not quite flawless with a little bit of a buzz on the nose and finish especially. But the rich mouthfeel and a pleasant, lush Garibaldi biscuit effect does ensure some very satisfying phases. *46%.*

Tomatin Caribbean Rum 2007 Edition db (89.5) n22 t23 f22 b22.5 Beautifully clean malt though, as is their wont, the rum casks keep everything tight. *46%.*

Tomatin Contrast Bourbon Casks from 1973, 1977, 1988, 2002, 2006 db (94.5) n24 t24 f22.5 b24 This is exceptionally fine malt whisky boasting an advanced degree of structure and complexity. If you don't have half an hour to spare to do it justice, don't even open the bottle... *46%. Packaged with sherry edition.*

Tomatin Contrast Sherry Casks from 1973, 1977, 1988, 2002, 2006 db (87) n21 t22 f22 b22. Certainly a contrast with the bourbon, not least on the complexity front. No damaging off notes, even if the nose is a little tight. But though the grape makes itself heard, it never spreads its wings and flies in this curiously muted offering. *46%. Packaged with bourbon edition.*

Tomatin Five Virtues Series Earth Peated Malt refill hogshead oak casks db (88) n22 t22.5 f21.5 b22 Can honestly say I have never seen Tomatin in this kind of shape before: enjoyable once you acclimatise... *46%.*

Tomatin Five Virtues Series Fire Heavily Charred Oak de-charred/re-charred oak fired casks db (94) n23.5 t24 f23 b23.5 High class malt with a sweet bourbon drizzle. *46%.*

Tomatin Five Virtues Series Metal Bourbon Barrels first fill bourbon barrels db (95) n24 t24 f23 b24 There's metal enough in the "Earth" bottling. Was wondering where the metal comes into things here. As these are first fill bourbon casks, wonder if it was the type of warehouse they came from in Kentucky... Anyway, talking metal: this is pure gold... *46%.*

Tomatin Five Virtues Series Water Winter Distillation sherry butts & bourbon barrels db (72) n18 t20 f16 b18 A small degree of molassed chocolate escapes the grim sulphured tightness of the sherry. *46%.*

Tomatin Five Virtues Series Wood Selected Oak Casks French, American & Hungarian oak casks db (90) n22.5 t23 f21.5 b23 A Franco-Hungarian truce means the malt and bourbon casks can work their magic...Some truly brilliant and unique phrases here. *46%.*

Tomatin Highland Grand Select db (92.5) n23 the style with which this distillery is most comfortable: healthy fresh barley and solid, though not too emphatic, oak. Pleasing light citrus, too; t23 excellent delivery: the two major players share equal billing but the muscovado sugars add a vague fruity piquancy; f23.5 some fabulous chocolate nut on the finish; b23 measured and elegant. *43%.*

Tomatin Highland Legacy db (88) n22 simplistic, untaxing malt and vanilla t22.5 best bit of the experience: the big malt and marzipan surge and interweaving of sharp tannins; f21.5 a light, malty buzz; b22 clean, nutty malt but beyond that unremarkable. *43%.*

Tomatin Warehouse 6 Collection 1971 db (87) n22 t22 f21.5 b21.5. Just one of those terribly frustrating malts where you just have to say: sorry, chaps, but you allowed this one to wallow in the warehouse a summer or two too long. Some superb vanilla and butterscotch, but the tannins have just a little bit too much of a scowl to their faces...That said, still plenty to savour and a fair bit of spice to show there's still life in the old dog... *45.8%*

◇ **Tomatin Warehouse 6 Collection 1972** db (92.5) n23.5 cinnamon, Chinese gooseberry and lychee...: now there's a combination you don't nose every day...; t23 the malt is offered up for delivery, the oak the rumbling aftershocks; f23 a salty soliloquy pays homage to the passing years; b23 I actually remember going through the Tomatin warehouse back in 1993 and tasting from some of the casks they were looking to make a 21-year-old malt from. Exactly 25 years on, could these be from that very same batch? *42.08%.*

Cù Bòcan 1988 db (89.5) n23 quite a dry smokiness; no shortage of herbal notes, too....; t22.5 soft oils encourage the vanillas as much as the light smoke; f21.5 reverts to its naturally dry stance; a few spices liven things up while some late mocha does offer a sweeter edge; b22.5 continually smoulders... *51.5%. nc ncf. 2,200 bottles.*

Cù Bòcan 2005 db (91) n22.5 t23.5 f22 b23 One of the most intriguing whiskies out there today: you never know quite what is going to land on your lap. Here the battle between a very young malt personality and spice is worth the entrance fee alone... Love it! *50%.*

◇ **Cù Bòcan 2006** db (77) n19 t20 f19 b19 Initially sweet, but significantly sulphur hit. *50%.*

Cù Bòcan The Bourbon Edition fully matured in bourbon casks db (84) n21.5 t22 f20 b20.5. The malt battles hard to overcome the poor cask bitterness. But fails. *46%*

Cù Bòcan Highland Single Malt virgin oak, bourbon & sherry casks db (85.5) n21 t21 f22 b21.5. An old fashioned dram: the type Pitt the Younger, or Pitt the Embryo might remember...and appreciate. Appears to be nearer new make than fully matured Scotch: the big player is the oak which, almost, bourbon-like, shovels cart loads of caramel and muscovado into the mix. Green...and engrossing. *46%*

Cù Bòcan Highland Single Malt 1989 Vintage db (95.5) n23 t24 f24.5 b24 the last Cu Bocan I got my nose around, I likened to Pitt the Younger. Well, the only pit here would be a peat one... This is not only absolutely superb whisky, but a bit of a shock, too...Indeed, I am stunned! *53.2%.*

Cù Bòcan The Sherry Edition fully matured in sherry casks db (83) n20 t22 f20 b21. For several magic seconds, the delivery and first four or five flavour waves after offer delicious malt polished by high grade grape. But it is all far too short-lived as off-key notes abound on the nose and finish. *46%*

Cù Bòcan The Virgin Oak Edition fully matured in virgin oak casks db (94.5) n23.5 t23.5 f23.5 b24 Don't expect a quiet little whisky to nuzzle into. This chap has attitude, and no little complexity. Magnificent use of differing honey styles: overall a delightful box of tricks. *46%*

The Cyprus Whisky Association Tomatin 2006 first fill bourbon barrel, cask no. 4191, dist 05 Oct 06, bott 18 Apr 16 (93) n23 t23.5 f23 b23.5 A very impressive choice of cask by the Cyprus Whisky Association: this is as much a pre-prandial loosener as it is a late night puzzler. Gorgeous. *58.9%. sc. 222 bottles.*

⟩⟩⟩ **Gordon & MacPhail Cask Strength Tomatin 2007** cask nos. 4920, 4921 & 4922, bott 13 Jun 17 (86.5) n21.5 t21.5 f22 b21.5 A curious, at times downright strange, Tomatin slightly at an angle from the normal concentrated barley style. Here it appears the tannins are on full throttle and polarised from the spirit which, especially on the delivery, does reveal a surprising degree of new make quality. *58.5%.*

Old Malt Cask Tomatin Aged 21 Years refill hogshead, cask no. 13268, dist Dec 95, bott Feb 17 (86) n22 t22 f20.5 b21.5 Atypical of a Tomatin with the malt playing a very silent second fiddle to the must-style fruit pips. Thin, pleasant but, by Tomatin standards, unconvincing. *50%. nc ncf sc. 309 bottles.*

Scotch Malt Whisky Society Cask 11.32 8 Year Old first fill ex-bourbon barrel, dist 6 Jun 08 (95.5) n23.5 t24 f24 b24 Give me a bottle of youthful, beautifully confident malt like this over an over-aged one any day...Brilliant...! *61.6%.*

⟩⟩⟩ **Spirit of Caledonia Tomatin 24 Years Old** dist 1991, bott 2015 (86) n23 t20.5 f21.5 b21 A little over oaked all round, except on the nose where the barley combines to help offer a nutty introduction and at the very death where some attractive cocoa signs off. *61.3%. sc.*

TOMINTOUL
Speyside, 1965. Angus Dundee. Working.

Tomintoul Aged 10 Years db (83.5) n21 t20 f21.5 b21. Has bucked up recently to offer a juicy, salivating barley thrust. Yet still a little on the thin side, despite some late oak. *40%*

Tomintoul Aged 10 Years bott code: L16 02149 CB2 db (84.5) n20.5 t22 f21 b21 A very consistent dram but far too much emphasis of the chocolate toffee rather than the big malt you feel is bursting to break free. *40%.*

Tomintoul Aged 12 Years Oloroso Sherry Cask Finish db (73.5) n18.5 t19 f18 b18. Tomintoul, with good reason, styles itself as "The Gentle Dram" and you'll hear no argument from me about that one. However, the sherry influence here offers a rough ride. *40%*

⟩⟩⟩ **Tomintoul Aged 12 Years Oloroso Sherry Cask Finish** bott code: L17 02772 CB2 db (74.5) n20 t19 f17.5 b18 A slightly cleaner sherry influence than the last of these I tasted, but the ungentle sulphur makes short work of the "gentle dram". *40%.*

Tomintoul Aged 14 Years db (91) n23.5 t23 f21.5. This guy has shortened its breath somewhat: with the distinct thinness to the barley and oak arriving a little flustered and half-hearted rather than with a confident stride; b23 remains a beautiful whisky full of vitality and displaying the malt in its most naked and vulnerable state. But I get the feeling that perhaps a few too many third fills, or under-performing seconds, has resulted in the intensity and hair-raising harmony of the truly great previous bottlings just being slightly undercooked. That said, still a worthy and delicious dram! *46%. nc ncf.*

Tomintoul Aged 15 Years Portwood Finish db (94) n23 t23.5 f23.5 b24 So rare to find a wine finish which maximises the fruit to the full without allowing it to dominate. Charming. And so clean. Probably a brilliant whisky to help repair my damaged palate after tasting yet another s******ed sherry butt. I'll keep this one handy...*46%. nc ncf. 5,820 bottles.*

⟩⟩⟩ **Tomintoul Aged 15 Years With A Peaty Tang** bott code: L17 02975 CB2 db (89.5) n23 a light Arbroath Smokie smokiness drifts across the malty plains...; t23 buttery to start with an ever intensifying maltiness. The smoke is at first a little lost, but comes out of hiding to give, well, a peaty tang...; f21.5 lightly smoked butterscotch tart, with perhaps a light sprinkling of salt; a fraction bitter as it disengages; b22 being a bit older than their original Peaty Tang, the phenols here a less forward. But, then, it calls itself "The Gentle Dram" and on this evidence with good reason. *40%.*

Tomintoul Aged 16 Years db (94.5) n24.5 t23.5 f23 b23.5 Confirms Tomintoul's ability to dice with greatness. *40%*

Tomintoul Aged 21 Years db (94) n24 t24 f22.5 b23.5 Just how good this whisky would have been at cask strength or even at 46 absolutely terrifies me. 40%.

Tomintoul Aged 25 Years db (95) n25 t24 f23 b23.5 A quiet masterpiece from one of Scotland's criminally underappreciated great distilleries. 43%

Tomintoul Aged 40 Years db (86) n22 t21 f21.5 b21.5. Groans every single one of its 40 years. Some lovely malty moments still, as well as butterscotch. But the oak has just jogged on past the sign that said 'Greatness' and carried straight on into the woods... 43.1%. nc ncf.

Tomintoul 1976 Vintage bott 2013 db (94.5) n25 t22 f23.5 b24 When you get that amount of exotic fruit on the nose, you know there is going to be a massive oaky kickback somewhere. However, this copes brilliantly and even has something fruitier up its sleeve further down the line. This can be taken as one of your five fruits a day... 40%

Tomintoul Five Decades bott Jul 15 db (94.5) n23.5 t24 f23 b24 Writing this Bible, and the inordinate amount of time it takes, day and night, night and day, week in, month out, means that I have to turn down most invites to attend the opening of distilleries and the celebration of anniversaries. Just can't fit it in. So glad the 50th anniversary of Tomintoul came to me in the shape of this luxurious dram. Another whisky which leaves you scratching your head to wonder why Whyte and Mackay sold this brilliant distillery: as though the manager wanted to get rid of the star player to harmonise the dressing room. Anyway, happy 50th birthday, Tomintoul distillery: you are in loving hands now and able to fulfil your enormous potential. 50%. nc ncf. 5,230 bottles.

Tomintoul With A Peaty Tang db (94) n23 t24 f23 b24. A bit more than a tang, believe me! Faultlessly clean distillate which revels in its unaccustomed peaty role. The age is confusing and appears mixed, with both young and older traits being evident. 40%

Old Ballantruan db (89.5) n23.5 t23 f21 b22 Profound young malt which could easily be taken for an Islay. 50%. ncf.

Old Ballantruan Aged 10 Years bott code 1706.15 db (94.5) n23.5 t23.5 f23.5 b24 Can't say this is a spectacular peated malt. But everything is brilliantly in proportion and so sublimely balanced. 50%. ncf.

◇ **Old Ballantruan Aged 15 Years** bott code: CBSC4 02976 db (95) n23.5 it takes a little while to exactly pinpoint the nucleus of the smoke, but once you get its bearings it is impossible to lose. A real salty, acidic bite to this yet with a sweetness of roast chestnuts to ensure a fabulous balance; t24 melt-in-the mouth sugars and then comes a degree of complexity uncommon among peated mainland malts. The succulence of the texture keeps your attention diverted, so you have to re-focus to discover the cleverness of the ulmo honey and its closely woven patterns with the peat. The mid-ground is neither sweet, nor dry – or maybe both as the oakier thrust is made with a little hickory joining the fray; f23.5 just a little bitterness from trig casks, but the pulsing, smoky spices and genteel vanillas compensate; b24 a Tomintoul classic. 50%. ncf.

Hepburn's Choice Tomintoul 10 Years Old refill butt, dist 2006, bott 2016 (81.5) n21.5 t21 f19 b20 Silky and malty. But never quite takes off or sits comfortably on the palate. A little furry and spiked on the finish. 46%. nc ncf sc. 654 bottles.

Kingsbury Gold Tomintoul 16 Year Old butt, cask no. 9525, dist 1999 (95) n23 t24 f24 b24 Suspect this sherry butt has done the rounds: no sulphur off notes whatsoever and enough fruit to make significant and enjoyable contribution. What a wonderful surprise this is! Technically faultless. 59%. 560 bottles. sc.

The Single Cask Tomintoul Aged 22 Years cask no. 2156, dist 1995 (93) n22.5 t23 f23.5 b24 One of those rare malts which just gets better as it goes along. Superb! 53.2%. nc ncf sc.

TORMORE

Speyside, 1960. Chivas Brothers. Working.

Tormore 12 Years Old db (75) n19 t19 f19 b18. For those who like whisky in their caramel. 40%

Tormore Aged 14 Years batch no. A1308, bott 2013 db (83.5) n21 t21.5 f20.5 b20.5. Toffeed, flat and inoffensive. Good dram to have last thing at night: chances are you'll be asleep before you finish the glass... 43% WB15/326

Tormore Aged 15 Years "Special Distillery Bottling" db (71) n17 t18 f19 b17. Even a supposed pick of choice casks can't save this from its fiery fate. 46%

Tormore Aged 16 Years batch no. B1309, bott 09 2013 db (95) n23.5 t24 f23.5 b24 Tormore as I have never seen it before. The label talks about the "long and dry" finish. It does the bottling such a disservice: this is magnificently complex with cocoa notes a thing of sheer beauty. A landmark bottling for Tormore. 48%

Alos Sansibar Whisky Tormore 1988 bott 2016 (86) n21.5 t23 f20 b21.5 If you do try this try not to concentrate too much on the tangy finish supplied by an unhappy oak note.

Instead concentrate on the delivery which boasts a fabulous boiled fruit and barley sugar candy mix. 50.4%.

⟐ **Cadenhead's Authentic Collection Tormore 33 Years Old** dist 1984 (87) n23.5 t22 f20 b21.5 Even after 33 years, the sins of the distillers way back in 1984 cannot be entirely forgiven and the fault lines of the original distillate are still evident and ready to rumble. However, these weaknesses are fully compensated on the nose which deserves full study: a wonderful butterscotch and subtlest imaginable coriander spice gives the unlikely feel of ice cream in a busy vegetable-packed kitchen. The delivery, likewise, is full of molten Demerara intent. Seek some delicious entertainment here and ye shall find. 51.7%. sc. 175th Anniversary bottling.

The Cooper's Choice Tormore Sweet & Smoky Islay cask, port finish cask finish, bott 2017 (96) n23.5 t24.5 f23.5 b24.5 Not a style of Tormore you really expect to see. Someone has done a very good job on this to produce probably the best Tormore I have ever encountered. A big surprise and genuine treat of a dram. And certainly one of my left field favourites of the year... 56.5%. nc ncf sc. The Vintage Malt Whisky Co.

The First Editions Tormore Aged 25 Years 1992 refill butt, cask no. 13311, bott 2017 (93) n23 t23.5 f23 b23.5 Not too bad a butt at all. Outstanding, in fact, and not an atom of sulphur to be seen. 55.9%. nc ncf sc. 434 bottles.

⟐ **Gordon & MacPhail Cask Strength Tormore 2004** cask nos. 901 & 902, bott 24 Mar 17 (91.5) n22.5 the gentlest smoke drifts over the standard barley; t23 that works! Big, intense delivery of the salivating kind, first thanks to the concentrated barley, then a much more muscular toasted oakiness; the spice which hits the middle is almost inevitable; f23 spice and hickory; b23 for a distillery which for years went out of its way to display little or no character, this bottling seems hell-bent on rewriting history. 59.6%.

⟐ **Gordon & MacPhail Discovery Range Tormore Aged 13 Years** (84.5) n21.5 t21.5 f20.5 b21 What you will discover is a malt pretty true to standard distillery character: malty but limited in scope and with a degree of aggressive bite 43%.

Old Malt Cask Tormore Aged 28 Years sherry butt, cask no. 13189, dist Nov 88, bott Jan 17 (77) n17 t21 f19 b20 Full credit here to Tormore which, though not being one of Scotland's more gifted distilleries, has put up a brave fight and offered some massively juicy barley to see off the worst excesses of the off-tune sherry butt. 50%. nc ncf sc. 403 bottles.

⟐ **Old Malt Cask Tormore Aged 28 Years** sherry butt, cask no. 14481, dist Nov 88, bott Nov 17 (93) n23.5 old-fashioned, dry, nose-puckering oloroso with the customary spices and slow infusion of burnt raisin; t24 a medium-oiled, mini-giant of a delivery with the fruit in proper moist fruitcake mode. Love the development of the nuttiness and dried orange peel and the slowest possible involvement of increasingly prickly spice; f22.5 dries appreciatively to become quite dusty; b23 a way above average sherry butt that does not have to have to see off any major obstacles to display its beauty. 50%. nc ncf sc. 106 bottles.

⟐ **The Single Cask Tormore 21 Years Old** cask no. 20313 (85.5) n21 t22.5 f21 b21 From a time when Tormore's distillate had less body than your average ghost, this one has picked up a creamier character than most, though the sweetness is more often aligned with chestnut casked spirits. 46.8%.

Spirits Shop Selection Tormore 1988 bourbon cask, bott 2016 (87) n21.5 t23.5 f20.5 b21.5 For a bourbon cask, this is one very confusing dram. Certainly Tormore is not a malt you normally align with complexity. But here there is so much going on with a fruity, muscovado, fresh date theme that it takes a little while for the cask's origins to make their mark. The finish is of the usual hard, unyielding house style. But the delivery, when peaking, is magnificent. 51.6%. 228 bottles. A joint bottling with Sansibar Whisky.

⟐ **The Whisky Cask Company Tormore 21 Year Old** bourbon hogshead, dist Aug 95, bott Feb 17 (94.5) n23.5 good grief...! Where did that come from? All kinds of orange-related bourbon tones cover this aroma. Spices begin to prickle, but then think better of it as a soothing orange blossom honey and liquorice mix eloquently and with satisfying complexity; t24 just a fabulous delivery: the tannins are rich, but such is the unerring accuracy in those chocolate-orange notes to hit the right spot, the mouth is awash with stirring juiciness. A light buttery sheen allows the spices to slip around the palate without any jarring whatsoever; f23 salted butter still and the slow fade of spiced ulmo honey; b24 not sure I've ever seen a Tormore in a bourbon cask of such high calibre before. Some elements of this almost blow the mind. 56.8%. nc ncf sc. 249 bottles.

TULLIBARDINE
Highlands (Perthshire), 1949. Tullibardine Ltd. Working.

Tullibardine Aged 20 Years db (92.5) n22.5 busy and can't decide which weight to adopt; ethereal hazelnut and citrus rise above the languid tannins; t24 no doubting the richness of body and the exceptional weight: first it is scorched yet juicy barley by the cartload, then thudding oak with just enough ulmo honey to oil the wheels. And then rampaging spice; f22.5

settles for more prosaic butterscotch but the spices continue to bristle; **b23.5** while there are whiskies like this in the world, there is a point to this book...*43%*

Tullibardine Aged 25 Years db (86.5) n22 t22 f21 b21.5. There can be too much of a good thing. And although the intricacies of the honey makes you sigh inwardly with pleasure, the overall rigidity and fundamentalism of the oak goes a little too far. *43%*

Tullibardine 1970 db (96.5) n25 ancient oak but the caress on the nose of the most profound exotic fruit – and the distinguished style with which it is effortlessly delivered makes this something extra special. There is a hint of pineapple and passion fruit but the acidity is kept in check by mango and the most genteel hint of smoke you are ever likely to encounter. Frankly, I could nose this all day long, like hours of foreplay without carrying out the act...; **t24.5** the malt and fruit dissolves on the palate without you having to do anything. The tannins possess the most subtle of spices which shape the mid-ground and offer unexpected life and activity. But before we reach that point we have already encountered the malts, thick in constitution and radiating as gently as possible a Manuka and ulmo honey blend of sweetness, tempered by a chalk dry but entirely delightful vanilla; from somewhere a little mocha can be found, too...; **f23** the chalkiness continues, with a little citrus joining the vanilla now...; **b24s** I am a professional wordsmith with a very long time in whisky. Yet words, any words, can barely do justice... *40.5%*

Tullibardine 225 sauternes cask finish db (85) n20 t22.5 f21 b21.5. Hits the heights early on in the delivery when the honey and Lubeck marzipan are at full throttle. *43%*

Tullibardine 228 Burgundy cask finish db (82) n21 t22 f18 b21. No shortage of bitter chocolate. Flawed but a wow for those looking for mega dry malt. *43%*

Tullibardine 500 sherry cask finish db (79.5) n19 t21 f19 b20.5. The usual problems from Jerez, but the grape ensures maximum chewability. *43%*

◇ **Tullibardine Custodians Collection 1962 52 Years Old** db (87.5) n22 t22 f21.5 b22 This oldie has gallantly fought in the great oak wars of 1987 to 2014 and shows some serious scars. Thankfully a little exotic fruit and citrus makes some impact on the austere tannins on the nose, but they aren't around to reduce the excesses of the finale, though a little chocolate does go a long way. The silky delivery doesn't quite hide the mildly puckering, eye-watering aggression of the tannin but butterscotch does its best to add a limp sweetness, as does the unexpected wave of juicy barley. Some fascinating old timer moments but, ultimately, a tad too ancient for its own good. *40.1%.*

Tullibardine The Murray dist 2004, bott 2016 db (94.5) n23.5 the most beautiful barley, still gristy and sugar-bound combine with the greenest greengages. Yet the fruit appears to be only an extension of the muscovado sugars which slowly yields to the ever-intensifying spice...wow! **t24** it had to be clean and salivating....and it is. Lovers of Glen Moray, Cardhu and Tomatin will recognise this barley style, as though sugars and vanillas are falling from the ever-expanding malt; **f23** the spices have to deal with a minor bitterness but the creamy butterscotch joins forces to see it off; **b24** beautiful, fulsome whisky which just pulses with personality. Still, I think my lawyers are twitching at this one: for the avoidance of doubt, this whisky has absolutely nothing to do with me and I make no money from any sales. *56.1%. The Marquess Collection.*

◇ **Tullibardine The Murray Châteauneuf-du-Pape Finish** dist 2005, bott 2018 db (91.5) n21.5 too much wine evident makes for a tart nose; the malt is restricted, though obviously trying to break free; **t23.5** now that, I admit, is very impressive. A real zeal to the intensity of the fruit and the marriage between the puckeringly spiced grape and multi-layered tannins. Some lovely chocolate raisin moments, but also a feel of the last heady mouthful of big aged, high voltage wine from the bottom of bottle...; for all the flavour complexity and Shenanigans on the palate, remains so beautifully clean, too...; **f23** the grape just never gives up. Still some endearing chocolate in the system...; **b23.5** not too sure my Trademark lawyer's too happy about this one (yes, my name is Trademarked)... Anyway, just for the record: no, I have no connection with this whisky and I don't make any money from sales or use of the Murray name. As I know I'll be slaughtered by the socially and intellectually challenged conspiracy theorist saddoes on the Internet somewhere along the line, thought I'd better make that crystal clear. Also, if I was to have my name linked to a whisky, a wine cask of any description would be the last thing it had matured in. Even one as good as this... *40.1%. ncf. The Marquess Collection.*

Tullibardine Sovereign bourbon barrel db (89.5) n22.5 a kind of 'what's what' of bourbon aromas: an entire regiment of delicate oaky tones from the standard butterscotch through to polished oak floors. But all tinged with a green-ish barley note. Always light and a little chalky; **t23** the nose is transferred almost in identical form to the delivery: more light sugars at play here and a little nutty, too; **f21.5** a slight tang to the fading milky Sugar Puffs; **b22.5** beautifully salivating despite the intricate oak notes. *43%*

◇ **Berry Bros & Rudd Tullibardine 24 Years Old** cask no. 942, dist 1993, bott 2018 (81) n21 t21 f19 b20 A decidedly odd cove, one minute wittering about baled hay and some such on the nose, the next hollering about the frightful and grimacing barley sugar on the palate.

Never for a moment settles down into a happy chappy and then caps it all by becoming deuced bitter of the finish. A borderline bounder, don't you know. *46%. nc ncf sc.*

◇ **The First Editions Tullibardine Aged 25 Years** refill hogshead, cask no. 14449, bott 2017 (88) n22.5 soft with lime and cucumber jostling with the vanilla and malt; t23 glorious! The most fragile of deliveries, by the melting of the delicate sugars, the re-emergence of the ulmo honey after several waves of tannin and then the light spices...just wonderful; f20.5 oh...! What happened there...? It's gone..! Just drops off the scale and dies quickly and quietly other than trace spice; b22 the sharp and unusual decline on the finish may have been due to the oxidisation of the sample sent to me rather than the whisky itself: a full bottle may well be a lot better than this. *46.3%. nc ncf sc. 90 bottles.*

◇ **The First Editions Tullibardine Aged 26 Years** refill hogshead, cask no. 14177, bott 2017 (89) n22 a curious and not entirely unattractive mix of barley grist and putty; t22.5 salivating barley displaying delicious stratum of red liquorice, muscovado and tannin; f22 dries oakily and with the lightest of spices; b22.5 not always a distillery which rewards years in the cask, this bottling certainly shines the malt in an attractive light. *44.4%. nc ncf sc. 143 bottles.*

◇ **Golden Cask Tullibardine Aged 10 Years** cask no. CM243, dist 2007, bott 2017 (86) n21 t22 f21.5 b21.5 Sharp, sugary and intense. Good malt depth. *57%. sc. 189 bottles.*

Hunter Laing's Old & Rare Tullibardine Aged 25 Years refill hogshead, dist Sept 90, bott Apr 16 (84) n23 t21.5 f19.5 b21 Sadly, the event doesn't live up to the hype on the nose. Where the aroma is a tone-poem in which orange blossom honey has a leading role, the oak-dominant, flat delivery and bitter finish is nothing like. *47.9%. nc ncf sc. 174 bottles.*

◇ **Old Malt Cask Tullibardine Aged 25 Years** refill hogshead, cask no. 14450, dist Sept 92, bott Nov 17 (86.5) n22 t22 f21 b21.5 Initially on the sweet, nutty side of single malt, but dries pugnaciously. *46.1%. nc ncf sc. 148 bottles.*

◇ **Old Particular Tullibardine 24 Years Old** refill hogshead, cask no. 12026, dist Mar 93, bott Aug 17 (93.5) n23.5 anyone who loves the smell of European bread shops when they first open will adore this sweet, doughy, crispy roll aroma; t23.5 malt concentrate polished even further by thin orange blossom honey; continuously succulent and juicy emboldened further by a light saltiness; f23 drier oak takes its place to offer a crusty, dry finish; b23.5 a glass of delights. *51.5%. nc ncf sc. 262 bottles.*

WOLFBURN

Highlands (Thurso), 2012. Aurora Brewing Ltd. Working.

Wolfburn Aurora sherry oak casks db (91.5) n22.5 t24 f22 b23 Early days at a distillery and still finding their feet with the still. The cut on this was wider than on the previous bottling I sampled, but there is no faulting the use of the 100% sulphur-free sherry butt. There is the odd aspect of genius attached to this dram, for sure. For the record: just vatted this with some OTT oak-hit sherry-cask 1954 malt in need of the kiss of life, or like a vampire in need of a virgin's blood: I suspect the first time a Wolfburn has been mixed with a 60-year-old Speysider. Result? One of the most complex and complete experiences of the last couple of months – a would-be award winner, were it commercially available! Stunning! *46%. nc ncf.*

◇ **Wolfburn Morven** db (91.5) n23 works better than its tender years would imply as the gentle strand of citrus broadens rather than lightens; nutty tannins and the clean phenols have locked together here to shut out the usual younger notes of such infant whisky; a t23 so much grist! The barley sugar carries a wonderful, understated smokiness which ensures intensity, though doesn't quite add extra depth. The spices buzz playfully as the demerara sugars arrive; a younger feel than the nose, but it doesn't matter: the elements are in place and fit together seamlessly; f22.5 a little bitterness from the oak b23 confirmation, were it needed, that lightly peated malt is a brilliant way of getting a distillery's whiskies out at a young age without the lack of development becoming too clear. This is a delicious and refined amble on the taste buds. *46%. nc ncf.*

◇ **Wolfburn Northland** db (88.5) n22.5 a very young, very attractive, if simple, entwining of light oaky caramels and lighter gristy malt; t22 very young: still has a gentle new make feel but the malt is juicy and the caramels delicate and softening; f22 more of the same, with a little late, half-hearted spice; b22 limited complexity but maximum charm for one so young. *46%. nc ncf.*

Wolfburn Single Malt Scotch Whisky db (91.5) n23 t23 f22.5 b23 This is a very young malt showing an intriguing wispy smokiness, its evenness more in line with having been matured in ex-Islay casks than using low phenol barley. Still, it might have been, and, if so, perhaps reveals a style that would not have been entirely unknown to the people of Thurso when they last drank this during Victorian times. It is probably 30 years ago I was shown to a spot in the town where I was told the original distillery had been. Now it is back, and eclipses Pulteney as the producers of the most northerly mainland Scottish whisky. For all its youth, its excellence of quality glimmers from the glass: a malt as beautifully flighted as a cricket ball delivered by the most crafted of spinners. And offers a delightful turn on the palate, too. The building of a new distillery, no matter how romantic its location or story, does not guarantee good whisky. So I am delighted for those involved in a project as exhausting as this that a very good whisky is exactly what they have in their hands. 46%. nc ncf.

◇ **Wolfburn Small Batch Release No. 128** half-sized first fill ex-bourbon barrels db **(88)** n22 toasty with a bourbon trace. Outlines of muscovado sugar with an almost apologetic hint of chickory; the vaguest hint of something smoky; t23 sturdy oil rounds up all the sugars present and holds them captive. The malt offers a juicy flourish; like the nose some phenols around, but not too well integrated; f21.5 as the oils lessen the tannins become a little discordant and tangy; b21.5 does very well until the home straight when balance is lost. 46%. nc ncf. 6,000 bottles.

◇ **Wolfburn Small Batch Release No. 270** half-sized first fill ex-bourbon barrels db **(92)** n23.5 delightful: sweetened custard powder matches up beautifully with the grapefruit and slightly crisp barley; t22.5 really good oils thicken the delivery where the malt intensifies. A light spice buzz through the mid points, but the vanillas are always holding the upper hand; f22.5 much bigger spice now, plus a a chalky vanilla fade; b23.5 you'd think from the lighter colour to Wolfburn 128 this would be less developed and offering fewer flavour options. Curiously, the reverse is true, the flavours more even, satisfying and elegant. 46%. nc ncf. 6,000 bottles.

UNSPECIFIED SINGLE MALTS (CAMPBELTOWN)

Cadenhead's Campbeltown Malt **(92)** n22 t24 f23 b23. On their home turf you'd expect them to get it right... and, my word, so they do!! 59.5%

UNSPECIFIED SINGLE MALTS (HIGHLAND)

Alexander Murray & Co Bon Accord Highland Single Malt **(82.5)** n21 t21.5 f20 b20. Fudge whisky. Pleasant, but way too simple. 40%

Alexander Murray & Co Highland Single Malt 1995 19 Years Old **(85)** n21 t22 f21 b21. Agreeably spiced toffee. 40%

◇ **Berry Bros & Rudd Orkney Islands 16 Years Old** cask no. 28, dist 1999, bott 2018 **(79)** n21 t20 f19 b19 Twenty years ago this would have been a cask that would be the answer to your whisky prayers. Now we have fire and brimstone. Those unable to pick out the obvious problem might enjoy the big chocolate signature. 53.6%. nc ncf sc.

◇ **Cave Aquila The Eagles Collection Highland Single Malt 10 Years Old** batch no. 1 **(85.5)** n21 t22 f21 b21.5 No amount of cajoling can get this tight and reserved malt to open fully and sing. Tangy towards the finish, but all a little too hefty even before then. 43%

◇ **Cave Aquila The Eagles Collection Highland Single Malt 10 Years Old** batch no. 2 **(89.5)** n22.5 gently nutty, with subtle citrus sharpening things slightly; t22.5 gorgeous texture on delivery: pure silk as the malt washes over all corners; a little not unexpected praline fills the middle; f22 dry toasty fudge; b22.5 this must be the Silky Nut Eagle... 43%

Glenwill RV rum cask finish **(80)** n21 t21 f19 b19 Mainly toffeed, characterless and just zzzzzzzzzz.... 40%. Quality Spirits International.

Glenwill S = 1 sherry butt finish **(73)** n19 t21.5 f16 b17.5 S = Sulphur. 40%. Quality Spirits International.

Grangestone Master's Selection Highland Single Malt bourbon cask finish **(87)** n22.5 t22 f21 b21.5 An attractive interplay between tannin and toffee, though the complexity is limited – especially on the simplistic finish. Good, though brief, molasses lift off on delivery. 40%. Quality Spirits International.

Hepburn's Choice Nice 'N Peaty 10 Years Old refill hogshead, dist 2006, bott 2016 **(87)** n21.5 t22 f21.5 b22 Well, that was nice 'n' peaty...! 46%. nc ncf sc. 355 bottles.

Hepburn's Choice Nice 'N Peaty 10 Years Old red wine finished barrique, dist 2006, bott 2016 **(89)** n22 t22 f22.5 b22.5 Well, that was nice 'n' fruity...! 46%. nc ncf sc. 352 bottles.

◇ **Hepburn's Choice Nice 'N Peaty 10 Years Old** refill hogshead, dist 2006, bott 2016 **(81)** n20 t21.5 f19 b20.5 Dry and tartly metal deficient in part. Rather flat and lifeless. 46%. nc ncf sc. 38 bottles.

Master of Malt Highland Single Malt **(86.5)** n21.5 t22 f21.5 b21.5 Pleasant, absolutely middle of the road malt with a juicy, nutty and toffee-rich character. 40%.

Muirhead's Silver Seal Aged 12 Years Highland Single Malt **(87.5)** n22 t22 f21 b21.5 Satisfyingly salivating. The vanillas arrive with a lemon escort from the first moment, ensuring a semi-ethereal element to this. Lightly oiled and a little nutty, just a tad too much caramel at the times you want the malt to begin to fly. 40%. Tullibardine Ltd.

Muirhead's Silver Seal Aged 16 Years Highland Single Malt **(86)** n21 t23 f20.5 b21.5 A hefty malt with a battling, earthy aroma. Hits its zenith about four or five flavour waves after delivery when it strikes up a stunning spicy walnut cake and date middle. Flags towards the finish, even becoming a little flat and furry, save for the wonderful spices.... 40%. Tullibardine Ltd.

Muirhead's Silver Seal Maturity Highland Single Malt (84) n19.5 t22 f21 b21.5 Though called "Maturity" the malt displays a youthful gristiness from time to time. Not technically the greatest nose, the malt recovers brightly on the palate with a volley of varied sugars and spice, including a light smothering of heather honey. 40%. Tullibardine Ltd.

Scotch Universe Kepler-186f 187° U.7.1' 1775.1" first fill Port pipe, dist 2001, bott 2016 (89.5) n23 t22.5 f21.5 b22.5 That Port pipe must have been very fresh, indeed... 59%.

◇ **Simon Brown Traders Bridge of Avon 2012** ex-bourbon cask, dist Mar 12, bott Aug 17 (83) n20 t21.5 f20.5 b21 A very young, nutty, slightly dense malt. Lots of sugars and oils but no great development beyond that. Will appeal to those who like the Fettercairns of this word. 40%. nc ncf sc.

Tesco Finest Aged 12 Years Highland Single Malt bott code L63353 (80.5) n20 t21 f19 b20.5 Quite possibly one of the most boring single malts of all time: not recommended as a night cap as you'll doze off by the time you reach the third step on your stairs, and it won't be the effect of the alcohol. Bland barely covers it. With the amount of cream toffee found on the nose and palate not sure if this should be stocked in the Spirits or Sweets aisles. Do I like it? No. Do I dislike it? No. But if I am putting 12-year-old malt into my body, I'd like it to have some semblance of character. I suppose it was designed to offend nobody: a mute hardly can. Trouble is, it is hardly likely to get new drinkers wanting to come back and discover more about single malt, either. Oh well, I suppose that buggers up any chance of getting The Bible stocked and sold by Tesco this year. But I'm afraid they need to hear the truth. 40%.

Trader Joe's Highland Single Malt 1996 17 Years Old (86.5) n21.5 t22 f21.5 b21.5. Some serious juiciness and spice on the delivery. The spices last the course. 40%.

◇ **Whisky-Fässle Orkney 13 Year Old** sherry butt, dist 2004, bott 2017 (93.5) n23 the mix of muscular tannin and exploding, fat sultana is delightful; t24 succulent and spicy on delivery. The malt is pretty concentrated, but the sweet muscovado sugar, sultana and pear juice does a great balancing act; f23 drier spices, but the maple syrup and sultanas keep the narrative going. Absolutely nothing off key at all... b23.5 did I expect a sherry butt quite this good? I'll be honest: I really didn't: bitter experience has taught me in recent years to be wary of the words sherry and Orkney in the same sentence. So my emergency palate cleaners were primed, but not needed. 50.5%.

UNSPECIFIED SINGLE MALTS (ISLAND)

Master Of Malt Island Single Malt (91.5) n22.5 t23 f22.5 b23.5. Don't know about Lord of the Isles. More like Lord of the Flies...Fruit flies, that is...! They would be hard pressed to find even an over-ripe mango any juicier than this gorgeous malt... 40%

UNSPECIFIED SINGLE MALTS (ISLAY)

Ben Bracken Islay Single Malt 22 Years Old dist 1993 (96) n24.5 t24 f23.5 b24 A real old timer showing its oaky scars with pride. A serious late night dram. And with an unspoiled palate, for this will be one of your smoky treats of the year... 40%

◇ **Cadenhead's Islay 9 Years Old** (94) n23 apparently docile and quiet; closer inspection makes you amend that to relaxed and even as some deeper phenol notes suggesting a possible change in character...; t24.5 the delivery just about represents perfection for the peatophile: the most extraordinary, rounded mouth feel and waves of intense peat, ever increasing in their lucidity. The sugars are pure grist...nothing else; f23.5 a simple linking of arms between the vanilla and the phenol; b23 only a degree of over simplicity has docked marks here. If it is prefect, clean, beautifully rounded, juicy all-enveloping peat you are after, then you might be tempted to give it a straight 100... 58.9%. sc. 175th Anniversary bottling.

Cask Islay (91.5) n22.5 t23 f22.5 b23 Does what it says on the tin. 46%. A.D. Rattray

◇ **Demijohn 8 Year Old Islay Region** (92.5) n23 oily and just pumped up with uncomplicated, smoky grist; a little citrus on the drier smoke elements; t23.5 all as it should be: the sugars burst forth with a mix of ulmo honey and molasses which eagerly counter the massive waves of smoke which surf the oil; f23 a little smoky spice buzz, but vanilla dominates; b23 clean, sweet and highly impressive youngster that has never mixed with undesirable company. 59.8%.

Eilan Gillan Islay Single Malt bourbon refill casks, dist 2010, bott 2015 (91.5) n23 t23 f22.5 b23 It's Leap Year's Day and a charming way to officially kick off tasting for the 2017 Bible! No doubting the youth and I especially chose a youngster hoping it would have enough bite and attitude to slap my taste buds back into action. It has not disappointed me in any way. A little belter! Ignore the descriptor on the label, though. It is nothing like...Oh well, one down, another 999 (at least!) to go... 43%. nc ncf.

Eiling Lim Bessie's Dram (88) n22.5 t22.5 f21 b22 A distinctly Laphroaigian type dram complete with Allied style bitter cask (oh, I have just spotted that this is Laphroaig...!!!), s plenty to enjoy. *51.3%.*

⬦ **Elements of Islay AR10** (93) n23.5 such typical dry sooty seaweedy notes. Oh, and that touch of citrus, of course....; t23 the oils coat the mouth like a warm blanket over your winter bed. Gristy sugars get sweeter still as the Demerara sugars kick in. This meets onrushing spices head on; f23 both you and the whisky now sigh...more peaceful vanillas arrive while the smoke caresses from near and afar; b23.5 not a fault, an off note, a flavour profile out of place, just sheer joy, though always on the lighter, less intense side of the distillery's spectrum. Well, just can't think what this might be... Ardbeg by any chance...? *52.4%.*

⬦ **Elements of Islay Cl8** (93) n23 the phenols are both ashy and in more weighty form; the confident vanillas an excellent counterpoint; t23.5 wow! The nose doesn't quite gear you up for the big blast of Manuka honey evidently dipped in peat concentrate, nor the spices which roar into action; f23 settles into a buzzing essay of molassed and smoky complexity with near perfect weight; b23.5 the natural sugars appears to have been piled in to create a real sweetie. This is a deceptively big dram. *55.2%.*

⬦ **Elements of Islay Cl10** (95) n23.5 dry anthracite and peat reek, sharp, dry, acidic and oily; t24 it's the clarity you notice first: the sugars dripping off the grist with any oak interference. Then the oils, followed by the entire enveloping of the mouth by multi-layered phenols. Those sugars, mainly of a Demerara hue, cover a lot of ground and maximise the juiciness which seeps out a barley maltiness despite the smoke; f23.5 long with the oak at last marking a delicate mark but the smoke and grist lingering and lingering some more; b24 one of those moments where my mind wondered, I nosed instinctively and without thinking said: "ah, Caol Ila!" Simply unmistakable and so true to the distillery. Beautiful. *58.2%.*

⬦ **Elements of Islay Lg7** (94.5) n23.5 the smoke signals are clear: "do not taste this whisky unless you want to be assaulted by massive peat"... A lovely, honeyed sweetness to this, with the phenols clinging to every nuance; t24 those smoke signals don't lie: truly enormous, muscular delivery, though again with the sugars in just the right proportions; f23.5 moderate oils stretch the gristy sugars into the slow crescendo of tannin; b23.5 does everything it says on the tin – and more. Some younger elements appear to be at work here, which means the peat intensity can sometimes fly, deliciously and dramatically, off the scale. *56.8%.*

⬦ **Elements of Islay LG8** (91) n22.5 firm phenols with a dash of lime; t23.5 surperb delivery as the texture seems perfectly formed to harmonise the muscular peat, spice, natural caramels and ulmo honey. The mid-ground begins to wobble slightly as a vague tang develop and the spices hot up a bit; f22 a dusty finish with a little Venezuelan chocolate latching onto the smoke. But the oak continues to have a minor yet slightly unsteadying influence; b23 against the back drop of excellence, some oak with attitude has a slightly too big a say. *59.5%.*

⬦ **Elements of Islay OC5** (95.5) n24 you have dived head-first into a concentrated peat factory...; t24.5 it is as if the phenols have squeezed out every last atom of sugary barley juice to impart a surprisingly juicy delivery...then soon lands on the grist and covers every last molecule with smoke...wow! f23 a vague bitterness on the oak actually momentarily upstages of the phenols, which is some achievement; the spices are now pinging around with untold glee; b24 anyone who drinks an overdose of this will have "peated to death" on their autopsy report. *59.8%.*

⬦ **Glen Castle Islay Single Malt 1990** dist 1990, bott 2017, bott code: L1 1520-2017 11 (94.5) n24 the manner in which the smoke and fruit dovetails is reason to pause over the aroma: this is not to be hurried. Age has withered the muscle of the peat, leaving it to gently embrace the oak without any attempt at dominance. In return, the tannins are polite and help infuse the ripe cherry and dried dates with the phenols; t24 silky and so beautifully orchestrated delivery with still an intense maltiness to be found, quite separate from the smoke. The oak pulses its resins in a form of toasty sugars; a lot of fudge fills the mid-ground; f22.5 a light citrus moment but the caramel becomes king; b24 had the toffee levels been down a bit, this might have carried off an award. Quite brilliant. *52.5%.*

Liquid Treasures Islay Malt 8 Year Old bourbon cask, dist 2008, bott 2016 (92.5) n23 t23.5 f23 b23 High ranking malt and very good cask makes for an excellent if simplistic 8-year-old. *58.5%. Fairy Tales Edition.*

Master of Malt Islay Single Malt (90.5) n22 t23 f22.5 b23 A smoky, gristy must for peat heads. *40%.*

Master of Malt Single Cask Williamson 6 Year Old dist 2009 (94.5) n24 t23.5 f23 b24 Is the 62.5 the strength or phenol level? Probably both. Williamson is a very smoky boy. And a very beautiful one, too. *62.2%. sc.*

⬦ **Peat's Beast** bott code: L 07 08 17 (92) n22.5 strikingly youthful. The peat is an unformed mishmash of phenols and varying hues and intensities; the spices and sugars are up in arms. Frankly, outrageously thrilling...; t23 thumping, uncompromising peat (as would be demanded after such a nose) – again showing youth as the phenol count has had little or no time to diminish. A gristy maltiness melds with an oily mocha sweetness where Manuka honey plays a keen role; **f23.5** a mix of praline and chocolate spread...smoked of course...; **b23** nosing this whizzed me back to the late 1980s and my old office in a national newspaper in Fleet Street where, by night, I was taking my first tentative steps into the then unknown and practically non-existent medium of whisky writing. And I remember opening up a Bowmore 5-years-old bottled by Oddbins. I'm not saying this is a Bowmore, but so many features on display in that landmark bottling 30 years ago are also to be found here... *46%. ncf.*

◈ **Peat's Beast Twenty Five** bott code: L1 1409-2017 11 **(88.5) n23** instead of a beast we have a bit of a cuddly kitten: gives the odd scratch but content just to sleep. The smoke has been rounded down by age and possibly other factors, so the phenols snuggle up to the nose, with a vague fruity, saltiness for company; **t23** your taste buds are gently embraced and caressed by the effusive smoke, the demerara and then muscovado sugars building in weight and purpose. A little bitterness begins to develop but a semi-bourbon style hickory and liquorice thread tries to divert your attention; **f20** a distinct furry weakness on the finale; **b22.5** there are far more beastly Islay whiskies than this out there – a quarter of a century in the cask means the teeth have been blunted, the claws clipped. And if you must "tame it" further, for God's sake ignore the daft advice on the label about adding water. Please use the Murray Method described on page 9. That will keep the thing alive while making it purr at full decibels... And this is so lovely (well, finish apart), it is worth listening to at full volume... which isn't very loud. *52.2%. ncf.*

◈ **Port Askaig 8 Years Old (85) n20 t22 f21.5 b21.5** Thankfully the slightly disappointing and sketchy nose isn't matched by the delivery which shows far greater harmony between the phenols and oaky vanillas. The finish, though, doesn't enjoy quite the same assuredness, despite the spice. *45.8%.*

◈ **Port Askaig 14 Year Old Bourbon Cask** dist 2004 **(95) n24** if I had time enough, I'd nose this all day. I don't but still have taken a few extra minutes for the genteel smoke to waft serenely around my nasal cavity, while at the same time noting the cleverness of the praline wafers which add both sweetness and a slightly different measure of weight; **t23.5** the delivery is no less delicate, except now the sugars have stepped up a gear or two. A mix of grist and acacia honey appears to deal with the malt, while a little Manuka honey appears on behalf of the smoke. By the mid-ground the spices assemble, louder than might normally be expected, thanks to the hush elsewhere on the palate; **f23.5** peat of such sensitivity can stretch only so far. So we reach a point where the phenols are now just background stars while back on earth the vanillas and persistent malty tones hold an earthy court; **b24** for those who prefer their peat to caress rather than kick. Elegant and so beautifully sensual. *45.8%.*

◈ **Port Askaig 15 Years Old** sherry cask **(87.5) n22.5 t22 f21.5 b21.5** I know, I know: I have a blind spot for this kind of whisky. Rather, not blind, but not an over developed appreciation of the big smoke notes slugging it out with and then being neutralised by equally big, occasionally eye-wateringly sharp, fruit ones. At least the sherry is clean and extra marks for that. But, for me, this is just too much of a tit-for-tat malt leaving a neutral toffee fruitiness to claim the big prize. Pleasant, I grant you. But I want it to be so much more.... *45.8%.*

◈ **Port Askaig 45 Years Old (90.5) n23** exotic fruit topped with a light dusting of smoke; a light spice nip; the vanilla almost bubbles in intensity, but the dull smoke keeps a lid on it; **t23** spices are up and at you early, but fade almost as quickly as they come. A vanilla and smoke facade takes its place; juicy with the smoke still making its mark. A bourbonesque hickory and demerara moment or two comes as relief; **f22** a degree of tiring tannins as the sweetness and smoke fags; **b22.5** even in my scaringly long career, I can probably count the number of peated malts that made it to this kind of age and then into a commercial bottling on one hand. Certainly by the end it is showing every year that has passed, but for an unexpected period the malt hangs together...sometimes surprisingly deliciously. *40.8%.*

Port Askaig 100 Proof (96.5) n24 can't ask for much more: the clarity matches the purity of the pale yellow colour, and that tint helps explain the nose. Deft vanillas can be heard here, alongside gristy malt; confident, yet never arrogant or boastful peat. Astonishing...; **t24** the sugars melt in the moth on impact. Just a light oiliness coats the mouth sufficiently for the citrus phenols to ensure there are two distinct weights on display. Yet, somehow, they seem equally poised...; **f24** what perfect oak must have been deployed here. No off notes or buzz. Just the insistent and steadying hand of vanilla/butterscotch to add a gentle counter to the spice and smoke; **b24.5** just exemplary, high quality Islay: a must experience malt. If you find a more beautifully paced, weighted and elegant Islay this year, I'd really like to hear about it.... *57.1%*

◇ **Romantic Rhine Collection Dun Naomhaig Bay Isle of Islay** bott 2017 (89) n22.5 a real industrial feel to this peat, as though anthracite smoke is added to give a big acidic kick; t23 that is one sharp, seemingly youthful but lovely delivery. Fishermen's Friend lozenges at first, but then the course changes to a more aggressive smokiness, though with darker sugars as a counter punch; gorgeously juicy throughout; f21.5 slightly slapstick feel to the finale as the oak fails to find its perch; b22 something a little raw and untamed about this. Which makes it rather fun. 55%. nc ncf.

◇ **Romantic Rhine Collection Dun Naomhaig Water Isle of Islay** batch no. 5 (87) n22 t22 f21 b22 A seemingly tamer, more sanitised version of their Naomhaig Bay but with more vanilla and caramel to blunt the peaty edges. 40%. nc ncf.

Scotch Universe Callisto I 110° R1.2′ 1846.4″ American bourbon hogshead, dist 2007, bott 2016 (92) n23 t23.5 f22 b23.5 The delivery is out of this world. 57.3%.

◇ **Single Cask Collection William & Son Aged 9 Years** bourbon barrel, cask no. 1887, dist 19 May 08, bott 21 Dec 17 (90.5) n22 exceedingly salty: a real earthy tang to the phenols; t23 early sweet grist, as expected, a light layering of citrus-infused oils and buttery Lincoln biscuits; f22.5 remains biscuity with gentle spices penetrating the vanilla; b23 from the sweaty armpit school of salty smokiness. 56.8%. nc ncf sc. 260 bottles.

Smokey Joe Islay Malt (94.5) n23 t24 f23.5 b24 A high quality Islay ticking all the required boxes. 46%

◇ **Smuggler's Vintage Cask Speyside Mystery 14 Years Old** sherry cask (89.5) n23 ostensibly a clean sherry butt at play. Massive over-ripe greengages, sultanas of rare juiciness, figs and molasses. The malt is a little conspicuous by its absence...; t23 delivers like a peach. Actually, no: a peach is one of the few fruits I can't locate on here. Sticks to the fruit salad of the nose while the molasses become drier and more liquorice minded; f21.5 anyone for a taste for Cadbury's chocolate raisin will be in ecstasy...; a vague furriness, alas...; b22 virtually no sulphur...! Now's there's a mystery... 56%. sc. 156 bottles.

That Boutique-y Whisky Company Williamson 6 Year Old batch 1 (86.5) n22.5 t22 f20.5 b21.5 Smoky, pleasant, easy going, friendly. But also, I'm afraid to say, a little boring, too. 50.2%.

The Whisky Chamber Buair An Diabhail Vol. XII (92.5) n23 t23.5 f23 b23.5 After the initial immense bite – something of Great White Shark proportions – eventually settles down into a much more docile and delicious beast. 58.1%. sc.

◇ **The Whisky Chamber Buair an Diabhail Vol. VIX** (88.5) n23 some serious nip to the major smoke. Highly attractive weight and pace with good tannin development; t22 far more sugars than expected: gristy with the commensurate smoke. Big oils, too, with burnt toast forming the mid-ground, with a little golden syrup to sweeten the impact; f21 bitters out further; very late cocoa b22.5 a busy, full-bodied, no-holds barred Islay. 58.3%. sc.

UNSPECIFIED SINGLE MALTS (LOWLAND)

Tweeddale Single Lowland Malt Scotch Whisky 14 Years db (89) n21.5 t23.5 f22 b22 busy, bustling, elegant and old-fashioned...like a small borders town. 62%. nc ncf sc. Stonedean Ltd.

UNSPECIFIED SINGLE MALTS (SPEYSIDE)

Alos Sansibar Whisky Speyside Region 1975 bott 2016 (96.5) n24.5 t24 f24 b24 Great malt plus magnificent cask multiplied by time equals an unforgettable whisky experience. Exquisite. 46.9%.

Ben Bracken Speyside Single Malt Aged 8 Years American white oak bourbon barrels (85.5) n21.5 t22.5 f20 b21.5. Juicy and pleasant, with an attractive honey and molasses middle. But the caramel wipes out any meaningful complexity. 40%

Ben Bracken Speyside Single Malt 28 Years Old dist 1987 (84.5) n22 t21 f21.5 b20. The early promise on delivery – where the malt powers through with spice on its coattails – isn't backed up quite as one may wish. Goes through a number of tangy turns, where even after 28 years the tannin appears to be uneasy with the malt, or perhaps the other way round, before it settles down for a light vanilla finish, tinged with the lightest coating of ulmo honey. 40%

Glenbrynth Aged 21 Years bott code L8W6323 2103 (86.5) n22.5 t22 f21 b21 What starts off as a super-sexy nose with apple tart aplenty, tails off into a more prosaic fudge fest as the caramels get a constrictor-like grip: a bit of a bore at the end... 43%. OTI Africa.

◇ **Glen Castle Speyside Single Malt Aged 12 Years** bott code: L6 7461-2017 10 05-21.14 (87) n22 t22 f21.5 b21.5 A really lovely sweet dram with a wonderful match between barley and spice. Ridiculously easy to drink and exceptionally more-ish. The only downside is the heavy toffee aspect which dulls the obvious vivacity of the barley itself. 40%.

◇ **Glen Castle Speyside Single Malt Aged 20 Years** bott code: L1 1419-2017 11 (89) n22.5 poached pear with spicy vanilla...yummy! t22.5 a silky mouth feel stirs up some early busy spices which fade surprisingly quickly. Some excellent oak begins to fill the middle ground, but a build of toffee is becoming a bit heavy on the palate; f22 Neapolitan ice cream...the chocolate in particular; b22 enjoyable malt which could be better still if the toffee could be tamed. 46.8%.

Glen Castle Aged 20 Years Sherry Cask Finish dist 1996 (94) n23.5 t23.5 f23 b24 Lucky Japanese! A really satisfying, high quality single malt. 54.1%. ncf. Quality Spirits International.

Glen Castle Aged 28 Years sherry cask, dist 1996 (96.5) n24.5 t24 f24 b24 A quality spirit from Quality Spirits: sherry butts from before the sulphur plague. Just look how magnificent this is...! Surely an award winner this year of some type... 59%. ncf. Quality Spirits International.

James King Aged 12 Years bott code L6Y 7422 2810 (84.5) n21 t22 f21 b20.5 "From one of the most revered distilleries in Scotland," crows the label. Glen Toffee, presumably. Chaps, please turn the caramel down – it is obvious that some stupendous notes are trying to get out and speak: give them – and the drinker - a chance. 43%. Quality Spirits International.

Master of Malt 60 Year Old Speyside (85) n24.5 t21 f19 b20.5 Such a brave try. The delivery for a moment keeps you hoping there is still enough malt at play to see off the pencil-shaving tannins...but it is not to be. That doesn't mean that you can't spend a good half hour to an hour simply worshipping the nose: name a fruit and it appears to be there. And as it oxidises, it is there – then gone to be replaced with another fruit. A carousel of citrus and mushy conference pear, a fleeting moment of cherry cake, then fruitcake; molasses comes and goes, as does the liquorice and hickory. Sadly, the taste doesn't have the same life force beyond the first few seconds. But that nose.... Just amazing... 42.2%.

Master of Malt Speyside Single Malt (88.5) n22 light and gristy with a delicate caramel thread; t22.5 clean delivery, salivating with the oak slowly becoming a match for the malt; f22 a relaxed, undemanding spiced toffee finale; b22 not the most exciting malt you'll find but certainly one of the most relaxed and comfortable. 40%.

Scotch Universe Mercury I 106° U.1.1′ 1897.2″ first fill American bourbon barrel, dist 2007, bott 2016 (95) n23.5 t24 f23.5 b24 For those who prefer a little whisky in their honey. stunning! 52.9%.

Scotch Universe Pollux I 97° U.2.2′ 1967.2″ Oloroso sherry butt, dist 2008, bott 2016 (72) n17 t20 f18 b17 Oh dear... OK if you like burnt raisin, but otherwise...oh, dear; oh dear.... 59%.

Spey River Aged 12 Years bourbon oak (88.5) n22.5 golden syrup weighed down with intense malt and toffee; t22.5 silky texture with toffee to the fore, a quick release of spice, but a slow intertwangling of caramel and vanilla; f21.5 butterscotch and light spice; b22 attractive. But you get the feeling the toffee notes are holding back a top-rate malt. 40%. Quality Spirits International.

Spey River Double Cask American oak casks, bourbon cask finish (76) n19 t21 f18 b18. I was fascinated to see how this unusual maturation technique panned out: but I was not expecting this, or anything like. Not dissimilar to some American micro distillery malts with a tobacco character attached to the sweet sugars. Seriously odd. 40%. Quality Spirits International.

Spirits Shop Selection Speyside Malt 1973 sherry cask, bott 2016 (92) n21.5 t24 f22.5 b24 A whisky that needs a good half hour in the glass to open and show its full potential. On the nose it appears close to extinction; the performance on the palate suggests otherwise. 52%. 240 bottles. A joint bottling with Sansibar Whisky.

Spirits Shop Selection Speyside Very Old Selection sherry butt, bott 2016 (90.5) n23 the grape is grappling still: moist fruitcake with dark cherries and raisins; t23.5 silk. Absolute silk. It is as though the sugars have melted to form a pool for the light spices to dive into and the fruits to bob around in...; f21.5 perhaps a little bitter and flat by comparison; b22.5 this little sweetie is not about complexity, but effect. And it certainly has a good effect upon me... 46.3%. 322 bottles. A joint bottling with Sansibar Whisky.

The Whisky Agency Speyside Region Single Malt 1973 (95.5) n24 t24.5 f23.5 b24 Yhose into the exotic fruit school of ye olde Speysiders will be pretty delighted with this: ticks every box....with a quilled flourish. 46.9%.

◈ **Whisky-Fässle Speyside Region 26 Year Old** sherry cask, dist 1991, bott 2017 (76) n18 t21 f18 b19 The odd fruit chocolate moment but a sulphurous sherry cask, alas.... 50.6%.

◈ **Whisky-Fässle Speyside Region 43 Year Old** sherry butt, dist 1973, bott 2017 (87.5) n21.5 t23 f21 b22 Solid, mouth-watering fruit mixes well with the richer bourbon-style notes liquorice notes. But just too heavy on the tannins late on as the passing 43 summers catch up. 51.3%.

UNSPECIFIED SINGLE MALTS (GENERAL)

◈ **Burns Nectar Single Malt** bott code: L17/8183 (77) n20 t19 f19 b19 An ode to toffee. 40%.

The Corriemhor Cigar Reserve sherry & bourbon casks (84.5) n21 t22 f20.5 b21.5. You must forgive me if I judge this as a whisky alone. I have never smoked a cigar in my life; not even taken as much as an unlit cigarette to my lips. Not once. Ever. Some doctors and medical specialists in the field reckon it is why my nose and taste buds are so synchronised and alert. So if this is brilliant with a cigar, Cuban or otherwise, I will take your word for it. As a single malt in its own right, it is nutty, lush and pleasant. But rather lacking in complexity, scope or excitement. Dull, in fact. 46%

Glen Castle Rum Cask Finish (81.5) n20 t21.5 f21 b19 It must have been over 25 years ago now that I brought to the world the first ever rum cask matured whisky, which I discovered in a long-forgotten corner of a Campbeltown warehouse. It deservedly gained great notoriety and thereafter I went out of my way to taste as many rum cask matured or finished malts as were out there. This one is unique, but for all the wrong reasons. As the sugars which normally define the crispness of the whisky appear to have been underdone by other sugars in toffee form, thus neutralising the effect. Pleasant enough. But so dull. 40%. *Quality Spirits International.*

Glen Castle Sherry Cask Finish (80) n21 t21 f19 b19 Clean sherry at work here, it appears, though so intense is the toffee the fruit (like anything else) can barely be heard. A malt neutered by caramel. 40%. *Quality Spirits International.*

Lotus Lord 20 Year Old 1996 sherry cask finish (91.5) n23.5 hugely enticing, come hither date and walnut tart, as well as a big lump bitten out of a crunchy toffee apple; a fabulous spiced molasses and maple syrup sub plot, softened by butterscotch; t23.5 the body is much lighter on delivery than expected, allowing those spices a quicker path on goal than normal. The vanillas are huge, then a slow laying down of toasty raisin and light liquorice; f21.5 just strays a little into a furry path, though the spices remain in top form; b23 the sherry butts do impart a degree of late sulphur, but by then your heart will have been won. 53.3%. ncf. 12,200 bottles. *Quality Spirits International.*

Lotus Lord 24 Year Old 1992 sherry cask finish (95) n24 lychee to the fore, helped along by stewed apple: superb; the vanillas are beautifully weighted; t24 textbook body, offering just enough oils to coat every inch of palate, but light enough for every nuance to come through unmolested. The malt is still evident despite the obvious fruit and oak influence; the toast and spices build slowly and politely into something substantial; the background butterscotch is never far from the surface, in either taste, sweetness or texture; f23 liquorice, mocha and muscovado sugars. The very vaguest of furry notes, but entirely forgivable; b24 what a delightful and classy malt. 53.3%. ncf. 6,200 bottles. *Quality Spirits International.*

Lotus Lord 28 Year Old 1988 sherry casks (96) n24.5 even the drips are drips with oloroso. Probably the most outrageously high church sherry and tannin you will find this year – and maybe for a few more. Totally over the top in the massiveness of the toasty grape...but it is a sniff for a sore nose...; t24 tastes identical to the nose or, rather, how the nose projects itself and defines the degree of expectation; we are talking Melton Hunt cake wallowing in a bowl of oloroso with burnt molasses sprinkled on top for good measure; the spice attack is short and surprisingly gentle; f23.5 difficult to get this hardcore toastiness without a feel of scorched oak and raisin, which the bitterness confirms; some extra high roast Java coffee sees out the finale; b24 some 20 years ago I might have given this malt a bit of a ticking off for being far too sherry dominant. But, my! How times have changed. I am so relieved to find absolutely no sulphur at work here, I am smothering with kisses what seems like a long-lost son... 58.4%. ncf. 5,000 bottles. *Quality Spirits International.*

Master of Malt New-Make Malt Spirit (93) n22.5 t23.5 f23 b23.5 The light body on the nose gives the lie to the splendour of the thickening malt on delivery. Pretty decent, mouth-filling new make. 63.5%.

Peat's Beast (88.5) n22 t22.5 f22 b22 "To tame the beast we recommend a dash of water." I don't. Recommend, instead, you use the Murray Method to warm up to body temp; otherwise you fracture the delicate oils and the sugars which hold this together vanish way too soon. 46%. ncf.

Raasay While We Wait finished in Tuscan red wine casks (77) n18 t21.5 f18.5 b19. I have always maintained that it is a dangerous tactic to link the name of a planned distillery with a malt which doesn't actually come from it. When in professional advisor mode, I always warn against it. I sincerely hope the distillery is built on Raasay one day by R&B, but to say that certain whiskies from other distilleries will taste like what theirs, not yet even constructed, one day might, is fraught with dangers: the truth is, you never know exactly what you'll get – with as much meticulous planning as you like - until you get it. However their whisky one day turns out, they must ensure they don't ruin it by putting it into wine casks as poor as these. 46%. nc ncf. *R&B Distillers.*

SaarWhisky Gruwehewwel Edition 3 dist 2007 bott 2015 (96) n24.5 t24 f23 b24.5 No problem giving this truly great whisky the high score and award it deserves. But, as a lifelong Millwall supporter, I just wish they'd drop the West Ham Utd motif... 50.3%.

Saar Whisky Malzbeisser ex-bourbon barrel, dist 2009, bott 2018 (90.5) n22.5 classic, simplistic Islay: gristy and smoky on the 35ppm level..; t23 a buttery delivery and a ridiculous degree of high propane vanilla stretching out across the taste buds, sweet and viscous. The smoke has good weight but not enough to crush the delicate work of the oak; **f22.5** oily, sweet, smoky and slightly warming...; **b22.5** if anyone wants to know what a very decent Islay whisky is all about, this will do rather well. *53.7%. ncf sc.*

◇ **Saar Whisky Mandelbachtal Edition No. 2** dist 2009, bott 2018 **(88) n22** loads of bourbon notes to tease you: red liquorice and molassed spice; crushed chocolate Malteser, too; strangely feinty; **t23** oily and massively more impactful than the nose: treacle and ulmo honey mixed to astonishing effect; the mid-ground sees a chocolate-rich maltiness take hold; **f21** slightly feinty again, almost of an European style, but the cocoa – now mocha – stays...; **b22** so much chocolate, not sure if this should be sold as a bottle or a bar... *53.7%. ncf sc.*

◇ **Spirit of Caledonia Cairn Guish 12 Years Old** cask no. 42 **(93) n23** very attractive brush with smoke, yet still retains a clean, light character. Good, playful spice nip; **t23.5** just brilliantly salivating: the barley cascades down in stunning grassy form. The phenols refuse to change in intensity or pace, forever present and adding base notes which refuse to drown out the treble; **f23** wonderful chocolate mint ice cream – tailed, of course, by those gentle phenols; **b23.5** a master class in the wearing of a light, smoky cloak, yet retaining your elegance. Beautifully made and matured without a single off note: of its type (a style not entirely dissimilar to Ledaig), exceptional. *61%. sc.*

That Boutique-y Whisky Company Secret Distillery No. 1 9 Year Old batch 2 **(79) n22 t22 f16 b19** Interesting case, this. High quality malt in partially top quality oak. But this is a malt, as a single malt rather than blend, that needs a good few years to bed down – more than given here. For a blend (I mean a real blend with grain whisky, not a vatted malt) you can work with this to utilise its meatier aspects. But as a single malt you have to ensure that all the big notes don't smother the underdeveloped smaller ones. And this, alas, is what has happened here. It helps if the dreaded S word isn't present, either...*51.7%. 1,220 bottles.*

That Boutique-y Whisky Company Secret Distillery 2 21 Year Old **(95) n24 t23.5 f23.5 b24** There is no secret to this malt's sparkling beauty. *49.7%. 420 bottles.*

◇ **The Whisky Embassy Green Meadows Aged 10 Years** cask no. 2914535, dist 2008, bott 2007 **(85.5) n21 t22 f21 b21.5** Despite the decade in cask there is a youthfulness to the malt which guarantees a lively, juicy vibrancy at first. But its integration with a cask slightly over-eager on the late bitterness is limited. *53.1%. nc ncf sc.*

Scottish Vatted Malts

(also Pure Malts/Blended Malt Scotch)

100 Pipers Aged 8 Years Blended Malt **(74) n19 t20 f17 b18**. A better nose, perhaps, and some spice on arrival. But when you consider the Speysiders at their disposal, all those mouth-wateringly grassy possibilities, it is such a shame to find something as bland as this. *40%*

Abrachan Triple Oak Matured **(77) n19 t21 f18 b19**. Some superb sugars on delivery, but a fuzzy, furry bitterness sadly gives the game away. *42%*

Acla Selection Burnside 23 Years Old bourbon hogshead, dist 1992, bott 2015 **(93) n23.5 t23 f23 b23.5** What a magnificent piece of oak this was given the chance to grow up in. As I taste this in my remote garden, a song thrush is celebrating the setting of the sun in spectacular triple-whistled fashion: between the whisky and the bird, nature's harmony cannot be better represented.*50.4%. nc ncf*

Angels' Nectar **(81) n21 t21 f19 b20**. This angel has a bitter tooth... *40%*

Angel's Nectar Blended Malt Rich Peat Edition **(90.5) n22.5 t23 f22.5 b22.5** Excellently-made malt: sticks unerringly to the script. *46%*

Ballantine's Pure Malt Aged 12 Years bott code. LKAC1538 **(88.5) n22.5 t23 f21 b22.** No sign of the peat being reintroduced to major effect, although the orange is a welcome addition. Remains a charmer. *40%. Chivas.*

Bell's Signature Blend Limited Edition **(83.5) n19 t22 f21 b21.5**. The front label makes large that this vatted malt has Blair Athol and Inchgower at the heart of it as they are "two fine malts selected for their exceptionally rich character". Kind of like saying you have invited the Kray twins to your knees up as they might liven it up a bit. Well those two distilleries were both part of the original Bell's empire, so fair dos. But to call them both fine malts is perhaps stretching the imagination somewhat. A robust vatting to say the least. And, to be honest, once you get past the nose, good back-slapping fun. *40%. 90,000 bottles.*

Ben Bracken Blended Malt Aged 12 Years **(85.5) n22.5 t21 f21 b21**. Quite a tight malt with a predominantly toffee theme. *40%*

◇ **Berry Bros & Rudd Islay Blended Malt** bott code: L18/8215 **(90.5) n22** a simplistic, beautifully rounded, zesty smokiness; **t23** you expect youthful, dissolving grist on delivery – and that exactly what is presented. The smoke is in gentle mode, more an accompaniment than star attraction; **f22.5** praline spread on toast. The lightest, slightly oily phenols kiss the dominant but vanilla and butterscotch tart as a little spice buzzes amiably; **b23** an endearing vatting which sums up the island's whiskies without any drama but still highly attractively and with no wrong turns. 44.2%. *The Classic Range.*

◈ **Berry Bros & Rudd Sherry Cask Matured Blended Malt** bott code: L18/8213 (74.5) **n19 t24.5 f14 b17** With Ronnie Cox's name all over this bottle, one can safely assume that the leading light in this vatting is Glenrothes. And, of course, with Glenrothes sherry butts at work, chances are so, too, will sulphur be. Well, it is – as can be picked out on the nose and the finish especially. But, for once, it is worth undergoing the pain of the massive sulphur simply to experience the delivery which scores absolutely maximum points for the lushest of mouthfeels and the extraordinary beauty of the richness of the fruit marrying some intense barley. Between the faulty sulphur start and end is sandwiched something which, for a few spellbinding, heavenly moments, touches perfection. 44.2%. *The Classic Range.*

◈ **Berry Bros & Rudd Peated Cask Matured Blended Malt** bott code: L18/8214 (92) **n22** a slight anthracite sharpness gives a nip and buzz. The smoke is healthy and full, but always soft; **t23** now, on delivery, finds a far better balance, the natural caramels spilling from the oak and making a graceful pairing with the phenols. Spices prickle half-heartedly; a slight youthfulness to the malt becomes apparent at the midway point; **f23.5** now the spices have warmed beautifully while the malt has shrugged off the peat and caramel to make a bigger pitch. All the time, though, so soft...; **b23.5** gentle and evenly paced. 44.2%. *The Classic Range.*

◈ **Berry Bros & Rudd Speyside Blended Malt** (85) **n20 t22.5 f21 b21.5** A lot of malt to get your teeth into. The oak isn't exactly sympathetic but the big wave of vanilla at the midpoint carries some attractive maple syrup. 44.2%. *The Classic Range.*

Big Peat Batch 31 (90.5) **n23** love it: superb mix of allotment bonfire and peat reek. Some young spirit offering great energy; **t22** gristy sweet delivery pounded by spicy attitude; a blast of hickory and cocoa; **f22.5** the smoke rumbles along, but there is no letting up in intensity of peat or spice; **b23** good to see it has maintained its cheery high standard. Youthful, boisterous and challenging throughout. 46%. nc ncf. Douglas Laing & Co.

Big Peat Bärlin Edition (91.5) **n23 t22.5 f23 b23** I imagine the Peat Heads of Berlin are, rightly, very happy fellows... 50%. ncf. Bottled for Big Market Berlin, 50th Anniversary bottling.

Black Face 8 Years Old (78.5) **n18.5 t22 f19 b19**. A huge malt explosion in the kisser on delivery, but otherwise not that pretty to behold. 46%. The Vintage Malt Whisky Co Ltd.

Blairmhor Aged 8 Years bott code L15/058 R15/5083 (86) **n22.5 t22 f20.5 b21** Probably a dram never drunk by people of a certain political persuasion who would have been more impressed had it been called Blairless... An attractive malt which suffers from a surfeit of caramel and a cramped finale, though there is a big juicy, ripe pear and malt surge through the middle. 40%. International Beverage Holdings Ltd.

Burns Nectar (89.5) **n22 t22 f23 b22.5**. A delight of a dram and with all that honey around, "Nectar" is about right. 40%

◈ **Cadenhead's Vatted Islay 25 Year Old** (89) **n23** coffee, then mocha, joining the phenolic liquorice. Some very jaded tannins join the show; **t22** a tart touch of the hickory and Fisherman's Friend to this, with back-up molasses aplenty; **f22** warming now, initially the oak remaining true and dark sugar coated; very late on the older tannins limp across the line...; **b22** may be wrong, but there is a feeling of something a little older than 25 in this: definitely shows its antiquity. 46%. 175th Anniversary bottling.

Carme 10 Years Old (79) **n21.5 t20 f18.5 b19**. On paper Ardmore and Clynelish should work well together. But vatting is not done on paper and here you have two malts cancelling each other out and some less than great wood sticking its oar in. 43%

Castle Rock Aged 12 Years Blended Malt (87) **n22.5 t23 f19.5 b22**. Stupendously refreshing: the finish apart, I just love this style of malt. 40%

◈ **Cave Aquila The Eagles Collection Westport 8 Years Old** first fill sherry cask (73.5) **n17 t20 f17 b18.5** What the odd blender might call "good sulphur". What this one calls "bad sulphur". Indeed, a Westport in a sulphur storm. A great shame because there is enough richness to the grape to confirm this must have once been a stupendous butt. 61.1%. sc.

Cearban (79.5) **n18 t21.5 f20 b19**. The label shows a shark. It should be a whale: this is massive. Sweet with the malts not quite on the same wavelength. 40%. Robert Graham Ltd.

◈ **Chapter 7 Island Blended Malt** (91.5) **n22** busy and layered. Citrus abounds but the chalkiness to the young-ish barley is very attractive; **t23.5** super-salivating. Astonishingly intense malt still showing here and there the odd sign of pre-pubescence but held in place by a really sturdy beam of vanilla; **f23** the fade is aided by light oils and a wonderful praline sign off; what a sublime build up of spices, also....wow! **b23** well done, chaps (or do I mean Chapts?).Vatting unpeated Island malt and getting the balance right is not one of the easier tasks in the whisky world. But this has been carried out wonderfully – the exclusive use of ex-bourbon helped. 49%.

⬙ **Chapter 7 Highland Blended Malt** (86) n21 t22 f22 b21 No serious age to this, which partly explains why the oak is in no-man's land here. It is trying to form enough character to make a positive impact but has strength enough only to disrupt the flow of the juicy barley. That said, the very simple, grassy impact of the malt itself is rather delightful. 46.8%.

Chapter 7 Peatside 2009 Barrique cask, Port finish, cask no. 5511 (94.5) n23.5 t23.5 f24 b23.5 There is a touch of genius to this... 46%. sc.

⬙ **Chapter 7 Simple Malt** batch no. 1 (90.5) n22 some younger notes on the phenols, making for a two-toned peat attack – though always a gentle one; t23 crispy Demerara sugars in league with gristy phenols: seriously salivating stuff; f22.5 a delicate fade of sweet, lightly smoked vanilla; b23 delightfully sweet and peated: as simple as that! 46%.

⬙ **Chapter 7 Simple Malt** batch no. 2 (93) n23 excellent depth: a genuine buzz to the integrated oak. Earthy yet vaguely fruity, too, without labouring the point; t23 after the complexity of the nose, we are met by a beautifully rounded mouthfeel, then a rich array of Demerara sugars and digestive biscuit; f23.5 creamy, with a vanilla thread but more coffee and walnut cake; b23.5 delightfully complex: nothing simple here at all... 48%.

⬙ **Chapter 7 Simple Malt** batch no. 3 (84) n20 t22 f21 b21 Very flat with the emphasis on tangy creamy toffee. 48%.

⬙ **Chapter 7 Simple Malt** batch no. 4 (93.5) n23.5 ultra-light but perfectly poised phenols; orange blossom and heather honey mix and spice; t23 chewy toffee and concentrated malt. More heather honey and the lightest of vaguely smoked cocoa notes; f23 long, buttery vanilla and pulsing spices to keep the building oak company; b24 like an old-fashioned Highland Park before the invention of sulphur casks. Fabulous. 46%.

⬙ **Chapter 7 Speyside Blended Malt** (82.5) n21.5 t22 f20 b19 Hardly a page turner. The plot doesn't make sense: mild smoke which does well on delivery but the remainder leads you nowhere. 46%.

Chivas Regal Ultis bott code LPNK1759 2016/09/16 (89.5) n22.5 t23 f21.5 b22.5 This vatted malt is the legacy of Chivas' five master blenders. But to pay real respect to them, just remove the caramel from the bottling hall. The whisky will be light coloured, for sure, but I suspect the flavour profile will blow us all away... 40%. Chivas Brothers Ltd.

Clan Campbell 8 Years Old Pure Malt (82) n20 t22 f20 b20. Enjoyable, extremely safe whisky that tries to offend nobody. The star quality is all on the complex delivery, then it's toffee. 40%. Chivas Brothers.

Clan Denny (Bowmore, Bunnahabhain, Caol Ila and Laphroaig) (94) n24 t23 f23 b24. A very different take on Islay with heavy peats somehow having a floating quality. Unique. 40%

Clan Denny Islay (86.5) n21.5 t23 f21 b21. A curiously bipolar malt with the sweetness and bitterness at times going to extremes. Some niggardly oak has taken the edge of what might have been a sublime malt as the peat and spices at times positively glistens with honey. 46.5%. nc ncf sc. Douglas Laing & Co.

Clan Denny Speyside (87) n22 t22 f21 b22. A Tamdhu-esque oiliness pervades here and slightly detracts from the complexity. That said, the early freshness is rather lovely. 46%

⬙ **Collectivum XXVIII** (96.5) n24 I have always been a sucker for gooseberry tart. Especially when the sugar is reduced and sharpness is at max...; t24.5 beyond salivating: the taste buds are simply plugged in to maximum stimulus as the tannins let rip, yet barely making a single impact on the grassy barley tones; f23.5 long, lightly oiled and determined to go down the cocoa route; b24.5 this, with boldness, vivaciousness and blinding sparkle is heading us brilliantly into the direction where blended Scotch needs to go. A Wurlitzer of a whisky...wow!!! 573%. Diageo Special Releases 2017.

Compass Box 3 Year Old Deluxe bott Aug 16 (96) n24 t24 f24 b24 Quite possibly the oldest three-year-old I have ever tasted. Being Compass Box, I have no doubt the flavour of irony is as powerful as any other here: surely this has to be a bunch of ancient malts with a tiny flash of something three years old, making up just a fraction of the composition. If so (and I strongly suspect it is), then it does much – as I am sure it has been designed – to both flag and undermine the utterly idiotic rules/laws set out by the appalling Scotch Whisky Association, that does not allow blenders to show what actually makes up their whisky - only the age of the youngest constituent no matter how large or, in this case, miniscule its contribution may have been. The SWA: perhaps the only trade body that has been able to get government backing to confuse the public and ensure they have no idea what they are paying for. So, a brilliant whisky on all counts. 46%. nc ncf. 3,282 bottles.

Compass Box Eleuthera Marriage married for nine months in an American oak Hogshead (86) n22 t22 f20 b22. I'm not sure if it's the name that gets me on edge here, but as big and robust as it is I still can't help feeling that the oak has bitten too deep. Any chance of a Compass Box Divorce...? 49.2%. Compass Box for La Maison du Whisky.

Compass Box Enlightenment bott Apr 16 (94.5) n24.5 t24 f22.5 b23.5 After the run of disappointing vatted malts I have tasted today, trust Compass Box to come to the rescue. This is not a whisky to have when in a hurry: the nose alone is worth a good 15 minutes... 46%. nc ncf. 5,922 bottles.

Compass Box Flaming Heart Fifteenth Anniversary bott Jul 15 (96.5) n24 t24.5 f23.5 b24.5 Really, John? Fifteen years? I mean: 15 years....??? Fucking hell! Oh, by the way, mate. It's a bloody masterpiece... 48.9%. nc ncf. 12,060 bottles.

Compass Box The Lost Blend (95.5) n23 t23.5 f24.5 b24.5 I may be wrong, but I have a feeling that when the nose and flavour profile was being constructed, a little extra smoke than first planned was added. Seems that way by the manner in which the phenols just pipe up a little louder than it first seems...46%

◇ **Compass Box No Name** bott Sept 17 (92.5) n23 a nose that repays five minutes in the glass. Then the complexity and dexterity of the smoke can be fully appreciated, especially the way it adds weight to the much sweeter cake mix, oaky background; t23 youthful and nubile on the palate, the controlled smoke meeting the glorious, understated and very clever mid-toast sugars and ulmo honey; f23 the smoke rumbles apologetically as the malt mounts up, natural caramel keeps it even while the vanilla dries; b23.5 I'll give it a name: Compass Box Bleedin' Delicious! 48.9%. nc ncf 15,000 bottles.

Compass Box The Peat Monster Cask Strength (89) n23.5 t23 f20.5 b22 Plenty of peat between your teeth but deserving of some better oak. 57.3%

Compass Box The Peat Monster Reserve (92) n23 t23.5 f22.5 b23. At times a bit of a Sweet Monster...beautiful stuff! 48.9%

Compass Box The Peat Monster Swedish Whisky Federation (91) n23 thumping peat in both dry ash and oily format. A little citrus tries to balance things; t23 big oils bring a tidal wave of Demerara sugars....all engulfed in phenols, of course; the spices have been patient but kick in now...; f22 a little oak bitterness seeps through but the smoke remains substantial; b23 what can you say? Its peaty. And it's a monster...! 46%. 2,000 bottles.

Compass Box The Peat Monster Tenth Anniversary Release bott Sept 13 (95) n24 t24 f23 b24 here we appear to see a mix, or compromise, between the sweeter bottling of two years ago and last year's searing dryness. And, unlike most compromises, this one works... 48.9%.

◇ **Compass Box Phenomenology** bott Sept 17 (92.5) n22 dense, ultra-thick malt with a little squeeze of citrus to lighten the barley and vanilla procession; t24.5 an incredible high ester delivery – not unlike Jamaican pot still rum – has the sweetness on full parade from the very first moment. Then comes shock waves of enormous malt that leaves you unable to move, just be blown away by the stunning beauty of the controlled intensity: amazing...! f22.5 a hard act to follow, that delivery and follow through. And while the malts and spices jostle, a little oak bitterness permeates through; b23.5 once upon a time, blenders took so much notice of the blend they actually forgot to really look at what it tasted like. Decades ago more than one blender told me that he didn't taste a whisky at final strength until a sample turned up in his lab from the bottling hall. This one appears to be almost the other way round. The nose is attractive and adequate without being anything special. The delivery and follow through, though: gee what a phenomenon...! 46%. nc ncf. 7,908 bottles.

Compass Box The Spice Tree first-fill and refill American oak. Secondary maturation: heavily toasted new French oak (95.5) n24.5 t24.5 f23 b23.5. Having initially been chopped down by the SWA, who were indignant that extra staves had been inserted into the casks, The Spice Tree is not only back but in full bloom. Indeed, the blossom on this, created by the use of fresh oak barrel heads, is more intoxicating than its predecessor – mainly because there is a more even and less dramatic personality to this. Not just a great malt, but a serious contender for Jim Murray Whisky Bible 2011 World Whisky of the Year. 46%

Compass Box Spice Tree Extravaganza bott Aug 16 (94.5) n24 there is a barely discernible oiliness to this which makes a huge difference to the shape of the nose: the acacia honey hangs as though in suspended animation, the diced lime peel dips in and out of consciousness, the aged tannins (no minor force) nip here and kiss there...; t23.5 a soft red carpet is laid out for the sugars and spices which arrive at a slow, measured pace, elegantly and hand-in-hand. First the lush malts lead the way and then move to one side to allow the star turn. Thinned golden syrup and a peppery, tannin-tinged double act in effortless harmony; f23 the oils have been reduced taking the sugars. The spices prevail and age becomes a factor once more...; b24 perhaps the most important factor to this whisky, which will be overlooked probably by about 99% of those who taste this, is not so much the taste itself but the mouth feel and balance. In other words, it is not always the words that are said which are most important, but the way they are delivered. That is the secret to this complex beauty. 46%. nc ncf. 12,240 bottles.

Cutty Sark Blended Malt (92.5) n22 t24 f23 b23.5. Sheer quality: as if two styles have been placed in the bottle and told to fight it out between them. What a treat! *40%*.

Deerstalker Blended Malt Highland Edition (94) n23.5 t23.5 f23 b24 A quite beautiful whisky by any standards. *43%*

Deerstalker Blended Malt Peated Edition (84.5) n22.5 t22 f19 b21 A slightly strange mixture: on one hand creamy, sweet and friendly, on the other somewhat metallic and harsh. Struggles to find either balance or a comfortable course. The finish is way off key and vaguely furry. *43%*.

Demijohn Islay Blended Malt 6 Year Old cask no. 5512, bott 10 Sept 15 (91) n23 t23 f22 b23 A very jolly kind of malt, the delicate fruit offering a chirpiness to the chipper young peats. Thoroughly enjoyable. *42.5%*.

◇ **Douglas Laing's Rock Oyster Aged 18 Years** (90.5) n23 salty and sensual: vague seaweedy phenols aids the distinct coastal feel; t22.5 mouth-watering with a youthful feel to the grist before the saltiness makes its slightly puckering mark; elsewhere an earthiness grounds the barley; f22 slightly salty coffee cake; b23 deserves a slug. *46.8%. nc ncf.*

◇ **Douglas Laing's Scallywag Aged 13 Years** (87.5) n21 t23 f21.5 b22 Well, for a bit of a scallywag, this strikes me as a remarkably well- behaved individual. The malt is at the centre of attention, recovering beautifully on the palate after a so-so nose. Salivating where you want it to be, too. *46%*.

◇ **Douglas Laing's Timorous Beastie Aged 18 Years** (89) n22.5 soft and exceptionally grassy; saved cucumber with a squeeze of lime, too; t22.5 as green on delivery as on the nose: gristy for all its years: a mousy malt to be sure; f21.5 dries towards a Lincoln biscuit, complete with sugary saltiness; b22.5 attractively sleekit. *46.8%. nc ncf. 7,258 bottles.*

Eiling Lim Older Than Old Blended Malt Whisky (87.5) n21.5 t22 f22 b22. Charming malt. Entirely non-taxing with a light Arbroath Smoky element as the main thread and genteel vanilla notes filling most of the gaps. *46.5%*

Elements of Islay Peat (91.5) n23 t24 f22 b22.5 This is rather more than elementary Islay, trust me.... *46%*

◇ **Elements of Islay Peat Islay Blended Malt** (94) n23 the smoke signals are clear: "do not taste this whisky unless you want to be assaulted by massive peat"... t24 those smoke signals don't lie: truly enormous, muscular delivery;f23.5 moderate oils stretch the gristy sugars into the slow crescendo of tannin; b23.5 does everything it says on the tin – and more. Some younger elements appear to be at work here, which means the peat intensity can sometimes fly, deliciously and dramatically, off the scale. *45%*.

◇ **Elements of Islay Peat Full Proof** (92.5) n23.5 impossible not to love that buzz of the spiced up peat against that almost crushed biscuit, gristy, doughy sweetness; t23.5 excellent oils work as well for the citrus notes as they do the main theme smoky ones, which both rumble and offer a more elementary TCP note; f22.5 dries surprisingly fast, the oak making its presence felt with a very dusty and dry finish; b23 a distinctly two-toned malt with the phenols seeming to be pitched quite differently. *59.3%*.

ePower Extra Old Blended Malt Whisky (93) n23 t23.5 f23 b23.5 This is beautifully constructed vatted malt and suggests some pretty good age, also. *45.2%*.

The Famous Grouse 10 Years Old Malt (77) n19 t20 f19 b19. The nose and finish headed south in the last Winter and landed in the sulphur marshes of Jerez. *40%. Edrington Group.*

The Famous Grouse 15 Years Old Malt (86) n21 t22 f21.5 b21.5. Salty and smoky with a real sharp twang. *43%. Edrington Group.*

The Famous Grouse 15 Years Old Malt (86) n19 t24 f22 b21. There had been a hint of the "s" word on the nose, but it got away with it. Now it has crossed that fine – and fatal – line where the petulance of the sulphur has thrown all else slightly out of kilter. All, that is, apart from the delivery which is a pure symphony of fruit and spice deserving a far better introduction and final movement. Some moving, beautiful moments. Flawed genius or what...? *40%*

The Famous Grouse 18 Years Old Malt (82) n19 t21.5 f21 b20.5. Some highly attractive honey outweighs the odd uncomfortable moment. *43%. Edrington Group.*

The Famous Grouse Malt 21 Years Old (91) n22 t24 f22 b23. A very dangerous dram: the sort where the third or fourth would slip down without noticing. Wonderful scotch! *43%*.

The Famous Grouse 30 Years Old Malt (94) n23.5 t24 f23 b23.5. Whisky of this sky-high quality is exactly what vatted malt should be all about. Outrageously good. *43%*

Five Lions Burnside 22 Years Old 2nd fill Oloroso sherry hogshead, dist May 93, bott Nov 15 (93) n23 t23.5 f23 b23.5 An unimpeachable sherry butt - amazing! *55.5%. nc ncf.*

Five Lions Westport 18 Years Old 1st fill sherry butt, dist Oct 97, bott Nov 15 (95) n23.5 t24 f23.5 b24 Brilliant! *59.7%. nc ncf.*

Gleann Mór Vatted Whisky Over 40 Years Old (92.5) n23.5 t23.5 f22.5 b23 An oldie and a goodie...Mor, please...!!! *47%*

Glenalmond Highland Blended Malt (84) n21 t22 f20.5 b20.5 Chugs along in safe, non-demanding caramel-rich fashion. 40%. *The Vintage Malt Whisky Co.*

Glenn (89.5) n22 t23 f22.5 A forceful malt. Seems as though at least two strands of the thread are trying to outdo each other. Enjoyable; erratic towards the end. 50%. *Svenska Eldvatten.*

Glenalmond 2001 Vintage (82.5) n22 t21.5 f19 b20. Glenkumquat, more like: the most citrusy malt I have tasted in a very long time. 40%. *The Vintage Malt Whisky Co Ltd.*

Glenalmond "Everyday" (89.5) n21.5 t23.5 f22 b22.5. They are not joking; this really is an everyday whisky. Glorious malt which is so dangerously easy to drink. 40%

Glen Brynth Aged 12 Years Blended Malt (87) n22.5 t23 f19.5 b22. Deja vu...! Thought I was going mad: identical to the Castle Rock I tasted this morning, right down to the (very) bitter end ..!!! 40%. *Quality Spirits International.*

Glenbrynth Blended Malt 12 Years (87.5) n22.5 t22.5 f21 b21.5. Heavyweight malt which gets off to a rip-roaring start on the delivery but falls away somewhat from the mid ground onwards. 43%. *OTI Africa.*

Glenbrynth Ruby 40 Year Old Limited Edition (94) n23.5 t24 f23 b23.5. Has all the hallmarks of a completely OTT, far too old sherry butt being brought back to life with the aid of a livelier barrel. A magnificent experience, full of fun and evidence of some top quality vatting at work, too. 43%. *OTI Africa.*

Glenbrynth Ruby 40 Year Old bott code L8V 7439 04/11/11 (95) n24 t23.5 f23.5 b24 You cannot ask much more from a 40-year-old vatted malt than this. Amazing what a lack of colouring (and sulphured sherry casks) can do – like let the whisky speak for itself and allow you to follow its myriad paths, its highways and byways, without the route being blocked by toffee or a rabid bitterness. Each and every cask included in this great whisky should be applauded, as should the blender. 43%. *OTI Africa.*

◇◇ **Glen Castle Blended Malt 1992 Sherry Cask Matured** bott code: L7 9595-2017 12 (96) n24 an outrageous mix of big oak – I mean pencil shavings and polished antiques furniture - and roasty, toasty fruit that could fill a thousand Christmas cakes...; t24.5 oh...my...word...! The most succulent of sherried impact. Molten muscovado sugars and molasses tumble down like lava from a fruity volcano taking all evidence of malt in its path. The oak is singed, a toastiness which matches the ripeness of the fruit. And, of course, the spices are loud and bristly; f23.5 long, languid and salty now. The fruit persists gamely, more dried dates now and black liquorice aplenty as well as hickory and cocoa. Manuka honey represents the lingering sweetness; b24 I have no official information into what makes up this vatted malt. But this is almost identical in style to the old fashioned Glendronach 12-year-old Sherry Cask that was on the market a quarter of a century ago and more. Then I was annoyed with its OTT characteristics which swamped everything in sight. Now I hug it affectionately like a long-lost friend back from the dead, because this is sulphur-free sherried whisky – such a delight and rarity. All is forgiven... For those who truly adore big, clean sherried whisky: this will take you to a grapey heaven. 51.8%.

◇◇ **Glen Castle Blended Malt 1992 Sherry Cask Matured** bott code: L7 9595-2017 12 (95.5) n24 anyone who has had a Melton Hunt Cake with extra Demerara sugar and little less – though still profound – fruit than usual, will recognise this...; t24 this isn't a delivery on the palate: it is pure seduction! The arrival is a series of light, fruity kisses before the oak begins to make an entry (ooh, err, Matron!), ramping up the roughness and thumping around its weight. But as a series of molasses and toasty notes – including slightly burnt cherry (ooh, I say!) – keeps the fruit on track; f23.5 a slightly bitter oaky residue is added to the slow fade; b24 just brilliant whisky to be savoured and cherished, restoring my faith in sherry – very few butts from this era survived the sulphury onslaught – and the perfect after dinner or very late night dram. 46.8%.

Glendower 8 Years Old (84) n21.5 t21 f20.5 b21 Nutty and spicy. 43%

The Glenfohry Aged 8 Years Special Reserve (73) n19 t19 f17 b18. Some of the malt used here appears to have come from a still where the safe has not so much been broken into, but just broken! Oily and feinty, to say the least. Normally I would glower at anyone who even thought of putting a coke into their malt. Here, I think it might be for the best.. 40%

Glen Talloch Blended Malt Aged 8 Years (85.5) n21 t23 f20.5 b21. An invigorating and engulfing vatting, full of intrinsic barley tones on delivery. But the caramel is too strident for further complexity. 40%

Glen Turner Heritage Double Wood Bourbon & Madeira casks, bott code. L311657A (85.5) n21.5 t22 f21 b21. A very curious amalgamation of flavours. The oak appears to be in shock with the way the fruit is coming on to it and offers a bitter backlash. No faulting the crisp delivery with busy sugar and spice for a few moments brightening the palate. 40%.

Glen Turner Pure Malt Aged 8 Years L525956A (84) n20 t22 f22 b20. A lush and lively vatting annoyingly over dependent on thick toffee but simply brimming with fabulously mouth-watering barley and over-ripe blood oranges. To those who bottle this, I say: let me into your lab. I can help you bring out something sublime!! 40%

Glen Orchy (80.5) n19.5 t21.5 f19.5 b20. Not exactly the most subtle of vatted malts though when the juicy barley briefly pours through on delivery, enjoyable. 40%. *Lidl*.

Glen Orchy 5 Year Old Blended Malt Scotch Whisky (88.5) n22 t22.5 f22 b22. Excellent malt plus very decent casks equals light-bodied fun. 40%. *Lidl*.

Glen Orrin (68) n16.5 t17.5 f17 b17. In its favour, it doesn't appear to be troubled by caramel. Which means the nose and palate are exposed to the full force of this quite dreadful whisky. 40%.

Glen Orrin Six Year Old (88) n22 t23 f21 b22. A vatting that has improved in the short time it has been around, now displaying some lovely orangey notes on the nose and a genuinely lushness to the body and spice on the finish. You can almost forgive the caramel, this being such a well balanced, full-bodied ride. A quality show for the price. 40%

Grand Macnish Six Cask Edition bott code L14/8867 (85.7) n21 t23 f19.5 b22 A late night chewathon: this is big, ballsy with little time for prisoners. Not exactly free from the odd flaw. But the delivery and middle have wonderful molten walnut and orange cake quality and a lush mouth feel to match. 40%. *MacDuff International Ltd*.

Hedges and Butler Special Pure Malt (83) n20 t21 f22 b21. Just so laid back: nosed and tasted blind I'd swear this was a blend (you know, a real blend with grains and stuff) because of the biting lightness and youth. Just love the citrus theme and, err...graininess..!! 40%

Highland Harvest Organic Blended Malt 7 Casks batch 002 (86.5) n21.5 t22.5 f21 b21.5 Not even remotely complex. But pleasant enough. 40% *WB15/371*

Highland Journey Blended Malt (94.5) n23.5 t23.5 f23.5 b24 I have been on some memorable Highland journeys in my life, but few have been quite as comfortable as this one. 46.2%. *Hunter Laing & Co.*

J & B Exception Aged 12 Years (80) n20 t23 f18 b19. Very pleasant in so many ways. A charming sweetness develops quickly, with excellent soft honeycomb. But the nose and finish are just so...so...dull...!! For the last 30 years J&B has meant, to me, (and probably within that old company) exceptionally clean, fresh Speysiders offering a crisp, mouth-watering treat. I feel this is off target. 40%. *Diageo/Justerini & Brooks*.

J & B Nox (89) n23 t23 f21 b22. A teasing, pleasing little number that is unmistakably from the J&B stable. 40%. *Diageo*.

John Black 8 Years Old Honey (88) n21 t22.5 f22.5 b22. A charming vatting. 40%

John Black 10 Years Old Peaty (91) n23 salty and peaty; t23 soft and peaty; f22 delicate and peaty; b23 classy and er...peaty. 40%. *Tullibardine Distillery*.

Johnnie Walker Green Label 15 Years Old (95) n24 t23.5 f23.5 b24. God, I love this stuff... this is exactly how a vatted malt should be and one of the best samples I've come across since its launch. 43%. *Diageo*.

Jon, Mark and Robbo's The Rich Spicy One (89) n22 t23 f22 b22. So much better without the dodgy casks: a real late night dram of distinction though the spices perhaps a little on the subtle side... 40%. *Edrington*.

Jon, Mark and Robbo's The Smoky Peaty One (92) n23 t22 f23 b24. Genuinely high-class whisky where the peat is full-on yet allows impressive complexity and malt development. A malt for those who appreciate the better, more elegant things in life. 40%. *Edrington*.

⬦ **Le Gus't Selection X Speyside Blended Malt 39 Years Old** sherry cask, cask no. 4 (94.5) n23.5 the rare kind of sherry nose these days where you know, instantly, that there is absolutely zero chance of some sulphur getting in on the act later down the line. Spiced glazed cherry and walnut fruit cake; t24 the amazing strength for the age 60% for a near 40-year-old whisky is something to truly marvel at − does no harm in guiding home the more potent flavour profiles, which in this case meanders between hugely intense grape and heroically soporific malt; f23 against all the odds the malt wins...though a little praline comes to the rescue; b24 truly X cellent. 60.4%. sc. 109 bottles.

⬦ **Le Gus't Selection XI Speyside Blended Malt** hogshead, cask no. 403 (91) n22.5 outwardly a flighty bananas and custard type, but closer inspection reveals a beautiful oak structure; t23 that big oak arrives early and makes its mark. Curious, as seemingly younger malts give a short, bright barley burst. However, the oak keeps its foot on the throat (literally) but softens to allow a friendlier praline note to develop; f22.5 the oily praline − backed now with richer malt − keeps on going; b23 appears to have good age to this and a little bit of class. 49.7%. sc. 262 bottles.

⬦ **Liquid Treasures Entomology Wardhead Over 21 Years Old** ex-bourbon hogshead, dist 1987, bott 2018 (88.5) n22 ah...a tiring cask. Attractive, superficially, but closer inspection reveals some tell-tale signs of distress. The oaky fissures are deep; tangy orange peel; t22.5 excellent texture: firm malty oils, salty also − which suggests big age. There is a moment of rich barley intensity before some light milky chocolate forms; f21.5 the tannins start heading in a vaguely astringent direction; b22.5 all the classic signs of a malt which really struggles with great age: so even at 21 the barley is fracturing to allow the oak an ungainly foothold. Lots to savour, though. 55.5%.

◇ **Liquid Treasures Entomology Williamson Over 6 Years Old** ex-bourbon hogshead, dist 2011, bott 2018 (87.5) n21.5 t22 f22 b22 A beautifully young and raw whisky which tears at your taste buds like a hawk's talon on its prey. Sound peat mingles with decent Demerara sugars and though a few tannin notes gets through, the malt's youth is never in doubt. 59.6%.

The Loch Fyne The Living Cask 1745 (94.5) n23.5 t23.5 f23.5 b24 One of the best whiskies ever created at quarter to six in the evening....and one quite impossible not to love. 46.3%

The Loch Fyne The Living Cask Batch One (92) n22 t23.5 f23 b23.5 Absolutely charming. 46.3%

The Loch Fyne The Living Cask Batch Two (78) n18 t21 f19 b20. A charming coincidence today: the first time I visited the Loch Fyne whisky shop, about 30 years ago, I spotted my first ever Spotted Flycatcher at Inveraray Castle. Just a few minutes before tasting this, a spotted flycatcher visited my garden for the first time this summer – and it is now late July. It must have known... Thirty years ago, though, the sherry-influenced bottlings available were so much better than today...43.6%

The Loch Fyne The Living Cask Batch Four (88) n21 an intriguing mix of Lincoln biscuits and oily vanilla...; t22.5 a real malt fest for the delivery: light castor sugar sprinkled on the tame vanilla; f22 the oily texture on delivery lasts the course, but reduces enough for the spice to make a meaningful entrance; b22.5 oh well, batch 3 gave us the slip but we caught up with Batch 4 which is a vast improvement on 2. A genuinely oily cove; and astonishingly malty, too... 43.6%

◇ **Loch Fyne Living Cask** batch no. 6 (88.5) n23 an oily Caol Ila-style smokiness holds the upper hand. Ridiculously yielding and sweet...; t22.5 ditto on delivery, except the sugars here really do take off. Nutty – Danish marzipan to be a little more precise; f21 loses Brownie Points for the furriness on the finish. Quite metallic, too; b22 well Batch 6 appears to be living and breathing peat... 43.6%.

The Lost Distillery Company Stratheden batch no. 2/II (86) n22 t21.5 f21 b21.5. A dry malt boasting sporadic muscovado fruity sweetness and the vaguest of underlying phenols. Pleasant, though by no means perfect. I wish the company well, but have to say that putting today's casks together to recreate a malt last distilled in 1926 (and which no-one living has probably ever tasted) is fanciful, to put it mildly. In those days bourbon casks weren't available so not in use, sherry ones were then of a significantly higher standard and the peat, almost certainly, would have been a little more punchy than here. 46%. nc ncf.

◇ **Macaloney's TWA Cask Series Benrinnes & Glenlossie** ex-bourbon casks, finished in re-toasted red wine barriques (89) n22.5 heady stuff: red and blackcurrants in a pungent match with full on barley; t22.5 a little demerara sugar puffs out its chest here and there, the spices punch hard but those big fruits dominate. Oak bites at last in the mid-ground, bringing with it a little cocoa and butterscotch; f22 blackberry tart with the pastry slightly overcooked..; b22 not a malt for the faint-hearted: the fruit dominates and makes little effort to integrate, leaving the oak to make a violent, forced entry. 57.2%. ncf. 1,198 bottles.

◇ **Macaloney's TWA Cask Series Blair Athol & Macduff** ex-bourbon casks, finished in re-toasted red wine barriques (88.5) n22.5 the distant smell of a breakfast table with jam smeared on overdone toast; t23 huge fruit delivery allows the malt to have its say for a juicy combo; a little ulmo honey formulates, and as it does the mouth feel changes to a little more oily format; f20.5 perhaps a touch too tangy...; b22.5 have to admit that those wine barrels, though not faultless, certainly have a charm and do all they can to accentuate any honey notes lurking. 58%. ncf. 797 bottles.

◇ **Macaloney's TWA Cask Series Caol Ila & Bunnahabhain** ex-bourbon casks, finished in re-toasted red wine barriques (93) n23 first a quick sighting of fresh fruit juice then basted away by Fisherman's Friend cough sweet phenols; t23.5 the smoke, though early on at times billowing, doesn't have the force this time to get the better of the salivating fruit which stays the course. There is still, though, a spiced Fisherman's Friend element which is truly satisfying and soft; and like that famous tablet melts in the mouth; f23 much drier with the spices now slight yet still keeping the rhythm; b23.5 about as juicy a peated malt as you'll ever find! Something for everyone. 55.6%. ncf. 918 bottles.

Mackinlay's Rare Old Highland Malt (89) n22 t22 f22 b23. Possibly the most delicate malt whisky I can remember coming from the labs of Whyte and Mackay. Though it still, on the palate, must rank as heavy medium. This is designed as an approximation of the whisky found at Shackleton's camp in the Antarctic. And as a life-long Mackinlay drinker myself, it is great to find a whisky bearing its name that, on the nose only, briefly reminds me of the defter touches which won my heart over 30 years ago. That was with a blend: this is a vatted malt. And a delicious one. In case you wondered: I did resist the temptation to use ice. 47.3%

Master of Malt Reference Series I (82) n19.5 t23 f19 b20.5. Not quite the happiest of bunnies at times, as it occasionally struggles to find a balance in the face of big, not entirely desired, oils.

That said, nothing to stop you embracing the enormity of the date & sugar-drizzled barley soon after dinner & during the period it has escaped a certain feintiness. 47.5% WB15/349

Master of Malt Reference Series I.1 (87.5) n21 t23 f21.5 b22. No enormous age – or at least oak involvement - as confirmed by the nose. But some wonderful moments as the juicy, clean barley hits the palate running. 47.5%

Master of Malt Reference Series I.2 (93) n23 t23 f23.5 b23.5 A charming marriage between Fisherman's Friend phenols and balletic barley. 47.4%

Master of Malt Reference Series I.3 (91) n22 dry, oak-steered with a nod towards mocha; t22.5 a deft, peaceful delivery with no drama but loads of development; f23.5 lightly sweetened cocoa powder makes for a fabulous ending: reminiscent of Merlin lollies of yesteryear; b23 it's all about the chocolate... 47.1%

Master of Malt Reference Series II (84.5) n20 t22 f21.5 b21. The oils have been toned down for this one, though the sugars have reached shrieking point. Malty, but perhaps a tad too cloying for its own good. 47.5% WB15/350

Master of Malt Reference Series II.1 (88) n21 nothing wrong with it: just dull and uninspiring; t23 a rich seam of malt appears to be of an oily disposition; f22 again, technically sound. Plenty of rich malt and all that plus a hint of spice; b22 an oily cove... 47.5%

Master of Malt Reference Series II.2 (87) n22 t22.5 f21 b21.5. Soft lemon drizzle on chunky malt plus an enjoyable volley of sugary grist early on. 47.4%

Master of Malt Reference Series II.3 (89) n21.5 floral – a dank bluebell wood; t22.5 mouth-filling malt. Playful oils and a steady ramping up of the malt intensity; f22.5 something of a malt cereal about the finale; a little butterscotch tart thickens the effect; b22.5 reminiscent of a Kentucky maltshake. 47.2%

Master of Malt Reference Series III (88) n22 t23 f21 b22 Still one for the sweet toothed, but you don't need a diagram at the back to tell you some decent age has been added to this vatting. The odd blemish, but great fun. 47.5% WB15/351

Master of Malt Reference Series III.1 (89.5) n22.5 a squeeze of blood orange and grapefruit set the malt off beautifully; t23 thrusts malt at the taste buds like a politician rams his party line down your earholes; f21.5 a little vanilla and spice, though the malt lingers; a tad bitter late on; b22.5 if you like your malt malty, vote for this. 47.7%

Master of Malt Reference Series III.2 (92.5) n22.5 earthy, yet enticingly malty. And thick...; t23 superb Malteser style delivery: massive malt with an attractive milk chocolate element; f24 good grief!! That malt just doesn't know when to call it a day. A little ulmo honey has joined in to intensify the sweetness slightly; even some late spice adds to the ultra late complexity; b23 similar to III.1, except without the bitter bits. 47.5%

Master of Malt Reference Series III.3 (78) n19.5 t21.5 f18 b19. Fruity, fat, sweet. A tad furry. And somewhat one-dimensional. 47.5%

Master of Malt Single Cask Peatside 5 Year Old dist 2011 (85) n21.5 t23 f20 b20.5 What an odd cove this is. Starts like a train, an express at that, then hits the buffers soon into its journey. The delivery makes a lie of the unkempt nose with an explosion of muscovado sugars, liquorice and thick malt and peat. The confounded thing then vanishes into a morass of toffee. So bloody annoying! 61.8%. sc.

Master of Malt Single Cask Wardhead 19 Year Old dist 1997 (94) n22.5 t24 f23.5 b24 So easy to mistake this for a Glenfiddich, which appears to peak around this age....the quality of the oak is just about perfection. 52%. sc.

Matisse 12 Year Old Blended Malt (93) n23.5 t23 f22.5 b23. Succulent, clean-as-a-whistle mixture of malts with zero bitterness and not even a whisper of an off note: easily the best form I have ever seen this brand in. Superb. 40%. Matisse Spirits Co Ltd.

Matisse Aged 12 Years (79) n17 t21 f20 b21. Not sure if some finishing or re-casking has been going on here to liven it up. Has some genuine buzz on the palate, but intriguing weirdness, too. Don't bother nosing this one. 40%. The Matisse Spirits Co Ltd.

Milroy's of Soho Finest Blended Malt (76) n18 t19 f20 b19. Full flavoured, nutty, malty but hardly textbook. 40%. Milroy's of Soho.

Mo'land (82) n21 t22 f19 b20. Extra malty but lumbering and on the bitter side. 40%.

Monkey Shoulder batch 27 (79.5) n21 t21.5 f18 b19. Been a while since I lasted tasted this one. Though its claims to be Batch 27, I assume all bottlings are Batch 27 seeing as they are from 27 casks. This one, whichever it is, has a distinctive fault found especially at the finale, which is disappointing. Even before hitting that point a big toffeed personality makes for a pleasant if limited experience. 40%. William Grant & Sons.

New Town Blends The Advocate's Batch (87.5) n21.5 t22.5 f21.5 b22. Attractive, pleasant and, though a vatting, simplistic. A youthful catch on the nose suggests development might be limited, but it makes amends by the sheer charm of the light, clean, earnest malt. A lovely dram before lunch, I suggest. 43%. Edinburgh Whisky Ltd.

Old St. Andrews Aged 10 Years Twilight batch no. L1058 G1048 (91.5) n22.5 lovely barley: sharp, fresh but with a spicy bite; t23.5 excellent viscosity gives the malt a real thickness and allows the barley to drive home a grassy, delicately sweet and then increasingly spicy element; f22.5 long cocoa and spice fade; b23 as clean a contact as you ever hope to make and travels a long way. 40%.

Old St. Andrews Aged 10 Years Twilight batch no. L3017 G2716 (91) n22 plenty of barley and flatter more toffeed notes; t23.5 thick and chewy, the barley has its moment in the sun before a far bigger oak backbone heaves itself firmly into place; light spices tease, then tickle, then prickle; f22.5 lots of coffee-caramel with a lightly spiced fade; b23 takes a different course from the previous batch, eschewing the sharper tones for a more rumbling, deeper and earthier character. Very much above par. 40%.

Old St. Andrews Aged 12 Years Fireside batch no. L2446 G2557 (89) n22.5 crisp malt... and juniper! t22 barley early on, a peck or two of juniper, then a light smearing of orange blossom honey; f22.5 more of the same, except the oak does now impact, even offering a light touch of liquorice; b22 perfect for those who can't make their mind up between a malt and a G&T in the 19th hole... 40%.

Old St. Andrews Aged 12 Years Fireside batch no. L2927 G2716 (93) n23 earthy, dry yet floral; t23 intense and rich: a slightly plummy side to this – a kind of chocolate cake with seasoned fruit included! Rejoices in its full- bodied texture; f23.5 spiced muscovado sugars, then a spent molasses; a delicate smokiness lengthens the finish considerably; b23.5 returns to its usual high quality brand which usually makes the cut. 40%.

Old St. Andrews Aged 15 Years Nightcap batch no. L2519 G2557 (86.5) n21.5 t22.5 f21 b21.5 A little more fizz on delivery than their last round but then again the finish ends up lost in the long grass. Just too much caramel effect from somewhere. 40%.

Old St. Andrews Aged 15 Years Nightcap batch no. L2976 G2716 (86) n22 t21.5 f21 b21.5 Well, this certainly is a nightcap: I fell asleep waiting for something to happen. Pleasant honey at times and chewy toffee but a bit short on the charisma front. 40%.

Poit Dhubh 8 Bliadhna (90) n22.5 t23.5 f21.5 b22.5. Though the smoke which marked this vatting has vanished, it has more than compensated with a complex beefing up of the core barley tones. Cracking whisky. 43%. ncf. *Pràban na Linne.*

Poit Dhubh 12 Bliadhna (77) n20 t20 f18 b19. Toffee-apples. Without the apples. 43%. ncf. *Pràban na Linne.*

Poit Dhubh 21 Bliadhna (86) n22 t22.5 f21 b20.5. Over generous toffee has robbed us of what would have been a very classy malt. 43%. ncf. *Pràban na Linne.*

The Pot Still Scotch Vatted Malt Over 8 Years Old (90) n22 t24 f22 b22. Such sophistication: the Charlotte Rampling of Scotch. 43.5%. ncf. *Celtic Whisky Compagnie, France.*

Prime Blue Pure Malt (83) n21 t21 f21 b20. Steady, with a real chewy toffee middle. Friendly stuff. 40%

Prime Blue 12 Years Old Pure Malt (78) n20 t20 f19 b19. A touch of fruit but tart. 40%

Prime Blue 17 Years Old Pure Malt (88) n23 t21 f22 b22. Lovely, lively vatting: something to get your teeth into! 40%

Prime Blue 21 Years Old Pure Malt (77) n21 t20 f18 b18. After the teasing, bourbony nose the remainder disappoints with a caramel-rich flatness. The reprise of a style of whisky I thought had vanished about four or five years ago 40%

Queens & Kings Kenneth I. MacAlpin (86) n22 t22 f20.5 b21.5 A brittle, unyielding vatting softened only by delicate smoke and a little but attractive Manuka honey, though the late vanilla is a bit aggressive. 53.7%.

Queens & Kings Mary, Queen of Scots (91.5) n22.5 t23 f23 b23 A very comfortable assembling of malt. Impressed. 55.6%. Mr. Whisky.

Queens & Kings Robert The Bruce (88) n21 t23.5 f21.5 b22 A bit of a wobbly vatting, where the part of the peat and its effects have not been thoroughly thought through. 54%. Mr Whisky

Rattray's Selection Blended Malt 19 Years Old Batch 1 Benrinnes sherry hogsheads (89.5) n22 t23.5 f21.5 b22.5. Absolutely love it! Offers just the right degree of mouth-watering complexity. not a malt for those looking for the sit-on-the-fence wishy-washy type. 55.8%. *Auchentoshan, Bowmore, Balblair & BenRiach. A.D. Rattray Ltd.*

Saar Whisky Gruwefreund sherry hogshead, dist 2009, bott 2018 (87) n22 t22.5 f20.5 b22 Though from a sherry hoggy, it is youthful, salivating malt which dominates, though the bitter-ish out of sync finish doesn't do much for the overall picture. 53.4%. ncf sc. *Vatted Malt from the Orkney Distilleries.*

Sansibar Whisky Very Old Vatted (74.5) n19 t19 f18 b18.5. Pretty smoky for a Speyside. But bitter and off key. 45.6%

Scotch Universe Voyager I 231˚ U.4.4˚F 1886.2"TS first fill Côte de Beaune wine barrique, dist 1997, bott 2016 (78) n20 t21 f18 b19 Voyager...that's me! A voyager through the universe of whisky having travelled on for what seems now like lightyears.And despite all the malty planets I have explored, I still don't like whiskies which are either sulphured or over fruity. Or both. *52.9%.*

Scottish Collie (86.5) n22 t23 f20.5 b21. A really young pup of a vatting. Full of life and fun but muzzled by toffee at the death. *40%. Quality Spirits International.*

Scottish Collie 5 Years Old (90.5) n22.5 t23 f22 b23. Fabulous mixing here showing just what malt whisky can do at this brilliant and under-rated age. Lively and complex with the malts wonderfully herded and penned. Without colouring and at 50% abv I bet this would have been given a right wolf-whistle. Perfect for one man and his grog. *40%.*

Scottish Collie 8 Years Old (85.5) n22 t21.5 f21 b21. A good boy. But just wants to sleep rather than play. *40%. Quality Spirits International.*

Scottish Collie 12 Years Old (82) n20 t22 f20 b20. For a malt that's aged 84 in Collie years, it understandably smells a bit funny and refuses to do many tricks. If you want some fun you'll need a younger version. *40%. Quality Spirits International.*

Scottish Leader Imperial Blended Malt (77) n20 t20 f18 b19. Now don't be confused here: this isn't Imperial malt from Speyside. And although it says Blended, it is 100% malt. What is clear, though, is that this is pretty average stuff. *40%. Burn Stewart.*

Scottish Leader Aged 14 Years (80) n21 t21 f19 b19. A cleaner, less peaty version than the no-age statement vatting, but still fails to entirely ignite the tastebuds *40%. Burn Stewart.*

⬨ **Selkie** batch no. 001, bott code: L13/9097 (94) n23.5 fingers of salted honey beckon you in. Rare to find oak so blithely doing its job in keeping everything grounded: wonderful harmony; t23.5 the body of this malt is firm, succulent and demands exploring: the barley is intense and focused and it hard to know exactly where the barley ends and ulmo honey starts; f23 sexy and spicy as that firm yet yielding body succumbs to a salty finish; b24 the label keeps abreast of this alluring whisky. I'd happily chew on a nip of this any day... *40%. House of MacDuff.*

⬨ **Selkie** batch no. 002 (80) n20 t23 f18 b20 Must be the ugly sister. The nose, finish and overall balance aren't a patch on batch 1. But impossible not to fall in love a little with the mid-point peak, which is rich, alive with creamy mocha and maintains that salty character. Now that bit gets my seal of approval... *50%. House of MacDuff.*

Sheep Dip (84) n19 t22 f22 b21. Young and sprightly like a new-born lamb, this enjoys a fresh, mouthwatering grassy style with a touch of spice. Maligned by some, but to me a clever, accomplished vatting of alluring complexity. *40%*

Sheep Dip 'Old Hebridean' 1990 dist in or before 1990 (94) n23 t24 f23.5 b23.5. You honey!! Now, that's what I call a whisky...!! *40%. The Spencerfield Spirit Co.*

Shetland Reel Batch No. 1 (72) n18 t22 f15 b17 I am just glad that the sulphur comes from dodgy casks used in this vatting of other distillery's malts and not their own. If this isn't a great lesson for the Shetland lads not to touch sherry butts with a pole that can stretch from Lerwick to Norway, I don't know what is. *47%. 1,800 bottles.*

Shetland Reel Batch No. 2 (90) n23.5 t23 f21 b22.5 A rogue sherry butt cannot entirely undo the many excellent qualities of this vatting. *47%. 1,800 bottles.*

⬨ **Shetland Reel Batch No. 3** (93) n23.5 a gentle caress of smoke plays second fiddle to the saline depth to this; a sawdusty dryness counters the vague beginnings of a honey influence; t23.5 malt has no place on the nose, but it makes its mark early here and with great intent; again the lightest smoke ensures depth and the ulmo honey, so quickly snuffed out on the nose, makes a better fist of it here; f22.5 citrus, salt and a little tangy; b23.5. It has been many a long year since I last visited the Shetlands but the salty bite to this, plus the peat reek on the breeze means someone has created a style well in keeping with the feel of those far off isles. A very satisfying dram. *47%. 1,800 bottles.*

Simon Brown The Captain's Pure Scotch Malt Islay bourbon casks, dist 2010, bott 2015 (91) n22.5 t23 f22.5 b23 A young malt delighted to display its sugary side. Exceptionally easy going. *43%. nc ncf.*

Simon Brown The Captain's Pure Scotch Malt Speyside Highlands sherry casks, dist 2009, bott 2015 (80) n18.5 t21.5 f20 b20. As present day sherry butts go, not too bad. It bounces back from a poor nose with some impressive honey on delivery – and this manages to keep going long into when the less attractive notes of the sherry return. *43%. nc ncf.*

S'Mokey (88) n22.5 t22 f21.5 b22. Delicate, sweet and more lightly smoked than the nose advertises. *40%.*

Smokey Joe Islay Malt (87) n21.5 t22 f21.5 b22. A soft, soporific version of a smoky Islay. No thumping of waves here: the tide is out. *46%. ncf Angus Dundee Distillers.*

⬨ **Son of a Peat** batch no. 01 (91) n23.5 so enticing! Young and alluring, the smoke, though on one level sharp and acidic, is not overplayed and the orange blossom honey plays no less an attractive part, as does the diced green apple; t23 soft with the gristy malts still apparent. The phenols are two handed, offering both weight and a lighter touch. In between, though, are young malts and dancing sugars determined to lighten the load; f22 the youngers malts land a little awkwardly at times but recover sufficiently to find their place among the caramels and spices; b23 peaty, but not just for peat's sake... 48.3%. nc ncf. Flaviar.

Spirit of Caledonia Flaitheanas 18 Years Old (94) n23.5 t24 f23 b23.5 Now that is a proper vatted malt...!!! 57.8%. Mr Whisky.

Svenska Eldvatten Blended Malt 1994 ex-sherry butt, dist Aug 94 (71) n18 t18 f17 b18. There is nothing I need to say... 54.5%. sc.

Tambowie (84.5) n21.5 t21.5 f20.5 b21. A decent improvement on the nondescript bottling of yore. I have re-included this to both celebrate its newly acquired lightly fruited attractiveness...and to celebrate the 125th anniversary of the long departed Tambowie Distillery whose whisky, I am sure, tasted nothing like this. 40%. The Vintage Malt Whisky Co Ltd.

That Boutique-y Whisky Company Islay Blended Malt No 1 23 Year Old batch 1 (94.5) n24 t23.5 f23 b24 Probably the most delicious cure for anything and everything... 46.3%. 419 bottles.

That Boutique-y Whisky Company Blended Malt Whisky No. 1 23 Year Old batch 2 (88.5) n21.5 t23 f22 b22 Pretty tired but hangs in there gamely and even shows some astonishing malty liveliness! 48.8%. 409 bottles.

That Boutique-y Whisky Company Blended Malt No. 2 batch 1 (72) n17.5 t19 f17.5 b18. Unmolested , the grape would have been spectacular, especially with the big cocoa finish. But the cask has done its damage. 48.3%. 370 bottles.

That Boutique-y Whisky Company Blended Malt No. 2 batch 2 (84.5) n21.5 t21 f21.5 b20.5. The sugars are a bit too flash and uncouth. Elsewhere, just a tad too tart and struggles to find a balance.43.1%. 415 bottles.

Treasurer 1874 Reserve Cask (90.5) n23 t23 f22.5 b22. Some judicious adding has been carried out here in the Robert Graham shop. Amazing for a living cask that I detect no major sulphur faultlines. Excellent! 51%. Live casks available in all Robert Graham shops.

Triple Wood Blended Malt Scotch Whisky (77) n17.5 t22 f18.5 b19. At least one wood too many. Tangy...for all the wrong reasons. 42%. Lidl.

Usquaebach Cask Strength 2016 Release (86) n21.5 t23.5 f20 b21 A curate's egg of a dram. The fruitiness is hit and miss: more miss than hit. But there is also a hugely attractive, shimmering sharpness, also, with the barley sparkling on the palate in fabulous fashion. Sadly, the caramels and then dull tanginess is hardly the progression hoped for. 57.1%. ncf.

Vintner's Choice Speyside 10 Years Old (84) n21.5 t22 f20 b20.5. Pleasant. But with the quality of the Speysiders Grants have to play with, the dullness is a bit hard to fathom. 40%.

Waitrose Pure Highland Malt (86.5) n22 t22 f20.5 b22. Blood orange by the cartload: amazingly tangy and fresh; bitters out at the finish. This is one highly improved malt and great to see a supermarket bottling showing some serious attitude...as well as taste!! Fun, refreshing and enjoyable. 40%

⬦ **Wemyss Family Collection Treacle Chest** 1st fill ex-sherry hogsheads, batch no. 2017/02 (84.5) n21.5 t22.5 f20 b20.5 There appears to be mainly clean sherry butts at work here: not perfect but by comparison to most, not too bad. And a mix of date and prune briefly fill the palate on delivery. But after that the lights appear to be switched off and though one can grope around in the dark and enjoy oneself to some extent, there is surprisingly little to stimulate the taste buds after. Just too flat by half. 46%. nc ncf. 6,300 bottles.

⬦ **Wemyss Family Collection Vanilla Burst** 1st fill ex-bourbon barrels, batch no. 2017/01 (86.5) n22.5 t22.5 f20 b21.5 A pleasant experience. But you can't help feeling that the casks are slightly neutralising each other rather than adding layers of complexity. The nose does express vanilla and the odd hickory note and the delivery, well, delivers. But by the time we reach the finale there is little in reserve. 46%. nc ncf. 4,800 bottles.

Wemyss Malts The Hive (87) n21.5 t22 f22 b21.5 A lush, easy-drinking dram but one with a surprising lack of high spots: it is as though someone has made the common but fatal mistake of putting together styles that have cancelled each other out – certainly at this strength - rather than bringing the best out of and enhancing the other. No lack of honey and spice, for sure, but also toffee aplenty. 46%. ncf.

Wemyss Malts The Hive Batch Strength batch 001 (90.5) n22 t23.5 f22 b23 A lovely malt which is heavily dependent on the honey and spice. And there is nothing wrong with that! 54.5%. ncf. 6,000 bottles.

Wemyss Malts Kiln Embers (94.5) n23.5 ashy, dry and acidic on one level; citrusy, muscovado-sweet and lightly oiled on another...charming; t23.5 the oils arrive first – and in greater intensity than the nose suggests. The nose is spot on though with the sweet-dry interplay, which here bounces around the palate until the sugar, all toasty and deep, finally win; f23.5 a manicured finale with the silky oily hanging on to the smoky embers...; b24 quite quite beautiful. 46%. ncf.

◇ **Wemyss Nectar Grove Madeira Wine Cask Finished** (88.5) n22.5 a hint of anthracite gives an acidic edge to the delicate fruit and dry marzipan; t22.5 silky, salivating start with no shortage of ulmo honey and toffee; f21.5 perhaps too much on the caramel front b22 soft and beautifully honeyed. 46%. nc ncf.

Wemyss Malts Peat Chimney (84.5) n21.5 t21.5 f21 b20.5 A sharp, muddled malt whose unbalanced kippery nose is a peaty indication of what is to follow. Each avenue explored appears to narrow into a dead end: a tight, restricted, frustrating experience. 46%. ncf.

Wemyss Malts Peat Chimney Batch Strength batch 001 (87.5) n22 t23 f21 b21.5 Much more comfortable and happy with itself than the 46% version, mainly thanks to the extra oils allowing the molasses to integrate to greater effect with the smoke. But the tinny, off kilter finale shows that some elements here simply refuse to bond. 57%. ncf. 6,000 bottles.

Wemyss Malts Spice King (90) n23.5 brilliant display of rich tannins: hickory, muscovado sugar and a nibbling, gently smoked spice link to excellent effect; t22.5 salivating and sweet delivery; a little grist thickens the mix; f22 classic vanilla and butterscotch fade; a very late and light sprinkling of spice...; b22 a lovely malt, but beyond the nose the spices of note are conspicuous by their absence and not a patch on those found on The Hive... 46%. ncf.

Wemyss Malts Spice King Batch Strength Batch 001 (95.5) n23.5 fruity muscovado, delicate smoke and confident, tingling spice do what they say on the label...; t24.5 magnificent delivery! Huge tannin thuds into the taste buds taking no prisoners. Enough sugars are present to prevent splinters and instead we get a huge spice blast with a gorgeous treacle and ulmo honey middle to sooth the battered nerve endings, the smoke arrives to minimise the storm f23.5 red liquorice, vanilla and now light orange blossom honey counter the tingling spices; b24 notably different in character and storyline to the 46% version...and here spices are in no shortage whatsoever...! Stunningly gorgeous. 56%. ncf. 6,000 bottles.

◇ **The Whisky Cask Company Peatside 7 Year Old** P.X. sherry cask, bott Feb 17 (84.5) n22 t21.5 f21 b20 This is my 1,110th new whisky for the 2019 Whisky Bible, and it seems like my 1,000th peat and PX sample. Very few of them particularly excite me. Usually, just too uncouth and showy I'm afraid...a bit like a young person staggering noisily along a Spanish resort in the early hours from one nightclub to another, deliberately wearing very little and no better for alcohol. 60.3%. 317 bottles.

◇ **Whisky D'arche 5 Ans D'âge** lot no. 250817 (90.5) n22.5 so young! Yet vibrant, well-made malt worn in tandem to offer a softy smoked (meaty smoky bacon), gristy, fun-spiced charmer; t23 ah! Didn't see that coming: the oak has promoted some vanillas further forward than you might expect. They sit comfortably with the gentle oil and then ever-expanding maltiness. Perfect salivation levels while a light phenol throb supplies the base notes f22 lighter now and more delicate with the vanilla; b23 what a joy of a whisky! Such is the joy of youth! 43% (86 proof).

Whisky-Fässle Blended Malt Whisky very old sherry butt, bott 2016 (87.5) n23 t23 f20 b21.5 Unquestionably some fruity- and fruit cakey - appeal on the nose with the grape showing both a catholic and zesty personality, and this is matched somewhat in the early moments of the rich delivery. But dulls and bitters out within a short period leaving a lopsided tale being told, all the interesting bits being in the opening chapters. 45.2%.

Whisky-Fässle Blended Malt Whisky very old sherry butt, bott 2016 (94) n24 t23.5 f22.5 b24 A much better balance to this with the oak having a welcome equal say in matters and giving the whisky an air of antiquity. 45.4%.

◇ **Whisky-Fässle Blended Malt 24 Year Old** sherry hogshead, dist 1993, bott 2018 (94) n23.5 massively attractive amalgamation of bristling oaky notes, big plummy fruit and molasses: classic Melton Fruit Cake with a tannin crust; t23 perfect mouth feel: the malt hangs together briefly before the sharp, salivating fruit gushes in, thickening all the while. Raisins and spice abound; f23.5 the raisins are a little more burnt, the spices a tad pricklier. Even a late hint of cocoa...then drops down to lighter vanilla; b24 sherry influence but elegant and clean as a whistle! 54.3%.

Whyte & Mackay Blended Malt Scotch Whisky (78) n19 t22 f18 b19. You know when the engine to your car is sort of misfiring and feels a bit sluggish and rough...? 40%. Waitrose.

Wild Scotsman Scotch Malt Whisky (Black Label) batch no. CBV001 (91) n23.5 t23.5 f21 b23. The type of dram you drink from a dirty glass. Formidable and entertaining. 47%

Wild Scotsman Aged 15 Years Vatted Malt (95) n23 t24 f24 b24. If anyone wants an object lesson as to why you don't screw your whisky with caramel, here it is. Jeff Topping can feel a justifiable sense of pride in his new whisky: for its age, it is an unreconstituted masterpiece... 46% (92 proof). nc ncf. USA.

William Grant & Sons Rare Cask Reserves 25 Years Old Blended Malt Scotch Whisky (82) n21 t22 f19 b20. Mouth-filling, chewy and mildly fruity, doesn't quite grow into the decent start offered and finishes untidily. 47%. Exclusive to The Whisky Shop.

Scottish Grain

It's a bit weird, really. Many whisky lovers stay clear of blended Scotch, preferring instead single malts. The reason, I am often told, is that the grain included in a blend makes it rough and ready. Yet I wish I had a twenty pound note for each time I have been told in recent years how much someone enjoys a single grain. The ones that the connoisseurs die for are the older versions, usually special independent bottlings displaying great age and more often than not brandishing a lavish Canadian or bourbon style.

Like single malts, grain distilleries produce whisky bearing their own style and signature. And, also, some display characteristics and a richness that can surprise and delight. Most of the grains available in (usually specialist) whisky outlets are pretty elderly. Being made from maize and wheat helps give them either that Canadian or, depending on the freshness of the cask, an unmistakable bourbony style. So older grains display far greater body than is commonly anticipated.

During the last year the grain whisky lover has been spoiled for choice. Especially those with deep pockets seeking the rarest of the grains, those which were seldom available to blenders even when those now lost distilleries were in full production. Top of the tree comes Garnheath, one of the lighter grains in its youth though now offering a unique charm whenever it surfaces. Two recent casks yielded just 300 bottles between them - each of them nectar.

Again, this year it has been the ancient bottlings which have been scoring particularly highly, though with a note of pathos because, usually, they are from distilleries now entirely lost to us. Topping the list is Cambus with a 26-year-old bottling from Berry Brothers which means this once small but perfectly formed distillery has been named Best Grain in the Whisky Bible three times in the last four years. The fact it is no more is just as much a matter of regret as any lost Scottish malt distillery.

Likewise, Dumbarton furnished a grain hitting a massive score of 96 this year - no surprise to any blender who has worked with this extraordinary and also vanishing grain.

Jim Murray's Whisky Bible Scotch Grain of the Year Winners	
2004-07	N/A
2008	Duncan Taylor Port Dundas 1973
2009	The Clan Denny Dumbarton Aged 43 Years
2010	Duncan Taylor North British 1978
2011	The Clan Denny Dumbarton Aged 40 Years
2012	The Clan Denny Cambus 47 Years Old
2013	SMWS G5.3 Aged 18 Years (Invergordon)
2014	The Clan Denny Dumbarton 48 Years Old
2015	The Sovereign Single Cask Port Dundas 1978
2016	The Clan Deny Cambus 25 Years Old
2017	Whiskyjace Invergordon 24 Year Old
2018	Cambus Aged 40 Years
2019	Berry Bros & Rudd Cambus 26 Years Old

Single Grain Scotch
CALEDONIAN

The Cally 40 Year Old refill American oak hogsheads, dist 1974 db **(88.5)** n23.5 t23 f20 b22 This poor old sod is tiring before your nose and taste buds. But it hangs on grimly to give the best show it can. Quite touching, really...we are witnessing first hand the slow death of a once great distillery. *53.3%. 5,060 bottles. Diageo Special Releases 2015.*

◇ **The Sovereign Caledonian 35 Years Old** refill hogshead, cask no. 14271, dist Feb 82, bott Oct 17 **(87)** n22 t22 f21 b22 Caledonian MacBrayn? Caledonian Canal? Caledonian Sea? Amazingly salty and coastal, more so than any grain I have encountered before. Has its unique and oddly delicious charm,but runs out of legs well before the finale. *46.9%. nc ncf sc. 154 bottles.*

That Boutique-y Whisky Company Caledonian 29 Year Old batch 2 **(96)** n24 t24.5 f23.5 **b24** The best Caledonian I have tasted in a very long time. A true classic! *47.7%. 310 bottles.*

CAMBUS

Cambus Aged 40 Years dist 1975 db **(97)** n24.5 not, perhaps the most wide-ranging of noses as far as different aroma traits are concerned. But it does what it sets out to do with something akin to perfection. Caramels simply don't come this intense yet pitch-perfect. The corn, oak, toasty sugars and all else to be found all seems wrapped one way or another in caramelised form with varying levels of honey and roast at work. So the feeling of age, great age. Yet as though preserved in caramel...extraordinary and beyond beautiful; t24 no surprises then that the delivery is firm to the point of crunchiness. And, again, it is concentrated caramel sweetened with honey, Manuka and ulmo, ensuring that the age doesn't take a turn for the sinister. It needs spices to balance the mouth experience away from deliciously sweet...and it arrives on schedule and with purpose; f23.5 long unravelling of the many elements and personalities which make up the caramel, especially the corn, with some late burnt toast and marmalade at the very death; b25 I chose this as my 600th whisky for Bible 2018: a tragically lost distillery capable of making the finest whisky you might expect to find at 40 years of age. And my hunch was correct: this is flawless. *52.7%. 1,812 bottles. Diageo Special Releases 2016.*

◇ **Berry Bros & Rudd Cambus 26 Years Old** cask no. 61972, dist 1991, bott 2018 **(96.5)** n24 a half hour nose: so many mercurial notes slip-sliding together, or merging, or re-merging, then slightly parting...; the oak influence is staggering with a warming, non-aggressive spice of a Jamaican rum style with a high estery fruit sweetness. Jackfruit, plantain, ulmo honey and molasses all at play; t24 salivating, and strictly sticking to the rum style. The sugars are lighter now: corn syrup yet a wheat-like spiciness makes it hard to pick the exact grain at play...though, when it is this sublime, who gives a damn! f24 more oak involvement now, as it dries – even a touch of dessicated coconut; the spices continue their busy Morse messages of complexity; b24.5 few whiskies this year have displayed so many beguiling twists and turns: a true gem of a grain, though always a bit of a rum do. I can imagine my dear friend of nearly three decades, Doug McIvor, leaping from his seat when he unearthed this sample....something as rare as any kind of satisfying Charlton Athletic experience... *55.1%. nc ncf sc.*

Best Dram Cambus 25 Year Old sherry hogshead, dist 1991, bott 2017 **(86)** n21 t22.5 f21 **b21.5** A bitter-sweet experience...literally! Quite a tangy finish. *55%.*

The Cooper's Choice Cambus 25 Year Old sherry wood, dist 1991, bott 2017 **(94)** n23.5 t23.5 f23 b24 Another of the parcel of Cambus 1991 to have hit the market this year...and of the sherry-matured this is by far the best. *51.5%. nc ncf sc. The Vintage Malt Whisky Co.*

◇ **The Cooper's Choice Cambus 1991** refill sherry butt, cask no. 61982, bott 2018 **(90)** n23.5 an old-fashioned British fruitcake, lightened by a degree of zest; a delicate offering of hickory from the oak; t24 fat, silky delivery, then a real outbreak of burnt raisin; the juicier notes ensure decent salivation levels; f20.5 a first, hunky dory, then a little bitterness develops; yes, there is a slight fault... b22 a very good whisky from the Swedish Whisky Fed which will probably make it to the quarter finals of any whisky competition – and then lose to an English malt... *58.5%. sc. Bottled for the Swedish Whisky Federation.*

◇ **Glen Fahrn Airline No. 17 Cambus 1991** hogshead, cask no. 79889, bott 2017 **(95.5)** n23.5 French toast – and I don't just mean the appalling Barnier in front of the British Brexit team...; t24.5 simply divine: yes, an outpouring of maple syrup, but balanced against the moist, buttery cake mix clinging to the side of the glass stirring dish; f23.5 bitters slightly as the tannins replicate that cake being slightly burnt; molasses and fudge towards the finale. Bitter? Fudge? Must be that dreadful Eurocrat Barnier again....; b24 my 999th whisky of the 2018 Bible gives up some of the secrets of this sadly lost gem of a distillery *54%. nc ncf sc. 279 bottles.*

Liquid Treasures Cambus 25 Year Old sherry butt, dist 1991, bott 2017 **(88)** n22.5 t22.5 f21 b22 A whisky not to be sneezed at.. *52.7%. Faces of Angkor Edition.*

MacAlabur Cambus 25 Years Old bourbon hogshead, cask no. 79900, dist 24 Sept 91, bott 10 Oct 16 (95.5) n24 t24 f23.5 b24 Should be in a frame and found in the Tate Modern... 62%. nc ncf sc. 221 bottles.

Old Particular Cambus 25 Years Old refill hogshead, cask no. 11353, dist Sept 91, bott Sept 16 (89) n23 t22 f22 b22 Quite a muted grain which seems to be working so extra hard to keep the oak under control that it forgets to expand its character. Always a joy, though. 55.4%. nc ncf sc. 282 bottles.

Old Particular Cambus 28 Years Old refill hogshead, cask no. 11607, dist Sept 88, bott Mar 17 (89.5) n22 t23.5 f21.5 b22.5 A gentle Cambus where just a little mischief from the cask makes a disproportionate impact on the delicate grain. 50.1%. nc ncf sc. 280 bottles.

Scotch Malt Whisky Society Cask G8.8 26 Year Old refill ex-bourbon hogshead, dist 18 Jun 90 (20) n23.5 t23.5 f22 b23 A slightly naughty cask tries to take the gloss off a brilliant grain: it fails. 56.7%.

The Sovereign Cambus 25 Years Old refill hogshead, cask no. 13051, dist Sept 91, bott Nov 16 (95) n24 t24 f23.5 b24 Substantial whisky: just packed to the last atom with character. Delicious! 55.5%. nc ncf sc. 271 bottles.

⬥ **The Sovereign Cambus 29 Years Old** refill hogshead, cask no. 15010, dist Sept 88, bott Apr 18 (86) n22 t22.5 f20.5 b21 Lots of fat and bubble gum at play here. Some superb moments on the corn, but never feels entirely at ease with itself, thanks to some stuttering oak. 45.6%. nc ncf sc. 299 bottles.

Whisky Broker Cambus 25 Year Old sherry butt, cask no. 62929, dist 08 Aug 91, bott 08 Mar 17 (88.5) n22 t23.5 f21 b22 So many positives here, but the slight sulphur taint does have a late effect. 56.9%.

The Whisky Chamber Cambus 25 Year Old refill sherry cask, dist 1991 (83) n22 t22 f19 b20 There appears to have been a run Cambus bottled this year thick with corn-oiled promise, but then crashing into small sulphured rocks. Not enough to sink the grain, but at least hole it... 53.1%.

Xtra Old Particular Cambus 40 Years Old refill hogshead, cask no. 11572, dist Sept 76, bott Nov 16 (97) n24.5 t24.5 f23.5 b24.5 When Cambus was still alive its output at standard blending ages was, for me, the finest of all the grains with Dumbarton following closely behind. As the grain matured towards middle and old age it lost the edge it had over the others...until now. For this bottling shines like a beacon and reveals in extraordinary detail just how truly great Cambus distillery was. 53.1%. nc ncf sc. 108 bottles.

CAMERONBRIDGE

Old Particular Cameronbridge 24 Years Old refill hogshead, cask no. 11225, dist Oct 91, bott Apr 16 (95) n24 t24 f23 b24 Very hard to ask any more of a grain whisky than that: beautiful. 51.5%. nc ncf sc. 461 bottles.

Old Particular Cameronbridge 25 Years Old refill hogshead, cask no. 11316, dist Oct 91, bott Oct 16 (94) n23.5 t23 f23.5 b24 If anyone says grain whisky is light and neutral, please put them in the direction of this. 54.5%. nc ncf sc. 276 bottles.

⬥ **Old Particular Cameronbridge 26 Years Old** refill hogshead, cask no. 12233, dist Oct 91, bott Dec 17 (93) n23 the nuzzling in of the red liquorice, cocoa and Demerara into the corn oils has a distinctive Kentucky burr; t23.5 as does the delivery which accentuates the oaky positives; ulmo honey and hickory make excellent bedfellows; f23 a serene butterscotch fade with a hint of light muscovado sugars; b23.5 A Scotch that wanted to be a bourbon when it grew up... 51.5%. nc ncf sc. 569 bottles.

⬥ **The Sovereign Cameronbridge 26 Years Old** refill butt, cask no. 14752, dist Oct 91, bott Feb 18 (79) n19 t22 f18 b20 Sweet and fruity but curiously tight on the nose and finish. 56.9%. nc ncf sc. 481 bottles.

That Boutique-y Whisky Company Cameronbridge 24 Year Old batch 1 (93.5) n23.5 t23 f24 b23 Takes its time to enter the super league – but gets there... 49.6%. 211 bottles.

Xtra Old Particular Cameronbridge 32 Years Old refill hogshead, cask no. 11342, dist Mar 84, bott Aug 16 (96.5) n24.5 t24 f23.5 b24.5 Quite indisputably magnificent. A contender for Scotch Grain of the Year. 56.2%. nc ncf sc. 254 bottles.

CARSEBRIDGE

Dramfool Carsebridge 52 Year Old cask nos. 89153, 89154, 89155 & 89157, dist 1964 (95) n23.5 t24 f23.5 b24 I doubt if you'll find a softer and more gentle whisky anywhere in the world this year... 40.8%. 50 bottles.

Old Particular Carsebridge 33 Years Old refill hogshead, cask no. 11339, dist Dec 82, bott Sept 16 (94.5) n23 t24.5 f23.5 b23.5 As grain whiskies go, what a stunning old rum this is...! 44.9%. nc ncf sc. 253 bottles.

The Sovereign Carsebridge 42 Years Old refill hogshead, cask no. 12366, dist May 73, bott Apr 16 **(77)** n18 t22 f18 b19 Very similar in style to old whiskies rounded off in sherry to take out the oaky claws with the nose and finish great disappointments. But I'm sure they wouldn't be that suicidal..! *53.1%. nc ncf sc. 167 bottles.*

The Sovereign Carsebridge 43 Years Old refill butt, cask no. 12653, dist May 73, bott Jun 16 **(86.5)** n21 t22 f21.5 b22 Despite being matured in an old sherry cask, this has much more rich caramel sloshing about the palate than fruit, complete with a tiring bitterness. It is if the two Sovereign Carsebridge samples I have been sent are in reverse... *54.3%. nc ncf sc. 345 bottles.*

◇ **The Sovereign Carsebridge 44 Years Old** refill hogshead, cask no. 14189, dist May 87, bott Sept 17 **(90)** n22.5 vanilla ice cream in a caramel wafer cone; t23 wow...! The sugars which skirt the nose hit the palate with unexpected force: oaky floorboards have had a couple of pounds of Tate and Lyle spilt on them; f22 vague bitterness, as expected, plus a little, manicured eucalyptus; b22.5 very attractive, but about as sweet as you'd like a whisky to go. *50.9%. nc ncf sc. 150 bottles. The Whisky Barrel 10th Anniversary bottling #7.*

That Boutique-y Whisky Company Carsebridge 52 Year Old batch 1 **(95)** n23.5 t24 f23.5 b24 Apart from the most minute extra tannin on the nose, an identical whisky to the Dramfool Carsebridge 52 above. *40.5%. 252 bottles.*

Xtra Old Particular Carsebridge 40 Years Old refill hogshead, cask no. 11529, dist Oct 76, bott Nov 16 **(93)** n23 t23.5 f23 b23.5 A surprisingly simplistic whisky considering its age, but what it does do is achieved with rare panache. *53.7%. nc ncf sc. 230 bottles.*

◇ **Xtra Old Particular Carsebridge 40 Years Old** refill hogshead, cask no. 11587, dist Oct 76, bott Feb 17 **(96)** n24 unlike, say, an Invergordon of this antiquity, the sugars are not blasted at you from point blank range. Instead they merge and/or intertwangle with a stupendously delicate series of oak tones, two or three of which, strangely, happen to perfectly match Neapolitan ice cream: chocolate, vanilla and strawberry...they certainly have the nose licked...! t24.5 great age creaks at you with every corn-stained nuance; the sugars are caked in both corn oil and corn dust; the slow melt of the vanilla and ulmo honey make you groan in delight; f23.5 more reserved oakiness, a little toasty with mocha and praline evident...then some late corn whisky once more; b24 not a bad way to celebrate my 1,001st whisky for the 2018 Bible. Sheer class. *49.9%. nc ncf sc. 148 bottles.*

DUMBARTON

◇ **Fadandel.dk Dumbarton 30 Years Old** cask no. 25241, dist 18 Mar 87, bott 27 Mar 17 **(86)** n22 t22.5 f20 b21.5 A clumsy grain festooned with honey and spice, but little ability to bring them happily together. Delicious early on but bitters out as the oak finally cracks. *57.2%. sc. 168 bottles.*

◇ **Single Cask Collection Dumbarton 30 Years Old** bourbon barrel **(96)** n24 pretty classic Dumbarton nose for the age. The corn refuses to be drenched in its own oils, instead offering a drier field on which the gentle spice, red liquorice and leathery tones can mingle without unnecessary disturbance; t24.5 a near perfect delivery: actually the first three or four waves ARE perfect! Just sufficient oils to coat the palate with a golden syrup and vanilla theme. Spices emerge quietly as do drier tannins, plus a few flakes of Brazil nut; f23.5 vanilla, butterscotch and ulmo honey work a ridiculously relaxed spell, sumptuously to round off something a little special...; b24 taste a whisky like this and you'll fully understand why I regard the destruction of this distillery as one of the greatest criminal acts ever perpetrated against the Scotch whisky industry. *52.1%. sc.*

◇ **The Sovereign Dumbarton 29 Years Old** refill barrel, cask no. 13049, dist Mar 87, bott Nov 16 **(96.5)** n25 t24.5 f23 b24 A mercurial, beautifully paced grain of the very highest order. Truly classic! *54.7%. nc ncf sc. 235 bottles.*

◇ **The Sovereign Dumbarton 30 Years Old** refill barrel, cask no. 14247, dist Mar 87, bott Sept 17 **(92)** n23 moist putty and well-aged Canadian whisky...; t23.5 sharp, salivating sugars: dissolving castor sugars and spices merge before the tannins gallop in with a volley of vanillas; f22.5 the ok tires, but is still able to mount a chocolate and mint finale; b23 beautiful stuff and those who appreciate Canadian will particularly benefit. But a little tiredness to the oak reminds you of its great age. *55.3%. nc ncf sc. 160 bottles. The Whisky Barrel 10th Anniversary bottling #6.*

◇ **The Sovereign Dumbarton 30 Years Old** refill barrel, cask no. 14327, dist Mar 87, bott Oct 17 **(94)** n23.5 dry corn and various oak spices make for surprisingly brittle nose; much closer to an ageing bourbon than scotch; t24 the well-known golden syrup theme to Dumbarton of this vintage with some excellent ok and nutty notes for balance; f23 the sugars a little more random here, still keeping the age at bay and bolstering the butterscotch; a slight bitterness late on; b23.5 practically a re-run of the Single Cask Dumbarton 30, except not all the dots on the sugars are joined. That said, still a whisky work of art. *50.2%. nc ncf sc. 135 bottles.*

The **Whisky Barrel Dumbarton 30 Year Old** barrel, cask no. 13436, dist 1987 **(96.5) n24 t24.5 f24 b24** Dumbarton at anything from 21to 30 is about as good as grain whisky gets (hence why Ballantine's can be sensational), providing it has lived in the right cask. And this is the right cask...56.7%. sc. 197 bottles.

GARNHEATH

The **Cooper's Choice Garnheath 28 Year Old** dist 1986, bott 2015 **(94.5) n23.5 t24 f23 b24** Garnheath at this relatively young age is tragically rare. And I'll be surprised if you'll see much more of this I the forthcoming years. High quality whisky at he peak of its range, rare or not... 55%. nc ncf sc. The Vintage Malt Whisky Co.

The **Cooper's Choice Garnheath 37 Year Old** dist 1978, bott 2015 **(91) n22 t23.5 f22.5 b23** Really shows none of its age. Surprisingly sweet and pliant for a grain so old. 46%. nc ncf sc. The Vintage Malt Whisky Co.

The **Cooper's Choice Garnheath 48 Year Old** dist 1967, bott 2016 **(96) n24 t24 f24 b24** It is an honour to experience a whisky both so rare and gorgeous. Perhaps not the most complex, but what it does io is carried out close to perfection. A must find grain. 41.5%. nc ncf sc. The Vintage Malt Whisky Co.

That **Boutique-y Whisky Company Garnheath 42 Year Old** batch 1 **(90) n22.5 t22.5 f22.5 b22.5** Attractive, but labours slightly under the weight of oils and oak. 44.3%. 120 bottles.

Xtra Old Particular Garnheath 42 Years Old refill butt, cask no. 11209, dist Feb 74, bott Jun 16 **(89.5) n22.5 t23 f21.5 b22.5** A kind of brighter version of the Boutique-y bottling, other than the finish... 44.5%. nc ncf sc. 130 bottles.

GIRVAN

The **Girvan Patent Still Over 25 Years Old** db **(84.5) n21.5 t21.5 f20.5 b21.** A pretty accurate representation of the character these stills were sometimes quietly known for at this time, complete with some trademark sulphury notes – presumably from the still, not cask, as I do pick up some balancing American white oak character. 42%. nc.

The **Girvan Patent Still No. 4 Apps** db **(87) n21.5 t22 f21.5 b22.** A first look at probably the lightest of all Scotland grain whiskies. A little cream soda sweetens a soft, rather sweet, but spineless affair. The vanillas get a good, unmolested outing too. 42% WB15/369

⌁ The **First Editions Girvan Aged 38 Years** refill hogshead, cask no. 14749, bott 2018 **(95) n23.5** a fascinating blend of sugars: molasses and muscovado lead the way but the heather honey also makes a fine contribution; a salty tang to the nose offers an unexpected coastal melody to this; **t24** oh, the succulence! Fabulous delivery and follow through, not least because the oak makes a classy contribution. The corn oils fatten, then the oak proffers a mix of spice and mocha. The balance between the sugars and the drying oak is exceptionally good; **f23.5** more very milky mocha, Demerara sweetened; **b24** wears its age and gravity lightly: this is wonderful grain whisky. 50.3%. nc ncf sc. 302 bottles.

⌁ **Liquid Treasures Entomology Girvan Over 28 Years Old** ex-bourbon barrel, dist 1989, bott 2018 **(86.5) n23 t22 f20.5 b21** A typical pea-souper of a Girvan, thick on the nose with sugary promise and no shortage of oak-encouraged vanilla depth then eye-smartingly sweet delivery with golden syrup mixing in with the oils. A warming sub plot as the spices build but a little disappointing as the oak gives way to bitterness. 52.7%.

⌁ **Old Particular Girvan 26 Years Old** refill hogshead, cask no. 11601, dist Dec 89, bott Feb 16 **(88.5) n22** a sticky, sweet nose punctuated by lively spice; **t22.5** green and sharp delivery but some ulmo honey moves in and quietens things; **f22** butterscotch tart with some mumbling spice; **b22** attractive, easy going and ridiculously simplistic. 51.5%. nc ncf sc. 224 bottles.

Old Particular Girvan 27 Years Old refill barrel, dist Jun 88, bott Nov 15 **(94.5) n23 t23.5 f24 b24** An any time of the day restorative... Truly beautiful. 62.6%. nc ncf sc. 192 bottles.

⌁ **Old Particular Girvan 27 Years Old** refill hogshead, cask no. 12191, dist Dec 89, bott Nov 17 **(91) n24** the corn pours off mixing with the light liquorice and hickory from the oak to set up the most outrageously delicious Kentucky nose in Scotland; **t22.5** more soporific on the palate: natural caramels run the show with an egg yolky, doughy sub strata; **f22** untaxing vanilla with a hint of butterscotch; **b22.5** it's all about the amazing nose, yesiree...! 51.5%. nc ncf sc. 148 bottles.

The **Sovereign Girvan 25 Years Old** bourbon barrel, cask no. 13285, dist Oct 91, bott Mar 17 **(91) n22.5 t23 f22.5 b23** With this degree of spice at work, presumably distilled from wheat. 58.9%. nc ncf sc. 342 bottles.

That **Boutique-y Whisky Company Girvan 52 Year Old** batch 2 **(95.5) n24 t24 f23.5 b24** Girvan is, of course, an anagram of raving... which is what this is from the moment you pour it into the glass. This has some very serious oomph....even after half a century! For its staggering age, one of the most amazing whisky forces of all time. 51.1%. 102 bottles.

INVERGORDON

◇ **Cadenhead's Single Cask International Invergordon 43 Years Old** dist 1973 (94.5) n23 something very dessert-ish about this: a kind of blend between a sherry trifle and crème brulé; t24.5 you have to be mean spirited to find any kind of fault with this delivery and follow through. I wasn't joking about the dessert: incredibly sweet, yet not even remotely cloying and simply fills the outh with the most delicious and succulent examples of ulmo honey and spice I have ever encountered; the maize also gives a slight corn whisky feel, too; f23.5 bitters slightly, as it was likely to do. Caramel and mocha do the repairs...; b23.5 you are more likely to find a jagged edge on a snooker ball than you are this luscious grain! 51.3%. sc. 175th Anniversary bottling.

◇ **Cave Aquila A Knight's Dram Invergordon 44 Years Old** cask no. 20, dist Dec 72, bott Mar 17 (95) n24 the cut-glass, crystalline demerara sugars versus the oak-laden, bourbon-edged prickly spice is nothing short of glorious; t24 just about perfect weight on the delivery, the corn oil captures every last input of the maple syrup and and Manuka honey mix; the spices buzz, neither too soft or loud; f23.5 remains gently toasty with an ever more noticeable nod towards a very classy Canadian/bourbon blend; b23.5 you almost want to give the spices a standing ovation... 46.7%. sc.

The Cooper's Choice Invergordon 30 Year Old dist 1984, bott 2015 (93) n23 t24 f22.5 b23.5 Invergordon benefitting from some exceptional oak these last three decades... 57%. nc ncf sc. The Vintage Malt Whisky Co.

ePower Invergordon 43 Year Old bourbon hogshead, dist 1972, bott 2016 (87) n21.5 t23 f21.5 b21.5 Absolutely no escaping the attitude to this. A slightly off-key cask has endowed a perceptible and unflattering tang which slightly undoes some of the good work carried out by the rampaging honey... 49%.

◇ **The First Editions Invergordon Aged 45 Years** refill barrel, cask no. 14772, bott 2018 (94) n23.5 the sugars seems at first to be delicate...then you realise they are intense, doing a great job of keeping the vanillas and citrus notes happily harmonised and the age of the tannins under control; t24 the delivery is confirmation of the nose: light, sweet corn oils with the icing sugar melting and making way of the caramelised biscuit; f23 unusually for a grain this age, not a bitter note in sight...but those vanillas...! b23.5 almost a halfway house between ancient grain and a simplistic liqueur. But not so sweet as to be beyond a thing of beauty. 49.6%. nc ncf sc. 230 bottles.

Old Particular Invergordon 18 Years Old refill barrel, cask no. 11197, dist May 97, bott May 16 (86.5) n22 t22.5 f20.5 b21.5 Sweet, a tad sappy, fat and a little one-dimensional. Bitterness at the death, though spices compensate slightly. 48.4%. nc ncf sc. 236 bottles.

Old Particular Invergordon 21 Years Old refill barrel, cask no. 11091, dist Oct 94, bott Feb 16 (94) n23.5 t24 f23 b23.5 A near faultless cask allows this Invergordon to confirm that few grain whiskies on the planet are anything like as yielding. 52.8%. nc ncf sc. 204 bottles.

◇ **Old Particular Invergordon 30 Years Old** refill butt, cask no. 12052, dist Aug 87, bott Sept 17 (83) n21 t23 f19 b20 Some do die for concentrated sultana, but right royally undermined by the dreaded S word... 55%. nc ncf sc. 278 bottles.

Saar Whisky Invergordon 1972 bott Sept 16 (94.5) n23.5 t24 f23 b24 A beautiful grain showing a style of whisky that will be lost to Scotland within the next decade. 49.1%. nc ncf sc.

Sansibar Whisky Invergordon 1973 bott 2016 (95) n24 t24 f23 b24 One for those with a sweet tooth. And probably no less a delight for those who haven't... 51.8%.

◇ **Single Cask Collection Invergordon 26 Years Old** rum barrel finish (87) n22 t22.5 f21 b21.5 Soft and sweet in the time-honoured Invergordon tradition. But with this amount of sugar at work, it needs to breathe and evolve. Rum casks have a tendency to clip a whisky's wings so, though a very decent and soothing grain, the fun comes to a slightly premature and bitter end. 57.4%. sc.

◇ **The Sovereign Invergordon 30 Years Old** refill hogshead, cask no. 15012, dist May 87, bott Apr 18 (88) n23 a trip to the candy store...or maybe a bourbon bar...; t23 the ultra-sweet delivery is predictable, though the muscovado sugars soon have a galaxy of tannin notes to deal with; f20.5 a tangy bitterness is at odds with the general theme; b21.5 promises so much, but the oak can't quite match the deal. 51.6%. nc ncf sc. 314 bottles.

The Sovereign Invergordon 40 Years Old refill hogshead, cask no. 13278, dist Jan 77, bott Feb 17 (92.5) n23.5 t23 f23 b23 Elegant, technically faultless and a grain which sticks to its theme. 47.8%. nc ncf sc. 390 bottles.

That Boutique-y Whisky Company Invergordon 43 Year Old batch 11 (86.5) n21.5 t23 f21 b21 Mixed feelings: part of me loves the fact the public gets a chance to see a single cask at this age. Putting my blender's hat on, what I could have done with this in a blend: accentuating its positives and disappearing its negatives. A poor barrel means there are a few too many negatives, but at least the delivery and first five or six waves of the follow through allow you to enjoy a brief glimpse of a corn oil and muscovado heaven. 48.2%. 186 bottles.

The Whisky Agency Invergordon 44 Years Old dist 1972 (94.5) n23.5 t24 f23 b24 Invergordon at its most unremittingly old Canadian... 49%. Bottled for La Maison du Whisky.

World of Orchids Invergordon 43 Year Old bourbon cask, dist 1973 (89) n22 t23 f21.5 b22.5 No great pretensions to greatness: an out and out blending grain which would have added to the desired honey-enriching effect. 46.7%.

LOCH LOMOND

Loch Lomond Single Grain db (93) n23 crisp sugars are willing to absorb the vanilla; t23.5 indeed, the sugars on the nose are indicative of a sweet grain, for the delivery centres around the maple syrup lead. The oak is something like most anchors at work: barely visible to invisible; f23 the oaks do have a say, though you have to wait a while on the long finale. A little spice arrives, too; b23.5 elegant grain; keeps the sweetness controlled. 46%

That Boutique-y Whisky Company Loch Lomond batch 2 (89) n22 t23 f22 b22 One of the softest grains ever produced in Scotland and here it shows all its accommodating sugars to the full... 47.8%. 91 bottles.

That Boutique-y Whisky Company Loch Lomond 19 Year Old batch 3 (88.5) n22 t23 f21.5 b22 A simplistic, lightly spiced, slightly flawed grain which ticks just enough boxes to make you want to explore at length. 49.7%. 267 bottles.

LOCHSIDE

The Cooper's Choice Lochside 44 Year Old dist 1964, bott 2015 (92.5) n23.5 not unlike a bourbon-Canadian blend (yes, I have encountered such a thing) where a muscular coconut-honey candy theme dominates the subservient vanilla; t24 salivating and soft, corn oils drift among the obliging sugars without a care in the world; you can hear the tannins knocking, but only the spices gain entry; f22 back to a coconut toffee thread; bitters late on; b23 it's hangs on in there, giving in to its age only in the final moments... 41.2%. nc ncf sc. The Vintage Malt Whisky Co.

NORTH BRITISH

◇ **Berry Bros & Rudd North British 20 Years Old** cask no. 224754, dist 1996, bott 2017 (94.5) n23.5 beautifully rich with a muscovado and orange blossom honey sweetness to match up with the drier vanilla and spices; t24 succulent and salivating. Spices arrive early but in control. The vanilla at the mid-point is as big as any you'll find anywhere, but before then the viscous ulmo honey and maple syrup makes you purr with joy...; f23 drier and toastier, but always with a sugary background. Light liquorice and slightly burnt fruitcake; b24 let's say you are a blender working on a high grade 21-year-old bend and a sample of this came into your lab as you worked out the next year's batch. You would be thrilled. This gives everything you'd want as it is far from neutral and a few casks of those would bolster your honey profile to sort out any oak from elsewhere which have gone a bit dry and gung ho early on. Exemplary. 54.8%. nc ncf sc.

Old Particular North British 21 Years Old refill barrel, cask no. 10996,, dist Oct 94, bott Nov 15 (91) n22 t23.5 f23 b23 You expect plenty of oomph on delivery...and my word, you get it!! 48.1%. nc ncf sc. 212 bottles.

◇ **The Sovereign North British 21 Years Old** refill hogshead, cask no. 14409, dist Oct 96, bott Nov 17 (87) n22.5 t22 f21 b21.5 A workmanlike grain keeping true to its age and type so far as a blender is concerned, the sharp clarity of the vanilla-tinged icing sugar more than useful. Likewise, the both lush yet underlyingly firm body would be of great use, especially with the marshmallow sweetness. The slight bitterness on the fade can be compensated for in a blend, though harder when a singleton like this. 54.8%. nc ncf sc. 219 bottles.

The Sovereign North British 55 Years Old refill butt, cask no. 13328, dist Dec 61, bott Feb 17 (85) n21 t23 f19 b21 Not sure if this has been "freshened up" as they call it these days in a newer sherry butt, as there is a more contemporary style of grape at play here... and a finish to match... When at its peak, is as succulent and sexy as they come... 55.1%. nc ncf sc. 144 bottles.

NORTH OF SCOTLAND

The Pearls of Scotland North of Scotland 1971 dist Dec 71, bott Apr 15 (95.5) n25 t23.5 f23 b24 What a beautifully elegant old lady...and one with virtually no wrinkles... 43.6%

PORT DUNDAS

◇ **Port Dundas 52 Year Old** refill American oak hogsheads db (96) n24.5 the corn is at its zenith, giving a show of corn whiskey but with an extra controlled firmness, with the most delicate crisp demerara sugar matching up to the oaky vanilla. Not a single off note, and everything in perfect harmony and pace. Wow...! **t24** just let this melt in your mouth: the corn-carrying sugars trace dreamy paths around the palate; **f23.5** slightly bitter as the oak tightens. But the soft vanilla is still on massage overdrive; **b24** note to all other grain whisky bottlers: bourbon casks every time to show the distillery in its true colours: NEVER sherry casks...! 44.6%. 725 bottles. Diageo Special Releases 2017.

Old Particular Port Dundas 12 Years Old refill barrel, cask no. 11340, dist Jun 04, bott Sept 16 (84.5) **n22 t22 f20 b20.5** Grain ordinaire. Plenty of sugary if one dimensional flavour on delivery but the finish is a bit clumsy and bitter. 48.4%. nc ncf sc. 247 bottles.

◈ **Old Particular Port Dundas 12 Years Old** refill barrel, cask no. 11758, dist Jul 04, bott Jun 17 (91) **n22.5** rich, spicy, exceptionally clean and just-so vanilla and citrus oak involvement; **t23** just as salivating as the nose promises, with extra sugars as a thin golden syrup covers the building butterscotch. The spices are delicate and in keeping; **f22.5** creamy butterscotch; **b23** when you wanted your blend to sparkle a little bit, this was the kind of grain you'd look out for. What an enormous loss this is to the industry... 48.4%. nc ncf sc. 357 bottles.

Old Particular Port Dundas 27 Years Old refill hogshead, cask no. 11333, dist Feb 91, bott Sept 16 (92) **n23.5 t23.5 f22 b23** At its best, as soft, sweet and slightly furry as a ripening peach. 51.5%. nc ncf sc. 206 bottles.

◈ **Old Particular Port Dundas 28 Years Old** refill hogshead, cask no. 11526, dist Oct 88, bott Nov 16 (92.5) **n23.5** exceptionally busy: corn oils and spices bubble gently; a little greengage and cut grass ensures a light touch; **t23** indeed, the delivery is lighter than can be possibly imagined for a grain so old: icing sugar and Demerara melt to reveal a surprisingly malty/caramel middle (this is grain, remember!) and sexy vanillas; **f22.5** must have been magnificent oak, as there is not a scar to the ultra-clean, light caramel finish; **b23.5** Port Dundas' uniquely rich yet delicate style is in full spate here. 51.8%. nc ncf sc. 205 bottles.

The Sovereign Port Dundas 27 Years Old refill hogshead, cask no. 12635, dist Oct 88, bott Jun 16 (93) **n23 t24 f22.5 b23.5** Curious one this: all the lush sweetness of corn oil but the bold spices of wheat. After 27 years, hard to detect exactly which is which, though I'll plump for corn. Whichever, superb! 56.1%. nc ncf sc. 191 bottles.

◈ **The Sovereign Port Dundas 27 Years Old** refill hogshead, cask no. 14451, dist Feb 90, bott Nov 17 (91.5) **n23** Fox's Party Rings biscuits; **t23.5** light corn oils can' distract from the German caramelised biscuit; **f22** most of the oils have burned off to leave roasty bourbon creams; **b23** simply takes the biscuit. 51.5%. nc ncf sc. 258 bottles.

The Sovereign Port Dundas 28 Years Old refill hogshead, cask no. 13046, dist Oct 88, bott Nov 16 (94.5) **n24.5 t24 f22.5 b23.5** Another lost distillery showing magnificently and why blended whisky is not going to improve anytime soon... 55.1%. nc ncf sc. 253 bottles.

That Boutique-y Whisky Company Port Dundas 25 Year Old batch 1 (95) **n24 t24 f23 b24.5** A little bit special... 48.2%. 115 bottles.

World of Orchids Port Dundas 24 Year Old bourbon cask, dist 1989 (92) **n22 t24 f23 b23** Don't expect great complexity...just a whole lot of technically faultless deliciousness. 56.1%.

STRATHCLYDE

Old Particular Strathclyde 11 Years Old sherry butt, cask no. 11484, dist Nov 05, bott Jan 17 (92.5) **n23.5** not only clean grape but even a hint of age on the sherry not unlike a superior late bottle vintage; **t23.5** teeming spices from the off...the ulmo honey and treacle is relentless; **f22.5** a little bit of oak bitterness gatecrashes at the end; **b23** well who'd've thought it: a near flawless sherry butt! Trouble is, it slightly subdues the original spirit, though still a superb experience. 55.5%. nc ncf sc. 306 bottles.

◈ **Old Particular Strathclyde 11 Years Old** sherry butt, cask no. 11952, dist Nov 05, bott Jul 17 (91) **n22** weighty fruitcake; **t23.5** a beautiful lilting sweetness to the exploding grape. Fresh and salivating in a manner few grain whiskies manage to achieve; **f22** slightly more bitter as the oak grabs the limelight; **b23.5** not just a sherry butt! But a clean, 100% untainted, entirely sulphur-free sherry butt! Fabulous! 55.5%. nc ncf sc. 638 bottles.

Old Particular Strathclyde 20 Years Old refill barrel, cask no. 11128, dist Apr 96, bott May 16 (86) **n21 t22.5 f20.5 b22** Sweet, chewy but has something of the Gorbals' roughhouse about it. 50.6%. nc ncf sc. 187 bottles.

Old Particular Strathclyde 25 Years Old refill barrel, cask no. 11335, dist Aug 90, bott Sept 16 (87) **n21.5 t22 f21.5 b22** A tangy beast with a metallic feel that subdues the sweetness which had gathered after delivery. Plenty of nip and bite, which is fun, but refuses to settle. 51.5%. nc ncf sc. 116 bottles.

◈ **Old Particular Strathclyde 26 Years Old** refill barrel, cask no. 11600, dist Aug 90, bott Mar 17 (94) **n23** an oscillating aroma: higher and lower notes arrive from all directions, making for both complexity and confusion. Both green apple and liquorice make telling contributions; t24 a stark, salivating, corn-fuelled, starchy delivery, then a second stage of intense muscovado sugars before the vanillas arrive; f23.5 busy and a little bitter, as though a metallic element is in short supply; b23.5 offers that peculiar complexity you get from old rums made on stills with perhaps slightly below average degrees of copper in the system. Uncanny. 55.5%. nc ncf sc. 174 bottles.

The Sovereign Strathclyde 25 Years Old refill barrel, cask no. 12281, dist Aug 90, bott Feb 16 (88) n21.5 t23 f21.5 b22 Many of the characteristics found in the OP of the same vintage (see above) but a far less accommodating cask. 51.7%. nc ncf sc. 176 bottles.

The Sovereign Strathclyde 26 Years Old refill barrel, cask no. 13045, dist Aug 90, bott Nov 16 (77) n19 t21 f18 b19 The pugnacious, lightly off-key nose offers fair warning of the Brillo pad delivery which scratches some unforgiving sugars onto the palate. The finish, though, suffers from a mixture of poor original distillate and a cask without the means to compensate. 54.5%. nc ncf sc. 241 bottles.

◇ **The Sovereign Strathclyde 30 Years Old** refill hogshead, cask no. 14448, dist Sept 87, bott Nov 17 (90) n22 pretty docile for Strathclyde: the natural caramels pleasant but domineering; t22 anyone remember Toffo toffee. This is just as creamy....and toffeed; f23.5 ah, at last wakes up from its pleasant slumbers as spices and citrus makes their mark for a beautifully complex finale; the oak offers some delightful layering and does so always with panache and not a single hint of bitterness; b22.5 it is as though the grain has fallen asleep after 30 years and finally wakes up late in the day. 50.7%. nc ncf sc. 175 bottles.

That Boutique-y Whisky Company Strathclyde 30 Year Old batch 1 (87.5) n22 t22.5 f21 b22 A grain that gives you a right punch in the throat on delivery. The sugars are profound but without structure and of very limited complexity. 53.1%. 228 bottles.

UNSPECIFIED SINGLE GRAIN

Borders finished in Oloroso sherry casks (66) n15 t18 f15 b18. Finished being the operative word. Has no-one been listening regarding the total mess sherry butts are in. I wonder why I bother sometimes. Jeez... 51.7%. nc ncf. R&B Distillers.

Haig Club toasted oak casks (89) n21.5 t23 f22.5 b22 When I first saw this, I wasn't quite sure whether to laugh or cry. Because 25 years ago bottles of single grain whisky were the unique domain of the flat cap brigade, the miners and other working class in the Kirkcaldy area of Scotland. Their grain, Cameron Brig, would be drunk with a splash, mixed with Coke or ginger, or even occasionally with Irn Bru, or straight and unmolested as a chaser to the ubiquitous kegged heavy, McEwan's lager or a bottle of Sweetheart stout. When I suggested to the hierarchy at United Distillers, the forerunners of Diageo, that in their finer grains they had a product which could conquer the world, the looks I got ranged from sympathy for my lack of understanding in matters whisky to downright concern about my mental wellbeing. I had suggested the exquisite Cambus, now lost to us like so many other grain distilleries in those passing years, should be brought out as a high class singleton. It was pointed out to me that single grain was, always had been and always will be, the preferred choice of the less sophisticated; those not wishing to pay too much for their dram. Fast forward a quarter of a century and here sits a gorgeously expensive bottle in a deep cobalt blue normally associated with Ballantine's and a very classy, heavyweight stopper. In it is a grain which, if the advertising is to be believed, is the preferred choice not of the back street bar room idlers carefully counting their pennies but of its major ambassador David Beckham: it is the drop to be savoured by the moneyed, jet-set sophisticates. My, oh my. Let's not call this hype. Let's just say it has taken some genius exec in a suit half a lifetime – and probably most of his or hers - to come around to my way of thinking and convince those in the offices on the floor above to go for it. Wonder if I qualify for 10 percent of profit for suggesting it all those years back...or, preferably, five percent of their advertising budget. Meanwhile, I look forward to watching David pouring this into some of his Clynelish and Talisker. After all, no-one can Blend it like Beckham... 40%. WB15/408

◇ **Haig Club Clubman** (87.5) n22 t22 f21.5 b22 A yieldingly soft and easy-as-you-like and at times juicy grain with a pleasant degree of light acacia honey to make friendlier still. 40%.

Svenska Eldvatten Grain 1964 ex-bourbon barrel, dist Dec 72, bott Mar 16 (95) n23.5 t24 f23.5 b24 I remember a couple of years back someone publicly poured scorn on me for saying blends now are vastly different to yesteryear because of the grain. Well, look at the way corn has shaped this baby: far closer to Canadian or even bourbon (or US Corn Whiskey to be more precise) than today's Scotch because of the extraordinary effect of the maize... 52.1%. sc.

Whisky-Fässle Lowland Single Grain 52 Year Old barrel, dist 1964, bott 2016 (90.5) n23 huge caramel...with a little squashed sultana for company; t23 soft and sensuous as a great grain should be. Salivating, too, after the initial caramel and vanilla surge has quietened. Some very serious chocolate through the middle section; **f21.5** the caramel continues, then takes a slightly fruitier pose – before constricting slightly; **b23** although from a barrel, the mystery fruitiness is there in all its strengths and weaknesses... *47.7%.*

WoodWinters The Five Distinguished and Rare Aged 39 Years (93) **n22.5** heavy duty oily corn whisky sexed up with a honeycomb, lime and spice complexity; **t24** now it enters a different league: the amalgamation of molasses and spice hits the palate with as much elegance as it does power – which is considerable. The corn fills the palate in the same way smoke envelopes a peated malt. But this is light enough for the acacia honey to embrace the meringue pie and red liquorice; **f23** dry vanilla but good, pulsing spice; **outstanding** oak leaves not a trace of tiredness; **b23.5** a grain of marvellous pedigree and integrity, at least equal to the vast majority of single malts whiskies you will find... *51%. sc. 330 bottles.*

Vatted Grain

Angus Dundee Distillers Blended Grain 50 Year Old (91.5) **n23** as old and creaking as a soon to retire Chelsea centre-half. Has given great service, but definitely a few cracks where there had been none a few years before. That said, the very light eucalyptus and heather honey work together charmingly; **t23.5** as silky as an Antonio Conte title winning side. Soaks up layers of tannins and counter attacks quickly with thrusting vanilla and ulmo honey; **f22** good spice helps deflect from the tiring oak; **b23** just champion...! *40.1%.*

Compass Box Hedonism first fill American oak cask, bott 20 Feb 13 (84) **n22 t22 f19 b20.** Just too fat, too sweet and too bitter at the finale to work to great effect. Some decent oak on both nose and delivery, though. *43%. nc ncf. Compass Box Whisky Company.*

Compass Box Hedonism Maximus (93.5) **n25 t22.5 f23 b23.** Bourbon Maximus... *46%*

◇ **Compass Box Hedonism The Muse** bott Feb 18 (89) **n23** a fat, roly-poly nose, a little lime putting an edge to the suet pudding and muscovado sugars. A little spicy, in a bourbon/ Canadian sense, though I don't expect this to come through loud on the palate; expect a little oak bitterness late on...; **t23** unlike the nose, there are shards and spikes here. A juicy fruitiness at first, again citrus-based, is tipped onto the mounting vanilla like sauce on an ice cream; **f21** the signs of bitterness evident on the nose come to fruition. Though, ironically, the spices I didn't expect were late to try to rectify; **b22** a fruit fly landing in a whisky while it is waiting to be tasted is always a good sign: these things know where to find sweetness. *53.3%. nc ncf.*

Compass Box Hedonism Quindecimus (88.5) **n22.5 t22 f22 b22** Sweet and refreshingly ordinary grain. Well made and unspectacularly delicious. *46%*

The Cooper's Choice Golden Grain 51 Year Old dist 1964, bott 2016 (87.5) **n22 t23.5 f20 b22** A lovely vatted grain with as many spoonfuls of honey as you like. Sadly, some tired oak radiates some significant bitterness at the death. *51%. nc ncf sc. The Vintage Malt Whisky Co.*

◇ **Count Cristo** bott code: L7117HA8 (89) **n22.5** a soft nose which only hints at sweetness while the spices are much more assertive; assorted green things, cucumbers especially, are diced and lightly seasoned; **t22.5** this count is clad in silk: the softest possible deliveries, yet it would have been softer still had the strength been higher and the oils intact. Instead, the tannins break the spell quickly to offer a substantial dose of vanilla; **f22** light, watery sugars balance out the oak's more bitter edge; **b22** "learning does not make one learned: there are those who have knowledge and those who have understanding. The first requires memory and the second philosophy." This is a whisky worth trying to understand. *40%.*

The Sovereign Blended Grain 28 Years Old bourbon barrel, cask no. 13327, dist Dec 64, bott Mar 17 (96) **n24.5** huge age on the nose; kumquats drying out in the bowl, liquorice both red and black with a little ground black pepper. More profound bourbon notes as each minute passes and as the air gets in. Praline and butterscotch, too...; **t24** soft, soft, soft... every element, be it the lightest sugar, the most fragile vanilla, thin walnut oil simply melts on the palate after landing with all the impact of a snowflake: no whisky on the planet can be more delicate; **f23.5** drier now as the light Demerara sugar gives way to the half-hearted vanilla; **b24** may be completely wrong, but a theory. There is a dryness here which suggests big age, maybe so big that the strength of a barrel fell below 40%abv... so had to be added to another to restore it back to whisky again. As I say: just a theory. But it'd fit the structure of this beautifully fragile old grain perfectly. *47.9%. nc ncf sc. 221 bottles.*

William Grant & Sons Rare Cask Reserves 25 Years Old Blended Grain Scotch Whisky (92.5) **n23 t23.5 f23 b23.** A really interesting one, this. In the old days, blenders always spent as much time vatting the grains together as they did the malts, for if they did not work well as a unit it was unlikely harmony would be found in their blend. A long time ago I was taught to, whenever possible, use a soft grain to counter a firmer one, and vice versa. Today, there are far fewer blends to choose from, though 25 years ago the choice was wider. So interesting to see that this grain is soft-dominated with very little backbone at all. Delicious. But screams for some backbone. *47%. Exclusive to The Whisky Shop.*

Scottish Blends

If any whisky is suffering an identity crisis just now, it must be the good old Scottish blend.

Once the staple, the absolute mainstay, of the Scotch whisky industry it has seen its market share increasingly buried under the inexorable, incoming tide that is single malt. But worse, the present-day blender has his hands tied in a way no previous generation of blenders has had before.

Now stocks must be monitored with a third eye, one that can judge the demand on their single malt casks and at increasingly varied ages. Worse, the blender cannot now, as was once the case, create blends with subtly shifting textures - the result of carefully using different types of grain. So many grain distilleries have closed in the last quarter of a century that now most blends seem remarkably similar to others. And there is, of course, the problem of sherry butts which has been fully documented over the years in the Whisky Bible.

For last year's Jim Murray's Whisky Bible I tasted or re-tasted 128 blends in total, a quite significant number. And there is no doubt that the lack of choice of grain for blenders is beginning to pose a problem for the industry. What was particularly noticeable was the number of blends which now lack a crisp backbone and have softened their stance, making them chewy and pliable on the palate but often lacking the crispness which can maximise the complexity of the malts on display. By the time you add in the caramel, the results can sometimes be just a little too cloying.

Naturally, it was the bigger blenders - those possessing by far the largest stocks - who best escaped this narrowing down of style among the younger blends in particular, as the always impressive Ballantine's Finest displayed its usual structured enormity with aplomb to once more pick up an award.

It is fascinating, and to the purist heartwarming, that after a short succession of either very old or very young blends being named as the Whisky Bible's Scottish Blend of the Year, once more it is the incomparable Ballantine's 17, whose default mode of understated and intricate complexty of the most delicate kind - which thankfully remained unaltered - that has breasted the tape ahead of the others. Perhaps it is a reminder that keeping to a tried and trusted formula is not always a bad thing; that there really is no substitute for true blending excellence.

Jim Murray's Whisky Bible Scottish Blend of the Year Winners	
2004	William Grant's 21 Year Old
2005	William Grant's 21 Year Old
2006	William Lawson Aged 18 Years
2007	Old Parr Superior 18 Years Old
2008	Old Parr Superior 18 Years Old
2009	The Last Drop
2010	Ballantine's 17 Years Old
2011	Ballantine's 17 Years Old
2012	Ballantine's 17 Years Old
2013	Ballantine's 17 Years Old
2014	Ballantine's 17 Years Old
2015	The Last Drop 1965
2016	The Last Drop 50 Years Old
2017	The Last Drop 1971
2018	Compass Box The Double Single
2019	Ballantine's 17 Years Old

Scottish Blends

100 Pipers (74) n18.5 t18 f19 b18.5. An improved blend, even with a touch of spice to the finish. I get the feeling the grains are a bit less aggressive than they for so long were. I'd let you know for sure, if only I could get through the caramel. 40%. Chivas.

100 Pipers bott code LKVK2677 2016/07/01 (74) n18 t19 f19 b18 These 100 Pipers deserve an award. How can they have played for so many years and still be so off key and out of tune? It is an art form, I swear. I feel like giving the blend a special gong for so many years of consistent awfulness. 40%. Chivas Brothers Ltd.

The Antiquary bott code L 02 08 16 (86) n20 t22 f22 b21 Appears to be going along the present day trend of spongy, super soft grain which doesn't always do the best of favours to the obviously high quality malt in here. Pleasantly sweet and chewy with an attractive base note. 40%. Tomatin Distillery.

Antiquary 12 Years Old (92) n23.5 t23.5 f22 b23 A staggering about turn for a blend which, for a very long time, has flown the Speyside flag. 40%. Tomatin Distillery.

The Antiquary Aged 12 Years bott code L 17 12 15 (87.5) n21.5 t22 f22 b22 The smoke I so well remember from previous bottlings appears to have dispersed. Instead we have an ultra-lush blend dependent on molasses and spice to punch through the major toffee. 40%. Tomatin Distillery.

Antiquary 21 Years Old (93) n23.5 t23.5 f23 b23 A huge blend, scoring a magnificent 93 points. But I have tasted better, and another sample, direct from the blending lab, came with even greater complexity and less apparent caramel. A top-notch blend of rare distinction. 43%

The Antiquary Aged 21 Years bott code 2016/02/29 LK30215 (92.5) n23 some very confident weight on the nose here: gentle, though slightly earthy, smoke mingles with the orange blossom honey; t23.5 excellent delivery: caramel and dates hold the fort until an oily smokiness turns up. Never less than succulent; f23 a beautiful lime note is the perfect match for the gently smoked mocha and spice; a very slight tang at the death; b23 if you are not sure what I mean by a beautifully paced whisky, try this and find out. 43%. Tomatin Distillery.

The Antiquary Aged 35 Years bott code L 24 08 15 (96.5) n24 absolutely classic Speyside-style exotic fruit on the top dressing malt, the sharpness amplified by the crisper, clean grain which shows no sign of tiring; t24 classic delivery: immediate spice but kept under control by the more sugary elements of the grain. The malt is pristine and sensationally three dimensional, really ramping up the light fruitiness and well as a distinctive sugar barley candy; f24 long and so relaxed you can only purr. The sugars remain of the boiled sweet/fruit candy type, though the malts and butterscotch intermingling at the end, and then dovetailing with the spices is a rare exhibition of how a great fade should really be...; b24.5 enjoy some of the grains involved in this beauty: their type and ability to add to the complexity is, tragically, a dying breed: the hardest whisky I have found so far to spit out...and I'm on dram number 530....! Antiquary's late, great blender, Jim Milne, would shed a tear of joy for this creation of unreconstructed beauty and brilliance, as this was just out of his school of elegance. 46%. Tomatin Distillery.

Ballaglass Blended Scotch Whisky (85) n21 t22 f21 b21. Perfectly enjoyable, chewy – but clean – blend full of toffee and fudge. Very good weight and impressive, oily body. 40%.

Ballantine's Aged 12 Years (84.5) n22.5 t22 f19 b21. Attractive but odd fellow, this, with a touch of juniper to the nose and furry bitter marmalade on the finish. But some excellent barley-cocoa moments, too. 43%. Chivas.

Ballantine's 12 Years Old (87) n21 t22 f21 b23. The kind of old-fashioned, mildly moody blend Colonel Farquharson-Smythe (retired) might have recognised when relaxing at the 19th hole back in the early '50s. Too good for a squirt of soda, mind. 40%. Chivas Bros.

Ballantine's 17 Years Old (97.5) n24.5 deft grain and honey plus teasing salty peat; ultra high quality with bourbon and pear drops offering the thrust; a near unbelievable integration with gooseberry juice offering a touch of sharpness muted by watered golden syrup; t24 immediately mouthwatering with maltier tones clambering over the graceful cocoa-enriched grain; the degrees of sweetness are varied but near perfection; just hints of smoke here and there; f24 lashings of vanilla and cocoa on the fade; drier with a faint spicey, vaguely smoky buzz; has become longer with more recent bottlings with the most subtle oiliness imaginable; b25 now only slightly less weighty than of old. After a change of style it has comfortably reverted back to its sophisticated, mildly erotic old self. One of the most beautiful, complex and stunningly structured whiskies ever created. Truly the epitome of great Scotch. 43%.

Ballantine's Aged 21 Years (94) n23.5 t24 f23.5 b24 Even though the strength has been reduced, presumably to eke out rare stocks, the beauty of this blend hasn't. 40%

Ballantine's Aged 30 Years (95.5) n24.5 t24 f23 b24 A fascinating malt, slightly underpowered perhaps, which I have had to put to one side and keep coming back to see what it will say and do next... 40%.

Ballantine's Aged 30 Years bott code LKRK1934 2016/05/16 **(96)** n24.5 t24 f22.5 b24 Practically a replay of the bottle I tasted last year, right down to that very late, barely perceptible furriness. Simply one of the world's most sensual drams... 40%. *Chivas Brothers Ltd.*

Ballantine's Finest (96) n24 t24 f23.5 b24.5 As a standard blend this is coming through as a major work of art. Each time I taste this the weight has gone up a notch or two more and the sweetness has increased to balance out with the drier grain elements. Take a mouthful of this and experience the work of a blender very much at the top of his game. 40%. *Chivas Bros.*

Ballantine's Finest bott code LKEK4068 2016/10/04 **(96)** n23.5 t24 f24 b24.5 The consistency and enormity of this blend fair staggers me. It is often my go to blend when travelling the world as I pretty much know what I'll get, within its normal parameters. This bottling has a little extra sweetness on the smoke but exceeds expectation on the finish with a slightly more clever use of the spices and Demerara sugars as they merge with the peat. Just such a big and satisfying experience. 40%. *Chivas Brothers Ltd*

Ballantine's Hard Fired (86.5) n22 t22 f21 b21.5. Despite the smoky and toasty elements to this, you're left waiting for it to take off....or even go somewhere. Perhaps just a little too soft, friendly and grain indulgent. Decent, enjoyable blend, of course, but a little out of the Ballantine's usual circle of high class friends. 40%

Ballantine's Limited release no. A27380 (96) n24 t24.5 f23.5 b24 Each Limited release has a slightly different stance and this one holds its posture with more debonair, lighter-on-foot poise. The vague furry note of recent bottlings is missing here or, rather, is of the least consequence. The fruit, also, is more of a sheen than a statement more room for the malt and vanilla to play and the spices to impart age. It may be soft on both nose and palate – especially the delivery – as the grains have obviously been vatted to create minimum traction, but it is a blend of quiet substance. Another Ballantine's brand this year hitting the 96 or more mark. Astonishing, absolutely astonishing...more a case of Ballantine's Unlimited... 40%. *Chivas Brothers Ltd.*

Ballantine's Master's (82) n21 t22 f19 b20. Excellent lively grain and chewy malt, but the always suspect, grain-drizzled finish has become even more nondescript in recent bottlings. 40%

Ballantine's Master's bott code LKAK1001 2016/03/09 (85) n21 t22 f21 b21 The label promises a "fresh take" on this blend. And I admit, it is far more agreeable than before with a little coconut oil and apple helping to give it a lift and the sugars herded into attractive use. But still far too dependent of caramel input, which may round the whisky but flattens it all rather too well. 40%. *Chivas Brothers Ltd.*

Ballantine's Rare Limited (89.5) n23.5 t22.5 f21.5 b22 A heavier, more mouth watering blend than the "Bluebottle" version. 43%. ncf. *Chivas.*

Bell's Original (91) n23 t22.5 f22.5 b23 Your whisky sleuth came across the new version for the first time in the bar of a London theatre back in December 2009 during the interval of "The 39 Steps". To say I was impressed and pleasantly surprised is putting it mildly. And with the whisky, too, which is a massive improvement on the relatively stagnant 8-year-old especially with the subtle extra smoky weight. If the blender asks me: "Did I get it right, Sir?" then the answer has to be a resounding "yes". 40%

Bells 8 Years Old (85) n21.5 t22.5 f20 b21. Some mixed messages here: on one hand it is telling me that it has been faithful to some of the old Bells distilleries – hence a slight dirty note, especially on the finish. On the other, there are some sublime specks of complexity and weight. Quite literally the rough and the smooth. 40%. *Diageo.*

Black & White (91) n22 t23 f22.5 b23.5 This one hasn't gone to the dogs: quite the opposite. I always go a bit misty-eyed when I taste something this traditional: the crisp grains work to maximum effect in reflecting the malts. A classic of its type. 40%. *Diageo.*

Black Bottle (74.5) n18 t20.5 f17 b18. Barely a shadow of its once masterful, great self. 40%.

Black Bottle bott code 2038310 L3 16165 **(94.5)** n23.5 complex: yes, there is a little earthy cabbage note in there. But the mix of hickory, Fisherman's Friend cough sweet, light smoke, molasses and even leather make for something attractively different; t23.5 wow! How succulent is that! The grains maybe of the stereotypically fluffy variety we find today, but the way it is moulded into a far richer and beautifully balanced mouth-filler is stunning. Maple syrup and liquorice work hard for maximum effect while the spices have a little edge to them; f23.5 long, lightly oiled and a slow evaporation of the sugars; no shortage of spiced butterscotch to complete the tale; b24 not the byword for macho complexity as it was 15 years ago but after a lull in its fortunes it is back to something that can rightfully boast excellence. Brilliant. 40%.

Black Bottle 10 Years Old (89) n22 t23 f22 b23 A stupendous blend of weight and poise, but possessing little of the all-round steaming, rampaging sexuality of the younger version... but like the younger version showing a degree less peat: here perhaps even two. Not, I hope, the start of a new trend under the new owners. 40%

Black Dog 12 Years Old (92) n21 t23 f24 b24. Offering genuine sophistication and élan. This minor classic will probably require two or three glass-fulls before you take the bait... 42.8%

Black Dog Century (89) n21 t23 f23 b22. I adore this style of no-nonsense, full bodied bruising blend which amid the muscle offers exemplary dexterity and finesse. What entertainment in every glass!! *42.8%. McDowell & Co Ltd. Blended in Scotland/Bottled in India.*

Black Grouse (94) n23 t24 f23 b24. A superb return to a peaty blend for Edrington for the first time since they sold Black Bottle. Not entirely different from that brand, either, from the Highland Distillers days with the smokiness being superbly couched by sweet malts. *40%*

The Black Grouse Alpha Edition (72.5) n17 t19.5 f17 b18. Dreadfully sulphured. *40%*

Black Hound (83) n21 t21.5 f21 b20.5 Here's to Max! Max grain in this but no complaints here as the relatively limited caramel doesn't spoil the enjoyment of what feels like (though obviously isn't) a single distillery output. Crisp at first, then succulent, chewy cream toffee. *40%. Quality Spirits International.*

Black Ram Aged 12 Years (85) n21 t23 f21 b20. An upfront blend that gives its all in the chewy delivery. Some major oak in there but it's all ultra soft toffee and molasses towards the finish. *40%. Vinprom Peshtera, Bulgaria.*

Black Stripe (77) n19 t20 f19 b19 Untidy without being characterful. *40%. Quality Spirits International.*

Blend No. 888 (86.5) n20 t21.5 f23 b22. A good old-fashioned, rip-roaring, nippy blend with a fudge-honey style many of a certain age will fondly remember from the 60s and 70s. Love it! *40%. The House of MacDuff.*

⬦ **Blend No. 888** bott code L15/8185 (84.5) n21 t22 f20.5 b21 Light, breezy and sweet, this is grain dominant and make no effort to be otherwise. Soft, untaxing and pleasant. *40%. House of MacDuff.*

Boxes Blend (90) n22.5 t23.5 f21 b23. A box which gets plenty of ticks. *40.9%. ncf.*

Buchanan's De Luxe 12 Years Old (82) n18 t21 f22 b21. The nose shows more than just a single fault and the character simply refuses to get out of second gear. Certainly pleasant, and some of the chocolate notes towards the end are gorgeous. But just not the normal brilliant show-stopper! *40%. Diageo.*

⬦ **Buchanan's Master** bott code: L7313CE001 (94.5) n24 oooh, so clever....this is a kaleidoscopic nose, a slightly different arrangement each time your shake it, the phenols playing the most tantalising peek-a-boo, a hidden fruit note here and there suddenly emerging. Especially impressive is the controlled degree of sweetness: enough to keep the tannins happy, but no more. Tantalising, stretching the organoleptic radar: a blender's blended nose, I'd say...; t23.5 as silky soft and as alluring as it beguiling. The chocolate notes, usually to be found at the back of whisky arrive early and with specific intent; malt is also compacted early. Then a more leisurely stroll through the tannins...;f23 the grains at last make their specific mark: it is simplistic and sweet and boosts the vanilla; a dull bitterness creeps in towards the finale; b24 some 40-odd years ago I was in love with Buchanans: it was one of the truly sophisticated blends from which I learned so much and this pays homage to the legacy. On the down side the grains are nowhere near so complex and the vague furry bitterness at the end tells its own tale. But I doff my Panama to blender Keith Law in genuine respect: works like this don't just happen and this is a blended Scotch worthy of the name. *40%.*

Cadenhead's Putachieside Aged 12 Years (91) n23 no shortage of citrus and vanilla: fresh, and the flaky, puff-pastry topping is fitting; t23 the sugars and oils make an early assault. A little bitterness from the oak creeps in; f22 malty-lemon sawdust; b23 not tasted for a while and delighted to re-discover this understated little gem. Also, has to be one of the best labels of any scotch going... *40% WB15/357*

Campbeltown Loch (94) n23 t24 f23.5 b23.5 Over 30 years ago, this blend was one of my preferred drams at home. Not seen it for a while, so disappeared from The Bible. Found again and though it has changed a little in structure, its overall excellence takes me back to when I was a young man. *40% WB15/355*

Campbeltown Loch Aged 15 Years (88) n22.5 t22.5 f21 b22 Well weighted with the age in no hurry to arrive. *40%. Springbank Distillers.*

Cambletown Loch 21 Years Old (83) n21 t23 f19 b20 Neither the nose or finish are much to write home about, the latter being a little tangy and bitter. But the delivery is rich and comforting: like a Digestive biscuit dunked in coffee. A seemingly decent malt content and a bit of toffee before the furry finale. *46%. WB15/102*

Castle Rock (81) n20 t20.5 f20 b20.5. Clean and juicy entertainment. *40%*

Catto's Aged 25 Years (85.5) n22 t22.5 f19.5 b21.5. A hugely enjoyable yet immensely frustrating dram. The higher fruit and spice notes are a delight, but it all appears to be played out in a padded cell of cream caramel. One assumes the natural oak caramels have gone into overdrive. Had they not, we would have had a supreme blend scoring well into the 90s. Elsewhere the increased furriness on the finale has not improved matters. *40%*

Catto's Aged 25 Years bott code RV9499 (94.5) n23 the accent, as one might hope, is on varying degrees of honey: here ulmo and orange blossom have joint star billing in this very soft and friendly performance; t24 excellent grains are at the vanguard of a glorious charm offensive: maple syrup, Lubek marzipan and barley sugar dissolves slowly into the vanillas; f23 even as the sugars fade enough light spices rises to meet the demands of the oak; b24.5 a far better experience than the last time I officially tasted a Catto's 25 seven or eight years ago. Both malts and grains are of the charming style once associated with Catto's Rare : so jaw-droppingly elegant... 40%. *International Beverage Holdings Ltd.*

Catto's Deluxe 12 Years Old (79.5) n20 t21.5 f18 b20. Refreshing and spicy in part, but still a note in there which doesn't quite work. 40%. *Inverhouse Distillers.*

Catto's Deluxe 12 Years Old bott code L 18 03 16 (86.5) n21.5 t22 f21.5 b21.5 A safe, sweet and sumptuous blend which places major emphasis to the molasses. Won't win any beauty contests but there is a weighty earthiness, also. 40%. *International Beverage Holdings Ltd.*

Catto's Rare Old Scottish (92) n23.5 t23.5 f22 b23 Currently one of my regular blends to drink at home. Astonishingly old-fashioned with a perfect accent on clean Speyside and crisp grain. In the last year or so it has taken on a sublime sparkle on the nose and palate. An absolutely masterful whisky which both refreshes and relaxes. 40%. *James Catto & Co.*

Catto's Rare Old Scottish bott code L 25 01 16 (83) n20.5 t21 f20.5 b21 Once fresh as dew on morning grass, this has changed in recent years with a different grain profile which no longer magnifies the malt. Adopted a rougher, more toffeed approach from its once clean cut personality: not even a close approximation of the minor classic it once was. 40%. *International Beverage Holdings Ltd.*

Chequers Deluxe (78.5) n19.5 t20 f19 b20. Charm, elegance, sophistication...not a single sign of any of them. Still if you want a bit of rough and tumble, just the job. 40%. *Diageo.*

The Chivas 18 The Ultimate Cask Collection First Fill American Oak (95.5) n24 t23.5 f24 b24 Immeasurably superior to any Chivas 18 I have tasted before. A true whisky lover's whisky... 48%. ncf.

Chivas Regal Aged 12 Years (83.5) n20.5 t22.5 f20 b20.5. Chewy fruit toffee. Silky grain mouth-feel with a toasty, oaky presence. 40%. *Chivas.*

Chivas Regal Aged 12 Years bott code 2017/01/31 LPAL 0162 (93) n23 t23.5 f22.5 b24 Last year I was in a British Airways Business Lounge somewhere in the world and spotted at the bar two different Chivas Regal 12s: the labels had differing designs. I asked for a glass of each and tried them side by side. The first one, from the older label, was the pleasant but forgettable blend I expected and knew so well. The newer version wasn't: had it not been time to get my flight I would have ordered a second glass of it....and I can't remember the last time I did that. What I have here is something very much like that surprise Chivas I discovered. This is, unquestionably, the best Chivas 12 I've encountered for a very long time (and I'm talking at least 20 years): pretty impressive use of the understated smoke, especially on the nose, which works well with that date and walnut toffee. I really could enjoy a second glass of this, though still a very different, delicate animal to the one I grew up with in the mid-70s. Actually, I just have had a second glass of this: delicious....! 40%. *Chivas Brothers Ltd.*

Chivas Regal Aged 18 Years (73.5) n17.5 t20 f17.5 b18.5. The nose is dulled by a whiff of sulphur and confirmation that all is not well comes with the disagreeably dry, bitter finish. Early on in the delivery some apples and spices show promise but it is an unequal battle against the caramel and off notes. 40%

Chivas Regal Aged 18 Years bott code LKRL0346 2017/01/30 (86) n22 t22 f21 b21 A great improvement on the last bottling I encountered with a pleasing chewiness and understated spiciness. But this remains far too dependent on a big caramel surge for both taste and structure. 40%. *Chivas Brothers Ltd.*

Chivas Regal 25 Years Old (95) n23 t23.5 f24 b24.5. Unadulterated class where the grain-malt balance is exemplary and the deft intertwangling of well-mannered oak and elegant barley leaves you demanding another glass. Brilliant! 40%

Chivas Regal Aged 25 Years bott code 2017/03/01 LPML0373 (95.5) n24.5 t24.5 f22.5 b24 This is quite brilliant whisky. Maybe just one sherry butt away from what would almost certainly have been among the top three whiskies of the year... 40%. *Chivas Brothers Ltd.*

Chivas Regal Extra (86) n20 t24 f20.5 b21.5. Chivas, but seemingly from the Whyte and MacKay school of thick, impenetrable blends. The nose may have the odd undesirable element and the finish reflects those same trace failings. But if chewy date and walnuts in a sea of creamy toffee is your thing, then this malt is for you. This, though, does show genuine complexity, so I have to admit to adoring the lush delivery and early middle section: the mouth-feel is truly magnificent. Good spice, too. Flawed genius comes to mind. 40%

Chivas Regal The Chivas Brother's Blend Aged 12 Years bott code 2016/04/12 LPEK0613 (81.5) n21 t21.5 f19 b20 Oh, brother! Fabulous texture but a furry finish... 40%. *Chivas Brothers Ltd.*

◈ **Chivas Regal Mizunara** bott code: LPBM0253 2018/02/06 **(89.5) n22.5** immediately as sharper tannin quality is apparent, almost like a vanilla note thickened and extended; over enthusiastic toffee dampens the effect slightly; **t23** at least those toffee tones ensure the delivery is soft and orderly before the body thins enough for a more discerning glimpse at the gathering complexity to become possible. Again a tannin note alien to Scotch bites, but not enough to draw blood while the malt offer a Speyside-style freshness for a short period before the caramel descends again; **f22** busy caramel and tannin interplay; **b22** for years the Japanese copied everything the Scotch whisky industry did, not quite realising – or perhaps willing to believe – that many of their indigenous whiskies were of world class standard deserving respect and discovery in their own right. Now the Scots have, for the first time I'm aware of, openly copied the Japanese– and celebrated the fact. The Japanese oak used within the marrying process does appear to have given an extra impetus and depth to this blend. Definitely offers an extra dimension to what you'd expect from a Chivas. *40%.*

Clan Campbell (86.5) n21.5 t22.5 f21 b21.5. I'll wager that if I could taste this whisky before the colouring is added it would be scoring into the 90s. Not a single off note; a sublime early array of Speysidey freshness but dulls at the end. *40%. Chivas.*

Clan Campbell bott code LR3 1047 13/09/05 **(89) n21.5** attractive sweet young grain, but a little Speyside grassiness grows on top; **t23** succulent delivery: a mouth-watering mix of light icing sugars, something vaguely gristier and a wonderful clean grain velvetiness. The mid ground is soft, slightly chalky with developing butterscotch; **f22** a gentle spiciness breezes in; **b22.5** amazing what happens when you reduce the colouring Last time I tasted this I could barely find the whisky for all the toffee. Now it positively shines in the glass. Love it! *40%. Chivas Brothers Ltd.*

◈ **Clan Campbell** rum barrel finish, bott code: 2018/04/04 **(90.5) n22** a full steam ahead blend, allowing a little spice nip to gee up the sturdier fudge and molasses; **t23.5** thick on delivery, this a chewer of the first order. Again, the toffee plays a big part but as the middle beckons the notes become more stretched and complex; some tannins enter the fray and the oils mount; the spices act more in keeping with rum than a blended scotch; **f22** drier and toastier yet still with an attractive viscous depth; **b23** this blend is all about impact and staying power. All kinds of rum and caramel incursions, but a really lovely broadside on the palate. *40%.*

Clan Campbell Dark rum barrel finish, bott code 2017/03/29 LPHL 0570 **(89.5) n22 t23 f22 b22.5** Putting my rum blender's hat on here, can't think which barrels they used to get this degree of colour and sweetness. Still, I'm not arguing; it's a really lovely, accommodating dram. *40%. Chivas Brothers Ltd.*

Clan Gold 3 Year Old (95) n23.5 t24 f23.5 b24. A blend-drinkers blend which will also slay the hearts of Speyside single malt lovers. For me, this is love at first sip... *40%*

Clan Gold Blended 15 Years Old (91) n21.5 t23 f23.5 b23 An unusual blend for the 21st century, which steadfastly refuses to blast you away with over the top flavour and/or aroma profiles and instead depends on subtlety and poise despite the obvious richness of flavour. The grains make an impact but only by creating the frame in which the more complex notes can be admired. *40%*

Clan Gold Blended 18 Years Old (94.5) n23 t24 f23.5 b24. Almost the ultimate preprandial whisky with its at once robust yet delicate working over of the taste buds by the carefully muzzled juiciness of the malt. This is the real deal: a truly classy act which at first appears to wallow in a sea of simplicity but then bursts out into something very much more complex and alluring. About as clean and charming an 18-year-old blend as you are likely to find. *40%*

Clan Gold 18 Years of Age bott code L6X 7616 0611 **(95) n24 t24 f23 b24** Nothing like as juicy and cleverly fruity as it once was, yet marriage between malt and grain seldom comes more happy than this... *40%. Quality Spirits International.*

Clan Gold Finest bott code L10Z 6253 1902 **(83) n20 t21 f21 b21** Sweet, silky, soft and caramel heavy. Decent late spice. *40%. Quality Spirits International.*

Clan MacGregor (92) n22 t24 f23 b23 Just gets better and better. Now a true classic and getting up there with Grant's. *43%*

Clan Murray bott code L9X 7694 1411 **(86) n20 t22.5 f21.5 b22** For the avoidance of doubt: no, this not my blend. No, I am not the blender. No, I do not get a royalty from sales. If I could have had a tenner for each time I've had to answer that over the last decade or so I could have bought my own island somewhere, or Millwall FC... Anyway, back to the whisky. Far better nose than it has shown in the past and the delivery has an eye-watering bite, the finish a roguish spice. Rough-ish but very ready... *40%. The BenRiach Distillery Co. Ltd.*

Clansman (80.5) n20.5 t21 f19 b20. Sweet, grainy and soft. *40%. Loch Lomond.*

Clansman bott code L3/170/15 **(84) n21 t22 f20 b21** More to it than of old, though still very soft, the dark sugars and spice have a very pleasant input. *40%. Loch Lomond Group.*

The Claymore (85) n19 t22 f22 b22. These days you are run through by spices. The blend is pure Paterson in style with guts etc, which is not something you always like to associate with a Claymore; some delightful muscovado sugar at the death. Get the nose sorted and a very decent and complex whisky is there to be had. 40%. Whyte & Mackay Distillers Ltd.

The Classic Cask 23 Year Old Caribbean Rum Barrels Finish European oak butt, batch no. #SW.110, dist 1992, bott 2016 **(92)** n23.5 t23 f22.5 b23 A beautifully crafted, satisfying blend. 43% (86 proof). 760 bottles.

The Classic Cask 23 Year Old Oloroso Sherry Butt European oak butt, batch no. #SW.109, dist 1992, bott 2016 **(78.5)** n18.5 t23 f18 b19 Damn and blast the mild sulphur on this – the sixth such tainted bottling I have tasted today and my taste buds are hoisting the white flag: that's me done for this session. The nose warns of what is to come, though the juicy, fruity vibrancy on delivery is sublime. The finish, though... 43% (86 proof). 771 bottles.

The Classic Cask 23 Year Old Original Cask European oak butt, batch no. #SW.108, dist 1992, bott 2016 **(88.5)** n22 t23.5 f21 b22 Yes, there is a small amount of sulphur here. Nothing fatal, though enough to knock what would have been an outstanding blend in a direction you'd prefer it didn't go. Curses! 43% (86 proof). 782 bottles.

The Classic Cask 23 Year Old Port Pipe Finish European oak butt, batch no. #SW.111, dist 1992, bott 2016 **(90.5)** n23.5 t23 f21.5 b22.5 Forget the slight blemish towards the end. Worth exploring as this complex blend takes you down countless avenues... 43% (86 proof). 769 bottles.

Compass Box Asyla 1st fill American oak ex-bourbon, bott May 10 **(93)** n24 t24 f22.5 b23.5 If you can hear a purring noise, it is me tasting this... 40%. nc ncf.

Compass Box Asyla Marriage nine months in an American oak barrel **(88)** n22 t23 f21 b22 A lovely blend, but can't help feeling that this was one marriage that lasted too long. 43.6%. Compass Box Whisky for La Maison du Whisky in commemoration of their 50th Anniversary.

Compass Box Delilah's Limited Release American oak, bott Jul 13 **(89.5)** n23 t22 f22 b22.5. A clean and satisfying blend which ramps up the sugars when need be. I'll be surprised if you get to the point where you couldn't take any more... 40%. 6400 bottles.

Compass Box Delilah's Limited Release Small Batch American oak **(92.5)** n23.5 t23 f23 b23 blends rarely come more honeyed, or even sweeter, than this with every last sugary element seemingly extracted from the oak. My only sorrow for this whisky, given its American theme, was that it wasn't bottled as a 101 (ie 50.5% abv) instead of the rather underpowered 80 proof – because you have the feeling this would have become pretty three dimensional and leapt from the glass. And then down your throat with serious effect. 40%. nc ncf. WB15/171

⬩ **Compass Box Delilah's XXV** American oak & sherry casks **(82)** n20.5 t22.5 f18 b21 A blend with an astonishing degree of natural caramels in play, giving the whole piece a soft, chewy feel with both sugars and spices coming off at a tangent. Sadly, the sherry input is distracting on the nose and distinctly tangy and furry towards the end. 46%. nc ncf.

Compass Box The Double Single bott Mar 17 **(97)** n24.5 one of those noses so delicate you daren't breath in too hard for fear of shattering it into a million pieces. The citrus, a kind of orange blossom honey thinned with the juices of Jaffa, is of the cleanest style imaginable; likewise the barley is fresh and gristy. One of the most ethereal and elegant noses of all time....; t25 perfection. This is faultless. This is exactly how whisky should be. A delivery you hope to encounter – or create – but suspect you probably never will. And here it is: in all its understated, genteel, feminine, seductive majesty. It is the nose all over again, but this time in liquid form, a physicality which curls against our taste buds and caresses them with the most erotic, arousing finger-tip touch...; f23.5 nothing can quite follow the delivery and follow through, but it tries. Though the oaks can now be heard, a little bitterly by comparison, while the spices up the tingling factor; b24 by no means the first time I have encountered a single malt and grain in the same bottle. But I am hard pressed to remember one that was even close to being this wonderful...This is Compass Box's finest moment...46%. nc ncf. 5,838 bottles.

Compass Box The Entertainer Limited Edition bott Aug 12 **(88.5)** n21.5 t22.5 f22 b22. A pleasant blend, though the tanginess is perhaps a little too sharp. 46%. Compass Box Whisky Company. 1000 bottles. Commissioned by Selfridges.

Compass Box Great King St. Artist's Blend **(93)** n24 t23 f22.5 b23.5. The nose of this uncoloured and non-chill filtered whisky is not dissimilar to some better known blends before they have colouring added to do its worst. A beautiful young thing this blend: nubile, naked and dangerously come hither. Compass Box's founder John Glaser has done some memorable work in recent years, though one has always had the feeling that he has still been learning his trade, sometimes forcing the issue a little too enthusiastically. Here, there is absolutely no doubting that he has come of age as a blender. 43%. nc ncf.

Compass Box Great King Street Experimental Batch #00-V4 bott Sep 13 **(93)** n22.5 t24 f23 b23.5. A blend combining astonishing vibrancy with oaky Russian roulette. Not a dram to do things by halves... 43%. 3,439 bottles.

Compass Box Great King Street Experimental Batch #TR-06 bott Sep 13 **(92)** n22 t23.5; f23 b23.5 I think this one's been rumbled... 43%.

Compass Box Great King Street Glasgow Blend (88.5) n22 t23.5 f21 b22 Just the odd note seems out of place here and there: delicious but not the usual Compass Box precision. 43%

Compass Box The Circus bott Mar 16 (93) n23 roll up, roll up and nose a fascinating juxtapositioning of the Fisherman's Friend-style smokiness with a sharp citric malt/grain mix...; t23.5 eye-wateringly tart start: a strange mix of undercooked and overcooked jam tarts, with a smoked liquorice middle; f23 remains, thick, dark and brooding: my worms here – these are all base notes; b23.5 Scotland's very own Clown Royal... 49%. nc ncf. 2,490 bottles.

Compass Box This Is Not A Luxury Whisky bott Aug 15 (81) n20 t21.5 f19.5 b20. Correct. 53.1%. nc ncf. 4,992 bottles.

Consulate (87) n21.5 t22 f22 b21.5 I assume this weighty and pleasant dram was designed to accompany Passport (whose chewiness it now resembles) in the drinks cabinet. I suggest, if buying them, use Visa. 40%. Quality Spirits International.

Crawford's (83.5) n19 t21 f22 b21.5. A lovely spice display helps overcome the caramel. 40%.

Cutty Black (83) n20 t23 f19 b21. Both nose and finish are dwarfed and flung into the realms of ordinariness by the magnificently substantial delivery. Whilst there is a taint to the nose, its richness augers well for what is to follow; and you won't be disappointed. At times it behaves like a Highland Park with a toffeed spine, such is the richness and depth of the honey and dates and complexity of the grain-vanilla background. But those warning notes on the nose are there for good reason and the finish tells you why. Would not be surprised to see this score into the 90s on a different bottling day. 40%. Edrington.

Cutty Sark (78) n19 t21 f19 b19. Crisp and juicy. But a nipping furriness, too. 40%

Cutty Sark bott code L60355 L7 (84.5) n21 t22 f20 b21.5 To some extent an improvement on a couple of years back when this blend was vanishing in character. But could still do with some urgent extra restorative work. For as long I can remember the grain on this was crisp and brought the sharpest, juiciest notes imaginable from the Speyside malts: indeed, that was its trademark character. Now, like so many standard blends, it is bubble gum soft and spreads the sugars evenly with the malts fighting to be heard. Only very mild sulphur tones to the crippling ones I had previously found. But it really does need to re-work the grain...if it can find it. 40%. .

Cutty Sark Aged 12 Years (92) n22 t24 f23 b23 At last! Cutty 12 at full sail...and blended whisky rarely looks any more beautiful! 40%. Edrington.

Cutty Sark Aged 15 Years (82) n19 t22 f20 b21. Attempts to take the honey route. But seriously dulled by toffee and the odd sulphured cask. 40%. Edrington.

Cutty Sark Aged 18 Years (88) n22 t22 f22 b22 Lost the subtle fruitiness which worked so well. Easy-going and attractive. 43%

Cutty Sark Aged 25 Years (91) n21 t23.5 f22.5 b23 Magnificent, though not quite flawless, this whisky is as elegant and effortlessly powerful as the ship after which the brand was named... 45.7%. Berry Bros & Rudd.

Cutty Sark Prohibition Edition American oak, bott code L0401W L4 11/18 (91) n21.5 t25 f20 b24.5 Probably the best label and presentation of any whisky in the world this year: sheer class. On the back label they use the word authentic. Which is a very interesting concept. Except authentic whisky sent to the USA back in the 1920s wouldn't have that annoying and debilitating rumble of sulphur, detectable on both nose and finish. And I suspect the malt content would have been higher – and the grain used showing far more of a corn-oily character. That all said, I doubt the blender of the day would have achieved better delivery or balance: indeed, this delivery has to be one of the highlights of the whisky year. You will not be surprised to discover my resolve cracked, and I swallowed a full mouthful of this special blend. And, gee: it was swell, bud... 50%. Edrington.

Cutty Sark Storm (81.5) n18 t23.5 f19.5 b20.5. When the wind is set fair, which is mainly on delivery and for the first six or seven flavour waves which follow, we really do have an astonishingly beautiful blend, seemingly high in malt content and reallyputting the accent on ulmo honey and marzipan: a breath-taking combination. This is assisted by a gorgeous weight to the silky body and a light raspberry jam moment to the late arriving Ecuadorian cocoa. All magnificent. However, as Cutty sadly tends to, sails into sulphurous seas. 40%. Edrington.

Demijohn Finest Blended Scotch Whisky (88) n21 strange, out of shape, but soft; t22 salivating delivery with an enveloping softness to the grain; the malts eventually mould into the style; f23 remains tangy to the end, even with a touch of marmalade thrown in; b22 OK, now that's spooky. You really don't expect tasting notes written ten years ago to exactly fit the bill today. But that is exactly what happens here: well maybe not quite exactly. Ten years ago I wrote of the "wonderful firmness of the grain" where today, like 90% of all blends, it is much more yielding and soft than before. Thankfully, it hasn't detracted from the enjoyment. 40%.

Dew of Ben Nevis Blue Label (82) n19 t22 f20 b21. The odd off-key note is handsomely outnumbered by deliciously complex mocha and demerara tones. Ditch the caramel and you'd have a sizzler! 40%. Ben Nevis Distillery. Replacement for Dew of Ben Nevis Millennium Blend.

Dew of Ben Nevis Special Reserve (85) n19 t21 f23 b22. A much juicier blend than of old, still sporting some bruising and rough patches. But that kind of makes this all the more attractive, with the caramel mixing with some fuller malts to provide a date and nuts effect which makes for a grand finale. 40%. Ben Nevis Distillery.

Dew of Ben Nevis Supreme Selection (77) n18 t20 f20 b19. Some lovely raspberry jam swiss roll moments here. But the grain could be friendlier, especially on the nose. 40%

Dewar's Special Reserve 12 Years Old (84) n20 t23 f19 b22. Some s... you know what... has crept onboard here and duffed up the nose and finish. A shame because elements of the delivery and background balance shows some serious blending went on here. 40%

Dewar's 18 Years Old (93) n23 t24 f22.5 b23.5 Here is a classic case of where great blends are not all about the malt. The grain plays in many ways the most significant role here, as it is the perfect backdrop to see the complexity of the malt at its clearest. Simply magnificent blending with the use of flawless whisky. 43%. John Dewar & Sons.

Dewar's 18 Year Old Founders Reserve (86.5) n22.5 t22 f20.5 b21.5. A big, blustering dram which doesn't stint on the fruit. A lovely, thin seam of golden syrup runs through the piece, but the dull, aching finale is somewhat out of character. 40%. John Dewar & Sons.

Dewar's Signature (93) n24 t23.5 f22 b23.5. A slight departure in style, with the fruit becoming just a little sharper and juicier. Top range blending and if the odd butt could be weeded out, this'd be an award winner for sure. 43%

Dewar's White Label (78.5) n19 t21.5 f19 b19. When on song, one of my preferred daily blends. But not when like this, with its accentuated bitter-sweet polarisation. 40%

Dhoon Glen (86) n21 t22 f21.5 b21.5 Full of big flavours, broad grainy strokes and copious amounts of dark sugars including chocolate fudge and now a little extra spice, too. Goes dhoon a treat... 40%. Lombard Scotch Whisky Ltd.

Dimple 12 Years Old (86.5) n22 t22 f21.5 b21. Lots of sultana; the spice adds aggression. 40%.

Dimple 15 Years Old (87.5) n20 t21 f24 b22.5. Only on the late middle and finish does this particular flower unfurl and to magnificently complex effect. The texture of the grains in particular delight while the strands of barley entwine. A type of treat for the more technically minded of the serious blend drinkers among you. 40%. Diageo.

The Famous Grouse (89) n22 t23 f21.5 b22.5 It almost seems that Grouse is, by degrees, moving from its traditional position of a light blend to something much closer to Grant's as a middle-weighted dram. Again the colouring has been raised a fraction and now the body and depth have been adjusted to follow suit. Have to say that this is one very complex whisky these days: I had spotted slight changes when drinking it socially, but this was the first time I had a chance to sit down and professionally analyse what was happening in the glass. A fascinating and tasty bird, indeed. 40%. Edrington Group.

The Famous Grouse bott code L4812TL1 25/08 (88.5) n22.5 t23 f21 b22 Changed its stance a few years back from light blend to a middle-weighted one and has worked hard to keep that position with thoughtful use of the phenols. Unlike many other brands it has not gone colouring mad and the little toffee apparent does nothing to spoil the narrative and complexity: I doff my hat. 40%.

The Famous Grouse Gold Reserve (90) n23.5 t23 f21.5 b22 Great to know the value of the Gold Reserve is going up...as should the strength of this blend. The old-fashioned 40% just ain't enough carats. 40%. Edrington Group.

The Famous Grouse Married Strength (82.5) n19 t22 f20 b21.5. The nose is nutty and toffeed. But despite the delightful, silky sweetness and gentle Speyside-style maltiness which forms the main markers for this soft blend, the nose, like the finish, also shows a little bitter furriness has, sadly, entered into the mix. Not a patch on the standard Grouse of a decade ago. 45.9% WB16/019

The Famous Grouse Mellow Gold sherry & bourbon casks (85) n20 t23.5 f20 b21.5. While the nose and finish tell us a little too much about the state of the sherry butts used, there is no harm tuning into the delivery and follow though which are, unquestionably, beautiful. The texture is silk normally found on the most expensive lingerie, and as sexy as who you might find inside it; while the honey is a fabulous mix of ulmo and orange blossom. 40%

The Famous Grouse Smoky Black (87) n22 t22 f21 b22. Black Grouse by any other name. Flawed in the usual tangy, furry Grouse fashion. But have to say there is a certain roughness and randomness about the sugars that I find very appealing. A smoky style that Bowmore lovers might enjoy. A genuinely beautiful, smoky, ugly, black duckling. Sorry, I mean Grouse. 40%

Firean blend no. 005, bottling line. 003, bott code. L17066 (91.5) n23 t23.5 f22 b23 Does the heart good encounter to encounter a blend so happy to embrace its smokier self. Deliciously impressive. 40%. Burlington Drinks.

Fort Glen The Blender's Reserve Aged 12 Years (88.5) n21.5 t23 f21.5 b22.5 An entirely enjoyable blend which is clean and boasting decent complexity and weight. 40%

Fort Glen The Distiller's Reserve (78) n18 t22 f19 b19. Juicy, salivating delivery as it storms the ramparts. Draws down the portcullis elsewhere. 40%. The Fort Glen Whisky Company.

Fraser MacDonald (85) n21 t21.5 f21 b21.5. Some fudge towards the middle and end but the journey there is an enjoyable one. 40%. Loch Lomond Distillers.

Gairloch (79) n19 t20 f20 b20. For those who like their butterscotch at 40% abv. 40%

Gleann Mór Blended Whisky 18 Year Old (87) n21.5 t23 f20.5 b22. A few passages in this are outstanding, especially when the delicate honey appears to collide with the softest smoke. A slight bitterness does jar somewhat, though the softness of the grain is quite seriously seductive 43.9%

Gleann Mór 40 Year Old Blend (94) n23 t23.5 f23.5 b24 Some 52-year-old Carsebridge makes up about a fifth of this blend, but I suspect the big oak comes from one of the malts. A supreme old whisky which cherishes its age. 44.6%.

Glenalba Aged 22 Years Sherry Cask Finish batch no. JS/322, lot no. 0745C, dist 1993 (90) n22 t23.5 f23.5 b21 A pristine sherry effect. No off notes whatsoever. If there is a downside, it is the fact that the sherry evens out the complexity of the blend. I mean, surely...that has to be the purpose of a blend: complexity and balance, right....? That said, for the experience alone...all rather lovely and deserving of further exploration...! 40%

Glenalba Aged 25 Years Sherry Cask Finish batch no. SE/425, lot no. 0274J, dist 1990 (89) n22 t23.5 f22.5 b21.5 A lovely whisky, though again the unreconstructed sherry effect does few favours to the overall layering and balance. Maybe the vaguest hint of something with the 'S' word, though very low key... 40%

Glenalba Aged 34 Years Sherry Cask Finish batch no. JM/012, lot no. 0862B, dist 1981 (95.5) n24 t24 f23.5 b24 A beautifully dry, sophisticated blend. Benefits from the use of what is about as good a sherry butt as I have encountered: not even the hint of a hint of an off-note. Where the 22 and 25 editions are rather overcome by the magnitude of the grape, this one has enough in reserve to take the sherry in its stride and out to it excellent effect. Truly superb Scotch. 40%

Glen Brynth (70.5) n18 t19 f16 b17.5. Bitter and awkward. 43%

Glenbrynth Premium Three Year Old (82) n19 t21 f21 b21 An enormously improved, salivating, toasty blend making full use of the rich muscovado sugars on display. Good late spice, too. 43%. OTI Africa.

Glenbrynth 8 Year Old (88) n21.5 t22 f22.5 b22. An impressive blend which improves second by second on the palate. 40%. OTI Africa.

Glenbrynth Pearl 30 Year Old Limited Edition (90.5) n22.5 t23.5 f21.5 b23 Attractive, beautifully weighted, no off notes...though perhaps quietened by toffee. Still a treat of a blend. 43%. OTI Africa.

Glenbrynth Pearl 30 Year Old bott code L8V 7410 28/11/11 (88) n22.5 t22.5 f21 b22 A genuinely strange blend. Not sure how ish whisky was mapped out in the creator's mind. A hit and miss hotchpotch but when it is good, it is very good.. 43%. OTI Africa.

The Glengarry bott code L3/301/15 (80) n19 t21 f20 b20 A brand that would once make me wince has upped its game beyond recognition. Even has the nerve to now possess an attractively salivating as well as silky disposition. 40%. Loch Lomond Group.

Glen Lyon (85) n19 t22.5 f22 b21.5. Works a lot better than the nose suggests: seriously chewy with a rabid spice attack and lots of juices. For those who have just retired as dynamite testers. Unpretentious fun. 43%. Diageo.

Glen Talloch Choice Rare & Old (85.5) n20.5 t22.5 f21 b21.5. A very pleasing sharpness to the delivery reveals the barley in all its Speyside-style finery, The grain itself is soothing, especially when the caramel notes kick in. 40%. ncf.

Glen Talloch Gold Aged 12 Years (85) n21 t22 f21 b21. Impressive grain at work insuring a deft, velvety caress to the palate. Mainly caramel speaking, despite the age, though there is an attractive spice buzz towards the thin-ish finish. 40%

Glen Talloch Peated (77) n18 t20 f20 b19 The awful tobacco nose needs some serious work on it. The taste is overly sweet, mushy and shapeless, like far too many blends these days. Requires a complete refit. 40%. Boomsma Distillery.

Glory Leading Aged 32 Years (88.5) n22.5 t22.5 f21.5 b22 At times a little heavy handed and out of sync. But the overall experience is one of stunningly spiced enjoyment. 43%

Glory Leading Blended Scotch Whisky 30 Years Old American oak casks (93) n22.5 t23 f23.5 b24 a big, clever, satisfying blend which just gets better and better... though not too sure about the Crystal Palace style eagle on the label. Even so, love it! 43%

Golden Piper (86.5) n22 t21 f22 b21.5. A firm, clean blend with a steady flush through of diverse sugars. The grain does all the steering and therefore complexity is limited. But the overall freshness is a delight. 43%. Whisky Shack.

◇ **Goldfield** bott code: L17 02796 CB1 (86) n21 t21.5 f21.5 b22 These days I am minded to give an extra mark to any blend that is not carrying a sulphur trace from the grain recepticals. So an extra mark here, for sure, for this fat and full-flavoured blend which, despite its unashamed cream toffee roundness, enjoys enough spice to punch through for bite, as well as some late hickory. 40%.

The Gordon Highlanders (86) n21 t22 f21 b22. Lush and juicy, there is a distinctive Speysidey feel to this one with the grains doing their best to accentuate the developing spice. Plenty of feel good factor here. 40%. *William Grant & Sons.*

Grand Macnish (79) n19 t21 f19 b20. Welcome back to an old friend...but the years have caught up with it. Still on the feral side, but has exchanged its robust good looks for an unwashed and unkempt appearance on the palate. Will do a great job to bring some life back to you, though. 43%. *MacDuff International Ltd.*

Grand Macnish bott code L16/8404 (85.5) n21.5 t22 f21 b21 Never a blend for the lily-livered this brand has always been a byword for a whisky with big character. It can still claim that, except now we have a much more absorbing grain at play which undermines the blend's former maltiness. 40%. *MacDuff International Ltd.*

Grand Macnish 12 Years Old (86) n21 t22 f21.5 b21.5. A grander Grand Macnich than of old with the wonderful feather pillow delivery maintained and a greater harmonisation of the malt, especially those which contain a honey-copper sheen. 40%. *MacDuff.*

Grand Macnish Black Edition charred Bourbon casks, bott code L15 8863 (94.5) n24 t23.5 f23 b24 A blended whisky classic. 40%. *MacDuff International Ltd.*

Grant's Aged 12 Years bott code: L6X 6682 1305 (96) n24 t24 f23.5 b24.5 There is no doubting that their 12-year-old has improved dramatically in recent years. Doubtless better grain than their standard blend, but also a slightly braver use of phenols has paid handsome dividends. Sits proudly alongside Johnny Walker Black as one of the world's must have 12-year-old blends. For me, the perfect daily dram. 40%.

Grant's Cask Editions No. 1 Ale Cask Finish bott code: L1X 7354 1809 (91) n22.5 attractive Demerara firmness and even a malty swirl; the green, youthful freshness charms; t23 juicy delivery and firmer than the Family Reserve with much more sharpness and clarity; big sugars build; f22.5 a pleasing spiced mocha fade; b23 a much cleaner, more precise blend than when this was first launched, with less noticeable beer character: impressive. 40%.

Grant's Cask Editions No. 2 Sherry Cask Finish bott code: L3Z 7760 0211 (84.5) n21.5 t22 f20 b21 A lovely fresh, fruity and salivating edge to this even boasting an early honeyed sheen. Complexity has been sacrificed for effect, however. 40%.

Grant's The Family Reserve bott code: L3A 8017 1711 (85) n21 t22 f21 b21 What was once the very finest, most complex nose in the entire Scotch whisky lexicon is now, on this evidence, a mushy shadow of its former self. Where once there was a judicious mix of softer and firmer grain to ensure the malts could make the most eloquent of speeches, now there is just a spongy sweetness which shouts loud enough to silence the poetry. If you like your blend fat, sweet, chewy, softer than quicksand and boasting a bitter, vaguely off-key finale here you go. But for those of us who once revered Grant's as the greatest of all standard blends, a whisky whose artistry once gilt-framed the very finest Scotland had to offer, this will not be a glass of cheer. I cannot blame the blender: he can work only with what he has available. And today, after a succession of nonsensical grain distillery closures (nonsensical to anyone who understands whisky, but not the soul-less bean counters who haven't the first clue) the choice in his lab is limited. It would be like blaming the manager of Bradford City for being a third tier football club because they won the FA Cup in 1910. Times change. And not, sadly, always for the better... 40%.

Grant's Signature bott code: L1Z 7468 1609 (79) n19 t22 f18 b20 Smudged. 40%.

The Great Macaulay (86.5) n22 t21.5 f21.5 b21.5 The character is one mainly of trudging, attractive caramel bolstered by busy, warming spice. The nose shows some degree of complexity. By no means unpleasant. 40%. *Quality Spirits International.*

Green Plaid 12 Years Old (89) n22 t23 f22 b22 Beautifully constructed; juicy. 40%.

Guneagal Aged 12 Years (85.5) n21 t22.5 f20.5 b21.5. The salty, sweaty armpit nose gives way to an even saltier delivery, helped along by sweet glycerine and a boiled candy fruity sweetness. The finish is a little roughhouse by comparison. 40%. *William Grant & Sons.*

Haddington House (81) n20 t21 f20 b20 Good grief! This has changed since I last tasted it over a decade ago. Gone is its light, bright juicy character and in its place a singularly sweet, cloying blend due, I suspect, to a very different grain input. 40%. *Quality Spirits International.*

Haig Gold Label (88) n21 t23 f22 b22 What had before been pretty standard stuff has upped the complexity by an impressive distance. 40%. *Diageo.*

Hankey Bannister (84.5) n20.5 t22 f21 b21. Lots of early life and even a malt kick early on. Toffee later. 40%. *Inverhouse Distillers.*

Hankey Bannister 12 Years Old (86.5) n22 t21.5 f21 b22. A much improved blend with a nose and early delivery which makes full play of the blending company's Speyside malts. Plenty of toffee on the finish. 40%. *Inverhouse Distillers.*

Hankey Bannister 21 Years Old (95) n23.5 a fruity ensemble, clean, vibrant and loath to show its age t24 as juicy as the nose suggests, except for the odd rumble of distant smoke; a firm, barley-sugar hardness as the grains keep control; f23.5 the arrival of the oak adds further weight and for the first time begins to behave like a 21-y-o; long, now with decent spice and with some crusty dryness at the very death; b24 with top dressing like this and some obviously complex secondary malts, too, how can it fail? 43%.

Hankey Bannister 25 Years Old (91) n22.5 t24 f21.5 b23 Follows on in style and quality to 21-year-old. Gorgeous. 40%

Hankey Bannister 40 Years Old (89) n22 t23 f22 b22. This blend has been put together to mark the 250th anniversary of the forging of the business relations between Messrs. Hankey and Bannister. And although the oak creaks like a ship of its day, there is enough verve and viscosity to ensure a rather delicious toast to the gentlemen. Love it! 44%. *Inverhouse.*

Hankey Bannister 40 Year Old (94) n23.5 t23.5 f23 b24. Pure quality. The attention to detail is sublime. 44.3%. *Inverhouse Distillers.*

Hankey Bannister Heritage Blend (92) n23 despite the evidence of sherry the spiced chocolate fudge keeps you spellbound; t24 at moments like this, one's taste buds are purely in love. They are being caressed, serenaded and kisses by the most glorious of old grains, encrusted with a Speyside-syle maltiness which makes you purr with pleasure; f22 the weakness on the nose returns, though sparingly. Outstanding late Malteser candy style confirms a very decent malt depth; b23 just so soft and sensual...46%. *Inverhouse Distillers.*

Harveys Lewes Blend Eight Year Old batch 4 (93) n23.5 t23 f23 b23.5 First tasted this in the front parlour of legendary Harvey's brewer Miles Jenner's home just after Christmas. It tasted quite different from their previous bottlings – and quite superb. Nosed and tasted now several months on in the cold analytical light of a tasting room...helped along with that deft addition of subtle peat, it still does. Superb! 40%

Hazelwood 18 Year Old (88) n23.5 top-notch dispersal of subtle notes: walnut cream cake with a pinch of vanilla. The malt is low key but distinctly Speyside-style in its clarity, despite the odd wisp of something a little heavier; t22.5 creamy-textured. Soft ulmo honey gives way to the thickening vanilla and toffee; f20.5 bitters slightly at the turned-up ending; b22 until the final furry moments, a genuine little, understated, charmer. 40%. *William Grant & Sons.*

Hazelwood 21 Year Old (74) n19 t20 f17 b18. Some decent acacia honey tries to battle against the bitter imbalance. 40%. *William Grant & Sons.*

Hazelwood 25 Year Old (89.5) n22 full on fruit underscored by the muscular tannins: simple, but satisfying; t23 wonderful delivery: a momentous mix of muscovado and maple syrup but with the toasty tannins offering an even more roasty depth; f22 a slight, non-spiced buzz to the finish. But that roastiness – akin to burnt fudge – gives much to chew over; b22.5 distinctly chunky. 40%. *William Grant & Sons.*

High Commissioner (88.5) n22.5 t22.5 f20.5 b22.5 Now I admit I had a hand in cleaning this brand up a couple of years back, giving it a good polish and much needed balance complexity. But I don't remember leaving it in quite this good a shape. Just a bitter semi-off note on the finish, otherwise this guy would have been in the 90s. What a great fun, three-course dram this is... 40%. *Loch Lomond Distillers.*

High Commissioner bott code L2/305/16 (87.5) n21.5 t22.5 f21.5 b22 Boasts an unusually well balanced disposition for a young blend, not at all cowered into being a one trick caramelled pony. Instead, we are treated to a fulsome array of huskier and duskier notes, especially the molasses mixing with a hint of phenol. Delicious. 40%. *Loch Lomond Group.*

Highland Baron (85.5) n21 t22 f21 b21.5. A very clean, sweet and competent young blend showing admirable weight and depth. 40%. *Loch Lomond Distillers.*

Highland Baron (88.5) n22 trace smoke works beautifully with the sweet and lithe grain; t22.5 outstanding mouth feel: chewy and sweet but always within the realms of balance and god taste. A little chocolate and honey arrives with that hint of smoke; f22 silky, lightly spiced, vaguely smoked, molassed mocha; b22 has seriously upped the smoke and honey ratio in recent years. Deserves its Baronetcy. 40%. *Lombard Scotch Whisky Ltd.*

Highland Bird (77) n19 t19 f19 b20. I've has a few of these over the years, I admit. But I can't remember one quite as rough and ready as this... 40%. *Quality Spirits International.*

Highland Bird bott code L9Z 6253 2302 (83.5) n21 t21 f20.5 b21 I've had a few of these over the years, I can tell you. Glasses of this whisky, as well. As for the blend, this is by far and away the cleanest, enjoyable and most well-balanced yet: a dram on the up. 40%. *Quality Spirits International.*

Highland Harvest Organic Scotch Whisky (76) n18 t21 f19 b18. A very interesting blend. Great try, but a little bit of a lost opportunity here as I don't think the balance is quite right. But at least I now know what organic caramel tastes like... *40%*

Highland Mist (88.5) n20.5 t23 f22.5 b22.5 Fabulously fun whisky bursting from the bottle with character and mischief. Had to admit, broke all my own rules and just had to have a glass of this after doing the notes... *40%. Loch Lomond Distillers.*

Highland Piper (79) n20 t20 f19 b20. Good quaffing blend – if sweet - of sticky toffee and dates. Some gin on the nose – and finish. *40%*

Highland Pride (86) n21 t22 f21.5 b21.5. A beefy, weighty thick dram with plenty to chew on. The developing sweetness is a joy. *40%. Whyte & Mackay Distillers Ltd.*

Highland Queen Blended Scotch Whisky (86.5) n22 t21 f21.5 b22. Lots of grains at play here. But what grains?! Clean and crisp with a superb bite which balances the softening mouth feel attractively. Old fashioned and delicious. *40%*

Highland Queen bott code L12 356 (87) n22.5 t22.5 f20.5 b21.5 If the caramels on this could be reduced slightly what a brilliant blend we'd have on our hands here. As it is, the nose is a hotbed of complex intrigue with earthier and lighter honeyed notes combining sublimely while the delivery allows the sugars, vanillas and spices room to make their cases. Bar the spices, just all dies off a little too soon. *40%. Tullibardine Ltd.*

Highland Queen Aged 8 Years bott code L15 071 (89.5) n23 beautifully rich and rounded in its time-honoured way, though less fruit now (though some boiled apples remain) and more honeyed; t22.5 gloriously succulent with its chewability going off the scale; muscovado sugars and spices force the agenda in the mid ground; f21.5 despite a caramel onslaught the spices win by a distance; b22.5 a classy blend showing great character and entertainment value. *40%. Tullibardine Ltd.*

Highland Queen Aged 12 Years Blended Scotch Whisky (87) n22 t22 f21 b22. A polite, slightly more sophisticated version of the 8-year-old...but without the passion and drama! *40%*

Highland Queen Aged 12 Years bott code L15 071 (90) n23 delicious gooseberry tart with an earthy, tannin undertone; t22.5 golden syrup majors on delivery, then a slow spreading of a vaguely phenolic but distinctly spicy vanilla theme; f22 caramel and spice: simple but wonderfully effective; b22.5 a much weightier blend than it used to be, displaying excellent pace of flavour development on the palate. Decent stuff! *40%. Tullibardine Ltd.*

Highland Queen Sherry Cask Finish bott code L16 201 (81.5) n19 t22 f19 b21.5 The sherry isn't exactly free from sin, and the grape easily overpowers the nuances of the blend itself. So, attractive to a degree, but... *40%. Tullibardine Ltd.*

Highland Queen 1561 bott code L16/80 28.01.16 (94) n23.5 t23.5 f23 b24. As it happens, I have a home where on a living room wall is an old oil painting of Fotheringhay, where the life of Mary Queen of Scots, the Highland Queen, ended on an executioners' block in 1561. Indeed, the house is quite close by and sits near the River Nene which passes through Fotheringhay. The village itself is quiet, particularly fragrant during Spring and Summer and with an unmistakable feel of history and elegance. Not at all unlike this excellent and most distinguished blend. *40%. Tullibardine Ltd.*

Highland Queen 1561 30 Years Old bott code LF13017261 261 (88.5) n23.5 the trick of an ancient blend is that you want it to show its age as a Victorian beauty might show her ankle: in a subtle, teasing and arousing way... The nose has pulled it off brilliantly, even if there is a hint of the dreaded S word to be caught on the fruit...; t23.5 perfect weight and sugary sheen to the delivery; the caramels and fruits are just about neck and neck in influence; the muscovado sugars are bright and crunchy; f19.5 becomes just a little too furry and tangy...; b22 shame about the finish. Until then we had one of the sweetest yet gentle blends of the year. *40%. Tullibardine Ltd.*

Highland Queen Majesty Classic bott code L14/8634 09.08.14 (92) n24, t23 f22 b23 The brilliant nose isn't quite matched by the pragmatism of the overall taste experience but a blend to savour nonetheless. *40%. Tullibardine Ltd.*

Highland Queen Majesty Aged 12 Years bott code L15/8538 19/08/15 (86.5) n22 t22 f21 b21.5 A pleasant but lazy blend considering its age. Lots of explosive malt on delivery, some with a lemon sherbet fizz. But a heavy dependence on caramel quietens the party, though a late spice surge gate-crashes with welcome effect. *40%. Tullibardine Ltd.*

Highland Queen Majesty Aged 16 Years bott code L15/8265 06 07 15 (88) n22.5 the house style of lemon sherbet is in full fizz...; t22.5 salivating, malty delivery with oaky reinforcements soon arriving; f21.5 caramel wafers and vanilla ice cream make for a simplistic finale; b22 enjoyable, yet leaves you with a feeling that it could have offered a little bit more. *40%. Tullibardine Ltd.*

Highland Reserve (80) n19 t21.5 f19.5 b20 See tasting notes for 43% below. *40%. Quality Spirits International.*

Highland Reserve bott code B154 **(80)** n19 t21.5 f19.5 b20 An easy quaffing, silky and profoundly grained, toffee-enriched blend. *43%. Quality Spirits International.*

Highland Warriors (82) n20 t21 f20.5 b20.5 This warrior must be wanting to raid a few grain stores... *40%. Quality Spirits International.*

The Highland Way (82.5) n20 t21 f21 b20.5 Grainy, with a big sweet toffee middle which makes for a slightly juicy dram of a class barely distinguishable from so many other standard blends. *40%. Quality Spirits International.*

The Highland Way bott code B445 **(83.5)** n20 t21.5 f21 b21 More Milky Way than Highland Way... Very similar to the 40% version, except some extra milk chocolate at the finish. *43%. Quality Spirits International.*

Islay Mist Aged 8 Years Amontillado Napoleon Cask Finish bott code L16/8826 **(76)** n19 t20 f18 b19 For those of you not carrying the sulphur recognition gene, I suspect this will be a delight. For those of us that do, well sorry: but not tonight, Napoleon. And this sulphur is a bit of a carry on, MacDuff... *43%. MacDuff International Ltd.*

Islay Mist Aged 8 Years Manzanilla La Gitana Cask Finish bott code L15/8293 **(85)** n21.5 t22 f20 b21.5 Lots of phenolic cough sweet properties but the fruit and smoke form a tight, enclosed union with little room for scope. The finish is rather too bitter. *40%.*

Islay Mist Aged 12 Years bott code L16/8089 **(86)** n22.5 t22 f20.5 b21 Slightly on the disappointing side by Islay Mist's high standards. The nose, with its smoked toffee apple, promises a playful complexity. But an overdose of dull caramel snuffs out any chance of that. *40%. MacDuff International Ltd.*

Islay Mist Aged 17 Years bott code L15/8826 **(96)** n24 t24 f23.5 b24.5 A truly brilliant blend that should have no water added and be spared as much time as you can afford. *40%. MacDuff International Ltd.*

Islay Mist Deluxe bott code L16/8283 **(87)** n22 t22 f21.5 b21.5 A charmingly brazen blend, offering young peat to you with far less reserve than it once did. More an Islay Fog than Mist... *40%. MacDuff International Ltd.*

Islay Mist Peated Reserve bott code L15 9:67 **(92.5)** n23.5 t23 f22.5 b23.5 The accent is on subtlety and balance: a very classy piece of whisky engineering. *40%. MacDuff International Ltd.*

Isle of Skye 8 Years Old (94) n23 t24 f23.5 b23.5. Where once peat ruled and with its grain ally formed a smoky iron fist, now honey and subtlety reigns. A change of character and pace which may disappoint gung-ho peat freaks but will intrigue and delight those looking for a more sophisticated dram. *40%. Ian Macleod.*

Isle of Skye 21 years Old (91) n21 t23.5 f23 b23.5 What an absolute charmer! The malt content appears pretty high, but the overall balance is wonderful. *40%. Ian Macleod.*

Isle of Skye 50 Years Old (82.5) n21.5 t21 f20 b20. Drier incarnation than the 50% version. But still the age has yet to be balanced out, towards the end in particular. Early on some distinguished moments involving something vaguely smoked and a sweetened spice. *41.6%*

The Jacobite (78.5) n18 t18.5 f22 b20. Neither the nose nor delivery are of the cleanest style. But comes into its own towards the finish when the thick soup of a whisky thins to allow an attractive degree of complexity. Not for those with catholic tastes. *40%. Booker.*

James Alexander (85.5) n21 t21.5 f21.5 b21.5. Some lovely spices link the grassier Speysiders to the earthier elements. *40%. Quality Spirits International.*

⬩ **James Buchanan's Special Reserve Aged 18 Years** bott code: L7237CE001 **(89)** n22.5 the smoke is such a clever cove here, apparently teasing you about its presence but actually forming the base notes; a slight weakness I expect to face towards the finish seems to be a curse of most blends these days; t24 texture and sweetness levels are just about in perfect mode, as is the smoke which wafts in to enrich the mid-point; f20.5 a sulphur kick dampens the fun; b22 a blend I have known and admired a very long time. Since indeed, my beard was black and I carried not an extra ounce of weight. And I am still, I admit, very much in love with, though she has betrayed me with a Spanish interloper... *40%.*

James King (81) n20 t19.5 f21 b20.5 A slightly more well balanced and equally weighted blend than it once was with better use of spice and cocoa. *43%. Quality Spirits International.*

James King Aged 5 Years (84) n19.5 t21 f21.5 b21.5 While the nose never quite gets going, things are quite different on the palate. And if you find a more agreeable chocolate fudge blend this year, please let me know. *43%. Quality Spirits International.*

James King Aged 8 Years (86) n21 t21 f22 b22 A far better constructed blend than of old, with the grains far more able to deal with the demands of the caramel. Fresh and salivating early on, despite the lushness, one can even fancy spotting the odd malt note before the spiced fudge takes command. *43%. Quality Spirits International.*

James King 12 Years Old (81) n19 t23 f19 b20. Caramel dulls the nose and finish. But for some time a quite beautiful blend soars about the taste buds offering exemplary complexity and weight. *40%. Quality Spirits International.*

James King Aged 12 Years bott code B289 (84.5) n21 t22 f20.5 b21 The malt has a far grander say than the 40% version, chipping in with an elementary Speyside note on both nose and delivery. It doesn't take long for the fudge-rich grain to take command, though. Easy, un-taxing whisky. 43%. *Quality Spirits International.*

J&B Jet (79.5) n19 t20 f20.5 b20. Never quite gets off the ground due to carrying too heavy a load. Unrecognisable to its pomp in the old J&B days: this one is far too weighty and never properly finds either balance or thrust. 40%. *Diageo.*

J&B Reserve Aged 15 Years (78) n23 t19 f18 b18. What a crying shame. The sophisticated and demure nose is just so wonderfully seductive but what follows is an open-eyed, passionless embrace. Coarsely grain-dominant and unbalanced, this is frustrating beyond words and not worthy to be mentioned in the same breath as the old, original J&B 15 which, by vivid contrast, was a malty, salivating fruit-fest and minor classic. 40%. *Diageo.*

J&B Rare (88.5) n21.5 t22.5 f22 b22.5 I have been drinking a lot of J&B from a previous time of late, due to the death of their former blender Jim Milne. I think he would have been pretty taken aback by the youthful zip offered here: whether it is down to a decrease in age or the use of slightly more tired casks – or both – is hard to say. 40%. *Diageo.*

Johnnie Walker Black Label 12 Years Old (95.5) n23.5 pretty sharp grain: hard and buffeting the nose; a buffer of yielding smoke, apple pie and delicate spice cushions the encounter; t24.5 if there is a silkier delivery on the market today, I have not seen it: this is sublime stuff with the grains singing the sweetest hymns as they go down, taking with them a near perfection of weighty smoke lightened by brilliantly balanced barley which leans towards both soft apple and crème broulee; f23.5 those reassuringly rigid grains re-emerge and with them the most juicy Speysidey malts imaginable; the lovely sheen to the finish underlines the good age of the whiskies used; b24 here it is: one of the world's most masterful whiskies back in all its complex glory. A bottle like this is like being visited by an old lover. It just warms the heart and excites. 40%. *Diageo.*

⬩⬩ **Johnnie Walker Aged 18 Years** bott code: L7276DN001 (92) n23 the earthy phenols have the biggest say, though admirably reserved, before delicate diced apple and relaxed spices offer a counter weight; t23.5 the palate is plunged into a morass of super-soft grain, light sugars filtering into the growing fruit; only towards the mid- point does the smoke, so evident on the nose, make its mark, working rather beautifully with the understated tannins; f22 a slight trace of a fruity furriness; b23.5 "the Pursuit of the Ultimate 18 year old Blend," says the label under the striding man. Well, they haven't reached their goal yet as, for all its deliciousness, this falls short of true Johnnie Walker brilliance thanks to an overly soft grain usage, when it was crying out for a variation which included a firmer, ramrod straight grain for extra mouth feel complexity, and give something for the malts to bounce off. That said, the extra but by no means over enthusiastic use of phenols ensures impressive depth to a genuinely lovely whisky. 40%.

Johnnie Walker Blenders' Batch Bourbon Cask & Rye Finish bott code L7219CA002 00034598 (89.5) n21.5 untaxing and even with emphasis on the caramel; t23 now comes alive on the palate with a sharp flourish of lively oak and vaguest of spice; this has hefty weight both from the caramels and the stodgy malt which balance well with the silky grains. Subtle orange blossom honey before much heftier chocolate fudge; f22.5 long, with the spices upped slightly; dry vanilla on the fade; b22.5 great to see someone have the good sense to try to make the most of rye. If they can tame the caramels the results will be better still. 40%. *Diageo.*

⬩⬩ **Johnnie Walker Blender's Batch Espresso Roast** bott code: L7233IH007 (86.5) n21 t23 f21 b21.5 Well, that was different! Can't really big up the nose or finish as it is just too tangy and furry. But the delivery – probably the softest and most well-rounded of any JW I have ever encountered - really does magic up some fabulously intense mocha notes – especially when the varying coffee and chocolate tones criss-cross or merge. The spices don't do any harm, either! 43.2%.

⬩⬩ **Johnnie Walker Blender's Batch Wine Cask Blend** bott code: L7179CD002 (91.5) n22.5 highly attractive weave of firm oak and earthy, jammy notes; very sharp, borderline aggressive in the arched intensity; t23.5 a brittle sharpness to the muscovado sugars leads to an excellent juiciness in which both malt and fruit lay an even hand; Jammy Dodger biscuit, or even strawberry Swiss Roll with no shortage of cream; f22 almost an old-fashioned cream sherry feel to this finish; the vaguest of furry finishes but no damage done; b23.5 an absolutely unique fingerprint to this member of the Walker family: none has such a fruity yt creamy profile. 40%.

Johnnie Walker Blue Label (88) n21 t24 f21 b22 What a frustrating blend! Just so close to brilliance but the nose and finish are slightly out of kilter. Worth the experience of the mouth arrival alone. 43%. *Diageo.*

Johnnie Walker Blue Label The Casks Edition (97) n24.5 t24.5 f23.5 b24.5. This is a triumph of scotch whisky blending. With not as much as a hint of a single off note to be traced from the tip of the nose to tail, this shameless exhibition of complexity and brilliance is the star turn in the Diageo portfolio right now. Indeed, it is the type of blend that every person who genuinely adores whisky must experience for the good of their soul....if only once in their life. 55.8%.

Johnnie Walker Double Black (94.5) n23 t23.5 f24 b24. Double tops! Rolling along the taste buds like distant thunder, this is a welcome and impressive addition to the Johnnie Walker stable. Perhaps not as complete and rounded as the original Johnnie Walker Black...but, then, what is? 40%.

Johnnie Walker Explorers' Club Collection The Gold Route (89) n23.5 t24 f19.5 b22. Much of this blend is truly the stuff of golden dreams. Like its Explorer's Club stable mate, some attention has to be paid to the disappointing finish. Worth sending out an expedition, though, just for the beautiful nose and delivery... 40%. Diageo.

Johnnie Walker Explorer's Club Collection 'The Royal Route' (93) n24.5 t24 f21.5 b23 A fabulous journey, travelling first Class most of the way. But to have discovered more, could have been bottled at 46% for a much more panoramic view of the great whiskies on show. 40%. Diageo

Johnnie Walker Explorers' Club Collection The Spice Road (84.5) n22 t23.5 f18 b21. Sublime delivery of exceptionally intense juiciness: in fact, probably the juiciest blend released this year. But the bitter, fuzzy finish reveals certain casks haven't helped. 40%.

Johnnie Walker Gold Label Reserve (91.5) n23 t24 f22 b23. Moments of true star quality here, but the finish could do with a polish. 40%. Diageo.

Johnnie Walker King George V db (88) n23 t22 f21 b22 One assumes that King George V is no relation to George IV. This has genuine style and breeding, if a tad too much caramel. 43%

Johnnie Walker Platinum Label Aged 18 Years (88) n22 t23 f21 b22. This blend might sound like some kind of Airmiles card. Which wouldn't be too inappropriate, though this is more Business than First... 40%. Diageo.

Johnnie Walker Red Label (87.5) n22 t22 f21.5 b22. The ongoing move through the scales quality-wise appears to suggest we have a work still in progress here. This sample has skimped on the smoke, though not quality. Yet a few months back when I was in the BA Business Lounge at Heathrow's new Terminal Five, I nearly keeled from almost being overcome by peat in the earthiest JW Red I had tasted in decades. I found another bottle and I'm still not sure which represents the real Striding Man. 40%. Diageo.

Johnnie Walker Select Casks Aged 10 Years Rye Cask Finish (90) n22.5 t23 f21.5 b23 With the use of first fill bourbon casks and ex-rye barrels for finishing, hardly surprising this is the Johnnie Walker with the most Kentuckian feel of them all. Yet it's even more Canadian, still. 46% (92 Proof)

Johnnie Walker X.R Aged 21 Years (94) n23.5 t24 f23 b23.5. How weird: I nosed this blind before seeing what the brand was. My first thought was: "mmm, same structure of Crown Royal XR. Canadian??? No, there's smoke!" Then looked at what was before me and spotted it was its sister whisky from the Johnnie Walker stable. A coincidence? I don't think so... 40%.

Kenmore Special Reserve Aged 5 Years bott code L07285 (75) n18 t20 f19 b18. Recovers to a degree from the poor nose. A must-have for those who prefer their Scotch big-flavoured and gawky. 40%

King Charles (82) n21 t21 f20 b20 From the salty, sweaty armpit nose (which I know some people absolutely love in a whisky!) to the OTT sugar attack before the bitter finish, this isn't quite one for the purists. Hard to imagine a grain any more soft and enveloping. 40%. Quality Spirits International.

King Glenorsen (81) n20 t21 f20 b20. Pleasant and easy drinking enough. But the young grains dominate completely. Designed, I think, to be neutralised by ice. 40%

King Robert II (77) n19 t19 f20 b19. A bustier, more bruising batch than the last 40 per cent version. Handles the OTT caramel much better. Agreeably weighty slugging whisky. 43%.

Label 5 Aged 12 Years bott code L515467C (90) n23 a lively nose, full of kumquat, raspberry cream Swiss Roll and deft smoke; clean for a blend these days and with the precision of an Exocet; t22.5 the vanillas wallow in the icing sugar for a while before the vanillas at last appear; f22 just a little tang, but still soft and sweet; the smoke arrives, thin and apologetically at the very end, though the late spice is much bolder; b22.5 one of the easiest drams you'll find this year with just enough complexity to lift it into the higher echelons. 40%. La Martiniquaise.

Label 5 Extra Rare Aged 18 Years bott code L5301576 (87.5) n21.5 t22.5 f22 b21.5 You have to say this is pleasant. But from an 18-year-old blend you should be saying so much more. Salivating and at times fresh and juicy, other than the late spice little gets the pulses racing in the vanilla and sugar morass. A tad too much toffee, alas. 40%. La Martiniquaise.

Label 5 Classic Black bott code L403055D (87) n22 t22 f21 b22 A malt famed for its indifferent nose now boasts an aroma boasting complexity, layering and spice. The mix of spice and muscovado sugars elsewhere is no less appealing, though the mouth feel is a little too fat and yielding. But what an improvement! 40%. La Martiniquaise.

Label 5 Gold Heritage (92) n22.5 t23.5 f22 b24 A very classy blend very skilfully constructed. A stunningly lovely texture, one of the very best I have encountered for a while, and no shortage of complexity ensures this is a rather special blend. I'll even forgive the dulling by caramel and light milkiness from the tired bourbon barrel. The overall excellence outweighs the odd blemish. *40%*

◇ **Label 5 Premium Black** bott code: L720856A (84.5) n21 t22 f20.5 b21 An, at first, luscious, then later on ultra-firm blend with the accent decidedly on the grain and caramels. *40%.*

Lang's Supreme Aged 5 Years (93.5) n23.5 t23.5 f23 b23.5. Every time I taste this the shape and structure has altered slightly. Here there is a fraction more smoke, installing a deeper confidence all round. This is blended whisky as it should be: Supreme in its ability to create shape and harmony. *40%. Ian Macleod Distillers Ltd.*

The Last Drop 1965 American Standard Barrel (96.5) n24 t24.5 f23.5 b24.5 Almost impossible to imagine a blended whisky to be better balanced than this. If there is a cleverer use of honey or less intrusive oak in any blended whisky bottled in the last year, I have yet to taste it. An award winner if ever I tasted one. Magnificent doesn't quite cover it... *48.6%. Morrison Bowmore. The Last Drop Distillers Ltd.*

The Last Drop 1971 Blended Scotch Whisky 45 Years Old (97) n24.5 t24 f24 b24.5 Even though I now know many of the people involved in the Last Drop, I am still not entirely sure how they keep doing it. Just how do they continue to unearth whiskies which are truly staggering; absolute marvels of their type? This one is astonishing because the grain used is just about faultless. And the peating levels can be found around about the perfect mark on the dial. Like an old Ballantine's which has sat and waited in a cask over four decades to be discovered and tell its wonderful, spellbinding and never-ending tale. Just mesmerically beautiful. *47%.*

The Last Drop 50 Year Old Sherry Wood (97) n24 t24.5 f24 b24.5 You'd expect, after half a century in the cask, that this would be a quiet dram, just enjoying its final years with its feet up and arms behind its head. Instead we have a fairly aggressive blend determined to drive the abundant fruitiness it still possesses to the very hilt. It is backed up all the way by a surprising degree of warming, busy spice. There is a hell of a lot of life in this beautiful ol' dog... *51.2%*

Lauder's (74) n18 t21 f17 b18. Well, it's consistent: you can say that for it! As usual, fabulous delivery, but as for the rest...oh dear. *40%. MacDuff International Ltd.*

Lauder's bott code L 08 10 14 4 BB (78.5) n19 t20 f19.5 b20 For those who like whisky with their cream toffee. Decent spice fizz, though. *40%. MacDuff International Ltd.*

Lauder's Aged 15 Years bott code L16/8189 (93) n23 hints of grape and sharper pear drop sink into a soft, grainy morass; t23.5 beautifully salivating delivery: thick, with structured fruit rather than the overbearing grape I was expecting; the mid-ground celebrates a wonderfully marriage between over-ripe pear and light spice; molasses and toasty fudge; f22.5 date, walnut, more fudge and molasses then, finally, a spiced butterscotch fade...; b24 not the big fat sherry influence of a decade ago...thank heavens...!! This is a gorgeous blend for dark, stormy nights. Well, any night really... *40%. MacDuff International Ltd.*

Lauder's Oloroso Cask bott code L 25 01 16 4 BB (86.5) n21.5 t24 f19 b22 A magnificent blend for those unable to nose or taste sulphur. For those who can, a nearly whisky as this is borderline brilliant. Yes, both nose and finish especially have their weakness, but the narrative of the delivery, not to mention the brilliance of the mouth feel and overall weight and pace of the dram is sublime. Before the sulphur hits we are treated to a truly glorious Jaffa cake mix of controlled fruity sweetness as good as any blend I have tasted this year. *40%. MacDuff International Ltd.*

Lauder's Ruby Cask bott code L 21 05 15 4 BB (94) n23 excellent spice prickle and oak layering; the clean fruit gives everything a polish; t24 mmmm! That is one outstanding mouth feel on the delivery: there is a sheen to the sharp Port-generated fruit plus a generous – though not too generous – sprinkling of muscovado sugar; a little ulmo honey thickens the middle. The trade-off between the crisp, crunchy fruit and sugars and the softer grains is sublime; f23 the spices are on slow burn but when they arrive they complement the oak perfectly; b24 a sophisticated little gem. *40%. MacDuff International Ltd.*

Lauder's Queen Mary bott code L 04 11 14 4 BB (86.5) n22.5 t21.5 f21 b21.5 The sweet oily aroma of Angel Cake and even some roast chestnut: the nose is certainly highly attractive. This almost translates through the body of blend when the caramel allows, the grains showing an oily strain and a slightly malty kick here and there. *40%. MacDuff International Ltd.*

The Loch Fyne (89.5) n22 t23 f21.5 b23. This is an adorable old-style blend....a bit of a throwback. But no ruinous sherry notes...just clean and delicious. Well, mainly... *40%*

Loch Lomond Blended Scotch (89) n22 t22.5 f22 b22.5 A fabulously improved blend: clean and precise and though malt is seemingly at a premium, a fine interplay. *40%*

Loch Lomond Reserve db (86.5) n21.5 t22 f21.5 b21.5. A spongy, sweet, chewy, pleasant blend which is more of a take as you find statement than a layering of flavours. *40%*

Loch Lomond Signature bott code L3/306/15 (86) n22 t21.5 f21 b21.5 Not quite the malty force it can be, though the sugar almonds are a treat. Succulent and gently spiced though the caramel has just a little too much force towards the end. 40%. Loch Lomond Group.

Lochranza (83.5) n21 t21.5 f21 b20. Pleasant, clean, but, thanks to the caramel, goes easy on the complexity. 40%. Isle of Arran.

Logan (78.5) n19 t19 f20 b19.5. Entirely drinkable but a bit heavy-handed with the grains and caramel. 40%. Diageo.

Lombard Gold Label (88) n22 t22 f22 b22 after evaluating this I read the tasting notes on the back of the label and for about the first time this year thought: "actually, the bottlers have the description pretty spot on. So tasted it again, this time while reading the notes and found myself agreeing with every word: a first. Then I discovered why: they are my tasting notes from the 2007 Whisky Bible, though neither my name or book have been credited... A gold label, indeed... 40%. Lombard Scotch Whisky Ltd.

⟜ **Long John Special Reserve** bott code: 2017/08/10 (87.5) n21.5 t22.5 f21.5 b22 An honest, non-fussy blend which makes a point of stacking the bigger flavours up front so it hits the ground running. The grains and toffee shape all aspects, other than this rich delivery where the malt offers both weight and a lighter, salivating quality also; an even a gentle thread of honey. The type of blend that an offer for a refill will be seldom refused. 40%.

Lord Elcho (83.5) n20 t22 f21 b20.5 Such a vast improvement on the last bottling I encountered: this has lush grain at the front, middle and rear that entertains throughout, if a little one dimensionally. A little bit of a tweak and could be a high class blend. 40%. Wemyss Malts.

Lord Elcho Aged 15 Years (89.5) n23.5 t22.5 f21.5 b22 Three or four years ago this was a 15-year-old version of the Lord Elcho standard blend today. So, small mercies, this has moved on somewhat and now offers up a genuinely charming and complex nose and delivery. One is therefore surprised to be disappointed by the denouement, taking into account the blend's history. Some more clever and attentive work on the middle and finish would have moved this into seriously high quality blend territory. But so much to enjoy as it is. 40%. Wemyss Malts.

Lord Scot (77.5) n18.5 t20 f19.5 b19.5. A touch cloying but the mocha fudge ensures a friendly enough ride. 40%. Loch Lomond Distillers.

Lord Scot (86.5) n20 t22 f22.5 b22. A gorgeously lush honey and liquorice middle. 43%

The Lost Distilleries batch 2 (94) n22.5 t24 f23.5 b24. Whoever lost it better find it again: this is how you dream every whisky should be. 53.2%.

The Lost Distilleries Blend Batch 6 (91) n23.5 t23 f22 b22.5 The Lost Malt as well: completely grain dominant – but wonderfully lush and tasty. 49.3%

The Lost Distilleries Blend batch 9 (91) n23 simplistic, gentle schmoozing of light citrus tones with more upfront vanilla; the grain has the bigger say; t23.5 big sugar blast on delivery – eyewateringly intense. Soft mocha and maltesers amble through the middle; f22.5 recedes back to a simple vanilla tale, though there is a a little tang, too; b23 the distilleries may be lost to us, but on the palate they are especially at home. 52.1%. 476 bottles.

Mac Na Mara (83) n20 t22.5 f20 b20.5. Absolutely brimming with salty, fruity character. But just a little more toffee and furriness than it needs. Enjoyable, though. 40%

Mac Na Mara bott code L 25 08 14 2 07 48 BB (84) n21.5 t22 f19.5 b21 As usual, a glass of tricks as the flavours come tumbling at you from every direction. Few blends come saltier and the dry vanilla forges a fascinating balance with the rampant caramel. A fraction furry at the death. 40%. Pràban na Linne Ltd.

Mac Na Mara Rum Finish (93) n22 t24 f23 b24 High quality blending, and the usage of the rum appears to have retained the old Mac Na Mara style. 40%. Praban na Linne.

Mac Na Mara Rum Cask Finish bott code L 23 05 16 3 BB (86) n22.5 t22 f21 b21.5 Lost a degree of the sugary crispness normally associated with this brand and after the initial rum embrace resorts far too quickly to a caramel-rich game-plan. 40%. ncf. Pràban na Linne Ltd.

MacArthur's bott code L16/L31 R16/5192 IB 1735 (87.5) n21.5 t22 f21.5 b22.5 Not quite the tricky and cleverly smoked blend of a few years back. But still a weightier chap than a decade ago, not least because of the softer grain type. The malts do come through with just enough meaning to make for a well-balanced and thoroughly enjoyable offering. 40%. International Beverage Holdings Ltd.

MacQueens (89) n21.5 t22.5 f22.5 b22.5. I am long enough in the tooth now to remember blends like this found in quiet country hotels in the furthest-flung reaches of the Highlands beyond a generation ago. A wonderfully old-fashioned, traditional one might say, blend of a type that is getting harder and harder to find. 40%. Quality Spirits International.

MacQueens of Scotland Aged 3 Years (86) n20.5 t22 f21.5 b22 Rare to find a blend revealing its age at 3 years, though of course many are that.... and a day. Enjoyable, with attractive weight and even an ulmo honey note to partner the spices which, combined, makes it distinctively a cut above for its type. 40%. Quality Spirits International.

MacQueens of Scotland Aged 8 Years (78.5) n18 t21.5 f19 b20 A little furry and off key. *40%. Quality Spirits International.*

MacQueens of Scotland Aged 12 Years (89.5) n23 certain exotic fruit notes suggest a usage of malts older than 12. Lots of marzipan and vanilla abound as well as a light kumquat note; t22.5 silky delivery with a slow procession of drier vanillas bolstered by muscovado sugars and spice; the spices grow in confidence and effect; f21.5 soft, though the caramel has too great a say; b22.5 some outstanding malts have gone into this charming blend. *40%. Quality Spirits International.*

Master of Malt Blended 10 Years Old 1st Edition (84.5) n21.5 t22.5 f20 b20.5. A pleasant enough, though hardly complex, blend benefitting from the lovely malty, then silky pick-up from delivery and a brief juicy barley sharpness. But unsettled elsewhere due, mainly, to using the wrong fit of grain: too firm when a little give was needed. *47.5%. ncf. WB15/353*

Master of Malt 30 Year Old Blended Scotch Whisky (86) n21.5 t23 f20 b21.5 Typical of Master of Malt blends it is the delivery which hits fever pitch in which myriad juicy notes make a mockery of the great age. Sadly, on this occasion both the nose and finish are undone by some ungainly oak interference and, latterly quite a tang. *47.5%.*

Master of Malt 40 Year Old Blended Scotch Whisky batch 1 (93.5) n24 magnificent! The subtlest hint of kiwi fruit gives extra life to something so ancient: the oaky notes have a threat of spice about them but butterscotch rues; t23.5 adorable barley sugars and grist on delivery with the usual salivating effect that bring. The lower oily grain and tannin notes rumble in as an afterthought and then take command; f22.5 those spices just keep on pulsing; b23.5 some outstanding oak at play here. For a blend the grains and malts appear a little isolated from the other, but the overall effect is still wonderful. *47.5%.*

Master of Malt 50 Year Old Blended Scotch Whisky (92.5) n24 the lightness of touch here is staggering. Malt and lightly spiced vanilla and ulmo honey appear to be polished by a lychee fruitiness; the very vaguest of smoke, too; t23.5 silk, melting in the mouth along with the sweet malty grist. A succession of boiled fruit sweet, especially pear and pineapple give way slightly as a little bitterness and sawdusty dryness seeps in from the oak; f22 a bitter-sweet fade; b23 hard to keep all the casks of over 50 years in line. But so much else is sublime. *47.5%.*

Master Of Malt St Isidore (84) n21 t22 f20 b21. Sweet, lightly smoked but really struggles to put together a coherent story. Something, somewhere, is not quite right. *41.4%*

Matisse 12 Years Old (90.5) n23 t23 f22 b22.5 Moved up yet another notch as this brand continues its development. Much more clean-malt oriented with a Speyside-style to the fore. Majestic and charming. *40%. Matisse Spirits Co Ltd.*

Matisse 21 Years Old (86) n23 t22 f20 b21. Begins breathtakingly on the nose, with a full array of exotic fruit showing the older bourbon casks up to max effect. Nothing wrong with the early delivery, which offers a touch of honeycomb on the grain. But the caramel effect on the finish stops everything in its tracks. Soft and alluring, all the same. *40%*

Matisse Old (85.5) n20 t23 f21 b21.5. Appears to improve each time I come across it. The nose is a bit on the grimy side and the finish disappears under a sea of caramel. But the delivery works deliciously, with a chewy weight which highlights the sweeter malts. *40%*

Matisse Royal (81) n19 t22 f20 b20. Pleasant, if a little clumsy. Extra caramel appears to have scuppered the spice. *40%. Matisse Spirits Co Ltd.*

McArthurs (89.5) n22 t22.5 f22 b23 One of the most improved blends on the market. The clever use of the peat is exceptional. *40%. Inverhouse Distillers.*

Monarch of the Glen (81) n20 t21 f20 b20 A youthful grainfest wallowing in its fat and sweet personality. *40%. Quality Spirits International.*

Monarch of the Glen Aged 8 Years (82.5) n19 t20.5 f21.5 b21.5 The initially harsh grain takes time to settle but eventually finds a decent fudge and spiced mocha theme. *40%. Quality Spirits International.*

Monarch of the Glen Aged 12 Years (88.5) n22 a lovely fudge note goes well with the mocha; t22.5 has kept its glorious silk texture, though the fruits have vanished. Demerara sugar and chocolate hazelnut; f22 long, soft, slow raising of spice and vanilla; b22 I always enjoyed this for its unusual fruity nature. Well, the fruit has gone and been replaced by chocolate. A fair swap: it's still delicious! *40%. Quality Spirits International.*

Montrose (74.5) n18 t20 f18 b18.5. A battling performance but bitter defeat in the end. *40%.*

Muirhead's Blue Seal bott code L15 138 780 21 (84.5) n21.5 t21 f21 b21 A clean, uncluttered and attractive blend with heavy emphasis on grain and no shortage of caramel and spice. A distinct wisp of malt can be located from time to time. *40%. Tullibardine Ltd.*

The Naked Grouse (76.5) n19 t21 f17.5 b19. Sweet. But reveals too many ugly sulphur tattoos. *40%.*

◈ **Nation of Scots** (92.5) n23 the most adroit use of smoke coupled with a vague saltiness – think Arbroath Smokies – sits comfortably with the chalky vanilla and sneezable black pepper;

t23 mouth-filling without being overly cloying or too soft. The smoke guarantees weight and backbone while a light, gristy sweetness ensures another level at work entirely; **f23** back to those spices now; smoke, vanilla and caramel make for a luxurious and satisfying fade; **b23.5** apparently, this is a blend designed to unite Scots around the world. Well, I'm not Scottish but it's won me over. If only more blends could be as deliciously embracing as this. *52%. Annandale Distillery.*

Northern Scot (68) n16 t18 f17 b17. Heading South bigtime. *40%. Bruce and Co. for Tesco.*

Oishii Wisukii Aged 36 Years (96) n24.5 t23.5 f24 b24 Normally, I'd suggest popping into the Highlander for a pint of beer. But if they happen to have any of this stuff there...break his bloody arm off: it's magnificent! *46.2%. The Highlander Inn, Craigellachie.*

Old Masters G (93) **n24** as this was formerly "Freemason's Whisky" the perfect nose to experience blindfolded: as the depth of the fruity muscovado sugar and grain – and their happy intermingling - is charming. Under-ripe gooseberries sits with the citrus; **t23** light, graceful with a fleeting caress of delicate and salivating Speyside malt before the silkier grain and spicier oak kicks in: superbly layered; **f23** long, succulent, beautifully spiced with the growing cocoa and vanilla ensuring balance; **b23** a high quality blend with enough clarity and complexity to suggest they have not stinted on the malt. The nose, in particular, is sublime. Thankfully they have gone easy on the colouring here, as it this is so delicate it could have ruined the artistry. *40%. Lombard Scotch Whisky Ltd.*

Old McDonald (83.5) n20 t22 f20.5 b21. Attractively tart and bracing where it needs to be with lovely grain bite. Lots of toffee, though. *43.%. The Last Drop Distillers. For India.*

Old Parr 12 Years Old (91.5) n21.5 t23.5 f23 b23.5 Perhaps on about the fourth of fifth mouthful, the penny drops that this is not just exceptionally good whisky: it is blending Parr excellence... *40%. Diageo.*

Old Parr Aged 15 Years (84) n19 t22 f21 b22. Absolutely massive sherry input here. Some of it is of the highest order. The nose, reveals, however, that some isn't... *43%*

Old Parr Classic 18 Years Old (84.5) n21 t21.5 f21 b21. A real jumbled, mixed bag with fruit and barley falling over each other and the grains offering little sympathy. Enough to enjoy, but with Old Parr, one expects a little more... *46%. Diageo.*

Old Parr Superior 18 Years Old batch no. L5171 (97) n25 t25 f23 b24. Year in, year out, this blend just gets better and better. This bottling struck me as a possible Whisky of the Year, but perhaps only an outsider. Familiarity, though, bred anything but contempt and over the passing months I have tried to get to the bottom of this truly great whisky. Blended whisky has long needed a champion. This grand old man looks just the chap. This is a worthy, if unexpected (even to me), Jim Murray' Whisky Bible 2007 World Whisky of the Year. *43%.*

Old Smuggler (85.5) n21 t22 f21 b21.5. A much sharper act than its Allied days with a new honeyed-maple syrup thread which is rather delightful. Could still do with toning down the caramel, though, to brighten the picture further. *40%. Campari, France.*

◈ **Old St. Andrews Clubhouse** batch no. L2519 G2362 (89) **n22** the grains are of the firm, bristling type: unusual these days. Spices, bananas and fudge represent the controlled sweetness; **t22.5** magnificently juicy kick to the delivery with malt shewing early before the grains join in and steer the remainder of the course; superb muscovado sugars at play; **f22** still spicy but the toffee-vanilla ensure a soft landing; **b22.5** very neat and tidy – and eminently quaffable. 40%.

◈ **Old St. Andrews Clubhouse** batch no. L2997 G2716 (87.5) n21.5 t22 f22 b22 Just a little extra grain bite to this one means the usual juiciness is down, though the slow spice build is pretty sexy. Lots of coffee-toffee tones to chew over. *40%.*

Passport (83) n22 t19 f21 b21. It looks as though Chivas have decided to take the blend away from its original sophisticated, Business Class J&B/Cutty Sark, style for good now, as they have continued this decently quaffable but steerage quality blend with its big caramel kick and chewy, rather than lithe, body. *40%. Chivas.*

Passport bott code LKBL0720 2017/02/24 (81.5) n20 t21 f20 b20.5 Still can't get used to the brash golden colour of the whisky that shines back at me. This was once the Passport to whisky sophistication: pale and glistening on the palate rather than from the bottle with its cut glass, precision flavour-profile – First Class in every way. Now it is fat, flat, chewy, and fudged in every sense of the word. *40%. Chivas Brothers Ltd.*

Parkers (78) n17 t22 f20 b19. The nose has regressed, disappearing into ever more caramel, yet the mouth-watering lushness on the palate remains and the finish now holds greater complexity and interest. *40%. Angus Dundee.*

Queen Margot (85.5) n21.5 t22 f21 b21. A clean, silky-textured, sweet and caramel-rich blend of disarming simplicity. *40%*

Queen Margot (86) n21 t22 f21.5 b21.5. A lovely blend which makes no effort to skimp on a spicy depth. Plenty of cocoa from the grain late on but no shortage of good whiskies put to work. *40%. Wallace and Young for Lidl.*

Queen Margot Aged 5 Years (89) n22 t22.5 f22 b22.5 A vey attractive blend with a most agreeable level of chewability. The chocolate orange which bolsters the yielding grain appears to suggest some good, clean sherry influence along the way. 40%

Queen Margot Aged 8 Years (85) n21 t22 f21 b21. Pleasant, untaxing, with a hint of oaky vanilla after the sugary crescendo. 40%

Reliance PL (76) n18 t20 f19 b19. Some of the old spiciness evident. But has flattened out noticeably. 43%. Diageo.

Robert Burns (85) n20 t22.5 f21 b21.5. Skeletal and juicy: very little fat and gets to the mouthwatering point pretty quickly. Genuine fun. 40%. Isle of Arran.

The Royal & Ancient (80.5) n20 t21.5 f19 b20. Has thinned out dramatically in the last year or so. Now clean, untaxing, briefly mouth-watering and radiating young grain throughout. 40%

Royal Park (87.5) n22 t22 f22 b21.5 A significantly improved blend which though still showing toffee appears to have cut down the amount, to the advantage of the busy vanilla, Demerara sugar and increased spices. Wholly enjoyable. Incidentally, the label helpfully informs us: "Distilled and Matured in Oak Casks." Who needs stills, eh...? 40%. Quality Spirits International.

Royal Salute 21 Years Old (92.5) n23 t23.5 f23 b23.5 If you are looking for the velvety character of yore, forget it. This one comes with some real character and is much the better for it. The grain, in particular, excels. 40%. Chivas.

Royal Salute 21 Years Old bott code LKSK2858 2016/07/13 (96) n24 a lovely, glinting degree of citrus which just seems to sparkle off the roundest grain imaginable. A little malt can, with care, be detected, adding a Speyside-style barley-biscuity spin; t23.5 succulent, though this time the malt is detectable earlier and more easily. The silky vanillas make for a soothing backdrop, though the spices are too half-hearted to be true; a mix of gristy sugars and muscovado makes for a light sweetness; f24 a very quiet finale with the grains again clearly leading the way. Vague spicing as the butterscotch slowly builds while the praline cannot be ignored; b24.5 elegant, sensual and the epitome of great blending. What else would you expect...? 40%. Chivas Brothers Ltd.

Royal Salute 21 Years Old The Polo Collection bott code 2017/04/25 LPNL0722 (95) n23.5 wow! A very different nose to the standard RS21: much earthier, warmer and bolder with a significant degree of tannin further adding weight; t23.5 an oilier texture than the norm helps embed the light smoke and tannins without them causing too much of a storm. The grain is slightly firmer and more prickly (actually, for anyone interested in this kind of thing this appears to have a slightly different grain structure to the standard RS21). Exceptionally chewy, again with an earthiness displayed on the nose and a bigger spice surge than usual; f24 long, with a wonderfully clever mix of Manuka honey with rich vanilla. That telling earthiness and spice continues its journey uninterrupted...; b24 a significantly different RS21 to the last standard bottling I came across, this being very much meatier – which is rather apt seeing that horses are involved. Mixes suave sophistication with a certain ruggedness: not unlike polo, I suppose. Not a dram to chukker away under any circumstances... 40%. Chivas Brothers Ltd.

Royal Salute 32 Years Old Union of the Crowns bott code 2017/01/17 LPNL0102 (96.5) n24 a glossy nose in part, a lively, slightly sharp and fruity aroma in another: beautifully weighted and intriguing; some of the lilting oak and grain notes appear significantly above the 32 years stated...; t24.5 magnificent...just so elegant. Allow it to sit on the palate, swirl it around gently and then just swoon as it melts in the mouth, leaving the most gorgeous deposits to be savoured. The honey is a blend in itself, with ulmo and heather at the forefront then a little orange blossom arriving towards the midway mark; the spices take their time to arrive, survey what they find and slowly begin to build in intensity, but only to a point. The texture is silk, helped along by a butteryness, the cream toffee...; f24 so long and remains elegant, eschewing the bitterness which often marks blends of this age. The spices still keep at their same pace and intensity; b24 I trust Nicola Sturgeon has given The Union of Crowns, this truly outstanding and worthy Scotch blend to celebrate the joining the kingdoms of England, Scotland and Ireland, her seal of approval and she will help promote it fervently as a great Scottish export... 40%. Chivas Brothers Ltd. ⊙

Royal Salute 38 Years Old Stone of Destiny bott code 2016/12/20 LPNK2479 (93.5) n24 oozes classic, understated ancient whisky notes, the grain in particular. Two toned in being seemingly soft but look closer and you'll find a much firmer crust beneath. The vast majority the aromas are oak-led, though this has been carefully and cleverly camouflaged by the lightest layering of ulmo honey which represents the malt with distinction but light enough to allow the more delicate kumquats and barely audible spices to underscore the great age; t23.5 there you go: the mouth feel as anticipated! So soft and delicate, the gentle sugars melting before making any great statement; this is a blend based on whispers and rumours, rather than bold speeches. Salivating thanks to both a trickle of malt and honey. The grain does all in its power not to be noticed, yet accommodate all...; f22.5 didn't see the light bitterness coming at the death, or such late arrival of spice; b23.5 knowing the blender and having a pretty educated guess at the range of stocks he would have to work from, I tried to picture in my mind's eye how this whisky would nose and taste even before I opened the bottle. In particular, I tried to pre-guess the mouth feel, a character vital especially in older blends but often overlooked by those who eventually taste it, though it actually plays a significant role without the drinker realising it. Well, both the nose and mouth feel were just as I had imagined, though some aspects of the finish were slightly different. An engrossing and elegant dram. 40%. *Chivas Brothers Ltd.*

Royal Salute 62 Gun Salute (95.5) n24.5 t24 f23 b24 How do you get a bunch of varying whiskies in style, but each obviously growing a grey beard and probably cantankerous to boot, to settle in and harmonise with the others? A kind of Old People's Home for whisky, if you like. Well, here's how...43%. *Chivas.*

Royal Salute The Diamond Tribute (91) n23.5 t23 f21.5 b23. Ironic that a diamond is probably the hardest natural creation, yet this whisky is one of man's softest... 40%. *Chivas.*

Royal Salute The Eternal Reserve (89.5) n23 t23.5 f21 b22 One of those strange whiskies where so much happens on the nose and delivery, but much less when we head to the finish 40%

Royal Silk Reserve (93) n22 t24 f24 b23 I named this the best newcomer of 2001 and it hasn't let me down. A session blend for any time of the day, this just proves that you don't need piles of peat to create a blend of genuine stature. A must have. 40%

Royal Silk Reserve Aged 5 Years (92.5) n23 t23 f23 b23.5 I was lucky enough to be the first person outside the tasting lab to sample this whisky when it was launched at the turn of this century. It was quite wonderful then, it still is so today though the grains aren't quite as brittle and translucent as they were back then. Still, I admire beyond words the fact that the current blenders have eschewed the craze for obscuration by ladelling in the colouring as though lives depended on it. What we can nose and taste here in this heart-gladdeningly light (both in colour and personality) blend is whisky. As an aside, very unusual for a blend to hide its age away on the back label. 40%.

Royal Warrior (86) n21 t22 f21.5 b21.5. An entirely pleasant grain-rich, young, old fashioned blend which masters the prevalent sugars well when they appear to be getting out of hand. Extremely clean and beautifully rounded. 40%

Sandy Mac (76) n18 t20 f19 b19. Basic, decent blend that's chunky and raw. 40%. *Diageo.*

Scots Earl (76.5) n18 t20 f19 b19.5. Its name is Earl. And it must have upset someone in a previous life. Always thrived on its engaging disharmony. But just a tad too syrupy now. 40%.

Scottish Collie (78) n18 t20 f20 b20 I thought I heard you saying it was a pity: pity I never had any good whiskies. But you're wrong. I have. Thousands of them. Thousands of them. And all drams.... 40%. *Quality Spirits International.*

Scottish Collie (80) n20 t21 f19 b20 A greatly improved bend with a far more vivacious delivery full of surprising juiciness and attractively controlled sweetness. Not as much toffee influence as had once been the case, so the spices cancels out the harsh finish. 43%. *Quality Spirits International.*

Scottish Leader Aged 12 Years bott code P037533 L3 09.18 16082 (89.5) n22 t23 f22 b22.5 A vast improvement on the last Leader 12 I encountered, this really finding a relaxed yet intriguing style. 40%.

Scottish Leader Original bott code P03 555 L 08.35 16342 (83) n19 t22 f21 b21 Had this been the "original" Scottish leader I tasted 20 or so years ago we'd have a lighter coloured, less caramel heavy, more malt sparkling whisky. As it is, overcomes a cramped nose to offer some excellent complexity on delivery. 40%.

Scottish Leader Signature bott code P038914 L316256 (90.5) n22 t23.5 f22 b23 Thoroughly enjoyable and beautifully constructed blend in which thought has clearly gone into both weight, texture and flavour profiling: not a given for blends these days. The nose and delivery are waxy with a vague honey richness; the delivery uses that honey to full effect by offering a growing firmness and then busy interplay between light oak, spices and weightier malts. Had they gone a little easier on the dumbing-down toffee, this might have bagged an award. 40%.

Scottish Leader Supreme bott code P039255 L3 14.21 16278 (77) n18.5 t20 f19 b19.5 Sticky, sweet and overly simple. 40%.

Scottish Piper (80) n20 t20 f20 b20. A light, mildly- raw, sweet blend with lovely late vanilla intonation. 40%

Scottish Piper bott code L17033 (82) n20 t20 f21.5 b20.5 Continues its traditional toffee drone, though with a spicier finale than before. 40%. *Burlington Drinks.*

Scottish Prince (83.5) n21 t22 f20 b20.5. Muscular, but agreeably juicy. 40%

Sia Blended Scotch Whisky (87) n21 t22.5 f21.5 b22. Rare to find a blend that's so up front with its smoke. Doesn't scrimp on the salivation stakes or sheer chewiness, either. 43% .

Sir Lawrence bott code: L17 03274 CB2 (87) n21 t22.5 f21.5 b22 An impressively clean blend having been matured in better quality oak. This allows you to enjoy the full-throttle delivery without fear of any tangy, off-note sub plots. The caramels do get a little too enthusiastic towards the end but before then the grain and Demerara sugars dig in for a delicious degree of mocha. 40%.

Something Special (85) n21.5 t22 f20.5 b21. Mollycoddled by toffee, any murderous tendencies seem to have been fudged away, leaving just the odd moment of attractive complexity. You suspect there is a hit man in there somewhere trying to get out. 40%. Chivas.

Something Special bott code LPFK 1116 2016/06/30 (90) n22 lifted dramatically by a gentle citrus note adding to the cream toffee: a very clean but soft nose...; t22.5 gorgeously lush without going down the cloyingly sweet route so many blends do, this enjoys a deliciously spiced honey middle and even the odd shaft of malt clearly bursting through; f23 the light tannins arrive with some toffee, but still that honey and spice continues; b22.5 one of the few blends that has actually improved in recent years. Always been an attractive, interesting if non-spectacular blend which I have enjoyed when meeting it at various bars with friends around the world. Now there is personality enough to punch through the toffee and leave you wanting more. 40%. Chivas Brothers Ltd.

Something Special Legacy (92) n23 t22.5 f23 b23.5 Good, solid blender is David Boyd. And here he has married substance with subtlety. Lovely stuff. 40%

Something Special Premium Aged 15 Years (89) n22 t23 f21 b23 Fabulous malt thread and some curious raisiny/sultana fruitiness, too. A blend-lover's blend. 40%.

Stag Hunter (79) n19 t20 f20 b20 Hard to get past the gin-type nose. Not sure if this is a bottling hall issue, or if we have a blend that celebrates a botanical-style personality. 40%. Burlington Drinks.

Stag's Head Blended Scotch Whisky (85.5) n21.5 t21.5 f21 b21.5. A thick, hefty nose and body, lush grain and lashings of caramel. Pleasant, sweet, nutty standard stuff. 40% (80 proof)

Stewart's Old Blended (93) n22.5 t24 f23 b23.5 Really lovely whisky for those who like to close their eyes, contemplate and have a damned good chew. 40%

Storm (94) n23 t23.5 t24 b23.5. A little gem of a blend that will take you by storm. 43%.

Talisman 5 Years Old (85.5) n22 t22 f20.5 b21. Unquestionably an earthier, weightier version of what was once a Speyside romp. Soft peats also add extra sweetness. 40%

Teacher's Aged 25 Years batch 1 (96.5) n24 t24.5 f23.5 b24.5 Only 1300 bottles means they will be hard pushed to create this exact style again. Worth a go, chaps: considering this is India bound, it is the Karma Sutra of blended scotch. 46%. Beam Inc. 1300 bottles. India & Far East Travel Retail exclusive.

Teacher's Highland Cream (90) n23 t23 f22 b22 Not yet back to its best but a massive improvement on the 2005 bottlings. Harder grains to accentuate the malt will bring it closer to the classic of old. 40%

Teacher's Origin (92) n23 t23 f23 b23 Almost brings a tear to the eye to taste a Scotch blend that really is a blend. With a better grain input (Dumbarton, say),this perhaps would have been one of the contenders of World Whisky of the Year. Superb! 40%

Teacher's Origin (88.5) n22 t23.5 f21 b22 A fascinating blend among the softest on the market today. That is aided and abetted by the exceptionally high malt content, 65%, which makes this something of an inverted blend, as that, for most established brands, is the average grain content. What appears to be a high level of caramel also makes for a rounding of the edges, as well as evidence of sherry butts. The bad news is that that has resulted in a duller finish than perhaps might have been intended, which is even more pronounced given the impressive speech made on delivery. Lovely whisky, yes. But something, I feel, of a work in progress. Bringing the caramel down by the percentage points of the malt would be a very positive start... 42.8%. ncf.

Té Bheag (86) n22 t21 f21.5 b21.5. Classic style of rich caramels and bite. 40%. ncf.

Té Bheag bott code L 06 12 16 3 (83) n19 t22 f21 b21 Reverted to its mucky nose of yore but though caramel has the loudest voice it has retained its brilliant spice bite. 40%. ncf.

Tesco Special Reserve Minimum 3 Years Old bott code L6335 16/04171 (83.5) n19 t22 f21.5 b21 Improved of late. Now unashamedly in the date and walnut school of blends, where before it had only dabbled; thick, uncompromisingly sweet and cloying but with enough spice and salivation to make for pleasant and characterful bit of fun. 40%.

That Boutique-y Whisky Company Blended Whisky No. 1 50 Year Old (96) n23.5 a blended whisky of box of chocolate liqueurs....? t25 as soft as a loving coo. Fruit then light, creamy fudgy caramels alight on the palate and then seems to magically transform into the milkiest chocolate mousse as a little Manuka and ulmo honey slowly dissolves into the mix: possibly the best delivery of any blend this year...; f23.5 just thins a little as the vanillas take up a more prominent position; b24 some of the moments encountered in this blend are the exact reason why no spirit on this planet comes close to whisky at its very finest. 46.6%. 2,000 bottles.

That Boutique-y Whisky Company Blended Whisky No. 2 18 Year Old (86.5) n20 t22.5 f22 b22 The caramels from the oak are quite startling. The off-key nose is best ignored but lovers of fruity fudge will have a field day. 46.7%. 1,132 bottles.

That Boutique-y Whisky Company Blended Whisky No. 3 23 Year Old (91) n21 t23.5 f23 b23.5 From the stuttering start on the nose this turns into rich, well-layered blend with no age scars whatsoever. 48.2%. 463 bottles.

The Tweeddale Blend Aged 10 Years (89.5) n22 t23.5 f21.5 b22.5 The first bottling of this blend since World War 2, it has been well worth waiting for. 46%. ncf. 50% malt. Stonedean.

The Tweeddale Blended Scotch Whisky Aged 14 Years batch 5 (92) n22.5 t23.5 f23 b23 I was salivating just at the prospect of this one, as I remember what a fresh article Batch 4 was. Well, this is even sharper in some places...yet curiously far more laid back and docile in others. 46%. nc ncf.

◇◇ **Tweedale 28 Year Old Evolution** (89) n22.5 robust fruit: clean and clear with a subtle blood orange nuance; t23 it's the malts which pin your attention first: there is just so much of it! Gristy despite the years, with the fruit slowing making its mark, threading cleverly into the barley; f21 bitters out slightly too enthusiastically; b22.5 a blend seemingly teeming in malt and helped greatly by the natural cask strength. A blended Scotch single malt lovers will miss at their peril. 52%. R & B Distillers.

Ushers Green Stripe (85) n19 t22.5 f21.5 b22. Upped a notch or two in all-round quality. The juicy theme and clever weight is highly impressive and enjoyable. 43%. Diageo.

VAT 69 (84.5) n20 t22 f21 b21.5. Has thickened up in style: weightier, more macho, much more to say and a long way off that old lightweight. A little cleaning up wouldn't go amiss. 40%

Walton Royal Blend Deluxe Reserve (91.5) n22.5 t23 f23 b23 It's amazing what a dose of good quality peaty whisky can do to a blend. Certainly ensures it stands out as a deliciously chewy – and smoky – experience.43%

White Horse (90.5) n22 t23 f22.5 b23 A malt which has subtly changed shape. Not just the smoke which gives it weight, but you get the feeling that some of Diageo's less delicate malts have been sent in to pack a punch. As long as they are kept in line, as is the case here – just – we can all enjoy a very big blend. 40%. Diageo.

White Horse Aged 12 Years (86) n21 t23 f21 b21. Enjoyable, complex if not always entirely harmonious. For instance, the apples and grapes on the nose appear on a limb from the grain and caramel and nothing like the thoroughbred of old. Lighter, more flaccid and caramel dominated. 40%. Diageo.

Whyte & Mackay Aged 13 Years bott code L6334 14/04116 (89.5) n22 attractive, tangy spiced kumquat; caramel....; t23.5 a toffee fruit bar with muscovado sugars lightening the load; still big and mouth-filling and even juicy; a little liquorice links with the date and walnut signature; f22 toffee and butterscotch, though with a late furry fade; b22 like the standard Whyte and Mackay...but thirteen years old and a little lighter... 40%.

Whyte & Mackay Triple Matured bott code 16/04120 L6329 (86.5) n21 t23.5 f20.5 b21.5 The kind of blend you can not only stand your spoon up in but your knife - table or carving - and fork – table or pitch - as well. The nose suggests something furry is in the offing which, sadly, the finale confirms. But the delivery really is such wonderful fun! Thick with intense toffee, which shapes both its flavour and mouth feel, and concentrated date and walnut cake. Roasty yet sweet thanks to the molasses this is about the chewiest blend on the market today. 40%.

William Lawson's Finest (85) n18.5 t22.5 f22 b22. Not only has the label become more colourful, but so, too, has the whisky. However that has not interfered with the joyous old-fashioned grainy bite. A complex and busy blend from the old charm school. 40%

William Lawson's Scottish Gold Aged 12 Years (89) n22 t23 f22 b22. For years Lawson's 12 was the best example of the combined wizardry of clean grain, unpeated barley and good bourbon cask that you could find anywhere in the world: a last-request dram before the firing squad. Today it is still excellent, but just another sherried blend. What's that saying about if it's not being broke...? 40%

Windsor 12 Years Old (81) n20 t21 f20 b20. Thick, walloped-on blend that you can stand a spoon in. Hard at times to get past the caramel. 40%. Diageo.

Windsor Aged 17 Years Super Premium (89) n23 t22 f22 b22. Still on the safe side for all its charm and quality. An extra dose of complexity would lift this onto another level. 40%

Windsor 21 Years Old (90) n20 t23 f24 b23. Recovers fabulously from the broken nose and envelopes the palate with a silky-sweet style unique to the Windsor scotch brand. Excellent. 40%. Diageo.

Ye Monks (86) n20 t23 f21.5 b21.5. Just hope they are praying for less caramel to maximize the complexity. Still, a decent spicy chew and outstanding bite which is great fun and worth finding when in South America. 40%. Diageo.

Irish Whiskey

Of all the whiskies in the world, it is Irish which probably causes most confusion amongst both established whisk(e)y lovers and the novices.

Ask anyone to define what is unique to Irish whiskey - apart from it being made in Ireland and the water likewise coming from that isle - and the answer, if the audiences around the world at my tastings are anything to go by, are in this order: i) it is triple distilled; ii) it is never, ever, made using peat; iii) they exclusively use sherry casks; iv) it comes from the oldest distillery in the world; v) it is made from a mixture of malted and unmalted barley.

Only one of these answers is true: the fifth. This is usually the final answer extracted from the audience when the last hand raised sticks to his or her guns after the previous four responses have been shot down.

And it is this type of whiskey, known as Irish Pot Still, which has again - indeed, for the eighth consecutive year - been named as Irish Whiskey of the Year. In 2016 it was the Midleton Dair Ghaelach, in 2014 and 2013 it was the Redbreast 12-years-old and in 2012 Power's John's Lane. Last year it was, just like 2017 and previously in 2015, the Jameson Redbreast 21-years-old. And this year....? Redbreast 12 once more! Considering that 25 years ago Irish Distillers had decided to end the bottling of Pure Pot Still, not bad. Just shows what a little campaigning can do.... Remarkable as it may seem, after the best part of a century of contraction within the industry, much of it as painful as it was brutal, there were only four distilleries operating on the entire island of Ireland in the autumn of 2011. Now there are 17. The question is: how many are planning to make a Pot Still to challenge Midleton's...?

Jim Murray's Whisky Bible Irish Whiskey of the Year Winners

	Irish Whiskey	Irish Pot Still Whiskey	Irish Single Malt	Irish Blend	Irish Single Cask
2004	Jameson	N/A	N/A	N/A	N/A
2005	Jameson	N/A	N/A	N/A	N/A
2006	Bushmills 21	N/A	N/A	N/A	N/A
2007	Redbreast 15	N/A	N/A	N/A	N/A
2008	Tyrconnel 10	N/A	N/A	N/A	N/A
2009	Jameson 07	N/A	N/A	N/A	N/A
2010	Redbreast 12	N/A	N/A	N/A	N/A
2011	Sainsbury's Dun Leire 8	N/A	N/A	N/A	N/A
2012	Powers John's Lane	N/A	Sainsbury's Dun Leire 8	N/A	Jameson 2007 Vintage
2013	Redbreast 12 Year Old	Redbreast 12 C.Strength	Bushmills Aged 21	Jameson	Tyrconnell 11 Year Old
2014	Redbreast 12 C.Strength	Redbreast 12 C.Strength	Bushmills Aged 21	Jameson	N/A
2015	Redbreast Aged 21	Redbreast Aged 21	Bushmills Aged 21	Jameson	N/A
2016	Midleton Dair Ghaelach	Midleton Dair Ghaelach	SMWS 118.3 Cooley 1991	Powers Gold Label	N/A
2017	Redbreast Aged 21	Redbreast Aged 21	Bushmills Aged 21	Jameson	Teeling S C 2004
2018	Redbreast Aged 21	Redbreast Aged 21	Bushmills Aged 16	Bushmills Black Bush	Dunville'sVR First Edition
2019	Redbreast 12 C.Strength	Redbreast 12 C.Strength	Bushmills Aged 12	Bushmills Black Bush	Irishman Aged 17

Pure Pot Still
MIDLETON (old distillery)

Midleton 25 Years Old Pot Still db (92) n24 t24 f21 b23. A really enormous whiskey that is in the truest classic Irish style. The un-malted barley really does make the tastebuds hum and the oak has added fabulous depth. Interesting when tasted against an American rye – the closeness of the character is there to be experienced, but also the differences. A subtle mature whiskey of unquestionable quality. Superb. 43%

Midleton 30 Years Old Pot Still db (85) n19 t22 f22 b22. A typically brittle, crunchy Irish pot still whiskey (a mixture of malted and unmalted barley) appears to absorb age better than most other grain spirits. This one is in its element. But drink at full strength and at body temp (it is pretty closed when cool) for the most startling – and memorable effects. I have no idea how much this costs. But if you can find one and afford it... then buy it!! 56%

Midleton 1973 Pure Pot Still db (95) n24 t24 f23 b24. The enormous character of true Irish pot still whiskey (a mixture of malted and unmalted barley) appears to absorb age better than most other grain spirits. This one is in its element. But drink at full strength and at body temp (it is pretty closed when cool) for the most startling – and memorable effects. I have no idea how much this costs. But if you can find one and afford it... then buy it!! 56%

MIDLETON (new distillery) County Cork.

Green Spot db (94.5) n23.5 t24 f23.5 b23.5. This honeyed state has remained a few years, and its sharpness has now been regained. Complex throughout. Unquestionably one of the world's greatest branded whiskies. 40%. *Irish Distillers for Mitchell & Son, Dublin.*

Green Spot bott code L622831252 db (95) n23.5 t23.5 f24 b24 A slightly different weight, pace and sugar emphasis to this bottling. But remains a true classic. 40%.

Green Spot Château Léoville Barton finished in Bordeaux Wine Casks db (83.5) n21.5 t22.5 f19 b20.5. Have a kind of proprietarily, fatherly feel about Green Spot, as it was an unknown whiskey outside Ireland until revealed to the world 21 years ago in my Irish Whiskey Almanac. And fitting this is finished in Ch. Leoville Barton as I have a fair bit of that from the 70s and 80s in my cellar – and the creators of Green Spot was Dublin's oldest wine shop. However, after all that, have to say that this is a disappointment. There are warning signs on the nose and confirmation on the finish that the wine barrel did not escape the dastardly sulphur treatment. Which means it is dull where it should be bright, though the delivery does reach out for complexity and there are some excellent light cocoa moments. But the sulphur wins. 46%

Green Spot Château Léoville Barton finished in Bordeaux wine casks, bott code L622331248 db (79) n20 t22 f18 b19 I'd so desperately like to see this work. But, once again, far too tight and bitter for its own good. The damaging sulphur note is worthy of neither the great Green Spot or Leoville Barton names... 46%.

Green Spot Chateau Montelena Zinfandel wine cask finished, bott code: L719331280 db (88) n23 a spicy, dry introduction, brittle muscovado sugars and butterscotch slowly coming into play; t23.5 ridiculously salivating. But that comes after the marriage of concentrated grape and muscovado sugars hit the palate. Dark cherry at play, sitting atop vanilla and light mocha; f19.5 not too sure about this. Definitely a bitterness is dragging through this for a little too long not too dissimilar to the problem we find from Jerez: no, please don't tell me...; b22 there is something fitting that Green Spot, an Irish Pot Still whiskey brand created many generations back by Dublin's Premier wine merchants, should find itself creating new ground...in a wine cask. Any European whisk(e)ys matured in American wine casks are thin on the ground. That they should be Chateau Montelena from Napa Valley makes this all the more remarkable. Does it work? Well, yes and no. The unique style of Irish Pot Still is lost somewhat under a welter of fruity blows and the fuzzy, imprecise finish is definitely off key. But there is no denying that it is a whiskey which does possess the odd magic moment. 46%.

Master Distiller's Selection Single Pot db (94) n23.5 t23.5 f23 b24 At the sweeter end of the Pot Still spectrum. The use of fruit as a background noise, rather than a lead, is a masterstroke. 46%. 500 bottles. ncf.

Method and Madness Single Pot Irish Whiskey bourbon barrels, finished in Virgin Hungarian oak (94) n23 a fascinating nose: the tannins feign to be fierce, yet tap the nose more playfully than you might expect. The pot still whisky, usually the centre of attention, for once plays a strict second fiddle; t23.5 a brilliant burst of dark sugars on delivery, all oak-inspired, then backed up handsomely by the firmness of the pot still...something very different, indeed; f23.5 the tannins return for an encore, perhaps this time a little more determined to make a spicy mark. But light caramels and firmer grins hang on in with the liquorice and chocolate to present a unusually long and complex finale; b24 now there was a nose! One that took me back almost 25 years to when I was visiting the Czech whisky distilleries soon after the fall of the communist regime. That whisky was matured in local oak, offering a near identical aroma to this Irish. 46%.

Method and Madness Single Pot Still Irish Whiskey sherry & American barrels, finished in French chestnut casks db (88) n22 t23 f21 b22.5 Ah...memories of the late 1970s or perhaps very early '80s. Walking in the lonely autumnal forests surrounding the tiny French village of Evecquemont, taking my girlfriend's family's soppy Alsatian for long walks, during which I would hoover up wild sweet chestnuts by the score. Never then figured it playing a part in whisky, especially Irish. Not sure it is the perfect marriage, but certainly adds to the whiskey lexicon. 46%.

Midleton Barry Crockett Legacy db (94) n23.5 t24.5 f22.5 b23.5. Another fabulous Pot Still, very unusual for its clever use of the varied ages of the oak to form strata of intensity. One very sophisticated whiskey. 46%. ncf.

Midleton Barry Crockett Legacy American bourbon barrels, bott code L623631258 db (95) n23.5 t24 f23.5 b24 Thank God for my dear old friend Barry Crockett. One of the top three most knowledgeable whiskey/whisky people I have known in my lifetime, you can at least be relieved that his name is synonymous with a truly great spirit. Fittingly, his whiskey is free of sherry butts, so I can just sit back and enjoy and not be on tenterhooks waiting for the first signs of a disastrous sulphur note to take hold. Indeed, the only thing that takes hold of you here is the Pot Still's stunning beauty... 46%. ncf.

Midleton Dair Ghaelach db (97) n23.5 t25 f24 b24.5 For heaven's sake. This is just too ridiculously beautiful...and so unmistakably Irish for all the virgin oak. Truly world class. 58.1%

Midleton Dair Ghaelach Bluebell Forest Castle Blunden Estate finished in virgin native Irish oak hogsheads, batch no. 1, tree number 1, bott code: L628033271 db (90.5) n22.5 a seemingly cordial and ultra-relaxed nose as the caramel floods in. But below the surface the bolder, nippier tannins thud home; t23.5 and it those slightly aggressive oak tones which grabs the palate – and your attention - first with a warming, tart, spiciness. The caramel on the nose is a true reflection of the reality on the palate, though the light maple syrup comes in like the 7th cavalry; f22 persistent caramel; once the sugars are exhausted the tannins become a little too forceful; b23 the vibrant pungency is matched equally by the grand dollops of natural caramel. 55.3%.

Midleton Dair Ghaelach Grinsell's Wood Ballaghtobin Estate American bourbon barrels, finished in Irish oak hogsheads, batch no. 1, tree no. 7, bott code L504031020 db (97.5) n24 t25 f24 b24.5 What we have here, if I'm not very much mistaken, is a potential World Whisky of the Year. Rarely these days am I given an entirely new flavour profile to chew on. Not only do I have that, but I am struggling to find any faults at all. Ireland is not known for its mountains: well, it certainly has one now. 57.9%. ncf.

Paddy Centenary Edition db (93) n22 t23.5 f24 b23.5. This 7-year-old Pure Pot Still whiskey really is a throwback. All Paddy's original whiskey from this era would have been from the old Midleton distillery which sits, in aspic, beside the one opened in 1975. Even with the likelihood of oats being in the mash in those days, still can't believe the original would have been quite as sweet on the palate — and soul — as this. 43%

Powers Aged 12 Years John's Lane Release db (96.5) n24 t25 f23.5 b24 This is a style of Irish Pot Still I have rarely seen outside the blending lab. I had many times thought of trying to find some of this and bottling it myself. No need now. I think I have just tasted Irish Whiskey of the Year, and certainly one of the top five world whiskies of the year. 46%

Powers Aged 12 Years John's Lane Release bott code L623731261 (96) n23.5 t24.5 f23.5 b24.5 A slightly different slant on the toffee and fudge — and now has a degree of rye-recipe bourbon about it - but firmly remains the go to Pot Still of quite staggering beauty. 46%. ncf.

Powers Signature Release bott code L433231240 (87.5) n21 t23 f21.5 b22 A much lazier version of this excellent Pot Still than I have become used to. Far too much fudge at play here, undermining the layering and complexity. Sexy and chewy for sure and a must for those into dried dates. But the usual Pot Still character is a little masked and the usual slightly off key sherry butt turns up at the very last moment. 46%. ncf.

Powers Three Swallow Release bott code L617051171 (83.5) n21 t21 f21.5 b20 Pleasant. No off notes. But vanishes into a sea of toffee. The fact it is pure Pot Still, apparently, is actually impossible to determine, In the last six months I have seen three swallows: a barn swallow, a Pacific and aa Wire-tailed. Wherever I saw them in the world, India, The Philippines, my back garden, they all swooped and darted in joyous abandon. This Three Swallow by Powers has, by vivid contrast, had its wings clipped. 40%. ncf.

Redbreast Aged 12 Years bott code L634031413 db (88.5) n22.5 t23 f21 b22 By far the flattest Redbreast I have tasted since...well, ever. Far too much reliance on obviously first-fill sherry, which had flattened out and virtually buried the unique personality of the Pot Still itself. Enjoyable, for sure. Beautiful, even, in its own way. But it should be so much better than this... 40%.

Redbreast Aged 12 Years Cask Strength batch B1/11 db (96) n24.5 t24.5 f23 b24 This is Irish pot still on steroids. And sporting an Irish brogue as thick as my great great grandfather John Murray's. To think, had I not included Redbreast in Jim Murray's Irish Whiskey Almanac back in 1994, after it had already been unceremoniously scrapped and discontinued, while championing the then entirely unknown Irish Pot Still cause this brand would no longer have been with us. If I get run over by a bus tomorrow, at least I have that as a tick when St Peter is totting up the plusses and minuses... And with the cask strength, he might even give me two... 57.7%. ncf. Irish Distillers.

Redbreast Aged 12 Years Cask Strength batch no. B1/13 db (95.5) n24 t24 f23.5 b24 Oh, for that bitterness. A potential World Whisky of the Year otherwise? Perhaps... 59.9%. ncf.

Redbreast Aged 12 Years Cask Strength Edition batch no. B1/16 db (86.5) n22.5 t23 f20 b21 Again, far, far too much sherry on this has completely skewed the character. The Pot Still does fight through for some beautiful and massive moments early on, but it simply can't win the battle against the overwhelming fresh grape. Sulphur builds up at the end to put the tin hat on it... 57.2%. ncf.

◇ **Redbreast Aged 12 Years Cask Strength** batch no. B1/17 db (97) n24 perhaps the ultimate pot still meets bourbon/rye nose. One of the hardest, flinty aromas on the market, yet somehow there is a secondary softness to encompass the fruit. The pot still simply pulses from the glass, the bourbon-style tannin on its tail all the way; t24.5 sensational delivery: the full strength of the whiskey allows the oils to cling with stunning purpose, maximising every last crunchy grain profile and ensuring the brown sugars absorb the oak with ease; f24 long with a significant build-up of spicy molasses, toasted raisin...and enormous pot still. Wow!! b24.5 a potential World Whisky of the Year 2019: the first in over a 1,000 tasted so far whiskies I could say that about. It really is that good...! 58.2%.

Redbreast 15 Years Old db (94) n23 t24 f23 b24. For years I have been pleading for Irish Distillers to launch a pot still at 46%, natural colour and unchillfiltered. Well, I've got two out of three wishes. And what we have here is a truly great Irish whiskey and my pulse races in the certain knowledge it can get better still... 46%. ncf. France.

Redbreast Aged 15 Years bott code L624931266 db (84) n21 t22 f20 b21 When you have this much sherry influence on a whiskey, it is likely that one day you will fall foul of the odd furry butt, as is the case here. 46%. ncf.

Redbreast Aged 21 Years db (96) n24 t25 f23 b24 I have tasted no shortage of 21-year-old pot still before in my career, but that was some time back when the whiskey in question was usually from the original Jameson distillery in Dublin, or Power's. I also managed to get my hands on some old stuff from the original Midleton as well as Tullamore Dew and few others. That old spirit had been made at a time when those distilleries were in the process of being closed down and the quality was nothing like it once was. This, I admit, is the first I can remember from Midleton's rebuilt distillery and it knocks the spots of the Jameson and Power's. Those did not have the balance or the insouciance so far as the honey involvement was concerned or the all-round world-class star quality which positively radiates from the glass. Hopefully this gentle giant amongst the world's truly great whiskies and near blue print for the perfect pot still Irish is here to stay. Only for the next bottling absolutely no need for the pointless caramel and the damaging sherry, both which contribute in tarnishing the dazzling sheen. There are times when less is so significantly more. 46%. ncf. WB15/417

Redbreast Aged 21 Years bott code L612731109 db (97) n24.5 t24 f24 b24.5 The mercifully restrained fruit and absolute total 100% absence of sulphur allows the Pot Still to display its not inconsiderable beauty unmolested and to the fullest extent. One of the world's most beautiful and iconic whisk(e)ys without doubt. The fact that so many facets of this whiskey are allowed to say their piece, yet never over-run their time and that the tenets are equally divided makes this one of the truly great whiskeys of the year. 46%. ncf.

◇ **Redbreast Aged 32 Years Dream Cask** db (96.5) n24 real old school sherry eclipsing the pot still depth. Metallic and firm, even when the thinned Manuka honey kicks in. Lightly toasty...as it should be; t24.5 can't ask for much more than that: a velvety arrival with the muscovado sugars and sultanas up front...then a slow march of the grain, firming things up considerably. Salivating from the first moment, and the age is underlined by the mix of old Guyana rum notes and rye-like sharpness, boring into the hickory and mocha; f23.5 finishes surprisingly swiftly, though the residual spice does extend the tail; b24 a fabulous pot still very comfortable in its ancient clothes. Marvellous! 46.5%.

Redbreast All Sherry Single Cask db (73.5) n17 t23.5 f15 b18. I mean: seriously guys....??? A single cask pure pot still whiskey and you bottle one with sulphur fingerprints all over it? I don't have the number of what cask this is from, so I hope yours will have come from clean sherry. If you have, you are in for a treat, because the sheer brilliance and magnitude of this whiskey was able to blot out the sulphur for a good seven or eight seconds as it reached heights of near perfection. A bowl of raspberries now and a 20 minute break to help cleanse my palate and relieve my tongue which is still seriously furred up. So frustrating, as I could see a clean butt of this getting Single Cask Whisky of the Year ... 59.9%. sc.

Redbreast Mano a Lámh db (85) n22.5 t22.5 f19 b21. Curious that on an all sherry butt bottling, the most enjoyable flavour profile is a spiced chocolate one which begins about four or five beats after the original big, soppy, lush delivery. No prizes for guessing why the score goes down towards the finish. By the way: love the robin on the label – a kind of weird cross between an immature and adult robin with the face of a white wagtail thrown in. Like the whiskey type: unique! 46%. ncf.

Redbreast Lustau Edition sherry finish, bott code L622131242 db (89.5) n22.5 t23.5 f22 b21.5 I somehow would have thought that, considering recent younger bottlings, going to the trouble of making a special sherry finish for a Redbreast is on a par with giving a gift of a barrel of sand to the Tuaregs... This bottling is attractive enough, with the fruit at its best on delivery when the whiskey goes through a spectacularly delicious phase. But this soon wears out, leaving a bitterness and slightly lopsided feel, especially at the death, as the balance struggles to be maintained. For those of you I know who refuse to touch anything sherry, this is entirely sulphur free I'm delighted to report. 46%. ncf.

Yellow Spot Aged 12 Years bourbon, sherry and Malaga casks db (88.5) n23.5 t22.5 f20 b22.5. If anything, just a shade too many wine casks used which somewhat drowns out the unique IP character. Reminds me of when Barry Walsh was working on the triple maturation theme of the Bushmills 16, probably about 15 years ago. Not until the very last days did all the components click. Just before then, it went through a phase like this (though obviously with malt, not IPS). Knowing current blender Billy Leighton as I do, I can see this whiskey improving in future batches as lessons are learned. not that there isn't already much to enjoy... 46%.

Yellow Spot Aged 12 Years bourbon barrels, sherry butts & Malaga casks, bott code L622431250 db (87) n22 t22 f21 b22 My previous comments stand for this, too. Except here we have a persistent bitterness towards the finish which reveals a weakness with one of the butts. An exceptionally bitty whiskey that does have its moments of soaring high, especially when the varying citrus note correlate. 46%. ncf.

OLD COMBER County Down.

Old Comber 30 Years Old Pure Pot Still (88) n23 t24 f20 b21. A classic example of a whiskey spending a few Summers too many in wood: increasing age doesn't equal excellence. That said, always very drinkable and early on positively sparkles with a stunning mouthfeel. Out of respect for the old I have made the markings for taste cover the first seven or eight seconds... 40%

Single Malt
COOLEY County Louth.

Connemara bott code L9042 db (88) n23 t22.5 f20.5 b22. One of the softest smoked whiskies in the world which though quite lovely gives the impression it can't make its mind up about what it wants to be. 40%

Connemara Aged 8 Years db (85) n22.5 t21.5 f20 b21. Another Connemara lacking teeth. The peat charms, especially on the nose, but the complexity needs working on. 46%

Connemara Aged 12 Years bott code L9024 db (85.5) n23 t21.5 f20 b21. The nose, with its beautiful orange, fruity lilt, puts the shy smoke in the shade. 40%

Connemara Cask Strength bott code L9041 db (90) n21.5 t23 f22 b22.5. A juicy negative of the standard bottling: does its talking on the palate rather than nose. Maybe an absence of caramel notes might have something to do with that. 57.9%

Connemara Distillers Edition db (86) n22 t22.5 f20 b21.5. When I give whisk(e)y tastings around the world, I love to include Connemara. Firstly, people don't expect peated Irish. Secondly, their smoked whisky stock is eclectic and you never quite know what is going to come out of the bottle. This is a particularly tight, sharp style. No prisoners survived... 43%

Inish Turk Beg Maiden Voyage db (91.5) n22 t23.5 f22.5 b22.5 Brooding and quite delicious. 44%

Tullamore Dew Single Malt 10 Years Old db (91.5) n23 t23 f22.5 b23. The best whiskey I have ever encountered with a Tullamore label. Furtively complex and daringly delicate. If only they could find a way to minimise the toffee... 40%. William Grant & Sons.

The Tyrconnell Aged 10 Years Madeira Finish bott code L8136 db (91) n23 t23 f22 b23. Not quite the award-winning effort of a few years back, as those lilting high notes which so complemented the baser fruit tones haven't turned up here. But remains in the top echelon and still much here to delight the palate. 46%

The Tyrconnell Single Cask 11 Year Old db (95.5) n23.5 t25 f23 b24. Well, if there weren't enough reasons to go to Dublin, you now have this... 46%. sc. Celtic Whiskey Shop Exclusive.

Clonmel Peated Aged 8 Years (86) n22 t23 f20 b21. Take the toffee away and you would have one hell of an Irish. Claims to be "Pure Pot Still". It isn't (in Irish terms): it's malt. 40%

Craoi na Mona Irish Malt Whiskey (68) n16 t18 f17 b17. I'm afraid my Gaelic is slipping these days: I assume Craoi na Mona means "Feinty, badly made smoky malt"... (that's the end of my tasting for the day...) 40%

Glendalough Single Malt Irish Whiskey Aged 7 Years bourbon casks (79) n18 t22 f20 b19. Disappointing on so many levels. Malt at Cooley at 7-year-old, should, if the casks are picked assiduously, be vibrant and brimming with barley and vitality. That only happens for the odd moment or two on delivery. The nose reveals some pretty poor barrels at work while two much toffee flattens the experience. Love the spice, though. 46%. ncf.

Glendalough Single Malt Irish Whiskey Aged 13 Years bourbon casks (90) n22.5 t23 f21.5 b23 A rather beautiful whiskey, spilling over with spices. A few tired casks evident, though. 46%. ncf.

Glen Dimplex (88) n23 t22 f21 b22. Overall, clean and classically Cooley. 40%

Liquid Sun Cooley 1999 bott 2012 (87) n22 t22 f21.5 b21.5 Awash with natural caramels and enjoyable in a horrible way...without the horrible. 53.2%. nc ncf sc. The Whisky Agency.

Magilligan Cooley Pure Pot Still Single Malt (91) n22 t22 f24 b23. A touch of honey for good measure ...or maybe not..!! 43%. Ian MacLeod Distillers.

Magilligan Irish Whiskey Peated Malt 8 Years Old (89) n21 t23 f22 b23. Such a different animal from the docile creature that formally passed as Magilligan peated. Quite lovely...and very classy. 43%. Ian Macleod Distillers.

Merry's Single Malt (83) n20 t22 f20 b21. Ultra-clean barley rich nose is found on the early palate. The finish is flat, though. 40%

Shannahan's (92) n23 t22 f24 b23. Cooley natural and unplugged: quite adorable. 40%

Slieve Foy Single Malt Aged 8 Years bott code L9108 (88) n23 t22.5 f21 b21.5. Never deviates from its delicate touch. 40%. Cooley for Marks & Spencer.

◇ **Tullamore Dew Aged 10 Years Four Cask Finish** bourbon, oloroso, port, madeira (89) n24 it is as though someone has distilled and matured in oak fruit pastel candy: the subtlety, interplay and weight distribution of varied fruit tones is nothing less than a work of art. Truly beautiful despite a dark note of warning...; t23 a very firm malt, its crunchy crispness at a variance with the salivating, succulent fruit; f19.5 annoyingly, the oloroso has the last very bitter word; b22.5 just a sherry butt or two away from complete brilliance. 40% (80 proof)

Tyrconnell 16 Year Old Single Malt (92) n22.5 t24 f22.5 b23 If anyone on here is old enough to remember Zoom lollies – and miss them as much as I after a gap of nearly half a century – then here's your chance to wallow down Memory Lane. So different. And so delicious! 46%

Vom Fass Cooley Irish Single Malt 8 Years Old (88) n22 t22.5 f21.5 b22. A very decent, if undemonstrative, example of the distillery at an age which well suits. 40%

The Wild Geese Single Malt (85.5) n21.5 t21 f22 b21. Just ignore the Wild Goose chase the labels send you on and enjoy the malt, with all its failings, for what it is (and this is pretty enjoyable in an agreeably rough and ready manner, though not exactly the stuff of Irish whiskey purists): which in this case for all its malt, toffee and delicate smoke, also appears to have more than a slight touch of feints - so maybe they were right all along...!!! 43%. Cooley for Avalon.

The Whisky Barrel Irish Single Malt 13 Year Old sherry hogshead, cask no. 200501, dist 2003 (82.5) n19 t21.5 f21 b21 Good grief....!!! This is my 1,151st whisk(e)y for the 2018 Bible... and I can safely say I have not encountered anything like this before...and very few in the near 20,000 samples for all the previous editions. It seems as though there is a strange unification or pact between some kind of skewed smoke and a sherry note the like of which I cannot even begin to describe. This is a gargoyle of a malt, strangely beautiful in its very ugliness. 52.7%. sc. 180 bottles.

MIDLETON County Cork.
Method and Madness Single Malt Irish Whiskey bourbon barrels, finished in French Limousin oak casks db (92) n22 t23.5 f23 b23.5 A very different Irish which is quietly uncompromising and seriously tasty... 46%.

OLD KILBEGGAN County Westmeath.
The Spirit of Kilbeggan 1 Month (90.5) n22 t23 f23 b22.5. Wow!! They are really getting to grips with the apparatus. Full bodied and lush small still feel to this but radiating complexity, depth, barley and cocoa in equal measures. The development of the oils really does give this excellent length. Impressed! 65.5%

The Spirit of Kilbeggan 1 Year (85) n20.5 t21 f22 b21.5. A veritable Bambi of a spirit: a typical one year old malt which, as hard as it tries, just can't locate its centre of gravity. Even so, the richness is impressive and some highly sugared chocolate mousse near the end is a treat. 62.7%

The Spirit of Kilbeggan 2 Years (84) n20 t21 f22 b21. A tad raw and a little thin. There is some decent balance between oak and malt, but the overall feeling is that the still has not yet been quite mastered. 60.3%

OLD BUSHMILLS County Antrim.
Bushmills Aged 10 Years matured in two woods db (92.5) n23 t23 f23 b23.5. Absolutely superb whiskey showing great balance and the usual Antrim 19th century pace with its favour development. The odd bottle of this I have come across over the last couple of years has been spoiled by the sherry involvement. But, this, as is usually the case, is absolutely spot on. 40%

⬦ **Bushmills Distillery Reserve Aged 12 Years** bott code: L7331IC002 db (95.5) n24 the usual chalky Bushmills trait has been usurped by the gentlest of cream sherry tones, augmented by a light blood orange and vanilla. Everything super-delicate, understated and ridiculously seductive; t24 you expect a silky delivery – and you get it with knobs on. A fruity caress is the prelude to a more meaningful spice note which tickles rather than warms. A light barley strand heads into first ulmo, then heather honey territory; f23.5 so unusual for a whiskey to offer full salivation towards the finale, but then this is not a usual whiskey. Late toast as the sultanas turn to raisin; b24 a sublime use of faultless sherry casks. Bushmills at the very height of its form and complexity. Truly outstanding. 40%.

Bushmills Select Casks Aged 12 Years married with Caribbean rum cask db (95) n23 t24 f24 b24 One of the most complex Bushmills in living memory, and probably since it was established in 1784. 40%

Bushmills Aged 16 Years db (71) n18 t21 f15 b17. In my days as a consultant Irish whiskey blender, going through the Bushmills warehouses I found only one or two sulphur-treated butts. Alas, there are many more than that at play here. 40%

Bushmills Aged 21 Years db (95.5) n24.5 t24 f23.5 b24 An Irish journey as beautiful as the dramatic landscape which borders the distillery. Magnificent. 40%

Bushmills Sherry Cask Reserve Single Malt Whiskey first-fill Oloroso sherry butts db (80) n20.5 t22 f18 b19.5. Although I am always 100% impartial, I would be lying if I didn't say I wanted this whiskey to be not just a high scorer, but a potential Bible world champion. Because in my tasting room stands a fine and very large - oil portrait of the Bushmills Distillery, and it is a place I have enjoyed special moments at - and love the people there dearly. And, also, in a few moments Northern Ireland's miracle-making football team are about to take on Wales in the last 16 of the Euros. But, sadly, the news, from here at least, is not good. Among the sherry butts selected has been one - and I am sure it is only one - that has been lightly sulphur treated. It means that the fruit, rather than taking off and going into complexity overdrive, crumples slightly as the vague bitterness and tightness spreads around the palate. There are some lovely fruit moments, so there are. But Bushmills should be so much better than this. As an Irish whiskey blender of old, I have been lucky enough to work with Bushmills sherry butts in pristine condition...and they can be among the best whiskeys you'll ever find on this planet. Sadly this is not fully representative. I just hope the boys in green rise to greater heights than this bottling and don't fall to an own goal like the one scored here.... 40%

◇◇◇ **Bushmills Single Malt The Steamship Collection #3 Bourbon Cask** db (95) n24.5 one of the most honeyed and intricate Bushmills aromas of all time: not a big ultra-sweet style – more a pollen and sugar number which allows the oak sufficient room to maximise its floral and spice notes...; t23.5 a reversal: oak shows first, initially with the distillery's trademark chalkiness mixing in with the delicate vanillas. Then molecule by molecule the honey returns, as if not to be noticed, until the mouth feel changes – it thickens and with it arrives the almost salty ulmo honey; t23 dry with a light rumbling of spice; b24 this steamship is sailing in calm seas of complexity...Take your time over this one: it is deceptively brilliant. 40%.

◇◇◇ **Acla Special Selection No. 5 County of Antrim 24 Years Old** sherrywood, dist 1991, bott 2016 (91.5) n23.5 wonderfully adroit spices flit in and out of the Jaffa Cake fruit and chocolate; the drier chalkiness is unmistakably Old Bushmills; t24 oh, yes...that delivery. Succulent and full bodied, the malt is not entirely lost under the welter of fruit, then a few phrases of blood orange and spice; f21 still succulent and some major caramels now but the cask bitterness just takes the edge of things slightly; the fruit just gets a little tangy very late on; b23 some brief moments of this malt defy belief for their beauty. 47.8%. sc. 158 bottles.

◇◇◇ **Acla Special Selection No. 6 County of Antrim 24 Years Old** bourbon barrel, cask no. 1073, dist 1991, bott 2016 (96) n23 gorgeous mix of rhubarb crumble and custard; a little hickory and spice make bourbon-style guest appearances; t24.5 sensational! A delivery you dream about: creamy with a distinctive Neapolitan ice cream character, the accent on the chocolate; f24 the oak finds its way into picture with a toasty encroachment onto the long chooolate and vanilla fade...; b24.5 truly an Antrim classic. Would love to see more of this in the actual Bushmills portfolio: well done Acla for showing the way. In other words: stopping mucking around with mixing casks types and look at some of the breathtaking bourbon barrels on your doorstep! This is indubitably world class. 44.7%. sc. 176 bottles.

Knappogue Castle Aged 12 Years bourbon cask matured (90) n23.5 t23 f21 b22.5. The massive toffee influence deflects from the huge character elsewhere which springs a few surprises. 40%. Castle Brands Group.

The Whiskey Cask Company Cù Chulainn 27 Years Old rum cask, dist 1988 (89) n22.5 t22.5 f22 b22.5 Apparently this is from Bushmills, so the whiskey I decided to taste before Northern Ireland's game against Poland, their first in international Finals since 1986. And the first time a player from my beloved Millwall, Shane Ferguson, has taken part since Tony Cascarino represented the Republic of Ireland in 1988. 45.7%

WEST CORK DISTILLERS County Cork.
◇◇◇ **West Cork Irish Whiskey Bog Oak Charred Cask Matured** db (88.5) n23 another tannin-topped aroma from West Cork, though a mix of dreamy malt and vanilla acts as a breakwater. The very faintest citrus note lightens things a little; t22 a hefty, though sharp, delivery in the distillery style, malt at the crux of all things at first, then caramel pours in; f21.5 the oils become a tad bitter here though the toffee counters; b22 a little known fact: I own a 100 to 125 year-old portable Irish pot still made entirely of copper with brass handles, once owned by a Victorian or Edwardian illicit distiller. Which would explain as to why it was found in an Irish bog over 20 years ago and has been in my possession ever since. Anyway, it is extremely unlikely it ever produced a spirit which ended up quite so heavy in natural caramels... 43%. West Cork Distillers Limited.

◇◇◇ **West Cork Irish Whiskey Glengarriff Peat Charred Cask Matured** db (90.5) n23 major tannin jolt from the off: we are halfway between bonfires and a half decent Kentucky bourbon...; t22.5 the delivery is no more subtle, either. A big whumph of eye-watering tannin and Demerara sugars are enough to thrust you back in your seat. Good oils, some barley peeping out here and there, but mainly they are bourbon noises we here, especially the caramels and liquorice; the lightest wisps of smoke circle around; f22 the toastiness of the oak finally creates bitterish residue, though the sugars deal with it comfortably; b23 well, Ireland is on the way to Kentucky from here... 43%. West Cork Distillers Limited.

◇◇◇ **Brean Tra Cask Strength Irish Whiskey** (91) n22.5 the malt digs deep and creates enough power to see off the cream toffee-vanillas of the oak; t23 so lush, thanks to their stills! In effect, the nose converted to the palate. And bejabers...that malt...!!! f22 happy to drift off down a simplistic vanilla path; **b22.5** doesn't bother too much about complexity: this is all about sheer intensity of flavour. Wow! 60%. West Cork Distillers Limited.

⬩ **Brean Tra Single Malt Irish Whiskey** db **(86.5) n21 t22 f21.5 b22** A very safe Irish. Distinctly oily and choc-a-bloc with intense if monosyllabic malt. The tannins take time to arrive but become moderately punchy. 40%. West Cork Distillers Limited.

⬩ **Dundalgan 10 Year Old Single Malt Irish Whiskey** db **(88.5) n22.5** enjoyable and attractive, the nose is oily, pushing the case for the barley. Grassy, though, if you look carefully enough; **t22** the house malt soup style: thick and intense; **f22** the concentrated mat form continues as the oils build further; **b22** enjoyable, though the complexity levels appear to be limited slightly by the oils from the still which fill in the gaps between the peaks and troughs. 40%. West Cork Distillers Limited.

⬩ **Mizen Head Cask Strength Single Malt Irish Whiskey** Bodega sherry casks db **(90.5) n22.5** the fruit is clean fresh and has much to say. The toffee tries to gag the grape, though. Great spices! **t23.5** top rate delivery: the fruit is fresh, juicy and impactful but the caramels and vanilla offer the perfect shock absorber **f22** toffee raisin fudge dipped in sea salt. A very slight furry murmur very late on – if you can spot it; **b22.5** well done chaps! Until the very death, barely a sulphur atom in sight! But such is the power of this distillery's love of caramel character, it even overtakes the fruit...which takes some doing! 60%. West Cork Distillers Limited.

UNSPECIFIED SINGLE MALTS

⬩ **Acla Special Selection No. 2 Somewhere in Ireland 24 Years Old** barrel, cask no. 10705, dist 1991, bott 2016 **(95) n23** some tired oak yawns and stretches across a chalky platform of malt and peppered French toast: a lovely sweetness defies the otherwise dry theme; **t24** the delivery at first stutters as the oak gasps for air. But as the malt finds its feet, the intensity of the barley steadies the ship and soon we are off into surprisingly grassy and salivating waters. The old oak nags, but the barley remains defiantly upbeat: a delicious journey which tells a spellbinding story; **f24** with spices now in place and the oils settles the finale finds an all-round peace and contentment the earlier stages had lacked, for all their beauty. The malt now shews a sublime degree of exotic fruits to cement that feeling of great age; **b24** a malt coming to the end of its life, but plucked from the warehouse while its greatness remains intact and unimpeached. 474%. sc. 212 bottles.

⬩ **Acla Special Selection No. 3 North of Ireland 27 Years Old** barrel, cask no. 16264, dist 1989, bott 2016 **(91.5) n24** having waited 27 years in the cask, it needs at least as many minutes in the glass before it really begins show its true colours. They are pastel shades of orange blossom honey, lime, Chinese gooseberry, vanilla and the juice of Maraschino cherry. Considering this is from a bourbon cask, it near defies belief that such sophisticated fruit tones can be heard...; **t23.5** the light oils stretch as far as possible to maximise the volume of the fudge and ulmo honey. Still a clear maltiness is intact and indeed blossoms; **f21.5** just enough lingering sugar dulls the excess of the oaky bitterness; **b22.5** this is the malt that has put "Old" into Old Bushmills. Very rarely does the distillery's whiskey get anywhere near this kind of age. This has withstood the test of time with remarkable fortitude and pride. 43.4%. sc. 163 bottles.

Barr an Uisce 1803 Irish Single Malt Aged 10 Years bourbon barrel **(92) n22.5 t23.5 f23 b23** Not sure if I have ever come across an Irish whiskey with such a pathetically weak phenolic signature. Even so, a delicious offering...! Unspecified, but Cooley for sure. 46%. ncf.

Chapter 7 Irish Single Malt 2001 13 Years Old sherry butt, cask no. 10836 **(67.5) n17.5 t18 f15 b18**. Sorry Chaps. Sweet as a nut it may be. But you have been seriously sulphured. 59.5%. sc. 293 bottles.

Chapter 7 Irish Single Malt 1999 16 Years Old rum cask, cask no. 5409 **(94) n23 t23.5 f23.5 b24** Genuinely impressive. 573%. sc.

Clontarf Single Malt (90.5) n23 t23 f22 b22.5. Beautiful in its simplicity, this has eschewed complexity for delicious minimalism; 40%. Clontarf Irish Whiskey Co.

Connemara Original Peated Single Malt db **(81.5) n21 t21.5 f19 b20** A bit of a while since the first thing I got off the nose and last thing on the finish was caramel. Not the Connemara I witnessed being launched in a blaze of defiant glory those decades back. This rather meek, pleasant, safe, lightly smoked version appears to have been sanitised. Today's Connemara it may sadly be. Original Connemara it is most certainly NOT...! 40%

Dublin in the Rare Ould Times Single Malt Irish Whiskey Aged 10 Years bourbon barrel **(81.5) n21 t21 f19 b20.5**. It was a rare old time when they made single malt whiskey like this in Dublin, for they hardly ever did. The city was the centre of Pot Still Irish and though single malt was not unknown there, it was a scarce order at the bar. When it did come along, it is hard to believe it would have been this kind of age. And, indeed, this malt would have been happier had it been a couple of years younger: the bourbon barrel at work here has allowed little malty punch to get through, while the toffee middle and finish is disappointingly dull. 40%. Bottled by Glendalough Distillery for Pete St John.

◇◇◇ **The Dubliner 10 Year Old Single Malt** bourbon casks, bott no. L17390-179 (89) n22 drying grass on a day before-mowed lawn; t23 malty, custard cream biscuit sweetness; juicy with a polite spice in the mid-ground leading to a brief burst of acacia honey; f21.5 dries exuberantly, but a lovely coppery tang, too; b22.5 'the real taste of Dublin' warbles the label in time-honoured Blarney tradition. Of course, the true, historic taste of Dublin is Irish Pot Still, that beguiling mix of malted and unmalted barley. But, in the meantime, this juicy little number will do no harm. 42%.

The Dublin Liberties Copper Alley 10 Year Old (88.5) n23 t22 f21.5 b22 About an easy drinking a malt as you'll find with no shortage of sugars. The caramels are a bit ham-fisted, though. 46%. ncf.

Dunville's Aged 10 Years Single Malt finished in ex-Pedro Ximénez sherry casks (78.5) n20 t21.5 f18 b19 Well, didn't quite see that coming. They may have launched a whisky with the best label of this and many years – a re-run of the old Classic Dunville's VR – but not quite the best whiskey with which to fill the bottle. The nose has a peculiar botanical note, juniper in particular, and this becomes a strange experience all round when the same note is picked upon the palate and then stretched and smothered – with everything else - by the furry PX. Lots of early flavours...but balance is at a serious premium. 46%. ncf.

◇◇◇ **Dunville's VR Aged 12 Years Single Malt** finished in ex-Pedro Ximénez sherry casks (87) n23 t22.5 f20 b21.5 The success story here is on the nose: despite its Spanish inquisition, there is a profound Kentucky note leading the way, a sharp almost rye-like note with its fruity crispness. The delivery also has its moments, the riot of date and molasses in particular. The rest of the tale, much of it bitterly told, doesn't go quite so well, alas. 46%. ncf.

Dunville's VR First Edition Aged 15 Years Single Malt Port Morant rum cask finish, cask no. 193 (96.5) n24 t24.5 f23.5 b24.5 Makes me wonder: it must have been about 15 years ago or so I was blending a high quality Pot Still rum and used some outstanding Port Morant for my creation. Some of the casks, I know, went on to be filled with Irish from Cooley (for some Irish I was blending at the same time)... Surely not... 57%. ncf sc.

◇◇◇ **Dunville's VR Aged 17 Years Single Malt** Port Mourant Estate rum cask finish, cask no. 195 (91.5) n22.5 unusually for where a PM cask is involved, the soft toffee tones find themselves up against an abrasive if curious fruitiness, under-ripe gooseberries to the fore; t22.5 a forthright delivery, puckering in its sharpness. Salivating, with a firm blast of barley, then again a non-specific fruit note, perhaps underscored by muscovado sugars; f23 at last settles down into a more complex and comfortable narrative as the PM begins to have some kind of influence. Light liquorice and chocolate form with the delicate spices; again a slightly off-key fruit note before the expected and long overdue mocha finally arrives; b22.5 putting my blending hat on (which is the same one as I wear when writing the Whisky Bible) Port Mourant – known by us rum blenders as PM – trumps PX every day of the week when it comes to maturation. PM is a bit special in the rum world: it is a Guyanan rum that you add for its depth and powering coffee flavour: indeed, if you work in a rum warehouse in Guyana you can locate where the PMs are situated just by the change in aroma. This comes about by the fact that caramel is already into the cask before the rum spirit is added to it for maturation. It is a style symbolic with British Naval Rum. So where PX can be sacharine sweet and occasionally turn a whisky into something bland and uninteresting, PM is brilliant for lengthening out the finish, especially with rich mocha notes. Here, there are some sharp features it has to contend with from the first cask and a little extra time in PM might have ensured an extra softness to the finale. 57.1%. ncf sc.

◇◇◇ **Egan's Single Malt 10 Aged Years** bott code: US001 244 (90) n22.5 enticing light fruit notes, mainly playing out on the melon and grapefruit spectrum; just a little stiffness to the oak; t23.5 ah...now that one very beautiful delivery. Orange blossom honey steels the show, but is perfectly backed by a rounded texture which almost oozes onto the palate; plenty of malt on show, and lazy spice, but still that honey blossoms...; f22 the slight tightness to the oak evident on the nose returns, but makes little headway against the excellence of the malty spirit; b22.5 rich, rounded and puts the "more" into this Tullamore-based bottler...47% (94 proof). ncf.

Eiling Lim Irish Single Malt 22 Years Old 1991 bott 2014 (95.5) n23.5 t24 f24 b24 After 22 years, this must have been one of the most highly smoked whiskeys ever produced at Cooley. A genuine landmark malt in Irish whiskey history. 48.6%. nc ncf sc. 116 bottles. 6th Release.

Glendalough 7 Year Old Irish Single Malt Black Pitts Porter Finish (81) n19 t21 f20 b21 Wearing my Panama Hattie, just got to say it's just Too Darn Hop! Would love to say You Do Something To Me and You're Sensational. But you don't and you aren't. Night and Day I hoped you'd Begin the Beguine...but there is no rhythm at all. I know in these whisky days Anything Goes but Make it Another Old-Fashioned, Please....That's enough Cole Porter references, thank you - Ed. 59%.

Glendalough 13 Year Old Irish Single Malt Mizunara Finish (96) n23.5 t24 f24 b24.5 Different and adorable. 56%.

Glendalough 24 Year Old Irish Single Malt Madeira Finish (86.5) n22.5 t22.5 f20.5 b20 OK, I know. The owners of this brand will be pretty pissed off with me. They have bought a 24-year-old malt. And what appears to be first use Madeira casks of the highest quality. Then put them together. Is there a sulphur fault with the wine cask? Not at all: it is perfect. So why the relatively low score compared to their Mizunara and Port Morant offerings? Well, if I can put my blender's hat on for a moment, allow me to explain. After 24 years, the malt will have a lot to say and deserves listening to. Some of the narrative will be cracked and in need of editing. So, yes, a finish of some sort might help. However, this Madeira cask is too fresh and pugnacious. It dominates bombastically and defines. Yes, it is delicious. But where is the 24-year-old malt? A few whispers can be heard...but it is me, me, me Madeira. Make no mistake: this whiskey enjoys some astonishing phrases of succulent beauty. But as a 24-year-old...it simply does not feel quite right or reverential enough... 54%.

Glendalough 24 Year Old Irish Single Malt Port Finish (89.5) n22.5 t23.5 f21 b22.5 If there were any cracks to this old whiskey, then the vivid Port certainly shored them up. 53%.

Glendalough 24 Year Old Irish Single Malt Sherry Finish (94.5) n24 t24 f22.5 b24 A sherry cask with only the odd, but forgivable, atom of renegade sulphur. Lovely people of Glendalough: allow me to shake your hands and kiss your foreheads... a very old fashioned (and now horrendously and tragically rare) style indeed: more like a lifetime top quality sherry held, rather than finished. 53%.

Hyde No.1 President's Cask Aged 10 Years Single Malt sherry cask finish (85.5) n23 t22 f20 b20.5 Pleased to report the sherry butt(s) used here offer no sulphur, so a clean malt with an outstanding fruity aroma. But it does quite literally fall flat because after the initial juicy, malty entry things go a bit quiet – especially towards the middle and finish where a dull vaguely fruity but big toffee note clings like a limpet. A wasted opportunity, one feels. 46%. ncf.

The Irishman Single Malt bottle no. E2496 (83) n20 t21 f21 b21. Highly pleasant malt but the coffee and toffee on the finish underline a caramel-style whiskey which may, potentially, offer so much more. 40%. Hot Irishman Ltd.

◇ **The Irishman Aged 12 Years** first fill bourbon barrels, bott 2017 (92) n23.5 presumably an Antrim malt from the intensity of the chalky signature: this brings down slightly the sharpness of the honeyed sugars – very much to the malt's advantage. A vague citrus tone adds leverage to the complexity; t23 the malt gets the odd look in, but really it is oak in command with a beautifully, roasty molassed feel to the ulmo honey; the mid-ground is akin to porridge with molten sugar f22.5 back, as expected, to its chalky old self..; b23 Old Bushmills like you have never quite seen her before in bottle. Works a treat. 43%. ncf. 6,000 bottles.

◇ **The Irishman 12 Years Old Florio Marsala Cask Finish** cask no. 2257 (90) n22 someone's left the Christmas Pudding in the oven too long...; toasty, slightly burnt raisin; t23 the malt has a brief foray onto the palate before being swamped by spiced dates and Melton Hunt Cake; the malt makes a brief re-appearance before vanishing under the timber; f22.5 dry and nutty; b22.5 a clean, unsullied cask but the grape allows the malt little room for manoeuvre. Very pleasurable though, and definitely a whisky rather than a wine..; 46%. ncf sc. 320 bottles.

The Irishman Single Malt 17 Year Old 1st fill Oloroso sherry casks (94) n23 t24 f23.5 b23.5 The sherry is far too dominant for this to be a well-balanced whiskey: it is all about effect. But this is a rare, as near as damn-it sulphur-free sherry influence and that ups the value and enjoyment of this malt greatly. 56%. ncf sc.

◇ **The Irishman Aged 17 Years** sherry cask, cask no. 6925, dist 2000 (95.5) n24.5 textbook oloroso whisky aroma: not just a fine, rich, nutty fruitiness, but the malt punches through to create its own balancing strand. The fruit fluctuates in depth, with the odd dark cherry popping into to sweeten and intensify even further. Perfectly weighted, brilliantly paced and topped off by the most teasing, mildly nipping spices. A half mark dropped because...oh, you'll see later, I suspect...; t24 so thick on the palate it could almost be a cough syrup. The grape's richness and mind-blowing layering is unmatched by any other sherried malt since the Yamazaki (also 17 years!) I gave the World Whisky Award to a few years back. Even so, for three or four waves the malt pours in, then a mix of vanilla and dried dates closes the gap; a beautiful fruit and nut chocolate occupies the midpoint; f23 long, now with a toffee raisin feel to it; a slight furriness begins to form here and there, shewing that this amazing butt didn't entirely escape the attentions of the sulphur candle lighter. Many most probably won't notice (lucky them!)...; b24 just a year or two after this was distilled, I was crawling around the warehouses of Old Bushmills doing some blending and sampling amazingly fine, completely un-sulphured or as near as damn it un-sulphured, sherry butts – better than any I had found in Scotland in the previous several years. This style of sherry has all the hallmarks of the Bushmills butts of that time. There is trace sulphur (so this is a as near-as-damn-it butt), but unless you know exactly what you are looking for it is in such small amounts it is unlikely to be detected or trouble you. This may not be from Bushmills, but if not then someone has made a good job of hiding some gems from me. If anyone can locate half a dozen of those entirely un-sulphured butts I located, then there is an Irish Whisky of the Year (at least!) in your hands... *56%. ncf sc. 600 bottles.*

Jack Ryan Single Malt Irish Whisky Aged 12 Years bourbon cask **(92.5)** n23.5 t23 f22.5 b23.5 Deft, very clean malt whisky where decent bourbon wood adds all kinds of beautifully paced complexity. Not even a hint of an off note. Impressive. *46%*

Liquid Sun Irish Single Malt XO (94) n23.5 t24 f23 b23.5 This morning a daughter of Ireland and friend of mine died. Had you seen Delores Meredith walking purposefully with shopping bags in hand you would not have given her a second look: from the other side of the street she appeared just an ordinary lady who had strayed, wearily, into late middle age like so many of us. But in those bags would, most likely, be the shopping of others too infirm to leave their chair or bed and Del, without a second thought, would round up those vital little bits and bobs which made the lives of others a little easier to bear, always in her own time and often by foot. I had first met Del at a time I was tasting the final whiskies of the 2017 Whisky Bible and it was she, a carer, who greeted my mother at the Care Home she had just entered, nervously, on her very first day. Delores with her bright Irish eyes, thick Irish midland brogue and bottomless wells of warmth and saintly patience tenderly tried to ease my mum into her new life. Stroking her hand, or gently brushing her hair, she would tell my mum not to worry for she would be there to look after her, which she did with a love and devotion which came as naturally to her as breathing does to you and me My mother, though admonishing her for minor perceived offences, demonstrably adored her and it was obvious my mum, her sharp wits still fully about her and at war with the world, meant much to Del. So often what started in tears of frustration for my mum would end as tears of laughter for them both. And every day, unfailingly, Delores would give me a detailed run down of how things were progressing, or not as the case may be, and try and spend as much time with her as she could; or head off to find her various things from the chemist that could give extra strength to a very fragile old lady. Then, a few months in, Delores was diagnosed with cancer. Not one of those where you fight and have a hope but one of the insidious variety which has crept up on you and, when you find it, it is most probably too late. As, indeed, it proved to be. So today, Easter Sunday, Delores who had so much to live for and give passed away, while my mother heads on towards a 96th birthday she does not wish to see. Life can be cruel and ironic. But it can be wonderful, also. Because it gave me the chance to meet Delores Meredith, one of the most beautiful people I ever knew. And here, with this gorgeous Irish whiskey, I toast your memory, Del, and say thank you for being one of those special people who restores or reinforces one's faith in human nature with every meeting thanks to your myriad kindnesses and bountiful love. *50.3%.*

Liquid Treasures Irish Malt bourbon barrel, bott 2016 **(91)** n22.5 t23 f22.5 b23 "Very old" it may be, but the "aged" oak involvement, other than some drying chalky moments, is negligible. Even so, unquestionably delicious. *496%. Summer Dram Edition.*

The Quiet Man 8 Year Old bourbon cask, Oloroso sherry finish **(84.5)** n23.5 t21.5 f19 b20.5 Pretty decent, though still slightly sulphured sherry butt been at play here. It is the nose which takes the plaudits, with its audacious lassoing of the bigger bourbon notes, fully-fledged tannins an' all, and then tying them to the orange blossom honey of the wine cask. The marriage on the nose is nowhere near matched on the bitty, untidy palate. *46%. ncf sc. 950 bottles.*

The Quiet Man 8 Year Old Single Malt Irish Whiskey bourbon casks **(89)** n22 t23 f21.5 b22.5 Had the finish not dulled quite so quickly this would have scored a lot higher. Nothing less than pleasant throughout. *40%*

⬦ **The Quiet Man 8 Year Old** bourbon cask, bott code L18080088 **(88.5)** n23 just love the spice which drifts up from the honeyed flatlands. Butterscotch tart, in a slightly overcooked pastry, augmented by maple syrup; t23 as silky and green as an Irish flag as rich, intense barley unfurls around the palate. Light Demerara sugars match the growing vanilla beautifully; f20.5 bitters out slowly, quietly, but with enthusiasm; b22 forget the finale: salute, quietly, the nose and delivery! *46%. ncf sc. 385 bottles.*

The Quiet Man 12 Year Old Kentucky bourbon casks **(93)** n23 t23.5 f23 b23.5 Odd, isn't it? The owner of this brand named this whisky The Quiet Man in memory of his father, John Mulgrew, who was known by that epithet. Yet, coincidentally, it was Maurice Walsh, the grandfather of one of the greatest Irish whiskey blenders of all time, Barry Walsh, who wrote the novel The Quiet Man from which the film was made. I feel another movie coming on: The Silence of the Drams. But sssshhhh: don't tell anyone... *46%. ncf.*

⬦ **The Quiet Man 12 Year Old Sherry Finished** bourbon casks, finished in oloroso sherry casks, bott code: L17304295 db **(73)** n18.5 t20 f16.6 b18 Ah. Sadly, the sulphur isn't quite as quiet as one might hope. *46%. ncf.*

⬦ **The Sexton Single Malt** batch no. L71861F001 (91) n23 a distinctive dry, chalky Bushmills style of malt and oak mix lets loose with a fabulously spicy fruitcake sub-strata; t23.5 superb, lush delivery with peppers pounding, backed by some excellent tannins. Mocha and gingerbread meet the fruitcake full on in midstream; f22 heads a little too easily towards a simplistic toffee raisin finale; b22.5 unmistakably malt from The Old Bushmills Distillery, and seemingly from sherry cask, also, as that distillery probably enjoys an above average number unsullied by sulphur. 40% (80 proof).

Single Cask Collection Old Dunluce 14 Year Old sherry hogshead, cask no. 10823, dist 18 Sept 01, bott 22 Jun 16 (93) n23.5 t24 f22.5 b23 Profound grape of the most luscious variety. 56.9%. 319 bottles. sc.

Teeling Whiskey Brabazon Bottling Single Malt Series 01 sherry casks, bott Mar 17 (92) n23.5 t23.5 f22 b23 Oooh, so close to a stupendous sherry influence. 49.5%. ncf.

⬦ **Teeling Whiskey Brabazon Bottling Single Malt Series 01** sherry casks, bott Feb 18, bott code: L18 001 059 (67) n16 t19 f15 b17 I'll let you guess what kind of sherry cask this is... 49.5%. ncf.

⬦ **Teeling Whiskey Brabazon Bottling Single Malt Series 02** port casks, bott Aug 17, bott code: L17 002 244 (95) n23.5 bold, expansive, expressive, and intrigues especially when the spices and fruits nibble at each other; t24 sublime mouth feel: absolutely perfect weight on both the malt and sugars, with a delicate oiliness ensuring a malt as rounded as you are likely to find; the fruit never travels far without a spicy accompaniment: there is much of the boiled sugar candy about this; f23.5 the spices fizz quietly while a little cocoa moves in with the plums; b24 an exemplary Port cask offering: such a beautiful whiskey experience. 49.5%. ncf.

Teeling Whiskey Single Cask port cask no. 12628, dist 9 Nov 07, bott 21 Feb 17 (94) n23 t24 f23.5 b23.5 The gentlest of fruity giants. 60%. nc ncf sc.

Teeling Whiskey Single Malt bott 07/2015 (87.5) n21.5 t23.5 f21 b21.5. Charming and, at times, intense malt impact with a lovely light fruit side-line. But a late bitterness confirms a degree of negativity from a tiring cask. The delivery, though, is pretty special. 46%. ncf.

Teeling Whiskey Single Malt bott Mar 17 (89) n22 t22 f23 b22 Ostensibly, a slightly over-simplified malt. But the subtlety of the finish is worth waiting for. 46%. nc ncf.

⬦ **Teeling Whiskey Single Malt** bott Nov 17, bott code: L17 016 333 (80) n19 t22 f19 b20 Never quite finds the right balance or rhythm. A furry note runs throughout the entire experience. 46%. nc ncf.

Teeling Whiskey Single Malt Aged 24 Years Sauterne & bourbon casks, bott Aug 16 (95.5) n24 t24.5 f23 b24 Well done, Jack Teeling: you caught me off guard there! Done me up like a kipper - literally. Wasn't expecting a smoky malt of this great antiquity (by Irish standards) and its marriage to a Sauterne influence makes it a complete one-off. Love to be sent the wrong way sometimes. Has all the craggy charm of an Irish character actor. 46%. ncf.

Teeling Whiskey Single Malt Aged 26 Years rum cask, cask no. 16231, bott 21 Feb 17 (96) n24 t24 f24 b24 Scratching my head, but this is probably the oldest Irish whiskey I have ever tasted from a distillery still working. All others of this antiquity – and beyond – have come from those which had closed many years before. Yes, the oldest – and one of the best... 57.9%. ncf sc.

Teeling Whiskey Single Malt Vol III Revival Aged 14 Years bourbon casks, finished in Pineau des Charentes barrels (76.5) n20.5 t21 f17 b18 'Tis a risky business, this cask finishing. Especially in French fortified wine, as well as sherry... 46%. nc ncf.

Teeling Whiskey Single Malt Vol IV Revival Aged 14 Years finished in ex-muscat barrels (95) n23.5 t23.5 f24 b24 ...Though this muscat appears to be bang on the money... indeed, this is a stunner! 46%. nc ncf.

⬦ **Teeling Whiskey Single Malt Vol V Revival Aged 12 Years** cognac & brandy casks, bott code: L18 001 088 (90.5) n23.5 now that takes you by surprise: too often cognac casks can dull a malt, but here the exact opposite has happened. The barley hits your nose like a pointy stick and the sugary grape is right behind to give you another joyful biff; t23.5 the stands of acacia honey dithering on the nose are broader and bolder here; intense butterscotch works beautifully with the spice and maple syrup; f21 a degree of bitterness amongst the vanilla; b22.5 sharper than a newly whetted knife. 46%. nc ncf.

⬦ **The Whistler Aged 7 Years Natural Cask Strength Oloroso Finished** batch no. 02-0360 (91.5) n22.5 pulsing fruit and malt. A real spiced moist fruitcake persona to this one with an attractive viscosity; t23.5 a big delivery, obviously helped along by the alcohol but most of all the oils which not only stick to the palate but keep safely in its orbit the little oak than can be detected; chewy, salivating and increasingly sexy as those spices spin a yarn or two, especially as it mixes with the molassed Melton Mowbray Hunt cake; f22 a real old grape skin bitterness to this, but again the oils work their magic by allowing enough molasses to minimise any damage; b23.5 if you are going to round your malt off using a sherry butt probably dripping in wine when it was filled, your best option is to make the tenancy in the second cask short and then bottle at cask strength. They may not have done the former, but certainly the latter action has helped no-end, as confirmed when tasted alongside Blue Note (below). Infinitely better structure and the spices here make a big difference. Very attractive whiskey, indeed. And helped no end by a clean, sulphur-free sherry butt of the old school. I doff my Panama in finding such unsullied sherry butts. *59%. nc ncf.*

◇ **The Whistler Aged 7 Years The Blue Note Oloroso Finished** (87) n22 t22 f21.5 b21.5 The great news: no sulphur! A clean sherry butt, which is a shock in itself. The less good news: the malt was a little too young and lacking in body to really be able to be much more than a vehicle for the grape. Enjoyable, rich sultana with attractive spice. But lacking in whisky-ish structure and complexity: just too much like a straight sweet sherry! *46%. nc ncf.*

◇ **The Whistler Aged 10 Years How The Years Whistle By Oloroso Finished** (92.5) n23 a much more complete nose than their 7-year-old, the extra oak laying a firm foundation on which the malt and grape is built. The most subtle spice, too, sitting prettily with the heather honey: impressive! t23.5 sensual and salivating, the grape is fat and explodes onto the plate bringing in its train and series of molasses and spice. The mid-ground dries as the oak has its say, forming a salty raisin biscuit depth; f22.5 trails off slightly, though the spices pound and throb; b23.5 a fabulously clean sherry butt which is much more at home with a broader-spectrumed malt... *46%. nc ncf.*

The Whisky Agency Irish Single Malt 1990 (92.5) n23 t23.5 f23 b23 One of the most gentle and juicy malts of the year – from any country! *48.1%.*

Whisky-Fässle Irish Single Malt extra old barrel, bott 2016 (88) n22 t24 f20 b22 A very uneven malt which has been let down by the oak. *50.6%.*

Writers' Tears Red Head Oloroso sherry casks (82.5) n21 t23 f18.5 b20 Always a dangerous game to play with sherry butts and this writer's tears are reserved for the light furry sulphur tones which, as will always be the case, stifle the enjoyment of the rich fruity delivery. *46%.*

Single Grain
COOLEY County Louth-
Greenore 6 Year Old bott code L9015 db (89) n23.5 t22.5 f21 b22. Very enjoyable whiskey. But two points: cut the caramel and really see the baby sing. And secondly, as a "Small Batch" bottling, how about putting a batch number on the label...? *40%. Cooley.*

Greenore 8 Year Old bott code L8190 db (86.5) n20 t22 f23 b21.5. The vague hint of butyric on the nose is more than amply compensated by the gradual build up to something rather larger on the palate than you might have expected (and don't be surprised if the two events are linked). The corn oil is almost a meal in itself and the degree of accompanying sugar and corn flour is a treat. *40%. Cooley.*

Greenore 15 Years Old bott code L8044 db (90) n23 t22.5 f22 b22.5. The advent of the Kilbeggan 15 reminded us that there must be some grain of that age around, and here to prove it is a superb bottling of the stuff which, weirdly, is a lot better than the blend. Beautiful. *43%*

Greenore 18 Years Old db (91) n22.5 t22.5 f23 b23. This continuous still at Cooley should be marked by the State as an Irish national treasure. One of the most complex grains you'll ever find, even when heading into uncharted territory like this one. *46%. ncf. 4000 bottles.*

Hyde 1916 No.3 Áras Cask Aged 6 Years Single Grain bott Feb 16 (87) n22 t23 f20.5 b21.5 Cooley grain probably ranks as the best being made right now, with the loss of Dumbarton and Port Dundas in Scotland. Sadly, as deliciously rich as this is, far too much toffee on the finish rather detracts from its normal excellence. Highly enjoyable, but the flag flies nowhere near full mast. By the way: the 1916 on the label doesn't represent year of distillation or bottling. Or is there to celebrate the year of my dad's birth. No, it is something a little more political than that. *46%. ncf. 5,000 bottles.*

GLENDALOUGH County Wicklow.
Glendalough 3 Year Old Irish Single Grain sherry & Madeira butts db (91) n22 t23.5 f22.5 b23 A much richer and more confident grain than their first, sherry-finished version. Excellent. *43%.*

Glendalough Double Barrel Irish Whiskey first aged in American bourbon casks, then Spanish oloroso casks (88.5) n22.5 t23 f21 b22 A very pleasant malt but rather vague and at times a little dull. *42%*

MIDLETON County Cork.
Method and Madness Single Grain Irish Whiskey bourbon barrels, finished in virgin Spanish oak casks db (89.5) n22 t22.5 f22 b23 If you've never tasted a sweet Spanish virgin before, here's your chance... *46%.*

TEELING Dublin.

Teeling Single Grain Irish Whiskey (94) n23.5 t23.5 f23 b24 Presumably Cooley grain – as good as anything of its ilk on this planet. And showing it has enough about it to combine to stunning effect with some high quality wine casks. I've just had that Teeling feeling.... wonderful! 46%. ncf.

Teeling Whiskey Single Grain wine cask finish, bott Aug 2015 (89) n22 t23 f22 b22 Exceptionally soft and satisfying. 46%. ncf.

Teeling Whiskey Single Grain Wine Casks Finish bott Jun 16 (87) n21.5 t22 f21.5 b22 Silky, friendly with an attractive wine gum simplicity. 46%. ncf.

◇ **Teeling Whiskey Single Grain** wine casks, bott Mar 17, bott code: L17 004 075 (94) n23 seemingly corn oil (OK, now tell me its wheat...!) pokes though with a Kentuckian drawl, though the light grape surround is most un-American; t24 fat, oily and then the most beautiful rise of complex sugars, ulmo honey and maple syrup at heading the cast. So much vanilla, too; f23 ah... spices, busy, battling and seeing off a slight oaky bitterness; b24 what a beautiful grain whisky this is. Thankfully the wine casks don't interrupt the already spellbinding narrative. 46%. ncf.

WEST CORK DISTILLERS County Cork.

◇ **Skibbereen Eagle Single Grain Irish Whiskey** Bodega sherry casks db (88.5) n21.5 the sherry is clean and untainted, but thick enough to silence the grain; t23 gorgeous delivery, both in flavour and texture. Sweet and viscous, some malt and a little oak enters the fray. Ulmo honey and caramel accompany the spotted dick pudding; f22 thick and chewy to the end as some other oils make a mark, though the grape still dictates play; b22 as frictionless as the post Brexit border between Britain and Ireland shall be... 43%. West Cork Distillers Limited.

UNSPECIFIED SINGLE GRAIN

◇ **Egan's Vintage Grain 10 Aged Years** bourbon casks, casked 2009, bott 2017, bott code: US001 244 (92.5) n23 not sure there is a softer nose on the market: your proboscis is kissed, stroked and coddled by a vaguely green and youthful sweetness. Nice biscuits, perhaps with a sugary coconut element plus natural caramels; t23.5 not sure if the silk traders out of China will have ever have found anything silkier than this. Melts in the mouth with a mix of Demerara and icing sugars plus light spices to remind you of the oak; f22.5 a light oak bitterness interjects into the juicy proceedings; b23.5 such a beautiful whiskey. Don't be put off by the fact this is grain: this is exceptionally high grade Irish. Very much of the Cooley style, who happen to make the best grain whisky in the British Isles. 46% (92 proof). ncf.

◇ **Hyde No. 5 Áras Cask 1860 Single Grain** burgundy cask finished, bott Jul 16 (86) n21 t22.5 f21 b21.5 When I first heard about this bottling I was intrigued: one of the softest yet most charismatic grain whiskies in the world rounded off in pinot noir grape casks. Would the grape add an intriguing flintiness to the proceedings, or be of a type to soften it further? Sadly, it was the latter. Yes, sulphur free and clean (itself a minor miracle) and with plenty of chewy fruit caramels and even a little spice. But the peaks have been levelled and what is left is a pleasant, easy drinking, sweet but mainly featureless malt. 46%. ncf. 5,000 bottles.

Blends

Barr an Uisce Wicklow Rare Blended Irish Whiskey bourbon barrel, sherry cask finish (87.5) n22.5 t22 f21 b22. Busy whiskey with a creamy nose and sugar-gorged middle. However, the finish turns a tad bitter. 43%. ncf.

Bushmills 12 Years Old Distillery Reserve db (86) n22.5 t22.5 f20 b21. This version has gone straight for the ultra lush feel. For those who want to take home some 40% abv fruit fudge from the distillery. 40%

Bushmills 1608 400th Anniversary (83) n21 t21.5 f20 b20.5. Thin-bodied, hard as nails and sports a peculiarly Canadian feel. 46%. Diageo.

Bushmills 1608 db (87) n22 t23 f20 b22. A blend which, through accident, evolution or design, has moved a long way in style from when first launched. More accent on fruit though, predictably, the casks aren't quite what they once were. Ignoring the furriness on the finish, there is much to enjoy on the grape-must nose and how the fruit bounces off the rigid grain on delivery. 46%

Bushmills Black Bush (91) n23 t23 f21.5 b23.5. This famous old blend may be under new management and even blender. But still the high quality, top-notch complexity rolls around the glass and your palate. As beautiful as ever. 40%

Bushmills Black Bush bott code L6140IB001 (95) n23.5 t24 f23.5 b24 Of all the famous old blends in the British Isles, this has probably bucked the trend by being an improvement on its already excellent self. The warehouses of Bushmills distillery boast the highest quantity of quality, unsulphured sherry butts I have encountered in the last 20 years, and this is borne out by a blend which has significantly upped the wine influence in the recipe but has not paid a price for it, as has been the usual case in Scotland. Indeed, it has actually benefitted. This is a belter, even by its normal own high standards. Truly classic and should be far easier to find than is normally the case today. *40%.*

Bushmills Original (80) n19 t21 f20 b20. Remains one of the hardest whiskeys on the circuit with the Midleton grain at its most unflinching. There is a sweeter, faintly maltier edge to this now while the toffee and biscuits qualities remain. *40%*

⬥ **Bushmills Red Bush** bourbon casks, bott code: L7161IB001 db (92) n22 working equally well on two levels: one dry and chalky, the second a little salty and with the shyest degree of vanilla sweetness; t23.5 immediately moistens on entry as shafts of honey rhythmically beat towards a sweet, pulsing climax, the mouth filling with golden syrup and acacia honey; f23 stiffens further as the wood enters the fray, culminating in a spicy finish...; in the afterglow it is liqueur chocolates all round; b23.5 a beautifully balanced and erudite blended Irish fully deserving of discovery. And after the preponderance of wine-finished Irish from elsewhere, it was great to taste one that hadn't already set my nerves jangling in fear of what was to come. A worthy and beautiful addition to the Bushmills range. I always knew I'd be a little bit partial to a Red Bush. *40%.*

Cassidy's Distiller's Reserve bott code L8067 (84.5) n21.5 t22 f20 b21. Some salivating malt on flavour-exploding delivery, but all else tame and gentle. *40%. Cooley.*

⬥ **The Dublin Liberties Oak Devil** bott no. L17 048 W3 (94) n23.5 fabulously toasty, the light coffee-roast char mixes sublimely with the ulmo honey and gentle spice; t23.5 every bit as lush as could be expected or hoped for. The ulmo honey steps down a gear into golden syrup, but the spices tap out an oaky code; f23 bitters slightly, but so much oily vanilla and spice to go round; b24 The Cooley grain at work here is of superstar status. So beautifully balanced and the word "lush" hardly does it justice... *46%.*

⬥ **The Dubliner Bourbon Cask Aged** batch no. 001, bott no. L0187F252 (87.5) n21.5 t22.5 f21.5 b22 A soft, clean attractive blend which peaks on delivery with a lilting juiciness which works brilliantly with the grain which is as yielding as a feathered silk pillow. Vague spices plot a course towards the bitter lemon finish. *40%.*

⬥ **Dundalgan Charred Cask Irish Whiskey** db (87) n21.5 t22 f22 b21.5 This is an interesting one: you have a spirit that produces a fair chunk of oil. You then char a cask, which produces caramel. The only result possible is a thick whiskey on both nose and palate with limited scope to develop. So although the end product is the antonym of complexity, the flavours and mouth feel are attractive and satisfying, especially if you are in to malt and toffee. There are even some very late spices to stir things up a bit. *40%. West Cork Distillers Limited.*

⬥ **Dundalgan Irish Whiskey** db (84) n21 t21 f21 b21.5 Pleasant, inoffensive, toffee-dominant and bland. *40%. West Cork Distillers Limited.*

Dunville's Three Crowns (80) n19 t22 f19 b20 Three casks and Three Crowns. So three cheers for the return of one of the great names in Irish whiskey! Somewhere in my warehouse I have a few original bottles of this stuff I picked up in Ireland over the years and at auction. None I opened tasted quite like this. Have to say that, despite the rich-lip-smacking delivery, certain aspects of the tangy nose and finish don't quite gel and are a little off key. The coronation remains on hold... *43.5%.*

Dunville's Three Crowns Peated (94.5) n23 t24 f23.5 b24 Even people purporting not to like peaty whisk(e)y will have a problem finding fault with this. This is a rare treat of an Irish. *43.5%.*

Feckin Irish Whiskey (81) n20 t21 f20 b20. Tastes just about exactly the feckin same as the Feckin Strangford Gold... *40%. The Feckin Drinks Co.*

Flannigans Blended Irish Whiskey (87.5) n21.5 t22.5 f21.5 b22 About as mouth-watering and easy going a blended Irish as you'll hope to find. Excellent sugars and velvety body ensure the most pleasant, if simple, of rides. Even a little spice peps up the flagging finish. *40%. Quality Spirits International.*

⬥ **Great Oaks Cask Strength Irish Whiskey** db (90.5) n22 distinctly coastal: salty rock pools; t23 a little raw in part, but the overall effect is terrific! Acceptable oils fail to hamper the grassy juiciness but succeed in spreading the light tannins and caramels gently around the palate; has a lively zestiness throughout; f22.5 salty again as the sweetened, gristy oils thicken and stick...; b23 a joyful whisky brimming with personality. *60%. West Cork Distillers Limited.*

⬥ **Great Oaks Irish Whiskey** db (87) n22 t22 f21.5 b21.5 Easy going, full of its signature caramel chewy sweetness. Pleasant and non-threatening. *46%. West Cork Distillers Limited.*

⬥ **Great Oaks New Frontiers Irish Whiskey** db (94) n23.5 much cleaner and crisper from the distillery, the oils entirely outgunned by enticing and complexing sweetness offered up by the oak: a light citrus marzipan and red liquorice. All rather bourbon...; t24 unusual clarity on delivery, too: molasses are first to arrive, then this thins to maple syrup. Wonderful spices counter, setting off a massive degree of juiciness as the barley also makes its case; f23 long, with just-so oils stretching out the sugars and vanilla; b23.5 very high class and inventive Irish. West Cork have seriously raised their game here and have entered a new quality dimension. 59%. *West Cork Distillers Limited.*

◇ **Hyde No. 6 President's Reserve 1938 Commemorative Edition** sherry cask finish, bott May 17 **(77)** n18 t22 f18 b19 Lush grape for sure. But the very last thing I'd commemorate anything in would be a sherry cask: unless you want sulphur to give you a good Hyding.... 46%. *ncf. 5,000 bottles.*

The Irishman Cask Strength 2016 1st fill bourbon casks **(90)** n21.5 t23 f22.5 b23 Doesn't try to overload the taste buds with too many flavour profiles: this one is all about shape, intensity and effect. 54%. *ncf. 1,800 bottles.*

Jameson (95) n24.5 24 f22.5 b24 I thought I had detected in bottlings I had found around the world a very slight reduction in the Pot Still character that defines this truly classic whiskey. So I sat down with a fresh bottle in more controlled conditions...and was blown away as usual. The sharpness of the PS is vivid and unique; the supporting grain of the required crispness. Fear not: this very special whiskey remains in stunning, truly wondrous form. *40%*

Jameson bott code L701012030 **(87)** n22 t22.5 f21 b21.5 Now, isn't that the way it always happens! Having tasted crisp, characterful true-to-form Jamesons around the globe for the last year or so, the one I get here for a re-taste is the "other" version. Suddenly the sexiest Irish on the market has become a dullard. Where it should be soaring with Pot Still it is laden with toffee. And a little sulphur nagging on the finish doesn't help, either. Does tick the other boxes, though. But hardly representative. *40%.*

Jameson 18 Years Old bott code L629231345 **(91)** n22 grain dominant and soft. Was expecting a much richer input from the barrels but we have a more marmalade-fruity incursion, instead; t23 excellent two tone mouth feel with both backbone and blubber. A definite fruit pastel sweetness – and juiciness - with the spices moving early...and fading a little; f23 the softer elements keep the game going; the fruits remain sharp and the spices re-form; b23 definitely a change in direction from the last Jameson 18 I analysed. Much more grain focussed and paying less heed to the oak. *40%.*

Jameson Black Barrel bott code L700431433 **(93)** n23 grain doesn't come more solid in character than this: a kind of White Bush on steroids. But, slowly, layers of sugars begin to become exposed, some as crisp as the grain, others soft and molten; t23.5 one of the most salivating deliveries of any Irish blend: little evidence of malt being at work here, again more the sugars and friendly, vaguely bourbon tannins producing the goods especially with the vivid, warming spices. Indeed, the spices become bolder by the second, but the uncompromising hardness of the grain never goes away; f23 spiced vanilla on a light oil; the spices stretch the whiskey further than had first seemed possible b23.5 an improved, more sugar-laden and spicy whiskey. *40%.*

Jameson The Blender's Dog (92) n23 t23.5 f22 b23.5 A clever blend, as this is just as much about mouth feel as it is flavour construction. You have made this dog do some entertaining tricks, Billy Leighton, my dear old friend... 43%. *ncf. The Whisky Makers Series.*

Jameson The Blender's Dog bott code L608231059 **(91.5)** n22.5 t23 f23 b23 A very slight variance on the previous sample (above) with the grain whiskey a little more dominant here despite the softer mouth feel. All the usual tricks and intrigues though a little less orange blossom honey a tad more maple syrup, which helps lengthen the finish. 43%.

Jameson Bold (92) n24 t23.5 f21.5 b23 Delicious stuff. But not to be confused with the excellent Indian malt, Bold, from Paul John, which is a lot Bolder than this... That said, a blender's blend with the nose making one purr with delight and appreciation. 40%. *The Deconstructed Series.*

Jameson Bold bott code L617431172 **(93)** n24 t23.5 f22.5 b23 Absolutely spot on with the tasting notes above. Only changes are slightly more fudge through the centre ground and a degree less bitterness on the finish, though still there. Crucially, however, the honey has a bigger late say. 40%. *The Deconstructed Series.*

◇ **Jameson Bow Street 18 Years Old** batch no. 1/2018, bott code: L804431050 **(88.5)** n22.5 dry, walnuty, chalky vanilla; t23.5 falls somewhere between treacle tart and Parkin Cake: enormous sweetness on delivery, though the roast sugars are soon muffed by a ginger-dry spiciness; f20 dries further still, though a little furry, too...; b22.5 few whiskies have such a wide flavour register between tooth-decayingly sweet and puckeringly dry. 55.3%. *ncf.*

Jameson Caskmates (91.5) n23.5 t23 f22 b23 Some serious elements of Jameson Gold involved in this, especially the acacia honey thread. Delightful. *40%*

◇ **Jameson Caskmates IPA Edition** bott code: L735315273 **(70.5)** n18 t18.5 f17 b17 And you want to ruin the taste of a fine whiskey by adding the bitter taste of hops is because...? Why exactly? Am I missing something here...? *40%. ncf.*

Jameson Caskmates Stout Edition bott code L629315085 **(93)** n22 t23.5 f24 b23.5 A very different experience to the Teeling equivalent. Here, the beer is far less prevalent on nose and taste, but makes a significant, highly positive, contribution to the mouth feel. A super lush experience. 40%.

Jameson The Cooper's Croze (95) n24 t23.5 f23.5 b24 This is one of the most softly spoken great orations on Irish whiskey in recent years. An understated masterpiece. *43%. ncf. The Whisky Makers Series.*

Jameson The Cooper's Croze bott code L608231057 (94.5) n23.5 t24 f22.5 b24 Huh! Near enough same final score as last time, though a gentle change in emphasis and shape means the scoring itself was slightly different. Remains the most astonishingly lush and richly-flavoured of whiskeys, except on this bottling there is a bigger toffee surge, especially towards the finish and a gentle bitter tail off which has cost a half mark. Just remember: whatever anyone ever tells you, no two bottlings are identical: it is impossible. *43%. The Whiskey Makers Series.*

Jameson Crested (90) n23 t24 f20.5 b22.5 When first introduced back in the early 1960s as Jameson's first-ever bottled whiskey, this was known as Crested 10. Now probably ditched the number so not to confuse with age. *40%*

Jameson Crested bott code L635731441 (91) n23 t23.5 f22 b22.5 That's curious. A slight upping of the caramels here has slightly reduced the overall complexity, and the depth of the fruit. However, the bitter, off-key finish from my last sample is missing here making, when all is said and done, a slightly more satisfying all round experience. Swings and roundabouts... *40%.*

Jameson The Distiller's Safe (95) n23.5 t24 f23.5 b24 Not sure if head distiller Brian Nation is any relation to former comedy scriptwriter Terry Nation, creator of The Daleks. Either way, this is Dalektable stuff and as beautifully timed as the funniest skits ever written. *43%. ncf. The Whisky Makers Series.*

Jameson The Distiller's Safe bott code L60331023 (93) n24 t24 f22 b23 This brand's safe, too...at least for another bottling! As near as damn it a re-run of the last bottle I tasted, though here the butteryness kicks in sooner and there is a vague bitterness on the now chocolate-flaked finale. Still a stunner. *43%. The Whiskey Makers Series.*

Jameson Gold Reserve (88) n22 t23 f20 b22. Enjoyable, but so very different: an absolute re-working with all the lighter, more definitively sweeter elements shaved mercilessly while the thicker oak is on a roll. Some distance from the masterpiece it once was. *40%*

Jameson Lively (84.5) n21 t21.5 f21 b21. The belligerent grain of Midleton appears to be coming at you at full throttle and from all direction. The nose appears to be all grain, though a little toffee apple does creep in. The delivery is uncompromising: as hard as nails. *40%. The Deconstructed Series.*

Jameson Lively bott code L617431174 (85.5) n21 t22 f21.5 b21 Well you have to applaud them for keeping to the script. A couple of thumbs up from the last bottling: the impact appears to have been softened very slightly (though, sadly, via toffee) and spices at the finish do no harm at all. *40%. The Deconstructed Series.*

Jameson Round bott code L625831239 (93.5) n22.5 the Midleton grain is there to more than make up the number sand forms the most rigid of backbones. A series of meagre- no-frills sugars furnish those grains with the bare essentials of sweetness; t24 ah...so that is where the roundness comes in! The delivery is like a sponge, revealing the softest molasses and maple syrup imaginable, even managing to remove the firmness from the grain; the mid-ground is a comfortable mix of half-hearted spice, coconut doused in golden syrup and an underlying vanilla...; f23.5 long, with the oak now taking a keener interest. The vanilla dries slightly, becoming almost sawdusty towards the finale. Just a hint of lime is attached to late spice resurgence; b23 just such a sensual whiskey... *40%. The Deconstructed Series.*

Jameson Jameson Signature bott code L617531177 (93) n24 what a stunning aroma: lime Swiss Roll, aided and abetted by orange blossom honey and a very curious, an almost inexplicable, anthracite phenol buzz; t23.5 soft as a the feather of quill, a light marmalade sharpness/sweetness diluted by what seems like a maltiness, though the gathering fudge makes it difficult to pick out exactly; a little mocha and spice fill the middle ground; f22.5 just a shade too much toffee on the still busy and spicy finish; b23 no longer Signature Reserve, though every bit as good. This, though, like some other Jamesons of late appears to have an extra dose of caramel. Bring the colouring down and whiskey – and the scores here - will really fly! *40%.*

Jameson Signature Reserve (93) n23.5 t23.5 f22.5 b23.5. Be assured with Signature, with its clever structuring of delicate and inter-weaving flavours, says far more about the blender, Billy Leighton, than it does John Jameson. *40%. Irish Distillers.*

Kellan American oak cask (84) n21 t22 f20 b21. Safe whisky which is clean, sweet and showing many toffeed attributes. Decent spices, too. *40% (80 Proof). Cooley.*

Kilbeggan bott code L7091 db (86) n21 t22 f21.5 b21.5. A much more confident blend by comparison with that faltering one of the last few years. Here, the malts make a significant drive towards increasing the overall complexity and gentle citrus style. *40%. Cooley.*

Kilbeggan 15 Years Old bott code L7048 db (85.5) n21.5 t22 f21 b21. My word! 15 years, eh? How time flies! And on the subject of flying, surely I have winged my way back to Canada and am tasting a native blend. No, this is Irish albeit in sweet, deliciously rounded form. However, one cannot help feeling that the dark arts have been performed, as in an injection of caramel, which, as well as giving that Canadian feel has also probably shaved off some of the more complex notes to middle and finish. Even so, a sweet, silky experience. 40%. Cooley.

Kilbeggan 18 Year Old db **(89)** n23 t21.5 f22.5 b22. Although the impressive bottle lavishly claims "From the World's Oldest Distillery" I think one can take this as so much Blarney. It certainly had my researcher going, who lined this up for me under the Old Kilbeggan distillery, a forgivable mistake and one I think he will not be alone in making. This, so it appears on the palate, is a blend. From the quite excellent Cooley distillery, and it could be that whiskey used in this matured at Kilbeggan... which is another thing entirely. As for the whiskey: apart from some heavy handedness on the toffee, it really is quite a beautiful and delicate thing. 40%

Kilgeary bott code L8063 **(79)** n20 t20 f19 b20. There has always, and still proudly is, something strange about this blend. Cold tea on the nose and a bitter bite to the finish, sandwiches a brief flirtation with something sweet. 40%. Cooley.

Locke's bott code L8056 **(85.5)** n21 t22 f21.5 b21. Now, there you go!! Since I last really got round to analysing this one it has grown from a half-hearted kind of a waif to something altogether more gutsy and muscular. Sweeter, too, as the malts and grains combine harmoniously. A clean and pleasant experience with some decent malt fingerprints. 40%

Michael Collins A Blend **(77)** n19 t20 f19 b19. Michael Collins was known as the "big fellow". This pleasant, impressively spiced dram, might have enjoyed the same epithet had it not surrendered to and then been strangled by caramel on the finish. 40% (80 proof). Cooley.

Midleton Distillery Reserve **(85)** n22 t22 f20 b21. A whiskey which, for all its muscovado sweetness offers some memorable barley moments. 40%. Irish Distillers Midleton Distillery only. Changes character slightly with each new vatting. This one is some departure.

Midleton Very Rare 30th Anniversary Pearl Edition db **(91)** n23.5 t24 f21 b22.5 The nose and delivery will go down in Irish whiskey folklore... 53.1%

Midleton Very Rare 1984 **(70)** n19 t18 f17 b16. Disappointing with little backbone or balance. 40%. Irish Distillers.

Midleton Very Rare 1985 **(77)** n20 t20 f18 b19. Medium-bodied and oily, this is a big improvement on the initial vintage. 40%. Irish Distillers.

Midleton Very Rare 1986 **(79)** n21 t20 f18 b20. A very malty Midleton richer in character than previous vintages. 40%. Irish Distillers.

Midleton Very Rare 1987 **(77)** n20 t19 f19 b19. Quite oaky at first until a late surge of excellent pot still. 40%. Irish Distillers.

Midleton Very Rare 1988 **(86)** n23 t21 f21 b21. A landmark MVR as it is the first vintage to celebrate the Irish pot-still style. 40%. Irish Distillers.

Midleton Very Rare 1989 **(87)** n22 t22 f22 b21. A real mouthful but has lost balance to achieve the effect. 40%. Irish Distillers.

Midleton Very Rare 1990 **(93)** n23 t23 f24 b23. Astounding whiskey: one of the vintages every true Irish whiskey lover should hunt for. 40%. Irish Distillers.

Midleton Very Rare 1991 **(76)** n19 t20 f19 b18. After the Lord Mayor's Show, relatively dull and uninspiring. 40%. Irish Distillers.

Midleton Very Rare 1992 **(84)** n20 t20 f23 b21. Superb finish with outstanding use of feisty grain. 40%. Irish Distillers.

Midleton Very Rare 1993 **(88)** n21 t22 f23 b22. big, brash and beautiful – the perfect way to celebrate the 10th-ever bottling of MVR. 40%. Irish Distillers.

Midleton Very Rare 1994 **(87)** n22 t22 f21 b22. Another different style of MVR, one of amazing lushness. 40%. Irish Distillers.

Midleton Very Rare 1995 **(90)** n23 t24 b21 b22. They don't come much bigger than this. Prepare a knife and fork to battle through this one. Fabulous. 40%. Irish Distillers.

Midleton Very Rare 1996 **(82)** n21 t22 f19 b20. The grains lead a soft course, hardened by subtle pot still. Just missing a beat on the finish, though. 40%. Irish Distillers.

Midleton Very Rare 1997 **(83)** n22 t21 f19 b21. The piercing pot still fruitiness of the nose is met by a countering grain of rare softness on the palate. Just dies on the finish when you want it to make a little speech. Very drinkable. 40%. Irish Distillers.

Midleton Very Rare 1999 **(89)** n21 t23 f22 b23. One of the maltiest Midletons of all time: a superb blend. 40%. Irish Distillers.

Midleton Very Rare 2000 **(85)** n22 t21 f21 b21. An extraordinary departure even by Midleton's eclectic standards. The pot still is like a distant church spire in an hypnotic Fen landscape. 40%. Irish Distillers.

Midleton Very Rare 2001 **(79)** n21 t20 f18 b20. Extremely light but the finish is slightly on the bitter side. 40%. Irish Distillers.

Midleton Very Rare 2002 **(79)** n20 t22 f18 b19. The nose is rather subdued and the finish is likewise toffee-quiet and shy. There are some fabulous middle moments, some of flashing genius, when the pot still and grain combine for a spicy kick, but the finish really is lacklustre and disappointing. 40%. *Irish Distillers.*

Midleton Very Rare 2003 (84) n22 t22 f19 b21. Beautifully fruity on both nose and palate (even some orange blossom on aroma). But the delicious spicy richness that is in mid launch on the tastebuds is cut short by caramel on the middle and finish. A crying shame, but the best Midleton for a year or two. 40%. *Irish Distillers.*

Midleton Very Rare 2004 (82) n21 t21 f19 b21. Yet again caramel is the dominant feature, though some quite wonderful citrus and spice escape the toffeed blitz. 40%.

Midleton Very Rare 2005 (92) n23 t24 f22 b23. OK, you can take this one only as a rough translation. The sample I have worked from here is from the Irish Distillers blending lab, reduced to 40% in mine but without caramel added. And, as Midleton Very Rares always are at this stage, it's an absolute treat. Never has such a great blend suffered so in the hands of colouring and here the chirpiness of the pot still and élan of the honey (very Jameson Gold Label in part) show just what could be on offer given half the chance. Has wonderful natural colour and surely it is a matter of time before we see this great whiskey in its natural state. 40%

Midleton Very Rare 2006 (92) n22 t24 f23 b23. As raw as a Dublin rough-house and for once not overly swamped with caramel. An uncut diamond. 40%

Midleton Very Rare 2007 (83) n20 t22 f20 b21. Annoyingly buffeted from nose to finish by powering caramel. Some sweeter wisps do escape but the aroma suggests Canadian and insufficient Pot Still gets through to make this a Midleton of distinction. 40%. *Irish Distillers*

Midleton Very Rare 2008 (88.5) n22 t23 f21.5 b22. A dense bottling which offers considerably more than the 2007 Vintage. Attractive, very drinkable and without the caramel it might really have hit the heights. 40%. *Irish Distillers.*

Midleton Very Rare 2009 (95) n24 t24 f23 b24. I've been waiting a few years for one like this to come along. One of the most complex, cleanest and least caramel-spoiled bottlings for a good few years and one which makes the pot still character its centre piece. A genuine celebration of all things Midleton and Barry Crockett's excellence as a distiller in particular. 40%. .

Midleton Very Rare 2010 (84) n21 t22 f20 b21. A case of after the Lord Mayor's Show. Chewy and some decent sugars. But hard to make out detail through the fog of caramel. 40%

Midleton Very Rare 2011 (81.5) n22.5 t20 f19 b20 Another disappointing version where the colour of its personality has been compromised for the sake of the colour in the bottle. A dullard of a whiskey, especially after the promising nose. 40%. *Irish Distillers.*

Midleton Very Rare Irish Whisky 2012 db (89.5) n22 t23 f22 b22.5. Much more like it! After a couple of dud vintages, here we have a bottling worthy of its great name & heritage. 40%.

Midleton Very Rare Irish Whisky 2014 db (78.5) n20.5 t22 f17 b19. Must say how odd it looks to see Brian Nation's signature scrawled across the label and not Barry Crockett's. Also, I was a bit worried by this one when I saw the depth of orange hue to this whiskey. Sadly, my fears were pretty well founded. Toffee creaks from every corner making for a mainly flat encounter with what should be an uplifting Irish. Some lift at about the midway point when something, probably pot still, throws off the shackles of its jailer and emerges briefly with spice. But all rather too little, especially in the face of a dull, disappointingly flawed, fuzzy finale. Midleton Very Rare should be, as the name implies, a lot, lot better than this safe but flabby, personality bypassed offering. The most frutrating aspect of this is that twice I have tasted MVR in lab form just prior to bottling. And both were quite stunning whiskeys. That was until the colouring was added in the bottling hall. 40% WB15/416

Midleton Very Rare 2016 (87.5) n22 t22.5 f21.5 b21.5 The grain, not exactly the most yielding, has the clearest mandate to show its uncompromising personality A huge caramel presence softens the impact and leads to a big show of coffee towards the finish. But between these two OTT beasts the Pot Still is lost completely soon after its initial delicious impact on delivery. 40%.

⬩⬩ **Midleton Very Rare 2017** (90.5) n22 a little spice nip and toffee; the grain dominates; t23.5 soft, juicy and sweet; a degree of orange blossom honey opens this up brilliantly; a little firm potstill type sharpness fills in the mid-ground and introduces the spices; f22 vanilla and toffee; b23 slightly less toffee than there has been, but still a fraction too much. But superb complexity levels nonetheless and one of the most attractively sweet MVRs for a little while. 40%.

⬩⬩ **Mizen Head Original Irish Whiskey** Bodega sherry casks db (87.5) n21.5 t22.5 f21.5 b22 Maybe this was a bit unlucky, in that I have just come from tasting Glenfarclas sherry casks of the 1980s to this. No damaging sulphur (though a little forms late on the finale), so some Brownie points there. But the lack of body to the spirit and shortage of complexity on the grape, beyond a delicious cinnamon spice, doesn't help the cause. Enjoyable, but thinner than you might expect or desire. 40%. *West Cork Distillers Limited.*

Paddy (74) n18.5 t20 f17.5 b18. Cleaned its act up a little. Even a touch of attractive citrus on the nose and delivery. But where does that cloying sweetness come from? As bland as an Irish peat bog but, sadly, nothing like so potentially tasty. 40%. *Irish Distillers.*

Powers (91) n23 t24 f22 b22. Is it any coincidence that in this bottling the influence of the caramel has been significantly reduced and the whiskey is getting back to its old, brilliant self? I think not. Classic stuff. 40%. *Irish Distillers.*

Powers Gold Label (87) n22 t22 f21 b22. The solid pot still, the very DNA of what made Powers, well, Powers is vanishing in front of our very noses. Yes, still some pot still around, but nothing like so pronounced in the way that made this, for decades, a truly one-off Irish and one of the world greats. Still delightful and with many charms but the rock hard pot still effect is sadly missed. What is going on here? 40%. *Irish Distillers.*

Powers Gold Label (96) n23 t24.5 f24 b24.5 A slightly dfferent breed. This is not all aboutminute difference in strength...this is also about weight distribution and flavour pace. It is a subtly different blend...and all the better for it...Make no mistake: this is a truly classic Irish. 43.2%

The Quiet Man Traditional Irish Whiskey bourbon casks (88.5) n22 t22 f22.5 b22 A gentle and genteel whiskey without an unfriendly voice. And with it I toast the memory of John Mulgrew. 40%

⬦ **Roe & Co** bourbon casks, bott code: L7173NB001 006084 (89.5) n22 caramel laden, but a lovely mix of delicate citrus, salt and spice offers balance and intrigue; t23 lush, sweet grain heads off in a heather-honey direction. The grains are improbably chewy; f22.5 the spices return, as does the fudge. Light muscovado sugars add an extra edge; b22 a joyful Irish blend, easy drinking and basking in some outrageously good grain. But the caramel levels could do with coming down slightly for greater complexity. 45%. ncf.

Teeling Small Batch Irish Whiskey (87.5) n21 t23 f21.5 b22. Pleasant enough, and again showing high class grain. But a sharper liquorice/phenol note is out of kilter here and disrupts the natural flow of things, especially on the finish. 46%. ncf.

Teeling Whiskey Small Batch rum casks, bott Feb 17 (89) n22 soft and with a sheen, as though burnished with sugar. A little spice juts out; t23 intensely sweet delivery. The mouth feel is massively sumptuous and yielding; f22 more sugars and spice on the vanilla; very slight bitter fade; b22 you have to be a little wary with rum casks as they can easily over-ride complexity, as is the case here. This, then, is all about effect and for that it can't be faulted. 46%. ncf.

⬦ **Teeling Whiskey Small Batch** rum casks, bott Jan 18, bott code: L18 001 031 (83.5) n21 t22.5 f19 b21 Some rum matured whisky works rather well. Others, like this bitter-sweet, monosyllabic offering, sadly I don't. 46%. ncf

Teeling Whiskey Stout Cask Small Batch 200 Fathoms Imperial Stout finish, bott Mar 17 (92.5) n22.5 certainly a unique nose among the world's whiskies: this has a peculiar empty Guinness glass effect, one that has been left out on the garden table in the sun for a few hours. Leather and Demerara sugar each play a role in balancing the roastiness...; t23.5 silky sugars land lightly, a little ulmo honey, too. But elsewhere there are much duskier tones, semi-toasty but incredibly soft; f23 the feeling that you had a mouthful of stout – oat stout especially - about two or three minutes ago, as this is without any lingering bitterness...; b23.5 whiskey and chaser in one go... The extra roastiness imparts a distinctive extra weight which works exceptionally well. 46%. ncf.

⬦ **Teeling Whiskey Stout Cask Small Batch** 200 Fathoms Imperial Stout finish, bott Jan 18, bott code: L18 001 018 (94) n23.5 a non-specific creamy roastiness (does anyone remember Mackeson Milk Stout?) benefits from a sweet mocha framework; t23.5 didn't expect the delivery to be anything like so sweet and beautifully balanced: again, I have to point you back to Mackeson, yet with the silky texture of a Sam Smith's Oatmeal Stout. And, I'm delighted to say, barely the hint of a hop in sight; f23 well there is now, but the creamy ulmo honey followed by a gorgeous chocolate mousse soon takes good care of it; late non-beer related spices are the icing on the cake; b24 a rare example of a beer finished whiskey not ruined by hops. An absolute beauty of its type. 46%. ncf.

Tullamore Dew (85) n22 t21.5 f20.5 b21. The days of the throat being savaged by this one appear to be over. Much more pot still character from nose to finish and the rough edges remain, attractively, just that. 40%. *Campbell & Cochrane Group.*

Tullamore Dew 10 Years Old (81.5) n21 t21.5 f19 b20. A bright start from this new kid on the Tullamore block. Soft fruit and harder pot still make some kind of complexity, but peters out at the death. 40%.

Tullamore Dew 12 Years Old (84.5) n21.5 t21.5 f20 b21.5. Silky thanks to some excellent Midleton grain: there are mouthwatering qualities here that make the most of the soft spices and gentle fruit. An improved whiskey, if still somewhat meek and shy. 40%.

Tullamore Dew Black 43 (85) n19 t22 f22.5 b21.5. "Black". Now there's an original name for a new whiskey. Don't think it'll catch on, personally: after all, who has ever heard of a whisky being called "This or That" Black...?? But the whiskey might. Once you get past the usual Tullamore granite-like nose, here even more unyielding than usual, some rather engaging and complex (and especially spicy) things happen, though the caramel does its best to neuter them. 43%. *William Grant & Sons.*

Tullamore D.E.W Cider Cask Finished bott code. L2 65TD, bott 05/05/2015 (85.5) n21.5 t22 f21 b21. Experienced Whisky Bible readers will know that over the years I have tasted whisky matured either in cider casks or, more usually, in an environment where cider brandy is also maturing. That has always been with a single malt, though, and without exception the apple shines through. Here, though, the apple has to work overtime to get any change out of the hardest, least yielding grain on the planet. The result is an, at times, attractive blend, but also one which has its more unforgiving moments... 40%

Tullamore Dew Heritage (78) n20 t21 f18 b19. Tedious going with the caramel finish a real turn off. 40.0%. Campbell & Cochrane Group.

Uisce Beatha Real Irish Whiskey ex-Bourbon cask (81) n21 t20.5 f19.5 b20. The label blurb claims this is soft and subtle. That is, about as soft and subtle as if distilled from granite. Hard as nails with dominant grains; takes no prisoners at the death. 40%

Walker & Scott Irish Whiskey (85) n21 t22 f21 b21. Oddly, sharper grain has helped give his some extra edge through the toffee. A very decent blend. 40%

⬦ **West Cork Black Cask Char #5** Level bott code: L17297 db (89) n22 huge amounts of natural caramel spill out, aided by a muscly viscosity. The barley plods quietly; t23 the fattest blend of all time, surely. Enough oil to fill a refinery, though for a blend the malt content appears massive as barley and vanilla combine enormously...; f22 more oil...; b22 good grief! This must be one of the most oil-rich, heavy duty blends I have encountered in my near 30 year whisky career. Either very little grain, or it is a grain distilled to a relatively low strength. Either way...good grief! 40%. West Cork Distillers Limited.

⬦ **West Cork Bourbon Cask** db (87.5) n22 t22.5 f21 b22 No-one does caramel like West Cork, and even in their blend – in which their own grain has attractively thinned their hefty malt, it comes through loud and clear. Indeed, had I not known the distillery, I would have marked this down as a Canadian or a young, unfulfilled bourbon. Wonderfully soft and proffers some seriously lovely moments. 40%. West Cork Distillers Limited.

⬦ **West Cork Cask Strength** bott code: L17293 db (87) n21 t23.5 f20.5 b22 Just love the power of this malt on the delivery, relentlessly, mercilessly driving home the barley, a little ulmo honey and vanilla offering a controlled sweetness. Neither the nose or finish work so well, but worth finding just for that beautiful launch. 62%. West Cork Distillers Limited.

The Wild Geese Classic Blend (80.5) n20 t21 f19.5 b19. Easy going, pretty neutral and conservative. If you are looking for zip, zest and charisma you've picked the wrong goose (see below). 40%. Cooley for Avalon.

The Wild Geese Rare Irish (89.5) n22 t23 f22 b22.5. Just love this. The Cooley grain is working sublimely and dovetails with the malt in the same effortless way wild geese fly in perfect formation. A treat. 43% Cooley for Avalon.

Writers Tears (93) n23.5 a glossy Pot Still character: rather than the usual fruity firmness, the recognisable Pot Still traits are shrouded in soft honey tones which dovetail with lightening kumquat-citrus tones. Quite a curious, but always deliciously appealing animal...; t24 works beautifully well: the arrival is an alternating delivery of hard and soft waves, the former showing a more bitter, almost myopic determination to hammer home its traditional pot still standpoint; the sweeter, more yielding notes dissolve with little or no resistance, leaving an acacia honeyed trail; towards the middle a juicier malt element mingles with soft vanilla but the Pot Still character never goes away; f22 relatively short with perhaps the Pot Still, with an old-fashioned cough sweet fruitiness, lingering longest, though its does retain its honeyed accompaniment for the most part; b23.5 now that really was different. The first mix of pure Pot Still and single malt I have knowingly come across in a commercial bottling, but only because I wasn't aware of the make up of last year's Irishman Blend. The malt, like the Pot Still, is, I understand from proprietor Bernard Walsh, from Midleton, but the two styles mixed shows a remarkably similar character to when I carried out an identical experiment with pure pot still and Bushmills the best part of a decade ago. A success and hopefully not a one off. 40%. Writers Tears Whiskey Co.

Writers' Tears Vintage Cask 2016 ex-bourbon barrels, bott Sept 2016 (89) n22 t23 f22 b22 A pleasant, but mildly muted version of Irishman Cask Strength 2016, though here the spices arrive later. 2016. 53%. ncf 2,640 bottles.

Poitin

Spirit of Dublin Irish Poitin batch. 02 db (88.5) n22 t23 f21.5 b22 A whole lot cleaner than some – if not all - of the Irish poitin I've tasted from jam jars, lemonade bottles and recycled bottles of Power's over the last 40 years or so. Has the obvious "new make" aroma of unmatured malt, except perhaps a little less discernible copper. Peaks with a big gristy sugar surge about four or five flavour beats after the delivery, but thins a little quickly thereafter. 52.5%.

American Whiskey

It had been eleven long years since a bourbon won the coveted title of Jim Murray's Whisky Bible World Whisky of the Year. And you might have thought that with Kentucky going a record-equalling three years without the top award the greatest days were in the past. Wrong. And wrong again.

Because Kentucky has done it again. Last year it was the ultra-complex Colonel E. H. Taylor. This year, from the same stable, the William Larue Weller a wheated bourbon of extraordiary consistency and intensity.

This is an amazing achievement by Buffalo Trace, that shrine and living museum to American whiskey-making sitting as resolutely on the banks of the Kentucky river in the same daunting way mediaeval castles would on the Rhine, Thames or Danube. For the fifth time in the last nine years their whiskey, be it bourbon or rye, has taken up two of the top three Whiskies in the World awards, a tale of near unbelievable consistency. It has got to the stage now where I try to mark Buffalo Trace whiskeys a little tougher than I do the others, which perhaps seems a little unfair. But, even so, still they end up seeing off the rest of the world's best. For Weller it is an even more remarkabe achievement: after two Third Best Whisky of the World Awards and three Runners-up spots, at last its perpetual genius has paid dividends.

And Buffalo Trace have not ended there. It was their bourbon which won Single Cask of the Year with a Blanton's Gold of improbable brilliance.

That is not to say other Kentuckians have been lying down and allowing the Buffalos to stampede all over them. The overall quality of the bourbons and ryes I tasted this year, both privately while in the USA and officially for Jim Murray's Whisky Bible, has been magnificent. One that was desperately unlucky not to come away with any award from the Whisky Bible was the glorious Knob Creek rye. Even that, though near faultless as it was, could not quite match the Thomas H. Handy which picked up Third Spot of all the world's whiskies.

And what of the smaller guys? Well, Texas is taking some beating at the moment. It was Balcone's with their massive Blue Corn last year, and now Garrison Brothers - not for the first time - this year, their Balmorhea eclipsing (or do I mean Trumping?) all others.

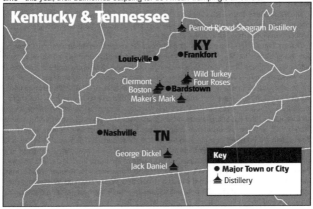

Kentucky & Tennessee

- Pernod Ricard Seagram Distillery
- **KY**
- Louisville ●
- ● Frankfort
- Wild Turkey
- Clermont ▲ Four Roses
- Boston ●Bardstown
- Maker's Mark ▲

- ●Nashville **TN**

- George Dickel ▲
- Jack Daniel ▲

Key
- ● Major Town or City
- ▲ Distillery

Bardstown	Woodford Reserve
Heaven Hill	**Louisville**
Tom Moore	Early Times
Frankfort	Bernheim
Buffalo Trace	Stitzel Weller

Bourbon Distilleries

Bourbon confuses people. Often they don't even realise it is a whiskey, a situation not helped by leading British pub chains, such as Wetherspoon, whose bar menus list "whiskey" and "bourbon" in separate sections. And if I see the liqueur Southern Comfort listed as a bourbon one more time I may not be responsible for my actions.

Bourbon is a whiskey. It is made from grain and matured in oak, so really it can't be much else. To be legally called bourbon it must have been made with a minimum of 51% corn and matured in virgin oak casks for at least two years. Oh, and no colouring can be added other than that which comes naturally from the barrel.

Where it does differ, from, say Scotch, is that the straight whiskey from the distillery may be called by something other than that distillery name. Indeed, the distillery may change its name which has happened to two this year already and two others in the last three or four. So, to make things easy and reference as quick as possible, I shall list the Kentucky-based distilleries first and then their products in alphabetical order along with their owners and operational status.

BUFFALO TRACE Leestown, Frankfort. Sazerac. Operating.

BROWN-FORMAN Shively, Louisville. Brown-Forman. Operating.

FOUR ROSES Lawrenceburg. Kirin. Operating

HEAVEN HILL BERNHEIM DISTILLERY Louisville. Heaven Hill. Operating.

JIM BEAM Boston and Clermont. Beam Suntory. Operating.

MAKER'S MARK Loretto. Beam Suntory. Operating.

WILD TURKEY Lawrenceburg. Campari Group. Operating.

WOODFORD RESERVE Near Millville. Brown-Forman. Operating.

Jim Murray's Whisky Bible American Whiskey Award Winners

	Overall Winner	Bourbon	Rye	Microdistilleries
2004	George T. Stagg	George T. Stagg	Sazerac Rye 18 Years Old	McCarthy's Oregan Single Malt
2005	George T. Stagg	George T. Stagg	Sazerac Rye 18 Years Old	McCarthy's Oregan Single Malt
2006	George T. Stagg	George T. Stagg	Sazerac Rye 18 Years Old	McCarthy's Oregan Single Malt
2007	Buffalo Trace Experimental	Buffalo Trace Experimental	Rittenhouse Rye 21 Barrel No.28	McCarthy's Oregan Single Malt
2008	George T. Stagg 70.3%	George T. Stagg 70.3%	Old Potrero Hotaling's 11 Essay	Old Potrero Hotaling's 11 Essay
2009	George T. Stagg (144.8 Proof)	George T. Stagg (144.8 Proof)	Rittenhouse Rye 23 Barrel No.8	Stranahan's Colorado 5 Batch 11
2010	Sazerac Rye 18 (Fall 2008)	George T. Stagg (144.8 Proof)	Sazerac Rye 18 (Fall 2008)	N/A
2011	Thomas H. Handy Rye (129 Proof)	William Larue Weller (134.8 Proof)	Thomas H. Handy Rye (129 Proof)	N/A
2012	George T. Stagg (143 Proof)	George T. Stagg (143 Proof)	Thomas H. Handy Rye (126.9 Proof)	N/A
2013	Thomas H. Handy Rye (128.6 Proof)	William Larue Weller (133.5 Proof)	Thomas H. Handy Rye (128.6 Proof)	Balcones Brimstone
2014	William Larue Weller (1234 Proof)	William Larue Weller (1234 Proof)	Thomas H. Handy Rye (132.4 Proof)	Cowboy Bourbon Whiskey
2015	William Larue Weller	William Larue Weller	Sazerac Rye 18 (Fall 2013)	Arkansas Single Barrel Reserve #190
2016	Pikesville Straight Rye (110 Proof)	William Larue Weller	Pikesville Straight Rye (110 Proof)	Notch 12 Year Old
2017	Booker's Rye 13 Years 1 Mo 12 Days	William Larue Weller (1346 Prof)	Booker's Rye 13 Years 1 Mo 12 Days	Garrison Brothers Cowboy 2009
2018	Colonel E.H. Taylor Four Grain	Colonel E.H. Taylor Four Grain	Thomas H. Handy Rye (126.2 Proof)	Balcones Texas Blue Corn
2019	William Larue Weller (128.2 Proof)	William Larue Weller (128.2 Proof)	Thomas H. Handy Rye (127.2 Proof)	Garrison Brothers Balmorhea

Bourbon

◇ **1792 Bottled In Bond** bott code: L172731504:465 db **(93) n23** red liquorice and hickory merge into the corn oils but lift as a light, tannic saltiness drifts through; **t23.5** there we go again! A very specific saline feel to this: sharp and three dimensional with massive hickory and molasses middle. The caramels make this a chewy chap, for sure; **f23** vanilla with an attractive tang; **b23.5** an unusually salty resonance to this which travels from the nose to the very last moments of the finish. Certainly does a job in sharpening up the flavour profile! 50% (100 proof).

1792 High Rye Kentucky Straight Bourbon db **(96) n23.5 t24.5 f23.5 b24.5** My word! What an exhibition of controlled and sometimes disguised big flavours...! Stupendous! 47.15% (94.3 proof).

◇ **1792 Small Batch** bott code: L173111514:395 **(94) n23** hefty and for once crammed with oilier corn notes. Makes for a soft aroma with a gentle parade of delicate honey tones elegantly countering the growing spice; **t24** a delivery of dreams: concentrated small grain emphasises a big toasty rye depth, though the vanillas try to outdo it with a surge of hickory enriched tannin; the corn gives a feeling of luxury with its velvety texture; the sugars melting to counter the oak; **f23.5** a long fade with those tannins at last building into something showing decent oak involvement; **b23.5** yet again a 1792 expression pulls off Whisky Bible Liquid Gold status. Astonishing. 46.85% (93.7 proof).

1792 Sweet Wheat Kentucky Straight Bourbon db **(94.5) n23.5 t24 f23 b24** Barton had long been one of the wasted distilleries of the world, its product once bottled and sold way before its intricate, busy bourbon was able to sing to its fullest potential. Under the new management of Sazerac, we are now consistently seeing the greatness from this distillery that for decades was found only in its 6-year-old. This is a wheated, honeyed stunner. 45.6% (91.2 proof)

◇ **Abraham Bowman Limited Edition Viriginia Sweet XVI Bourbon** dist 4-26-02, bott 4-26-18 **(95.5) n23.5** insane amounts of liquorice and hickory make for as much a dry as it is sweet 16-year-old...; **t24.5** hold on to your hats! This is not taking prisoners. Nor is it letting up on complexity. We have so many different sugar types it is hard to keep count. Molasses leads, then Manuka honey thinned with maple syrup and Demerara, yet all the while the tannins are pounding out their basest, toastier notes: this is so loud it is like being standing by the speakers at a concert...; **f23.5** the toastier element has the upper hand towards the end, though the sugary underbelly is never far away. A pinch of spice, but little more: a bit like that quiet moment after a body-shattering orgasm...; **b24** probably the most outrageously complex and full-flavoured Virginia whiskey I have ever encountered in bottled form...Just amazin'! 58% (116 proof). Release No. 17.

◇ **Ancient Age** bott code: 03072163212:09F **(94) n24** not sure if you can get a more classic aroma for a bourbon so seemingly young. A sublime blend of acacia and ulmo honey appears to absorb the tannins with ease and comfort, balancing beautifully the ripe pear, butterscotch and marzipan...wow! **t23.5** melts-in-the-mouth with a mix of golden syrup and corn oil before a spicy surge blasts a path through, like a highway thorough a Kentucky limestone hill; **f22.5** the honey is still around, now duskier, almost roasty in its make-up. Dries as a chalky oakiness arrives; **b24** though at times a little youthful and proudly possessing a little nip to the delivery, this still exudes Buffalo Trace character and class and a lot more inner oomph than when I first encountered this brand decades ago – indeed, when the distillery was still called Ancient Age. Enough oak to make a comfortable foil for the busy small grain. Salivating, complex and deeply satisfying, especially when the burnt honey begins to make itself heard .A classic name and my word, this bottling shows it in a classic light. 40% (80 proof)

Ancient Age Bonded **(92) n23 t24 f23 b23.** Unmistakably Buffalo Trace... with balls. 50%

Ancient Ancient Age 10 Star **(94.5) n23 t24 f23.5 b24.** A bourbon which has slipped effortlessly through the gears over the last decade. It is now cruising and offers so many nuggets of pure joy this is now a must have for the serious bourbon devotee. Now a truly great bourbon which positively revels in its newfound complexity: a new 10 Star is born... 45%

◇ **Ancient Age 10 Star** bott code: B1704707:294 **(86) n21 t22.5 f21 b21.5** Plenty of action but struggles to find a rhythm and balance while the finish is just plain dull. The spiced chocolate and liquorice surge is the highlight but slightly disappointing for an Ancient Age. 45% (90 proof)

Ancient Ancient Age 10 Years Old **(96) n23.5 t24 f24 b24.5.** This whiskey is like shifting sands: same score as last time out, but the shape is quite different again. Somehow underlines the genius of the distillery that a world class whiskey can reach the same point of greatness, but by taking two different routes...However, in this case the bourbon actually finds something a little extra to move it on to a point very few whiskeys very rarely reach... 43%

◇ **Ancient Age 90** bott code: 03072173209:38W **(88.5) n22** dry and roasty with black pepper nip; **t22** big, thumping delivery with the non-specific honeys and chunky oak outgunned only by the massive spice; **f22.5** settles down for a more subtle and complex finale. The layering excels: the oak and sugars interplay for a very long time, though again it is the spice which wins; **b22** an emboldened bourbon showing little of genteel complexity of the standard Ancient Age. Delicious, though! *45% (90 proof)*

Baker's Aged 7 Years Kentucky Straight Bourbon Whiskey batch no. B-90-001 (95) **n24 t23.5 f23.5 b24** One of those uncompromisingly delicious bourbons which makes spitting, as I have to do with each sample tasted, a very unnatural act... *53.5% (107 proof)*

Basil Hayden's Kentucky Straight Bourbon Whiskey bott code L5222 (87) **n22.5 t22 f21 b21.5**. Bigs up the bitter marmalade but a relatively thin bourbon with not enough depth to entirely manage the flattening and slightly unflattering vanilla. The usual rye-based backbone has gone missing. *40% (80 proof)*

Big Bottom Straight Bourbon 91 (95) **n23** tight, in that small grain dominates over the corn, while making the most of its oils, and the oak is chunky, salty and chocolaty; **t24** again, a big salty tang to this, but this then serves to bring out the enormity of the grains, in which the corn has fought back pole position; the middle is full of honey, liquorice and burgeoning spices; **f24** and now the small grains are back behind the wheel for a tantalisingly complex finale; **b24** stupendous bourbon. *45.5% (91 proof) ncf.*

Big Bottom Straight Bourbon 111 (85.5) **n21.5 t20.5 f22.5 b21**. An aggressive bourbon and that has nothing to do with the strength. The delivery is tart and lopsided. The sharpness recedes towards the middle and, finally, the lights shine as the praline and mocha enter the fray on the spicy finish. *55.5% (111 proof) ncf.*

Blade & Bow batch SW-B1 (84) **n21.5 t21.5 f20 b21**. A simple, if at times massively sweet, offering which minimises on complexity. *45.5%*

Blade and Bow 22 Year Old (95.5) **n24 t24 f23.5 b24** This may not be the oldest bourbon brand on the market, but it creaks along as though it is. Every aspect says "Old Timer". But like many an old 'un, has a good story to tell... in this case, exceptional. *46% (92 proof)*

Blade & Bow DeLuxe batch WLCFSS-2 (88.5) **n22.5** major liquorice contribution; **t22.5** manuka honey and molasses counter the big toasty notes; **f21** as the sugars fade, the toast burns...; **b22.5** a steady ship which, initially, is heavy on the honey. *46%*

Blanton's (92) **n21.5 t24 f23 b23.5**. If it were not for the sluggish nose this would be a Whisky Bible Liquid Gold award winner for sure. On the palate it shows just why little can touch Buffalo Trace for quality at the moment... *40%*

Blanton's Gold Original Single Barrel (96.5) **n24 t24.5 f24 b24**. It is improbable that a whiskey this enormous and with so many star turns can glide so effortlessly over the palate. One of the best Blanton's in years, this is true Gold standard... *46.5% (93 Proof)*

Blanton's Gold Edition Single Barrel barrel no 40 dumped 3-6-17 Warehouse H Rick 79 (96.5) **n24.5** think Mercedes. The cut of a Savile Row suit. The contours of a Georgian house in a London square. The workings of a Blancpain watch. Undisputed elegance and given excellence. As is this nose: a quiet show of genteel complexity with a just so squeeze of orange to freshen the muscovado sugars and varied strata of poised tannin....; **t24.5** the nose – liquified. Only now perfectly-measured spices enter the fray, and do so with panache, of course...; **f23.5** long, soft oils and plenty of natural caramels making for a slightly simplified though still delicious finale; **b24** it does not seem possible that so much beauty, such incomprehensible complexity could be tied up in a single barrel. As astonishing as it is beautiful. *40% (80 proof)*

Blanton's Single Barrel barrel no 44 dumped 8-31-17 warehouse H Rick 1. (95.5) **n24** such a subtle aroma: beautiful interplay between thinned Manuka and orange blossom honey stirred out of its serenity by delicate spices; **t24** not many bourbons can be cut to 43% and yet keep so many of the oils intact. But a judicious choice of cask means that the roof of the moth plays host to a stunning exhibition of opulent underacting: the sugars are measured yet profound, the spices follow suit while the oak quietly broods...; chocolate here....coffee there....all quietly done, of course...; **f23.5** improbably long with the spices bidding farewell to the exiting stars; **b24** if you can find a bourbon with more sublime mocha notes this year, let me know about it. As gentle as a bluegrass rolling field... *46.5% (93 proof)*

Blanton's Single Barrel barrel no 224 dumped 5-12-17 warehouse H Rick 51 (94.5) **n23.5** if you are nutty for Blanton's, this is about as nutty as it gets; **t24** as on the nose the toffee and nut show early, then the massive tannin begins to take over. The molasses make a grand entrance and stays awhile; **f23.5** think burnt fudge, overcooked toast, Italian coffee...; **b23.5** for the odd moment you think the tannin has gone too far. Then you realise there is a choreographed movement of oaks which ensures the sugars to get a fair hearing. Massive is perhaps a bit of an understatement... *66.6% (133.2 proof)*

Blanton's Single Barrel barrel no 1943 dumped 10-17-17 Warehouse H Rick 48 (95) **n23.5** one of those whiskeys which leaves you groping thin air: is it heavy or light...? It's both. Sweet or dry...? Both. More honey accented or scorched oak? Neither. Both. Oiled? Perhaps. Fruity...? Yes...but wait a bit...no. Sexy and desirous...? Without question...; **t23.5** first a kind of sherbet fizzy sweetness allows the vanillas to dissolve s fine style. Then spices immediately pop up and grab the attention. For a moment the liquorice appears hefty, then the dark sugars and ulmo honey sort that one out...; f24 what an essay in how a bourbon should be: instead of lazily fading away, it holds its ground grabbed by both oils and spices and that continuous thread of golden syrup. Sublime...; b24 just a random bottling of the many they do of this single cask. Yet it somehow seems to summarise Buffalo Trace's high pedigree and complexity with effortless aplomb. Another thoroughbred and odds on favourite. 46.5% (93 proof)

Blanton's Takara (91.5) n24.5 t23 f22 b22. Not quite how many people might envisage a bourbon: certainly not butch enough to keep the wild west gunslingers happy. No this is a bourbon which searches for your feminine side. And being so light, leaves itself open for any off-key bitter notes which might just happen along the way. 49% (98 proof)

Blanton's Uncut/Unfiltered (96.5) n25 t24 f23.5 b24. Uncut. Unfiltered. Unbelievable. 65.9%

Booker's Bourbon 6 Years, 11 Months, 0 Days batch no. 2016-01 db (92.5) n24 t23.5 f22 b23 An usually fast tail off barely detracts from another beguiling bourbon. 63.95% (1279 proof)

Booker's 7 Years 2 Months 28 Days batch no. 2015-03 db (92.5) n23 t23.5 f22.5 b23.5 One very gentle giant. 63.6% (1272 Proof)

Booker's 7 Years 5 Months batch no. C2014-05 db (95) n24 t24 f23 b24 Not for the simpering or squeamish. There's an oaky ambush to deal with. And if you ain't man (or woman) enough, then best to mosey on over to the sarsaparilla counter... 63.95%

Booker's Big Man, Small Batch 7 Years 2 Months 16 Days batch no. 2015-01 db (89.5) n22 t23 f22 b22.5 The driest Booker's I've happened across for a good while: probably ever. Matured for seven years in a warehouse located somewhere near the centre of the sun, one assumes... 64.35% (128.7 Proof)

Bowman Brother's Virginia Straight Bourbon (90) n21 t23 f23 b23. Quietly confident and complex: a bit of a gem waiting to be discovered. 45% (90 proof)

◊ **Bowman Brothers Virginia Straight Bourbon Small Batch** bott code: 71600080ASB08:22 (88.5) n22 a little Arabica coffee at play here with firm tannin and spiced dates; t23 a firm, no-nonsense delivery which is full of salivating promise. The tannins do appear a little uncompromising but the starchy sugars counter with liquorice and Java coffee; f21.5 a little too firm as the vanilla digs deep; b22 a lovely bourbon, though the sugars are thinly spread. 45% (90 proof)

Buffalo Trace (92.5) n23 t23 f23.5 b23. Easily one of the lightest BTs I have tasted in a very long while. The rye has not just taken a back seat, but has fallen off the bus. 45%

Buffalo Trace Experimental Collection Organic 6 Grain Whiskey 7 Years, 1 Month dist 3-3-2010, bott 4-6-17, warehouse/floor H/3, rick/row/slot 4/2/4-11, sour mash type db (96) n23.5 t24.5 f24 b24 Always great to start the working day off with an entirely new experience. And with this containing corn, buckwheat, brown rice, sorghum, wheat and rye it was certainly that: indeed, I have nosed and tasted the bourbon blind of the label or even the title entry above, for the sheer fun of trying to work out what this particular experiment was up to. I figured, easily, that it was a new grain recipe but I'd be lying if I said I recognised the constituent parts. Probably because while I have tasted whiskies and whiskeys containing all these individual grains, it was the first time I had encountered one where they had all been thrown together. I hope it won't be the last time that they do, because those who love their bourbons weighty and impossibly busy will be clamouring for more of this. 45% (90 proof)

Buffalo Trace Single Oak Project Barrel #132 (r1yKA1 see key below) db (95) n24 t23.5 f23.5 b24. This sample struck me for possessing, among the first batch of bottlings, the classic Buffalo Trace personality. Afterwards they revealed that it was of a profile which perhaps most closely matches their standard 8-year-old BT. Therefore it is this one I shall use as the tasting template. 45% (90 Proof)

Key to Buffalo Trace Single Oak Project Codes

Mash bill type: r = rye; w = wheat
Tree grain: 1 = course; 2 = average; 3 = tight
Tree cut: x = top half; y = bottom half
Warehouse type: K = rick; L = concrete

Entry strength: A = 125; B = 105
Seasoning: 1 = 6 Months; 2 = 12 Months
Char: All #4 except * = #3

Buffalo Trace Single Oak Project Barrel #1 (r3xKA1*) db (90.5) n22 t23 f23 b22.5. Soft corn oil aroma, buttery, big sugars building, silky texture, long. 45% (90 Proof)

Buffalo Trace Single Oak Project Barrel #2 (r3yKA1*) db (91.5) n23 t23 f22.5 b23. Bright rye on nose and delivery. Juicy red liquorice and soft corn oil to chew on... 45%

Buffalo Trace Single Oak Project Barrel #3 (r2xKA1*) db (90.5) n22.5 t23 f22.5 b22.5. Nutty, dry aroma; apple fruitiness and brown sugars. 45% (90 Proof)

Buffalo Trace Single Oak Project Barrel #4 (r2yKA1) db **(92)** n23 t23 f23 b23. Exceptionally crisp; sharp rye, honeycomb, big liquorice. *45% (90 Proof)*

Buffalo Trace Single Oak Project Barrel #5 (r2xLA1*) db **(89)** n23 t22.5 f21.5 b22. Dullish after a rye-intense and busy nose. Early muscovado followed by vanilla and spice. *45%*

Buffalo Trace Single Oak Project Barrel #6 (r3yLA1*) db **(90)** n22.5 t22 f23 b22.5. Toast with salted butter and maple syrup. Prickly, mildly aggressive spice throughout. *45%*

Buffalo Trace Single Oak Project Barrel #7 (r3xLA1) db **(92)** n23 t22.5 f22.5 b22.5. Prominent rye on nose and delivery; tannin rich, toasty with big liquorice fade. *45%*

Buffalo Trace Single Oak Project Barrel #8 (r3yLA1) db **(92.5)** n23 t23 f23.5 b23. Crisp rye aroma. Fruity, firm, salivating. Spiced toffee and muscovado; toasty.45% (90 Proof)

Buffalo Trace Single Oak Project Barrel #9 (r3xKA2*) db **(90)** n22 t22.5 f23 b22.5. Marmalade on singed toast. Soft oils: slow release of natural caramels and mocha. *45%*

Buffalo Trace Single Oak Project Barrel #10 (r3yKA2*) db **(93)** n23.5 t23.5 f22.5 b23.5. Rich, delicate rye. Complex, busy body; rye oils, tannins; slow sugar build. Bitters. *45%*

Buffalo Trace Single Oak Project Barrel #11 (r3xKA2) db **(94.5)** n23 t24 f23.5 b24. Pronounced accent on rye, especially on delivery. Oak nose upfront; good muscovado fade. *45%*

Buffalo Trace Single Oak Project Barrel #12 (r3yKA2) db **(92)** n24 t23 f22.5 b22.5. The floral, supremely balanced nose isn't matched on the palate in weight or complexity. *45%*

Buffalo Trace Single Oak Project Barrel #13 (r3xLA2*) db **(89.5)** n22 t23 f22 b22.5. Soft, yielding tactile. Early juicy, rye stance, slow build of duller light vanilla. Late spice. *45%*

Buffalo Trace Single Oak Project Barrel #14 (r3yLA2*) db **(95)** n24 t24 f23 b24. Chocolate rye nose and body; silky texture; brown sugar and vanilla; rye-rich sweet finish. *45%*

Buffalo Trace Single Oak Project Barrel #15 (r3xLA2) db **(90.5)** n22.5 t23 f22 b23. Mouth feel concentrates on sugars and spices, which grow well. Fruity on nose and finish. *45%*

Buffalo Trace Single Oak Project Barrel #16 (r3yLA2) db **(91.5)** n22.5 t23.5 f22.5 b23. Explosive delivery: big spices, juicy, firm rye. Silky middle butterscotch & ulmo honey finish. *45%*.

Buffalo Trace Single Oak Project Barrel #17 (r3xKB1*)db **(88.5)** n21.5 t22.5 f22.5 b22. Liquorice nose; oily body sweetens; big vanilla, caramel; dull spice. *45% (90 Proof)*

Buffalo Trace Single Oak Project Barrel #18 (r3yKB1*) db **(92.5)** n23 t23.5 f23.5 b23.5. Full bodied from nose to finish. Cocoa mingles with rye and rich corn oil. Deep, intense, even. *45%*

Buffalo Trace Single Oak Project Barrel #19 (r3xKB1) db **(93)** n23 t23.5 f23 b23.5. Solid, crisp rye hallmark on nose, delivery. Sugars firm and fractured. Precise whiskey. Salivating. *45%*.

Buffalo Trace Single Oak Project Barrel #20 (r3yKB1) db **(95)** n23.5 t24 f23 b23.5. Buttery nose; profound rye kick on delivery, ulmo honey body; complex toasty fade. *45%*

Buffalo Trace Single Oak Project Barrel #21 (r3xLB1*) db **(92)** n23 t23 f23 b23. Estery, clipped rye nose; salivating delivery, dark sugars, moderate spice. *45%*

Buffalo Trace Single Oak Project Barrel #22 (r3yLB1*) db **(91)** n22 t23.5 f22.5 b23. Corn/rye mix nose with manuka honey; silky corn oil throughout. Sweet, soft.45%.

Buffalo Trace Single Oak Project Barrel #23 (r3xLB1) db **(89)** n21 t22.5 f22.5 b23. Massive spices throughout; juicy, rye-dominated middle. Soft corn oil and rounded. *45%*.

Buffalo Trace Single Oak Project Barrel #24 (r3yLB1) db **(90)** n22 t23 f22.5 b22.5. Big liquorice nose and delivery; toffee raisin; big corn oil; medium spice; even ulmo honey. *45%*

Buffalo Trace Single Oak Project Barrel #25 (r3xKB2*) db **(90.5)** n22.5 t23 f22.5 b22.5. Much more accent on the rye and a slow revealing of rich caramels and Demerara. *45%*

Buffalo Trace Single Oak Project Barrel #26 (r3yKB2*) db **(89.5)** n22 t23.5 f22 b22. A sugary volley follows a shy nose. Quietens quickly; small grains add complexity. *45%*

Buffalo Trace Single Oak Project Barrel #27 (r3xKB2) db **(95.5)** n23 t24 f24.5 b24. Bold timber on nose and delivery; hickory and liquorice evident; a big spiced honey finale. *45%*

Buffalo Trace Single Oak Project Barrel #28 (r3yKB2) db **(94.5)** n23 t24 f23.5 b24. Sublime balance between sugars and grains on body. Controlled spice; layered cocoa. *45%*

Buffalo Trace Single Oak Project Barrel #29 (r3xLB2*) db **(91)** n23 t22.5 f23 b22.5. Crisp rye nose; more precise grain. Excellent spices. *45% (90 Proof)*

Buffalo Trace Single Oak Project Barrel #30 (r3yLB2*) db **(95.5)** n23.5 t24 f24 b24. One of the most delicate yet: crisp rye and sugars, minty forthright oak. Clean yet deep. *45%*

Buffalo Trace Single Oak Project Barrel #31 (r3xLB2) db **(87.5)** n22 t22 f21.5 b22. Dull, rumbling and herbal; oily caramel and sugars. Soft. *45% (90 Proof)*

Buffalo Trace Single Oak Project Barrel #32 (r3yLB2) db **(90.5)** n23.5 t23 f21.5 b22.5. Soft corn oils dominate. Buttery, molten muscovado. Late hickory. Bitterish finish. *45%*

Buffalo Trace Single Oak Project Barrel #33 (w3xKA1*) db **(94.5)** n24 t23.5 f23 b24. Huge, busy baking spiced cake; muscovado sugar delivery; remains sweet, silky and spicy; *45%*

Buffalo Trace Single Oak Project Barrel #34 (w3yKA1*) db (90) n21.5 t23.5 f22.5 b22.5. Lazy nose but big succulent spiced molasses on delivery, with a mint cocoa finale. 45%

Buffalo Trace Single Oak Project Barrel #35 (w3xKA1) db (89.5) n22 t22 f23 b22.5. Soft mint, yeasty; soft toffee delivery, builds in spice. 45% (90 Proof)

Buffalo Trace Single Oak Project Barrel #36 (w3yKA1) db (91.5) n23 t23 f22.5 b23. Vague rum and toffee; bold, salivating, slow spice. 45% (90 Proof)

Buffalo Trace Single Oak Project Barrel #37 (w3xLA1*) db (90) n21 t23 f22 b22. Typical big spice beast. Complex, doughy middle with accent on butterscotch and citrus. 45% (90 Proof)

Buffalo Trace Single Oak Project Barrel #38 (w3yLA1*) db (87.5) n22 t23.5 f20.5 b21.5. Fizzy, busy nose matched by massive spice attack on delivery. Bitter, thin finish. 45% (90 Proof)

Buffalo Trace Single Oak Project Barrel #39 (w3xLA1) db (87) n21.5 t22 f21.5 b22. Oak dominated: a degree of bitterness runs from nose to finish. Spices build slowly. 45%

Buffalo Trace Single Oak Project Barrel #40 (w3xLA1) db (93) n23 t23 f23.5 b23.5. Soft, spiced cake, big citrus; silky, oily, bananas and golden syrup; late spice, balancing bitters. 45%

Buffalo Trace Single Oak Project Barrel #41 (w3xKA2*) db (92.5) n22 t23 f23.5 b24. Less spice than expected. Docile start, builds in intensity. Buttery, big sugars. Balanced. 45%

Buffalo Trace Single Oak Project Barrel #42 (w3yKA2*) db (85.5) n22 t21.5 f21 b21. Tight nose opens slowly; sultana pudding with maple syrup. Sweet, late bitterness. 45%

Buffalo Trace Single Oak Project Barrel #43 (w3xKA2) db (89) n22 t23 f22 b22. Dates & plum nose; succulent fruit with broad maple syrup & molasses flourish. Big late spice. 45%.

Buffalo Trace Single Oak Project Barrel #44 (w3yKA2) db (89) n23 t23 f21 b22. Spice rack nose; superb warm liquorice eruption on palate but dull finale. 45%

Buffalo Trace Single Oak Project Barrel #45 (w3xLA2*) db (87) n23 t22 f21 b21. Ginger and allspice nose; body thick corn oil and toffee. Short finish.45%.

Buffalo Trace Single Oak Project Barrel #46 (w3yLA2*) db (88) n21.5 t22 f22.5 b22 Doughy aroma. Big corn oils and sugars. Late spice growth. Big vanilla. Quietly complex. 45%

Buffalo Trace Single Oak Project Barrel #47 (w3xLA2) db (88.5) n22.5 t22 f22 b22. Floral, waxy aroma; sugars dominate on palate with vanilla-butterscotch-ulmo theme. 45%.

Buffalo Trace Single Oak Project Barrel #48 (w3yLA2) db (90.5) n22 t23 f22.5 b23. Sound, rounded from first to last. Greater accent on sugar intensity and vanilla inclusion. 45%

Buffalo Trace Single Oak Project Barrel #49 (w3xKB1) db (93) n24 t23 f23 b23. Chocolate spice, apples, oaky aroma; treacle pudding, soft oils; banana and custard; bitters. 45%

Buffalo Trace Single Oak Project Barrel #50 (w3yKB1*) db (88) n21.5 t23 f21.5 b22. Flat nose. Muscovado delivery. Slow spices. Late liquorice. Even. Limited depth. 45% (90 Proof)

Buffalo Trace Single Oak Project Barrel #51 (w3xKB1) db (89.5) n23 t23 f21.5 b22. Firm and well spiced from start. Oils play bigger role as sugar develops. 45%.

Buffalo Trace Single Oak Project Barrel #52 (w3yKB1) db (87.5) n21.5 t22 f22 b22. Yeasty nose; blend of molasses and toffee on delivery then slow spice increase.45%

Buffalo Trace Single Oak Project Barrel #53 (w3xLB1*) db (91) n22 t23 f23 b23. Full bodied on nose and palate. Toasty, big liquorice and molasses. Even and elegant. 45%

Buffalo Trace Single Oak Project Barrel #54 (w3yLB1*) db (89) n22 t23 f22.5 b22.5. Crisp sugars and coconut nose; big molassed delivery, nutty and gentle oil. Late vanilla. 45%

Buffalo Trace Single Oak Project Barrel #55 (w3xLB1) db (89) n22 t23 f23 b22. Mocha nose with sturdy tannin and vanilla early on delivery. Red liquorice and vanilla late on. 45%.

Buffalo Trace Single Oak Project Barrel #56 (w3yLB1) db (91) n24 t22.5 f22 b22.5. Chocolate vanilla and tannins; soft, slow build up of spice, oily; bitters. 45% (90 Proof)

Buffalo Trace Single Oak Project Barrel #57 (w3xKB2*) db (94) n23 t23.5 f23.5 b24. Immediate spice kick on nose and delivery. Caramels and marmalade. Busy, balanced. 45%

Buffalo Trace Single Oak Project Barrel #58 (w3yKB2*) db (90.5) n22.5 t23 f22.5 b22.5. Liquorice and Fisherman's Friend nose; molassed middle and big spice finish. 45%

Buffalo Trace Single Oak Project Barrel #59 (w3xKB2) db (92) n22 t23.5 f23 b23.5. Lighter Fisherman's Friend; roasted fudge; busy small grains attack. Mega complex. 45%

Buffalo Trace Single Oak Project Barrel #60 (w3yKB2) db (87.5) n22 t22.5 f21 b21.5. Aggression to spice nose; tame delivery and body. Soft corn oil and muscovado. 46%

Buffalo Trace Single Oak Project Barrel #61 (w3xLB2*) db (94.5) n24 t23 f23.5 b24. Classic spiced wheat; Demerara sugars and spices abound.Big. 45% (90 Proof)

Buffalo Trace Single Oak Project Barrel #62 (w3yLB2*) db (88) n22 t22.5 f21.5 b22. Caramel is leading theme; soft, big wheated spice. Oily. 45% (90 Proof)

Buffalo Trace Single Oak Project Barrel #63 (w3xLB2) db (95.5) n24 t23 f24 b24.5. Subtle dates, spice, cocoa; gentle, oily, perfectspice build. Ultra complex. 45% (90 Proof)

Buffalo Trace Single Oak Project Barrel #64 (w3yLB2) db (91) n22.5 t23.5 f22.5 b23. Citrus nose. Big oak and spice delivery; treacle tart and liquorice. Softens into caramel. 45%

Buffalo Trace Single Oak Project Barrel #65 (r2xKA1) db **(91)** n23.5 t22 f23 b22.5. Small grain nose; crunchy muscovado, corn oil; liquorice, vanilla; late spice. Complex. *45%*

Buffalo Trace Single Oak Project Barrel #66 (r2yKA1*) db **(88.5)** n22.5 t22.5 f21.5 b22. Dry tannin dominates on nose and palate; good spice kick and treacle. Short finish. *45%*

Buffalo Trace Single Oak Project Barrel #67 (r2xKA1) db **(89.5)** n22 t23 f22 b22.5. Blandish nose; tart, tight, sharp, some toffee raisin. *45% (90 Proof)*

Buffalo Trace Single Oak Project Barrel #68 (r2yKA1) db **(92)** n22.5 t23 f23.5 b23. Rye depth; deeper, warmer spices, liquorice and light molasses. *45% (90 Proof)*

Buffalo Trace Single Oak Project Barrel #69 (r2xLA1*) db **(94.5)** n23 t24 f23.5 b24. Crisp, sharp rye on nose and delivery. Jagged muscovado and spice. Goes down a treat... *45%*

Buffalo Trace Single Oak Project Barrel #70 (r2yLA1*) db **(91.5)** n22.5 t23 f23 b23. Yielding caramel and vanilla. Rye and hot spice breaks up the sleepy theme. *45% (90 Proof)*

Buffalo Trace Single Oak Project Barrel #71 (r2xLA1) db **(92)** n22.5 t23 f23.5 b23. Busy, small grain and citrus nose; rye backbone then darker sugars and tannin. *45%*

Buffalo Trace Single Oak Project Barrel #72 (r2yLA1) db **(89)** n22.5 t23 f21.5 b22. Floral nose; juicy, tangy, citrus. Liquorice, sugary vanilla. Bitter marmalade finish. *45%*

Buffalo Trace Single Oak Project Barrel #73 (r2xKA2*) db **(87.5)** n21.5 t22 f22 b22. Tight, unyielding nose. Initially crisp rye then thick vanilla and baked apple blanket. *45%*

Buffalo Trace Single Oak Project Barrel #74 (r2yKA2*) db **(88)** n22 t22 f22 b22. Corny nose; more corn oil early on; syrup, huge rye sure on finish; bitters slightly. *45% (90 Proof)*

Buffalo Trace Single Oak Project Barrel #75 (r2xKA2) db **(91.5)** n23 t22.5 f23 b23. Clean with accent firmly on grain throughout. Spiced minty mocha middle and fade. *45%*

Buffalo Trace Single Oak Project Barrel #76 (r2yKA2) db **(89)** n22.5 t22.5 f22 b22. Bristling rye on nose and delivery; fruity edge then dullish spiced fudge and mocha. *45%*

Buffalo Trace Single Oak Project Barrel #77 (r2xLA2*) db **(88)** n22 t23 f21 b22. Busy, bitty nose; sugary blast on delivery; spice follow through then vanilla overload. *45%*

Buffalo Trace Single Oak Project Barrel #78 (r2yLA2*) db **(89)** n22.5 t22 f22.5 b22. Small grain busy nose; light spice to oils; light rye, late sugars; chewy caramels. *45% (90 Proof)*

Buffalo Trace Single Oak Project Barrel #79 (r2xLA2) db **(93)** n23 t23.5 f23 b23.5. Juicy crisp sugars. Toasty with slow liquorice burn. Creamed spiced hickory fade. Complex. *45%.*

Buffalo Trace Single Oak Project Barrel #80 (r2yLA2) db **(91.5)** n23 t22.5 f23 b23. Broad oily strokes on nose, delivery. Simple vanilla tannins and ulmo honey. *45%.*

Buffalo Trace Single Oak Project Barrel #81 (r2yKB1*) db **(94)** n23 t23 f24 b24. Candy shop fruitiness; delicate oils and flavour development; big yet subdued brown sugars. *45%*

Buffalo Trace Single Oak Project Barrel #82 (r2yKB1*) db **(91.5)** n22.5 t23.5 f22.5 b23. Liquoice, manuka honey; lurid rye bite and lychee fruitiness; mocha and Demerara. *45%*

Buffalo Trace Single Oak Project Barrel #83 (r2xKB1) db **(92)** n22.5 t23 f23.5 b23. Sharp, angular grain, rye dominant. Softer salty praline fade. *45%.*

Buffalo Trace Single Oak Project Barrel #84 (r2yKB1) db **(94)** n23.5 t24 f23 b23.5. Hefty nose mixing tannin, rye and hickory. Huge sugar and corn oil theme. *45%.*

Buffalo Trace Single Oak Project Barrel #85 (r2xLB1*) db **(88.5)** n21.5 t22.5 f22 b22.5. Shy nose of soft vanilla; firm body with more vanilla and butterscotch; low level sugar. *45%*

Buffalo Trace Single Oak Project Barrel #86 (r2yLB1*) db **(92)** n22.5 t23 f23.5 b22.5. Salty, sweaty nose; sharp delivery with rye, red liquorice dominant; spiced mocha finish. *45%*

Buffalo Trace Single Oak Project Barrel #87 (r2xLB1) db **(93.5)** n22.5 t23.5 f23.5 b23.5. Citrus-led nose; slow, corn oil start then explosive grain; rye, liquorice & honey to the fore. *45%.*

Buffalo Trace Single Oak Project Barrel #88 (r2yLB1) db **(89)** n23.5 t22 f21.5 b22. Hickory, rye nose; liquorice delivery big caramel surge; bitters on finish. *45% (90 Proof)*

Buffalo Trace Single Oak Project Barrel #89 (r2xKB2*) db **(89.5)** n22 t22.5 f22 b22.5. Rye radiates on nose and delivery. Big spice surge to the middle. Late mocha, liquorice. *45%*

Buffalo Trace Single Oak Project Barrel #90 (r2yKB2*) db **(94)** n23 t24 f23 b23.5. Big tannin, cocoa and caramel throughout. Major peppery spice. Complex. *45% (90 Proof)*

Buffalo Trace Single Oak Project Barrel #91 (r2xKB2) db **(86.5)** n21.5 t22 f21.5 b21.5. Half-cooked: dull caramel throughout. Short spice peak. Sweet, oily, lacking complexity. *45%*

Buffalo Trace Single Oak Project Barrel #92 (r2yKB2) db **(91)** n22 t23 f23 b23. Silky texture. Big corn oil but intense tannin thinned by beech honey. Hickory and maple syrup. *45%*

Buffalo Trace Single Oak Project Barrel #93 (r2xLB2*) db **(89)** n22.5 t22 f22 b22.5. Soft rye and sugars; juicy grain, tangy citrus, muscovado. *45% (90 Proof)*

Buffalo Trace Single Oak Project Barrel #94 (r2yLB2*) db **(92.5)** n22.5 t24 f23 b23. Rich, hefty. Slightly salty, crisp rye. Light caramel, hint of Guyanese rum. Delicate spice. *45%*

Buffalo Trace Single Oak Project Barrel #95 (r2xLB2) db **(94)** n23 t23.5 f23.5 b24. Citrus, banana; soft vanilla, profound rye sharpness, spices. Big. *45% (90 Proof)*

Buffalo Trace Single Oak Project Barrel #96 (r2yLB2) db (89) n22 t23.5 f21.5 b22. Bright, grainy delivery in contrast to oily nose and finish. Heavy, dry molasses at the death.45%

Buffalo Trace Single Oak Project Barrel #97 (w2xKA1*) db (87) n22.5 t22 f21.5 b21.5. Toffee apple nose; heavy corn oil, light muscovado sugar, bitters out; 45% (90 Proof)

Buffalo Trace Single Oak Project Barrel #98 (w2yKA1*) db (93) n23 t23.5 f23 b23.5. Peppers on at full blast on nose and delivery; big oily liquorice and treacle counter. 45%

Buffalo Trace Single Oak Project Barrel #99 (w2xKA1) db (86.5) n22 t22 f21 b21.5. Malty, vanilla; thin maple syrup, caramel. Dull. 45% (90 Proof)

Buffalo Trace Single Oak Project Barrel #100 (w2yKA1) db (94) n23 t23.5 f23.5 b24. Busy, green, fresh; big juicy, vanilla, muscovado, spices. 45% (90 Proof)

Buffalo Trace Single Oak Project Barrel #101 (w2xLA1) db (96) n23.5 t24 f23.5 b25. Unerring chocolate and mint aided by even muscovado, vanilla and spice. Hugely complex. 45%

Buffalo Trace Single Oak Project Barrel #102 (w2yLA1*) db (88.5) n22 t22 f22.5 b22. Insane tannin on nose; overcooked caramel. Massive sugar-spice mix. 45% (90 Proof)

Buffalo Trace Single Oak Project Barrel #103 (w2xLA1) db (89) n22.5 t22 f22 b22.5. Early spice on nose; prominent brown sugars on deliver; corn oil follow through. 45%

Buffalo Trace Single Oak Project Barrel #104 (w2xLA1) db (91) n23 t23 f22.5 b22.5. Apple, cinnamon; light spice; corn oil; vanilla and ulmo honey; spices, bitters out. 45%

Buffalo Trace Single Oak Project Barrel #105 (w2xKA2*) db (89) n22.5 t22 f22.5 b22. Spiced, lively nose; hot cross buns; oils and sugars build slowly; spices intensify at end. 45%

Buffalo Trace Single Oak Project Barrel #106 (w2yKA2*) db (92.5) n24 t23 f23 b23.5. Mega complex nose: busy sugars and spices; silky texture; nougat, caramel. 45%

Buffalo Trace Single Oak Project Barrel #107 (w2xKA2) db (93.5) n23.5 t23 f23 b24. Bold, rich nose; pepper bite; thick body; maple syrup, molasses, cocoa. Classic wheat recipe. 45%.

Buffalo Trace Single Oak Project Barrel #108 (w2yKA2) db (94) n22.5 t24 f23.5 b24. Soft, delicate. Ulmo honey leads the sugars; corn oil but complex liquorice and lavender. 45%

Buffalo Trace Single Oak Project Barrel #109 (w2xLA2*) db (87.5) n21.5 t23.5 f21 b21.5. Dull nose and finish. Delivery lush, souped-up spiced caramel-toffee fudge. 45%.

Buffalo Trace Single Oak Project Barrel #110 (w2yLA2*) db (90) n22 t22.5 f22.5 b23. Intense caramel; liquorice and toffee middle, citrus and salt; caramel finish. 45% (90 Proof)

Buffalo Trace Single Oak Project Barrel #111 (w2xLA2) db (89) n22.5 t22.5 f22 b22. Intriguing sugar operatic. Varies from castor to muscovado. Countering spices make it work. 45%.

Buffalo Trace Single Oak Project Barrel #112 (w2yLA2) db (90) n21.5 t23 f22.5 b23. Caramel fudge lead. Usual whited spice before heavier, liquorice development. 45%.

Buffalo Trace Single Oak Project Barrel #113 (w2xKB1*) db (88) n22.5 t22 f22 b21.5. Big vanilla nose; minor spice, oily, buttery vanilla. Simple. 45% (90 Proof)

Buffalo Trace Single Oak Project Barrel #114 (w2yKB1*) db (90) n22 t23 f22 b23. Elements of citrus. Oily corn. Controlled spice. Earthy and sweet. 45% (90 Proof)

Buffalo Trace Single Oak Project Barrel #115 (w2xKB1) db (88.5) n22 t22 f22.5 f22 b22. An even mix of corn oil and persistent light sugars. Low level spice until finish. A tad dull. 45%.

Buffalo Trace Single Oak Project Barrel #116 (w2yKB1) db (90.5) n22 t22 f23.5 b23. Caramelised biscuit nose; polite, corny start; finish rich with hickory, manuka honey. 45%

Buffalo Trace Single Oak Project Barrel #117 (w2xLB1*) db (82.5) n20 t20.5 f22 b20. Weird pineapple nose; fruity delivery with spices trying to escape. Entirely different. 45%

Buffalo Trace Single Oak Project Barrel #118 (w2yLB1*) db (86) n20.5 t21.5 f22 b22. Fruity (less than 117); big toffee body, busy spice, developing ulmo honey. Soft. 45%

Buffalo Trace Single Oak Project Barrel #119 (w2xLB1) db (93.5) n22.5 t24 f23.5 b23.5. Spices from nose to fade, accompanied by chewy burnt fudge. French toast finale. Big. 45%.

Buffalo Trace Single Oak Project Barrel #120 (w2yLB1) db (89.5) n23 t22 f22.5 b22. Controlled oak throughout. Intermittent dry vanilla. Delicate sugars. 45% (90 Proof)

Buffalo Trace Single Oak Project Barrel #121 (w2xKB2*) db (89) n22.5 t23 f21.5 b22. Citrusy corn oil apparent and dominates. Sugars rampant, spices shy. Rather flat finale. 45%

Buffalo Trace Single Oak Project Barrel #122 (w2yKB2*) db (93) n22 t23.5 f23.5 b24. Serious wheat-spice with cocoa back up. Demerara sugars evenly spread. Complex. 45%

Buffalo Trace Single Oak Project Barrel #123 (w2xKB2) db (85.5) n21 t22 f21 b21.5. One of the dullest yet: limited sparkle despite light spice. Big caramel. 45% (90 Proof)

Buffalo Trace Single Oak Project Barrel #124 (w2yKB2) db (90.5) n22.5 t23 f22.5 b22.5. The startling, extra sugars over #123 impact hugely. Juicy; oak (liquorice) support.45%

Buffalo Trace Single Oak Project Barrel #125 (w2xLB2*) db (93) n24 t22 f22.5 b22.5. Heavy oak, spices; firm, juicy. Softer caramel fade. 45% (90 Proof)

Buffalo Trace Single Oak Project Barrel #126 (w2yLB2*) db (90) n22 t23 f22.5 b22.5. Floral nose (primroses); elaborate delivery of spice and creamed mocha plus molasses. 45%

Buffalo Trace Single Oak Project Barrel #127 (w2xLB2) db (85.5) n21.5 t22 f21 b21. Off balance, citrus; juicy at first, bitters later. 45% (90 Proof)

Buffalo Trace Single Oak Project Barrel #128 (w2yLB2) db (89) n21.5 t22 f22.5 b22.5. Conservative nose, OTT spice on delivery.Molassed dates and walnut. 45% (90 Proof)

Buffalo Trace Single Oak Project Barrel #129 (r1xKA1*) db (88) n22.5 t22 f22 b22. Firm grainy, tannin nose; nougat, nutty, corn oil; clean but dim vanilla fade. 45% (90 Proof)

Buffalo Trace Single Oak Project Barrel #130 (r1yKA1*) db (92.5) n22 t23.5 f23 b24. Macho: cloaked in oak. Kumquats on nose, oily, punchy tannins on sharp, silky delivery. 45%

Buffalo Trace Single Oak Project Barrel #131 (r1xKA1) db (92.5) n23 t23 f23.5 b23. Relaxed vanilla, light tannin; corn oily, icing sugars, marzipan. 45% (90 Proof)

Buffalo Trace Single Oak Project Barrel #132
See above.

Buffalo Trace Single Oak Project Barrel #133 (r1xLA1*) db (89) n22.5 t23 f21 b22.5. Small grain busyness does the business: rye leads the dark sugar procession. Bitters out. 45%

Buffalo Trace Single Oak Project Barrel #134 (r1yLA1*) db (91.5) n22 t23.5 f23 b23. Velvet delivery: big spice cushioned by muscovado and butterscotch. Mixed honey finale. 45%

Buffalo Trace Single Oak Project Barrel #135 (r1xLA1) db (92.5) n23 t23 f23.5 b23. Chocolatey theme, except on firm, grainy nose. Silky oils, intense flavours, rye rigidity. 45%

Buffalo Trace Single Oak Project Barrel #136 (r1yLA1) db (92) n23.5 t22.5 f23 b23. Liquorice on nose and delivery. Spicy. Richer oils. Demerara. Spice. 45% (90 Proof)

Buffalo Trace Single Oak Project Barrel #137 (r1xKA2*) db (90.5) n23 t23.5 f22 b23. Fruity opening with a hardening rye presence and emphasis on muscovado. Late cocoa. 45%

Buffalo Trace Single Oak Project Barrel #138 (r1yKA2*) db (87) n23 t21.5 f21.5 b21.5. Marzipan, citrus nose; dull delivery, slow build of muscovado and vanilla. Soft. 45%

Buffalo Trace Single Oak Project Barrel #139 (r1xKA2) db (88) n22.5 t22 f21.5 b22. More or less flatlines throughout. Big corn oil with limited spice and cocoa. 45%

Buffalo Trace Single Oak Project Barrel #140 (r1yKA2) db (93) n23 t24 f23 b23. Classic bourbon: citrus-rich nose, thumping spicy molassed liquorice-hickory delivery. 45%

Buffalo Trace Single Oak Project Barrel #141 (r1xLA2*) db (90) n23.5 t22 f22.5 b22. Busy nose & finish. Corn dominates the mid ground. Sugar, spice growth. Complex finale. 45%.

Buffalo Trace Single Oak Project Barrel #142 (r1yLA2*) db (89.5) n22.5 t22.5 f22 b22.5. Light tannin nose; oils, liquorice, spice bite. More corn oil. Sugars, spicy vanilla. 45%

Buffalo Trace Single Oak Project Barrel #143 (r1xLA2) db (88.5) n22.5 t22.5 f21.5 b22. Hickory drifts in and out of narrative. Light rye & vanilla. Very soft – overly gentle. 45%.

Buffalo Trace Single Oak Project Barrel #144 (r1yLA2) db (91) n23 t23 f22.5 b22.5. Tannin led. Bristling dark sugars. Oily with comforting vanilla.45%.

Buffalo Trace Single Oak Project Barrel #145 (r1xKB1*) db (91) n22.5 t22 f23.5 b23. Nougat, cocoa; busy small grains; oily corn; spiced chocolate. 45%

Buffalo Trace Single Oak Project Barrel #146 (r1yKB1*) db (93) n23 t24 f22 b24. Rye dominates with clarity and aplomb. Crystal clean nose and delivery: Dundee cake. 45%

Buffalo Trace Single Oak Project Barrel #147 (r1xKB1) db (93) n23.5 t23 f23.5 b23. Macho rye & tannins. Toasty & dry delivery; liquorice, sugars, soft spice gain ascendency.45%.

Buffalo Trace Single Oak Project Barrel #148 (r1yKB1) db (94) n22.5 t24 f23.5 b24. Quiet aroma but intense delivery. Big sugar up front, liquorice and manuka honey fade. 45%

Buffalo Trace Single Oak Project Barrel #149 (r1xLB1*) db (92) n22.5 t23.5 f23 b23. Massive tannin influence. Heavy nose; heavier body with toasty liquorice and cocoa.45%

Buffalo Trace Single Oak Project Barrel #150 (r1yLB1*) db (93) n23 t23.5 f23 b23.5. Huge tannin softened by big dark sugars, hickory, sharp rye notes. Long, chewy finish. 45%

Buffalo Trace Single Oak Project Barrel #151 (r1xLB1) db (91.5) n22 t23 f23.5 b23. Diced citrus; light body with busy grains. Powerful dark sugars gain upper hand. 45%.

Buffalo Trace Single Oak Project Barrel #152 (r1yLB1) db (81.5) n21 t20.5 f20 b20.5. Vaguely butyric; harsh, hot fat corn, light rye; bitters out. 45% (90 Proof)

Buffalo Trace Single Oak Project Barrel #153 (r1xKB2*) db (94) n23.5 t23.5 f23 b24. Complex nose, delivery. Big spice with crisp, juicy rye. Praline, delicate oils. Big but elegant. 45%

Buffalo Trace Single Oak Project Barrel #154 (r1yKB2) db (92) n23 t23 f23 b23.5. Rye dominates. Hard on palate; yet burnt raisin, lychee and muscovado soften. 45% (90 Proof)

Buffalo Trace Single Oak Project Barrel #155 (r1xKB2) db (93) n23 t24 f22.5 b23.5. Fierce spice. Dynamic rye shapes all directions. Hickory and manuka honey combine. 45%

Buffalo Trace Single Oak Project Barrel #156 (r1yKB2) db (85.5) n22 t21 f21.5 b21. Doesn't work. Spices too hot. Caramels and oils negate development. 45% (90 Proof)

Buffalo Trace Single Oak Project Barrel #157 (r1xLB2*) db (84.5) n21 t21.5 f20.5 b21. Vague butyric; sharp, juicy corn with slow rye build. Bitter. 45% (90 Proof)

Buffalo Trace Single Oak Project Barrel #158 (r1ylB2*) db (88) n22 t22 f22 b22. Another brawny, corn-oily, oaky effort. Excellent cocoa, citrus and spice development. 45%

Buffalo Trace Single Oak Project Barrel #159 (r1xLB2) db n20.5 t22.5 f22 b22.5. Vague butyric; firm sugars then watery, confident spices, soft honey. Complex. 45%

Buffalo Trace Single Oak Project Barrel #160 (r1ylB2) db (92.5) n23.5 t23 f22 b23. A salty style with fruity, crisp rye right behind. Steady and firm. 45%

Buffalo Trace Single Oak Project Barrel #161 (w1xKA1*)db (87) n21 t22 f22 b22. Cream caramel candy; juicy corn, oily; more caramel, Light spice. 45% (90 Proof)

Buffalo Trace Single Oak Project Barrel #162 (w1yKA1*) db (88.5) n22 t22 f22.5 b22. Cream soda and minty fudge. Early treacle kick then settles for simple life. 45% (90 Proof)

Buffalo Trace Single Oak Project Barrel #163 (w1xKA1) db (90) n23 t22.5 f22 b22.5. Citrus, bubble gum; spiced muscovado sugars at first, bitters. 45% (90 Proof)

Buffalo Trace Single Oak Project Barrel #164 (w1yKA1) db (94.5) n23.5 t23 f24 b24. Citrus and vanilla; massive spice, building. Demerara. Warm and complex. 45% (90 Proof)

Buffalo Trace Single Oak Project Barrel #165 (w1xLA1*) db (91.5) n22.5 t23 f23 b23. Lively, spice dominated. Ulmo honey offers superb back up.45% (90 Proof)

Buffalo Trace Single Oak Project Barrel #166 (w1ylA1*) db (91) n22 t23 f23 b23. Heady, leathery. Sublime spice middle; molasses and liquorice enrich the tail.45% (90 Proof)

Buffalo Trace Single Oak Project Barrel #167 (w1ylB1) db (94) n23.5 t23.5 f23 b24. Demerara, rummy; intense liquorice, hickory; dark sugars and big spice. 45% (90 Proof)

Buffalo Trace Single Oak Project Barrel #168 (w1xLA1) db (89.5) n22 t23 f22 b22.5. Clean, spiced nose; juicy grains with toffee and raisin. Mocha and liquorice on finish. 45%

Buffalo Trace Single Oak Project Barrel #169 (w1xKA2*) db (94) n23.5 t23.5 f23 b24. Spice, lavender & leather on delivery; spicy nose. Honey & corn oil follow through. 45% (90 proof)

Buffalo Trace Single Oak Project Barrel #170 (w1yKA2*) db (92.5) n22.5 t23 f23.5 b23.5. Sweet, spiced nose; firm, spicy delivery; Demerara and ulmo honey. 45% (90 Proof)

Buffalo Trace Single Oak Project Barrel #171 (w1xKA2) db (88.5) n22 t23 f21.5 b22. Friendly corn oils dominate. Estery. Dry finish after sugar and spice crescendo. 45%.

Buffalo Trace Single Oak Project Barrel #172 (w1yKA2) db (90.5) n22.5 t23 f22.5 b22.5. Tannins prevalent on nose and spiced delivery. Good bite, esters and oils. Late mocha. 45%

Buffalo Trace Single Oak Project Barrel #173 (w1xLA2*) db (91) n23.5 t23 f22 b22.5. Bold nose & delivery: honeycomb, tannins. Liquorice & vanilla middle; good spice balance. 45%.

Buffalo Trace Single Oak Project Barrel #174 (w1ylA2*) db (89) n22 t22.5 f22.5 b22. Delicate oak; juicy corn, liquorice, light spices, buttery corn. Bitter marmalade. 45% (90 Proof)

Buffalo Trace Single Oak Project Barrel #175 (w1xLA2) db (91.5) n21.5 t23 f24 b23. Lazy nose, juicy delivery. Big vanilla profile. Buttery caramel; light honey & spice. Long. 45%.

Buffalo Trace Single Oak Project Barrel #176 (w1ylA2) db (89) n21.5 t22.5 f22.5 b22.5. Light caramel aroma; sharp, juicy (rye-esque) delivery with mocha & butter toffee finale. 45%.

Buffalo Trace Single Oak Project Barrel #177 (w1xKB1*)db (87) n21.5 t22 f22 b21.5. Vaguely spiced corn oil; soft, nutty, marzipan sweetness, citrus. Late mocha. 45% (90 Proof)

Buffalo Trace Single Oak Project Barrel #178 (w1yKB1*) db (88.5) n22.5 t23 f21.5 b21.5. Complex marzipan and Demerara nose and delivery; runs out of things to say. 45%

Buffalo Trace Single Oak Project Barrel #179 (w1xKB1) db (91) n22 f22.5 b22.5 Dull caramel nose. Toffee caramel continues on palate. Late fudge sweetness. Growing spice. 45%

Buffalo Trace Single Oak Project Barrel #180 (w1yKB1) db (92) n22 t23.5 f23 b23.5. Molasses/cough sweet nose; scrambled grains and citrus; thickens with corn at end. 45%

Buffalo Trace Single Oak Project Barrel #181 (w1xLB1*) db (94.5) n22.5 t24.5 f23 b23.5. Silky chocolate fudge delivery with perfect spice. Nose more austere, finish intense. 45%

Buffalo Trace Single Oak Project Barrel #182 (w1ylB1*) db (86) n21.5 t21.5 f22 b21. Nose over fruity; profound sugars but tart, thin body. Vanilla and mocha on finish. 45%

Buffalo Trace Single Oak Project Barrel #183 (w1xLB1) db (95.5) n24 t24 f23.5 b24. Intense. Brilliant fudge/honey/molasses delivery; cocoa finish; perfect spices: mini Weller! 45%.

Buffalo Trace Single Oak Project Barrel #184 (w1ylA1) db (93) n23.5 t23 f23 b23.5. Tannins, walnut oil; nutty, corn oils. Light spice, firm Demerara. Late fruity spice. Complex. 45%

Buffalo Trace Single Oak Project Barrel #185 (w1xKB2*) db (92.5) n23 t23.5 f23 b23. Dry, riveting nose; liquorice dominates the palate. Cocoa, hickory enlivened by sugars. 45%

Buffalo Trace Single Oak Project Barrel #186 (w1yKB2*) db (90) n23 t22.5 f22 b22.5. Rampant spice from delivery onwards. Burnt fudge and toasted raisin. 45% (90 Proof)

Buffalo Trace Single Oak Project Barrel #187 (w1xKB2) db (88) n22 t22 f22 b22. Exceptionally even and caramel rich. Unbalanced tannin and lack of spice. 45% (90 Proof)

Buffalo Trace Single Oak Project Barrel #188 (w1ykB2) db (90) n21.5 t23.5 f22.5 b22.5. Lazy nose. Bright delivery; citrusy corn oil and muscovado. Late mocha and liquorice. 45%

Buffalo Trace Single Oak Project Barrel #189 (w1xLB2*) db (88.5) n24 t22 f21 b21.5. Complex citrus, delicate yet big; tart, sweet, fresh, strangely off balance. *45% (90 Proof)*

Buffalo Trace Single Oak Project Barrel #190 (w1ylB2*) db (94) n23.5 t24 f23 b23.5. Ulmo/manuka honey mix on nose and delivery; silky corn oil; spiced mocha. Complex. *45%*

Buffalo Trace Single Oak Project Barrel #191 (w1xLB2) db (94.5) n23 t23.5 f24 b24. Big, spicy, classic; firm wheaty spiciness, juicy, thick caramels. Complex. *45% (90 Proof)*

Buffalo Trace Single Oak Project Barrel #192 (w1ylB2) db (94.5) n23 t24 f23.5 b24. Demerara rum nose; heavy, dry liquorice body; late spice; molassed butterscotch finish. *45%*

Buffalo Trace Experiment #7 Heavy Char Barrel charred white oak, dist 21 Jan 97, bott Oct 12 db (77) n20 t21.5 f17 b18.5. The very nature of experiments means that, sometimes, they go wrong. Perhaps a bit harsh for this one which, to be more precise, has not gone right. The nose has an almost bizarre sherry feel to it, the fruitiness really striking home on the attractive delivery. From then on, it's downhill, leaving an unattractive tang at the death. *45%*

Buffalo Trace Experimental Collection 15 Minute Infrared Light Wave Barrels dist 10/13/09, barrelled 10/14/09, bott 03/31/16, still proof: 140, entry proof: 125, warehouse/floor: I/5, rick/row/slot: 1/5/1-4, age at bottling: 6 Years, 5 Months, evaporation: 32% db (92) n24 t23 f22 b23 Astonishing that it is now some 25 years since I first discussed infrared cask treatment with a Scottish distiller (and was sent samples of maturing spirit in such treated barrels) but it is only now that I have seen it commercially available. Good ol' Buffalo Trace for keeping the public on its toes! *45% (90 proof)*

Buffalo Trace Experimental Collection 30 Minute Infrared Light Wave Barrels dist 10/13/09, barrelled 10/14/09, bott 03/31/16, still proof: 140, entry proof: 125, warehouse/floor: I/5, rick/row/slot: 1/5/1-8, age at bottling: 6 Years, 5 Months, evaporation: 32% db (91) n23 t23 f22.5 b22.5 Has quite a different gait to the 15 minute version, being far more oak dependent as well as aggressive. *45% (90 proof)*

Buffalo Trace Experimental Collection Old Fashioned Sour Mash Entry Proof 105 dist 05/01/02, barrelled 05/01/02, bott 08/20/15, still proof: 135, warehouse/floor: I/7, rick/row/slot: 22/2/1, age at bottling: 13 Years, 3 Months, evaporation: 66.2% db (93) n23.5 t23.5 f23.5 b23.5 Fascinating comparison to the 125 entry. Much more liquorice and tannin, much less acacia honey. Seems older and hairier, which I would not necessarily have expected. *45% (90 proof)*

Buffalo Trace Experimental Collection Old Fashioned Sour Mash Entry Proof 125 dist 05/01/02, barrelled 05/01/02, bott 08/20/15, still proof: 135, warehouse/floor: I/7, rick/row/slot: 50/2/1, age at bottling: 13 Years, 3 Months, evaporation: 54.8% db (95) n24 t24 f23 b24 An experiment which should be turned into reality... *45% (90 proof)*

Bulleit Bourbon (87) n21.5 t22 f21.5 b22. Vanilla-fashioned on both nose and flavour development. If it was looking to be big and brash, it's missed the target. If it wanted to be genteel and understated with a slightly undercooked feel yet always friendly, then bullseye... *45% (90 proof)*

Bulleit Bourbon 10 Year Old (90) n23 t22.5 f22 b22.5 Not remotely spectacular. But does the simple things deliciously. *45.6% (91.2 proof)*

Bulleit Bourbon Barrel Strength (91.5) n22.5 t22.5 f23.5 b23 The extra oils at full strength make such a huge difference in seeing the fuller picture. *59.6% (119.2 proof)*

Calhoun Bros Straight Bourbon (84.5) n20.5 t22 f21 b21. Very different! A much wider cut than the norm on straight bourbon whisky results in an oily fellow which you can chew until your jaws ache. Massively toasty, vanilla gorged and intense. *43% (86 proof)*

Charter 101 (95.5) n23.5 t24.5 f23.5 b24. Now here is a whiskey which has changed tack dramatically. In many ways it's like the Charter 101 of a year back. But this bottling suggests they have turned a warehouse into a giant beehive. Because few whiskeys offer this degree of honey. You can imagine that after all these years, rarely does a whiskey genuinely surprise me: this one has. No wonder there is such a buzz in the bourbon industry right now... *50.5%*

Clarke's Old Kentucky Straight Sour Mash Whisky Bourbon (88.5) n22.5 t22 f22 b22. Honest and hugely impressive bourbon. The rich colour – and remember straight bourbon cannot be falsely coloured – tells its own tale. *40%. Aldi.*

Colonel E H Taylor Barrel Proof (91) n23.5 t23 f22 b22.5. A big boy which turns out to be a bit ofa softy in the end... *67.25% (134.5 Proof). nc ncf.*

◇ **Colonel E.H. Taylor Barrel Proof** bott code: B1319909:44M (93) n23 nutty with a gentle sweet-dry interplay. The lightest tannin-induced spices plus delicate hickory; t23.5 intense natural caramels are blasted against the palate and stay there for some time thanks to the big corn oil in play. The molasses are intense, as is the liquorice...then those natural toffee – and sometimes toffee and nut – all the way; f23 the briefest Blue Mountain Jamaican coffee note glides over the delicate vanilla; a little demerara sugar keep the sweetness onside but it is caramel all the way...; **b23.5** it is as though every last trace of natural caramel has been sucked from the barrel... 67.7% (135.4 proof).

Colonel E H Taylor Cured Oak (93.5) **n23 t24 f23 b23.5** Not sure about the oak being cured: coming from Buffalo Trace, I doubt if there was anything wrong with it in the first place...In many ways a much quieter than normal and delicate bourbon with the tannins harnessed and led to a path quite different from the normal toasty/liquorice style. 50%. (100 Proof)

Colonel E.H. Taylor Four Grain Bottled in Bond Aged 12 Years db (97.5) **n24.5 t24.5 f24 b24.5** Unquestionably one of the greatest whiskeys bottled worldwide in the last 12 months, simply because of the unfathomable depths of its complexity. Every aspect of great whisky making clears its respective hurdle with yards to spare: brewing, distilling, maturation...the nose and taste confirms that a team of people knew exactly what they were doing...and achieved with rare distinction what they set out to do. Forget about the sheer, undiluted beauty of this bourbon: for me, it is simply a true honour – and thrill – to taste. 50% (100 proof).

Colonel E. H. Taylor Old Fashioned Sour Mash (94) **n24 t23.5 f23 b23.5.** When they say "old fashioned" they really aren't joking. This is a style which takes me back to my first bourbon tasting days of the mid 1970s. And, at the moment, it is hard to name another bourbon offering this unique, technically brilliant style. Outstanding! 50% (100 Proof)

Colonel E.H. Taylor Seasoned Wood db (93.5) **n25 t24 f21.5 b23** I am sitting in my garden in near darkness tasting and writing this, the near-thousand-year-old church just 75 yards or so behind me clanging out that it is ten of the clock. Although mid-July, it is the first day warm enough in this apology of a British summer where I have been able to work outside. Oddly, it reminded me when I used to write my books and chapters on bourbon in the grounds of Buffalo Trace in the 1990s, the sun also set and a warm breeze kissing my face. No possums here for company, although the bats are already circling me, kindly protecting me from midges. And as I can't read the label of the whiskey, it makes my senses all the more alive. A whiskey, though not perfect, for when the sun sets but your day is really about to begin... 50% (100 proof)

⟡ **Colonel E.H. Taylor Single Barrel Bottled in Bond** bott code: L172190110:45K (96.5) **n24** close on a classic BIB bourbon nose: the character doesn't come through either too aggressively or like a wilting flower, either. The liquorice is precise and firm, the small grains impact with a fascinating busy-ness and the molasses are controlled and proportionate... superb...! **t24.5** well, if you think the nose is good, get a handle on this delivery! One of those rare whiskeys – of any persuasion – where the tale told on the nose is played out almost word-for word on the palate...borderline incredible. And even more beautiful, as now there are reverberations and variations of intensity to be savoured; **f24** the small grains had upheld a crispness by which the toastier notes hang. This still continues into the finish despite the toastiness rising on cue and the molasses feeling a little more burnt. Even so, at no time is the rhythm or balance lost, or a strain put on either the dryness or sweetness. It just fades with hat-doffing style...; **b24** a single barrel has no right to be this incredibly good: how can so much complexity yet balance be stored in one cask alone? Simply mind-blowingly mesmerising.... 50% (100 proof).

Colonel E.H. Taylor Small Batch (94.5) **n23 t24 f23.5 b24** From first nose, to last, the exemplary high quality of this bourbon is not for a second in dispute. 50% (100 Proof)

⟡ **Colonel E.H. Taylor Small Batch Bottled in Bond** (no bottling number) (94.5) **n23.5** a dreamy, soft butterscotch tart on a nose; a little ulmo honey mixes in with the gentle, half-heartedly toasted oak-vanilla. But for a BIB, this really is a real softie...; **t23.5** again the caramels rule the roost. A mix of ulmo and Manuka honey make a thin strike for sweetness before a surge of roasty tannins: toasted fudge and lightly burnt mallow; **f23.5** more caramels with the corn oils finally petering out to give the toastiness a much drier feel at the death; **b24** just balances out so beautifully. 50% (100 proof).

Cougar Bourbon Aged 5 Years (95) **n25 t24 f23 b23.** If Karl Kennedy of Neighbours really is the whisky buff he reckons he is, I want to see a bottle of this in his home next to Dahl. By the way: where is Dahl these days...? (And by the way, Karl, the guy who married you and Susan in London is a fan of mine. So you had better listen up...!) 37% (74 proof). Foster's Group, Australia.

Daniel Stewart 8 Years Old (92.5) **n22 t23 f23.5 b24.** Stellar sophistication. Real complexity here, and, as 8-year-olds go, probably among the most complex of them all. A deep notch up on the previous bottling I encountered. 45%

⟡ **Eagle Rare Aged 10 Years** bott code: L172800119:194 (95.5) **n23.5** at first a lilting toffee note which just gets creamier. Next a little thinned Manuka honey makes way for light spices, kumquats and low rumbling oak...; **t24** technically sublime: the two-toned delivery both caresses with the cream promised on the nose, but scorches slightly also with a confident spice which appears to be at the vanguard of the haughty liquorice which follows in its wake. The texture is nigh on perfect....; **f24** just sit tight and let those spices and vanillas do their job: almost perfect sweet/dry nuancing, though the hickory-led roastiness wins out in the end...as it should...; **b24** to the British and Europeans Eagle Rare means Crystal Palace not losing a game...very rare indeed. In the US it will probably mean a lot more to those who once hankered after Ancient Age 10, as this is not the Single Barrel incarnation. And while Crystal Palace may be pointless, literally, this striking whiskey most certainly isn't... That's one soaring, beautiful eagle... 45% (90 proof)

Eagle Rare Aged 10 Years Single Barrel (89) n21.5 t23 f22 b22.5. A surprising trip, this, with some dramatic changes en route. 45%

Eagle Rare 17 Years Old bott Spring 2015 db (94.5) n24 t23.5 f23.5 b23.5 One very consistent, big and serious bourbon... 45% (90 proof)

Eagle Rare 17 Years Old bott Spring 2016 db (95) n24 t23 f24 b24 An eagle with a slightly different plumage, this one really determined to display its tannin – though never at the cost of compromising its excellent complexity. 45% (90 proof).

⟨⟩ **Eagle Rare 17 Years Old** bott Summer 2017 db (94.5) n24 cream toffee with a delicate chocolatey edge; a little liquorice and hickory is stirred into the mix, but just enough for a hint of both: complex, balanced and satisfying; t23.5 after the initial caramel wave, a little extra bite on delivery which is a tad unusual. But it doesn't take long for the corn oils to settle and the molasses and Manuka honey to break free; the hickory and liquorice pick up spices to make the mid-ground impactful; f23 dry and very roasty; b24 just goes a fraction easier on both the sugars and cocoa here. But the toastiness always remains in control and impressively underscores the big age. 45% (90 proof).

⟨⟩ **Early Times Bottled-in-Bond Straight Bourbon** bott code: A146171040 3131550 (94) n23 fabulous nip to the tannin, which is both tight and yet at times expansive as it reaches out to touch every facet on the nose. A real Manuka honey and molasses mix, but with a gentle orangey citrus tone, too; t23.5 talk about salivating! The delicate spices mix in early with the fizzing maple syrup and Manuka to get the juices flowing. Good corn oil glade over the palate to ensure maximum intensity, the tannins bight deeper and with ever more intense liquorice; f23.5 incredibly long, beautiful mocha fad with delicate spice and still the toasty sugars do their job; b24 they call this "Old Style", and it really is. A blast from the past bourbon, oozing personality. A bit of a stunner. 50% (100 proof).

Elijah Craig Barrel Proof Kentucky Straight Bourbon batch no. A117 db (94.5) n23.5 t23.5 f24 b23.5 An old-fashioned bourbon full of joy. 63.5% (127 proof).

Elijah Craig Barrel Proof Kentucky Straight Bourbon batch no. B517 db (91) n23.5 t23 f22 b22.5 Not exactly the most complex EC, but really makes the most of the big liquorice intervention. 62.1% (124.2 proof).

⟨⟩ **Elijah Craig Barrel Proof Kentucky Straight Bourbon** batch no. C917 db (95) n23.5 no shortage of natural caramel here. But a light coconut swirl, along with a blood orange ensures subtle complexity; t24 the texture is enough to make you purr: it is hard to imagine the heather-honey-tinged oils being any more luxurious. One of the most honeyed deliveries from Craig for a very long time: meadow blossom honey offering a soft, waxy and most gentle of sweetnesses and still stands its round even as the oak makes its caramel and liquorice-led entry; f23.5 vague spices, but that waxy honeyed sheen persists...thankfully! b24 a bourbon which is winner just for much for its rich texture as it is the subtle complexities of its nose and delivery. A real honey – in every sense! 65.5% (131 proof).

Elijah Craig Barrel Proof Bourbon 12 Years of Aging db (95.5) n23.5 t24 f24 b24 Not sure when I saw a darker bourbon at 12 years commercially available. Remember that in straight bourbon colour represents interaction between spirit and barrel. So expect big oak presence and you will not be disappointed! A bourbon for bourbon lovers with very hairy chests – male or female.. 671% (134.2 proof) ncf.

Elijah Craig Small Batch Kentucky Straight Bourbon db (89.5) n22.5 t22.5 f22 b22.5 About as quiet and unassailable as Elijah Craig ever gets. 47% (94 proof).

Elmer T Lee Single Barrel (91) n22 t23.5 f(22.5) b23. A sturdy, dense bourbon with above average sweetness. So effortless, it is hard to immediately realise that greatness has entered your glass. 45%

⟨⟩ **Elmer T Lee Single Barrel** bott code B1622821:38K (89.5) n23 a procession of caramel notes, each extracted from a slightly different depth of the oak sets up the minty, richer tones beautifully; t22.5 salivating delivery, but a harder edge to the mouth feel than normal; the creaminess to the liquorice and toffee is too charming; f22 a little quick to lose the sugars but the milky toffee stands its ground; b22.5 one of the more caramel dominant of the Elmers. 45%

⟨⟩ **Elmer T Lee Single Barrel** bott code: L172400121:26K (94.5) n24 how does one barrel do it...? How can a single barrel be so soft and yielding on the nose, so teasing in its character with its little hints and whispers of a dab of honey here, a little cream caramel there; just the odd dry leaf diced in for good measure, so elegant in its deportment...yet still forging subtle weight and depth... Glorious! t23.5 the creaminess on the nose is translated on delivery to a beautiful cream toffee. Light muscovado sugars counter the questioning oak; f23.5 long and as delicate as the nose. At last a little spice arrives and with it a toasty liquorice which has held off a remarkably long time. Satisfying...; b24 if my dear old friend Elmer was still with us and visited my tasting room today, I think he'd be going home with cap tightly on head and the bottle this sample came from held even more firmly under his arm.... 45% (90 proof)

Elmer T. Lee Single Barrel Bourbon 1919 - 2013 db (96.5) n24.5 t24 f24 b24 I left this as the 1,145th and final new whisk(e)y to be tasted for the 2015 Jim Murray's Whisky Bible. Elmer, once a neighbour of mine, loved his garden and more than once I helped him safely remove squirrels without them being hurt in any way. Which makes this whiskey, seemingly gentle but with a backbone of American steel - yet on the nose flowing with floral notes, a touching and entirely apposite marker to his memory. And it delights me to say that I know, with absolute certainty, he would have been blown away by this barrel of glorious complexity. Elmer: with a glass of this rare genius I salute your memory, my friend. 46.5%

Evan Williams 23 Years Old (94) n22 t23.5 f24.5 b24. Struts his stuff, refusing to allow age to slow him or dim the shine from his glowing grains. Now oak has taken its toll. This seems older than its 23 years... Or so I first thought. Then a light shone in my soul and it occurred to me: hang on...I have wines going back to the last century. For the older ones, do I not allow them to breathe? So I let the whiskey breathe. And, behold, it rose from the dead. This Methuselah of a whiskey had come alive once more...and how!! 53.5%

George T. Stagg (97.5) n24 t25 f24 b24.5. Astonishing how so much oak can form and yet have such limited negative impact and so few unpleasant side effects. These tasting notes took nearly four hours to compile. Yet they are still in a simplified form to fit into this book... George T Stagg is once again... staggering. 71.5% (143 Proof). ncf.

George T. Stagg (Barrel Proof) db (95) n24 t24 f23 b24 Quite beautiful bourbon of the top order. But not quite so breathtakingly complex and brain-shatteringly vivid as Staggs of past times. 64.1%. Buffalo Trace Antique Collection.

George T. Stagg (96.5) n24.5 t24 f24 b24 The alcohol by volume of one of the sexiest whiskeys on the planet is 69...and it goes down a treat. Much harder to spit than swallow...69.05% Buffalo Trace Antique Collection.

George T. Stagg Limited Edition (96.5) n24 t24.5 f24 b24.5 As spectacular as a sunset from the hilltop village of Coldharbour in my beloved Surrey 71.4% (142.8 proof). ncf

George T. Stagg db (96.5) n24 t24 f24 b24.5 It is impossible not to finish a mouthful of George T without letting out a long, contented, slightly awe-felt and entirely fulfilled sigh, just as one might make after listening to the final strains of Vaughan Williams' London Symphony or Strauss' Tod und Verklarung. Most of the usual traits to be had in abundance, plus one or two slight differences as the pot was stirred for another dip into one of world's whisky's deepest caverns... 69.1% (138.2 proof)

George T. Stagg db (97) n24 t24.5 f24 b24.5 Amazing consistency: this is the fourth year running it has been given a score of 96.5 or above - a Stagg-ering achievement. 72.05% (144.1 proof).

◇ **George T. Stagg** db (97) n24 only Stagg can do this: rock hard rye and Demerara on stalks, coming at you at first like some kind of Picasso-inspired dream, then toned down slightly by the corn oils, yet always that wonderfully nagging golden syrup-sweet toastiness...; t24.5 only Stagg can do this: rock you back in your chair both with sheer power but always with the dazzling wonderment of a cosmic explosion being played out in your mouth. And there are stars everywhere, the liquorice and hickory shooting to all parts of the palate; the blend of golden syrup and treacle mingling with thick corn oil to sooth the spicier, toastier tannins. The bitter-sweet, dry-oily juxtaposition throughout...only a Stagg...; f24 moist, ridiculously long, with the sugars keeping their feet on the throat of the ever-threatening toastier notes...; b24.5 funny: I nosed this and I thought: "T-bone steak." Huge whiskey deserving to be the warm-up act for a meal at either RingSide Steakhouse, Portland or Barberian's Steak House in Toronto or even some outdoor parrilla in Uruguay. It is the kind of whiskey that demands something very special: it just refuses, point-blanc, to do ordinary... 64.6% (129.2 proof).

◇ **Hancock's President's Reserve Single Barrel** bott code: B1710117:26K (90.5) n22.5 playful dark sugars meld with untaxing toasted oak; t23 as on the nose, the sugars are out of the traps fast. The corn oil is limited, allowing the darker toasted fudge notes a disproportionate say. A little drying hickory meets the vanilla as we head towards the finish; overall a little fluffy and ridiculously relaxed; f22.5 light but busy spices arrive late on the scene, though the vanillas still dominate; b22.5 a joyous Bourbon that gives the impression that it is performing well within itself. 44.45% (88.9 proof)

Hancock's Reserve Single Barrel (92) n25 t23 f21.5 b22.5. A slightly quieter example of this consistently fine brand. The nose, though, is the stuff of wet whiskey dreams... 44.45%

Hogs 3 Bourbon Aged Over 3 Years (86.5) n22.5 t21.5 f21 b21.5 A bang on standard mid-towards upper warehouse Kentucky 3-year-old with plenty of juicy but ungainly vanilla, Demerara sugar and citrus.... and absolutely no frills. *40% (80 proof). Quality Spirits International.*

I.W. Harper Kentucky Straight Bourbon (87.5) n22 t22 f21.5 b22. The puckeringly dry delivery and finish forms the toast for the well spiced light sugar sandwich. *41% (82 Proof)*

I.W. Harper Kentucky Straight Bourbon 15 Year Old (94.5) n23.5 t23.5 f24 b23.5 Class in a glass. *43% (86 Proof)*

Jefferson's Reserve batch no. 84 (91) n23 t23.5 f22 b23. Once a 15-year-old, no age statement here. But this has seen off a few Summers, sweetening with each passing one. *45.1%.*

Jim Beam Black Double Age Aged 8 Years (93) n23 t24 f22.5 b23.5. Rather than the big, noisy, thrill-seeking JB Black, here it is in quiet, reflective, sophisticated mode. Quite a shift. But no less enjoyable. *43% (86 proof)*

Jim Beam Bonded 100 Proof db (92.5) n22.5 t23.5 f23 b23.5 Takes its time to get going. But when it does, it just won't shut up.... Complex and compelling, the toastiness takes time to make itself felt but does so with panache. *50%*

Jim Beam Signature Craft Aged 12 Years db (92.5) n23 gorgeous roasted coffee and liquorice. The rye pokes through gamely; t23.5 soft delivery with a wonderful toasted fudge quality. Takes time for the rye to arrive but it does as the spices mount; f23 softly spiced with plenty of creamy mocha; b23 classic Beam: big rye and massive fruit. Quite lovely. *43% WB15/386*

John B. Stetson Straight Bourbon Whiskey (92) n23.5 t23.5 f22 b23. Absolutely love it! Quality: I take my hat off to you...*42%*

Jim Beam Signature Craft Brown Rice 11 Year Old db 45% (78) n20.5 t21 f18 b18.5 A whiskey I nosed and tasted before looking to see what it was. And immediately alarm bells rang and I was reaching to inspect the bottle in a state of panic and shock. RICE!!! Well that explains the unsatisfying simplicity to the finish where, really, only oak can be heard....apart from the wallpaper paste, that is. And the fact the whiskey never quite gets off the ground despite an attractive cocoa thread. Or was that actually real cocoa...? Sorry, but in the great name of Jim Beam, this is one that should have just stayed in the lab. *(90 Proof)*

Jim Beam Signature Craft Soft Red Wheat 11 Year Old db (92) n22 t23.5 f23 b23.5 A beautifully weighted bourbon making a big deal of the sugar-spice interplay. Hugely enjoyable and at times fascinating. *45% (90 Proof)*

Jim Beam Signature Craft Small Batch Quarter Cask Finished 3rd Release db (92) n23.5 23.5 f22 b23 Quarter casks are not normally associated with deftness and poise. This one certainly is. Elegant, if a little lightweight at the end. *43% (86 Proof)*

John E. Fitzgerald Larceny (94) n23 t23.5 f23.5 b24. If this doesn't win a few converts to wheated bourbon, nothing will. A high quality, stunningly adorable whiskey, pulsing with elegance and personality. Every drinks cabinet should have this wonderful new addition to the bourbon lexicon. *46%*

John E. Fitzgerald Very Special Reserve Aged 20 Years (93) n22.5 t24 f23 b23.5 A bourbon lover's bourbon! *45% (90 proof)*

John J Bowman Virginia Straight Bourbon Single Barrel (94) n23 t24 f23 b24. One of the biggest yet most easily relaxed and beautifully balanced bourbons on the market. *50%*

◈ **John J Bowman Virginia Straight Bourbon Single Barrel** bott code: L172010507:28B (93) n23 manuka honey meets moist muscovado sugar...all atop toasted Hovis. Liquorice and hickory are no strangers, either... t23.5 those with a sweet tooth should be heading to Virginia pronto: a veritable avalanche of dark sugars and Manuka honey cascades on to the palate though the dark, vaguely bitter oak tones soon counter and then balance. The result is a spiced bourbon surge, sweet and salivating. The drier oak tones are just what the doctor ordered; f23 more warming spices and ever drying vanilla: a superb mix; b23.5 this is very high quality bourbon making the most of both its big toastiness and its more intrinsic honey tones. Simple...yet devastatingly complex... *50% (100 proof)*

Johnny Drum (Black Label) (89.5) n22 t23 f21.5 b23. How often does that happen? The same whiskey, different strength, virtually same quality (though this has a little more depth) but gets there by a slightly different route. *43%*

Johnny Drum (Green Label) (89) n22.5 t23 f21 b22.5. Much more honey these days. Worth making a bee-line for. *40%*

Johnny Drum Private Stock (90.5) n22.5 t22.5 f23 b22.5. One of those bourbons where a single glass is never quite enough. Great stuff! *50.5% (101 proof)*

Kentucky Owl Kentucky Straight Bourbon Whiskey batch no. 2 (91) n22.5 t23.5 f22.5 b22.5 A big, corn-led bourbon but with some extra oaky depth. *58.6% (117.2 proof). 1,380 bottles.*

Kentucky Vintage batch 08-72 (94.5) n23.5 t24.5 f23 b23.5 Staggered! I really didn't quite expect that. Previous bottlings I have enjoyed of this have had hair attached to the muscle. This is a very different Vintage, one that reaches for the feminine side of a macho whiskey. If you want to spend an hour just getting to know how sensitive your taste buds can be, hunt down this batch... 45%

Knob Creek Aged 9 Years bott code L6154 (95.5) n23.5 t24 f23.5 b24.5 Seems like more barrels have been included from the lower echelons of the warehouse. Lighter, sweeter and more feminine. One of the most complex Knob Creeks I have ever encountered: a true Kentucky belle! 50% (100 proof)

Knob Creek Aged 9 Years (94.5) n23.5 t24 f23.5 b23.5 No whiskey in the world has a more macho name, and this is not for the faint-hearted. Big, hard in character and expansive, it drives home its point with gusto, celebrating its explosive finish. 50%

Knob Creek Single Barrel Reserve Aged 9 Years bott no L6133 (95) n24 f24 b24 A macho bourbon of a wonderfully high standard. Just a degree juicier than you normally find with a Knob Creek. 60% (120 proof)

◇◇◇ **Knob Creek 25th Anniversary Single Barrel** barrelled 2/25/2004 db (93) n23 takes time for the caramels to calm, but then we have a solid delivery of liquorice and chicory-led camp coffee; t24 again, early caramels but underneath can be found slabs of treacle and liquorice; both the rye small grain and accompanying spices are well mannered; f23 lovely low-level spices pave the way for more of the same; b23 a caramel-rich critter, yes-siree! But let it hang around the glass a bit and a rich liquorice edginess will develop... 62% (124 proof). sc.

Maker's 46 (95) n23.5 t24.5 f23 b24 Some people have a problem with oak staves. I don't: whisky, after all, is about the interaction of a grain spirit and oak. This guy is all about the nose and, especially, the delivery. With so much controlled honey on show, it cannot be anything other than a show-stopper. Frankly, magnificent. I think I've met my Maker's... 47% (94 proof)

◇◇◇ **Maker's 46** barrel finished with oak staves, bott code: L6155MMB 00651 1233 (89) n22.5 a gentle breeze of vanilla is in contrast to the localised storm of wheat-induced spice; t22.5 and yep: it's the spices first out the traps on the palate, also. Lightly and gently evolving sugars offer a contrast, with the usual suspects of liquorice, hickory and vanilla all making an entrance, but wiping their feet first; f22 incredibly quiet and sober, a few heavier tannins sticking around to the end; b22 Maker's at its most surprisingly genteel. 47% (94 proof).

Maker's Mark (Red Seal) (91) n22.5 t23.5 f22 b23. The big honey injection has done no harm whatsoever. This sample came from a litre bottle and the whiskey was darker than normal. What you seem to have is the usual steady Maker's with a helping hand of extra weight. In fact this reminds me of the old Maker's Gold wax. 45%

Mayor Pingree Aged 9 Years Straight Bourbon Whiskey batch no. 16-314 (96) n23.5 t24 f24 b24.5 This is my second darling Valentine from Indiana... 58.6% (117.2 proof). ncf.

Mayor Pingree Aged 10 Years Straight Bourbon Whiskey Single Barrel barrel no. 2-1 (89) n22.5 t22.5 f22 b22 Compare this to the 9-years-old to see what happens when the oak and grains are just very slightly off beat... 52.7% (105.4 proof). ncf. 159 bottles.

◇◇◇ **McAfee's Benchmark Old No 8 Brand** bott code: 03072193223:04W (89) n22.5 charming, nutty, mocha-rich aroma which climbs in intensity with surprising dexterity; t23 a brilliant delivery which is thick in Venezuelan chocolate and Demerara sugars; a solid oily accompaniment allows the liquorice good purchase; f21.5 thins and dries with the vanilla becoming a little dry and flaky towards the finish; b22 above average standard bourbon full of chewy riches but which can't quite keep up with its exceptional nose and delivery. 40% (80 proof)

◇◇◇ **Michter's 10 Years Old Single Barrel** barrel no. 174/1135 (93) n23.5 excellent small grain busy-ness to accompany the maple syrup and manuka sweetness. Dense and very attractive; t23.5 seems to have wrung all the caramels from the oak as it could, as the soft toffee notes dominate from the very first mouthful; the sugars are thin but lightly toasty; f23 red liquorice and hickory make some small but attractive marks, with a little corn oil still keeping the sugars in place; b23 like the rye, has a slight metallic persona which adds a degree of lustre to both the nose and taste. 47.2% (94.4 proof). sc.

Michter's No. 1 Bourbon (87) n23 t22.5 f20 b21.5. This one is mainly a nose job: all kinds of heavy liquorice and diced kumquat. But there is also a brooding tannin menace lurking in the shadows, which reveal themselves more fully – and with a tad of bitterness - on delivery and finish. 45.7%

Noah's Mill batch 13-81 (93.5) n23 gorgeous glazed almonds; a little citrus & cold coffee; t23.5 oddly enough, doesn't taste like the nose: much more macho, with the full blooded hickory & Demerara; enormous weight & depth; assorted honey notes begin to form; f22.5 gentle finale, reverting back to the style of the aroma. Excellent vanilla on sugars & weightier liquorice; b23.5 a full bodied classic bourbon which undulates over the palate. 57.15% (114.3 proof)

❖ **Old Charter 8** bott code: B170871 10:094 (**91**) n22.5 almost perfumed in the delicate sweetness of the liquorice, hickory and thinned honey. Repays time in the glass to maximise the gentle layering of sugars; t23 surprising weight on delivery with the corn oils lightly coating the mouth and the spices arriving more in a wheated bourbon style than rye. The small grains fix beautifully on mid palate; f22.5 those oils come into their own and maximise the tannins which now offer a mocha and light liquorice finale, a bit like a Bassett's Allsorts candy; b23 a wonderfully oily affair which sticks to the palate like a limpet. From taste alone, appears no longer to be an 8-year-old but has retained the number 8. Probably a mix of years as the layering and complexity is significant. 40% (80 proof)

❖ **Old Forester** bott code: A083151035 db (**94.5**) n23.5 an object lesson in the busy-ness of small grains: the rye element dances brightly and crisply over the more ponderous hickory and overbaked fruitcake body; t23.5 as silky as they come, the corn oil put to full use to accentuate the molasses and red liquorice; f23 magnificent spice and honey fade, topped off with a latte coffee...complete with a crisp rye fruitiness; b24 solid as a rock: a classic and criminally under-rated bourbon which is wonderfully true to the distillery. 43%.

❖ **Old Forester Statesman** bott code: L2337123:49 db (**92.5**) n23 slightly duller than the standard Forester thanks to extra natural caramels filling in the highs and lows: still plenty of high ryes, though; t23.5 indeed, the delivery confirms that big caramel kick. Manuka honey in abundance with muted spices and no shortage of creamy shortbread and fudge; f23 long, corn soaked and gentle, the spices massage rather than attacking the taste buds; b23.5 a very laid back and relaxed Forester. 47.5% (95 proof)

Old Fitzgerald Very Special 12 Years Old (**93**) n24 t23.5 f22.5 b23. There is always something that makes the heart sing when you come across a whiskey which appears so relaxed in its excellence. At the moment my heart is in the shower merrily lathering itself... 45%

Old Grand-Dad (**90.5**) n22 t23 f23 b23.5. This one's all about the small grains. A busy, lively bourbon, this offers little to remind me of the original Old Grand-Dad whiskey made out in Frankfort. That said, this is a whisk(e)y-lover's whiskey: in other words the excellence of the structure and complexity outweighs any historical misgivings. Enormously improved and now very much at home with its own busy style. 43%

Old Grand-Dad Bonded 100 Proof (**94.5**) n22.5 t24 f23.5 b24.5 Obviously Old Grand-dad knows a thing or two about classy whiskey: this is a magnificent version, even by its own high standards. It was always a winner and one you could bet your shirt on for showing how the small grains can impact upon complexity. But this appears to go a stage further. The base line is a touch deeper, so there is more ground to cover on the palate. It has been a whiskey-lover's whiskey for a little while and after a few barren years, has been inching itself back to its great Frankfort days. The fact that Beam's quality has risen over the last decade has played no insignificant part in that. 50% (100 proof)

Old Rip Van Winkle 10 Years Old (**93**) n24 t23 f23 b23. A much sharper cookie than it once was. And possibly a Maryland Cookie, too, what with the nuts and chocolate evident. As graceful as it is entertaining. 45% (90 Proof). Buffalo Trace.

❖ **Old Rip Van Winkle Aged 10 Years** bott code: B17053113:497 (**91.5**) n23 pungent, earthy – even slightly vegetable noted. Not an aroma to be trifled with and confirms its wheaty depth with some ill-tempered spice; t23.5 quite beautiful: a real depth to the chocolate which accompanies the nuts perfectly: anyone who has chewed happily into a bar of Cadbury's Chocolate Nut will be more than content with this; f22 a light finish as the oils give up a little too easily. The oak has a freer hand to dry things than one might expect...; b23 those who know the Weller Antique 107 will find this enjoyable, but just a little lacking in body by comparison. 53.5% (107 proof)

❖ **Old Taylor 6** (**89.5**) n22.5 who needs to add fruit to a bourbon for a cheap thrill or some hare-brained marketing ploy when a helpful yeast kicks in with the rye to do the job beautifully...and naturally? Understated class; t23 a dazzling delivery: salivating brown sugar at first, then a gorgeous impact of busy spice followed quickly by cocoa; f21.5 slightly over thins so the big vanilla has little to hold on to; some late hickory still offers limited body; b22.5 a relaxed, stylish and surprisingly complex bourbon with a distinctly fruity edge. 40% (80 proof)

❖ **Old Virginia Aged 6 Years Kentucky Bourbon** bott code: L632901C (**85.5**) n22 t21.5 f21 b21 A pleasant if slightly thin bourbon with casks plucked, seemingly, from the bottom of the warehouse. The most delicate tannins offer gentle vanillas and spices. 40%.

Old Weller Antique 107 (**96**) n24.5 t24 f23.5 b24 This almost blew me off my chair. Always thought this was pleasant, if a little underwhelming, in the past. However, this bottling has had a few thousands volts passed through it as it now comes alive on the palate with a glorious blending of freshness and debonair aging. One of the surprise packages of 2012. 53.5% (107 proof)

Orphan Barrel 'Barterhouse' 20 Years Old (91) n22.5 t22.5 f23 b23 To think: this was still white dog when I first visited Old Stitz! 45.1%.

Orphan Barrel Forged Oak (87) n22 t22 f21 b22. Decent bourbon, but a little stiff and mechanical in its development. The finish has a tad too much toast for its own good. Still, a good chewing bourbon. 45.25%

Orphan Barrel Lost Prophet batch tul-tr-1 (92) n22.5 hickory and butterscotch pair off beautifully; t23.5 and in steams the liquorice, the old fashioned way, with molasses as its sidekick; f23 comfortable as the spices rise; b23 markedly more relaxed than Forged Oak and understands the value of good sugar-spice interplay. 45.05%

Orphan Barrel 'Old Blowhard' 26 Years Old (95) n23.5 t24 f23.5 b24 I do get my hands on a few samples of very old bourbon, but this seems to have a style more recognisable in the 1980s and early to mid '90s than now. Time warp whisky in every sense. Wonderful! 45.35%. Bottled in Tullahoma, aged 26 years, "found in Stitzel Weller".

Orphan Barrel Rhetoric 21 Year Old batch 0109-67 (94.5) n23.5 t24 f23 b24 A bourbon drinker's bourbon. How's that for rhetoric...? 45%

Orphan Barrel Rhetoric 22 Year Old batch no. L6063J3 (87) n20.5 t23.5 f21 b22. Certainly has a few proud war wounds to show for 22 searing hot Kentucky summers. Some outstanding tannins and roasty sugars at play on delivery, and a few grapefruit notes for good measure. But some bitterness, also, as the oak gives up a degree of its less impressive qualities. Very hard to call it right on whiskeys this age. This comes home just the right side of very good, but another summer might have done some fair damage. 45.2% (90.4 proof)

⬥ **Orphan Barrel Rhetoric Aged 24 Years** bott code: L8059K1002 (95) n24 a surprising degree of ulmo honey and caramel makes for one of the softest geriatric bourbons I have ever encountered: whether in a warehouse, lab, or from a commercial bottling. Almost redefines the term delicate...; t24 such silkiness on the palate is probably the last thing you'd expect...but there it is. A mix of demerara sugars, maple syrup and molasses give an initial feeling of toasty oak-activation but then the vanilla and caramel take control, limiting the build-up of spice; f23.5 and there we have it: the softest finish of any pensionable age bourbon on the planet: its vanilla and caramel all the way, the tannins left far behind...; b23.5 an unusual bourbon for this kind of great age. Usually they head down a heavy duty tannin route. Instead this one almost drowns in natural creamy caramels. Almost as meek as Theresa May when facing the EU bully boys though, of course, nothing on the planet is that pathetic. 45.4% (90.8 proof).

Pappy Van Winkle's Family Reserve 15 Years Old (96) n24.5 t23.5 f24 b24 At a book signing in Canada a Bible enthusiast asked me which well-aged, wheated bourbon he should look for. I told him Pappy 15. He looked at me quizzically and said: "Well, that's what I thought, but in the Bible you have it down as rye-release." I told him he was wrong...until I checked there and then. And discovered he was right. Of course, Pappy has always been wheated and the lushness on the palate and spices radiating from it has always confirmed this. I'll put it down to not spitting enough. Or perhaps the speed at which I type whilst tasting. Sometimes you mean one thing – then another word comes out. Like when a member of my staff asks for a pay rise. I mean no. But somehow say yes. So apologies to any other I fooled out there. For not only is this a wheated bourbon. With its improbable degree of deftness for something so big, it has edged up a notch or two into a truly world great whiskey...whatever the recipe. 53.5%

⬥ **Pappy Van Winkle Family Reserve 15 Years Old** bott code: L172520110:237 (96) n24 not sure you can ask much more of a 15-year-old bourbon ...rye recipe or wheated. The honey has been set on maximum and buries itself into the most toasty notes of them all. The spices are profound, yet controlled. Hard to find a better- balanced aroma...; t23.5 silky, soft yet exuding power. The oils are magnificently rich and the toastier notes cling to them like a child to its mother's breast. The spices start with a jolt and grow into something that appears to involve its own universe...; f24 ridiculously long, with those honey tones at last released to counter the chest- beating oak...; b24.5 Weller Antique fans will possibly find a closer match here structure-wise than the 10-year-old. While those in pursuit of excellent bourbon should just linger here awhile. Anyone other than true bourbon lovers need not sample. But there again... 53.5%

⬥ **Pappy Van Winkle's Family Reserve 20 Years Old** bott code: L172640108:18N (95) n24 very much in the red liquorice school of tannins: soft, slightly fruity, kiwi fruit especially, and muscovado sugars; the spices, not unlike those found in Caribbean sweets, are crucial to the balance; t22.5 a duller middle than you might expect after a reserved delivery, the quicksand corn oil dominating above all but holding the darker sugars well; f24.5 here now the bourbon comes into its own with a sublimely long and complex finish. Vanilla and butterscotch lead, but the all the usual high quality bourbon traits - and, like the nose, some extra fruity ones, too - duck and dive and bob and weave to magical effect; the spices are, like on the nose, the work of fairies...; b24 an ancient bourbon, so should be a flavour powerhouse. But this is all about understatement and complexity. 45.2% (90.4 proof).

◇ **Pappy Van Winkle's Family Reserve 23 Years Old** bott code: L1707013:20N (94.5) n24.5 massive esters, like an old West Indian pot still rum. So toasty, yet the deep, thickset honey seems to be with one with the higher than average copper richness. And then there's the coconut, mint, liquorice and so much more... A nose of bourbon legend...; t23 the gentle gush of early corn oil, and again that coppery sheen, is a bit of a surprise. But such lightness means the more OTT oak is brought out in sharper relief, and not always to the whisky's fullest advantage, especially at the bittering midpoint; f23.5 ah, that's better. The finish is no less toasty, in fact a little burnt, but the sugars have caught up now and the balance is the better for it. Some major hickory and distant Manuka honey are accompanied by growing prickly spice; b23.5 I well remember the first Pappy boasting this kind of age: it was horrifically over-oaked and lacked any form of meaningful structure. Well, this also has the odd moment where the tannins are slightly out of control, especially just after delivery. But the structure to this is sound, the complexity a joy. And as for the nose....wow! 47.8% (95.6 proof).

◇ **Parker's Heritage Collection 11 Year Old Single Barrel Bourbon** barrel no. 5027255, OED: 4/10/2006, rickhouse : DD, Floor: 6, Rick: 39 db (84.5) n19.5 t23 f20.5 b21.5 Now there's a rarity: a cask kink apparent with the milkiness on the nose and bitterness at the death. But at least the middle is a joy with cream toffee perked up by moderate spices and the obligatory molasses as well as a little cocoa butter and liquorice. 61% (122 proof). sc.

Parker's Heritage Collection 24 Year Old Bottled in Bond Bourbon dist Fall 90 (95.5) n24 t24 f23.5 b24 For my 999th whisky for the 2018 Bible, thought I'd take on the oldest commercially bottled Kentucky bourbon I can ever remember seeing. Had no idea how this one would go, as the heat of the Midwest means there is little room for the whiskey to manoeuvre. What we actually have is a bourbon in previously uncharted territory and clearly experiencing new, sometimes mildly bewildering, sensations, having proudly gone where no bourbon has gone before... 50%.

Parker's Heritage Collection 24 Year Old Bottled in Bond Bourbon dist Spring 91 (96) n24 t24 f24 b24 Straight 24s all the way through for the 24-year-old: how fitting. Wears its crown a little easier than the Fall 1990 version. Superb! 50%.

Parker's Heritage Collection Wheated Mash Bill Bourbon Aged 10 Years (97) n24 t24 f24.5 b24.5. Hard to find the words that can do justice. I know Parker will be immensely proud of this. And with every good reason: I am working exceptionally hard to find a fault with this either from a technical distillation viewpoint or a maturation one. Or just for its sheer whiskeyness...A potential World Whisky of the Year. 62.1% (124.2 Proof). ncf.

Redemption High Rye Bourbon (74.5) n19 t20 f17.5 b18. Hugely disappointing bottling. Vaguely butyric, and its failure to reach any high point of quality is really driven home by the car-crash finish, complete with less than pleasant tang. Seriously needs to redeem itself next time round. 46%

Ridgemont Reserve 1792 Aged 8 Years (94.5) n23.5 t24 f23.5 b23.5 Now here is a whiskey which appears to have come to terms with its own strengths and, as with all bourbons and malts, limitations. Rarely did whiskey from Barton reach this level of maturity, so harnessing its charms always involves a bit of a learning curve. Each time I taste this it appears a little better than the last...and this sample is no exception to the rule. Excellent. 46.85% (93.7 Proof)

◇ **Rock Hill Farms Single Barrel Bourbon** bott code: B1717118:40K (95) n24 deft fruit, raspberry and plum preserve most likely, offers a softening note for the mix of tannin-shaped liquorice and molasses to land upon; one of the most gentle yet rich noses you'll locate this year; t24 the delivery oozes in honey – three different styles become apparent – and class. But it is the immediate volley of spice which catches the eye – well, taste buds – not least because its juxtaposition with the honey makes for an astonishing yet majestically controlled entrance. A much sturdier Fisherman's Friend/hickory middle confirms the oak's big input but still the corn remains intact to oil the wheels as required. Brilliant! f23.5 long, with the hickory playing its part for all its worth. Still the spices prickle and buzz while a little caramel joins forces with the hickory and light cocoa; b24 almost impossible to find fault with this. Anyone who loves whisky, bourbon in particular, will simply groan in pleasure in the same way your leg might jolt out when the knee is tapped. The only fly in the ointment is that I cannot tell you the barrel or bottling, because it isn't marked on the bottle. This really is bourbon at its sexiest. 50% (100 proof)

Russell's Reserve Single Barrel (94) n23.5 t24 f23 b23.5. Old-fashioned, thick as treacle bourbon. Delicious. 55%. ncf. Wild Turkey.

Russell's Reserve Small Batch 10 Year Old (92.5) n24.5 t23 f22 b23. Had the quality and complexity on the palate followed on from the nose I may well have had the world's No 1 whisky for 2012 in my glass. Just slum it with something quite wonderful, instead. Still waiting for an official explanation as to why this is a miserly 90 proof, when Jimmy Russell's preferred strength is 101, by the way... 45%. Wild Turkey.

Stagg Jn (91.5) n22.5 t24 f22.5 b22.5. A whiskey of staggering brinkmanship. Who will blink first? The massive oak or the taste buds. To be honest, this is the kind of bourbon that sorts out the men from the boys, the women from the girls. Doesn't have quite enough covering sweetness of varying type and intensity to match the complexity found in the original Stagg. One that needs a very long time to get to the bottom of. 67.2% (134.4 proof)

◇ **Stagg Jr** bott code: B170310457 (96) n24 no apologies that the huge personality is ladled on with a trowel, though the elements are much more delicately proportioned. A mixing of treacle and Manuka honey is only the start: the spices are sprinkled in just so, but there is a meaty, earthy element also: a kind of menacing beauty...; t24.5 this is where it comes into its own: the oils are profound carrying not just intense corn but the complex roastiness of the oak, the Peruvian coffee in particularly fine fettle. But the Manuka honey, Demerara sugars and liquorice quickly follow in its footsteps and before too long the dance is in perfect harmony; f23.5 dries as the oak pulses. Toasty with drying hickory and scurrying spices; b24 I well remember the first Stagg Junior I encountered. Which though truly excellent, skimped a little too much on the sugars and struggled to find its balance and, thus, full potential. Certainly no such worries with this bottling: indeed, the honey is remarkable for its abundance. Staggering... 64.75% (129.5 proof)

That Boutique-y Whisky Company Heaven Hill batch 1 (94) n23 t23.5 f24 b23.5 Now that's what I call bourbon! Travel back 30 years and taste some Heaven Hill, and – though a different distillery - you wouldn't be too far off! This bottling does the HH name proud! 50%. 240 bottles.

Trails End Bourbon 8 Year Old (87) n21.5 t22.5 f21.5 b21.5. A light bourbon, where the end of the trail begins early. The citrus outpoints the tannins all too easily. 45% (90 Proof). Hood River Distillers, Inc.

◇ **Van Winkle Special Reserve 12 Years Old Lot "B"** bott code: L172550110:147 (93.5) n23 an unusual buttery element coupled with less than common aroma of baked prunes helps lift this into a zone you might not previously expected to locate. The spices nip playfully, reminding us we are back in the land of wheated bourbon but the sugars are a force unto themselves; t23 a stunningly sexy texture really does maximise the intensity of the molasses and liquorice. The oils guarantee the required sheen while the spices nibble rather than bite; f24 long thanks to the oils. And improbably layered with the oak showing half a dozen nuances stretching between praline and hickory. Always creamy, though. And the spices never give up the fight...; b23.5 those looking for comparisons between certain Weller products and Van Winkle's might find this particular bottling a little better weighted, less forthright and more complex. 45% (90 proof)

◇ **Very Old Barton** bott code: L17/60111:104 (87.5) n22 t22 f21.5 b22 Attractive, brittle and with a delicious slow burn of first delicate, then broader hickory tones. The small grains fizz and dazzle in typical VOB style. If anything, slightly undercooked at this strength, and missing the extra oils, too. 40% (80 proof)

◇ **Very Old Barton 6** bott code: 907:104 (93) n22 toasty – even for a moment or three manuka on brown. Some sparring muscovado sugar notes momentarily blind you from the creeping spices. For VOB, exceptionally understated; t24 those sugars playing hide and seek on the nose are nowhere near so shy on delivery! Beautiful corn oils help spread the fabulously weighted spice which counter the sweeter notes with uncanny precision; f23.5 this is a long-un. More hickory and liquorice build and stand their ground while the drier tannins circle but refuse to strike; b23.5 the VOB 6, when the number stood for the years, has for the last quarter of a century been one of my bourbons of choice: an understated classic. This version has toned down on the nose very slightly and the palate underlines a far less definite oak-to-grain parry and counter-thrust. That said, still a bourbon which mesmerises you with its innate complexity and almost perfect weight and pace on the palate. One that has you instinctively pouring a second glass. 45% (90 proof)

Very Old Barton 6 Years Old (92) n23 t23 f23 b23. One of those seemingly gifted bourbons that, swan-like, appears to glide at the surface but on closer inspection has loads going on underneath. 43%

◇ **Very Old Barton 86** Proof bott code: B1635619:024 (89) n21.5 a far from confident nose, seemingly hesitant in just how firmly to turn the toasty screw. The lack of oils makes for thin gruel but sufficient breathing will allow the more complex grains to finally battle through. It is the half-hearted vanilla which stills holds the upper hand; t22.5 complex and salivating from the first mouthful. Again, surprisingly oil light, leaving the rye notes to really make themselves heard with crackling, crisp volley of vague fruit tones; f22.5 the diffident oak sauntering around on the palate has far more positive effect here with a delightful vanilla undertone to the rye and liquorice fade; b22.5 it is not the three percent extra alcohol which makes the difference here: simply the marriage of barrels. These ones have allowed the rye tones within the small grain to positively shine...; 43% (86 proof)

Very Old Barton 90 Proof (94) n23 t24 f23.5 b23.5. One of the most dangerously drinkable whiskeys in the world... 45% (90 proof)

◇ **Very Old Barton 100 Proof** bott code: L17/640102:074 **(96)** n23.5 orange blossom honey offers a compelling start to this most delicate and complex of noses. The small grains abound but are docile yet articulate and ordered as opposed to the traditional VOB helter- skelter and anarchy. The liquorice here is of the red and slightly creamy variety, the sugars crisp Demerara; **t24.5** the undiluted bourbon allows the corn oil to spread voluptuously about the palate; a stunning sharpness in the grain triggers massive salivations, then a big display of spices. The oak is toasty and builds in intensity, but never to the costs of the grain; **f23.5** a more simplistic throbbing of spice; the liquorice hangs and hangs to ensure depth; **b24.5** here's a challenge for you: find fault with this whiskey... Brilliant bourbon of the intense yet sophisticated variety. 50% (100 proof)

Virgin Bourbon 7 Years Old (96.5) n24 t24.5 f24 b24 This takes me back nearly 40 years to when I first began my love affair with bourbon and was still a bit of a whisky virgin. This was the very style that blew me away: big, uncompromising, rugged...yet with a heart of honeyed gold. It is the type of huge, box-ticking, honest bourbon that makes you get on your hands and knees and kiss Kentucky soil. 50.5% (101 proof)

Virgin Bourbon 15 Years Old (92.5) n23.5 t23 f23.5 b23. The kind of bourbon you want to be left in a room with. 50.5% (101 proof)

Virginia Gentleman (90.5) n22 t23 f23 b23.5. A Gentleman in every sense: and a pretty sophisticated one at that. 40% (80 Proof)

Weller 12 Years Old (93) n24 t23.5 f22.5 b23. Sheer quality. And an enormous leap in complexity and grace from the 7-y-o. 45%

◇ **Weller Aged 12 Years** bott code: B17081 20:56 **(91)** n22.5 the oak takes few hostages but has a tender, sweeter side to it also: a kind of spiced Manuka an acacia honey, liquorice mix; **t23** chewy, then a little crunchy and the oils firm up slightly. Big hickory and even a slight teasing of camp coffee. Curling oils help pile on the sugars; **f22.5** long with the honey staying its ground, though the oak now drifts into drier, vaguely sawdusty territory; **b23** firm, crunchy, sweet bourbon and very warming... 45% (90 proof)

◇ **Weller Antique 107** bott code: B17044 17:374 **(95.5)** n23.5 a nose thick enough to block draughty doors with. A little blood orange had bled into the aroma to lighten that hickory and liquorice oak lead. The wheat is evident with a muted spiciness that promises to do some damage once it hits the palate...; **t24.5** one of the best deliveries you'll find in all Kentucky. It is an almost miraculous mix of mouth feel and perfectly balanced sugar and spice which leaves you speechless. All compartments: the sugar segment, spice, oak and grain all appear to be singing to the same hymn sheet - an improbably well-structured bourbon. The key, though, is the oil which as well as guaranteeing that highly satisfying mouth feel, also ensures the plates keep spinning for a very long time...; **f23.5** more of the same, though fade allows in some extra drying oak; **b24** the higher strength has helped bring the best from the great whiskey as the oils are left unchecked and allowed to help the other elements cast their magic spells. To add water to this, especially, would be sacrilege. 53.5% (107 proof)

◇ **Weller Special Reserve** bott code: L172080115:014 **(93)** n23 a warm, nutty mocha lead heads slowly towards liquorice; a light Demerara background; **t23.5** salivating and surprisingly firm for a wheated bourbon. The spices are intact, though, and acts as fanfare to the more muscular oak notes; **f23** dry and toasty with **b23.5** imperiously excellent, yet somehow given to understatement. 45% (90 proof)

Western Gold 6 Year Old Bourbon Whiskey (91.5) n22 t23 f22.5 b23 Taken from barrels sitting high in the warehouse, that's for sure. You get a lot for your six years... 40%.

Whiskey Thief Straight Bourbon (87) n22 t22 f21.5 b21.5. Straight as a die, unwavering bourbon which sticks to an uncomplicated, intense vanilla theme. Very pleasant. 40%

Wild Turkey 101 (91) n22 t23.5 f22.5 b23. By far the best 101 I have tasted in a decade: you simply can't do anything but go weak at the knees with that spice attack. 55.5% (101 proof)

Wild Turkey American Spirit Aged 15 Years (92) n24 t22.5 f22.5 b23. A delightful Wild Turkey that appears under par for a 100 proofer but offers much when you search those nooks and crannies of your palate. 50.0% (100 proof)

Wild Turkey Rare Breed bott code L0049FH **(94)** n22.5 t24.5 f23 b24. It is hard to credit that this is the same brand I have been tasting at regular intervals for quite a long while. Certainly nothing like this style has been around for a decade and it is massively far removed from two years ago. The nose threatens a whiskey limited in direction. But the delivery is as profound as it is entertaining. Even on this bottling's singular though fabulous style, not perhaps quite overall the gargantuan whiskey of recent years. But, seeing as it's only the nose which pegs it back a point or two, will make this one that would leave a big hole in your whiskey experience if you don't get around to trying. 54.1%

Willett Pot Still Reserve barrel no. 2421 **(95.5)** n24.5 t23 f24 b24. Another fabulous whiskey from Willett. You can so often trust them to deliver and here they have given us a bourbon showing serious oak injection, yet a sweetness which counters perfectly. 47%.

William Larue Weller (97.5) n24 t24.5 f24 b25 For any whiskey with a proof of 123.4, the only way is up...! Last year's Whisky Bible World Whisky of the Year Runner-up is going for the full title big time, no holds barred. Again, this is absolutely supreme class. *61.7% (123.4 proof). ncf. Buffalo Trace Antique Collection.*

William Larue Weller dist Spring 2001 db (97.5) n24.5 t24.5 f24 b24.5 I always save this as one of the last whiskeys I taste for each Bible. In life you always need something to look forward to... *68.1%.*

William Larue Weller (97) n24 t24.5 f24 b24.5 Just one of those whiskeys which makes sense of life, of whiskey. A collection and collaboration of flavours and shapes on the palate which simply beguile... *70.1% (140.2 proof).*

William Larue Weller db (96) n24 t24.5 f23.5 b24 the most relaxed and lightly spiced Weller since its first launch. May lack its inherent oomph, but the deft, complex notes are still one of life's great pleasures... *67.7% (135.4 proof).*

⟡ **William Larue Weller** db (97.5) n24 just like last year's the fruity undertone has vanished and we are left to concentrate instead on a headier nose, more weighty but a little flatter. Though this can hardly be deemed a complaint when the mix of cocoa and liquorice notes are this rich and complex, its unique brilliance can only be worshipped over a good half hour period; t25 now we go into territory only William Larue Weller knows: no other whisk(e)y on the planet gives you so complete a delivery as this. The mouth is not just filled, but every nook and cranny of the palate is searched for, found and then tested with the most astonishing array of mocha notes any whisky, anywhere can produce. The light molasses and stronger demerara sugars are the perfect complement to an amalgamation of toasty tannins which never for a moment look like going too far and smaller grains, the wheat especially which radiate spice to a literally perfect pitch...; f24 for any blender out there looking to learn how to finish a great whisky after a perfect delivery without it being a let down by comparison, then they should study this in detail. This is more than just a tapering of the unique elements which went to make up the glory we witnessed before. Now we see how specific flavour points – here especially the corn oil – fill in any gaps being created by the retreating sugars or the more exposed oak. We see how the sugar residue, itself, still of a toasty and light liquorice nature, blends into and tones down the char from the barrel. It is... b24 ...the most delicious lesson in whiskey structure imaginable. This was my 1,263rd and final new whiskey for the Jim Murray Whisky Bible 2019. Did I leave the very best until last....? *64.1% (128.2 proof).*

⟡ **Woodford Reserve Distiller's Select Batch 296** bott code: L197611812 db (88.5) n22 a little praline, lime and spice barely lays a glove on the thick caramels; t22.5 the nose certainly forewarns what's coming next: caramel! A little spice tries to liven things up a bit, but the creamy oak-rich procession stays the course; the of hazelnut note pops in and out to balance with the light cocoa; f22 slightly toastier, but the natural caramels persist; b22 soft, nutty and not keen to change gears too often. *43.2% (86.4 proof).*

Woodford Reserve Double Oaked (95) n24.5 t23.5 f23 b24 The old Labrot and Graham Distillery has just entered a new phase of excellence since its reopening. Well done blender on creating a bourbon not just of beauty but of great significance. *43.2% WB16/052*

Woodford Reserve Master's Collection Four Grain (95) n24 t24 f23 b24. Sod's law would have it that the moment we removed this from the 2006 Bible, having appeared in the previous two editions without it ever making the shelves, it should at last be belatedly released. But a whiskey worth waiting for, or what? The tasting notes are not a million miles from the original. But this is better bourbon, one that appears to have received a significant polish in the intervening years. Nothing short of magnificent. *46.2%*

Tennessee Whiskey

⟡ **Whisky Krüger American Edition No. 1 Straight Tennessee Whiskey 5 Years Old** bott 2017 (89) n22 cinnamon and hickory with a creamy texture; t22 same cinnamon on delivery with cream toffee; f22.5 ups in spice despite the caramel build up; b22.5 soft, untaxing and sweet Tennessee with a delightfully gentle nature. *46%. nc ncf. 100 bottles.*

BENJAMIN PRICHARD

Benjamin Prichard's Tennessee Whiskey (83) n21.5 t21 f20 b20.5. Majestic fruity rye notes trill from the glass. Curiously yeasty as well; bounding with all kinds of freshly crushed brown sugar crystals. Pleasant enough, but doesn't gel like Prichard's bourbon. *40%*

GEORGE DICKEL

George Dickel Aged 17 Years bott code: L6154K1001 db (94) n24 t24 22.5 b23.5 The oldest George Dickel I have ever encountered has held its own well over the years. A defiant crispness to the piece makes for memorable drinking, though it is the accommodating and comfortable nose which wins the greatest plaudits... *43.5% (87 proof).*

George Dickel Barrel Select (90.5) **n21 t23 f23.5 b23** The limited nose makes the heart sink. What happens once it hits the palate is another story entirely. Wonderful! *43%*

George Dickel Distillery Reserve Collection 17 Year Old (91.5) **n23.5 t23.5 f21.5 b23** Outside of a warehouse, I'm not sure I've encountered a Tennessee whiskey of this antiquity before. I remember one I tasted some while back, possibly about a year older or two older than this, was black and like tasting eucalyptus concentrate. This is the opposite, showing extraordinary restraint for its age, an almost feminine charm. *43.5%*

George Dickel No. 12 bott code: L7034R60011402 db (89) **n21.5 t23.5 f22 b22** In a way, a classic GD where you feel there much more still in the tank... *45% (90 proof).*

George Dickel Rye (95.5) **n24 t23.5 f24 b24** Dare I say it? On this evidence, they do rye probably a fraction better than they produce straight Tennessee. This is a belter! *45%*

George Dickel Superior No 12 Brand Whisky (90.5) **n22.5 t23 f22.5 b22.5.** A different story told by George from the last one I heard. But certainly no less fascinating. *45%*

Eiling Lim Tennessee Whisky (92.5) **n23.5 t23.5 f22.5 b23** The full strength of the whiskey does this no harm whatsoever as some of the sugars take on extraordinary dimensions. Beautifully made Tennessee. *51.5%.*

◇ **Gleann Mor George Dickel Aged Over 13 Years** dist 2003 (89) **n22** classic hickory and corn nose...; **t23** big lift off on the molasses, then a volley of toasted grain. Liquorice and molasses reach ever corner; **f22** dries despite the natural caramels; **b22** steady, deliciously straightforward and not a hair out of place. *53.7%.*

◇ **Whisky Krüger Taubi Edition No. 2 American Sour Mash Whiskey 5 Years Old** bott 2017 (89.5) **n22** the odd vegetable note, but plenty of liquorice and hickory, too.; **t23** mouth-grabbing oil, then a huge arrival of molasses. Manuka honey sweetness further before the liquorice kicks back in; **f21.5** a little tangy and unkempt as a slightly bitter vanilla arrives; **b23** if you like your corn oil sweet, then get a mouthful of this! *60.5%. nc ncf. 100 bottles.*

JACK DANIEL

Jack Daniel's 120th Anniversary of the White Rabbit Saloon (91) **n22.5 t23.5 f22 b23** On its best-behaved form. After the delivery, the oils are down a little, so not the usual bombastic offering from JD. Nonetheless, this is pure class and the clever use of sugars simply make you drool... *43%. Brown-Forman.*

Jack Daniel's Old No.7 Brand (Black Label) (92) **n23 t23 f22.5 b23.5.** Actually taken aback by this guy. The heavier oils have been stripped and the points here are for complexity...that should shock a few old Hell's Angels I know. *40%*

Jack Daniel's No. 27 Gold Double Barrelled extra matured in maple barrels (82) **n21 t21.5 f19 b20.5.** Pleasant enough. But it appears the peculiar tannins from the maple barrels have just done slightly too good a job of flattening out the higher, more complex notes from the grains themselves. Slightly bitters towards the finish also. Tennessee Gold with precious little sparkle at all... *40%*

Jack Daniel's Master Distiller Series No 1 db (90.5) **n24** wonderful dose of extra tangy kumquat over the normal JD signature; something of the fruity cough sweet about this one; **t22** a massive, pleasantly oiled mix of molassed fudge and liquorice; **f22** drier, toastier hickory; **b22.5** no mistaking the JD pedigree. Just a few telling degrees of fruit. *43%*

Jack Daniel's Rested Tennessee Rye batch 2 (88.5) **n22 t23 f21 b22.5** Possibly the most intriguing whiskey of the year: America's most flavour-enhancing stills take on the world's most flavoursome grain. The result is surprisingly well mannered, though the oils from both the stills and grain do help obliterate any meaningful complexity. Probably the only world whiskey type I have never tasted in a warehouse at full strength (though I now intend to correct that). Instinct tells me a trick has been missed by not making this a 101...Oh, and one important thing. Normally I suggest you take your whiskey at body temperature. This is one whiskey which needs to be tasted at normal room temperature to keep the oils to a minimum and allow the rye maximum airtime. *40% WB16/022*

Jack Daniel's Single Barrel Proof Tennessee Whiskey barrel no. 16-2572, rick no. L-19, bott 14 Apr 16 db (94.5) **n23.5 t23.5 f24 b23.5** Now that is what you call Tennessee whiskey... *66.25% (132.5 proof). sc.*

Jack Daniel's Single Barrel Tennessee Rye Whiskey barrel no. 16-1340, rick no. L-3, bott 24 Feb 16 db (86.5) **n21 t22 f21.5 b22.** I remember tasting a JD Rye last year which didn't come at me the way I expected. This, too, is surprisingly flat and oily in the places you expect it to sing. Yes, the burnt honey notes are lovely and it does have some of that heavyweight JD swagger we all love. But somehow the finer points of the grain are lost amid it all and we end up with a pretty muted whiskey. *45%. sc.*

Corn Whiskey

Dixie Dew (95) n22.5 t24 f24 b24.5 I have kept in my previous tasting notes for this whiskey as they serve a valuable purpose. The three matured corn whiskeys I have before me are maybe the same distillers. But, this time round, they could not be more different. From Mellow Corn to Dixie we have three whiskeys with very differing hues. This, quite frankly, is the darkest corn whiskey I have ever seen and one of world class stature with characteristics I have never found before in any whiskey. Any true connoisseur of whisk(e)y will make deals with Lucifer to experience this freak whiskey. There is no age statement... but this one has gray hairs attached to the cob... 50%

Georgia Moon Corn Whiskey "Less Than 30 Days Old" (83.5) n21.5 t22 f20 b20. If anyone has seen corn whiskey made – either in Georgia or Kentucky – then the unique aroma will be instantly recognisable from the fermenters and still house. Enjoyable stuff which does exactly what it says on the jar. 50%

J. W. Corn (92.5) n23 t23.5 f23 b23. In another life this could be bourbon. The corn holds the power, for sure. But the complexity and levels are so far advanced that this – again! – qualifies as very high grade whiskey. Wonderful that the normal high standard is being maintained for what is considered by many, quite wrongly, as an inferior spirit. 50%

Mellow Corn (83) n19 t21 f22 b21. Dull and oily on the nose, though the palate compensates with a scintillating array of sweet and spicy notes. 50%

Single Malt Rye
ANCHOR DISTILLERY

Old Potrero Single Malt Straight Rye Whiskey Essay 10-SRW-ARM-E (94) n24 t23 f24 b23 The whiskey from this distillery never fails to amaze. With the distillery now under new management it will be fascinating to see what lands in my tasting lab. Even at 75% quality we will still be blessed with astonishing whiskeys. 45% (90 proof)

Straight Rye

Basil Hayden's Rye Whiskey 2017 Release re-barreled in charred oak quarter casks, bott code: L7129CLA 153330822 (88.5) n23 t22 f21.5 b22 You can have too much of a good thing and it appears here the quarter casks have managed to over dose this rye with a surfeit of caramel. 40% (80 proof).

Benjamin Prichard's Tennessee Rye Whiskey (86) n20 t21.5 f23 b21.5. Bit of a scruffy nose, but polishes up pleasantly. The rye itself is not of the sharp variety and at times is hard to identify. But the ulmo honey and lush butterscotch offer the gloss at the finish. 43%

Booker's Rye 13 Years, 1 Month, 12 Days batch no. 2016-LE db (97.5) n25 t24 f24 b24.5 This was a rye made in the last days of when Jim Beam's Yellow Label was at its very peak. Then, it was the best rye commercially available. Today, it is simply a staggering example of a magnificent rye showing exactly what genius in terms of whiskey actually means. If this is not World Whisky of the Year for 2017, it will be only fragments of molecules away... 68.1% (136.2 proof)

Bulleit 95 Rye (96) n25 t24.5 f22.5 B23.5 This is a style of rye, indeed whiskey, which is unique. Buffalo Trace makes an ultra high-quality rye which lasts the course longer. But nothing compares in nose and delivery to this...in fact few whiskies in the world get even close... 45%. Straight 95% rye mash whiskey.

Bulleit 95 Rye bott code: L6344R60010848 (83) n20.5 t22 f20 b20.5 In some 30 years of tasting rye from the great Lawrenceburg, Indiana, distillery, this has to be the weirdest batch I have yet encountered. The highly unusual and mildly disturbing tobacco note on the nose appears to be a theme throughout the tasting experience. A rye which rallies briefly on delivery but ultimately falls flat on its face. 45% (90 proof).

Colonel E.H. Taylor Straight Rye (97) n24 t24.5 f24 b24.5 reminds me of the younger ryes when Sazerac Handy first hit the shelves, with the emphasis on the clarity of the grain and the fallout of oak and spice. Really, a bottle which should never be left on a liquor store shelf. 50%

Colonel E.H. Taylor Straight Rye Bottled in Bond bott code: L1728501 (94.5) n23.5 a low voltage nose where the grain and natural caramels are just about on equal terms; t24 succulent delivery, sweet and salivating. Yet, you scratch your head for a moment, as it isn't automatically clear where this delicious stimulation is coming from. The mouth feel is soft, with the whisky moulded to the palate, rather than crisp and radiating crunchy fruity sugar. Slowly it dawns that some of the sweetness is from the oak, the grain ensuring a slightly more channelled intensity; f23.5 soft red liquorice, a little caramel and butterscotch and at last a vague, nagging spice; **b23.5** nothing like the big rye lift I found on the previous E. H.Taylor rye: this is happier to play the subtle game with a slow build rather than a naked graininess. A genuine surprise package. *50% (100 proof).*

Cougar Rye (95) n25 t24 f23 b23. The Lawrenceburg, Indiana Distillery makes the finest rye I have ever tasted - and that is saying something. Here is a magnificent example of their astonishing capabilities. Good luck hunting the Cougar. *37%. Foster's Group, Australia.*

Crater Lake Rye Whiskey Batch no. JA 08 db (83.5) n20 t22 f20.5 b21. A distinctly warming, peppery whiskey with an obvious high rye content. Would do itself better justice as a 100 proof whiskey as here the oils are broken down a little too enthusiastically, allowing unhelpful freedom to a tobacco note. Good early use of dark sugars, though. One to keep an eye on. *40%.*

Devil's Bit Seven-Year-Old Single Barrel (93.5) n22.5 t24 f23 b24. A must-find rye from one of the most impressive small distilleries in the world. *47.7%. Edgefield Distillery.*

Governor's Reserve Lightning Straight Rye Whiskey (94.5) n24 t24 f23 b23.5 Now this is rye, believe me!!! Those who love the Lawrenceburg, Indiana, type rye (and who doesn't?!?) will adore this... *45% (90 proof). sc. Bottled by KGB Spirits LLC.*

High West 12 Years Old Rye (92.5) n22 t24 f23 b23.5. A very clever rye which will hit a chord of appreciation for those who savour this whiskey style. *46%*

High West Whiskey Rendezvous Rye Batch 12431 db (94.5) n23.5 t24 f23 b24 After a few disappointing batches, this one appears to have found that vital spark. It could be a whole new set of whiskeys, a change of one barrel, or even the same whiskey re-stirred before bottling. It doesn't matter: something has clicked. *46%. ncf. WB15/176*

Jim Beam Pre-Prohibition Style Rye db (95) n23 t24.5 f23.5 b24 Very similar to how Jim Bean Yellow Label was over 20 years ago. In other words: simply superb! *45% (90 Proof)*

John David Albert's Taos Lightning Straight Rye Whiskey batch no. A1 (96) n24 t24.5 f23.5 24 Some decent age to this has really ensured enormous complexity. And astonishing beauty. *45% (90 proof). sc. Bottled by KGB Spirits LLC.*

◇ **Knob Creek Cask Strength** warehouse A, barreled 2009, 2018 release, bott code: L8106CLA (96.5) n24 anyone who drank Jim Beam Yellow Label Rye two decades ago wil immediately recognise the incisor-like sharpness. But there is much more: the deeper resonance within fruitiness of the grain is not entirely dissimilar to the freshly plucked corked of a better Bordeaux; t24 you could almost punch the air with delight as the highly concentrated rye explodes upon impact, sending shards of oak-toughened grain to every corner of the palate. Yet, simultaneously, the crisper element of rye produced maximum salivation, liquid Demerara sugar and rye swamping the taste buds and thinning out the red liquorice tannin; f24 so much dark chocolate. And what goes better together than rye mixed into dark chocolate mousse...? b24.5 Knob Creek rye has always been excellent, but having tasted Jim Beam's rye output for some 40 years I always thought it delivered within itself. Now this one is much closer to what I had been expecting. Brilliant! And the first rye to give the great rye of Buffalo Trace a serious run for their money. Indeed; this is going for a head to head... *59.8% (1196 proof).*

Knob Creek Straight Rye Whiskey (92.5) n23.5 t23.5 f22.5 b23 a slightly more genteel rye than I expected, if you compare standard Knob Creek to their usual bourbon. *50% (100 proof).*

Knob Creek Straight Rye Whiskey batch L5349CLA (92.5) n23.5 t23.5 f22.5 b23 Curious: just checked: I scored a batch from last year at 92.5 also. Can't say this isn't consistent quality...! *50%*

Michter's 10 Years Old Single Barrel Straight Rye barrel no. 16A113 (88) n22.5 t23 f20.5 b22 Michter's and rye go together like all the great names of America and success: like David Beckham and football, Christopher Nolan and Hollywood directing, Hugh Laurie and Hollywood acting, my old Fleet Street colleague Piers Morgan and chat shows, my girlfriend's old chum Simon Cowell and talent shows. This, though, isn't quite in the same league as the bottle I tasted from them last year, which was in a Saville Row suit compared to the dowdy hand-me-down here. Enjoyable, but by Michter's high standards... *46.4% (92.8 proof).*

Michter's No. 1 Straight Rye (95.5) n23.5 t24 f24 b24 Truly classic rye whiskey. The stuff which makes one write swoonerisms... *42.4%*

◇ **Michter's Single Barrel Kentuck Straight Rye 10 Years Old** barrel no. 18E559 (95.5) n24 not sure if new stills are at play here, whether it was distilled extra slow...or both factors are at work. Because he copper coming off this is phenomenal and sits very comfortably with the big, firm, fruity thrust of the rye; t24.5 silky delivery with first big caramels from the oak forming a barrier for the rye. This in turn backs up, getting more honeyed by the moment with heather honey and Manuka honey mixed to the fore; f23 the tangy copper really does take command towards the finish, though the caramels softens things slightly; b24 rye lovers have never had it so good. Another astonishingly beautiful rye – this time from Michter's. This one is notable for its big flavours but lack of spice. *46.4% (92.8 proof).*

Pappy Van Winkle's Family Reserve Rye 13 Years Old (94) n24 t23.5 f23 b23.5 Uncompromising rye that successfully tells two stories simultaneously. A great improvement on the Winkle rye of old. *47.8%*

Pikesville Straight Rye Whiskey Aged at Least 6 Years (97.5) n24.5 t24.5 f24 b24.5 The most stunning of ryes and the best from Heaven Hill for some time. *55% (110 Proof)*

Redemption Riverboat Rye (78) n19 t21 f19 b19. Dry, weirdly off key and oily – and holed below the water line. *40%*

Redemption Rye (85.5) n22 t22.5 f20 b21. The tobacco nose is a bit of a poser: how did that get there? Or the spearmint, which helps as you try to chew things over in your mind. The big rye wave on delivery is supported by mixed dark sugars yet something ashy about the finish. *46%*

Rittenhouse Very Rare Single Barrel 21 Years Old (91) n25 t23 f21 b22. I may be wrong, but I would wager quite a large amount that no-one living has tasted more rye from around the world than I. So trust me when I tell you this is different, a genuine one-off in style. By rights such telling oak involvement should have killed the whisky stone dead: this is like someone being struck by lightning and then walking off slightly singed and with a limp, but otherwise OK. The closest style of whisky to rye is Irish pot still, a unique type where unmalted barley is used. And the closest whiskey I have tasted to this has been 35 to 50-year-old pot still Irish. What they have in common is a massive fruit base, so big that it can absorb and adapt to the oak input over many years. This has not escaped unscathed. But it has to be said that the nose alone makes this worthy of discovery, as does the glory of the rye as it first melts into the tastebuds. The term flawed genius could have been coined for this whisky alone. Yet, for all its excellence, I can so easily imagine someone, somewhere, claiming to be an expert on whiskey, bleating about the price tag of $150 a bottle. If they do, ignore them. Because, frankly, rye has been sold far too cheaply for far too long and that very cheapness has sculpted a false perception in people's minds about the quality and standing of the spirit. Well, 21 years in Kentucky equates to about 40 years in Scotland. And you try and find a 40-year-old Scotch for £75. If anything, they are giving this stuff away. The quality of the whiskey does vary from barrel to barrel and therefore bottle to bottle. So below I have given a summary of each individual bottling (averaging (91.1). The two with the highest scores show the least oak interference...yet are quite different in style. That's great whiskey for you. *50% (100 proof). ncf.*

Barrel no. 1 (91) n25 t23 f21 b22. As above. *50%*
Barrel no. 2 (89) n24 t23 f20 b22. Dryer, oakier. *50%*
Barrel no. 3 (91) n24 t23 f22 b22. Fruity, soft. *50%*
Barrel no. 4 (90) n25 t22 f21 b22. Enormous. *50%*
Barrel no. 5 (93) n25 t23 f22 b23. Early rye surge. *50%*
Barrel no. 6 (87) n23 t22 f20 b22. Juicy, vanilla. *50%*
Barrel no. 7 (90) n23 t23 f22 b22. Even, soft, honeyed. *50%*
Barrel no. 8 (95) n25 t24 f23 b23. The works: massive rye. *50%*
Barrel no. 9 (91) n24 t23 f22 b22. Sharp rye, salivating. *50%*
Barrel no. 10 (93) n25 t24 f22 b22. Complex, sweet. *50%*
Barrel no. 11 (93) n24 t24 f22 b23. Rich, juicy, spicy. *50%*
Barrel no. 12 (91) n25 t23 f21 b22. Near identical to no.1. *50%*
Barrel no. 13 (91) n24 t24 f21 b22. Citrus and toasty. *50%*
Barrel no. 14 (94) n25 t24 f22 b22. Big rye and marzipan. *50%*
Barrel no. 15 (88) n23 t22 f21 b22. Major oak influence. *50%*
Barrel no. 16 (90) n24 t23 f21 b22. Spicy and toffeed. *50%*
Barrel no. 17 (90) n24 t23 f22 b22. Flinty, firm, late rye kick. *50%*
Barrel no. 18 (91) n24 t24 f21 b22. Big rye delivery. *50%*
Barrel no. 19 (87) n23 t22 f21 b21. Major coffee input. *50%*
Barrel no. 20 (91) n23 t24 f22 b22. Spicy sugar candy. *50%*
Barrel no. 21 (94) n24 t23 f24 b23. Subtle, fruity. *50%*
Barrel no. 22 (89) n23 t22 f22 b22. Mollased rye. *50%*
Barrel no. 23 (94) n24 t23 f24 b23. Soft fruit, massive rye. *50%*
Barrel no. 24 (88) n23 t22 f21 b22. Intense oak and caramel. *50%*
Barrel no. 25 (93) n25 t22 f23 b23. Heavy rye and spice. *50%*
Barrel no. 26 (92) n23 t23 f23 b23. Subtle, delicate rye. *50%*
Barrel no. 27 (94) n25 t23 f23 b23. Delicate rye throughout. *50%*
Barrel no. 28 (96) n25 t24 f23 b24. Salivating, roasty, major. *50%*
Barrel no. 29 (88) n23 t22 f21 b22. Hot, fruity. *50%*
Barrel no. 30 (91) n24 t23 f22 b22. Warming cough sweets. *50%*
Barrel no. 31 (90) n25 t22 f21 b22. Aggressive rye. *50%*

Rittenhouse Rye Single Barrel Aged 25 Years (93.5) n24.5 t24 f22 b23. This is principally about the nose: a thing of rare beauty even in the highest peaks of the whiskey world. The story on the palate is much more about damage limitation with the oak going a bit nuts. But remember this: in Scottish years due to the heat in Kentucky, this would be a malt well in excess of 50 years. But even with the signs of fatigue, so crisp is that rye, so beautifully defined are its intrinsic qualities that the quality is still there to be clearly seen. Just don't judge on the first, second or even third mouthful. Your taste buds need time to relax & adjust. Only then will they accommodate and allow you to fully appreciate and enjoy the creaky old ride. At this age, though, always worth remembering that the best nose doesn't always equal the best tasting experience... 50% (100 proof).

Barrel no. 1 (93.5) n24.5 t24 f22 b23. As above. 50%
Barrel no. 2 (88) n22 t24 f20 b22. Intense. Crisp, juicy; a tad soapy, bitter. 50%
Barrel no. 3 (89.5) n23 t23.5 f21.5 b21.5. Fabulously crisp. Fruity. Mollassed. 50%
Barrel no. 4 (85) n21.5 t21.5 f21 b21. Subdued fruit. Massive oak. 50%
Barrel no. 5 (90.5) n25 t22.5 f21.5 b21.5. Complex. Mega oaked but spiced, fruity. 50%
Barrel no. 6 (91.5) n24.5 t22 f23 b22. Tangy. Honeyed and hot. Spiced marmalade. 50%
Barrel no. 7 (83.5) n20 t22 f20.5 b21. Treacle toffee amid the burnt apple. 50%
Barrel no. 8 (90) n23.5 t23.5 f21 b22. Flinty, teeth-cracking rye. Crème brulee. 50%
Barrel no. 9 (91) n23.5 t23.5 f22 b22. Massive ryefest. Mocha coated. 50%
Barrel no. 10 (86.5) n22 t23 f20 b21.5. Early zip and juice. Tires towards caramel. 50%
Barrel no. 11 (89) n24 t22 f21 b22. Honeycomb. Hickory. Caramel. Oil. 50%
Barrel no. 12 (84.5) n22.5 t21 f20 b21. Delicate. Vanilla and caramel. Light. 50%
Barrel no. 13 (89.5) n22.5 t23 f22 b22. Succulent. Yet rye remains firm. 50%
Barrel no. 14 (88) n22 t23 f21 b22. Very similar to 13 but with extra caramel. 50%
Barrel no. 15 (86) n21 t23 f20.5 b21.5. Lazy grain. Warming but flat. Caramel. 50%
Barrel no. 16 (92) n23 t23 f23 b23. Sculpted rye: sugared fruit; a twist of juniper. 50%
Barrel no. 17 (86.5) n22.5 t21.5 f21 b21.5. Fizzy, fruity spice calmed by caramel. 50%
Barrel no. 18 (91) n23.5 t23.5 f21.5 b22.5. Pristine rye. Spice. Juicy molasses. Crisp. 50%
Barrel no. 19 (96) n24 t23.5 t24.5 b23.5. Concentrated honeycomb and chocolate. 50%
Barrel no. 20 (89.5) n23 t22 f22.5 b22. Cream toffee. Fruit and spice. 50%
Barrel no. 21 (85) n21 t20 f23 b21. Severe oak delivery. Recovers with mocha toffee. 50%
Barrel no. 22 (81) n20 t20 f21 b20. Mild sap. Fruity. Oily. 50%
Barrel no. 23 (94) n23.5 t24 f23.5 b23. Rich. Fruity. Juicy. Clean. Corn oil. Cocoa. 50%
Barrel no. 24 (88.5) n22.5 t22 f21 b22. Huge vanilla. Slow spice. 50%
Barrel no. 25 (88) n22.5 t21.5 f22 b22. Custard and sugared fruit. Sharpens. 50%
Barrel no. 26 (90.5) n22 t23 f23 b22.5. Classic crisp rye. Big, manageable oak. 50%
Barrel no. 27 (88) n23 t22 f21.5 b21.5. Huge, honeyed oak. Oily. Dries at end. 50%
Barrel no. 28 (91) n22.5 t23.5 f22.5 b22.5. Exemplary honeycomb-rye delivery. Spices. 50%
Barrel no. 29 (94) n23.5 t24 f23 b23.5. Juicy rye; crisp sugar-vanilla-hickory fade. 50%
Barrel no. 30 (94.5) n23 t24 f24 b23.5. Thick rye. Cocoa. Spices. 50%
Barrel no. 31 (79) n21 t20 f19 b19. Lethargic. Bitter. 50%
Barrel no. 32 (88) n21.5 t22.5 f22 b22. Relaxed honeycomb. Hint of mint. 50%
Barrel no. 33 (88.5) n22.5 t22 f22 b22. Powering oak-rye battle. 50%
Barrel no. 34 (84) n23 t21 f20 b20. Thick oak throughout. Corn oil. 50%
Barrel no. 35 (93.5) n22.5 t23.5 t24 b23.5. Big rye. Demerara-hickory. Complex. 50%
Barrel no. 36 (77) n21 t19 f18 b19. Bitter oak. 50%

Russell's Reserve Rye 6 Year Old Small Batch bott. code L0194FH) (93.5) n24 t23.5 f22.5 b23.5. Lost none of its wit and sharpness: in fact has improved a notch or two in recent times. 45%

⟐ **Sazarac Rye** bott code: L172540108: 414 ref 1A 5C VT 15C (96) n24 firm but also a softer massing of muscovado sugars and spices in equal measure...strangely warming an sexily alluring; almost a blueprint for exactly how a clean, unambiguous, faultless straight rye should nose...; t24.5 instantly salivating and though the backbone of the grain is erect, firm and proud (well, I think it's the backbone...) there is enough give on the sugars to make this a stunningly juicy and salivating experience; sharp and fabulously three dimensional grain without ever getting aggressive, a little creaminess as a sub plot forms the perfect base for that flinty theme; f23.5 just thins out a little as the flavours fade. But the crunchiness never seems to go away; the very late spices enters almost as an afterthought; b24 the nose and delivery are just about as good as it gets. Anyone thinking of making a clean and succulent rye whiskey should plant this on a dais and bow to it every morning before heading into the stillroom... 45% (90 proof).

Sazerac Kentucky Straight Rye Whiskey 18 Years Old bott 2012 (95.5) n24 t23 f24 b24.5. Unquestionably showing a different side to its personality this time out, allowing the rye to show its fruity personality to the full. 45%

Sazerac Rye 18 Year Old bott Fall 2013 db (97) n24.5 t24.5 f24 b24 Another stir of the pot and up comes Sazerac 18 polished and wallowing in its own enormity. Rye whiskey exactly how it should be. 45%.

Sazerac Rye 18 Year Old bott Spring 2014 db (96.5) n24.5 t24.5 f23.5 b24 Always one of the great and most fascinating whiskeys on the planet - essentially the same stuff year after year - plays out with each roll of the bottling dice. Here someone has cut off much of the oil... with stunning results. Way better than than last year's offering and much closer to its old self. 45%. Buffalo Trace Antique Collection

Sazerac 18 Years Old bott Spring 2015 db (97) n25 t24 f24 b24 It is as though all excess oils have been drained from this whiskey in the last year or two and we are seeing something stark, naked and even more desirable than before. Technically sublime. 45% (90 proof).

Sazerac 18 Years Old bott Spring 2016 db (95.5) n24 t24 f23.5 b24 Simply a classic, gilt-edged rye. 45% (90 proof).

⬦ **Sazerac 18 Years Old** bott Summer 2017 db (96) n24 fruity, as every good straight rye should be. But there is far more orange and lighter citrus – including weak grapefruit - tones on this than normal, almost disorienting you for a moment. Such a subtle, clever sweetness – rye induced, mainly – allows the spices to mount but with limited aggression. Complex? Not half...! t24.5 mouth-watering, mouth-filling, mouth kissing, and mouth resuscitating: the delivery both seduces you and stirs you back to life with a superb display of grainy impulses, the majority granite hard, the others silkier and softer than Casanovas cravat....; f23.5 just a little bitterness creeps into the toastier elements. The vanilla and molasses are both refined, the spices already spent; b24 brilliant! What else do you expect from a Sazerac 18...? 45% (90 proof).

Smooth Ambler Old Scout Straight Rye Aged 7 Years batch 17, bott 9 Nov 13 (82) n21 t22 f19 b20. Now this is odd. What do you get when you combine the characteristics of rye and gin? Something, probably, like this. Never been to these guys in West Virginia, though I'll try and make a point of paying a visit when next in that stunning state. No idea if they are involved with gin. But something about the botanical feel to the nose and finish in particular suggests they might. Perhaps a bottling problem for this single batch? Intrigued. 49.5% WB15/373

Sonoma County Rye pot distilled from grain db (83.5) n21 t21.5 f20 b21. Sweet nougat, heavy duty, wide-cut oily. Quite German in style. 48%. 1512 Spirits. WB15/384

Thomas H. Handy Sazerac db (95.5) n23.5 t24.5 f23.5 b24 With each bottling, the style of the Thomas Handy moves away from the Sazerac 18 in style 63.45% (126.9 proof).

Thomas H. Handy Sazerac Straight Rye Whiskey (97.5) n24 t24.5 f24.5 b24.5 This was World Whisky of the Year last year and anyone buying this on the strength of that will not be disappointed. Huge whiskey with not even the glimmer of a hint of an off note. Magnificent: an honour to taste and rye smiles all round... 66.2%. ncf.

Thomas H. Handy Sazerac Straight Rye db (95) n24 t24 f23.5 b24 Perhaps because this has become something of a softie, without all those usual jagged and crisp rye notes, it doesn't quite hit the spot with quite the same delicious drama. Still a beauty, though. 64.6%

Thomas H. Handy Sazerac db (96.5) n24 t25 f23.5 b24 When Thomas Handy hits the very height of its powers, which for a significant period it does here, very few whiskeys can match its eloquence and sheer force of nature. A whiskey to be as much worshipped as savoured... 63.1% (126.2 proof).

⬦ **Thomas H. Handy Sazerac** db (97) n24 the trademark crisp rye notes dance rigidly as though ready to shatter if challenged. A light black pepper encompasses both the delicate tannins and a gentle minty note; t24.5 just stunning! So, so beautiful. Dramatic, expansive, and seemingly expensive like Verdi 's Requiem, the choir issuing forth on a silver disc. The rye crunches up against the roof of the mouth, meets even crunchier demerara sugars and bounces back down to crash into the more giving tannin and oils: the result is maximum salivation and then a harmonisation to remember as the tannins drift with a delightful mocha theme to mingle with the fruitier aspects of the grain; f24 after the drama, delightful simplicity – relatively. The grain has at last softened enough to become one sensual stream, rather than explosion. The light cocoa and vanilla is understated but when it comes to balancing with the rye, works like a dream; b24.5 just one of those must have whiskeys. Dramatic. And dreamy. All in one. 63.6% (1272 proof).

Turley Mill Straight Rye Western Whiskey aged 6 years, batch no. 12 (94) n23.5 t24 f23 b23.5 So, with this from KGB Spirits, here's my Cold War: don't add ice to this superb rye under any circumstances...58% (118 proof). sc. Bottled by KGB Spirits LLC.

⬦ **Van Winkle Family Reserve Rye 13 Years Old** batch Z2221 (90) n22.5 a two-toned nose: the usual crisp fruit edge as expected but also a slightly yeasty softness, also; t23.5 that hard edge on the nose hardens further on delivery: granite like entry with a massive degree of salivation; this is all about the grain with the oak tones there, but side-lined; f22 bitters out slightly both on the tannin side and the chocolate; spices gather slowly then stick around; b22 a hard-as-nails, uncompromising rye with a slightly tangy finale. A whiskey to break your teeth on... 47.8% (95.6 proof)

Whistlepig Aged 10 Years db (88) n21 t22 f23 b22. Having tasted this after the Sazarac beasts, this could have disappeared without trace. But had enough sharpness and rye freshness to make for a very pleasant and worthwhile experience. 50% (100 proof)

WhistlePig Old World 12 Year Old European casks (87) n23 t23.5 f20 b20. What a tragedy! The spirit itself is magnificent. The grain positively glistens on both nose and delivery and is on a par with Kentucky's finest. Sadly, a pretty rough finish thanks to the cask...which is always the danger when dealing with European wine barrels. 45% (90 Proof)

Straight Wheat Whiskey

Bernheim Original (91.5) n22 t23 f23 b23.5. By far the driest of the Bernheims I have encountered showing greater age and perhaps substance. Unique and spellbinding. 45%

Parker's Heritage Collection Original Batch Kentucky Straight Wheat Whiskey Aged 13 Years db (95.5) n23.5 t24 f23.5 b24.5 Not sure if they get Bassett's Liquorice Allsorts in the US. But, if they did, they would immediately recognise the brown ones in this...though in an insanely beautiful mutated form. So, so delicious....! 63.7%. ncf.

American Microdistilleries

10TH MOUNTAIN WHISKEY & SPIRIT COMPANY Vail, Colorado

10th Mountain Rocky Mountain Bourbon Whiskey Aged 6 Months db (92) n22 t23 f23.5 b23.5 The youth of the spirit is apparent on the nose where slightly more hostile tannins have not yet had a chance to say howdy to the corn. But once on the palate the entire story changes and, amazingly, even liquorice already – makes a far better attempt to find a happy medium with the grain. Beautifully made and a really sumptuous and spice-ridden offering. 46% (92 proof).

10th Mountain Rye Whiskey Aged 6 Months batch 10, bott 11.28.16 db (94.5) n23.5 t24 f23.5 b23.5 The grain is crisp, allowing its friable, fruity personality to star from nose to finish. It also infiltrates the sexy and sultry oily sub-plot in which most of the ulmo honey stars. But what makes this a star turn is the roasty, cocoa aspect to this which works so well with the rye-laden crispness. What a treat this is... Now, good people of 10th Mountain, you are holding out on us: the barrel strength version, if you please... 43% (86 proof).

Colorado Clear Mountain Moonshine 100% Corn Whiskey db (92.5) n23 t23.5 f23 b23 Whenever I pick up a pickle jar full of clear corn moonshine, it is near impossible to wipe the smile off my face...yesiree! So many happy moments over the last 30 years in some wilderness spots of the US where the local hooch has been handed to me in near identical receptacles... and by so many wonderful people. At a mere 80 proof, this weighs in at about the friendliest of them all – and possible the cleanest and sweetest. But the corn comes through as it should and it is hard not to pour yourself a refill...even in a tasting lab 3,500 miles from where I should be. 40% (80 proof).

ALASKA DISTILLERY Wasilla, Alaska.

Alaska Proof Bourbon db (86) n22 t22.5 f20 b21.5. It must be Alaska and the lack of pollution or something. But how do these guys make their whiskey quite so clean....? For a rugged, wild land, it appears to concentrate on producing a bourbon which is borderline ethereal and all about sugary subtlety. The downside is that such lightness allows any weakness in the wood or distillation to be flagged up, though with nobody saluting. 40% (80 proof)

ALCHEMY DISTILLERY Arcata, California.

⬥ **Boldt Blue Corn Whiskey** batch no. 27 db (89.5) n23 t23.5 f21 b22 Cleanly made, mega intense, sweet as a nut white dog corn whiskey which hits you like a Boldt from the Blue...Shade more copper on the finish will enrich it even further. 62.5% (125 proof).

ALLTECH Lexington, Kentucky.

Pearse Lyons Reserve (85) n22 t21 f21 b21. A fruity, grainy, pleasant whisky with the higher notes citrus dominant. Never quite finds a place to land or quite tells its story. Attractive but incomplete. 40% (80 proof)

Town Branch Kentucky Straight Bourbon (88.5) n22.5 t21.5 f23 b22 A delicious Kentucky bourbon of considerable depth and charm. I think they have found their niche: bourbon. In Kentucky. Go for it, guys! 40% (80 proof)

AMERICAN CRAFT WHISKEY DISTILLERY Redwood Valley, California.

Low Gap Bavarian Hard Wheat Aged 2 Years dist 31 Dec 10, bott 23 Jan 13 (76.5) **n18 t21 f18.5 b19**. There appears to be butyric on the nose and the finish bitters uncompromisingly. Despite the odd juicy, spicy high spot, not this distillery's finest moment. 43.1%

ARIZONA DISTILLING Tempe, Arizona

Desert Durum Wheat Whiskey Batch no. 2 db (87.5) **n21.5 t23 f21.5 b21.5**. Another hairy-chested gung-ho whiskey which pins you back in your chair. And my notes for the first edition fits this one equally as well. Except here it loses out slightly by having a slightly too wide cut, meaning the feints bite on the nose and finish. But still about as macho as a whiskey gets. And as chocolatey, too. 46%.

AXE AND THE OAK Colorado Springs, Colorado

Axe and the Oak Bourbon Whiskey batch no. 20 db (86.5) **n20.5 t22.5 f21.5 b22** Although this is batch number 20, you still get the feeling this is a work in progress. The nose at times displays some most unbourbon-like traits with far more of the still and/or fermentation room than opened cask. But the whiskey recovers with admirable calm: on the palate the corn oils establish themselves and the rye present kicks in with a firm sweetness while the tannins crank up the light liquorice and spice. The soft chocolate mousse on the finish works well with the molasses. Promising. 46% (92 proof).

Axe and the Oak Cask Strength Bourbon Whiskey batch no. 1 db (87.5) **n21 t23 f21.5 b22** Big, bustling, no-prisoners whiskey which reveals quite a wide cut. That adds extra weight for sure, but a tanginess interrupts the flow of the excellent liquorice and molasses tones which had made the delivery and immediate aftermath something genuinely to savour. Get the cut right on the run and this will be one hell of a bourbon. 64.4% (128.8 proof).

BAINBRIDGE ORGANIC DISTILLERS Bainbridge Island, Washington

◇ **Bainbridge Battle Point Organic Wheat Whiskey** db (87.5) **n21.5 t23 f21 b22** A charming if single-paced wheat whiskey with only a modest degree of the usual spice one associates with this grain type. The delivery, with its mix of silky tannins, lightened molasses and caramel is its high point by a distance; the finish has a slightly bitter edge at the death. Very well distilled without doubt. 43% (86 proof).

◇ **Bainbridge Battle Point Two Islands Organic Wheat Whiskey** Islay cask db (95) **n23.5** the lightness of the distillate certainly helps the smoke get a loftier place in the pecking order than might be expected; gentle and elegant phenols; **t24** not sure any smoky whiskey (or whisky) this year has such a delicate touch: like peaty snowflakes landing on the palate and melting on impact; **f23.5** still sweet with a little smoky hickory and Demerara sugar; **b24** now the Japanese cask (below) may not work quite as had been hoped, but this certainly does! Has to be one of the surprise packages of the year. An exercise in poise and balance: just so effortlessly and gracefully beautiful. 43% (86 proof).

◇ **Bainbridge Yama American Single Grain Barley Whiskey** Mizunara Japanese oak cask db (87) **n21 t23 f21 b22** Before tasting this, in my mind's eye I tried to picture what was to come. I settled on a sweet and spicy number bursting out all over the palate. Well, it wasn't quite like that: the sugars light and profound early on and the spices peak modestly and then buzz lightly. Elsewhere, though, it is if the grain and the tannin have cancelled each other out a little. 45% (90 proof).

BALCONES DISTILLERY Waco, Texas.

Balcones Baby Blue Corn Whisky Aged At Least 6 Months in Oak batch no. BB17-1, bott 3-7-17 db (87) **n22.5 t23 f20.5 b21** Spill a drop of this on your foot and you'll end up with a few broken toes. This is heavy corn whisky, just feeling the effects of a slightly wider cut than is the norm for this great distillery. The result is a profound whisky with some serious sugars but a lack of the usual balance. 46% (92 proof). nc ncf.

Balcones Brimstone Texas Scrub Oak Smoked Whisky Aged At Least 1 Day in Oak batch no. BRM17-1, bott 1-19-17 db (92.5) **n23.5 t23 f22.5 b23.5** A truly unique flavour profile that will be too much of a challenge for some but like ultimate surfing for the peat head. Once you become acclimatised you soon realise the balance is very impressive. 53% (106 proof). nc ncf.

◇ **Balcones Brimstone Texas Scrub Oak Smoked Whisky Aged At Least 1 Day In Oak** batch no. BRM18-1, bott 1-23-18 db (93) **n23.5 t23.5 f22.5 b23.5** I can neither add nor subtract from my tasting notes to the previous bottling. Actually, upon reflection, I can. A half extra point for some clever extra spices on delivery... 53% (106 proof). nc ncf.

◇ **Balcones Brimstone Redux Aged 33 Months in American Oak** barrel no. 4880 db (94) **n23.5** it is nearly 55 years ago and I am being carried in my Dad's wheelbarrow up the road to his Surrey allotment...and there he sets off a fascinating bonfire, as all bonfires are fascinating to six or seven-year-olds, and the smoke smells just like...this! **t24** just so much tannin. Yet unlike whiskies which have aged 30 or 40 years and passed their peak, this contains high levels of natural (very dark) sugars to balance out the creaking dryness of the oak, so together form an unlikely but flavour-exploding partnership which makes you salivate rather than suck; **f22.5** a comfortable fade of cough sweet hickory and cocoa; **b24** welcome to Texas's very own Tannin Fest...in a bottle... Phew...! One of a kind, for sure. *64.9% (129.8 proof). sc.*

⬥ **Balcones FR.OAK Texas Single Malt Whisky Pot Distilled Aged At Least 35 Months In Oak** batch no. FROAK18-1, bott 4-27-18 db (92.5) n21.5 pungent tannin but lacking balance; t24 ah...that's much better! The delivery is immediately back on an even keel, though there is as much caramel at play here as I've ever seen in a Balcones whiskey. Maybe it is the barley reacting to the intense molasses to create this delicious effect; the mid-point liquorice/treacle is stunning; f23.5 a red liquorice and ulmo honey fade; excellent late spice; b23.5 discernible barley gets lost in a forest of sweet tannin. *59.9% (119.8 proof). nc ncf. Tenth Anniversary.*

⬥ **Balcones Peated Texas Single Malt Aged 26 Months in American Oak** barrel no. 10472 db (96) n24 the phenols and tannins move as though with linked arms and eyes for each other...; t24 if there is a state of harmony and bliss on the nose, then what about the delivery? This is the consummation: the powerful, but entirely placid peat shews early but the maple syrup and spice embraces the smoke tenderly. The result is a lot of spice; f24 long, chocolate and vanilla, the smoke padding out the experience without threat, the light honey without reducing the overall intensity or upsetting the balance; b24 there's no smoke without fire...and this has both. Enormous and really cleanly and beautifully made. Rarely has peated malt and new oak been so happily married. One of the greatest malt whiskeys ever produced in the USA. *63% (126 proof). sc.*

Balcones Texas Blue Corn Straight Bourbon Whisky Aged At Least 24 Months in Oak batch no. BCB 16-1, bott 7-7-16 db (96.5) n24 t24.5 f24 b24 Whatever you do, don't add anything to this. Not a drop of branch water: the adding of ice deserves a custodial sentence. Hard labour, in fact. I'll give you on the rocks: you should spend time smashing them...! No, the only thing this needs is time: a good half hour, undisturbed. A clean glass, warmed. And the ability to sit and listen to a great Texan tale as it speaks to you with both force and eloquence. This is an alpha male of a bourbon and when it tells you to listen up, you listen up good... *64.9% (129.8 proof). nc ncf.*

⬥ **Balcones Texas Blue Corn Bourbon Aged At Least 30 Months** batch no. BCB17-1, bott 10.5.17 db (94.5) n23 irresistible balance between honey and spice as the liquorice leads; t24 huge delivery: red liquorice now as it is thinned after the initial thumping, spicy arrival by a succession of honey and maple syrup notes; serious vanilla at midway; f23.5 long, ridiculously lush even now; the liquorice dn hickory just keep on going...; b24 a typically muscular Balcones dripping with bourbony brilliance. Cavernous in depth and just as dark in character. *64.6%. nc ncf.*

⬥ **Balcones Texas Rye 100 Proof Pot Distilled 100% Straight Rye Whiskey Aged At Least 15 Months** batch no. RYE10018-1, bott 2-28-18 db (85) n20 t21 f22.5 b21.5 By Balcones astonishingly high standards, this is an underwhelming rye. Neither the nose nor delivery get off the ground, or feel particularly comfortable. Only once the big cocoa finish hoves into view do we get some idea of the distillery's usual excellence, though the very last off key notes of the fade tell a story *50% (100 proof). nc ncf.*

⬥ **Balcones Texas Rye Cask Strength Pot Distilled 100% Straight Rye Whiskey Aged At Least 30 Months** batch no. 12CS17-1, bott 12-7-17 db (89.5) n23 the rummiest rye known to whiskeykind. Some serious esters at play, but so attractive; t23 again, the grain appears to be playing second fiddle here to the sugary esters. Like the nose, sampled blind I'd have marked this as Jamaican rum; f21.5 spicy and a distinctly oily, with the odd feint apparent; b22 if I was marking this purely as a rye, it'd probably shed a few points as, beyond the initial delivery, the grain adds little of the fruitiness and unique profile one would expect. However, there is no faulting its overall intensity and entertainment. *55% (110 proof). nc ncf. Tenth Anniversary.*

Balcones Texas Single Malt Whisky Classic Edition Aged At Least 18 Months in Oak batch no. SM17-3, bott 4-19-17 db (93) n23 t23.5 f23 b23.5 Most of the micro distillers have a bit of a problem when it comes to producing a single malt; but not these boys! Superb. *53% (106 proof). nc ncf.*

⬥ **Balcones Texas Single Malt Whisky Classic Edition Aged At Least 19 Months In Oak** batch no. SM18-2, bott 2-8-18 db (93) n22.5 none of the trademark biff! ker-pow! and thud! of the usual Balcones, instead opting for a drier, vaguely grape-seedy infusion with spice; gentle hickory guarantees weight; t23.5 salivating and by no means overwhelming. Indeed, the malt really does have a big say here, making the most of its rare outing. The light treacle grows only slowly and with a degree of elegance, the spices coming along on a parallel thread; f23.5 excellent finale: a blend of Manuka and ulmo honey lays the foundations for the vanilla and butterscotch; b23.5 a deceptive Balcones: it is like coming out of the dark into the light, being blinded and then slowly adjusting to what is around you. Easy to underestimate in its excellence. 53% (108 proof). nc ncf.

◇ **Balcones Texas Single Malt Whisky Pot Distilled Rum Cask Finished Aged At Least 32 Months** batch no. SMR18-1, bott 4-6-18 db (92) n23.5 liquorice and molasses on steroids: yep – Balcones...; t23.5 the silky soft caress on delivery still cannot entirely absorb the impact of the powering maple syrup, butterscotch and spice. The oils are something to be worshipped; f22 the vanillas up their game as the rum holds back the more pungent personalty traits; b23 not even a rum cask, capable of clipping some bigger whiskies' wings, can get a look in here, perhaps until the final fade. Typically enormous. 55% (110 proof). nc ncf. Tenth Anniversary.

Balcones True Blue Straight 100 Proof Corn Whisky Aged At Least 24 Months in Oak batch no. TB-100 16-1, bott 8-4-16 db (90.5) n23.5 t22.5 f22.5 b22.5 big! 50% (100 proof). nc ncf.

◇ **Balcones True Blue Straight 100 Proof Corn Whisky Aged At Least 24 Months** batch no. TB10018-1, bott 3-26-18 db (94.5) n23.5 those corn oils sing lustily: melted salted butter and butterscotch; oh, and such sweet tannins; t23.5 massive mouth-watering, coppery properties throughout. Like the nose a bit salty, upping the flavours significantly. Light liquorice and treacle in tandem give a more bourbon-style edge than a corn one...; the mouth feel is never less than silky, the poise of the sweetness against the more guttural tannins never less than perfect; f23.5 throbbing, pulsing tannins darkening in character, increasing in weight. But a light maple syrup shadow proves the perfect foil; b24 the type of whiskey which just makes you sigh with contentment. 50% (100 proof). nc ncf.

Balcones True Blue Cask Strength Straight Corn Whisky Aged At Least 24 Monthsbatch no. TB 16-1, bott 8-3-16 db (95) n24 t24 f23.5 b23.5 Their True Blue 100 Proof is big. This is a whole lot bigger... 65.7% (131.4 proof). nc ncf.

◇ **Balcones True Blue Cask Strength Straight Corn Whisky Aged At Least 39 Months** batch no. TB17-1, bott 10-13-17 db (96) n24.5 beautifully defined, almost taut nose, free from excess oils, allowing the cross rum and bourbon aroma to take corn whisky into slightly new territory. Gentle esters hang on the heather honey/maple syrup/molasses blend. Fruity, too. Almost erotically satisfying...; t24 oilier and weightier here than on the nose, the delivery almost a mix of intense blackcurrant juice and concentrated liquorice; the spices pulse evenly and warmly, the vanillas building by the second; even late on there is a enough juiciness to take on the growing drier notes; f23.5 long with a brilliant chocolate mousse tail; b24 here we go again: Balcones at its most Balcones. Profound and glorious. 68.3% (136.6 proof). nc ncf.

BENJAMIN PRICHARD'S DISTILLERY Kelso, Tennessee.

Benjamin Prichard's Lincoln County Lightning Tennessee Corn Whiskey (89) n24 t22.5 f21 b22. Another white whiskey. This one is very well made and though surprisingly lacking oils and weight has more than enough charm and riches. 45%

BERKSHIRE MOUNTAIN DISTILLERS Great Barrington, Massachusetts.

Berkshire Bourbon Whiskey (91.5) n23 t23.5 f23 b23. A bourbon bursting with character: I am hooked! Another micro-gem. 43%

BLAUM BROS Galena, Illinois

◇ **Blaum Bros Bourbon Aged 3 Years** db (81) n19.5 t22 f19 b20.5 A curious bourbon, this. Has the complex spice make up of a cake mix. Exceptionally sweet and leaves the tongue buzzing... 50% (100 proof).

◇ **Blaum Bros Fever River Rye Aged 2 Years** new American oak, finished in Port and Madeira barrels db (86.5) n21.5 t21.5 f22 b21.5 Less bizarre spices at play here, the wine casks making for a friendlier, after experience with an attractive complexity that now makes sense. 40% (80 proof).

BLUE RIDGE DISTILLING CO. Golden Valley, North Carolina.

Defiant American Single Malt Whisky db (80.5) n19 t21 f20.5 b20. A wide cut ensures a chewy, honey and nougat feel to this. Barley, though, does not have the same flavour compounds to compensate for the oils. Undeniably tasty, if a little flawed!41% (82 proof)

Blue Ridge Rye Whisky db (87) n21.5 t22.5 f21 b21. This is heavy and feinty, though the intensity of the rye papers over the smaller to medium sized cracks. And the sugars are intense. This is big, imperfect rye with character spilling out of the glass. But great fun and more than a nod to America's distilling past. 46% (92 proof)

BRECKENRIDGE DISTILLERY Breckenridge, Colorado.

Breckenridge Colorado Bourbon Whiskey Aged 2 Years (86) n22.5 t22 f20.5 b21. Full of character, big-hearted, chewy, slightly rugged bourbon where honey and cocoa thrives; spices make a telling impact. How apposite that probably the one and only town in Colorado named after a Kentuckian should end up making bourbon. Being close on 10,000 feet above sea level you'd think ice would come naturally with this. But it does pretty well without it, believe me... 43%

◇◇◇ **Breckenridge Colorado Whiskey Aged a Minimum of at least Three Years Port Cask Finish** batch no. 4 db (87.5) n21 t23 f22 b21.5 Here's the problem: you have a high rye bourbon mash made, so it seems, rather beautifully. But can you tell it's a high rye bourbon mash? Well, no...because the fruit has taken over completely. Yes, the delivery is as soft, succulent and delicious as could be hoped for. But, spice apart, it is hard to get much more out of it. Do I like this? Yes. Would it have been sexier still if the port input had been more subdued? Indubitably. The truth is, it is easier to drink this like an over-fortified port than a whiskey. And that isn't quite where we should be. 45% (90 proof).

◇◇◇ **Breckenridge Colorado Whiskey Aged a Minimum of at least Three Years PX Cask Finish** batch no. 1 db (86.5) n21 t22.5 f22 b21 And we have the same problem with PX: it could not be any other way. PX casks are the hardest of any to manage, as the sweet wine residue has a horrible tendency to clog up a whisky's arteries, rendering it flat with little or no undulations. The delivery is sublime and the spices are scintillating. But there is just too little going on elsewhere. 45% (90 proof).

◇◇◇ **Breckenridge Colorado Whiskey Single Barrel Bourbon Whiskey** barrel no. 12H31-1, bott 1-17-18 db (90) n22 an extraordinary degree of blood orange...; caramel covers the back drop; t23 sumptuous, soft yet bristling with a busy spice and red liquorice. This is sweet and salivating stuff, the weightier tannin tones bringing things back to earth before it headed into too sweet a direction; f22 back to those orangey citrus tones now like fudge with tangy orange peel; b23 highly unusual, intense bourbon with hefty tannins, but that blood orange/kumquat thread never far away. 48% (96 proof). sc.

◇◇◇ **Breckenridge Dark Arts** batch no. 3 db (87) n20.5 t23 f21.5 b22 Some of the passages on this are a sheer delight, the warming vanilla and caramel in particular. Undone slightly by a very wide cut which offers unwanted oils. The delivery though,is spectacularly beautiful. 46% (92 proof). Whiskey distilled from malt mash.

BREUCKELEN DISTILLING Brooklyn, New York.

◇◇◇ **77 Whiskey Bonded Rye Aged 4 Years** American oak barrels db (86.5) n21.5 t22 f21.5 b21.5 Big flavoured and butch, but a few too many nougat and tobacco notes point an accusing finger towards the cut. Plenty to enjoy, but perhaps not up to Breuckelen's usual very high standards. 50% (100 proof).

◇◇◇ **77 Whiskey Bonded Rye & Corn Aged 4 Years** American oak barrels db (95) n23.5 oddly enough, the rye is crystalline, sharp and sweet here in a way it fails with their new rye whiskey. Sublime spice counters perfectly; t24 ooooh, just soooo sexy! Again the rye leads the way: demerara sugar concentrate, the crispness of the grain in stark and beautiful contrast to the quicksand corn; spices rise like a full moon and shine s brightly; f23.5 a more amalgamated finale with more tannin present, offering a light toffee mocha; b24 there you go: Breuckleyn back on track with a spot edition of their signature brand. Sings from the glass like a barber-shop quartet. 50% (100 proof).

◇◇◇ **77 Whiskey Local Corn 700 Days Old** db (92) n23 sweetened coconut almost, salty and roasty with a light corn oil balance; t23.5 good grief....! Yes, though sugars on the nose manifest themselves here to startling effect, though some fabulous, earthier oakiness rushes in to accompany. Red liquorice and a little sweetened hickory fill the middle ground excellently; f22.5 long corn oils keep the sweet and dry notes in a state of contant flux; b23 it is as if very single atom of sugar has been sucked out of the oak though, thankfully, baser tannins give balance. Remarkable and delicious! 45% (90 proof).

77 Whiskey Local Rye & Corn 483 Days Old, American oak barrels, db (95) n24 t24 f23 b24 An absolute gem of a whiskey just dripping with rye. 45%

77 Whiskey Local Rye & Corn 538 Days Old American oak barrels db (92.5) n22.5 t23.5 f23 b23.5 The 377th whisky tasted for my Bible 2018 just had to be this. I remember last year tasting a younger version of this which was quite astonishing. Here the rye, which was so prominent last time, has been overtaken by the corn which has clipped its brittle wings. Still an astounding experience, nonetheless... 45% (90 proof).

77 Whiskey New York Wheat 519 Days Old American oak barrels db (89.5) n22 t23 f22 b22.5 Just looked up my tasting notes for this whiskey from last year: identical score and very similar description. This is one very consistent whiskey!! 45% (90 proof).

77 Whiskey New York Wheat 622 Days Old American oak barrels db (89.5) n22 t23 f22 b22.5 A very busy whiskey which never quite decides which direction it wishes to take. Still, there's something to say for a mystery tour... 45%

◇ **Project No 1: Wheated Straight Bourbon Bottled in Bond Aged 4 Years** dist 2013 db (88) n22 a hefty nose: corn appears to dominate but the nip from the wheat is unmistakable; t22.5 salivating delivery. Tannins have a slight upper hand in the first few waves, before that attractive corn oil and wheat spice combine again to fill in the middle; f21.5 a few feints kick in late on, but there is vanilla and spice enough to compensate; b22 a bit heavy on the oils, but the wheat and associated spices make their mark. 50% (100 proof).

◇ **Project No 2: Single Malt Whiskey Bottled in Bond Aged 4 Years** dist 23 Mar 13, bott 26 Feb 18 db (84.5) n21 t21 f21.5 b21 Sweet and widely cut. A project still in development, I suspect... 50% (100 proof).

CADÉE DISTILLERY Clinton, Washington.

Cadée Distillery Cascadia Rye Whiskey finished in Port barrels db (87) n21.5 t23 f21 b21.5. Works quite well. A vaguely wide cut does ramp up the oils. But the rye has enough crystalline firmness to cut through the fruit. Think this pretty high quality rye actually deserves better than being masked by the Port which, though clean and juicy, has a flattening effect. 43.5% (87 proof)

Cadée Distillery Deceptivus Bourbon Whiskey finished in Port barrels db (87) n21 t22 f22.5 b22. The sweet corn and the fruit combine to form a formidable chewiness. Attractive with some lovely ulmo honey also. The spiced chocolate fruit and vague nougat really does ensure an entertaining finale. 42.5% (85 proof)

◇ **Cadée Distillery Medusa** db (71) n18 t18 f17 b18 Stone me! A seriously hair-raising experience. Curiously flat and what notes it does offer are not particularly attractive. 40% (80 proof).

◇ **Cadée Distillery Rye Whiskey** (93) n23.5 classic intense rye, full of ginger and Demerara sugars. Light spice touches the vanilla and the grainy fruity crispness; t23 such an attractive mix of crisp rye and vanilla wafer; f23.5 brilliant spice explosion and a long, juicy grain fade; b23 have to admit, when I tasted this a rye type crossed my mind: then I looked at the label and spotted where it was actually made.... 42% (84 proof). Distilled in Indiana.

CATOCTIN CREEK DISTILLERY Loudoun County, Virginia.

Braddock Oak Single Barrel Rye Whisky batch B17K1 db (90) n22.5 t23 f22 b22.5 It is heart-warming to see a distillery dedicated to making rye. Still the odd technical off-note but I am sure this will be corrected with time and experience. Plenty here to savour. 46% sc.

Catoctin Creek Cask Proof Roundstone Rye Whisky batch B17A2, charred new oak barrels db (88) n21.5 t22.5 f22 b22 So much flavour. But needs to get those cuts cleaner to maximise the rye profile. 57.8% (115.6 proof). ncf.

Catoctin Creek Roundstone Rye Single Barrel Whisky batch B1IE43Y, new white oak barrels db (87) n22 t22 f21 b22 The thing that has to be said about Catoctin is the amazing consistency (and close scoring) of their brands. Oddly enough, for a single barrel this perhaps does the distillery least justice as it is the work of the stills rather than complexity of the grain which is most noticeable. But, as with the others, no shortage of personality. 40% (80 proof). sc.

Catoctin Creek Roundstone Rye Whisky batch B17G1, charred new oak barrels db (88) n21.5 t23.5 f21 b22 The brighter end of the distillery's narrow spectrum: the rye here really is deliciously on song! 46% (92 proof). ncf.

CEDAR RIDGE DISTILLERY Swisher, Iowa.

Twelve Five Rye recipe: rye, corn & malted barley, batch no. 131304-A db (87.5) n23 t22.5 f20.5 b21.5. Some seriously big rye at work here and the nose is something to enjoy if not marvel at. Once the distillers can just narrow the middle cut, this will be a rye of serious magnitude. As it is, the feints just take the edge off an otherwise impressive rye. 47.5%

CHAMBERS BAY DISTILLERY University Place, Washington.

Greenhorn Bourbon aged for a minimum of 1 year, batch 1, bott 13 Dec 15 db (74.5) n18.5 t21 f17 b18. A sharp, eye-watering experience where an interesting fermentation has given the distiller little room for manoeuvre. 44% (88 proof)

CHARBAY DISTILLERY Napa Valley, California.

Charbay Hop Flavoured Whiskey release II, barrels 3-7 (91) n22 t22 f23 b24. Being distilled from beer which includes hops, it can – and will - be argued that this is not beer at all. However, what cannot be disputed is that this is a rich, full-on spirit that has set out to make a statement and has delivered it. Loudspeaker and all. 55%

◇ **Charbay 1999 Pilsner Whiskey Release III Double Alambic Charentais Pot Distilled Whiskey** aged 6 years in new American white oak barrels and 8 additional years in stainless steel tanks db **(84.5) n21 t22 f21.5 b20** Just a point: you can't age for 8 years in stainless steel tanks. The moment it leaves the barrel the aging process stops: the term makes no sense. Lots of sugars at play and a distinctive fruity and spicy edge, though harmonisation is at a premium. *66.2% (132.4 proof).*

⟨⟩ **Charbay Lot S 211A Hop Flavored Whiskey Aged 29 Months** French oak barrels, distilled from Bear Republic Black Bear Stout db **(74) n18 t20 f18 b18** Hop, but no glory. *49.5% (99 proof).*

⟨⟩ **Charbay R5 Lot No. 4 Hop Flavored Aged 28 Months** French oak barrels, distilled from Bear Republic Racer 5 IPA db **(72) n17 t19 f18 b18** I'm sure Charbay once did a distillation from a hopped beer which worked agreeably well: I remember it, as it is an unusual occurrence. Most hopped whiskeys (if, indeed they are whiskeys, which I dispute) really don't work. This is one such failure, though there is a pleasant round of chocolate on the delivery. *49.5% (99 proof).*

CLEAR CREEK DISTILLERY Portland, Oregon.
McCarthy's Oregon Single Malt Aged 3 Years batch W16-01, bott 6 May 16 db **(88.5) n22 t23 f21.5 b22** For the first time since I tasted their first bottlings – in the days when my beard was still black – this whiskey has changed. Appears to have far less copper in the system to give the normal all-round richness; this is quite apparent on the nose and finish in particular. But they appear to have upped the peat ratio to good effect. *42.5% (85 proof)*

CLEVELAND WHISKEY Cleveland, Ohio.
⟨⟩ **Cleveland Underground Bourbon Whiskey Finished with Black Cherry Wood** batch no. 05 db **(88) n22.5** a busy nose, dependent mainly on an ulmo honey-vanilla theme. The complex tannins brood, threaten even; a burnt mallow note underscores the baser toasty notes; **t22.5** a sweet, welcoming start. Natural caramels extracted from the wood lays the foundation for the busy spices, a type of Yorkshire Parkin cake, though saltier and, latterly, less dependence on sugars; **f21** spicy, bitter, a tad off key. **b22** in the blurb on the back of this bottle they claim their methods of maturation are regarded sacrilegious to some. But these methods "adds a series of flavors and aromas never before experienced in traditional whiskies." Well, let's take the first claim for a start: there is nothing in this whiskey I have never tasted hundreds, indeed, thousands of times before. Sorry about that. Only one whisky of this year's intake of over 1,000 whiskies gave me something I had never encountered before: and it wasn't this. I have no idea what these maturation techniques might be, and I am really keen to find out: I am truly fascinated. But I don't regard any whiskey finished (as well as started and middled) in anything other than virgin oak to be bourbon. Sorry. Back to the whiskey: pleasant with an intriguing layering structure to the nose which certainly points to something other than a species of Quercus. However, these notes have, over the last 25 years, cropped up many times elsewhere in the USA and around the globe. More importantly, the finish, so vital in any whiskey, needs some serious attention as it is bitter and unbalanced and undoes a lot of good work. *47% (94 proof). Uncommon Barrel Collection.*

COLORADO GOLD DISTILLERY Cedaredge, Colorado.
Colorado Gold Rye charred oak barrel no. 23, bott 31 Oct 15 db **(80) n20 t21 f19.5 b19.5.** Insane sugars – Manuka honey concentrate – still can't fully overcome the tobacco bitterness. A certain dirtiness when a rye should sparkle. *45% (90 proof). sc.*

Colorado Gold Straight Bourbon aged 3 years, new oak barrel no. 43, bott 1 Dec 15 db **(91) n22.5 t23 f23 b22.5** If you have a sweet tooth, buy a case...!! *45% (90 proof). sc.*

Colorado Gold Straight Bourbon Over Two Years Old Single Barrel bott 8 Oct 11 **(86.5) n21 t23 f21 b21.5.** A bit of a whippersnapper of a bourbon. The nose and finish may lack depth. But it is a whiskey bursting with personality and the delivery is an understated treat. A light mocha thread weaves in and out of the muscovado. Fun. *40%*

COOPERSTOWN DISTILLERY Cooperstown, New York.
⟨⟩ **Cooper's Classic American Whiskey** bourbon mash finished in French oak barrels, bott code. 148 10 db **(90.5) n22.5** a beautifully clean distillate with exemplary cut points. A light citrussy hue to the icing sugar; **t22.5** those sugars on the nose weren't a false signal...! Light maple syrup pours like lava from a hacked off volcano. Spices tingle on two fronts, one ethereal and playful, the other deeper – very unusual; **f23** with the tannins gaining greater weight the marriage with the syrup is spot on; a little chocolate orange marzipan at the very death; **b22.5** plugs into the sugars and takes full voltage. *45%.*

⟨⟩ **Cooper's Legacy Bourbon Whiskey Grant's Recipe** bott code. 147 02 db **(95) n23.5** a real Kentucky feel to this little beauty: wonderfully clean distillation, allowing the liquorice, hickory and manuka honey full scope to show their magic; t24 sweet as a nut! The corn oils are gentle enough to encourage a busy small grain complexity at around the mid-point. As on the nose, the hickory, liquorice and honey are there is attractive quantities; f23.5 so long and sweet. The caramels from the oak begin to pile up, but the spices puncture them at regular intervals; b24 I'd like, with this exceptional bourbon, to raise a toast to my son, James', new (indeed, first) dog: Cooper. Named, naturally, after Dale Cooper of Twin Peaks fame. Dale whippet. Dale bourbon. 50% (100 proof).

⟨⟩ **Cooper's Ransom Rye Whiskey** db (86.5) n21 t22 f21.5 b22 If they could just keep the cut points a little more tight, they'd really have some rye here. Despite the light feints the rye does at times sparkle with commendable crispness. 51% (102 proof).

COPPER FOX DISTILLERY Sperryville, Virginia.

Copper Fox Rye Whisky Aged 21 Months bott 18 Jan 17 db (94.5) n23.5 t24 f23 b24 Had this bottle on my tasting lab table ready to explore when I decided I needed to break off, rest my palate for a while and get some exercise. So, I went for a walk, and just as I reached the highest point of the remote countryside around me, I espied a fox crossing a field heading straight for me. Darker than usual, like unburnished copper. It stopped and stared at me as I stared at it, just a few yards separating us. It slunk off downhill in no great hurry and stopped with only its head showing above a hollow: again we regarded each other eye to eye for a few precious minutes. If only I had had this fabulous bottle with me... 47.5% (95 proof).

Wasmund's Single Malt Whisky 24 Months Old batch no. 135 db (89) n22 t22.5 f22 b22.5 Quite a different style from Rick Wasmund this time. 48% (96 proof). ncf.

COPPERWORKS Seattle, Washington

Copperworks American Single Malt Whiskey Release No. 001 Aged 30 Months new American oak casks db (91) n23 t22.5 f22.5 b23 Congratulations! An impressive first bottling for a new distillery in Seattle. Going along the lines of Stranahan Distillery, they are maturing their single malt in virgin American oak. This is a lighter, far less in-your-face version. Instead elegance appears to be the goal. Well, it has been achieved. 52% (104 proof). 1,530 bottles.

Copperworks American Single Malt Whiskey Release No. 002 Aged 30 Months new American oak casks db (95) n24 t23.5 f23 b24 A higher part of the warehouse? More summer months within the 30? Somehow Copperwork has raised the game considerably with much broader and enveloping malt which has flourished in the extra oak. A three course single malt if ever there was one...! 53% (106 proof). 1,753 bottles.

Copperworks American Single Malt Whiskey Release No. 003 Aged 34 Months new American oak casks db (92.5) n24 t23.5 f22 b23 The closest style to a rye I have ever found a single malt barley. Phenomenal...! 52% (104 proof). 1,559 bottles.

Copperworks American Single Malt Whiskey Release No. 004 Aged 31 Months cask no. 44, new American oak cask db (88.5) n22 t22 f22.5 b22 A very gin-like feel to this which casts a heavy shadow over the whiskey character. Maybe be wrong, but suspect some gin was bottled not long before this whiskey was using some of the same equipment. 61.75% (123.5 proof). 219 bottles.

⟨⟩ **Copperworks American Single Malt Whiskey Release No. 005 Aged 33 Months** new American oak casks, pale malt recipe db (90.5) n22.5 intense malt and so beautifully clean. Gentle Brazilian biscuit flour, then a light oaky and apple-y undercurrent; t22 busy and fizzing malt with plenty of grist and sappy sugars intertwangling; f23 spices at play as the toastiness increases: classic crossover between malt and bourbon styles with late burnt fudge; b22.5 some clever sugars at play here. 50% (100 proof). 1,563 bottles.

⟨⟩ **Copperworks American Single Malt Whiskey Release No. 006 Aged 24 Months** new American oak & oloroso sherry casks, five malt recipe db (89) n23 there may be only 10% sherry butt at work, but its clean grapey tones appear to dominate 90% of the nose; t22 early fruit met by a certain bitterness; f22 good oaky spice buzz and late malt; b22 a surprisingly bitter fellow. I know they don't have hops here, but there is a certain hint of hop throughout. Very curious. 47.5% (95 proof). 2,037 bottles.

⟨⟩ **Copperworks American Single Malt Whiskey Release No. 007 Aged 35 Months** new American oak cask, cask no. 53, five malt recipe db (89) n22.5 a light hint of eucalyptus – not something you usually find with a whiskey barely three years old! Mint humbugs, too; t23 fabulous delivery: the first four or five flavour waves crash down meaning business, along with that cool, minty note detected on the nose. Toffee begins to stream in, then a little bitterness; f21.5 minty bitterness; b22 could this be the world's first chewing gum whiskey? It is certainly the mintiest! 59% (118 proof). sc. 210 bottles.

⟨⟩ **Copperworks American Single Malt Whiskey Release No. 008 Aged 35 Months** new American oak cask, cask no. 59, five malt recipe db (89.5) n23 the meeting of various firm sugars and malt, amid a mix of hay bales and malt is a joy; t23 a strange coming together of varied sugars (grist at the fore), honey and a bitter note one normally associates with beer: odd, but enjoyable; f21 that persistent bitter note in there bothers me...; b22.5 no doubts about this being a malt whiskey: good grief...! 58.85% (1177 proof). sc. 215 bottles.

◇◇◇ **Copperworks American Single Malt Whiskey Release No. 009 Aged 40 Months** new American oak cask, cask no. 43, five malt recipe db (86.5) n21 t23.5 f20.5 b21.5 It has been a few years since I last rode, but this is like being on a horse determined to make the jumps: you grip on tight (with knees and everything else) and let it enjoy the course. The highest hurdle is in delivery with a plethora of dark sugars. But a few hurdles are dislodged with that house hop-like bitterness which seems starker still against the sugars. 62.5% (125 proof). sc. 122 bottles.

◇◇◇ **Copperworks American Single Malt Whiskey Release No. 010 Aged 39 Months** new American oak casks, five malt & pale malt recipe db (88) n21.5 sweet but strangely untidy; t23 now that is big! The sugars are of varying levels of sweetness, the gristier notes to the fore and soon in concentrate; the mid-ground is strange: some beautiful vanilla and barley notes, but a vague bitter tone seeps into every corner; f21.5 malt and butterscotch, but with a residual, mysterious bitterness; b22 so, so odd. The house style appears to have a fruity, languid hop note. But hops aren't used. I am bewildered... 52.5% (105 proof). 1,380 bottles.

◇◇◇ **Copperworks American Single Malt Whiskey Release No. 011 Aged 32 Months** new American oak & sherry oloroso casks, five malt & pale malt recipe db (87) n21 t22.5 f21.5 b21.5 The lush fruit dulls the majority of that irritating bitterness, but not all. Also, the sugars are welcome but need toning down. A malt that keeps threatening to hit the high notes, but then goes off key. 49% (98 proof). 1,460 bottles.

CORNELIUS PASS ROADHOUSE DISTILLERY Hillsboro, Oregon.
McMenamins C.P.R. White Owl Distillery (93) n23.5 t23 f23 b23.5. Top dollar White Dog. Huge amount of copper helps expose all the honey available, especially on the nose. Superbly distilled and surging with barley and spice. 49.3%

CORSAIR ARTISAN DISTILLERY Nashville, Tennessee.
Corsair Triple Smoke (92.5) n24 t23 f22 b23.5. The odd technical flaw, to pick nits. But, overall, a lovely whiskey with a curiously polite smoke style which refuses to dominate. Teasingly delicate and subtle...and different. 40%

DAD'S HAT RYE DISTILLERY Bristol, Pennsylvania
Dad's Hat Pennsylvania Straight Rye Whiskey Aged Minimum 3 Years db (91.5) n23 t23.5 f22 That persistent vague bitterness does gather momentum towards the end; b23 the truest rye I have seen from you yet: I take my hat off to you guys...quite literally...! 47.5% (95 proof).

DARK CORNER DISTILLERY Greenville, South Carolina
Dark Corner Moonshine Corn Whiskey (77.5) n18.5 t22 f18 b19. Full blooded sweet corn on delivery. But could do with some extra copper elsewhere. 50%

DARK HORSE DISTILLERY Lenexa, Kansas
Dark Horse Reserve Bourbon Less Than Four Years Old Batch 2 (93) n23 t23.5 f23 b23.5 Even though they appear to have used oak chips to bolster the overall richness of this bourbon, there is no taking away that this is the closest any whiskey produced by a microdistiller comes to the true Kentucky style. But even there, there are few which display so much vanilla. 44.5% (89 proof)

DEERHAMMER DISTILLING COMPANY Buena Vista, Colorado.
Deerhammer American Single Malt Whiskey virgin oak barrel #2 char, batch no. 32 db (87.5) n21.5 t23.5 f20.5 b22 This, like most Colorado whiskeys, is huge. Had the cut been a little less generous, the oils a little less gripping and tangy, this would have scored exceptionally highly. For there is no doubting the deliciousness of the big toasted malt, the kumquat citrus element, the moreishness of the heavyweight dark fudge and the magnificent Java coffee. All these make a delivery and follow through to remember. I look forward to the next bottling where hopefully the cut is a little more careful: a very significant score awaits as this is borderline brilliant... 46% (92 proof). 870 bottles.

DELAWARE PHOENIX DISTILLERY Walton, New York.
Rye Dog Batch 11-1 (78.5) n19 t21.5 f18 b19. Sweet, distinctive rye tang but a little short on copper sheen. 50% (100 proof)

DISTILLERY 291 Colorado Springs, Colorado.

◇◇◇ **291 Bad Guy Colorado Bourbon Whiskey Aged 311 Days** distilled from a bourbon mash, American oak barrel, aspen stave finished, batch no. 3 db **(92)** n23.5 yet another compelling nose from 291: the liquorice, hickory and golden syrup have been slapped on with great confidence; **t23.5** all the usual toasty notes present and correct, with a polished honey counter, the disciplined oils impartial in boosting both factions; the slightly dry intensity of the toasted fudge, liquorice and hickory is quite special; **f22** acceptable late bitterness to the tannins; **b23.5** gorgeous, as usual! 60.4% (120.7 proof). 785 bottles.

291 Bad Guy Colorado Bourbon Whiskey Aged 525 Days distilled from a bourbon mash, American oak barrel, aspen stave finished, barrel no. 2 db **(93)** n23.5 t23.5 f23 b23 Even though this Bad Guy socks you one right between the eyes, raise a glass of this and toast a massive and desirable whiskey: in fact, everything about this is toasted....!! 59.7% (119.4 proof). sc. 644 bottles.

291 Barrel Proof Colorado Whiskey Aged Less Than 2 Years distilled from a rye malt mash, American oak barrel, aspen stave finished, barrel no. 90 db **(95)** n23.5 t24 f23.5 b24 That a distillery can produce a young rye malt whiskey of this standard and something as magnificent as their 333 days bottling shows that Distillery 291 are way up there among the elite of the US micro-distillery movement. 63.1% (126.3 proof). sc. 48 bottles.

◇◇◇ **291 Barrel Proof Colorado Whiskey Aged Less Than 2 Years** distilled from a rye malt mash, American oak barrel, aspen stave finished, barrel no. 255 db **(92.5)** n23 heather honey matches the tannins; the spiced-up rye grain is aloof from it all; **t23.5** scintillating and salivating. Those poker hot spices and intensity of the cooler crisp rye means it is a little while before you notice the toasty tannins and honey lurking around; **f22.5** some lingering oils allow you to chew the last of the rye; **b23.5** their rye mash is getting noticeably better. This bristles with the grain. 63% (126 proof). sc. 49 bottles.

◇◇◇ **291 Barrel Proof Colorado Whiskey Aged Less Than 2 Years** distilled from a rye malt mash, American oak barrel, aspen stave finished, barrel no. 195 db **(95)** n24 the rye element has moved away from its usual crisp, lonely, fruity course to be part of a much richer, more lush tapestry involving involving fudge and chocolate. This has the potential to be huge whiskey...; just love the liquorice and overcooked blackcurrant tart; **t24** ...and my word it is! There is a degree of brittleness to the rye small grains which ensures a pulsating juiciness. But those chocolate fudge notes are equal to the challenge and offer a deliciously chewy alternative; the spices are profound but always in control and perfectly paced with the main heady, toasty bourbon flavour development; **f23.5** so much chocolate...! **b24** you know these boys will come up with a blockbuster among their latest releases...this is it! 63.1% (126.1 proof). sc. 45 bottles.

291 E Colorado 100% Rye Malt Whiskey Aged 291 Days American oak barrel, aspen stave finished, batch no. 3 db **(95.5)** n23.5 t24 f23.5 b24.5 What a treat for the taste buds! Substantial and as full flavoured as they come. 62.3% (124.6 proof). 368 bottles.

291 E Colorado Bourbon Whiskey Aged 333 Days American oak barrel, aspen stave finished, batch no. 2 db **(96)** n24 t24 f24 b24 Exceptional, enthralling, eclectic, engrossing, engaging, edifying, enticing, entirely extraordinary...encore! The whiskey which puts the E into three threes.... (the author would like to assure the public that no thesaurus, electronic or otherwise, was used in the writing of these tasting notes.... 63.4% (126.8 proof). 191 bottles.

291 E Colorado Whiskey Aged 405 Days American oak barrel, aspen stave finished, batch no. 1 db **(90.5)** n22.5 t23.5 f22 b22.5 Wlegant. 62.9% (125.9 proof). 198 bottles. Barrel select for The Stanley.

291 M Colorado Whiskey Rye Malt Mash Aged Less Than 2 Years Aspen Stave Finished barrel no. 1, American oak barrel db **(95.5)** n24 t24 f23.5 b24 The nose promises something quite immense. And not for a second does it let you down. A whiskey which needs not just a knife and fork, but a carving set, too...Bravo Disitillery 291! 63% (126.1 proof)

291 M Colorado Whiskey Rye Malt Mash Aged Less Than 2 Years Aspen Stave Finished barrel no. 3, American oak barrel db **(86)** n21.5 t22 f21 b21.5. Quite dapper rye appears through the slight mustiness on both nose and delivery. A little murky by comparison to Barrel 1's outlandishly high standards. 63.1% (126.2 proof)

291 M Colorado Whiskey Rye Malt Mash Aged Less Than 2 Years Aspen Stave Finished batch no. 1, American oak barrels db **(92.5)** n22 t24 f23b23.5 A surprisingly subtle rye considering its undoubted intensity. 62.9% (125.9 proof). 190 bottles.

291 M Colorado Whiskey Rye Malt Mash Aged Less Than 2 Years Aspen Stave Finished barrel no. 5, American oak barrels db **(89.5)** n22.5 t23 f21.5 b22.5 When they say there's a high rye content in the mash recipe, they just ain't kidding, nosiree! A slightly cleaner cut would have piled on the points... 50% (100 proof). 55 bottles

291 Single Barrel Colorado Bourbon Whiskey Aged Less Than 2 Years distilled from a bourbon mash, American oak barrel, aspen stave finished, barrel no. 33 db **(87.5)** n22 t23 f20.5 b22 Lots of fruit jelly at play here, working well with the big spice kick and profound vanilla. Enjoyable and correct other than a nagging bitterness which just skews the overall message. 50% (100 proof). sc. 60 bottles.

◇◇ **291 Single Barrel Colorado Bourbon Whiskey Aged Less Than 2 Years** distilled from a bourbon mash, American oak barrel, aspen stave finished, barrel no. 196 db (88) n22.5 an attractive, heady mix of nougat and honey; t22 chewy corn oils – and others – give immediate weight on delivery f21.5 lightly sugared spices; b22 perhaps a little too much oil from the still for greatness, but not too much to spoil it. 50% (100 proof). sc. 53 bottles.

◇◇ **291 Single Barrel Colorado Rye Whiskey Aged Less Than 2 Years** distilled from a bourbon mash, American oak barrel, aspen stave finished, barrel no. 231 db (92) n22 busy small grains pepper the nose – not the usual rye fruity or crisp type; a little earthy and not unlike some oilier West Indian rums; t23.5 surprising degree of dark sugars first up; softens with the vanilla into a more ulmo honey style sweetness; never loses its bigness of body but the weight is beautifully distributed; f23 very attractive spice rumble; b23.5 would gladly down one of these after a T Bone steak...or if I fancied a decent rum and there wasn't one around. 50.8% (101.7 proof). sc. 60 bottles.

◇◇ **291 Single Barrel Colorado Rye Whiskey Aged Less Than 2 Years** distilled from a bourbon mash, American oak barrel, aspen stave finished, barrel no. 261 db (77) n18 t22 f18 b19 Well, didn't expect that! On the palate the rye is profound: crisp, sweet and as juicy as it comes. But the nose displays a degree of a butyric-style aroma – exceptionally unusual for this on the money distillery. The finish is, as expected, less than up to scratch, either. 50.8% (101.7 proof). sc. 55 bottles.

DOWNSLOPE DISTILLING Centennial, Colorado.
Double Diamond Whiskey cask no. WR-283 db (86) n21 t22 f21.5 b21.5 The aroma of new-baled hay suggests a whiskey a long way from stating its original intentions. Some lovely light and citrusy sugars at play, nonetheless. 40% (80 proof). sc.

Double Diamond Whiskey Aged 4 Years Cognac Finish cask no. WR-290 db (93) n23 t23 f23.5 b23. An old British advert from the 1960s for a beer warbled: "A Double Diamond Works Wonders, Works Wonders. A Double Diamond Works Wonders. So drink some today..." It could equally apply to this hugely different whiskey! 41% (82 proof). sc.

Downslope Malt Whiskey Aged 2 Years Cognac Finish cask no. WR-260 db (77.5) n19.5 t21 f18 b19 The Cognac cask makes little headway into the feints. 48.5% (97 proof). sc.

Downslope Malt Whiskey Aged 3 Years Sherry Finish cask no. WR-184 db (87) n20 t21 f24 b22 Doesn't really gel until towards the finish when the most brilliant chocolate mousse kicks in. Then, out of nowhere, it suddenly becomes something rather special... 50% (100 proof). sc.

Downslope Rye Whiskey cask no. WR-235 db (90.5) n23.5 t22 f22.5 b22.5 OK, not quite technically on the money but the flavour profile is a delight. 46% (92 proof). sc.

DRY FLY DISTILLING Spokane, Washington.
Dry Fly Bourbon 101 (88) n21.5 t23 f21.5 b21.5. A well made bourbon which, with a bit of extra complexity, would stand above some of its Kentucky colleagues. 50.5%

Dry Fly Cask Strength Straight Wheat Whiskey (94.5) n23 t24 f23.5 b24 Quite beautiful whiskey. One every whisky lover should experience to further their understanding of this multi-faceted spirit. 60%

Dry Fly Port Finish Wheat Whiskey (89) n22 t23 f22 b22. If you mixed whiskey and jam you might end up with this little charmer. 50% (100 proof)

Dry Fly Straight Triticale Rye Wheat Hybrid (86) n22 t22 f21 b21. Pleasant and easy going. But very surprising degree of natural caramels fill in the gaps and shaves off the higher notes expected from the rye. 44% (88 proof)

Dry Fly Washington Wheat Whiskey (89) n22 t22 f22.5 b22.5. Hugely impressive, well weighted and balanced and a much better use of wheat than bread, for instance... 40%

EASTSIDE DISTILLING Portland, Oregon.
Burnside Bourbon 4 Year Barrel-Aged bott 2012 (92) n24 t23.5 f22 b22.5. "Put some sideburns on your face!" screams the back label. Well, a whiskey far too gracious to put hairs on your chest though it would be a close shave to choose this or a Kentucky 4-y-o as one of the best young bourbon noses of the year...Just bristles with charm. 48%

EDGEFIELD DISTILLERY Troutdale, Oregon.
Edgefield Hogshead Whisky 100% malted barley, batch 12-B (94) n23.5 t24 f23 b23.5 Been a little while since I lasted tasted Edgefield. At that time they were seriously getting their act together. Now they deserve star billing in any bar. This is sheer quality and even though the cut is very fractionally wide, the two years in new oak has ensured something bordering magnificence. 46%

FEW SPIRITS DISTILLERY Evanston, Illinois.

◇◇ **FEW Bourbon Whiskey** batch no. 17]20 db (89.5) n22 charming hickory-liquorice mix; t23 superb salivation levels on delivery. For once the house oils have been lost, leaving the liquorice and Manuka honey clean to make a delicious impression; f22 ah, the oils turn up at last, though no damage is done and a sweet and spicy theme sees us out; b22.5 FEW can definitely vary in its quality. This bourbon is very comfortable and though rich, seems to operate well within itself. 46.5% (93 proof).

◇◇ **FEW Rye Whiskey** batch no. 17B24 db (87.5) n21.5 t23.5 f21 b22 Definitely a step up from the last batch of FEW rye I tasted, having reduced most – though not all – of the cabbage effect from the distillation. More spices at play here, the rye still beautifully clipped and juicy. If only the finish were as excellent at the midpoint... 46.5% (93 proof).

That Boutique-y Whisky Company FEW 2 Year Old batch 2 (94.5) n23.5 t24 f23.5 b23.5 By far and away the best thing I have ever seen from this distillery, sticking so close to a Kentucky style it is impossible to tell them apart. So easy to have a Few 2 many... 51.8%. 275 bottles.

FINGER LAKES DISTILLING Burdett, New York.

Glen Thunder Corn Whiskey (92.5) n23.5 t23 f23 b23. Beautifully distilled, copper rich, Formula 1 quality, absolutely classic corn white dog. 45% (90 proof)

FISH HAWK SPIRITS Gainesville, Florida.

◇◇ **Sui Generis Conquistador 1513** batch no. 6 db (68) n21 t20 f12 b15 I had learned the hard way, from tasting their other two whiskies first, to wait until the finish kicked in before even beginning to form a view. And, again, the awful finish makes what goes on before almost irrelevant. 40% (80 proof).

◇◇ **Sui Generis Silver Queen** batch no. 2 db (70) n17 t18 f17 b18 There are no words. Perhaps other than "fish".... 40% (80 proof).

◇◇ **Sui Generis Siren Song** batch no. 6 db (78) n21 t22 f17 b18 Where the Silver Queen was dethroned (and hopefully guillotined), at least this Siren Song has some allure. The big salty nose and big sweet delivery make some kind of sense. But this song goes horribly out of tune as the fade beckons. 40% (80 proof).

FLORIDA FARM DISTILLERS Umatilla, Florida

Palm Ridge Reserve Handmade Micro Batch Florida Whiskey orange and oak wood Less the 1 Year Old batch 29 (94.5) n23 t24 f23.5 b24 I can see why everyone heads to Florida in the winter: obviously to try and grab one of the meager 6,000 bottles of this on offer each year. This is beautifully crafted, truly adorable whiskey where fruit appears to constantly have its hand on the tiller. And rather than blast in like a Hurricane from the sea, it breezes gently around the glass and palate with an easy elegance. I have relatives in Florida: about time I gave them another visit... 45% (90 proof)

GARRISON BROTHERS Hye, Texas.

◇◇ **Garrison Brothers Balmorhea Texas Straight Bourbon Whiskey** db (96.5) n24 where do you start...? With the French toast? The molasses on sour dough bread? The spices which simultaneously prickle yet sooth? The Manuka honey smeared over the overcooked fruitcake? The salty, deep tannin...? t24.5 incredible...just incredible....! The sugars form a toasty, sonorous shield that looks as though they are to batter all before them...then melt into a buttery softness. The molasses are in concentrated form, the toastiness profound yet the bitter-sweet balance always spot on; f24 softens in intensity and lowers in weight, as a good finale should but never loses its shape or integrity with the characteristics shown earlier there until the very final fade; b24 the quality of their whiskey is simply ridiculous. The smaller independent distilleries from outside Kentucky are just not supposed to be this good.... If it doesn't win some kind of Whisky Bible gong, then the standard this year must be extraordinary... 575% (115 poof).

Garrison Brothers Cowboy Bourbon Barrel Proof Aged Four Years #1 panhandle white corn, corn harvest 2011, dist 2012, bott 2017 db (96) n24 t24 f24 b24 These guys have proved once again that they do a mighty mean four-year-old... another improbably spectacular bourbon from Garrison Brothers. 68.5% (137 poof).

Garrison Brothers Single Barrel Texas Straight Bourbon Whiskey Aged Three Years #1 panhandle white corn, corn harvest 2011, cask no. 3306, dist 2012 db (94.5) n23 t23.5 f24.5 b23.5 Oh, my word! What a finale...! Seems at first to be going quietly, then flickers back into life with the most sublime Manuka honey and molasses crescendo, trailing off into softer ulmo honey: almost perfect...! 47% (94 poof). sc. 55 bottles.

◇◇ **Garrison Brothers Single Barrel Texas Straight Bourbon Whiskey Aged Three Years** #1 panhandle white corn, corn harvest 2011, cask no. 3433, dist 2012 db (93.5) n23 a saline edge to the light hickory and liquorice lead...; t23.5 salivating, the oils fragment slightly to allow the chalkier elements of the tannins a bigger say than normal; the sugars are still intense, though and of the darkest, toastiest hue on the palate; f23.5 the molasses and maple syrup redouble their efforts to keep the toastiness at bay b23.5 delicious, but Garrison's whiskey at this strength always seems a fraction under par. 47% (94 poof). sc.

Garrison Brothers Texas Straight Bourbon Whiskey Aged Three Years #1 panhandle white corn, corn harvest 2011, dist 2012, bott 2016 db (88.5) n22 t22.5 f22 b22 This is the first time any whiskey by Garrison has shown the remotest hint of a wide cut. So not quite the usual brilliance, but still plenty to be getting on with... 47% (94 poof).

Cadenhead's Garrison Brothers 4 Years Old dist 2012, bott 2016 (94.5) n24 t23.5 f23 b24 A great move by Cadenhead to bottle a whiskey from a distillery I have raved about for quite a long time. This cask does nothing to undermine the distillery's excellence. 47%. 60 bottles. *Chosen by Peter Siegenthaler.*

GLENNS CREEK DISTILLERY Frankfort, Kentucky.

⋙ **Millville Malt barrel 1** db (91.5) n23 one of those rare aromas where malt whiskey meets bourbon and it is hard to tell which has given way, or if the two worlds have happily teamed up. Golden syrup on the nose sits well with an earthier tannin; t23.5 fabulous. Just fabulous. The delivery does a great job of aping the nose with the sugars arriving early and thickly. There is a light prune fruitiness wandering around while the tannins arrive first quietly then get noiser as the spices take off; the mouth fell is never less than full, beautifully weighted oil-wise and sumptuous; f21.5 there is a slight bitterness here, as well a vague furry quality which may suggest a slight lack of copper. But compared to what has gone on before, a mere detail; b23.5 a distillery located just a mile or two from my house on Glenn's Creek has come up with a malt that defies belief. Massive attention to detail on the cuts has paid dividends and has ensured a clean yet majestically rich addition to the malt whisky lexicon. 57.1% (114.2 proof)

⋙ **OCD #5 Kentucky Bourbon** barrel 16 Aged at least 6 months db (93) n22.5 massive oak presence. Yet the natural sugars are relaxed and sprawl quietly, their Manuka honey notes occasionally catching the odd oak-free moment; t23.5 now that is one superb delivery – almost faultless. At once toasty and juicy, the palate is on full salivation alert as both the tannins and the muscovado sugars do their work. Outstanding layering with flavour wave after flavour wave crashing into the taste buds; f23 dries towards a Jamaican Blue Mountain coffee complexity (with a touch of cream added).a little spice late on as the oak really does ramp up its presence; b24 what a gorgeous bourbon which revels in its exceptional layering. A little gem of a whiskey. 52.2% (114.4 proof)

⋙ **Ryskey** barrel 4 single barrel double oaked db (92.5) n23.5 punchy, solid, spicy rye of the top order. The tannins, literally, float around with a degree of randomness but the ginger and delicate nutmeg move us into new territory...; t23.5 a unique delivery: the grains are screeching at full throttle and matched note for note by the tannin. A blistering, eye-popping start which settles into a spicy and juicy rye fest...; f22 the oak begins to bite now and creates an usually dry finale to this style of rye; b23 the usual excellence from the Lawrenceburg, Indiana, distillery but given a curious twist but the stirring in of some muscular tannin. Attractive and intriguing. 59.3% (118.6 proof) distilled Indiana – oak staves added at Glenns Creek.

⋙ **Stave + Barrel Bourbon** single barrel, double aged db (88.5) n22 full bodied; a little boiled tomato suggests a fruitiness to the grain and probably high rye in the mash bill; good spice, crispy and the lightest hint of mocha; t23 the big rye and sugars flavours explode on delivery. The more hickory and fudgy elements of the bourbon take time to arrive; salivating; f21.5 over bitter, though some very late molasses recovers the situation slightly; b22 full flavoured and salivating, but as well balanced as their Ryskey. 57.9% (115.8 proof) distilled Indiana. Toasted staves added at Glenns Creek.

GOLDEN NORTHWEST DISTILLERY Bow, Washington.

Golden Artisan Spirits Single Barrel Cask Strength (88) n20.5 t22.5 f23 b22 Much more like it! Not exactly textbook but excellent body and some lovely honey touches. 62.3%

GRAND TRAVERSE DISTILLERY Traverse City, Michigan

Bourbon Whiskey (88.5) n21 t22 f23 b22.5 an absolute charmer which just gets better as it goes along. 46% (92 proof)

Ole George Straight Rye Whiskey (80) n19 t21 f20 b20. Hard to mark this one. As a rye, it marks relatively low. As a gin, it would be higher. Not sure why, but there seems to be all kinds of botanical aromas and flavours involved here. Pleasant as a spirit – and I love the mouth feel. But the flavour make up is skewed. 46.5% (93 proof)

GREAT LAKES DISTILLERY Milwaukee, Wisconsin.
KinnicKinnic A Blend of American Whiskies (87) n21.5 t22.5 f21 b22. The bitterness is replaced by an extra dollop of nougat and honey. *43% (86 proof)*

HAMILTON DISTILLERS Tuscon, Arizona.
Whiskey Del Bac Classic Unsmoked Single Malt batch US15-16, bott 19 Aug 15 db **(91) n23 t23 f22 b23** These guys know how to make mighty fine whiskey. Literally, a cut above... *42% (84 proof)*

Whiskey Del Bac Clear Mesquite Smoked Single Malt batch MC15-4, bott 2 Dec 15 db **(91) n21.5 t23 f23.5 b23.** I was in Arizona recently, but sadly didn't make it to this distillery.Shame: I would have loved to have seen how the smoking is carried out for one of the sweetest and most surprisingly soft, idiosyncratic and attractive white dogs currently barking. *45% (90 proof)*

Whiskey Del Bac Dorado Mesquite Smoked Single Malt batch MC16-1, bott 29 Feb 16 db **(94) n23 t23.5 f24b23.5** Dang! I'd sure like to see a bottle of this come sliding up to me next time I'm-a-drinkin' in the Crystal Palace Saloon Bar in Tombstone, yesiree! And I'd take my own dirty glass – one smoked with mesquite!! *45% (90 proof). ncf.*

HIGH WEST DISTILLERY Park City, Utah.
High West Silver Oat (86) n20 t22 f22 b22. A white whiskey which at times struggles to find all the copper it needs. But so delicious is that sweet oat – a style that has enjoyed similar success in Austria – that some of the technical aberrations are forgiven. Soft and friendly. *40%*

HILLROCK ESTATE DISTILLERY Hudson Valley, New York.
Hillrock Double Cask Rye Whiskey American oak barrels, barrel no. Port-4, aged under 4 years db **(88) n22.5 t21.5 f22 b22** A rare case of a Port finish working amid bourbon or rye, mainly because it eliminates the more aggressive vegetable notes and allows the attractive rye a relatively free hand. *45%*

Hillrock Single Malt Whiskey American oak barrels, finished in sherry casks, barrel no. HS-1, aged under 4 years db **(95.5) n23.5 t24 f24 b24** Smoke and fruit rarely make happy bedfellows from a balancing viewpoint. Here they do, doubtless helped by the fact that, for once, the sherry butt does not possess a sulphur-stained edge. You won't get it until about the fifth mouthful: then is all clicks. The classiest of class acts. *48.2%*

Hillrock Solera Aged Bourbon Whiskey American oak barrels, finished in sherry casks, barrel no. 48 db **(89) n22.5 t23 f21.5 b22** A rare case of the wine finish working with a bourbon, but probably because the grape remains subtle. *48.2%*

HOUSE SPIRITS DISTILLERY Portland, Oregon
Westward Oregon Straight Malt Whiskey 2 Years Old batch 1 **(92.5) n23 t23.5 f23 b23.5** Two years old, perhaps. But absolute star quality with the barley pulsing at every turn: just so satisfyingly mouth-filling and palate teasing. Another great whiskey from Portland. *45%*

◇ **Westward American Single Malt Whiskey** new American oak barrels, bott 06.28.17 db **(91.5) n23** rich: not unlike a spiced treacle sponge cake; **t23** sweet and intense. Spices nip and throb while tannins bark out its weight. The molasses and ulmo honey keep things on a sweet, malty keel; **f22.5** a little oily bitterness can't disrupt the comfortable yet complex flow; **b23** interesting how in the years since I lasted tasted this it has moved from an Oregon Straight malt to American Single Malt, perhaps reflecting the greater interest in the USA of home grown single malts. However they see it, this is a big and enjoyable whiskey. *45% (90 proof). ncf.*

IRON SMOKE WHISKEY Fairport, New York.
Iron Smoke Apple Wood Smoked Whiskey batch no. 9, bott 4/2/16 db **(94.5) n23.5 t23.5 f23.5 b24** An unconventional whiskey from Fairport. Though by no means the first apple wood smoked, it has less vigour than its Virginian forefather and no shortage of class...With it having a little more body than the skeletal 40%abv, handle with care as this would be too easy to get smashed out of your skull... Love it! *40% (80 proof)*

Iron Smoke Apple Wood Smoked Whiskey batch no. 10, bott 7/8/16 db **(95.5) n24 t24 f23.5 b24** This is extraordinary whiskey. Normally I'd advise that a distiller ups from 40 to 46% abv minimum in order to keep the oils intact. Yet this barely needs it and shows a heftier personality that their last, excellent bottling. Genuinely sublime. *40% (80 proof).*

Iron Smoke Apple Wood Smoked Whiskey batch no. 11, bott 3/28/17 db **(93.5) n23 t23 f23.5 b24** Quite a step down in terms of weight and intensity to their last batch, as though this is a little younger. But most rewarding to see two different styles, yet both of the highest standard. Congratulations to these guys for really taking care with their whiskey. 40% (80 proof).

⬩ **Iron Smoke Four Grain Bourbon With Apple Wood Smoked Wheat Aged A Minimum of Two Years** barrel no. 196, bott 4/11/18 db (**94**) n23.5 unusually for this distillery, the apple wood appears to have thrown up an unexpected but not unwelcome orangey kumquat facet to the nose, lightening the style slightly but not so much that the heavier phenols don't have an important and delicious say; t23.5 improbably salivating on delivery, the spices and sugars from the wheat kicking in early and with meaning. Demerara sugars and liquorice develop and then dissolve; f23 wheat is still on the radar even late on while the lingering smoke and spice just, well, linger...; b24 just all fits together like a hand-made shoe and no less comfortable. 45% (90 proof). sc. Bottled for DW Select.

JOHN EMERALD DISTILLING COMPANY Opelika, Alabama.

⬩ **John's Alabama Single Malt Whiskey Aged Less Than 4 Years** batch no. 59 db (**87.5**) n22 t22 f21.5 b22 Interesting they have a horse on their label as this pleasant offering never quite reaches a trot. The natural caramels offer only an outline of the pecan and peach smoke. Instead it is the mix of barley and toffee which dominate...slowly and drowsily. 43% (86 proof).

⬩ **John's Alabama Single Malt Whiskey Aged Less Than 4 Years** batch no. 63 db (**86**) n21 t21 f22.5 b21.5 Far more oil abroad here, unmistakably from the distillation. That pays off on the finish which is longer and more intense than normal, and very comfortable, too. Again, no great complexity to speak of, just an enjoyable degree of malt and toffee at large with the smoke stirring up light spices. 43% (86 proof).

⬩ **John's Alabama Single Malt Whiskey Aged Less Than 4 Years** batch no. 65 db (**89.5**) n23 by far the smokiest of the three bottlings here. A real buzz to this, slightly acidic and with depth like a bonfire toffee chew...; t22 usual big caramel surge, but with some extra spicy zing; malt thrives at the midpoint, as does the spice; f22 a lovely black pepper buzz; b22.5 the extra surge of smoke has added a degree of dynamism to the charming house simplicity. 43% (86 proof).

JOURNEYMAN DISTILLERY Three Oaks, Michigan.

Journeyman Buggy Whip Wheat Whiskey batch 38 db (**94.5**) n24 t23.5 f23 b24 I'll climb aboard this buggy any day. What a beautiful wheat whiskey this is...cracking, in fact...! 45% (90 proof).

Journeyman Featherbone Bourbon Whiskey batch 72 db (**84**) n21 t21.5 f20 b21.5 The first mouthful of this flung me back 50 years to when I was a kid tucked up in bed and having to swallow a couple of spoons-worth of cherry-flavoured cough syrup. I can picture their salesmen getting people to gather round and peddling this as Dr Journeyman's Elixir for Coughs and Colds. In truth, though, a forceful corn-rich, oily, muscovado-sugared bag of tricks. 45% (90 proof).

Journeyman Last Feather Rye Whiskey batch 72 db (**91**) n22.5 t23.5 f22 b23 Truly a unique rye whiskey profile and one, that despite the odd fault, literally carries you on a delicious journey. 45% (90 proof).

Journeyman Silver Cross Whiskey batch 61 db (**86**) n22 t22 f20.5 b21.5 I am a fan of this fascinating distillery, that's for sure, and wondering what they are up to next. Not sure if this was designed to ward off vampires, but to be on the safe side I tasted this long after the sun set. A serious mish-mash of a whiskey which celebrated a rich ulmo-honey sweetness, but is ultimately undone by a bitterness which, sadly, no amount of sugar can keep fully under control and gets you in the neck in the end... 45% (90 proof).

KINGS COUNTY DISTILLERY Brooklyn, New York.

Kings County Distillery Barrel Strength Straight Bourbon Whiskey Aged Two Years or More batch no. 6, dist Fall 2012, bott Fall 2016 db (**84**) n22.5 t22 20.5 21 Tannin and liquorice on steroids: the palate gets more splinters than a pole dancer straddling and spinning round a plank of tinder wood.... This is insane whiskey but a must for sap suckers... 63%.

Kings County Distillery Bottled-in-Bond Straight Bourbon Whiskey Four Years Old batch no. 3 db (**94**) n24 t23 f23.5 b23.5 Easy to mistake as a fine old Kentucky bourbon: there is no higher praise than that...!! 50%.

Kings County Distillery Peated Bourbon Whiskey aged one year or more, batch no. p4 db (**94**) n23.5 t24 f23 b23.5 No problem with this. You can use peat-smoked grain and still produce bourbon, which is how I assume this was produced. Just not a bourbon finished in a peated cask. That ain't bourbon. Whatever this is – and it appears to be the former – it is quite stunningly lovely. 45%

⬩ **Kings County Distillery Straight Bourbon Whiskey Aged Two Years or More** batch no. 142 db (**89**) n22 demerara sugars on liquorice; t23 this distillery knows how to kick off with a Kentucky style liquorice and hickory volley. Lovely treacle and caramel follow up; f22.5 a real lingering bourbony liquorice stamp as the tannins keep their shape; b22.5 keeps it simple and satisfying. 45% (90 proof).

◇◇ **Kings County Distillery Straight Rye Whiskey Aged Two Years or More** batch no. 1 db **(88)** n22.5 the crispness of the rye is matched only by the spice; t23 superb delivery, soft oils balancing the crunchiness of the grain. Fruity muscovado sugars drift and meet a warm pepperiness; f20.5 a shade too bitter; b22 KC's first entry into rye is a success: the grain is profound and every bit as salivating as it should be. Room for improvement, but some great moments. 51% (101 proof).

KOVAL DISTILLERY Chicago, Illinois.

◇◇ **Koval Single Barrel Malt Whiskey** barrel no. 4009 db **(91)** n22.5 such a complex nose: slightly surreal, too. I could swear I'm getting that lightly peppery sweat smell of boiled crab amid the rich malt; t23 one of the most intense malt deliveries I've experienced from the USA. The balance of those husky, gristy notes with the firm tannin is delightful; f22.5 light molasses and spikey tannins; b23 these guys really know how to distil really good whiskey... Of all America's whiskeys I have ever sampled only a single malt I tasted in Maryland in 1974 boasted a more concentrated maltiness than this. 40% (80 proof). sc.

KOZUBA & SONS DISTILLERY INC. St. Petersburg, Florida.

Mr. Rye Straight Rye Malt Whisky virgin American oak barrels db **(91)** n23 big, impressive, unmistakable rye character, intensified and thickened by it being malt, so a little less crisp. Technically not quite perfect but the spices clear the nose beautifully; t23.5 fabulous delivery! No prisoners taken, no shelter offered. Just pounding rye which offers a massive degree of layering; so many layers, in fact, almost impossible to count. Just so thick and chewy; f22 the oils from the wide cut begin to create a bit of a slick; the spices carry on regardless; b22.5 Okay, the cut has been maximised, but forgivably so. The quality of the rye malt is very high. 45%. ncf.

LAS VEGAS DISTILLERY Las Vegas, Nevada.

Nevada 150 Bourbon Whiskey American white oak barrels, aged 2 years, 4 months db **(92)** n24 t22.5 f22.5 b23.5 Who would have thought that the loudest, brashest city in the world could conjure the most delicate, intricate and shy bourbon for many a year? Don't let this whisky fool you: it has much to say...but all in whispers...45% (90 proof). 2,014 bottles.

LAWS WHISKEY HOUSE Denver, Colorado.

A.D. Law Four Grain Straight Bourbon Whiskey Aged No Less Than 3 Years batch no. 10 db **(87)** n21 t22.5 f21.5 b22 So close to being a magnificent whiskey. It is all there: the marzipan, the maple syrup, the chocolate-liquorice. Acting like a ball and chain are gentle feints which - now you see it, now you don't – have crept stealthily into the mix. Still plenty to delight. 47.5% (95 proof).

A.D. Law Four Grain Straight Bourbon Whiskey Aged No Less Than 3 Years batch no. 11 db **(82)** n20.5 t21 f20 b20.5 If Batch 10 is borderline with the cut, this one has strayed openly into feints territory, the dull bite and spice confirming the nose's hefty tones. 47.5% (95 proof).

A.D. Law Four Grain Straight Bourbon Whiskey Aged No Less Than 3 Years Cask Strength barrel no. 316 db **(94)** n22 t24.5 f23.5 b24 How can you not slightly fall in love with this distillery's whiskey...? 56.7% (113.4 proof).

◇◇ **A.D. Law Four Grain Straight Bourbon Whiskey Aged Over 3 Years** batch no. 15, 53 gallon white American oak char 3 barrels db **(85.5)** n20.5 t22.5 f21 b21.5 On the feinty side of right. Top rate demerara sugars, light caramels and mocha on the plus side but those errant oils are a bit of a hurdle. 47.5% (95 proof).

◇◇ **A.D. Law Four Grain Straight Bourbon Whiskey Aged 5.2 Years** batch no. 174, 53 gallon white American oak char 3 barrels db **(90)** n23 a real sense of scorched oak at work here, the tannins salty and business like. Red liquorice, thin Manuka honey and, strangely, sweet crab meat...; t23 concentrated everything: oak, corn oils, rye. This is juicy and deep, treacle seeping into the hickory; f21.5 flattens as caramel moves in; b22.5 very good aged oakiness to the big bourbon. 59.3% (118.6 proof).

A.D. Law Four Grain Straight Bourbon Whiskey Aged 5.5 Years barrel no. 1 db **(92.5)** n24 t23 f22.5 b23 The textbook nose is not a perfect match with the more cumbersome delivery and follow through. That said, what a fabulous experience...; 47.5% (95 proof).

A.D. Law Four Grain Straight Bourbon Whiskey Bottled in Bond Aged No Less Than 4 Years batch no. 1 db **(93)** n23 t24 f22.5 b23.5 Only a fractionally wide cut means the corn oils don't become too stodgy while the honey gets a good hearing. 50% (100 proof).

A.D. Law Four Grain Straight Bourbon Whiskey Bottled in Bond Aged No Less Than 4 Years batch no. A17 db **(92)** n23.5 t23 f22.5 b23 Its minor sin can be easily forgiven after such a heavenly experience. *50% (100 proof).*

◈ **A.D. Law Four Grain Straight Bourbon Whiskey Bottled in Bond Aged Over 4 Years** batch no. B-17-S, 53 gallon white American oak char 3 barrels db **(94)** n22.5 a right busybody: the small grains have a lot to chat about and let you hear it...; t24 seriously grandee and mega-complex, salivating delivery: again a real twittering of grains with the palate at full stretch to intercept and decode all the messages which come through at some volume. The chocolate fudge middle acts as lovely backdrop, but it is the rye and muscovado sugars which take centre ground; the slow build of spice is sublime; f23.5 the spices still pulse and the grains still natter and chatter; more vanilla now but with cocoa, too; b24 really impressive and complex whiskey. *50% (100 proof). Summer Season.*

◈ **A.D. Law Four Grain Straight Bourbon Whiskey Ruby Port Finish Aged Over 4 Years** db **(82.5)** n20 t21.5 f21 b20 Not sure how a straight bourbon (requiring virgin oak) can be finished in a ruby port cask. Still, it hardly matters as this is no gem, the dull fruit flattening the complexity of the grains like an out of control steamroller. *47.5% (95 proof).*

A.D. Law Hordeum Straight Malt Whiskey Aged No Less Than 3 Years batch no. 1 db **(79)** n18 t20 f21 b20 Improves as it goes along – it has to. The nose is a shock to the system, the delivery, initially, a little odd. Has a few moments in the sun with malt and golden syrup to the fore. But never mind: there is always the bourbon and corn! *42.5% (85 proof).*

A.D. Law Secale Straight Rye Whiskey Aged No Less Than 4 Years batch no. A17 db **(87)** n22 t21 f22.5 b21.5 A relatively lightweight rye considering the feints with a distinct tartness which I think I have encountered in Law's whiskey before. The chocolate is a late treat. *50% (100 proof).*

A.D. Law Secale Straight Rye Whiskey Aged No Less Than 4 Years batch no. B17 db **(89.5)** n23.5 t23.5 f21 b21.5 Some ryes are crisp and blow you away with their mix of power and dazzling finesse. There are others which are chunky and too hefty to really allow the grain to fly and sing. This bottling is stuck about halfway between the two... Give it a few minutes for the feints to burn off slightly and the nose and delivery really are special. *50% (100 proof).*

◈ **A.D. Law Secale Straight Rye Whiskey Aged 4.5 Years** batch no. 172, 53 gallon white American oak char 3 barrels db **(95)** n23.5 beautifully defined, brittle rye, shewing some very sexy contours; t24 brilliant! The rye arrives crisp and bursting with fresh, juicy character even more pronounced when about five minutes of the Murray Method burns off and evaporates the worst of the excess oils. A fabulous blend of Manuka and muscovado sugar is the result while the spices pile in with an orange and blue flame; f23.5 the juicy crispness of the rye has not remotely softened: 10% true to the grain, through the death; b24 a mixture of indigenous oils and The Murray Method makes this the easiest 70+% abv whiskey you'll ever taste. Talk about a gentle giant...! By far the best rye I've seen from A D Law and deserves to stand proudly beside America's finest. This is, truly, a Law unto itself... *71.5% (143 proof).*

◈ **A.D. Law Secale Straight Rye Whiskey Bottled in Bond Aged Over 4 Years** batch no. C-17-F, 53 gallon white American oak char 3 barrels db **(86)** n20.5 t23 f20.5 b22 A more usual Law rye: technically not quite the full shilling, but for sheer, unadulterated ryeness it has few peers. *50% (100 proof). Fall Season.*

A.D. Law Straight Corn Whiskey Bottled in Bond Aged No Less Than 4 Years batch no. 1 db **(94.5)** n23.5 t23.5 f23.5 b24 Just returned from a two mile walk in the country with the spring sun setting: it reminded me of many such walks in Kentucky. Oddly enough, so, too, does this excellent and magnificently distilled corn whiskey. I'm really impressed with this! *50% (100 proof).*

A.D. Law Triticom Straight Wheat Whiskey Aged No Less Than 3 Years batch no. 1A db **(91.5)** n22 t23.5 f22.5 b23.5 A sticky bread pudding of a whiskey where the sugars and spices enter a previously unknown universe...Unique..? I should say so... A must try once in a lifetime experience. *50% (100 proof).*

◈ **A.D. Law Triticom Straight Wheat Whiskey Aged Over 3 Years** batch no. 2, 53 gallon white American oak char 3 barrels db **(92.5)** n22 not as outwardly spicy as their first batch, thanks to a little extra vanilla. But they are there, all right, busily nipping away; t24 now that is stunning: a firmer delivery than I remember with molasses and Manuka honey arriving earlier two and in greater force. The spices take time to make their mark, but once established they continue turning up the heat...wow! f23 a deeply satisfying finale: the whiskey has kept its shape and order and it is just a question of the sweetness and fires fading away; b23.5 fans of Wheat Whiskey will be delighted with this deliciously bold and memorable offering. *50% (100 proof).*

A.D. Law Two Grain Straight Bourbon Whiskey Bottled in Bond Aged No Less Than 4 Years batch no. 1A db **(92.5)** n23 t24 f22.5 b23 Beautifully distilled. *50% (100 proof).*

LOST SPIRITS DISTILLERY Monterey County, California.

Abomination The Crying of the Puma Heavily Peated Malt (93) n23.5 t24 f22.5 b23 An utterly baffling experience. This is, for all intents and purposes a Scotch whisky: at least in personality. If this was distilled in the US, then they have cracked it. The thing I particularly couldn't work out was an unrecognisable fruit edge. And after tasting I dug out the bottle and read the small print (so small, the detail was left off the heading by my researchers) that Riesling seasoned oak staves had been used. From the bizarre label and even brand name to the battle on your palate this is a bewildering and nonsensical whisky – if it is whisky at all, as the term is never used. But wholly delicious if raw... and boasting an impact that blows the taste buds' doors down... 54%. nc ncf.

Abomination The Sayers of the Law Heavily Peated Malt (94) n23 t23.5 t24 b23.5 More of the same as The Crying of the Puma. Except, despite the identical strength, this has a softer all-round feel and a much more Caol Ila-style oiliness to sooth and maximise the length of the sugars and lighten the smoky load. The fruit here is negligible other than muscovado sugar mixing in with the liquorice and ulmo honey. Feels older than the Puma and the spices are far more accentuated yet controlled, especially towards the complex coffee-stained finale. 54%. nc ncf.

MIDDLE WEST SPIRITS Columbus, Ohio

OYO Dark Pumpernickel Rye Whiskey db (77) n20 t21.5 f17.5 b18 Too many tangy, bitter notes to ever feel comfortable, though the intensity of the rye for a brief spell after delivery has much going for it. Very similar to a number of central European distilleries who have yet to completely master their stills. But it is that tangy bitterness on the finish that most urgently needs eradicating. 45% (90 proof).

OYO Michelone Reserve Bourbon Whiskey db (86) n22.5 t22 f20 b21.5 A mainly attractive, restrained bourbon showing limited age and therefore depth. Lovely small grains to the busy nose and the sugars rise early before the buttery spices begin, but runs out of steam quite soon after. Not too happy with the tangy finish. 45% (90 proof).

OYO Oloroso Wheat Whiskey db (88) n23.5 t22.5 f20 22 As any good wheat whiskey should, this radiates spices with abandon. The fruit helps paper over some cracks in the distillate, especially towards the weak finish. 51% (102 proof).

OYO Sherry Finished Bourbon Whiskey db (86.5) n22 t22 f21 b21.5 My experience with sherry-finished whisky over the last two decades meant it was a case of "oh, no!" when I saw this, rather than OYO. However, the wine cask here is entirely sulphur free and clean, and instead of dirtying the whiskey, as is tragically so often the case in Scotland, actually goes a long way to overcoming some contentious elements of the distillate. Good spice and even better sweet grape theme. 43.25% (86.5 proof).

MISSISSIPPI RIVER DISTILLERY Le Claire, Indiana

Cody Road Rye 2013 Batch 4 (86.5) n23 t22.5 f20 b21. The clean, fruity unambiguous rye on the nose is stunning. There is nothing too shoddy about the crisp, juicy grain on delivery, either. Just bitters out a little too enthusiastically from the midpoint onwards. 40%

MOYLAN'S DISTILLING COMPANY Petaluma, California.

Moylan's American Cask Strength Single Malt Whisky Aged 4 Years finished in orange brandy, stout & French oak chardonnay barrels db (80) n19 t23 f19 b19. Ladies and Gentlemen of Moylan. I cannot fault you for your kaleidoscopic delivery which enthrals and entertains with a wild and delicious a cross section of fruity riches as you are likely to find. But remember: it is about balance. So don't lose sight of what a wide cut and hops from the stout can do... 58.7% (117.4 proof)

NELSON'S GREEN BRIER DISTILLERY Nashville, Tennessee.

Belle Meade Aged 9 Years Sherry Bourbon finished in Oloroso sherry casks, batch no. 3 (87) n22 t22 f21 b22 A far better sherry bottling than I tasted before from these guys. The actual bourbon itself is able to poke through the smothering fruit with far greater energy. The fruit is clean and clear enough to offer a second dimension, though still not too keen on that soupy flavour profile. 45.2% (90.4 proof). Bottled by Nelson's Green Brier Distillery.

Belle Meade Cognac Bourbon finished in XO Cognac casks, batch no. 2 (78.5) n21 t20 f18.5 b19 Very frustrating. This distillery makes a very high class bourbon which is a joy to experience, and here it is being muzzled by the restrictive limitations of a poor Cognac cask. Seriously and untidily bitter from the midpoint onwards. 45.2% (90.4 proof).

Belle Meade Madeira Bourbon finished in Malmsey Madeira casks, batch no. 6 (89) n23 t22 f21.5 b22.5 Give me a straight bourbon over a cask finished job any day. But this works as well as they come and even offers a degree of sophistication. 45.2% (90.4 proof). Bottled by Nelson's Green Brier Distillery.

NEW HOLLAND BREWING COMPANY Holland, Michigan.
New Holland Beer Barrel Bourbon American white oak db (83) n21.5 t21.5 f20 b20 For those who aren't the greatest fans of lightly hopped whiskey, slightly more bearable than their rye bottling... 40% (80 proof).

New Holland Beer Barrel Rye American white oak db (80) n21 t21 f19 b19 Were this from Speyside, I daresay it would be called hopscotch... The hoppiest whisk(e)y I have tasted anywhere in the world. Apart from a brief chocolate intervention, this is seriously not my kind of thing. I mean: I love whisky and I love beer. But just not together. Less befuddled by it than befuggled... 40% (80 proof).

New Holland Zeppelin Bend Reserve American Single Malt sherry cask finish db (87) n22 t21.5 f22 b21.5 My Panama off to the chaps at Zep Bend for finding some outstanding sherry casks to help infuse the most wonderful, succulent grape note to this mouth-filling malt and slow-burning cocoa. Rich fruit cake at its most moist and spicy, though a slight, off-key hop note somewhat paddles against the style and grain. Otherwise, close to being a stunner. 45% (90 proof).

Pitchfork Wheat Michigan-Grown Wheat Whiskey aged 14 months, American oak barrels db (93) n22.5 t23.5 f23.5 b23.5 So love it! Like a digestive biscuit you want to dunk in your coffee...By far and away the best thing I have ever seen from this distillery: this really is top drawer microdistillery whiskey just brimming with flavours and personality. Genuinely impressed. 45% (90 proof).

Zeppelin Bend Straight Malt Whiskey American oak barrels db (84.5) n21 t21.5 f21 b21 The Zep is back!! Not seen it for a while and this is a new model. Actually, in some ways barely recognise it from the last one I saw about five years ago. Much more effervescent than before, though that curious hop note I remember not only persists but appears to have been upped slightly. 45% (90 proof).

OLD LINE SPIRITS Baltimore, Maryland.
◈ **Old Line Single Malt American Whiskey Aged at Least One Year** (87.5) n22 t22 f21.5 b22 A beautifully calm and majestic malt whisky which suffers a little from being a touch too round and elegant. Beautifully distilled, the thinned Manuka honey and natural caramels appear to fill every gap, other than a slight bitterness at the death. At times, though, spends a little too much time in the doldrums. 43% (86 proof). Distilled at Middle West Spirits.

◈ **Old Line Single Malt American Whiskey Cask Strength Aged at Least One Year** batch no. 1M (92) n22.5 molasses and dates to the fore; t23.5 superb delivery, the big Manuka honey and malt heaving and pitching in the storm. Tannins are also biting deep as the mouth chews and chews this one until it aches; f23 vanilla and caramel at the aft and no little spice, either; b23 an altogether more impressive sailing than their 43% version. Not least because of the oils, destroyed at the weaker strength, are able to encourage the richer segments of the malt to work full speed ahead. Excellent. 60% (120 proof). Distilled at Middle West Spirits.

PALMETTO DISTILLERY Anderson, South Carolina.
◈ **Palmetto Moonshine Bootlegger Proof Corn Whiskey** db (92) n23.5 t23 f22.5 b23 As one might expect, this is along the same lines as their Lightning white dog (see below) except the oils are more intact ensure greater length and a cocoa powder finish demanded of new make of this strength. Beautifully made, the corn gets every opportunity to shine. 65% (130 proof).

◈ **Palmetto Moonshine White Lightning Corn Whiskey** db (91) n23 t23.5 f22 b22.5 Apart from a slight thinning of the copper effect on the finish, this is near flawless white dog. Sweet and exceptionally well distilled the corn profits by the cleanness of the cut. 52.5% (105 proof).

◈ **Palmetto Whiskey** new French oak db (84) n20.5 t22.5 f21 b20 Despite the high rye content this simply overdoses on chocolate caramel. Has been bottled at a time when the balance isn't quite right. 44.65% (89.3 proof).

PARLIAMENT DISTILLERY Sumner, Washington.
Ghost Owl Pacific Northwest Whisky db (88.5) n21.5 t22.5 f22 b22.5 On the sugary side of matters. But keeps just enough heavier tannin in reserve to ensure balance. 45% (90 proof)

Ghost Owl Pacific Northwest Rye Whisky db (94.5) n23 t23.5 f24 b24 Simply outstanding rye. Can't lose, really: my favourite grain (rye) being distilled in one of my favourite places on the planet (the Pacific north west of USA) and one of my favourite birds on the label (a barn owl). Actually, quite recently, I was doing some work in a lab at a distillery in India when I walked into a nearby wood to stretch my legs, rest my nose and enjoy 15 minutes of bird watching. There was suddenly a clattering above my head, strange shadows on the forest floor before me and then a crashing sound and soft thud. Astonishingly, a barn owl had fallen dead from the sky just three or four feet from where I stood. Spooky. And almost as dramatic as this stunning rye. 45% (90 proof)

PEACH STREET DISTILLERS Pallisade, Colorado.

Colorado Straight Bourbon Aged More Than Two Years batch 40 **(92.5) n22.5 t23.5 f23 b23.5** The last bottle I tasted was around the batch 20 mark and was an impressive intro to this distillery. Remarkably, this batch enjoys an almost identical thumb print. But now there is much more sharpness and definition. Superb! 46% (92 proof)

RANGER CREEK DISTILLING, San Antonio, Texas

Ranger Creek .36 Texas Bourbon (93) n23 t23.5 f23 b23.5 I would so love to get back to Texas and have this wash down a plate-filling, half cooked ribeye. It's pretty obvious they have used small barrels to create a gentle giant like this – even before you find confirmation on the bottle. This comes under their Small Caliber series of whiskeys. Don't you believe it: this is a howitzer of a bourbon. 48% (96 proof)

Ranger Creek .36 White db **(84) n21 t22 f20 b21**. A white dawg whose tail doesn't always wag. A deliciously jaw-dropping, juicy array of grain on delivery. But needs to get the copper content up to ensure a better pedigree. 50% (100 proof)

Ranger Creek Rimfire Mesquite Smoked Texas Single Malt batch 1 **(85) n21.5 t22 f20.5 b21**. As I have never tasted anything smoked with mesquite before – especially whiskey – I will have to guess that it is the tree of the semi-desert which is imparting a strange, mildly bitter tang on the finish. Whether it is also responsible for the enormous degree of creamed toffee, I am also not sure. Enjoyable, fascinating even...but something the ol' taste buds need a bit of acclimatising to. 43% (86 proof)

RANSOM SPIRITS Sheridan, Oregon.

◇ **Ransom The Emerald 1865** batch no. 005 db **(86.5) n21 t23 f21 b21.5** "This whiskey rings a bell", thought I. Brilliant delivery, magnificently complex grains at play, but OTT feints. I've tasted this one before, I concluded. And, on checking in a previous Bible, I see I had a couple of years back, though an earlier bottling and then not called The Emerald. Brilliant Irish style mix of malted and unmalted barley. But just need to sort that cut out. 43.8%.

◇ **Ransom Rye, Barley, Wheat Whiskey Aged a Minimum of 2 Years** batch no. 003 db **(85.5) n21 t22 f21 b21.5** A little too much earthiness to this for its own good, meaning the wheat has to fight hard to get its sweet and spicy message out there. Needs a tad more copper in the system to get the most out of this whiskey, as a metallic spark appears missing. Just love this distillery's labels, by the way: real class. 63.4%.

RESERVOIR DISTILLERY Richmond, Virginia.

Reservoir Distillery Bourbon Whiskey batch no. 1, bott 2017 db **(93) n24 t23.5 f22 b23.5** Big, buxom, bang on the money bourbon! 50% (100 proof).

Reservoir Distillery Bourbon Whiskey batch no. 2, bott 2017 db **(92.5) n23** lighter tannins with plenty of moist date; **t23** corn oil drenched in maple syrup. A little ulmo honey tones the sweetness down; soft caramels lighten things further; **f23** much more relaxed finale than batch 1 with far less oak intrusion; **b23.5** no shrinking violet. But nothing like so muscular as the last batch, making the most of the natural caramels. 50% (100 proof).

◇ **Reservoir Distillery Bourbon Whiskey 100% Corn** batch no. 18, bott 2017 db **(88.5) n22.5** they claim 100% corn for this "bourbon" and the nose doesn't disagree...; **t23** sweet delivery and oily textured. A distinct custardy personality here, though a lot more juicy than most 100% corn whiskeys; **f21** bit of a strange hoppy bitter, beery kick to the finale, though the butterscotch tart finale is divine; **b22** OK, this is my 595th whiskey for Bible 2019 and either I am getting punch drunk or physically drunk, though the latter – seeing as I spit every whiskey – is highly unlikely. But how can a bourbon be 100% corn? By definition that is Corn Whisky, surely.... 50% (100 proof).

◇ **Reservoir Distillery Holland's Blade Rummer** batch no. 1, bott 2017 db **(86) n21.5 t22 f21 b21.5** Feisty at first, then full of fudge, though the chocolate element redeems it a little. 53.5% (107 proof).

Reservoir Distillery Bourbon Whiskey Holland's Brew batch no. 1, bott 2017 db **(83.5) n21 t22 f20 b20.5** A wider cut ramps up the sugars and oils. But loses some of the overall balance and excellence of their standard bourbon. 50% (100 proof).

◇ **Reservoir Distillery Holland's Ghost** batch no. 1, bott 2017 db **(87) n22 t21 f22 b22** Steeped high with personality. But for some reason the sharp, angular flavour doesn't quite ring true until it steadies itself into a more docile and delicious chocolate mousse finale. 53.5% (107 proof).

◇ **Reservoir Distillery Hunter & Scott Bourbon Whiskey** batch no. 4, bott 2018 db **(84) n21 t22 f20 b21** The feints are over cooked here making hard work of what might have been a sweet and chewy bourbon full of small grain complexity. 45% (90 proof).

◈ **Reservoir Distillery Mash-Up Series Ardent IPA** batch no. 2, bott 2017 db (62) n15 t17 f15 b15 In whisky, hops are hops and malt is malt: and never the twains should meet... more a fuck up than a mash up. *45% (90 proof).*

◈ **Reservoir Distillery Mash-Up Series Hardywood Park Gingerbread Stout** batch no. 1, bott 2017 db (67) n15 t18 f17 b17 Pretty awful, especially the nauseating nose. Please good people of Reservoir Distillery, you are able to produce seriously good whisky, so I beg of you, give up this beer cask folly: it is doing your reputation – and my constitution – no good whatsoever. And if anyone is telling you they like this Mash-Up stuff, they either have no taste or are lying. *45% (90 proof).*

◈ **Reservoir Distillery Reserve Rye Whiskey 100% Rye** batch no. 4, bott 2017 db (91) n23 no mistakin' this grain... any more crisp and it'll smash into a 1,000 fruity pieces...; t23.5 the beautifully crafted fruity rye hits the palate as it does the nose: sure-footed and ridiculously crisp; f22 the tannins and oils make matters a tad more soft and vanilla-rich, though the rye fights on proudly; b22.5 an incorrigible rye with the grain leaking out of every pore. *50% (100 proof).*

Reservoir Distillery Rye Whiskey batch no. 1, bott 2017 db (91.5) n23.5 t23 f22 b23 Made a little bit of a rod for its own back last year by releasing one of the best rye whiskeys of the year. The 2017 bottling remains delicious but the extra oils from the distillate make it harder for the grain to make the same dashing performance. *50% (100 proof).*

Reservoir Distillery Rye Whiskey batch 2, bott 2016 db (95.5) n24 t24 f23.5 b24 There must be something in the DNA of the average Virginian in knowing how to make rye whiskey. I adore Richmond and I no less adore very good rye: indeed, I will always be proud to be its first advocate. I have some of my happiest memories of all time travelling in Virginia (the first time way back in 1967, now 50 years ago), and once with someone who was, still is and forever will be, very, very special. A truly great bitter-sweet whiskey to rekindle some beautiful, bitter-sweet memories... *50% (100 proof).*

Reservoir Distillery Wheat Whiskey batch no. 1, bott 2017 db (91) n23 t23 f22.5 b22.5 A beautiful, understated wheat whiskey and a clear step up from the previous bottling. *50% (100 proof).*

◈ **Reservoir Distillery Wheat Whiskey 100% Wheat** batch no. 2, bott 2018 db (92) n24 spices galore! t23.5 spices ashore...! The delivery is a series of high octane spices crashing onto the taste buds with a brilliant brown, crusty bread – Hovis – back up. Vanilla and toasted mallows fill in any void; f21.5 biters out annoyingly; b23 some of the better moments are as good as a micro-distillery gets. *50% (100 proof).*

ROCK TOWN DISTILLERY Little Rock, Arkansas.

◈ **Rock Town Arkansas Straight Bourbon Whiskey Aged 3 Years** db (85) n21.5 t22 f21 b21 Has its butterscotch and molasses moments, but too much mysterious bitterness intervenes here. *46%.*

◈ **Rock Town Arkansas Four Grain Sour Mash Bourbon Whiskey Aged 20 Months** batch no. 5 db (91.5) n23 a lovely mix of late evening summer flower and bolder bourbony notes: a hickory and maple syrup mix starring; t23 despite the surprisingly big oils on delivery there is a pleasing ruggedness to the oak and small grain mix. There appears to be rye at the cutting edge, offering a sharp fruitiness which burrows deep into the palate; light caramels and and mch follow through; f22.5 the mocha has found its home; b23 a satisfyingly intricate and impressively complex whiskey. *46%.*

◈ **Rock Town Arkansas Bourbon Whiskey Aged 19 Months** batch no. 49 db (94) n22.5 masses of natural caramel; quite chocolatey, too; the tannins are present but under control; t24 a delivery to die for: the weight and texture of the mouth feel is exemplary. Oily, yes. But such is the richness of the flavour profile, all is forgiven. Here we have a ridiculous degree of chocolate fudge; salivating, especially when the red liquorice gets going, too; f23.5 just more and more of the same. Amen...; b24 I really do love this distillery... *46%.*

◈ **Rock Town Arkansas Bourbon Whiskey Flavour Grain Series Chocolate Malt Aged 12 Months** db (89.5) n22 big oaky statement with accompanying spice. It is the vanilla which carries the light cocoa strands; t23 beautifully mouth-filling. The soft oils carry the tannins and molasses with aplomb but it is not until the sun is about to set do the rays of chocolate finally light the palate; f22 a sensuous praline note plus oil; b22.5 when Glenmorangie brought out the first whisky I was ever aware of containing chocolate malt, its character was such I was able to identify the grain to their blender even before he admitted it was in there. This version is not quite so clear cut due to both the impact of the oak, the extra oiliness from the stills and the fact it is here a secondary grain. But it is there for sure and a good test of your nosing and tasting skills... *46%.*

◈ **Rock Town Arkansas Bourbon Whiskey Flavour Grain Series Golden Promise Aged 12 Months** db (88.5) n22 the barley gets a decent hearing despite the rich oak tones. A little hay and honey, too; t22 soft and best buddy friendly. Big toasted honeycomb centre dominates; f22 another sighting of the grain late on; b22.5 an intense feller, and certainly golden. 46%.

⬙ **Rock Town Arkansas Bourbon Whiskey Flavour Grain Series Peated Malt Aged 12 Months** db (92) n22.5 bitty and busy, harmonising rather beautifully only after a little effort; t23 much more together here, tranquil even. The oak is a shade arrogant, but a pretty succession of honey and caramel waves brings it back in line; f22.5 gentle vanillas and a slow build of ulmo honey; b23 a complex, almost disorganised bourbon, which tries to send you on several different routes simultaneously. Fully worth the effort of getting to understand. 46%.

⬙ **Rock Town Arkansas Rye Whiskey Aged 18 Months** batch no. 19 db (94) n23.5 the rye is so well defined and fruity! You could cut diamonds with this...; t23 salivating, the rye works on both a crisp and fruity level despite the obvious oils around; intricate spices and subtle vanilla and chocolate; f23 the oils do kick on slightly, but the marriage of castor sugar and juicy rye is built to last; b24 Arkansas is slowly becoming a major rye destination: this is excellent! Better, in fact, than some ryes made by the established distilleries of Kentucky. 46%.

⬙ **Rock Town Single Barrel Bourbon Whiskey Aged 18 Months** cask no. 422 db (94) n23.5 spiced molasses, anyone...? No? How about red liquorice, then...? t23.5 sumptuous and spicy delivery, rich Manuka honey and corn oil marry brilliantly. Despite the age, impressive tannins join the throng with a big liquorice surge; f23 the spices pulse while a butterscotch and fudge softness try to bring things to a gentle close: some hope...! b24 this bourbon Rocks...! 57.9%. sc.

⬙ **Rock Town Single Barrel Bourbon Whiskey Aged 18 Months** cask no. 430 db (87) n22 t22 f21.5 b21.5 Plenty happening: sugars crashing like dodgems around the palate, tannins blindly bumping around the place not sure where they are going, spices with no rhythm or consistent intensity or a game plan. Enjoyable whiskey in so many ways. But confusing and frustrating, too. 55.3%. sc.

⬙ **Rock Town Single Barrel Bourbon Whiskey Aged 22 Months** cask no. 494 db (90) n22.5 bold and oaky, tannins flex their muscles and reveal their body hair. The classic bourbon tones are well chiselled and impressive, especially the liquorice which appears set in stone; t23 surprisingly, delightfully, salivating with the small grains kicking in early to ensure complexity. A mix of corn and distillate oil make for a rich mouth feel and possibly accounts for the intensity of the liquorice-molasses-cocoa surge about two thirds the way in; f22 a long, chewy fade; b22.5 an oily but entirely delicious bourbon. 578%. sc.

⬙ **Rock Town Single Barrel Rye Whiskey Aged 16 Months** cask no. 99 db (89) n22 you need a bit of a stick to prod the rye into action. Very relaxed and fruit fudgy; t22.5 the rye is more emboldened on delivery with some sharper notes accompanied by spice in the slow motion lift off. A cream toffee succeeds in quietening the grainy uprising f22 chocolate fudge; b22.5 a pleasant if subdued affair, especially if compared to cask 90. Has less of the crisp grain which propels that towards the elite and instead depends upon a fudgy effect with the lovely rye flavours growing slowly by degree. 60.01%. sc.

⬙ **Rock Town Single Barrel Rye Whiskey Aged 23 Months** cask no. 90 db (91) n23.5 the rye sparkles in its most crisp and fruity mode: almost a lesser Sazerac in style. Impressive; t23.5 monumental rye on delivery, and then for four or five flavour waves it just gets better with the dark sugars entering to add an extra dimension to the grain. Fruity caramel middle, though some feint is starting to seep in; f21.5 a more even fruity rye persona though a tad too oily for comfort... b22.5 probably one of the truest and most impressive ryes made outside Kentucky and Indiana. The high spots are very high, indeed. 59.01%. sc.

⬙ **Rock Town Whiskey from Wheat Mash** sherry cask finish db (94) n22 the grape surprisingly flattens all except the spice which gradually reveal their wheaty credentials; t24.5 and grape is first to show, but only briefly. Then the unmistakably toasty, spicy, unique personality of a wheat whiskey powers through with an almost obscene deliciousness. The mouth feel is like no other, with spices heading off snarling in all directions like Medusa's hair. Frankly, this is truly brilliant; f23.5 just carries on with more of the same, but more quietly; b24 yay...!!! No sulphur!! This mention of sherry cask gets me worried, but without cause here.... and, beyond the nose, it plays only a bit part anyway. A strange fish, this, but one which grows on you until you are fatally in its thrall. 50%.

ROGUE SPIRITS Newport, Oregon

Rogue Chipotle Whiskey ocean aged in oak barrels at least 6 months db (84.5) n21.5 t22 f21 b20. Peppery. Which, considering it has apparently been distilled with peppers, is hardly surprising. Interesting, chaps (especially with the countering honey). And entertaining. But using a vegetable disqualifies it from being a whiskey....!!! Does anyone happen to have a spare tortilla....? 40% (80 proof)

Rogue Dead Guy Whiskey ocean aged in oak barrels at least 1 year db (86) n22.5 t22 f20.5 b21. Ah, I remember this guy from a year or two back: I had a bone to pick with him about his finish. Well, not the preferred drink of the Grim Reaper now, and makes good use of its malty, peppery structure. The finish is still a bit tangy and salty. But a big improvement.*40% (80 proof)*

Rogue Farms Oregon Rye Whiskey ocean aged in new oak barrels at least 4 months db (74) n18 t21 f17 b18. Rogue? You ain't joking... *40% (80 proof)*

Rogue Farms Oregon Single Malt Whiskey ocean aged in oak barrels at least 3 months db (81.5) n22 t22 f18 b19.5. Malty, gristy and pleasant at first. But like many of their whiskeys, it feels as though the Pacific ocean has leaked into the cask. I'm not sure what "ocean-aged" means exactly, but whatever it is, I do wish they'd stop it... *40% (80 proof)*

ROUGHSTOCK DISTILLERY Bozeman, Montana.

Roughstock Black Label (92.5) n22.5 t23.5 f23 b23.5. A very beautiful malt whiskey very well made which underlines the happy marriage between barley and virgin oak. A stunner! *64%*

ST GEORGE SPIRITS Alameda, California.

St Georges Single Malt Lot 15 db (89) n22 t22.5 f22.5 b22 Hah! Even in the pitch dark, sitting in my garden on the first warm evening of the year with the church about to strike midnight, I know, St George, that this is your whiskey. Because, nobody – nobody, I tells yer!! -has this delicate fruity edge to the malt (I'm sure it is malt). So, although it is now too dark to even properly see the label in the dull glow of this computer, let alone read it, I am writing this in your pre-set space, just knowing it is you. Have to say, normally this distillery has a slightly more impressive tone: this is just a little too young and flaky – yet still great fun! *43%*

SAINT JAMES SPIRITS Irwindale, California.

Peregrine Rock (83.5) n21 t20.5 f21.5 b20.5. Fruity and friendly, the wine and smoke combo work well-ish enough but the thumping oak injection highlights that maybe there isn't quite enough body to take in the ageing. Perhaps less time in the barrel will reduce the bitter orange finale. *40%*

SANTA FE SPIRITS Santa Fe, New Mexico.

Colkegan Single Malt Whiskey American white oak barrels, batch no. 8 db (87) n22 t23.5 f20 b21.5 Once you get used to Mesquite-smoked malt it can become mildly addictive. So I have to concentrate hard and put my analyst's and blender's hats on here. The problem is the finish: it is just too much and numbs the tongue. But before it reaches that point I cannot other than heap praise on this: it has that unmistakable smoked almond tang on both nose and delivery and the muscovado sugars are profound. But once the Mesquite hits, the barley is lost to us. The mouth feel, though, really is pretty impressive. *46% (90 proof).*

Colkegan Single Malt Whiskey American white oak barrels, batch no. 9 db (90) n23 t23.5 f21 b22.5 They have learned to control the Mesquite...! Much better! *46% (90 proof).*

Colkegan Single Malt Whiskey American white oak barrels, batch no. 10 db (91) n23 t23.5 f22 b22.5. Yep! Toning down the smoke has been a good move, but that finish still needs some attention...That said...superb! *46% (90 proof).*

SONOMA COUNTY DISTILLING CO. Rohnert Park, California.

Sonoma County Cherrywood Rye Whiskey batch 4, bott 12/07/2016 db (81) n19 t21.5 f20 b20.5 I so wanted to fall in love with this whiskey: a magnificent label; the makers using the right ingredients and cask. I could even have put on Vivaldi at his most romantic as the rye had been matured for a minimum of Four Seasons. But sadly the tobacco grip on this is simply too tight. The grain, though unmistakable, bursts out and sparkles spasmodically, but little more than that. *47.8% (95.6 proof).*

Sonoma County West of Kentucky Bourbon Whiskey No.1 batch 7, bott 08/31/2016 db (95) n23.5 t24 f23.5 b24 Californian bourbon a la Sonoma County. And it really is worth experiencing. *47.8% (95.6 proof).*

Sonoma County West of Kentucky Bourbon Whiskey No.2 batch 4, bott 12/16/2016 db (87) n21.5 t23.5 f20 b22 A big, bold bourbon benefitting from a reduced tobacco trespass... though it does mount up late on. The delivery and middle, though, concentrates on the oily, succulent maple syrup and molasses mix, the following butterscotch theme and spices which enthusiastically punctuate the sweet narrative. *47.5% (95 proof).*

Sonoma County West of Kentucky Bourbon Whiskey No.3 batch 2, bott 01/20/2017 db (77.5) n21 t21.5 f17 b18 Can't really make head nor tail of this. There is a custardy sweetness filling up some of the mid ground. But, some molasses apart, the recognisable bourbon landmarks are few and far between. Certainly as hot as Hades, especially on the tongue-torchingly aggressive finale. *46.5% (93 proof).*

SONS OF LIBERTY Rhode Island, New England.
↠ **Battle Cry American Single Malt Whiskey** db (77.5) n19 t21 f18 b19.5 A sweet, nutty whisky weakened by the butyric-like off notes. *46% (92 proof).*

↠ **Battle Cry American Single Malt Whiskey** finished in Sauternes wine barrels db (71) n18 t19 f16 b18 When even something as magical as a Sauternes cask fails to deal with the fire on the throat and the persistent weaknesses of the spirit, you know it's back to the drawing board. Less Battle Cry: more hara kiri... *46% (92 proof).*

↠ **Battle Cry American Single Malt Whiskey** finished in oloroso sherry barrels, batch no. 2 db (80) n20 t21 f19 b20 An acceptable malt which does little to entertain other than allow the richer notes of the oloroso to show a sweet, fruit cake intensity. Still a bit of flame-thrower late on, though. *46% (92 proof). 625 bottles.*

↠ **Uprising American Single Malt Whiskey** finished in Pedro Ximenez sherry barrels, batch no. 4 db (83.5) n21.5 t21 f20 b21 A hot, mildly aggressive whisky where for once the PX is a force for good by sculpting an intensely rich, sugary grapeyness to fill in the plot holes of the malt itself. *46% (92 proof). 900 bottles.*

SPIRIT HOUND DISTILLERS Lyons, Colorado.
↠ **Spirit Hound Straight Malt Whisky 2 Years Old Single Barrel** no. 57 db (91) n22.5 sweet and gristy with a quiet surge of caramels and vanillas; t23 a succulent delivery rich in ulmo honey and marzipan; more vanilla hits the mid-ground; f22.5 the last of the ulmo honey vies with the vanilla for quiet domination; b23 a very comfortable malt, bigging up the vanilla with no howling from this particular hound. *45%. sc. 244 Bottles.*

↠ **Spirit Hound Straight Malt Whisky Cask Strength 2 Years Old** barrel no. 40 db (88) n22 sweet, honeyed aroma, though a mystery bitter surround, too; t23 gosh...! The intensity of the delivery stuns one for a moment: a blend of ulmo and heather honey mix with malt concentrate to offer one of the most startling deliveries of the year...; f21.5 the out of sync bitterness of the nose returns; b21.5 honey hound, more like... *63.7%. sc. 27 Bottles. Distilled & bottled exclusively for Hazel's Beverage World.*

↠ **Spirit Hound Straight Malt Whisky Cask Strength 2 Years Old** barrel no. 60 db (87.5) n22 t22.5 f21.5 b21.5 In style from the same litter as barrel 40 with an outrageous sweetness stopped in its tracks by a gnawing bitterness. For sheer impact, it should get 100 out of 100...!!! *63.1%. sc. 31 Bottles.*

STEIN DISTILLERY Joseph, Oregon.
Straight Rye Whiskey Aged 2 Years cask no. 7 (88) n23 t22 f21 b22. A whiskey which offers up the grains to the full spotlight. A little more care with the cut and we have something special on our hands. *40%*

STONE BARN BRANDYWORKS DISTILLERY Portland, Oregon.
Hard Eight Unoaked Rye Whiskey (86.5) n22.5 t21.5 f21 b21.5. The excellent fruity-rye nose does not quite show the width of the cut which creates a buzzing oiliness. Good brown sugar balance. *40%*

STRANAHAN DISTILLERY Denver, Colorado.
Stranahan's Colorado Whiskey Batch #110 (91.5) n22 t23 f23 b23.5 Lovely interplay between crispy grain and even crispier sugars. Two-toned . Juicy and gorgeously spiced.47%
Stranahan's Snowflake Cab Franc (95.5) n24 t24.5 f23 b24. A celebration of great whiskey, and a profound statement of what the small distilleries of the USA are capable of. *47%. sc.*

SQUARE ONE BREWERY & DISTILLERY St. Louis, Missouri
J J Neukomm Missouri Malt Whisky Single Barrel (88.5) n21 t23 f22 b22.5 it was like being transferred back to Sperryville, Virginia, where Copper Fox whiskey is made. The cherry wood smoked malt has a highly distinctive voice, and here it is again. Except this really does appear to have dark cherry notes at work on the palate. Annoyingly, although single barrel, there is no distinguishing reference number. *45% (90 proof)*

TACONIC DISTILLERY Stanfordville, New York.
Taconic Dutchess Private Reserve Straight Bourbon Whiskey db (86) n21.5 t22 f21 b21.5. A pretty bourbon, with the sugars sitting in the right place, if sometimes over

enthusiastically. Good spice balance, roastiness and generous oils. Also, some decent rye in that mash bill it seems. *45% (90 proof)*

Taconic Founder's Rye Whiskey db **(90.5)** n22.5 t23.5 f22 b22.5 Well done, people of Taconic distillery. You sure know how to make a rye whiskey..! *45% (90 proof)*

Taconic Straight Bourbon Whiskey db **(92.5)** n23 t23.5 f23 b23 I well remember their bourbon from last year: this appears to have upped a gear...not only in strength but in far better usage of the sugars. *57.5% (115 proof).*

Taconic Straight Rye Whiskey db **(91.5)** n22.5 t23.5 f22.5 b23 If memory serves, this is the same distillery which came up with a resounding rye last year. This, though, has a different feel with the oak enclosing in on the grain like a python gets all up close and personal to a lamb. *57.5% (115 proof).*

TOM'S FOOLERY Chargin Falls, Ohio.

Tom's Foolery Ohio Straight Bourbon Whiskey aged 3 Years, batch 6, dist 2012 db **(83)** n19 t22 f21 b21. Not sure if Tom's fooling or feinted. Superb arrival on palate with some pretty smart spices, well backed up by maple syrup. But the cut needs to be narrowed considerably. *45% (90 proof)*

Tom's Foolery Ohio Straight Rye Whiskey finished in an apple brandy barrel, aged 3 Years, batch 2, dist 2012 db **(92.5)** n22.5 t24 f22.5 b23.5 Does finishing it in an apple brandy barrel mean this is a straight rye...? Either way, the extra fruit on top of the rye's already fruity nature appears to work. A beautifully vivid and memorable rye...which isn't quite as straight as Tom thinks... *45% (90 proof)*

TOMMYROTTER DISTILLERY Buffalo, New York.

⟫ **Tommyrotter Triple Barrel American Whiskey** batch no. 3 French oak Finish **(88.5)** n22 hardly surprisingly, gentle tannin makes its mark playing anchor, no end of vanilla takes up a lighter role; t22.5 sweet and silky delivery the malt and vanilla appear joined at the hip. The oaky spices certainly aren't; f22 the spices form a jagged edge to the gentle caramels; b22 despite using three barrels, it as though the caramel has merged many of the facets to create a continuous flavour stream. Not as a complex as I hoped for, but not a whiskey to turn down a second glass to. *46% (92 proof). nc ncf.*

TRIPLE EIGHT DISTILLERY Nantucket, Massachusetts.

The Notch Aged 12 Years cask no. 026-055 dist 2002, bott 2014 db **(96.5)** n24 t24.5 f23.5 b24.5 Interesting to see this great whisky cope, as we all must do, with the passing of time. The quiet understatement and elegance of the 10-y-o has given way to a more brash and assertive, oak-stained version. Not that that is a criticism, as it does it with the usual Triple Eight panache. On the 8th of August 2008 (just two days after I had completed the 2009 Whisky Bible) I gave a speech at the distillery predicting that, from the samples I had tasted in their warehouses, this new venture was on course to be one of the great malt whisky distilleries of the world. I am heartened that, for once in my life, I got something right... *48%*

TUTHILLTOWN SPIRITS Gardiner, New York.

Hudson Baby Bourbon Year 13 Batch E1 **(86)** n21 t21.5 f22 b21.5. A big, heavy duty bourbon. Feinty, though nothing like as oily as some previous bottlings I've encountered from these guys over the years. Enough toasted honeycomb and liquorice for this to make a few lovely noises. *46%. WB15/174*

VAN BRUNT STILLHOUSE Brooklyn, New York.

Van Brunt Stillhouse Bourbon db **(81.5)** n19 t21 f21 b20.5. For a bourbon, this has a peculiarly malty kick to it. Distinct whiff of the hay ricks about this, before the fledgling liquorice becomes involved. *42%*

Van Brunt Stillhouse Rye db **(86)** n20.5 t22 f22 b21.5. Technically wins few awards. But something, seemingly instinctually, seems to have dragged out the very best from this distillery with its rye. The oils are a bit of a problem, yet the grain rises above it enough to tap out a delightfully fruity and spicy message, and even confident enough to, late on, stray into mocha land.... *42%*

VALENTINE DISTILLING CO. Ferndale, Michigan.

Mayor Pingree Small Batch Bourbon Whiskey batch no. 39 db **(89.5)** n23.5 t22.5 f21.5 b22 A very different animal, or mayor, and obviously distilled in different stills from their 9- and 10-year-old Mayor Pingree brands. A little confusing for the punter but a very attractive if under-stated micro-bourbon without doubt. *45% (90 proof).*

VIRGINIA DISTILLERY CO. Lovinston, Virginia.
Virginia Highland Malt Whisky Port Finished batch no. 03 (87) n22 t22.5 f21 b21.5 A vibrant malt, youthful and sharp in places. Exceptionally crisp and clean but sporting an unusually thin body also which means that there is a slight jarring on the grain-fruit transmission. Displays an attractive consistent sweetness until the death when a vague bitterness develops. 46% (92 proof).

WESTLAND DISTILLERY Seattle, Washington.
Westland American Single Malt Garryana 2/1 bott 2017 db (89.5) n23 t22 f22 b22 This second bottling proves Westland have created a universally unique whisky style, though the cut from the still is a little generous. 50% nc ncf.

Westland American Single Malt Peat Week db (92) n23 t23.5 f22.5 b23 A distillery which does understated smoky whiskey rather well... 50% nc ncf.

Westland American Single Malt Winter 2016 db (88) n22 t22.5 f21.5 b22 A straight up and down maltfest. 50% nc ncf.

◇ **Westland Peat Week 4th Year** db (94) n23 impressive for the evenness of the smoke: it doesn't try to be dramatically peaty, instead allowing just as much hickory to take centre stage as peat; t24 fabulously soft, the light oils spread the smoke far and wide. A brilliant, melt-in-the-mouth gristy, sugary quality which underlines just how clean the distillate was; f23 long, now with a touch of liquorice and toasted treacle to keep the sweetness going as the drier, biscuity vanillins arrive; b24 one of the best smoke signals to come out of Washington State for a very long time...and surely destined for consumption at The Old Highland Stillhouse in Oregon City! 54.4% (108.8 proof).

WIDOW JANE DISTILLERY Brooklyn, New York.
◇ **Baby Jane Bourbon Whiskey** batch no.1 db (85.5) n21 t22 f21 b21.5 Jane is a chubby little thing, displaying plenty of baby fat. Sweet, though, with an enjoyable molasses and nougat theme. 45.5% (91 proof).

◇ **Widow Jane Straight Bourbon Whiskey Aged 10 Years** barrel no. 1609, bott 2017 db (90.5) n23 ticks every bourbon box, especially the honey and molasses ones. A big dollop of corn oil means the peppery spices stick and stick hard; a slow build-up of liquorice and mint completes the happy scene; t23 the corn oil so prevalent on the nose takes little time to make its mark on delivery. Big, but now with a real burnt feel to the molasses; huge amount of caramel in mid-stream; f22 dry and toasty: lots of oaky vanilla; b22.5 good, honest, rock solid if oily, old-fashioned bourbon. 45.5% (91 proof). sc.

◇ **Widow Jane Whiskey Distilled From A Rye Mash** batch no. 15 db (83) n21 t21.5 f20 b20.5 So good to see a distiller call a whiskey exactly what it is: kudos to you and let me shake you warmly by the hand. That said, a slightly less wide cut would allow the rye to have a bigger and much sharper say. 45.5% (91 proof).

◇ **Widow Jane Whiskey Distilled From A Rye Mash Oak & Apple Wood Aged** batch no. 13 db (86) n22 t21.5 f21 b21.5 Sweet, firm, has a few teeth that aren't afraid to nip – and a slight tobacco note on the nose. Plenty to chew on, for sure. 45.5% (91 proof).

WOOD'S HIGH MOUNTAIN DISTILLERY Salida, Colorado.
◇ **Wood's Alpine Rye Whiskey Aged 2 Years** batch no. 9 db (88) n21.5 the oils and spices point towards an over-generous cut. But the rye really stands up to be counted, showing commendable fruity crispness in the face of so much oil; t23.5 now that is a superb delivery: a huge tannin surge is softened by the maple syrup and Manuka honey blend. The rye cuts through all the fat to offer its simultaneously deep and shrill tones loud and clear; f21 the return of the feint...; b22 a knife and fork whiskey. But has nailed the rye quite beautifully. 49% (98 proof).

◇ **Wood's Tenderfoot American Malt Whiskey Aged 18 Months** batch no. 50 db (84.5) n20 t22.5 f21 b21 Perhaps not technically a world beater, but an attractive, sweet malt which has taken the freshly cut hay route, especially on the nose. Juicy delivery rich in both malt muscovado sugars. Oddly enough, for a mountain whiskey it reminds me of lowland pastures! 45% (90 proof).

WOODINVILLE WHISKEY CO. Woodinville, Washington
Woodinville Straight 100% Rye Whiskey db (95) n24 t23.5 f23.5 b24 /rye distilling and maturation to a very high standard, especially for a micro distillery. 45% (90 proof).

Woodinville Straight Bourbon Whiskey db (93) n24 t23.5 f22.5 b23 A few years back I highlighted this then fledgling distillery as one to watch. This latest, magnificent bottling alongside its sister rye shows you exactly why. What a joy! 45% (90 proof).

WOODSTONE CREEK DISTILLERY Cincinnati, Ohio.

Woodstone Creek 10 Year Old Peated Malt (92) 24 23 22 23. Just read the previous tasting notes. There is nothing I can either add or subtract. Quite, quite wonderful... 46.25%

WYOMING WHISKEY Kirby, Wyoming.

Wyoming Whiskey Double Cask Straight Bourbon Whiskey finished in sherry casks db (87.5) n23 t22 f21 b21.5 Kind of leaves me scratching my head, this. Yes, the grape infusion is clean and profound, suffering not an atom of the sulphur pollution which wrecks so much scotch. But this is bourbon – which needs unsullied virgin oak. And here we get virtually no meaningful bourbon contribution but masses of delicious grape. Yes, some glorious fruit notes, but this needs more balance so the bourbon has a telling say. 50% (100 proof).

Wyoming Whiskey Single Barrel barrel no. 1840 db (87) n22 t22 f21 b22 If you like your whiskey to have a big cream caramel and ulmo honey charge, then this guy is for you. Doesn't quite gel towards the end, though. 44% (88 proof).

Wyoming Whiskey Small Batch batch no. 42 db (86.5) n22 t22.5 f20.5 b21.5 Another Wyoming which has so much going for it but (annoyingly!) falters at the final step towards the finale. Here the accent is on the vanilla and a rich, spicy fruity suet pudding middle. Hard not to like. 44% (88 proof).

Wyoming Whiskey Outryder db (88.5) n22.5 t22.5 f21.5 b22 Perhaps should be called Easy Rider, as this is as gentle as it gets... 50% (100 proof).

YELLOW ROSE DISTILLING Houston, Texas.

Yellow Rose Outlaw Bourbon Whiskey Over 6 Months batch 24 db (87) n20 t22.5 f23.5 b21. The closest whiskey in style found to this anywhere in the world is European, where chestnut casks have been deployed for finishing (at least!). A tannin-dominated whiskey, where the normal liquorice and honey tones don't really apply, though close relatives may be found. Delicious when it settles down towards the end but, overall, little balance to be had. Very different...and like a yellow rose, grows on you. 46%

YAHARA BAY DISTILLERY Madison, Wisconsin.

Sample No 1 (87) n22.5 t22 f20.5 b22. A disarmingly elegant whiskey. 40%

American/Kentucky Whiskey Blends

Ancient Age Preferred (73) n16.5 t19 f19.5 b18. A marginal improvement thanks mainly to a re-worked ripe corn-sweet delivery and the cocoa-rich finish. But still preferred, one assumes, by those who probably don't care how good this distillery's whisky can be... 40%

Beam's Eight Star (69.5) n17 t18 f17 b17.5. If you don't expect too much it won't let you down. 40%

Bellows (67) n17 t17.5 f16 b16.5 Just too thin. 40%

Calvert's Extra (79) n19 t20 f20 b20. Sweet and mega-toffeed. Just creaking with caramel but extra marks for the late spice. 40%

Carstair's White Seal (72) n16.5 t18.5 f19.5 b17.5 Possibly the cleanest blend about even offering a cocoa tang on the finale. Pleasant. 40%

◇ **High West American Prairie Bourbon** batch no. 17F02 (92.5) n23 though blended, this brand does favour that sweet hickory note in its make-up and it comes though like a train here; t23 a camp coffee and liquorice delivery, with spices kicking in with intent; the sugars, dark, buttery and toasty, hang suspended in the oils; f23 long with a serious vanilla and butterscotch thread; the tannins have no intention of letting go; b23.5 this is big and sweet with massive chewability. 46% (92 proof). nc ncf. Blend of straight bourbon whiskies.

◇ **High West Campfire** batch no. 17F29 (95.5) n24 a Fisherman's Friend cough sweet-Bowmore-style smokiness envelops the leading, crisp rye notes. Liquorice and hickory link to a buttery saltiness until your jaw aches... Seriously fat in part, but the star turn is the myriad sugar tones ranging from delicate ulmo honey to an earthier molasses depth; the smoke looks down serenely, filling in any gaps when required; f23.5 that buttery saltiness returns as the rye and smoke linger; b24 like something straight out of my blending lab! Beautifully and skilfully constructed...! And proves that the USA and Britain can work together despite Britain's feeble Prime Minister May's duplicity over Europe. 46% (92 proof). nc ncf. Straight rye whiskey, straight bourbon whiskey, blended malt Scotch whiskey.

◇ **High West Double Rye** batch no. 18A11 (96) n24 just adore that intensity to the grain: as fruity and muscovado-rich as it gets. The cutglass crispness of the rye feels as though it could shatter at any moment; t24 this is big...very big...!! A blend of ulmo honey, butter and molten muscovado soon explodes into glorious rye concentrate; f23.5 so much happening here: the fade allows the cinnamon and mint easier access while the spices show commendable restraint, despite their obvious power; **b24.5** complex and bang on the money: one of the most intense and true ryes on the market. *46% (92 proof). nc ncf. Blend of straight rye whiskies.*

⌖ **High West Rendezvous Rye** batch no. 17F16 **(93) n24** a sublime nose: complex with the rye pitching it at different degrees of sharpness and intensity, seemingly a mix of malted and unmalted, the latter magnifying the the sharper edges. Fruity with distinct cinnamon and orange peel, mint and lavender; **t23** delightfully two-toned: excellent oils mixing it with the flintier aspects of the grain; **f23** the oak bites in at last to deliver a slight bitterness but the muscovado and demerara sugars counter perfectly. Late hickory and cinnamon; **b23** a rye-lovers dream. *46% (92 pro of). nc ncf. Blend of straight rye whiskies.*

Kentucky Dale (64) n16 t17 f15 b16. Thin and spineless, though soft and decently sweet on delivery. The grain spirit completely dominates. *40%*

Kessler (84.5) n20 t21 f22 b21.5. "Smooth As Silk" claims the label. And the boast is supported by what is in the bottle: a real toffee-mocha charmer with a chewy, spicy depth. *40%*

⌖ **Little Book Blended Straight Whiskey (87.5) n22 t22.5 f21 b22** A silky, sweet whiskey with a small grain sharpness that keeps the taste buds salivating. Even at this strength, easy, semi-complex and very pleasant drinking with the accent on a maple syrup sweetness. Whiskey snobs will turn their noses up at this at their peril. *60.24% (120.48 proof).*

⌖ **Little Book Chapter 02: Noe Simple Task Blended Straight Whiskey (91) n22.5** excellent bite to the nose with the small grains fizzing; **t23** now it really comes into its own with a cascade of maple syrup and molasses notes upping the sweetness to max; earthier, drier tannin checks further progress superbly; **f22.5** liquorice and mocha..and big spice, too; **b23** very distinctive Beam-like elements which is taking blended American whiskey into higher, more rarified atmosphere. *60.55% (121.1 proof).*

PM Deluxe (75) n18 t18 f19 b18. Pleasant moments as the toffee melts in the mouth. *40%*

Sunny Brook (79.5) n20 t21 f19 b19.5. An entirely agreeable blend with toffee and lightly oiled nuts. Plus a sunny disposition... *40%*

Straight Malt Whiskey

Parker's Heritage Collection Kentucky Straight Malt Whiskey Aged 8 Years db **(93) n23 t23.5 f23 b23.5** From the distillery which brought you wheat whisky, now comes malt – Kentucky style. As delicious as it is fascinating. *54% (108 proof)*

Whiskey Distilled From Bourbon Mash

Angels Envy Bourbon Finished in Port Barrels (84) n20 t22 f21 b21. Almost like a chocolate raisin candy and fruitcake. Silky textured and juicy. *43.3% (86.6 proof)*

Whiskey Distilled From Rye Mash

Angels Envy Rye Finished in Caribbean Rum Casks (78) n18.5 t20.5 f20 b19 Frankly, I was hardly expecting to have any teeth left after this sample. The hardest, most crisp of all whiskeys is rye. And if you want to give any whisk(e)y an extra degree of exoskeleton, then just finish it in a rum cask. And here we have the two together : yikes! Some twenty years ago I gave then Jack Daniel's blender Lincoln Henderson his first-ever taste of peated whisky: a Laphroaig. He hated it! I think he's waited a long time to return the compliment by showing me a style I did not know could exist. Beyond fascinating. Weird, even - hence the full tasting notes. One for the ladies with this liqueur-style smoothie. *50%.*

White Dog

⌖ **Buffalo Trace White Dog Mash #1 (94) n23 t24 f23 b24** This is the DNA of Buffalo Trace and it is not difficult to see why it goes on to make a bourbon that challenges al the world's whiskeys. You cannot be a shrinking violet to withstand the onslaught of virgin oak, and here the full muscular framework is exposed. Oddly enough, there is a little less copper now than when I first tasted the new spirit – the White Dog – some 25 years ago. But the sublime balance of the grains themselves – offering a sweetness as vague as da Vinci smile – sits beautifully with the late chocolate mousse finale. *62.5% (125 proof).*

⌖ **Buffalo Trace White Dog Rye Mash (96) n23.5 t24.5 f24 b24** When the Russians and Finns created their version of whisky back in the day, they distilled from rye...but just never got round to putting it in a barrel. They called it vodka. Find a time machine on ebay and head back into the past – then offer those same people this. Doubtless you will be treated to the finest cut of elk. For the rye is almost three dimensional in its crisp, ever-building enormity. Absolutely faultless white dog. Or should that be Siberian Husky...? *62.5% (125 proof).*

⌖ **Buffalo Trace White Dog Wheated Mash (94.5) n23 t24 f23.5 b24** Wheated bourbon tends to have a spicier kick than rye mash bourbon...and this sticks to the script. Rich, borderline lush and chewy. Every box ticked and a few more thrown in for good measure. *57% (114 proof).*

Other American Whiskey

Abraham Bowman Sequential Series 2nd Use Barrels dist 11-17-04, bott 5-1-17 db **(92.5)** n23 t23 f23.5 b23 'S'funny, I thought. Doesn't nose right for a bourbon. Wrong kind of tannin: too quick on the naked brown sugars and spice instead of heavier liquorice and caramel frame. So checked the header and spotted the 2nd use barrels bit. Just shows, doesn't it, how unique and delicate true bourbon actually is, despite its enormity of flavour. 50% (100 proof). Release No. 16.

Abraham Bowman Sequential Series 4th Use Barrels dist 11-17-04, bott 5-1-17 db **(86.5)** n22 t22 f21 b21.5 An early hint of honey quickly vanishes and we are quickly thrust into a straight-laced, bittering narrative. A bit like dating an ex-girlfriend's twin sister and finding she just doesn't have the same depth of character. And is only half as passionate. 50% (100 proof). Release No. 16.

◇◇◇ **Basil Hayden's Two by Two Rye (95)** n23.5 as usual, the rye grain dominates in this kind of set up – the chiselled sugars working well alongside an earthier, leafier backdrop; t23.5 soft sugars rise early, then a big vanilla surge – almost like custard on a rocky rye outcrop; salivating from first to last; f24 the spices flit around with mild abandon; the sugars are crisp and collected. Light liquorice, ulmo honey and vanilla notes underscore the late bourbon swish; b24 a beautiful blend. I remember some 20 years ago or so asking the good people of Jim Beam why they didn't produce a blend of their fabulous ryes and bourbon and their answer was three fold: they didn't have enough rye, it wasn't a traditional or acceptable whiskey category. And they didn't think anyone would drink it. Well, having upped rye production they now can do this. And so beautiful is it, people would be mugs to turn their back on this massively flavoured whiskey as something inferior. 40% (80 proof). Kentucky Straight Rye whiskies blended with Kentucky Straight Bourbon whiskies.

◇◇◇ **Cascade Blonde American Whiskey** bott code: L8081ZX222 1458 **(85.5)** n22 t22 f20.5 b21 An exceptionally easy ride, soft and avoiding any big flavours without ever lacking character. The thin finish apart, abounds with tannin and roasty promise. 40% (80 proof).

◇◇◇ **Early Times Kentucky Whisky** bott code: A027161143 3125362 **(89)** n22.5 charmingly sweet with crisp Demerara, taking the edge off the firmer tannins. Much hickory on show, too; t22.5 soberly layered with vanilla, light liquorice, delicate hickory and earthier molasses; f21.5 happy to sign off with a chalkier vanilla fade; b22.5 the fact they are using what they term on the label as "reused cooperage" means this is Kentucky Whisky as opposed to Kentucky Bourbon, which requires virgin oak (and before you ask, YES, bourbon is a whisky...!). So, while may not be a mighty fine Kentucky bourbon, brimming as it is with all kinds of liquorice and molasses this is still mighty fine Kentucky whisky...!! 40% (80 proof).

◇◇◇ **Isaac Bowman Straight Bourbon Whiskey Port Barrel Finished** bott code: L173050513:42B 168 db **(81)** n20 t21 f20 b20 Pleasant in its own way, I s'pose. But, after the sweet fruit, flatter than your average witch's tit. If God had really wanted this kind of whiskey he would have planted Virginia in Portugal. 46% (92 proof).

Jim Beam Double Oak db **(86)** n22 t22.5 f20.5 b21. Attractive, caramel-soaked whiskey with a little too much fade after a big spice and liquorice delivery. 43%

Knob Creek Smoked Maple (35) n10 t10 f10 b5. How can this be called a " Kentucky straight bourbon"? What is straight about this? Am I missing something here? About 98% closer to maple syrup than bourbon, this would make a pleasant spread on your breakfast toast. It may be whiskey, Jim (Beam), but not as we know it. 45% (90 proof)

Michter's No. 1 American Whiskey (84.5) n21 t21.5 f21 b21 Sugar-coated, oily and easy going. About as friendly as any whiskey you'll find this year 41.7%

Michter's No. 1 Sour Mash (86) n22 t22 f21 b21 A pleasant, clean, light whiskey: perhaps too clean at times. Good mocha throughout, with the accent on the coffee. 43%

◇◇◇ **Ten High Bourbon With Natural Flavors (61)** n18 t18 f10 b15 Not sure what those natural flavours are (though a grotesque vanilla note keeps coming to mind), but seeing as they are not as natural as good old fashioned bourbon, don't see the point of them. Or it. Not exactly pleasant and the finish is almost Herculean in its grimness. 40% (80 proof).

Trail's End Batch No 002 Kentucky Bourbon finished in Oregon Oak (92) n23.5 t23 f22.5 b23 So, here we are: at the Trail's End. This is my final official day of tasting, having spent the last few months working six days a week to bring you Jim Murray's Whisky Bible 2018 in on time. The romantic in me meant that this had to be my last whisk(e)y: what else would fit the bill? Especially as both Kentucky and Oregon are my two adopted states in the US. For the record, it is the 1,199th new whisky for Bible 2018, though there had been a couple of dozen additional re-tastes. And as I write the front of the Bible and we edit and finally put this book to bed, the odd straggler will come in to take the total over 1,200. But for me this, officially, is it...the Trail's End for another year.... 45% (90 proof).

WhistlePig Old World 12 Year Madeira Finish European casks **(88)** n21.5 t23.5 f21 b22 Not sure how this can be called a straight rye. But as a whiskey experience, certainly has its merits. 45%. (90 Proof)

Canadian Whisky

The vastness of Canada is legendary. As is the remoteness of much of its land. But anyone who has not yet visited a distillery which sits serenely on the shores of Lake Manitoba more or less bang in the middle of the country and, in early Spring, ventures a few miles out into the wilderness has really missed a trick.

Because there, just a dozen miles from the remotest distillery of them all, Gimli, you can stand and listen to the ice crack with a clean, primeval crispness unlike any other thing you will have experienced; a sound once heard by the very first hunters who ventured into these uncharted wastes. And hear a distant loon call its lonely, undulating, haunting song, its notes scudding for miles along the ice and vanishing into the snow which surrounds you. Of all the places on the planet, it is the one where you will feel a sensation as close to nature - and insignificance - as you are likely to find.

It was also a place where I felt that, surely, great whisky should be made. But in the early days of the Gimli distillery there was a feeling of frustration by the blenders who used it. Because they were simply unable to recreate the depth and complexity of the legendary Crown Royal brand it had been built to produce in place of the old, now closed, distilleries to the east. When, in their lab, they tasted the new Crown Royal against the old there were furrowed brows, a slight shaking of heads and an unspoken but unmistakable feeling of hopeless resignation.

To understand why, we have to dispense with the nonsense which appears to have been trotted out by some supposed expert in Canadian whisky or other

Yukon

BRITISH COLUMBIA

ALBERTA

MANITOBA

Shelter Point ▲ Okanagan ▲
● Vancouver

▲ Alberta
▲ Highwood
Calgary

▲ Palliser

Gimli ▲

Key
● **Major Town or City**
▲ Distillery

290

who has, I have been advised by quite a few people I meet at my tastings, been writing somewhere that Canada has no history of blending from different distilleries. Certainly that is now the perceived view of many in the country. And it is just plain wrong: only a maniac would write such garbage as fact and completely undersell the provenance of Canadian whisky. Crown Royal, when in its pomp, was a meticulous blending of a number of different whiskies from the Seagram empire and by far the most complex whisky Canada had to offer.

The creases in the furrowed brows deepened as the end of the last century approached. Because the key distilleries of LaSalle, Beupre and Waterloo were yielding the very last of their stocks, especially top quality pure rye, and although the much lighter make of Gimli was of a high standard, they had not yet been able to recreate the all round complexity as when adding the fruits of so many great distilleries together. The amount of experimentation with yeasts and distilling speeds and cutting times was a wonder to behold. But the race was on: could they, before the final stocks ran dry, produce the diversity of flavours to match the old, classic distilleries which were now not just closed but in some cases demolished?

When I had sat in the LaSalle blending lab for several days in the 1990s and worked my way through the near extinct whiskies in stock I recognised in Beupre a distillery which, had it survived, probably might have been capable of producing something as good, if not better, than anything else on this planet. And it was clear just what a vital contribution it made to Crown Royal's all round magnificence.

So I have monitored the Crown Royal brand with interest, especially since Gimli and the brand was acquired by Diageo some 15 years ago. And anyone doubting that this really was a truly great whisky should have accompanied me when I visited the home of my dear and now sadly lost friend Mike Smith and worked our way through his astonishing Crown Royal collection which showed how the brand's taste profile had evolved through the ages.

And, at last, it appears all that hard work, all those early days of experimentation and fine tuning at Gimli have paid off. For while the standard Crown Royal brand doesn't yet quite live up to its starry past, they have unleashed upon us a whisky which dazzles, startles and engulfs you in its natural beauty like an early spring morning on Lake Manitoba. The whisky is called Crown Royal Northern Harvest Rye. It is not only the best Canadian to be found in the market, it was Jim Murray's World Whisky of the Year 2016: batch L5085 N3 had redefined a nation's whisky.

The fact it should have achieved this at a time when Canadian whisky is at a nadir, with far too many brands dependent on adding too many unacceptable things as accepted flavouring agents, is providential. It shows that keeping the grains at a maximum and allowing them to be the flavouring agents - like Alberta Premium - is not just keeping true to the old Canadian traditions, but the way to go to drag it back onto the world's stage and give it a leading role. Walter Jonke and the other old Canadian blenders I knew understood this. Let this be a lesson to the present generation. And so many so-callled whisky experts.

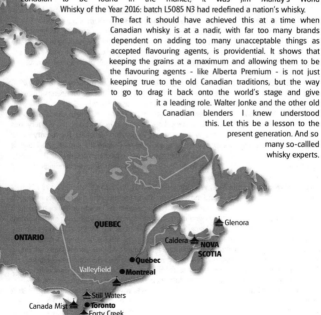

QUEBEC

ONTARIO

Glenora

Caldera NOVA
SCOTIA

Valleyfield   •Quebec
           •Montreal

           Still Waters
Canada Mist •Toronto
           Forty Creek
           Kittling Ridge
  Walkerville

Jim Murray's Whisky Bible Canadian Whisky of the Year Winners	
2004	Seagram's VO
2005	Seagram's VO
2006	Alberta Premium
2007	Alberta Premium 25 Years Old
2008	Alberta Premium 25 Years Old
2009	Alberta Premium
2010	Wiser's Red Letter
2011	Crown Royal Special Reserve
2012	Crown Royal Special Reserve
2013	Masterson's 10 Year Old Straight Rye
2014	Masterson's 10 Year Old Straight Rye
2015	Masterson's 10 Year Old Straight Rye
2016	Crown Royal Northern Harvest Rye
2017	Crown Royal Northern Harvest Rye
2018	Crown Royal Northern Harvest Rye
2019	Canadian Club Chronicles: Issue No. 1 41 Year Old

Canadian Single Malts

CENTRAL CITY BREWERS & DISTILLERS LTD. Surrey, British Columbia.

◇ **Lohin McKinnon Chocolate Malt Single Malt Whisky** Sauternes barrels db (80) n19 t23 f17 b21 Chocolate malt and Sauternes Barrels...? Sound like something straight out of the Glenmorangie blending lab. To taste, this is truly amazing: the closest thing to liquid Jaffa Cake biscuits I have ever encountered. So orangey...so chocolatey... Sadly, the nose and finish tell their own tale: if you are going to use wine casks from Europe, make sure they have not been sulphur treated first. 43%.

◇ **Lohin McKinnon Lightly Peated Single Malt Whisky** oloroso sherry barrels db (69.5) n17.5 t19 f16 b17 A polite tip to any micro distillery planning on using European wine casks. Just don't. Or you might end up with a sulphur-ruined disaster like this. 43%.

◇ **Lohin McKinnon Peated Single Malt Whisky** db (95.5) n23.5 light bands of smoke and hickory, with a slightly more acidic back drop; t24 that is really classy: the delivery tries not to force the issue but instead allows the smoke to develop gracefully. The hickory works in tandem with the grist, the barley showing great poise despite the smoke; f23.5 such a lovely echo to the phenols...; even at this late stage the gristy sugars still melt in the mouth; b24.5 I think they have found their forte. This is genuinely top rate, outstandingly distilled and matured peated whisky 43%.

Lohin McKinnon Single Malt Whisky batch no. LOT 0001 db (89.5) n23.5 t23 f21 b22 Always one of the favourite – and most treasured - moments in the many facets of my job is to taste a brand new whisky. I am always a little nervous, as I really don't like breaking it to new whisky makers that they need to get back to the drawing board. No such problem here: this malt is a noble first release. The cuts need adjusting very slightly to lessen the feints (indeed, how it sweetens when you nose a glass after it has been warmed for a good ten minutes and the higher oils evaporate underlines that the excess feints are pretty minor) and I'd work with a cannier mix of first and second fill ex-bourbon barrels to help up the honey character which so perfectly suits this malt. But this is a highly drinkable whisky and they are not that far away from producing an excellent one. Hearty congrats. 43%.

◇ **Lohin McKinnon Wine Barrel Finished Single Malt Whisky** finished in B.C. VQA Okanagan Valley Back Sage Vineyard Pipe wine barrels db (90.5) n22 blackberries and black pepper; t23 the silky disposition, helps the fruit to wallow around the palate relaxed enough to show no opposition to the gathering spice and mocha; f22.5 spiced fruit chocolate with a late surge of friendly vanilla; b23 impressive balance here with the fruit doing enough but not too much. 43%.

DEVINE SPIRITS Saanichton, British Columbia.

Glen Saanich Single Malt batch no. 1, bourbon barrels db (**94**) n22.5 t24 f23.5 b24 As a first bottling, genuinely superb. What it may lack in out and out complexity it more than makes up for with the unfettered brilliance of the malt and the all-round joy of the intense experience. Hope they can keep this standard going. Congratulations to all at deVine! 45%.

⟜ **Glensaanich Single Malt** batch no. 2 db (**86**) n21.5 t22 f21 b21.5 An unexpected tobacco note on the nose mixes it with the malt. The oil wades in to soften, releasing an attractive degree of bruyere honey which covers the slightly more bitter notes with aplomb. 45%.

⟜ **Glensaanich Quarter Cask Ancient Grains** batch no. 1 db (**91.5**) n23 lovely interplay between the full on spice, acacia honey and a very complex small grain-style attack which gives it a distinct bourbon persona; t23 the nose flags some extra oils and these arrive post-haste on delivery; then we are back to those beautiful grains – a kind of malted barley plus which fits in with the growing tannin to confirm that bourbon-type complexity; little acacia honey and molasses melt together at the midway stage; f22 toasty fudge...but still with that complex grain buzz; b23.5 a beautiful little essay in complexity. The varied grains spelt, emmer, einkorn, khorosan and, of course, locally grown organic BC barley have been put together to delicious and fascinating effect. A real entertainer, especially when warmed for a while. 45%.

GLENORA Glenville, Nova Scotia.

Glen Breton Rare Aged 10 Years bott 10 db (**89.5**) n22 t23 f22 b22.5. An impressive whisky: one of the best bottlings of this age for some while and showing the malt at full throttle. 43%

HIGHWOOD DISTILLERS High River, Alberta.

Highwood Distillers Centennial Whisky db (**84.5**) n21.5 t22 f20 b21 Toffee and raisin. Tangy, though the finish dries significantly. 40%.

Highwood Distillers Ninety 5 Year Old Whisky db (**86.5**) n21.5 t22 f21.5 b21.5 A sweet, simplistic whisky which, despite its thin body and big toffee theme, ramps up some very attractive spices. 45%.

Highwood Distillers Ninety 20 Year Old Whisky db (**90**) n23.5 superb aroma which beautifully encapsulates the age – and country - without there being a single fading note to be heard: a stunning array gentle sugars augment the lightest of vanilla and butterscotch themes. Naturally, the spices are a low key as possible, but hints of wheat; t22.5 a fragile, skeletal frame; the muscovado sugar muscle is undeveloped and any fattiness carries that prominent vanilla; f22 more of the same, though quieter and a little spicier; b22 this is a grand old man of Canadian whisky yet sprightly and full of very simple Canadian tales... 45%.

Canadian Rockies 10 Year Old (**84.5**) n21.5 t22 f20.5 b20.5. Resplendent in all its chewy one-dimensional caramel. 40%. Taiwan Exclusive.

⟜ **Canadian Rockies Aged 17 Years** bott code: 8127 (**92**) n23 typical light and gentle aroma with the accent on lightly sweetened vanilla; t23.5 gorgeous mouth feel: again, light and fragile but enough oils to soften the impact. A mix of light ulmo honey and vanilla, before soft natural caramels and spices fill the mid-ground; f22. Delicate even on the finale with the vanillas showing just a little extra tannin; b23.5 so true to Highwood's style, this could be their signature whisky. Elegant. 50%.

Canadian Rockies 21 Year Old (**88**) n22 so light, with a mix of apple crumble and vanilla ice cream; t22 soft and simple as you like: vanilla and docile spice; f22 more of the same...; b22 not sure you can find a straighter, simpler whisky... 40%. Taiwan Exclusive.

Canadian Rockies 21 Year Old (**91.5**) n22.5 t23.5 f22.5 b23 Surely it just can't be a matter of 6% abv. This has far more personality and joie de vivre. 46%. Canadian Exclusive.

Canadian Rockies 34 Year Old (**92.5**) n23 t23 f23.5 b23 The most fun I've had with a 34-year-old Canadian for quite a few years now...though that was a little hotter than this... 79.3%. Taiwan Exclusive.

OKANAGAN SPIRITS CRAFT DISTILLERY Vernon, British Columbia.

Laird of Fintry Single Malt Whisky French & American oak. db (**84**) n21 t22 f20 b21. A tangy, aromatic whisky where the oak appears to have a disproportionate say. Interesting marmalade depth. 40%. First Batch. 264 bottles.

PEMBERTON DISTILLERY Pemberton, British Columbia.

Pemberton Organic Single Malt Whisky 2010 ex-bourbon cask, cask no. 1, dist Aug 10, bott May 17 db (**89**) n22 solid grist holds its place tight and sees off the hint of wide cut but polishing up the malt; t22 superb sugars popping and fizzing all over the palate, some with a light citrusy feel; f22.5 less feint noticeable here (which is unusual in a whisky) as the sugars and oaky vanilla form a happy union; **b22.5** I think 2010 was a classic vintage for Pemberton: this is rather lovely! 44%. nc ncf sc.

Pemberton Organic Single Malt Whisky 2010 ex-bourbon cask, cask no. 3, dist Oct 10, bott May 16 db (88) **n21.5 t22.5 f22 b22** Massively malty. And they really can claim their very own idiosyncratic style: deliciously different. 45.6%. nc ncf sc.

Pemberton Organic Single Malt Whisky 2013 ex-bourbon cask, cask no. 1, dist 11 Apr 13, bott May 17 db (85.5) **n21 t21.5 f22 b21** I was thinking: "peat and nougat...I've encountered this before". And checking the Bible, I see I have...from Pemberton, with their 2011 bottling! Lots of sweet charm from the grist, but this is a malt which struggles to go to the next step of integration. 44%. nc ncf sc.

Pemberton Organic Single Malt Whisky Lightly Peated 2011 ex-bourbon cask, cask no. 1, dist 2011, bott May 16 db (84.5) **n20.5 t22 f21 b21.** The mix of peat and nougat make slightly uncomfortable bedfellows. Apparently, the first ever peated malt from this distillery north of Whistler – a tough art to master. 45%. nc ncf sc.

Pemberton Organic Single Malt Whisky Medium Peated 2012 ex-bourbon cask, cask no. 3, dist Aug 12, bott May 16 db (87.5) **n21 t22.5 f22 b22.** This one is all about the delivery: colossal barley on show despite the smoke. Again, a very wide cut from the stills means the oils tighten the sugars and experience and make for a challenging, tangy dram. 45.3%. nc ncf sc.

POTTER DISTILLING CO. Kelowna, British Columbia.

Cadenhead's World Whiskies Canada Potter Distilling Co. Aged 24 Years Bourbon barrel, bott Feb 14 (94.5) **n23 t24 f23.5 b24** a true classic of the Canadian rye style...though of course without any rye at all. As a whisky, a little bit of a mystery. When at Potter distillers in British Columbia about 17 years ago, I remember they then had no maturing stock of their own as they did not distil large enough quantities. But they did have casks of maturing Canadian whisky they had bought in from the nearby Okanagan Distillery which, for a while, had made Canadian Club for the west coast and Far East market. No guarantees, but chances are it could be that – and they did make very good whisky there, evidenced by the outstanding old Bush Pilot single cask brand. 56.5%. 126 bottles. WB15/178

SHELTER POINT DISTILLERY Campbell River, British Columbia.

Shelter Point Distillery Artisanal Cask Strength Whisky American oak, finished in French oak db (91) **n22.5** the European tannin makes a statement here and a point of turning the vaguely wide cut into a thick chocolate malt: fascinating and increasingly enticing... **t23.5** light delivery for about a third of second in which you can spot the sweet barley, then...crash..! Just a few minutes before tasting this whisky I was attacked at lightning speed by a sparrowhawk which came at me from nowhere talons fully extended. Well, the huge tannin here arrives at the same velocity and with the same murderous intent. Wrapped up in those oaky notes is a mix of spice, molasses and Nutella which roar onto the taste buds with extraordinary effect, capturing and conquering all before it; **f22** the slightly wide cut is faintly detectable but the malts come out to play; **b23** looks as though the law in Canada now says you even have to have the barrels from both English and French language... A beautifully complex and intense malt. 54.8%. 1,200 bottles.

Shelter Point Single Malt Whisky db (89.5) **n22 t23 f22.5 b22** A charming and very promising malt made by lovely people at a gorgeous distillery – and best when served very much at body temperature. I have been watching progress at Shelter Point – a remote distillery on Victoria Island in stunning British Columbia – since before it was actually built. And having looked at many of the early casks as they matured, I can tell you even better is to come, especially when more sugars are absorbed from the oak and a wider collection of barrels can be vatted for even greater complexity. Like the distillery, this is a whisky – even at this tender age - which just oozes personality. Congratulations to all concerned. 46%

STILLWATERS DISTILLERY Concord, Ontario.

Stalk & Barrel Single Malt Whisky cask 13 db (77) **n20 t21 f17 b19**. Not quite the delight that is cask 11. Not sure if that is because the weaker strength means the water has broken up the oils a little bit too much for their own good, exposing a few feints. Or if the cut wasn't quite as carefully made this time round. Still plenty of malt to get on with, though. 46%. sc.

VICTORIA CALEDONIAN DISTILLERY Victoria, British Columbia

◇ **Mac na Braiche Single Malt Spirit** db (79) **n18 t22 f20 b19** From my home from home town, Victoria in BC. Would like to talk it up, but not that easy with the flavours and balance being all over the place. Some redeeming chocolate on delivery but the rest is very hard work. Wobbles about the palate like a satisfied customer leaving the Garrick's Head...Has the basis for something very good. But some hard work needed to get there. 50%. nc ncf.

YUKON BREWING Whitehorse, Yukon.

Two Brewers Yukon Single Malt Release 03 Peated db (86) n22 t21.5 f21 b21.5 Not the kind of smoke to get the peat heads up all excited and battering down doors to find a bottle. But a friendly and attractive phenol input, especially on the nose, though the delivery and follow though is far more about the Demerara sugars, light cocoa powder and oils. 46%.

Two Brewers Yukon Single Malt Release 04 Special Finishes db (89) n22 t22.5 f22 b22.5 Takes a while to pick up what this malt is trying to do, but once you find its rhythm, it's joy. 43%.

Two Brewers Yukon Single Malt Release 05 Innovative db (94) n23.5 t23.5 f23 b24 What a classy, complex, truly brilliant whisky this is. Take a bow, good people of the Yukon... 43%.

⬙ **Two Brewers Yukon Single Malt Release 06 Classic** db (86.5) n22.5 t22 f20.5 b21.5 Soft and understated, the accent falls on the barley which, when in tandem with the light tannin, offers a custard tart sweetness. The finish, though, is undone by some rogue bitter oak. 43%. 1,050 bottles.

⬙ **Two Brewers Yukon Single Malt Release 07 Peated** db (94) n23.5 such a wonderful mix of peat reek and garden bonfire: simultaneously dry and sweet; t23.5 one of those fascinating malts where for a brief moment you wonder where the smoke is...and then you soon know! Grist at first, seemingly sans peat, then in it steams, for a moment appearing belligerent then backing off into a far more relaxed mode; the mouthfeel is outwardly soft, yet a firm backbone is evident; f23 some real high toast Venezualan cocoa at work here... wow! b24 elegant and making the most of restrained smoke – cleverly showing just how less can mean more. What a massive leap in quality since the last peated malt of their I tasted. Two previous planned trips to this part of Canada to give whisky tastings had been snowed off over the years. I really have to get to the Yukon now... 43%. 1,740 bottles.

⬙ **Two Brewers Yukon Single Malt Release 08 Innovative** db (84.5) n21.5 t21 f21 b21 Sweet, slightly oily and with a citrusy hop character. Reminds me of Marston's New World bitter: an attractive style for a beer, but not so much for a whisky. 43%. 920 bottles.

Canadian Blended Whisky

Alberta Premium (95.5) n24 t25 f22.5 b24 It has just gone 8am and the Vancouver Island sky is one of clear blue. My windows are open to allow in some chilly, early Spring air and, though only the first week of March, an American robin sits in the arbutus tree, resplendent in its now two-toned leaves, calling for a mate, as it has done since 5.15 this morning, his song blending with the lively trill of the house finches and the doleful, maritime anthem of the gull. It seems the natural environment of Alberta Premium, back here to its rye-studded best after a couple I tasted socially in Canada last year appeared comparatively dull and restrained. I am tasting this from Bottle Lott No L93300197 and it is classic, generating all I expect and now demand. A national treasure. 40%

Alberta Premium 25 Years Old (95) n24 t23 f23 b25. Faultless. Absolutely nothing dominates. Yet every aspect has its moment of conquest and glory. It is neither bitter nor sweet, yet both. It is neither soft nor hard on the palate yet both elements are there. Because of the 100% rye used, this is an entirely new style of whisky to hit the market. No Canadian I know has ever had this uncompromising brilliance, this trueness to style and form. And, frightening to think, it could be improved further by bottling at least 46% and un-chillfiltered. For any whisky lover who ever thought Canadian was incapable of hitting the heights among the world's greats. 40%. Alberta Distillers.

Alberta Premium 30 Years (88.5) n23 t23.5 f20 b22. It doesn't take much to tip the balance of a whisky this delicate on the nose and delivery. Five extra years in the cask has nudged the oak just a little too far. However, savour the nose and delivery which are to die for. 40%

Alberta Premium Dark Horse (84) n18 t22 f22 b22. The nose is not great: it really does seem as though fruit cordial has been given the lead role. But the taste really does challenge, and I have to say there are many aspects I enjoy. It is as though some peated malt has been added to the mix as the finish does have distinctive smokiness. And the balance has been expertly worked to ensure the sugars don't dominate while the spices are persistent. But if it falls down anywhere, the over reliance on the fruit apart, it is the fact that Alberta makes the best spirit in Canada by a very great distance....yet someone has forgotten to ensure that fact is made clear in the taste and the nose especially. 45%

Alberta Rye Whisky Dark Batch Blended Rye (86) n19 t23 f22 b22. A veritable fruitcake of a whisky – and about as moist and sultana-laden as you'll ever find. Not sure about that bitter-tobacco most un-Canadian nose, though. 45% (90 Proof)

Alberta Springs Aged 10 Years (83) n21 t21 f20 b20. Really appears to have had a bit of a flavourectomy. Sweet but all traces of complexity have vanished. 40%.

Barton's Canadian 36 Months Old (78) n19 t20 f19 b20. Sweet, toffeed, easy-going. 40%

Bowman's Canadian Whisky (90.5) n22 t22 f23.5 b23. A delicious blend for chocoholics. 40%

Black Velvet (78) n18 t20 f20 b20. A distinctly off-key nose is compensated for by a rich corn and vanilla kick on the palate. But that famous spice flourish is a distant memory. Another big caramel number. 40%

Caldera Distilling Hurricane 5 Whisky batch no. 0001 (87.5) n21.5 t22 f22 b22. Silky, soft. But lashings of toffee and sugars. Decent spices balance things up a little. 40% (80 proof)

Campbell & Cooper Aged a Minimum of 36 Months (84.5) n21.5 t22 f20 b21. Huge flavour profile. An orchard of oranges on the nose and profound vanilla on delivery. 40%

Canadian Club 100 Proof (89) n21 t23 f22 b23. If you are expecting this to be a high-octane version of the standard CC Premium, you'll be in for a shock. This is a much fruitier dram with an oilier body to absorb the extra strength. An entertaining blend. 50%.

Canadian Club 100% Rye (92) n23 t23.5 f22.5 b23 Will be interesting to see how this brand develops over the years. Rye is not the easiest grain to get right when blending differing ages and casks with varied histories: it is an art which takes time to perfect. This is a very attractive early bottling, though my money is on it becoming sharper in future vattings as the ability to show the grain above all else becomes more easily understood. Just so wonderful to see another excellent addition to the Canadian whisky lexicon. 40% (80 proof)

Canadian Club Chairman's Select 100% Rye (81.5) n21 t21.5 f20 b19. A bemusing whisky. The label proudly announces that here we have a whisky made from 100% rye. Great news: a Canadian eagerly anticipated. But the colour – a deep orange – looks a bit suspicious. And those fears prove well founded when the taste buds, as well as the nose, go looking for the rye influence in vain. Instead we have a massive toffee effect, offset by some busy spice. Colouring has ruined many a great whisky...and here we have a painful example. What a waste of good rye... 40%

⬩⬩⬩ **Canadian Club Chronicles: Issue No. 1 Water of Windsor Aged 41 Years** (97) n24.5 one of the greatest, most classic, non-high-rye noses ever experienced with a Canadian: it has it all...and every bit of it good. It is as though the nose has been fashioned on an architect's drawing board, the framework of the rich corn, itself seemingly created from freshly-baled straw, ulmo honey and Brazilian sequilhos, interwoven into a deeper oak body. Lightened, it seems by something flitting and grainy, the tannins are stunningly deft and delicate, at times chalky, at others sweeter and vaguely molassed. This is a nose which never sits still, or comes across twice identically. As mesmerising as it is beautiful; t24 after the nose you expect the flavours to be almost too delicate to fully appreciate. Well, they could be if you are not prepared to give this whisky the Murray Method and at least 20 minutes of your time. At body temperature the sugars are entirely in sync with the tannins: the corn oils forming the most luscious, salivating coating, not remotely too thick but sticky enough for the red liquorice and thinned Manuka honey to last an improbably long time, tangling and untangling, landing, taking off and landing again... Spices hint rather than perform; a light hickory note blends into the sweetening butterscotch; f24 now the spices at last make a genuine move and...oh, just look at that amazing Belgium chocolate finale...and now praline, too....; b24.5 have I had this much fun with a sexy 41-year-old Canadian before? Well, yes I have. But it was a few years back now and it wasn't a whisky. Was the fun we had better? Probably not. It is hard to imagine what could be, as this whisky simply seduces you with the lightness and knowledgeable meaning of its touch, butterfly kissing your taste buds, finding time after time your whisky erogenous zone or g spots ... and then surrendering itself with tender and total submission. 45% (90 proof).

Canadian Club Premium (92) n23 t22.5 f23 b23.5. A greatly improved whisky which now finds the fruit fitting into the mix with far more panache than of old. Once a niggardly whisky, often seemingly hell-bent on refusing to enter into any form of complexity: but not now! Great spices in particular. I'm impressed. 40%

Canadian Club Aged 6 Years (88.5) n21.5 t22 f22.5 b22.5. Not at all bad for a Canadian some purists turn their nose up at as it's designed for the American market. Just brimming with mouth-watering enormity and style. Dangerously moreish. 40%

Canadian Club Reserve Aged 10 Years (86) n20 t22 f21.5 b22. Odd cove, this. The nose is less than welcoming and offers a hotchpotch of somewhat discordant notes giving a jumbled message and less than well defined statement of intent. Decent delivery, though, shifting through the gears with some impressive and sultry fruit tying in well with a rare grain onslaught found in Canadian these days. The finish, though, just can't steer away from the rocks of bitterness, alas. Again, as so often appears to be the case with CC, the spices star. 40%

Canadian Club Classic Aged 12 Years (91.5) n22 t24 f21.5 b23.5. A confident whisky which makes the most of a honeycomb theme. 40%

Canadian Club Aged 20 Years (92.5) n24 t21 f23.5 b23. In previous years, CC20 has ranked among the worst whiskies I have tasted, not just in Canada, but the world. Their current bottling, though, is not even a distant relation. Sure, it has a big sherry investment. But the sheer elan and clever use of spice make this truly magnificent. Possibly the most pleasant surprise in my latest trawl through all Canada's whiskies. *40%*

Canadian Five Star Rye Whisky (83) n21 t22 f20 b20. An entirely tame, well behaved Canadian which celebrates the inherent sweetness of the species. That said, the immediate impact on the palate is pretty delicious with a quick, flash explosion of something spicy. But it is the deft, satin-soft mouthfeel which may impress most. *40%*

Canadian Hunter (85.5) n20.5 t21 f22 b22. Remains truly Canadian in style. The toffee has diminished, allowing far more coffee and cocoa to ensure a delightful middle and finish. *40%*

Canadian Mist (78) n19 t20.5 f18.5 b20. Much livelier than previous incarnations despite the inherent, lightly fruited softness. *40%*

◈ **Canadian Mist At Least 36 Months Old** bott code: L 171007 3133317 (87.5) n21.5 t22.5 f21.5 b22 An old-fashioned style of Canadian which is big on the grain and softens out further with the moderate intervention of fruit and caramel. Doesn't stint on the late spice, either. A lovely every day kind of Canadian. *40% (80 proof)*.

Canadian Pure Gold (82) n21.5 t20.5 f20 b20. Full-bodied and still a notably lush whisky. The pure gold may have more to do with the caramel than the years in cask but the meat of this whisky still gives you plenty to chew over. I especially enjoy the gradual building of spices. *40%*

Canadian Spirit (78) n20 t20 f19 b19. A real toffee-fest with a touch of hard grain around the edges. *40%. Carrington Distillers (Alberta Distillers).*

Centennial 10 Year Limited Edition (88.5) n21.5 t23 f22 b22. Retains its usual honey-flavoured breakfast cereal style, but the complexity has increased. Busy and charming. *40%*

Century Reserve 8 Years Old Premium (82) n20 t21 f20 b21. Clean vanilla caramel. *40%*

Century Reserve Custom Blend 15 Years Plus (88.5) n21.5 t22 f23 b22. After two days of being ambushed in every direction, or completely steamrollered by Canadian caramel, my tastebuds are in total shock. Caramel kept to an absolute minimum so that it hardly registers at all. Charming and refined drinking. *40%*

Century Reserve 21 Years Old (91.5) n23.5 t23 f23 b22. Quite beautiful, but a spirit that is as likely to appeal to rum lovers as whisky ones. *40%*

Century Reserve Custom Blend lot no. 1525 (87) n21.5 t22 f21.5 b22. An enjoyable whisky which doesn't quite reach its full potential. *40%*

Corby's Canadian 36 Months Old (85) n20 t21 f22 b22. Attractive with a fine bitter-sweet balance and I love the late spice kick-back. *40%. Barton*

Crown Royal (86) n22 t23.5 f19.5 b21. The Crown has spoken and it has been decreed that this once ultra grainy old whisky is taking its massive move to a silky fruitiness as far as it can go. It was certainly looking that way last time out; on this re-taste (and a few I have unofficially tasted) there is now no room for doubt. If you like grape, especially the sweeter variety, you'll love this. The highpoint is the sublime delivery and starburst of spice. The low point? The buzzy, unhappy finale. The Grain Is Dead. Long Live The Grape! *40%*

Crown Royal bott code: 318 B4 2111 (87.5) n22 t23 f21 b21.5 Carries on in the same style as above. But at least the finish is a lot happier now with welcome ulmo honey extending further and the spices also working overtime. Still a little residual bitterness shows more work is required but, unquestionably, keep on this course and they'll soon be getting there. *40%*

Crown Royal Black (85) n22 t23 f18.5 b21.5. Not for the squeamish: a Canadian which goes for it with bold strokes from the off which makes it a whisky worth discovering. The finish needs a rethink, though. *45%*

◈ **Crown Royal Bourbon Mash Bill** bott code: L8 N04 N7 db (94.5) n23.5 what'd be regarded as a small grains special in ol' Kentuck'. Spices and crisp fruit dance around the glass to the tune of the delicate vanilla and brittle sugars; t23.5 the delivery offers the softest moment, when the oils slowly slide around the palate seemingly moving the flavour elements into a position to attack. Then about three or four flavour waves in, the spices begin the mount – from all directions, while a sweeter, firmer, juicier thrust makes its mark; f23.5 now you get the full busy-ness of the grain, flicking and teasing the palate, never sweet, verging on the dry, always toasty; b24 whiskies like this do so much to up the standing of Canadian whisky. *40% (80 proof). The Blenders' Series.*

Crown Royal Cornerstone Blend (85.5) n21 t22 f21 b21.5. Something of a mish-mash, where a bold spiciness appears to try to come to terms with an, at times, random fruity note. One of the most curious aspects of this quite different whisky is the way in which the weight of the body continues to change. Intriguing. *40.3% (80.6 proof)*

Crown Royal DeLuxe (91.5) n23.5 t23 f22.5 b22.5 Some serious blending went into this. Complex. *40% (80 proof)*

Crown Royal Hand Selected Barrel (94.5) n23.5 t24 f23.5 b23.5 If this is a single barrel, it boasts extraordinary layering and complexity *51.5% (103 proof)*

Crown Royal Limited Edition (87) n22 t22.5 f20.5 b22. A much happier and productive blend than before with an attractive degree of complexity but the more bitter elements of the finish have been accentuated. 40%

◇ **Crown Royal Noble Collection 13 Year Old Bourbon Mash** bott code: L8037 2S 00108:06 db (96) n24.5 one of the best noses in the world this year. Its secret is the extraordinary juxtaposition of evenness and complexity. So delicate it should be arrested for showing off! The small grains whizz through their set pieces, busily buzzing between periods of roasty sweetness...and even roastier dryness; t24 oh, that is just so fine... The nose in liquid form, the taste buds mesmerised by the movement of the grain, its amazing ability to pop and fizz around the palate, rye in particular showing an angular firmness which you might have thought would have reduced the possibility of complexity. But not a bit of it, for a gorgeous hickory and liquorice sub strata appears to summon up spices at will; f23.5 long, with light oils now shewing a light corn and vanilla thread. So ridiculously satisfying...; b24 it's Canadian, Jim: but not as we know it... Deliciously going places where no other Canadian has gone before... 45% (90 proof).

Crown Royal Noble Collection Wine Barrel Finished lot no. 0100-43-B1245 (87) n21 t22.5 f21.5 b22 A friendly, juicy Canadian. Because Canada is allowed to add things into their whisky – and fruit has (sadly) been a popular choice for the last 20 years – it is hard to see how a wine barrel finish will make a notable difference to a blend. So, perhaps the little cleverly diffused spice apart, it is a major ask to tell the difference between this and standard practice. My guess is the spice. Unquestionably pleasant, though. Despite the late bitterness. 40.5%.

Crown Royal Northern Harvest Rye bott code L5085 N3 (97.5) n25 t24.5 f23.5 b24.5 This is the kind of whisky you dream of dropping into your tasting room. Rye, that most eloquent of grains, not just turning up to charm and enthral but to also take us through a routine which reaches new heights of beauty and complexity. To say this is a masterpiece is barely doing it justice. 45%

Crown Royal Northern Harvest Rye bott code L5099 (94) n23 t24 f23.5 b23.5 Superb whisky but just missing the magic of its all-conquering sister bottling. 45%.

Crown Royal Northern Harvest Rye bott code L5134 (97) n24 t24.5 f24 b24.5 A close relation to last year's whisky sensation: Jim Murray's Whisky Bible World Whisky of the Year 2016. Not quite as truly incredible, but the link can very obvious and much more than bottling L5099 and a few others I have subsequently tasted, though not in controlled conditions like this. And, having just this moment tasted last year's winner, I can can confirm that it is a close-ish miss. Absolutely brilliant and helps carry on the work of its sister bottling in waking up the world to how good the very top Canadian whiskies can be... 45%.

Crown Royal Northern Harvest Rye bott code: L6022 N5 (96) n24.5 t23.5 f24 b24.5 Breathtakingly clean rye with not a single note out of place, or the odd bitter note where not required: indeed, this is the sweetest Northern Harvest Rye I have yet encountered. Beautifully weighted and paced, this bottling does lack the stunning grain intensity which won it worldwide acclaim two years ago. 40.5%.

◇ **Crown Royal Northern Harvest Rye** bott code: 095 B1 0247 db (95.5) n24 though the rye is crisp and Demerara coated, it holds back on the weightier notes, preferring a more fragile and ethereal feel. The tannins are relaxed, but given the lighter personality of the grain, still play an important part; t24 so sweet! Brilliant double jointed delivery with some softer vanillas cushioned by grain taking the weight of the far crisper rye, which, just like on the nose, positively celebrates the companionship of the demerara sugar; f23.5 spicier now, a little bitter as the tannins fill in where grain has has left off; b24 not quite the same beguiling intensity as the batch which once won the Whisky Bible's World Whisky of the Year, but what an absolute salivating treat of a whisky this remains...as sprightly and fresh as any NHR I have tasted yet. 45% (90 proof).

◇ **Crown Royal Reserve** bott code: 3046A52219 db (88) n22 surprisingly crisp: lots of toasty sugars at play; t23 no less toasty on the medium sweet delivery: only medium weight to the corn thrust, then a vanilla and liquorice middle; f21 a slightly untidy, tangy and furry finish; b22 not sure if this is complex or just confusing. The excellent moments are as good as the lesser moments are not. 40% (80 proof).

Crown Royal Special Reserve (96) n24 t24 f24 b24 Complex, well weighted and simply radiant: it is like looking at a perfectly shaped, gossamer clad Deb at a ball. The ryes work astonishingly well here (they appear to be of the malted, ultra-fruity variety) and perhaps to best effect after Alberta Premium, though now it is a hard call between the two. 40%

Crown Royal XR Extra Rare lot no. L7064 N4 (93.5) n24 t23 f23 b23.5. Just about identical to the previous bottle above. The only difference is on the finish where the rye, fortified with spice, decides to hang back and battle it out to the death; the toffee and vanilla make a controlled retreat. Either the same bottling with a slightly different stance after a few years in the bottle, or a different one of extraordinary high consistency. 40%

Crown Royal XO (87.5) n22 t21 f22.5 b22. With an XO, one might have hoped for something eXtraOrdinary or at least eXOtic. Instead, we have a Canadian which carried on a little further where their Cask No 16 left off. Always a polite, if rather sweet whisky, it falls into the trap of allowing the Cognac casks a little too much say. Only on the finish, as the spices begin to find channels to flow into, does the character which, for generations, set Crown Royal apart from all other Canadians begin to make itself heard: complexity. 40% WB15/398

Danfield's Limited Edition Aged 21 Years (95) n24 t24 f23.5 b23.5. A quite brilliant first-time whisky. The back label claims this to be small batch, but there is no batch number on the bottle, alas. Or even a visible bottling code. But this is a five star performer. 40%

Danfield's Private Reserve (84.5) n20 t21.5 f22 b21. A curious, non-committal whisky which improves on the palate as it goes along. An overdose of caramel (yawn!!) has done it no favours, but there is character enough for it to pulse out some pretty tasty spice. Seamless and silky, for all the toffee there underlying corn-rich clarity is a bit of a turn on. 40%

8 Seconds Small Batch (86) n20 t22 f22.5 b21.5. Fruity, juicy, luxurious. Perhaps one of the few whiskies on the market anywhere in the world today which could slake a thirst. 40%

Forty Creek Barrel Select (86.5) n21.5 t22 f21 b21.5. Thank goodness that the sulphur taint I had found on this in recent years has now vanished. A lush, enjoyable easy-goer, this juices up attractively at the start and ends with an almost sophisticated dry pithiness. 40%

Forty Creek Confederation Oak Reserve lot 1867-B (94.5) n23.5 t24 f23.5 b23.5. Those who tasted the first batch of this will be intrigued by this follow up. The shape and intensity profile has been re-carved and all now fits together like a jigsaw. 40%

Forty Creek Copper Pot Reserve (91.5) n23 t23.5 f22 b23. One of the beauties of John Hall's whiskies at Forty Creek is that they follow no set pattern in the whisky would: they offer flavour profiles really quite different from anything else. That is why they are worth that bit of extra time for your palate to acclimatise. Here you are exceptionally well rewarded... 43%

Forty Creek Double Barrel Reserve lot 247 (86) n21.5 t22.5 f20.5 b21.5. Juicy ride with plenty to savour early on. But something is slightly off balance about the finish. 40%

Forty Creek Port Wood Reserve lot 61 (95.5) n24.5 oh my word! Very highest quality Turkish Delight with some pretty top score chocolate; the fruit hangs off the frame full of juice and muscovado sugars. It demands spices...and gets them – with the right pizzazz! t24 the delivery is pure silk in texture and the most stunning fruit and spice on delivery. Hard to know whether to suck as it melts in the mouth, or chew the background depth is outrageously nutty, with more cocoa to thicken. It is the astonishing spice that really mesmerises, as it is of almost perfect intensity; f23 dries into an attractive crushed grape pip dryness, again with the spices lingering; b24 John P Hall has got his ducks in a row. Magnificent! 45%

Forty Creek Three Grain (76) n19 t20 f18 b19. Not quite as well assembled as some Three grains I have come across over the last few years. There is a lopsidedness to this one: we know the fruit dominates (and I still haven't a clue why, when surely this of all whiskies, just has to be about the grains!) but the bitterness interferes throughout. If there have been sherry casks used here, I would really have a close look at them. 40%

Fremont Mischief Whiskey batch MPJ-0803, bott 11 (77) n19 t20 f19 b19. Though this was from the Mischief distillery in Seattle, USA, the whiskey was produced in Canada. Overly sweet, overly toffeed and bereft of complexity. Like Alberta Springs on a very bad day. 40%

Gibson's Finest Aged 12 Years (77) n18 t20 f19 b20. Unlike the Sterling, going backwards rather than forwards. This is way too syrupy, fruity and toffee impacted. Despite the very good spice, almost closer to a liqueur than a true whisky style. 40%

Gibson's Finest Rare Aged 18 Years (95.5) n24 t24.5 f23.5 b23.5 So far ahead of both Sterling and the 12, it is hard to believe they are from the same stable. But make no mistake; this is pure thoroughbred: truly world class. 40%

Gibson's Finest 100th Grey Cup Special Edition (87) n21 t23 f21 b22. When the label tells you there is a hint of maple, they aren't joking... 40%

Gibson's Finest Canadian Whisky Bourbon Cask Rare Reserve (89) n23 t21 f23 b22. A much better version than the first bottling, the depth this time being massively greater. 40%

Gibson's New Oak (88) n22 t21 f23 b22. Distinctly different from any other Canadian doing the rounds: the oak influence makes a wonderful and clever impact. 40%

Gooderham & Worts Four Grain blend no. A.A1129 (94) n23 t24 f23.5 b23.5 Four there's a jolly good whisky...worts and all...! 44.4%

⟫ **Gooderham & Worts 11 Souls** (94) n23.5 buzzes with small grain complexity. The rye fizzes and cuts with a slightly fruity edge, but there is more besides. If that isn't wheat in there bigging up the spice, then something is giving a good impression; t23.5 I stand by my assertion on the nose. Beautiful layering of acacia honey and barley, then a real chattering buzz of grain – the rye in particular now a three dimension essay; f23 the vanillas are now left to their own devices, a little butterscotch making up for the spent grain; b24 this wouldn't be named after Frank Saul, who once famously wore the Millwall number 11 shirt, would it...? Absolutely have no idea what this whisky consists of, but the leading element appears to be small grain complexity with rye, barley and perhaps others, especially wheat, causing all kinds of delicious mayhem. Controlled, of course. Love it! And by far the most exciting whisky I've tasted today – and I'm now more than seven hours into my shift! 49%.

Gooderham & Worts Little Trinity Three Grain Blend (94) n23.5 t24 f23 b23.5 Beautifully complex but will still suit those with catholic tastes... 45%. *Ultra-Rare Craft Series.*

⟳ **Hiram Walker Legends Series Guy Lafleur** (87.5) n21.5 t22.5 f21.5 b22 A kind of classic present day style Canadian with plenty of fruit muscling in on the corn. Easy going and very drinkable. 40%. *Legends Whisky Series.*

⟳ **Hiram Walker Legends Series Lanny McDonald** (85) n21.5 t21.5 f21 b21 Looks like they are taking a maple leaf out of the Welsh Whisky Company's books by launching whiskies in honour of great fellow countrymen. A friend informs me Lanny McDonald was an ice hockey player. So I suspect he had a touch more personality than this rather sweet straight up and downer. 40%. *Legends Whisky Series.*

⟳ **Hiram Walker Legends Series Wendel Clark** (94) n23.5 rye drips from the glass. Firm and fruity with a cinnamon edge. Beautifully two-toned it is both soft and rigid...or neither...or both...! Wow! t23.5 and there it goes again: salivating with a spicy spark now. The fruit reverberates around the palate alongside the Demerara sugars; more cinnamon and red liquorice, too; f23 long, very delicately oiled with extra cinnamon on French toast; light butterscotch accompanies the persistent spices b24 being English, don't know about Wendel Clark being a legend...but this whisky certainly is... 41.6%. *Legends Whisky Series.*

Hiram Walker Special Old (93) n22.5 t24 f23 b23.5. Even with the extra degree of all-round harmony, this remains the most solid, uncompromising Canadian of them all. And I love it! Not least because this is the way Special old has been for a very long time with obviously no intentions of joining the fruity bandwagon. Honest, first class Canadian. 40%

Hiram Walker Special Old Rye Whisky bott code L16123 (90.5) n22.5 t23 f22.5 b22.5 Once one of my daily drinking ryes when in Canada, this has changed course a little in recent years, going easier on the classic old rye itself and making up for it with a richer, sweeter, fatter mouth feel. Not the same magic, but still hard not to love... 40%.

J.P. Wiser's 18 Year Old db (94) n22.5 dusty, fruity, busy. Soft, fruity sawdust to the sugars; t24 excellent early bite, though the oils make their mark early. Salivating and silky despite the spice build and a little cocoa to accompany the fruit; f23.5 comfortable, with a pleasing acceleration of spice; b24 exceptionally creamy but maintains the required sharpness. 40%.

J.P. Wiser's 18 Years Old bott code 54SL24 L16341 (94) n23 t24 f23 b24 Some great blending here means this is a slight notch up on the bottling above, though the styles are almost identical. Main differences here concern the fruit aspect: more prolific and spicier on the nose and then added moist date on the delivery. Significantly, there is more honey on the longer finish, also. Remains a deliciously rounded and satisfying whisky. 40%.

J. P. Wiser's 35 Year Old (96) n23.5 spices abound and, thrillingly, at varying pitches and intensities. The softer tones are supplied by apple pie as well as rhubarb and custard, giving the most gentle fruitiness while a mix of black and red liquorice mixes comfortably with the molasses to underline the age; t24 that is rather wonderful: the landing is soft, but the grains are not lost in a sea of bland as could so easily happen. Instead, the palate is peppered with some of the spices so rampant on the nose but also layers of ulmo honey and muscovado sugars, ensuring a serious juiciness despite the years; f24 a slow burn of spice, something akin to rye in both crispness and fruitiness and vanilla; a little bitterness reveals some tiring oak; b24.5 many, many years ago I tasted Canadian older than this in the blending lab. But I have never seen it before at this age as an official bottling. What I had before me on the lab table could not have engineered this style, so this is as fascinating as it is enjoyable. 50%. *Ultra-Rare Craft Series.*

⟳ **J. P. Wiser's Canada 2018 Commemorative Series** bott code: L18064EW1332 (94) n23.5 it is not just the complexity that works so well here, it is the weight of the flavours. The vaguest plumy note acts as a buffer between a slightly biting tannin and sweeter vanillas; t23.5 the corn oil, which you can glimpse only now and then on the nose, is much more fulsome on delivery, though a salivating toffee-apple delivery ensures a controlled sharpness; the mid-ground offers light, nibbling spice and a blend of molasses and fudge; f23 such an old-fashioned Canadian face of vanilla, spice, corn and caramel...; b24 this whisky, as the front label confirms, has been created to mark the 200th anniversary of the 49th Parallel, the line on which much of Canadian border sits. And this would be the perfect drinking whisky, not just to celebrate, in effect, Canada's birthday. But also to watch the brilliant film The 49th Parallel, by the most extraordinary pairing in cinematic history: Michael Powell and Emeric Pressburger. This 1941 film, designed to help persuade the USA to join in the battle against Germany, picked up an Academy Award for Powell; and many a time have I had the honour of sitting next to another of their Oscars when dining at my club, The Savile, of which both Powell and Pressburger were members. Pressburger was a Jew who had escaped Germany before the war and very famously said of this film: "Goebbels considered himself an expert in propaganda; but I thought I'd show him a thing or two." I can imagine Powell and Pressburger toasting their work – and Canada's special anniversary - with a glass or two of this classical Canadian. I already have. Next time I pop in to my Club, I will do it again from there...on their behalf. 43.4%.

J.P. Wiser's De Luxe (86) n20 t22.5 f21.5 b22. Still nothing like the classic, ultra-charming and almost fragile-delicate Wiser's of old. But this present bottling has got its head partly out of the sand by injecting a decently oaked spiciness to the proceedings and one might even fancy detecting shards of fruity- rye brightness beaming through the toffeed clutter. Definitely an impressive turn for the better and the kind of Canadian with a dangerous propensity to grow on you. If they had the nerve to cut the caramel, this could be a cracker... 40%

J. P. Wiser's Dissertation (89) n22 t22 f22 b22.5 A distinctive and quite different style being handsome, a little rugged but always brooding. 46.1%.

J.P. Wiser's Double Still Rye (94) n23.5 the rye is gorgeously crisp, its natural fruity notes augmented by spearmint; t23.5 every bit as salivating and full-flavoured as the nose predicts. Not as crunchy, maybe, until the Demerara sugars ram themselves home. But the spices arrive in the first few moments and continue building until they become quite a force; f23.5 long, oily, with that spice still impacting positively; b23.5 big, superb rye: a genuine triumph from Wiser's. 43.4%

J.P. Wiser's Hopped Whisky (77) n18 t21 f19 b19. Sorry chaps: one has to draw the line somewhere. But, despite my deep love for great beer, as a whisky this really isn't my kind of thing. Oh, and by the way: been tasting this kind of thing from Germany for the last decade... 40%

J.P. Wiser's Last Barrels Aged 14 Years (94.5) n24.5 t23.5 f23.5 b23.5 You don't need to be pulsing with rye to ensure a complex Canadian of distinction. 45%

J.P. Wiser's Legacy (95) n24 t24.5 f22.5 b22.5. When my researcher got this bottle for me to taste, she was told by the Wiser's guy that I would love it, as it had been specially designed along the lines of what I considered essential attributes to Canadian whisky. Whether Mr Wiser was serious or not, such a statement both honoured and rankled slightly and made me entirely determined to find every fault with it I could and knock such impertinence down a peg or two. Instead, I was seduced like a 16-year-old virgin schoolboy in the hands of a 30-year-old vixen. An entirely disarming Canadian which is almost a whisky equivalent to the finest of the great French wines in its rich, unfolding style. Complex beyond belief, spiced almost to supernatural perfection, this is one of the great newcomers to world whisky in the last year. It will take a glass of true magnificence to outdo this for Canadian Whisky of the Year. 45%

J. P. Wiser's One Fifty (86) n22 t21.5 f21.5 b21 The nose gives hope as heather honey and spices stir. But another Canadian too jammed packed with caramel to enjoy to the fullest, though there is an attractive, if slightly bland, golden syrup thread running through the piece. 43.4%. Commemorative Series.

J.P. Wiser's Red Letter 2015 Release Virgin oak finish (90.5) n22.5 t22.5 f23 b22.5 Stubbornly refusing to return to its complex grain past, electing instead to stick to the silky route of more recent years. The sugars are kept in control – just. At times, a little touch and go: this style has been taken as safely as it can go... A backbone to this would be worth so many more points... 43.4%. ncf.

J.P. Wiser's Reserve (75) n19 t20 f18 b18. The nose offers curious tobacco while the palate is uneven, with the bitterness out of tandem with the runaway early sweetness. In the confusion the fruit never quite knows which way to turn. A once mighty whisky has fallen. And I now understand it might be the end of the line with the excellent Wiser's Small Batch coming in to replace it. So if you are a reserve fan, buy them up now. 43%

J.P. Wiser's Rye (84.5) n21 t22 f20.5 b21 Sweet, soft and easy going. The delivery is classic Canadian, with an enjoyable corn oil-vanilla oak mix which initially doesn't go easy on the sugars. The finish, though, is more brittle toffee. 40%

J. P. Wiser's Rye 15 Year Old (89) n22 the nose owes much more to a rum style than rye: the golden syrup and molasses make their mark; t22.5 chewy. Very chewy. More golden syrup and toffee with a late spice development; again a rum-type sheen; f22.5 simple spice and toffee; b22 doesn't do too much. But what it does do, it does big... 40%.

J.P. Wiser's Rye Triple Barrel bott code L16331 54SL24 (85.5) n22 t21.5 f21 b21 Three types of toffee barrel by the looks of it. Pleasant but lacking complexity. 45%.

J.P. Wiser's Small Batch (90.5) n21.5 t24 f22 b23. A real oddity with the nose & taste on different planets. The fruity onslaught promised by the drab nose never materialises and instead we are treated to a rich, grainy explosion. It's the spices, though, that take the plaudits. 43.4%

◈ **J. P. Wiser's Seasoned Oak Aged 19 Years** seasoned 48 months, bott code L18114EW0814 (87.5) n22.5 t23 ff20.5 b21.5 Some high- octane tannin trumps all, though some rich fruit – moist dates especially - rounds off the peppery oak. Enjoys a glossy, coppery but unravels somewhat at the death with a furry, off-key finale. Some lovely, lilting moments but the balance seems controlled. 48%. *Rare Cask Series. Exclusive to the LCBO.*

J.P. Wiser's Special Blend (78) n19 t20 f19 b19. A plodding, pleasant whisky with no great desire to offer much beyond caramel. 40%

J.P. Wiser's Spiced Whisky Vanilla db (51) n16 t12 f11 b12. The policy of the Whisky Bible is not to accept any spiced distillate as, by definition, being whisky. Only Canadian can escape that ban, as they are allowed to put up to 9.09% of whatever into their spirit and still call it whisky. That does not mean to say I am going to like it, though. And, believe me when I tell you I really can't stand this cloyingly sweet liqueur-like offering. Indeed, it may have "whisky" on the label, but this is about as much that great spirit as I am the next Hollywood pin up. 43%

J.P. Wiser's Triple Barrel (85.5) n22 t21.5 f21 b21. The barrels, whatever their number, appear to be no match for the big caramel theme. 40% (80 proof)

⬩ **J. P. Wiser's Triple Barrel Aged 10 Years** bott code: L17258 (89) n22 the softest nose imaginable: gentle vanilla...a kind of sherry trifle... but without the sherry; t23 here it excels: the delivery retains an endearing juiciness despite the marriage in heaven between caramel and vanilla; alert spices ensure you don't get too comfortable; f21.5 slightly bitter and a tad out of balance; b22.5 the finale apart, this is a celebration of the gentler side of whisky 40%.

James Foxe (77.5) n20 t19.5 f19 b19. James could do with putting some weight on... 40%

Lot 40 Cask Strength (88.5) n23.5 t24 f20 b22 At last! Lot 40 at full strength! You will not read this anywhere (or anything to do with my many whisky creations over the last 25 years as journalists can sometimes be a pathetically narrow-minded and jealous bunch disinclined to tell the true story if it doesn't suit their own agenda) but when I first created the style for Lot 40 a great many years back the first thing I proposed was that it should be a rye at cask strength. The idea was liked in principle but regarded way too radical for its time and dropped. So I helped come up with a weaker but still excellent rye. This is a different style to what I had in mind as the oak gives a slant I would have avoided. But it gladdens my heart to see it nonetheless. 53%. *Ultra-Rare Craft Series.*

Lot No. 40 Rye Whisky bott code 54SL24 L16344 (96) n24 t24 f23.5 b24.5 Now this is very close to the rye I had in mind when first involved in putting this whisky together the best part of a couple of decades ago. Much more complex and satisfying than the previous re-introduced bottling I encountered...which in itself was magnificent. Here, though, the honey I had originally tried to lasso has been brilliantly recaptured. Happy to admit: this is better than my early efforts. There really is a Lot going on... Classic! 43%.

Masterson's 10 Year Old Straight Rye Whiskey barrel finished in American oak, batch no. P5A3 (94.5) n24 t24 f23 b23.5 Lovely, as always. But this batch of Alberta does not have three dimensional grain sharpness which can, on its day, set it apart. That said, just sit back and try and unravel the extraordinary complexity of this: a bit like peeling an onion. But any tears that form here will be ones of joy... 45% (90 proof).

Masterson's 10 Year Old Straight Rye Whiskey barrel finished in French oak, batch no. P573 (92) n22.5 t24 f23 b22.5 Just a question here about the terminology of straight rye here: matured in a pre-used bourbon barrels and finished in another oak entirely. Really? Something to ponder while enjoying this barn-storming, slightly over oaked rye. 45% (90 proof).

Masterson's 10 Year Old Straight Rye Whiskey barrel finished in Hungarian oak, batch no. P5H3 (95.5) n23.5 t24 f24 b24 A complex and truly delicious rye with a quick unique fingerprint. Spectacularly beautiful. 45% (90 proof).

Okanagan Spirits Rye (88.5) n23 t22.5 f21 b22. A crisp, quite beautiful whisky with a youthful strain. Sort the thin finish out and we'd have something to really remember! Not, by the way, a whisky distilled at their new distillery. 40%

Pendleton 1910 Aged 12 Years Rye (83) n21 t22 f20 b20. Pleasant enough. But if it wasn't for the small degree of spice pepping up this fruitfest, it would be all rather too predictable. 40%

Pendleton Director's Reserve 2017 Aged 20 Years (90) n22.5 t22 f22.5 b23 If you don't enjoy this super-soft blend I'll eat my Pendleton Fedora hat. But don't worry, I never have less than three or four of them at any one time... 40% (80 proof).

Pendleton Midnight (78) n20 t21 f18 b19. Soft and soothing. But far more rampant fruit than grain. In fact, hard to detect the grain at all... 45% (90 Proof).

Pike Creek (92) n22 t23.5 f23 b23.5 A whisky that is more effect over substance, for this really has to be the softest, silkiest world whisky of 2015. And if you happen to like your taste buds being pampered and chocolate is your thing, this Canadian has your name written all over it. 40%

⬩ **Pike Creek** French, Hungarian & American oak casks (89) n23 this is all about the varied intensity and rhythm of the tannin: deep, toasty and rich, a malty sweetness helps keep the lid on the oak. Manuka honey and green tea also give this a slightly medicinal quality; **t22.5** the delivery would need an injection of sugars to work...and they duly arrive in the form of toasty molasses. Slight coffee fudge; **f21.5** back to green tea tannins again; **b22** you know you have a great nose on your hands when a fly drowns in your whisky even before you get a chance to taste it... Decent stuff keeping your taste buds at full stretch. 45%.

Pike Creek 10 Years Old finished in port barrels (80) **n21.5 t22.5 f17 b19**. The delivery is the highlight of the show by far as the fruit takes off backed by delicate spices and spongy softness. The nose needs some persuading to get going but when fully warmed, gives a preview of the delivery. The furry finish is a big disappointment, though.40%

Pike Creek 10 Year Old Rum Barrels Finish bott code 54SL24 L16174 EW07:30 (86.5) **n22 t22.5 f20 b22** A far happier fellow than the Port finish, for sure – even though the slight furriness on the finale is a bit of a bore. Before reaching that point, though, there is a velvet revolution involving much honey. 42%.

Pike Creek 21 Year Old Single Malt Cask Finish (87.5) **n21 t23.5 f21.5 b21.5** Pleasant and fruity. As silky as you like with a moist date and spiced theme. But, doubtless, through the cask finish, the age and accompanying complexities seems to have been lost in translation somewhere... 45%. *Ultra-Rare Craft Series.*

Potter's Special Old a blend of 5 to 11 year old rye whisky (91) **n23.5 t23 f22 b22.5**. More Canadian than a hockey punch-up – and, for all the spice, somewhat more gentle, too. 40%

Rich and Rare (79) **n20 t20 f20 b19**. Simplistic and soft. One for toffee lovers. 40%

Rich and Rare Reserve (86.5) **n19.5 t21 f23.5 b22.5**. Actually does what it says on the tin, certainly as to regard the "Rich" bit. But takes off when the finish spices up and even offers some ginger cake on the finale. Lovely stuff. 40%

Royal Reserve Gold (94.5) **n24 t23.5 f23 b24**. Retains its position as a classy, classy Canadian that is an essay on balance. Don't confuse this with the much duller standard bottling: this has been moulded in recent years into one of the finest – and among its country's consumers - generally most underrated Canadians on the market. 40%

Sam Barton Aged 5 Years (83.5) **n19 t21.5 f22 b21**. Sweet session whisky with a lovely maple syrup glow; some complexity on the finish. Friendly, hospitable: impossible not to like. 40%.

Schenley Golden Wedding (92) **n22 t24 f22 b23**. Like a rare, solid marriage, this has improved over time. Always consistent and pleasant, there now appears to be a touch of extra age and maturity which has sent the complexity levels up dramatically. Quite sublime. 40%

Seagram's Canadian 83 (86.5) **n21 t22 f21.5 b22**. A vastly improved blend which has drastically cut the caramel to reveal a melt-in-the-mouth, slightly crisp grain. There are some citrusy edges but the buttery vanilla and pleasing bite all go to make for a chic little number. 40%

Seagram's VO (91) **n22 t23.5 f22.5 b23**. With a heavy heart I have to announce the king of rye-enriched Canadian, VO, is dead. Long live the corn-dominant VO. Over the years I have seen the old traditional character ebb away: now I have let go and have no option other than to embrace this whisky for what it has become: infinitely better than a couple of years back; not in the same league as a decade ago. But just taking it on face value, credit where credit is due. This is an enjoyably playful affair, full of vanilla-led good intention, corn and complexity. There is even assertive spice when needed and the most delicately fruity edge...though not rye-style. Thoughtfully blended and with no little skill, I am impressed. And look forward to seeing how this develops in future years. A treat which needs time to discover. 40%

Union 52 (90.5) **n23 t23 f22.5 b23** A very different type of Canadian which is as busy as it gets. 40%.

Western Gold Canadian Whisky (91) **n23 t23 f22.5 b22.5**. Clean and absolutely classic Canadian: you can't ask for much more, really. 40%

White Owl (77.5) **n19 t19.5 f20 b19**. White whisky: in others words, a whisky the same colour as water. To both nose and taste somewhat reminds me of the long gone Manx whisky which was casks of fully matured scotch re-distilled and bottled. Sweet and pleasant. But I doubt if connoisseurs will give two hoots... 40%

Windsor (86) **n20 t21 f23 b22**. Pleasant but the majority of edges found on the Canadian edition blunted. Some outstanding, almost attritional, spice towards the middle and finale, though. Soft and desirable throughout: a kind of feminine version of the native bottling. 40%.

Canadian Wheat Whisky

Masterson's 12 Year Old Straight Wheat Whiskey batch 001 (92) **n23 t23 f22.5 b23.5** Chose this as my 1,000th new whisk(e)y for Jim Murray WB 2015 because a couple of years back I uncorked their Rye...and tasted everything a great Canadian should be: indeed, it was a contender for my World Whisky of that year. Here I have their new wheat bottling. Not the blockbuster the rye bottling was: rye when distilled and matured to its fullest possibilities probably cannot be touched by any other grain. But this is a soft, melodious whisky, perfect for ending any day on a quiet high... 50%WB15/380

Japanese Whisky

How fitting that in the age when the sun never sets on where whisky is produced it is from the land of the Rising Sun that the finest can now be found.

Recently Japan, for the first time ever, won Jim Murray's World Whisky of the Year with its insanely deep and satisfying Yamazaki Sherry Cask(s) 2013, a result which caused predicted consternation among more than a few. And a degree of surprise in Japan itself. The industry followed that up by commanding 5th spot with a very different but truly majestic specimen of a malt showing a style unique to Japan. How impressive.

It reminded me of when, some 20 years ago, I took my old mate Michael Jackson and a smattering of non-friends on a tour of the Yoichi distillery on Hokkaido, pointing out to them that here was a place where a malt could be made to mount a serious challenge to the best being made anywhere in the world. While there, a local journalist asked me what Japanese distillers could learn from Scotland. I caused a bit of a sharp intake of breath – and a pathetically gutless but entirely characteristic denial of association by some whisky periodical executive or other who had a clear idea which side his bread was buttered – when I said it was the other way round: it was more what the Scots could learn from the Japanese.

The reason for that comment was simple: the extraordinary attention to detail and tradition that was paid by Japanese distillers, those at Yoichi in particular, and the touching refusal to cut costs and corners. It meant that it was the most expensive whisky in the world per unit of alcohol to produce. But the quality was astonishingly high – and that would, surely, eventually reap its rewards as the world learned to embrace malt whisky made away from the Highlands and islands of Scotland which, then, was still to happen. Ironically, it was the Japanese distillers' habit to ape most things Scottish – the reason why there is a near century-old whisky distilling heritage there in the first place - that has meant that Yoichi, or the magnificent Hakushu, has yet to pick up the Bible's World Whisky of the Year award I expected for them. Because, sadly, there have been too many bottlings over the last decade tainted by sherry butts brought from Spain after having been sulphur treated. So I was also pleasantly surprised when I first nosed – then nosed again in near disbelief – then tasted the Yamazaki 2013 sherry offering. There was not even the vaguest hint that a single one of the casks used in the bottling had been anywhere near a sulphur candle. The result: something as close to single malt perfection as you will have found in a good many years. A single malt which no Scotch can at the moment get anywhere near and, oddly, takes me back to the Macallans of 30 years ago.

A Japanese custom of refusing to trade with their rivals has not helped expand their export market. Therefore a Japanese whisky, if not made completely from home-distilled spirit, will instead contain a percentage of Scotch rather than whisky from fellow Japanese distilleries. This, ultimately, is doing the industry no favours at all. The practice is partly down to the traditional work ethics of company loyalty and an inherent, and these days false, belief, that Scotch whisky is automatically better than Japanese. Back in the late 1990s I planted the first seeds in trying to get rival distillers to discuss with each other the possibility of exchanging whiskies to ensure that their distilleries worked more economically. So it can only be hoped

Yamazaki

●Osaka

●Fukuoka

Key	
●	**Major Town or City**
▲	Distillery

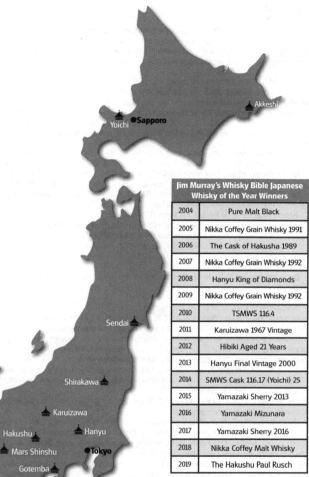

Jim Murray's Whisky Bible Japanese Whisky of the Year Winners	
2004	Pure Malt Black
2005	Nikka Coffey Grain Whisky 1991
2006	The Cask of Hakusha 1989
2007	Nikka Coffey Grain Whisky 1992
2008	Hanyu King of Diamonds
2009	Nikka Coffey Grain Whisky 1992
2010	TSMWS 116.4
2011	Karuizawa 1967 Vintage
2012	Hibiki Aged 21 Years
2013	Hanyu Final Vintage 2000
2014	SMWS Cask 116.17 (Yoichi) 25
2015	Yamazaki Sherry 2013
2016	Yamazaki Mizunara
2017	Yamazaki Sherry 2016
2018	Nikka Coffey Malt Whisky
2019	The Hakushu Paul Rusch

that the deserved lifting of the 2015 Jim Murray's Whisky Bible World Whisky of the Year crown, and the hitherto unprecedented international press it received has helped put the spotlight back on the great whiskies coming from the east. Because unless you live in Japan, you are likely to see only a fraction of the fabulous whisky produced there. The Scotch Malt Whisky Society should have a special medal struck as they have helped in recent years with some memorable bottlings from Japan, single cask snapshots of the greatness that is still to be be fully explored and mapped.

Yet Jim Murray's Whisky Bible has provided a double-edged sword for the Japanese whisky industry. The amazing news for them was their World Whisky of the Year award precipitaed sales worth billions of yen. And, consequently, a near exhaustion of stocks. The Hibiki 17 and Hakushu 12 have now vanished as brands altogether. But it means that, at long last and deservedly, whisky drinkers around the globe finally recognise that Japanese single malt can be second to no other. Their probem is how to satisfy the thirst for Japanese whisky and knowledge on what it has to offer: at the moment they cannot. But Forsyths, the Speyside-based Scottish still manufacturers, are working overtime to supply more distilling equipment for the land of the rising sun. And rapidly setting whisky stocks.

Single Malts
AKKESHI 2016. Kenten Co., Ltd.

⬦ **The Akkeshi New Born 2018 Single Malt Spirit** bourbon barrel, bott Jan 2018 db **(88.5)** n22 t22 f22.5 b22 Young, clean, nutty and malty but with a very fragmented and thin body. This spirit's fragility means it will absorb the oak's influence quicker than most, a point worth bearing in mind in not too many years hence. 60%.

CHICHIBU 2004. Venture Whisky.

Chichibu 'The Peated' 2013 dist 2010 bott 2013 db **(96.5)** n24.5 t24.5 f23 b24.5 Clean, elegant, does exactly what it says on the tin...and a lot, lot more besides... 53.5%.

ePower Chichibu Double Barrel Mizunara heads hogshead & hard charred new barrels, dist 2012, bott 2015 **(88)** n21.5 t23.5 f21 b22 Were it not for the spices, the sugars might have proved a little too much. Though not always hitting quite the right notes, this is big, profound malt. 61.1%.

Ichiro's Malt Chichibu Chibidaru dist 2010, bott 2014 db **(92)** n22.5 t23.5 f23 b23 This distillery certainly understands the meaning of "intense"... 53.5%. Number One Drinks Company.

Ichiro's Malt Chichibu Floor Malted 2009 **(85.5)** n22 t22.5 f20 b21. Big, pre-pubescent malt and barley statement, but barely in unison. Bitterness on the finish is unchecked. 50.5%.

Ichiro's Chichibu Peated 2009 **(91.5)** n23 t23.5 f22 b23. You can stand your chopsticks up in this one...works so beautifully in so many department. 50.5%

Ichiro's Malt Chichibu Peated 2015 dist 2010, bott 2015 db **(95)** n23.5 t24 f23.5 b24 Had I tasted this blind, I would have mistaken it for an Islay. Quite sublimely made malt. As astonishing as it is beautiful... 62.5%. Number One Drinks Company.

Number One Asama 1999/2000 **(71)** n17 t19 f16 b19. Sulphured. 46%

FUJI GOTEMBA 1973. Kirin Distillers.

The Fuji Gotemba 15 Years Old db **(92)** n21 t23 f24 b24. Quality malt of great poise. 43%. Kirin.

HAKUSHU 1973. Suntory.

Hakushu Single Malt Whisky Aged 12 Years db **(91.5)** n22.5 t23.5 f22.5 b23. About identical to the 43.3% bottling. Please see those tasting notes for this little beauty. 43.5%

Hakushu Single Malt Aged 12 Years db **(91)** n22 t23 f23 b23. An even more lightly-peated version of the 40%, with the distillery's fabulous depth on full show. 43.3%

The Hakushu Single Malt Whisky Aged 15 Years Cask Strength db **(95)** n24 t23 f24 b24. Last time round I lamented the disappointing nose. This time perhaps only a degree of over eagerness from the oak has robbed this as a serious Whisky of the Year contender. No matter how you look at it, though, brilliant!! 56%

The Hakushu Single Malt Whisky Aged 25 Years db **(93)** n23 t24 f23 b23. A malt which is impossible not to be blown away by. 43%

The Hakushu Single Malt Whisky Sherry Cask bott 2014 db **(96.5)** n24.5 t24 f24 b24 Theoretically, this should have been World Whisky of the Year. After all, Yamazaki – a distillery I regard as very slightly eclipsed in quality by Hakushu – won it last year using, like this, strictly unsulphured sherry butts. This is magnificent. One of the great whiskies of the year, for sure. However, the intensity of the grape has just strayed over that invisible line by a few molecules between being a vital cog and a shade too dominant. It is the finest of lines between genius and exceptional brilliance. 48%. ncf.

⬦ **The Hakushu Paul Rusch 120th Anniversary of Birth** bourbon barrel, bott code LX7CJV db **(96)** n24 serious tannin: antique furniture which has not been polished for several decades: creaky and dry. But the lightest spearmint and eucalyptus join forces to help give shape to the oak, allowing the malt a way in even at this late stage; t24.5 exactly the same as the nose – except now there are some very serious sugars on the radar. A little heather honey seems to carry something a tad smoky – not unlike an ancient Orkney cask. Except this has far greater weight as the tannins re-establish themselves, injecting natural caramels, spice and toasted honeycomb; f23.5 toasty, dry, spicy and very long...; b24 there is a tipping point where a barrel has just gone over the edge, like one might at the Niagara Falls: there is no turning back and the ending is catastrophic. There is the odd moment here where you pick up a note where you realise it has moved close to that point, then myriad flavours come to the rescue to show this whisky is still very much alive and well and, like an old cowboy, basking in its great age and sun-burned charisma. Brilliant. 58%.

Suntory Pure Malt Hakushu Aged 20 Years db **(94)** n23 t24 f23 b24. A hard-to-find malt, but find it you must. Yet another huge nail in the coffin of those who purport Japanese whisky to be automatically inferior to Scotch. 56%

HANYU 1941. Toa Shuzo Co. Ltd.

Ichiro's Malt Aged 20 Years (95.5) n24 t24 f23.5 b24. No this finish; no that finish. Just the distillery allowed to speak in its very own voice. And nothing more eloquent has been heard from it this year. Please, all those owning casks of Hanyu: for heaven's sake take note... *575%.*

Ichiro's Malt Aged 23 Years (92.5) n23 t23.5 f23 b23. A fabulous malt you take your time over. *58%*

KARUIZAWA 1955. Mercian.

Karuizawa Pure Malt Aged 17 Years db (90) n20 t24 f23 b23. Brilliant whisky beautifully made and majestically matured. Neither sweetness nor dryness dominates, always the mark of a quality dram. *40%*

The Spirit Of Asama sherry cask (75) n18 t20 f18 b19. Lots of sultanas. Sweet. Pleasant in part. But it isn't just Scotland suffering from poor sherry butts. *55%*

KIRIN 1969. Kirin Group.

Kirin 18 Years Old db (86.5) n22 t22 f21.5 b21. Unquestionably over-aged. Even so, still puts up a decent show with juicy citrus trying to add a lighter touch to the uncompromising, ultra dense oak. As entertaining as it is challenging. *43%. Suntory.*

MIYAGIKYO 1969. Nikka.

Nikka Coffey Malt Whisky db (96) n23.5 t25 f23.5 b24 Not quite the genius of the 12-year-old. But still one of the most tactile and sensual whiskies on the world whisky stage today. *45%.*

Nikka Whisky Single Coffey Malt 12 Years db (97) n23.5 t25 f24 b24.5. The Scotch Whisky Association would say that this is not single malt whisky because it is made in a Coffey still. When they can get their members to make whisky this stunning on a regular basis via their own pots and casks, then perhaps they should pipe up as their argument might then have a single atom of weight. *55%*

Nikka Whisky Single Malt Miyagikyo db (91.5) n22 vanilla blancmange; t23 excellent early malt thrust on delivery, then thickens and allows in all kinds of fudgy sugars; f22.5 light spice, tannin and fudge; b23 thick, clumsy but deliciously malty. *45%.*

SENDAI 1969. Nikka.

Scotch Malt Whisky Society Cask 124.4 Aged 17 Years 1st fill butt, dist 22 Aug 96 (94) n24 t24 f23 b23 If there is a complaint to be made, it is that, at times, one might forget that this is a whisky at all, resembling instead a glass of highest quality oloroso.*60%. sc. 479 bottles.*

SHINSHU MARS 1985. Hombo Shuzo Ltd

Mars Whisky Single Malt Komagatake Sherry & American White Oak 2011 db (79.5) n19 t22 f18.5 b20. My heart bleeds, as the high class – and intensity – of the malt is outstanding. Sadly, the sherry butt does not match the excellence of the distillate and results in a Mars that is slightly out of orbit... *57%*

ePower Komagatake American Puncheon, dist Mar 13, bott Sept 16 (96) n23.5 t24 f24 b24.5 Just fabulous for Japan's most malty whisky to be able to show its most intense and unique form without it being wrecked by awful sherry butts. What a malty treat this is! You could not ask for more. Well, actually you could...another glass, that is... *56.9%.*

WHITE OAK DISTILLERY 1984. Eigashima Shuzo.

White Oak Akashi Single Malt Whisky Aged 8 Years bott 2007 db (74.5) n18.5 t19.5 f17.5 b19. Always fascinating to find a malt from one of the smaller distilleries in a country. And I look forward to tracking this one down and visiting, something I have yet to do. There is certainly something distinctly small still about his one, with butyric and feintiness causing damage to nose and finish. For all the early malty presence on delivery, some of the off notes are a little on the uncomfortable side. *40%*

YAMAZAKI 1923. Suntory.

The Yamazaki Single Malt Whisky Aged 12 Years bott 2011 db (90) n23 t22 f22.5 b22.5. A complex and satisfying malt. *43%*

The Yamazaki Single Malt Aged 18 Years db (96) n23 a sublime blend of Java and Sumatra coffees, enriched by vanilla and even toastier tannins. The sugars, a mix of treacle and maple syrup try not to steal the show, but nearly do...; t24.5 oh, oh, oh...!!!! Possibly the softest yet most compelling delivery this year: the grape is doused in busy, ever intensifying spice, the toasty vanillas in those subtle sugars spotted on the nose. Overripe plums, juicy dates, stewed prunes...and all the time the spice buzzes, the sugars salivate; f24 long, with just a slow wind down of the previously intense fruit notes. The juices just keep on gushing, but met almost perfectly with toasty, slightly milky mocha notes; the final strands are praline wafer...with chocolate fruit and nut, too; **b24.5** for its strength, probably one of the best whiskies in the world. And one of the most brilliantly and sexily balanced, too... All told,one glass is equal to about 45 minutes of sulphur-free satisfaction... *43%*

Suntory Pure Malt Yamazaki 25 Years Old db (**91**) n23 t23 f22 b23. Being matured in Japan, the 25 years doesn't have quite the same value as Scotland. So perhaps in some ways this can lay claim to be one of the most enormously aged, oak-laden whiskies that has somehow kept its grace and star quality. *43%*

The Yamazaki Single Malt Whisky Mizunara Japanese oak cask, bott 2014 db (**97**) n25 t24 f23.5 b24.5 No other malt offers this flavour profile. And as there are now very few Japanese oak casks still in the industry it is a malt worthy of as long a time as you can afford it. A very special whisky of very high quality. *48%*

The Yamazaki Single Malt Whisky Sherry Cask bott 2013 db (97.5) n24.5 t24.5 f24 b24.5 One of the first sherry casks I have seen from Japan not in any way, shape or form touched by sulphur for a very long time. It is as if the oloroso cask was still half filled with the stuff when they filled with Yamakazi spirit. If anyone wants to find out roughly what the first Macallan 10-year-old I had in 1975 tasted like, then grab a bottle of this... *48%. ncf. WB15/180*

Yamazaki Single Malt Sherry Cask 2016 Edition db (96.5) n24.5 t24 f24 b24 A work of art. The oils, though, are markedly younger in style than the imperious 2013 edition. *48%*

The Yamazaki Single Malt Whisky db (**86**) n22 t22 f21 b21. A tame, malty affair which, after the initial barley burst on delivery, plays safety first. *43%*

◇ **Suntory Single Cask WhiskyL!** sherry cask, cask no. AJRY30041 db (**88**) n21.5 t22.5 f22 b22 Question: what happens when you get sublimely distilled Yamazaki new make and mature it for four years in a faultless sherry butt? Answer: You get this! A fun single malt which reveals the absolute beauty of Yamazaki in sherry in its most basic form. Ridiculously juicy with a delightful degree of sweetness. *48%. Selected for CWS.*

YOICHI 1934. Nikka.

Nikka Whisky Single Malt Yoichi db (**91**) n24 t24 f21 b22 When 20 years ago I declared this as one of the top five distilleries in the world, I was considered quite mad: it was not sitting in Scotland. Indeed, the fact I had named a Japanese whisky at all, irrelevant of it being Yoichi, made a lot of people question my sanity and professionalism. Until they tasted this then unheard of malt for the first time, that is. In the last decade Yoichi have helped neither me nor themselves by bringing out far too many bottlings which have betrayed a sulphur weakness from a sherry butt. This bottling may have a borderline flaw, also – even I am struggling to be sure. But what I know for a fact is that of all the single malts worldwide I have tasted for this Bible 2018, this was the first to make me yelp and then stretch with pleasure, glass in hand raised as I rode the ecstasy. Yes, there is the most minor blemish on the very end of the finale, and for that it will not be contending for World Whisky of the Year. But, it was a very close run thing... *45%*.

Yoichi Key Malt Aged 12 Years "Peaty & Salty" db (**95**) n23 t25 f23 b24. Of all the peated whiskies of the world, only Ardbeg can stand shoulder to shoulder with Yoichi when it comes to sheer complexity. Here is an astonishing example of why I rate Yoichi in the best five whiskies in the world. Forget the odd sulphur-tarnished bottling. Get Yoichi in its natural state with perfect balance between oak and malt and it delivers something approaching perfection. And this is just such a bottling. *55%. Nikka.*

Yoichi 15 Years Old batch 06I08B db (91.5) n22 t23.5 f23 b23. For an early moment or two possibly one of the most salivating whiskies you'll get your kisser around this year. Wonderfully entertaining yet you still suspect that this is another Yoichi reduced in effect somewhat by either caramel and/or sherry. When it hits its stride, though, becomes a really busy whisky that gets tastebuds in a right lather. But I'm being picky as I know that this is one of the world's top five distilleries and am aware as anyone on this planet of its extraordinary capabilities. Great fun; great whisky – could be better still, but so much better than its siblings... *45%*

Yoichi 20 Years Old db (**95**) n23 t23 f25 b24. I don't know how much they charge for this stuff but either alone or with mates get some for one hell of an experience. What makes it all the more remarkable is that there is a slight sulphury note on the nose: once you taste the stuff that becomes of little consequence. *52%. Nikka.*

Vatted Malts

All Malt (**86**) n22 t21 f21 b22. The best example by a mile of an almost unique style of vatted whisky: both malt and "grain" are distilled from entirely malted barley, identical to Kasauli malt whisky in India. Stupendous grace and balance. *40%. Nikka.*

All Malt "Pure & Rich" (89) n22 t24 f21 b22. Not unlike some bottlings of Highland Park with its emphasis on honey. If they could tone down the caramel it'd really be up there. 40%. Nikka.

Hokuto Pure Malt Aged 12 Years (86) n20 t22 f22 b22. An oaky threat never materialises: excellent mixing. 40%. Suntory.

Ichiro's Malt Double Distilleries bott 2010 (86.5) n22.5 t22 f21 b21. Some imperious barley-rich honey reigns supreme until a bitter wood note bites hard. 46%. Venture Whisky Ltd.

Ichiro's Malt Mizunara Wood Reserve (76) n19 t21 f18 b19. I have my Reservations about the Wood, too... 46%. Venture Whisky Ltd.

Malt Club "Pure & Clear" (83) n21 t22 f20 b20. Another improved vatting, much heavier and older than before with bigger spice. 40%. Nikka.

Mars Maltage Pure Malt 8 Years Old (84) n20 t21 f21 b22. A very level, intense, clean malt with no peaks or troughs, just a steady variance in the degree of sweetness and oak input. Impossible not to have a second glass of. 43%. Mars.

Nikka Malt 100 The Anniversary Aged 12 Years (73) n18 t19 f18 b18. The depressing and deadly fingerprint of sulphur is all over this. Shame, as the spices excel. 40%

Nikka Pure Malt Aged 12 Years batch 10I24C db (84) n21.5 t21 f20 b21.5. The nose may be molassed, sticky treacle pudding, but it spices up on the palate. The dull buzz on the finish also tells a tale. 40%

Nikka Pure Malt Aged 21 Years batch 08I18D db (89) n23 t22.5 f21.5 b22. By far the best of the set. 43%

Nikka Pure Malt Aged 17 Years batch 08I30B db (83) n21 t21 f20 b21. A very similar shape to the 12-years-old, but older - obviously. Certainly the sherry butts have a big say and don't always do great favours to the high quality spirit. 43%

Pure Malt Black batch 06F54B (92) n24 t24 f21 b23. Not the finish of old, but everything else is present and correct for a cracker! 43%. Nikka.

Pure Malt Red batch 06F54C (84) n21 t22 f20 b21. Oak is the pathfinder here, but the oily vanilla-clad barley is light and mouth-watering. 43%. Nikka.

Pure Malt White batch 06J26 (91) n22 t23 f22 b24. A sweet malt, but one with such deft use of peat and oak that one never really notices. Real class. 43%

Pure Malt White batch 10F46C (90) n23 t23 f22 b22. There is a peculiarly Japanese feel to this delicately peated delight. 43%

Southern Alps Pure Malt (93) n24 t23 f22 b24. This is a bottle I have only to look at to start salivating. Sadly, though, I drink sparingly from it as it is a hard whisky to find, even in Japan. Fresh, clean and totally stunning, the term "pure malt" could not be more apposite. Fabulous whisky: a very personal favourite. 40%. Suntory.

Suntory Pure Malt Whisky Kiyosato Field Ballet 25th Anniversary (88) n23.5 gentle: over-ripe plums, green apple and red liquorice; t22.5 the malt surges on delivery for a very sharp introduction; soon calms down with a vague Indian candy sweetness and a more assertive bourbon style; goes tits up as the end approaches; f20 an annoying tang as the balance is compromised; b22 so frustrating: a whisky destined for greatness is side-tracked by some off-kilter casks. 48%

Super Nikka Vatted Pure Malt (76) n20 t19 f19 b18. Decent and chewy but something doesn't quite click with this one. 55.5%. Nikka.

Taketsuru Pure Malt 12 Years Old (80) n19 t22 f19 b20. For its age, heavier than a sumo wrestler. But perhaps a little more agile over the tastebuds. Lovely silkiness impresses, but lots of toffee. 40%. Nikka.

Taketsuru Pure Malt 17 Years Old (89) n21 t22 f23 b23. Not a whisky for the squeamish. This is big stuff – about as big as it gets without peat or rye. No bar shelf or whisky club should be without one. 43%. Nikka.

Taketsuru Pure Malt 21 Years Old (88) n22 t21 f22 b23. A much more civilised and gracious offering than the 17 year old: there is certainly nothing linear about the character development from Taketsuru 12 to 21 inclusive. Serious whisky for the serious whisky drinker. 43%. Nikka.

Zen (84) n19 t22 f22 b21. Sweet, gristy malt; light and clean. 40%. Suntory.

Japanese Single Grain
CHITA 1972. Suntory.

Suntory Single Grain Chita Distillery db (92.5) n23.5 t23 f22.5 b23 Now that's more like it! Far more down the track of the Chita I have tasted through the years than the SMWS bottling. Then again, this is the brand new official distillery version, so perhaps no surprises there... 43%. Available only in Nagoya Prefecture, Japan.

The Chita Single Grain bott code L1610R db (91.5) n23 a very old-fashioned style of Scottish grain whisky now entirely lost. Soft, with the grain radiating light sugars and vanilla in equal amounts; t23 big, fat corn oils fills the mouth, allowing soft marzipan and golden syrup to lulls around the palate; f22.5 long, thanks to those oils with a slow spice build; b23 spot on Corn Whiskey-type grain: could almost be a blueprint. Simple, but deliciously soft and effective. 43%.

MIYAGIKYO 1969. Nikka.

Nikka Coffey Grain Whisky db (94.5) n23.5 molten muscovado sugar; t24 soft oils carry the thinned golden syrup aloft. Almost a semi-liqueur, but with that indefinable whiskyness which sets it apart..; f23 the slight bitterness of the cask jolts the serenity of the oily sugars; b24 whisky, from any part of the globe, does not come more soft or silky than this... 45%

Blends

◇ **25th Anniversary Kiyosato Field Ballet Ichiro's Malt & Grain Japanese Blended Whisky** (90.5) n22.5 amazing: last time I nosed anything quite like this I was at a German Christmas market in Köln. Plenty of oak but the stollen really dominates; t23.5 a three-pronged delivery sees the softer, custardy grain combine with spices and a mix of maple syrup and Manuka honey to dominate for the first ten flavour waves; f21.5 bitters out unevenly as the spices dry; b23 if spice is the variety of life, then this whisky certainly adds variety. 49%. 359 bottles.

Black Nikka Aged 8 Years (82) n20 t21 f21 b20. Beautifully bourbony, especially on the nose. Lush, silky and great fun. Love it! 40%. Nikka.

The Blend of Nikka (90) n21 t23 f22 b24. An adorable blend that makes you sit up and take notice of every enormous mouthful. Classy, complex, charismatic and brilliantly balanced. 45%

Evermore (90) n22 t23 f22 b23. Top-grade, well-aged blended whisky with fabulous depth and complexity that never loses its sweet edge despite the oak. 40%. Kirin.

Ginko (78.5) n20.5 t20 f19 b19. Soft – probably too soft as it could do with some shape and attitude to shrug off the caramel. 46%. Number One Drinks Company.

Golden Horse Busyuu Deluxe (93) n22 t24 f23 b24. Whoever blended this has a genuine feel for whisky: a classic in its own right and one of astonishing complexity and textbook balance. 43%. Toa Shuzo. To celebrate the year 2000.

Hibiki (82) n20 t19 f23 b20. The grains here are fresh, forceful and merciless, the malts bouncing off them meekly. Lovely cocoa finale. A blend that brings a tear to the eye. Hard stuff – perfect after a hard day! Love it! 43%. Suntory.

◇ **Hibiki Japanese Harmony** bott code LG7F04 db (93) n23 a blend, all right: there appears to be rum, Cognac and lightly smoked malts melded together. Wonderfully busy and impressively balanced; t23 sweet and estery on delivery. A big corn oily surge, then back to malt and spices, the later hitting a crescendo before dropping back to a vanilla plain and light molasses; f23.5 now we really get harmony! The spices trundle along busily with German caramelised biscuit and delicate malts hanging on the oils and seemingly unwilling to end; b23.5 immaculately spiced and as complex a bag of tricks on the palate as you're likely to find. 43%.

◇ **Hibiki Japanese Harmony Master's Select** bott code LN6CKK db (89) n22.5 a kind of spiced-up grain whisky with a little under-ripe banana and golden syrup; t22.5 again golden syrup on delivery, though pepped up with black peppers. The grain forms a soft spine while the vanillas mount up; f22 an unassuming procession of caramels; b22 as silky as a kimono, the grains dominate on this blend 43%.

Hibiki 50.5 Non Chillfiltered 17 Years Old (84) n22 t22 f20 b20. Pleasant enough in its own right. But against what this particular expression so recently was, hugely disappointing. Last year I lamented the extra use of caramel. This year it has gone through the roof, taking with it all the fineness of complexity that made this blend exceptional. Time for the blending lab to start talking to the bottling hall and sort this out. I want one of the great whiskies back...!! 50.5%. Suntory.

Hibiki Aged 30 Years (88) n21 t22 f22 b23. Still remains a very different animal from most other whiskies you might find: the smoke may have vanished somewhat but the sweet oakiness continues to draw its own unique map. 43%

Hokuto (86) n22 t24 f19 b21. A bemusing blend. At its peak, this is quite superb, cleverly blended whisky. The finish, though, suggests a big caramel input. If the caramel is natural, it should be tempered. If it is added for colouring purposes, then I don't see the point of having the whisky non-chillfiltered in the first place. 50.5%. ncf. Suntory.

Imperial (81) n20 t22 f19 b20. Flinty, hard grain softened by malt and vanilla but toffee dulled. 43%. Suntory.

Kakubin (92) n23 t23 f22 b24. Absolutely brilliant blend of stunningly refreshing and complex character. One of the most improved brands in the world. 40%. Suntory.

Kakubin Kuro 43° (89) n22 t23 f22 b22. Big, chewy whisky with ample evidence of old age but such is the intrusion of caramel it's hard to be entirely sure. 43%. Suntory.

Kakubin New (90) n21 t24 f21 b24. Seriously divine blending: a refreshing dram of the top order. 40%.

Kirin Whisky Tarujuku 50° (93) n22.5 t24 f23 b23.5. A blend not afraid to make a statement and does so boldly. A sheer joy. *50%. Kirin Distillery Co Ltd.*

Master's Blend Aged 10 Years (87) n21 t23 f22 b21. Chewy, big and satisfying. *40%.*

New Kakubin Suntory *(see Kakubin New)*

Nikka Master Blend Blended Whisky 12 Years Old 70th Anniversary (94) n24 t23 f24 b23. An awesome blend swimming in top quality sherry. Perhaps a fraction too much sweetness on the arrival, but I am nit-picking. A blend for those who like their whiskies to have something to say. And this one just won't shut up. *58%. Nikka.*

Nikka Whisky From The Barrel db (91) n22.5 happy to coast on the caramels but allowing a sharper malt punctuation; t23 salivating, and masterfully intense... as usual. Excellent molasses sub theme, then that sublime layering of lighter malts; the spices and honey come into play about halfway through and dovetail sublimely; f22.5 long, with rich spiced toffee; b23 I have been drinking this for a very long time – and still can't remember a bottle that's ever let me down. *51.4%.*

Nikka Whisky Tsuru Aged 17 Years (94) n23 t24 f23 b24. Unmistakingly Tsuru in character, very much in line, profile-wise, with the original bottling and if the caramel was cut this could challenge as a world whisky of the year. *43%*

Robert Brown (91) n22.5 t23 f22.5 b23. Just love these clean but full-flavoured blends: a real touch of quality here. *43%. Kirin Brewery Company Ltd.*

Royal 12 Years Old (91) n23 t23 f22 b23. A splendidly blended whisky with complexity being the main theme. Beautiful stuff that appears recently to have, with the exception of the nose, traded smoke for grape. *43%*

Royal Aged 15 Years (95) n25 t24 f22 b24. Unquestionably one of the great blends of the world that can be improved only by a reduction of toffee input. Sensual blending that every true whisky lover must experience: a kind of Japanese Old Parr 18. *43%*

Shirokaku (79) n19 t21 f20 b19. Some over-zealous toffee puts a cap on complexity. Good spices, though. *40%. Suntory.*

Special Reserve 10 Years Old (94) n23 t24 f23 b24. A beguiling whisky of near faultless complexity. Blending at its peak. *43%. Suntory.*

Special Reserve Aged 12 Years (89) n21 t24 f21 b23. A tactile, voluptuous malt that wraps itself like a sated lover around the tastebuds, though the complexity is compromised very slightly by bigger caramel than the 10-y-o. *40%. Suntory.*

Suntory Old (87) n21 t24 f20 b22. A delicate and comfortable blend that just appears to have over-simplified itself on the finale. Delicious, but could be much better than this. *40%*

Suntory Old Mild and Smooth (84) n19 t22 f21 b22. Chirpy and lively around the palate, the grains soften the crisp malts wonderfully. *40%*

Suntory Old Rich and Mellow (91) n22 t23 f23 b23. A pretty malt-rich blend with the grains offering a fat base. Impressive blending. *43%*

Super Nikka (93) n23 t23 f23 b24. A very, very fine blend which makes no apology whatsoever for the peaty complexity of Yoichi malt. Now, with less caramel, it's pretty classy stuff. However, Nikka being Nikka you might find the occasional bottling that is entirely devoid of peat, more honeyed and lighter in style (21-22-23-23 Total 89 – no less a quality turn, obviously). Either way, an absolutely brilliant day-to-day, anytime, any place dram. One of the true 24-carat, super nova commonplace blends not just in Japan, but in the world. *43%. Nikka.*

Super Nikka Rare Old batch 02I18D (90.5) n22 t23 f22.5 b23. Beautiful whisky which just sings a lilting malty refrain. Strange, though, to find it peatless. *43%. Nikka.*

Torys (76) n18 t19 f20 b19. Lots of toffee in the middle and at the end of this one. The grain used is top class and chewy. *37%. Suntory.*

Torys Whisky Square (80) n19 t20 f21 b20. At first glance a very similar blend to Torys, but very close scrutiny reveals slightly more "new loaf" nose and a better, spicier and less toffeed finale. *37%.*

Tsuru (93) n23 t24 f22 b24. Gentle and beautifully structured, genuinely mouthwatering, more-ish and effortlessly noble. If they had the confidence to cut the caramel, this would be even higher up the charts as one of the great blends of the world. And with Japanese whisky becoming far more globally accepted and sought after, now would be a very good time to start. As it is, in my house we pass the ceramic Tsuru bottle as one does the ship's decanter. And it empties very quickly. *43%. Nikka.*

The Whisky (88) n22 t22 f21 b23. A rich, confident and well-balanced dram. *43%. Suntory.*

White (80) n19 t21 f20 b20. Boring nose but explodes on the palate for a fresh, mouth-watering classic blend bite. *40%. Suntory.*

Za (79) n19 t21 f19 b20. Some lively boisterous grain offers a suet-pudding chewiness. A little bitter on the finish. *40%. Suntory.*

English & Welsh Whisky

When, exactly, do you decide that a new whisky region is born? Is it like the planets forming after the Big Bang, cosmic dust gathering together to form a solid, recognisable whole?

That is the question I have had to ask myself for a long time and, since the Whisky Bible began 15 years ago, look for an answer that is beyond the hypothetical. At last I have come to a conclusion: it is, surely, when a country or region produces sufficient whisky of high enough consistency and character that its contribution to the lexicon of the world's greatest whiskies cannot be ignored. Or should that whisky be lost for any reason its effects would be greatly felt. There is no denying that this is now the case in the varied and often glorious lands to be found south of the Scottish Border.

When in 2003, on the cusp of world whisky's very own Big Bang, I sat down and tasted the whiskies for the inaugural 2004 edition of Jim Murray's Whisky Bible, Ireland boasted just three distilleries, four if you included Cooley's grain plant. Today, England and Wales provide us with three distilleries producing exceptionally high class whiskies: Penderyn, St George's and The Cotswolds. The latter is still very much in its infancy, but the quality is already beyond doubt. Penderyn and St. George's have won numerous awards in the Whisky Bible and are remarkable for the consistency and excellence of their maturing spirit.

These three distilleries are not micro distilleries. They are set up to make whisky on an industrial scale and have forged markets all over the world. On their skirt tails comes The Lakes in the beautiful Lake District while dotted around the region comes a plethora of other distilleries of varying shapes and sizes, some being built, others waiting for their maturing spirit to pass the three year mark and become whisky.

Over the last year I have been busy actively enouraging the larger English and Welsh distillers to create their own Whisky Association, especially as Britain leaves the EU during 2019. Why not? They are now their own region: they demand respect as their very own entity.

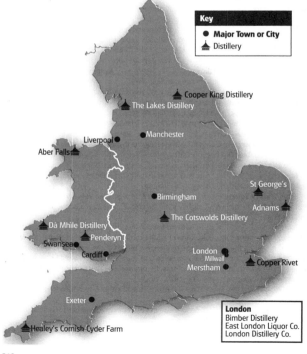

Key
- ● **Major Town or City**
- ⛪ Distillery

⛪ Cooper King Distillery
⛪ The Lakes Distillery
● Liverpool   ● Manchester
Aber Falls ⛪
St George's ⛪
● Birmingham
Adnams ⛪
Dà Mhile Distillery ⛪
⛪ The Cotswolds Distillery
⛪ Penderyn
Swansea ●
Cardiff ●
London ●
Millwall
Merstham
⛪ Copper Rivet
● Exeter
⛪ Healey's Cornish Cyder Farm

London
Bimber Distillery
East London Liquor Co.
London Distillery Co.

ENGLAND
ADNAMS Southwold, Suffolk. 2010. Working.

Adnams Southwold Triple Grain Whisky No 2 American oak, bott 2013 (87) n22 t22 f21 b22. The most remarkable thing to report is the nose. It is, and I really have to find out how, the closest whisky I have ever encountered on nose that matches a decent biryani in its subtle Asian spicy complexity. To taste it is a lot more straightforward: a tad feinty, but those oils conjure up the spices which sit well with the intense sugars. The finish, naturally enough, is a little bitter and foggy from the feints...but with no uncomfortable edges. For now I shall stick to their almost incomparable bitter beer. But I shall be keeping a close eye... 43%. ncf. WB15/407

BIMBER DISTILLERY London. 2015. Working.

Bimber Single Malt 1 Year Old ex-bourbon 190 litre casks, cask no. 8, filled 06 Jun 16, bott 5 Jun 17 db (84) n21.5 t21.5 f20 b21 As the distillers at Bimber will discover, the path of maturation of any whisky is not a perfect upward curve. Instead, early maturing spirit – and whisky - peaks and troughs, sometimes violently, while different forces come into play and there is insufficient time for a courtship, let alone a marriage to take place. Most spirits around a year old are right slap bang in the middle of that wobble and we can see it here to a degree, and I expect it to see it in the others they have bottled. Some barrels at this age may be riding the wave and carrying out all kinds of stunning tricks; others might be in a trough with the wave about to crash over them. Here, none of the sugars or barley notes appear too confident in their handling of their other flavour profiles. So a whisky to enjoy watching trying to walk and sometimes falling – a bit like a toddler taking its first steps. 62.9%. sc.

Bimber Single Malt 1 Year Old ex-port 225 litre casks, cask no. 40, bott 5 Jun 17 db (72.5) n17.5 t19 f18 b18 Oh dear... 62.2%. sc.

Bimber Single Malt 1 Year Old ex-P.X. 250 litre casks, cask no. 31, filled 06 Jul 16, bott 5 Jun 17 db (85) n21 t22 f21 b21 A jumbled message of sticky fruit, big sugar, bigger barley... and tobacco... 62.8%. sc.

Bimber Single Malt 1 Year Old Virgin American oak 190 litre casks, cask no. 7, filled 06 Jun 16, bott 5 Jun 17 db (89) n22.5 t23 f21.5 b22 Eye-wateringly sharp barley in part, but the extra caramels and molassed sugars provided by the virgin oak helps bulldoze some of the less pesky off-key peaks into submission. Mildly brutal but entirely delicious. 62.2%. sc.

⬦ **Bimber Single Malt Test Batch Sample 22 Months Old** ex-bourbon cask, cask no. 8 db (91.5) n22.5 t23 f22.5 b23.5 With still another 14 months to go before this can be called whisky, this is already taking on impressive proportions....and is whisky in everything other than legal definition. The caramels extracted from the oak have had a highly attractive softening effect on both nose and palate. The sugars pose beautifully with the rich malt while the spices do much to reduce the youthfulness in perception. Beautifully distilled and matured, this is a gorgeous malt spirit experience. 63%. sc.

⬦ **Bimber Single Malt Test Batch Sample 22 Months Old** ex-port cask, cask no. 39 db (80) n21 t21 f19 b19 So much better than the last sample Port Cask offering from Bimber. However, there is very limited balance to this and the bitterness, as though from sour grape skin, goes largely unanswered. 63%. sc.

⬦ **Bimber Single Malt Test Batch Sample 22 Months Old** ex-sherry cask, cask no.31 db (88) n20 t24 f22 b22 A great example of a malt still finding its feet and balance because at times, and on the nose especially, the grape does lurch about out of control. But this is a clean butt free from sulphurous negativity and when the grain and the grape do match up the result is some eye-watering beauty of quite staggering proportions: indeed, the delivery is one of almost carnal bliss. Elements of the late fruit chocolate finish isn't shoddy, either. 62.5%. sc.

⬦ **Bimber Single Malt Test Batch Sample 22 Months Old** virgin oak cask, cask no.7 db (95) n23.5 t23.5 f24 b24 For a single malt spirit of this age, it is probably impossible to ask for more. The nose makes no apology for its strong tannin accent, a little hickory combining with the caramels to massage the sugars into the broader oak. While to taste there are no rough edges at all, cleanly distilled yet mouth-filling with a thick Malteser richness, the malt combining with the milk chocolate. The oils round of the experience, softening further... if that seemed possible. A Five Star wow! 62%. sc.

⬦ **Bimber Single Malt Test Batch Sample 22 Months Old** Signature Cask bourbon, sherry & virgin oak casks, batch no.1 db (85.5) n21 t22.5 f20.5 b21.5 With the lighter strength seems make the oils fragment resulting in a slightly disharmonised nose followed by a distinctly bitter and off- key finish. The delivery, though, possesses a fair degree of charm which just before the bitterness arrives is at its zenith thanks to a superb malt and sultana crescendo. 46%.

⬦ **Bimber Single Malt Test Batch Sample 22 Months Old Signature Cask** bourbon, sherry & virgin oak casks, batch no.1 db (89) n22.5 t23 f21 b22.5 The fruit has been outmuscled at every turn by the bountiful cream toffee. Youthful it may be, but those bourbon and virgin oak casks have been dug deep into to extract such pleasing sugars which sit with the intense malt superbly, though the slight late bitterness does create a moment of late discord. 62.5%.

Bimber Single Malt New-Make Test Batch Sample batch no. 25, bott 17 Nov 16 db **(95.5) n24 t24 f23.5 b24** Quite possibly the best new make from a fledging distillery I have ever encountered: off the top of my head I cannot recall its master. Gorgeously rich despite being entirely feints-free with an astonishing castor sugar melt on the tail of the ultra-intense grist. Stylish and simply brilliant. 63%.

COPPER RIVET DISTILLERY Chatham, Kent. 2016. Working.

⬥ **Son of a Gun Cask Finished English Grain Spirit** db **(82.5) n20 t22 f19.5 b21** Nothing wrong with whoever is running the stills, as the body and pace of this grain spirit is impressive – especially on delivery. However, the curious feature is that despite the name of the distillery, this feels as though not enough copper has come into contact with the spirit, leaving a slightly tangy finale. At the time of writing this, I'd not yet been to the distillery, but looking forward to seeing how this was created. 47.4%.

COTSWOLDS DISTILLERY Shipton-on-Stour, Warwickshire. 2014. Working.

Cotswolds Distillery Single Malt 25 Months Peated Quarter Casks cask no. 221, bott 4 Jun 17 db **(93.5) n23.5 t23 f23.5 b23.5** A malt which has no right to boast this kind of depth, and even-ness at this age. No doubt the smaller casks have helped by injecting sufficient tannin to stabilise a malt's natural tendency at this age to buck around in the barrel. But the big smoke has assisted, also, as that has added further weight and enriched a rather lovely toasty and roasty chocolate element that would be recognisable in the wonderful Double Stout brewed just up at the road at arguably Britain's finest brewery, Hook Norton. 62.4%. sc.

Cotswolds Distillery Single Malt Prototype 29 Months bott 6 Jun 17 db **(90.5) n21.5 t24 f22.5 b22.5** This remarkable malt is all to do with oak: cut the spirit and it'll have rings on it.... Tannins screech at you on both the nose and finish and were they any louder they might be problematic. However, such is the staggering intensity of the barley and sugar delivery it never gets to that point... and one is able to forgive anything. Again, the sweet notes have been plucked from the barrel, a kind of distilled maple syrup in richness. The red liquorice and drier chalkiness towards the finish is also an oaky giveaway. What an experience...! 62.4%.

Cotswolds Distillery Single Malt Spirit 20 Months Old bourbon cask, cask no. 47, bott 11 Jul 16 db **(91) n21.5 t23 f23.5 b23** Coming along rather beautifully... 61.8%

Cotswolds Distillery Single Malt Spirit 20 Months Old ex-red wine cask (shaved, toasted & recharred), cask no. 58, bott 11 Jul 16 db **(94) n22.5 t24 f23.5 b24** If they don't put the brakes on this, it'll be too old by the time it reaches 36 months. At this moment, simply stunning! 62.7%

Cotswolds Distillery Single Malt 30 Months Re-rack cask no. 4, bott 4 Jun 17 db **(89.5) n22 t23.5 f21.5 b22.5** A thick malt, creamy textured and brimming with muscovado sugars and eye-watering tannin. To taste, a happy, agreeable mix of cream soda and chocolate raisin with a slow, almost, apologetic spiciness and a light degree of bitterness on the finish. One of those malts which hasn't quite found its feet as a fair bit of tannic turbulence is encountered on both nose and in in the aftershocks of delivery. But overall...wow! 62.4%. sc.

⬥ **Cotswolds Single Malt Whisky 3 Years Old** STR cask, cask no. 236 db **(94) n23.5** unadulterated elegance: the malt has gathered into an intense ball, thick but with enough give to allow sublimely delicate cinnamon to revel in its unexpected oakiness; **t23.5** again it is the malt that surges through with major intent, a plethora of treacle and Manuka honey notes giving astonishing oaky depth for a malt so young; **f23.5** long, just more of the same thought the spices are now warming to the task; **b24** if you require proof that brilliance can be achieved even when a whisky is only just legally old enough to be called whisky, then here you go. For its age, the depth to this malt is truly stunning. 62%. nc ncf sc. Bottled for That Boutique-y Whisky Company.

⬥ **Cotswolds Single Malt Whisky 3 Years & 3 Months** bott 4 Apr 18 db **(91) n23** the tannins stand proud and upright, as though covered solid in a crispy Demerara sugar coating; **t23** there we go again: amazing sweetness to the delivery. A blend of ulmo honey and maple syrup accompany the intensely gristy malt, though by the mid-point we have moved into darker, toastier territory; **f22** burnt fudge plus honey-covered burnt toast; **b23** who would have though, a quarter of a century ago, when I gave my first of many whisky tasting at Fortnum and Mason, the pantry of Piccadilly would one day have their very own label (and beautifully distilled and matured) English single malt whisky for sale. St James's may still look the same, but the whisky world has moved on beyond recognition. 46%. nc ncf sc. Bottled for Fortnum & Mason.

⬥ **Cotswolds Single Malt Whisky 3 Years & 6 Months** bourbon 1st fill cask, cask no. 82 db **(92.5) n23** profound oaky caramel with a delightful sub-layering of malt; **t23.5** beautifully rich.

The oils gather and nail the barley to the spot. More layers than an average onion, and every bit as warming, too. The mid-point hit maximum complexity, with oaky stratum varying from toasty to light praline; **f23** ridiculously long. Vanilla, starting lightly gathers in intensity just as the malt and caramels did earlier; **b23** about as oily as Cotswolds malt gets, ensuring the barley is spread not just to all distant corners of the palate, but stays there for a long time, also. 60.5%. nc ncf sc.

◇ **Cotswolds Single Malt Whisky Inaugural Release** first fill barrels, batch no. 01/2017 db (**95**) **n23.5** an adorable nuttiness has its fingerprints all over this nose, ensuring a measured dryness the Demerara sugars and outline gristiness; murmurs of spice and echoes of something a little chocolatey; **t24** indeed, strains of the chocolate are evident on the delivery, which is soothed with light oils and ever growing malt intensity; the value of the oak grows, first as simple vanillas, then broader, backboned tannins with a light liquorice hue; youthful, but with adult shoulders; **f23.5** back again to the oily vanilla and a slow mocha development; **b24** just before I officially tasted this, my 1,000th new whisky for the Jim Murray Whisky Bible 2018, (I had initially and unofficially tasted it when I spoke at the distillery's opening ceremony last Spring) I turned my telescope to the sky to see with excellent clarity the banded giant Jupiter with four moons in almost perfect alignment (one to the left, three to the right); then swung my scope slightly to the south east and there was Saturn, its rings as clear and breathtaking as I had ever witnessed, at an angle of ten past eight. In an hour or so, Mars will rise and shine as brightly as it has done in 17 years and will not do again until the 2036 Whisky Bible. The portents were good for this malt, hopefully the distillery. And with this universally beautiful whisky, I was not remotely let down. 46%. nc ncf. 4,000 bottles.

◇ **Cotswolds Single Malt Whisky 2014 Odyssey Barley Batch No. 02/2017** first fill oak barrels db (**95**) **n23.5** the softness from the natural caramels charms; the light citrus note intrigues, the evenness of the malt soothes; the subtlety of the heather honey and its harmony with the headier tannins blows you away; **t24** a real surprise package of hefty sugars on delivery, with thinned molasses and maple syrup leading the way; outstanding oils of near perfect weight ensure the spices and chocolate fudge cling together beautifully at the midpoint; **f23.5** those now delicate oils guarantee a beautifully sculpted and elongated finish, highlighting, in shadowed form, the shape and substance of the delivery; **b24** only two bottlings into The Cotswolds' doubtless long history and you think: "yep, this is going to be one very substantial, high class and important distillery". With less than 2,000 bottles of this improbably precocious masterpiece produced, this will be one of the most collectable whiskies for years to come. 46%. nc ncf. 1,920 bottles.

◇ **Cotswolds Single Malt Whisky 2014 Odyssey Barley Batch No. 03/2017** first fill oak barrels db (**88.5**) **n22.5** a drier, denser version of 02/2017, with a more date and walnut style emphasis; **t22.5** less oils but more early spice and Manuka honey; **f21** has taken more time for the complexity to begin to show but a slight bite and furriness interrupts the flow. Some lovely chocolate, though; **b22.5** plays down its usual sweetness. 46%. nc ncf. 6,800 bottles.

◇ **Cotswolds Single Malt Whisky 2014 Odyssey Barley Batch No. 04/2017** first fill oak barrels db (**94**) **n23** serious depth: heather honey and barley sugar candy in a jar (with a few fizzy cola ones for good measure); **t23.5** beautiful array of malt tones, of varying depth and weight: always warms the heart to see the barley shewing what it can do; the intertwangling of light toasty tannins and delicate ulmo honey makes an engaging side show; **f23.5** only late on do the spices begin to surface. The ulmo honey, delicate vanilla and inexhaustible malt made the fade a drawn-out joy; **b24** a return to form and its more expansive, complex and sweet framework. What a treat of a dram! 46%. nc ncf. 10,800 bottles.

◇ **Cotswolds Single Malt Whisky 2014 Odyssey Barley Batch No. 01/2018** first fill barrels db (**93**) **n23** dense with a Manuka honey fringe; a lighter and softer fruit salad caress; **t23.5** it isn't the flavour which blows you away first, but the mouth feel: simultaneously firm and lush – not the easiest trick to pull off. Salivating, too, as soon as the malt gets to work with roasty intent. A little blood orange peels away in the background; **f23** mocha and molasses, there is a furry buzz to the residual spice; **b23.5** whisky of this age matured in the British Isles has no right to be this beautifully rounded. 46%. nc ncf. 7,150 bottles.

◇ **Cotswolds Single Malt Whisky 2014 Odyssey Barley Batch No. 02/2018** first fill barrels db (**88**) **n23** hefty and thick – one of their date and walnut specials. Attractive prickly spice; a tad chalky and dry; **t22** early burst of Demerara sugars, then a muddled, though malty, mid ground; **f21** toasty, but a little bitter and out of alignment also; **b22** an enjoyable malt, though not quite up to the distillery's hitherto very high standards. The exact storyline to this malt has you scratching your head. 46%. nc ncf. 8,600 bottles.

◇ **Cotswolds Single Malt Whisky 2014 Odyssey Barley Batch No. 03/2018** first fill barrels db (**95**) **n23.5** butterscotch tart, anyone? Sticky barley sugar, then? All found on a polished Victorian oak Welsh dresser. Wow...! **t24** Cotswolds at its most tactile and sumptuous:

the malt spreads enquiring fingers around the palate. Cake mix direct from the bowl, compete with Demerara sugar and caramel. Then...just count the layers of malt...it's obscene...! f23.5 dries and becomes markedly toastier as the oak finds a voice; even a date and walnut cake sweet chewiness very late on as light spices rise; b24 The Cotswolds is an understatedly beautiful place: it has just become more beautiful still... 46%. nc ncf. 8,550 bottles.

Cotswolds Single Malt Whisky 2014 Odyssey Barley Batch No. 04/2018 first fill barrels db (92.5) n23 playfully nippy, though the chocolate fudge has a dreamy, creamy quality by contrast; the malt is full on; offers a reserved sweetness; t24 mmmm... about as full bodied and salivating a delivery as Cotswolds have yet produced, allowing the toasty tannins to puff out their chest from the very first moment, yet the malt to be around in force; a spiced Manuka honey mixed with a modicum of liquorice...and much to chew on; a slight echo of fruitcake can just be heard; f22.5 the spices still quietly fizz while the sweeter oak tones revert to a more mocha-rich persona; b23 a delicious, confident whisky not frightened of letting the oak play a leading role. 46%. nc ncf. 7,050 bottles.

Cotswolds Distillery New Make Spirit batch no. WC 22:2:2, dist 29 May 16, bott 11 Jul 16 db (89) n20 t23.5 f23 b22.5. Slightly different character to the last new make bottling I tasted from them. Here, they have allowed the cut to be just a little too wide, impacting on the nose. Though that can mean a massive personality on delivery, which is in evidence here. Loads of malt and chocolate notes later on, and astonishing sugars in between. Yummy doesn't quite cover it. Though with my blender's technical hat on, a few marks dropped. Anyway, thought I'd taste this English whisky – made just a short journey from my tasting room - on the very day our new Prime Minister, Theresa May, formed a brand new cabinet which includes the Whisky Bible's local MP as Environment Secretary: here's to you, Andrea! 63.5%

Cotswolds Distillery New Make Spirit Plumage Archer bott 6 Jun 17 db (95) n23.5 t24 f23.5 b24 Absolutely top-notch, ultra-salivating and characterful new make which enjoys a stunning fruity flair (and, of course, not a wine cask in sight) before it settles down to the more basic business of radiating quite beautiful malt. Gorgeously weighted and excellent residual cocoa and spice. By quite peculiar coincidence, the last time I tasted the Cotswold's new make for The Bible, it was on the very day Theresa May was announced as Prime Minister. This sample for the 2018 Bible arrived today: on the morning, slightly less than a year later, that a chastened and greatly weakened Theresa May was confirmed at Buckingham Palace as Prime Minister again after limply and loosely "winning" a snap election. As this New Make would in barrel discover, a year is not very long in the life of a whisky. However, it can be a lifetime in British politics... 63.5%.

Cotswolds Test Batch Series New Make batch no. 01/2017, bott 13 Oct 17 db (94.5) n23 t24 f23.5 b24 A Test Batch Special. As English as a game of cricket, old chap, and as barley rich as mid-June sun-drenched Cotswold field... 63.5%. nc ncf.

Cotswolds Test Batch Series Peated Cask Aged 25 Months cask no. 221, bott 13 Oct 17 db (91.5) n22.5 t22.5 f22 b22.5 By no means the finished article. Yet even at this tender age the marriage between the phenols, the barley and the oak is taking on a shape which a bit of a turn on. The smoke is more meaningful than many such similar cask maturation phenolic whiskies, but still allows a delightful citrus note to wander through the entire piece. Lovely gristy sugars ensures a light touch throughout, though a hefty tannin and love heart combination gives a brief pulse. 62.4%. nc ncf sc.

HEALEY'S CORNISH CYDER FARM Penhallow. 1986. Working.
Hicks & Healey Cornish Whiskey 2004 Cask #32 dist 13 Feb 04, bott Feb 12 db (96) n24 t24.5 f23.5 b24. I picked this one up absent-mindedly, nosed...and was carried to Cornwall. I knew what it was without even opening my eyes. Unmistakable. And just so stunningly beautiful... 60.2%. ncf

LAKES DISTILLERY Cockermouth, Cumbria. 2014. Working.
The Lakes Malt Spirit db (90) n23 t22 f22.5 b22.5. I have chosen this as the 999th new "whisky" for the 2017 Jim Murray's Whisky Bible as a tribute to my dear old friend Harold Currie who was recently lost to us. Harold was behind the building of the Isle of Arran Distillery and a close bond, based mainly on mutual respect and fondness for the simple things in life – like St Mirren and football in general - formed between us. Both his sons played a part in getting this distillery off the ground, so though not yet a whisky, it is a special moment for me to taste their new-ish make. With the very first sip I ever have of this ground-breaking malt, I shall toast a very special old fiend: Harold Currie.... A lovely developing malt with a very puritanical cut ensuring the citrus has a big part to play. Massively promising as this is clean and characterful. But, my dear old friends, you have to bottle this stuff at something closer to cask strength: you have broken up the oils so we cannot quite see its full potential. 40%

ST. GEORGE'S Rowdham, Norfolk. 2006. Working.

The English Whisky Co. Chapter 7 Rum Cask cask nos. 471 & 472 db (92.5) n23 t23.5 f23 b23 What an amazingly consistent malt this is: the Chapter 7 Rum Cask has become one of highlights of my tasting year, simply because you suspect what you going to get...and never end up disappointed. Slightly more youthful than before, but still another minor gem from St George. 46%. nc ncf.

The English Whisky Co. Chapter 14 Not Peated cask no. 120, 121, 122 & 123, dist Apr 11, bott Jun 16 db (96) n24 t24 f24 b24 There are less than 200 bottles of this unambiguously world-class and faultless nectar, apparently. What a bugger...!58.8%. ncf nc. 192 bottles.

The English Whisky Co. Chapter 14 ASB Casks 5 Year Old cask nos. 290, 291, 292 & 293, dist Nov 11, bott Nov 16 db (92) n23 t23.5 f22.5 b23 An intense, satisfying malt that keeps you guessing in which direction it is heading next. 46%. nc ncf.

The English Whisky Co. Chapter 14 Single Malt (unpeated) cask no. 205, 181, 182, 183, dist Apr 10, bott May 15 db (92.5) n23 t23.5 f23 b23 How can a malt at nearly 60%abv be so silky soft and sexy? A ridiculously gentle and genteel whisky. 58.8%. nc ncf.

The English Whisky Co. Chapter 16 peated sherry casks db (95) n23.5 t24 f23.5 b24 Quite superbly vatted: the marriage between smoke and grape is a rare success for the style and there is not a single atom of sulphur to be bought. Truly brilliant! 46%. nc ncf.

The English Whisky Co. Chapter 17 Small Batch Release batch no. 01/2017, dist Jun 12, bott Jun 17 db (87) n22 t23.5 f20 b21.5 A typical St George's malt explosion, the delivery being something of a grist convention. But there is a tang to this with the tannins never quite being on the same song sheet as the malt. That all said, worth finding just for the spiced barley-caramel extravaganza on delivery alone...! 46%. nc ncf. 1,641 bottles.

The English Whisky Co. Founders Private Cellar 2010 bourbon & virgin cask, cask 365, dist Dec 10, bott Mar 16 db (94) n23 t24 f23 b24. Whisky snobs will put this comment down as an insult to this distillery (which it most certainly isn't), but certain elements of this malt – especially on the nose - have remarkable similarities with the long discontinued no age-statement Glenfiddich which, in its day, offered one of the most thrilling and pugnacious malt signatures on the world stage. This is a slightly more honey rich and magnificent version. 59.7%. nc ncf sc. 285 bottles.

The English Whisky Co. Original bourbon cask db (89) n22.5 t22.5 f22 b22 when I first tasted this an odd thing happened. For a moment I thought I was tasting an old Scottish blend still in lab form and pre-bottled from over 25 years ago. I certainly didn't recognise it as Norfolk's finest. Pleasant, hugely enjoyable and friendly. But by EWC standards, pretty basic, too. 43%.

⟡ **The English Whisky Co. Original** batch no.003 18, bourbon casks db (94.5) n24 just like the partner of your dreams, this has a nose you slowly fall in love with. And it is, invariably, unique. This is different, like a parcel of malt wrapped in freshly cut moist Spring grass; t23.5 the grass suggests high grade salivation –and bang on cue, there it is. Gorgeous melt-in-the-mouth grist with a spicy accompaniment works in tandem with a light muscovado fruitiness; f23 vanilla and grist all the way; b24 annoyingly, I appear to have missed out on batch 2, but I remember the original version of this – batch 1 – was a little undercooked. What you have here, I delighted to report, is the Full English....thoroughly recommend for breakfast. 43%. ncf.

⟡ **The English Whisky Co. PX Sherry Cask Matured** db (85.5) n22 t22 f20.5 b21 While their Unpeated Peated Bourbon cask is the distillery's most honeyed ever whisky, this is their most sugared. There is a difference and it's all about balance and complexity,neither of which are up to this distillery's normal high standards here... 46%. ncf.

⟡ **The English Whisky Co. Small Batch Release Rum Cask Matured** batch no.01/2018, dist Mar 13, bott Feb 18 db (91.5) n23 a more sugar-coated rum version than the norm: a lovely green leaf and heather honey mix ensured a fresh softness; t23 as on the nose, the sugars deliver early but for all their Demerara crunchiness, the salivating quality of the grist takes centre stage; f22.5 toastier, more spicy oak fade than expected; b23 a classic rum-matured style with a crisp, sugary outer shell and softer malt-rich middle. 46%. ncf.

⟡ **The English Whisky Co. Single Cask Peated Triple Distilled** cask no. B1/154, dist Aug 10 db (93) n23.5 thumping, ribald, no-prisoners-taken peat; t23 big peat and sugar explosion of delivery: Manuka honey tires to make an impact, but the phenols are too quick for it; f23.5 a better finale as a gorgeous and unexpected chocolate and liquorice element enters the smoky fray; b23 almost as aggressive a peated malt as their "Smokey" bottling is relaxed. 57.4%. ncf sc.

⟡ **The English Whisky Co. Single Cask Portuguese Cabernet Sauvignon** cask no. B1/832, dist Jun 07 db (77) n19 t20 f19 b19 The closest thing to an English Whisky Liqueur. Excessively sweet, and off key on the finish, also. Hopefully a one off. 56.8%. ncf sc.

⟡ **The English Whisky Co. Single Cask Unpeated Bourbon Cask** cask no. B1/593, dist May 08 db (95) n23.5 neat and tidy layering involving concentrated malt, heather honey, chalk, vanilla, butterscotch and lightly sweetened allspice; **t24** it is the honey which is first out of the gun, immediately ramping up its sweetness to scintillating effect. The spices are also now in full flow, though the oak is making dry, chalky waves as the balance stays on an even keel; **f23.5** still gristy, but the heather honey stays the course with some late red liquorice pairing beautifully with the spice; **b24** the most honeyed whisky ever produced by this distillery. An English single malt classic. *58.1%. ncf sc.*

The English Whisky Co. Smokey bourbon cask db **(93.5) n23 t23 f23.5 b24** They could have also written "smoky bacon cask".... *43%.*

The English Single Malt Whisky Smokey bourbon casks, batch no. L001 16 db **(90.5) n23** smoky; **t23** oily and smoky; **f22** smoky and bittering; **b22.5** smoky... *43%. nc ncf.*

English Single Malt Whisky Smokey The Original bourbon casks, batch no. L002 16 db **(91) n22.5 t23.5 f22 b23** ery much a simplified version over the previous Original thanks to a significant upping on the oak-drained sugars... *43%. nc ncf.*

⬦ **The English Whisky Co. Smokey** batch no.002 18, bourbon casks db **(94) n24** really...? There is almost an arrogance to the faultless, seamless weight plied by the peat on the nose: substantial smoke without for a moment becoming heavy or aggressive; sweet without **t23.5** salivating, gristy, gently spiced...and that smoke never for a moment changes pace, intensity of pace: is in total control; **f22.5** very late oak bitterness, but the peat...well, it just gently rumbles on with the spices regardless; **b24** this has to be one of the most relaxed peaty whiskies on the planet: the way it gets its smokiness across borders on the indolent. But, my word, it is so lovely... *43%. ncf.*

The Norfolk Single Grain Farmers American oak, batch no. 01/2016, bott 1 Nov 16 db **(91) n23 t24 f21.5 b22.5** I know that St George's outstanding distiller, David Fitt, has a partiality to this particular multi-grain (yes, multi-grain: not single grain, as seven different grain types are in the recipe...don't ask!) creation. I can see why, as it is a grand departure from their norm. It is engaging and intriguing, but falls very slightly towards the end as the harmonisation between grain and oak hasn't quite peaked... *45%. nc ncf sc. 1,998 bottles.*

⬦ **The Norfolk Farmers Single Grain Whisky** batch no. 02/2018, bourbon cask, bott 28 Feb 18 db **(96.5) n23.5** I was told, prior to sampling this, that malted oats were in the grain mix. They needn't have bothered: the oat, with its unique footprint, is the noisiest incumbent in there, just ahead of the rye; **t24.5** there is so much flavour in this whisky, you start to wonder if there might be a law against it: surely nothing this delightful can be legal... For a start you need a machine to measure the salivation levels...and then send the results to the Guinness Book of Records. And while you are at it, find out from them the record number of bitter-sweet flavour waves ever detected on a whisky; so juicy, so crisp, slightly yielding, too; just adore that latent sharpness which keeps the taste buds on constant edge; **f24** late chocolate, perhaps a mix of the barley and oak; **b24.5** some people might be a little confused by the labelling of this whisky, and you have my sympathy. It is called a "single grain whisky" which kind of suggests that only one grain type has been used. Well, no, there are four: in no particular order, rye, wheat, oats and several styles of malted barley. In fact, all the grains are malted, but they didn't want to call it a "Malt Whisky" in case people automatically assumed it was a single malt like Scotch, made from 100% barley. While the "single" term reflects it is from just the one distillery, St George's in Norfolk. Complicated? Well, not half as complex as this truly beautiful and gloriously idiosyncratic malt whisky. *45%. ncf sc. 392 bottles.*

The Norfolk Single Grain Malt 'N' Rye American oak, batch no. 01/2017, bott 23 Jan 17 db **(88) n22** hefty and oily, the usual sharp fruity rye note is silenced by both barley and vanilla; **t22.5** chewy, salivating and increasingly firm in texture as it progresses. Big oils, a light buzz of spice and ever-increasing butterscotch through the middle; **f21.5** a little sharp, though oily; **b22** a strange beast, absolutely bursting with flavour yet never quite finds the rhythm it seeks. *45%. nc ncf sc. 1,962 bottles.*

The Norfolk Single Grain Parched db **(96.5) n24.5 t24 f23.5 b24.5** A classic Irish "mod pot" style Irish pot still whiskey...from Norfolk! Nosed this when it was just a few months old...and it has moved on magnificently; indeed, beyond hope and expectation. Only the cat's bowler on the label and a green bottle seems to give the faintest hint towards anything Irish... For the record, by far the best Pot Still I have ever encountered made outside Ireland's shores... *45%. nc ncf sc.*

WALES
PENDERYN Penderyn, Aberdare. 2004. Working.

Penderyn Celt bott code 70474 db **(95) n23.5 t24 f23.5 b24** This is like a malt for peat addicts trying to wean themselves off the phenols, but needing a lighter fix to keep them going. I doubt if any smoked whisky bottled anywhere in the world is as delicate as this... *41%. ncf.*

⬦ **Penderyn Celt** bott code 71172 db **(91) n22.5** a gentle mix of Nesquick chocolate milkshake powder, spices, vague phenols and possibly vaguer citrus; **t23** malt, which doesn't appear on the nose, certainly does on delivery. So soft, sensual and always chewy, Light Demerara and sherbet meet in the middle; **f22.5** the softest spices breathe life into the vanilla; **b23** if a whisky got any more laid back and lighter it'd be carrying out levitation... *41%. ncf.*

⬦ **Penderyn Celt** bott code 72773 db **(92.5) n23** it is though the malt is talking to you in whispers, listen hard – with your nose – for once you are attuned so clearly comes the message of lightly smoked bacon and freshly squeezed lemon – from the back kitchen of your local eatery; **t23** an emphatic use of light sugars, first gristy and malt intense, then of a more citrus bent – thinly spread marmalade, perhaps; **f23.5** what little noise there was on the palate has died down now as the modest spices are heard clearly; a little cream toffee and butterscotch continues the soft theme; **b23** ssshhh! Don't drink this malt too loudly...you'll never hear what it's saying... *41%. ncf.*

⬦ **Penderyn Celt** bott code 73491 db **(94) n23.5** one of the most citrusy noses I've encountered on a Penderyn: its acidic punch actually hits you as you pour into the glass; there are also phenols to add a no less acidic tang, but earthier now; **t23.5** the nose warns you that this is going to be as salivating as they come – and it is! The malt may not be that apparent on the nose, but it turns up in force in about the fourth favour wave and stays; the mid-ground plays host to gentle oaky visitations; **f23** a real softy with phenol trace and ridiculously lazy spice; **b24** an impossibly attractive whisky which just seems to understate everything – emphatically. *41%. ncf.*

⬦ **Penderyn Celt** bott code 80735 db **(88.5) n22** little of the usual lilting fruit, though the phenols do give the nose a slight tweak; **t22.5** hmmm....curiously docile delivery. The malt and toffee are at first on different wavelengths, then meld, harmlessly, into one; **f22** vanilla and spice; **b22** a little flat this one: Wales without the hills and valleys. *41%. ncf.*

Penderyn Icons of Wales No 5/50 Bryn Terfel bourbon casks db **(96.5) n24 t24.5 f23.5 b24.5** Having seen Bryn Terfel perform live – many years ago now, I admit – I can vouch for this man's power on stage; his rare, uncanny ability to resonate with the soul. See Bryn and you get your full tenor's worth... So, this must be his alto-ego, for this is the most delicate malt ever bottled by Penderyn: ethereal, closer to the angelic voices in the closing movement of Faure's Requiem than Bryn's bass-baritone. To get that you would have needed to have added a lot of peat – and we would have ended up with Bryn Turfel....and that would never do... *41%. ncf.*

Penderyn Legend bott code 61375 db **(94.5) n24 t23.5 f23 b24** The blender is a lady? You don't say.... *41%. ncf.*

Penderyn Legend bott code 62873 db **(92.5) n23 t23 f23 b23.5** A much plainer, crisper version with the emphasis on the sugars. *41%. ncf.*

Penderyn Legend bott code 63223 db **(87.5) n21.5 t22 f22 b22** An entirely pleasant boyo, though by the almost unbelievably high standards now set by Penderyn this bottling seems overly content to chug along on a simplistic fruit and vanilla theme buoyed (or is that buoyoed?) by knuckle-dusting spice. *41%. ncf.*

Penderyn Legend bott code 70057 db **(91) n22** peach, apricot and playful vanillas; **t23** salivating and so clean! The fruits are much grapier here: squashy sultanas and even that distinctive grape juice sweetness; **f22.5** a little tangy as the spices and tannins hit harder; a little golden syrup ensures a sweet finale; **b23.5** a delightful procession of fruit and subtle sugars. *41%. ncf.*

⬦ **Penderyn Legend** bott code 72618 db **(92.5) n23** dried apricots on a red currant and marmalade base; **t23** chewy delivery with, initially, massive malt then a slow unveiling of delicate fruits – essence of apricot leading the way; **f23** sexy spices jazz up the light fruits; **b23.5** by no means the most taxing Penderyn. But what it does, it does just right... *41%. ncf.*

⬦ **Penderyn Legend** bott code 72965 db **(95.5) n23.5 t24 f23.5 ...b24.5** Not sure whiskies under 46% abv are meant to be quite this complex, rich and satisfying. A truly brilliant whisky, underlining Penderyn's world class credentials. *41%. ncf.*

⬦ **Penderyn Legend** bott code 80593 db **(93.5) n23.5** what's this...? Phenols? Yep – the very lightest smokiness adds a bit of extra weight to the superlight citrus tones; **t23** as we now come to expect from Penderyn, a delivery to savour. The malt cascades onto the palate with a divine barley sugar and lemon sherbet mix; light phenols buzz and tingle; **f23** the barley stays the course beautifully; the spices nip graciously and the oils keep the gristy sugars going to the last; **b24** a luscious malt which offers greater oils than most 41% whiskies and, mysteriously from somewhere, the lightest hint of phenol more associated with their Celt bottlings. Works here, though! *41%. ncf.*

Penderyn Madeira Finish bott code 61734 db **(93.5) n23** one of those super-dry noses Penderyn throws into the mix from time to time: curiously fruity, yet the sugars have taken the day off...; **t23.5** yep, a dry one! That said, the sugars, in hiding on the nose, slowly reveal themselves here and are of a gristy, muscovoado variety; the mid-ground reverts to a drier vanilla with a threat of spice which takes time to arrive...; **f23** well, the spices are here now, as is a dry, chalky crushed pip tone; **b24** the most sophisticated thing to emerge from Wales since Shirley Bassey. *46%. ncf.*

Penderyn Madeira Finish bott code 61851 db (92.5) n22.5 t23 f23.5 b23.5 Every trait of this whisky displays a friendly aspect. 46%. ncf.

Penderyn Madeira Finish bott code 63503 db (96) n24 t24 f24 b24 A whisky which just flows, effortlessly, from nose to finish without any recognisable flaws or cracks. My old mate, Jim Swan, who created this unique flavour profile, would have been proud... 46%. ncf.

Penderyn Madeira Finish bott code 70395 db (92) n23 t23.5 f23 b23.5 A fascinating yet still delicious shift in oaky emphasis. 46%. ncf.

Penderyn Madeira Finish bott code 71021 db (87) n21 t22.5 f21.5 b21.5 Full of mouth-filling fruit, chalky tannins and spice. Plenty to chew on and enjoy, but just lacking that usual Penderyn harmony. 46%. ncf.

Penderyn Madeira Finish bott code 72705 db (90.5) n21.5 slightly imbalanced with some creaking ultra-dry chalkiness; t23 this is the cheese to the nose's chalk. And a big cheese at that. The malt is huge; about as concentrated as Penderyn has yet amassed. The light fruits take some time to gather and even by the midpoint can barely make a scratch on the barley and honeycomb; f23.5 just love that glorious chocolate mousse finale. With the accompanying light spices, that is just a very classy sign off...; b23 a slightly different Penderyn in type but makes up for indifferent nose in spades. 46%. ncf.

Penderyn Madeira Finish bott code 73282 db (93) n22.5 slightly chalky and dry with some firm pith notes, too. A secondary bourbon note can be detected before the fruits quietly get going; t23.5 a sumptuous mouth-feel belies the drier outline of the nose. A beautiful mix of ulmo and Manuka honey gives way to liquorice and grape; the spices offer just the right thrust; f23 soft oils spin out the cocoa and lightest of fruits; b24 the end of an era: the last batch in the original tall bottle that launched a thousand sips. And what a way to bow out..! Truly exceptional balance makes this the kind of whisky that just demands a refill. When you consider the average, very decent quality of the first bottlings of Penderyn in this trademark bottle and compare it to the excellence of this, well: now there's a story... 46%. ncf.

Penderyn Madeira Finish bott code 73196 db (92.5) n23 all the usual Welsh gold hallmarks which distinguish this from the rest, especially that pithy dryness; t23 followed by a juicy eruption of dark cherry and intense malt; the sub-plot of dry oak is well marked here; f23 late liquorice and hickory to accompany the light spice delicate muscovado; b23.5 and so a rocket-shaped bottle for the whisky that really has taken off around the world... how apt! 46%. ncf.

Penderyn Madeira Finish bott code 803912 db (91) n22 dry enough to trigger a hosepipe ban...; t22.5 early sugars are a stark contrast to the aroma: gristy and moistened by chocolate limes; as usual, the oak and dried fruits plays an accompanying, more sophisticated tune; f23.5 the lime may have gone, but the chocolate hasn't...; b23 very elegant, indeed. 46%. ncf.

Penderyn Madeira Finish bott code 81036 db (94) n23.5 much more tannin on the nose gives an immediate bourbon-style lift; the drier notes are there, but this time playing second fiddle; t23.5 intense and oily with a real splash of Kentucky colour to this. The malt remains intact and rich but we are now in molasses territory, rather than the fruiter muscovado...; f24 the chocolate is intense, the spices are busy, the fuit is just the od raisin here and there – but it works so well; b23 that extra dose of oak has gone a very long way. Not perhaps how I'd like to see every Penderyn, but the extra cocoa injection makes for a delightful detour. This is the biggest Madeira Finish Penderyn ever bottled, and make no mistake. 46%. ncf.

Penderyn Myth bott code 70193 db (93.5) n23 t24 f23 b23.5 Perplexing how a whisky at a lower strength can have more body than bottlings which are higher. But Penderyn is nothing if not different...! 41%. ncf.

Penderyn Myth bott code 70732 db (91) n22 t22.5 f23.5 b23 A complex malt which just grows and grows... 41%. ncf.

Penderyn Myth bott code 73342 db (94) n23 just such a lovely and endearing mix of fruit notes, and on an unusually dry axis, too. Gorgeous pithy apricot plus diced pear and a lovely red liquorice note to offer a delicate sweetness; t23.5 good oils embolden the melt-in-the-mouth sugars on delivery. But the mid-ground is not unlike a tropical fruit and vanilla ice cream at work with a little bourbon stirred in to add extra edge; f23.5 such a lovely Manuka honey, hickory and spice fade...; b24 once, a Penderyn this good and so complex would stand out amongst the rest. Now it is almost becoming the norm... 43%. ncf.

Penderyn Myth bott code 80821 db (92.5) n24 I actually started salivating just from nosing this...that premature act is something almost unknown to me. Needless to say, the malts and fruits have combined to create something fresh and teasingly provocative; t23 soft and floaty...like driving across the Severn Bridge from Wales to England with a gentle tail wind behind you (something that happens all too rarely.!); the fruit ducks out early leaving an intense malty body; f22.5 spiced butterscotch, added by a glistening bourbon-style sugar and tannin effect; b23 a myth? No-way Hothay. Ith a hit...!! 43%. ncf.

Penderyn Portwood bott code 63185 db **(95)** n23.5 t23.5 f24 b24 Doubtless, some people will taste these two Portwood whiskies side by side and wonder why one scores an OK, the other very highly. Well, they may be similar in myriad ways, but they are different where it matters. Just look at the chemical composition of salt and sugar: not much in it, is there...? 46%. ncf.

⬦ **Penderyn Portwood** bott code 80471 db **(79)** n21.5 t22.5 f17 b19 One of the more understated Port matured malts on the market with an almost Chardonnay feel to it. Sadly, the sulphury finish confirms all is not what it should be. 46%. ncf.

Penderyn Rich Oak db **(93)** n23 t24 f23 b23 A curious, even unique, line-up of flavours makes for a massively enjoyable and occasionally head-scratching experience. 50%. ncf. 1,113 bottles.

⬦ **Penderyn Rich Oak** bott Nov 17 db **(94.5)** n23.5 the tannins are here to make a point and not just mix in quietly with the fruit. Dry and chalky but wearing a Stetson, too as there is some Kentucky-type liquorice and hickory to contend with, too...; t24 the mouth feel makes you groan with delight. The big malt and muscovado sugars then make you purr and the liquorice and concentrated spiced dates teases a contented sigh: this is one very noisy single malt; f23 a toasted, roasty fade – breathtakingly long, still lush, still over-ripe fruity and brilliantly spiced; b24 the famous Penderyn style seemingly on steroids. Any richer and it'll be buying Swansea City FC... 50%. ncf. 1,349 bottles.

Penderyn Sherrywood bott code 70232 db **(81.5)** n20 t22.5 f19 b20 Big spice and magnificent creamy toffee raisin. But all rather tight and constricted. On nose and finish especially. 46%. ncf.

⬦ **Penderyn Sherrywood** bott code 73381 db **(76)** n19 t21 f17 b19 Flat and off key thanks to a dose of sulphur. Again, their Sherrywood bottling proves the Achilles heel in this distillery's seemingly inexorable rise towards greatness. 46%. ncf.

⬦ **Penderyn Single Cask Ex-Ruby Port 2007 Vintage** cask no. PT88, bott Feb 18 db **(94.5)** n23.5 a thick soup of a nose – a well-peppered soup at that. A bowl of over-ripe fruit, for sure, but much else besides. A mix of orange blossom honey and strawberry jam accounts for the sweeter element. But there is a darker side, semi-phenolic with a hefty vanilla on slightly burnt toast offering, too., t24 eye-wateringly succulent, the malt making a surprise, intense early incursion. The fruits are a tease, a nibble of the taste buds here, a lick there. Mainly on a greengage and loganberry theme. But it is the mix of Manuka honey and light treacle which really grabs the attention, guiding the malt towards a rich fruit cake feel; f23.5 dark, hefty and brooding the spices play pretty patterns; a high cocoa dark chocolate note has just the right degree of accompanying raisins...; b23.5 a truly premium malt for a Premium company. 58%. ncf sc. Bottled for Premium Spirits, Belgium.

Penderyn Single Cask Portwood cask no. PT255 db **(94)** n23.5 t23.5 f23 b24 The most ruby to claret-hued whisky I have ever encountered in bottled form: it like a Ch. Margaux. Only a whisky for after a fine meal, not during... 58.9%. ncf sc.

⬦ **Penderyn Single Cask Rich Madeira** cask no. M729 db **(95.5)** n23.5 no mistaking the provenance: so heavy and heady there is even a degree of phenol weight to this – smoke coming off the burnt raisin, perhaps... Both the fruit and the oak make massive contributions, and there is even an estery note usually far more associated with heavy Pot Still Jamaican rum than whisky, Welsh or otherwise; t24.5 good grief! The grey hairs on my chest have turned black and doubled in number. One of the deliveries of the year: a blitzkrieg of massive fruit from succulent over-ripe plums and sugary dates, through to heavily toasted raisin and slightly overcooked Melton Hunt Cake. That would all be too much, except the oak does make a balancing contribution with light hickory and liquorice filling in the gaps; f23.5 the taste buds are in shock for a few seconds after that onslaught, then re-focus to find vanillas and currents in much less assertive mood. A little late bitter tang; b24 when they say "Rich Madeira" they really aren't joking. Huge. And very, very rich. 58.8%. ncf sc. Bottled for Charles Hofer SA, Switzerland.

Penderyn Single Cask Rich Oak cask no. D161 db **(91)** n22 t24 f22 b23 A deliciously thick and intense whisky which is not too bothered about narrative or detail but knows how to create an effect. 59.8%. ncf sc. 289 bottles.

⬦ **Penderyn Single Cask Tawny Portwood** cask no. PT261/1 db **(96)** n23.5 crushed ripe elderflower, cherry candy and robust spice as the oak makes a very heathy statement; t24.5 been transported back to my childhood and my old mum pouring out a thick reddish cough mixture into a spoon. God, how I loved it...it made it a pleasure to be ill. There is certainly something of the tincture in this, especially the mix of friendly sugars – here a lovely mixture of muscovado and molasses – and the business end of prune juice and spicy sultanas. The late mid-ground also boasts a toasty butterscotch tart, moving now towards a chocolate torte; f24 the cocoa criss-crosses with more dried fruits: bread pudding, complete with light oil: childhood days, indeed...; b24 just ridiculously good! And mind-bogglingly complex. 59.7%. ncf sc. Bottled for Bresser & Trimmer BV, The Netherlands.

European Whisky

The debate about what it means to be European was one that seemingly never ended. That was until June 23rd 2016 when the people of Britain firmly decided that it should and they weren't. By contrast, the discussion on how to define the character of a European whisky is only just beginning.

And as more and more distilleries open throughout mainland Europe, Scandinavia, even Israel the styles are becoming wider and wider. Those of the British Isles have even grown large enough to warrant their own chapter in the Whisky Bible, though their awards shall be linked in with Europe for now.

Small distillers in mainland Europe, especially those in the Alpine area, share common ground with their US counterparts in often coming late into whisky. Their first love, interest and spirit had been with fruit brandies. It seemed that if something grew in a tree or had a stone when you bit into it, you could be pretty confident that someone in Austria or California was making a clear, eye-watering spirit from it somewhere.

So perhaps it is not surprising that the whiskies which each year seem now to get the highest and most consistent marks are those built purely with whisky in mind. Mackmyra in Sweden. Penderyn in Wales. The aged whiskies representing Gold Cock in the Czech Republic came from state-built distilleries when the land was still Czechoslovakia. The most impressive whisky I have enountered in Europe this year has come from the continuous stills of Nestville in Slovakia, nestled in the hills close to the Polish border. Their sound policy of linking clean whisky with superb casks was enough to win them an major award in this year's Whisky Bible.

There is a pattern now: every year I taste certain whiskies and I know there will be a professionalism to their consistency. They tend to be from distilleries which have invested heavily in both their stills, usually (though not always) moving away from the German type which is harder to control, and their casks. Langatun of Switzerland, Belgium Owl, Kornog of France, Domaine Mavela of Corsica, Sweden's Mackmyra, Stauning of Denmark and certain others have set the bar.... and just keep increasing the height.

	Jim Murray's Whisky Bible European Whisky of the Year Winners	
	European Whisky Multiple Casks	**European Whisky Single Cask**
2004	**Waldviester Hafer Whisky 2000**	N/A
2005	**Hessicher Whisky**	N/A
2006	**Swissky Exklusiv Abfullung**	N/A
2007	**Mackmyra Preludium 03 Svensk**	N/A
2008	**Mackmyra Privus 03 Svensk**	N/A
2009	**Old Buck 2nd Release (Finland)**	N/A
2010	Santis Malt Highlander Dreifaltigheit	**Penderyn Port Wood Single Cask**
2011	**Mackmyra Brukswhisky**	The Belgian Owl Aged 44 Months
2012	Mackmyra Moment "Urberg"	**Penderyn Bourbon Matured S C**
2013	**Penderyn Portwood Swansea**	Hicks & Healey 2004
2014	**Mackmyra "Glod" (Glow)**	Santis Malt Swiss Highlander
2015	**English Whisky Co. Chapter 14 N.P**	The Belgian Owl '64 Months'
2016	English Whisky Co. Chapter 16	**Kornog Chwee'hved 14 BC**
2017	**English Whisky Co. Chapter 14**	Langatun 6YO Pinot Noir Cask
2018	Penderyn Bryn Terfel	**The Norfolk Parched**
2019	Nestville Master Blender 8YO	**The Norfolk Farmers**

AUSTRIA

ACHENSEE'R EDELBRENNEREI FRANZ KOSTENZER Maurach. Working.

Whisky Alpin Grain Whisky Hafer 3 Years Old bott code L1/2013 db (86) n21 t22.5 f21.5 b21. A distinctly bitter-sweet affair. Good body and molasses kick. 40%

ALPEN WHISKY DISTILLERIE Frastanz. Working.

Alpenwhisky Single Malt Crocodile Toast new barrel, dist May 13, bott 14 Feb 17 db (88) n21.5 t23 f21.5 b22 Yes, I know: technically it is far from perfect with a good smattering of feint, but there is something just irresistible about the richness of the malt and coffee... 55%.

Alpenwhisky Single Malt Double Wood port cask, dist Feb 11, bott 06 Mar 17 db (77) n18 t20 f20 b19 Fruity, for sure. But only for the feint-hearted...46%

ALTE HAUSBRENNEREI A. WECKLEIN Arnstein. Working.

⬦ **Wecklain A.53 Frankonian Single Malt** barrels 4, 3 & 9, bott code LN 1004-17 db (89) n22 deceptive weight: slightly oily but toffee apple, too; t22.5 sugars group early and stay on that toffee apple theme: enormous fudge sweetness with a juicier sub element; f22 well weighted spice, a like fudge and nougat then more precise malt tones; b22.5 an amiable, sweet malt. 50%. 560 bottles.

⬦ **Wecklain A.54 Rushburn Frankonian Single Malt** barrels 8 & 19, bott code LN 1005-17 db (90) n23.5 an aroma – unique to the world's whiskies – which has just catapulted me over 50 years back into my childhood. But to where; doing what? It is linked to my childhood home in Surrey. Is it the straw drying in the field at the bottom of my garden, or the vanilla wafers holding my Walls Ice Cream block...a mixture of both perhaps, with praline, too...? Or ice cream cones by the sea, a light saltiness in every childhood sniff...? It is an aroma, uniquely beautiful, innocent and non-threatening that will haunt me...; t23 I was expecting a kind of grassy delivery after the nose, and it has arrived. Salivating, malt with husk and stem...the lot; f21.5 a little too bitter on the oils, good redeeming spices; b23 a very different, highly evocative whisky. 43%. 650 bottles.

BRENNEREI GUGLHOF Hallein. Working.

Tauern Rogg Single Malt Whisky Sauternes cask no. 93, dist 2011 db (88.5) n21 t23 f22 b22.5 Soft, sweet and satisfying. 42%. sc.

BRENNEREI ROSSETTI Kolsassberg. Working.

Rossetti Young & Fine Pure Single Malt bott code L582 db (89.5) n22 t23 f22 b22.5 I remember well the previous Rossetti I tasted: a bit of a gaunt, pasty lad: youthful and undernourished. The boy has grown. Perhaps a slight buzz on the finish, but an altogether burlier and more rounded character altogether. 43.5%

BROGER PRIVATBRENNEREI Klaus. Working.

Broger Burn Out Single Malt Whisky bott code L BO-12 db (95) n23.5 t24 f23.5 b24 When I saw I was faced with six new samples of Broger, I strapped myself in. I remember from old, that this is a distillery of extremes, with wildly varying quality. So I went for this one first – taking the bull by the horns. Closed my eyes...took a mouthful...and lived! Actually, the label should be one of billowing smoke, as you want as little flame as possible when smoking malt. And perhaps one, also, of sugar cane. Because the Demerara on this is highly impressive. A very pleasant surprise. Oh, and didn't I mention it? This is a mini masterpiece... 42%

Broger Distiller's Edition Single Malt Whisky Madeira cask db (66) n16 t17 f16 b17. Oh dear... The S word in abundance. 60.7%. 165 bottles.

Broger Medium Smoked Single Malt Whisky bott code L MS-09 db (94) n23.5t23.5 f23 b24 There is no doubt that this distillery knows exactly how to make smoky whisky...because this is a very different, more subtle, style to their peated efforts. 42%

DACHSTEIN DESTILLERIE Radstadt. Working

Mandlberggut Rock Whisky 5 Years bott code LWh11 db (87) n21 t22.5 f21.5 b22 A distillery on the rise! Massive improvement since I last tasted them and here the malt positively shimmers on the palate. Still so delicate the oils have a slightly over-important say but the grassy-lemon effect is truly delicious. 40.3%.

⬦ **Mandlberggut Rock Whisky Single Malt 5 Years** bott code LWh13 db (86) n20 t22 f22 b22 From the nougat school of German whisky, enjoying a slow but marked light honey development. No quicker to make itself felt is the malt, but finally does – and in tandem with toasty oak – quite impressively. 40.8%.

DESTILLERIE GEORG HIEBL Haag. Working.

George Hiebl Mais Whisky 2004 db (93) n23 t23.5 f23 b23.5. More bourbon in character than some American bourbons I know...!! Beautifully matured, brilliantly matured and European whisky of the very highest order, Ye..haahhhh!! 43%

DESTILLERIE ROGNER Rappottenstein. Working.

Rogner Waldviertel Whisky 3/3 db (86.5) n20 t22 f22.5 b22. A beautiful display of crisp sugars and come-back-for more grainy juiciness. Lovable stuff, for all its gliches. 41.7%. ncf.

DESTILLERIE WEIDENAUER Kottes. Working

◇ **Waldviertler Dinkelwhisky** bott code L10 db (90) n22 a slightly wide cut but a good chocolate fudge catch; t23 wow...eye-wateringly rich and glorious delivery. Again it goes straight into cocoa mode –not unlike Merlin chocolate and mint lolly – while the tannins beef themselves up beautifully; f22 so much molasses...! b23 a cleaner (though not perfect) distillation by comparison to the last dinkelwhisky I tasted from here, though the build-up of chocolate mousse is something to behold... one for the taste buds...! 42%.

◇ **Waldviertler Dinkel Whisky 2/3 Dinkelwalz Süßweinfass** finish, bott code L08 db (90.5) n22 pleasant, clean, delicate sweetness, but unusually uneventful by Weidenauer standards, depending entirely on subtlety; t23 wakes from its slumbers on the nose with some at first dainty fruitiness, which soon turns into something that makes your pips squeak. Good grief...! f22.5 settles down into a more sane, yet fabulously busy, infusion of spice and vanilla; b23 has to be tasted using the Murray Method to make sense of this! Deceptively complex. 48.6%.

◇ **Waldviertler Einkorn-Whisky 100% Bio-Urweizen** bott code L09 db (88) n22 good grief: lemon zest; t22.5 the arrival is as light as the nose, arriving on tip toe. Busy, vaguely fruity and increasingly warming; f21.5 lightly spiced vanillas carrying a hint of lime; bitters slightly late on; b22 an unusually light and citrussy offering from this distillery: wonder if it was the yeast at play here. 42%.

◇ **Waldviertler Haferwhisky Classic** bott code L10 db (94) n23.5 a busy, distinctly bourbony nose with a fabulous mix of maple syrup and small grains – in this case oat. Light honeycomb, too...; t23 succulent, melt-in-the-mouth with the oats and oaks in magnificent harmony from the get go. A mix of ulmo honey and Demerara; f23 I had been waiting for the spice – it arrives now. Couched by vanilla; b24 truly classic oak whisky from the very man who created it. Always one of the treats of the year when Weidenauer's Haferwhisky turns up on my tasting room table.. 42%.

◇ **Waldviertler Haferwhisky Classic** bott code L11 db (91) n22.5 a distinctly porridgy stance, with light tannin and molten Demerara sugars for company; t23 dry delivery, again the tannins having a freer role than the last bottling. A touch of bourbon as the liquorice and spices arrive; f22.5 stays spicy with an excellent sweet-dry intertwangling at the finale; b23 as ever, a pleasure to get my oats. 42%.

◇ **Waldviertler Hafer-Whisky Single Malt Dunkel** bott code L10 db (87) n21 t22 f22 b22 Just a slight technical faltering on the nose, but the sugars move in quickly compensate; the chocolate on the finish is superb. 42%.

◇ **Waldviertler Hafer Whisky Unit 2/3 Hafermalz** bott code L10 db (92.5) n22.5 oat and fruit health bars with a helping of fudge; t23.5 sensuous in its medium oils, the sugars are given a free hand here which, thankfully, is not abused. Stupendously rich and chewy muscovado sugars are stirred into the thick porridge; f23 pleasing, pulsing spice and a slow build of chocolate fudge; b23.5 like a sensuous massage in oaty oils... 42%.

◇ **Waldviertler Intensiv Getorfter Hafermalzwhisky** bott code L09 db (88.5) n20 now that is very different. The smoke is, as it says on the tin, intense. Very! It is an acrid, burnt note which clears the sinuses beautifully; t22 the delivery is a bit of a car crash, those bitter burnt notes smashing head-first into disjointed sugars and jagged oak. Then, at about the halfway point, the smoky clouds clear and oak-rich sun appears, dispensing Manuka honey on slightly burnt bread; f24 fabulously complex, with the Manuka dovetailing with the grains while the sweet vanillas jostle for a positon; b22.5 I don't think I've experienced a peated malted oat whisky before, so how wonderful for my whisky experiences to be stretched even after all these years. Forget the nose and delivery, which take some getting used to: from the midpoint onwards we are in some kind of oaty Eden.... 42%.

DESTILLERIE WEUTZ St. Nikolai im Sausal. Working.

Franziska bott code. L070206/02 db (93) n23.5 t23 f23.5 b23. The 5% elderflower means this is 100% not whisky. But a fascinating and eye-opening way to create a spirit very much in the young Kentucky rye style, especially in the nose. They certainly can do delicious... For the record, the scoring for enjoyment alone: 48%.

DISTILLERY ZWEIGER Mooskirchen. Working.

Zweiger Single Malt Whyskey Sherryfasslager bott code SH/L0601/17 db (76.5) n18 t21 f18 b19.5 No sulphur, you'll be pleased to know. But this feinty malt lurches around the palate like a man around the desert with no map or compass, only some attractive gristy sugars to keep it going. Finally collapses entirely lost. 43%.

Zweiger Smoked Prisoner bott code SH/L0601/17 db (89) n22 t22 f22.5 b22.5 Probably not the whisky of choice for officials of the European Court of Human Rights. 44%.

EDELBRENNEREI FRANZ KOSTENZER Maurach, Working.

⬦ **Whisky Alpin Single Malt Double Wood 11 Years Old** bott code L1/2005 db (88) n22 what the...? Head-scratching stuff as you try to translate this into descriptors tangible to the English language. OK – a wide cut giving a kind of nougat style – nougat dipped in blood oranges, perhaps, that have been smoked lightly on a bonfire...; t22.5 a less formidable delivery – at first. Certainly the wide-ish cut is confirmed, then a sudden burst of slightly over the top kumquat: bitter and slightly bruising but a salty Manuka honey to mend things; f21 feints and fudge; b22.5 one thing that cannot be levelled against this distillery is that it has no idea how to conjure up malt personalities previously unknown to the whisky world. It has done so again... 40%.

⬦ **Whisky Alpin Single Malt Peaty 5 Years Old** bott code L1/2013 db (89) n22 good grief...! I mean...bloody hell! Think of the driest, most ashy peat you can imagine. Done it..? Well, you're not even close...; t22.5 the powdery peat raises just enough gristy collateral to find a sweetening balance; f22 vague nougat oils buzz in the distance, hushed and shocked by the smoky battering they have received; b22.5 one of the most brutally peaty whiskies I have ever encountered. The phenols hammer the palate into merciless submission, using the same force of will that tames the oily distillate. Kind of brilliant, in a truly terrifying kind of way. Outside my lab I hear the sound of distant thunder. Well, I think it's the thunder: it could well be this whisky... 46%.

⬦ **Whisky Alpin Single Malt Roggen Amarone Cask Finish 7 Years Old** bott code L1/2010 db (85) n19 t22 f21.5 b21.5 Though some of this distillery's other work is – like this - technically unsound, I enjoy it because of the sheer entertainment value provided and the sensation of exploring unknown worlds. The one- dimensional quality of the grape, though offering moments of true deliciousness, reduces that last element without entirely seeing off the excesses of the overly generous cut. 46%.

⬦ **Whisky Alpin Single Malt Sherry Cask Finish 9 Years Old** bott code L2/2008 db (84) n18.5 t22 f21.5 b22 Enjoy the grape: this is an excellent sherry cask at work and at its zenith akin to a sultana fest. The usual feinty gremlins elsewhere. 40%.

⬦ **Whisky Alpin Single Malt Smoky 6 Years Old** bott code L2/2011 db (87.5) n21.5 t22.5 f21.5 b22 The distillery's distinctive nougat rich style is in full voice here. But hats off to the sturdiness of the peat which impresses in the way it is able to gather up the balm of the ulmo honey for a charming mid session. The heavier oils fur up the finish slightly. 42%.

⬦ **Whisky Alpin Single Malt Tiroler Whisky** organic Obernberger black oats, bott code L1/2014 db (80) n22 t21.5 f17.5 b19 Not sure last time I encountered a nose and finish singing off such different hymn sheets. An eye-wateringly bitter finale after a green, refreshing and promising aroma and sweet start on the palate. 42%.

LAVA BRÄU Feldbach. Working.

Mehr Leben Brisky Single Malt Eiche dist 2013, bott code H 02|13 db (87) n22 t22.5 f21.5 b22 "Brisky". Thought this was the first whisky made in Britain after the people had decided to get the hell out of Europe. But apparently not... A very well made malt with some serious loganberry on the nose – not exactly the most usual of aromas. But eventually disappears under its own weight of caramel on the palate. 40.8%.

Mehr Leben Genesis Brisky Single Cask Rare Malt dist 2010, bott code G 04|10 db (88.5) n22 t23 f22.5 b21 A delicious must have (and I mean must in both senses of the word) for those who love a little whisky in their fruit... 48.7%. sc.

LEBE & GENIESSE Lagenrohr. Working

Bodding Lokn cask no. 8, dist 2010, bott 2014 db (88) n22 t22.5 f21.5 b22. Tight and toasty. But very young. 42%.

Bodding Lokn Golden Wheat Single Malt Lagerung Double Cask fass nr. 1120 & 111, gebrannt 2008 db (91.5) n22.5 t23 f23 b23 Though perhaps a little too sweet for some, this is truly one of a kind. Almost too beautiful and demure to drink... 45%. ncf.

⬦ **Bodding Lokn Single Malt Blended Malt Nr. 2** refilled bourbon & sherry casks, dist 2011, bott 2018 db (94) n23 caramelised biscuit, with maybe some garibaldi thrown in for good measure; t23.5 mmmm...now that is rather tasty...! Seemingly light in body, a little Manuka honey and gig roll combine to thicken things beautifully. Such delicate spices, too;

f23.5 as this type of whisky has a tendency, once the fruit and malt are spent it is now the turn of the oak for its solo: so much butterscotch, and a little nod to some sultana, also; **b24** confusingly, the label describes itself as both a single malt and a blended malt. I presume they mean it is from a single distillery but from more than one barley or perhaps cask type... though I could be wrong. Whatever it is, there is no doubting its high quality. 43%. ncf.

⬨ **Bodding Lokn Single Malt Double Cask** American white oak & a 50 Litre Oloroso sherry cask, dist 2010, bott 2018 db **(88) n22** clean, intense grape rules; a semi-sweet edge to this, too, as the spiced tannins make their mark; **t22.5** not just impressive weight, but the measured pace of flavour development scores brownie points; never exactly succulent, but the fruit when combined with the spice does a salivating personality; **f21.5** toasty with late molasses; **b22** a generous cut give the big grape something to work on. 49.5%. ncf.

⬨ **Bodding Lokn Single Malt Double Cask Classic** French Limousine oak & American white oak casks, dist 2012, bott 2018 db **(92) n22.5** the tannins think about firm dominance, but compromise by bringing in light muscovado sugars; **t23.5** just adore that mouth feel! Gorgeous weight, with the barley having an oaky stage to say its complex and salivating piece; **f22.5** long, with impressive spices to add to the gingerbread; **b23.5** the limousine takes you on a very pretty journey... 43%. ncf.

Bodding Lokn Single Malt Lagerung Double Cask Sherry Finish Amerikan Weisseiche & Oloroso sherry fass, fass nr. 11,14 & 372, gebrannt 2010 db **(95) n24 t24 f23 b24** A mildly aggressive, oak-biased malt but beautifully made and matured. The sulphur-free sherry plays second fiddle to the American oak from first to last. High class malt. 43.5%. ncf.

Bodding Lokn Single Malt Smoky Lagerung Single Cask Amerikan Weisseiche fass, fass nr. 9, gebrannt 2011 db **(86) n22 t22.5 f20.5 b21** A malt awash in the early stages with natural caramels and sweet, nutty phrasing to the barley. Also, satisfyingly lush on delivery. But just a little rough and ready on the very uneven and sugar-derived finish. 51%. ncf.

Bodding Lokn White Bull Spirit Malt gebrannt 2010 db **(85.5) n21 t22.5 f21 b21** Malty and gristily sweet. But also a little copper starved, leading to a degree of tanginess. 46%. ncf.

MARILLENHOF DESTILLERIE KAUSL Mühldorf. Working.

⬨ **Wachauer Whisky Single Pure H** bott code L:1WH db **(88.5) n21.5** an odd nose: very unusual tannin tones, not within the normal Quercus spectrum and the grains show a more oaty personality than barley; **t22.5** lush, again with an oat-style softness to the grain and a slightly porridge and molten sugar feel, too. The tannins offer a thumping burnt fudge and cocoa middle; **f22** dry despite the molasses; **b22** attractive but a real odd fish. 40%.

⬨ **Wachauer Whisky Malt Royal** bott code L:1malt db **(87.5) n22 t22 f21.5 b22** The slightly wide cut on this certainly has a kick on delivery and finish. But the extra oils ensure a comfortable ride for the most part, as does the big cream toffee presence. 40%.

⬨ **Wachauer Whisky Malt Royal** bott code L:1mR db **(92) n23** oats, surely...and as big and rich as they ever get; **t23.5** told this isn't an oat whisky, yet this just appears to scream that grain – actually sing loudly and rather beautifully would be a better way of putting it; **f22.5** porridge with molten demerara sugar atop; **b23** even a little bitterness at the death cannot undermine the brilliant character of this malt. And those who love oat or oak-style whisky...just dig in...!!! 40%.

MARKUS WIESER GMBH Woesendorf in der Wachau. Working.

Wieser Wahouua Single Malt WIESky Pinot Noir bott code L1015 db **(87) n21 t22 f22 b22.** A curious malt. Always soft, always polite and at times positively charming. But the fruit never makes much of a stand while the toffee has no such reservations. 40%. nc.

MICHELEHOF Vorarlberg. Working.

Micheles Single Malt 6 Years Old 100% barley, dist 2008, bott code L8121 db **(78.5) n19 t21 f19 b19.5.** An oily, nutty affair which struggles hard to get over the effect of the wide cut. A few attractive salivating fudgy moments at about the halfway point. 43%

PETER AFFENZELLER Alberndorf in der Riedmark. Working.

Peter Affenzeller Single Malt Whisky 7 Years Old dist 2008, bott code: L-0841201 db **(95.5) n23.5 t24.5 f23.5 b24** I defy any malt whisky lover, wherever you are in the world, not to entirely fall head over heals for this stunning whisky. 42%

PFANNER Vorarlberg. Working.

Pfanner Single Malt dist 2009, bott code L 212 db **(74) n19 t20 f16.5 b18.5.** Nutty and some hefty feints late on puts a Pfanner in the works... 43%

⬨ **Pfanner Single Malt Single Barrel 2011** first fill sherry oak cask, cask no. 5, dist 16 Jun 11, bott 09 Oct 17 db **(93.5) n23** generous helping of plum pudding; **t23.5** the malt forms into a neat intensity early on but, as the spices mount their own warming challenge; slowly gives way to the clean fruit, mainly an over-ripe greengage and toasted sugar mix; **f23** remains toasty, Muscovado and molasses sugars underlining the lightly burnt fruit effect; **b23.5** delightful whisky benefitting from an entirely clean sherry cask. *56.2%. sc. 412 bottles.*

🔸 **Pfanner Single Malt Smokey Whisky** bott code L217 db **(87.5) n21.5 t22 f22 b22** I'd love to know what they used to smoke the malt with. Rather than peat, it reminds me of some of the weird and wonderful aromas concocted over flame in distilleries in America's west coast. An engulfing, rounded mouth feel where the sugars are maybe just a little too enthusiastic. Not a bad shout for someone with a sweet tooth, though. *43%.*

REISETBAUER Axberg, Thening. Working.

🔸 **Reisetbauer 7 Year Old Distillers Choice Single Malt Whisky** Chardonnay & Trockenbeerenauslese casks, bott code. 180120 db **(89) n22.5** a far from straightforward, complex aroma. Seemingly flat and at oak dominant at first, slow and careful investigation unravels a bits and pieces nose: an intense muscovado note alongside polished oak floors; **t22.5** genuinely bitter-sweet. The tannins bite, the sugars follow a peculiarly bitter path to ensure balance; **f22** malt at last...; **b22** I suppose the grape style used with the chardonnay, TBA, is Austria's answer to Spain's PX or maybe Slovakian Tokay – and, having tasted quite a few over the years, you can really stand your spoon up in the darker ones. It was inevitable, then, that they would end up maturing whisky at one point. I think there is no secret of the fact that I am no great fan of PX in relation to whisky, as the intense sweetness has a tendency to kill subtlety and complexity. Because of this, this is a whisky that takes a lot longer than normal for all the nuances to filter through. A hard work whisky.. *43%.*

🔸 **Reisetbauer 12 Year Old Single Malt Whisky** Chardonnay & Trockenbeerenauslese casks, bott code. 180120 db **(80) n19 t20.5 f20 b20** Despite the cask yet, hard to get away from the feinty nose revealing a weakness in the distillate. No amount of patience sees the TBA improve matters. *48%. 1,253 bottles.*

Reisetbauer 15 Years Old Single Malt db **(80.5) n18.5 t22.5 f19 b20.5** Those feints are still there in force, even after 15 years, which is some achievement. But, not for the first time, their malt recovers from a dodgy start to present an attractive chocolate nougat middle before succumbing to the oils for a second time. *48%.*

🔸 **Reisetbauer 15 Year Old Single Cask Single Malt Whisky** dist 2001 db **(86.5) n20 t21.5 f23 b22** From the earliest days of this distillery, the technical flaws of the distillate are obvious. However, the malt has reacted favourably with some high class oak. The result is a whisky that grows in confidence as it goes along, like the girl who thought she was too plain to go to the ball, only to find she was as pretty as many. Late on the mix of chocolate nougat and treacle tart is rather compelling and worthy of drinking from a glass shoe.... *48%. sc. 500 bottles.*

STBG BRAUEREI SCHLOSS STARKENBERG Tarrenz. Working.

STGB Tiroler Single Malt Whisky Aged 3 Years db **(94.5) n23.5 t23.5 f23.5 b24** A charmingly relaxed single malt which has been beautifully crafted. You cannot really ask for more from a three-year-old single malt. *40%*

WHISKY-DESTILLERIE J. HAIDER Roggenreith. Working.

🔸 **J H. 12 Years Single Malt Single Cask** bott code L SM 05 SL db **(94) n23** light orange blossom honey mixes well with the vanilla and toffee: as intricate as it is intimate; subtle hints of bourbon; **t23.5** early spices lose none of their power even as a rampant fudge offers massive chewability; **f23.5** the distillery oils at last settle, making for a long finish. So much molasses and juicy, too, with the barley arriving very late. The spices have never faltered; **b24** not quite in the same Super League as their unforgettable 13-year-old but this is a huge, uncompromising but always classy Austrian, again making the most of their generous cut. *46%. ncf sc.*

J.H. 13 Years Old Single Malt bott code L SM 03 FS db **(96) n24 t23.5 f24 b24.5** One of the beauties of feints in whisky, is that the longer the spirit hangs around the more chance there is that they'll be burnt off. And I suspect this has happened here because this astonishing malt, doubtless from a cask they have matured for one of their longest periods, has little interference from the dark side of distilling. Its colossal malt, this distillation of genius, is honeyed uplands all the way... *69%. ncf sc.*

🔸 **J.H. Dark Single Malt Peated Single Cask 7 Jahre** bott code L SMP 10 BRM db **(93) n23.5** even the most hardened peatophiles will be blasted through the back of their chairs by this Austrian monster...; **t23** the intense acidity on the nose is almost matched on the palate though, amazingly, distinct gristy sugars emerge like barley ghosts out of the dense peat fog...; slowly a toasty sweetness emerges; **f23.5** vanilla – smoked. Barley – burnt. Sugars – incinerated...; **b23** not sure if they have bothered about the malt: it just seems like peat-smoked peat turf. No, not really! But it takes a while to acclimatise to phenols this toasty, this intense. What's the Austrian for bloody hell!...? 46%. ncf sc.

⬧ **J.H. Original Rye 12 Jahre** bott code L3S05 db (91) n22.5 their unique nougat and chocolate style on display, here with a firmer rye fruitiness; t23 the usual oils make for one of the softest of all deliveries. The first wave or two are confused. But a delicious nougat and rye mix formulate before we head into the most magnificent regions of Chocolateland....; f22.5 minty chocolate now, though the rye always bites; b23 PS. Deploy the Murray method for best results by far. 46%. ncf sc.

J.H. Rare Selection Dark Rye Malt bott code L DRR 09 SG db (89.5) n20 t23 f23.5 b23 Still utterly unique and true to itself. 46%. ncf sc.

J.H. Rare Selection Original Rye Whisky bott code L RR 12 MÜ db (94) n23.5 t23.5 f23 b24 One of the cleanest and most technically correct J.H. whiskies I have ever encountered. What a treat! 46%. ncf sc.

⬧ **J.H. Rare Selection Rye Malt 6 Jahre Fassfinish Likörwein Portewinmethode** bott code L 1R 11 db (92) n23 proud, brittle rye: intense and no mistaking the grain. Builds in Demerara sugars; a light citrus note; t23 again, the rye crackles through solidly on impact. A slower build of light plum pudding and custard; f22.5 essentially nougat-free and playing on the rye spice; b23.5 J.H. whisky without nougat is akin to the World Cup being without one of Germany, Brazil or Spain in the semi-finals. Oh, hang on a minute... 46%. ncf sc.

⬧ **J.H. Rare Selection Rye Malt TBA Chardonnay 4 Jahre** bott code L RM 13 MÜ db (86.5) n19 t22 f23.5 b22 Takes an age to find its niche. Unless you are willing to leave the glass open in a hot environment for an hour, the nose, sadly, doesn't work – the oils and grape make everything claustrophobic, while at least the dense delivery does allow the rye to plant its flag. The finish, though, is sublime with a rich chocolate nougat intensity aided by a two-tone fruit from the grain and grape. 46%. ncf sc.

⬧ **J.H. Rare Selection Single Malt TBA Chardonnay 4 Jahre** bott code L SM 13 MÜ db (87) n22 light nougat and spiced heather honey; t22 rye is first up, but soon vanishes under a dull wave of caramel; f21.5 spices up pleasantly; b21.5 an enjoyable whisky but never seems to get the shackles off the rye. 46%. ncf sc.

DESTILLERIE WEIDENAUER Kottes. Working.

Waldviertler Hafer-Malz (2007 Gold Medaille label on neck) db (91) n22 t22.5 f23 b23.5. One of those whiskies that just gets better the longer it stays on the palate. Also, a master class in achieving near perfection in the degree of sweetness generated. 42%

BELGIUM
THE BELGIAN OWL Grâce-Hollogne. Working.

⬧ **Belgian Owl Single Malt 11.5 Years Old** first fill bourbon cask, cask no. 4275920 db (90.5) n23 old school Belgium Owl, a stupendous, concentrated nuttiness – or perhaps fruit stone as there is a fruitiness to this despite the bourbon cask history; some thick Belgium chocolate it seems, too...; t23.5 yikes! I had almost forgotten how eye-wateringly astringent some of the early makes could be on delivery; but there is also over a decade's worth of natural caramels beefing up the party – yet still the malt has a say; f22 very burnt fudge; b22 an owl which takes no prisoners... 71.4%. nc ncf sc.

⬧ **Belgian Owl Single Malt 12 Years Old** first fill bourbon cask, cask no. 4275897 db (93.5) n23.5 the usual concentrated nutty trait but more relaxed sugars, too – a little maple syrup softening the process; lovey praline spread fits in beautifully; t23.5 so intense and salivating: the malt and vanillas are in some kind of sado-masochistic overdrive, the mouth-shrivelling from the onslaught of the huge flavours; a big malty-chocolate middle retains a firm, fruity edge; f23 mmm... so much chocolate, and still a little honey, too; b23.5 an owl that hangs on to its sugars like some others owls hang on to their mice... 71.9%. nc ncf sc.

⬧ **Belgian Owl Single Malt 12.5 Years Old** first fill bourbon cask, cask no. 4275928 db (95) n23.5 a distinctive fruity touch: green apple and under-ripe greengage: not perhaps what one might expect from such an old malt, though the parched strands of cinnamon might be; deft muscovado sugars and ulmo honey balance things out beautifully; t24 malty and salivating from the start before a spicy left takes into a deeper liquorice and cinnamon territory; light malt is scattered throughout with hefty, heavily toasted molasses offering a fruitcake touch; f23.5 the tannins are left to their own complex and spicy devices; b24 a surprisingly wise and gentle old owl considering its alcoholic strength after the passing of a dozen years... 72.5%. nc ncf sc.

Belgian Owl Single Malt Whisky Aged 36 Months first fill bourbon casks, bott code LB036282 db (89.5) n22.5 t22 f23 b22 A strange, unconvincing start is more than compensated for by the moreish finish. 46%. ncf.

Belgian Owl Single Malt Whisky Aged 36 Months first fill bourbon casks, bott code LC036341 db **(92.5)** n23 t23 f23.5 b23 What a hugely satisfying whisky and a distinct notch up from its sister bottling. *46%. ncf.*

Belgian Owl Single Malt Whisky The Private Angels Aged 36 Months first fill bourbon casks, cask no. 035/200 db **(88)** n22 t22.5 f22 b21.5 A pleasant though directionless malt which seems to make it up as it goes along. *46%. ncf sc.*

Belgian Owl Single Malt Whisky The Private Angels Aged 36 Months first fill bourbon casks, cask no. 036/200 db **(96)** n24 t24.5 f23.5 b24 A malt of outstanding weight and complexity that is much more well suited to these higher strengths. A Belgian Owl of the old school and which I can give far more than two hoots for... *70.3%. ncf sc.*

Belgian Owl Flavours of Nature The Private Angels Aged 36 Months first fill bourbon casks, cask no. 040/200 db **(87)** n22 t22.5 f22 b22 Another pleasant malt with all kinds of attractive if half-hearted themes. But absolutely refuses to show any degree of firmness or confidence... *46%. ncf sc.*

◁▷ **Belgian Owl Single Malt 42 Months** first fill bourbon barrel, cask no. 1523509 db **(94.5)** n23.5 quite adorable: praline wafer and spiced Manuka honey act only as background music to the malty symphony!) celebrates the big, gristy malt inclusion to the full. A little lime also though slowly the spicier tannins make their play, a little treacle and liquorice representing the oak; f23 long, with a moderate oils spreading both malt and tannin in roughly equal measure b24 slightly less proactive oak involvement means not just a bigger say for the malt but great alcohol bite. Both gentle and big whisky at one and the same moment. *73.7%. nc ncf sc.*

◁▷ **Belgian Owl Single Malt «By Jove» Collection No. 1 48 Months** first fill bourbon cask db **(88)** n21.5 a little rough-edged in part with quite a metallic kick; t22.5 ah, the malt is back on track now. A cross between barley sugar and red liquorice laces. Outstanding middle as light butterscotch tart takes the full weight of the malt to ensure the balance stays true; f22 that metallic tang returns to harden the softer malts; as ever, the spices are late but arrive before closing time; b22 may this malt be a tribute to British comedy legend and proud Englishman Ken Dodd. His career was lost to us during the writing of this book. By Jove, missus, what a fine day to say to that Guy Verhofstadt fellow: if you want More Europe stick a bottle of this where the sun doesn't shine and then try whistling Ode to Joy! By Jove yes, Mr Verhofstadt. What a fine day to keep pouring this excellent whisky into your diddy pal Jean-Claude Juncker's glass and see what comes first: proper Brexit or the word "when". By Jove, missus! That hair. Have you seen that Mr Verhofstadt's hair? Well, at least something's straight about him. By Jove! Tatty bye! Yes tatty bye, Mr Verhofstadt! See you at my dentist's. If we let you back in the country. Tatty bye! *46%. nc ncf.*

◁▷ **Belgian Owl Single Malt Distillery Intense 42 Months** first fill bourbon cask, cask no. 6033600, edition 2017-02 db **(86.5)** n22 t22 f 21 b21.5 The nose sticks vehemently to the cream toffee theme but the palate unmasks this as a warm and relatively aggressive bottling. Younger in style to some with a vague new make lightness to measure against the wall of natural caramels. The late bitterness points an accusatory finger at the cask. *72.5%. nc ncf sc.*

◁▷ **Belgian Owl Single Malt Distillery Passion 39 Months** first fill bourbon cask, cask no. 1519105, edition 2017-01 db **(88)** n22 as darker bottling for its age and strength with lustier tannins already apparent and larger gaps allowing the relatively youthfulness to be underscored; t23 a robust delivery with manuka and ulmo honey flying in from the off and a big dollop of toffee following on behind; f21.5 ah...falls apart here somewhat. Like on the nose, holes appear and youth has its day; b21.5 it is as if the whisky has yet to work out exactly where to put the extra tannin: flavoursome, but disjointed. *46%. nc ncf. sc*

◁▷ **Belgian Owl Single Malt Intense 40 Months** first fill bourbon cask, cask no. 5558589, edition 2018-02 db **(92)** n23 ignore the alcohol nip which not even the Murray Method can completely control: intense, lightly lemon-drizzled, grist buffers against the usual bourbon-rich caramel front; Rich Tea biscuits portray the drier element; t23.5 sublime oils at work here doing a first-class job on coating the palate and spreading an intensely malty word; the citrus hinted at on the nose also adds to the juiciness; f22.5 spices, naturally, linger and at last the cream toffee feels safe and at home; b23 one of Belgium Owl's famous plaque dissolvers, though also a celebration of all things malt and caramel. *72.6%. nc ncf sc.*

◁▷ **Belgian Owl Single Malt Intense 41 Months** first fill bourbon cask, cask no. 6033608, edition 2017-04 db **(96)** n24 you know when a distillate has been taken off the still at exactly the right point, and this has. The aroma is whole, nothing missing and nothing added. The oak has made just the right degree of impression on the barley. A little orange blossom honey mixes with the toastier tannins and the odd hint of mint sweetens shyly and unobtrusively; t24 and you know when you are in the midst of greatness: you don't for a moment realise the enormous alcohol strength here as the softness of the toffee caresses and gently lays the malt before you; the sugars, ranging from Demerara to light golden syrup, melt; f24 the spices had been prickling away for a little while and now come to the fore. Old Fox's Butter Crinkle biscuits melt beautifully to ensure a consistency to the creamy sweetness; **b24** truly world class whisky: amazing from a dram so young. Magnificently made, magnificently matured. Simple as that. *72.4%. nc ncf sc.*

◇ **Belgian Owl Single Malt Intense 42 Months** first fill bourbon cask, cask no. 1519134, edition 2018-07 db **(94.5) n23.5** dazzles with its confident nose: toasted fudge is the order of the day; **t23.5** wow! Uncompromising explosion of gristy sugars and a blend of ulmo and Manuka honey, all this taken a step further by some blistering liquorice notes; **f23.5** the slowest, most beautifully oiled and orchestrated climb down from the dizzy heights of the mid-point; **b24** what a delightfully consistent distillery this is. *72.6%. nc ncf sc.*

◇ **Belgian Owl Single Malt Intense 42 Months** first fill bourbon cask, cask no. 5560227, edition 2017-06 db **(88) n23** polished oak floorboards mix with concentrated cream toffee; **t22** ah...! A little youthfulness on delivery, which means that the tannins bunch up a bit, intensifying, then another surge of young malt. The honey, mainly ulmo, is thick and is subject to the same surges as the tannins; **f21.5** over the earlier yips and is drawn towards a toasted fudge finale; some very late bitterness; **b21.5** sometimes the casks at Belgian Owl appear to be emptied at a point when the growing pains can still be felt. *73%. nc ncf sc.*

◇ **Belgian Owl Single Malt Intense 42 Months** first fill bourbon cask, cask no. 5698086, edition 2018-08 db **(92.5) n23** more polished oak floors – something this distillery does quite well. But here with a green leaf, Spring forest freshness and a light basting of heather honey; **t23.5** such an incredible overdose of cream toffee; **f23** bitters very slightly, but the sugar-spice combo see off any danger; **b23** a substantial and complex malt of greatly conflicting personality. *72.4%. nc ncf sc.*

◇ **Belgian Owl Single Malt Intense 42 Months** first fill bourbon cask, cask no. 6033554, edition 2018-04 db **(93.5) n24** I know Kentucky has a Paris. But a Clocher...? Thought that was in Belgium. The malt is playing lip – or should I say nose? - service here as the malt heads towards a Kentuckian idyll of nutty caramels, a gentle Manuka honey and molasses blend, a background of spice and red liquorice. Oh, and lightly polished leather; **t23** a salivating delivery par excellence, though the more youthful malt notes are a surprise as they don't come up on the nose's general radar; some juicy fruity tones, too, all barley related; **f23** Milky Way candy, anyone...? **b23** another delightful malt from one of Europe's great distilleries. *72.4%. nc ncf sc.*

◇ **Belgian Owl Single Malt Passion 39 Months** first fill bourbon cask, cask no. 5673151, edition 2017-03 db **(93) n23.5** the sugars which gently rise from the glass are ones that are sometimes encountered in Kentucky: a slightly glazed Demerara at first, then gently moving into muscovado territory as a light, non-specific fruitiness hoves into view; **t23.5** just a fabulous array of sugars on delivery, starting with the most delicate grists, then moving into a thin molasses; a chocolate and hazelnut middle fits the bill perfectly; **f22.5** a slight toasty bitterness is apparent, but this disappears as the praline ends the tale; **b23.5** the kind of whisky of which a glassful can send you to sleep – before you've drunk it! It is that laid back... *46%. nc ncf sc.*

◇ **Belgian Owl Single Malt Passion 40 Months** first fill bourbon cask, cask no. 5643556, edition 2017-05 db **(92.5) n23** a beautiful gentle balance between the light caramels gathered from the oak and a greener, sharper kiwi fruit nip; **t23** the silky house style really does capitalise of the gentle nature of the cream toffee caramel which abounds; **f23** spicier towards the finish, but we are talking fine margins. The elegant caramel heads more towards a milky mocha finale; **b23.5** probably one of the most relaxing and easy going single malts you'll find this year. *46%. nc ncf sc.*

◇ **Belgian Owl Single Malt Passion 40 Months** first fill bourbon cask, cask no. 5698143, edition 2018-01 db **(91) n22.5** a lovely mix between gentle toffee and Love Heart sweets; a little slate celery, too; **t22.5** off it goes on its now famous cream toffee escapades: a few fragments of caramelised biscuit offer a degree of midlife crunchiness; **f23** some soft barley regroups, while the spices build an a little molasses adds weight; **b23** pretends to be a little toffee dominant...but look carefully and much more else going on besides. *46%. nc ncf sc.*

◇ **Belgian Owl Single Malt Passion 42 Months** first fill bourbon cask, cask no. 1519110, edition 2018-09 db **(91) n22.5** soft, salty and nutty; **t23** a delicious malty sheen to this, but the caramel and spice from the oak probably has a slightly bigger say; **f22.5** cream toffee; **b23** such a sweet natured owl. *46%. nc ncf sc.*

◇ **Belgian Owl Single Malt Passion 42 Months** first fill bourbon cask, cask no. 5558604, edition 2018-06 db **(87) n21.5 t22 f21.5 b22** As youthful as the England team that lost to Belgium in the World Cup (twice, sob...!). The occasional flash of inspirational brilliance, especially early in the second half. But the first touch lets it down a little too often. A little raw at the end. *46%. nc ncf sc.*

◇ **Belgian Owl Single Malt Passion 42 Months** first fill bourbon cask, cask no. 5665829, edition 2018-05 db **(94) n23** sublime citrus notes coast along easily with the youthful grist; **t23.5** you cannot but purr – or maybe hoot with delight – as the astonishing balance between the early oak and the sumptuous, lightly oiled barley grist. The sugars ping around with gay abandon; **f23.5** such a wonderful of darker tannins and toffee: so rare to find these two combine an complexity maintained; **b24** a really graceful owl. *46%. nc ncf sc.*

 Belgian Owl Single Malt Passion 47 Months first fill bourbon cask, cask no. 5660299, edition 2018-03 db (**94**) **n23** something of a December pine forest mixing with a late April Bluebell wood. Earthy for an Owl with the malt a little suppressed and sugars hiding in the dark forest...; **t23** return to a toffee norm. Ulmo honey provides the most gentle of sweet nudges while the malt really does intensify an expands; **f24** back comes that malt, now in its most intense form yet. A slight coppery shimmer towards the very finale but, with that light milk chocolate note, it is impossible not to think of Malteser sweets...; spices take their time to assemble but stretch the finish some distance; **b24** heading now towards 400 whiskies for this year's Bible and the entire day spent tasting the whiskies of the Belgian Owl has been by far the most enjoyable yet. This really is a very special distillery. *46%. nc ncf sc.*

 Belgian Owl Spirit Drink Unaged bott code. Ld 000101 db (**92**) **n22 t23.5 f23 b23.5** I'm presuming this new make malt spirit is from the old Caperdonich stills as there is an ethereal quality to this that used to found in the days when they operated in Speyside. Whoever is handling them now is probably doing a better job than in its Scotch days as every nuance of the delicate malt appears to have been squeezed out. Exceptionally pleasing, with just the right degree of gristy sweetness. *46%. nc ncf.*

BROUWERIJ PIRLOT Zandhoven, Working.

 Golden Carolus Single Malt first fill bourbon cask, Het Anker cask finish db (**88**) **n22** anyone remember Toffees cream toffee candy? Well, here it is in whisky form...; the malt does offer a juicy edge, thankfully; **t22.5** a brief barley hit, then things become very sweet with a dose of maple syrup followed by... cream toffee...; **f21.5** a little spiced toffee and burnt fudge..; **b22** cream toffee, anyone? *46%. nc ncf.*

 Kempich Vuur Single Malt Aged 3 Years Laphroaig quarter casks, cask no. L5, bott 24 Jan 17 db (**91**) **n22** the influence of the cask is left in no doubt. An acidic, dry peatiness stamps its authority on the malt, but just enough delicate sugars are on hand to fight back. Busy...; **t23** mouth-watering with a biscuity feel to the proceedings as the malt finds weight a slight saltiness. The smoke drifts around keeping close tabs on the demerara sugars; **f23** reverts to its drier self; excellent depth and layering; **b23** well, those quarter casks weren't wasted! What a joy of a malt! *46%. sc.*

 Stokerij De Molenberg 4th Anniversary Muscad'or 2017 db (**82.5**) **n20 t22 f20 b20.5** A haphazard whisky (lots of Hazards in Belgium...) revealing a slight distilling flaw on the nose which the outrageous grape does its best to conceal. But the palate is accosted by some maniacal fruit before the wide cut is re-exposed on the finish. *46%.*

DESTILLERIE RADERMACHER Raeren. Working.

Lambertus Single Grain Aged 10 Years db (**44**) **n12 t12 f10 b10**. This is whisky...? Really???!!!!???? Well, that's what it says on the label, and this is a distillery I haven't got round to seeing in action (nor am I now very likely to be invited...). Let's check the label again... Ten years old...blah, blah. Single grain... blah, blah. But, frankly, this tastes like a liqueur rather than a whisky: the fruit flavours do not seem even remotely naturally evolved: synthetic is being kind. But apparently, this is whisky: I have re-checked the label. No mention of additives, so it must be. I am stunned. *40%*

IF GOULDYS FILLIERS DISTILLERY Deinze. Working.

Goldly's Belgian Double Still Whisky Aged 10 Years db (**88**) **n21.5 t23 f21.5 b22.** Having actually discovered this whisky before the distillers — I'll explain one day...!! — I know this could be a lot better. The caramel does great damage to the finish in particular, which should dazzle with its complexity. Even so, a lovely, high-class whisky which should be comfortably in the 90s but falls short. *40%*

 Goldys Distillers Range 14 Years Old Belgian Single Grain Whisky Madeira cask finish, bott code: L16240900 db (**90.5**) **n22.5** at first the grape appears a little too dense to allow through light. But, slowly, the palate acclimatises and the grains peep through: first a shaft of rye, then a busier, industrious smattering of spices and small grain. A distinct Guyanese Coffey Still rum side to this, also...; **t23** the nose poined towards the lushest of delivery, and reality offers something rounder still. A multitude of dark sugars and Manuka honey quietens before a plummy fruitiness takes hold; **f22.5** lots of spicy coffee notes; **b22.5** a big whisky, but one without muscle or threat. The Madeira cask is a little too rich to allow this whisky to move up into the next level of excellence: in whisky less is often more... *43%.*

◈ **Sunken Still 4 Years Old Belgian Single Rye Whisky** bourbon barrels, bott code: L16450900 db (85.5) n21 t22 f21.5 b21 There is no escaping that a degree of Genève character has leaked into this rye, affecting both nose and taste. Whether it was from the filters in the bottling hall, or some other reason I can't say. Lots of positive, busy flavours at play but the incursion of the local spirit is just a little too distracting. 45%.

CORSICA
DOMAINE MAVELA Aléria. Working.

◈ **P & M Red Oak Corsican Single Malt Whisky** bott code L1783 db (91.5) n22.5 a busy, striated aroma bursting forth with warm spices and enjoying a fascinating interplay between cucumber and fruitcake; t23.5 a beautifully succulent delivery: red currents and plums fill the mouth, helped by healthy oils and far from shy spice. The secret, though, is the low profile of the muscovado sugars. The mid-ground has a distinct sherry trifle feel to it.; f22.5 drier, but retains a pulsing fruitiness; b23 a wonderfully understated, complex malt, despite the voluptuousness of the fruit. 42%. nc ncf. 567 bottles.

◈ **P & M Signature Corsican Single Malt Whisky** bott code L1684 db (89.5) n21.5 tangy marmalade-esque notes merges with buttery toast: a breakfast malt, surely...; t23 typical full bodied Mavela malt, impacting in lush style with sugary, melt-in-the-mouth grist erupting all over the palate. The intense malt recedes slightly for a light mocha note to move in without missing a beat; f22 long, thanks to the oils. A feeble spice buzz radiates its gentle warmth while the mocha becomes a little more vanilla rich; b23 a very charming malt which at its peak sings like a Corsican Finch. 42%. nc ncf. 6,600 bottles.

◈ **P & M Tourbé Corsican Single Malt Whisky** bott code L1682 db (92) n22.5 a charming, indeed unique, peatiness here: a minty edge helps boost the sweetness while a delicate black pepper spice ensures all is not serene; t23 fabulous mouth feel greets the delivery: a lovely rough edge mixing with the rounder Demerara sugars; the smoke drifts aimlessly at first but gathers forces to ramp up the spices. The sugars are darker, now, much more molassed with a superb hickory undertone; f23 the sublime oils carry the finish a long way. The sugars remain intact, yet never too overbearing, while the smoke and spices whirl around like a Golden Eagle on the mountains which frame the distillery b23.5 a beautifully paced, gentle malt which always carries a threat on the peaty wind. 42%. nc ncf. 1,700 bottles.

CZECH REPUBLIC
Single Malt
RUDOLF JELÍNEK DISTILLERY Vizovice. Working.

Gold Cock Single Grain Whisky 2008 Czech oak barrels, dist Feb 08, bott Mar 17 db (87) n22.5 t22 f21 b21.5 Being one of only a handful of people to have visited the old distillery in Tesetice in its operational days some two decades ago I can gauge with some accuracy the differences between the output of its original and new stills. Usually, when new stills are deployed for the first year or so an extra degree of copper gives a sharp, metallic feel to a spirit; this dies down after time. Here, quite the opposite seems true: there is less copper than was found in the original stills, so this is a lighter whisky which by the end is struggling to cope with the unique richness of the Czech oak. The nose does offer an attractive citrus note that was also absent from Tesetice's old King Barley brand. The early maple syrup found on the delivery can spread only so far before the oak takes control. 49.2%. nc ncf sc.

Gold Cock Single Malt Whisky 8 Years Old Czech oak barrels db (93) n23 t23.5 f23 b23.5 A delightful whisky making full use of the wheat content to ramp up the oils and spices while the sugars missing on the 8-year-old appear to have found their way here... 49.2%. nc ncf.

Gold Cock Single Malt Whisky 2008 Virgin Oak Czech oak barrels, dist Feb 08, bott Mar 17 db (96) n24 no other aroma on the planet boasts a signature which celebrates the sweeter, fruitier elements of bourbon alongside the creamier, treacle tart tones of an obviously non-American oak: the must subtle sweetness to any whisky this year; t24 for the first few moments we are transported to Kentucky as wave upon wave of liquorice and molasses crashes into the palate. Next a sexy buttery note thins things out and allows a barley-sugar/butterscotch middle to take hold; f24 long with more Worther's original butter candy and a slow reverting to the toasty liquorice and molasses...as though going full circle: amazing! b24 not often you get gold cocks and virgins mentioned in the same sentence in a drinks guide. Or anywhere else, come to that. Equally few rampant cocks can crow so loudly; no virgin give so passionately. A consummate whisky consummated... 61.5%. nc ncf sc. 270 bottles.

STOCK PLZEN - BOZKOV S.R.O. Plzen. Working
Hammer Head 1989 db (88.5) n22 t22.5 f22 b22. Don't bother looking for complexity: this is one of Europe's maltiest drams...if not the maltiest... 40.7%

Blends

Gold Cock Aged 3 Years "Red Feathers" bott 22/06/09 (86) n22 t21 f21.5 b21.5. Sensual and soft, this is melt-in-the-mouth whisky with a big nod towards the sweet caramels. 40%.

Granette Premium (82) n21 t22 f19 b20. Lighter than the spark of any girl that you will meet in the Czech Republic. Big toffee thrust. 40%

Printer's Aged 6 Years (86.5) n21.5 t22.5 f21 b21.5. Blended whisky is something often done rather well in the Czech Republic and this brand has managed to maintain its clean, malty integrity and style. Dangerously quaffable. 40%

DENMARK

BRAENDERIET LIMFJORDEN Øster Assels. Working.

Island of Mors Single Malt Danish Whisky db (87) n21.5 t22 f22 b21.5. A most curious – and delicious – whisky from Denmark. Though a single malt, it has the bite, underlying firmness, slimness of body, and thick line of caramel which one normally associates with a blend. Some lovely spices at play, as well as malt, but just needs to complex out slightly. 46%. ncf. 462 bottles.

◇ **Lindorm Danish Single Malt Whisky 1st Edition** db (90) n22 a breakfast cereal maltiness to this one –with some marmalade on toast sitting nearby...; t22.5 super-salivating, again with a delicate interplay between malt and citrus; f22.5 extra complexity as the oak gives the malty mix a light chocolate stir; some lovely late spices, too; b23 this distillery appears to have created its very own understated and elegant style. Most enjoyable. 46%. ncf. 899 bottles.

BRAUNSTEIN DISTILLERY Køge. Working.

Braunstein Danish Single Malt Cask Edition no. 2 db (94) n23.5 t23.5 f23 b24 Seriously high quality distillate that has been faithfully supported by good grade oak. Complex, satisfying, and for its obviously tender years, truly excellent malt. A welcome addition to the Scandinavian – and world! – whisky lexicon. 62.4%

FARY LOCHAN DESTILLERI Give. Working.

Fary Lochan Forår db (90) n22 t23 f22.5 b22.5 Denmark's most delicate whisky...by a distance. Youthful but quite lovely. 47%.

◇ **Fary Lochan G25 Summer** cask no. 2011-15, dist 26 Nov 11, bott 4 Sept 17 db (90.5) n22.5 the spices are sublime: complex, beautifully weighted tannins fly around the nose; t23 those spices pile in on delivery. Delicious treacle tart to chew on; the weight and pace of the flavour development is spot on; f22 long, thanks to excellently controlled oils; toasty in all the right places; b23 a moody, brooding whisky balancing out the sugars and muscular tannins delightfully. 50%. 74 bottles. sc.

◇ **Fary Lochan Rum Edition** ex- bourbon barrels, casks no. 2012-15 & 2012-16, dist 18 Oct 12, bott 6 Nov 17 db (85.5) n21 t22 f21 b21.5 Not entirely sure I understand the narrative of this whisky. Impressed by the odd honeyed high point. But there is an innate bitterness which runs through all sections, a wideness to the cut which offers extra oils and a general all round confusion. 64.7%. 639 bottles.

◇ **Fary Lochan Summer** batch no. 2, ex-bourbon barrels, cask nos. 2013-05, 2013-09, 2013-10 & 2013-11, bott 13 Feb 18 db (84.5) n21 t21.5 f21 b21 Plenty of brown sugars to stir into the background coffee. But a degree of bitterness betrays a weakness in the cut. 46%. 1,715 bottles.

MOSGAARD DISTILLERY Oure. Working.

◇ **Mosgaard New Make Spirit Organic** db (94.5) n23.5 t24 f23 b24 Outstanding new make malt. Truly exemplary, bursting with the cleanest and most intense grist you could hope for. What a fine piece of distilling this is. Put this on the market and none will mature long enough ever to reach whisky...! 68%.

◇ **Mosgaard Peated New Make Spirit Organic** 25 ppm db (92.5) n23 t24 f22.5 b23.5 More superb new make from Mosgaard. There is a sharp interaction between the copper and phenols which offers a slight edge to this, a phenomenon which will probably pass within 18 months. But enjoy it while you can...! 66.8%.

◇ **Mosgaard Peated Young Malt** batch no. 18-02, production date. 060218, 25 ppm, bourbon barrels db (90) n22 lashings of tannins hold sway here, not the smoke which is confined to a subordinate role and also one to soften the oaky impact; t22.5 like the nose, very youthful for all the oaky interruptions. But so salivating as the barley bites deep. Creamy toffee tannin mingle with the peat; no shortage of smoked Demerara in the mid-ground; f22.5 smoked butterscotch with a touch of ulmo honey; b23 the phenols come across as about half the stated dose while the oak has whipped up quite a storm. As curious as it is enjoyable. And rather beautifully made. 48%.

⌖ **Mosgaard Port Young Malt** batch no. 18-03, production date. 200318 db **(84) n21 t22 f21 b20** A big whisky, but the flavour profiles are far from relaxed. The tannins are gargantuan and feel a little forced, thus knocking the fruit out of kilter. Plenty of big enjoyable flavours and spice. But balance is at a premium. *41%.*

⌖ **Mosgaard Young Malt** Pedro Ximenez cask finish, batch no. 18-01, production date. 170118, 25 ppm db **(86.5) n21 t22 f22.5 b21** A very pretty whisky with plenty of fruit and nut. Technically well made. And also filled into a decent and not overly-sweet PX. However, has been bottled at a point where both the young spirit and the oak influence are at times a little at cross purposes, perhaps not helped by lazy, slightly incoherent peat. That said, the chocolate towards the finale is sublime. *41%.*

NYBORG DESTILLERI Nyborg. Working.

⌖ **Nyborg Destilleri Ardor Isle of Fionia** batch no. 117 db **(92.5) n23** youthful, clean and gristy, the sugars luxuriate in their delicate citrus tones; **t23** sweet and mouth-watering on delivery, this could easily be mistaken for a Speyider as the grain is imbued with the light vanillas of a high quality, previously used cask. Admirably simple, yet what it does is done with panache; **f23** really classy fade: again gristy, but a little mocha and spice moves in just as it is meant to; **b23.5** as sweet and well controlled as Sweden's vital World Cup victory over Switzerland today. Technically, a right little beauty... *46.8%.*

SMALL BATCH DISTILLERS Holstebro. Working

Small Batch Distllers Peat by Peat db **(86.5) n21 t22.5 f21 b22** Angular and forceful. From the very green, sugary and lightly smoked nose, through the eye-wateringly sharp and puckering delivery to the postulating, tangy finish there is no peace for the senses. *62%.*

Small Batch Distillers Peat by Peat 3rd Edition American white oak virgin barrels, db **(89) n22.5 t23 f21 b22.5** It is probably this whisky's foibles that make this so attractive. *60%.*

Small Batch Distillers Peated Mystery 2nd Edition French virgin oak barrels db **(88) n21.5 t23 f21 b22.5** Again, drops a few points for a few technical weaknesses, on the nose and finish especially. But the over-all picture is very pretty. *56%.*

Small Batch Distllers Peated Rye db **(90) n23 t22 f22.5 b22.5** Playing around my lab over the years I have experimented with amalgamating the intense aroma and flavour of rye with the depth of a smoky malt. I had come up with some interesting concoctions but none, to my memory, quite matched the unique shape of this remarkable whisky, especially on the nose. Memorable...and very beautiful. *58%.*

Small Batch Distillers RugBy db **(91.5) n22.5 t23.5 f22.5 b23** A profound rye which, if cleaned up a bit would represent the grain with a touch of classicism. *58%.*

Small Batch Distillers RugBy Extend French virgin oak barrels db **(86.5) n21.5 t23.5 f21 b20.5** No denying the impact of the rye, or its high class crisp fruitiness, which can be fully enjoyed on the astonishing delivery and for a short while beyond. But a combination of the wide cut off the still and the unforgiving tannin means the balance of the whisky is lost far too early and easily. *60%.*

STAUNING WHISKEY Skjern. Working.

Stauning Bourbon Oak Virgin Oak dist 2012, bott Feb 17 db **(80.5) n20 t22.5 f19 b19** Slightly too feinty. Definitely too oaky. Plenty of sugars and spice to suck on, especially on delivery, but creates scant harmony. *478%.*

⌖ **Stauning Heather** dist 2013/14, bott Sept 17 db **(87.5) n22 t22 f22 b21.5** When I was a teenage trainee reporter my first girlfriend was called Heather – and she was every bit as sweet as the delivery on this malt. However, a wisp of a thing, she was nothing like so stodgy nor so inelegant. Intense and chewy (this whisky, not Heather) there are some beautiful moments to savour (both the Stauning and Heather) but ultimately let down by a feinty bitterness (again, the whisky, not Heather). And kisses quite beautifully (Heather, not the Stauning). 48.7%.

⌖ **Stauning Kaos** dist 2013/14, bott Apr 17 db **(90.5) n23.5** just adore the confident, yet seemingly understated smoke to this: quiet elegance; a little youthful and sweet; **t22.5** again, young at heart, delicate gristy sugars melt on impact; the smoke, lazy at first, builds, though proportionately; **f22** light smoky oils amid thriving vanilla; **b22.5** youthful and orderly to me... *473%.*

Stauning Kiesp dist 2011-2013, bott Nov 16 db **(91) n21.5 t23 f24 b22.5** Wins few prizes – or points – for its technical prowess. But for sheer flavour explosivity, this is some whisky...! *474%.*

⌖ **Stauning Peated 7th Edition** dist 2012, bott May 18 db **(91) n23** impossible not to be either charmed or seduced by the inexplicit peat at work here: big phenols, for sure, but gentle vanillas blunt the edge; **t23** malt, vanilla, molasses and caramel dominate the deliver; the smoke, getting nothing like the foothold of the nose, only slowly forges a presence; **f22** slightly bitter; **b23** understated peat at work here: indeed, when I last visited Stauning, it was still a working farm and the earthiness of the animals there had a more rugged phenolic quality than this sexy, gentle teaser. 48.4%.

◇ **Stauning Traditional** rum cask finish, dist 2014, bott Nov 17 db (80) n21 t20 f19 b20 When I did some of the first experimentation with rum cask maturation some 20 years ago, one of the first things I noticed, very early on, was the danger of the sugars closing down development and conversation within the whisky. This tight and limited expression is a good example of what I mean. 48.2%.

◇ **Stauning Web Kaos** dist 2013/14, bott Apr 17 db (95) n24 a more acidic, punchier display of phenols compared to the other Kaos: a touch of anthracite smoke, too; t23.5 brilliant, explosive delivery, the phenols firing into all direction with different pace and intensity; the gristy sugars are more complete and concentrated than in the standard chaos, while the mid-ground fills with Lubek marzipan and chocolate coffee Swiss roll; f23.5 long, abounding in spice still and the phenols ensuring the satisfactions continues for a very long time: the very lightest feints are harnessed to work to full advantage; b24 it seems wonderfully perverse to mark a whisky which is supposedly chaotic so highly for its balance. But rather than Kaos, perhaps this should be regarded as a controlled explosion...! One of the best whiskies I have ever experienced from Stauning: an absolute classic by any standards. 49.9%.

Stauning Young Rye 2013 bott Nov 16 db (92) n22.5 t23.5 f23 b23 A five course meal of a rye with the grain at its most intense. 52.3%.

◇ **Stauning Young Rye** dist 2014, bott Oct 17 db (93.5) n23.5 on early bottlings of Stauning rye, it was sometimes difficult to pick out the rye grain amid the oils: no such problem here. Crisp, fruity and precise; t23.5 ah, a much more oily delivery. Though the grain is heard loud and clear from the first moment, the texture is gorgeous, the taste buds wrapped in a cloak of rye-studded coffee; f23 long with wonderful mocha and rye interplay, lengthened by the gentle oils; b23.5 the mark of a very good distillery is that they learn from their mistakes. They had noted and acknowledged that their earlier cuts with the rye was too wide. The result is this: a true rye whisky, as clean and clear as a penny whisky and just as penetrating. 51.1%.

◇ **Stauning Young Rye** dist 2014, bott Feb 18 db (92) n23.5 the delicate oils accompanying the grain do nothing to marginalise the sharpness of the rye: there is a very seriously fruity crispness to this; t23.5 so salivating: the rye is brittle enough to shatter is jagged shards around the palate, light traces of Demerara sugars accompanying them; f22 attempts to bitter out, but fails...mostly; b23 does what it says on the tin: a substantial young rye! 43.3%.

◇ **Stauning Young Rye** rum cask finish, dist 2014, bott Jan 18 db (87.5) n23 t22.5 f20 b22 Some magnificent clipped honey tones really does bring out the more fragile and fruity elements of the rye. Annoyingly let down by a poor finish which leaves the bitterness unchecked. 46.5%.

THY WHISKY Snedsted. Working.

Thy Whisky No. 4 Kræn Klemme Single Malt ex-bourbon fass, dist 10 Dec 12, tappet 15 Jul 16 db (86) n21 t22.5 f21 b21.5 What a strange creature this is! A nondescript citrus note infiltrates the nose and early stages of the exceptionally clammy and sweet delivery. Soft and friendly natured, the vanilla ice cream finish is a bit odd at first but grows on you, as do the very late spices. 52%. nc ncf sc. 95 bottles.

Thy Whisky No. 5 Kræn Kusk Single Malt ex-bourbon, PX finish fass, dist 27 Aug 11, tappet 17 Oct 16 db (92.5) n23 t23.5 f22.5 b23.5 Not often you find a whisky where PX is particularly at home. But it certainly is here... 60.7%. nc ncf sc. 82 bottles.

Thy Whisky No. 6 Kræn Kræmmer Single Malt ex-Olorosso, PX finish fass, dist Oct 13 to Mar 14, tappet Mar 17 db (86.5) n21 t22 f21.5 b22 Well done, chaps! You have sourced a clean, unspoiled oloroso cask. That means the grape adds a fruity edge to the incredibly dense, sometimes juicy malt. A wide cut here results in a little off-key tang but the sultanas work overtime to make amends. Attractive. 50.4%. nc ncf. 642 bottles.

TROLDEN DISTILLERY Kolding. Working.

Trolden Nimbus The Kolding Single Malt No 3 dist 2012, bott 2016 db (94) n24.5 t23.5 f22.5 b23.5 Denmark offers grey skies like no other country I know, or to use the distiller's own confusing term when describing their whisky: "unlike no other". Yet the sun is shining on this wonderful new malt with serene benevolence. Impressed! 46%. nc ncf.

◇ **Trolden Nimbus The Kolding Single Malt Nimbus** cask no. 4 db (89) n22 something of a cough syrup to this: all is intense as green fruit, malt and oak form a thick union; t22.5 soft, mercurial delivery: an incredible saga of improbable dark sugars and even darker juicy fruits. Muscovado abounds as though trying to take over the world...well, errr...Kolding, anyway...; f22 after such a sweet delivery the finish has to be drier, bitter even. It is, and spicy, too. The oak can here at last be heard; b22.5 happy memories of many a tasting I conducted at Kolding back in the day. Before even there was a Whisky Bible! None of those bottles we tasted as Denmark slowly woke up to whisky was anything like this idiosyncratic little beauty, though. 46%. nc ncf sc.

FINLAND
THE HELSINKI DISTILLING COMPANY Helsinki. Working.

The Helsinki Distilling Co. Prelude 23 Months Single Malt 190 litre American virgin oak, cask no. 105, dist 23 Jun 15, bott 19 May 17 db **(89) n21.5 t22.5 f23 b22** Fabulous experience for the most part with a concentrated malt component you have to use a pneumatic drill to get through. Again, the signs are that the cut times are slightly more generous than their earlier distillations which affords a degree of extra flavour but does nothing for the overall precision and quality of the malt. Once more a wonderful coffee character, but this also boasts rich molasses and Manuka honey for good measure. 61%.

The Helsinki Distilling Co. Prelude 24 Months 100% Rye 55 litre French virgin oak, cask no. 91, dist 13 May 15, bott 19 May 17 db **(77) n19 t20 f19 b19** Mon Dieu! Stick to bourbon barrels: the cabbage-laden tannins here are so powerful they render the rye practically silent. And that seriously takes some doing. 62.7%.

The Helsinki Distilling Co. Prelude 26 Months Straight Rye 190 litre American virgin oak, cask no. 83, dist 19 Mar 15, bott 19 May 17 db **(88.5) n21.5 t23 f22 b22** A significantly wider cut than their earlier distillations and they'll have to watch this. Predictably, it mingles with the huge sugars off the grain and cask to create a coffee effect. Don't want that to distract from the mind-exploding and palate-pulsating rye which gives its all in one of the most full blooded samples I have tasted this year. A cleaner version would score a very high mark, indeed. 59.5%.

The Helsinki Distilling Co. Prelude 31 Months Straight Rye 28 litre French virgin oak, cask no. 27, dist 20 Oct 14, bott 19 May 17 db **(81.5) n21 t18 f23.5 b19** You can have too much of a good thing, I'm not sure the French oak was a good thing to start with... Still, no denying the stunning deliciousness of the coffee on the finish. But it is a bloody battle to get there... 61.5%.

➣ **Helsinki Whiskey 100% Rye Malt Release #2** new French oak casks db **(80) n19 t21.5 f20.5 b19** A wide cut on the distillate is accentuated by the oak's inability to compromise. But there is a massive onrushing of icing sugars and golden syrup which for a moment or two takes the pressure off the taste buds. The rye, however, is lost without trace...; 45%.

➣ **Helsinki Whiskey Rye Malt Release #3** small new French oak casks db **(82.5) n21 t20 f21.5 b20** Probably ideal for drinking nude in a sauna while being flagellated with birch. Like this, it will be enjoyable and painful at the same time. I just hope whoever does the whipping shows more mercy than the French oak... 47.5%. 350 bottles.

➣ **Helsinki Whiskey Rye Malt Release #4** new American oak casks db **(78.5) n20.5 t20 f19 b19** Not what I was expecting, or looking forward to. Earlier "test" bottlings of maturing spirit using American oak had been positive. This, surprisingly, takes the same route as the French casks with over aggressive tannins. The oils don't help, either. Having tasted their recent new make, which was good, a different wood profile is now a matter of urgency. 47.5%.

KYRÖ DISTILLERY COMPANY Isokyrö. Working.

➣ **Rye Whisky #1** bott 10 Aug 17 db **(83.5) n19 t21.5 f21.5 b21.5** No doubting the grain: the rye turns up big and loud, especially at the crescendo on about the fourth flavour wave. But too much oil at work here dulls the sparkle. Recovers beautifully late on with some chocolate milkshake. 47.8%.

PANIMORAVINTOLA KOULU Turku. Working.

Sgoil Sherry Cask db **(90) n23 t23.5 f21.5 b22.5** Sherry...and clean as a whistle! A sulphur-free dram from Finland. 59%. sc. 80 bottles.

TEERENPELI Tahti. Working.

➣ **Teerenpeli Islay Cask** db **(95) n24** ridiculously beautiful. The earthiness of an Islay whisky but without the drama: lightly salted, even a fraction minty; **t24** typical Teerenpeli controlled intensity and juiciness. Now with subtle waves of smoke taking it a stage further; the malt has a wonderfully gristy feel – and peated grist: that is some illusion! **f23** light with smoky coffee and hickory notes **b24** they have pulled this one off brilliantly. The cleanness of the spirit means there is a glorious impression of a lightly, and delightfully peated malt. Really, after so many years nothing this wonderful distillery does should surprise me. 61.7%

➣ **Teerenpeli Peated New Make** db **(94.5) n24 t23.5 f23 b24** Finland's finest now in fabulous phenols and.... fantastic! 63.5%.

➣ **Teerenpeli Savu** db **(85.5) n21 t22.5 f21 b21** Unusual to find a Teerenpeli at such a relatively weak strength, and it does little to help this whisky. The oils have fractured, resulting in a dry, chalky offering which struggles to find a rhythm or purpose. Pleasant in part and some intriguing phenol tones. But Finns aren't as they should be. 43%.

Teerenpeli Single Malt 10 Year Old bourbon & sherry casks db (80) n20 t21 f19 b20. Very hard to see what an average sherry butt can add to a malt as good as Teerenpeli's. And, sad to say, this is very average sherry wood, indeed...43%

Teerenpeli Suomi 100 Single Malt Whisky bott 26 Aug 16 db (95) n23.5 t24 f23.5 b24 Brilliant: a Megastar...! 43%.

Teerenpeli Tallink Silva Megastar Single Malt Whisky bott 13 Feb 17 db (93.5) n23.5 t24 f23 b23 Underpowered at 43%. But technically sublime... 43%.

FRANCE
Single Malt
DISTILLERIE ARTISANALE LEHMANN Obernai. Working.

Elsass Whisky Single Malt Whisky Alsacien Gold db (84.5) n21.5 t22 f20 b21. The family of my old French girlfriend, Dominique, had an Alsacien. Dog, not whisky. And despite the breed's ferocious nature, I bonded with it more than any other dog before or since. For it was just a friendly as this caramel-rich offering. But had a lot more energy and personality. 40%. ncf.

Elsass Whisky Single Malt Whisky Alsacien Origine bott code. LF02 db (83) n19 t22 f21 b21. The soft feintiness on the nose warns of the riches of the oils to come. But before they reassemble on the finish, there is a lovely barley moment about two thirds of the way through the passage which does impress. 40%. ncf.

Elsass Whisky Single Malt Whisky Alsacien Premium db (86) n20.5 t21.5 f22 b22. This is about as close as you'll get to an abstract single malt. The early discordant notes of the distillate are thrown against the canvas of the malt, and then fruit is randomly hurled at it, making a juicy, then spicy, splash. The overall picture when you stand back is not at all bad. But getting there is a bit messy. 50%. ncf.

DISTILLERIE BERTRAND Uberach. Working.

Uberach db (77) n21 t19 f18 b19. Big, bitter, booming. Gives impression something's happening between smoke and grape... whatever it is, there are no prisoners taken. 42.2%

DISTILLERIE CASTAN Villeneuve-sur-Vère. Working.

Vilanova Berbie db (80) n20 t21 f19 b20 For what it boasts in intensity it lacks in grace and elegance. Uncomfortable on both nose and finish thanks to less than impressive oak, it just has too much of everything. Some will doubtless find the concentrated prunes and molasses very much to their liking. 44%. ncf.

Vilanova Berbie Single Cask batch no. 13 db (89.5) n22.5 t22 f22.5 b22.5 A classic and very enjoyable pre-prandial whisky which sharpens up the taste buds without overly exercising them themselves. 42%. ncf sc.

Vilanova New Spirit Single Malt Classic db (90.5) n23 t23 f22.5 b22 A well-made, light bodied and clean new made showing distinct signs of gristy barley and, surprisingly, vanilla. 45.1%. ncf.

Vilanova New Spirit Single Malt Terrocita db (91.5) n23.5 t23 f22 b23 The peat adds both weight and sweetness to this lean white dog. Plenty of gristy chewiness; the toasty smoked molasses lingers. 45.1%. ncf.

Vilanova Terrocita db (91.5) n23 t23.5 f22 b23 Have to admit that this is a nose and flavour profile I have never quite encountered before. What a shame it wasn't at about 55% ab .think we might have been heading off the planet from terra firma to terro cita... 43%. ncf.

DISTILLERIE DE MONSIEUR BALTHAZAR Hérisson. Working.

Hedgehog Straight Whisky Bourbonnais bott code. L2.16 db (85.5) n20 t22.5 f21.5 b21.5. You'd expect this to be a prickly little beast. Yet it is anything but: it celebrates the oils and honeys generated by the ample cut to the full and with only a minimum degree of spice. Eye-watering at its height, an unmistakable rye tartness maximises the flavour profile and dominates deliciously to the end. Get that cut a little tighter and what a magnificent whisky we would have here. 45%. ncf.

DOMAINE DES HAUTES GLACES Saint-John-d'Hérans. Working.

Domaine des Hautes Glaces Flavis Single Cask Organic Whisky db (84.5) n21 t20 f22.5 b21. Well, you can't say it doesn't have personality. Actually, the maltiness, which improves as it goes along, does hit impressive proportions. And the gathering cocoa also shows the oak plays an important part. But one or two verses of this are well out of tune. 46%. sc.

Domaine des Hautes Glaces Moissons Single Malt Organic Whisky db (86.5) n20.5 t22 f22 b22. Warming this to body temperature is vital as, when cool, it is not the most attractive proposition and scores badly. But when it is opened by body heat, the most delicate phenols show a subtlety and weight which were not before apparent, as do the tannins which reveal a more generous and inclusive element. The sugars are decidedly of an oaky bent with a dark toastiness which melt towards the tannins. 42%

DISTILLERIE DES MENHIRS Bretagne. Working.

Eddu Gold db (93) n22 t23 f24 b24. Rarely do whiskies turn up in the glass so rich in character to the point of idiosyncrasy. Some purists will recoil from the more assertive elements. I simply rejoice. This is so proud to be different. An exceptionally good, to boot!! 43%

Eddu Grey Rock db (87.5) n21.5 t22 f22 b22. A docile whisky reliant on friendly muscovado sugars which match the vanilla-oak very attractively.40%

Eddu Grey Rock Affinage Porto db (83) n19 t21 f22 b21 Tasting whisky from this distillery is like taking part in a lucky dip: no idea if you'll pick a winner or the booby prize. This has the uncontrollable nose of a dud, but the fruit helps it pick up on the palate to an acceptable level. Good late spices, too. 40%

Eddu Grey Rock Brocéliande db (86.5) n22 t22.5 f20.5 b21.5. Dense whisky which enjoys an enjoyable molassed fruitcake theme. A bit thin and wonky towards the finish.40%

Eddu Silver db (81) n20 t22 f19 b20. A curiosity of a whisky, though not up to the distillery's normal high standards. The base spirit hasn't been cut to advantage, so the feints tend to damage both nose and finish. Some astonishing sugars on deliver, though. 40%.

Eddu Silver Broceliande db (92.5) n23 t23 f23 b23.5 Pure silk. A beautiful and engaging experience. 40%.

Eddu Grey Silver The Original db (92.5) n23 t23 f23.5 b23 J'adore! 40%.

Eddu Grey Silver Sherry Cask Finish db (81.5) n20 t21 f21.5 b19 Sherbet cask finish, surely. Fizzes in a lemon sherbet kind of way. No sulphur: no off notes like that, all. And even a degree of mocha at the finish. But there is not a semblance of balance here. Attractively weird. 46%.

DISTILLERIE DU PÉRIGOLD Sarlat. Working.

Lascaw Aged 12 Years Blended Malt Whisky bott 2-12-15 db (87) n21 t22 f22 b22. A very pleasant blend, very much of a Scotch style. Super soft, safe though sometimes juicy, this is perhaps held back by a constant caramel theme which tames the expected high points. 40%

DISTILLERIE GILBERT HOLL Ribeauvillé. Working.

Lac'Holl 8 Year Old Single Malt Whisky db (69) n19 t20 f14 b16 If memory serves, this is the youngest Lac'Holl I have tasted. But without doubt it is the most singular and disappointing. The profile of their whisky is usually far from conventional but attractive; this one is utterly bizarre and ugly. The peculiar scenting on the Swedish aquavit-style nose, which appears to include coconut sunscreen and orange liqueur, is matched only by the finish which reminds me, late on, of Milk of Magnesia. This has not been a good tasting day: it just got a whole lot worse... 42%.

Lac'Holl Vieil Or 10 Years Old Single Malt Whisky db (92.5) n22.5 t23.5 f23 b23.5 A malt which gives one's taste buds a real working over. Superb balance. 42%

Lac'Holl Junior 13 Years Old Single Malt Whisky db (89) n22 t22.5 f22 b22.5 Wow!! Bursts from the glass with so much charisma and charm. Perhaps not technically the finest of all time, but such fun! Delicious!! 43%

Lac'Holl 15 Years Old Single Malt Whisky db (90.5) n23.5 t22.5 f22 b22.5 Such a rare display of barley and gristy sugars. Very impressive malt. And fabulously refreshing. 42%

DISTILLERIE GLANN AR MOR Larmor-Pleubian. Working.

⬩ **Glann Ar Mor 2018** db (94.5) n23.5 a light lemon sherbet fizz to the seemingly youngish grist; t23.5 indeed, this is a fizzy dram: the barley flickers around the palate with intense yet always teasing maltiness; a blend of heather and ulmo honey accounts for the sweetness. The salivating qualities kick in about halfway through, light spices aiding the effect and a toasted fudge middle displaying the oak's interest; f23.5 some late oils but the intense malt pulses alongside the delicate spice; b24 there is always something alluring and sexy about effortless elegance...what a classy act. 46%.

⬩ **Glenn ar Mor Maris Otter Barley 2017** bourbon barrels db (94.5) n23 a youthful, citrussy freshness to this but tannin enough to ensure depth t24 wow...! So rare that the malt enjoys such centre of attention no matter the occasion: concentrated grist, both juicy salivating and powdery; red liquorice and light hickory fashioned further by delicate molasses and spice; a degree of oiliness intensifies the higher points; f23.5 amazingly gristy and zesty even at the death; the late chocolate is too good to be true; **b24** she was only the brewer's daughter, as she sat by the mill. Maris otter was in the mash tun, but she was 'otter still... The kind of malt that moves you to poetry.. *46%. nc ncf.*

> **Glann Ar Mor Maris Otter Barley** batch. Autumn 2017 db **(95)** **n23.5** concentrated malt and lighter praline: soft and sexy; **t24** astonishing clarity to the malt on delivery ensures a mouth-watering start. Vanillas slowly build up and begin a relaxed drying process. The spices threaten to sizzle, but are content to rumble; **f23.5** back to a light praline and marzipan finale, the nuttiness the key to its longevity; **b24** this is a cleaner version their other Maris Otter bottling with less oil. Every nuance involves subtlety. Simply great whisky as technically excellent as Pavard's sweetly struck volley against Argentina this afternoon... *46%.*

> **Kornog Côteaux du Layon** db **(87.5)** **n22** **t22** **f22** **b21.5** I am rapidly coming to the conclusion that this is a distillery that benefits from bourbon cask above all else. Nothing unattractive about the peppery grape. But it does fill in the many of the natural contours as the malt develops, so the instead of complexity we have a constant (though very attractive) toffee-fruit note. Maybe this distillery has now become so well established as one of the finest, if not the finest, on mainland Europe, I have become hyper critical. Such is the price of excellence. *52.8%. sc.*

> **Kornog PX Finish 2016** bourbon barrel & PX butt db **(87)** **n21.5** **t22** **f22** **b21.5** Some people will adore this whisky, I know. But, for me, getting a PX cask with a vaguely smoky malt to gel is one of the hardest tricks in the book. Often, as this malt does, it can come across as a little disjointed and aggressive. There is no denying there are some delightfully succulent and attractive phrases, the delivery the pick of the lot. But, despite the idiosyncratic type of wine cask, this is a little too thin and angular for its own good. Enjoyable...but with caveats. *58.1%. nc ncf.*

> **Kornog Roc'h Hir 2017** bourbon barrels db **(87)** **n21** **t21.5** **f23** **b21.5** Spoke a little too soon about Roc'h Hir's feinty days being over. Distinct tobacco on the nose – perfectly acceptable if you smoke, I suppose – and a bit of an oily mishmash on the delivery and follow up. On the subject of mash, there is no escaping the gristiness, nor the chocolate mint finale. *46%. nc ncf.*

> **Kornog Roc'h Hir 2018** db **(88.5)** **n22** a light feint kicks in, as does the most apologetic smoke. Sweet with a dab of citrus; **t22.5** yep, again a slight feint on the delivery, but the extra oils offer attractive weight to the intense malt; **f22** long, thanks to the oils. With gentle strands of malt, vanilla and marmalade to be found along the way; **b22** very straightforward malt, eschewing a path of twists and turns for a pleasant simplicity. *46%.*

> **Kornog Saint Erwan 2017** first fill bourbon barrel db **(96)** **n24** the gentle smoke drifts in as slowly and mysteriously as sea mist over a coastal village...; **t24** so lush. The house style of melt-in-the-mouth gristiness has never been more profound than in this bottling. The peat is sweet and malty, while the oils offer a buttery sheen. The spices are warming and match the light ulmo honey beat for beat; **f23.5** the new house style of praline kicks in, but of course now with the peaty edge to it. The tannins also lap gently on the palate, a little hickory going a long way; **b24.5** if you don't succeed first time, try and try again.... Previous editions of this lightly smoked rendition of Kornog has been found just short of the mark: pleasant but not quite there. Eureka! They've cracked it: this is truly beautiful. Big time... *50%. nc ncf sc. 277 bottles.*

> **Kornog Saint Ivy 2017** bourbon barrel db **(94.5)** **n23.5** chunky malt, clean yet intriguingly angular. Beautiful gristy tones, complete with understated citrus; **t23.5** ohhh... such depth! Light oils scrunch up the intensity of the malt while the blend of muscovado and icing sugars deal with the encroaching tannins...; spices prickle while a vanilla and malt milkshake mix fills the middle ground; **f23.5** not a hint of bitterness, a fault with so many malts these days, as the grist and oaky vanilla play out their gentle end game: walnut whip chocolate at its most whippy...; **b24** beautifully made and matured: satisfying in every respect. Back in November I celebrated my 60th birthday in London's magnificent Ivy Restaurant: this malt should be a fixture there. I, for one, would have savoured a glass to mar my special day... *59.9%. nc ncf sc. 259 bottles.*

> **Kornog Sauternes Cask 2016** db **(88.5)** **n22** one of the most intensely thick and fruity Sauternes noses I have found anywhere in the world: the sultana – spotted dick pudding – quality leaves little room for the malt to manoeuvre; **t23** as expected, spices cascade from the delivery and it is only after a few flavour waves crash onto the palate it settles enough for the rich grape to stand on its own feet; **f21.5** some hefty oils from the distillate and ever-warming spices reveal a mild flaw which the grape continues to mainly conceal; **b22** the excellence of the cask patches up some unhappy oils. *46%. nc ncf sc.*

> **Kornog Sauternes 2018** db **(88)** **n21.5** just a little ungainly as the wide cut and muscular grape joust; **t22** hot and spicy kick off – a real burn to this. The muscovado sugars and grape try to douse the flames; **f22** at last the tannins gets a fair hearing; **b22.5** eye-wateringly intense. *46%.*

⬦ **Kornog Sherry Oloroso Finish** db **(92)** n23 beautifully manicured smoke topped off with clean and sympathetically balanced sultana; t23 impressive delivery: soft yet bursting with a mix of confident smoke and competent grape; f22.5 a buttery textured shortbread and vanilla trait but the smoke lengthens matters impressively; b23.5 how heart-warming to find not only a clean oloroso butt at work, but the smoke and fruit entirely harmonised. 46%.

DISTILLERIE GRALLET-DUPIC Rozelieures. Working.

G.Rozelieures Whisky De Lorraine Single Malt Whisky bott code: L446 db **(87)** n21.5 t22.5 f21 b22. Exceptionally nutty. The blossoming of the sugars on delivery is always attractive, as are the complex nougat/caramel/cocoa tones. Though the feints are always a threat, the genteel pace and softness of the malt makes it well worth a look. 40%

G.Rozelieures Whisky De Lorraine Single Malt Whisky Fumé Collection bott code: L415 db **(91.5)** n23 t24 f22 b22.5 But for a lingering offnote, this would have scored very highly indeed. A vague smokiness gives this a lovely weight. 46%

G.Rozelieures Whisky De Lorraine Single Malt Whisky Rare Collection bott code: L446 db **(88.5)** n19.5 t23.5 f22.5 b23 One of the sweetest and most lush malts this year, but always delicious. 40%

G.Rozelieures Whisky De Lorraine Single Malt Whisky Tourbé Collection bott code: L416 db **(92)** n22 t23.5 f23 b23.5 There is a feinty flaw to this, and even perhaps a slight lack of copper in the system; but the overall picture is a very pretty one. 46%

DISTILLERIE GUILLON Louvois. Working.

Guillon No. 1 Single Malt de la montagne de Reims db **(87)** n22 t21 f22 b22. Right. I'm impressed. Not exactly faultless, but enough life here really to keep the tastebuds on full alert; By and large well made and truly enjoyable. Well done, Les Chaps! 46%

DISTILLERIE HEPP VUM MODERTAL Uberach. Working.

⬦ **Authentic Whisky D'Alsace Whisky Single Malt Doble Fût No. 6** db **(82.5)** n19 t22.5 f20 b21 Well, that was different! The nose is vaguely on the soapy side and the dry finish conjures up a late burn. The delivery, though, does have a brief spasm of enjoyably intense barley at its heart, and a little cocoa to follow through. 42%. ncf.

⬦ **Authentic Whisky D'Alsace Whisky Single Malt Doble Fût No. 7** db **(87)** n21 t23 f21 b22 A much more complete malt than their No.6. The nose is a tad austere and, again, the finale requires a fire extinguisher as the degree of burn increases. But there is no doubting the beauty and integrity of the delivery, a kind of malt and chocolate bonbon, even with a Milky Way element. My word it's hot, though. 40%. ncf.

⬦ **Authentic Whisky D'Alsace Whisky Single Malt Pinot Noir & Pinot Gris** db **(85)** n21.5 t22.5 f20 b21 The unspoiled grape offers a magnificent salivating juiciness. But even barrels as excellent as these cannot completely cover the flame-throwing traits of the original spirit. 47%. ncf. 640 bottles.

⬦ **Authentic Whisky D'Alsace Whisky Single Malt Russian Imperial Stout #01** db **(76)** n19 t22 f16 b19 I adore malt whisky. And my cellars are never without a case of Harvey's Russian Imperial Stout. But would I drink the two together? Never! The nose, though sweet, is undone by hop and there is not enough cover on the attractive, viscous malt to see off the incendiary tendencies of the spirit. 43%. ncf.

⬦ **Authentic Whisky D'Alsace Whisky Single Malt Squaring the Circle** Pinot Noir & Pinot Gris casks db **(86.5)** n22 t23 f20 b21.5 Hot as Hades. But at least the nose and the delivery does offer us an all to brief vision of Pinot perfection... 48.6%. ncf. 890 bottles.

⬦ **Authentic Whisky D'Alsace Whisky Single Malt Timeless Intemporel** db **(81)** n20 t21.5 f19 b20.5 Something a little beery about this. The late burn is as unforgiving as usual but the maltiness does have a little extra sweetness to counter the flames. 47%. ncf.

DISTILLERIE J.ET M. LEHMANN Obernai. Working.

⬦ **Elsass Single Malt Whisky Gold Aged 7 Years** Bordeaux Blanc finition db **(90)** n23 two-toned: the barley is ethereal, the grape rich enough to fill a fruitcake; t22.5 and here we go again: a fabulously two-toned delivery, with a repeat from the nose on the palate. Beautifully clean, allowing the grape to offer untold succulence; f22 very light oils; even lighter marzipan; b22.5 deceptive and delicious. 40%.

⬦ **Elsass Single Malt Whisky Origine Aged 7 Years** Bordeaux Blanc barrel db **(90.5)** n23 thin cantaloupe melon brushed by grape juice and barley – any lighter and the glass would float off...; t23 just like the nose, there is no fire or violence here. Just a teasing brush of young malt fortified with a must background offering weight and chewability; f22 a little thin and strained as the vanillas dominate...gently...; b22.5 a picture of understated elegance. 40%.

Elsass Single Malt Whisky Premium Aged 8 Years Sauternes barrel db (**94.5**) **n23** it's all about the grape! This is like a moist, sweet Sultana cake on heat...; **t24** what a delivery! Supercharged muscovado sugars join seamlessly with the concentrated sultana and – later - toasty raisin for an unforgettable entry; the midpoint sees plenty of spices in action and still the salivation continues; **f23.5** wonderfully long, a little praline mixing in with the grape and molasses; the spices tingle to the very end; **b24** there is no finer wine cask in which to mature whisky than a clean Sauternes one. This does nothing to undermine my argument. Truly superb. 50%.

DISTILLERIE MEYER Hohwarth. Working.

Meyer's Le Whisky Alsacien Blend Superieur db (**90**) **n22.5** moist date and walnut cake; **t23** house style of yielding silk and then further fruit and nut tones, almost vaguely sherry trifle; **f22** more of the same, though just with the volume down slightly; **b22.5** not a whisky you can easilly say no to...Really charming. 40%

Meyer's Le Whisky Alsacien Blend Superieur bott code: L1808595 db (**87.5**) **n21.5 t22.5 f21.5 b22** Some feints kick in early here but recovers for a date and walnut chewiness on the delivery in particular. Not quite as well constructed as their last blend but at least here we see a fine example of extra oils being put to good use. And the malt making its mark deliciously and with gusto. 40%.

Meyer's Whisky Alsacien Blend Superieur db (**88.5**) **n22.5 t22.5 f21.5 b22**. Impressively clean, barley-thick and confident: a delight. 40%

Meyer's Le Whisky Alsacien Blend Superieur Affinage En Fut De Sauternes Finition Pinot Noir bott code: L179895 db (**91.5**) **n23** the malt element may be a little heady but the freshness to the fruit, and its accompanying honey and spice, is superb...; **t23** a thick set blend: both the malt and fruit are rich and intense but marry far more happily than the last such blend from Meyer's I tasted. The sweetness of the Sauternes is crucial to the balance and helps thin things out slightly; **f22.5** a little oily, still, but the fruit is untainted and carry the increasingly crisp, muscovado-like sugars to their vanilla-clad conclusion; **b23** now, I may just have mentioned that I have a Meyer's Parrot called Percy. Percy likes raspberries and cherries. And he also likes grapes. As well as grains. I'd better not tell him I've tasted this whisky today or there might just be one very upset bird. This is mine...all mine...! 40%.

Meyer's Le Whisky Alsacien Blend Superieur Pinot Noir Finish db (**83.5**) **n21.5 t21.5 f20 b21.** Slightly sticky on the palate as the fruit tries to take charge. Though pleasant, imbalanced somewhat by the late feints and lack of give from the grape. 40%

Meyer's Le Whisky Alsacien Pur Malt No. 05169 db (**92**) **n22 t23.5 f23 b23.5** My old Budgie, Borat, used to help himself to whatever whisky was going if no-one was watching. Sadly, he is no more and is buried in the garden overlooked by my tasting room. By contrast, my parrot, Percy, has never had a single drop of whisky in all his four years. Though he might be interested in this one, because he is a pure Meyer's. He has a sweet tooth, has Percy. Or do I mean beak? Anyway, I am sure he would bob his head up and down in appreciation of the sugary gristiness which pervades throughout this impressive dram. Who's a pretty whisky, then....? 40%

Meyer's Le Whisky Alsacien Pur Malt No. 06857 bott code: L173469667430 db (**84**) **n20.5 t21.5 f21 b21** Now, I won't be offering this one to Percy my Meyer's Parrot. He would have been mightily impressed with the gristy sweetness of their last pure malt I encountered. But this has a feinty edge which limits the scope of the sugars and overall development. Pleasant, oily of course, but lost its chirpiness. 40%.

Meyer's Le Whisky Alsacien Pur Malt 12 Ans db (**92.5**) **n23** love that nose: so nutty, with both marzipan and praline in the mix; **t23.5** firm and sweet, the malt flows around the palate, activating the sensors which trigger the saliva. Juicy beyond belief; the mid-ground at last reveals the nuttiness apparent on the nose; **f23** long, still malty and light praline nuttiness **b23** an astonishing role reversal: usually it the older whiskies of the microdistilleries which are weaker as the distiller has yet to learn to master his stills. Yet this is as clean as a whistle, unlike their younger malt. A wonderfully precise and nutty experience. Percy....!!! Daddy's got a treat for you...! 53%.

DISTILLERIE WARENGHEM Lannion. Working.

Armorik db (**91**) **n23 t22 f23 b23**. I admit it; I blanched, when I first nosed this, so vivid was the memory of the last bottling. This, though ,was the most pleasant of surprises. Fabulous stuff: one of the most improved malts in the world. 40%

Armorik Double Maturation finished in oloroso casks db (**75**) **n18.5 t20 f18 b18.5**. Dull and decidedly out of sorts. 46%. ncf.

Armorik Millésime Matured for 10 Years cask no. 3261 db (**92**) **n22.5 t23 f23 b23**. Never quite know what you are going to get from these messieurs. Didn't expect this bottle of delights, I must say. The sweetness is a bit OTT at one point, but just copes. 56.1%. sc.

Armorik Sherry Finish db **(92)** n22.5 t23.5 f23 b23.5. The first sherry finish today which has not had a sulphur problem...and I'm in my eighth working hour...! Bravo guys! If their Classic was a note on sophistication, then this was an essay. 40%

KAERILIS Le Palais. Working.

Kaerilis l'Aube du Grand Dérangement 15 Ans db **(83.5)** n20 t22.5 f20 b21. Misfires when the revs are up, but purrs for moment on two on delivery as the sugar and barley kicks in to delicious effect. An enigmatic fruitiness enriches. 57%. nc ncf sc.

WAMBRECHIES DISTILLERY Wambrechies. Working.

Wambrechies Single Malt Aged 8 Years db **(83)** n20 t21 f21 b21. There's that aroma again, just like the 3-y-o. Except how it kind of takes me back 30 years to when I hitchhiked across the Sahara. Some of the food I ate with the local families in Morocco and Algeria was among the best I have ever tasted. And here is an aroma I recognize from that time, though I can't say specifically what it is (tomatoes, maybe?). Attractive and unique to whisky, that's for sure. I rather like this malt. There is nothing quite comparable to it. One I need to investigate a whole lot more. 40%

UNSPECIFIED

◇ **Brenne French Single Malt Whisky Estate Cask** finished in Cognac barrels, batch no.001, bott 2017 **(80.5)** n19 t21.5 f19.5 b20.5 In over 25 years of professionally tasting whisky, I cannot recall a single sample that has this profile. Firstly, had I tasted blind I would not have recognised this as a single malt. The nose has an almost synthetic quality, candy floss and pear drops. The body is thin, though not unpleasant when the sugars settle, and the vanilla makes its mark. Once you are over the peculiar nose, there is nothing to fear... or be particularly excited about, either. 40%.

◇ **Brenne Ten French Single Malt Whisky Aged 10 Years** bott 2016 **(85.5)** n21 t22.5 f21 b21 I'd love to know what kind of warehouse this whisky has spent the last ten years maturing in: the most dominant trait is fruit. Indeed, the malt is lost entirely, as though it has lived exclusively in the environment of cider brandy and Armagnac, to the extent that it has changed character into the content of its brother casks. Have to enjoy the mega-fruity delivery, though it doesn't possess an atom of whisky character; and quite a bite, too. 48%.

Vicomte Single Malt Whisky Aged 8 Years Cognac barrels **(86)** n22 t22 f21 b21. Just like so much Cognac, this whisky has a distinctive toffee theme which makes for a rather too easy going malt. Just not enough peaks and troughs to add "interesting" to "enjoyable" in the description of this caramel-laden malt. From the attractive silky texture, I would not be surprised to learn the Cognac barrels in which this whisky laid were hand made by Asterix. 40% (80 proof)

Blends

Moon Harbour Pier 1 Sauternes cask finish (86.5) n20 t22.5 f22 b22. A sticky toffee, chewy number with a beautiful flavour spike as the apricot on the Sauternes kicks in and lingers. Shame about the nose, though, which cannot disguise far from peerless malt. 45.8%. ncf.

Vatted Malts
KAERILIS

Kaerilis Ster Vraz No 9 4 Year Old db **(80)** n22 t21 f18 b19. Plenty of salt and no little citrus. But undone by an oaky bitterness. 45%. nc ncf.

Kaerilis Ster Vraz No 9 4 Year Old db **(87)** n21.5 t23.5 f20 b22. What the hell was that...??? Something different, for sure. At its best, quite stunning. At its worst – at the death – hmmm, not great. Get your bucket and spade out for this one. 61.8%. nc ncf.

GERMANY
BAULAND BRENNEREI ALT ENDERLE ROSENBURG. WORKING.

Alt Enderle Neccarus 8 Years Old Single Malt Whisky db **(90.5)** n22 t23 f23 b22.5 A gently complex, delightful malt.Had it been scotch, I would have thought it was a coastal dram. Odd...! 43%

Alt Enderle Neccarus 12 Years Old Single Malt Whisky db **(94)** n23.5 t23.5 f23 b24 Technically, among the best malt I have ever encountered from Germany. 43%

Alt Enderle Neccarus 15 Years Old Port Fass Single Malt Whisky db **(92.5)** n23 another salty Neccarus: dry grape skin comes over in waves; t23.5 eye-watering fruit and saline mix; the sugars are subdues and of a fudgy style before mocha begins to soften the moment; f23 a lovely chocolate and raisin fade; b23 a chocolate mousse is on the loose. 51%

Alt Enderle Neccarus 15 Years Old Sherry Fass Single Malt Whisky db (86.5) n21 t22 f21.5 b22. Clean sherry. But, after the mouth-watering delivery, relatively sweet and simple with just not enough gear changes. Pleasant, if not up to the standard of the other Neccarus. 49%

BIRGITTA RUST PIEKFEINE BRÄNDE Bremen. Working.
Van Loon 5 Year Old Single Malt Whisky batch 2012 db (85) n21.5 t22 f20 b21.5 Usually, a little extra strength will greatly enhance a complex whisky - if give it time in the glass. The exception is when the cut is already a little too wide, resulting in a lumpy, ultimately bitter effort. Where this does benefit is in the richness of the fruit and the light mocha effect. 55%.

BRENNEREI BERGHOF RABEL Owen-Teck. Working.
⟐ **Whisky Stube Spirit of the Cask OWEN Albdinkel** Jamaika rum fass finish, destillert am 01/2012, abgefüllt am 11/2017 (90) n21.5 untidy, but some acacia honey sails to the rescue...and it needed to; t23 huge delivery with the rum having a bigger say early on than any Jamaican cask I have encountered for a very long time. Enthralling esters spin out the sugars and honey, the spices squawking like a parrot on a pirate's shoulder; f22.5 excellent spices and oils; a slow fade of heather honey, combining beautifully with the spices, vanilla, mallow and red liquorice; b23 the spirit is not exactly faultless. But a stupendous rum cask has generated a treasure chest of untold honeyed riches. 46%.

BRENNEREI DANNENMANN Owen. Working.
Danne's Single Malt Schwäbischer Whisky Vom Bellerhof dist 09, cask strength, bott code L 0017 db (87) n20 t23 f22 b22. A huge whisky which kicks a lot harder than its 55% abv. Works a lot better than its sister 43% bottling, making the most of the golden syrup and grist mix, and the spiced cocoa fade. Pretty enjoyable. 54.9%

BRENNEREI FELLER Dietenheim-Regglisweiler. Working
⟐ **Augustus Dinkel Port Single Grain** port cask finish, bott code los 903 db (89) n21.5 entirely haphazard and out of sync...yet intriguing. The fruit is profound, but its seems to act like a dodgem, smashing into to the spelt grain and knocking it askew; t22.5 good grief...! Well, a wide cut from the still generates hefty, vaguely off-key oils. But again the impact of the concentrated grape and spelt focuses the mind – and taste buds which are slowly hammered into submission; juicy and chewy, if nothing else...; f23 more intense grape: remarkable; there is an inevitability to the spice and cocoa; b22 the odd Feller whisky I have tasted of late has been found guilty of going easy on the character front. No such charge can be levelled at this peculiar feller...enjoy the ride! 46%.
⟐ **Augustus Single Grain** port cask finish, bott code los 1001 db (85.5) n21 t22 f21 b21.5 I seem to remember their last Port pipe being slightly on the faulty side. No such problem this time, but the grain and spirit make hard work of gelling. Peculiarly angular on both nose and delivery there is a spirit note which doesn't quite ring true. A real mixed bag. 58.8%
⟐ **Valerie Rye Malt** bott code los 901 db (88.5) n22 the general noise from the caramel means the rye takes its time to be heard: once it arrives, it stays; t22.5 gorgeously distilled, the rye quickly taking as much caramel and tannin from the cask as possible. Again, the rye takes its time to emerge, but presents itself stiffly; f22 more cream toffee with a light spice; b22 highly attractive but you seriously implore the grain to take firmer control. 46%.
⟐ **Valerie Rye Malt** bott code los 901 db (91.5) n22.5 the rye is quicker out of the blocks and crisper, too; t23.5 a satisfying delivery: the rye reveals and revels in a greater crispness to its character and a far juicier intensity. Light oils further the toffee cause; a mix of spice and liquorice help create the outline of Kentuckian feel to this...; f22.5 mildly creamy chocolate toffee; some harder grains still loiter; b23 the extra strength and oils offer a sharper edge to the rye and greater overall depth and length. 59.9%.
Valerie Single Malt Amarone Cask Strength bott code 114 db (95.5) n24 t24 f23.5 b24 They don't come more voluptuous and buxom than Valerie... 59%.
⟐ **Valerie Single Malt** bott code los 113 db (87.5) n22 t22 f21.5 b22 A sweet, silky and malty dram guilty perhaps of resting on its laurels and allowing the ever-intensifying caramels to have far too great a say. 40%.

BRENNEREI FRANK RODER Aalen - Wasseralfingen. Working.
Frank's Suebisch Cask Strength 2008 db (91) n22 t23 f23 b23. Frank has really got the hang of how to make the most of his still...a little stunner! And his cleanest yet. 57%

BRENNEREI HENRICH Kriftel, Hessia. Working.

Gilors Port Cask sherry, bott code L13033, dist 2010, bott 2013 db (86) n20 t22 f22.5 b21.5.
Thoroughly enjoyable and full of depth and no little fruit and spice. But the wide cut, apparent
in the sherry version, is not tamed in quite the same effortless way. 44%. sc.

BRENNEREI HÖHLER Aarbergen, Kettenbach. Working.

Whesskey Hessischer Barley-Whisky bott code GW 01-15 db (84) n19 t22 f21.5 b21.5.
Follows a similar path to the corn whisky, except this has a dried grass/hay edge and never
quite reaches those same heights of chocolatey deliciousness. 44%

Whesskey Hessischer Blend-Whisky bott code BW 01-15 db (90.5) n23 t22 f23 b22.5 A
typical Hohler slightly flawed stunner. 44%

Whesskey Hessischer Corn-Whisky bott code MW 01-15 db (87.5) n20.5 t23 f22 b22.
Though the nose leaves you in no doubt about the feints at work, the beauty of the chocolate
wafer and Nutella is there to be savoured. 44%

Whesskey Hessischer Rye-Malt-Whisky bott code MW 01-15 db (84.5) n19 t22 f21.5 b22.
After the usual less than impressive nose, this is an earthy beast which grows on you. Hefty
hardly touches it: the chunky sugars aids the clanking rye no end. 44%

Whesskey Hessischer Single Malt Whisky bott code CA 01-15 db (81) n18.5 t21 f21 b20.5.
Despite the fact it has all kinds of flavour permutations, it is hard to get beyond the butyric. 44%

Whesskey Hessischer Whisky au Dinkel bott code DW 01-14 db (86) n21 t21.5 f22 b21.5.
Brimming with character, the oils ensure the flavours keep building to the sweet end. Gristy
at times, then more spicy as the oils accumulate. Plenty of burnt fudge as it progresses. 40%

BRENNEREI MACK, Gütenbach. Working

Kilpen Single Malt Malt Whisky Single Barrel bott code L14092108 (88) n21.5 the vague
heaviness of the still is perfectly countered by toffee and dates; t22.5 gorgeous spice and
barley mix. The sugars are half Demerara and half molasses; f22 more creamy toffee, but
beautifully spiced up; b22 attractively distilled and delightfully matured whisky. 40%

BRENNEREI ZIEGLER Freudenberg, North Württemberg. Working.

Aureum 1865 5 Year Old db (87) n21.5 t22 f21.5 b22. A tad feinty and nutty, but the huge
barley makes this entertaining and sweet in all the right places. 43%

Aureum 1865 2008 Cask Strength db (84.5) n21 t21.5 f21 b21. A massive whisky, in no
little part due to the very wide cut back in 2008. The usual nougat, hazelnut and cocoa gang
up in the thick oils. 53.9%

Aureum 1865 Château Lafite Rothschild casks, dist 2008, bott 2015 db (85) n20.5 t23 f20
b21.5. Tight, hard, grapey, beautifully sweet on delivery but with some furriness. 47%

Aureum 1865 Grave Digger 6 Year Old db (88) n22 salty and oily. Layers of molasses;
t22.5 a yielding delivery, soft with fertile malt. Mocha arrives early, a light feint buzz a little
later; f22 excellent spice; the mocha notes persist; b22 this grave digger goes deep. 43%

DESTILLERIE ARMIN JOBST E.K.Hammelburg. Working.

◇ **Single Malt Whisky 4 Jahre Holzfass** bott code: L SM Whisky 12 db (82) n19 t21 f21
b21 Incredibly sweet malt, as though the grist has been distilled into intense barley sugar candy.
The spirit suffers from a too generous cut, though the feinty nose proves a bark worse than
its bite. 43%.

◇ **Single Malt Whisky 5 Jahre Holzfass** bott code: L SM Whisky 16 db (80.5) n18 t20
f21.5 b21 Big feints means it takes a while before the rich malt is able to settle things down.
By comparison a lovely finish, but the nose and start leave something to be desired. 43%.

◇ **Whisky 5 Jahre Holzfass Sherry Cask** bott code: L 5 WhisSher 01:11 db (85) n20 t22
f22 b21 This distillery appears to specialise in remarkable whiskies that are loud, brash wrong
in so many ways yet strangely compelling and attractive. A clean sherry cask does all in its
power to inject an intense fruitiness, and succeeds. The spices are insane and the base spirit
is obviously eccentric. The result is a whisky you want on technical grounds to dislike but can't
help being dangerously attracted to. 46%.

◇ **Whisky 6 Jahre Holzfass Madeira Cask** bott code: L 6 WhisMad 06:10 db (82.5) n18.5
t22.5 f20 b21.5 Jolly well done and take a bow that Madeira cask. The grain itself offers little
that is positive but the soft golden syrup and grape carries a distinct charm. 46%.

◇ **Whisky 6 Jahre Holzfass Moscatel Cask** bott code: L 6 WhisMos 06:10 db (85) n19.5
t22 f21.5 b22 We know what to come to expect by now: a nose a few pfennigs short of a
Deutsche Mark, the entire currency of the whisky propped up by an outstanding cask. It really
is all about the grape here, which is clean and succulent, the oils and oak giving a kind of
chocolate and jam Swiss roll combo. 46%.

Whisky 9 Jahre Barrique Barrel Strength bott code: L 9 Whisky 17 db **(85.5) n19 t23 f22 b21.5** Another poor nose. But the delivery is like receiving a cherry pie bang in the kisser. Technically a bit of a miss, but for sheer chutzpah, a resounding hit. Outrageous fruity juiciness on delivery that has to be experienced to be believed, and spices are pretty bold, too. And there really is a degree of chocolate cherry tart to this... 48.7%.

DESTILLERIE HERMANN MÜHLHÄUSER Oberwälden. Working.
Mühlhäuser Oberwalder Single Grain bott code L0612 db **(86.5) n22 t22 f21 b21.5.** Enjoyable, showing sturdy and at times sophisticated oak and good early sugar structure. The grain is a bit on the shy side, though: may have had a better chance to shine at 46%. 40%
Mühlhäuser Schwäbischer Whisky aus Korn db **(90) n22.5 t23 f22 b22.5.** So different! If you are into this, it'll be pastoral perfection. 40%

DESTILLERIE & BRENNEREI MICHAEL HABBEL Sprockhövel. Working.
Hillock 4 1/2-12 bott code L4512 db **(88.5) n23.5 t22 f21 b22** On the nose I thought: wow! They've come up with a peatiness as close to an Islay style as I've ever seen in mainland Europe – watch out Scotland! Later I discovered that the whisky had been matured in ex-Islay casks. Either way, all rather lovely. 45%

DESTILLERIE RALF HAUER Bad Dürkheim. Working.
Saillt Mór Peated Torf Single Malt Whisky ex bourbon fass, fass-nr. 43, jahrgang 2013, gefüllt am 11/17 db **(92) n22** spices appear to be on equal par with the smoke, though they in turn trail the caramelised biscuit; **t23.5** ah, there we go....! As though someone has bottled the grist: the smoky malt is in its most dissolvable and sugary form. Vanillas and hearty, busy spices pad in the gaps; **f23** excellent oak counter play ensures a light treacle heaviness pins down the flightier phenols; **b23.5** at the best of times this distillery thinks it is planted in the Highlands of Scotland producing, as it does, one of the most Scottish of mainland European whiskies. It appears now to have removed itself to Islay – though it doesn't appear to have picked up the inherent saltiness on the way. Even so, another malty treat from Ralf Hauer – this time peated. Very. 59.8%. sc.
Saillt Mór Pfälze Eiche Single Malt Whisky ex-bourbon casks, fass-nr. 18 & 19, Jahrgang 2012, gefüllt m 11/16 db **(93) n23 t24 f22.5 b23.5** This distillery certainly knows how to make an impact. Gorgeous! 59.3%.
Saillt Mór Pfälze Eiche Single Malt Whisky fass-nr. 3 & 4, Jahrgang 2012, gefüllt m 1/16 db **(89.5) n21.5 t23.5 f22 b22.5** Not technically as well gifted as other malts I have encountered from this distillery. But enjoys a big, expansive personality. 46%.
Saillt Mór Pfälze Eiche Single Malt Whisky fass-nr. 21 & 22, Jahrgang 2013, gefüllt m 05/17 db **(91.5) n22.5 t23.5 f22.5 b23** A departure from the normal style with a massive oak injection here. Superb, though. 46%.
Saillt Mór Pfälzer Eiche Single Malt Whisky new Palatinate oak, dist 4-8 Sept 12, bott 2 Nov 2015 db **(94) n24 t23.5 f23 b23.5** One of the most Scottish of all European malts, having something of a Dalwhinnie/Clynelish/Highland Park constitution. Or maybe constitution is not a good term to use regarding anything European at the moment... 46%

DESTILLERIE RIEGER & HOFMEISTER Fellbach. Working.
Rieger & Hofmeister Schwäbischer Malt & Grain Whisky bott code LWMG06062016 db **(89.5) n21.5** not entirely happy, as the disjointed light nougat reveals; **t22.5** incredibly busy: a kind of small grain buzz with a gentle spice prickle adding shape to the chocolate nougat; **f23** now comes into its own as the malt goes up several notches in intensity; light milk chocolate and Demerara sugar, too; **b22.5** anyone who loves Milky Way chocolate will be a sucker for this 42%.
Rieger & Hofmeister Schwäbischer No. 4 sherryfass finished, bott code LWSF281117 db **(83.5) n21 t21.5 f20.5 b21** A wider cut than usual results in extra oils which make it hard work for the fruity notes to knit together as they might. 42%.
Rieger & Hofmeister Schwäbischer Rye Roggenmalz-Whisky bott code LWR281117 db **(95) n23.5** huge: the rye is of an intensity and weight only the malted variety can bring; a touch of green tea, too; **t24** fills the mouth with not just uncompromising, unambiguous rye – and all the juicy fruitiness that entails – but the startlingly brilliant grain simply pulses its single-minded intent; **f23.5** long with some Demerara notes still ensuring a degree of juiciness even this far in; late chalkier oak notes fit in with the master plan delightfully; **b24** a deliciously macho rye of the highest order. 42%.
Rieger & Hofmeister Schwäbischer Single Malt Whisky bott code LWSM26082015 db **(85) n21.5 t21 f21.5 b21** The malt hangs together well, improving in its stature as the intensity increases. Some mocha notes amid the late bitterness. 40%.

DESTILLERIE THOMAS SIPPEL Weisenheim am Berg. Working.

⬦ **Palatinatus Single Malt Whisky American Oak Peated 6 Years Old** db (92.5) n22.5 the smoke rolls in with confidence. Some spikey spices nip, but the peat kisses, sweetly...; t23.5 what can you say? But it is like being caressed by a thousand peaty wings...presumably from the angel's share. So soft...; f23 that feeling of gentle peat grist melting all over your taste buds continues; b23.5 a sure fire winner amongst peat lovers. Simplistic, maybe. But wonderfully effective and beautifully made. 45%. 218 bottles.

⬦ **Palatinatus Single Malt Whisky Bordeaux Single Cask 5 Years Old** db (81.5) n21.5 t21 f19.5 b20.5 Oddly enough, the wine cask may be sulphur-free, but not so sure about the original distillate. When the fruit shines, all is well. 57.8%. sc.

⬦ **Palatinatus Single Malt Whisky German Oak Single Cask 2013** db (85.5) n20.5 t22.5 f20.5 b22 Still a little cabbage water on the nose but the oak appears to already be ramping up the sugars. From the first moment that distinctive melt-in the mouth icing sugar bursts through, followed up by a more measured, gristier charm; long strands of vanilla and barley sugar; bitters out towards the end. Even so, thrilled that Thomas Sippel is still using German oak which I can now see does impart a unique sweetness to maturing malt. 45%. sc.

⬦ **Palatinatus Single Malt Whisky Port Single Cask 2013** db (81) n19 t21 f21 b20 You know all that effortless beauty and harmonisation displayed by their stunning, peated whisky. Well, this hasn't got it. The cut from the still was too wide and the big grape's attempt to find a balance with it has become like an Argentine football striker: a little messy. 45%. sc.

EDELBRÄENDE-SENFT Salem-Rickenbach. Working.

Senft Whisky bott code L-SW43, dist 2012, bott 2016 db (83.5) n19 t21 f22 b21.5 You have to laugh when you absent-mindedly nose a whisky, having mechanically opened it and poured... and then thought: "Senft!" without knowing what it actually was. This distillery does possess a unique character, especially on the nose, though here there is a little extra cabbage over the nougat. Recovers really well on the palate as the sugars claw back the balance. 42%. nc.

Senft Whisky bott code L-SW44, dist 2013, bott 2017 db (88) n22 t22 f22 b22 Boasts the usual Senft foibles, but light years ahead of their previous bottling. 42%. nc.

⬦ **Senft Whisky Edition 78** dist 2013, bott 2017, bott code: L-WE178 db (85) n19 t22.5 f21.5 b21.5 Absolutely true to the Senft house style, especially on the nose. Plenty of nougat knocking around but that wide cut has also grabbed some oils which beef up the sugars almost towards a meaty molasses. A very good chewing whisky. 47%. nc.

EDELBRENNEREI BISCHOF Wartmannsroth. Working.

Stark & Eigenwillig Rebell Der Whisky Single Grain Chestnut Barrel Finish db (93) n23 a series of spices and sugars not normally associated with oak, especially the mix of praline and marzipan; t23 seriously thick on the palate: again intense, vaguely nutty sugars moving towards a lighter Milky Way creaminess. The spices are precise, and also with a sweet edge; f23.5 heavy tannin late on but this morphs into a series of rich, high quality cocoa notes, accompanied perfectly by molasses; b23.5 I didn't need to be told chestnut maturation was involved here: just one sniff tells you all you need to know. 44%

EDELBRENNEREI DIRKER Mömbris. Working.

Dirker Blended Whisky Aged 3 Years bott code L L 15 db (87.5) n21 t22.5 f22 b22. Beautifully soft and viscous with a highly attractive fruit and nut theme. Even some rather excellent spices late on to keep the show going. Impressed. 45%

Dirker Whisky Aged 3 Years bourbon cask, bott code L E 15 db (81.5) n18 t22 f20.5 b21. After the boiled sprouts, unfriendly nose, recovers quickly and nimbly on the palate. The burst of sugars and gristy oils attractively repairs some of the damage. 53%

Dirker Whisky Aged 4 Years Sassicaia cask, bott code L A 16 db (80.5) n18.5 t22.5 f19 b20.5. A deeply frustrating whisky. This is one exceptionally beautiful cask at work here and - in the mid ground - offers all kinds of toffee apple and muscovado-sweetened mocha. Sadly, the initial spirit wasn't up to the barrel's standard. This really needs some cleaning up. 53%

EIFEL DESTILLATE Koblenz. Working.

⬦ **Eifel Whisky Duo Malt & Peat 2018** ex-Bordeaux American oak barrique, dest 2012, bott 2018 db (89) n22 the peat has the feel of very distant smoke drifting over a Scottish coastal village; t23 huge fruit delivery: moist sultana cake...perhaps having once been aflame...; f22 back to that saltiness evident on the nose; b22 rarely subtle. But always delicious. 50%.

⬦ **Eifel Malt Whisky Regional Serie Hohes Venn Quartett** first fill Bordeaux cask, dest 2012, bott 2017 db (80.5) n21 t20.5 f19 b20 Good cask. The spirit, sadly, doesn't quite match it. 46%.

◇◇ **Eifel Roggen Whisky Regional Serie Ahrtaler** first fill Pinot Noir Barrique db **(94)** n23 the rye has plays a surprisingly big part here, despite the richness of the grape; t24 the best delivery of the day! Sweet ultra-ripe grape and maple syrup part for a moment for the grain to have its firm, clean say. The mid ground is the rye reasserting its presence...superb! f23.5 fruit chocolate; b23.5 Eifel have found a number of ways for their rye whisky to appear in some fascinating and delicious situations. 46%.

◇◇ **Eifel Whisky Signature Serie Single Rye** ex-Rotwein cask db **(86)** n21.5 t22 f21 b21.5 A little disappointing as the rye doesn't sparkle as usual, save for the odd moment about third or flavour fourth wave in. The fruit is enormous, but a shade too loose. 50%.

◇◇ **Eifel Whisky Single Malt 2018** refill bourbon barrels, oloroso finish dest 2012, bott 2018 db **(91)** n22.5 quite a few bourbon pointers with the tannins sharp, business-like and hickory minded. The grape which washes over it rounds the more jagged edges; t22.5 like some kind of flying carpet, the fruit magically floats above the deeper, eye-wateringly intense tannin. When the lush grape lands we find peppery addition to the fruit and chocolate middle; f23 keeps on a beautiful mocha course; b23 unlike the sherry and peat combination, which struggles for balance, this combination works far more dextrously, the big tannin feeling at home in grapey company. 50%.

◇◇ **Eifel Whisky Single Malt & Peat 2018** ex-Bordeaux barrique, dest 2012, bott 2017 db **(86.5)** n23 t21 f21.5 b21 On the nose, outwardly similar to their Duo bottling, except the peat is crustier, drier and sootier; but that is one brutal fruit and peat explosion on delivery...youch! This is a towering malt from Eifel: a not remotely subtle whisky designed for those looking for effect over beauty. 50%.

Eifel Whisky Single Rye rum cask, dist 2012, bott 2017 db **(93)** n23 t23.5 f23 b23.5 There is probably only one thing that can make a whisky more brittle on the palate than distilling from rye. And that is to put it in a rum cask... What an inspired idea this is! Oh, and this is the 778th whisky I have tasted for my 2018 Bible...and the first to make me cough..! 50%. nc ncf sc.

◇◇ **Eifel Whisky Single Rye 2018** ex-Bordeaux American oak barrique, dest 2013, bott 2018 db **(92.5)** n23 a busy fruitiness with mainly over-ripe plums at work, but the distant squawk of crisp rye fruit, too...; t23 enormous. The palate is engulfed by muscovado sugars and Manuka honey, both thinned by the madcap juiciness of the exploding grape. The rye's own fruity contribution is mainly lost in the onslaught; f23 still a lot of wine hanging around...; b23.5 after a succession of poor whiskies from elsewhere, I needed a restorative so made a beeline for this: Eifel do rye rather well. The rye grain itself is not so vividly expressed as in the past, perhaps because of an over-enthusiastic wine barrique. But after some of the whiskies of before, this is nectar... 50%.

◇◇ **Eifel Whisky Triple Malt 2018** refurbished French oak barrique, dest 2012, bott 2018 db **(86.5)** n21.5 t22 f21 b22 Relentlessly fruity, the entertainment comes from the complexity on delivery where spices take on the grape, backed further by a toasty oakiness. The grape wins. 50%.

◇◇ **Eifel Weizenmalz Whisky Regional Serie Moseltaler** first fill Weisswein Barrique db **(87)** n20.5 t23 f21.5 b22 Though the off-key nose promises little, the delivery and follow through are a pleasant surprise. Indeed, the very first notes offer a satisfying and beautifully balanced intensity, allowing the grape and spice full freedom. The finish reveals an expected patchiness. 46%.

FEINDESTILLERIE BÜCHNER Langenbogen. Working

Büchner Single Malt db **(89)** n22.5 superb malt: clean and alive with gristy sugars. Refreshing and sexy; t22 light oils, but never enough to discourage the barley from showing to full effect; f22.5 those oils confirm the wider cut, but celebrate their extra body with a malty, spicy display of defiance; b22 a wonderfully characterful and enjoyable malt. 43%

FINCH WHISKYDESTILLERIE Nellingen, Alb-Donau. Working.

Finch Schwäbischer Highland Whisky Dinkel Port bott code LA0011 db **(85)** n20.5 t22.5 f21 b21 Finch, usually, offers a whisky which either flies pretty high or crash lands. This year we have two additions to their range which do neither, or both –depending how you look at it. This one gets off to a faltering start with far too much oil from the cut apparent on the nose. But the lush Port helps fills the cracks though those big oils return late on. 42%.

◇◇ **Finch Schwäbischer Hochland Whisky Barrel Proof** bott code LA0006 db **(92)** n23 seems as though some wine finishing has been indulged in here: port springs to mind as there is a just-so spice nip accompanying the grape; superb weight and balance; t23 at last! A Finch with a texture that does it justice. Heather honey and muscovado sugars combine brilliantly to accompany the fruitcake; the spices initially take no prisoners, but calm down...; f22.5 evidence of more than one cask at play here as a light liquorice tag offers extra depth to the vanilla and fruity butterscotch; b23.5 I think Finch have cracked it. Previous bottlings had been a 42% abv, allowing the oils to shatter and the narrative of the whisky to become disjointed when the water was added for reduction. This whisky is far happier at full strength...and now so am I... 54%.

Finch Schwäbischer Hockland Whisky Destillers Edition bott code LA0013 db **(87)** n22 t22 f21 b22 Firm and busy, all kind of muscovado sugars and caramels fill the palate with lush good intent. The finish bitters quite abruptly, but the clever sugar-spice mix leading up to this is worth experiencing. 42%.

⬦ **Finch Schwäbischer Hochland Whisky One Decade** bott code L18026 db **(87.5)** n21 t23 f21.5 b22 A slight weakness to the distillate – evident on both nose and finish - is royally compensated for by the lush sugars and chewable oils which act more than just sticking plaster. Big and fun! 51%. sc. 372 bottles.

⬦ **Finch Single Malt Kronberger Genuss-Messe 2017 4 Years & 353 Days** sherry cask db **(94.5)** n23.5 so rare to find sherry influence this intense and intact: a youthful freshness to the grape matched only by the grain; no shortage of diced Granny Smith apples and light honey, also..; t23.5 the palate is instantly coated with gratuitous grape, but this soon calms so a narrative is devised. Wonderful, sensual intertwangling between the almost must-like grape and concentrated barley making for a thick and brooding middle; a blend of Manuka honey and muscovado sugar fills in the late middle... f23.5 ...and start of the finish. The taste buds are massaged with gentle spices, though the grape, clean and still confident, is never far away; b24 a clean sherry butt to be applauded and an overall experience to be savoured. 58%. sc. 81 bottles. Bottled for Taste-ination.

GUTSBRENNEREI JOH. B. GEUTING Bocholt. Working.

J.B.G Münsterländer Single Grain Aged 6 Years American white oak, cask nos. 26,27 & 28, dist 12 Nov 10, bott 20 Mar 17 db **(86)** n21 t22 f21.5 b21.5 The house nougat and chocolate style is out in force here: the wide cut does offer a verdant note but the delivery is massively juicy and chewy. 42%. 1,000 bottles.

⬦ **J.B.G Münsterländer Single Grain Whisky Aged 7 Years** oloroso casks, cask nos. 9,10 & 29, dist 12 Nov 11, bott 20 Feb 18 db **(89.5)** n22 acceptable light nougat bursts at the seams with raisin and sultana; good oak structure; t23 as soft a delivery as it is possible to find. Rich textured, salivating with a gentle build of cream sherry tones, mingling with the polite vanillas: not unlike a sherry trifle, in fact... f22 even a little late feint can't detract from the spice and custard...; b22.5 probably the best distillation I have seen from this distillery with the cuts being more on the mark, while the oloroso butts are clean and drip enticingly with grape. 42%. 1,036 bottles.

J.B.G Münsterländer Single Malt American white oak, cask nos. 148, 149, 150 & 151, dist 12 Mar 13, bott 27 Apr 17 db **(87.5)** n22 t22 f21.5 b22 By the time they had got round to distilling malt for this, it is obvious that they had learned to control their cuts a bit better. So not so much nougat and chewy oils here. A lighter malt altogether with the barley far more vocal though the dry, spiced finale does offer something for the nougat fans to grip on to. 43%. 1,319 bottles.

J.B.G Münsterländer Single Malt sherry Oloroso & sherry Pedro Xienez, cask nos. 3 0 & 2 PX, dist 22 Jan 14, bott 13 Mar 17 db **(85)** n19 t23 f21 b22 This is a bit like a puppy which really wants you to like it. The delivery is playful and charming, the faultless grape making all the right noises; your palate is licked by lovable fruit notes and the spices are lovely. But none of this can make up for the feints which do few favours for the finish and even less for the nose. Excellent non-sulphured sherry casks, though. 43%. 1,692 bottles.

HAMMERSCHMIEDE Zorge. Working.

⬦ **The Alrik Harz Mountain Single Malt The Handfilled** triple cask, bott 7 May 18, bott no.1827 db **(91)** n22 one of the most fruity yet salty aromas I have encountered for a while: deliciously different; t23 again, this screams the sea: light saline compounds work beautifully with a mix of heather honey and intense malt; really impressive oaky-vanilla tones, also...; f22.5 salty milk chocolate with a malty twist; b23.5 mountains...? Germany...? This is one of the most coastal–style whiskies I have tasted in weeks...! Very different. But never less than delightful. 53%. nc ncf sc. 145 bottles.

⬦ **The Glen Els Château d'Yquem Sauternes Casks Aged 5 Years** dist 2012, bott 2017, bott code. 1795 db **(69)** n16 t19 f17 b17 A d'Yquem mass required: this has been murdered by sulphur. 56%. nc ncf. 384 bottles.

⬦ **The Glen Els Claret Aged 5 Years** cask 439, dist 15 Apr 13, bott 17 Apr 18, bott code. 1871 db **(95.5)** n24.5 a deep nose, one not given to cliché. Unusual in its weight and depth and seemingly changing its stance with each separate sniff. At times the spices appear to be an appendage, at others its leads; likewise the grape appears to be full-hearted, lusty and rich, at other moments lighter and sugar dominant; the malt may sometimes snaffle around, or it may come in a more intense, subtly phenolic cloud. One of my favourite European noses this year; t23.5 see my nosing notes: now translate that to taste, except add a brilliant degree of juiciness...and a surprising life to spice middle; f23.5 fades on the same theme, with spices slightly more acute and the chocolate making delicious inroads; b24 heartily recommended by me to my many old friends at Burnley Football Club. One of the most complex and beautiful European whiskies this year. 57.7%. nc ncf sc. 258 bottles.

◆ **The Glen Els Edition Boudoir** db **(92.5)** n23 date and walnut soup; t23.5 a luxurious mouth feel, further developed by treacle tart: it was always likely a tart might find its way into this whisky...; the mid ground is occupied by a massive spice explosion; f23 some oak bitterness late on but the palate is diverted by a continuation of the big spice; b23 if you find anything spicier in the sack than this, good luck to you... 51.73%. 695 bottles.

◆ **The Glen Els The Handfilled Sherry Firkin Ltd Release** cask no. 872, bott 5 Apr 18, bott code. 1807 db **(91)** n23 there's some spice in that fruitcake..; fruit, too...; t23 succulent and attractive mouth feel: chewy despite the big juiciness. The fruit gets sweeter and matters juicier as the malt progresses; f22; decent spice; the malt is expected but an oaky bitterness arrives; b23 big, clean and fruity and very big, but makes only limited efforts to the complexity front. 53.2%. nc ncf sc. 62 bottles.

◆ **The Glen Els The Journey Distiller's Cut** bott code. 1807 db **(73)** n18 t19.5 f17 b18.5 Glen Els has done the European whisky project proud this year with some malts of exquisite beauty. A poor cask at work here means, sadly, this isn't one of them... 57.7%. nc ncf. 1,000 bottles. 2018 Edition.

◆ **The Glen Els PX Sherry Casks Aged 10 Years** bott code. 1708 db **(94)** n22.5 forceful, rich grape; slightly off key and awkward but enough grain and grape interacting to make this interesting; t24 no doubting the sherry type now: the intense sugars fills every hole vacated by either grain or oak; thick-textured and pleasingly lush, though the malt has its moment towards the late middle; f23.5 settles into a fruity treacle persona; b24 anyone who regularly reads the Whisky Bible is well acquainted with my views on PX casks: a lot more trouble than they are worth. Have to say, though, that this little (or perhaps I should say big) charmer dramatically bucks the trend: this must have been one hell of an unsullied PX butt..; 49.6%. nc ncf. 750 bottles.

◆ **The Glen Els Tokaji Casks Aged 5 Years** dist 2012, bott 2017, bott code. 1798 db **(76)** n19 t20 f18 b19 Before tasting this, I think I could count the number of successful Tokaji-matured whiskies from around the world on one hand. Sadly, I still can. Incredibly tight, the sugars and salt – and something else besides - bite hard. 55.5%. nc ncf. 472 bottles.

HAUSBRAUEREI ALTSTADTHOF Nürnberg. Working.

Ayrer's Bourbon Barrel Aged Organic Single Malt db **(87)** n22.5 t22.5 f21 b21. A slightly wide cut here has undone some supreme work by the casks. And at 51% abv, close to a Kentucky 101, has just the right mouth feel for the light liquorice and ulmo honey on display. But when so little metal is apparent in the spirit, those cuts have to be as clean as a whistle. 51%

Ayrer's PX Sherry Cask Finished Organic Single Malt dist 2009 db **(90)** n22 t22.5 f23 b22.5 Always brave to use PX, as the intensity of the sugars can sometimes put the malt into the tightest of straight-jackets. However, this is fine, sulphur-free butt and is eventually relaxed enough for the malt to share equal billing once it finds its rhythm. 56%

Ayrer's Red Organic Single Malt db **(86)** n21.5 t22 f21 b21.5. Quite dry and niggardly in places, a degree of chalkiness on the nose and delivery slightly undoing the sugars as they attempt to soar. Pleasant enough, but never quite gets into stride. 43%

Ayrer's Red Organic Single Malt db **(90.5)** n22.5 t22.5 f22.5 b23 An impressive malt, probably benefitting from the full strength, as the unbroken oils play a leading role in length and balance. 58%

Ayrer's White Organic Single Malt db **(86)** n21.5 t22 f21 b21.5. An attractive enough new make with good cut points, particularly hitting the heights with a big sugar surge in the mid-ground. But in this naked form, reveals a slight shortage of copper in the system. 46%

HINRICUS NOYTE´S-BRAUHAUS AM LOHBERG Wismar. Working.

Baltach Wismarian Single Malt Whisky db **(83)** n20.5 t21 f20.5 b21. Needs a defter touch on the still to ensure those hefty oils don't get through. Some decent redeeming honey, though. Fascinating light curry on the nose! 43%

KAUZEN-BRÄU Ochsenfurt. Working.

◆ **Old Owl Feinster Fränkischer Single Malt Whisky** dest 08/2013, abgef 11/2017 **(87.5)** n22 t22.5 f21 b22 The barley is attractive and intense; enormous caramels coat the palate, a little spiced molasses offering an alternative, darker sweetness. A little oily late on (unlike a previous bottling of theirs I tasted), this is an attractive, untaxing single malt. 46%.

KINZIGBRENNEREI MARTIN BROSAMER Biberach. Working.

Kinzigtäler Whisky Single Malt Smoke db (88.5) n21.5 t22.5 f22 b22.5 The phenols have much to say. 42%

KLEINBRENNEREI FITZKE Herbolzheim-Broggingen. Working.

Derrina Dinkelmalz Schwarzwälder Single Malt Whisky bott code L 5512 db (87.5) n21.5 t22.5 f21.5 b21.5 Lovely whisky of the salivating – indeed, eye-watering - kind, though struggles to find a way of completely controlling the distinctive spelt sharpness. 43%

⬩ **Derrina Emmermalz Schwarzwälder Single Malt Whisky** bott code L 6812 db (87) n22 t22 f21 b22 An usual flight path for the fascinating, occasionally wheat-spiced, sough dough flavours. Grounded slightly, though, by a little excess oil; 43%

Derrina Gerstenmalz Schwarzwälder Single Malt Whisky bott code L 5412 db (74) n18 t19 f18 b19 You know this distillery, for all its usual brilliance, is going to bottle you a fail at some stage...and this is it! 43%

⬩ **Derrina Gerstenmalz Torfrauch "Leicht" Schwarzwälder Single Malt Whisky** bott code L 11313 db (89.5) n23 a light smokiness to the intense barley sugar; t22 soft and chewy, a charming gristiness keeps the proceedings sweet and fluffy; f22 a mild house bitterness has crept in. But the light phenols ensure a delightful earthiness and impressive length; a light liquorice depth, also; b22.5 understated yet quietly resolute complexity. 43%

⬩ **Derrina Hafermalz Schwarzwälder Single Malt Whisky** bott code L 6712 db (89) n23 around my remote village are many fields of oats: and this has the sweet, evocative aroma of walking through them after harvest; a mixture of straw and crushed grains between your finger and thumb; t22.5 salivating and two toned: a bit like a rye in being both hard and soft simultaneously, wheat for burst pepperiness and barley for its juiciness; f21.5 a little dry and bitter; b22 oats for lunch, oats for my whisky but, sadly, as this is prime Whisky Bible time, when a headcold has to be avoided like the plague, no oats when I get to bed tonight.... 43%

Derrina Kamut Ur-Weizen Schwarzwälder Single Grain Whisky bott code L 12112 db (93.5) n23.5 t23.5 f23 b23.5 Give this whisky time in the glass, let it breathe, apply a little heat and....wow! 43%

Derrina Purpur Ur-Weizen Schwarzwälder Single Grain Whisky bott code L 14012 db (95.5) n23.5 t24 f24 b24 This distillery does wheat whisky a lot better than most... 43%

⬩ **Derrina Roggenmalz Schwarzwälder Single Malt Whisky** bott code L 5613 db (91) n22.5 fat and oily but the fruity rye bathes also in a sea of oak-dried butterscotch and honey tart (I once got a chef to make this to my instruction – sublime and very whisky-ish) t23 much sweeter on delivery than the oak threatens on the nose, though this honeyed gloss soon dulls as the oils kick in...then the building rye; f22.5 long, surprisingly nutty with a liquorice lick to the oily grain; b23 a slightly wider cut than their last improbably beautiful rye, but the grain still shines through like a beacon. 43%

Derrina Waldstauden Ur-Roggen Schwarzwälder Single Grain Whisky bott code L 13612 db (85) n19 t21.5 f23 b21.5 The one thing I will say about the Derrina Rye, is that is not just an odd fellow, but a unique one for its type. The house green style does few favours to the nose. But at least this version opens out on the palate, though through a big oily wall. The Manuka honey and recognisable rye on the finish works beautifully well with the late spices. 43%

Derrina Weizenmalz Schwarzwälder Single Malt Whisky bott code L 5712 db (89.5) n22.5 t22 f22.5 b22.5 What I adore about this distillery is that you never quite know what is coming out of the bottle – but with the incentive that when it is good it is truly magnificent. This is a slightly unusual mid-range for them – but veering towards brilliant. 43%

KYMSEE WHISKY Grabenstätt. Working.

Kymsee Der Chiemsee Single Malt Whisky cask no. 2, dist Dec 2012 db (87.5) n21 t23 f22 b21.5. A fascinating malt. When sweet, it is very sweet with the molasses piled on thick. When it is bitter, it is so in a way which undermines the sweetness, rather than balancing with it. And the spices are borderline aggressive. Pleasant, and impressively distilled. But still a bit of an odd ball. 42%. sc.

⬩ **Kymsee Der Chiemsee-Whisky Single Malt** fass nr. 12, dest Dec 14 db (87) n22 t22 f21.5 b21.5 As usual, an attractive and competent malt from Kymsee. The barley and oak support each other deliciously early on but the increasing dryness does reveal an overall lack of sugars. 42%

Kymsee Der Chiemsee-Whisky Single Malt Quarter Cask Finish fass nr. 1, dest May 13 db (88) n22 earthy and floral - like walking through woods that the sun can rarely penetrate; t22.5 a gabbling sweetness – semi-lurid white sugar in a French-toasty kind of way...; f22 an amazing degree of natural caramels before a little bitterness closes in...; b21.5 Kymsee have a very unusual way of doing things in the bottle. The marks as much for fascination as effect... 42%

Kymsee Der Chiemsee-Whisky Single Malt Quarter Cask Finish fass nr. 2, dest Dec 13 db (82.5) n19 t21 f21.5 b21 Malty and nutty. But perhaps not Kymsee's finest-ever distillate. 42%.

Kymsee Der Chiemsee-Whisky Single Malt Sherry Cask Finish fass nr. 1, dest May 13 db (85) n20 t22 f21.5 b21.5 The sherry, though rich and profound in its sultana and sticky suet pudding intent, plays second fiddle to the generous oils from the cut. 42%.

Kymsee Der Chiemsee-Whisky Single Malt Sherry Cask Finish fass nr. 2, dest Dec 14 db (91) n22.5 massive clean grape: thickset nose with a slightly salty edge; t23 delightful delivery: both malt and grape are at full throttle, the spices helping to set up a juicy, salivating element despite the mid-ground drying by the moment; f22.5 dry, vaguely salty marzipan with the lightest hint of sultana; b23 well balanced, elegant and satisfying. 42%.

MARDER EDELBRÄNDE Albbruck-Unteralpfen. Working.

Marder Single Malt Whisky Aged 3 Years bott 2015 db (92) n22.5 t23.5 f23 b23 Very attractive whisky with plenty of character and complexity. 43%

Marder Single Malt 3 Years Old bott 2017, bott code L 2017 MARDER db (88) n22 has kept the house marmalade style, which I remember so clearly from the last time I tasted this malt a couple of years back; salty, too; t23 immediate spice kick, even before the big malt has had a chance to settle; f21.5 a little oily now with caramel and vanilla joining forces; a tad bitter, also; b21.5 pleasant, though the vague bitter thread does knock the sugars out of true slightly. 43%.

Marder Single Malt Black Forest Reserve Cask No. 90 Single Malt 5 Years Old db (91) n22.5 exceptionally nutty and malty; orange blossom honey sweetens; t23 some serious spiced chocolate, pepped up with a huge malty middle; f22.5 an attractive late treacle injection counters a late bitterness; b23 this malty monster sits prettily on the palate. 54.6%. 369 bottles.

MÄRKISCHE SPEZIALITÄTEN BRENNEREI Hagen. Working.

DeCavo Handcrafted Single Malt Höhlenwhisky Fass-Nr. L 3 db (89) n22 t23.5 f21 b22.5 Certainly knows how to make an impact...! 43%. sc. 262 bottles.

DeCavo Handcrafted Single Malt Fass-Nr. L 13 db (87) n22 t22 f21 b22. A tame malt. First gristy, then a more complex development of vanilla and lighter, friendly sugars.46%. sc.

DeCavo Handcrafted Single Malt Fass-Nr. L 13 db (91) n22 t23 f23 b23 An astonishingly lush malt with an almost three dimensional sugar attack. Wow! 55%. sc.

Edelstahl Moonshiner White Single Malt bott code. L1/2015 db (87) n20.5 t23 f21.5 b22. The nose reveals just a little less copper than is desired, but the cut is a sound one: feint free and teaming with delicious, viscous malt and light ulmo honey. Attractive. 50%. sc.

DeCavo Single Malt Höhlenwhisky fassbelegung 2/2014, fass-nr L 22 db (82) n20 t21.5 f21 b20.5 Malty but the bitterish sub plot is never far from the surface. 473%.

DeCavo Single Malt Höhlenwhisky fassbelegung 3/2014, fass-nr L 14 db (89.5) n22.5 a little coconut on the gristy sweetness; t23 even bigger grist on the delivery: icing sugar at work before the malt kicks in with a healthy and confident surge: thick and tasty middle; f21.5 just bitters slightly despite the sugary attention; b22.5 sugars n so many levels and at different intensities. Impressive! 59.7%.

NORDPFALZ BRENNEREI Höning. Working.

Taranis Pfälzer Single Malt Whisky 3 Years Old port cask finish, dist Aug 13 db (88.5) n21 t22.5 f22.5 b22.5 A deliciously rich and juicy malt benefitting from an outstanding port cask. 50.1%. 213 bottles.

Taranis Pfälzer Single Malt Whisky 3.5 Years Old chestnut cask finish, dist Sept13 db (92.5) n22.5 chocolate nougat par excellance...; t23.5 this is where the cask type kicks in – forcibly, without apology - and comes into its own. As it settles, chocolate digestive biscuit. Milk, of course...; f23 the more blatant tannins still hold office and while the cocoa now fades – slowly – a saltier ginger element comes in to play; b23.5 very different and strikingly attractive in its own right. 51.4%. 480 bottles.

NUMBER NINE SPIRITUOSENMANUFAKTUR
Leinefelde-Worbis, Working.

The Nine Springs Single Malt Whisky Age 3 Years batch no. 5 db (86.5) n19 t23 f22 b21.5 An attractive whisky, though the nose isn't entirely happy. Exceptionally sweet delivery with some serious maple syrup moments. Some red and black liquorice which underlines the bourbon-style which by the time it is in full flow late on, makes up a lot of the ground lost by the off- key nose and delivery. One careful cut away from being a classic. 45%. nc ncf.

⬦ **The Nine Springs Single Malt Whisky Cask Pineau Des Charentes** cask no. 119 db **(87.5) n20 t23.5 f22 b22** The wine gives a charming polish to this malt −once on the palate. The grape is too light to make a telling difference to the off-key nose. But the spices fizz and marmalade covers the buttered toast rather beautifully. *57.9%. nc ncf sc.*

⬦ **The Nine Springs Single Malt Whisky Peated Breeze Edition** Muscatel wine cask db **(95) n23** such clean grape: aligned to a mix of maple syrup and muscovado sugars; and as the clarity of the grape grows so, too, does the smoke element, which makes it mark with commendable subtlety; **t24** such a sumptuous mouth feel: it is impossible to ask for more. The grape merges with the malt without a single join noticeable; the fruit of a moist Milton Hunt cake disposition, especially as the toastier notes grow in stature. Meanwhile, the smoke massages...; **f24** long, the spices working through the varying levels of fruit and smoke as the complexity, if anything, increases; **b24** this is how fruit and peat can work together - just exploding with flavour. Beautiful! *49%. nc ncf.*

SAUERLÄNDER EDELBRENNEREI Ruthen-Kallenhardt. Working.
Thousand Mountains Mc Raven Single Malt Whisky cask no. L1003 03.2012 db **(74.5) n16 t21 f18.5 b19**. A massively wide cut means this is a gluepot of a whisky. Best ignore the nose and concentrate on the delivery which has its magnificently sugared moments. But, as is to be expected, an oily, untamed beast. *46.2%*

SCHLENKERLA Bamberg, Working.
Schlenkerla (79.5) n21 t18.5 f21 b19. Very much more like German lebkuchen biscuit/cake than whisky. Soft, vaguely phenolic, gingery and friendly − and the finish is surprisingly lovely, especially after the chaotic and confusing opening. A challenging whisky to say the least. *40%*

SEVERIN SIMON Alzenau-Michelbach, Aschaffenburg. Working.
Simon's Bavarian Pure Pott Still db **(86) n21 t22 f21 b22**. Always great to renew acquaintances with this idiosyncratic malt. I remember lots of pine last time out. Here the pine is remarkable for its almost lack of interest in this whisky after the nose. Which means this is a better bottling, with the malt − man marked by crisp sugars − having a much louder say than normal. Some soft, creamy toffee and nougat at play. But the spices and barley are most enjoyable. *40%*

SLYRS Schliersee-Neuhaus. Working.
Slyrs Bavarian Single Malt Sherry Edition No. 1 finished in Oloroso, lot no. L00354, bott 2013 **(86) n20 t22 f22 b22**. Anyone out there who loves cream toffee and spice? This malt has your name on it. *46%*

That Boutique-y Whisky Company Slyrs 3 Year Old (94.5) n24 beautifully clean, thumping, in-your-face barley; the light citrus background adds even more clarity; **t23.5** good grief! I'm not sure I have ever seen Slyrs in more malt-dominating mode; a background of grist and lemon drops enlivens the palate further; **f23.5** the vanillas rise slightly, but it is all about the fading malt; **b23.5** from the ultra-intense school of whisky. A malt-lover's dream and the most Scottish style dram they have yet produced. *52.5%. 691 bottles.*

SPERBERS DESTILLERIE Rentweinsdorf. Working.
Sperbers Destillerie Malt Whisky Anno 2010 los-nr. 40 db **(86.5) n21.5 t22 f21.5 b21.5**. One gets the distinct feeling this was distilled to a pretty high strength before being put into cask. Hard to spot the malt, but plenty of tannins from the oak. Still, quite delicious! *59%*

SPREEWÄLD BRENNEREI Schlepzig. Working.
Spreewälder Sloupisti Single Malt Whisky dist Oct 11, bott Mar 16 db **(94) n23 t23.5 f24 b23.5** Absolutely my best whisky of the day! And with its portrayal of a stork in a bow tie and top hat, probably the best label of the year! My kind of whisky; my kind of distillery...!! *68.5%*

SPREEWOOD DISTILLERS GMBH Schlepzig. Working.
⬦ **Stork Club Single Cask Whiskey 1207 Days** ex Bordeaux cask, cask no. 173, bott 13-11-17 db **(82.5) n20 t21.5 f20 b21** A tight, eye-watering whisky which steadfastly refuses to open beyond the gripping sugars and the restricting fruit. A little late coffee does it no harm at all, especially as the weakness of the cask become more evident. *55%. ncf sc. 860 bottles.*

⬦ **Stork Club Single Malt Whiskey** ex-bourbon, ex-sherry & ex-Weißwein casks, lot no. 008543 L002 db **(88.5) n22.5** the grape hangs off the nose like an apple hangs from the tree: easy to spot and full of tempting possibilities, some of them dangerous...; **t22.5** again, bit soft fruit on delivery: muscovado sugars about, then a praline and vanilla wafer middle; f21 a late off note from the sherry; plenty of delicate spice buzz, though..; b22.5 not a faultless sherry butt. But one that offers more ticks than crosses. 47%. ncf.

⬥ **Stork Club Straight Rye Whiskey** ex-bourbon & ex-Weißwein casks, batch no.2, lot no. 001030 5317 db (92) n23 some dulcet fruit and honey tones sit comfortably with the sharper grain notes; some decent oaky marzipan, too; t23.5 so salivating! lots of copper in the system here, as though a new still is at work. That metallic kick sits comfortably with the crisp grain; f22 a little tang on the finale; b23.5 despite the spelling of whiskey not to be confused with the American definition of a Straight Rye: the Weisswein cask sees to that! And I doubt if it is virgin American oak in play, either. That said, no faulting the overall composition of a rather lovely rye whisky – straight or otherwise 55%. ncf.

ST. KILIAN DISTILLERS GMBH Rüdenau. Working.

St. Kilian Distillers Turf Dog los-nummer: 161115 db (91) n23 t23 f22 b23 The smoke, naturally, dominates like a hill-topping Schloss looking benevolently down upon the cowering village below. But there appears to be something of an uprising as first a metallic then a cocoa and molasses intensity begin to look for parity. Entertaining new make. 49.9%. 499 bottles.

St. Kilian Distillers White Dog los-nummer: 160630 db (91.5) n23.5 t23 f22.5 b22.5 A very competently made malt spirit. Reducing the new make – the white dog – to 43%abv means that the oils are broken down and the metallic element is a little more naked, resulting in a slightly lumpy finish and the grain not quite so in tune. Even so, very good indeed! 43%.

St. Kilian Distillers White Dog Cask Strength los-nummer: 160801 db (94.5) n23.5 t24 f23.5 b23.5 At near natural strength the oils ensure a fabulous harmony between the barley and copper, ensuring a rich, chewy, salivating experience and uninterrupted, balancing, sugars. Whoever manned – or womaned – the still certainly knew exactly where the centre cut was. A real thoroughbred doggie! 63.5%.

⬥ **The Spirit of St. Kilian Single Malt Batch No. 1 18 Months Old** Garrison Brothers Distillery bourbon quarter casks, dist Apr 16, los-no 17 11 08 db (92) n22.5 t22.5 f23.5 b23.5 when, 15 years ago, I began writing the first-ever edition of the Whisky Bible, there were very few American microdistilleries and hardly many more European ones. And the appalling whisky establishment which existed in those days – predominantly arrogant, snobbish Scotch whisky know-nothings - rounded on me for daring to include this little known dram in the same book as their fabled single malts. Well, looks as though we have come full circle in a way: a European micro maturing whisky in casks from an American micro. Now that's what I call a neat whisky...or would be if it were twice the age. However this maturing malt spirit is an absolute charmer: youthful, for sure, but has picked up enough buttery notes to five the intense barley a beautiful lustre. The praline spread finish is sublime. What in impressive distillery this is. 47%.

⬥ **The Spirit of St. Kilian Single Malt Batch No. 2 15 Months Old** American standard barrels, dist 2016, los-no 180222 db (94.5) n23 t23.5 f24 b24 Another astonishing example of deliciously complex maturing mate make which suggests this distillery has what it takes to become one of the finest on mainland Europe. The secret is the integrity of the spirit – beautifully cut with little or no feints to be found. Next, they have sourced great oak. Put the two together – and you get this: a proudly and unambiguously malty young number full of barley passion and luxuriating in an oak-fed chocolate fest. Brilliant. 46%.

⬥ **The Spirit of St. Kilian Single Malt Batch No. 3 8 Months Old** 30 Liter Jamaica rum casks, dist 2017, los-no 180312 db (94) n23.5 t22.5 f24 b24 Seriously: who needs a spirit to travel three years in a cask to be called whisky when at eight months something beautiful and dynamic is fit for savouring? The esters on shew remind me of a mix between Long Pond and Hampden, starting boringly and with a hint of honey on the nose, quietening on delivery, but then tht stunning mix of esters and malt taking off for a late middle and finish that will blow you away. Glorious! 44.5%. 832 bottles.

STEINHAUSER 1. BODENSEE-WHISKY-DESTILLERIE Kressbronn. Working.

Brigantia 3 Years Old bott L-12/12 db (79) n19 t21 f19 b20 Huge malt statement, as is the distillery style. But it appears someone decided to try and extract as much spirit as possible, because the cut seems to be a little too wide for comfort here: the oils are unforgiving. 43%

WEINGUT MÖßLEIN Kolitzheim. Working.

M Mößlein Fränkischer Single Malt Whisky 5 Jahre fass nr. 5, bott code. L730-1-15 db (85) n21 t22 f21 b21. More comfortable with the single malt than with the grain, though better cut point selection has helped. Even so, the oils are still big on this while the light liquorice works well with the buzzing spices. 41%. sc.

WHISKY-DESTILLERIE DREXLER Arrach. Working.

Bayerwold Pure Rye Malt Whisky dest Aug 13, abge Sept 17 db **(83) n19.5 t22.5 f20 b21** The feints steer much of the course for this sweet rye but when the grain itself is heard loud and clear there are moments rye lovers will cherish. Just could do with them lasting a bit longer... *42%. 215 bottles.*

Bayerwold Single Malt Whisky dest Aug 13, abge Sept 17 db **(86) n19 t22.5 f22.5 b22** Right out of the Drexler school of ultra-intense whiskies. The feintiness is a bit too much on the nose, but I doff my Panama to the way they have orchestrated the delicious chocolate nougat delivery and finish without the feints ever becoming too cloying - a rare feat. *42%. 356 bottles.*

Drexler Arrach No 1 Aged 10 Years Bayerwold Single Cask Malt Whisky sherryfass, fass nr. H44, dest Sept 07, abge Oct 17 db **(88.5) n22** cherry brandy mixed with straight rye, bourbon and cough drops; **t22** the silkiest of deliveries: we are back to the cough drops r, rather, syrups, in this case. Again, dark cherry liqueur mixed with molasses; **f22** spices now and more structured degree of oak and fruit; **b22.5** as soft a whisky is it comes. A little bit of the cough syrup about his early on, but on the third of fourth mouthful the quiet richness of this malt does begin to win your heart over. Decidedly idiosyncratic. *46%. sc.*

WHISKY-DESTILLERIE GRUEL Owen/Teck. Working.

Tecker Single Malt Whisky Port Cask Matured db **(82.5) n19 t21.5 f21 b21.** A toffee-raisin whisky with a big degree of burnt sugar. *43%. ncf.*

Tecker Single Grain Whisky Aged 5 Years db **(84) n21.5 t22 f20 b20.5.** Somewhere in the five years between the ten and this five-year-old, someone appears to have made the cut a little wider. *40%. ncf.*

Tecker Single Grain Whisky Aged 10 Years Chardonnay casks db **(93) n23.5 t23 f23 b23.5** Now, that is all rather beautiful... *53.2%. ncf.*

WHISKY DESTILLERIE LIEBL Bad Kötzting. Working.

Coillmór Bavarian Single Malt Bordeaux Cask cask no. 398, dist Oct 09 db **(87) n21.5 t21.5 f22 b22.** A stable bottling allowing the fruit to make the best use of the light nougat to offer a rich, rounded, lightly fruited malt.Well balanced, salivating and a joy to experience. *46%.*

Coillmór Bavarian Single Malt Port Cask 8 Years Old cask no. 351, dist 4 May 07 db **(79.5) n21 t20 f19 b19.5.** Even a Port cask has problems seeing off the excesses of the massively heavy nougat. Rough. *46%. 1080 bottles.*

Coillmór Bavarian Single Malt Alabanach Peat American oak, cask no. 47, dist 17 Jul 10 db **(81.5) n20 t21 f20 b20.5.** I'll give the peat from this distillery one thing: it really is idiosyncratic. No other smoked whisky is so jarring and a liquid antonym of "rounded". An absolute must for any serious collector or student of peated whisky. *46%. 392 bottles.*

Coillmór Bavarian Single Malt American Oak cask nos. 60,214,229,268339, dist May 10 db **(83) n21 t20 f21 b21.** A malt with a huge nougat input. Lots of toffee, but curiously little sweetness. *43%. 1895 bottles.*

WHISKY DESTILLERIE BLAUE MAUS Eggolsheim. Working.

Blaue Maus New Make los nr. 516, destilliert May 16 db **(96) n23.5 t24 f24.5 b24** No chance of smelling a rat with this young mouse. Worth investing in a bottle of this so you can see the indescribably complex and stunningly beautiful skeleton on which their whiskies hang. And this really is complex indeed, not unlike the metal composition of the old Lammerlaw, New Zealand, new make in its day, which has to be its closest relative in style. The amount of chocolate on this is almost obscene. Easily one of the best new makes on the market in the world. *87.2%.*

Blaue Maus Single Cask Malt Whisky 14 Years Old German oak casks, fass/los nr. 1, destilliert Apr 04, abgefüllt Jun 18 db **(83) n20 t22 f20 b21** Feinty at first and then an outbreak of slightly bizarre spice. The sticking plaster honey is superb! *45.7%. sc.*

Blaue Maus Single Cask Malt Whisky 30 Years Old German oak casks, fass/los nr. 1, destilliert May 88, abgefüllt Jun 18 db **(89) n22** a powering nose with a mix of straw bales, orange blossom honey and burnt toast; **t23.5** sensuous, soft and melt-in-the-mouth honey-rich delivery with a superb malt development; **f21.5** a fraction bitter as the oak and spices dig deep; **b22.5** not quite as memorable as some of the older Blaue Maus whiskies of the past, the spices curtailing development early. But the sweetness to this is beautifully controlled and elegant. *40.4%. sc.*

Grüner Hund Single Cask Malt Whisky 16 Years Old German oak casks, fass/los nr. 1, destilliert Feb 02, abgefüllt Jun 18 db **(92.5) n23** big oils and even bigger oak and acacia honey; **t23.5** the honey and malt turn up arm-in-arm on delivery, forming a sumptuously delicious wall of light oil and sugars; spices are next on the agenda, burning brightly early then dimming as the tannins move towards a Kentucky backbone; **f22.5** malt and vanilla fade: mild for this distillery's standards....; **b23.5** there are a lot of Germans in Kentucky (or at least people from German descent) and there is a lot of Kentucky in this German. Beautifully bourbony in style. 49.5%. sc.

◇ **Mary Read Single Cask Malt Whisky 20 Years Old** German oak cass, fass/los nr. 1, destilliert Apr 98, abgefüllt Jun 18 db **(86) n21.5 t23 f20.5 b21.5** When the nose offers you something of an Indian Balti curry in style you know you are in strange territory. Uniquely Blaue Mauss with spices, presumably from the German oak, which send you into places where no other European whisky has gone before. 46.8%. sc.

◇ **Jubiläums Abfüllung 2018 Single Cask Malt Whisky 16 Years Old** German oak cass, fass/los nr. 1, destilliert May 02, abgefüllt Jun 18 db **(87) n21.5 t22.5 f21 b22** One of the most feinty offerings from this distillery for a while. But in typical style recovers with a big honeyed volley of malt. The finish is slightly bitty, though. 40%. sc.

◇ **Spinnaker Single Cask Malt Whisky 20 Years Old** German oak cass, fass/los nr. 1, destilliert May 98, abgefüllt Jun 18 db **(89.5) n21.5** big on the chocolate nougat; **t23** the extra oils do a brilliant job ramping up both the malt and the ulmo honey and intense toffee mix; mocha strikes the midpoint; **f22.5** light spices on butterscotch; **b22.5** a sublime cask makes the most of a wide cut on the stills. 40%. sc.

Sylter Tide Whisky dest 2011, bott 2017 db **(90.5) n22 t23 f22.5 b23** Ever heard of Crusted Port? Well, here's the world's first Crusted Whisky... Truly unique flavour profile. 40%.

Blends

Kahlgrund Whisky Blend (86.5) n21.5 t22 f21 b22. A well balanced, impressively weighted whisky full of enjoyable sugars. But definitely from the nougat school of German distilling. 46%

German Vatted Malt

Germania 2016 Malt Whisky bott code L01B03R17 **(73) n18 t19 f18 b18** Off key and off target. 40%.

ISRAEL
THE MILK & HONEY DISTILLERY

◇ **The Milk & Honey Distillery Single Malt Whisky** db **(91.5) n23** oddly enough – so very fittingly - both milk and honey appear on the nose: milk from the creamy caramels and the mix of ulmo and heather honeys which jon the vanilla to create a delicate sweetness; **t23** a silky entrance, again with the caramels ensuring a cream oiliness while the barley eventually juices up into a salivating delight; **f22** vanilla and most playful of spices; **b23.5** some years back I made a film about whisky in Israel – and they weren't then even making their own malt! So a reason to return. For this is a beautiful country...now with a beautiful whisky. Well done people of Milk and Honey with this charming malt: you have set yourself a high standard. Mazel Tov. And Lechaim! 46%. nc ncf sc. 391 bottles.

ITALY
PUNI WHISKY DISTILLERY Glurns, Bozen. Working.

◇ **PUNI Nero Italian Single Malt** bott code LE/2017, Pinot Nero casks db **(88) n23.5** that is a lot of grape...and even more layering. Multi-textured on the nose, lovers of Opal Fruits will appreciate this most of all...; **t22** a busy – perhaps too busy – delivery which takes its time to formulate and find its bearings: the fruit comes come every direction, though; **f21.5** bitters as the grape skin and toastier oak intensifies; perhaps a shade fuzzy, too; **b21.5** it is to my shame and chagrin that, even after they forged a magnificently complex 95 pointer the last time I tasted it, I still have not been able to sculpt my diary in a way that has made a visit to their distillery possible: there are simply too many distilleries in the world!! This bottling, for all its intermittent charm, doesn't come close to the clever use of marsala and phenols which made their last expression so extraordinary. But the grape on show here does at times revel in a certain élan... 46%. nc ncf. 3,000 bottles. Limited Edition 2017.

◇ **PUNI Sole Italian Single Malt** batch no. 01, bourbon barrels & Pedro Ximénez sherry casks db **(92.5) n23** has that uniquely PX obliqueness: attractive, yet a kind of dead end as the sugars meld with the malt but refuse to discuss matters further; **t23** probably the most PX of PX deliveries I've ever encountered: the sugars, if any thicker, could replace the receding polar ice caps. In their favour, they have picked up some intense maltiness along the way; **f23** almost minty and cool as butterscotch represents the oak with aplomb; **b23.5** have to say that that is an intriguing take on the PX theme, not making any effort to disguise the outrageous sugariness. A must experience malt. 46%. nc ncf.

LATVIA
LATVIJAS BALZAMS Riga. Working.
L B Lavijas Belzams db (83) n20 t22 f20 b21. Soft and yielding on the palate, this is said to be made from Latvian rye, though of all the world's rye whiskies this really does have to be the softest and least fruity. I'll be astonished if there isn't a fair degree of thinning grain in there, too. 40%

LIECHTENSTEIN
TELSER DISTILLERY Triesen. Working.
◇◇ **Telser Liechtenstein Single Malt L'Ultimo Grappa Berta Cask Finish** db (89) n22 an almost relaxed mix of grist and vivid grape; t22.5 starts gently with a series of malty kisses before the throat is seized by an aggressive grape bite; the mid-ground is sharpe grape and garibaldi biscuit; f22 bitters slightly, but finds a commonality between grape and straw-like barley; b22.5 like Grappa, it has its schizophrenic, throat-gripping moments. But the soft sensuality of the gristy barley makes a very decent whisky out of it. 60%. sc.

Telser Liechtenstein Single Malt Whisky IX - Pinot Noir Edition Aged 7 Years db (94.5) n23.5 t24 f23 b24 The Burgundian edge to this is clean and almost fascinating: this distillery does Pinot Noir-matured malt probably better than any other in the world. A big treat from a small country. 42.5%. nc ncf.

◇◇ **Telser Liechtenstein Single Malt X+1 Pinot Noir** db (95.5) n23.5 lots of cream toffee but the fruit, though seemingly soft, possesses a must depth, also; t24 as I write this, at my home where often more horses pass my window than cars (and would not be out of place beside Vaduz castle), a motorbike has just passed by, backfiring as it went. There is no hint of a backfire here: the barley is intense yet beautifully scored; the grape has an even bigger impact but lightens quickly to ensure a fabulous juiciness; fudge fills the middle with a light chocolate frame; f24 before it was strands now it a very happy and equal mix of flavours and intensities. The muscovado sugars late on hold sway...and still you salivate right at the death: remarkable...; b24 just brilliant that I have looked to see my last Telser score: and it was 95.5 for virtually an identical whisky. You have to say this is one very consistent distillery. Another massive whisky from this tiny country... 52.9%. sc. 350 bottles.

◇◇ **Telser Liechtenstein Single Malt XII Salamandra** db (88.5) n22.5 presumably if and when cornfields are cut and threshed in this remote principality, the air will be thick with this delightful straw-laden graininess; where the delicate fruit comes from, I'm not quite so sure; t23 an intensely malty, salivating, cream soda; f21 bitters slightly, but remains ludicrously malty and hick; b22 a malt personality you may never have quite seen before. 44.6%. sc.

LUXEMBOURG
DISTILLERIE DIEDENACKER Niederdonven. Working.
Diedenacker Number One Aged 5 Years Rye & Malt 2011 db (89.5) n22 t22.5 f23 b22 Luxembourg's single cask for 2011 – literally! – has come up trumps: similar to first bottling where the grains serve up a feast of flavours. 42%.

Diedenacker Number One Aged 5 Years Rye & Malt 2012 db (85.5) n21.5 t22 f21 b21 With flavour this complex, it is too easy to misfire slightly. The extra feints wipe out much of the complexity. 42%.

THE NETHERLANDS
ZUIDAM BAARLE Nassau. Working.
Millstone Aged 12 Years Sherry Cask dist 26 Feb 99, bott 22 Mar 13 db (95) n24 t23.5 f23.5 b24 After last year's disappointing sherry bottling, thought I'd need some Dutch courage to tackle this one. But, instead, an excellent cask at work here which ensures an overflow of character. Just underlines the difference between putting a good quality spirit into a less than impressive cask or filling into top quality oak So, so elegant... 46% WB15/399

SLOVAKIA
NESTVILLE DISTILLERY Hniezdne. Working.
◇◇ **Nestville Master Blender 8 Years Old Whisky** barrel nos. 509208, 509825, 509859 & 509872, dist 20 May 09, bott 19 Sept 17 db (95.5) n23.5 gentle tannins caress, seasoning nibbles and dark sugars kiss: this is a glorious and seductive introduction to a whisky; t24 magnificent mouth feel: so soft that silk would seem like a scouring pad by comparison. The most subtle fruit notes tease further, then melt, allowing the salivating grains and light spices to dance their complex little routine; f24 a crescendo of warming vanilla plus the most sensual chocolate toffee fade; the delicate spices take their time to fade; b24 this is

as slick and sublime as they come. Stupendous layering and rare to find a European malt so well structured and balanced. 46%. 1,386 bottles.

⟫ **Nestville Master Blender 9 Years Old Whisky** barrel nos. 504894, 504895, 504896 & 517380, dist 2009, bott 20 Jun 18 db (93) n23 a peppery spice punctuates the layered fruit. Boiled apples and ripe sultana play gently together, taking turns in delicate dominance; a little marzipan sweetens subtly; t23.5 the usual Nestville silky texture makes the perfect foil for the mouth-watering qualities of the fruit, especially the accompanying muscovado sugars. The mid-ground, though, is all about the grain, the corn in particular which melds with the tannins for a brief glimpse of something distinctly bourbony; f23 late, beautiful chocolate; the cocoa effect intensifies with the broader spices; b23.5 my initial thoughts on tasting this was an extraordinary marriage between malt and bourbon styles. So it came as no surprise to learn that the grains involved in this clever vatting of barrels include both wheat and corn. You need to listen carefully to this whisky, as its subtlety means much can too easily go unheard, as some of what it says is shyly and gently spoken. And such is its unique style, in foreign tongue. The never-to-be forgotten beauty and elegance, however, comes in the translation... 46%. 1,475 bottles.

⟫ **Nestville Single Malt 2013 Single Barrel** cask no. 509707, bott 20 Jun 18 db (92) n23 tannins thrive but without a hint of over dominance and aggression. Soft and yielding in the house style, the vanillas boast a light muscovado touch, with the merest hint of something fruity; as those tannins build, so too does a vague, liquorice-rich bourbon theme; t23.5 a no less tantalising delivery. The sugars are more profound here: a mix of ulmo honey and muscovado with spices at first sleepy and then slowly stirred into action; f22.5 the finale offers that same tantalising now-you-see-it, now-you-don't glimpse of light fruitiness b23 curious: while much of the music was loud, this whisky bottled to celebrate the event, was anything but... 43%. 427 bottles. sc. For Nestville Open Fest 2018

⟫ **Nestville Cast Strength Single Barrel 2011** cask no. 502011, bott 20 Jun 18 db (94) n23 the full strength ensures extra oils not normally associated with Nestville, giving the bold sugars extra lustre; when warmed sufficiently, attractive vanillas pours from the glass; t24 succulent date and walnut but boosted by a big oak-spicy surge. Muscovado sugars and molasses offer a drying fruitiness but those spices hammer their point home; f23 good oils spread the sugars far and wide. Butterscotch adds a sweeter note to the vanilla; long, deeply satisfying and a distinctive bourbon-style finale; b24 another beautiful cask from the only distillery I know on the planet which has an active white stork's nest in the middle of its operation. The young storks appear to thrive on the angel's share, while the distillery appears to thrive on outstanding wood management. 63.9%. 227 bottles. sc. For Nestville Open Fest 2018.

SPAIN
DYC Aged 8 Years (90) n22 t23 f22.5 b22.5. I really am a sucker for clean, cleverly constructed blends like this. Just so enjoyable! 40%

DYC Selected Blended Whisky (85.5) n21.5 t22 f21 b21. One of the cleanest and perhaps creamiest whiskies in Europe. Some gooseberry, like the malt, occasionally drifts in, ramping up the flavour profile which is anything but taxing. 40%

DYC Single Malt Whisky Aged 10 Years (91) n22 t23 f23 b23 Far more complex than it first seems. Like Segovia, where the distillery is based, worth exploring...40%

SWEDEN
BOX DESTILLERI Bjärtrå. Working.
Box Single Malt The 2nd Step Collection 03 bott Oct 16 db (95) n23.5 t24 f23.5 b24 In football terms, does my tasting this straight after their American New Oak Finish make me a Box to Box writer...? Whatever, this is a joyous offering much more subtle and worthy of study: superb! 51.3%. nc ncf.

Box Single Malt American Oak new American oak finish db (88.5) n22 t22.5 f22 b22 Hardly a malt for those with lily-livered palates. This is a near enough unique flavour profile in world whisky where smoke and tannin smash head-first into the other. Beware of the flying fragments... 50.8%. nc ncf.

Box Single Malt Dálvve batch no. 2 db (86.5) n22 t22.5 f21 b21 Nothing particularly wrong with this whisky...but there is something just not right. The nose has its attractively nutty moments and the delivery enjoys a gripping intensity. But though gentle sugars and spices are present, there is a thinness to the finish in particular which underlines whisky's inability to sew together and balance satisfactorily. 46%. nc ncf.

Box Single Malt PX Pedro Ximénez sherry cask finish db (93) n23 t24 f23 b23 This bottling should be used as the industry standard to show exactly how to make perfect use of a non-sulphured PX cask...! 56.7%. nc ncf.

Swedish Whisky Federation Box Distillery (94) n23.5 t23 f23.5 b24 Box's aim was to create an elegant, lightly peated, high class malt. Mission accomplished. 56.4%. 2,000 bottles.

GUTE DESTILLERI Havdhem. Working.

Gute Single Malt Whisky db (95.5) n24.5 t24 f23 b24 This is really quite weird. Back in the late 1970s and early 1980s, I used to comb old village stores looking for 1960s bottlings by Gordon and MacPhail single malts of Speyside and Highland whiskies as they were distilled just after the Second World War and early 1950s. Then, those whiskies had a little more smoke than was being used in the later 1950s. This malt has just hurled me back nearly 40 years. A malt very much in tune with a lost style in Scotland from some 60 years ago: I am stunned...!! 40%

MACKMYRA Gästrikland. Working.

Mackmyra Midvinter Single Malt Art No MC-001 db (94.5) n23.5 t24 f23 b24 How fitting: probably the most Swedish of all the Mackmyra whiskies yet: reminds me of light-challenged days in that country when, at night, you would retreat to a restaurant and finish the evening with an aquavit, spiced to the owner's liking. The seasoning and smoking here takes us very close to that uniquely Swedish style. The sophistication takes the breath away... 46.1%

Mackmyra Reserve "Queen of Fucking Everything" recipe: Rök, Bourbon barrel, Cask no. 32, dist 24/03/2010, bott 04/09/2014 db (94) n24 t24 f22.5 b23.5 After over 40 years of tasting whisky – some 25 of them professionally – this is the first time I have ever encountered a brand which includes in its title the word "Everything"... 53.4%

NORRTELJE BRENNERI Norrtälje. Working.

◇ **Roslagswhisky EKO Cask Strength** batch no. bourbon fat 23-200, dest Nov 13, fatfylld 9 Apr 14, bott 19 Dec 17 db (90.5) n22.5 clean, concentrated malt grist; t22.5 salivating, sweet, chewy concentrated malt grist; f23 even sweeter concentrated malt grist, though now with spice and cocoa; b22.5 my word: Cinderella will have a ball with all this barley: possibly in the top two or three most malty whiskies of the year. Much better distilled and matured than their last rural offering. 61.6%. ncf sc. Bottled for the Cinderella Whisky Fair 2018 10th Anniversary.

◇ **Roslagswhisky EKO Dubbel Single Cask** sherry Oloroso fat nr. 13-50/2013, fatfylld 29 Apr 13, bourbon fat nr. 13-200/2013, fatfylld 19 Sept 13, bott 4 Oct 17 db (85.5) n20.5 t22 f21.5 b21.5 One of the rare occasions in world whisky when an oloroso cask doesn't stand an earthly chance against the barley! Back to its usual giant haystack self with the grape merely getting in the way! 48.3%.

SMÖGEN WHISKY Hunnebostrand. Working.

◇ **Smögen Single Malt Barrique 7 Years Old** db (87) n22 t22 f21.5 b21.5 Pretty straightforward fare, big on the juicy grape but low on subtlety and development. Lots of toffee and raisin, but a shade too bitter at the death. 60.3%.

◇ **Smögen Svensk Single Malt Single Cask 18** dist 2012 db (96) n24 it appears Islay has been towed out to join the multiple islands which help form Sweden. Somewhere between light and medium peated, but a delicate coastal persona; too gristy too be true... I'm in love...; t24.5 oh...my ...word...! This is like a slow orgasm being played out on the taste buds: the peat gathers in slow motion, the sugars form and gang together, then dissipate and move around the mouth in a way which....well...I'll let you describe it for yourself; f23.5 the slight youthfulness on delivery has gone now. Instead a few oaky notes wash in and offer vanilla to the gristy peat. It is constructed or choreographed, as so many aspects of this Anacreontic whisky, like a love poem, or a dance of the seven veils...; b24 on this evidence, previous Smogen whiskies I had tasted had criminally underperformed. This is not only a superstar single malt, but probably the sharpest rise in quality at a distillery I have ever witnessed. Very well one! If you have never been seduced by a beautiful Swede by now, you will after experiencing this. It should carry an X-certificate... 61.3%. sc.

SPIRIT OF HVEN DISTILLERY Sankt Ibb. Working.

Spirit of Hven Organic Single Malt 7 Stars No. 4 Megrez db (94) n23 t24 f23.5 b23.5 Hven sent! A malt which doesn't pull a single punch. 45%

Spirit of Hven Seven Stars No. 5 Alioth Single Malt db (94.5) n23.5 t24 f23.5 b23.5 Another Russian roulette European distillery where you have no idea of the quality you are about to face. This, though, is Hven. 45%.

◇ **Spirit of Hven Seven Stars No. 6:1 Mizar Single Malt Whisky** db (94.5) n23.5 the playfulness and elegance of the phenols takes some believing: indeed, you begin to wonder if they are there at all; t24 fills the mouth with pastel shades of chocolate raisin,

Bruyere honey, marzipan and mocha; f23.5 thins somewhat, but allows the oak a bigger stage; the complex dark sugars just keep on melting as the most delicate of translucent smoky tones drifts around; b23.5 doesn't this distillery know how to make very ordinary whisky....? An exhibition of complexity....again! 45%.

SWITZERLAND
ANDREAS VON OW DISTILLERY Busingen. Working.
Munot Malt dist Aug 10, bott 19 Sep 13 db (87.5) n22 t22 f21.5 b22. Sturdy and steady. The nose appears to offer more as a bourbon than malt and there is plenty of oak to chew on the palate. But the youthfulness is hinted at by firm oils and the light cocoa finish. 46%. sc.

BAUERNHOF BRENNEREI LÜTHY Muhen. Working.
◇ **Herr Lüthy Pure Swiss Corn Böörbon** cask no. 554, dest 2014, abge 2018 db (91) n23 beautiful in part: sweet lavender and spearmint combine to excellent effect; t23 wow...that mint..! Cool on delivery, then a slow melt of icing sugar and spice; light corn oil bathes the palate; f22 gentle build of vanilla and caramel; b23 a surprising Swiss bourbon offering a chance to draw delicious flavour map of previously uncharted territory. 43%. sc.

Herr Lüthy Pure Swiss No. 10 cask no. 508, destilliert 2011, abgefüllt 2015 db (89.5) n22.5 t23 f21.5 b22.5 A firm, impressively made and matured whisky worth finding. 43%

◇ **Herr Lüthy Pure Swiss N° 11 Single Malt** dest 2012, abge 2016 db (87.5) n21 t22.5 f22 b22 Impressively chewy. Make no apology for its chocolate fudge persona and comes up with a few choice dark sugar notes as well as vanilla. Plays a little loose with the cut, but gets away with it! 43%. 889 bottles.

◇ **Herr Lüthy Pure Swiss N° 12 Single Malt** dest 2013, abge 2017 db (86.5) n21.5 t21.5 f22 b21.5 One of the driest malts I have encountered for a little while. Perhaps the nougat pointing to a generous cut may explain some of the reason, the expected chocolate back up arriving on cue. Rich and attractively resonating. 43%. 878 bottles.

◇ **Herr Lüthy Pure Swiss Rye Rogge** cask no. 639, dest 2014, abge 2018 db (85) n20.5 t22 f21.5 b21 Not the first – and won't be the last – rye whisky where the cut off the still has gone slightly askew, resulting in an over indulgence of oils. The grain dazzles briefly on delivery. Great spices, though. 56.6%. sc.

◇ **Herr Lüthy Pure Swiss Spelt UrDinkel** cask no. 501, dest 2013, abge 2018 db (87) n20.5 t23 f21.5 b22 The nose may not be too promising – and spelt is a bit of a challenge for any distiller – but the heather honey and butterscotch explosion on delivery more than makes up for the early problems. Hefty oils on the finale ensure the weakness is truly spelt out, but there is no shame in enjoying that beautifully sensuous arrival. 43%. sc.

BRAUEREI FALKEN Schaffhausen. Working.
Munot Malt Single Cask Limited Edition 2015 red wine cask no. 1-111 db (87) n22 t21.5 f22 b21.5. Has the thin feel of a whisky distilled initially to pretty high strength. The oak has by far the biggest script to learn here and only slowly does a balancing fruitiness emerge, though it remains gentle. Clean but warming. 57.1%. sc.

BRENNEREI HANS ERISMANN Bülach-Eschenmosen. Working.
Tsyri Zürcher Swiss Single Cask Malt Whisky Aged 5 Years db (86) n21.5 t21.5 f21 b22. Quite a sharp, clean malt with tangy tannin. Big caramels soften the impact. The molasses do a good balancing job. 40%. sc.

BRENNEREI KOBELT Marbach. Working.
Glen Rhine Whiskey 2011/4J db (85) n21.5 t22 f20 b21.5. A welter of sugary, soft, toffee tones with a squeeze of citrus to the malt to lightly freshen the experience. A vague burn on the finish. Pleasant and as untaxing as a Monaco bank account. 40%. sc. 181 bottles.

BRAUREREI LOCHER Appenzell. Working.
Säntis Malt Himmelberg Edition oak beer casks, finished in wine casks db (88) n22 malt from the spirit? Or malt from the beer barrel, I wonder...Either way it is the mega intense fruit which balances out more comfortably; t22.5 powering sugars on delivery from a dessert wine type grape with light spices and a vague hop undertone; f21.5 a few extra hops from the beer barrel appear to blast their way through; b22 make mine a pint...! 43%

BRENNEREI SCHWAB Oberwil. Working.
Buechibärger Whisky Single Malt Fassstärke 2006 Chardonnas Fass Nr. 27 db (94.5) n23 t24 f23.5 b24 A whisky to cherish... 55%. sc.

Buechibärger Whisky Single Malt Fassstärke 2009 Chardonnas Fass Nr. 34 db (75.5) n19 t19.5 f18 b19. The cask cannot entirely overcome the severe limitations of the distillate. 42%. sc.

BRENNEREI STADELMANN Altbüron. Working.

⟡ **Dorfbachwasser Single Malt 10 Years Old** Moschtfass Eiche cask, dist Sept 05, bott Mar 16 db (90.5) n22.5 a curious, vaguely phenolic note plays along with a more explicitly fruity text: yet the result is one of subtlety and complexity – not unknown to this distillery; t23 crisp bold sugars abound on the delivery, then it's all about the barley and the malt takes off with a big kick. Muscovado sugars blend with a touch of Manuka honey and liquorice; f22 some mocha; stays chewy and toasty, though a little bitterness seeps in; b23 this distillery really does know how to distil! Another above average example of the art. 40%. ncf. Bottled for the Whisky Club Melchnau.

Luzerner Hinterländer Whiskey Nr. 6 db (89.5) n22 t22 f23 b22.5 Unspectacular, but doesn't try to be a superstar. Just offers a lovely malty narrative without a cross word or hint of attitude. 40%

Luzerner Hinterländer Whiskey Nr. 7 db (91) n21.5 t23.5 f23 b23 Very much along the same lines as their Nr. 6 in many respects. Except this is softer still and, despite the restrictions of the natural caramel, has an extra degree of complexity. 40%

⟡ **Luzerner Hinterlander Single Malt Whiskey Old Nr. 7** Jack Daniel's cask db (92) n22.5 an enjoyable and pronounced oak presence, both deep and liquorice-laden and of a lighter vanilla hue, too; t24 bright and buzzy: firm malt to start, then a light, controlled ulmo honey sweetness moving into heather honey – all tied down with drier tannins: superb! f22.5 beautiful vanilla and cocoa; the lovely spice buzz carries on; b23 a beautifully distilled, clean, highly complex and busy malt. 45%.

BRENNEREI-ZENTRUM BAUERNHO Zug. Working.

Swissky db (91) n23 t23 f22 b23. While retaining a distinct character, this is the cleanest, most refreshing malt yet to come from mainland Europe. Hats off to Edi Bieri for this work of art. Moving stuff. 42%

DESTILLERIE EGNACH Egnach. Silent.

Thursky db (93) n24 t23.5 f22.5 b23. Such a beautifully even whisky! I am such a sucker for that clean fruity-spice style. Brilliant! 40%

DISTILLERIE ETTER Zug. Working.

⟡ **Johnett Whisky Aged 7 Years** dist May 10, bott Aug 17 db (93) n22.5 earthy and green: that unmistakable sweet dankness of a bluebell wood in Spring; t23.5 a ridiculously soft delivery with gentle oils massaging the vanilla and moch into the taste buds; the spices grow beside the increasing chocolate milk tones (beautifully distilled, so no chance of a nougat, Toblerone note); f23.5 a mocha, spice, vanilla and malt fade...and still as soft as the delivery; b23.5 yet another sublime whisky from Switzerland. It's not just cuckoo clocks, you know... 44%. ncf.

DESTILLERIE HAGEN-RÜHLI Hüttwilen. Working.

Hagen's Best Whisky No. 2 lot no. 00403/04-03-08.08 db (87) n19 t23.5 f22 b22.5. Much more Swiss, small still style than previous bottling and although the nose isn't quite the most enticing, the delivery and follow through are a delight. Lovely whisky. 42%

DESTILLERIE MACARDO Strohwilen. Working.

⟡ **Macardo 10th Anniversary Single Malt** db (87) n19.5 t24 f21.5 b22 Were it not for the feinty, off-kilter nose, this would have scored so much higher – and would have deserved to. The complexity of the malt deserves a round of applause alone: the delivery is the stuff of dreams. The maltster-style intensity comes complete with cocoa plus light spices. The finish, though, confirms the weakness of the nose. Even so, the 10th anniversary is marked with some stupendous whisky moments. 42%. 999 bottles.

⟡ **Macardo Bourbon** dist 2010, bott code 6020 db (84.5) n20.5 t21.5 f21.5 b21 You can see where this is coming from – and where it is trying to go. But it gets stuck, literally, with bubble gum clogging up the works – on both delivery and finish. A little too sticky and indistinct. 42%.

⟡ **Macardo Single Malt** dist 2010, bott code 7002 db (92.5) n22.5 a light malt and wheat style breakfast cereal; light muscovado sugars in place, too...; t23.5 brilliantly intense delivery: the sugars work wonders both intensifying the impact of the grain but equally thinning out the mid-ground oaky effect in order to keep balance; f22.5 remains grainy, vanilla-rich and honest, emphasising just how good the distiller did in making this such a clean cut; b23.5 an honest and attractive, beautifully distilled, single malt squeezing out every last barley note. 42%.

EDELBRENNEREI BRUNSCHWILER Oberuzwil. Working.
B3 Fürsterländer Single Malt Whisky Los Nr. 2015 db (88.5) n22 t22 f22 b22.5 Does a great job of elevating the malt to prominence and keeping it there. Understatedly lovely. 40%

FREIHOF BRAUEREI Gossau. Working.
Gossauer Single Malt Whisky sherry cask no. 6, dist 23 Feb 13, bott 18 Jun 16 db (92.5) n23.5 t23 f23 b23 Can't argue with that: a clean cask and a profusion of fruit. 43%. sc. 50 bottles.

HIGHGLEN WHISKY DISTILLERY Santa Maria Val Müstair. Working.
HighGlen Raetia Prima Single Malt Swiss Whisky db (92) n22.5 t23 f23.5 b23 Worth getting a spoon for this. Amazing! 54.9%. 25 bottles.
HighGlen Raetia Secunda Single Malt Swiss Whisky db (93) n23.5 t24 f22 b23.5 Magnificent whisky of Alpine beauty. 64.1%. 30 bottles.
HighGlen Raetia Terza Single Malt Swiss Whisky db (88) n22 t23 f21 b22 Another mainly sweet malt, but this time barley-based and less oak oriented. 58.5%. 64 bottles.

HUMBEL DISTILLERY Stetten Aargau. Working.
OURBEER Aged 36 Months Single Malt Whisky Tokaj Finish dist 2002 db (88.5) n22 t22 f22.5 b22 A friend of mine who lives just a few villages from me was one of the people who successfully got Tokaj wine back on the map and he was a little surprised when I told him that for the whisky lover that has been something of a mixed blessing: most Tokay-finished or matured casks have been wrecked beyond redemption by sulphur. Thankfully, not this offering. Though, like its distant cousin, PX, the improbable intensity of the sugars do restrict the overall development of the malt. 50%
OURBEER Single Malt Whisky dist 10, bott 23 Jul 14 db (82) n20 t21.5 f20 b20.5. A pretty unique aroma and flavour profile, strongly scented with spiced citrus and with a late herbal tang to the standard toffee. 43%

KOBELT Marbach, St. Gallen. Working.
Glen Rhine Whiskey db (88) n21 t22.5 f21.5 b22. Try and pick your way through this one...can't think of another whisky in the world with that kind of fingerprint. 40%. Corn & barley.

LANGATUN DISTILLERY Langenthal, Kanton Bern. Working.
Langatun 10 Years Langatun Distillery Single Malt Whisky Châteauneuf-du-Pape cask, cask no. 5, dist Mar 08, bott Mar 15 db (96.5) n23.5 t24 f24.5 b24.5 Just a few miles from where this distillery, with its ancient walls and in the shadow of a mediaeval schloss, now sits is the old town of Langenthal. But it is ancient village of Aarwangen that provides the perfect setting now, with the distillery close to the river from which the community takes its name and where, if you are lucky like me, you might even spot a Hoopoe on its summer visit. And with outstanding cheese made there as well, it is some kind of whisky heaven which the gods have sprinkled a little magic on. 49.12%. nc. 499 bottles.
Langantun 400 Years Kornhaus Single Malt db (94.5) n23 t24 f23.5 b24 Whisky is a derivation of the Gaelic meaning "water of life". Tasting this after their Hell Fire, the accent here appears very much on the water... And, no, this isn't 400-year-old whisky...thankfully. Though the stunningly beautiful building in which the distillery is housed is of that vintage. Oh, and did I mention stunningly beautiful? Perfectly describes this malt... 49.12%.
◇ **Langatun Cardeira Cask Finish Single Malt** dist 25 Oct 10, bott 2 May 17, bott code L 0291 db (95.5) n23.5 from the heart of Switzerland comes the salty freshness of the Atlantic: the saline properties of the grape are so beautifully in tune with the list gristy threads of malt. There is also a decidedly winey must effect here, too, upping the complexity further still; t25 quite possibly the most full-flavoured malt to be produced on mainland Europe in the last year or so. There is an almost unbelievable amount of chocolate at play here – arriving much earlier than you would even dare to suspect possible. The earliest moments deal with the improbably layering of the beautiful fruit: grape of course, but backed by muscovado sugar, tomatoes, Chinese gooseberries, chocolate fruit and nut, and all along a brittle barley spine; f23 just a mild bitterness: nothing sinister or threatening and grape rather than cask related. A degree of youth in the malt is now slightly evident, but the complexity rumbles on, now with soft spices; b24 trust Langatun to come up with something very different, indeed. The effect of this less than common Portuguese wine dovetails with rare precision with the malt. The first ten seconds of the delivery is as delicious as any whisky on the planet this year. 61.4%. nc. 100 bottles.

Langantun Hell Fire cask nr. 666, sherry cask, dist Sept 10, Bott Okt 16 db **(93)** n22 t24 f23.5 b23.5 Use the Murray method of tasting and it becomes a mere pussycat (OK, one with a few sharp claws) – even with no water added. I was going to make this the 666th whisky tasted for the 2018 Bible...but I forgot. So it is the 1,111th. Oh, hell...!!!! *81%*. 444 *bottles*.

Langatun Jacob's Dream Single Malt Whisky pinot noir cask, cask no. 97, dist 23 Mar 09, bott 15 Jun 15 db **(92.5)** n23.5 t24 f22 b23 Quite astonishing how this malt has the presence to comfortably fit into the shoes of such big wine casks.

Langatun Old Bear Single Malt bott code L 0116 db **(88)** n21.5 t22.5 f22 b22 Langatun whisky is such a force of nature, it doesn't seem natural to taste it much below natural strength, let alone at 40%. *40%*

Langatun Old Deer Single Malt bott code L 0116 db **(87.5)** n21.5 t22.5 f21.5 b22. This is one of the great distilleries of Europe, make no mistake. But here the cut strays just onto the wide side of things, though it is still brimming with hay and marmalade notes. The sugars are of the heather-honey variety. But those feints, a rarity - a collectors' item - for Langatun, just stifle the overall complexity. *40%*

Langatun Old Deer Cask Strength Single Malt bott code L 0116 db **(95.5)** n24 t24 f23.5 b24 Now that is what I was expecting...not the character of the 40% bottling. This is, quite simply, brilliant. *62.1%*

◈ **Langatun Quinta do Zambujeiro Cask Matured** dist 17 Dec 11, bott 12 Oct 17 db **(90.5)** n22.5 coconut biscuit...with sultana; t23.5 succulent, salivating and mouth filling, the grape possesses an attractive degree of viscosity, so clinging to the plate as though its life depends on it; muscovado sugars and ulmo honey work brilliantly in the middle stages before the vanilla goes into auto drive; f22 a slight bitterness where none is desired but the vanilla ups its game as a late chalkiness counters the sweeter notes; b22.5 a curious stop-start malt which when it manages to hit top gear genuinely purrs along the palate. *49.12%*.

◈ **Langatun Sherry Cask Finish** Oloroso cask, cask no. 319, dist 12 Dec 11, bott 14 Aug 17 db **(95.5)** n24 good grief...! I am back in Scotland during the 1970s and sniffing one of those single malt whiskies which are so very much out of fashion and favour with its dark, deep intensity to the grape, yet still subtle enough to allow the malt to come through and play. In others words: matured in a perfect sherry butt; t24 here we go again: how can the most beautiful, unreconstructed sherry note still have enough space to allow the whisky to be...well, whisky! f23.5 drier now, a tad bitter – though not in a negative way, b24 if anyone tells you there has been nothing wrong with the sherry butts which have blighted Scottish whisky for the last 20 years, they should find a bottle of this. It is the closest thing to a time machine I know: a former member of the Gentleman's Club to which I belong, Mr H. G. Wells, would have approved with gusto. What a privilege to experience a whisky like this... *49.12%*. sc.

◈ **Langatun White House Single Malt** db **(88)** n22.5 a generous cut doesn't underplay the barley, but restricts the sweetness slightly; some soft toffee nougat and mocha, nonetheless t22.5 beautiful malt: intense and thick enough to stand a spoon in; f21 hmm, tangy and unusually out of sync; b22 trumps many other European whiskies, but not quite up to many of its predecessors... *45%*.

RUGENBRAU AG Matten bei Interlaken. Working.

Interlaken Swiss Highland Single Malt "Classic" oloroso sherry butt db **(95)** n23.5 t24 f23 b24. Hugely impressive. I have long said that the finest whiskies made on mainland Europe are to be found in Switzerland. Game, set and match... *46%*

SANTISBLICK DESTILLERIE Niederbüren. Working.

Santisblick 3 Jahre alt, im Sherryass ausgereift bott code 447 von 600 db **(60)** n22.5 t22.5 f5 b10 The delivery has a fabulous density to the dark muscovado fruitiness and structured malt; some spices begin to take off. But the finish shows its fabled fiery harshness of before. My taste buds were burning from this one some 24 hours after tasting. *43%*

Whisky 3 Years Old bourbon cask, bott code L-130001 db **(83.5)** n21 t22 f21.5 b19. An odd but attractive whisky where the maltiness has been ramped up to nuclear strength. Best of all, though, is the body and overall mouth feel which is highly satisfying. A peculiar experience, though. *43%*

SPEZIALITÄTENBRENNEREI ZÜRCHER Port. Working.

Weidhöfler Single Malt Whisky sherry casks, dist 05 May 11 db **(87.5)** n22 t22.5 f21 b22. Some sharp, lively fruit – not unlike pastels – on the nose, the delivery is much fatter and flatter. There are a few wonderful moments where the grape offers up its head in a defiant, bright-eyed pose, before dull vanillas flatten it. *41%*. 114 *bottles*.

WEINGUT CLERC BAMERT Ruteli im Buobental. Working.

Weingut Clerc Bamert Whisky Finest Pure Malt 8 Years Old db (87) n22 t22 f21 b22. Splutters and misfires on the finish, though not as badly as the single engine plane that has just gone, worryingly, overhead. Elsewhere some lovely malt, black cherry and caramel makes for a soft landing. *40%. sc nc.*

WHISKY CASTLE Elfingen. Working.

Whisky Castle Single Malt Edition Käser cask no. 468 db (93) n22 t24 f23.5 b23.5 / immense, magisterial and a castle for which there is no breaching... 68%. sc.

Whisky Castle Single Malt Family Reserve cask no. 17 db (91) n22 t23 f22.5 b23.5 It is a great many years now since I met the lovely family who are behind the Family Reserve at Whisky Castle. I was highly impressed with their whisky then; I am impressed now: this isbeautifully and very carefully distilled without a single trace of feints. So I selected this as the malt of choice prior to Switzerland playing France in the European Championships. I think it will score a lot higher than the boys in red. *43%. sc.*

British Blends

The One British Blended Whisky (84.5) n22 t21.5 f20 b21. Although it doesn't say so on the bottle, I understand this is made from a blend of malts from England, Ireland, Scotland and Wales. It says "blend" which implies the use of grain, though this is probably not so...another example of the confusion caused by the brainless and arrogant change of terminology from "vatted" to denote a blend of malts insisted upon by the Scotch Whisky Association. Not yet checked, but would have thought that as not scotch, they still would have been entitled to call it a vatting. The mind boggles over what they will do with this whisky if Scotland votes for independence in a few weeks' time. Doubtless the SWA will make some kind of noise... Anyway, back to the action. The label does claim this is a whisky of "intriguing complexity". If true, the term will have to be redefined. The nose, sure enough, does offer just enough smoky and citrus twists and turns to wonder what will happen next. But the delivery on the palate is a disappointment, with any complexity desired submerged under a welter of dull caramels. Just too flat and soft for its own good: back to the drawing board....and possibly without scotch... 40% WB15/406

⇨ **Steel Bonnets** bott code: L 13 06 18 (83) n19 t23 f20 b21 This would have been so much better had, presumably, sherry butts not been involved... The nose is a classic case of smoke and fruit neutralising the other, leaving a tangy note to rule. Such a contrast to the big and boisterous palate: nothing like the white-flag-ishness of the nose. A serious tannin-induced spice prickle kicks in from the very first moment and keeps its foot on the throat of the roast fudge and raisin delivery; light wisps of smoke mingle with mocha at the mid-point. The furriness on the finale underscores where things have gone slightly awry. 46.6%. ncf. The Lakes Distillery. Blend of English & Scottish Malts.

European Blends

Black Mountain Excellence Whisky Selection No. 1 (85) n21.5 t22 f20.5 b21. Thin, delicate, clean, toffeed and with an early sweet peak. 42%

Black Mountain Premium Whisky Sélection No. 2 (85.5) n21 t21.5 f22 b21. Just like the No 1 bottling, this is grain dominant and simplistic. Though less sweet and more vigorously spiced throughout. Not at all unpleasant. 40%

⇨ **Black Mountain Notes Fumées** (87) n21 t22.5 f21.5 b22 You half expect to see starfish and sea anemonies crawling out the glass here. A remarkable tidal rock pool on the nose and this saltiness translates throughout the tasting experience. Lush, silky soft and caramel rich and easy drinking, there is something a little unnerving about that incessant coastal persona. 45%.

MISCELLANEOUS

Michel Couvreur Very Sherried 25 Year Old Single Malt Whisky sherry cask (86.5) n22 t22 f21.5 b21. No off-notes from the sherry here. But the strange thing about this malt is that the grape is so single-minded and bossing proceedings with such dominance, it is hard to recognise the quarter of a century of maturation. A whisky with such a lack of balance is always a bit unnerving, especially when the sugars – or date concentrate - are so cloying. 45%

Nomad Outland Whisky (82) n21 t22 f20 b19. The entire shape of the whisky is lost under the tsunami of the PX casks. So first comes the scary sugars...followed by a very bitter finish with no happy midpoint. All-in-all, I have tasted whisky liqueurs less sweet than this... 41.3% WB16/006

Deciphered and Distilled. The Bible's European Guide to Whisky Labels

English	German	French
Malt	Malz	Malt
Grain	Getreide	céréales
Wheat	Weizen	blé
Barley	Gerste	orge
Rye	Roggen	seigle
Spelt	Dinkel	épeautre
Corn	Mais	maïs
Oat	Hafer	avoine
Peated	getorft	tourbé
Smoked	geraucht	fumé
Organic	biologisch	biologique
Cask	Fass	fût
Matured in/Aged in	gereift in	vieilli en
Finish	Nachreifung	déverdissage
Double Maturation	Zweitreifung	deuxième maturation
Oak	Eiche	chêne
Toasted	wärmebehandelt	grillé
Charred	ausgeflammt, verkohlt	carbonisé
Years	Jahre	ans
Months	Monate	mois
Days	Tage	journées
Chill Filtration	Kühlfiltration	filtration à froid
Non Chill Filtered	nicht kühlgefiltert	non filtré à froid
No Colouring	nicht gefärbt	non coloré
Cask Strength	Fassstärke	brut du fût
Single Cask	Einzelfass	single cask
Cask No.	Fass-Nummer	numéro du fût
Batch	Charge	Lot/charge
Distillation Date	Destillations-Datum	date de distillation
Bottling Date	Abfüll-Datum	date de mise en bouteille
Alcohol by Volume/abv	Volumenprozente/% vol.	teneur en alcool/abv
Proof (American)	amerikanische Einheit für % vol.	unité américaine

Danish	Dutch	Swedish
Malt	Gerst	Malt
Korn	graan	säd
hvede	tarwe	vete
byg	gerst	korn
rug	rogge	råg
spelt	spelt	speltvete
majs	mais	majs
havre	haver	havre
tørv	geturfd	torvrökt
røget	gerookt	rökt
organisk	biologisch/organisch	ekologisk
fad	vat	fat
modning i	gerijpt in	mognad på/lagrad på
finish	narijping/finish	slutlagrat
dobbelt modning	dubbele rijping	dubbellagrat
egetræ	eik	ek
ristet	getoast	rostad
forkullet	gebrand	kolad
år	jaren	år
måned	maanden	månader
dage	dagen	dagar
kold filtrering	koude-filtratie	kylfiltrering
ikke kold filtreret	niet koud gefilderd	ej kylfiltrerad
ikke farvet	niet bijgekleurd	inga färgämnen
fadstyrke	vatsterkte	fatstyrka
enkelt fad	enkel vat	enkelfat
fad nr.	vat nummer	fatnummer
parti/batch	serie/batch	batch
destillations dato	distillatie datum	destilleringsdatum
aftapnings dato	bottel datum	buteljeringsdatum
volumenprocent	alcoholpercentage/% vol	volymprocent/% vol.
Proof	amerikaanse aanduiding voor % vol	Amerikanska proof

Australian Whisky

I t is not surprising that Australia, cast adrift it seems from the rest of the world until Captain James Cook thrust his triangulation apparatus at it some 240 years ago, has many indigenous species. The result of biodiversity having to get on with it alone, often bravely and against the odds.

From the kangaroo to the koala, the wombat to the platypus, the kookaburra to the bearded Lark. Now it is the bearded Lark (Billius Distillus) in its native Tasmanian habitat, a small creature found mainly flying around darkened buildings in the vicinity of Hobart, that has had the greatest impact on Australian whisky, and without whom there would be no new chapter given only to that singular scion of the world's malt distillation family.

Bill Lark is a one man force majeure who took a country out of a starch-knickered Victorian reactionism, so far as distilling was concerned, into one that now proudly boasts over 25 distilleries either operating or in the process of being built. And a standard achieved by many so far that is way above the norm.

We must go back to 1992, seemingly recent in the grand scheme of whisky matters but a year before many of the people I met attending a recent Shanghai whisky festival were actually born. It was the year I gave up my work as a national newspaper journalist to become the world's first full-time whisky writer. And was the year Bill Lark began taking on the Australian government to change a law that forbade private distilling in Australia. Having got sympathetic politicians on board – always a wise move – he found his battle shorter and less bloody than expected and it was not long before he and his wife Lyn were hard at work distilling an unhopped mash made at the local – and historic – Cascade brewery. Soon their daughter, Kristy, was on board showing exceptional skill as a distiller. And next a family affair became a national one, as, inspired by the Larks, small distilleries began rising around the country, first Dave Baker across the Tasman Straight in Melbourne and then onwards along and up the coast. A new whisky nation was born. And is growing prodigiously.

Now, 26 years on, I have given Australia its own section in Jim Murray's Whisky Bible, perhaps not before time. It is a form of award well merited, because Australian malt has constantly proved to be something worth finding: often as bold and brave as Bill Lark's vision. And, like the great man and dear friend himself, you always feel better for its company.

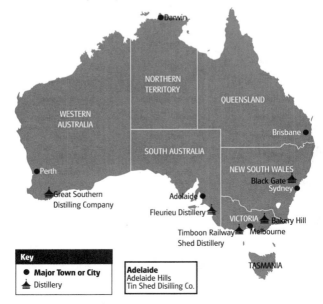

Key
- ● **Major Town or City**
- ⏥ Distillery

Adelaide
Adelaide Hills
Tin Shed Disilling Co.

AUSTRALIA

ADELAIDE HILLS DISTILLERY Nairne, South Australia. 2014. Working.

⟩⟩⟩ **Native Grain Project Wattleseed & Malt** db (88) n22 t21.5 f22.5 b22 Well, for a start, this isn't whisky. However, how can wattleseed not deserve its place in my Whisky Bible when its Latin name is acacia murrayana? This confirms it a member of the acacia tree or shrub family, rather than a grain....thus rendering anything distilled from it a non-whisky. Also, it is from the stunningly beautiful Adelaide Hills, one of my favourite parts of Australia. So far as nose and taste goes, sampled blind it is no different from some of the American whiskeys smoked over native woods and certainly pokes out a spiciness not to be sniffed at...or, rather, to be. Dry with precise background sugars plus a decent cocoa finish. An enjoyable whisky cousin. 46.2%.

BAKERY HILL North Bayswater, Victoria. 1999. Working.

Bakery Hill Classic Malt cask no. 1015 db (91.5) n23 t23 f22.5 b23. A beautiful malt for sure. Compared to its cask strength sister bottling, this has a far more sawdusty, dry feel though the cocoa finale is an extra bonus. 46%

Bakery Hill Classic Malt cask no. 1015 db (95) n23.5 t24 f23.5 b24 Emphasis on a fruit character, but always stunningly subtle in its execution. But it pays off because it never falls out of sync or balance. 60%

Bakery Hill Classic Malt cask no. 1415 db (93.5) n23 t23 f24 b23.5. As the 60% version below, except here there is far less emphasis on the light phenols and more, especially late on, on the bready sugars. 46%

Bakery Hill Classic Malt cask no. 1415 db (94.5) n23.5 t24 f23.5 b23.5 This is the seventh Bakery Hill whisky I have tasted today. And in the many years I have been sampling this stuff, I cannot remember when I was faced with such a long line of outstanding whisky from this Melbourne distillery. This is truly stunning malt, the light smokiness doing it no harm whatsoever. 60%

BELGROVE DISTILLERY Kempton, Tasmania. 2010. Working.

Belgrove Distillery Oat Whisky bott 19 Apr 17 db (95) n23.5 t24 f23.5 b24 Oats and whisky was long ago associated with the Irish. And many Irish ended up in Australia. So there was something inevitable about this whisky turning up in my tasting room one day. What could not be so easily predicted was the outstanding quality of the product. This is top quality whisky and make no mistake: anyone wanting to get their oats every night will now be left with a very satisfied glow, indeed... 58%.

Belgrove Distillery Peated Rye Whisky bott 17 Mar 17 db (95) n23.5 t24.5 f23 b24
It is a well-known fact that Denmark and Australia have so much in common they are viewed as parallel, if not identical, countries. For instance, both nations cover almost the same number of square miles and are entirely surrounded by seas (except for a bridge to their neighbouring state, Belgium and Japan respectively) yet admit all-comers to live no matter from where they hail, no questions asked; both countries share an almost identical population and climate, are governed by blood-lusting, expansionist Emperors, while each country's national emblems are birds that bound around the place with eggs in their pockets and animals that cannot fly but stick their heads in the sand (Denmark being particularly noted for its deserts); the national language of both countries is New Zealandish, their currencies the Euro and national sports Darts. Both countries drive neither on the left nor right side of the road, but straight down the middle and, like Ireland, they are entirely free of venomous snakes. They also, amazingly, both make a peated rye whisky. Huh! I knew you wouldn't believe the last one, but it is true; I have them here in my lab side by side. But here the two countries part: Australia's version wins by a nose...not to mention taste, finish and balance.... 64.8%.

⬩ **Belgrove Distillery Peated Rye Whisky** bott 17 Apr 18 db (96.5) n24.5 one of the most distinctive and beautiful noses of the year. Rare to find such natural harmonisation between two proudly individual and biggest styles in the whisky lexicon: peat and rye. The fact it works so well is marked by the fact you can still recognise the grain, the smoke and where, deliciously, they have merged together, neither ruling the other; there is one word only that sums up the sweet-dry balance here: perfection... t24 the oils from the rye coat the mouth on impact, in so doing both setting up a juicy base and making more gentle the impact of the major phenols; smoked Manuka honey is reinforced with cut glass, crisp Demerara sugars; f24 the smoke softens and then drifts, changing shape and emphasis; as it clears a light Fisherman's Friend cough sweet evolves, sweetened slightly by a little mocha but the oak digs in and a little eucalyptus seeps into the mix; b24 my two favourite whisky styles combining in a way that, before, I have ever only achieved in a lab. A truly great whisky: unquestionably stupendous. 60%.

⬩ **Belgrove Distillery Rye Whisky** aged in ex-Heartwood "Release the Beast" barrel PB 020, bott 27 Apr 18 db (95.5) n24 something distinctly bourbony about this, well, apart from the fruit and phenol effect, that is... t24 bravo! Against all the odds the rye stands firm, shoehorning the fruitier, muscovado sugars into the midpoint which the grain pounds remorselessly against the taste buds; surrounding the fruit a wonderful bend of heather and ulmo honey ensures a satisfying sweetness to match the toastier oaks; f23.5 good spice on the finish, over varying temperature and pace; the grain is still present and correct b24 a whisky of mind-blowing complexity from what is emerging as one of the world's great distilleries. 65.4%.

⬩ **Belgrove Distillery Rye Whisky 100% Rye** Shiraz casks, bott 10 Nov 17 db (95) n23.5 complex nose: bold and heavy with tannins, hefty grape and firm grain combining to create a thumping combination; a little heather honey in the mix, also; t24 dark, firm Demerara sugars herald in the juicier, crisp rye compounds. Toasted raisins hang from every corner; f23.5 spicy, slightly burnt, Melton Hunt fruitcake; b24 a very rare case of where certain, lusty elements are at almost full throttle yet somehow all is kept in formation. Brilliant. 60%. ncf.

⬩ **Belgrove Distillery Rye Whisky 100% Rye** Pinot casks, bott 29 Sept 17 db (89) n23 the rye has a firm input, but the overwhelming nose configuration here is of a First Growth Bordeaux cork just pulled from the bottle it had called home for the past 40 years. A magnificent nose in its own right. But not one I'm sure I'm looking for in a whisky...; t22 the rye is first out of the blocks, but I have seen more give in a taxman. The fruit is immediately behind and it is huge and all-consuming: indeed this is more a fortified wine than a whisky; f22 big fruit cake with plenty of sherry but little sugar; b22 I think the last time I tasted Belgrove's Pinot cask rye, I advised caution, though they had got away with it. This time they were not quite so lucky as the domination of the grape is over-egged, leaving the rye to make occasional cameo appearances... Still very enjoyable, but in whisky, as I have so often reiterated, less, often means more... 61%. ncf.

⬩ **Belgrove Distillery Single Malt Peated Whisky** bott 25 Jul 17 db (92) n23 clean, delicately peated barley: the oak stands back and lets the phenols do all the earthier work; t23 soft, though increasingly intense, peat with strands of barley sometimes youthful in its persona; f22.5 unusually for a finish the vanillas, just making their mark at the mid-point, drop in intensity leaving a smoky, dry and slightly bitter finish; b23.5 an interesting difference between this and the peated rye is the apparent lack of age: maybe the rye can cover a more youthful spirit with its boisterous, juicy personality, whereas the light barley can't. Or, maybe, this is a just a bit younger... 50.5%.

BLACK GATE DISTILLERY Mendooran NSW. 2012. Working.

⬩ **Black Gate Single Malt Whisky** first fill 100% litre Port cask, cask no. BG022 db (92) n22.5 thick fruit yet sweet, almost like an old-fashioned jar of boiled candy in a sweet shop;

t23.5 satisfying, fulsome mouth-feel. The malt has a bigger say than the fruit, revelling in its beautifully concentrated intensity; f23 spice, light fruitcake juicy dates star, but still the malt leaves no doubt that this is a whisky, not a wine; b23 Port casks are certainly all the rage in Australia at the moment, some working better for certain distilleries over others. This is a success story. *50%. sc.*

CRADLE MOUNTAIN DISTILLERY Legana, Tasmania. 1989. Working.
Cradle Mountain Pure Tasmanian Malt db (87) n21 t22 f21 b23. A knock-out malt from a sadly now lost distillery in Tasmania. Faultlessly clean stuff with lots of new oak character but sufficient body to guarantee complexity. *43%*

DEVIL'S DISTILLERY Hobart, Tasmania. 2015. Working.
◇ **Hobart Whisky Tasmanian Single Malt First Release** American oak ex-bourbon cask, bott Aug 18 db (94) n23.5 so buttery! One of the creamiest noses of the year sees the rich barley and even richer caramels from the bourbon casks form a partnership made in heaven...rather than hell, as you might fear...; t23.5 just so salivating! The barley is in tip-top form and dishes out a measured juicy sweetness. But there is also a fascinating to-ing and fro-ing of tannins, though of varying densities as though some have melded with the copper...and others haven't. This is in turn means the fudge-like caramels also vary in weight and pace: we are talking complexity...; f23 the astonishing creaminess of the delivery and mid-point dissipates only up to a point; mild chocolate fudge then moves in...before the spices go into overdrive. Some lack of copper tang at the very death...but by this point, who cares...? b24 it always does the soul good when I can report the success of a distillery's bottling of their very first whisky. And for Devil's Distillery, that's exactly what I can do as this, as they might say in that little corner of the planet, is a beaut! Oddly enough, the distillery's very weakness has become, in part, its strength. The lack of evident copper (confirmed on the very last moments of the finish) contributes to a delightful and easily overlooked complexity – a phenomenon we saw with another antipodean whisky two decades ago - Willowbank in New Zealand – and with many rums from around the globe. Their trick, though, has been to distil cleanly and use outstanding American oak. And the Tasmanian sun... A treat of a dram, I must say. *51%.*

◇ **Tasmanian Moonshine Company Tasmanian Malt Barrel Aged New Make** db (87) n21.5 t21.5 f22 b22 The distillery's distinctive shortage of metal within the spirit is apparent on the nose and delivery. But the spirit itself has been well tended to with good cuts and now an excellent oak involvement ensuring a very tasty degree of natural caramels at play. The malt, also, plays a big part. All topped off with decent and busy spice. Attractive. *43%.*

◇ **Tasmanian Moonshine Company Tasmanian Malt Barrel Aged New Make** port cask db (91.5) n23 t23 f22.5 b23 Big almost jammy fruit. But that is only half of it: a huge injection of hefty tannin has ensured backbone to the plummy muscle. And as for the spices....? Wow! A huge dose of flavours: this youngster isn't mucking about! *50%.*

Tasmania Moonshine Company Tasmania Malt Spirit batch 80001, bott 15 Mar 17 db (84.5) n21 t22 f20.5 b21 Would probably benefit from being at full strength: there is a thinness to the spirit which reducing to 43% accentuates. A little copper-poor but sweet caramel rich. *43%.*

DEVIANT DISTILLERY Sandy Bay, Tasmania. Working.
◇ **Deviant Distillery Anthology 10 Single Malt Spirit** Pinot Noir F.O. cask db (88.5) n22 subtle smoke, sweet and with a minty hue disguises a lack of copper on the spirit; t22.5 thin delivery at first, then that really outstanding peat works its magic, bringing into play gristy sugars; f22 sugar and vanilla see us comfortably home, despite some nagging from the still; b22 a high class bit of eating going on there. *47.5%.*

FANNYS BAY DISTILLERY Lulworth, Tasmania. 2014. Working.
◇ **Fannys Bay Tasmanian Single Malt** Port cask, barrel no. 9 db (93) n23 a dry, nose-pinching salty aroma. Almost like dessicated plums; a little grassy in part – thankfully; t23.5 that's more like it: outstanding oils gang together early on to bring the most sublime marriage of concentrated prunes and mouth-peppering spices; a lovely intertwangling of austere tannin and carefree Manuka honey; f23 you expect major spices – and you're not disappointed...; b23.5 there is no fannying around with this big boy... *59%. sc.*

◇ **Fannys Bay Tasmanian Single Malt** Port cask, barrel no. 11 db (85.5) n21.5 t21.5 f21.5 b21 A lack of oils appear to allow this malt to fall apart a little. The limited sugars available find little to grip onto, allowing a sawdusty dryness to mingle with the bitter grape. Pleasant in part, but the balance just isn't there. *46%. sc.*

◇ **Fannys Bay Tasmanian Single Malt** sherry cask, barrel no. 6 db **(85)** n21.5 t21.5 f21 b21 If anything, the grape – seemingly pleasant enough - appears to restrict intricacy allowing a bitter thread to dishevel the piece. *47%. sc.*

◇ **Fannys Bay Tasmanian Single Malt** sherry cask, barrel no. 8 db **(90)** n22.5 far better structure than the 47% version, the fruit appearing to have substance – a concoction of under-ripe and gooseberries and over-ripe greengages for a start – and a slight coconut oil to the sweetness; t23 eye-watering delivery: tart yet satisfying with a few waves of intense malt filling the middle; the tannins have a brief optimum period of liquorice-led sharpness; f22 a distinct sherry trifle finale, though a tad bitter late on; b22.5 now that's much more like it... *60%. sc.*

FLEURIEU DISTILLERY Goolwa, South Australia. 2004. Working.

◇ **Fleurieu Distillery Atlantic Crossing** ex-Seppeltsfield Port barrels db **(91)** n22.5 though lightly smoked, this is their cleanest nose of the four, the fresh grape having no battles to fight at all; t23 a beautiful array of sugars on delivery, muscovado heading the cast. The fruit and spice begin by holding hands, but it is the spice which takes the bolder strides; f22.5 lovely fruit and praline chocolate; b23 that's better: much better spirit as a starting point, ensuring a more even taste profile. Excellent complexity and weight. *52%. 800 bottles.*

◇ **Fleurieu Distillery Bogart & Bacall** Aus "Apera" sherry barrels db **(90.5)** n22.5 the loose cut shews its face briefly, before a thick cloud of peat reek descends upon it. Moist fruit cake does the mopping up; t23 sweet, tingly, spicy, hickory-rich delivery with a surprisingly thin body; the peat really does to take hold...roughly...a bit like how Bogart used to kiss Bacall...; f22.5 dries like ash falling from a two bit cigar...but the grape does enough to breathe some late life into it; b22.5 great name for a whisky; though having seen every single film Bogart and Bacall ever made together (several times) I think I would have reserved it for a traditional rye matured in virgin oak. Though I suspect this heavily peated number might allude to the fog of cigarette smoke in which the pair were often enshrouded. Anyways, you know how to taste, don't you? You just put your lips together... and suck. *61.2%. 270 bottles.*

◇ **Fleurieu Distillery River's End** ex-Seppeltsfield Port barrels db **(83.5)** n21 t21.5 f20 b21 The Port does the business early on, but even some robust grape has problems dealing with some average make. *53%. 200 bottles.*

◇ **Fleurieu Distillery The Rubicon** ex-Seppeltsfield Port barrels db **(89)** n22.5 the is almost a chocolate edge to the smoke which forms a semi-dense layer over the thick grape; t22.5 explosive delivery: a real date and walnut thrust at first, though the fruit gets plummier, silkier and warmer; the big peat surge hits the midpoint; f22 dries and bitters slightly as those peat notes insist on the final say; b22 a muscular whisky with some big flavour egos at work. When they gel, there are some magical moments. *55%. 500 bottles.*

HEARTWOOD DISTILLERS North Hobart, Tasmania. Working.

The Good Convict Port cask, cask no. HH0543, dist Nov 00, bott Jun 15 db **(96)** n24 t24 f24 b24 No problems with this cask. Has done its time, and has come away even and rounded. Massively impressive distilling and maturation: just beautiful! *71.3%. sc. 100 bottles.*

Heartwood 3of/3 cask no. LD 643, vatted Jan 14, bott Jan 17 **(94)** n24 t23.5 f23 b23.5 Seemingly distilled by Zeus...this comes across as significantly older than Bill Lark's jokes... which until now hadn't seemed possible. *675%. sc. 125 bottles.*

Heartwood @#$% &* 2nd fill Port cask, 2 x 1st fill sherry finish, cask no. TD0124, filled Aug 06, bott May 17 **(96)** n23.5 &%%*+A!$ ∙ &%$% ** ∙ $+A fruit; t24 fruit * ∙ $((£ £A ∙$& %!* ∙ *; f24 $%&A)_ ∙ spices ∙ ∙ A(£++* ∙ ; b24.5 just f*£%ing &%A*)+$ *62.5%. sc. 337 bottles.*

Heartwood The Beagle 4 **(94.5)** n23.5 t23.5 f24 b23.5 Bloody hell...! *61%. 187 bottles.*

Heartwood Spiritual Journey sherry cask no. LD300, dist Apr 07, bott Mar 16 **(94)** n23.5 t24 f22.5 b24 When I read "sherry" on a Scotch, Irish and Japanese, my heart sinks and I bring the glass to my nose as might a man bring a gun to his head, with five loaded chambers and one empty. With Oz whisky, though, sulphur is never, thankfully, an issue. *679%. 100 bottles.*

HELLYERS ROAD Havenview, Tasmania. 1999. Working.

Hellyers Road Henry's Legacy Wey River American oak casks, Pinot Noir finish db **(88.5)** n22.5 t23 f21 b22 Wey River...? Thought for a moment we had our first whisky from my native county of Surrey...! Mouth-watering and entirely presentable single malt enlivened and enriched by an exceptionally healthy wine cask which has imparted just the right degree of sharpness and weight. Good spices, also. *60.8%.*

◇ **Hellyers Road Slightly Peated Aged 10 Years** db **(91.5)** n23 soft cream toffee with the most genteel smokiness – how elegant is that...? t23 a succession of melt in the mouth sugars – first grist, then a number of oak-toffee ones and even a mild strand of heather honey;

f22.5 long with competent oils and a slow build-up of phenols, give both an earthy depth and further length; b23 Hellyers Road has come of age in every sense: the lack of copper in their system that held them back for so long has now been mostly overcome by a mix of peat and extremely high quality oak. This is a quietly spoken little beaut. Congratulations all round: it has been a long journey... 46.2%.

Hellyers Road Port Cask Matured Aged 12 Years French oak db (85.5) n22 t22.5 f20 b21 Certainly has the required chutzpah from the Australian port to carry a fruity strut, but let down slightly by the noticeable lack of copper depth. 48.9%.

Hellyers Road Single Malt Whisky 12 Year Old Original db (84.5) n19 t22 f21.5 b22. Forget the nose and get stuck into the massive malt. 46.2%.

Hellyers Road Single Malt Whisky Henry's Legacy 'The Gorge' db (83) n21.5 t21 f20 b20.5. Eye-wateringly sharp in places, its best bits hang on a vaguely smoky, molasses-sweetened coffee note. 46.2%.

Hellyers Road Single Malt Whisky Original db (84) n20.5 t22 f20.5 b21. Bolstered on last year's bottling thanks to a profound malt surge on delivery. Citrus fruity in part, but both nose and the tingle at the finish demands more copper. 46.2%.

Hellyers Road Single Malt Whisky Port Matured db (88) n22.5 spiced, juicy fruitcake; t23 superb delivery with the grape ripping home onto the throat with spice, then soothing and kissing better with its salivating freshness; f20.5 a tad off key but the spices are busy and biting; b22 without question the direction this distillery should take. Some wonderful moments. 46.2%.

Hellyers Road Single Malt Whisky Port Matured db (89.5) n23 t23 f21 b22.5 An absolutely top dog wine cask has done a splendid job on this malt. Impressive. And, what's more, Australia haven't lost a wicket – and even scored 28 runs - in all the time it took me to taste this... 48.9%

Hellyers Road Single Malt Whisky Saint Valentine's Peak db (85.5) n22.5 t22 f20 b21 Regular readers of Jim Murray's Whisky Bible know that I traditionally taste the Australian whisky during the First Test of an Ashes series, if one is being played – which seems like every six months in recent years. So it is fitting I tasted St Valentine's on the day of a massacre – the Aussies are currently 128-6 in their second innings, still needing almost 300 more runs to win. This malt has done a lot better than Clarke's sorry mob. Still pretty rough towards the finish, the gorgeous fruit effect on the nose works well into the delivery. At least the last embers show some coffee cake attractiveness. Now, I'd better hurry up with the remaining Aussie whiskies before Broad and Co bring the game to an early close on just the 4th day...60.1%

LARK DISTILLERY Hobart, Tasmania. 1992. Working.

The Beagle Tasmanian Vatted Malt Whisky batch no. 2, bott Aug 14 db (95) n23 t24 f23.5 b24.5 Another ridiculously fine whisky from Australia. 68.3%. 160 bottles.

Heartwood Calm Before The Storm 2009 Oloroso sherry cask, cask no. LD588, filled Nov 09, bott Nov 16 (96) n24 t24.5 f23.5 b24 Chose this as my 500th whisky for the Whisky Bible 2018 – part out of respect to Bill Lark and also, as there is Oloroso involvement, I like to live dangerously... 66.4%. sc. 292 bottles.

Heartwood Dare To Be Different Oloroso sherry cask, cask no. LD 542, filled Nov 08, bott Nov 16 (94.5) n23.5 t24 f22.5 b23.5 As you know, Bill Lark, when it comes to oloroso casks, I Dare Not To Be Diffident. But as I know you are one of the few whisky people who, like me , can spot sulphur from 100 paces, was completely confident this would be a first rate bottling...! 65.5%. sc. 330 bottles.

Heartwood Darkest Before Dawn Single Malt Oloroso sherry cask, cask no. LD559, filled May 09, bott Nov 17 (90.5) n23 surprisingly simplistic grape: flat, though very attractive; t22.5 enormous grape with a mild spice buzz; f23 at last some interplay as one aspect of fruit takes on a more boiled sugar candy while another has a burnt fruitcake persona. Simple tannins dovetail in their intensity; b22 high class malt but lacking the usual Lark spark and panache. 64%. sc. 242 bottles.

Heartwood Heart of Darkness Oloroso sherry cask, cask no. LD567, filled Aug 09, bott Sept 17 (93) n23 that familiar concentrated grape effect; salty, too, as the tannin bears down hard; t23.5 puckering fruit, initially dry on contact but soon relaxes to allow a restrained muscovado and molassed sugar combination into play; f23 here the chocolate oakiness fits well with the burnt raisin; b23.5 very muscular grapiness. 67.1%. sc. 260 bottles.

Heartwood Mediocrity Be Damned Oloroso sherry cask, cask no. LD 530, filled Sept 08, bott Aug 16 (94) n24 t23.5 f23 b23.5 This bottling, the label tells us, is dedicated to Lyn Lark, an extraordinary woman who, like this whisky, is much loved, admired and appreciated by at least two middle aged beardies... 67.2%. sc. 280 bottles.

⬦ **Heartwood Shade of Night Single Malt** sherry cask, cask no. LD 653, filled Sept 10, bott Mar 18 **(96) n24** the grape not so much radiates onto the nose, but pulses. Almost a cream toffee raisin...; **t24** ah...and it's that cream toffee on lift off, though by degrees it transmogrifies into cream sherry. The mid-ground enjoys a slow build of ulmo honey and rich vanilla; **f24** complex and exceptionally well layered. The oak has come into play now, the tannins giving a throaty roar of hickory and liquorice; **b24** another enormous whisky of great beauty and from Bill Lark. Think I'll be sending Bill a bill for the extraordinary likeness of me on the label... though when you look at the exact strength, no doubt he'll be telling me to go to the (Tasmanian) devil... 66.6%. sc. 280 bottles.

LAUNCESTON DISTILLERY Western Junction, Tasmania. 2013. Working.

⬦ **Launceston Distillery Tasmanian Single Malt Whisky** batch no. H17-01, ex-Apera (Australian sherry) cask db **(89) n23** a nose of great promise: some intense tannin pulses in and out of the equation; cocoa and grape are the other main players; **t21** oh...right. A disjointed eye-watering delivery offers all of the above. But very little harmony...; **f23** now we're getting there. The round pegs find their rounds holes as the jumble on the palate settles to make sense. The cocoa and late spice stars; **b22** perhaps bottled at a time when a promising malt was in a state of flux. Many points to enjoy, though. 46%.

⬦ **Launceston Distillery Tasmanian Single Malt Whisky** batch no. H17-02, ex-Tawny (Australian port) cask db **(92) n23** a gentle, playful and moderately sweet grape effect sits prettily with the gentle phenol and oak core; **t23** salivating fruit kick off, but soon the malt has made its mark and the oak makes a bigger one still; **f22.5** a little tang to the distillate but the cocoa and spice fade compensates; **b23.5** how fitting: a tawny owl is outside my tasting room widow hooting to its youngster. I'm sure you'll give two hoots about this unusual and busy creature. 46%.

LIMEBURNERS Albany, Western Australia. 2014. Working.

Limeburners Single Malt Whisky American Oak refill American oak bourbon barrels db **(86) n22; t22 f20 b22** Just a hint of feint here and there – and especially at the finish - unsettles the generous sugars. Though, from the lemon curd tart nose to the acacia honey late middle, the good far outweighs the bad. 43%.

Limeburners Single Malt Whisky Darkest Winter ex-bourbon American oak cask, barrel no. M348 db **(96.5) n24 t24.5 f24 b24** Whatever you do, DON'T add water: you'll absolutely wreck the intricate oils which set this whisky apart and makes this fabulous malt tick, as well as ensuring a rougher ride. 65.1%. ncf sc.

Limeburners Single Malt Whisky Directors Cut Australian port cask finish, barrel no. M230 db **(95) n23.5 t24 f23.5 b24** A little bit of Western Australian magic with not a single tang, off-note or any sense of disproportion. Magnificent! 59.5%. ncf sc. 202 bottles.

Limeburners Single Malt Whisky Heavy Peat 200 litre ex-bourbon American oak, barrel no. M226 db **(94.5) n23.5 t24 f23 b24** The third world-class malt I have tasted from Limeburners in a row. This distillery has single-handedly put Western Australia up there in the great whisky-making regions of the world. 61%. ncf sc. 212 bottles.

Limeburners Single Malt Whisky Port Cask second fill bourbon barrels, port cask finish, barrel no. M283 db **(88) n22 t23 f21 b22** 100% fruit, 0% subtlety. This insanely fortified wine (or so it seems!) is a must for grape lovers out there....literally! 61%. ncf sc. 244 bottles.

Limeburners Single Malt Whisky Sherry Cask second fill bourbon barrels, sherry cask finish, barrel no. M269 db **(91.5) n22 t23.5 f23 b23** A fascinating and delicious structure and complexity the port cask finish is unable to match. 60.4%. ncf sc. 199 bottles.

OLD HOBART DISTILLERY Hobart, Tasmania. 2007. Working.

Overeem Single Malt Whisky Port Cask Matured cask no. OHD-096 db **(84) n21 t21.5 f20.5 b21.** Big, but doesn't have the excellence of the Port cask as in OHD-104 to get away with a few technical frailties. 43%. sc.

Overeem Single Malt Whisky Port Cask Matured cask no. OHD-104 db **(91.5) n22.5 t23 f23 b23** Just dig that chocolate, digger...! 43%. sc.

Overeem Single Malt Whisky Sherry Cask Matured cask no. OHD-098 db **(95) n23 t23.5 f24.5 b24** Confirms this is a malt very much more at home at natural high strength. A late night dram of rare magnificence. 60%. sc.

REDLANDS ESTATE DISTILLERY Redlands, Tasmania. 2013. Working.

⬦ **Redlands Distillery Single Malt** bourbon cask, cask no. RD114 #8 db **(96) n24** the malt is so clean and intense I could almost weep: Malteser candy in concentrated form – even with a hint of milk chocolate – with the tannins so delicate and respectful, happy to go with a gentle vanilla and butterscotch mix. Sublime...; **t24** this is so beautifully distilled malt : not a single mark from the still, so the oils are as delicate as the gristy sugars that melt to match the intensity of the caramel on the nose; **f23.5** medium length, unerringly malty with a subtle hint of purple love hearts amid the increasingly spicy tannins; **b24.5** that rarest of whiskies out of Australia: a malt whisky matured exclusively in ex-bourbon cask with no wine cask interference. Who would have thought of such a novel way of maturing beautiful whisky? Just wish it would happen more often. Don't suppose that such an outrageous maturation method will catch on, though... 64%. sc.

⬦ **Tasmania Independent Bottlers Redlands Release Single Malt 2** Port cask, cask no. TIB RD 009, bott Feb 18 (78) **n19 t19.5 f20.5 b19** A little while since I last tasted Redlands. I certainly don't remember the feints which play such a prominent role on both the nose on delivery. The Port cask does its best to heal the wounds. The worst of the feints disappear with a little continuous warming. 49.6%. sc.

⬦ **Tasmania Independent Bottlers Redlands Single Malt Release 3** Muscat cask, cask no. TIB RD 002, bott Feb 18 (90.5) **n22.5** that unique spiced fruitiness of a Muscat cask comes through loud and clear; **t22.5** beautifully thick and chewy. Whichever Aussie designed this must have a love for good old fashioned British spotted dick pudding: suety thanks to the oils and charmingly fruity; **f22.5** sticks n course delightfully, some butterscotch and vanilla representing an increased oak presence; **b23** at times thick enough to stand a spoon in. Unconventional, yet the results are beautiful. 49.1%. sc.

SKENE ESTATE DISTILLERY Pontville, Tasmania. 2014. Working.

⬦ **Mackey Tasmanian Single Malt** Port cask db (85.5) **n21 t22 f21. b21.5** A big malt taking few prisoners. However, not quite up to the dizzy heights of previous bottlings I have experienced from this distillery, the cut, though triple distilled, being a little looser allowing some oils and bitterness to wander into places they shouldn't go. No faulting the wine cask, though, which imparts an intense, almost sticky, grape residue thought the impact of the sugars is thwarted. 49%. 297 bottles.

SOUTHERN COAST DISTILLERS Adelaide, South Australia. 2014. Closed.

Southern Coast Single Malt Batch 006 db (95) **n24 t24 f23.5 b24**. When I saw these Southern Coast Whiskies before me, my eyes lit up. Here was my journey to Demerara. Much cheaper and less problem-riddled than any trip I normally make to Guyana..and with less chance of coming away with my normal stomach complaint. Batches 4 and 5 let me down. But Batch 6.... even the sun has come out for the first time in three days as I nose this... Georgetown, here I come... 46%

SPRING BAY DISTILLERY Spring Beach, Tasmania. 2015. Working.

⬦ **Spring Bay Tasmanian Single Malt Whisky** bourbon cask, cask no. 9, dist 31 Oct 15 db (88) **n22.5** the barley is distinctive and upfront; light orange blossom honey and slight vanilla; **t22** the tannins are slightly more confident on the nose and quickly interrupt the early malty procession; light oils carry the tannin-induced tang; **f21.5** a little spice and caramel; **b22** a two-sided malt: one is delicate and malty, the other is increasingly oak-laden. 46%. sc.

⬦ **Spring Bay The Rheban Cask Strength Tasmanian Single Malt Whisky** Port cask, cask no. 15, dist 13 Mar 16 db (91) **n21.5** no amount of cajoling can prise open the very tight (by, for once, I don't mean sulphur-spoiled) grape and semi-bourbon liquorice mix; **t23.5** unlike the nose, this opens up – and opens up quickly. Revealing notes of complex fruit, unceasingly sugary and salivating. Indeed, the fruit intensity drops as it opens, while barley and vanilla peak through the gaps; **f22.5** bitters slightly but spices abound; vaguely salty at the death; **b23.5** a beautiful puzzle of a malt. Deft complexity is the key here... 58%. sc.

SULLIVANS COVE DISTILLERY Cambridge, Tasmania. 1995. Working.

⬦ **Sullivans Cove American Oak** 200 litre American oak bourbon cask, barrel no. HH0502, dist 29 Sept 00, bott 09 Jun 17 db (88.5) **n22.5** beautiful mix of rich malt, cream toffee, light citrus and mint; **t22.5** silky, and off it goes again with a re-run of the nose to very juicy effect; **f21** quite oily, rendering the toffee even chewier; **b22.5** tasting this directly after watching France beat Australia 2-1 in the World Cup. Ironic Sullivan's Cove uses a convict's badge as their motif, as the Aussies were clearly robbed: VAR used to get make an initially correct decision wrong. The defender touched the ball, so no penalty. Football needs intrusive technology like whisky needs sulphur. Anyway, don't need technology to tell me this is a highly enjoyable if slightly over-oiled dram. 46%. sc.

⬦ **Sullivans Cove American Oak** 200 litre American oak bourbon cask, barrel no. TD0172, dist 16 Nov 06, bott 01 May 17 db (84) **n20 t22 f21 b21** Lots of nougat on this SC: unusual as their cuts are usually pretty spot on. Much better on delivery where the malt and light acacia honey gel well. 47.5%. sc.

◇◇ **Sullivans Cove American Oak Cask Strength** 200 litre American oak bourbon cask, barrel no. TD0126, dist 11 Aug 06, bott 07 Nov 17 db (93.5) n23.5 wonderful: full bodied malt mingling beautifully with a toasted fudge and hazelnut inspired oakiness, Manuka honey and more chocolate fudge...: a semi-bourbon character; t24 so beautiful... Ulmo honey at its most intense, broadcasting the big vanilla theme; really big spice plus thinner Demerara sugars; a beautiful stratum of malt is never out of sight; f23 long, the oak still in league with the malt; b23.5 hard to believe that this whisky and that of cask TD0172 are in any way related... sheesh! This is the real Tasmania Distillery standing up...! 69.1%. sc.

◇◇ **Sullivans Cove Double Cask** batch no. DC085, dist 16 Jan 01, bott 22 Feb 16 db (89.5) n24 this could quite possibly the most delicate and complex nose I've ever experienced on an Australian whisky: no harshness, with the malt and fruit whispering fragile, busy, little sugary notes like a warbler in the bush; t22.5 totally melts in the mouth: barley first, the malt juicy and gristy. Then the fruit, more melon than grape in its gentle sweetness; f21 bitters out slightly; b22.5 a lightweight, fragile and sophisticated malt. Just so un-Australian...! 40%.

◇◇ **Sullivans Cove Double Cask** batch no. DC095, dist 29 May 08, bott 06 Oct 17 db (78) n19 t21 f19 b19 Apart from the sweet rise on the delivery and a later odd chocolate note, this one just doesn't work. The casks and spirit only make for an unhappy combination. 49.6%. ncf.

◇◇ **Sullivans Cove French Oak** 300 litre French oak Tawny Port cask, barrel no. HH0516, dist 12 Dec 00, bott 14 Apr 17 db (87) n22.5 t23 f20.5 b21 An unfortunate late furry bitterness undoes some great work by the fruity muscovado sugars and firm oak. 47.5%. sc.

◇◇ **Sullivans Cove French Oak** 300 litre French oak Tawny Port cask, barrel no. TD0312, dist 22 Aug 08, bott 01 May 17 db (93) n23 huge tannin but no aggression. There is a Guyanan rum-like quality to the crisp sweetness. At times the oak looks a little too confident, but it holds back, softening to a vanilla and lime chorus; t23.5 softening oils absorb the oaky impact helped by toasted honeycomb and butterscotch; f23 long with light oily vanillas; b23.5 few can handle French oak better than Sullivan's Cove: these bottlings are always one of my highlights of the year! 47.5%. sc.

◇◇ **Sullivans Cove Special Cask** 300 litre French oak Chardonnay cask, barrel no. TD0202, dist 06 Jun 07, bott 20 Jan 17 db (85) n21 t23 f20 b21 Charmingly sweet on delivery and a beautiful texture, too: light muscovado sugars at play, giving the gristy malt real boost. But the finish is a little too dry and bitter. 47.5%. sc.

TIMBOON RAILWAY SHED DISTILLERY Timboon, Victoria. 2007. Working.
Timboon Single Malt Whisky 2010 dist 05/09/10, bott 03/06/15 db (96) n24 t24 f24 b24 How can any critic fault a whisky this magnificent and mega...? A late night dram...but don't leave it too late to give it the full half hour treatment it deserves. 69%

Timboon Single Malt Whisky Christie's Cut dist 29 Aug 12, bott 30 Mar 17 db (90.5) n22.5 t23.5 f21.5 b23 Christie 1, Tom 0. 60%.

◇◇ **Timboon Single Malt Whisky Christie's Cut** dist 14 Apr 14, bott 01 Mar 18 db (95) n24 such a beautiful nose, it is a challenge to get on to the next stage of tasting: a blend of acacia honey and maple syrup combined perfectly with deeper tannin notes, especially red liquorice. A strand of muscovado highlights a subtle, fruitier thread; elsewhere the backdrop is of soft vanilla; t24 a surprisingly soft landing, light oils breaking the fall. The fruit element is more in play here, a mix of dates and plums mixing with a a vanilla and treacle tart; f23 excellent spice, and we are on the darker, toastier side now; b24 a way better version than the last Christie's Cut I sampled, the balance and all round oomph coming up trumps big time. 60%.

◇◇ **Timboon Single Malt Whisky Governor's Reserve** dist 2 May 14, bott 22 Jan 18 db (71) n18 t19 f17 b17 Most un-Timboonish. The intense citrus on the nose is way too severe and is completely off road from the moment it touches the palate. Every bit as awful as their Christie's Cut is delicious. 48.8%.

Timboon Single Malt Whisky Port Expression dist 5 Sept 10, bott 25 Jul 16 db (96) n24 t24 f24 b24 Such a profound whisky I thought to myself: "I've tasted this before". And, indeed, looking through previous Whisky Bibles I see I have had the great fortune to come face-to-face with Timboon's distillate of 5th Sept 2010 on a previous occasion. And what do you know...? Just like this, it scored straight 24s... Even more remarkable (as I don't think this has ever happened before in the history of the Whisky Bible), despite two extra years in the cask, my tasting notes above fit this bottling to the slightest nuance. It is a stunning again.... 66.7%.

Timboon Single Malt Whisky Tom's Cut dist 15 May 13, bott 25 Jul 16 db (84.5) n21.5 t22 f20 b21 Tim's cut, surely.... Just a little on the young and imbalanced side, where the massive components have yet to snugly find place and order in their whisky world... 58%.

TIN SHED DISTILLING COMPANY Adelaide, South Australia. 2013. Working.
Iniquity Gold Label Single Malt Batch 001 db (92.5) n23 clean, intense fruit: a hint of spice but the muscovado sugars help the balance no end; t23.5 the taste buds are smothered in the

most gorgeously soft and tactile fruit notes, especially over-ripe plum and dates; a little oily but the molasses helps with that rich fruitcake experience; f23 remains chewy and as it fades the roastiness intensifies dramatically; b23 less a whisky, more of a journey.... 60%. ncf.

Iniquity Gold Label Single Malt Batch 002 db (87.5) n22 t22.5 f21.5 b21.5 The nose is tannin rich and threatening but some diluted maple syrup keeps it safe and honest...while the delivery throws you back across the room with its explosive spices. But in the back of your mind you fear for the tannin intensity. And with justification for, despite the mocha element, the oak plays just too great and aggressive a part for greatness. That all said, my Blender's instincts kicked in automatically: buy both bottles and make a mix of about 75% Batch 1 and 25% Batch 2. The lush, ultra-complex and amazingly gentle chocolate fruit bar result scores a good 94-95 points... 60%. ncf.

⬦ **Iniquity Gold Label Single Malt Batch 003** db (92) n23 TGE (see below); t23 the palate is awash with juicy grape, casing max salivation; the odd malty moment is slipped in as well; f22.5 a slight oiliness due to the wide cut adds the delicate chocolate nougat to the raisin; b23.5 the Australians appear to have buttoned that amazing Total Grape Effect, right down to the pips: no other country produces anything even close. So if you like that mega grape effect (and, yes: entirely sulphur free!) then here's another uncompromising belter for you. 60%. ncf.

Iniquity Single Malt Batch 006 db (89.5) n21.5 a tad on the nougat side; t22 black cherries in chocolate...but only after a predictable nougat landing; f23.5 wow! That delicious black cherry travels a long way and fades alongside melt-in-the-mouth praline and vanilla wafer; b22.5 this whisky is a one stop candy store... 46%. ncf.

Iniquity Single Malt Batch 007 db (89) n22 so many rich bourbon notes! A few oils, but these appear to help the honey and liquorice fuse; t23 an immediate tingle on delivery then a build of rich toffee and molasses; f22 well spiced and full of roasted fudge; b22 a better distilled malt, oddly, with this eschewing the staggering black cherry of Batch 6 to give this a more Kentuckian feel. 46%. ncf.

Iniquity Single Malt Batch 008 db (82) n20 t21 f20.5 b20.5 When the heavy nougat out performs the fruit, then you know they didn't quite have the cuts on the still right. 46%. ncf.

⬦ **Iniquity Single Malt Batch 009** db (87) n21.5 t22 f21.5 b22 Much more like it! Just enough oils off the still to really give weight and length. The mid-point offers an intriguing and delicious chocolate fruit cake. 46%. ncf.

⬦ **Iniquity Single Malt Batch 010** db (88) n21.5 attractively nutty. Almost dense to the point of impenetrability, though some hefty fruit vapours are able to escape this whisky's own gravitational pull...; t22.5 a kind of minimally liquidised toffee fruit and nut; sweetened by a light layer of Manuka honey; f21.5 a little bitter as the heavier oils get even heavier; still nutty to the last; b22.5 hard to know whether to drink it, chew it or name an astronomer after it... A malt of substance. 46%. ncf.

⬦ **Iniquity Single Malt Batch 011** db (90.5) n22 fabulously intense malt; t23 oh...just adore that big heather honey vibe on delivery; thick with natural caramels from the oak and sublime accompanying spices; f22.5 long with the mocha intensifying by the moment; superb echoes of molasses and spice; b23 a beautifully distilled whisky bursting from the bottle with character. 46%. ncf.

Unspecified Single Malts

⬦ **Tasmania Independent Bottlers A Renowned NSW Distillery Release 2** sherry cask, cask no. TIB TIB ?? (sic) 005, bott Apr 18 (93) n23 not sure if I'm in Australia, Jerez or Guyana; t23 with those coffee notes and light esters, Guyana, surely... f23.5 remains brilliantly rich and complex with all kinds of Demerara, treacle and spiced coffee (or is that Coffey?) notes...; b23.5 now that was a bit of a rum do... 49.1%. sc.

Vatted Malts

Heartwood 2 of /3 Tasmanian Malt Whisky distilled at Lark 8 & 6 Years and Tasmania Distillery 16 Years, Port, peated & sherry casks, bott Apr 16 (95.5) n23.5 t24 f24 b24 Make no mistake: the vatting of these casks from these two distilleries and over such wide ages really is a work of art: a study of fruit, as well. 68.1%. 189 bottles.

Unspecified Grain

3Souls Small Batch Australian Single Malt Whisky Batch 2 Port cask, cask no. SC35, dist Oct 09, bott Aug 15 (90.5) n22 t23 f22.5 b23 Apparently, an unspecified Australian. If the finish was anything to go by, made in Victoria, I'd say.... 46.3%. sc.

3Souls Small Batch Australian Single Malt Whisky Batch 3 Pedro Ximenez cask, cask no. SC41, dist Dec 10, bott Aug 15 (79) n20 t21 f19 b19. Either too sweet or too bitter. Like many a PX whisky, comes to a sticky end... 52.1%. sc.

World Whiskies

I have long said that whisky can be made just about anywhere in the world; that it is not writ large in stone that it is the inalienable right for just Scotland, Ireland, Kentucky and Canada to have it all to themselves. And so, it seems, it is increasingly being proved. Perhaps only sandy deserts and fields of ironstone can prevent its make physically and Islam culturally, though even that has not been a barrier to malt whisky being distilled in both Pakistan and Turkey. Whilst not even the world's highest mountains or jungle can prevent the spread of barley and copper pot.

Outside of North America and Europe, whisky's traditional nesting sites, you can head in any direction and find it being made. Australia, in particular, has gained a deserved reputation for magnificent malt though, like its finest wines, it can be hard to locate outside its own country. Indeed, Australian whiskies are of such high quality and relatively abundant that it has, like England and Wales now been rewarded with its own section in the Whisky Bible, though Australian whisky will still be found in the World Whisky awards section. World class whisky can be found in other surprisingly lush and tropical climes with Taiwan leading the way thanks to the wonderful Kavalan distillery, no stranger to the Whisky Bible awards.

Japan has long represented Asia with distinction and whisky-making there is in such an advanced state and at a high standard Jim Murray's Whisky Bible has given it its own section - and World Whisky of the Year for 2015! But while neighbouring South Korea has ended its malt distilling venture, further east, and at a very unlikely altitude, Nepal has forged a small industry to team up, geographically, with fellow malt distillers India and Pakistan. The main malt whisky from this region making inroads in world markets is India's Amrut single malt, though Paul John is also now beginning to forge a deserved following of fans. Inroads is hardly doing Amrut justice. Full-bloodied trailblazing, more like. So good now is their whisky they were, with their fantastically complex brand, Fusion, deservedly awarded Jim Murray's Whisky Bible 2010 Third Finest Whisky in the World. That represented a watershed not just for the distillery, but Indian whisky as a whole and in a broader sense the entire world whisky movement: it proved beyond doubt that excellent distilling and maturation wherever you are on this planet will be recognised and rewarded.

Jim Murray's Whisky Bible World Whiskies of the Year Winners

	Asian Whisky	Southern Hemisphere Whisky
2010	**Amrut Fusion**	N/A
2011	**Amrut Intermediate Sherry Matured**	N/A
2012	Amrut Two Continents 2nd Edition	**Kavalan Solist Fino Single Cask**
2013	N/A	**Sullivan's Cove Single Cask HH0509**
2014	Kavalan Podium Single Malt	**Timboon Single Malt Whisky**
2015	Kavalan Single Malt Whisky	**NZ Willowbank 1988 25 years Old**
2016	**Amrut Greedy Angels 46%**	Heartwood Port 71.3%
2017	**Kavalan Solist Moscatel**	Heartwood Any Port in a Storm
2018	Paul John Kanya	**Limeburner's Dark Winter**
2019	Amrut Greedy Angels 8 Years Old	**Belgrove Peated Rye**

ARGENTINA
Blends
Breeders Choice (84) n21 t22 f21 b20. A sweet blend using Scottish malt and, at the helm, an unusually lush Argentinian grain. *40%*

BRAZIL
HEUBLEIN DISTILLERY
Durfee Hall Malt Whisky db (81) n18 t22 f20 b21. Superbly made whisky; the intensity of the malt is beautifully layered without ever becoming too sweet. Very light bodied and immaculately clean. Good whisky by any standards. *43%*

UNION DISTILLERY
Barrilete db (72) n18 t19 f18 b17. Nothing particularly wrong with it technically; it just lacks vitality. Thin but extremely malt intense. *39.1%*

Blends
Cockland Gold Blended Whisky (73) n18 t18 f19 b18. Silky caramel. Traces of malt there, but never quite gets it up. *38%. Fante.*

Gold Cup Special Reserve (84.5) n21 t22.5 f20 b21. Ultra soft, easily drinkable and, at times, highly impressive blend which is hampered by a dustiness bestowed upon it by the nagging caramels on both nose and finish. Some lovely early honey does help lift it, though, and there is also attractive Swiss roll jam towards the finish. Yet never quite gets out of third gear despite the most delicate hint of smoke. *39%. Campari, Brasil.*

Gran Par (77) n19.5 t22 f17.5 b18. The delivery is eleven seconds of vaguely malty glory. The remainder is thin and caramelled with no age to live up to the name. And with Par in the title and bagpipes and kilt in the motif, how long before the SWA buys a case of it...? *39%*

BHUTAN
K5 Premium Spirit Himalayan Whisky bott 2013 (88) n22 t23 f21 b22 Absolutely nothing wrong with the Bhutan grain but more judicious cask selection (i.e remove the odd one or two sub-standard Scotch barrels) and this really could be an irresistible little charmer. As a first attempt, really impressive. This whisky is a mix of Scotch malt and grain made in Bhutan. So it was fitting that seeing as parts of that mysterious, land-locked mountainous country rises to some 23,000 feet, I was just slightly above that height when I first learned of the whisky. While on board a flight to Asia I witnessed the brand's manager trying to talk an airline into carrying it. He then assured me I'd love it. Actually, clean that malt up a bit and I really could! *40%*

INDIA
AMRUT DISTILLERY
Amrut Double Cask batch no. 3, ex-bourbon & port pipe casks, Scottish peated barley, cask nos. 3189 & 2715, dist Mar/May 12, bott Jun 17 db (94.5) n23.5 forget any fruity edge to the port pipes: this nose belongs to the peat and the tannins. Together they combine for a distinctively sharp Love Heart candy bite, the phenols indulging with the tannins in a no-holds barred show; t23.5. For a few moments the plummy fruits of the port intervenes, creating a super-soft no-man's land where little happens. Slowly the phenols emerge, as do the muscovado sugars...in force; f23.5 spicier now with a vanilla, malt and smoky backdrop; b24 a deeply complex, satisfying and high quality Indian whisky. *46%. 1,050 bottles.*

Amrut Fusion batch 10, bott Mar 11 db (94.5) n24 t24 f22.5 b23.5. Superb whisky, though to be plotted on a different map to the now legendary Whisky Bible award-winning Batch 1. This is a much more delicate affair: more hints and shadows rather than statements and substance. Still, though, a fabulous malt whisky in Amrut's best style. *50%. nc.*

Amrut Greedy Angels 8 Years Old batch no. 2, unpeated Indian barley & Scottish peated barley, bott Jun 17 db (96) n23 the two years dropped on the last Greedy Angels I encountered is noticeable. But the gentle swirl of smoke to soften the tannin kick has all the usual Amrut charm; t24.5 such a beautiful delivery! The mouth-feel is the stuff of dreams – lightly honeyed with silky-textured oils creating just a light glaze to the palate. The Demerara sugars are gentle, working beautifully in tandem with the liquorice-tannin. Again, as on the nose, the smoke swirls elegantly adding a just-so weight; the salivation levels are absolutely perfect! Spices and tannins, prickle before finally settling down...; f24 there is almost a zen-like quality to the finale: after all the intricacies, now there is a quiet, delicious platform for contemplation as the flavours mingle as though now at last at one. A light butterscotch, ulmo honey and unsalted, buttery quality makes for a finale of astonishing intimacy; b24.5 had the nose just been as in tune as the unforgettable sequence of favours and counter-flavours on the palate, we would have had a contender for World Whisky of the Year... *50%.*

Amrut Greedy Angels 10 Years Old batch no. 1, bott Sept 14 db (96.5) n24.5 t24 f23.5 b24.5 when I visited my first Indian distillery, some 20 years ago, the last thing I thought I would ever experience would be a native malt reaching double figures in age. All those I tasted showed decline to the point of undrinkability at only half that age. However, cellared warehousing and far more judicial oak selection means that not only is there now an Indian malt whisky reaching double figures in age, it has reached a stage of magnificence on its maturation road. I first tasted this at the distillery itself in the Spring of 2015. But waited until August 2015, making this the second to last whisky sampled for the 2016 Bible, before officially reviewing it under neutral conditions in the UK. What is apparent is that wherever in the world you experience this, you are being royally entertained- bewitched and mesmerised, to be nearer the truth - by one of the most remarkable whiskies of all time. 46%. 284 bottles.

Amrut Greedy Angels 10 Years Old batch no. 1, bott Sept 14 db (96) n24 t24 f24 b24. As above. Except at this strength it is all a little oilier; tighter in its delivery and demeanour, with a bit more shouting where there were once whispers. All the same flavours are present and correct, though they all rush through at a greater pace to get to the finale. Beautiful, salivating...and dazzlingly brilliant. 71%

◇ **Amrut Kadhambam** batch no. 10, bott Jun 17 db (89.5) n22 pleasantly spiced. Flat by Amrut's usual standards, though a lot of natural caramels hit the mark; t23 rich and salivating delivery. Again, cream toffee dominates, then a fruity spice buzz; f22 more of the same, though more vanilla now than caramel; b22.5 almost as though the rum, sherry and brandy casks, rather than adding complexity, have neutralised each other somewhat: in blending more can often lead to less A pleasant malt, all the same. 50%.

◇ **Amrut Naarangi** batch no. 3, bott Jun 17 db (90) n21 the zesty orange peel is definitely a little too OTT for this bottling, dominating rather than gently permeating the fruit, as was the case with their first bottling; t23 but my word it certainly makes up for the nose on delivery! Again, the mouth feel is truly stunning with just the right degree of oils to grease the palate and ensure smooth running. The orange infuses here rather than dictates, like an orange blossom honey in concentrated form, softened by butterscotch tart and spice; f23.5 marmalade on lightly salted buttered toast...; b22.5 the whisky with peel appeal... 50%.

Amrut 100 Peated Single Malt ex-bourbon/virgin oak barrels db (92) n23 t23 f23.5 b22.5. Ironically, though one of the older whiskies to come from this distillery, the nose shows a little bit of youth. A quite different style from Amrut's other peated offerings and it was obviously intended. Further proof that this distillery has grown not only in stature but confidence. And with very good reason. 57.1%. nc ncf.

◇ **Amrut Spectrum 004** batch no. 1, ex-oloroso, new French oak, new American oak & ex-PX sherry casks, bott Apr 17 db (81) n20 t23 f19 b19 I admit I feared the worst when I saw the make-up of this malt: using such casks is like jumping around in a minefield. Even had all the barrels been top notch, to create something that would make sense and balance out would either be the most enormous luck or some of the greatest blending ever known in whisky history. But there are flaws to the casks which you may well pick up on both nose and finish. And though elsewhere, especially on delivery, there are a few moments of balmy, insanely intense beauty, they are fleeting. Maybe, though, enduring a day of stormy seas and lightning is worth the dazzling beauty of the brief rainbow. 50%.

JOHN DISTILLERIES

Paul John Brilliance db (94.5) n23.5 t24 f23.5 b23.5 Yet another astonishing malt from India. 46%

Paul John Brilliance batch no. 3, bott July 16 db (94) n24 t24 f22.5 b23.5 It is impossible not to be impressed. Complexity is the key word here. And though it has moved on a little – mainly through tannin – from its earliest rendition, the layering and structure remains superb. The tail needs a little attention, but I am being ultra-strict: this is excellent whisky and make no mistake. 46%

◇ **Paul John Chairman's Reserve** db (89) n22 sharp and aggressive: big peat, bigger fruit and hurled at you at 60% abv. Some decent Manuka honey gets a work in edgeways but...ouch! t23 an eye-popping, ultra-salivating delivery: both the smoke and grape hurtle themselves into your taste buds...; f22 spices buzz and PJ's irrepressible malt still battles through, though the smoke and fruit appear to have cancelled the other out; b22 I cannot say I am much of a fan of the mixing of PX and peat. Sometimes it works, usually it doesn't: often it is a case of two heavyweight fighters landing punches simultaneously, each knocking the other out. Well, both contestants hit the deck here but, thankfully, got up again briefly for a becalmed finish. Oh, and the really good news: 100% sulphur free...! 59.7%. ncf.

Paul John Edited db (96.5) n24.5 t24.5 f23.5 b24 A new Indian classic: a sublime malt from the subcontinent. To be more precise: a world classic! Think of Ardmore at its most alluring: one of Scotland's finest and most complex single malts, yet somehow possessing a saltiness and depth more befitting Islay. Then stir in a small degree of ulmo honey and bourbon-style hickory and liquorice. Plus subtle chocolate mint. And there you have it...the smoke drifting around stirring up spicy tales of the east. A world class whisky to be talked about with reverence without doubt... *52.9%*.

Paul John Exceptional db (95) n23 t24 f24 b24 The sheer elan of the controlled intensity is something to behold: Indian malt at its maltiest and most charmingly expressed. *47%. ncf.*

Paul John Kanya db (96) n23.5 t24 f24 b24.5 When a distillery can find honey at the very end of the its flavour range and profile, you know they have cracked it. Superb! *50%. ncf.*

Paul John Mars Orbiter db (95) n24 t23.5 f23.5 b24 We have lift off!! Out of this world whisky! *57.8%*

Paul John Olorosso Sherry Cask Finish db (94.5) n23.5 t23.5 f23.5 b24 Oh, for the rare joy of a sulphur-free malt. And as complex a one as this, to boot. *57.4%. ncf.*

Paul John Peated Single Malt db (89) n23 t22 f21.5 b22.5. A delicately peaty guy which gangs up on you slowly. The smoke-infused layering of sugars is the star turn, though. *55.5%*

⬦ **Paul John PX** db (90.5) n22.5 PJ malt has a decent weight at the best of times: with this impenetrable fruit this is as heavy as Indian whisky ever gets. Subtlety isn't the key here...; t23.5 the distillery's light metallic firmness cuts through the fruit pudding. The barley also battles through gamely. At times eye-watering and salivating; at others, it is like chewing a plum pudding with a Demerara sugar topping; f21.5 just a little tangy and disjointed, as is so often the case after PX influence; b23 the plan was to write these tasting notes while England were playing India during the first Test match in Birmingham. England, as usual, collapsed after previously having their foot on India's throat and potentially all out for a very low score...but then blew it. So with India now favourites to win, thought I'd better get these tasted today, rather than tomorrow, while there is still a Test match. For the cricket: why do England have only one Surrey player, Sam Curran? And not surprisingly the only one to show any resistance. And as for the whisky: enjoyable with a truly brilliant delivery. But not showing the true subtlety and colours of PJ's excellent malt. *48%. ncf.*

Paul John Single Malt-Classic (Un Peated) db (95) n23.5 t24 f23.5 b24 Further evidence that Indian whisky is on the rise. Just so charming...and irresistible. *55.2%*

Paul John Select Cask Peated (96) n24 a sexy, sultry, sympathetic exhibition of smoke on varying levels...though all of them soft. A tantalising chocolate mint hangs of the embers, which glow both sweet and dry. Peated whisky from outside Islay rarely comes as complex and beautiful as this, or as deliciously gristy; t24 a massive delivery. Massive yet tender and subtle. How does that happen? Again, cocoa quickly fills the middle but there is more than enough molasses to counter. The weight and depth are spot on, as are the spices which get off to a delicate start but soon get into the swing of things; f24 long, fabulously oiled and just-so amounts of gristy sugars clinging to the smoke. As charming and impressionistic as an Indian kitchen fire wafting its smoke over a remote village in the nearby valleys; b24 a peated malt whisky which will make a few people sit up and take even further notice of Indian whisky. World class... *46%*

⬦ **Cadenhead's Paul John 5 Years Old** dist 2012 (94.5) n23 huge malt topped with the unique JP spicy, dusty intensity; t24 mmmm!! So mouth-filling and satisfying. The malt seems to be perfectly proportioned with ulmo honey and maple syrup: sweet but totally in balance with the underpinning vanilla-rich tannins; f23.5 long, vaguely metallic with a spice, barley and ulmo honey glow...; b24 typical of the outstanding Cadenhead brand to celebrate for their 175th anniversary an Indian whisky that many others in their sector of the market would prefer to rubbish. As ever, Cadenhead's have called it right for this is a superb single malt. *57.4%. 175th Anniversary bottling.*

PONDA DISTILLERY

Stillman's Dram Single Malt Whisky Limited Edition bourbon cask no. 11186-90 (94) n23 t23 f24 b24. Well, I thought I had tasted it all with the Amrut cask strength. And then this arrived at my lab...!! I predicted many years back that India would dish out some top grade malt before too long. But I'd be stretching the truth if I said I thought it would ever be this good... *42.8%. McDowell & Co Ltd, India.*

RAMPUR DISTILLERY

Rampur Vintage Select Indian Single Malt Whisky batch no. 383, bott Jun 16 db (89) n22.5 a curiously scented malt, as though it has run from stills through the wardrobe of a millionaire and into the cask. Mainly malty, but the gentle fruits, mango in particular, are quite a sexy surprise...; t23 much more like it: this is more like the rich, well-weighted malt I discovered all those years back. Good cask management means the tannins harmonise with the malt effortlessly; f21 some serious spice builds, but there is that scented tang again...; b22.5 although I first went to this distillery over 20 years ago, it is the first time I have ever tasted it in my own lab back here in the UK. In those days, it was 100% designated for blended whisky: I argued it should be a single malt. On this evidence, you can see why... 43%. ncf.

Blends

Peter Scot Malt Whisky (84) n20 t21 f22 b21. Enjoyable balance between sweetness and oak and entertainingly enlivened by what appears to be some young, juicy malt. 42.8%.

Rendezvous (95.5) n24 t24 f23.5 b24.5. A sublime malt from the subcontinent. 46%

Royal Stag Barrel Select batch 212, bott 17 Feb 12 (75.5) n20.5 t19 f17 b18. Thin and sweet. But should be shot to put it out of its misery. 42.8% Mix of Scotch malt and India grain spirit.

Seagram's Blenders Pride Reserve Collection (77) n19 t20 f19 b19. Way too reliant on the grain and the malt submerged under the caramel.Soft, clean and painfully non-committal. 42.8%. Mix of Scotch malt and India grain spirit.

Signature (81.5) n22.5 t22 f17.5 b19.5. Excellent, rich nose & delivery helped along with a healthy display of peat reek. But more attention has to be paid to the brutally thin finish. 42.8%

NEW ZEALAND
THE NEW ZEALAND WHISKY COMPANY

High Wheeler 3070 Singlewood Aged New Zealand Whisky (88.5) n23 t22.5 f21 b22 This is 30% grain (which has a very different, much thinner feel to the grain found in Scotland, for instance) and 70% malt. As soft and friendly as you like. 43%.

The New Zealand Whisky Collection 25 Years Old Single Malt dist in Dunedin, matured in Oamaru, Ex-Bourbon casks (94.5) n23 t24 f23.5 b24 Around the time this was made, some of the malt was very lightly peated. Though it doesn't mention so on the bottle, I strongly suspect that – after 25 years wear and tear in the cask – this is one of them. Seriously charming malt. And historic – and for me, at least, as one of the very few to see it in operation – touchingly memorable. 46%

THE SOUTHERN DISTILLING CO LTD

The MacKenzie Blended Malt Whiskey (85) n20 t22 f21 b22. A vaguely spicier, chalkier, mildly less honeyed version of Coaster. Quite banana-laden nose. 40%

THOMSON WILLOWBANK

Thomson Single Malt 21 Years Old (84) n21 t22.5 f20.5 b20. Bit of a bimbo whisky: looks pretty and outwardly attractive but has picked up very little in its 21 years... 46%. sc.

WILSON DISTILLERY

Cadenhead's World Whiskies Lammerlaw Aged 10 Years bourbon, bott 07 (91.5) n22 t23.5 f23 b23. Stunning bottlings like this can only leave one mourning the loss of this distillery. 48.9%

Blends

Wilson's Superior Blend (89) n22 t23 f21 b23. Apparently has a mixed reception in its native New Zealand but I fail to see why: this is unambiguously outstanding blended whisky. On the nose you expect a mouthwatering mouthful and it delivers with aplomb. Despite this being a lower priced blend it is, intriguingly, a marriage of 60% original bottled 10-y-o Lammerlaw and 40% old Wilson's blend, explaining the high malt apparent. Dangerous and delicious and would be better still at a fuller strength...and with less caramel. 37.5%.

MISCELLANEOUS

The New Zealand Whisky Collection Doublewood Aged 16 Years (87.5) n22 t22 f22.5 b21 Light, silky, fruity and an all-round lovely experience. But as a whisky leaves one somewhat frustrated as it is a bit of a one trick pony with variation and complexity very much at a premium. 40%.

SOUTH AFRICA
JAMES SEDGWICK DISTILLERY

Three Ships 10 Years Old db (83) n21 t21 f20 b21. Seems to have changed character, with more emphasis on sherry and natural toffee. 43%

Three Ships Aged 10 Years Single Malt Limited Edition db (91) n22.5 t22.5 f23 b23.5. If you are looking for a soft, sophisticated malt whose delicate fingers can sooth your troubled brow, then don't bother with this one. On the other hand, if you are looking for a bit of rough, some entertaining slap and tickle: a slam-bam shag of a whisky - a useful port in a storm - then your boat may just have sailed in... Beware: an evening with this and you'll be secretly coming back for more... 43%

Bain's Cape Mountain Single Grain Whisky db (85.5) n21 t22 f21 b21.5. A lively, attractively structured whisky with more attitude than you might expect. Some lovely nip and bite despite the toffee and surprising degree of soft oils. 43%

Blends

Drayman's Solera (86) n19 t22 f23 b22. For a change, the label gets it spot on with its description of chocolate orange: it is there in abundance. If they can get this nose sorted they would be on for an all round impressive dram. As it is, luxuriate in the excellent mouthfeel and gentle interplay between malt and oak. Oh and those chocolate oranges... 43%.

Harrier (78) n20 t20 f19 b19. Not sure what has happened to this one. Has bittered to a significant degree while the smoke has vanished. A strange, almost synthetic, feel to this now. 43%. South African/Scotch Whisky.

Knights (83) n20.5 t21 f20 b20.5. While the Harrier has crashed, the Knights is now full of promise. Also shows the odd bitter touch but a better all-round richer body not only absorbs the impacts but radiates some malty charm. 43%. South African/Scotch Whisky.

Knights Aged 3 Years (87) n22 t22 f22 b22. This now appears to be 100% South African whisky if I understand the label correctly: "Distilled Matured and Bottled in South Africa." A vast improvement on when it was Scotch malt and South African grain. Bursting with attitude and vitality. When next in South Africa, this will be my daily dram for sure. Love it. 43%.

Three Ships Bourbon Cask Finish (90) n22 t23 f22.5 b22.5. A soft, even whisky which enjoys its finest moments on delivery. Clean with a pressing, toasty oakiness to the sweeter malt elements. Always a delight. 43%

Three Ships Premium Select Aged 5 Years (93) n23 t23.5 f23 b23.5. What a fabulous whisky. The blender has shown a rare degree of craft to make so little smoke do so much. Bravo! 43%. James Sedgwick Distillery.

Three Ships Select (81) n19 t21 f20 b21. Busy and sweet. But I get the feeling that whatever South African malt may be found in Knights does a better job than its Scotch counterpart here. 43%. James Sedgwick Distillery.

TAIWAN
KAVALAN DISTILLERY

Kavalan Distillery Reserve peaty cask, dist 2007, bott 23 Jan 2015 db (95) n23.5 t24.5 f23 b24 What a crackerjack cask this malt spent seven worthwhile and highly active and productive years maturing in. Starts so quietly, then becomes pretty loud. 55%.

Kavalan Distillery Reserve Single Malt rum cask, cask no. M111104073A db (93) n23 more fruit than the norm for a rum cask malt with soft hints of physallis, apricot, date and even banana all making delicate contributions. Traces of muscovado and molasses, also...; t24 this is where the malt comes into its own: a big delivery but always under control. The malt flies around the palate and thickens in intensity, spices are busy and at times startle slightly; f22.5 a little bitterness – note an unknown problem with ex-rum casks – just slightly downplays the tangy barley; b23.5 I have always regarded rum maturation at one of the most severe tests for any distillery: it is often a challenge for a malt to shows the depth of its personality in an environment which is perfectly set to clip its wings. Though this may not soar quite like some other Kavalans, it has still passed its test with flying colours... 57.1%. 448 bottles.

Kavalan Single Malt butt code: 2016:03:14 (92) n23 intense, slightly salty maltiness. The caramels are active but there is no damping down the diced pears and peaches; t23.5 soft and sensuous, the delivery first grips, then caresses and slowly, the malt, radiates juicily across the palate. The caramels dig in deep for a while, then the mid-palate comes back to life with a succession of vague, non-specific fruit notes, mingling with the thickening oak; spices arrive early but no more than keep the muscovado sugars company; f22.5 chocolate fudge fruit and nut candy, with a malty sign off; b23 an elegant and succulent malt which would do even greater justice to this wonderful distillery if they could find a way to harness the caramel... 40%.

Kavalan Single Malt Amontillado Sherry Cask cask no. S100623016A db (97) n24 t24.5 f24 b24.5 Given the right bottling, Amontillado is probably my favourite sherry style. How many times, though, have I discovered its delicate, complex, understated nature perfectly transferred onto a singe malt? In some 35 years, this must be only the fourth or fifth time, and I doubt any quite displayed such truth to its style, such panache. Forget the unique and intriguing bottle design (though it is hard!). This is a classic whisky on so many levels that it will stay indelibly stamped on both taste buds and memory. What a magnificent whisky experience this is...!!! 56.3%. sc. 744 bottles. Limited edition 2014_1402.

Kavalan Single Malt Manzanilla Sherry Cask cask no. S100716002A db (95.5) n23 t24 f24 b24.5 A mouth-watering jape from Kavalan. The nose appears a tad tight and introverted. But as it relaxes on the palate it certainly lets the malt the freedom to take on the grape. Or is it the other way round? A sublime surprise package.... *578%. sc. 744 bottles. Limited edition 2014_1402.*

Kavalan Solist Fino Sherry Cask db cask no. S060814021 (97) n24.5 t24 f24 b24.5 The Solist. And this is what we have here: a perfect fino sherry selected by the maestro Dr Jim Swan. But able to display its full magnificence only because the host spirit is so beautifully composed. Good whisky is, without question, a work of art; great whisky is a tone poem. And here, I beg to insist, is proof. *58.4%. nc ncf sc. 513 bottles.*

Other Brands Available In Taiwan

Eagle Leader Storage Whisky (81.5) n20 t21 f21 b20.5. Attractively smoky with a surprisingly long finish for a whisky which initially appears to lack body. By no means straightforward, but never less than pleasant. *40%*

Golden Hill Single Malt (75) n18 t20 f19 b18. An unwieldy heavyweight. *40%*

Sea Pirates (77) n18 t21 f19 b19. More Johnny Depp than Errol Flynn. *40%*

URUGUAY

Dunbar Anejo 5 Anos (85.5) n20 t22.5 f21.5 b21.5. A clean, mouth-wateringly attractive mix where the grain nips playfully and the Speyside malts are on best salivating behaviour. Decently blended and boasting a fine spice prickle, too. *40%*

MISCELLANEOUS

Precinct No. 6 Kentucky Sour Mash spirits distilled from 50% corn & 50% cane, batch no. 2 db (60) n12 t18 f14 b16. If you were to say, this seems like half whisky and half rum, you'd be right. Because it is both. And neither. Similar to so-called and self-styled "whiskies" of the Far East and some South American countries where either cane or molasses is used. Except this has much more oak involvement and spice. *478% (956 proof).*

CROSS-COUNTRY VATTED WHISKIES

◇◇ **Golfer's Shot Barrel Aged Whisky** blend of Indian malts & Scotch (84) n21 t22 f20 b21 An immaculately preened whisky with a lovely initial softness replaced by ever-increasing spice. Its main handicap is the big toffee kick and a sometimes skewed flavour register consistent with flavour additives. If additives are being used, then there is no need: the basics are good enough, If not, my apologies. *42.8%. Alcobrew Distilleries India Pvt. Ltd.*

Jim Beam Kentucky Dram (89) n22.5 t22.5 f21.5 b22.5 There may be some of you reading this who will remember tastings I did 15 or 20 years ago where, for fun and to show balancing effects, I vatted bourbon with smoky Scotch. At last someone has done it commercially. I suspect this is more for the American palate as the peat has been used sparingly. *40% (80 Proof)*

◇◇ **Virginia Distilling Co. Brewers Batch** batch no. 1, beer cask finished (78) n19 t21.5 f18.5 b19 Hugely intense, almost glutinous, malt on the palate after a stale beer nose. But the hop bitterness is just a little too vigorous for its own good. I know some like this kind of whisky – I'll leave it to them. *46% (92 proof). Stage Road Wee Heavy Ale. Bottled by the Virginia Distilling Co, USA.*

◇◇ **Virginia Distilling Co. Chardonnay Cask Finished** batch no. 2 (83) n20.5 t21 f21 b20.5 From both an unpromising nose and delivery, both of which are tight and lacking fluidity of development, it recovers sufficiently for a few attractively penetrating fruit strokes. The finish is again off key, but the odd cocoa note revives the interest. *46% (92 proof). Bottled by the Virginia Distilling Co, USA.*

◇◇ **Virginia Distilling Co. Cider Cask Finished** batch no. 2 (88.5) n22 Incredibly spicy. Not exactly in tune, but the nibbling fruit is fascinating; t22.5 fat and chewy, the malt does beat its chest of a good while. Some heftier, slightly feinty notes do swirl about, but the combination of bit malt, teasing fruit and prickly spices diverts the attention; f22 continues to warm, with lots of chocolate fudge, too; b22 now that was a bit weird. Sometimes delicious, but always intriguingly odd. *46% (92 proof). Bottled by the Virginia Distilling Co, USA.*

◇◇ **Virginia Distilling Co. Port Cask Finished** batch no. 7 (87.5) n21 t22.5 f22 b22 Dense and dusky, the fruit works ceaselessly to bring about a rewardingly sweet personality to the big oily structure. Technically not quite the best, but the chocolate fruit and nut character that does eventually emerge is charming and at times quite delicious. *46% (92 proof). Bottled by the Virginia Distilling Co, USA.*

◇◇ **White & Blue** blend of Indian malts & Scotch (68) n17 t18 f16 b17 OK, certain this one is riddled with flavour additives – my tongue is buzzing. Good people of Alcobrew: the world has moved on and Indian malt deserves better respect. A decent blend can be created just from the whisky itself – I'll come and show you! If I'm wrong and this is all natural, I apologise unreservedly. But I don't think am I. *42.8%. Alcobrew Distilleries India Pvt. Ltd.*

Slàinte

This is the point where I say a warehouse-sized thank you to all those who have helped me write the Whisky Bible, showing my appreciation to the many who have chipped in with their time, help and kindnesses, small and large, one way or another.

Also, of course, my usual thanks to my team of Vincent Flint-Hill, Peter Mayne, Robin Pulford, David Rankin and the brilliant and matronly Jane Garnett. As well as Julia Nourney and my support team of Tim and Sue Nicholson, Paul and Denise Egerton, Linda Mayne, David Hartley and Julie Barrie, the purveyor of the World's Finest Breakfast. As always, a massive hug to Heiko Thieme. And, finally, thanks to those below who have provided assistance and samples for the 2013 Bible onwards. For all those who have assisted in the previous decade, we remain indebted.

Mitch Abate; Andrew Abela; Hayley Adams; Emma Alessandrini; Mary Allison; Mike Almy; Ally Alpine; Nicole Anastasi; Tommy Andersen; Wayne Anderson; Gareth andrews; Kristina Anerfält-Jansson; Clint Anesbury; Jane & Martin Armstrong; Hannah Arnold; Teemu Artukka; Scott & Sam Ashforth; Paul Aston; Kevin Atchinson; Ryan Baird; David Bakery; Duncan Baldwin; Clare Banner; Keith Barnes; Lauren Barrett; Hans Baumberger; Stefan Baumgart; Steve Beam; Lauren Beck; Stefan Beck; Jan Beckers; Kirsteen Beeston; Sarah Belizaire-Butler; Becky Bell; Annie Bellis; Sigurd Belsnes; Franz Benner; Alexander Berger; Akash Beri; John Bernasconi; Barry Bernstein; Stuart Bertra; Jodi Best; Marilena Bidaine; Peter Bignell; Menno Bijmolt; Lee Bilsky; Sonat Birknecker Hart; Franziska Bishof; Rich Blair; Olivier Blanc; Mike Blaum; Elisabeth Blum; René Bobrink; Andreas Boessow; Anna Boger; Arthur H. Boggs, III; Amy & Steve Bohner; Hans Bol; Mark Boley; Yvonne Bonner; Keith Bonnington; Etienne Bouillon; Borat, Birgit Bornemeier; Phil Brandon; Caroline Brel; Stephen Bremner; Rebecca Brennan; Franz Brenner; Cam Brett; Stephanie Bridge; Chris Brown; James Brown; Sara Browne; Chris Bryne; Ralf Brzeske; Michael Brzozowski; Alexander Buchholz; Ryan Burchett; Amy Burgess; Nicola Cameron; Andrew Campbell Walls; Euan Campbell; Nathan Campbell; Kimla Carsten; Lauren Casey-Haiko; Bert Cason; Stuart Cassells; Jim Caudill; Danilo Cembrero; Lisa Chandler; Thomas Chen; Yuseff Cherney; Ashok Chokalingam; Julia Christian; Morten Christensen; Michelle Clark; Claire Clark; Nick Clark; Anne-Marie Clarke; Joseph Clarkson; Fredi Clerc; Dr Martin Collis; Shelagh Considine, Peter Cooney; Mathew & Julie Cooper; Christina Conte; Gabriel Corcoran; Lynn Cross; Lauren Crothers; Rosie Cunningham; Brian Cox; Jason Craig; David Croll; Molly Cullen; Nathan Currie; Larry Currier; Benjamin Curtis; Danni Cutten; Dave Cuttino; Larry Currier; Mike DaRe; Alan Davis; Bryan Davis; Stephen Davies; Alasdair Day; Dick & Marti; Scott Dickson; Martin Diekmann; Sharton Deane; Dixon Dedman; Conor Dempsey; Paul Dempsey; Lauren Devine; Marie-Luise Dietich; Holly Forbes; Hugo Diez; Arno Josef Dirker; Caroline Docherty; Oscar Dodd; Korrie Dodge; Angela D'Orazio; Georgia Donmall; Jean Donnay; Kellie Du; Tim Duckett; Camille Duhr-Merges; Mariette Duhr-Merges; Gemma Duncan; Shane Dunning; Christophe Dupic; Jens Drewitz; Reinhard Drexler; Jochen Druffel; Michael D'souza; Kellie Du; Jonas Ebensperger; Lenny Eckstein; Ray Edwards; Winston Edwards; Bernd Ehbrecht; Carsten Ehrlich; Ben Ellefsen; Rebecca Elliott-Smith; Lucie Ellis; Thimo Elz; Maximilian Engel; Camilla Ericsson; Beanie Espey; James Espey; Brad Estabrooke; Patrick Evans; Jennifer Eveleigh; Selim Evin; Thomas Ewers; Charlotte Falconer; Lauren Fallert; Bruce Farquhar; David Faverot; Joanna Fearnside; Angus Ferguson; Walter Fitzke; Roland Feller; Andrea Ferrari; Bobby Finan; Brigette Fine; Holly Forbes; Tricia Fox; Jean-Arnaud Frantzen; Sascha Frozza; Barry Gallagher; Hans-Gerhard Fink; Sarah Fisher; David Fitt; Walter Fitzke; Kent Fleischman; Mara Flynn; Martyn Flynn; Holly Forbes; Carole Frugier; Danny Gandert; Arno Gänsmantel; Patrick Garcia; Dan Garrison; Ralph Gemmel; Stefanie Geuting; Carole Gibson; Jonathan Gibson; Daniel Giraldo; John Glaser; John Glass; Emily Glynn; Emma Golds; Rodney Goodchild; Chloe Gordon; Jonathon Gordan; Tomer Goren; Bob Gorton; Lawrence Graham; Kelly Greenawalt; Hannah Gregory; Andrew Grey; George Grindlay; Rebecca Groom; Jason Grossmiller; Jan Groth; Viele Grube; Immanuel Gruel; Barbara Grundler; Katia Guidolin; Stefanie Geuting Josh Hafer; Jasmin Haider; Jamie Hakim; Georgina Hall; Georges Hannimann; Denis Hanns; Claire Harris; Scott E Harris; Alistair Hart; Andrew Hart; Donald Hart; Stuart Harvey; Ralf Hauer; Elizabeth Haw; Steve Hawley; Ailsa Hayes; Ross Hendry; Lianne Herbruck; Thomas Herbruck; Nils C. Herrmann; Bastian Heuser; Jennifer Higgins; Jason Himstedt; Brian Hinson; Roland Hinterreiter; Paul Hletko; Eva Hoffman; Marcus Hofmeister; Tom Holder; Julie Holl Rebsomen; Genise Hollingworth; Arlette Holmes; Bernhard Höning; Jason Horn; Mike Howlings; Emma Hurley; Alex Huskingson; Thomas B. Ide; Jill Inglis; Rachel Showalter Inman; Victoria Irvine; Hannah Irwin; Kai Ivalo; Emma Jackson; Caroline James; Richard Jansson; Amelia James; Ulrich Jakob; Andrew Jarrell; Don Jennings; Pascal Jobst; Michael John; Celine Johns; Eamonn Jones; Robert Joule; Aista Jukneviciute; Emiko Kaji; Jeff Kanof; Raphael Käser; Alfred Kausl; Christina Kavanaugh; Serena Kaye; Colin Keegan; Joy Kelso; James Kiernan; Kai Kilpinen; Jessica Kirby; Daniel Kissling; Sara Klingberg; Martina Krainer; Franz Kostenzer; Pavlos Koumparos; Matt Kozuba; Martina Krainer; Larry Krass; Armin

Krister; Karen Kushner; Sophie Lambert-Russell; Ryan Lang; Oliver Lange; Jürgen Laskowski; Sebastian Lauinger; Alan Laws; Darren Leitch; Christelle Le Lay; Danguole Lekaviciute; Cédric Leprette; Eiling Lim; Bryan Lin; Lars Lindberger; Mark T Litter; Tom Lix; Steven Ljubicic; Kelly Locker; Vincent Löhn; Richard Lombard; Alistair Longwell; Dorene Lorenz; Claire Lormier; Sarah Ludington; Valentin Lutikov; Urs Lüthy; C. Mark McDavid; James Macdonald; Jane Macduff; Jenna Macfarlane; Myriam Mackenzie; Julia Mackillop; Bethan Mackenzie; Damian & Madeleine Mackey; John Maclellan; Rosalyn MacLeod; Derek Mair; Dennis Malcolm; Jari Mämmi; Sarah Manning; Stefan Marder; Ole Mark; Amaury Markey; Gene Marra; Tim Marwood; Jennifer Masson; Gregor Mathieson; Leanne Matthews; Josh Mayr; Roxane Mazeaude; Stephen R McCarthy; Mark McDavid; Christy McFarlane; Angela Mcilrath; Catherine McKay; Mark McLaughlin; Jonny McMillan; Douglas McIvor; Heinz Meistermann; Sarah Messenger; Uwe Meuren; Raphael Meuwly; Herman C. Mihalich; Joanna Miller; Maggie Miller; Gary Mills; Tatsuya Minagawa; Clare Minnock; Ashish Misra; Euan Mitchell; Jacqueline Mitchell; Paul Mitchell; Jeroen Moernaut; Stephan Mohr; Henk Mol; Kim Møller-Elshøj; Nick Morgan; Celine Moran; Katy Moore; Maggie Morri; Elyse Morris; Michael Morris; Brendan J. Moylan; Miroslav Motyčka; Fabien Mueller; Raphael Meuwly; Dennis Mulder; Mike Müller; Tarita Mullings; Tom-Roderick Muthert; Michael Myers; Simone Nagel; Arthur Nägele; Andrew Nelstrop; Sandra Neuner; Stuart Nickerson; Alex Nicol; Jane Nicol; Jennifer Nicol; Jens Nielsen; Thorsten Niesner; Sharon Nijkerk; Zack Nobinger; Soren Norgaard; Julia Nourney; Michael Nychyk; Nathan Nye; Tom O'Connor; Sinead Ofrighil; Richard Oldfield; Linny Oliphant; Jonas Östberg; Casey Overeem; Ted Pappas; Lauri Pappinen; Allison Parc; Jason Parker; Richard Parker; Katie Partridge; Sanjay Paul; Pascal Penderak; Percy; Nadège Perrot; Jörg Pfeiffer; Alexandra Piciu; Amy Preske; Phil Prichard; Rupert Ponsonby; Andreas Poulsen; George Quiney; Rachel Quinn; George Racz; Robert Ransom; Nidal Ramini; Sarah Rawlingson; Julie Holl Rebsomen; Michael Reckhard; Guy Rehorst; Michel Reick; Lutz Reifferscheid; Marco Reiner; Drexler Reinhard; Carrie Revell; Frederic Revol; Kay Riddoch; Massimo Righi; Nicol von Rijbroek; Karen Ripley; Patrick Roberts; James Robertson; Dr. Torsten Römer; Mark Rosendal Steiniche; Casey Ross; Anton Rossetti; Fabio Rossi; David Roussier; Ronnie Routledge; Stephane Rouveyrol; Matthias Rosinski; Ken Rose; Miriam Rune; Michal Rusiňak; Jim Rutledge; Caroline Rylance; Simi Sagoo; Paloma Salmeron Planells; Kiran Samra; Jasmine Sangria; Carla Santoni; Colette Savage; John Savage-Onstwedder; Kirsty Saville; Manuela Savona; Ian Schmidt; Fred Heinz Schober; Lorien Schramm; Becky Schultz; Birgitta Schulze van Loon; John Scott; Chris Seale; Mick & Tammy Secor; Tad Seestedt; Tanya Seibold; Marina Sepp; Paul Shand; Steven Shand; Mike Sharples; Lorien Schramm; Rubyna Sheikh; Caley Shoemaker; Lauren Shayne Mayer; Jamie Siefken; Peter Siegenthaler; Fred Siggins; Sam Simmons; Alastair Sinclair; Thomas Sippel; Sukhinder Singh; Thomas Sippel; Thomas Smidt-Kjaerby; Aidan Smith; Barbara Smith; Beccy Smith; Gigha Smith; Phil Smith; Marianna Smyth; Gunter Sommer; Orlin Sorensen; Oliver Späth; Cat Spencer; Colin Spoelma; Alexander Springensguth; Tom Stacey; Jolanda Stadelmann; Silvia Steck; Guido Stohler Jeremy Adam Spiegel; Jolanda Stadelmann; Silvia Steck; Marlene Steiner; Vicky Stevens; Karen Stewart; Jakob Stjernholm; Katy Stollery; Greg Storm; Jarret Stuart; Jason Stubbs; Nicki Sturzaker; Peter Summer; Michael Svendsen; Henning Svoldgaard; Tom Swift; Cameron Syme; Daniel Szor; Solene Tailland; Shoko Takagi; Cheryl Targos; Chip Tate; Marko Tayburn; Elizabeth Teape; Emily Tedder; Marcel Telser; Celine Tetu; Kevyn Termet; Sarah Thacker; Johanne Theveney; Ryan Thompson; Laura Thomson; Kelly Tighe; Brian Toft; Jarrett Tomal; Katy Took; Hamish Torrie; Louise Towers; Hope Trawick; Matthias Trum; Anne Ulrich; Jessie Unrah; Jens Unterweger; Richard Urquhart; Stuart Urquhart; CJ Van Dijk; Rifino Valentine; Zvi A. Vapni; Lisandru Venturini; Rhea Vernon; Adam Vincent; Mariah Veis; Aurelien Villefranche; Lorraine Waddell; Josh Walker; Grace Waller; Emma Ware; Katharina Warter; Patrick Wecklein; Oswald Weidenauer; Micheal Wells; Katrin Werner; Arne Wesche; Zoe Wesseon; Anna Wilson; Georgia Wilson; Nick White; Peter White; Robert Whitehead; Lucy Whitehall; Stephanie Whitworth; Daniel Widmer; Markus Wieser; Julien Williems; George Wills; James Wills; Rinaldo Willy; Georgia Wilson; Ken Winchester; Arthur Winning; Ellie Winters; Lee Wood; Stephen Worrall; Kate Wright; Frank Wu; Tom Wyss; Junko Yaguchi; Laura Young; Kiyoyuki Yoshimura; Bettina Zannier; Jörg Zahorodnyj; Ruslan Zamoskovny; Ulrich Jakob Zeni; Rama Zuniga; Ernst Zweiger. And, as ever, in warm memory of Mike Smith.